Frommer's

Japan

by Beth Reiber

with Janie Spencer

Macmillan • USA

About the Authors

Beth Reiber worked for several years in Tokyo as the editor of the *Far East Traveler.* Now a freelance travel writer residing in Lawrence, Kansas, she is the author of several Frommer guides: *Tokyo, Hong Kong, Berlin, Berlin from $50 a Day,* and *St. Louis & Kansas City.* She also has contributed to *Europe from $50 a Day.*

Janie Spencer also spent several years in Japan, working for *Tokyo Journal* and the Kyodo News Service. A freelance travel writer and mother, she divides her time between France and Santa Barbara. Her coverage of the Burmese theater (*pwe*) has been praised in *Discovery* magazine.

MACMILLAN TRAVEL

A Simon & Schuster Macmillan Company
1633 Broadway
New York, NY 10019

Find us online at **http://www.mgr.com/travel**
or on America Online at **Keyword: Frommer's**

ISBN 0-02-860927-1
ISSN 1045-6899

Editor: Michael Feist
Design by Michele Laseau
Digital Cartography by Devorah Wilkenfeld
Maps copyright © by Simon & Schuster, Inc.

Special Sales

Bulk purchases (10+ copies) of Frommer's travel guides are available to corporations at special discounts. The Special Sales Department can produce custom editions to be used as premiums and/or for sales promotion to suit individual needs. Existing editions can be produced with custom cover imprints such as corporate logos. For more information write to: Special Sales, Simon & Schuster, 1633 Broadway, New York, NY 10019.

Manufactured in the United States of America

Contents

9 The Rest of Honshu 339

10 Shikoku 435

11 Kyushu 449

12 Northern Japan—Hokkaido 505

Appendix 544

Index 554

List of Maps

ACKNOWLEDGMENTS

I would like to thank several fine and very special people who graciously offered their help in the preparation of this book: Toshinobu Ikubo, Grace Herget, and Seiko Tanigushi; as well as Larry Estes, Debbie Howard, and Evelyn Lenzen for the moral support and editorial advice.

—*Beth Reiber*

I would like to express my appreciation to those who assisted in the preparation of this book and without whom it would not have been possible: Tetsuya Sato, Takashi Nagaoka, Seiko Taniguchi, Satsuki Watanabe, Tomoko Matsuo, Tomoko Inuishi, Setsuko Morita, Kazuhiro Sakaue, Fumiko Izumi, Keiko Miki, and Yoshihiko Nakagawa for their knowledge, efforts, and kindness; Shinichi Tomioka and Julia Nolet for invaluable secretarial and office support; and Debbie Howard, Zita Ohe, Nicole Terisse and Naoko Tsunoi for information and advice.

—*Janie Spencer*

An Invitation to the Reader

In researching this book, we discovered many wonderful places—hotels, restaurants, shops, and more. We're sure you'll find others. Please tell us about them, so we can share the information with your fellow travelers in upcoming editions. If you were disappointed with a recommendation, we'd love to know that, too. Please write to:

Beth Reiber and Janie Spencer
Frommer's Japan, 3rd Edition
Macmillan Travel
1633 Broadway
New York, NY 10019

An Additional Note

Please be advised that travel information is subject to change at any time—and this is especially true of prices. We therefore suggest that you write or call ahead for confirmation when making your travel plans. The authors, editors, and publisher cannot be held responsible for the experiences of readers while traveling. Your safety is important to us, however, so we encourage you to stay alert and be aware of your surroundings. Keep a close eye on cameras, purses, and wallets, all favorite targets of thieves and pickpockets.

What the Symbols Mean

✪ Frommer's Favorites

Hotels, restaurants, attractions, and entertainment you should not miss.

$ Super-Special Values

Hotels and restaurants that offer great value for your money.

The following abbreviations are used for credit cards:

AE	American Express	EU	Eurocard
CB	Carte Blanche	JCB	Japan Credit Bank
DC	Diners Club	MC	MasterCard
DISC	Discover	V	Visa
ER	enRoute		

1

The Best of Japan

Each destination in this book was chosen to provide you with a rich itinerary. No doubt each traveler to Japan will discover favorites based upon personal interests and fond memories. Of course, my favorite destinations are based on years of experience. To make your travel plans a little easier, I've listed here the kind of place to which I always enjoy returning year after year because it's such a good deal, or so luxurious, or so Japanese, or because there's no other place like it anywhere in the world—the best in its category.

1 The Most Scenic Towns & Villages

- **Tsumago,** nestled in the Japan Alps, is a village of authentic wooden structures virtually untouched by the 20th century. Once a stop for *daimyo* (lords) and their samurai on the old Nakasendo Highway linking Kyoto with Edo (Tokyo) when walking was the means of transport, today it offers you a walk back in time. See chapter 8, section 4.
- **Shirakawa-go,** with its thatch-roofed farmhouses, rice paddies trimmed with flowerbeds, roaring river, and pine-covered mountains rising on all sides, is one of the most picturesque regions of Japan. Many of the large farmhouses with their typical *irori* (open-hearth fireplaces) are now *minshuku* (family-run inns) where you can stay and taste the local mountain cuisine. See chapter 8, section 2.
- **Takayama,** an isolated town surrounded by 10,000-foot peaks, offers friendly people, excellent museums, sake breweries, beautiful crafts, and 18th-century merchant homes. One highlight is Hida no Sato, an open-air museum of more than 30 old, thatched farmhouses, showing how local farmers and artisans used to live. See chapter 8, section 1.
- **Kurashiki,** with its willow-lined canal along which cluster distinctive 17th-century warehouses, is perhaps the most picturesque locale in Japan. In addition, Kurashiki is known for its art museums and present-day artisans. See chapter 9, section 9.

2 The Best Temple Destinations

- **Koya-san,** a sacred 3,000-foot mountain of wooden temples, head-shaven monks, towering cypress trees, the most famous samurai burial ground, and chanting in the early morning mists, is far removed from the rest of Japan. Of the 120 Shingon sect temples, some 50 offer accommodations, where you can eat artfully prepared vegetarian cuisine and even study Buddhism. See chapter 9, section 6.

- **Kyoto,** the ancient capital, is home to 1,700 Buddhist temples and 300 shinto shrines, including Ryoanji, with its famous Zen rock garden; Kinkakuji, with its three-story pagoda covered in gold leaf; and Ginkakuji, whose pavillion and garden are designed for the enjoyment of the tea ceremony, moon viewing, and similar aesthetic pursuits. See chapter 7.

3 The Best Landscaped Gardens

- **Kenrokuen in Kanazawa,** begun in 1670 by the once-powerful Maeda clan, took 150 years to create. Its flowers, greenery, ponds, trees, streams, rocks, and footpaths have been tastefully combined to delight even indoor types. This is the largest of the three best gardens in Japan. See chapter 9, section 3.
- **Korakuen Garden** artfully landscapes a pond, running streams, pine trees, plum and cherry trees, bamboo groves, grassy areas, and tea plantations and uses the surrounding hills, as well as Okayama's famous black castle, for a backdrop to its superior design. The 28-acre park is considered one of Japan's most beautiful. See chapter 9, section 8.

4 The Best Shrine of Buddha

The 50-foot tall (15.4m) Daibutsu (Great Buddha), originally built in the 700s, is the largest in Japan. It took 437 tons of bronze, 286 pounds (130kg) of pure gold, 165 pounds (75kg) of mercury, and 7 tons of vegetable wax to build. It is housed in the largest wooden structure in the world, and you can see it by taking an excursion from Kyoto. See chapter 7, section 9.

5 The Best National Parks

- **Daisetsuzan,** with its tall mountains covered with fir and birch trees and sprinkled with wild flowers, its river gorge dotted with waterfalls and spectacular hiking trails, and its natural healing hot-springs waters, is the rare Japan—unspoiled. See chapter 12, section 4.
- **Akan,** where you'll find Kussharo, one of Japan's largest mountain lakes; Mashu, a clear, deep crater lake considered the most beautiful; and Lake Akan, famous for the two volcanoes that rise out of it, for marimo (a spongelike ball of duckweed found in only a few places in the world), and for the hot-springs spa resorts that hug its shores. See chapter 12, section 4.

6 The Best Active Vacations

- In **Akan National Park,** you can hike, canoe, snowmobile, ski, fish, and hunt. Your best bet for personally designed nature vacations is to make arrangements with Dameon Takada in Akan-ko. See chapter 12, section 4.
- **Shinyi Ski Club** organizes weekend trips at a variety of ski areas throughout the ski season, designed for maximum time on the slopes. You could make all the arrangements yourself, but then you'd have to make train reservations as much as six months in advance. See chapter 3, section 4.

- **Mount Fuji,** at 12,388 feet, is the highest mountain in Japan—not surprising then that this symmetrical cone of almost perfect proportions has been described in poetry and painting, widely revered, and, of course, climbed. See chapter 6, section 5.

7 The Best Ryokan (Traditional Japanese Inn)

This is the most difficult of categories to choose from because almost any ryokan worthy of the name (these days many places are called ryokan but shouldn't be) combines beauty, good food, and excellent service. One could make the case for many more to be included, yet the following ryokans are, in my opinion, exceptional because of their superior service, beautiful setting, and/or history.

- **Hiiragiya** is the archetypal ryokan, featuring artfully traditional rooms of wood, bamboo, stone, and lacquer with garden views, and offering elaborate cuisine in the heart of old Kyoto. It opened in 1818, and six generations of the same family have given impeccable service and hospitality here to countless guests, including Charlie Chaplin and Pierre Cardin. See chapter 7, section 4.
- **Wakamatsu** is 110 years old and soothes you with the sound of waves lapping at the shore, scenic views, fresh seafood (right from the boats), stunning traditional interiors (pebble and burl wood corridors, handmade paper shoji, cedar wood baths, carved transoms), healing hot-springs waters, and, of course, personal, attentive service. See chapter 12, section 2.
- **Shusuien** has consistently won top place for cuisine and is listed among the top 10 for service in annual competitions rating the 100 best accommodations in Japan. Located in Ibusuki at the southern tip of Kyushu, it has a staff of 120 employees to pamper you and hot-springs baths to soak your tension away. Need I say more? See chapter 11, section 8.
- **Shigetomiso** was once a villa for the Shimazu clan, making it resonate with history—even recent history, as a sequence of the James Bond movie *You Only Live Twice* was filmed in one of the rooms. Set on a hill sporting a flowering garden and a waterfall, it overlooks Kagoshima Bay and Mt. Sakurajima, an active volcano. See chapter 11, section 7.
- **Kurashiki,** in an antique-filled converted sugar warehouse, features a calm inner garden and smiling, friendly service. Each room is uniquely furnished, and it's fun just to wander the corridors and peek into nooks and crannies, admiring all the antiques. See chapter 9, section 9.

8 The Best Minshuku (Inexpensive, Small, Family Inns)

- **Matsubaya,** run by the verbose and friendly Mrs. Hayashi, is a 180-year-old, 11-room inn at the very heart of old Kyoto. I wouldn't miss a meal at her table and a conversation in Japanese—there's no language barrier here where warmth makes up for vocabulary. See chapter 7, section 4.
- **Sosuke** makes you forget you're on the road; make yourself at home around the irori in the traditional living area and at the low dining table where you'll eat local delicacies. Spotlessly clean, run by a smiling couple, and only $70 a day including two meals, this 160-year-old inn is sure to delight the visitor. See chapter 8, section 1.

9 The Best Spas

- **Hakusuikan** is an elegant ryokan that sprawls along the Ibusuki shoreline in southern Kyushu. You'll soak in the hot springs in a wood-and-stone, Edo period (1603–1867) bathing area with pools of varying temperatures, a *rotenburo* (outdoor pool), and a period steam room. You can also savor the luxury of hot sand baths. Expect excellent service—and beauty. See chapter 11, section 8.
- **Thalassa Shima** set right at the entrance to breathtaking Ise Shima Bay, combines the Japanese love for taking the waters with French thalassotherapy (seawater, sea mud, and seaweed treatments). A sauna, whirlpool bath, lounge, library, salon, elegant interiors with expensive artwork, and French or Japanese restaurants, along with a pool overlooking the bay, make this a great getaway. See chapter 9, section 2.
- **Suginoi Palace** is one of the largest and most remarkable baths in all of Japan, filled with lush tropical plants and pools of various sizes and temperatures. There's also a steam room, sauna, Korean-style heated floor to lounge on, and a hot sand pit. What's more, Acqua Beat, in an annex, is a huge simulated beach, bath, and amusement area—designed to keep the young ones happy while you soak. See chapter 11, section 2.
- **Dogo Onsen Honkan** and **Takegawara** are the most traditional spas in Japan. Dogo Onsen Honkan, in Dogo Onsen, is 3,000 years old—the oldest. This bath house was built in 1894 as a three-story wooden structure with shoji screens, tatami rooms, and creaking wooden stairways. Takegawara, in a traditional wooden structure dating to 1879, is the oldest pubic bath in Beppu, a hot-springs town gushing out 130,000 tons of water daily. You'll receive a relaxing hot sand bath here and soak in hot springs for $6.50. See chapter 10, section 2; chapter 11, section 2.
- **Noboribetsu Spa** boasts 11 different types of hot water containing minerals, including sulfur, salt, iron, and gypsum, and it spews forth 10,000 tons of it a day. See chapter 12, section 4.

10 The Best Castles

- **Himeji-jo,** began in the 14th century and nicknamed White Heron Castle, is probably the most beautiful castle in all of Japan and also one of the few original, undamaged ones. With its extensive gates, moats, turrets, and maze of passageways, some ending in deadends, it is one of the best surviving medieval fortifications. See chapter 9, section 7.
- **Nijo** in Kyoto is considered the quintessence of Momoyama architecture. Built by the first Tokugawa shogun, Ieyasu, it has a protective moat and stone walls, as well as ingenious corridors that warned of any enemy's approach. See chapter 7, section 6.
- **Matsumoto-jo,** built in 1504, is a fine example of a feudal castle and boasts the oldest donjon (keep) in Japan. The outside walls, surrounded by a moat, are black, earning it the name Karasu-jo (Crow Castle). See chapter 9, section 8.
- **Matsue-jo,** built in the 16th century, is one of Japan's few remaining original castles, not a reconstruction. See chapter 9, section 10.

11 The Best Experiences of Old Japan

- **Gion,** Kyoto's geisha entertainment district, where one can stroll through austere alleyways unchanged by time, catch a glimpse of an elaborately made-up *maiko* (apprentice) rushing to an appointment, or hear strains of shamisen played behind closed doors. See chapter 7, sections 1 & 6.
- **Asakusa,** the old downtown of Tokyo, where one can taste the *matsuri* (festival) atmosphere, browse in traditional shops, and visit Sensoji Temple—Tokyo's oldest—where a statue of Kannon, the Buddhist goddess of mercy and happiness, still resides. See chapter 5, Walking Tour 1.
- **Uchiko** on the island of Shikoku, with some fine old homes dating to the Edo period and to the turn of the century, including a Kabuki theater. You can also visit the atelier of a man who carries on the local tradition of candlemaking and represents the sixth generation of such artisans. See chapter 10, section 2.

12 The Best Japanese Performing Arts

- **Kabukiza** is Tokyo's most famous Kabuki theatre, staging about eight productions a year. The plays are dramatic, the costumes gorgeous, and the themes universal—love, revenge, and the conflict between personal desire and duty. See chapter 5, section 6.
- **The National Bunraku Theatre** in Osaka presents unique Japanese puppets six times a year. Dressed in black, the puppeteers are right on stage and are highly skilled in making the intricate puppets seem especially lifelike. See chapter 9, section 4.

13 The Best Museums

- **Tokyo National Museum,** the largest museum in Japan, holds the biggest collection of Japanese art in the world. Though the museum has some 86,000 items, only some 4,000 priceless antiques are displayed at one time, including kimono, screens, scrolls, pottery, lacquerware, and bronzes. See chapter 5, section 1.
- **Shikoku Mura Village** is an open-air museum of the Edo period, complete with authentic thatched homes, artisans' workshops, a tea ceremony house, and a 150-year-old rural Kabuki stage. It is located near Takamatsu on Shikoku Island, on the picturesque slope of Yashima Hill. See chapter 10, section 1.
- **Japan Ukiyo-e Museum** is the largest collection of its kind in the world, displaying more than 100,000 prints that include masterpieces of all the well-known ukiyo-e artists. See chapter 8, section 3.
- **The Inro Museum** displays Japan's largest collection of 18th-century *inro* (a small, portable medicine pouch) and *netsuke* (a counterweight). Located in a *kura* (old warehouse), the private collection is comprised of some 300 inro carved from boxwood, ivory, ceramic, and lacquerware. See chapter 8, section 1.

14 The Best Offbeat Experiences

- **Cormorant fishing** is held in July and August near Kyoto and near Nagoya. You board a narrow, wooden boat gaily decorated with paper lanterns to watch the cormorants with rings around their necks (so that they don't swallow their catch) dive under the water for *ayu,* a small river fish. See chapter 7, section 6.

- **Ugiusa no kona,** a facial cosmetic said to soften the skin, can still be bought at a 200-year-old shop in Tokyo's Asakusa district, where Kabuki or geisha come in to buy their makeup. What is *ugiusa no kona?* Nightingale droppings. See chapter 5, section 5.
- **Pachinko** is a kind of pinball machine into which ball bearings are flung and points are amassed based on where they fall. How to find a pachinko parlor? Easy,the game is so popular that they are everywhere in Japan. See chapter 5, section 6.

15 The Best Festivals

- **The Snow Festival** in Sapporo, Hokkaido, features international competitors, huge elaborate statues, and figures carved vividly in snow and ice.
- **Hinamatsuri,** celebrated all over Japan, fetes the future happiness of young girls. Dolls dressed in ancient costumes representing the emperor, empress, and dignitaries with their miniature household articles are set up on tiers.
- **Aoi (hollyhock) Matsuri** is one of Kyoto's largest pageants commemorating imperial processions to the city's shrines.
- **Gion Matsuri,** near Kyoto, a monthlong festival climaxing in a procession of floats, was organized to ask the gods for an end to plague. It dates from the 9th century.
- **Sanja Matsuri** features a parade of 100 portable shrines carried through the streets of Asakusa in old downtown Tokyo.
- **Jidai Masuri** is held in commemoration of the founding of Kyoto and features a procession of 2,000 people dressed in traditional costumes.
- **Tenjin Matsuri** is one of Osaka's biggest festivals, and it dates to the 10th century. A boat procession with more than 100 sacred boats floating down the river is re-enacted.

Getting to Know Japan

2

Japan—3rd Edition—is designed to guide you through your own discoveries of Japan, however brief—or extended—your visit may be. According to the Japan National Tourist Organization (JNTO), the average length of stay for tourists visiting Japan is 12.3 days. To see all the places I describe, however, you would need approximately three *months.* So, in planning your itinerary, you should be selective. Decide beforehand what your priorities are—whether you want to concentrate on temples, hot-spring spas, landscaped gardens, or breathtaking mountain scenes. Brief introductions to each destination chapter should give you an idea of whether the destination suits your itinerary. Although the Japanese archipelago consists of more than 3,000 islands, I've limited the scope of this book to the main islands of Hokkaido, Honshu, Shikoku, and Kyushu. On these four islands you'll find all of Japan's major cities and historical sights.

1 The Regions in Brief

Separated from mainland China and Korea by the Sea of Japan, the nation of Japan stretches in an arc about 1,800 miles long from northeast to southwest but it is only 250 miles wide at its broadest point. Japan consists primarily of four main islands—Hokkaido, Honshu, Shikoku, and Kyushu. Surrounding these large islands are more than 3,000 smaller islands and islets, most of them uninhabited; farther to the south are the Okinawan islands, perhaps best known for the fierce fighting that took place there during World War II. If you were to superimpose Japan's four main islands onto a map of the United States, they would stretch all the way from Maine down to northern Florida, which should give you an idea of the diversity of Japan's climate, flora, and scenery.

Of the four main islands, Honshu is the largest and the most important historically and culturally—the place where most visitors spend the bulk of their time. Honshu is the home of the ancient capitals of Nara, Kyoto, and Kamakura, in addition to such bustling metropolises as Osaka, Nagoya, Hiroshima, and Tokyo, the modern capital of Japan. Hokkaido, the next-largest island, lies to the north of Honshu and is regarded as the country's last frontier, with its wide-open pastures, wildlife, and national parks of mountains, woods, and lakes. Nature lovers will want to head to Hokkaido.

The southernmost of the four main islands is Kyushu, with a mild subtropical climate, active volcanoes, and hot-spring spas. Because it's the closest to Korea and China, Kyushu served as a gateway to the continental mainland throughout much of Japan's history, later becoming the springboard for both traders and Christian missionaries from the West. Shikoku, the smallest of the four islands, remains fairly undeveloped and is famous for its 88 Buddhist temples, founded by one of Japan's most interesting historical figures, the Buddhist priest Kukai, known posthumously as Kobo Daishi.

As much as 75% of Japan consists of mountains, most of them volcanic in origin. Altogether, there are some 265 volcanoes, more than 30 of them still considered active. Mt. Fuji (on Honshu), now dormant, is Japan's most famous volcano, while Mt. Aso (on Kyushu) is the largest volcano in the world. In 1991 the eruption of Mt. Unzen (in southern Kyushu) killed more than 30 people. Because of its volcanic origins, the country has been plagued by earthquakes throughout the centuries (including a huge destructive 1993 earthquake and the Great Hanshin Earthquake, which hit in 1995).

Even though Japan is only slightly smaller than California in area, it has about *half* the population of the United States. And because three-fourths of the nation is mountainous and therefore uninhabitable, its people are concentrated primarily in only 10% of the country's landmass, with the rest of the area devoted to agriculture. In this island nation—isolated physically from the rest of the world; struck repeatedly through the centuries by earthquakes, fires, and typhoons; and possessed of only limited space for harmonious living—geography and topography have played a major role both in determining its development and in shaping its culture, customs, and arts.

2 Japan Today

Hardly a day goes by that one doesn't hear something about Japan, whether the subject is trade and fair competition or Japan's increasingly prominent role in world affairs. Yet, although Japan is constantly in the news, it remains something of an enigma to people in the Western world. What best describes Japan? Is it the giant producer of cars and computers and a whole array of sleek electronic goods that compete favorably with the best in the West? Or is it still, behind its phenomenal economic growth, the land of the geisha and bonsai, the punctilious tea ceremony and delicate art of flower arrangement? Has it become, in its outlook and popular culture, a country more Western than Asian; or has it retained its unique ancient traditions as it assumes a central place in the modern industrialized world?

Japan, in fact, is an intricate blend of East *and* West, and therefore not an easy nation for Westerners to comprehend. Discovering Japan is like peeling an onion—you uncover one layer only to discover more layers underneath. Thus, no matter how long you stay in Japan, you never stop learning something new about it, and to me that constant discovery is one of the most fascinating aspects of being there. An American journalist who has lived in Japan more than 20 years, and written several books on the land and its people, has told me that she still doesn't understand all the nuances of Japanese culture and customs, and is amazed to find new aspects of the country almost daily.

Even if you have difficulty with the language, however, you'll find Japan navigable. It's one of the safest countries in the world. In general you don't have to worry about

Japan

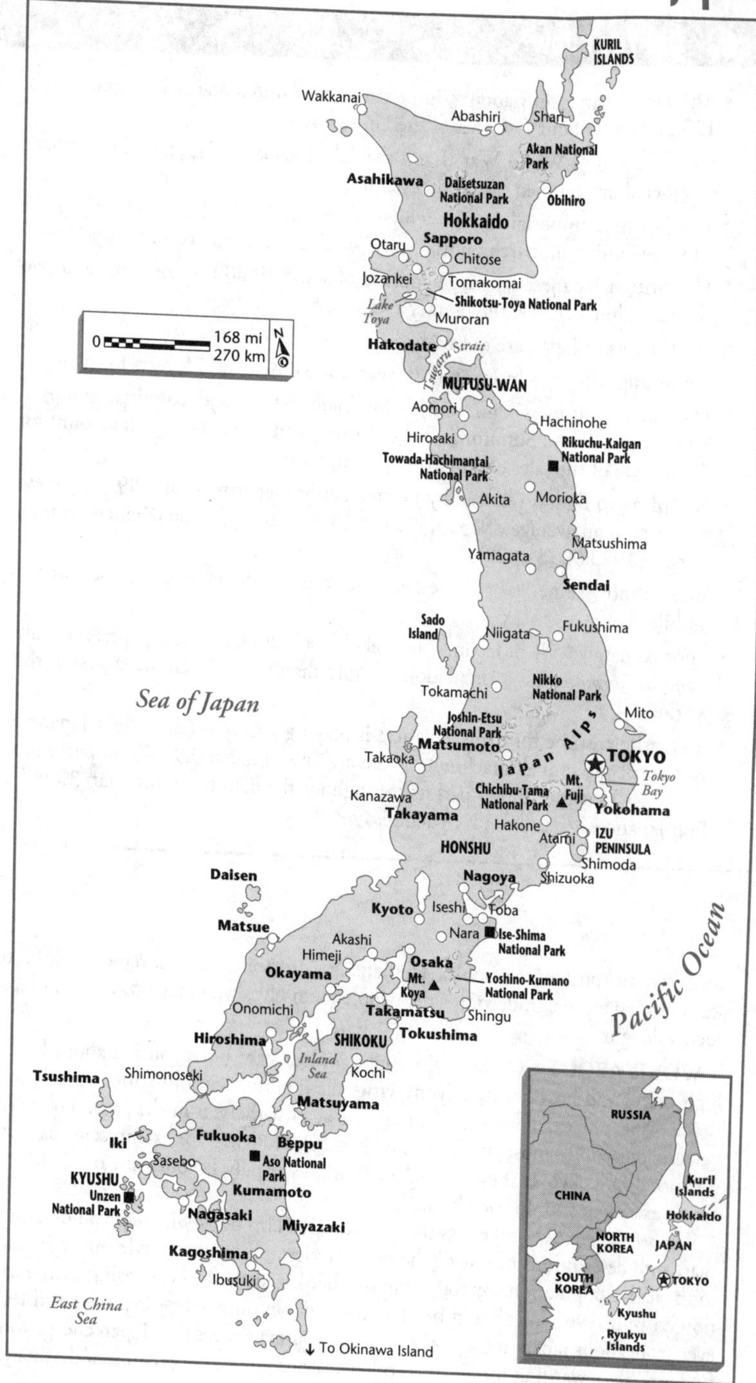
KURIL ISLANDS
Wakkanai
Abashiri
Shari
Akan National Park
Asahikawa
Daisetsuzan National Park
Obihiro
Hokkaido
Sapporo
Otaru
Chitose
Jozankei
Tomakomai
Shikotsu-Toya National Park
Lake Toya
Muroran
0
168 mi
270 km
N
Hakodate
Tsugaru Strait
MUTUSU-WAN
Aomori
Hachinohe
Hirosaki
Rikuchu-Kaigan National Park
Towada-Hachimantai National Park
Akita
Morioka
Matsushima
Yamagata
Sendai
Sado Island
Niigata
Fukushima
Sea of Japan
Tokamachi
Nikko National Park
Mito
Joshin-Etsu National Park
Matsumoto
Japan Alps
TOKYO
Takaoka
Tokyo Bay
Mt. Fuji
Chichibu-Tama National Park
Kanazawa
Yokohama
Takayama
Hakone
Atami
IZU PENINSULA
HONSHU
Shimoda
Nagoya
Shizuoka
Daisen
Kyoto
Iseshi
Toba
Matsue
Nara
Ise-Shima National Park
Akashi
Himeji
Osaka
Okayama
Mt. Koya
Yoshino-Kumano National Park
Onomichi
Takamatsu
Shingu
Pacific Ocean
Hiroshima
SHIKOKU
Tokushima
Inland Sea
Kochi
Tsushima
Shimonoseki
Matsuyama
Fukuoka
Iki
Beppu
Sasebo
Aso National Park
KYUSHU
Unzen National Park
Kumamoto
Nagasaki
Miyazaki
Kagoshima
Ibusuki
East China Sea
To Okinawa Island
RUSSIA
CHINA
Kuril Islands
Hokkaido
NORTH KOREA
JAPAN
SOUTH KOREA
TOKYO
Kyushu
Ryukyu Islands
2090

Did You Know?

- Although Japan is only about 1/25 the size of the United States, its population of 125 million is about *half* that of the United States.
- Until the end of World War II and the Allied invasion, Japan had never been conquered or occupied by another nation.
- The Japanese imperial family, which traces its line back to 660 B.C., is the longest-reigning monarchy in the world, with a succession of 125 emperors.
- The written Japanese language consists of some 10,000 pictographs and two phonetic alphabets, yet the literacy rate in Japan is 99%.
- Most streets in Japan are not named.
- The average life span in Japan is 80 years for women and 75 years for men.
- The Japanese business community is dominated by six major corporate groups—Mitsubishi, Mitsui, Sumitomo, Fuyo, Sanwa, and Ichikan—which account for about 16% of the sales of all Japanese companies.
- According to figures released by Japan's Labor Department in 1993, Japanese men earned an average of ¥313,500 ($3,135) monthly, while Japanese women earned ¥192,800 ($1,928).
- Surveys show some 90% of the Japanese consider themselves members of the middle class.
- Approximately 95% of Japanese households subscribe to a newspaper; the daily *Yomiuri Shimbun* has a circulation of more than 9.7 million, the largest in the world.
- A favorite pastime for many Japanese is playing *pachinko* (an upright Japanese version of the pinball machine). There are an estimated 3.9 million pachinko machines in some 17,000 parlors throughout the country; more than 30 million Japanese are said to play pachinko regularly.

muggers, pickpockets, or crooks. The Japanese are honest and extremely helpful toward foreign visitors. Indeed, it's the people themselves who make traveling in Japan such a delight.

A WORD ABOUT COSTS No doubt you've heard horror stories about Japan's high prices and how hardly anyone visits the country without suffering an initial shock. With the dramatic fall of the dollar against the yen in the '90s, Tokyo has become the world's most expensive city. Food and lodging, for example, are as costly (or more) in Tokyo as they are in New York, especially if you insist on living and eating exactly as you do back home.

The secret is to live and eat as the Japanese do. This book will help you do exactly that, with descriptions of out-of-the-way eateries and Japanese-style inns that cater to the native population. By following this book's advice and exercising a little caution on your own, you should be able to cut down on needless expenses and learn even more about Japan in the process. While you may never find Japan cheap, you'll find it richly rewarding for all those other reasons you chose Japan as a destination in the first place.

3 A Look at the Past

ANCIENT HISTORY (ca. 30,000 B.C.–A.D 710)

According to mythology, Japan's history began when the sun goddess, Amaterasu, sent one of her descendants down to the island of Kyushu to unify the people of Japan. Unification, however, was not realized until a few generations later, when Jimmu, the great-grandson of the goddess's emissary, succeeded in bringing all of the country under his rule. Because of his divine descent, Jimmu became emperor, in 660 B.C. (the date is mythical), thus establishing the line from which all of Japan's emperors are said to derive. However mysterious the origin of this imperial dynasty, it is acknowledged as the longest-reigning such family in the world.

Legend begins to give way to fact only in the 4th century A.D., when a family by the name of Yamato succeeded in expanding its kingdom throughout the country. At the core of the unification achieved by the Yamato family was the Shinto religion. Indigenous to Japan, Shintoism is marked by the worship of nature and the spirits of ancestors and by the belief in the divinity of the emperor.

Although the exact origin of the Japanese people is unknown, we know Japan was once connected to the Asian mainland by a land bridge, and the territory of Japan was occupied as early as 30,000 B.C. From about 10,000 to 300 B.C., hunter-gatherers, called Jomon, thrived in small communities primarily in central Honshu. They are best known for their hand-formed pottery, decorated with cord patterns. The Jomon Period was followed by the Yayoi Period, marked by metalworking, the pottery wheel, and the mastering of irrigated rice cultivation. The Yayoi Period lasted until about A.D. 300, after which the Yamato family unified the state for the first time. Yamato (present-day Japan) began turning cultural feelers toward its great neighbor to the west, China.

In the 6th century, Buddhism, which originated in India, was brought to Japan via China and Korea, and the large-scale Chinese cultural and scholarly influence, including art, architecture, and the use of Chinese characters, began. In 604 the prince regent, Shotoku, greatly influenced by the teachings of Buddhism and Confucianism, drafted a document calling for political reforms and a constitutional government. By 607 he was sending multitudes of Japanese scholars to China to study Buddhism and building Buddhist temples. The most famous is

Dateline

- **660 B.C.** According to tradition, Japan's first emperor, Jimmu, accedes to the throne.
- **A.D. 538–52** Buddhism is introduced into Japan via China and Korea.
- **607** Prince Regent Shotoku sends the first Japanese envoy to China; Horyuji Temple is completed.
- **710** Nara becomes the country's capital.
- **752** The Great Buddha at Todaiji Temple in Nara is completed.
- **794** Kyoto is declared the national capital.
- **806** Kukai (Kobo Daishi) establishes the Shingon sect of Buddhism.
- **1001** Sei Shonagon completes the *Pillow Book*, her collection of court-life impressions.
- **1011** Murasaki Shikibu completes the world's first major novel, *The Tale of Genji.*
- **1192** Minamoto Yoritomo becomes shogun and establishes his government in Kamakura.
- **1274** Mongolian forces, under Kublai Khan, attack Japan but are repelled.
- **1281** The Mongols attack again and are driven back, this time with the help of a typhoon.
- **1333** The Kamakura shogunate falls, and the imperial system is restored.
- **1336** The turbulent but culturally fecund Muromachi Period begins.
- **1397** The Kinkakuji, or Golden Pavilion, is built in Kyoto.

continues

- **1489** The Ginkakuji, or Silver Pavilion, is built in Kyoto.
- **1543** Portuguese ships land in Japan, introducing firearms.
- **1549** St. Francis Xavier arrives in Kyushu to spread the teaching of Christianity.
- **1573** Nobunaga Oda overthrows the Muromachi shogunate and tries to unify the country.
- **1582** Nobunaga is assassinated.
- **1585** General Hideyoshi Toyotomi defeats his enemies and begins a campaign to unify the country; later, he will build a magnificent castle in Osaka.
- **1597** A group of 26 Japanese and European Christians is crucified in Nagasaki.
- **1598** Hideyoshi dies.
- **1600** Tokugawa Ieyasu defeats Hideyoshi's followers and seizes power.
- **1603** Tokugawa becomes shogun and establishes his shogunate in Edo (present-day Tokyo), marking the beginning of a 264-year-long rule by the Tokugawa clan.
- **1615** Tokugawa captures Osaka Castle and wipes out the remaining members of the Hideyoshi clan.
- **1626** Christianity is banned in Japan.
- **1639** Japan closes its doors to the rest of the world, barring all foreigners from landing and all Japanese from leaving; the policy of isolation will last more than 200 years.
- **1853** Commodore Matthew C. Perry of the U.S. Navy arrives in Japan.
- **1854** Perry persuades the Japanese to sign a trade agreement with the United States.

continues

Horyuji Temple, near Nara, said to be the oldest existing wooden structure in the world.

THE NARA PERIOD (710–94) Before the 700s, the site of Japan's capital changed every time a new emperor came to the throne. In 710, however, a permanent capital was established at Nara. Although it remained the capital for only 74 years, seven successive emperors ruled from Nara. The period was graced with the expansion of Buddhism and a flourishing of temple construction throughout the country. Buddhism also inspired the arts, including sculpture, metal casting, painting, and lacquerware. It was during this time that the huge bronze statue of Buddha was cast and erected in Nara. Known as the Daibutsu, it remains Nara's biggest attraction.

THE HEIAN PERIOD (794–1192) In 794 the capital was moved to Heiankyo (present-day Kyoto), and following the example of cities in China, Kyoto was laid out in a grid pattern, with broad roads and canals.

Heiankyo means "capital of peace and tranquillity," and the Heian Period was a glorious time, a time of luxury and prosperity, during which court life reached new heights in artistic pursuits. Chinese characters were blended with a new Japanese writing system, allowing for the first time the flowering of Japanese literature and poetry. The life of the times was captured in the works of two women: Sei Shonagon, who wrote a collection of impressions of her life at court known as the *Pillow Book*, and Murasaki Shikibu, who wrote the world's first major novel, *The Tale of Genji*.

Because the nobles were completely engrossed in their own luxurious lifestyles, however, they failed to notice the growth of military clans in the provinces. The two most powerful warrior clans were the Taira and the Minamoto, whose fierce civil wars tore the nation apart until a young warrior, Minamoto Yoritomo, established supremacy. (*Note:* In Japan, a person's family name—here, Minamoto—comes first, followed by the given name.)

THE KAMAKURA PERIOD (1192–1333) Wishing to set up rule far away from Kyoto, Minamoto Yoritomo established his capital in a remote and easily defendable fishing village called Kamakura, not far from today's Tokyo. He created a military government, ushering in an era in Japan's history in which the power of the country passed from the aristocratic court into the hands of the warrior class. In becoming the nation's first *shogun,* or military dictator, Yoritomo laid the groundwork for 700 years of military governments, until the imperial court was restored in 1868.

The Kamakura Period is perhaps best known for the unrivaled ascendancy of the warrior caste, or *samurai.* Ruled by a rigid honor code, samurai were bound in loyalty to their feudal lord, and they became the only caste allowed to carry weapons. They were supposed to give up their lives for their lord without hesitation, and if they failed in their duty they could regain their honor by committing ritualistic suicide, or *seppuku.* Spurning the soft life led by the Kyoto court nobles, samurai embraced a spartan lifestyle. When Zen Buddhism, with its tenets of mental and physical discipline, was introduced into Japan from China in the 1190s, it appealed greatly to the samurai.

In 1274, Mongolian forces, under Kublai Khan, made an unsuccessful attempt to invade Japan, returning in 1281 with a larger fleet. But a typhoon destroyed the whole fleet. Regarding the cyclone as a gift from the gods, the Japanese called it *kamikaze,* meaning "divine wind," which took on a different significance at the end of World War II, when Japanese pilots flew suicide missions in an attempt to turn the tide of war. More important, however, is the fact that until U.S. and other Allied forces entered Japan at the end of World War II, the country had never been invaded or occupied by a foreign nation.

THE MUROMACHI & AZUCHI-MOMOYAMA PERIODS (1336–1603) After the fall of the Kamakura shogunate, a new feudal government was set up at Muromachi, in Kyoto. The next 200 years, however, were marred by bloody civil wars as daimyo (feudal lords) staked out their fiefdoms. Similar to the barons of Europe, the daimyo owned tracts of land with complete rule over the people who lived on them. Each lord had his retainers, the samurai, who fought his enemies.

These centuries of strife also saw a blossoming of art and culture. Kyoto witnessed the construction of the extravagant Golden and Silver pavilions, as well as the artistic arrangement of Ryoanji Temple's famous rock garden. Noh drama, the tea ceremony, flower arranging, and landscape gardening became the passions of the upper class. At the end of the 16th century, a number of castles were built, both to demonstrate the daimyo's strength and to defend against the firearms introduced in 1543 by the Portuguese.

- **1867** The Tokugawa regime is overthrown, bringing Japan's feudal era to a close.
- **1868** Emperor Meiji assumes power, moves his capital to Edo (renamed Tokyo), and begins the industrialization of Japan.
- **1870** Japan's class system is abolished.
- **1877** Saigo Takamori, a disgruntled samurai, leads a rebellion in Satsuma province, but he is defeated and commits ritual suicide with his followers.
- **1894–95** Japan wins a war against China.
- **1904–5** Japan wins a war against Russia.
- **1910** Japan annexes Korea.
- **1914** World War I breaks out in Europe; Japan sides with the Allies (Great Britain and France) against the Central Powers (Germany and Austria).
- **1923** Tokyo and Yokohama are devastated by a major earthquake.
- **1926** Crown Prince Hirohito succeeds his father, Taisho, as emperor.
- **1931** Japan seizes Manchuria.
- **1933** Japan withdraws from the League of Nations.
- **1937** Japan goes to war against China, occupying Peking (Beijing), Shanghai, and Nanking (Nanjing).
- **1940** As World War II flares in Europe, Japan forms a military (Axis) alliance with Germany and Italy and attacks French Indochina.
- **1941** Japan bombs Pearl Harbor, provoking a declaration of war by the United States; Germany and Italy respond by declaring war on the United States.
- **1945** Hiroshima and Nagasaki suffer atomic bomb attacks by American war

continues

planes; Japan surrenders unconditionally to Allied forces, which then occupy the country under the command of U.S. Gen. Douglas MacArthur.
- **1946** Hirohito renounces the imperial claim to divinity; Japan adopts a new, democratic constitution; women gain the right to vote.
- **1952** The Allied occupation of Japan ends; Japan regains its independence.
- **1956** Japan becomes a member of the United Nations.
- **1964** The XVIII Summer Olympic Games are held in Tokyo.
- **1972** The XI Winter Olympic Games are held in Sapporo; the Okinawan islands are returned by the United States to Japan.
- **1989** Emperor Hirohito dies, after a reign of 63 years.
- **1990** Hirohito's son and heir, Crown Prince Akihito, formally ascends the Japanese throne, proclaiming the new "Era of Peace" (*Heisei*).
- **1993** Crown Prince Naruhito marries Masako Owada, a Harvard-educated commoner, in ancient ceremony.
- **1995** The Great Hanshin Earthquake destroys Kobe. A religious sect releases deadly sarin gas on three commuter subway lines.

In the second half of the 16th century, a brilliant military strategist by the name of Nobunaga Oda almost succeeded in ending the civil wars. Upon Nobunaga's assassination (by one of his own retainers), one of his best generals, Hideyoshi Toyotomi, took up the campaign, built the magnificent Osaka castle, and crushed rebellion to unify Japan.

THE EDO PERIOD (1603–1867) But alas, Hideyoshi died (1598), and power was seized by Tokugawa Ieyasu, a statesman so shrewd and skillful in eliminating enemies that his heirs would continue to rule Japan for the next 250 years. In 1603, Tokugawa set up a shogunate government in Edo (present-day Tokyo), leaving the emperor intact but virtually powerless in Kyoto.

Meanwhile, European influence in Japan was spreading. The first contact with the Western world had occurred in 1543, when Portuguese merchants arrived, followed by Christian missionaries. St. Francis Xavier landed in Kyushu in 1549, remaining for two years and converting thousands of Japanese. By 1580 there were perhaps as many as 150,000 Japanese Christians. Although Japan's rulers at first welcomed foreigners and trade, they gradually became alarmed by Christian missionary influence. Hearing of the Catholic church's power in Rome and fearing expansionist policies of European nations, the shogunate banned Christianity in the early 1600s. In 1597 a group of 26 Japanese and European Christians was crucified in Nagasaki.

The Tokugawa shogunate intensified the campaign against Christians in 1639, when it closed all ports to foreign trade. Adopting a policy of total isolation, the shogunate subsequently forbade foreigners from landing in Japan and Japanese from leaving. Even those Japanese who had been living abroad in overseas trading posts were not allowed to return, but were forced to live the rest of their days in exile. Those who defied the strict decrees were killed. The only exception to this policy of isolation was in Nagasaki, where there was a colony of tightly controlled Chinese merchants and a handful of Dutch, who were confined to a trading post on a tiny island.

Thus began an amazing 200-year period in Japanese history, during which Japan's doors were virtually closed to the rest of the world. It was a time of political stability but also a time when personal freedom was strictly controlled by the Tokugawa government. Japanese society was divided into four distinct classes: the court nobles, the samurai, the farmers, and the merchants. Although nobles occupied the most exalted social position, the real power lay with samurai, and it was probably during the Tokugawa Period that the samurai class reached the zenith of its glory. At the bottom of the social ladder were the merchants, but peace and prosperity led to the development of new entertainment forms to occupy their time. Kabuki drama and woodblock prints became the rage, while stoneware and porcelain, silk brocade for elaborate and gorgeous kimono, and lacquerware improved in quality.

To ensure that no daimyo in the distant provinces would overrun the shogun's power, the Tokugawa government ordered each daimyo to leave his family in Edo (effectively a hostage) and required he spend every other year in Edo. In expending so much time and money traveling back and forth and maintaining residences both in the provinces and in Edo, the daimyo had no resources left over with which to wage a rebellion. Inns and townships sprang up along Japan's major highways to accommodate these elaborate processions of palanquins, samurai, and footmen traveling back and forth between Edo and the provinces through the rough terrain of Japan's mountains.

Yet, even though the Tokugawa government took measures to ensure its supremacy, by the mid-19th century it was clear that the feudal system was outdated and economic power was in the hands of the merchants, with money rather than rice the primary means of exchange. Many samurai families were impoverished, and discontent with the shogunate became widespread.

In 1853, American Commodore Matthew C. Perry sailed to Japan, seeking to gain trading rights. The Japanese, however, were unwilling, and Perry departed, his mission unaccomplished. Returning a year later, he succeeded in forcing the shogun to sign an agreement despite the disapproval of the emperor, thus ending Japan's two centuries of isolation. In 1867, some powerful families succeeded in toppling the Tokugawa regime and restoring the emperor as ruler, thus bringing the feudal era to a close.

MODERN JAPAN (1868 TO THE PRESENT) In 1868, Emperor Meiji moved his imperial government to Edo, renamed it Tokyo (Eastern Capital), and designated it as the official national capital. During the next few decades, known as the Meiji Restoration, Japan rapidly progressed from a feudal agricultural society of samurai and peasants to an industrial nation. The samurai were stripped of their power and no longer allowed to carry swords. A prime minister and a cabinet were appointed, a constitution was drafted, and a parliament, called the Diet, was elected. With the enthusiastic support of Emperor Meiji for Japan's modernization and Westernization, the latest in technological know-how was imported, including railway and postal systems, along with specialists and advisers. Between 1881 and 1898 as many as 6,177 British, 2,764 Americans, 913 Germans, and 619 French were retained by the Japanese government to help modernize the country.

Meanwhile, Japan made incursions into neighboring lands. In 1894–95 it fought and won a war against China; in 1904–5 it attacked and defeated Russia; and in 1910 it annexed Korea. After militarists gained control of the government in the 1930s, these expansionist policies continued and Japan went to war with China in 1937.

On December 7, 1941, Japan attacked Pearl Harbor, entering World War II against the United States. Although Japan went on to conquer Hong Kong, Singapore, Burma, Malaysia, the Philippines, the Dutch East Indies, and Guam, the tide eventually turned and American bombers reduced to rubble every major Japanese city, with the exception of historic Kyoto. On August 6, 1945, the United States dropped the world's first atomic bomb over Hiroshima, followed on August 9 by a second, over Nagasaki. Japan submitted to unconditional surrender on August 14, and soon thereafter American and other Allied occupation forces arrived in the country, where they remained until 1952. For the first time in its history, Japan had suffered defeat and occupation by a foreign power.

The experience had a profound effect on the Japanese people, yet they emerged from their defeat and began to rebuild. In 1946, under the guidance of the Allied military authority, headed by U.S. Gen. Douglas MacArthur, they adopted a democratic constitution renouncing war and divesting the emperor of divinity. A parliamentary system of government was set up, and in 1947 the first general elections held. The following year, many Pacific War militarists were tried and convicted. To the younger generation, the occupation was less a painful burden to be suffered than an opportunity to remake their country, with American encouragement, into a modern, peace-loving, and democratic state.

A special relationship developed between the Japanese and their American occupiers. In the early 1950s, as the cold war between the United States and the Communist world erupted in hostilities in Korea, that relationship grew into a firm alliance, strengthened by a security treaty. In 1952 the occupation ended, and Japan joined the United Nations as an independent country.

Avoiding involvement in foreign conflicts, the Japanese concentrated on economic recovery. Through a series of policies favoring domestic industries and shielding Japan from foreign competition, they achieved rapid economic growth. By the mid-1960s, they had transformed their nation into a major industrialized power.

But since the early 1970s, a snowballing trade surplus has created friction between Japan and the United States, its chief trading partner. In the 1980s especially, as Japanese automobile sales in the United States soared while foreign sales in Japan continued to be restricted, disagreements between Tokyo and Washington heated up.

In the 1990s the demand by the United States—as well as the European Community, another major trading partner—that Japan liberalize its trade policies has been coupled with the appeal that Tokyo take a more active role in world affairs, consonant with its economic power. A principal reason for Tokyo's reluctance to go beyond what Washington calls "checkbook diplomacy" (in 1991, Japan contributed about $13 billion to the Allied effort in the Persian Gulf War but refused to send a token military force) is the constitution's 1967 restriction on the use of Japanese military forces for any purpose other than national defense. But in 1992, bowing to international pressure, Japan agreed to take part in United Nations peacekeeping operations in Cambodia. It sent a small contingent of troops (the first to serve outside Japan since World War II), as well as civilian police instructors. In doing so, the government went against strong public opposition.

As to politics, under the constitution, adopted in 1946, supreme power resides with the people, who elect the National Diet. The prime minister and his cabinet are members of the Diet and are chosen generally from the majority party. There are six major political parties, the largest of which is the Liberal Democratic Party (LDP). Founded in 1955, the LDP held power uninterruptedly for nearly four decades, giving Japan the kind of political stability it needed to grow economically and compete in world markets. By mid-1993, however, a series of political and financial scandals involving top LDP officials eroded public confidence; in hastily called elections, the LDP lost control of the Diet to a coalition of reform-minded parties. Since then, the government has floundered as prime ministers from various parties were elected, but few remained above political scandal. Two events in 1995 further weakend confidence in the government: the damage of the Great Hanshin Earthquake, and the poor handling of the rescue and rebuilding; and the Aum Shinrykyo gas attack. The 90s in Japanese government may well be remembered as helmless.

Usually upbeat, sure of their culture and customs, the Japanese received two shocks in 1995 that weakened the very confidence of the nation. In the aftermath of the

Great Hanshin Earthquake, which destroyed Kobe and killed nearly 5,000 people on January 24, 1995, it not only became evident that Japanese buildings, railway lines, and highways were *not* earthquake-proof as the government (in a Confucian society, the "father") had led them to believe, but rescue efforts were almost laughably inadequate and inefficient.

Two months later the Japanese suffered another national blow: On March 20 an obscure religious sect, Aum Shinrykyo (Supreme Truth), with a penchant for scientific know-how, made history as it released the deadly nerve gas sarin on three different commuter lines at rush hour, killing at least 12 people and injuring nearly 6,000. That such a crime, the first of its kind in the history of the world, should occur in Tokyo left people bewildered. The attack was followed by the murder of one of the Aum suspects and the attempted murder of the National Police Agency (NPA) chief.

These cultural shocks are not easy to overcome for the Japanese, who pride themselves on the safety and orderliness of their society, and one cannot help but notice a new wariness.

4 Famous Japanese

Basho (1644–94) Japan's most famous haiku poet. Basho spent much of his life traveling the country. He left a rich legacy of haiku written about its various regions.

Chikamatsu Monzaemon (1653–1724) Japan's greatest dramatist of the Edo Period. Chikamatsu wrote plays for Kabuki and Joruri (puppet theater). His works reflect the everyday social life of Edo townspeople, including the popular theme of *shinju,* double suicide committed by lovers.

Hokusai Katsushika (1760–1849) A notable and prolific *ukiyo-e* (woodblock print) artist of the late Edo Period, thought to have influenced the French Impressionists. He is especially famous for his 36 landscape paintings of Mt. Fuji.

Ichikawa Danjuro (1660–1704) Kabuki actor of the early Edo Period and originator of red-and-black facial paint and exaggerated movements. In his memory, Kabuki actors through the centuries have adopted his name and acting style; thus, today's star actor is the 12th Ichikawa Danjuro.

Izumo-no-Okuni (16th to 17th century) An actress, credited with founding Kabuki. According to folklore, she and a troupe of female dancers began performing rather lewd dances in Kyoto, gaining a wide, appreciative audience. However, the shogun eventually forbade women performers on the stage. It therefore became necessary for men to assume female roles, and today all Kabuki roles are performed by men.

Kawabata Yasunari (1899–1972) Winner of the Nobel Prize for Literature in 1968 and considered the foremost novelist of modern Japan. Among his most famous works are *Yukiguni* (*Snow Country*) and *Izu-no-Odoriko* (*The Izu Dancer*). He committed suicide at the age of 73.

Kitagawa Utamaro (1753–1806) One of the foremost ukiyo-e painters of his time. He is famous for depictions of beautiful women, use of limited colors, and backgrounds.

Kukai (774–835) Known posthumously as Kobo Daishi and regarded as Japan's most important Buddhist religious figure. After studying Buddhism in China, Kukai returned to found the Shingon Esoteric sect of Buddhism, establishing a seminary on Mt. Koya. He traveled to various parts of the country, teaching, and left behind many temples, some of which remain today, especially on Mt. Koya and Shikoku.

Emperor Meiji (1852–1912) Japan's 122nd emperor, credited with leading his nation from a feudalistic society into the industrial age. He ascended the throne at 15 and was only 17 at the time of the Meiji Restoration, which returned the imperial family's power. He went on to create a modern constitution and lead Japan in the Sino-Japanese War (1894–95) and the Russo-Japanese War (1904–5).

Mishima Yukio (1925–70) One of Japan's most prominent modern writers, both at home and abroad. Among his most famous works is *Kinkakuji* (*The Temple of the Golden Pavilion*), about a young priest who sets fire to Kinkakuji Temple to visualize what he thinks must surely be the most beautiful scene in the world. Shocking the literary world, Mishima formed a radical right-wing movement, attempted a coup, and failing, committed seppuku (disembowelment, followed by decapitation by one of his followers).

Miyamoto Musashi (?–1645) Foremost swordsman of the Edo Period and author of *Gorin-no-sho*, which advises that in order to master the sword, one must first master one's spirit. Miyamoto originated a new technique in fencing, in which a long sword is held in the right hand, a short sword in the left.

Murasaki Shikibu (980–1014) Court lady to the emperor's wife. Her life at the imperial court provided her with much insight for her classic work, *The Tale of Genji*. Regarded as the world's first major novel, it describes the life and love affairs of Hikaru Genji and provides a fascinating look at Japanese nobility in the 11th century.

Natsume Soseki (1867–1918) One of Japan's most prominent literary figures of the Meiji Period, whose portrait appears on the ¥1,000 note. Among his many works, *I Am a Cat* is best known; it is a humorous commentary on human society, written from the viewpoint of a cat.

Saigo Takamori (1828–77) A popular hero of the Meiji Restoration, who as a samurai subsequently became disgruntled and led a group of fellow warriors in the Seinan Civil War, in Kyushu, in 1877. Defeated, he and his followers committed suicide. He remains, however, a popular historical figure; all Japanese are familiar with his statue in Ueno Park in Tokyo.

Sen-no-Rikyu (1522–91) Master of the tea ceremony, Rikyu elevated it to an art, utilizing such Zen principles as *wabi* (quiet elegance) and *sabi* (quaintness). Teaching simplistic beauty over gaudy pompousness, Rikyu placed great importance on both the environment and one's mental state during the tea ceremony; the tearoom, the garden, even the tea utensils, he asserted, are significant. Rikyu taught the tea ceremony to both Nobunaga Oda and Hideyoshi Toyotomi and therefore wielded tremendous influence, but after overstepping his boundaries by placing a likeness of himself atop Daitokuji Temple's main gate, he was ordered to commit suicide. After his death, Rikyu's sons founded three different schools of the tea ceremony, all in existence today.

Shotoku Taishi (574–622) Serving as prince regent to the emperor, Shotoku is remembered for his intelligence and virtue and for his promulgation of the Seventeen Articles Constitution, an administrative ethics code for court officials, which served to strengthen imperial power. Making Buddhism a cornerstone of his government policies, he ensured the religion's growth throughout Japan and ordered construction of Horyuji Temple near Nara.

5 Japanese Culture

TRADITIONAL JAPANESE THEATER

KABUKI Probably Japan's best-known traditional theater art, Kabuki is also one of the country's most popular forms of entertainment. Visit a performance and it's easy to see why. In a word, Kabuki is fun! The plays are dramatic, the costumes are gorgeous, the stage settings are often fantastic, and the themes are universal—love, revenge, and the conflict between duty and personal feelings. Probably one of the reasons Kabuki is so popular even today is that it developed centuries ago as a form of entertainment for the common people in feudal Japan, particularly the merchants. And one of Kabuki's interesting aspects is that all roles—even those depicting women—are portrayed by men.

It didn't start out that way. In Kyoto in the early 1600s, a group of women originated Kabuki by giving performances of erotic dances. Needless to say, the dances were enthusiastically received by the audience, and it wasn't long before there were troupes of women of rather questionable repute giving all kinds of lewd performances. Finally, the shogun decided that the dances were too vulgar, and he banned all women from performing. Kabuki was then taken over by all-male companies, who transformed it into the drama it is today.

Kabuki has changed little in the past 100 years. Altogether, there are more than 300 Kabuki plays, all written before this century. For a Westerner, one of the more arresting things about a Kabuki performance is the audience itself. Because this has always been entertainment for the masses, the audience can get quite lively, with yells, guffaws, and laughter from spectators. In fact, old woodcuts of cross-eyed men apparently stemmed from Kabuki—when things got a little too rowdy, actors would stamp their feet and strike a cross-eyed pose in an attempt to get the audience's attention.

Of course, you won't be able to understand what's being said. Indeed, because much of Kabuki drama dates from the 18th century, even the Japanese sometimes have difficulty understanding the language. But it doesn't matter. Many theaters have programs and earphones that describe the plots in minute detail, often in English as well. Thus, you can follow the story and enjoy Kabuki just as much as everyone around you.

NOH Whereas Kabuki developed as a form of entertainment for the masses, Noh was a much more traditional and aristocratic form of theater. In contrast to Kabuki's extroverted liveliness, Noh is very calculated, slow, and restrained. The oldest form of theater in Japan, it has changed very little in the past 600 years. The language is so archaic that the Japanese cannot understand it at all, which explains in part why Noh does not have the popularity that Kabuki does. *Note:* Don't expect programs in English.

As in Kabuki, all the performers are men. The subject matter of Noh's some 240 surviving plays is usually supernatural beings, beautiful women, mentally confused people, or tragic-heroic events. Performers usually wear masks.

Because the action is slow, watching an entire evening can be quite tedious unless you are particularly interested in Noh dance and music. You may just want to drop in for a short while. In between Noh plays, there are short comic reliefs called *kyogen,* which usually make fun of life in the 1600s.

BUNRAKU Bunraku is traditional Japanese puppet theater. But contrary to what you might expect, Bunraku is for adults, with themes centering on love and revenge, sacrifice and suicide. Many dramas now adapted for Kabuki were first written for th Bunraku stage.

Impressions

It has always seemed a grave reflection on the Japanese character that their language, with the exception of the word "fool"—and "countrified fool" is extremely strong—should contain no opportunities for invective.

—Peter Quennell, *A Superficial Journey Through Tokyo and Peking,* 1932

Popular in Japan since the 17th century, and at times even more popular than Kabuki, Bunraku is fascinating to watch because the puppeteers are right onstage with their puppets. Dressed in black, they're wonderfully skilled in making the puppets seem like living beings. Usually, there are three puppeteers for each puppet, which is about three-fourths human size. One puppeteer is responsible for movement of the puppet's head, as well as for the expression on its face, and for the movement of the right arm and hand. Another puppeteer operates the puppet's left arm and hand, while the third moves the legs. Although at first the puppeteers are somewhat distracting, after a while you forget they're there as the puppets assume personalities of their own. The narrator, who tells the story and speaks the various parts, is an important figure in the drama. The narrator is accompanied by a traditional three-stringed Japanese instrument called a *shamisen.* By all means try to see Bunraku if possible. The most famous presentations are at the Osaka Bunraku Theater, but there are performances in Tokyo and other major cities as well.

THE TEA CEREMONY

Tea was brought to Japan from China more than 1,000 years ago. It first became popular among Buddhist priests as a means of staying awake during long hours of meditation. Gradually, its use filtered down among the upper classes, and in the 16th century the tea ceremony was perfected by a merchant named Sen-no-Rikyu. Using the principles of Zen and the spiritual discipline of the samurai, the tea ceremony became a highly stylized ritual, with detailed rules on how tea should be prepared, served, and drunk. The simplicity of movement and tranquility of setting are meant to free the mind from the banality of everyday life and allow the spirit to enjoy peace. In a sense, it is a form of spiritual therapy.

The tea ceremony, *cha-no-yu,* is still practiced in Japan today and is regarded as a form of disciplinary training for mental composure, and for etiquette and manners. There are many schools with different methods for performing the tea ceremony throughout the country. Several of Japan's more famous landscape gardens have teahouses on their grounds where you can sit on tatami, drink the frothy green tea (called *maccha*), eat some sweets (meant to counteract the bitter taste of the tea), and contemplate the view.

IKEBANA

Whereas a Westerner is likely to put a bunch of flowers into a vase and be done with it, the Japanese consider the arrangement of flowers tantamount to an art. Most young girls have at least some training in flower arranging, known as *ikebana,* and there are various schools and differing methods on the subject. First becoming popular among the aristocrats during the Heian Period (A.D. 794–1192) and spreading to the common people in the 14th to the 16th centuries, traditional ikebana, in its simplest form, is supposed to represent heaven, man, and earth. Department store galleries sometimes have ikebana exhibitions; otherwise, check with the local tourist office.

GARDENS

Nothing is left to chance in a Japanese landscape garden. The shape of hills and trees, the placement of rocks and waterfalls—everything is skillfully arranged in a faithful reproduction of nature. To the Westerner, perhaps, it may seem a bit strange to arrange nature to look like nature. But to the Japanese, even nature can be improved upon to make it more pleasing, with the best possible use of limited space. The Japanese are masters at this, as a visit to any of their famous gardens will testify.

In fact, they have been sculpting gardens for more than 1,000 years. At first the gardens were designed for walking and boating, with ponds, artificial islands, and pavilions. As with almost everything else in Japanese life, however, Zen Buddhism exerted an influence, making gardens simpler and attempting to create the illusion of boundless space within a small area. To the Buddhist, a garden was not for merriment but for contemplation—an uncluttered and simple landscape on which to rest the eyes. Japanese gardens often use the principle of "borrowed landscape"—that is, using the surrounding mountains and landscape by incorporating them into the overall design and impact of the garden.

Basically, there are three styles of Japanese gardens. One style, called *tsukiyama*, uses ponds, hills, and streams to depict nature in miniature. Another style, known as the *karesansui*, uses stones and raked sand in the place of water and is often seen at Zen Buddhist temples. It was developed during the Muromachi Period as a representation of Zen spiritualism, with the most famous rock garden being Ryoanji Temple's in Kyoto. The third style, called *chaniwa*, emerged with the tea ceremony and is built around a teahouse, with an eye toward simplicity and tranquility. Such a garden will often feature stone lanterns, a stone basin filled with water, and water flowing through a bamboo pipe.

Famous gardens in Japan include Kenrokuen and Suizenji Parks in Kanazawa, Korakuen Park in Okayama, and Ritsurin Park in Takamatsu. Kyoto alone has about 50 gardens, including the famous Zen rock gardens at Daitokuji and Ryoanji Temples, the gardens at both the Golden and Silver Pavilions, and those at Heian Shrine, Nijo Castle, and the Katsura Imperial Villa.

MARTIAL ARTS

Japan's three most popular martial arts—judo, karate, and kendo—all have roots stretching back to the age of the samurai. **Judo,** the best-known martial art, originated in Japan and is based on jujitsu, a deadly martial art practiced by the samurai as a means of defense. Founded in 1882 by Jigoro Kano, who established the Kodokan Dojo, judo became popular throughout the world after World War II. Judo trains both the body and the mind, with bouts won by one's throwing the opponent or getting hold of him, through several techniques.

Karate, on the other hand, was used as a means of defense and attack, at a time when common people were forbidden to carry weapons. It developed in ancient China and was imported to Japan via Okinawa. In karate, hands and feet are used to strike vulnerable areas of the opponent, with power achieved through speed and concentration. Although it is generally thought to be an aggressive sport, karate master Gichin Funakoshi, who popularized it, emphasized there is no "first strike" in karate.

The oldest of Japan's martial arts is **kendo,** an embodiment of the samurai's philosophy of life, combined with swordmanship. Practiced today with bamboo swords and protective clothing, it, too, emphasizes the training of the mind and body as opponents try to strike each other's mask, arm, or body, using the correct combination of force, bodily posture, and sword position.

Another popular martial art is **aikido,** which stresses the spiritual aspect of the sport and is said to be "zen in motion." Using the correct breathing and meditation, opponents try to throw or disable each other by attacking weak points.

6 Religion

The main religions in Japan are Shintoism and Buddhism, and many Japanese consider themselves believers in both. Whereas Westerners might find it difficult to belong to two completely different religious organizations, the Japanese find nothing unusual about it and incorporate both into their lifestyle. Most Japanese, for example, are married in a Shinto ceremony and have a Buddhist funeral.

Japanese generally visit a temple or shrine only for a specific purpose. On New Year's, for example, many of them throng to shrines to pray for good fortune in the coming year, while in mid-July or mid-August they go to pay their respects to their ancestors. As such, neither religion has a great influence on everyday life. Rather, religion is more a way of thinking, a way of relating to one's world, environment, and family. The Japanese appreciation of natural beauty and strong sense of duty and obligation, for example, have religious roots.

SHINTOISM A native religion of Japan, Shintoism is the worship of ancestors and national heroes, as well as of all natural things, both animate and inanimate. These natural things are thought to embody gods, called *kami,* and can be anyone or anything—mountains, trees, the moon, stars, rivers, seas, fires, animals, rocks, even vegetables. In this respect, the beliefs of Shintoism resemble those of Native American tribes. Shintoism also embraces much of Confucianism, which entered Japan in the 5th century and stressed the importance of family and loyalty. There are no scriptures in Shintoism, as there is no ordained code of morals or ethics.

The most important goddess in Shintoism is Amaterasu, the sun goddess, who is considered the progenitor of the Japanese imperial family. Thus emperors held the revered position of a living god for more than 1,500 years, until the end of World War II, when Emperor Hirohito was forced to renounce the claim to divinity and admit that he was an ordinary mortal. At this time, Shintoism also lost its official status as the national religion, a position it had held since the Meiji Restoration (1868). However, Shintoism has not lost its popularity and claims more than 80 million followers in Japan. As for the imperial family, it still occupies a special place in the hearts of the Japanese.

The place of worship in Shintoism is called a *jinja,* or shrine. Every city, town, village, and hamlet has at least one shrine, and to most inhabitants it embodies the soul of their district. The most famous shrines are Meiji Shrine in Tokyo, the Ise Shrines in the Ise-Shima National Park (dedicated to the sun goddess), and Itsukushima Shrine on Miyajima Island.

The most obvious sign of a shrine is its *torii,* an entrance gate, usually of wood, consisting of two tall poles topped with either one or two crossbeams. Sometimes there will be several torii spread along the path leading to the shrine, reminding visitors they are approaching a shrine and giving them time to achieve the proper frame of mind. Before reaching the shrine itself, you'll pass a water trough with communal cups where the Japanese will rinse out their mouths and wash their hands. Purification and cleanliness are important in Shintoism because they show respect to the gods, aspects that have carried over even today in the Japanese custom of bathing and removing shoes indoors.

At the shrine itself, worshippers will throw a few coins into a money box, clap their hands three times to get the gods' attention, and then bow their heads and pray. Sometimes there will be a rope attached to a gong that's even louder in calling the gods. Worshippers pray for good health, protection, the safe delivery of a child, and that sons get into good universities and daughters find good husbands. Some shrines are considered lucky for love, while others are good against certain ailments. You can ask any favor of the gods. Shrines are also the sites of many festivals and are visited on important occasions throughout one's life, including marriage and certain birthdays. New Year's is also a popular time to visit famous shrines around the country.

BUDDHISM Shintoists have shrines (*jinja*); Buddhists, temples (*otera*). Instead of torii, temples will often have an entrance gate with a raised doorsill and heavy doors. Temples may also have a cemetery on their grounds, which Shinto shrines never have, and a pagoda.

Founded in India in the 5th century, Buddhism came to Japan in the 6th century via China and Korea, bringing with it the concept of eternal life. By the end of the 6th century, Buddhism had gained such popularity that Prince Regent Shotoku, one of Japan's most remarkable historical figures, declared Buddhism the state religion and based many of his governmental policies on its tenets. Another important Buddhist leader to emerge was a priest called Kukai, known posthumously as Kobo Daishi. After studying Buddhism in China in the early 800s, he returned and founded the Shingon sect of Buddhism, establishing a retreat atop Mt. Koya. The temples he built throughout Japan, including the famous 88 temples on Shikoku Island and those on Mt. Koya, continue to attract millions of pilgrims today.

Probably the Buddhist sect best known to the West, however, is Zen Buddhism. Considered the most Japanese form of Buddhism, Zen is the practice of meditation and a strictly disciplined lifestyle to rid one of desire so that one can achieve enlightenment. There are no rites in Zen Buddhism, no dogmas, no theological conceptions of divinity. You do not analyze rationally but are supposed to know things intuitively. The strict and simple lifestyle of Zen appealed greatly to Japan's samurai warrior class, and many of Japan's arts, including the tea ceremony, arose from the practice of Zen.

As in Shintoism, there are several popular festivals relating to Buddhism. Probably the most widely practiced is O'bon, celebrated in July or August, depending on the region and the time when the spirits of departed ancestors are thought to return. Many Japanese return to their home towns for O'bon, to visit their ancestors' graves and partake in O'bon dances held at shrines or temples or other public places.

ZAZEN *Zazen*, or meditation, is practiced by Zen Buddhists as a form of mental or spiritual training. Laymen meditate to relieve stress and clear the mind.

Zazen is achieved if one sits down in a cross-legged lotus position, with the neck and back straight and the eyes slightly open. Usually done by a group—in a semidark room with cushions, facing the wall—meditation is helped along by a monk, who stalks noiselessly behind the meditators. If someone squirms or moves, he is whacked on the shoulders with a stick to help him get back to meditating.

There are several Zen temples where foreigners can join in zazen (see chapter 7). Through a notice in the *Japan Times*, I spent a weekend at a Zen temple outside Tokyo and tried zazen, ate vegetarian meals, and helped in household chores. If you'd like to try zazen yourself, contact the Tourist Information Center in Tokyo or Kyoto. Check the *Japan Times* also to see whether a session of zazen is being organized with instruction in English for foreigners.

7 Minding Your P's & Q's

SOCIAL LIFE & CUSTOMS

As an island nation with few natural resources, Japan's 123 million people are its greatest asset. Hard-working, honest, and proud about performing a task well no matter how insignificant it may seem, the Japanese are well known for their politeness and helpfulness to strangers. Indeed, hardly anyone returns from a trip to Japan without stories of the extraordinary goodness and kindness extended by the Japanese.

With approximately 99% of the population consisting of ethnic Japanese, Japan is one of the most homogeneous nations in the world. Originally of Mongoloid stock, with strains of a few other Asian peoples thrown in, the Japanese have had remarkably little influx of other gene pools into the country since the 8th century. That, coupled with Japan's actual physical isolation as an island nation, has more than anything else led to a feeling among the Japanese that they belong to a single huge tribe that is different from any other people on earth. You'll often hear a Japanese preface a statement or opinion with the words "We Japanese," implying all Japanese think alike and all people can basically be divided into two categories, Japanese and non-Japanese.

A characteristic of the Japanese that has received much publicity in recent years, and is seen as (at least by some) a reason why Japan's so economically powerful, is their group mentality. In Japan, consideration of the group always wins out over the desire of the individual. In fact, I have had Japanese tell me they consider individuality to be synonymous with selfishness and a complete disregard for the feelings of others.

Whereas in the West the attainment of "happiness" is the elusive goal for a full and rewarding life, in Japan it's satisfactory performance of duty. From the time they are born, the Japanese are instilled with a sense of duty that extends toward parents, spouses, bosses and co-workers, neighbors, and the society as a whole.

FAMILY LIFE In a nation as crowded as Japan, consideration of others is essential. The average Japanese family lives in what Westerners would regard as intolerably tiny living quarters, especially in the larger cities, such as Tokyo and Osaka, where space is at a premium. And in many cases it's still customary for retired parents to live with their eldest son.

The son, however, has very little time to spend at home. If he lives in Tokyo, he spends an average of three hours a day commuting on the city's trains and subways. Commonly called a "salaryman" (a description that includes all white-collar company employees), he works long hours. In 1994 the average Japanese worker spent 1,903 hours on the job, according to the Japanese Labor Ministry. But while it used to be customary for the salaryman to work until 7 or 8 pm, then spend a necessary evening out drinking with fellow workers in order to promote understanding, closeness, and more harmonious working conditions, the recent Japanese recession has curtailed this custom. Now, companies are no longer willing to pay overtime or costly nights out on the town. One-pot family dinners, such as *nabe*, have become popular, showing that father has come home to eat with the family.

Impressions

According to a popular Japanese saying, the four most fearsome things in human life are: earthquake, thunder, fire, and father.

—James Kirkup, *Heaven, Hell and Hara-Kiri*, 1974

Most likely the salaryman will work for the same company during his entire career, taking only national holidays off and one week of vacation a year. In return, he is assured of lifetime employment (unless his company goes bankrupt), a pay raise according to his age, and promotion according to the number of years he has worked for the company. Although he may secretly complain of the long hours he has to work, he basically accepts the situation because everyone else is doing the same thing.

As for Japanese women, being a housewife and full-time mother is considered the most honored position. Although more women are working outside the home than ever before, they are generally confined to low-paying menial and part-time jobs. Take a look at the employment opportunities in the classified section of the *Japan Times.* There, you'll see that employers can discriminate on the basis of sex, age, and race. Jobs for women are typically as secretaries, waitresses, and teachers, with few jobs open to those over 30. It's still pretty much a man's society, and a woman's primary obligation is in the home. The main goal of most Japanese women is to get married and have children. Those who fail to find a mate during college or the early working years can find one through arranged marriages (if she's not too old), which still make up about 12% of Japanese marriages. The Japanese go all out when it comes to weddings—believe it or not, the cost of an average wedding, including the honeymoon, is a whopping $79,000.

Of course, the situation is changing in Japan, as elsewhere. In 1986 the Equal Employment Opportunity Act went into effect, overturning an earlier law that limited the number of overtime hours women could work (and if you don't work overtime in Japan, there's hardly any chance for promotion). Day-care centers for children are on the increase; young people are moving away and living far from their hometowns; and some young couples are determined to lead different, and separate, lives from their parents. You can now find, though they are rare, female politicians, doctors, and lawyers who juggle both family and career. In a recent trend, some young Japanese women are putting off marriage until later years; some even say they never wish to marry or have children, a choice that would have been unthinkable just a decade ago.

But change evolves slowly in Japan. Those who advocate it are in danger of ridicule or, even worse, rejection from the group. Such resistance to change is especially difficult for Japanese who have lived abroad and then return home; unless they slip quietly back into their old mold, they are regarded with suspicion and resentment, as though they have somehow become tainted and are no longer quite Japanese.

MEETING THE JAPANESE On a personal level, the Japanese are among the most likable people in the world. They are kind, thoughtful, and adept in perceiving another person's needs. The Japanese have an unerring eye for pure beauty, whether it be in food, architecture, or landscaped gardens. I don't think it would be possible to visit Japan and not have some of the Japanese appreciation of beauty rub off. Quite a few foreigners originally go to Japan with the intention of staying only a short while—and they end up living there for years. I was one of them.

As for foreigners, even though they're treated with extreme kindness during a visit, they soon realize that they will never be totally accepted in Japanese society. They will always be considered outsiders, even if they speak the language fluently. In fact, Japanese-speaking foreigners will tell you that they are sometimes met with suspicion and coldness simply because, to the Japanese mind, foreigners aren't supposed to be able to speak their language. Among the groups most discriminated against are probably the Koreans, many of them second and third generation and the descendants of Koreans who were brought to Japan as forced labor before World War II.

If you're invited to Japan by some organization or business, you'll receive the royal treatment and most likely be wined and dined so wonderfully and thoroughly that you'll never want to leave. If you go to Japan on your own as an ordinary tourist, however, chances are that your experiences will be much different. Except for those who have lived or traveled abroad, few Japanese have had much contact with foreigners. In fact, even in Tokyo there are Japanese who have never spoken to a foreigner and would be quite embarrassed and uncomfortable if they were confronted with the possibility. And even though most of them have studied English, few Japanese have had the opportunity to use the language and cannot communicate in it. That's one reason why you may find the seat empty beside you in the subway is the last one to be occupied—most Japanese are deathly afraid you'll ask them a question they won't be able to understand.

In many respects, therefore, it's much harder to meet the inhabitants in Japan than in many other countries. The Japanese are simply much more shy. Although they will sometimes approach you to ask whether they might practice some English with you, for the most part you're left pretty much on your own, unless you make the first move.

I've found one of the best ways to meet Japanese is to visit a so-called English-conversation lounge. Such lounges, which are informally set up and often attached to English schools, are intended to give the Japanese an opportunity to converse freely in English. Most are open in the evening and offer the chance to play games or read magazines and drink coffee or beer. Usually, foreigners are admitted free of charge; at some lounges you must pay an entrance fee of $5.00 or so, but it's always less than what the Japanese pay. At any rate, the Japanese who come to these lounges often speak excellent English and will be delighted to talk to you. When I first went to Japan, I visited one of these lounges several times, learning much about Japanese society in the process—everything from the role of women to homosexuality and interracial marriage. I was told that the Japanese feel much more comfortable talking about such subjects in English and would be unable to express themselves as openly in their own language. The *Tokyo Journal*, published monthly to describe what's going on in the capital city, lists conversation lounges in its classified section.

Another way to meet Japanese is to go where they play—namely, the country's countless bars and eateries. There, you'll encounter Japanese who will want to speak to you if they understand English, and some slightly inebriated Japanese who will speak to you even if they don't. If you're open to them, such chance encounters may prove to be the highlight of your trip.

And finally, I found that traveling with children opened up the Japanese like a magic key. Their children will talk to your children (and they never have a language barrier), and parents can always talk about their children. I had complete strangers I met on the train invite me home when I traveled with my three-year-old, while Japanese I have known for years have never invited me.

ETIQUETTE

Much of Japan's system of etiquette and manners stems from its feudal days, when the social hierarchy dictated how a person spoke, sat, bowed, ate, walked, and lived. Failure to comply with the rules could bring severe punishment, even death.

Of course, nowadays it's quite different, although the Japanese still attach much importance to proper behavior. As a foreigner, however, you can get away with a lot. After all, you're just a "barbarian" and, as such, can be forgiven for not knowing the rules. There are two cardinal sins, however, you should never commit. One is you should never wear your shoes inside a Japanese home, traditional inn, or temple; the other is you should never wash with soap inside a Japanese bathtub. Except for these two horrors, you will probably be forgiven any other social blunder (like standing with your arms folded or in your pockets).

As a sensitive traveler, however, you should try to familiarize yourself with the social etiquette in Japan, the basics of which are given below. The Japanese are very appreciative of foreigners who take the time to learn about their country and are quite patient in helping you learn. Remember, if you do commit a faux pas, apologize profusely and smile. They don't chop off heads anymore.

Most forms of behavior and etiquette in Japan developed to allow relationships to be as frictionless as possible—a pretty good idea in a country as crowded as Japan. The Japanese don't like confrontations, and fights are extremely rare.

The Japanese are very good at covering almost all unpleasantness with a smile. Foreigners find the smile hard to read—a smiling Japanese face can mean happiness, sadness, embarrassment, or even anger. My first lesson in such physiognomic inscrutability happened on a subway in Tokyo, where I saw a middle-aged Japanese woman, who was about to board the subway, being brutally knocked out of the way by a Japanese man rushing off the train. She almost lost her balance, but she gave a little laugh, smiled, and got on the train. A few minutes later, as the train was speeding through the tunnel, I stole a look at her and was able to read her true feelings on her face. Lost in her own thoughts, she knitted her brow in consternation and looked most upset and unhappy. The smile had been a put-on.

Another aspect of Japanese behavior that sometimes causes difficulty for foreigners, especially in business negotiations, is the reluctance of the Japanese to say no when they mean no. They consider such directness poor manners. As a result, they're much more apt to say your request is very difficult, or they'll simply beat around the bush without giving a definite answer. At this point, you're expected to let the subject drop. Showing impatience, anger, or aggressiveness rarely gets you anywhere. Apologizing sometimes does. And if someone does give in to your request, you can't say thank you often enough.

If you're invited to a Japanese home, you should know that it's both a rarity and an honor. Most Japanese consider their homes too small and humble for entertaining guests, which is why there are so many restaurants, coffee shops, and bars. If you're invited to a home, don't show up empty-handed. Bring a small gift, such as candy, fruit, or flowers. Alcohol is also appreciated. You don't have to fly to Japan more than once to realize that every Japanese on board is laden down with his or her three-bottle quota of alcohol. Take your cue from them and stock up on a few bottles on the flight over, especially if you know you'll be visiting someone. Whiskey and brandy seem to be the favorites.

When the Japanese give back change, they hand it back to you in a lump sum rather than counting it out. Trust them. It's considered insulting for you to sit there and count it in front of them, because it insinuates you think they might be trying to cheat you. The Japanese are honest. It's one of the great pleasures of being in their country.

Don't blow your nose in public if you can help it, and never at the dinner table. It's considered most disgusting. On the other hand, even though the Japanese are very hygienic, they're not at all averse to spitting on the sidewalk. And, even more peculiar, the men urinate when and where they want, usually against a tree or a wall and most often after a night of carousing in the bars.

This being a man's society, men will walk in and out of doors and elevators before women, and in subways they will sit down while women stand. Some Japanese men who have had contact with the Western world will make a gallant show of allowing a Western woman to step out of the elevator first. For the sake of Western women living in Japan, thank them warmly.

BOWING The main form of greeting in Japan is the bow rather than the handshake. Although, at first glance, it may seem simple enough, the bow—together with its implications—is actually quite complicated. The depth of the bow and the number of seconds devoted to performing it, as well as the total number of bows, depend on who you are and to whom you're bowing and how they are bowing back. In addition to bowing in greeting, the Japanese also bow upon departing and to express gratitude. The proper form for a bow is to bend from the waist with a straight back and to keep your arms at your sides, but if you're a foreigner, a simple nod of the head is enough. Knowing foreigners shake hands, a Japanese may extend his hand, although he probably won't be able to stop himself from giving a little bow as well. I've even seen Japanese bow when talking on the telephone. Although I've occasionally witnessed Japanese businessmen shake hands among themselves, the practice is still quite rare.

VISITING CARDS You're a nonentity in Japan if you don't have a visiting card, called a *meishi*. Everyone—from housewives to plumbers to secretaries to bank presidents—carries meishi to give out during introductions. If you're trying to conduct business in Japan, you'll be regarded suspiciously—even as a phony—if you don't have business cards. As a tourist you don't have to have them, but it certainly doesn't hurt, and the Japanese will be greatly impressed by your preparedness. The card should have your address and occupation on it. You might even consider having your meishi made in Japan, with the Japanese syllabic script (*katakana*) written on the reverse side.

DINING As soon as you're seated in a Japanese restaurant, you'll be given a wet towel, which will be steaming hot in winter or pleasantly cool in summer. Called an *oshibori*, it's for wiping your hands. In all but the fancy restaurants, men can get away with wiping their faces as well, but women are not supposed to (I ignore this if need be). The oshibori is a great custom, one you'll wish would be adopted back home.

The next thing you'll probably be confronted with are chopsticks. The proper way to use them is to place the first chopstick between the base of the thumb and the top of the ring finger (this chopstick remains stationary) and the second one between the top of the thumb and the middle and index fingers. This second chopstick is the one you move to pick up food. The best way to learn to use chopsticks is to have a Japanese show you how. It's not difficult, but if you find it impossible, some restaurants might have a fork as well. How proficiently foreigners handle chopsticks is a matter of great curiosity for the Japanese, and they're surprised if you know how to use them; even if you were to live in Japan for 20 years, you would never stop receiving compliments on how talented you are with chopsticks.

As for etiquette involving chopsticks, if you're taking something from a communal bowl or tray, you're supposed to turn your chopsticks upside down and use the part that hasn't been in your mouth. After transferring the food to your plate, you turn the chopsticks back to their proper position. Never stick your chopsticks down vertically into your bowl of rice and leave them there—that is done only when a person has died. Also, don't pass anything from your chopsticks to another person's chopsticks, as that's done only to pass the bones of the cremated.

If you're eating soup, you won't use a spoon. Rather, you'll pick up the bowl and drink from it. It's considered in good taste to slurp with gusto, especially if you're eating noodles. Noodle shops in Japan are always well orchestrated with slurps and smacks.

You won't find many nonsmoking areas in restaurants. Some 60% of Japanese men smoke (15% of women), and although this figure is down from 85% in 1965, those who do smoke have little consciousness of nonsmokers' rights.

By the way, it's considered bad manners to walk down the street in Japan eating or drinking (except at a festival). You'll notice if a Japanese buys a drink from a vending machine, he'll stand there, gulp it down, and throw away the container before going on.

If you're drinking in Japan, the main thing to remember is that you never pour your own glass. Bottles of beer are so large that people often share one. The rule is that, in turn, one person pours for everyone else in the group, so be sure to hold up your glass when someone is pouring for you. Only as the night progresses do the Japanese get sloppy about this rule. It took me a while to figure this out, but if no one notices your empty glass, the best thing to do is to pour everyone else a drink so that someone will pour yours. If someone wants to pour you a drink and your glass is full, the proper thing to do is to take a few gulps so that he or she can fill your glass. Because each person is continually filling everyone else's glass, you never know exactly how much you've had to drink, which (depending on how you look at it) is very good or very bad.

SHOES Nothing is so distasteful to the Japanese as the bottoms of shoes. Therefore, you should take off your shoes before entering a home, a Japanese-style inn, a temple, and even some museums and restaurants. Usually, there will be some plastic slippers at the entranceway for you to slip on, but whenever you encounter tatami, you should take off even these slippers—only bare feet or socks are allowed to tread upon tatami.

Restrooms are another story. If you're in a home or Japanese inn, you'll notice another pair of slippers—again plastic or rubber—sitting right inside the restroom door. Step out of the hallway plastic shoes and into the bathroom slippers, and wear these the whole time you're in the restroom. When you're finished, change back into the hallway slippers. If you forget this last changeover, you'll regret it—nothing is as embarrassing as walking in wearing toilet slippers and not realizing what you've done until you see the mixed looks of horror and mirth on the faces of the Japanese. Although it might seem like a lot of bother to go through all this ritual with shoes, it actually does make sense once you get used to it.

BATHING On my very first trip to Japan, I was certain I would never get into a Japanese bath. I was under the misconception that men and women bathed together, and I couldn't imagine getting into a tub with a group of smiling and bowing Japanese men. I needn't have worried. The good news (or, I suppose, bad news for some of you) is that in almost all circumstances bathing is gender-segregated. There are some exceptions, primarily outdoor hot-spring spas in the countryside, but the women who go to these are usually grandmothers who couldn't care less. Young Japanese women wouldn't dream of jumping into a tub with a group of male strangers.

Japanese baths are delightful—and I, for one, am addicted to them. You find them at Japanese-style inns, at hot-spring spas, and at neighborhood baths (not everyone has his or her own bath in Japan). Sometimes they're elaborate affairs with many tubs, plants, and statues, and sometimes they're nothing more than a tiny tub. The procedure at all of them is the same. After completely disrobing in the changing room and putting your clothes in either a locker or a basket, hold your washcloth in front of you so that it covers the vital parts and walk into the bath area. There, you'll find a plastic basin (they used to be wood), a plastic stool, and faucets along the wall. Sit on the stool in front of a faucet and repeatedly fill your basin with water, splashing it all over you. If there's no hot water from the faucet, it's acceptable to dip your basin into the hot bath. Soap yourself down; then rinse away completely—and I mean *completely*—all soap traces. After you're squeaky clean, you're ready to get into the bath. When you've finished your bath, do *not* pull the plug.

Your first attempt at a Japanese bath may be painful—simply too scalding for comfort. It helps if you ease in gently and then sit perfectly still. You'll notice all tension and stiffness ebbing away, a decidedly relaxing way to end the day. The Japanese are fond of baths, and many take them nightly, especially in winter, when a hot bath keeps one warm for hours afterward. With time, you'll probably become addicted too.

8 The Language Barrier

Without a doubt, the hardest part of traveling in Japan is the language barrier. Suddenly you find yourself transported to a crowded land of 120 million people, where you can neither speak nor read the language. To make matters worse, few Japanese speak English. And outside the major cities, the menus, signs at train stations, and shop names are often in Japanese only.

However, millions of foreign visitors before you who didn't speak a word of Japanese have traveled throughout Japan on their own with great success. Much of the anxiety travelers experience elsewhere is eliminated in Japan, because the country is safe and the people kind and helpful to foreigners. In addition, the Japan National Tourist Organization (JNTO) does a super job of publishing various helpful brochures, leaflets, and maps and staffing information centers, usually at train stations. Finally, Japan itself has done a mammoth job during the past few years in updating street signs, subway directions, and addresses in Roman letters, especially in Tokyo and the very visitor-friendly Osaka.

If you need to ask directions of strangers in Japan, your best bet is to ask younger people. They have all studied English in school and are most likely to be able to help you. Japanese businessmen also often know some English. And as strange as it sounds, if you're having problems communicating with someone, write it down so that he or she can read it. The emphasis in schools is on written rather than oral English (many English teachers can't speak English themselves), so Japanese who can't understand a word you say may know all the subtleties of syntax and English grammar. If you still have problems communicating, you can always call the "Travel-Phone," a toll-free nationwide English-language helpline set up by the JNTO. (Information on the Travel-Phone is given in "Fast Facts: Japan" at the end of chapter 3.) It also doesn't hurt to arm yourself with a small pocket dictionary.

If you're heading out for a particular restaurant, shop, or sight, have your destination written out in Japanese by someone at your hotel. If you get lost along the way, look for one of the police boxes, called *koban,* found in virtually every neighborhood. They have maps of particular districts and can pinpoint exactly where you want to go if you have the address with you. Remember, too, train stations in major cities and tourist-resort areas have tourist information offices (*kanko annaijo*), which can help you with everything from directions to hotel reservations. The staff may not speak any English, but I don't think you'll have trouble communicating your needs.

Realizing the difficulties that foreigners have with the language barrier in Japan, the JNTO has put out a nifty booklet called "The Tourist's Handbook." It contains basic sentences in English, with their Japanese equivalents, for almost every activity, from asking directions and shopping to ordering in a restaurant and staying in a Japanese inn. Foreigners traveling around Japan on their own should pick up a copy of this valuable booklet at the Tourist Information Center in either Tokyo or Kyoto. Appendixes A and B in the back of this guide also list some common phrases and words in Japanese to help you get around on your own. *Note:* Japanese nouns do not have plural forms; thus, for example, *ryokan,* a Japanese-style inn, can be both singular and plural. Plural sense is indicated by context.

No one knows the exact origins of the Japanese language, but we do know that it existed only in spoken form until the 6th century. It was then that the Japanese borrowed the Chinese characters, called *kanji,* and used them to develop their own form of written language. Later, two additional character systems, *hiragana* and *katakana,* were added to kanji to form the existing Japanese writing system. Thus, Chinese and Japanese use some of the same pictographs, but otherwise there is no similarity between the languages. While they may be able to recognize some of each other's written language, the Chinese and Japanese cannot communicate verbally.

There are about 10,000 Japanese characters, but the average adult knows only 2,500 or so, which is enough to read newspapers, most books and novels, and other everyday material. Hiragana and katakana, phonetic alphabets consisting of 46 symbols each, came into use because kanji was considered inadequate to express everything in Japanese thought. Hiragana is used for writing words not expressed in kanji and for verb endings. Katakana is the alphabet used for all foreign words and for telegrams. As a foreigner, for example, if you have visiting cards made up in Japanese, your name will be written in the katakana syllabary.

The Japanese written language—a combination of kanji, hiragana, and katakana—is probably one of the most difficult systems of written communication in the modern world. As for the spoken language, there are many levels of speech and forms of expression relating to a person's social status and sex. It's little wonder that St. Francis Xavier, a Jesuit missionary who came to Japan in the 16th century, wrote that Japanese was an invention of the devil designed to thwart the spread of Christianity. And yet, astoundingly, adult literacy in Japan is estimated to be 99%.

There are at least two (often four) ways of pronouncing most kanji in Japanese—one is a Chinese pronunciation from the 6th century, and the other is a Japanese pronunciation. This means that, except by context, one often can't tell by looking at the characters which pronunciation is the proper one. Similarly, if one doesn't know the characters of, say, a restaurant, it may be impossible to find out the telephone number.

If you're having difficulty communicating with a Japanese, it may help to pronounce an English word in a Japanese way. Foreign words, especially English, have penetrated the Japanese language to such an extent they are now estimated to make up 20% of everyday vocabulary. The problem is that these words change in Japanese pronunciation, because words always end in either a vowel or an *n,* and because two consonants in a single syllable are usually separated by a vowel. Would you recognize *terebi* as "television," *koohi* as "coffee," or *rajio* as "radio"?

I'd like to mention here that English words are quite fashionable in Japanese advertising, with the result that you'll often see it on shop signs, posters, shopping bags, and T-shirts. However, words are often wonderfully misspelled, or used in such unusual contexts you can only guess at the original intent. I don't know how many times my day has been brightened by the discovery of some zany or unfathomable English. What, for example, could possibly be the meaning behind "Today birds, tomorrow men," which appeared under a picture of birds on a shopping bag? In Okayama I saw a shop whose name was a stern admonition to customers to "Grow Up," while in Kyoto there's the "Selfish" coffee shop and the "Pitiful Pub."

Certainly, the most amusing sign I've seen was at the Narita airport, where each check-in counter displayed a notice advising passengers they would have to pay a service-facility charge at "the time of check-in for your fright." I was unable to control my giggles as I explained to the perplexed man behind one counter what was wrong with the sign. Two weeks later, when I went back through the airport, I noticed all the signs had been corrected. That's Japanese efficiency!

9 Sports

BASEBALL

Baseball, introduced into Japan from the United States in 1873, is as popular among Japanese as it is among Americans. Even the annual high school play-offs are avidly followed on television.

As with other imports, the Japanese have added their own modifications: The playing fields are smaller, and, borrowing from American football, each team has its own cheerleaders. There are several American players, who have proved very popular with local fans; but according to the rules, no more than two foreigners may play on any team.

While playing one's hardest is at a premium in the United States, in Japan any attempt at excelling individually—as by stealing bases—is frowned upon. As in other aspects of life, it is the group, the team, that counts. To what extent that's so may be illustrated by the case of an American player: When he missed opening day at training camp, because he was at the hospital with his son, who was undergoing a life-or-death operation, his contract was immediately canceled. And rather than let a foreign player break the hitting record set by a Japanese, American Randy Bass was thrown only balls and walked.

There are two professional leagues, the Central and the Pacific, which play from April to October and meet in final play-offs. In Tokyo the home teams are the Yomiuri Giants and the Yakult Swallows of the Central League and the Nippon Ham Fighters of the Pacific League. If you want to take in a game and compare it with games you've attended back home, you can purchase advance tickets at the stadium or, for Tokyo teams, at city Playguide ticket offices.

For Tokyo teams, the locations are:

Yomiuri Giants, Tokyo Dome, 1-3-61 Koraku, Bunkyo-ku (☎ 03/3811-2111). Station: Suidobashi.

Yakult Swallows, Jingu Stadium, 13 Kasumigaokamachi, Shinjuku-ku (☎ 03/3404-8999). Station: Gaien-mae, on the Ginza Line; then a five-minute walk.

Nippon Ham Fighters, Tokyo Dome, 1-3-61 Koraku, Bunkyo-ku (☎ 03/3811-2111). Station: Suidobashi.

Two other major teams, outside Tokyo, are:

Chiba Lotte Marines, Chiba Marine Stadium, 1 Mihama, Chiba City, Chiba Prefecture (☎ 043/296-1189). Station: Kaihin Makuhari Station on the JR Keiyo Line; then a 15-minute walk.

Seibu Lions, Seibu Lions Stadium, 2135 Kami Yamaguchi, Tokorozawa City, Saitama Prefecture (☎ 0429/25-1151). Station: Seibu Kyujo-mae Station, on the Seibu Sayama Line.

SUMO

The Japanese form of wrestling known as sumo began perhaps as long as 2,000 years ago, becoming immensely popular by the 6th century. Today, it's still popular, and the best wrestlers are revered as national heroes, much as baseball players are in the United States. Often taller than six feet and weighing well over 300 pounds, sumo wrestlers follow a vigorous training period, which usually begins in their teens and includes eating special foods to gain weight. Unmarried wrestlers even live together at their training schools, called sumo stables.

A sumo match takes place on a sandy-floored ring less than 15 feet in diameter. Before each bout, the wrestlers scatter salt in the ring, to purify it from the last bout's loss. They also squat and then raise each leg, stamping it into the ground to crush, symbolically, any evil spirits. They then squat down and face each other, glaring to psych each other out. Once they rush each other, the object is for a wrestler either to eject his opponent from the ring or to cause him to touch the ground with any part of his body other than his feet. This is accomplished by shoving, slapping, tripping, throwing, and even carrying the opponent. Altogether, there are 48 holds and throws, and sumo fans know all of them. Most bouts are very short, lasting only 30 seconds or so.

There are six 15-day sumo tournaments in Japan every year. Three are held in Tokyo (in January, May, and September); the others are held in Osaka (in March), Nagoya (in July), and Fukuoka (in November). Matches are widely covered on television. If no match is being held during your stay, you may want to drop in on a sumo stable to watch the training.

10 What to Dig Your Chopsticks Into

Whenever I leave Japan, it's the food I miss the most. Sure, there are sushi bars and other Japanese specialty restaurants in most major cities elsewhere, but they don't offer nearly the variety available in Japan. For just as America has more to offer than hamburgers and steaks—and England, more than fish and chips—Japan has more than just sushi and teppanyaki. For both the gourmet and the uninitiated, Japan is a treasure trove of culinary surprises.

CUISINE

Altogether, there are more than a dozen different and distinct types of Japanese cuisine, plus countless regional specialties. A good deal of what you eat may be completely new to you, as well as completely unidentifiable. No need to worry—sometimes the Japanese don't even know what they're eating, so varied and so wide is the range of edibles. The rule is simply to enjoy, and enjoyment begins even before you raise your chopsticks to your mouth. To the Japanese, presentation of food is as important as the food itself, and dishes are designed to appeal not only to the palate but to the eye. In contrast to the American way of piling as much food as possible onto a single plate, the Japanese use lots of small plates, each arranged artfully with bite-size morsels of food. After you've seen what can be done with maple leaves, flowers, bits of bamboo, and even pebbles to enhance the appearance of food, your relationship with what you eat may be changed forever.

Below are explanations of some of the most common types of Japanese cuisine. Generally, only one type of cuisine is served in a given restaurant—for example, only raw seafood is served in a sushi bar. There are some exceptions to this, especially in those restaurants where raw fish may be served as an appetizer. In addition, some Japanese drinking establishments offer a wide range of foods, from soups to sushi and skewered pieces of chicken.

For a quick rundown of the various types of Japanese foods, refer to the menu terms in the appendix.

FUGU Known as blowfish, pufferfish, or globefish in English, fugu is one of the most exotic and adventurous foods in Japan—if it's not prepared properly, it means almost certain death for the consumer! In the past decade, some 50 people in Japan have died from fugu poisoning, usually because they tried preparing it at home. The fugu's ovaries and intestines are deadly and must be entirely removed, without puncturing them. So why eat fugu if it can kill you? Well, for one thing, it's delicious, and for another, fugu chefs are strictly licensed by the government and greatly skilled in preparing fugu dishes. You can eat fugu either raw (*sashimi*) or in a stew (*fugu-chiri*) cooked with vegetables at your table. The season for fresh fugu is from October or November through March, but some restaurants serve it throughout the year.

KAISEKI The king of Japanese cuisine, kaiseki is the epitome of delicately and exquisitely arranged food, the ultimate in Japanese aesthetic appeal. It's also among the most expensive and can cost ¥25,000 ($250) or more per person; some restaurants, however, do offer more affordable mini-kaiseki courses. Kaiseki is expensive because so much time and skill are involved in preparing each of the many dishes, with the ingredients cooked to preserve natural flavors. Even the plates are chosen with great care, enhancing the color, texture, and shape of each piece of food.

Kaiseki cuisine is based on the four seasons, with the selection of food and its presentation dependent on the time of the year. In fact, so strongly does a kaiseki preparation convey the mood of a particular season, the kaiseki gourmet can tell what season it is just by looking at a meal. (The roots of kaiseki go back to the development of the tea ceremony, when monks ate small morsels of food to protect the stomach against strong tea.)

A kaiseki meal is usually a lengthy affair, with various dishes appearing in set order. First come the appetizer, clear broth, and one uncooked dish. These are followed by boiled, broiled, fried, steamed, heated, and vinegared dishes, and finally by another soup, rice, pickled vegetables, and fruit. Since kaiseki is always a set meal, there's no problem in ordering. Let your budget be your guide.

KUSHIAGE Kushiage foods (also called *kushikatsu* or *kushiyaki*) are deep-fried on skewers and include chicken, beef, seafood, and lots of seasonal vegetables (snow peas, gingko nuts, lotus root, and the like). The result is delicious, and I highly recommend trying it. I don't understand why this style of cooking isn't better known—maybe someday it will be. Ordering the set meal is easiest, and what you get is often determined by both the chef and the season.

OKONOMIYAKI Okonomiyaki, which originated in Osaka and literally means "as you like it," could be considered a Japanese pizza. Basically, it's a kind of pancake to which meat or fish, shredded cabbage, and vegetables are added. Since it's a popular offering of street vendors, restaurants specializing in this type of cuisine are very reasonably priced. At some places the cook makes it for you, but at other places it's do-it-yourself, which can be quite fun if you're with a group.

RICE There are no problems here—everyone is familiar with rice. The difference, however, is that in Japan it's quite sticky, making it easier to pick up with chopsticks. It's also just plain white rice (called *gohan*)—no salt, no butter, no soy sauce (it's thought rather uncouth to dump a lot of sauces in your rice). As in other Asian countries, rice has been a Japanese staple for about 2,000 years, although not everyone in the old days could afford the expensive white kind. The peasants had to be satisfied with a mixture of brown rice, millet, and greens. Today, some Japanese still eat rice three times a day, although they're now just as apt to have bread and coffee for breakfast.

ROBATAYAKI Robatayaki refers to restaurants in which seafood and vegetables are cooked over a *robata* grill. In the olden days an open fireplace (robata) in the middle of an old Japanese house was the center of activity for cooking, eating, socializing, and simply keeping warm. Therefore, today's robatayaki restaurants are like nostalgia trips back into Japan's past and are often decorated in rustic farmhouse style, with the staff dressed in traditional clothing. Robatayaki restaurants, many open only in the evening, are popular among office workers for both eating and drinking.

There's no special menu in a robatayaki restaurant—rather, it includes just about everything eaten in Japan. The difference is that most of the food will be grilled. Favorites of mine include gingko nuts, asparagus, green peppers, mushrooms, potatoes, and just about any kind of fish. You can usually get skewers of beef or chicken, as well as a stew of meat and potatoes (*nikujaga*), delicious in cold winter months. Since ordering is à la carte, you'll just have to look and point.

SASHIMI & SUSHI It's estimated that the average Japanese eats 83.6 pounds (38kg) of seafood a year, six times the American consumption. Although this seafood may be served in any number of ways, from grilled to boiled, a great deal of it is eaten raw. Granted, the idea of eating raw fish might seem a little strange at first, but if try it, you'll probably like it.

Sashimi is simply raw seafood. If you've never eaten it, a good choice to start out with is *maguro*, or lean tuna. Contrary to what you might think, it doesn't taste fishy at all and is so delicate in texture that it almost melts in your mouth. The way to eat sashimi is first to put *wasabi* (pungent green horseradish) into a small dish of soy sauce and then dip the raw fish in the sauce.

Sushi comes in many varieties. The most known is *nigiri-zushi:* raw fish, seafood, or vegetables placed on top of vinegared rice with just a touch of wasabi. It's also dipped in soy sauce. Use chopsticks or your fingers to eat sushi; remember you're supposed to eat each piece in one bite—quite a mouthful, but about the only way to keep it from falling apart. Another trick is to turn it upside down when you dip it in the sauce, to keep the rice from crumbling.

Typical sushi includes flounder (*hirame*), sea bream (*tai*), squid (*ika*), octopus (*tako*), shrimp (*ebi*), and omelet (*tamago*). Ordering is easy because you usually sit at a counter, where you can see all the food in a refrigerated glass case in front of you. You also get to see the sushi chefs at work. The typical meal begins with sashimi and is followed by sushi, but if you don't want to order separately, there are always various set courses.

By the way, the least expensive sushi is **chiraishi,** which is a selection of fish, seafood, and usually tamago on a large flat bowl of rice. Because you get more rice, those of you with bigger appetites may want to order chiraishi.

SHABU-SHABU Similar to sukiyaki, shabu-shabu is also prepared at your table and consists of thinly sliced beef cooked in a broth with vegetables. (It's named for the swishing sound the beef supposedly makes when cooking.) The main difference

Impressions

There is a saying that the Chinese eat with their stomachs and the Japanese with their eyes.

—Bernard Leach, *A Potter in Japan,* 1960

between the two dishes is the broth. Whereas in sukiyaki it consists of stock flavored with soy sauce and sake and is slightly sweet, in shabu-shabu it's relatively clear and has little taste of its own. The pots used are also different.

Using their chopsticks, diners hold pieces of meat in the watery broth until they are cooked. This usually takes only a few seconds. Vegetables are left in longer, to swim around until fished out. For dipping, there is either sesame sauce with diced green onions or a more bitter fish stock sauce. Restaurants serving sukiyaki usually serve shabu-shabu as well.

SOBA & UDON The Japanese love eating noodles, but I suspect at least part of the fascination stems from the way they eat them—they slurp, sucking in the noodles with gravity-defying speed. What's more, slurping noodles is considered proper etiquette. Fearing it would stick with me forever, however, slurping is a technique I've never quite mastered.

There are many different kinds of noodles—some are eaten plain, some in combination with other foods, some served hot, some served cold. *Soba*, made from buckwheat flour, is eaten hot or cold. *Udon* is a thick, white noodle originally from Osaka; it's usually served hot. *Somen* is a fine, white noodle eaten cold in the summer and dunked in a cold sauce.

SUKIYAKI Until about a hundred years ago, the Japanese could think of nothing so disgusting as eating the flesh of animals (fish was okay). Considered unclean by the Buddhists, meat consumption was banned by the emperor way back in the 7th century. Imagine the horror of the Japanese to discover that Western "barbarians" ate bloody meat! It wasn't until Emperor Meiji himself announced a century ago his intentions to eat meat that the Japanese accepted the idea. Today, the Japanese have become skilled in preparing a number of beef dishes, and according to a survey conducted a couple of years ago by the Japan Fisheries Association, grilled meat, curried rice, and hamburger were the three favorite dishes among senior high school boys living in Tokyo. The girls, by the way, still preferred sushi.

Sukiyaki is among Japan's best-known beef dishes, and is one many Westerners seem to prefer. Actually, its origins are more Western than Japanese (it was introduced in the last century as a new Western cuisine). To the Western palate, however, it seems distinctly Japanese and today enjoys immense popularity in Japan. Whenever I'm invited to a Japanese home, this is the meal most often served. Like fondue, it's cooked at the table, which makes for an intimate and cozy setting.

Sukiyaki is thinly sliced beef cooked in a broth of soy sauce, stock, and sake, along with scallions, spinach, mushrooms, tofu, bamboo shoots, and other vegetables. All diners serve themselves from the simmering pot and then dip their morsels into their own bowl of raw egg. You can skip the raw egg if you want, but it adds to the taste and also cools the food down enough so that it doesn't burn.

TEMPURA Today a well-known Japanese food, tempura was actually introduced by the Portuguese, who came to Japan in the 16th century. Tempura is fish and vegetables coated in a batter of egg, water, and wheat flour, and then deep-fried; it's served piping hot. To eat it, dip it in a sauce of soy, fish stock, radish (*daikon*), and grated ginger, or in some restaurants salt or powdered green tea are provided for dipping. Various tempura specialties may include eggplant, mushroom, sweet potato, green pepper, sliced lotus root, shrimp, squid, and many kinds of fish. Again, the easiest thing to do is to order the set meal, the *teishoku*. If you're still hungry, you can always order something extra à la carte.

TEPPANYAKI A teppanyaki restaurant is a Japanese steakhouse. As in the famous Benihana restaurants in many U.S. cities, the chef slices, dices, and cooks your meal of tenderloin or sirloin steak and vegetables on a smooth hot grill right in front of you. Because beef is relatively new in Japanese cooking, some people categorize teppanyaki restaurants as "Western." However, I consider this style of cooking and presentation special enough to be referred to as Japanese.

TONKATSU The Japanese word for "pork cutlet," made by dredging pork in wheat flour, moistening it with egg and water, dipping it in breadcrumbs, and deep-frying it in vegetable oil. Since restaurants serving tonkatsu are generally inexpensive, they are popular with office workers and families. The easiest order is the *teishoku*, which usually features either the pork filet (*hirekatsu*) or the pork loin (*rosukatsu*). In any case, your tonkatsu is served on a bed of lettuce or shredded cabbage, and two different sauces will be at your table.

UNAGI I'll bet that if you ate unagi without knowing what it was, you'd find it very tasty. In fact, you'd probably be very surprised to find out you had just eaten eel. Popular as a health food because of its high vitamin A content, eel is supposed to help fight fatigue during hot summer months but is eaten year-round. Broiled eel (*kabayaki*) is prepared by grilling filet strips over a charcoal fire; the eel is repeatedly dipped in a sweetened barbecue soy sauce while cooking. A favorite way to eat broiled eel is on top of rice, in which case it's called *unaju*. Do yourself a favor and try it.

YAKITORI Yakitori is chunks of chicken or chicken parts basted in a sweet soy sauce and grilled over a charcoal fire on thin skewers. A place that serves yakitori (sometimes called a *yakitori-ya* and often identifiable by a red paper lantern outside its front door) is technically not a restaurant but, rather, a drinking establishment; it usually doesn't open until 5pm. Most yakitori-ya are popular with workers as inexpensive places to drink, eat, and be merry.

You can order a set course of various yakitori, which will often include various parts of the chicken like the skin, heart, and liver. Set courses are cheaper, but à la carte gets you exactly what you want. If you're ordering by the stick, you might want to try chicken meatballs (*tsukune*), green peppers (*piman*), chicken and leeks (*negima*), mushrooms (*shiitake*), gingko nuts (*ginnan*), or chicken breast (*sasami*).

OTHER CUISINES During your travels you might also run into these types of Japanese cuisine. ***Kamameshi*** is a rice casserole with different kinds of toppings that might include seafood, meat, or vegetables. ***Nabe,*** a stew cooked in an earthenware pot at your table, consists of chicken, sliced beef, pork, or seafood; noodles; and vegetables. ***Oden*** is a broth with fish cakes, tofu, eggs, and vegetables, served with hot mustard.

Although technically Chinese fast-food restaurants, ***ramen*** shops are so much a part of dining in Japan, I feel compelled to include them. Serving what I consider to be generic Chinese noodles, soups, and other dishes, ramen shops can be found everywhere, easily recognizable by red signs, flashing lights, and quite often pictures of various dishes displayed right by the front door. Many are stand-up affairs, just a high counter to rest your bowl on. In addition to ramen (noodle and vegetable soup), you can also get such things as ***yakisoba*** (fried noodles) or—my favorite—***gyoza*** (fried pork dumplings). What these places lack in atmosphere is made up for in price: Most dishes average about 500 ($5).

Impressions

It is the man who drinks the first cup of sake, then the second cup of sake drinks the first; then it is the sake that drinks the man.

—Japanese proverb

DRINKS

All Japanese restaurants serve complimentary green tea with meals. If that's a little too weak, you may want to try ***sake,*** an alcoholic beverage made from rice and served either hot or cold. It goes well with most forms of Japanese cuisine. Produced since about the 3rd century, sake is an integral part of Shinto wedding ceremonies, celebrations, and festivals. Sake varies by region, the production method, alcoholic content, color, aroma, and taste. Altogether, there are about 2,000 brands of sake produced in Japan. Miyabi is a prized classic sake; other popular brands are Gekkeikan, Koshinokanbai, Hakutsuru (meaning White Crane), and Ozeki.

Japanese **beer** is also very popular. The biggest sellers are Kirin and Sapporo, and each brand has a variety of brews. In an attempt to capture the newest drinking market—Japanese women—beer companies continually come out with new products. Ironically enough, Budweiser is also a big hit among young Japanese. Businessmen are fond of **whiskey,** which they usually drink with ice and water. Although **cocktails** are available in discos, hotel lounges, and fancier bars, most Japanese stick with beer, sake, or whiskey.

Popular in recent years is ***shochu,*** an alcoholic beverage usually made from rice but sometimes from wheat or sweet potatoes. It used to be considered a drink of the lower classes, but sales have increased so much that it's threatening the sake and whiskey businesses. A clear liquid, it's often combined with soda water in a drink called *chuhi,* but watch out—the stuff can be deadly.

11 Recommended Books & Films

BOOKS

Japanese society, history, and culture are so rich and extensive that I've been able to give only a short overview in this book. Fortunately, vast numbers of books in English cover every aspect of Japan, so you shouldn't have any problem reading up on various subjects in more detail. In particular, Kodansha International, a Japanese publisher, has probably brought out more books on Japan in English than any other company. Available at major bookstores in Japan, its books are distributed in the United States through HarperCollins, 10 E. 53rd St., New York, NY 10022.

For an introduction to Japan's history, a standard work is George B. Sansom's *Japan: A Short Cultural History* (Prentice Hall, 1962), which ranges from antiquity to modern times. A former U.S. ambassador to Japan, Edwin O. Reischauer, gives a detailed look at its history in *Japan: The Story of a Nation* (Knopf, 1974). If you're interested in Japan since World War II, *A History of Postwar Japan* (Kodansha, 1982), by Masataka Kosaka, takes in the enormous changes of the past few decades.

A general overview of Japanese history, politics, and society is provided in Reischauer's study *The Japanese* (Harvard University Press, 1977). Delving deeper into Japanese society and psychology are Kurt Singer's *Mirror, Sword and Jewel: The Geometry of Japanese Life* (Kodansha, 1981) and Chie Nakane's *Japanese Society* (University of California Press, 1970). A classic description of the Japanese and their culture is found in Ruth Benedict's brilliantly written book *The Chrysanthemum and the Sword: Patterns of Japanese Culture* (New American Library, 1967), first published in the 1940s but reprinted many times since. For a more contemporary approach, look into *The Japanese Mind: The Goliath Explained* (Linden Press/Simon & Schuster, 1983), by Robert C. Christopher. I consider this book compulsory reading for anyone traveling to Japan because it describes so accurately the Japanese, the role history has played in developing their psyche, and the problems facing the nation today.

In a more lighthearted vein, there's *Dave Barry Does Japan* (Random House, 1992). Trust the inimitable Dave Barry to solve the mystery of the success of the Japanese car industry (they use steel!). A delightful account of the Japanese and their customs is given by the irrepressible George Mikes in *The Land of the Rising Yen.* Because it was published in the early 1970s and is now out of print, I doubt you'll be able to find the book in the United States; it's in major bookstores in Japan, however, and would make enjoyable reading during your trip.

Likewise, the Japan Travel Bureau puts out some nifty pocket-size booklets on things Japanese, including "Eating in Japan," "Living Japanese Style," and "Festivals of Japan." My favorite, however, is *Salaryman in Japan* (JTB, 1986), which describes the private and working lives of those guys in the look-alike business suits—Japan's army of white-collar workers who receive set salaries. With chapters devoted to life in the salaryman's company, the etiquette of business cards, company trips, the wife of a salaryman, and even the "salaryman blues," this book is both entertaining and enlightening.

If you're interested in women's issues in Japan, read Alice Cook and Hiroko Hayashi's *Working Women in Japan: Discrimination, Resistance and Reform* (ILR Press, 1980). A book seemingly from another era is *Geisha* (Kodansha, 1983), by Liza C. Dalby; it describes her year living as a geisha in Kyoto as part of a research project.

For information on Japanese religions, two beautifully illustrated books are *Shinto: Japan's Spiritual Roots* (Kodansha, 1980) and *Buddhism: Japan's Cultural Identity* (Kodansha, 1982), both by Stuart D. B. Picken, with introductions by Edwin O. Reischauer.

If you find yourself becoming addicted to Japanese food, you might want to invest in a copy of *Japanese Cooking: A Simple Art* (Kodansha, 1980), by Shizuo Tsuji. Written by the proprietor of one of the largest cooking schools in Japan, this book contains more than 220 recipes, as well as information on food history and table etiquette. The history and philosophy of the tea ceremony, beginning with its origins in the 12th century, are given in *The Tea Ceremony* (Kodansha, 1983), by Sen'o Tanaka.

An introduction to Japanese art is provided in Langdon Warner's *Enduring Art of Japan* (Grove Press, 1958). *Japan, A History of Art* (Doubleday, 1971), by Bradley Smith, offers a beautifully illustrated overview and makes an elegant coffee-table book, too. *A Net of Fireflies: Japanese Haiku and Haiku Paintings* (Charles E. Tuttle, 1960) is a charming collection of these typical Japanese art forms. Kabuki and other stage arts are covered in Faubion Bowers's *Japanese Theater* (Greenwood Press, 1976).

Two other informative books are *The World of the Shining Prince: Court Life in Ancient Japan* (Knopf, 1964), by Ivan Morris, and—if you're planning to stay at a ryokan—*The Japanese Inn: A Reconstruction of the Past* (University of Hawaii Press, 1982), in which Oliver Statler takes you through 400 years of Japanese social history with the family that owned one.

Whenever I travel in Japan, I especially enjoy reading fictional accounts of the country; they put me more in tune with my surroundings and increase my awareness and perception. The world's first major novel was written by a Japanese woman, Murasaki Shikibu, whose classic, *The Tale of Genji* (Knopf, 1978), dating from the 11th century, describes the aristocratic life of Prince Genji. Lafcadio Hearn, a prolific writer about things Japanese in the late 19th century, describes life in Japan around the turn of the century in *Writings from Japan* (Penguin, 1985), while Isabella Bird, an Englishwoman who traveled alone to Hokkaido in the 1870s, wrote a vivid account of what life was like for rural Japanese in *Unbeaten Tracks in Japan* (Virago Press Limited, 1984). An overview of Japanes classical literature is provided in *Anthology of Japanese Literature* (Grove Press, 1955), edited by Donald Keene. In Tokyo bookstores, you'll find whole sections dedicated to English translations of Japan's best-known authors, including Mishima Yukio, Soseki Natsume, Abe Kobo, Tanizaki Junichiro, and Nobel Prize winner Kawabata Yasunari.

Finally, because it was also made into a television miniseries, most Westerners are familiar with James Clavell's *Shogun* (Dell, 1975), a fictional account based on the lives of Englishman William Adams and military leader Tokugawa Ieyasu around 1600. In addition, a vivid history of Japanese woodblock prints from the 17th to the 19th century comes alive in a first-person account written by James Michener in *The Floating World* (University of Hawaii Press, 1983). Nicholas Bouvier, the Swiss travel writer, mixes personal accounts and art with Japanese history that reads as easy as fiction in his vivid and sensual *The Japanese Chronicles* (Mercury House, 1992).

For other personal accounts of what it's like for Westerners living in Japan, two entertaining novels are *Ransom* (Vintage, 1985), by Jay McInerney, and *Pictures from the Water Trade* (Harper & Row, 1986), by John D. Morley. Robert J. Collins describes life in Tokyo in *Max Danger: The Adventures of an Expat in Tokyo* (Charles E. Tuttle, 1987). Pico Iyer taps into the mysterious juxtaposition of the old Japan versus the new in *The Lady and the Monk: Four Seasons in Kyoto* (Knopf, 1991).

FILMS

Samurai flicks, which resemble the American western, have never lost their appeal to the Japanese audience. The classic samurai film is probably Kurosawa Akira's *The Seven Samurai.* Other Kurosawa films that deal with feudal Japan include *Kagemusha,* which was cowinner of the Grand Prize at the 1980 Cannes Film Festival, and *Ran,* an epic drama set in 16th-century Japan, based on Shakespeare's *King Lear.*

Kurosawa, the grandfather of Japanese directors, is probably the best known and certainly one of the finest in his field. His films—from such early ones as *Stray Dog,* a revelation on Japan immediately after the war (it begins with a shot of a dog carrying a human hand in its mouth), to his more recent *Dreams,* said to be autobiographical—have never failed to interest an international audience.

For a look at Japan's mountain people in the 1880s, nothing can beat Shohei Imamura's *The Ballad of Narayama,* with its unsentimentalized portrait of an elderly woman who goes off into the snowy countryside to die, as was the custom of her people.

Another film providing insight into the Japanese psyche is Nagisa Oshima's *Merry Christmas, Mr. Lawrence,* about a P.O.W. camp in Java in 1942; the cast includes rock stars David Bowie and Ryuichi Sakamoto. Oshima created a stir in the film world with *In the Realm of the Senses,* a story of obsessive love between a prostitute and the master of the house. Considered too erotic, it was banned from its première at the New York Film Festival in 1976. Today accepted as an "erotic masterpiece," it even has a sequel, *Passion of the Senses.* These are obviously very adult fare.

Mishima, produced by Francis Ford Coppola and George Lucas and directed by Paul Schrader, relates the bizarre life and death of Mishima Yukio, one of Japan's most famous writers.

Juzo Itami, a well-known Japanese director, has recently done some very funny films, which, though the finer points may be lost in the subtitles if you don't understand Japanese, have no trouble translating to an international audience. Itami's *Tampopo* is about a Japanese woman who achieves success with a noodle shop, while *The Funeral* is a comic look at death in Japan, including the surviving family's helplessness when it comes to arranging the complex rituals of the Buddhist ceremony. Itami's *A Taxing Woman,* about a gung-ho tax collector and her prey, a consummately devious tax evader, was so popular in Japan that he quickly came up with a sequel, *A Taxing Woman II.*

3 Planning a Trip to Japan

It's quite natural, when you're preparing for a trip abroad, to feel a certain anxiety, especially if your trip is to the other side of the planet, to a country whose language you do not speak and whose customs and traditions may be strange to you. Such fear of the unknown can give even the most seasoned traveler butterflies.

This chapter and the next, therefore, are intended to allay your anxiety by advising you, step by step, on how to plan your trip properly, both before you leave home and after you arrive in Japan. They are designed to answer any questions you may have concerning the what, when, where, and how of travel to Japan—from what documents and clothes you should take with you to how to get around easily and economically, despite the language barrier.

In the conviction, however, that familiarity breeds confidence, I recommend you also read other chapters in this guide before embarking. They will advise you on what to expect of accommodations and dining choices, on the best places in which to do your shopping, and on the many attractions this fascinating country has to offer. The breakdown by price categories will enable you to plan your budget ahead of time.

1 Information & Entry Requirements

VISITOR INFORMATION

The **Japan National Tourist Organization (JNTO)** publishes a wealth of free, colorful brochures and maps covering Japan as a whole, Tokyo, and various regions of the country. For general information about Japan, ask for *Budget Traveller,* with money-saving advice on traveling, lodging, and dining; and *The Tourist's Handbook,* a phrase booklet to help foreign visitors communicate with the Japanese.

THE JNTO OVERSEAS If you'd like more information on Japan before leaving home, write to or call one of the JNTO offices:

In the United States: 401 N. Michigan Ave., Suite 770, Chicago, IL 60611 (☎ 312/222-0874); 624 S. Grand Ave., Los Angeles, CA 90017 (☎ 213/623-1952); 1 Rockefeller Plaza, Suite 1250, New York, NY 10020 (☎ 212/757-5640); and 360 Post St., Suite 601, San Francisco, CA 94108 (☎ 415/989-7140).

In Canada: 165 University Ave., Toronto, ON M5H 3B8, Canada (☎ 416/366-7140).

In the United Kingdom: Heathcoat Hours, 20 Savile Row., London W.1X 1AE, England (☎ 0171/734-9638).

In Australia: Level 33 the Chifley Tower, 2 Chifley Sq., Sydney, NSW 2000, Australia (☎ 02/232-4522).

THE JNTO IN JAPAN In Japan, you'll find tourist offices in nearly all the cities and towns, most of them located at or near the main train station. Although the staff at a particular tourist office may not speak English (many do) and may not be able to provide you with maps in English, it can point you in the direction of your hotel and, in many cases, it can even make bookings for you. Your best bet for information is the Tourist Information Center (TIC). Operated by the Japan National Tourist Organization, the TIC has offices in Tokyo, as well as at the Narita airport outside Tokyo, and in Kyoto. It distributes leaflets on destinations throughout Japan, along with information on train, bus, and ferry schedules. Unfortunately, the leaflets are almost never available at the destinations themselves, so you must pick them up at the TIC before leaving Tokyo or Kyoto. The TIC also has leaflets on major attractions and sights—for example, *Japanese Gardens, Japanese Hot Springs,* and *Museums and Art Galleries.* For more information on tourist information centers, see the individual listings for cities.

ENTRY REQUIREMENTS

Americans traveling to Japan as tourists with the intention of staying 90 days or less need only a valid passport to gain entry into the country; visa requirements have been waived by a reciprocal visa-exemption agreement.

Note that only American tourists don't need a visa—those in the country for sightseeing, sports activities, family visits, inspection tours, meetings, or short study courses. In other words, you cannot work in Japan or engage in any remunerative activity, including the teaching of English (though many young people ignore the law). No extensions of stay are granted, which means American tourists must absolutely leave the country after 90 days. If you're going to Japan to work or study and plan on staying longer, you'll need a visa; contact the Japanese embassy or consulate nearest you.

Australians must possess a passport and a three-month visa for entry to Japan, and can apply for extensions for longer stays. Canadians and New Zealanders do not need a visa for stays of up to 90 days, while citizens of the United Kingdom and Ireland can stay for up to 180 days without a visa.

If you qualify for an extension of stay in Japan (for example, you are on a working visa or are a Canadian on a tourist visa), you can apply at the nearest immigration bureau in Japan. In Tokyo, go to the **Hakozaki Immigration Office** at Tokyo City Air Terminal (TCAT), 42-1 Nihonbashihakozaki-cho, Chuo-ku (☎ 03/3665-7157) or the **Shibuya Immigration Office,** 1-3-5 Jinnan, Shibuya-ku (☎ 03/5458-0370), or the **Tokyo Regional Immigration Information Center** (☎ 03/3286-5245) at 1-3-1 Otemachi, Chiyoda-ku, near the Otemachi subway station. The facilities are open Monday through Friday from 9am to 4pm (closed from noon to 1pm for lunch). After you've extended your visa, you must also apply for an alien registration card, which all foreigners must carry if they stay in Japan longer than 90 days. Apply at the ward office closest to your home or hotel. (All cities in Japan are divided into wards, called *ku.*) The registration card is free, but you'll need two passport-size (45mm × 34mm) photos.

IMPORTANT NOTES Foreigners are required to carry with them at all times either their passports or alien registration cards. The police generally do not stop foreigners, but if you're caught without the proper identification, you'll be taken to the local police headquarters. It happened to me once, and believe me, I can think of better ways to spend an hour and a half. I had to explain in detail who I was, what I was doing in Japan, where I lived, and what I planned on doing for the rest of my life. I then had to write a statement explaining how it was that I rushed out that day without my passport, apologizing and promising never to do such a thoughtless thing again. The policemen at the station were very nice and polite—they were simply doing their duty.

If you intend to drive in Japan, you'll need either an international or—if you stay longer than a year—a Japanese driver's license.

2 Money

CURRENCY The currency in Japan is called the **yen,** symbolized by **¥.** Coins come in denominations of ¥1, ¥5, ¥10, ¥50, ¥100, and ¥500. Bills come in denominations of ¥1,000, ¥5,000, and ¥10,000. Although the conversion rate varies daily, the prices in this book are based on the rate of ¥100 to U.S. $1. You can easily figure what things cost by remembering $10 to every ¥1,000.

The Japanese Yen

For American Readers At this writing $1 = approximately ¥100 (or ¥10 = 10 cents), and this was the rate of exchange used to calculate the dollar values given in this chapter.

For British Readers At this writing £1 = approximately ¥150 (or ¥10 = 6.6 pence), and this was the rate of exchange used to calculate the pound values in the table below.

Note: The most difficult task of writing a guide is to set the rate of exchange. If I could advise accurately the future exchange rate, I'd be too rich to be a guide book writer. These rates may change and, therefore, you should check the rate again when you travel to Japan and use the table as a guide:

¥	U.S.$	U.K.£	¥	U.S.$	U.K.£
10	.10	.07	1,500	15.00	9.90
25	.25	.16	2,000	20.00	13.20
50	.50	.33	2,500	25.00	16.50
75	.75	.50	3,000	30.00	19.80
100	1.00	.66	4,000	40.00	26.40
200	2.00	1.32	5,000	50.00	33.00
300	3.00	1.98	6,000	60.00	39.60
400	4.00	2.64	7,000	70.00	46.20
500	5.00	3.30	8,000	80.00	52.80
600	6.00	3.96	9,000	90.00	59.40
700	7.00	4.62	10,000	100.00	66.00
800	8.00	5.28	15,000	150.00	99.00
900	9.00	5.94	20,000	200.00	132.00
1,000	10.00	6.60	25,000	250.00	165.00

What Things Cost in Tokyo	U.S. $
Taxi from the Narita airport to the city center	200.00
Subway ride from Akasaka to Roppongi	1.40
Local telephone call	.80
Double room at the Imperial Hotel (deluxe)	350.00
Double room at the Gajoen Kanko Hotel (moderate)	180.00
Double room at the Kikuya Ryokan (inexpensive)	82.00
Lunch for one at Chinya (moderate)	25.00
Lunch for one at Genrokusushi (inexpensive)	5.00
Dinner for one, without drinks, at Inakaya (deluxe)	100.00
Dinner for one, without drinks, at Ichimon (moderate)	50.00
Dinner for one, without drinks, at Irohanihoheto (inexpensive)	15.00
Glass of beer	5.00
Coca-Cola	6.00
Cup of coffee	2.80–10.00
Roll of ASA 100 Fujichrome film (36 exposures)	4.20
Admission to the Tokyo National Museum	4.00
Movie ticket	19.05
Theater ticket to Kabuki	25.00

What Things Cost in Kyoto	U.S. $
Express train from Kansai International Airport to Kyoto	34.30
Subway ride from Kyoto Station to Karasuma Station	1.80
Local telephone call	.80
Double room at the Miyako (deluxe)	210.00
Double room at the Kyoto Kokusai Hotel (moderate)	160.00
Double room at the Matsubaya Ryokan (inexpensive)	90.00
Lunch for one at Okutan (moderate)	30.00
Lunch for one at Musashi (inexpensive)	8.00
Dinner for one, no drinks, at Minoko (deluxe)	130.00
Dinner for one, no drinks, at Tagoto (moderate)	60.00
Dinner for one, no drinks, at Gontaro (inexpensive)	35.00
Glass of beer	5.00
Coca-Cola	5.00
Cup of coffee	2.80–10.00
Roll of ASA 100 Fujichrome film (36 exposures)	5.00
Admission to Kinkakuji Temple	4.00
Movie ticket	19.00
Theater ticket to Gion Corner	25.00

Personal checks are virtually useless in Japan. Even if you had an account at a Japanese bank (foreign travelers cannot have Japanese bank accounts), processing a personal check costs about $40 and takes about three weeks. Most Japanese pay with either credit or charge cards or cash—and because the country has such a low crime rate, you can feel safe walking around with lots of money (although, as a rule, you should always exercise caution whenever you're traveling). When I worked as editor of a travel magazine in Tokyo, I was paid in cash; I often left the office for a night on the town with a whole month's salary in my purse. Never once was I afraid of being mugged, and I certainly wasn't the only one. Because the Japanese feel so safe in their own society and carry lots of cash with them, sadly enough they're often easy targets when they travel abroad. The only time you should be alert to possible pickpockets in Japan is when you're riding a crowded subway during rush hour.

CURRENCY EXCHANGE If you need to exchange money outside of banking hours, inquire at one of the larger first-class hotels—some of them will cash traveler's checks or exchange money, even if you're not their guest. If you're arriving at the Narita airport outside Tokyo, you can exchange money there from 6am until the arrival of the last flight that day.

TRAVELER'S CHECKS Traveler's checks can be exchanged for yen at most banks with exchange services. They generally fetch a better exchange rate than cash. Note however that in remote areas, even banks won't cash them. Before taking off for small towns, be sure you have enough cash.

CREDIT & CHARGE CARDS As an example of how adaptable the Japanese are, just five years ago you'd have been hard-pressed to find establishments outside hotels, tourist shops, and well-known restaurants that accepted credit or charge cards. Even the most expensive kaiseki meals, which could easily cost upward of ¥20,000 ($200), would be paid for in cash.

No longer. Credit and charge cards have taken Japan by storm, the most readily accepted cards being American Express, Visa, and the Japanese credit card JCB (Japan Credit Bureau). Many tourist-oriented facilities also accept MasterCard and Diners Club. Shops and restaurants accepting credit and charge cards will usually post which cards they accept at the door. However, some establishments may be reluctant to accept cards for small purchases. Inquire beforehand. In addition, note that the majority of Japan's smaller businesses, including many restaurants, noodle shops, fast-food joints, and ma-and-pa establishments, do not accept credit or charge cards.

3 When to Go

The Japanese have a passion for travel, and generally they all travel at the same time, resulting in jam-packed trains and hotels. The worst times of year are the New Year's period, from December 28 to January 4; Golden Week, from April 29 to May 5; and the Obon Festival time, in mid-July or mid-August—avoid traveling on these dates at all costs.

CLIMATE

Most of Japan's islands lie in a temperate seasonal wind zone similar to the East Coast of the United States, which means there are four distinct seasons.

Summer, which begins in June, is heralded by the rainy season, which lasts from about mid-June to mid-July. Although it doesn't rain every day, it does rain a lot and umbrellas are imperative. As you walk through all those puddles, remember this is when Japan's farmers are out planting rice seedlings. After the rain stops, it turns very hot (in the 80s) and uncomfortably humid throughout the country, with the exception of the northern island of Hokkaido, such mountaintop resorts as Hakone, and the Japan Alps.

The period from the end of August through September is typhoon season, although most storms stay out at sea and generally vent their fury on land only in thunderstorms. Autumn, which lasts until about November, is one of the best times to travel in Japan. The days are pleasant and slightly cool, with the changing reds and scarlets of leaves giving brilliant contrast to the deep-blue skies. A photographer I know says that autumn is the best season for landscape photography.

Lasting from December to March, winter is marked by snow in much of Japan, especially in the mountain ranges, where the skiing is superb. The climate then is generally dry, and on the Pacific coast the skies are often blue. Tokyo, where the mean temperature is about 40°F, doesn't get much snow.

Spring arrives with a magnificent fanfare of plum and cherry blossoms in March and April, an exquisite time when all Japan is set ablaze in whites and pinks. The cherry-blossom season starts in southern Kyushu toward the end of March and reaches northern Japan in about mid-April. The blossoms themselves last only a few days, symbolizing to the Japanese the fragile nature of beauty and of life itself.

Remember that because Japan's four main islands stretch from north to south at about the same latitudes as Boston and Atlanta, you can travel in the country virtually any time of the year. Winters in southern Kyushu are mild, while summers in Hokkaido, in the north, are cool. In addition, there is no rainy season in Hokkaido.

Tokyo's Average Daytime Temperatures and Rainfall

	Jan	Feb	Mar	Apr	May	June	July	Aug	Sept	Oct	Nov	Dec
Temp. (°F)	37	39	45	54	62	70	77	79	73	62	51	41
Temp. (°C)	3	4	7	13	17	21	25	26	23	17	11	5
Days of Rain	4.3	6.1	8.9	10	9.6	12.1	10	8.2	10.9	8.9	6.4	3.8

HOLIDAYS

National holidays are January 1 (New Year's Day), January 15 (Adults' Day), February 11 (National Foundation Day), March 20 or 21 (Vernal Equinox Day), April 29 (Greenery Day), May 3 (Constitution Memorial Day), May 5 (Children's Day), September 15 (Respect-for-the-Aged Day), September 23 or 24 (Autumn Equinox Day), October 10 (Health and Sports Day), November 3 (Culture Day), November 23 (Labor Thanksgiving Day), and December 23 (Emperor's Birthday). When a national holiday falls on a Sunday, the following Monday becomes a holiday.

Although government offices and some businesses are closed on public holidays, restaurants and most stores remain open. The exception is during the New Year's celebration, January 1 through 3, when almost all restaurants, public and private offices, and stores close up shop; during that time you'll have to dine in hotels.

As for museums, major museums remain open during public holidays. If a public holiday falls on a Monday (when most museums are closed), most museums will remain open but will close instead the following day, on Tuesday. Note that privately owned museums, such as art museums or special-interest museums, generally close on public holidays.

FESTIVALS

With Shintoism and Buddhism the major religions in Japan, it seems as though there's a festival going on somewhere in the country almost every day. Every major shrine and temple has at least one annual festival, with events that might include traditional dances, archery, or colorful processions in which portable shrines are carried through the streets by groups of chanting Japanese dressed in traditional costumes. Such festivals are always free, though admission may be charged for special exhibitions.

There are also a number of national holidays observed throughout the country, as well as such annual events as cormorant fishing and cherry-blossom viewing. During the summer, festivals are held seemingly everywhere, and you may stumble onto a neighborhood festival just by accident.

As for the larger, better-known festivals, they may be exciting for the visitor but do take some planning, since hotel rooms may be booked six months in advance. If you haven't made prior arrangements, you may want to let the following schedule be your guide in avoiding certain cities on certain days. You won't find a hotel room anywhere near Takayama, for example, on the days of its two big festivals. If you plan your trip around a certain festival, be sure to double-check the exact dates with the Japan National Tourist Organization, since these dates can change. And remember, if a national holiday falls on a Sunday, the following Monday becomes a holiday.

JAPAN CALENDAR OF EVENTS

January

- **New Year's Day,** the most important national holiday in Japan. Like Christmas in the West, it's a time of family reunions, as well as a time when friends get together to drink sake and eat special New Year's dishes. Streets and homes are decorated with straw ropes and pine or plum branches. Because this is a time when Japanese are together with their families, and because almost all businesses, restaurants, and shops close down, it's not a particularly rewarding time of the year for foreign visitors. January 1.
- **Tamaseseri** (Ball-Catching Festival), Hakozakigu Shrine, Fukuoka. The main attraction here is a struggle between two groups of youths who try to capture a sacred wooden ball. The winning team is supposed to have good luck the whole year. January 3.
- **Dezomeshiki** (New Year's Parade of Firemen), Harumi Chuo Dori, Tokyo. Agile firemen dressed in traditional costumes prove their worth with acrobatic stunts atop tall bamboo ladders—you'd certainly feel safe being rescued by one of them. January 6.
- **Usokae** (Bullfinch Exchange Festival), Dazaifu Temmangu Shrine, outside Fukuoka. The trick here is to get hold of the bullfinches made of gilt wood that are given away by priests—they're supposed to bring good luck. January 7.
- **Toka Ebisu Festival,** Imamiya Ebisu Shrine, Osaka. Ebisu is considered the patron saint of business and good fortune, so this is the time when businesspeople pray for a successful year. The highlight of the festival is a parade of women dressed in colorful kimonos and carried through the streets in palanquins. January 9–11.
- **Adults' Day,** a national holiday. This day honors young people who have reached the age of 20, when they can vote and assume other responsibilities. January 15.
- **Grass Fire Ceremony,** Wakakusayama Hill, Nara. As evening approaches, Wakakusayama Hill is set ablaze and fireworks are displayed. The celebration marks a time more than a thousand years ago when a dispute over the boundary of two major temples in Nara was settled peacefully. January 15.
- **Toshi-ya,** Sanjusangendo Hall, Kyoto. A traditional Japanese archery contest. January 15.

February

- **Oyster Festival,** Matsushima. Matsushima is famous for its oysters, and this is the time they're considered at their best. Oysters are given out free at booths set up at the seaside park along the bay. First Sunday in February.
- **Setsubun** (Bean-Throwing Festival), held at leading temples throughout Japan. According to the lunar calendar, this is the last day of winter, and people throng to temples to participate in the traditional ceremony of throwing beans to drive away imaginary devils. February 3 or 4.
- **Lantern Festival,** Kasuga Shrine, Nara. A beautiful sight, in which more than 3,000 stone and bronze lanterns are lit. February 3 or 4.
- **National Foundation Day** (*Kigensetsu*), a national holiday. February 11.
- ✪ **Snow Festival.** This famous Sapporo festival features huge, elaborate statues and figurines carved in snow and ice, with competitors from around the world. Second week of February.

March

- **Omizutori** (Water-Drawing Festival), Todaiji Temple, Nara. This festival includes a solemn evening rite in which young ascetics brandish large burning torches and draw circles of fire. The biggest ceremony takes place on March 12, and on the next day the ceremony of drawing water is held to the accompaniment of ancient Japanese music. March 1–14.
- **Hinamatsuri** (Doll Festival), observed throughout Japan. It's held in honor of young girls to wish them a future of happiness. In homes where there are girls, dolls dressed in ancient costumes representing the emperor, empress, and dignitaries are set up on a tier of shelves, along with miniature household articles. March 3.
- **Kasuga Matsuri,** Kasuga Shrine, Nara. With a history stretching back 1,100 years, Kasuga Matsuri features traditional costumes and classical dances. March 13.
- **Vernal Equinox Day,** a national holiday. Throughout the week Buddhist temples hold ceremonies to pray for the souls of the departed. March 20 or 21.
- **Cherry-blossom season.** This rite of spring begins in late March on the southern islands of Kyushu and Shikoku, travels up Honshu through April, and reaches Hokkaido by the beginning of May. Early to mid-April is when the blossoms burst forth in Tokyo and Kyoto. Popular cherry-viewing spots in Kyoto include Maruyama Park, the garden of Heian Shrine, the Imperial Palace, Nijo Castle, Kiyomizu Temple, and Arashiyama, while in Tokyo people throng to Ueno Park, Yasukuni Shrine, and the moat encircling the Imperial Palace. Late March to May.

April

- **Buddha's Birthday,** observed throughout Japan. Ceremonies are held at all Buddhist temples. April 8.
- **Kamakura Matsuri,** Tsurugaoka Hachimangu Shrine, Kamakura. This festival honors heroes from the past, including Yoritomo Minamoto, who made Kamakura his shogunate capital back in 1192. Highlights are horseback archery (truly spectacular to watch), a parade of portable shrines, and sacred dances. Second to third Sunday.
- **Takayama Festival,** Takayama. Supposedly dating back to the 15th century, this festival features a procession of huge, gorgeous floats that parade through the village streets. April 14–15.
- **Gumonji-do** (Firewalking Ceremonies), Miyajima. These rites and ancient shrine dances called *bugaku* are held atop Mt. Misen. Walking on fire is meant to show devotion and is also for purification. Mid-April.
- **Yayoi Matsuri,** Futarasan Shrine, Nikko. Yayoi Matsuri also features a parade of decorated floats. April 16–17.

- **Greenery Day,** a national holiday. The birthday of the former emperor, Hirohito. April 29.
- **Golden Week,** a major holiday period throughout Japan. Many Japanese offices and businesses close down, and families go on vacation. It's a crowded time to travel; reservations are a must. April 29 to May 5.

May

- **Constitution Memorial Day,** a national holiday. May 3.
- **Hakata Dontaku,** Fukuoka. Citizens dressed as deities ride through the streets on horseback to the accompaniment of flutes, drums, and traditional instruments. May 3–4.
- **Children's Day,** a national holiday. This festival honors young boys, and the most common sight throughout Japan is colorful streamers of carp flying from poles. These fish symbolize attributes desirable for young boys—perseverance and strength. May 5.
- **Cormorant fishing,** Nagara River near Gifu. Visitors board small wooden boats at night to watch cormorants dive into the water to catch *ayu,* a kind of trout. Cormorant fishing is also held on the Katsura (also called Oi) River outside Kyoto. Begins May 11, extending to October 15.
- **Takigi Noh performances,** Kofukuji Temple, Nara. These Noh plays are presented outdoors after dark, under the blaze of torches. May 11–12.
- **Kanda Festival,** Kanda Myojin Shrine, Tokyo. Held every other year. Portable shrines are carried through the district. Saturday and Sunday closest to May 15.
- ✪ **Aoi Matsuri (Hollyhock Festival).** This is one of Kyoto's biggest events, a colorful pageant commemorating the days when the imperial procession visited the city's shrines. It supposedly dates from the 7th century, when a ceremony was held to appease the gods following severe storms. May 15.
- **Kobe Matsuri,** Kobe. This relatively new festival celebrates Kobe's international past with fireworks at Kobe Port, street markets, and a parade on Flower Road, with participants wearing native costumes. Mid-May.
- **Grand Festival of Toshogu Shrine,** Nikko. This festival commemorates the day in 1617 when Tokugawa Ieyasu's remains were brought to his mausoleum in Nikko, accompanied by 1,000 people. This festival re-creates the drama, with more than 1,000 armor-clad people escorting three palanquins through the streets. May 17–18.
- **Sanja Matsuri,** Asakusa Shrine, Tokyo. About 100 portable shrines are carried through the district on the shoulders of men and women in traditional garb. Third Saturday and Sunday in May.
- **Mifune Matsuri,** Arashiyama, on the Oi River outside Kyoto. A reproduction of an ancient boat festival. The days of the Heian Period, when the imperial family used to take pleasure rides on the river, are reenacted. Third Sunday in May.

June

- **Takigi Noh performances,** Heian Shrine, Kyoto. Evening performances of Noh are presented on an open-air stage in the shrine's compound. June 1–2.
- **Sanno Festival,** Hie Shrine, Tokyo. This festival, which first began in the Edo Period (1603–1867), features the usual portable shrines, transported through the busy streets of the Akasaka district. June 10–16.
- **Rice-planting Festival,** Sumiyoshi Shrine, Osaka. In hopes of a successful harvest, young girls in traditional farmers' costumes transplant rice seedlings in the shrine's rice paddy to the sound of music and traditional songs. June 14.
- **Hyakuman-goku Festival,** Kanazawa. Held only since 1952, the Hyakuman-goku Festival commemorates the arrival of Maeda—a feudal lord who laid the foundations

of the Kaga clan—in this castle town. The highlight of the festival is a procession, and in the evening paper lanterns float down the Asano River. Mid-June.

July

- **Hakata Yamagasa,** Fukuoka. The main event takes place on the 15th, when a giant fleet of floats, topped with elaborate decorations, is paraded through the streets. July 1–15.
- **Tanabata** (Star Festival), celebrated throughout Japan. According to myth, the two stars Vega and Altair, representing a weaver and a shepherd, are allowed to meet once a year on this day. If the skies are cloudy, however, the celestial pair cannot meet and must wait another year. July 7.
- ✪ **Gion Matsuri.** One of the most famous festivals in Japan, it dates back to the 9th century, when the head priest at Kyoto's Yasaka Shrine organized a procession in an attempt to ask the gods' assistance against a plague that was raging in the city. Although the festival is actually celebrated during the whole month of July, the highlight is on the 17th, when spectacular floats wind their way through the city streets. Many foreigners plan their trip to Japan around this event. July 16–17.
- **Obon Festival.** This national festival, which takes place in either mid-July or mid-August, commemorates the dead, who, according to Buddhist belief, revisit the world during this period. Many Japanese return to their hometowns for the event, especially if a member of the family has died recently. As one Japanese, whose grandmother had died a few months before, told me, "I have to go back to my hometown—it's my grandmother's first O'bon." Mid-July or mid-August, depending on the area in Japan.
- **Tenjin Matsuri,** Osaka. One of the city's biggest festivals, it dates back to the 10th century, when the people of Osaka visited Temmangu Shrine to pray for protection against the diseases prevalent during the long, hot summer. They would take pieces of paper cut in the form of human beings and, while the Shinto priest said prayers, would rub the paper over themselves in ritual cleansing. Afterward, the pieces of paper were taken by boat to the mouth of the river and disposed of. Today, the festival reenacts the boat procession with a fleet of more than 100 sacred boats making its way down the river, followed by a fireworks display. July 24–25.
- **Kangensai Music Festival,** Itsukushima Shrine, Miyajima. There are classical court music and bugaku dancing, and three barges carry portable shrines, priests, and musicians across the bay, along with a flotilla of other boats. Because this festival takes place according to the lunar calendar, the actual date changes each year. Late July or early August.
- **Hanahi Taikai** (Fireworks Display), Tokyo. This is Tokyo's largest summer celebration, and everyone sits on blankets along the banks of the Sumida River near Asakusa. Great fun! Last Saturday of July or early August.

August

- **Oshiro Matsuri,** Himeji. Famous for its Noh dramas, performed on a special stage constructed on the Himeji Castle grounds. On Sunday there's a procession from the castle to the city center, with participants dressed in traditional costumes. First Saturday and Sunday of August.
- **Waraku Odori,** Nikko. This is a good opportunity to see some of Japan's folk dances. August 5–6.
- **Peace Ceremony,** Peace Memorial Park, Hiroshima. Held annually in memory of those who died from the atomic bomb dropped over Hiroshima on August 6, 1945. A similar ceremony is held on August 9 in Nagasaki. August 6.

- **Tanabata Festival,** Sendai. Sendai holds its Star Festival one month later than the rest of Japan. It's the country's largest, and the whole town is decorated with colored paper streamers. August 6–8.
- **Matsuyamam Festival,** Matsuyama. Festivities include dances, fireworks, and a night fair. August 11–13.
- **Takamatsu Festival,** Chuo Dori Avenue, Takamatsu. About 6,000 people participate in a dance procession that threads its way along the avenue. Anyone can join in. August 12–14.
- **Toronagashi and Fireworks Display,** Matsushima. Held in the evening. First there's a fireworks display, followed by the setting adrift on the bay of about 5,000 small boats with lanterns. Another 3,000 lanterns are lit on islets in the bay. The lanterns, which illuminate the water, are meant to console the souls of the dead. August 15.
- **Daimonji Bonfire,** Mt. Nyoigadake, Kyoto. A huge bonfire in the shape of the Chinese character *dai,* which means "large," is lit near the peak of the mountain as part of the O'bon Festival in mid-August.

September

- **Respect-for-the-Aged Day,** a national holiday. September 15.
- **Yabusame,** Tsurugaoka Hachimangu Shrine, Kamakura. Archery performed on horseback recalls the days of the samurai. September 16.
- **Autumnal Equinox Day,** a national holiday. September 23 or 24.

October

- **Okunchi Festival,** Suwa Shrine, Nagasaki. This festival illustrates the influence Nagasaki's Chinese population has had on the city through the centuries. A parade of floats and dragon dances are highlights. October 7–9.
- **Marimo Matsuri,** Lake Akan, Hokkaido. Marimo is a spherical green weed that grows in Lake Akan. This festival is put on by the native Ainu population. October 8–10.
- **Great Festival of Kotohiragu Shrine,** near Takamatsu. The climax of this festival is a parade of *mikoshi* (portable shrines). October 9–11.
- **Takayama Matsuri,** Takayama. Similar to the festival held here in April, with huge floats paraded through the streets. October 9–10.
- **Health and Sports Day,** a national holiday. October 10.
- **Oeshiki Festival,** Hommonji Temple, Tokyo. In commemoration of Buddhist leader Nichiren (1222–82), people march toward the shrine carrying large lanterns decorated with paper flowers. October 11–13.
- **Mega Kenka Matsuri** (Roughhouse Festival), Matsubara Shrine, Himeji. Youths shouldering portable shrines jostle each other as they attempt to show their skill in balancing their heavy burdens. October 14–15.
- **Autumn Festival,** Toshogu Shrine, Nikko. Armor-clad parishioners escort a sacred portable shrine. October 17.
- **Fire Festival,** Yuki Shrine, Kyoto. Long rows of torches are embedded along the approach to the shrine to illuminate a procession of children. October 22.

✪ **Jidai Matsuri (Festival of the Ages).** Another of Kyoto's grand festivals, this is one of its most interesting. Held in commemoration of the founding of the city in 794, it features a procession of more than 2,000 people dressed in ancient costumes representing different epochs of Kyoto's 1,200-year history. October 22.

November

- **Ohara Matsuri,** Kagoshima. About 15,000 people parade through the town in cotton *yukata,* dancing to the tune of popular Kagoshima folk songs. A sort of

Japanese Mardi Gras, this event attracts several hundred thousand spectators a year. November 2–3.

- **Culture Day,** a national holiday. November 3.
- **Daimyo Gyoretsu,** Hakone. The old Tokaido Highway that used to link Kyoto and Tokyo comes alive again with a long parade that is a faithful reproduction of a feudal lord's procession in the olden days. November 3.
- **Shichi-go-san** (Children's Shrine-Visiting Day), held throughout Japan. Shichi-go-san literally means "seven-five-three" and refers to children of these ages who are taken to shrines by their elders to express thanks and pray for their future. November 15.
- **Labor Thanksgiving Day,** a national holiday. November 23.

December

- **On-Matsuri,** Kasuga Shrine, Nara. This festival features a parade of people dressed as courtiers, retainers, and wrestlers of long ago. December 17.
- **Emperor's Birthday,** a national holiday. December 23.
- **New Year's Eve.** At midnight many temples ring huge bells 108 times to signal the end of the old year and the beginning of the new. Many families visit temples and shrines on New Year's Eve to pray for the coming year. December 31.

TOKYO CALENDAR OF EVENTS

January

- **Dezomeshiki** (New Year's Parade of Firemen), Harumi Chuo Dori. This annual event features agile firemen dressed in traditional costumes who prove their worth with acrobatic stunts atop tall bamboo ladders. January 6.

February

- **Hari-kuyo.** Women bring broken pins and needles to Awashimado near Sensoji Temple in Asakusa on this day, a custom since the Edo Period. February 8.

April

- **Jibeta Matsuri,** Kanayama Shrine, Kawasaki (just outside Tokyo). This festival extols the joys of sex and fertility, featuring a parade of giant phalluses. Needless to say, not your average festival, and you can get some unusual photographs here. Mid-April.

May

- **Kanda Festival,** Kanda Myojin Shrine. Held every other year on odd-numbered years. It began during the feudal era as the only time townsmen could enter the shogun's castle and parade before him. It features a parade of dozens of portable shrines, plus a tea ceremony. Saturday and Sunday closest to May 15.

June

- **Sanno Festival,** Hie Shrine. This festival, dating from the Edo Period (1603–1867), features the usual portable shrines, transported through the busy streets of the Akasaka district. June 10–16.

July

- **Ueki Ichi** (Potted Plant Fair), Fuji Sengen Shrine, near Asakusa (on the Ginza subway line). This fair displays different kinds of potted plants and bonsai (miniature dwarfed trees), as well as a miniature Mt. Fuji that symbolizes the opening of the official climbing season. July 1.
- **Hozuki Ichi** (Ground Cherry Pod Fair), Sensoji Temple, Asakusa. It features hundreds of stalls selling ground cherry pods and colorful wind bells. July 9–10.

October

- **Oeshiki Festival,** Hommonji Temple. This is the largest of Tokyo's commemorative services held for Nichiren, a Buddhist leader. People march to the temple carrying large lanterns decorated with paper flowers. October 11–13.

November

- **Tori-no-Ichi** (Rake Fair), Otori Shrine, Asakusa. This fair features stalls selling rakes lavishly decorated with paper and cloth, which are thought to bring good luck and fortune. Based on the lunar calendar, the date changes each year. Mid-November.

December

- **Hagoita-Ichi** (Battledore Fair), Sensoji Temple, Asakusa. Popular since Japan's feudal days, Hagoita-Ichi features decorated paddles of all types and sizes. Most have designs of Kabuki actors—images made by pasting together padded silk and brocade—and make great souvenirs and gifts. December 17–19.
- **New Year's Eve.** Meiji Shrine is the place to be in Tokyo for this popular family celebration, as thousands throng to the shrine to usher in the new year at midnight. December 31.

4 Special Interest & Sports Vacations

For those of you who want to get more involved with the culture and/or take a more active approach to your visit, here are some ideas for out-of-the-ordinary vacation planning.

EDUCATION/STUDY TRAVEL

Many U.S. universities have campuses in Japan offering courses in English, or study programs ranging from summer school to graduate exchange fellowships. Contact your nearest university to inquire about such programs.

In addition, the **National Registration Center for Study Abroad** (NRCSA), a consortium of more than 100 universities, foreign-language institutes, adult-education colleges, and activity centers located in 20 countries around the world, welcomes North Americans to its three member schools in Japan. The LIC Kokusai Kaiwa Gakuin in Tokyo provides intensive Japanese-language instruction for five weeks, while the Eurocentre in Kanazawa offers a four-week course consisting of language classes, cultural instruction (ranging from flower arranging to life in Japan), and the opportunity to live with a Japanese family. The Japanese Division of the Kyoto English Center offers four-week to six-month Japanese courses and homestay or guesthouse lodging. The Japan Homestudy program in the Tokyo and Hiroshima areas provides the chance to live and study in the teacher's home, with weekly rates. For more information on these programs, contact the NRCSA, 823 N. 2nd St., Milwaukee, WI 53203 (☎ 414/278-0631).

If you're interested in learning about specific aspects of Japanese culture but prefer to make arrangements on your own upon arrival in Japan, contact the Tourist Information Center in Tokyo, Narita, or Kyoto for more information.

HOMESTAYS

One good way to meet the Japanese is to stay in a *minshuku,* inexpensive lodging in a Japanese home. Usually small, with only a handful of rooms, minshuku often afford the opportunity to meet both the family running the place and the other guests, since meals are usually served in a communal dining room.

Home-Visit System Recognizing the difficulty foreigners may face in meeting the Japanese, the Japan National Tourist Organization has launched a super program called the Home-Visit System, which offers overseas visitors the chance to visit an English-speaking Japanese family at home. It doesn't cost anything, and the visit usually takes place for a few hours in the evening (dinner is not served). It's a good idea to bring a small gift, such as flowers, fruit, or a souvenir of some kind from your hometown. The system operates in 18 cities. I've provided a few of the contact telephone numbers: **Tokyo** (☎ 03/3502-1461), **Narita** (☎ 0476/32-8711 or 24-3198), **Yokohama** (☎ 045/641-5824), **Nagoya** (☎ 052/581-5678), **Otsu** (☎ 0775/23-1234), **Kyoto** (☎ 075/752-3511), **Osaka** (☎ 06/345-2189), **Kobe** (☎ 078/303-1010), **Okayama** (☎ 0862/22-0457), **Kurashiki** (☎ 0864/22-5141), **Hiroshima** (☎ 082/247-8007), **Fukuoka** (☎ 092/733-2220), **Nagasaki** (☎ 0958/24-1111), and **Kagoshima** (☎ 0992/24-1111). To apply, call the appropriate city at least one day in advance of your intended visit. Address other questions to the **Tourist Information Center** in Tokyo (☎ 03/3502-1461).

OUTDOOR VACATIONS

Want to go on a vacation where hiking, canoeing, skiing or hunting is the focus? Head straight for Hokkaido, Japan's wilderness. Dameon Takada, who speaks English, organizes active vacations, including airfare (from Tokyo), accommodations, and meals, at his Japanese-style hot-springs resort on volcanic Lake Akan (see the chapter on Hokkaido for more details). Write to him with a proposal; he'll tailor a trip to suit you (Hotel Ichikawa, Aza Akankohan, Akancho, Akan-gun 085-04, ☎ 0154/67-2011).

SKIING

With about 75% of Japan's land space consisting of mountains, you can bet that skiing is the country's most popular winter sport. In fact Hokkaido, Japan's big northern island, was selected as the site of the 1972 Winter Olympics and Nagano, in the Japan Alps, has been chosen as the site of the 1998 Winter Olympics. With the ski season generally lasting from about mid-December to early April, keep in mind the slopes—especially those close to a large city—can be very crowded during weekends and holidays and transportation to the slopes booked six months in advance. Also, although shops where you can rent skis, boots, and poles for about $50 a day are plentiful, most don't have shoes larger than about a man's size 11 (27cm). Day passes for ski lifts generally run about $40. A great plus of many Japanese ski resorts is that they're situated around hot springs—what could be better than soaking in a hot tub after a day out on the slopes? For more information, the Tourist Information Centers in both Tokyo and Kyoto have a pamphlet called "Skiing in Japan."

When I lived in Japan, I skied with the Shin-yi club. Created in the early 1970's by avid foreign skiers, the club organizes weekend to five-day trips designed for minimum hassle and maximum time on the slopes. Trips average ¥35,000 to ¥75,000 ($350 to $750) and include all transportation and lodging (usually in minshuku with two meals). With your ¥5,000 ($50) membership fee, you'll receive a phamplet with detailed information on skiing in Japan (ski areas, lift prices, preseason conditioning, etc.), as well as complete details for the trips. The train and plane seats are reserved, they've arranged the best accommodations, and the ski slopes chosen have enough variety to ensure skiers of all levels can enjoy themselves, plus the train rides and meal times are fun in a friendly international group with a common purpose: to ski! Contact Julia Nolet, 3-6-4 Nishi Azubu, Minato-ku, Tokyo 106, or call 03/3423-8858 (between 10am and 10pm Tokyo time) or fax 03/3423-8859.

SPECIAL INTEREST VACATIONS

Rather than follow the throng, you may be a visitor with a purpose in mind; if so, this may help you to tailor your vacation to your goals. If you're interested in **feudal castles,** you'll find them in Osaka, Nagoya, Matsue, Matsumoto, Himeji, Kumamoto, Okayama, Hiroshima, and Matsuyama. Japan's most famous **gardens** are Kenrokuen Garden in Kanazawa, Korakuen Garden in Okayama, and Kairakuen Garden in Mito. Other beautiful gardens are Ritsurin in Takamatsu, on the island of Shikoku; Suizenji Garden in Kumamoto and Iso Garden in Kagoshima, both on the island of Kyushu; and the gardens at the Heian Shrine and Saihoji (Moss Temple), both in Kyoto. Japan's most famous rock garden is probably the one at Ryoanji Temple in Kyoto.

If you're a camera buff, you may want to make a special effort to visit some of the many **picturesque towns and villages** in Japan. My own personal list includes Kamakura, Takayama, Shirakawa-go, Tsumago, Kurashiki, and the hamlet of Chiran, south of Kagoshima, as well as Mt. Koya. As for towns with historical significance, nothing can beat Kyoto, Nara, and Kamakura, three ancient capitals of Japan. These three towns are also where you'll find a majority of the country's **temples and shrines.** Other important Shinto shrines in Japan include Meiji Jingu Shrine in Tokyo, the Ise Jingu Shrines located in Ise-Shima National Park, and Itsukushima Shrine on Miyajima Island. Mt. Koya is the place to head if you're interested in spending the night in a genuine Buddhist temple.

If you're considering visiting a spa, you'll find Japan is blessed with many **hot-spring spas.** In fact, tourism in Japan began when bathing enthusiasts started traveling to hot springs simply for the joys of the bath. There are open-air spas in forests, sand baths, gigantic public baths, mud baths, sulfur baths, and just plain hot tubs. Now you can even try thalassotherapy in Ise-Shima. This relaxing and allegedly therapeutic treatment with sea water, seaweed, and sea mud is gaining popularity with the bath-conscious Japanese. The hot springs closest to Tokyo are at Hakone and on the Izu Peninsula. Other famous hot springs include Matsuyama's Dogo Spa on Shikoku; the spas at Beppu, Ibusuki, and Unzen, on Kyushu; Toyako Spa and the spas at Noboribetsu, Sounkyo, and Akanko Onsen, on Hokkaido.

5 Health & Insurance

HEALTH

You don't need any inoculations for entry into Japan. As for drug prescriptions, they can be filled at Japanese pharmacies. However, it's always better to bring along extra supplies of special medications, especially if you prefer name brands from your own country.

Another consideration for visitors flying to Japan, especially on long flights from North America, is the effects of jet lag. For some reason, flying west has slightly less effect than flying east, which means the hardest flight to overcome is the journey from Japan back to North America.

To minimize the adverse effects of jet lag—primarily fatigue and slow adjustment to your new time zone—refrain from smoking and from consuming carbonated drinks or alcohol during the flight. In addition, eat light meals high in vegetable and cereal content the day before, during, and the day after your flight. Further, exercise your body during the flight by walking around the cabin every so often and by flexing your arms, hands, legs, and feet. It also helps to set your watch (and your mental clock) to the time zone of your destination as soon as you board the plane.

Once you reach your destination, schedule your day according to your new time zone. Put in a normal day, even if you're tired. Go for a walk in the sunlight, and once in your hotel, turn on the lights as brightly as you can until it's time to go to bed in the evening. If you follow these instructions, your body should be back to normal within two days.

INSURANCE

Medical and hospital services are not free in Japan, and they can end up being quite expensive. Before leaving home, therefore, you'd be wise to check with your health-insurance company to see whether you're covered for a trip to Japan. If not, you may wish to take out a short-term traveler's medical policy that covers medical costs and emergencies.

You may also want to take extra precautions with your possessions. Is your camera or video equipment insured anywhere in the world through your home insurance? Is your home insured against theft or loss if you're gone longer than a month (some insurance companies will not cover loss for homes unoccupied for a specified length of time)? If you're not adequately covered, you may wish to purchase an extra policy to cover losses.

6 Tips for Special Travelers

FOR TRAVELERS WITH DISABILITES

For the disabled, traveling can be a nightmare in Japan, especially in Tokyo and other large metropolises, despite the fact we are beginning to see changes. In Tokyo, for example, most subways are accessible only by stairs; many sidewalks can be so jam-packed that getting around on crutches or in a wheelchair is exceedingly difficult. Although Tokyo's subway trains have seating for handicapped passengers—located in the first and last compartments of the train and indicated by a white circle with a blue seat—subways can be so crowded that there's barely room to move. In addition, the seats for the handicapped are almost always occupied by commuters; so unless you look handicapped, no one is likely to offer you his or her seat. Even Japanese homes are not very accessible, since the main floor is always raised about a foot above the entrance-hall floor. Not surprisingly, disabled persons are a rare sight in the larger cities. When I mentioned this once to a Japanese friend, she agreed, saying she was very surprised by the number of disabled people she had seen on a trip to the United States. In Japan, handicapped people are likely to be kept at home and cared for by family members.

When it comes to facilities for the blind, however, Japan has a very advanced system. Throughout subway stations and on many major sidewalks in Tokyo and other cities, there are raised dots and lines on the ground to guide blind people at intersections and toward subway platforms. In some cities, street lights chime a certain song when the signal turns green east-west and another for north-south greens. Even Japanese yen notes are identified, by a slightly raised circle—the ¥1,000 note has one circle in a corner, while the ¥10,000 note has two. And finally, many elevators have floors indicated in Braille.

Because Tokyo can be confusing and frustrating even for the able-bodied, disabled travelers may wish to travel to Japan's smaller cities and rural villages. Those using a wheelchair should travel with a compact one.

FOR SENIORS

Senior citizens do not receive discounts in Japan for admission to museums or other places charging an admission fee. So be prepared to pay full price.

FOR SINGLES

Traveling alone in Japan poses no difficulty, even for women. The main obstacle, however, is expense, since the price of accommodations is cheaper for couples and groups. Single travelers, therefore, should do what traveling businessmen do: stay at so-called business hotels. With their large number of single rooms, they cater almost exclusively to solo businessmen.

FOR FAMILIES

The Japanese are very fond of children, which makes traveling in Japan with children a delight. All social reserve seems to be waived for children. While the average Japanese will not approach foreign adults, if you bring a child with you the Japanese will not only talk with you but even invite you home.

While children may not like such foreign customs as eating raw fish, they will find many other Japanese customs to their taste. What child could resist taking baths *en famille* and actually getting to splash? If you go to a ryokan, chances are your children will love wearing *yukata* (cotton kimono) and slapping around in *geta* (sandles). Your children will be pampered and played with and receive presents and lots of attention. Udon and soba shops are inexpensive and ubiquitous, and the transition from children's favorite spaghetti to udon is easy.

By the way, taking along some small and easy-to-carry gifts to give out to other children you meet is a great icebreaker. We found such gift giving could escalate into a "war of gifts," with children running back and forth between parents to deliver candy or trinkets.

Children 6 to 11 years old generally are charged half price for everything from temple admission to train tickets, while children under 6 are free. (Where I have indicated an admission price for children in this book, it means children 6 to 11, unless otherwise indicated.) If your child under 6 sleeps with you, you generally won't even have to pay for him or her in most hotels and ryokans (in Japan, it's common practice for children to sleep with their mothers usually until six, but even until the age of 12 in some cases). However, it's always advisable to ask in advance.

Another reason Japan is a good destination for families is safety. Still, you must plan your itinerary with care. To avoid crowds, visit tourist sights on weekdays. Never travel on city transportation during rush hour or on trains during popular public holidays. And remember that with all the stairways and crowded sidewalks, strollers are less practical than baby backpacks.

FOR STUDENTS

Students sometimes receive discounts at museums, though occasionally discounts are available only to students enrolled in Japanese schools. Furthermore, discounted prices are often not displayed in English. Your best bet is to bring along an **International Student Identity Card** (ISIC; you can apply for one at your university), along with your university student ID, and show them at museum ticket windows.

7 Getting There

BY PLANE

Most visitors to Japan arrive by air. There are several major carriers flying from the United States, England, Australia, and New Zealand to Japan. In choosing which airline to fly, you'll want to consider such factors as safety, ticket price, available destinations and departure points, in-flight service (there's nothing quite so frustrating as being stuck in a small space for 12 hours or more with inadequate service), and even mileage programs.

The Airlines

Northwest Airlines (☎ 800/447-4747) is the largest American carrier out of Japan, offering the traveler a wider choice of destinations as well as departure points. Ranked fourth worldwide in terms of overall passenger volume, Northwest boarded one million passengers at Tokyo's Narita airport alone in 1995. Northwest services Tokyo, Osaka, Nagoya, and Fukuoka from Honolulu, Los Angeles, San Francisco, Seattle, Detroit, New York, Minneapolis–St. Paul, and Chicago. Japan-bound flights also depart from Singapore, Manila, Bangkok, Taipei, Seoul, Beijing, Shanghai, Guam, Saipan, and Hong Kong. The fact that Northwest flies to so many destinations in Asia makes coordinating travel plans to go on to, say, Hong Kong or Beijing simple, and the wide range of departure points makes it easy to get to Asia from wherever you start off.

Flights landing in Osaka's Kansai International Airport (KIX) are more convenient to Osaka, Kobe, Nara, or Kyoto. If you have a limited stay in Japan and want mainly to see the ancient capital, you may want a flight landing at KIX. Northwest provides the most service to KIX of any airline.

As the longest-operating U.S. carrier in the Pacific (since 1947), Northwest has tailored its services to meet the specific needs of tourists and business travelers to Asian destinations. Flight attendants and on-board service to Japan are based on traditional Japanese cuisine and style, including starting out with *oshibori,* the Japanese hot steaming towels, to refresh yourself with. Northwest's service has attracted even the hard-to-please Japanese—some 65% of its passengers out of Japan and 55% out of the States are Japanese.

One of the benefits of flying Northwest—especially important to the business traveler—is the carrier's strong on-time record. Northwest has been the number one on-time airline among the seven largest U.S. carriers since 1990.

You'll appreciate the extra on-board services, as flying time to Tokyo is about 12 hours from Los Angeles and 13½ hours from Chicago or New York. Service is important on these long hauls and especially if you're flying with children. Northwest provides bassinets (reserve in advance), warms baby bottles, and stocks baby food on all international flights at no extra charge.

Some people I know fly Northwest simply for its great mileage program, WorldPerks, which has one of the lowest requirements for free trips. There's no fee to enroll, and with your first 20,000 (or 25,000 depending on season) miles you earn a free trip within the continental United States (if you fly from the States) or within Asia on Northwest's extensive route system. Round-trip mileage Los Angeles–Tokyo is 12,000 miles, while New York–Tokyo, at 18,000 miles, is almost a free trip. If you fly business or first class, you're awarded bonuses of 25% and 50%, respectively. There are also lots of other ways to earn mileage (MCI, car and hotel rentals, etc.), including flying Northwest's global alliance partner KLM Royal Dutch Airlines (more convenient to Japan from Europe). Check with Northwest WorldPerks (in the U.S. ☎ 800/447-3757) for details.

Air Canada (in Canada ☎ 800/268-7240) has one flight a day five days a week to KIX (Osaka) from Toronto and Vancouver.

Air New Zealand (☎ 800/262-1234) flies from Auckland to Tokyo and Nagoya; see your travel agent for details.

All Nippon Airways (☎ 800/235-3663) is Japan's largest domestic carrier, flying more people annually (some 35 million) than any other Japanese airline. It's also the ninth-largest passenger carrier worldwide. ANA operates more than 500 flights a day on 91 domestic routes connecting 34 major cities in Japan, making it *the* airline to fly within Japan. In 1986, Japan Airlines's monopoly on Japanese overseas air routes was challenged, and ANA began international flights. Although 45 years old, ANA was little known outside Japan, so it has had to try harder to please, and it does. ANA now offers 101 round-trip flights a week, including daily round-trip service from New York and Los Angeles and three flights a week from Washington, D.C., to Tokyo, daily flights from London to Tokyo, and flights from Sydney to Tokyo (six a week) and Osaka (two a week). Passengers can also receive free baggage transfer and discounts at ANA Hotels in Japan, and booking domestic destinations in conjunction with international flights is less expensive, so it makes sense to discuss your travel plans with ANA.

British Airways (in England ☎ 03/4522-2111) flies from London to Tokyo twice a day except Wednesdays, while it services Osaka three times a week and flies to Nagoya as well.

Japan Airlines (in the U.S. and Canada ☎ 800/525-3663), Japan's flagship carrier, is noted for its excellent service. JAL flies from New York, Chicago, San Francisco, Atlanta, Vancouver, and Washington, D.C., to Tokyo and from Los Angeles to Tokyo and Osaka. From Honolulu, JAL also flies to Osaka, Fukuoka, and Sapporo. JAL also operates JALTOURS offering a variety of complete travel packages to Japan. It also has flights from New Zealand and Australia to Tokyo and Osaka. Contact JAL or your travel agent for more details.

Qantas (☎ 800/227-4500) flies from some 13 Australian cities to Tokyo and from five cities to Osaka, so if you're reading this from down under, Quantas may be the best way for you to go.

United Airlines (in the U.S. ☎ 800/538-2929) has daily flights from San Francisco and Los Angeles to Tokyo. United also has a good mileage program called Mileage Plus; contact United for details.

Airline Fares

BUSINESS & FIRST CLASS Northwest's World Business Class offers one of the roomiest business class compartments in the skies and an excellent personal video entertainment system, as well as entrance to WorldClub, a luxurious lounge located in airports in 24 cities. WorldClub representatives provide boarding passes, seat assignments, flight information, reservations, WorldPerks account status, and general travel assistance. Amenities include complimentary beverages and snacks; business machines, including fax and photocopiers; flight monitors; newspapers, magazines, and television; conference rooms; and credit-card telephones. Once on the plane, World Business Class travelers are treated to a separate cabin, with seats that recline 48°. Meals feature Western and Japanese cuisine, and for health-conscious passengers, there's a special low-calorie menu. Northwest's round-trip business-class fares to Tokyo are $3,522 from New York, $3,370 from Chicago, and $2,664 from Seattle, San Francisco, or Los Angeles. Northwest's royal **first class** treatment begins with special check-in and luggage handling and, of course, complimentary entrance to the WorldClub. On board in a separate cabin, rest comfortably in electronically operated seats that recline to a 60° angle. I love the personal five-inch video screen in the seat armrest, which shows movies without interruption on several channels. Food and beverage service is top-class, with a generous choice of cuisines. Northwest's round-trip first-class fares to Tokyo are $6,432 from New York, $6,274 from Chicago, and $5,058 from Seattle, San Francisco, or Los Angeles.

ECONOMY & APEX Economy class tickets offer little in terms of pampering on board but have few purchase restrictions and are certainly less expensive than first and business class. For example, on Northwest, a round-trip fare is $2,788 from New York or Chicago, and $2,038 from the West Coast. APEX (Advance Purchase Excursion) fares are less expensive still, but are usually loaded with restrictions and based on seasons. Northwest's APEX fare ranges from $2,880 (for a summer weekend flight from New York) to as low as $2,000 (for a winter weekday flight from Los Angeles). There are three fare seasons: peak season (summer) is the most expensive, basic season (winter) is the least expensive, and shoulder season is between the other two in time and in price. In all three seasons, APEX fares are a little higher on weekends. Reservations, ticketing, and payment for the nonrefundable APEX fare usually must be completed no later than 21 days prior to departure and limited stay, usually not less than one week and not more than six months. A few airlines offer inexpensive last-minute tickets with all the APEX restrictions except the advance-purchase time limit, in order to achieve full-passenger capacity.

OTHER GOOD-VALUE CHOICES There are also companies providing deeply discounted tickets (some more than 50% less on economy fares and around 30% less on APEX fares), with no restrictions, depending on availability. You can buy your ticket through them well in advance or, if you're lucky, at the last moment. Among the firms that deal with travel to Japan are **Nippon Travel,** 3408 Wisconsin Ave., Suite 208, Washington, DC 20016 (☎ 202/362-0039); **Japan Associates Travel,** 2000 17th St. NW, Washington, DC 20009 (☎ 202/939-8853); and **Japan Express Travel,** 1150 17th St. NW, Suite 408, Washington, DC 20036 (☎ 202/347-7730). Consolidators, such as **Pacific Gateway, C. L. Thomson Express International, CNH International,** and **Star Tours, Inc.,** also sell discounted tickets, but only through travel agents.

Many airlines and tour operators also offer occasional promotional fares, with tight restrictions, as well as package tours, which might be the cheapest way to go, since packages include hotels, transfers, some meals, and more.

Certainly, the best strategy for securing the lowest airfare is to shop around. Consult the travel sections of major newspapers—they often carry advertisements for low fares. You may, for example, find bargains offered by so-called bucket shops, which sell discounted tickets at reductions of about 20% to 30%. Tickets are usually restrictive, valid only for a particular date or flight, nontransferable, and nonrefundable.

A warning: Remember that all fares, rules, and regulations are subject to change. Be sure to contact your travel agent or the airlines for current information.

BY SHIP

There is infrequent **ferry service** connecting ports in Japan with Shanghai, South Korea, Taiwan, and Nakhodka in Russia. From Shanghai, ferries travel to Kobe or Osaka in 46 hours and to Yokohama in 60 hours, with fares starting at around ¥23,000 ($230) for Kobe or Osaka and ¥29,900 ($299) for Yokohama. From Pusan, South Korea, ferries take 21 hours to Osaka and cost ¥14,400 to ¥25,000 ($144 to $250) one way. Travel time to Keelung in Taiwan from Osaka is about 53 hours, including a 12-hour stop in Naha on Okinawa. Fares start at about ¥33,000 ($330). Contact the JNTO for fact sheets and further information. There is a ship that leaves Niigata, a three-hour train ride from Tokyo by Shinkansen train, for Vladivostok, which is the trans-Siberian terminus for the train from Moscow, on Tuesday from June to September. The two-day trip costs ¥32,600 ($326) one way. For more information on travel to Russia, contact Japan-Soviet Travel Service, 5F Daihachi Tanaka Bldg., 5-1 Gobancho, Chiyoda-ku, Tokyo (☎ 03/3238-9101). Located near the JR Ichigaya Station, it's open Monday through Friday from 9am to 8pm and on Saturday from 9am to 5pm.

PACKAGE TOURS

If you're the kind of traveler who doesn't like leaving such arrangements as accommodations, transportation, and itinerary to chance, you may wish to join an organized tour of Japan. Among the many companies offering group tours are **American Express,** American Express Plaza, New York, NY 10004 (☎ 212/323-2291 or 800/241-1700); **Pacific Best Tours,** 228 Rivervale Rd., Rivervale, NJ 07675 (☎ 201/664-8778 or 800/688-3288); **TBI Tours,** 787 Seventh Ave., Suite 1101, New York, NY 10019 (☎ 212/489-1919 or 800/223-0266); and **Visitours, Inc.,** Olympic Tower, 645 Fifth Ave., 61st Floor, New York, NY 10022 (☎ 212/355-6077 or 800/367-4368).

8 Getting Around

Japan has an extensive public transport system. To help you get around and find hotels, restaurants, and sights, I've listed train, bus, tram, and subway stations, followed in parentheses by the number of minutes it takes to get from the station to your destination.

BY PLANE

Because it takes the better part of a day and night to get by train from Tokyo down to southern Kyushu or up to northern Hokkaido, you may find it more convenient to fly at least one stretch of your journey in Japan. You may, for example, fly into Tokyo and in conjunction with your in-bound flight fly to Kagoshima, then take a leisurely two weeks to travel by train from Kagoshima through Kyushu and Honshu arriving in Tokyo. I don't advise flying for shorter distances—say, from Tokyo to Osaka—because of the time spent getting to and from airports. By the way, domestic flights from Tokyo leave from the much more conveniently located Haneda Airport, reached by monorail from Hamamatsucho Station on the Yamanote Line.

Two major domestic airlines are **Japan Airlines** and **All Nippon Airways (ANA),** with networks that stretch all the way from Okinawa to northern Hokkaido. ANA carries more than half of all domestic passengers in Japan and flies to 30 cities throughout the country, including Tokyo, Sapporo, Fukuoka, Hakodate, Takamatsu, Nagasaki, Kagoshima, and Osaka.

Although it's subject to change, the cost of flying on ANA from Tokyo to Sapporo in Hokkaido runs about ¥23,850 ($238) one way, while the flight from Tokyo to Kagoshima is about ¥29,100 ($291). It's cheaper, however, if you plan ahead and purchase your domestic flight in conjunction with your international flight to Japan. For example, if you plan to visit Tokyo and Sapporo from Los Angeles, then you should purchase a Los Angeles–Sapporo ticket with a Tokyo stopover. Such through fares on ANA are available to the following cities from the United States: Tokyo, Osaka, Sapporo, Nagoya, Fukuoka, and Okinawa. Contact ANA or your travel agent.

BY TRAIN

The most convenient way to travel around Japan is by train. Whether you're being whisked through the countryside aboard the famous Shinkansen bullet train or are winding your way up a wooded mountainside in a two-car electric tram, trains in

Japan are punctual, comfortable, dependable, safe, and clean. All trains except locals have washrooms, toilets, and drinking water. And because train stations are usually located in the heart of the city, next to the city bus terminal, arriving in a city by train is usually the most convenient. What's more, most train stations in Japan's major cities and resort areas have tourist offices to help with hotel directions. The staff may not speak English, but it often has maps or brochures in English. Train stations also often have a counter where hotel reservations can be made free of charge. Most of Japan's trains are run by the **Japan Railways (JR) Group,** which operates as many as 26,000 trains daily, including more than 500 Shinkansen bullet trains.

The **Shinkansen** is probably Japan's best-known train. With a front car that resembles a space rocket, the Shinkansen hurtles along at 170 m.p.h. (275kmph) through the countryside on its own special tracks. Among the most luxurious Shinkansen trains are the *Grand Hikari,* a double-decker train that travels between Tokyo and Kyushu, and the *Twilight Express,* a luxury hotel on wheels that runs from Osaka to Sapporo.

Three Shinkansen lines operate in Japan. The most widely used line for tourists is the **Tokaido-Sanyo Shinkansen,** which runs from Tokyo Station west to such cities as Nagoya, Kyoto, Osaka, Kobe, Himeji, Okayama, and Hiroshima before reaching its final destination of Hakata/Fukuoka, on the island of Kyushu. The **Tohoku Shinkansen** line runs from Tokyo and Ueno stations to Morioka in northern Japan. The **Joetsu Shinkansen** connects Tokyo and Ueno stations with Niigata, on the Japan Sea coast. There are two types of Shinkansen running along these tracks, one stops only at the major cities and one makes more stops and is therefore slightly slower. If your destination is a smaller city on the Shinkansen line, make sure the train you take stops there. As a plus, information on stops is broadcast in English, and telephone calls can be made to and from bullet trains. To reach someone on a bullet train, you can call 107 from anywhere in Japan, provided you know the exact train; announcements are made only in Japanese.

There are also two long-distance trains that operate on regular tracks. The **limited-express trains** (*Tokkyu*) are the fastest after the Shinkansen, while the **express trains** (*Kyuko*) are slightly slower and make more stops. To serve the everyday needs of Japan's commuting population, **local trains** (*Futsu*) stop at all stations and are the trains most widely used for side trips outside the major cities. A bit faster are the **rapid trains** (*Kaisoku*), which stop only at major stations.

There are also some privately owned lines that operate from major cities to tourist destinations.

No matter which train you ride, be sure to hang on to your ticket—you'll be required to give it up at the end of your trip as you exit through the gate. And pack lightly, since porters are virtually nonexistent, overhead luggage space is small, and most rail stations have multitudes of stairs. Even if you're a woman traveling alone, don't expect anyone to help you with your luggage—it's happened to me twice in 15 years.

The Tourist Information Center in Tokyo has a *Condensed Railway Timetable* giving details, in English, for the Shinkansen and some other major lines. If you plan to do a lot of traveling by train, however, I recommend you purchase the Japan Travel Bureau's *Mini-Timetable* (*Speedo Jikokuhyo*) for ¥350 ($3.50); it's published monthly and is available at bookstores or at Japan Travel Bureau offices in big cities. It covers the schedules, in both English and Japanese, for all JR long-distance trains, including Shinkansen, and for private trains, planes, ferries, and even express buses. It also has maps of Japan, in English and Japanese, showing train stops. I find this handy little guide invaluable during my Japan trips.

TRAIN DISTANCES/TRAVELING TIME Distances in Japan can be deceiving, since the country is much longer than most people imagine. Its four main islands, measured from the north to the south, cover roughly the distance from Maine to northern Florida. Thank goodness for the Shinkansen bullet train!

The chart below measures the distances and traveling times from Tokyo to principal Japanese cities. Since Tokyo is located approximately in the middle of Japan, you'll most likely change trains there when traveling from north to south and vice versa. Traveling times do not include the time needed for transferring and are calculated for the fastest trains available, excluding the *Nozomi Super Express.* I have expressly left out these times because most travelers will be traveling on a JR Rail Pass and the pass is valid on all JR trains except the *Nozomi.*

Train Travel from Tokyo to Principal Cities

City	Distance (Miles)	Travel Time
Aomori*	458	4 hr. 43 min.
Atami	65	52 min.
Beppu*	762	7 hr. 00 min.
Fukuoka (Hakata Station)	730	6 hr. 00 min.
Hakodate*	557	6 hr. 51 min.
Hiroshima	554	4 hr. 37 min.
Kamakura	32	56 min.
Kanazawa*	386	4 hr. 20 min.
Kumamoto*	803	7 hr. 15 min.
Kyoto	318	2 hr. 39 min.
Matsue*	571	6 hr. 25 min.
Matsumoto	146	2 hr. 48 min.
Matsuyama*	587	6 hr. 47 min.
Miyazaki*	897	10 hr. 25 min.
Nagasaki*	825	8 hr. 3 min.
Nagoya	227	1 hr. 49 min.
Narita	42	1 hr. 13 min.
Niigata	207	1 hr. 39 min.
Nikko	93	1 hr. 29 min.
Okayama	454	3 hr. 51 min.
Sapporo*	731	10 hr. 17 min.
Shimoda	75	2 hr. 40 min.
Kobe (Shin-Kobe Station)	366	3 hr. 12 min.
Osaka (Shin-Osaka Station)	343	2 hr. 30 min.
Takamatsu*	499	5 hr. 00 min.
Takayama*	330	4 hr. 52 min.
Toba*	289	3 hr. 59 min.
Yokohama	18	27 min.

*Destination requires a change of trains.

TRAIN RESERVATIONS You can reserve a seat in advance for the Shinkansen, as well as for limited-express and express trains, at any major Japan Railways station for a small fee. The larger stations have special reservation counters or offices that are easily recognizable by their green signs with RESERVATION TICKETS written on them. They're open daily from 10am to 6pm. If you are at a JR station with no special reservation office, you can reserve your seats at one of the regular ticket windows. I recommend you reserve your seats for your entire trip through Japan as soon as you know your itinerary, especially if you'll be traveling during peak times. However, you can only reserve one month in advance. Note that all trains also have nonreserved cars that work on a first-come, first-seated basis.

You can obtain information and buy tickets at any Japan Railways station for JR trains going throughout Japan, including those along the Yamanote Line, which loops around Tokyo. For specific train times and routing information, call the Tourist Information Center (**03/3502-1461**) or call JR's English-Language Telephone Service in Tokyo directly for information (**03/3423-0111**), Monday through Friday from 10am to 6pm (no reservations are accepted by telephone).

JAPAN RAIL PASS The Japan Rail Pass is without a doubt the most convenient and most economical way to travel around Japan. With the rail pass you don't have to worry about buying individual tickets, and you can reserve your seats on all JR trains for free. The rail pass entitles you to unlimited travel on all JR train lines, including the Shinkansen (except the *Nozomi Super Express*), as well as on JR buses and ferries.

The Japan Rail Pass is available only to foreigners visiting Japan as tourists and can be purchased only outside Japan from an authorized travel agent or from Japan Airlines. *You cannot buy a rail pass once you're in Japan,* so you must arrange for one before you leave home. You'll be issued a voucher, which you'll then exchange for the pass itself after you arrive in Japan. You can exchange it either at the JR Information and Ticket Office at the Narita airport or at some 42 other stations with Japan Rail Pass exchange offices, including Tokyo, Osaka, Kyoto, Hiroshima, and Sapporo.

There are two types of Japan Rail passes available—one for ordinary coach class and one for the first-class Green Car—and you can purchase passes good for one, two, or three weeks. Rates for the ordinary pass, as of August 1995, are ¥27,800 ($278) for 7 days, ¥44,200 ($442) for 14 days, and ¥56,600 ($566) for 21 days. Rates for the Green Car are ¥37,000 ($370) for 7 days, ¥60,000 ($600) for 14 days, and ¥78,000 ($780) for 21 days. Children (under 12, over 6) are charged half fare. Even if you plan to do just a little traveling, you can save quite a bit by purchasing a rail pass. For example, if you were to buy a round-trip reserved-seat ticket on the Shinkansen from Tokyo to Kyoto, it would cost you ¥24,940 ($249.40), which is almost as much as a week's ordinary rail pass. If you plan to see more than just Tokyo and Kyoto, it pays to use a rail pass.

BY BUS

Buses often go where trains don't, and thus may be the only way for you to get to the more remote areas of Japan—such as, for example, Shirakawa-go, a picturesque hamlet in the Japan Alps. In Hokkaido and other places, buses are used extensively. When you board a bus, you'll generally find a ticket machine by the entry door. Take a ticket, which is number-coded with a board displayed at the front of the bus. The board shows the various fares, which increase with the distance traveled. You pay your fare when you get off.

In addition to serving the remote areas of the country, long-distance buses (called *chokyori basu*) also operate between major cities in Japan. Although Japan Railways operates almost a dozen bus routes eligible for JR rail pass coverage, the majority are run by private companies. Many long-distance buses travel during the night, saving passengers the price of a night's lodging. For example, a special bus leaves Tokyo Station every night for Nagoya (¥6,300/$63), Kyoto (¥8,030/$80.30), and Osaka (¥8,450/$84.50), arriving the next morning. Similarly, there's also a night bus from Osaka, Kyoto, and Nagoya to Tokyo. If you're on a limited budget, this is certainly the cheapest way to travel.

BY CAR

Except perhaps in the Izu Peninsula and Hokkaido, driving is not the best way to tour Japan. In cities, streets are often hardly wide enough for a rickshaw, let alone a car, and many roads don't have sidewalks, so you have to dodge people, bicycles, streetlights, and telephone poles. But that's not all—it's not even economical to drive in Japan. Not only is gas expensive, but all of Japan's expressways charge high tolls. The one-way toll from Tokyo to Kyoto, for example, is almost the same as the price of a ticket to Kyoto on the Shinkansen. But whereas the Shinkansen takes only three hours to get to Kyoto, driving takes about eight hours. So unless there are four of you to split the costs and you aren't limited by time, it doesn't make sense to drive.

Note: If you intend to drive in Japan, you'll need either an international or a Japanese driving license.

Car-rental rates vary, but the average cost for 24 hours with unlimited mileage (but not including gasoline) is ¥8,800 ($88) for a sub-compact car. Hertz accepts reservations for its affiliated car-rental companies in Japan. **Gas** (or petrol) stations are found readily along Japan's major highways. As of this writing, the average cost for gasoline is about ¥120 per liter or about $4.80 per gallon. Cars are driven British style, *on the left side of the road,* and signs on all major highways are written in both Japanese and English. You should not have even one drink of alcohol if you plan to drive, and you should wear seat belts at all times.

A profusion of maps of Japan are readily available at the major bookstores in Tokyo (see "Fast Facts: Tokyo," in chapter 4). Be sure to purchase a bilingual map, since back roads often have names of towns written only in Japanese.

BREAKDOWNS/ASSISTANCE The Japan Automobile Federation (JAF) maintains emergency telephone boxes along Japan's major arteries to assist drivers whose cars have broken down or drivers who need help. Calls from these telephones are free and will connect you to the operation center of JAF.

BY FERRY

Because Japan is an island nation, it has an extensive ferry network linking the string of islands. Although it takes longer to travel by ferry, it's also cheaper. For example, you can take the ferry from Tokyo all the way to Hokkaido (Tomako-mai)—a 30-hour trip—for ¥11,840 ($118.40). Ferries also ply the waters of the Seto Inland Sea. From Osaka you can take a ferry in late evening and arrive in Beppu, on Kyushu, the next morning for ¥6,900 ($69). Contact the Tourist Information Center for more details concerning ferries, prices, and schedules.

HITCHHIKING

Hitchhiking is not common in Japan; in fact, some drivers stop simply because they're curious about what a foreigner could possibly want. But even though hitchhiking is uncommon, Japan is probably one of the safest countries in the world for hitchhiking. Once, a couple picked me up when I was hitchhiking in Sado Island and took me the entire circuit around the island, though it was hours out of their way—and I'm not the only one with such a story.

SUGGESTED ITINERARIES

Japan, with its rich culture and varied geography, has much to offer the curious visitor, not only in and around the major cities but in many of the outlying regions as well. If you want to see *everything,* however, you should plan on spending at least a year in Japan. More likely, your time will be limited to a week or two. So you'll have to be selective in planning your itinerary. You'll have to decide *beforehand* what your priorities are—whether, for example, you'll want to spend all your time in Tokyo or divide your time between a stay in Tokyo or another large city and extensive travel around the country. This section offers you some choices that will help you decide on an itinerary.

If you visit only one city in Japan, make it Kyoto. In addition to having served as the nation's capital for more than 1,000 years, it has more temples, shrines, and historical sights than any other Japanese city. Other top cities you might include in your travels are Nara, another ancient capital, and Tokyo, for its wealth of museums, design, and fashion. Depending on how much time you have, you might also want to visit Mt. Koya, Japan's most revered religious center, where you can sleep in a Buddhist temple; Nikko, site of Shogun Tokugawa Ieyasu's mausoleum; Takayama and Shirakawa-go, two picturesque villages in the Japan Alps; Hiroshima, with its famous Peace Memorial Park and museum of the atomic bomb; and Beppu, a spa renowned for its hot springs. There are, of course, other important destinations.

Note: With the exception of Tokyo and Kyoto, few Japanese cities have tours conducted in English. This book is designed for the individual traveler who prefers sightseeing on his or her own, but if you're pressed for time or don't want to deal with public transportation to sights spread throughout a city, consider joining a Japanese day tour. It's certainly the easiest way to get to the various attractions, and perhaps a Japanese tourist may be able to provide some translations.

If You Have 1 Week (Plan 1)

Day 1 Arrive at the Narita airport, from which it's about a two-hour trip to your hotel in Tokyo. Recuperate from your flight, settle in, and get a feel for the city. Top off the day with a meal in a traditional restaurant.

Day 2 Because of the difference in time zones, you'll probably be wide awake in the wee hours of the morning, so get up and head for Tsukiji Fish Market. After a breakfast of fresh sushi, take the Hibiya Line to Ueno, where you'll find the Tokyo National Museum. From Ueno, hop on the Ginza Line for Asakusa and its famous Nakamise Dori lane, with shops selling traditional products, and its popular Sensoji Temple. If you have time, stroll down Ginza's fashionable shopping district or head toward Harajuku, with its inexpensive clothing boutiques and Oriental Bazaar. Spend the evening in Shinjuku, Roppongi, or another of Tokyo's famous nightlife areas.

Day 3 Take the three-hour Shinkansen bullet train to Kyoto early in the morning. Spend the afternoon on a self-guided walk from Kiyomizu Temple to Heian Shrine and the Silver Pavilion, followed by shopping at the Kyoto Handicraft Center. Spend the night in one of Kyoto's many traditional Japanese-style inns.

Day 4 Take in Nijo Castle, Ryoanji Temple, the Golden Pavilion, and a few other sights of your choosing. If you want to see more temples in one of Japan's ancient capitals, head for Nara, where you'll want to spend at least two to three hours seeing the Great Buddha, Nara Park, and Kasuga Shrine.

Day 5 Leave Kyoto very early in the morning. If you want to spend the night in a Buddhist temple, take the Kintetsu Railways private line (there are only a couple of departures daily, so plan ahead) to Kintetsu Namba Station in Osaka, transferring there to the Nankai Koya Line for the two-hour trip to Mt. Koya. If you'd rather spend the night in a picturesque town with some museums, board the Shinkansen for Kurashiki—less than two hours away; along the way, make a two-hour stopover in Himeji, where you'll find Himeji Castle. If all you want to do is relax at a hot-spring resort, take the Shinkansen back toward Tokyo to Odawara, where you should transfer to a local train bound for Hakone.

Day 6 Spend the day sightseeing, departing by late afternoon for Tokyo. If your plane leaves early the next morning, you may wish to spend the night at Narita.

Day 7 Departure.

Now that the Kansai International Airport in Osaka makes access to Kyoto even easier, if you're more interested in the Japan of temples and history than the capital, you may consider this alternative week:

If You Have 1 Week (Plan 2)

Day 1 Arrive at Kansai International Airport and go into Osaka (a 30-minute trip). Settle into your hotel, then head for the Floating Garden Observatory near Umeda to get a bird's eye view of the city. Do some shopping and have a meal in the area.

Day 2 If you wake up early, visit the Korean market or Tempozan and the aquarium, then head for Osaka Castle. Have lunch nearby, then head to Shittenoji temple, after which you can wander in the Dotonburi area, have a Japanese meal, and later explore the nightlife or take in a Bunraku performance.

Day 3 From Kintetsu Namba Station take the Nankai Koya Line to Mt. Koya to spend the night in a Buddhist temple.

Day 4 Return early in the morning to Osaka and change for the train to Kyoto. Spend the rest of the day as in Day 3 (Plan 1) above.

Day 5 Spend the day as in Day 4 (Plan 1) above.

Day 6 Board the Shinkansen for Kurashiki, a picturesque town with musuems two hours away. Along the way make a stopover at Himeji Castle. Spend the night in a ryokan.

Day 7 Take the Shinkansen back to KIX for departure.

If You Have 2 Weeks

Day 1 Arrive at the Narita airport, settle into your hotel, and become acclimated to Tokyo.

Day 2 Spend the day as you would on Day 2 in the one-week itinerary, above.

Day 3 Spend another day in Tokyo—refer to the Tokyo chapters. Or take a day trip to either Kamakura, with its many temples, or Nikko, famous for the mausoleum of Shogun Tokugawa Ieyasu.

Day 4 Early in the morning, take the Shinkansen to Nagoya (about two hours), then a three-hour train ride to Takayama, in the Japan Alps. Explore the picturesque, narrow streets of this old castle town.

Day 5 Before departing Takayama, visit the morning market by the river. Take the $2^1/_2$-hour bus ride along a winding mountain road to Shirakawa-go, a tiny village of rice paddies and thatched farmhouses. Spend the night in one of these farmhouses.

Day 6 From Shirakawa-go it takes the better part of a day to reach Kyoto, but the scenery is magnificent. From Shirakawa-go you can take a bus back to either Takayama or Nagoya, then transfer to a train for Kyoto.

Days 7 and 8 Spend the two days in Kyoto as you would in the one-week itinerary, above.

Day 9 Early in the morning, set out for Nara, visiting the Great Buddha, Nara Park, and Kasuga Shrine. From Nara you can take the Kintetsu Railways private line (departing from Nara Kintetsu Station) to Kintetsu Namba Station in Osaka, transferring there to the Nankai Koya Line bound for Mt. Koya. If you have a rail pass, you can take Japan Railways trains to Hashimoto, transferring there to the private Nankai Koya Line. Spend the night on Mt. Koya in a Buddhist temple.

Day 10 After visiting Okunoin, the burial grounds of Kobo Daishi, return to Osaka and transfer to the Shinkansen bullet train at Shin-Osaka Station or to a JR train at Osaka Station bound for Kurashiki. Make a two-hour stopover in Himeji to see the beautiful Himeji Castle. Spend the night in Kurashiki and take an evening stroll along the canal.

Day 11 Take in the sights of Kurashiki, including its many museums. Leave for Hiroshima late in the day (about an hour away by Shinkansen).

Day 12 Spend the morning at Peace Memorial Park, with its museum and statues. Take an afternoon excursion to the tiny island of Miyajima, with its famous Itsukushima Shrine. Take the overnight ferry from Hiroshima to Beppu.

Day 13 Spend a relaxing day in the hot-spring resort of Beppu and either visit the huge baths of Suginoi Palace or take a sand bath at Takegawara Bathhouse. Visit the Hells, boiling ponds created by volcanic activity.

Day 14 Take an early-morning flight from nearby Oita airport to Haneda Airport in Tokyo, transferring to the Narita airport for the flight home.

Needless to say, this is something of a whirlwind trip, but it allows you to take in some of the best that Honshu Island has to offer. If you want to get off the beaten track and if you have more time, refer to the chapters on Shikoku, Kyushu, and northern Japan for more ideas on planning your itinerary.

If You Have 3 Weeks

Days 1–3 Spend the first three days in Tokyo, as outlined in the one- and two-week itineraries, above.

Day 4 Go to Takayama, a picturesque town in the Japan Alps.

Day 5 Spend the day in Takayama.

Day 6 Depart Takayama for Shirakawa-go early in the morning. Spend the night in a thatched farmhouse in a rural setting.

Day 7 Go from Shirakawa-go to Kyoto.

Days 8–10 Spend the days in Kyoto and Nara, visiting the many famous gardens, temples, and traditional shops.

Day 11 From Kyoto take an excursion to Mt. Koya, where you can spend the night in a Buddhist temple.

Day 12 From Mt. Koya go to Kurashiki, with a stopover at Himeji Castle.

Day 13 Spend the day in Kurashiki. Leave for Hiroshima late in the day (about an hour away by Shinkansen).

Day 14 After spending the day at Hiroshima's Peace Memorial Park and nearby Miyajima Island, board an overnight ferry for the trip from Hiroshima to Beppu.

Day 15 Spend a relaxing day in the hot-spring resort of Beppu.

Day 16 Take an early-morning direct flight from Oita to Sapporo, on Hokkaido (not available every day, so plan ahead). Take an afternoon stroll through Odori Park and the underground shopping arcades of Aurora Town and Pole Town. Dine on crab, corn on the cob, and other Hokkaido specialties.

Day 17 Start the day with an early-morning tour of the Sapporo Beer Museum, topped off with lunch and a beer at the beer hall or garden. In early afternoon, head for Daisetsuzan National Park.

Day 18 Spend the day at Sounkyo Onsen, skiing, bicycling, or hiking through Daisetsuzan National Park.

Day 19 Take the early morning bus, then train to Hakodate. In the evening, head for Mt. Hakodate, where you can enjoy a great view of the city.
Day 20 Visit the morning market of Hakodate before boarding a train for Matsushima, considered one of the three most scenic spots in Japan.
Day 21 From Matsushima, take a return train ride to Tokyo, about a three-hour trip.

FAST FACTS: Japan

American Express There are several American Express offices in *Tokyo* (see "Fast Facts: Tokyo," in chapter 4, for offices in the capital). In addition, there are American Express offices in *Osaka* (☎ 06/264-6300), *Kobe* (☎ 078/392-3431), *Sapporo* (☎ 011/251-0057), *Nagoya* (☎ 052/204-2246), and *Fukuoka* (☎ 092/272-2111). Most are open Monday through Friday from 9am to 5pm and on Saturday from 9am to 1pm.

Business Hours *Banks* are open Monday through Friday from 9am to 3pm; closed Saturday and Sunday. *Government offices* and *private companies* are generally open Monday through Friday from about 9am to 5pm. In reality, however, Japanese businessmen in the private sector tend to work long hours, and it's not unusual to find someone in the office as late as 10pm. To be on the safe side, however, it's best to conduct business before 5pm.

Most *stores* in Japan don't open until 10am, and they close about 8pm. Often they're closed one day a week, and it's not unusual for almost all the shops in a particular neighborhood to be closed on the same day. Some shops, especially those around major train stations and entertainment areas, stay open until 10pm; some convenience stores are open 24 hours. *Department stores* are open from 10am to 6 or 7pm. They close one day a week, but it's different for each store, so you can always find one open, even on Sunday.

Here, *restaurants* close at exactly the time posted, with the last order taken usually a half hour before closing time (even earlier in kaiseki restaurants). To enjoy your meal fully, therefore, always arrive at a restaurant at least an hour before closing.

Similarly, *museums* and *attractions* in Japan close ticket windows a half hour before closing time.

Calendar Years The Japanese have a unique system for counting years, based on an emperor's reign. The Meiji Period, for example, ran from 1868 to 1912, which translates in the Japanese calendar to Meiji 1–44. Thus, Meiji 10 refers to the 10th year of Emperor Meiji's reign, or 1878. Subsequent periods are Taisaho (1912–26), Showa (1926–89), and Heisei, which began in January 1989, at the beginning of Emperor Akihito's reign. The year 1996, therefore, is Heisei 8.

Cigarettes A wide variety of both domestic and imported brands are readily available throughout Japan. There are even outdoor vending machines on what seems to be every city street. (See also "Customs," below.) Unfortunately for nonsmokers, Japan has never had much of an antismoking campaign. Few restaurants, therefore, have no-smoking sections, and only a few enlightened hotels have designated no-smoking floors. The Tokyo Prince even has a no-smoking lounge. If you want to sit in the no-smoking car of the Shinkansen bullet train, ask for the *kinensha.*

Crime See "Safety," below.

Customs You can take duty-free into Japan up to 400 non-Japanese cigarettes or 500 grams of tobacco or 100 cigars; three bottles (760cc each) of alcoholic beverages; and two ounces of perfume. You can also bring in gifts and souvenirs whose total market value is less than ¥200,000 ($2,000).

A word of caution: Make sure you don't take any pornographic material with you: American magazines, such as *Playboy* and *Penthouse*, that show pubic hair are not allowed into Japan. The Japanese equivalents of these magazines either are much more modest or have the offensive parts blacked out. As for drugs, don't even think about it; penalties for offenders are severe and are strictly imposed (see also "Drug Laws," below).

On your return home, you're allowed by U.S. Customs to bring back duty-free $400 worth of goods purchased abroad. Beyond that, the next $1,000 worth of goods is assessed at 10% duty. If you're shipping purchases home by mail, you're allowed to send up to $50 per package duty-free. Incidentally, you might want to keep a record of your purchases in Japan, in order to be able to declare the exact value of each item.

Driving Rules See "Getting Around," earlier in this chapter.

Drug Laws Drug abuse is not a problem in Japan, simply because there aren't many drugs. Nevertheless, the drug laws are stringent. You'll be fined and deported if you're caught with drugs; if you're caught with harsher drugs, such as cocaine, penalties will be more severe. Don't risk it!

Drugstores Drugstores, called *kusuri-ya,* are found readily in Japan, and they can fill American prescriptions. Nevertheless, it's always best to carry an adequate supply of important medicines with you, particularly since drugstores in Japan do not stay open 24 hours. Convenience stores, which are open day and night, carry such nonprescription items as aspirin.

Electricity The electricity throughout Japan is 100 volts AC, but there are two different cycles in use. In Tokyo and in regions northeast of the capital, it's 50 cycles, while in Nagoya, Kyoto, Osaka, and all points to the southwest, it's 60 cycles. Leading hotels in Tokyo often have two outlets, one for 110 volts and one for 220 volts; many of them also have hair dryers that you can use for free. Actually, you can use many American appliances, such as radios and hair dryers, in Japan, because the American standard is 110 volts and 60 cycles. The only difference is that the appliances may run a little more slowly; the prongs are the same. For sensitive equipment, either have it adjusted or use batteries if it's also battery-operated.

Embassies and Consulates The embassies of most countries are located in Tokyo and are generally open Monday through Friday from 8:30 or 9am to about 5 or 5:30pm. Most of them close for an hour or so for lunch; their visa or passport sections are open at certain times during the day. It's best to call in advance. The *U.S. Embassy,* 1-10-5 Akasaka, Minato-ku (☎ 03/3224-5000), close to the Toranomon subway station, is open Monday through Friday from 8:30am to noon and 2 to 5pm. The *Canadian Embassy,* 7-3-38 Akasaka, Minato-ku (☎ 03/3408-2101), near Aoyama-Itchome Station, is open Monday through Friday from 9am to 12:30pm and 1:30 to 5:30pm. The *British Embassy,* 1 Ichibancho, Chiyoda-ku (☎ 03/3265-5511), close to Ichigaya, Kojimachi, and Hanzomon Stations, is open Monday through Friday from 9am to noon and 2 to 5:30pm. The *Australian Embassy,* 2-1-14 Mita, Minato-ku (☎ 03/5232-4111), is open from 9am to noon and from 2 to 5pm. The *Embassy of Ireland,* 8-7 Sanbancho, Chiyoda-ku

(☎ 03/3263-0695), a 15-minute walk from either Ichigaya or Hanzomon Station, is open Monday through Friday from 9am to 4:30pm. The *New Zealand Embassy,* 20-40 Kamiyama-cho, Shibuya-ku (☎ 03/3467-2271), a 15-minute walk from Shibuya Station, is open Monday through Friday from 9am to noon and 1:30 to 5pm.

The U.S. Embassy and the British Embassy have consular services in Tokyo as well. They also maintain consulates in some major cities, as do several other embassies; for information regarding location, inquire at the respective embassies.

Emergencies The national emergency numbers are **110** for calling *police* and **119** both for calling an *ambulance* and for reporting a *fire.* Be sure to speak slowly and precisely.

Help A number of services offer help and counseling; most of them are based in Tokyo. *Alcoholics Anonymous* has a program in Japan (☎ 03/3971-1471). *Tokyo English Life Line* (☎ 03/5841-4347) is an English-speaking, volunteer service providing free, confidential counseling over the phone. *Japan Helpline* does not offer counseling but provides emergency services nationwide, such as interpreting at hospitals; it handles English-language inquiries to the police and fire departments and provides general information related to travel and living. *Japan Hotline* (☎ 03/3586-0110), open Monday through Friday from 10am to 4pm, gives out general information about daily life problems you might encounter. The *Counseling Center of Tokyo* (☎ 03/3953-2495) and *TELL Community Counseling Service* (☎ 03/5481-4455) offer professional face-to-face counseling, therapy sessions, and workshops; the latter works on a sliding-scale-fee basis.

Holidays See "When to Go," in chapter 3.

Information See "Information & Entry Requirements" in chapter 3, as well as individual city chapters for local information offices.

Language See "The Language Barrier," in chapter 2.

Laundry All the upper-bracket hotels and even some of the hotels for business travelers have laundry service. Since such service tends to be expensive, you may want to wash your clothes yourself. Not everyone has a washing machine in Japan, so self-service laundries are abundant. The cost is about ¥200 to ¥400 ($2–$4) per load for the washer; the dryer is about ¥100 ($1) for 10 minutes. Some of the inexpensive Japanese inns that cater to young travelers also have coin-operated laundry machines on their premises.

Liquor Laws The legal drinking age is 20. You'll find vending machines dispensing beer and whiskey in almost every neighborhood in Japan, but they close down at 11pm. *Note:* If you intend to drive in Japan, you are not allowed even one drink.

Mail Citizens of Canada, the United Kingdom, the Republic of Ireland, Australia, and New Zealand can have mail forwarded to their respective embassies in Japan. The U.S. Embassy, however, will not hold mail. If you don't know where you'll be staying, you can always have your mail sent to the central post office of the major cities you'll be visiting. In Tokyo, have your mail sent c/o Poste Restante, Central Post Office, Tokyo, Japan, which is located just southwest of Tokyo Station.

Although all *post offices* are open Monday through Friday from 9am to 5pm, international post offices are open much later, often until 7 or 8pm, and also on Saturday from 9am to 5pm. It's only at larger post offices that you can mail packages abroad, and these are often found close to the city's main train station.

Conveniently, these branches sell cardboard boxes in three sizes, with the necessary tape and string. Packages mailed abroad cannot weigh more than 20 kilos (about 44 pounds). A package weighing 10 kilos (about 22 pounds) will cost ¥8,000 ($80) if sent to North America via surface mail. As you see, it's very expensive to ship packages abroad.

If you're *mailing a letter,* your hotel may be able to do it for you or direct you to the nearest post office. Airmail letters weighing up to 10 grams cost ¥110 ($1.10) to North America and Europe and postcards are ¥70 (70¢). Domestic letters weighing up to 25 grams are ¥80 (80¢); postcards are ¥50 (50¢). It takes approximately five to seven days for letters and postcards to reach North America.

Post offices are easily recognizable by the red symbol of a capital T with a horizontal line above it. *Mailboxes* in Japan are painted a bright orange-red.

If you have questions telephone 03/5472-5851 for postal information in English, available from Monday to Friday 9:30am to 4:30pm.

Maps Maps are readily available at major bookstores that have sections in English. A recent check of Jena bookstore in Tokyo, for example, revealed at least a dozen different maps of the capital city. Some zero in on sightseeing attractions, while others give postal addresses for the various Tokyo wards and are in both Japanese and English. However, unless you're living in Japan or plan on doing extensive sightseeing, I personally believe that the free maps offered by the Tourist Information Center and local city offices are adequate for trips through the country. Free maps at the Tourist Information Center include maps of Japan, Tokyo, and Kyoto.

Measures Before the metric system came into use in Japan, the country had its own standards for measuring length and weight. There's no reason for you to learn these nowadays, but you will hear one way of measuring that is still common—rooms are still measured by the number of tatami straw mats that will fit in them. A six-tatami room, for example, is the size of six tatami mats, and a tatami is roughly three feet wide and six feet long.

Newspapers and Magazines Five English-language newspapers are published daily in Japan. They are the *Japan Times,* the *Mainichi Daily News,* the *Daily Yomiuri,* the *Asahi Evening News,* and the *International Herald Tribune.* Hotels and major bookstores also carry the international edition of such newsmagazines as *Time* and *Newsweek.* For regional publications detailing what's going on in a city, check with the local tourist information office listed in the individual city chapters.

Pets There is no regulation for bringing a cat into Japan. If you intend to bring a dog with you, however, you must obtain a rabies certificate from the U.S. Department of Agriculture or, if you're a citizen of another country, from the appropriate ministry in your government. For more information, contact the Japanese Embassy or consulate nearest you.

Photographic Needs Japan is the right country to be in if you're looking to buy *cameras* and other photographic equipment. Japanese products are, of course, among the finest in the world, and for that reason they're not cheap. (In fact, you can probably obtain Japanese cameras cheaper in the United States by ordering from one of the many camera catalogs available.) Check "Shopping A to Z," in chapter 5, to find out the location of good camera stores in the capital.

As for *film,* you won't have trouble finding Kodak or the Japanese brand Fuji in Tokyo or other major cities. Outside the big cities, particularly around tourist attractions, it's sometimes difficult to find any film other than Fuji for color prints.

If you intend to take a lot of slides, be sure to stock up on the film of your choice *before* setting out for remote areas. To have Kodak film processed, you should wait until you return to Tokyo or home; shops outside Tokyo often send Kodak film to the capital for development, which can take a week.

Police The national emergency telephone number for police is *110.*

Radio and Television For English-language radio programs, the *Far East Network,* or *FEN* (at 810 kHz), is the U.S. military station, with broadcasts of music, talk shows, and sports events from the United States, as well as Tokyo sumo matches. *J-Wave* (81.3 FM) is a Tokyo radio station that broadcasts programs in English, with a wide range of music. Upper-bracket hotels in Tokyo also have *KTYO,* a cable radio station broadcasting music, news, and sports around the clock.

If you enjoy watching television, you've come to the wrong country. Almost nothing is broadcast in English; even foreign films are dubbed in Japanese, and the only way to hear them in English is if you have what's called a bilingual television. A few of the best hotels in Tokyo and other major cities do have bilingual televisions, and there are generally several English movies on television each week. Major hotels in Tokyo, Osaka, Kobe, and Kyoto also have cable TV with English-language programs, including *CNN* broadcasts from the United States. But even if you don't understand the language, I suggest that you watch television in Japan at least once. Maybe you'll catch a samurai series, which is very popular. Commercials are also worth watching—often they're what I call "mood" advertising, in which the scenery simply sets a mood that has very little to do with the actual product.

By the way, during your travels you may come across rooms in both Western- and Japanese-style establishments that offer video programs with their TVs. These programs are either coin-operated or charged automatically to your bill. Since the descriptions of these programs are usually in Japanese only, I'll clear up the mystery—they're generally "adult entertainment" programs. Now you know. *Note:* If you're traveling with children, you'll want to be extremely careful about selecting your television programs: Many adult video pay channels appear with a simple push of the channel-selector button, and they can be difficult to get rid of.

Restrooms If you're in need of a restroom, your best bet is at train and subway stations, big hotels, and department stores. Many toilets in Japan, especially those at train stations, are Japanese style: They're holes in the ground over which you squat facing the end that has a raised hood. Men stand and aim for the hole. Although Japanese lavatories may seem uncomfortable at first, they're actually much more sanitary because no part of your body touches anything. Who knows, you may even come to prefer them over Western-style toilets. To find out whether a stall is empty, knock on the door. If it's occupied, someone will knock back. Similarly, if you're inside a stall and someone knocks, answer with a knock back or else the person will just keep on knocking persistently and try to get in.

Don't be surprised if you go into some restrooms and find men's urinals and individual private stalls in the same room. Women are supposed to simply walk right past the urinals without noticing them.

Safety Japan is one of the safest countries in the world, and the people, for the most part, are honest. These twin attributes of safety and honesty make Japan a particularly attractive place for the tourist. Nevertheless, crime does exist, for every society has its criminals, but it's negligible compared with that of the United States.

As a general policy, therefore, whenever you're traveling in an unfamiliar country, stay alert. Be aware of your immediate surroundings, especially in heavily touristed areas. Wear a moneybelt and don't sling your camera or purse over your shoulder. Men should carry their billfolds in an inner pocket. These elementary precautions will minimize the possibility of your becoming a victim of theft.

Taxes In 1989 the Japanese government introduced a 3% *consumption tax* on goods and services, including hotel rates and restaurant meals. If you stay overnight in accommodations that cost ¥15,000 ($150) or less per person, a 3% government consumption tax will be added to your bill; if your accommodations cost more than ¥15,000 per person, both a 3% consumption tax and a 3% *local tax* will be added to your bill. Some hotels, particularly business hotels, include the tax in their tariff, while others don't. Be sure to ask, therefore, whether rates include tax. In restaurants, a 3% consumption tax is levied on meals costing ¥7,500 ($75) or less per person, while meals costing more than ¥7,500 are subject to a 6% tax (which includes both consumption and local taxes).

In addition to these taxes, a 10% to 15% *service charge* will be added to your bill in lieu of tipping at most of the fancier restaurants and at many hotels. Thus, the 16% to 21% in tax and service charge that will be added to your bill in the more expensive locales can really add up. Most ryokan, or Japanese-style inns, include a service charge but not a consumption tax in their rates. If you're not sure, ask.

As for shopping, a 3% consumption tax is also levied on most goods (some of the smaller vendors are not required to levy tax). Travelers from abroad, however, are eligible for an exemption on goods taken out of the country, although only the larger department stores and specialty shops seem equipped to deal with the procedures. In any case, most department stores grant a *refund* on the consumption tax only when the total amount of purchases exceeds ¥10,000 ($100). You can obtain a refund immediately by having a sales clerk fill out a list of your purchases and then presenting the list to the tax-exemption counter of the department store. You will need to show your passport. Note that no refunds for consumption tax are given for food, drinks, tobacco, cosmetics, film, and batteries.

If you depart Japan from the Narita airport outside Tokyo, you will be charged a ¥2,000 ($20) *service facility fee,* or ¥1,000 ($10) for children (over 2, under 12). There are vending machines selling departure-tax tickets just past the airline counters, before you descend downstairs to Customs. Kansai International Airport also charges a service facility fee of ¥2,600 ($26) for adults and ¥1,300 ($13) for children (over 2, under 12).

Telephone, Telegram, Telex, and Fax If you're staying in a medium- or upper-range hotel, most likely you can make local, domestic, and international calls from your room. However, you'd be prudent to ask first whether you can make the call directly, whether you must go through the operator, and whether a surcharge will be added to your bill.

There are several different kinds of *public telephones* in Japan, all color-coded. You can find them virtually everywhere—in telephone booths on the sidewalk, on stands outside little shops, on train platforms, in restaurants and coffee shops. There are even telephones in Japan's bullet trains. Some older pink telephones take only ¥10 coins, while the yellow, green, purple, and gray ones accept both ¥10 and ¥100 coins. All gray ones are equipped for international calls. A *local call* costs ¥10 (10¢) for the first minute, after which a warning chime will ring to tell you to insert more coins or you'll be disconnected. I usually insert two or three coins when I make a telephone call so that I won't have to worry about being disconnected; ¥10 coins that aren't used are always returned at the end of the call.

If you don't want to deal with coins, you can purchase a *telephone card,* which can be inserted into a slot on green and gray telephones. Telephone cards are given as gifts and sold at vending machines (located right beside many telephones), at telephone offices, at station kiosks, and even at tourist attractions, where cards are imprinted with photographs of temples, castles, and other sights. The cards come in values of ¥500 and ¥1,000 ($5 and $10). Ask about the value of the tourist attractions cards, as some are sold for double the telephone value as collector cards.

Telephone rates for **international calls** have become more competitive as Japan's one-time monopoly Kokusai Denshin Denwa (KDD) has had to make room for competitors, International Telecom Japan (ITJ) and International Digital Communications (IDC). In fact, at press time, KDD was considering lowering its rates, since it had lost about 30% of the market to the two newcomers. For *international calls* made from public telephones, you can make a collect call or place a call through an operator anywhere in Japan by dialing 0051. An operator-assisted *station-to-station call* to the United States costs ¥1,740 ($17.40) for the first three minutes. Cheaper, however, are calls made without the assistance of an operator, either through an international gray public telephone or through telephones that offer *direct-dial service* (most medium- and upper-range hotels in larger cities offer direct dial, but remember to ask about the surcharge). All gray telephones are equipped to handle international calls. This is when those telephone cards really come in handy. You can make a direct-dial call by dialing 001 (KDD), 0041 (ITJ), or 0061 (IDC), followed by the code of the country you're calling, the area code, and the telephone number. The direct-dial number for calls to the United States, for example, is 001 (or 0041 or 0061) + 1 + area code + telephone number. The cheapest time to call is between 11pm and 8am Japan time, when a three-minute call to the United States costs as little as ¥350 ($3.50).

If you wish to be connected with an operator in your home country, you can do so from green international telephones by dialing 0039, followed by the country code (for the United States, dial 0039-111). These calls can be used for collect calls or credit-card calls. Some hotels and other public places are equipped with special telephones that will link you to your home operator with the push of a button, and there are instructions in English.

The telephone *area codes* for all of Japan's cities begin with a zero. Tokyo's area code, for example, is 03, while Osaka's is 06. For other area codes, check the "Orientation" section of each city in this guide. Use the area code only when dialing from outside the area. When calling Japan from abroad, it may be necessary to drop the zero in the area code. When calling from the United States, for example, dial only 3 for Tokyo (not 03) and 6 (not 06) for Osaka. If you have questions, call the international operator in the country from which you are placing your call.

As for *telegrams* and *faxes* (facsimiles) your hotel probably can handle such services. If not, you can send a telegram or a fax from a Kokusai Denshin Denwa office. (The name is equivalent to International Telephone & Telegraph.) Ask the hotel clerk where the office nearest your hotel is. KDD offices can also handle phototelegrams, and have booths for international telephone calls and *telex* service. The cost of sending a telegram to the United States is ¥120 ($1.20) per word. To send an international *telegram* 24-hours a day dial 03/3344-5151 toll free.

Incidentally, Japan leads the way when it comes to faxes. Almost all my friends in Tokyo have a home fax machine, and most businesses cannot survive without one.

Time Japan is 9 hours ahead of Greenwich mean time, 14 hours ahead of New York, 15 hours ahead of Chicago, and 17 hours ahead of Los Angeles. Since Japan does not go on daylight saving time, subtract one hour from the above times if you're calling the United States in the summer. Because Japan is on the other side of the international dateline, you lose a day when traveling from the United States to Asia. Returning to North America, however, you gain a day, which means that you arrive on the same day you left. In fact, it often happens that you arrive in the States at an earlier hour than you departed from Japan.

Tipping One of the delights of being in Japan is that there's no tipping, not even to waitresses, taxi drivers, or bellboys. If you try to tip them, they'll probably be confused or embarrassed. Instead of giving individual tips, you will have a 10% to 15% service charge added to your bill at the higher-priced hotels and restaurants.

Tourist Offices See "Information & Entry Requirements," in chapter 3.

Travel-Phone If you're having problems communicating with someone in Japan, are lost, or need information, the Japan National Tourist Organization operates a nationwide telephone system, called Travel-Phone, that provides service every day throughout the year from 9am to 5pm. If you're outside Tokyo or Kyoto, all you have to do is insert a ¥10 coin or card into a telephone (it will be returned to you at the end of the call) and dial one of two numbers. If you want to know something about eastern Japan (Tokyo, Yokohama, Matsumoto, the island of Hokkaido), dial 0120-222800; if you have any questions pertaining to western Japan (Nagoya, Kanazawa, Kyoto, western Honshu, Shikoku, Kyushu), dial 0120-444800. Toll-free calls can be made only if you're outside Tokyo or Kyoto. If you're in Tokyo, the number to dial is 3503-4400; in Kyoto it's 371-5649. In these two cities you have to pay for the call, which is ¥10 (10¢) per minute.

Water The water is safe to drink anywhere in Japan, although some people claim it's too highly chlorinated. Bottled water is also readily available.

Weather The *Japan Times* carries nearly a full page of weather information daily, including forecasts for Tokyo and other major Japanese cities and a weekly outlook. In addition, local weather information can be obtained anywhere in Japan by dialing 177. If you wish to know what the weather is in another part of the country, you must first dial that region's area code. Information is given in Japanese only.

9 Tips on Accommodations

Accommodations available in Japan range from inexpensive Japanese-style to large Western-style hotels. Although, theoretically, you can travel throughout Japan without making reservations beforehand, it's essential to do so if you're traveling during peak travel seasons, and recommended at other times. These peak times are the end of April through the first week of May (called Golden Week); the New Year's holiday, from about December 27 to January 4; and mid-July through August, particularly around mid-August.

If you find all my recommendations for a certain city fully booked, there are several ways to find alternative accommodations; book through a travel agency, or book a room through one of three **Welcome Inn Reservation Centers,** located at the Tourist Information Centers in Tokyo and Kyoto and at the Narita airport outside Tokyo. Some 650 modestly priced hotels, business hotels, and Japanese-style inns are members of Welcome Inn and are located throughout Japan. Room rates are ¥8,000 ($80) or less per person per night. No fee is charged for the reservation service, but applicants must appear in person at one of the three centers. The Tokyo and Kyoto centers are open Monday through Friday from 9am to 5pm; the Narita center is open Monday through Friday from 9am to 8pm. All centers are closed on public holidays. Reservation requests are accepted for up to five locations for one party. Reservations can also be made from abroad before your departure for Japan, but note you must have a confirmed booking on a flight to Japan. For more information, contact your nearest Japan National Tourist Organization office.

If you arrive at your destination and need help obtaining accommodations, you may inquire about a place to stay at the hotel and ryokan reservation office or tourist information office found in most train stations. Although policies may differ from office to office, you generally don't have to pay a fee for their services, but you usually do have to pay a percentage of your overnight charge as a deposit. The disadvantage is that you don't see the locale beforehand, and if there's space left at a ryokan even in peak tourist season, there may be a reason for it. The two worst places I've stayed in Japan were booked through one of these reservation offices at a train station (don't worry, I don't recommend them in this book). Although these offices can be a real lifesaver in a pinch, and in most cases may be able to recommend quite reasonable and pleasant places in which to stay, it certainly pays to plan in advance.

JAPANESE-STYLE INNS

A stay at a ***ryokan*** or Japanese inn, you may be surprised to learn, can prove very expensive. Yet the unique experience makes it worth it. For nothing quite conveys the simplicity and beauty, indeed the very atmosphere, of old Japan more than these inns with their gleaming polished wood, tatami floors, rice-paper sliding doors, and meticulously pruned gardens. Personalized service, offered by kimono-clad hostesses, and exquisitely prepared meals are the trademarks of such inns, some of them of ancient vintage. Staying in one of these inns is like taking a trip back in time.

If you want to experience a Japanese-style inn but can't afford the prices of a ryokan, there are a number of other types of accommodations available. Although they don't offer the personalized service and beautiful setting of a ryokan, they do offer the chance to stay in a simple tatami room, sleep on a futon, and in some cases eat Japanese food. As at a ryokan, prices are per person and include service charge and often two meals as well. English is rarely spoken.

RYOKAN Traditionally, ryokan are small, only one or two stories high and containing about 10 to 30 rooms, and are made of wood, with a tile roof. The entrance to a ryokan is often through a gate and small garden. When you enter, you're met by a bowing woman in a kimono. Take off your shoes, slide on the proffered plastic slippers, and follow your hostess down long wooden corridors until you reach the sliding door of your room. After taking off your slippers, step into your tatami room, which is almost void of furniture: a low table in the middle of the room, floor cushions, an antique scroll hanging in an alcove, a simple flower arrangement, and best of all, a view past rice-paper sliding screens of a Japanese landscaped garden with bonsai, stone lanterns, and a meandering pond filled with carp. Notice there's no bed in the room.

Almost immediately your hostess brings you welcoming hot tea and a sweet, served at your low table so that you might sit there for a while and appreciate the view, the peace, and the solitude. Next comes your hot bath, either in your own room (if you have one) or in the communal bath. (Be sure to follow the procedure outlined in the section on Japanese etiquette in "Minding Your P's & Q's," in chapter 2—soaping and rinsing yourself *before* getting into the tub.) After bathing and soaking away all tension, aches, and pains, change into your yukata, a cotton kimono provided by the ryokan.

When you return to your room, you'll find the maid ready to serve your dinner, which consists of locally grown vegetables, fish, and various regional specialties, all spread out on many tiny plates. There is no menu in a ryokan but, rather, one or more set meals determined by the chef. Admire how each dish is in itself a delicate piece of artwork, adorned with slices of ginger, a maple leaf, or a flower. It all looks too wonderful to eat, but finally hunger takes over. If you want, you can order sake or beer to accompany your meal.

After you've finished eating, your maid will return to clear away the dishes and to lay out your bed. The bed is really a futon, a kind of mattress with quilts, and is laid out on the tatami floor. The next morning the maid will wake you, put away the futon, and serve a breakfast of fish, pickled vegetables, soup, dried seaweed, rice, and a raw egg to be mixed with the rice. Feeling rested, well fed, and pampered, you are then ready to pack your bags and pay your bill. Your hostess sees you off at the front gate, smiling and bowing as you set off for the rest of your travels.

Such is life at a good ryokan. Sadly, however, the number of upper-class ryokan diminishes each year. Unable to compete with more profitable highrise hotels, many ryokan in Japan's large cities have closed down, with the result that very few are left in such cities as Tokyo and Osaka. If you want to stay in a Japanese inn, it's best to do so in Kyoto or at a resort or hot-spring spa.

Altogether, there are approximately 90,000 ryokan still operating in Japan in a variety of different price ranges. Although, ideally, a ryokan is an old wooden structure at least 100 years old and perhaps once the home of a samurai or a wealthy merchant, many—especially those in hot-spring resort areas—are modern concrete affairs with as many as 100 or more rooms. What they lack in intimacy, however, is made up for in such amenities as modern bathrooms and perhaps a bar and outdoor recreational facilities. Most guest rooms are fitted with a color TV, a telephone, and a safe for locking up valuables.

In a ryokan, **rates** are based on a per-person charge rather than, as in Western-style hotels, on a straight room charge, and include breakfast, dinner, and service charge. Tax is usually extra.

Although rates can vary from ¥6,000 to ¥150,000 ($60 to $1,500) per person, the average cost is generally ¥10,000 to ¥20,000 ($100 to $200). Even within a single ryokan the rates can vary greatly, depending on the room you choose, the dinner courses you select, and the number of people in your room. If you're paying the highest rate, you can be certain you're getting the best view of the garden, or perhaps even your own private garden, as well as a better meal than lower-paying guests. All the rates for ryokan in this book are based on double occupancy; if there are more than two of you in one room, you can generally count on a slightly lower per-person rate.

Although I have heartily recommended you try spending at least one night in a ryokan, there are a number of **disadvantages** to this style of accommodation. The most obvious problem may be that you will find it uncomfortable sitting on the floor. And because the futon is put away during the day, there's no place on which to lie down for an afternoon nap or rest, except on the hard tatami-covered floor. In addition, some of the older ryokan, though quaint, are bitterly cold in the winter and may have only Japanese-style toilets. As for breakfast, some foreigners might find it difficult to swallow raw egg, rice, and seaweed in the morning (I've even been served grilled grasshopper—quite crunchy). Sometimes you can get a Western-style breakfast if you order it the night before, but more often than not the fried or scrambled eggs will arrive cold, leading you to suspect they were cooked right after you ordered them.

A ryokan is also quite rigid in its **schedule.** You're expected to arrive sometime after 4pm, take your bath, and then eat at around 6 or 7pm. Breakfast is served early, usually by 8am, and checkout is by 10am. That means you can't sleep in, and because the maid is continually coming in and out, you have a lot less privacy than you would in a hotel.

The main drawback of the ryokan, however, is that the majority of them will not take you. They simply do not want to deal with the problems inherent in accepting a foreign guest, including the language barrier and differing customs. I've seen a number of beautiful old ryokan I'd like to include in this book, but I've been turned away at the door. Every year I lose ryokans to the antics of foreigners (climbing in the window at midnight, wild partying, etc.), so please try to be courteous. The ryokan in this guide, therefore, are those willing to take in foreigners.

You should always make a **reservation** and check details if you want to stay in a first-class ryokan, and even in most medium-priced ones, because the chef has to shop for and prepare your meals. The ryokan staff members do not look kindly upon unannounced strangers turning up on their doorstep. You can make a reservation for a ryokan through any travel agency in Japan, or by calling a ryokan directly, although it's best if the call is conducted in Japanese or by fax, as the written language is always easier to understand (this goes for all types of accommodations). You may be required to pay a deposit.

JAPANESE INN GROUP The Japanese Inn Group is a special organization of more than 60 Japanese-style inns throughout Japan offering inexpensive lodging and catering largely to foreigners. Although you may balk at the idea of staying at a place filled mainly with foreigners, remember many inexpensive Japanese-style inns are not accustomed to guests from abroad and may be quite reluctant to take you in. I have covered many of these Japanese Inn Group members in this guidebook and have found the owners for the most part to be an exceptional group of friendly people eager to offer foreigners the chance to experience life on tatami and futon. In many cases, these are good places in which to exchange information with other world travelers, and they are popular with both young people and families.

Although they call themselves ryokan, they are not ryokan in the true sense of the word, because they don't offer personalized service and many of them don't serve food. However, they do offer simple tatami rooms that generally come with a coin-operated TV and sometimes with a coin-operated air conditioner as well. Some of them have towels and a cotton yukata kimono for your use. Facilities generally include a coin-operated washer and dryer and a public bath. The average cost of a one-night stay is about ¥4,000 ($40) to about ¥8,000 ($80) per person, without meals.

Upon your arrival in Japan, you can pick up a pamphlet at the Tourist Information Center in Tokyo called "Japanese Inn Group," which lists the members of this organization. You should make reservations directly with the ryokan in which you wish to stay (many have faxes). In some cases, you'll be asked to pay a deposit (equal to one night's stay), which you can do with a personal check, traveler's check, money order, or bank check, but the easiest way is with American Express. If you want more information, the Inn Group's headquarters is at Sawanoya Ryokan, 2-3-11 Yanaka, Taito-ku, Tokyo 110 (☎ 03/3822-2251, Fax 03/3822-2252), and a Kyoto office is at 314, Hayao-cho, Kaminoguchi-agaru, Ninomiyacho-dori, Shimogyo-ku, Kyoto 600 (☎ 075/351-6748). You can often make your reservation through the local JNTO office, but will pay about $5 more.

MINSHUKU Technically, a minshuku is an inexpensive lodging in a private home. The average per-person cost for one night is ¥6,000 to ¥7,000 ($60 to $70), including two meals. Because minshuku are family-run affairs, you're expected to lay out your own futon at night, supply your own towel and nightgown, and tidy up your room in the morning. Rooms don't have their own private bathroom, but there is a public bath, and meals are served in a communal dining room. Minshuku can range from thatched farmhouses and rickety old wooden buildings to modern concrete structures. Although, officially, what differentiates a ryokan from a minshuku is that it is more expensive and provides more services, the difference is sometimes very slight. I've stayed in cheap ryokan providing almost no service and in minshuku too large and modern to be considered private homes.

Since minshuku cater primarily to Japanese travelers, they're often excellent places to meet the locals, and I've included in this guide a number of minshuku willing to take in foreigners. For more information, contact the **Japan Minshuku Center,** Kotsu Kaikan Building, Basement 1, 2-10-1 Yurakucho, Chiyoda-ku, Tokyo (☎ **03/3216-6556**). It's open Monday through Friday from 10am to 6pm and on Saturday from 10am to 5pm (closed holidays), and you can make reservations here for member minshuku across the country. Note, however, that reservations are accepted only for two or more people during July and August, from December 25 to January 4, and on weekends.

KOKUMIN SHUKUSHA A kokumin shukusha is public lodging found primarily in resort and vacation areas. Established by the government, there are more than 300 of these facilities throughout Japan. Catering largely to Japanese school groups and families, they offer basic, Japanese-style rooms at an average daily rate of about ¥5,000 ($50) per person, including two meals. Although you don't have to have a reservation to stay in these places, they're usually quite full during the summer and peak seasons. Reservations can be made through a travel agency. The drawback to many of these lodges is that because they're often located in national parks and in scenic spots, the best way to reach them is by car.

KOKUMIN KYUKA MURA Similar to a kokumin shukusha, the kokumin kyuka mura is a "vacation village" that's government-run and located in a national park, but the difference is that it's more expensive—generally around ¥6,000 to ¥10,500 ($60 to $105) per person, with two meals—and offers more recreational facilities. Apply through a travel agency.

SHUKUBO These are lodgings in a Buddhist temple. Providing Japanese-style rooms, they're similar to inexpensive ryokan, except that they're attached to temples and serve vegetarian food. There's usually an early-morning service at 6am, which you're welcome—and in some shukubo, required—to join. Probably the best place to experience life in a temple is at Mt. Koya (described in chapter 10). Prices at a shukubo range from about ¥5,500 ($55) to about ¥11,000 ($110) per person, including two meals.

WESTERN-STYLE ACCOMMODATIONS

Lodging in this category ranges from large first-class hotels to inexpensive ones catering primarily to Japanese businessmen. In figuring out your bill, remember that in accommodations costing more than ¥15,000 ($150) per person per night, a 6% local/consumption tax will be added, while in accommodations costing less than ¥15,000, a 3% consumption tax will be added. There will also be a 10% to 15% service charge added to your bill. Although ryokan and some of the less expensive types of lodgings include service and sometimes tax in their prices, most hotels do not. Unless otherwise stated, therefore, you can assume that 16% to 21% will be added to the prices quoted in this book for hotels costing more than ¥15,000 ($150) per person per night. Incidentally, a twin room refers to a room with twin beds, and a double room refers to one with a double bed.

HOTELS Both first-class and medium-priced hotels in Japan are known for excellent service and cleanliness. The first-class hotels in the larger cities can compete with the best hotels in the world and offer a wide range of services, which may include a health club and massage services (for which there's an extra charge), an executive business center with secretarial services, a guest relations officer to help with any problems you may have, a travel agency, a shopping arcade, cocktail lounges with live music, and fine Japanese- and Western-style restaurants. Rooms have their own private bathroom with a tub and shower combination (since Japanese are used to soaping down and rinsing off before bathing, it would be rare to find tubs without showers; similarly, showers without tubs are practically nonexistent in this nation of bathers). Because they're accustomed to foreigners, most hotels in this category employ an English-speaking staff. Services provided include room service (usually until midnight, although some Tokyo hotels have 24-hour room service), laundry and dry-cleaning service (note that some hotels do not provide this service on Sunday), and often a complimentary English-language newspaper, such as the *Japan Times,* delivered to guest rooms.

The most expensive hotels in Japan are in Tokyo, where you'll pay at least ¥20,000 ($200) for a single room in a first-class hotel. Outside Tokyo, single rooms in this category generally range from about ¥12,000 ($120) to about ¥15,000 ($150), while in medium-priced hotels rooms are usually about ¥2,000 ($20) less.

BUSINESS HOTELS Catering primarily to traveling Japanese businessmen, a "business hotel" is a no-frills establishment with tiny, sparsely furnished rooms, most of them singles, but usually with some twin or double rooms also available. Primarily just a place to crash for the night, these rooms usually have everything you need, but in miniature form—minuscule bathroom, tiny bathtub, small bed (or beds), and barely enough space to unpack your bags. If you're a large person, you may have trouble sleeping in a place like this. There are no bellhops, no room service, and sometimes not even a lobby or coffee shop, although usually there are vending machines. The advantage of staying in business hotels is price—starting as low as ¥5,500 ($55) for a single—and they are often conveniently located next to train and subway stations. Check-in is usually not until 3 or 4pm and checkout is usually at 10am; you can leave your bags at the front desk. The most sophisticated business hotels can be found in Tokyo, where, because of high prices, they make up the bulk of medium-priced accommodations.

PENSIONS If you see an accommodation listed as a pension, you know that it's the Western equivalent of a minshuku. Usually containing no more than 10 rooms, these Western-style lodges come with beds and, on the average, charge ¥6,500 to ¥8,500 ($65 to $85) per person, including two meals. Many seem geared to young Japanese girls and are thus done up in rather feminine-looking decor, with lots of pinks and flower prints. They're most often located in ski resorts and in the countryside, sometimes making access a problem.

YOUTH HOSTELS There are more than 450 youth hostels in Japan, most of them privately run and operating in locations ranging from temples to concrete blocks. There's no age limit, and although most of them require a youth hostel membership card from the Japan Youth Hostel Association, they often let foreigners stay without one for about ¥600 ($6) extra per night. Such restrictions as a 9 or 10pm curfew, meals at fixed times, and rooms with many bunk beds or futon apply. Youth hostels are quite cheap, costing about ¥3,500 ($35) per day, including two meals. They're certainly the cheapest accommodation in Japan. A Norwegian I met compared life in a youth hostel to that in the military—perhaps not that regimented, but you get the picture.

I've included youth hostels in case you want to try some of them to keep down costs. If you plan on staying exclusively in youth hostels, you should pick up a pamphlet called "Youth Hostel Map of Japan," available at the Tourist Information Center in Tokyo or Kyoto. You should also get a youth hostel membership card. If you fail to obtain one in your own country, you can get one in Japan for ¥2,800 ($28). The **Japan Youth Hostel Association** is located in the Suidobashi Nishguchi Kaikan, 2-20-7 Misaki-cho, Chiyoda-ku, Tokyo 101 (☎ **03/3288-1417**). You can buy a youth hostel card in Tokyo at the Youth Hostel information counter in the second basement of Sogo Department Store in front of Yurakucho Station, and on the eighth floor of Seibu Department Store in Ikebukuro.

INTERNATIONAL VILLAS

These small country inns are financed and maintained by the Okayama prefectural government, and are open only to foreigners, although accompanying Japanese guests are welcome. The idea for the inns originated with Okayama's governor, who wanted to repay the kindness of foreigners during his trips abroad as a youth. Each villa is small, with half a dozen or so guest rooms, and equipped with the latest in bathroom and kitchen facilities. You can cook your own meals or visit one of the local restaurants. There are six International Villas, most of them in small villages or rural settings. They're located in Fukiya, Koshihata, Ushimado, Hattoji, Shiraishi Island, and Takebe. The cost for staying at one of the villas is ¥3,000 ($30) per person for nonmembers and ¥2,500 ($25) for members. To become a member, simply pay ¥500 ($5) for a membership card upon check-in at any villa. For more information, refer to the section on Okayama.

10 Tips on Dining

The biggest problem facing the hungry foreigner in Japan is ordering a meal, because few restaurants have English menus. This book alleviates the problem to a large extent by giving some sample dishes and prices for specific restaurants throughout Japan. One aid to simplified ordering is the common use of plastic food models in glass display cases either outside or just inside the front door of restaurants. Sushi, tempura, daily specials, spaghetti—they're all there in mouth-watering plastic replicas, along with the corresponding prices. The use of such food models began after Japan opened its doors a century ago and was inundated by all kinds of strange, foreign things. Food was one of them, and the models eased the problems of ordering strange Western dishes. Today, those plastic dishes work in reverse, saving the lives of hungry visiting foreigners. Simply decide what you want and point it out to your waitress.

Unfortunately, not all restaurants in Japan have plastic display cases. In such a situation, the best thing to do is to look at what people around you are eating and order what looks best. An alternative is simply to order the *teishoku,* or daily special meal (also called "set course" or simply "course"). These are fixed-price meals that consist of a main dish and several side dishes, including soup, rice, and Japanese pickles. Although most restaurants have special set courses for dinner as well, lunch is the usual time for the teishoku, and you can help keep your costs down by eating your big meal in the middle of the day. Even a restaurant that may be prohibitive to your budget at dinnertime may be perfect for a lunchtime treat, when specials may cost as little as a fourth of what a dinner would be. The usual time for the teishoku is from about 11 or 11:30am to 1:30 or 2pm. Keep in mind that restaurants will add a 6% tax to bills costing ¥7,500 ($75) and more, while a 3% tax will be added to bills costing less than ¥7,500. First-class restaurants will also add a 10% to 15% service charge, as do restaurants located in many hotels.

For those of you who may not want to eat Japanese food every day, I've included suggestions throughout this book for non-Japanese restaurants as well. The most popular Western-style restaurants in Japan are Italian and French, although more often than not they cook for the Japanese rather than the Western palate. French nouvelle cuisine matches well the Japanese style of cooking, since both stress presentation, textures, and flavor, and the most expensive foreign restaurants in Japan are nearly all French. Other popular restaurants are Indian, Thai, and Chinese, as well as numerous steakhouses.

The usual opening hours for restaurants in Japan are from about 11am to 10 or 11pm. Of course, some establishments close as early as 9pm, while others stay open past midnight; some close for a few hours in the afternoon. The main thing to remember is that if you're in a big city like Tokyo or Osaka, you'll want to avoid the lunchtime rush, which is from 1 to 2pm. In addition, the closing time posted for most restaurants is exactly that—everyone is expected to pay his or her bill and leave. A general rule of thumb is that the last order is taken about a half hour before closing time. To be on the safe side, therefore, try to arrive at least 30 minutes before closing time. An hour would be even better, giving you time to relax and enjoy your meal.

INEXPENSIVE CHOICES During your first few days in Japan—particularly if you're in Tokyo—money will seem to flow out of your pockets like water. In fact, money has a tendency to disappear so quickly that many people become convinced they must have lost some of it somehow. At this point, almost everyone panics (I've seen it happen again and again), but then slowly realizes that since prices are markedly different here (steeper), a bit of readjustment in thinking and habits is necessary. Coffee, for example, is something of a luxury, and some Japanese are astonished at the thought of drinking four or five cups a day. By following the advice here, you'll be able to cut down on needless expenses, saving your money for special things.

If you're on a tight budget, avoid eating breakfast at your hotel. Coffee shops offer what is called "morning service" until 10 or 11am; it generally consists of a cup of coffee, a small salad, a boiled egg, and toast for about ¥450 ($4.50). That's a real bargain when you consider that just one cup of coffee costs $2.80 to $10, depending upon where you order it. If you drink coffee or black tea in the morning, you can save money by purchasing instant coffee or tea bags and drinking it in your hotel room. Most hotels and inns in Japan provide a thermos of hot water or a water heater. Since jars of instant coffee tend to be heavy and bulky, you might want to buy individual packets of coffee, available in cubes, tubes, or so-called coffee sticks, complete with powdered cream and sugar. You'll find instant coffee or tea in the food department of major department stores and in the now ubiquitous *supa,* or mini-supermarket chain stores.

Eat your biggest meal at lunch. Many restaurants offer a daily set lunch, or teishoku, at a fraction of what their set dinners might be. Usually ranging in price from ¥700 to ¥1,500 ($7 to $15), they're generally available from 11 or 11:30am to 2 or 3pm. A Japanese teishoku will often include the main course (such as tempura, grilled fish, or the specialty of the house), soup, pickled vegetables, rice, and tea, while the set menu in a Western-style restaurant usually consists of a main dish, salad, bread, and coffee. Places in which to look for inexpensive restaurants include department stores (often one whole floor will be devoted to various kinds of restaurants), underground shopping arcades, nightlife districts, and around train and subway stations. Some of the cheapest establishments for a night out on the town are the countless yakitori-ya across Japan—drinking establishments that also sell skewered meats and vegetables.

Noodle shops are generally inexpensive, ranging from stand-up stalls seen around train stations to more traditional restaurants, where guests sit at low tables on tatami. Although noodle and ramen shops are already rock-bottom choices, you can save even more money by avoiding restaurants altogether. There are all kinds of pre-prepared foods you can buy; some of them are complete meals in themselves, perfect for picnics in the park or right in your hotel room.

Perhaps the best known is the *obento,* or box lunch, commonly sold on express trains, on train-station platforms, and at counter windows of tiny shops throughout Japan. In fact, the obento served on trains and at train stations are an inexpensive way to sample regional cuisine, since they often include food typical of the region. In Hiroshima, for example, an obento may include oysters. Costing usually between ¥800 and ¥1,500 ($8 and $15), the basic obento contains a piece of meat (generally fish or chicken), various side dishes, rice, and pickled vegetables. Sushi boxed lunches are also available.

Department stores usually sell pre-prepared foods in their basements, in the food and produce sections; they include such items as tempura, yakitori, sushi, salads, and desserts. There are numerous samples available, and some travelers have been known to "dine" in department-store basements for free. These places are very popular with housewives. By the way, most department stores also have inexpensive restaurants, usually on one of the top floors. Since they almost always have plastic food displays, ordering is easy.

Street vendors are also good sources for inexpensive meals. They sell a variety of foods, including *oden* (fish cakes), *okonomiyaki* (pancakes with different ingredients), and *yakisoba* (fried noodles). If you find yourself in real financial woes, you can always subsist on "cup noodle," which you can buy in any food store. Eaten by poor students and workingmen who don't have the time to sit down to a real meal, it's a dried soup that springs to life (well, sort of) when you add hot water—usually readily available if you're staying in a ryokan. The cup noodle comes in a variety of choices, such as curry or chili tomato, and usually costs less than ¥300 ($3). Eat too much of it, though, and you'll probably disintegrate.

Japan also has American fast-food chains, such as McDonald's (where Big Macs cost about ¥400/$4), Wendy's, and Kentucky Fried Chicken, as well as Japanese chains—Morninaga, Lotteria, and First Kitchen, among them—that sell hamburgers and french fries.

11 Tips on Shopping

ANTIQUES & CURIOS Antiques are another good buy in Japan, simply because most are unique to Japan and therefore make memorable souvenirs of your trip. Cast-iron teapots, secondhand kimonos, china, religious statuary, furniture, *hibachi* (charcoal braziers), masks, dolls, mirrors—the list goes on and on. Tokyo is one of the best places in which to pick up antiques, since it has the greatest number of weekend flea markets and antique shops.

POSTCARDS Unless you have a photographic memory and can remember places and names, and how to spell them, chances are that all those snapshots of temples, shrines, and gardens will look distressingly alike once you get your film developed. My mother's solution: Buy postcards of every place you visit. That way you can match snapshots with postcards, many of which may have such useful information as name, location, and correct spelling of the place or object in question. And if your pictures don't turn out well, you'll always have those postcards.

TRADITIONAL CRAFTS Produced throughout Japan, traditional crafts are often distinctive of a region. Those readily available include ceramics and pottery, toys, textiles, products made from Japanese paper (*washi*), Japanese dolls, carp banners, kites, swords, fans, masks (including Noh antique and reproduction masks), lacquerware, items made from bamboo, knives, and artwork. Many prefectural government offices maintain a display room where the local products are offered for sale; otherwise, they can be found in city shops. Refer to the individual city listings for more information. In addition, there are many prefectural display shops grouped together around Tokyo Station, where you can shop for crafts from around Japan. (See chapter 5 for more information.) And finally, when it comes to traditional crafts, no city can outdo Kyoto, where many shops have been passed down from generation to generation.

4 Getting to Know Tokyo

To the uninitiated, Tokyo may seem like a whirlwind of traffic and people, so confusing that visitors might swear they had somehow landed on another planet. This chapter should make getting settled in Tokyo not only less confusing but more enjoyable as well.

First-time visitors to Tokyo are almost invariably disappointed. They come expecting an exotic Asian city, but instead they find a Westernized and modernized city—to the point of ugliness, much of it a drab concrete jungle of unimaginative buildings clustered so close together there's hardly room in which to breathe.

Simply stated, Tokyo is a crush of humanity. Its subways are often packed, its sidewalks are crowded, its streets are congested, and its air is filled with an irritating amount of noise, pollution, and what can only be called "mystery smells." Almost 12 million people live in its 770 square miles, many of them in bedroom towns, from which they have to commute to work an average of two to three hours every day. No matter where you go in Tokyo, you're never alone. After you've been here for a while, Paris, London, and even New York will seem like deserted cities.

Tokyo's crowds and ugliness, however, are what you'll see only if you don't bother to scratch beneath the surface. Beautiful in its own way, Tokyo is most definitely a state of mind, and if you open yourself to it you'll find a city humming with energy and vitality, a city unlike any other in the world. People rush around here with such purpose, with such determination, it's hard not to feel that you're in the midst of something important, that you're witnessing history in the making.

1 Tokyo Past & Present

Though today the nation's capital, Tokyo is a relative newcomer to the pages of Japanese history. For centuries it was nothing more than a rather unimportant village called Edo, which means simply "mouth of the estuary." Then, in 1603, Edo was catapulted into the limelight when the new shogun, Tokugawa Ieyasu, made the sleepy village the seat of his shogunate government. From then on, the town developed quickly, and by 1787 the population had grown to 1.3 million, making Edo even then one of the largest cities in the world.

The Tokugawas ruled Japan for about 250 years, adopting a policy of isolation from the rest of the world. When they were overthrown in 1868, the Japanese emperor, virtually exiled in Kyoto, was restored to power and moved the capital to Edo, now renamed Tokyo, "Eastern Capital." Thus, Japan's feudal era came to an end. The country put an abrupt halt to its isolation policy and flung its doors wide open to the West in a concerted effort to modernize.

As the nation's capital, Tokyo was the hardest hit in this new era of modernization, with fashions, architecture, food, department stores, and even people imported from the West. West was best, and things Japanese were forgotten or ignored. It didn't help that Tokyo was almost totally destroyed twice in the first half of this century. In 1923 a huge earthquake struck the city, followed by tidal waves. Almost 150,000 people died, and half of Tokyo was in ruins. Disaster struck again in 1945, toward the end of World War II, when Allied incendiary bombs destroyed most of the city.

I guess that's why most visitors are disappointed with Tokyo—there's almost nothing of historical importance to match Kyoto or Kamakura. So put your notions of "quaint Japan" out of your mind and plunge headfirst into the 21st century, because that's what Tokyo is all about. The city is so wired and electric you can feel it in the air.

As the financial nerve center of Japan, Tokyo is where it's happening in Asia. In a nation of overachievers, Tokyo has more than its fair share of intellectuals, academics, politicians, and artists, and it's the country's showcase for technology, media, fashion, art, music, and advertising.

But even though the city has a fast-paced, somewhat zany side, get up early and take a walk in one of its gardens and you'll experience another, more peaceful side. Although formidable at first glance, Tokyo is nothing more than a series of small towns and neighborhoods clustered together, each with its own narrow, winding streets, ma-and-pa shops, fruit stands, and stores. Look for the small things, and you'll notice the carefully pruned bonsai adorning the sidewalks, women in kimonos bowing and shuffling down the streets, an ikebana arrangement on a station shelf, old wooden houses, neatness and order.

Tokyo is both old and new, both Japanese and Western—but it's definitely more Japanese than Western. The harmonious blending of its two aspects gives it a unique charm and character. I love Tokyo. Although the city is overcrowded, and despite the occasional frustrations one is bound to feel as a foreigner, I find Tokyo exhilarating and fun. It never ceases to be interesting. Best of all, it's one of the safest cities in the world; you can walk without fear anywhere, anytime, night or day. The only thing you may have to watch out for sometimes is the alacrity with which Japanese businessmen who have had a little too much to drink will approach you to practice their English on you. Their reserve thrown off after an evening of conviviality, they may prove surprisingly friendly.

2 Orientation

ARRIVING

BY PLANE

There are two airports serving Tokyo, but most likely you'll arrive at the **New Tokyo International Airport** in Narita (usually referred to as the Narita airport), 40 miles outside Tokyo. If you're arriving in Tokyo from elsewhere in Japan, your flight will probably land at **Haneda Airport,** used primarily for domestic flights.

Facilities at Narita Once you've gone through Customs, you'll exit through automatic doors into the arrival waiting lobby of either Terminal 1 or Terminal 2. Arrival lobbies in both terminals have counters for hotel reservations, limousine bus service into Tokyo, and the Keisei Skyliner train to Ueno Station. Both terminals connect to all ground transportation.

If you've purchased a Japan Rail Pass, you can turn in your voucher at one of the Japan Railways (JR) Travel Service Centers (☎ 04/7634-6008), located on the arrival or Level B1 of Terminal 1 and on Level B1 of Terminal 2. Both are open daily from 7am to 9pm.

Tourist Information Centers (TIC), managed by the Japan National Tourist Organization, is located in the arrival lobby of Terminal 2 and is open daily from 9am to 8pm. You can pick up a map here and ask for directions to your hotel or inn. If you don't yet have a hotel room and want one at a modest price, you can make reservations here free of charge Monday through Friday between 9am and 7:30pm.

If you need to change money, you can do so at a **bureau de change,** which you'll come across just after you clear Customs and before you enter the arrival lobby in both terminals. If you forget to change money there, you can do so at counters in the arrival lobby and at a bank in the departure lobbies of Terminal 1 (fourth floor) and Terminal 2 (second floor).

Other facilities include four **post offices:** two in Terminal 1 (one in the departure lobby, open daily from 9am to 8:30pm, and the second in the basement, open Monday through Friday from 9am to 5pm and on Saturday from 9am to 12:30pm); and two in Terminal 2 (one in the third-floor departure lobby, open daily from 9am to 8:30pm, and the second on the second-floor domestic departures level, open Monday through Friday from 9am to 5pm and on Saturday from 9am to 12:30pm).

There are also **Kokusai Denshin Denwa (KDD)** offices in both terminals, where you can make an international telephone call or send a telegram. The office on the fourth floor of Terminal 1 is open daily from 9am to 8pm; the office in the third-floor departure lobby in Terminal 2 is open daily from 7am to 9:30pm.

Getting from Narita Airport into Tokyo Everyone grumbles about the Narita airport because it's so far away from Tokyo, compared with the distance of other airports from the capital cities they serve.

Obviously, jumping into a **taxi** and driving straight to your hotel is the easiest way to get to Tokyo, but it's also the most expensive—and may not even be the quickest if you happen to hit rush hour. Expect to spend ¥22,000 to ¥24,000 ($220 to $240) for a one- to two-hour taxi ride from the Narita airport.

The most popular way to get from Narita to Tokyo is via the **Airport Limousine Bus** (☎ 03/3665-7232). Buses, which depart from just outside the arrival lobbies of both terminals, operate most frequently to the Tokyo City Air Terminal (TCAT), and the trip takes about 70 minutes. Buses also go to Tokyo and Shinjuku Stations and to more than a dozen of Tokyo's major hotels, but service to these places is slightly less frequent. Check with the staff at the Airport Limousine Bus counter in the arrival lobbies to inquire which bus stops nearest your hotel. Fares for the limousine bus range from ¥2,700 to ¥3,800 ($27 to $39), based on distance traveled; children 6 to 12 are charged from ¥1,350 ($13.50); children under 6 ride free.

If you take a limousine bus to the TCAT or one of the other destinations, there are plenty of taxis available. And the subway is convenient, since improvements in the central-city Hanzomon Line now connect its last stop, Suitengu-mae, directly to the TCAT with moving walkways and escalators.

Tokyo At A Glance

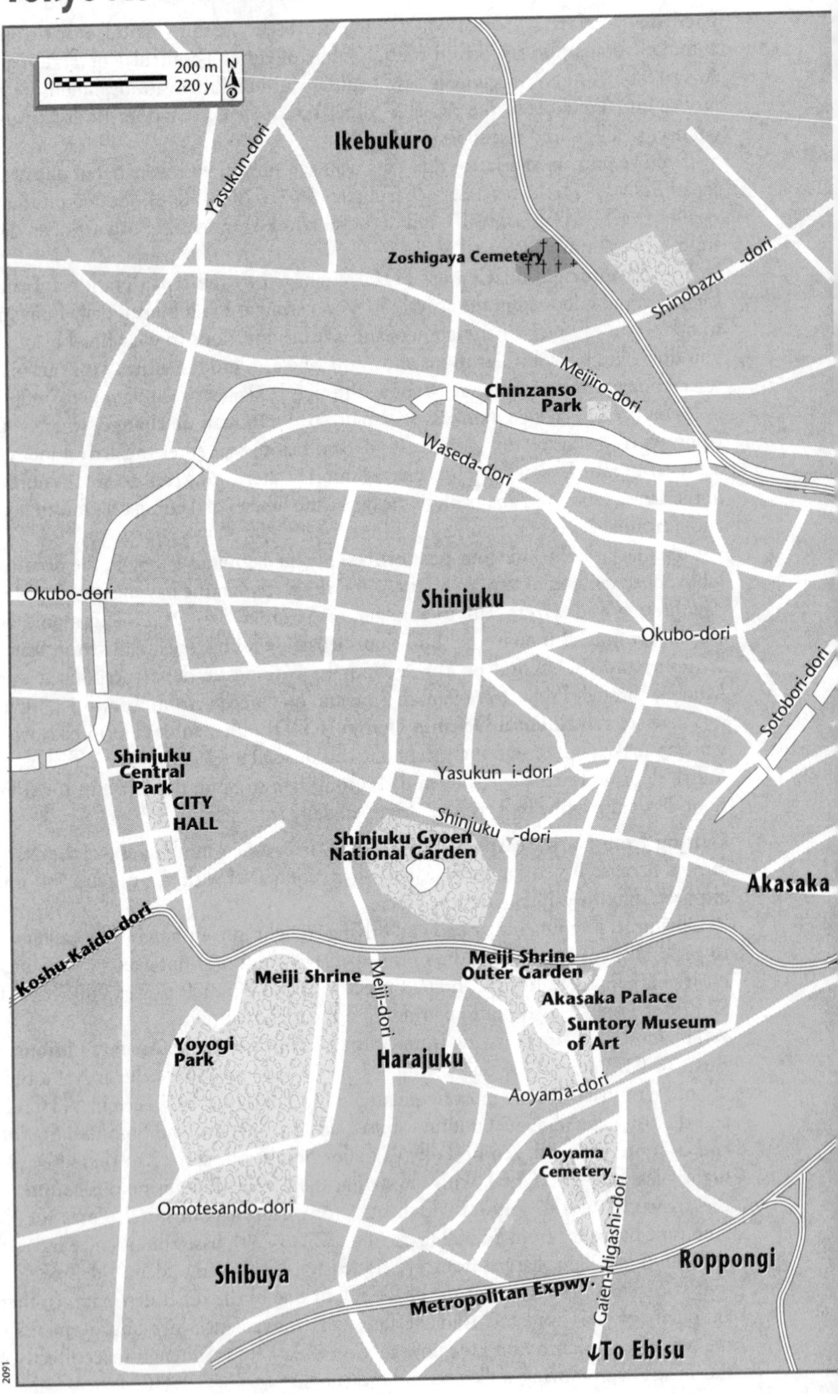

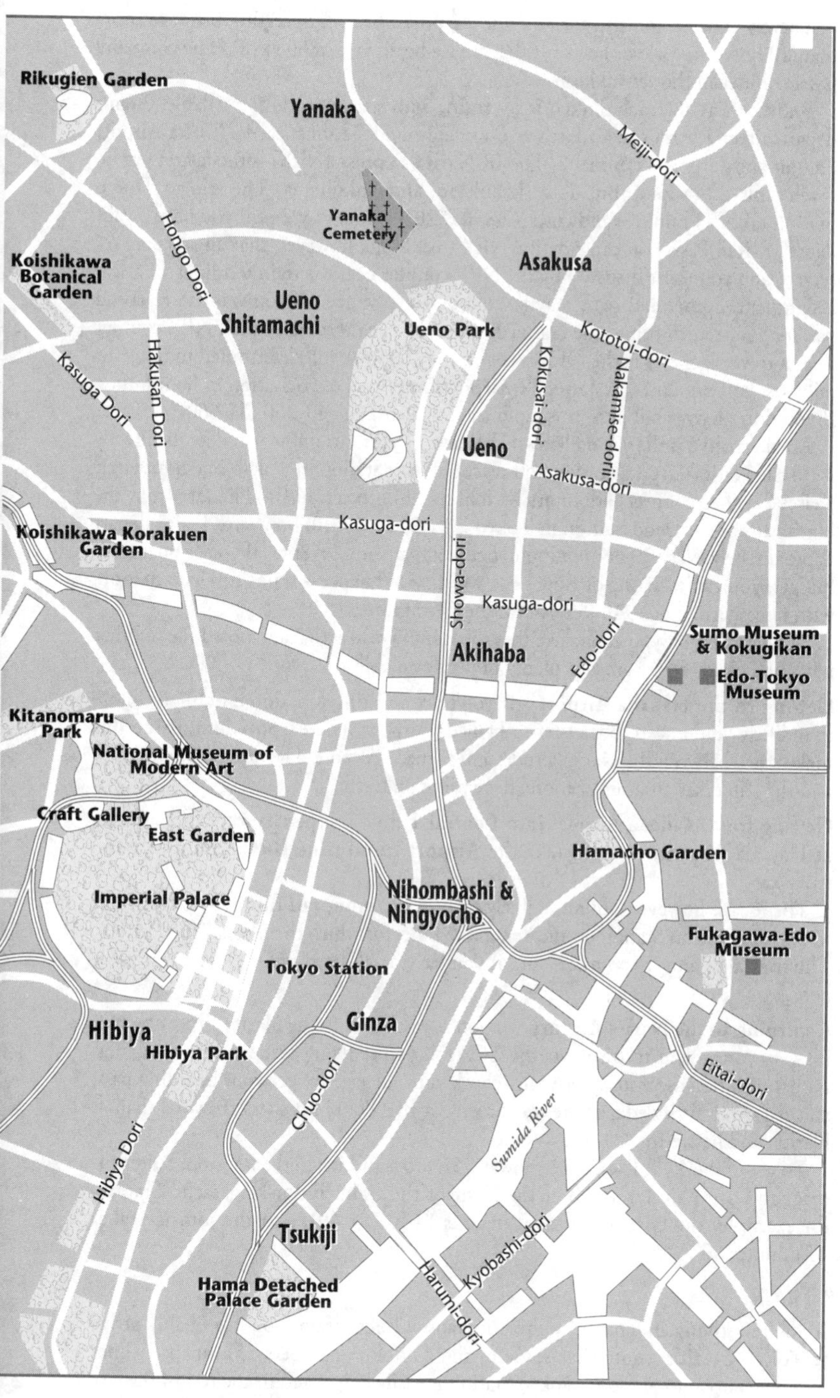

Rikugien Garden
Yanaka
Yanaka Cemetery
Meiji-dori
Koishikawa Botanical Garden
Hongo Dori
Asakusa
Ueno Shitamachi
Ueno Park
Kototoi-dori
Kasuga Dori
Hakusan Dori
Kokusai-dori
Nakamise-dorii
Ueno
Asakusa-dori
Kasuga-dori
Koishikawa Korakuen Garden
Showa-dori
Kasuga-dori
Edo-dori
Sumo Museum & Kokugikan
Akihaba
Edo-Tokyo Museum
Kitanomaru Park
National Museum of Modern Art
Craft Gallery
East Garden
Hamacho Garden
Imperial Palace
Nihombashi & Ningyocho
Fukagawa-Edo Museum
Tokyo Station
Ginza
Hibiya
Hibiya Park
Eitai-dori
Chuo-dori
Sumida River
Hibiya Dori
Tsukiji
Kyobashi-dori
Harumi-dori
Hama Detached Palace Garden

There's another company, called the **Airport Shuttle,** operating buses to more than 20 hotels in Tokyo. Fares for this service begin at ¥2,800 ($28). The company has a counter in the arrival lobby.

Another way to reach Tokyo is by **train,** with several options available. Trains depart directly from the airport's two underground stations, called Narita Airport Station and Airport Terminal 2. The JR **Narita Express (NEX)** is the fastest way to reach Tokyo Station, Shinjuku, Ikebukuro, and Yokohama. The trip to Tokyo Station takes 53 minutes and costs ¥2,890 ($28.90) one-way, but if you have a validated JR Rail Pass, you can ride the NEX free. Note, however, that all seats are reserved, and you must first stop by the NEX counter near the train terminal for a seat assignment. Sometimes seats may be sold out in advance. (If you want to reserve a seat for your return trip to the Narita airport, you can do so here at the NEX counter or at a travel agency.) If the NEX is sold out and you're still determined to use your rail pass, you can take the slower JR **Airport Liner** to Tokyo Station in 80 minutes. If you don't have a rail pass, this rapid train will cost you ¥1,260 ($12.60).

An alternative is the privately owned **Keisei Skyliner** train, which departs directly from the Narita Airport Station and reaches Ueno Station in Tokyo one hour later. Keisei Skyliner counters are in arrival lobbies of both terminals. The fare from the Narita airport to Ueno Station in Tokyo is ¥1,740 ($17.40) one-way. Trains depart approximately every 30 or 40 minutes between 9am and 9:58pm. If you're on a strict budget, you can take one of Keisei's slower **limited express** trains to Ueno Station, with fares starting at ¥940 ($9.40) for the 75-minute trip.

At Ueno Station you can take either the subway or the JR Yamanote Line to other parts of Tokyo. There are also plenty of taxis available.

Getting to the Haneda Airport If you're connecting to a domestic flight, more than likely you'll need to transfer to Haneda Airport. The **Airport Limousine Bus** makes runs between the Narita airport and Haneda Airport. The fare is ¥2,900 ($29) and the trip takes an hour or more, depending on traffic.

Getting from Haneda Airport into Central Tokyo If perchance you're arriving at Haneda Airport, you can take the **Airport Limousine Bus** to Shinjuku and Akasaka.

The locals, however, are more likely to take the **monorail** from Haneda Airport to Hamamatsucho Station on the Yamanote Line, for which the fare is ¥460 ($4.60). The trip takes only 15 minutes, and if you have a validated rail pass, you can use it here.

Returning to the Narita Airport If you're returning to the Narita airport by bus, it's very convenient to travel via the TCAT if you're flying certain airlines, such as Northwest, because you can actually check your luggage in, get your boarding pass, and pay your airport departure tax directly at the TCAT. It's less crowded than at Narita, and hassle-free.

To get to the TCAT, take the subway's Hanzomon Line to the last stop, Suitengu-mae, and use Exit 1A or 1B at the front of the train. From Nagatacho Station, for example, the cost to Suitengu-mae is ¥140 ($1.40), and the journey takes 15 minutes.

BY TRAIN

If you're arriving in Tokyo by the Shinkansen bullet train, you'll probably arrive at **Tokyo Station** (note that some of the Tohoku and Joetsu Shinkansen lines terminate at Ueno Station). Tokyo Station is easily connected to the rest of the city via JR commuter trains and the subway. If you need assistance or information on

Tokyo, stop by the **Information Bureau of Tokyo** (run by the Tokyo Metropolitan Government), located in Tokyo Station at the Travel Plaza, near the Yaesu Exit. It's open Monday through Saturday from 9am to 6pm, closed Sunday and holidays.

By Bus

Long-distance bus service from Hiroshima, Nagoya, Osaka, Kyoto, and other major cities delivers passengers to **Tokyo Station,** from where the city's extensive transportation system can be used. Other bus terminals serving the region outside Tokyo include Shinagawa and Shinjuku Stations, both of which are served by the JR Yamanote Line, which loops around the city.

By Car

The **Chuo Expressway** is the major artery leading into Tokyo from Osaka, Kyoto, Nagoya, and other major cities on the island of Honshu. In any case, all expressways lead toward the heart of the city, Hibiya and Ginza. Parking spaces, however, are scarce, although major hotels have parking garages.

By Ferry

Long-distance ferries arrive in Tokyo at the **Tokyo Ko Ferry Futo (Tokyo Port Ferry Terminal).** From there, passengers can board a bus for Shinkiba JR Station and catch a train to town.

VISITOR INFORMATION

The **Tourist Information Center (TIC),** 1-6-6 Yurakucho, Chiyoda-ku (☎ 03/3502-1461), can answer all your questions regarding Tokyo and can give you a map of the city, plus various sightseeing materials. They are courteous and efficient; I cannot recommend them highly enough. The office also has more information than any other tourist office on the rest of Japan, including pamphlets and brochures on major cities and attractions. Be sure to stop off here if you plan to visit other destinations, since information in English may not be available at the destination itself.

The TIC is open Monday through Friday from 9am to 5pm and on Saturday from 9am to noon; closed Sunday and national holidays. The office is near both Hibiya and Yurakucho subway stations (if you're arriving at Hibiya Station, take Exit A4 or A5.

If you want to have a quick rundown of what's happening in Tokyo, you can call 03/3503-2911 for a taped recording in English of what's going on in the city and its environs in the way of special exhibitions, performances, festivals, and events.

Finally, the Nippon Telegraph Corporation and the Kokusai Denshin Denwa Company sponsor a telephone service, the **Japan Hotline** (☎ 03/3586-0110), which advises callers on Japanese customs and etiquette, gives tips on such aspects of Japanese daily life as education and health services, and answers questions ranging from the availability of instruction on flower arranging to obtaining tickets for Kabuki. Advisers are on duty Monday through Friday, except holidays, from 10am to 4pm.

Tourist Publications The best publication for finding out what's going on in Tokyo in terms of contemporary and traditional music and theater, exhibitions in museums and galleries, films, and special events is the *Tokyo Journal.* Published monthly and available for ¥600 ($6) at foreign-language bookstores, restaurants, and bars, it also has articles of interest to foreigners in Japan. It even lists department store

Impressions

That street was typical of the modern Tokyo—not of its main arteries, mushroom offices, and towering department stores, but of the Tokyo which lies always around the corner, an easy stone's throw from the bright lights and the grinding trams. Vague and slatternly, a sprawling skyline of wooden houses overlooked by a massive procession of telegraph poles that marched—or rather staggered—up its slope, linked together by loose wires in a drooping curve.

—Peter Quennell, *A Superficial Journey Through Tokyo and Peking,* 1932

sales, photography exhibitions, apartments for rent, schools for learning Japanese, and much else. Living in Tokyo was certainly much more difficult before this publication made its debut in the early 1980s.

There are other English-language publications of interest to tourists, but they come and go (probably can't compete with *Tokyo Journal*), so I hesitate to mention them. One that's been around a while is the *Tour Companion's Tokyo City Guide,* a monthly tabloid distributed free to hotels, travel agencies, and the TIC; it tells of upcoming events and festivals, as well as other information useful to the visitor.

English-language newspapers such as the *Japan Times* also carry information on the theater, films, and special events.

CITY LAYOUT

Your most frustrating moments in Tokyo will probably occur when you find you're totally lost. Maybe it will be in a subway or train station, when all you see are signs in Japanese, or on a street somewhere as you search for a museum, restaurant, or bar. At any rate, accept here and now, you *will* get lost if you are at all adventurous and strike out on your own. It's inevitable. But take comfort in the fact Japanese get lost, too, even taxi drivers! And don't forget most of the hotel and restaurant listings have the number of minutes (in parentheses) it takes to walk there from the nearest station. If you take note, you will at least know the radius from the station to your destination.

STREETS One difficulty in finding your way around is that hardly any streets are named. Think about what that means—12 million people living in a huge metropolis of nameless streets. Oh, major thoroughfares and some well-known streets in areas like Ginza and Shinjuku have names received after World War II at the insistence of American occupation forces, but for the most part Tokyo's address system is based on a complicated number scheme that must make the postal worker's job here a nightmare. To make matters worse, most streets in Tokyo zigzag—an arrangement apparently left over from olden days (to confuse potential attacking enemies). Today, streets in Tokyo confuse not only foreign tourists but even city residents themselves.

Among Tokyo's most important named streets are **Meiji Dori,** which runs from Ebisu through Shibuya, Harajuku, Shinjuku, and Ikebukuro; **Yasukuni Dori** and **Shinjuku Dori,** which connect Shinjuku with Chiyoda-ku in the heart of the city; and **Sotobori Dori, Harumi Dori,** and **Showa Dori,** which pass through Ginza. By the way, *dori,* as you probably guessed, means avenue or street, as does *michi.*

ADDRESSES A typical Tokyo address might read 7-8-4 Roppongi, Minato-ku, which is the address of the Inakaya restaurant. Minato-ku is the name of the ward, which encompasses a large area (Tokyo has 23 wards, or *ku*). Within that area is the district, in this case Roppongi. Roppongi is further broken down into *chome,* here 7-chome. Number 8 refers to a smaller area within the chome, and 4 is the actual building (but don't expect to find 9 next to 8; they were numbered when built). Addresses are usually posted on buildings, beside doors, on telephone poles, and by streetlights. In recent years Roman letters have been added to street (and other) signs in Tokyo, but usually addresses are written only in Japanese.

As you walk around Tokyo, you will notice maps posted beside sidewalks giving a breakdown of the number system for the area. The first time I tried to use one, I stopped first one Japanese, then another, and asked them to point out on the map where a particular address was. They both studied the map and pointed out the direction. Both turned out to be wrong. Not very encouraging, but if you learn how to read these maps, they're invaluable.

Another invaluable source of information is the numerous police boxes, called *koban,* throughout the city. Police officers have area maps and are very helpful. You should also never hesitate to ask a Japanese the way, but be sure to ask more than one. You'll be amazed at the conflicting directions you'll receive. Apparently, the Japanese would rather hazard a guess than impolitely shrug their shoulders and leave you standing there. The best thing to do is ask directions of several Japanese and then follow the majority opinion. You can also duck into a shop and ask someone where a nearby address is, although in my experience employees do not even know the address of their own store.

MAPS Before setting out on your own, arm yourself with a few maps. Maps are so much a part of life in Tokyo they're often included in a shop or restaurant advertisement, on a business card, and even in private party invitations. Even though I've spent several years in Tokyo, I rarely venture forth without a map. The Tourist Information Center issues a *Tourist Map of Tokyo* which includes smaller, detailed maps of several districts (such as Shinjuku), as well as subway and greater Tokyo train maps. With this map you should be able to locate at least the general vicinity of every place mentioned in the Tokyo chapters of this book.

If you want a detailed map, head for Tower Books (see "Shopping A to Z," in chapter 6) or another English-language bookstore. In my sack I carry Kodansha's *A Bilingual Atlas,* a book with rail and subway maps, district maps, and an index to important buildings, museums, and other places of interest. Because it is bilingual, it will help you find addresses or ask others. *A Great Detailed Map,* published by Nippon Kokuseisha, gives the postal addresses for neighborhoods throughout Tokyo and includes bus routes and a subway map.

NEIGHBORHOODS IN BRIEF

Taken as a whole, Tokyo seems formidable and unconquerable. It's best, therefore, to think of it as nothing more than a variety of neighborhoods scrunched together, much like the pieces of a jigsaw puzzle. Holding the pieces together, so to speak, is the Yamanote Line, a commuter train loop around central Tokyo, passing through such important stations as Yurakucho, Tokyo, Ueno, Shinjuku, Harajuku, and Shibuya.

Hibiya This is one of the financial hearts of Tokyo, together with nearby Marunouchi and Nihombashi. This is where the Tokugawa shogun built his magnificent castle, and was thus the center of old Edo. Today, Hibiya is where you'll find the Imperial Palace and—important for tourists—the Tourist Information Center. Hibiya is located in the Chiyoda-ku ward.

Ginza Ginza is the swankiest and most expensive shopping area in all Japan. When the country opened to foreign trade in the 1860s, following two centuries of self-imposed seclusion, it was here Western imports and adopted Western architecture were first displayed. Today, Ginza is where you'll find a multitude of department stores, boutiques, exclusive restaurants, art galleries, hostess clubs, and drinking establishments. On the edge of Ginza is Kabukiza, venue for Kabuki productions.

Tsukiji Located only two subway stops from Ginza, Tsukiji is famous for the Tsukiji Fish Market, Japan's largest wholesale fish market and one of the largest in the world.

Asakusa Located in the northeastern part of central Tokyo, Asakusa served as the pleasure quarters for old Edo. Today it's known throughout Japan as the site of the famous Sensoji Temple, one of Tokyo's top attractions. It also has a wealth of tiny shops selling traditional Japanese crafts. When Tokyoites talk about *shitamachi* (old downtown), they are referring to the traditional homes and tiny narrow streets of the Asakusa and Ueno areas.

Ueno Located not far from Asakusa, on the northern edge of Tokyo, Ueno is also part of the city's old downtown. Ueno boasts Ueno Park, a huge green space comprising a zoo, a concert hall, and several acclaimed museums. Among them, the Tokyo National Museum has the largest collection of Japanese art in the world. North of Ueno is **Nippori,** a residential area of traditional old homes and temples.

Shinjuku An upstart in Tokyo and a district that has been attracting businesses away from the more established Hibiya, Shinjuku is located on the western edge of the Yamanote Line loop. Shinjuku Station, the nation's busiest, separates Shinjuku into an east and a west side. Western Shinjuku boasts Tokyo's greatest concentration of skyscrapers and a number of hotels, as well as the new Tokyo Metropolitan Government Office (TMG). Eastern Shinjuku is known for its shopping and nightlife, particularly Kabuki-cho, a thriving amusement center.

Harajuku The mecca of Tokyo's younger generation, Harajuku swarms throughout the week with teenagers in search of fashion and fun. Omotesando Dori is a fashionable tree-lined avenue flanked by trendy shops, sidewalk cafes, and restaurants. At one end of Omotesando Dori is Takeshita Dori, a narrow pedestrian lane packed with young people looking for the latest in inexpensive clothing. At the other is the most exclusive block of designer fashions from Comme des Garçons to Issey Miyake and a clientele to match. Near Harajuku Station is Meiji Jingu Shrine, built in 1920 to deify Emperor and Empress Meiji. Not far from Omotesando Station is a street lined with top-name fashion boutiques.

Ikebukuro Located north of Shinjuku on the Yamanote Line loop, Ikebukuro is the working man's Tokyo, less refined and a bit rougher around the edges. Crowded with commuters who live past Ikebukuro in less expensive areas of the metropolis, Ikebukuro is where you'll find Seibu and Tobu, two of the country's largest department stores, as well as the Sunshine City Building, one of Tokyo's tallest skyscrapers and home of a huge indoor shopping center.

Akihabara Tokyo's center for electronic and electrical appliances, with more than 600 shops offering a look at the latest in gadgets and gizmos. This is a fascinating place for a stroll, even if you aren't interested in buying anything.

Shibuya Located on the southwestern edge of the Yamanote Line loop, Shibuya serves as an important young nightlife and shopping area. There are as many as a dozen department stores here, specializing in everything from designer clothing to housewares, and Bunkamura, a cultural center. **Daikanyama** is Shibuya's hipper southern neighbor. Not only are fashion ateliers here, but their boutiques, too. Used-clothing and antique shops, trendy restaurants, interesting storefronts, and the Hillside Terrace area galleries make Daikanyama a nice place to stroll.

Impressions

Frequent outbreaks of fire constitute one of the greatest perils to life in Japan. In Tokyo, burning houses are given the poetic name of "the flowers of Edo."

—James Kirkup, *Heaven, Hell and Hara-Kiri,* 1974

Roppongi Tokyo's best-known nightlife district for young Japanese and foreigners, Roppongi has more discos and bars than any other district, as well as a multitude of restaurants serving international cuisine. The action here continues until dawn. **Nishi-Azabu,** once a residential neighborhood (many foreign residents live here), has turned into a restaurant and nightclub venue, too.

Akasaka Another important nightlife district of Tokyo, this one caters more to businessmen. In addition to its expensive hostess bars, Akasaka also has many restaurants and several large hotels.

3 Getting Around

The first rule of getting around Tokyo: It will always take longer than you think. Tokyo is huge, and its attractions are far-flung. Learning to gauge the time needed to get to a destination can take quite a while. In fact, old Tokyo hands pride themselves on being able to calculate travel time perfectly—arriving late is an unpardonable sin in Tokyo.

For short-time visitors, calculating travel times in Tokyo is tricky business. Taking a taxi is expensive and involves the probability of getting stuck interminably in traffic. (Nothing can be more upsetting than to watch the meter jumping higher and higher and not even being able to arrive on time.) Taking the subway is usually more efficient, even though it's more complicated and harder on your feet: choosing which route to take isn't always clear, and transfers between lines are sometimes quite a hike in themselves. However, if I'm going from one end of Tokyo to the other by subway, I usually allow anywhere from 30 to 60 minutes, depending on the number of transfers and walking distance to the final destination. The journey from Roppongi or Shibuya to Ueno, for example, takes approximately a half hour because it's a straight shot on the subway, but the trip from Toranomon to Ueno can take three-quarters of an hour because it requires transfers.

At any rate, the best policy for getting around Tokyo is to take the subway or Japan Railways commuter train to the station nearest your destination. From there you can either walk, asking directions along the way, or take a taxi.

BY PUBLIC TRANSPORT

Tokyo's population is served by subway, JR commuter trains (including the Yamanote Line loop), and buses. Of these, the subway is probably the most convenient for visitors. Children younger than 6 can ride free; children 6 to 11 pay half the adult fare.

BY SUBWAY To get around Tokyo on your own, it's imperative that you learn how to ride its subways. Fortunately, the subway system is efficient, modern, clean, and easy to use, and all station names are written in English. Altogether, there are 12 subway lines crisscrossing underneath the city, and each line is color-coded. The Ginza Line, for example, is orange, which means all its coaches are orange. If you're transferring to the Ginza Line from another line, just follow the orange signs and circles to the Ginza Line platform.

Vending machines at all subway stations sell tickets, which begin at ¥140 ($1.40) for the shortest distance and increase according to how far you're traveling. Vending machines give change, and some even accept ¥1,000 notes. To purchase your ticket, insert coins into the vending machine until the fare buttons light up, then push the amount for the ticket you want. Your ticket and change will drop onto a little platform at the bottom of the machine. Fares are posted on a large subway map above the vending machines, but it's in Japanese only. Major stations also post a smaller map listing fares in English, but you may have to search for it. An alternative is to look at your Tourist Information Center subway map—it lists stations in both Japanese and English. Once you know what the Japanese characters look like, you may be able to locate your station and the corresponding fare.

If you still don't know the fare, just buy a **basic-fare ticket** for ¥140 ($1.40). When you exit at the other end, the ticket collector will tell you how much you owe. In any case, be sure to hang on to your ticket, since you must give it up at the end of your journey. In recent years, an automated ticketing system has been installed at most subway entrances and exits—simply insert your ticket and the doors to the wicket swing open. Once you reach your destination, if you're confused about which exit to take from the station, ask the ticket collector (there's always one). Taking the right exit can make a world of difference, especially in Shinjuku, where there are more than 60 station exits.

Most subways run from about 5am to midnight, although the times of the first and last trains depend on the line, the station, and whether it's a weekday or weekend. There are schedules posted in the stations, and through most of the day trains run every three to five minutes. Avoid taking the subway during the morning rush hour, from 8 to 9am. The stories you've heard about commuters packed into trains like sardines are all true. There are even "platform pushers," men who push people into compartments so that the doors can close. If you want to witness Tokyo at its craziest, go to Shinjuku Station at 8:30am—but go by taxi unless you want to experience the crowding firsthand.

BY TRAIN In addition to subway lines, electric trains operated by Japan Railways (JR) run above ground. These are also color-coded, with fares beginning at ¥120 ($1.20). Buy your ticket the same as you would for the subway. The **Yamanote Line** (green-colored coaches) is the best-known and most convenient JR line. It makes a loop around the city, stopping at 29 stations along the way. In fact, you may want to take the Yamanote Line and stay on it for a roundup view of Tokyo. The entire trip around the city takes about an hour, passing stations like Shinjuku, Tokyo, and Ueno on the way.

Another convenient JR line is the **Chuo Line,** whose coaches are orange-colored. It cuts across Tokyo between Shinjuku and Tokyo Stations.

Transfers You can transfer between subway lines without buying another ticket, and you can transfer between JR train lines on one ticket. However, your ticket does not allow a transfer between subway lines and JR train lines. You usually don't have to worry about this, though, because if you exit through a wicket and have to give up your ticket, you'll know you have to buy another one. There are instances, however, when you pass through a ticket wicket to transfer between subway lines (for example, when you transfer from the Yurakucho Line to the Hibiya Line at Hibiya Station). In this case, simply show your ticket when you pass through the wicket. The general rule is that if your final destination and fare are posted above the ticket vending machines, you can travel all the way to your destination with only one ticket. But don't worry about this too much—the ticket collector will set you straight if you've made a miscalculation. Note, however, that if you pay too much for your ticket it is not refundable, so, again, the easiest thing to do is to buy the cheapest fare.

Passes Each system of transport in Tokyo has its own one-day pass fare. If you think you're going to be using the subways a lot, you can purchase a **one-day economy ticket** (¥700/$7 for an adult, ¥350/$3.50 for children 6 to 12), which allows unlimited travel on the Eidan Lines: Ginza, Marunouchi, Hibiya, Tozai, Chiyoda, Yurakucho, Namboku, and Hanzomon subway lines. These lines pass through more than 140 stations in Tokyo, including Hibiya, Ginza, Shinjuku, Tsukiji, Ueno, and major sightseeing destinations. One-day tickets are valuable, however, only if you plan on using the subways for very long distances or more than five times in a day. The pass can be purchased at more than two dozen subway stations, including Ginza, Shinjuku, Shibuya, Suitengu-mae, and Akasaka-mitsuke.

If you're really going to be traveling extensively, you may wish to buy the **Tokyo Furii Kippu Pass** (¥1,460/$14.60 adults, children half price), which allows one-day unlimited travel on all Eidan and Toei subway lines, all metropolitan bus lines (except double-decker), all metropolitan streetcars, and all JR lines within the 23 wards of Tokyo. However, if you have a valid Japan Rail Pass, you can travel on JR trains in Tokyo for free. Note that you'll have to pass by the one wicket with a human being in it to show your pass on entering and exiting. Contact the TIC for more information.

BY BUS Buses are difficult to use in Tokyo because destinations are often written only in Japanese and most bus drivers don't speak English. If you're feeling adventurous, board the bus at the front and drop the exact fare into a box by the driver. If you don't have the exact fare (usually ¥200/$2), another machine located next to the driver will accept coins only; your change will come out below, minus the fare. When you wish to get off, press one of the buttons on the railing near the door or the seats.

BY TAXI

Taxis are fairly expensive in Tokyo, starting at ¥650 ($6.50) for the first 2km (1¼ miles) and increasing ¥80 (80¢) for each additional 280 meters (910 feet). You can hail a taxi from the street or go to a taxi stand. A red light will show above the dashboard if a taxi is free to pick up a passenger; a green light indicates the taxi is already occupied (just another one of those things that are backwards in Japan). Be sure to stand clear of the door—it swings open automatically. Likewise, it shuts automatically once you're in.

Unless you're going to a well-known landmark or hotel, it's best to have your destination written out in Japanese, since most taxi drivers don't speak English. But even that may not help. Tokyo is so complicated even taxi drivers may not know a certain area, although they do have detailed maps. If a driver doesn't understand where you're going, however, he may refuse to take you. (By the way, notice the taxi drivers' white gloves and the way the drivers are always writing things down on a roster—Japanese taxi drivers must write down more information than any other taxi drivers on earth.)

There are so many taxis cruising Tokyo that one is always around and available—except when you need it most. That is, when it's raining and late at night on weekends, after all subways and trains have stopped. Nightlife areas such as Shinjuku, Roppongi, Ginza, and Akasaka used to be especially bad, but one important measure of the recession is the number of available taxis. One used to have to stay out until 2 or 3am to find a taxi, but not since companies are no longer paying for employees' expensive after-the-last-train taxi fares. (Some Tokyoites lament the passing of the good old days, when no taxis to be found gave them an excuse to get home in the wee hours.) Also it's worse for foreigners, whether it's the fact that most foreigners live close-in and are therefore cheaper fares, or whether taxi drivers just don't want to deal with us. I've been passed by time and again by drivers who pick up the next waiting Japanese. Note that from 11pm to 5am, an extra 30% is added to your fare.

The telephone numbers of major taxi companies are 3586-2151 for Nihon Kotsu, 3491-6001 for Kokusai, 3563-5151 for Daiwa, and 3814-1111 for Hinomaru. Note, however, that only Japanese is spoken and you will be required to pay extra (usually not more than ¥550/$5.50).

BY CAR

Driving a car in Tokyo can be a harrowing experience. For one thing, the maze of one-way streets are crowded and unbelievably narrow. Also, street signs are often only in Japanese, and driving is on the left side of the street (okay for you British). Parking spaces can be hard to find, and garages are expensive. Parking meters along the street cost ¥300 ($3) an hour, and parking garages ¥500 to ¥600 ($5 to $6) per hour. If you still want to drive, see "Rentals," below.

Rentals As I've stressed before, driving a car in Tokyo can make a roller-coaster ride at the local amusement park seem like tame stuff. If you're still not convinced, there are approximately a dozen major **car-rental** companies in Tokyo, with branch offices throughout the city and at the Narita airport, including **Nissan Reservation Center** (☎ 03/3587-4123), **Nippon Rent-A-Car Service** (☎ 03/3485-7196 for the English Service Desk), and **Toyota Rent-A-Car** (☎ 03/3264-2834). Rental prices start at around ¥8,800 ($88) for 24 hours. You'll need either an international or a Japanese driver's license.

Tokyo residents must have proof of off-street **parking** before they can buy a car, and yet finding a parking space is still a challenge in Tokyo. You'll pay about ¥500 ($5) an hour for the privilege of a metered parking space on the street, and more than ¥600 ($6) per hour in a parking garage. Because space is at a premium, parking garages are usually tall and narrow, with cars transported by elevatorlike devices, and some are completely automated. In many garages, drivers drive onto a platform that rotates because there isn't even enough room to turn around.

Driving Rules Remember, driving in Japan is on the *left* side of the street, and you'll need either an international or a Japanese driver's license. Signs for expressways and major streets are written in English. Because traffic is so horrendous, you should have plenty of time to read them along the way.

FAST FACTS: Tokyo

American Express The only American Express handling client mail and emergency card-replacement services is located in Yurakucho on the ground floor of the Yurakucho Denki Building, 1-7-1 Yurakucho, Chiyoda-ku (☎ 03/3214-0280). It's open Monday through Friday from 9am to 7pm and on Saturday and Sunday from 10am to 5pm. Another office is located in Shinjuku, in the Shinjuku Gomeikan Building, 3-3-9 Shinjuku (☎ 03/3352-1555), open daily from 10am to 6pm. Note that both offices have 24-hour access to American Express cash machines.

Area Code If you're calling a number in Tokyo from outside the city but within Japan, the area code for Tokyo is 03. If you're calling Tokyo from abroad, it may be necessary to drop the zero and dial only 3, as is the case if you're calling from the United States. If you have any questions, contact your local international operator.

Baby-sitters Many major hotels, like the Imperial in Tokyo, provide baby-sitting services (expect to pay $80 for 2 hours). Tokyo Domestic Service (☎ 03/3584/4769) can provide bilingual sitters (3 hour/¥5,000 or $50 minimum, then ¥1,500/$15 per hour, plus transportation, plus meals).

Bookstores Check the "Shopping A to Z" section of chapter 6 for a good selection of bookstores with English-language books.

Currency Exchange You can exchange money in major banks throughout Tokyo, often indicated by a sign in English near the front door. The *Bank of America* is located in the Arc Mori Building, 1-12-32 Akasaka, Minato-ku (☎ 03/3587-3111), and the *Chase Manhattan Bank* is at 1-2-1 Marunouchi, Chiyoda-ku (☎ 03/3287-4000). Generally speaking, banks give a better exchange rate for traveler's checks than for cash. If you need to exchange money outside banking hours, inquire at one of the larger first-class hotels—some of them will cash traveler's checks or exchange money even if you're not their guest. If you're arriving at the Narita airport, you can exchange money from 9am until the arrival of the last flight.

Dentists and Doctors Your embassy can refer you to English-speaking doctors, specialists, and dentists. Otherwise, listed here are some clinics popular with foreigners living in Tokyo where some of the staff speak English. The *Tokyo Medical & Surgical Clinic,* close to Tokyo Tower in the 32 Mori Building, 3-4-30 Shiba-koen, Minato-ku (☎ 03/3436-3028), is open Monday through Friday from 9am to 5:30pm (closed 1 to 2pm for lunch) and on Saturday from 9 to 11am. Appointments are necessary. The *International Clinic,* within walking distance of Roppongi Station, is at 1-5-9 Azabudai, Minato-ku (☎ 03/3582-2646), open Monday through Friday from 9am to noon and 2:30pm to 5pm and on Saturday from 9am to noon. Only walk-ins accepted here. You can also make appointments to visit doctors in the hospitals listed below under "Hospitals."

Drugstores There is no 24-hour drugstore in Tokyo, but ubiquitous convenience stores carry things like aspirin. (If it's an emergency, I suggest going to one of the hospitals listed below.) If you're looking for specific pharmaceuticals, a good bet is the *American Pharmacy,* Hibiya Park Building, 1-8-1 Yurakucho, Chiyoda-ku (☎ 03/3271-4034). Open Monday through Saturday from 9am to 7pm and on Sunday and holidays from 11am to 7pm, it has most of the drugs you can find at home (many of them imported from the United States) and can fill American prescriptions.

Embassies and Consulates The addresses, telephone numbers, and business hours for the United States, Canadian, British, Australian, Irish, and New Zealand embassies are given in "Fast Facts: Japan," in chapter 3.

Eyeglasses There are optical shops throughout Tokyo, so ask at your hotel which store is nearest you. Otherwise, try the *Tokyo Optical Center,* 6-4-8 Ginza (☎ 03/3571-7216). An English-speaking staff will assist you in replacing eyeglasses or contact lenses.

Hairdressers and Barbers Most first-class hotels have beauty salons and barbershops. In addition, check the advertisements and classified section of the *Tokyo*

Journal for more listings of hairdressers used to dealing with foreigners. In any case, you will be pampered to death in a Japanese salon, making it a delightful experience.

Hospitals In addition to going to a hospital for an emergency, you can also make an appointment at a hospital's clinic to see a doctor. The *International Catholic Hospital (Seibo Byoin),* 2-5-1 Naka-Ochiai, Shinjuku (☎ 03/3951-1111), has clinic hours from 8:30 to 11am Monday through Saturday (closed the fourth Saturday of each month). The closest subway station is Meijiro on the Yamanote Line.

Other hospitals include *St. Luke's International Hospital (Seiroka Byoin),* 1-10 Akashicho, Chuo-ku (☎ 03/3541-5151), with clinic hours from 8:30 to 11am Monday through Saturday (closest subway station is Tsukiji on the Hibiya Line); and the *Japan Red Cross Hospital (Nisseki Iryo Center),* 4-1-22 Hiroo, Shibuya-ku (☎ 03/3400-1311), with hours from 8:30 to 11am Monday through Friday and from 8:30 to 10:30am on the second and fourth Saturdays of the month (closest subway stations are Roppongi, Hiroo, and Shibuya, from which you should take a taxi). No appointments taken here.

Hot Lines At the end of your rope? Have some problems? The *Tokyo English Life Line (TELL)* (☎ 03/5721-4347) gives free confidential counseling over the telephone and will listen to your problems and gripes. It's available daily from 9am to 4pm and 7 to 11pm. A similar service is provided by *Japan Helpline* (☎ 01/2046-1997), a 24-hour voluntary service for the foreign community. *TELL HIV/AIDS* (☎ 03/5721-4334) is an AIDS hotline.

For questions in English on anything relating to Japan, call the *Japan Hotline,* (☎ 03/3586-0110), sponsored by KDD, NTT, and IBM. Its staff advises callers on Japanese etiquette and customs; gives tips on daily life, such as health services and transportation; and can answer questions ranging from the availability of instruction in flower arranging to where to obtain tickets to Kabuki. Advisers are on duty Monday through Friday (except national holidays) from 10am to 4pm.

The Tokyo *Tourist Information Center* (TIC) (☎ 03/3502-1461) can answer questions relating to tourism and sightseeing in Tokyo and Japan. Its phone service is available daily from 9am to 9pm.

Lost Property If you've forgotten something on a subway, in a taxi, or on a park bench, you don't have to assume it's gone forever. In fact, if you're willing to trace it, you'll probably get it back. If you've lost something on the street, go to the nearest police box (*koban*). Items found in the neighborhood will stay there for about three days. After that, you should contact the *Central Lost and Found Office of the Metropolitan Police Board,* 1-9-11 Koraku, Bunkyo-ku (☎ 03/3814-4151).

If you've lost something in a taxi or subway, you need to contact the appropriate office: for taxis, it's the *Taxi Kindaika Center,* 7-3-3 Minamisuma, Koto-ku (☎ 03/3648-0300); for JR trains, it's the *Lost and Found Section* at Tokyo JR Station (☎ 03/3231-1880) or at Ueno JR Station (☎ 03/3841-8069); and for Tokyo Metropolitan buses, subways, and streetcars, it's at 1-35-15 Hongo, Bunkyo-ku (☎ 03/3818-5760). If you've lost something on one of the subways belonging to the Teito Rapid Transit Authority (for example, the Ginza, Marunouchi, Yurakucho, Tozai, or Hanzoman Line), call 03/3834-5577.

Luggage Storage/Lockers Coin-operated lockers are located at all major JR stations, such as Tokyo, Shinjuku, and Ueno, as well as at most subway stations. Lockers cost ¥200 to ¥300 ($2 to $3) per day.

Newspapers and Magazines Five English-language newspapers are published daily in Japan. They're the *Japan Times,* the *Mainichi Daily News,* the *Daily Yomiuri,* the *Asahi Evening News,* and the *International Herald Tribune.* The international editions of both *Time* and *Newsweek* are also available. For city magazines that describe what's going on in Tokyo, pick up a copy of *Tokyo Journal.*

If you're interested in seeing the latest edition of your favorite magazine back home, check Tower Books (listed in "Shopping A to Z" of chapter 6. Otherwise, your best bet is to drop in on the *World Magazine Gallery,* 3-13-10 Ginza (☎ 03/3545-7227). Located behind the Kabuki-za near Higashi-Ginza Station, it displays more than 1,200 magazines from 40 countries around the world. Magazines are for reading here only, and are not for sale. It's open Monday through Saturday from 11am to 7pm; closed Sunday and public holidays.

Photographic Needs There are many camera shops on both sides of Shinjuku Station offering a wide variety of film. As for film development, a reliable store used by professional photographers is East West Sigma, 3-2-6 Roppongi, Nishi Azabu, Minato-ku (☎ 03/3479-3931). Located about a five-minute walk from Roppongi Station, it's open Monday through Saturday from 9am to 7pm; closed the second and fourth Saturdays of the month, every Sunday, and public holidays. See also "Fast Facts: Japan," in chapter 3.

Police The national emergency telephone number is 110.

Post Office If your hotel cannot mail letters for you, ask the concierge where the nearest post office is. The *Central Post Office* is located just southwest of Tokyo Station at 2-7-2 Marunouchi, Chiyoda-ku (☎ 03/3284-9527). It's open Monday through Friday from 9am to 7pm, on Saturday from 9am to 5pm, and on Sunday and public holidays from 9am to 12:30pm. If you need information on postage or mail, contact the *Information Office of the Tokyo International Post Office,* 2-3-3 Otemachi (☎ 03/3241-4891), located north of Tokyo Station. See also "Mail" in "Fast Facts: Japan," in chapter 3.

Restrooms If you're in need of a restroom in Tokyo, your best bet is at train and subway stations, big hotels, department stores, and fast-food chains like McDonald's. For an explanation of Japanese toilets, refer to "Fast Facts: Japan," in chapter 3.

Safety Tokyo is one of the safest cities in the world. Yet there are precautions you should take whenever you're traveling in an unfamiliar city or country. Stay alert and be aware of your immediate surroundings. Be especially careful with cameras, purses, and wallets—all favorite targets of thieves and pickpockets—particularly in crowded subways. Every society, even one as relatively safe as Japan's, has its criminals. It's your responsibility to exercise caution at all times, even in the most heavily touristed areas.

Shoe Repairs All department stores have a shoe-repair counter, usually a Mister Minit. In addition, stations such as Yurakucho and Shibuya have streetside shoe repairs. Hotels also often offer such services.

Taxes For an explanation of taxes on accommodations, food, and goods, refer to "Fast Facts: Japan," in chapter 3.

Telephones, Telegrams, and Telex You can make local and long-distance calls from your room in most tourist hotels in Tokyo. Otherwise, there are public telephones, as well as telephone and telegraph offices throughout the city. The *Kokusai Denshin Denwa (KDD)* office, 1-8-1 Otemachi (☎ 03/3275-4343), close to Tokyo Station, is open Monday through Friday from 9am to 6pm and on Saturday, Sunday, and holidays from 9am to 5pm. It can handle facsimiles, phototelegrams, ISD calls, and telexes, in addition to telegrams and telephone calls. In Shinjuku there's a telephone and telegraph office at 2-3-2 Nishi Shinjuku (☎ 03/3347-5000).

There are several English telephone directories providing addresses and telephone numbers for many businesses, companies, shops, and restaurants in Tokyo. They're *City Source,* the *English Telephone Directory,* the *Japan Times Directory,* and the *Japan Telephone Book Yellow Pages.* If your hotel does not have one of these and you're interested in buying one, they're available at the bookstores listed in chapter 6. For assistance on directory telephone listings in Tokyo, English-speaking operators can help you if you call 03/3347-9222. See also "Fast Facts: Japan," in chapter 3.

4 Accommodations

Tokyo has no old, grand hotels and not many old hotels, period. But what the city's hotels may lack in quaintness or old grandeur is more than made up for by excellent service, for which the Japanese are legendary, and cleanliness and efficiency. Be prepared, however, for small rooms. Space is at a premium in Tokyo, so with the exception of some of the upper-range hotels, rooms seem to come in only three sizes: minuscule, small, and adequate.

Unfortunately, Tokyo doesn't have many ryokan, or Japanese-style inns. You may want to wait for your travels around the country to experience a ryokan. However, I've listed moderate and inexpensive ryokan willing to take in foreigners. In fact, if you're traveling on a tight budget, a simple Japanese-style inn is often the cheapest way to go. As for upper-range ryokan in Tokyo, none of them accepts foreigners. They prefer guests be introduced through someone they know and simply don't want to deal with the inconveniences caused by cultural and language barriers.

Most of the upper-bracket hotels (like the Miyako) offer at least a few Japanese-style rooms, with tatami mats, a Japanese bath-tub (deeper and narrower than the Western version), and futon. Although these rooms tend to be expensive, they're usually large enough for four people.

For each hotel or ryokan listed, I've given the nearest subway station and in parentheses the walking time required.

Hotels are arranged according to geographical location, starting with the areas of Ginza and Hibiya in the heart of the city and fanning out. Each neighborhood is subdivided by price based upon two people per night: **Very Expensive** hotels charge ¥31,000 ($310), **Expensive** hotels charge ¥21,000 to ¥30,000 ($210 to $300), **Moderate** hotels offer rooms for ¥12,000 to ¥20,000 ($120 to $200), and **Inexpensive** accommodations offer rooms for ¥11,000 ($110) and less.

Remember that in addition to quoted prices, upper-class hotels and most medium-range hotels will add a 10% to 15% service charge. Further, rates of more than ¥15,000 ($150) per person per night will require an additional 6% tax; rates of less than ¥15,000 per person will require an additional 3% tax. Unless otherwise stated, the prices given below do not include tax.

Tokyo's very expensive and expensive hotels can rival upper-range hotels anywhere in the world. Although many of the city's best hotels may not show much character from the outside, inside they're oases of subdued simplicity where service and hospitality reign supreme. Rooms in this category are adequate in size—some of them even large by Tokyo standards (notably the Park Hyatt and Four Seasons)—and they all come with such amenities as a minibar, bilingual TV with English-language cable and CNN broadcasts, a clock, a radio, cotton kimono, hot water for tea, and countless other personal touches. Note, however, that while many hotels in this bracket have a health club and a swimming pool, an extra (often exorbitant) use fee is charged (an exception is the Four Seasons, where there's no fee for guests).

As for the moderately priced hotels, they vary from Western-style hotels to business hotels to ryokan, with business hotels making up the majority in this category. Popular with Japanese businessmen, these hotels are generally quite small and offer just the basics—a private bathroom, TV, and a telephone—but are usually situated in a convenient location. If you're interested simply in a clean and functional place to sleep rather than in roomy comfort, a nondescript business hotel may be the way to go.

If you're looking for rock-bottom prices for rooms, you've come to the wrong city. It's difficult to find inexpensive lodging in Tokyo. The price of land is simply too prohibitive. You can, however, find rooms—tiny though they may be—for two people for $80 a night, which is pretty good considering you're in one of the most expensive cities in the world. Accommodations in this category are basic: a bed and usually a phone, TV, heating, and air-conditioning. Facilities are generally spotless, and prices often include tax and service charges. Inexpensive Japanese-style rooms make up the bulk of this category.

RESERVATIONS Although Tokyo doesn't suffer from a lack of hotel rooms during peak holidays (when most Japanese head for the hills and beaches), rooms may be in short supply because of conventions and other events. And in summer, when there are many foreign tourists in Japan, the cheaper accommodations are often the first to fill up. It's always best, therefore, to make your hotel reservations in advance, especially if you're arriving in Japan after a long transoceanic flight and don't want the hassle of searching for a hotel room. Many listed hotels belong to reservations services or have their own international reservations services, and you can easily make reservations in advance by dialing the hotel's local representative or toll-free number. Reservations for the major hotels can also be made through travel agents. And since most hotels have fax numbers, you can also reserve your room by facsimile. Once you're in Japan, call immediately to reconfirm your reservation.

LOVE HOTELS Finally, a word about Tokyo's so-called love hotels. Usually found close to entertainment districts and along major highways, such hotels do not provide sexual services themselves; rather, they offer rooms for rent by the hour to lovers. Altogether, there are an estimated 35,000 such love hotels in Japan, usually

A Note on Prices

The prices quoted in this book were figured at ¥100 = $1 U.S. Because of fluctuations, however, in the exchange rate of the yen (it was ¥106 to the dollar at press time), the U.S. dollar equivalents given will probably vary during the lifetime of this edition. Be sure to check current exchange rates when planning your trip. In addition, the rates given below may increase, so be sure to ask the current rate when making your reservation.

Accommodations & Dining In Ginza & Hibiya

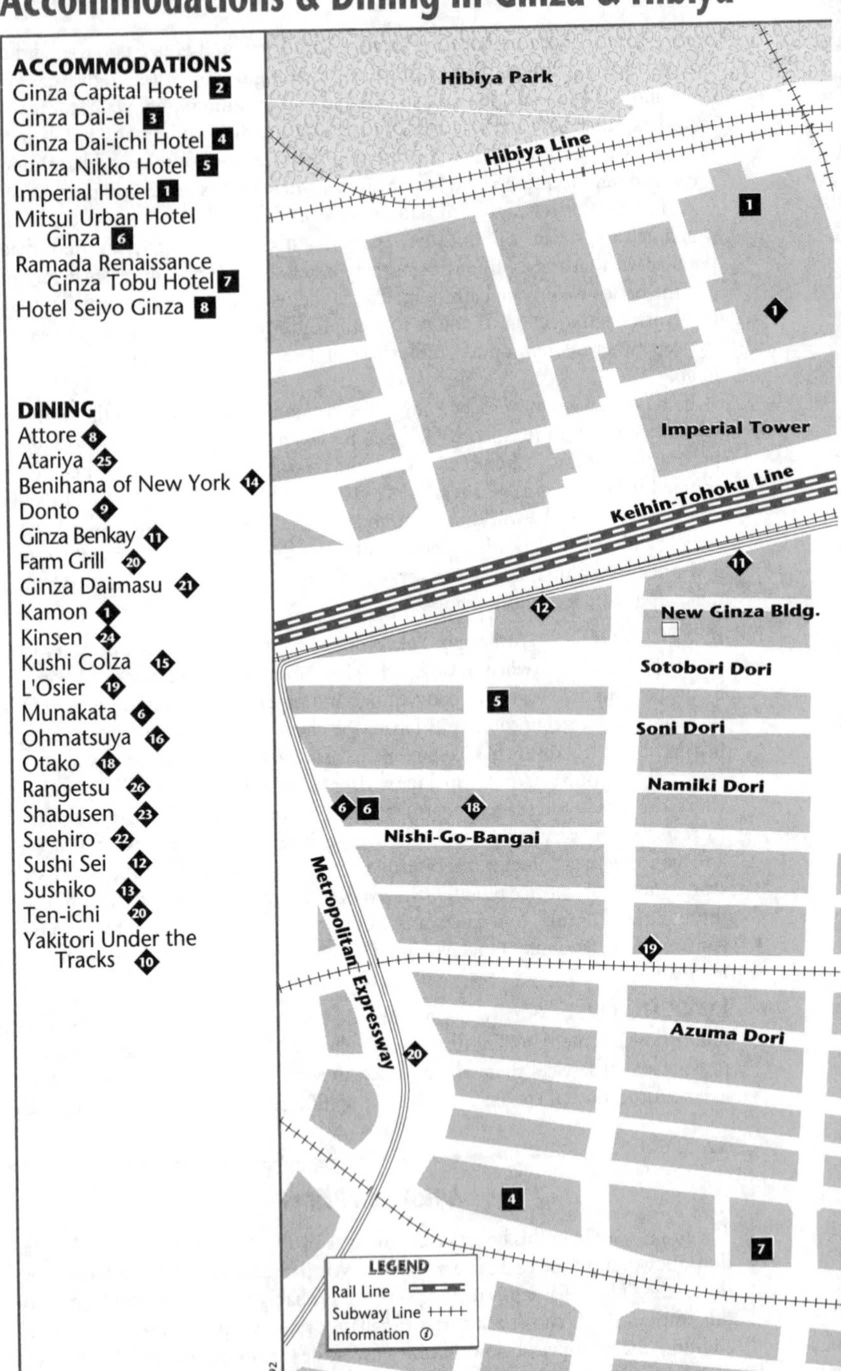

ACCOMMODATIONS
Ginza Capital Hotel 2
Ginza Dai-ei 3
Ginza Dai-ichi Hotel 4
Ginza Nikko Hotel 5
Imperial Hotel 1
Mitsui Urban Hotel Ginza 6
Ramada Renaissance Ginza Tobu Hotel 7
Hotel Seiyo Ginza 8
DINING
Attore 8
Atariya 25
Benihana of New York 14
Donto 9
Ginza Benkay 11
Farm Grill 20
Ginza Daimasu 21
Kamon 1
Kinsen 24
Kushi Colza 15
L'Osier 19
Munakata 6
Ohmatsuya 16
Otako 18
Rangetsu 26
Shabusen 23
Suehiro 22
Sushi Sei 12
Sushiko 13
Ten-ichi 20
Yakitori Under the Tracks 10
Hibiya Park
Hibiya Line
Imperial Tower
Keihin-Tohoku Line
New Ginza Bldg.
Sotobori Dori
Soni Dori
Namiki Dori
Nishi-Go-Bangai
Metropolitan Expressway
Azuma Dori
LEGEND
Rail Line
Subway Line
Information
2092

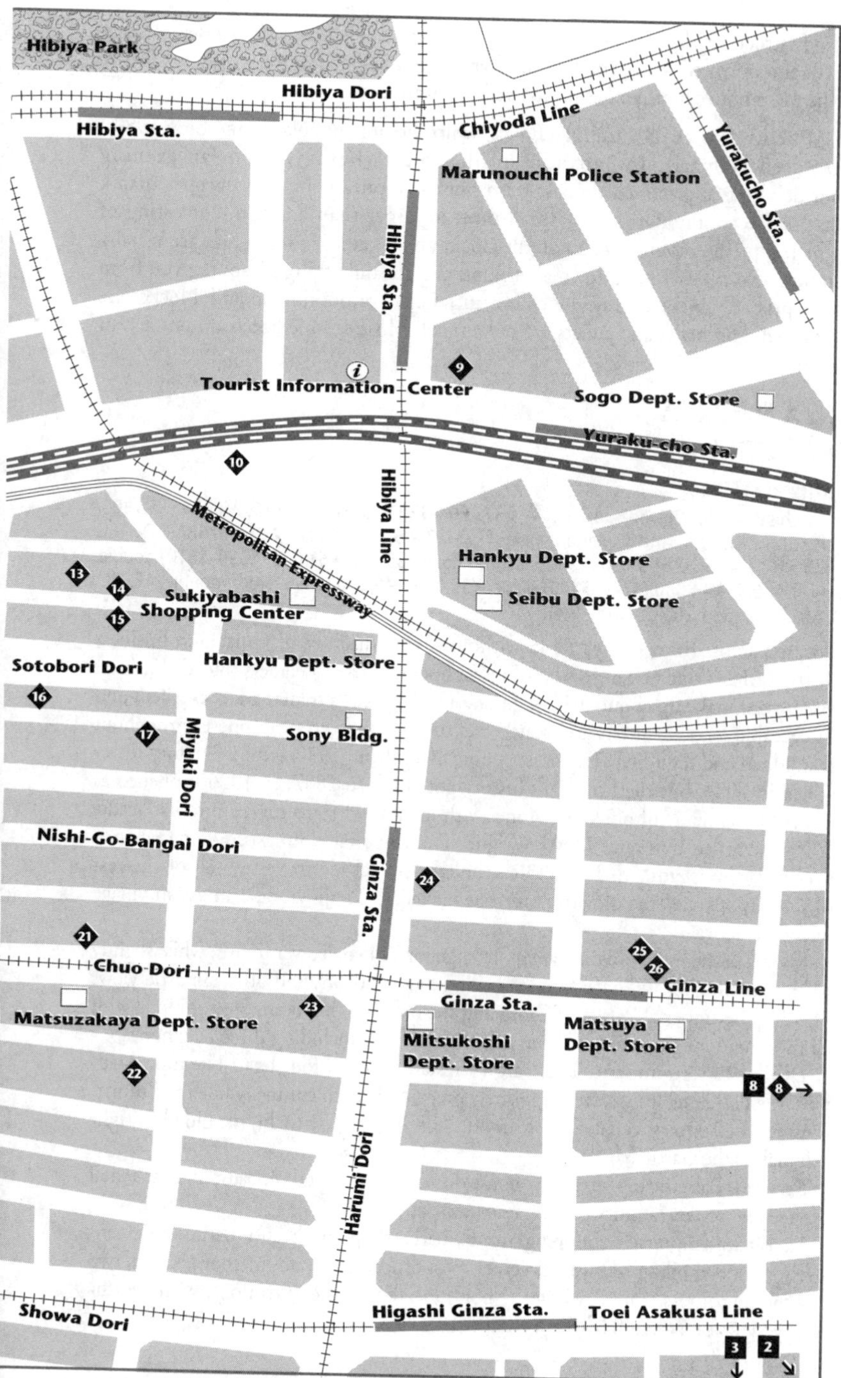
Hibiya Park
Hibiya Dori
Hibiya Sta.
Chiyoda Line
Marunouchi Police Station
Yurakucho Sta.
Hibiya Sta.
Tourist Information Center
9
Sogo Dept. Store
Yuraku-cho Sta.
10
Metropolitan Expressway
Hibiya Line
Hankyu Dept. Store
Seibu Dept. Store
13
14
15
Sukiyabashi Shopping Center
Hankyu Dept. Store
Sotobori Dori
16
17
Miyuki Dori
Sony Bldg.
Nishi-Go-Bangai Dori
Ginza Sta.
24
21
25
26
Chuo-Dori
Ginza Line
Ginza Sta.
23
Matsuzakaya Dept. Store
Mitsukoshi Dept. Store
Matsuya Dept. Store
22
8
8
Harumi Dori
Showa Dori
Higashi Ginza Sta.
Toei Asakusa Line
3
2

gaudy structures shaped like ocean liners or castles and offering such extras as rotating beds and mirrored walls. You'll know that you've wandered into a love-hotel district when you notice hourly rates posted near the front door.

CAPSULE HOTELS Capsule hotels, which became popular in the early 1980s, are used primarily by Japanese businessmen who have spent an evening out drinking and missed the last train home—a capsule hotel is cheaper than a taxi. An accommodation is a small unit no larger than a coffin, consisting of a bed, a private color TV, an alarm clock, and a radio. These units are usually stacked two deep in rows down a corridor, and the only thing separating you from your probably inebriated neighbor is a curtain. A cotton kimono and a locker are provided, and baths and toilets are communal. Most capsule hotels do not accept women.

GINZA & HIBIYA

VERY EXPENSIVE

✪ Imperial Hotel

1-1-1 Uchisaiwaicho, Chiyoda-ku 100. ☎ **03/3504-1111,** or 800/223-5652 in the U.S., 800/223-6800 in the U.S. and Canada. Fax 03/3581-9146. 1,059 rms. A/C MINIBAR TV TEL. Main building: ¥30,000–¥56,000 ($300–$560) single; ¥35,000–¥61,000 ($350–$610) double. Tower: ¥34,000–¥44,000 ($340–$440) single; ¥39,000–¥49,000 ($390–$490) double. AE, DC, JCB, MC, V. Station: Hibiya (1 minute).

Located across from Hibiya Park, within walking distance of Ginza and business districts, this is one of Tokyo's best-known hotels, where foreigners (mostly business executives) make up about 50% of guests. The Imperial's trademark is excellent and impeccable service. Guests are treated like royalty, and the atmosphere throughout is subdued and dignified. The present hotel dates from 1970, with a 31-story tower added in 1983, but the Imperial's history goes back to 1887. In 1920 it opened as a small hotel made of brick and stone, with intricate designs carved into its facade. It was designed by Frank Lloyd Wright. The Imperial won lasting fame when it survived, almost intact, the 1923 earthquake, which destroyed much of the rest of the city. Part of the old structure was moved to Meiji-Mura, a museum village outside Nagoya.

Rooms in the main building are quite large for Tokyo. Tower rooms, while slightly smaller, are higher up, have floor-to-ceiling bay windows, and offer fantastic views of either the Imperial Palace or Ginza and the harbor. The rooms are equipped with all the amenities you'd expect from a first-class hotel, including three telephones.

Dining/Entertainment: There are 13 restaurants and four bars. The top restaurant, the Fontainebleau, serves exquisitely prepared French cuisine, while the Prunier, founded in 1936, specializes in seafood. The Imperial with Frank Lloyd Wright originals is the classic bar.

Services: Baby-sitting service, in-house doctor and dentist, limousine and car-rental services, same-day laundry service, free newspaper.

Facilities: Impressive shopping arcade, barbershop and beauty parlor, an extensively equipped bilingual business center, post office, tea-ceremony room, sauna, two no-smoking floors, and a swimming pool, located on the 20th floor, with breathtaking views of Tokyo Bay (fee: ¥1,000/$10).

Hotel Seiyo Ginza

1-11-2 Ginza, Chuo-ku 104. ☎ **03/3535-1111.** Fax 03/3535-1110. 80 rms and suites. A/C MINIBAR TV TEL. ¥28,000–¥72,000 ($280–$720) single or double; ¥85,000–¥280,000 ($850–$2,800) suite. AE, CB, DC, JCB, MC, V. Station: Ginza-Itchome (2 minutes).

The Seiyo Ginza is a luxury hotel with expensive room rates that targets personalities, royalty, and top executives. With only 80 guest rooms and suites, service is at a premium. The hotel is not open to the public—that is, you must either be a hotel guest or have a reservation at one of its exclusive restaurants to go in the main entrance.

Rooms are large and come with humidity-control dials, a safe, and a videocassette player. With the busy executive in mind, telephones have two lines, and computerized DO NOT DISTURB and MAID SERVICE buttons prompt immediate response to guests' desires. Large bathrooms have separate shower and tub units and a mini-TV.

Dining/Entertainment: There are a tea lounge, a private guest and members bar, and three restaurants serving French, Japanese, and Italian cuisine. Attore serves northern Italian specialties and is a good place for a business lunch.

Services: 24-hour room service, a personal secretary to organize business needs, travel arrangements, shopping, and sightseeing, among other services.

Facilities: Fitness room, two theaters.

EXPENSIVE

Ginza Dai-Ichi Hotel

8-13-1 Ginza, Chuo-ku 104. ☎ **03/3542-5311.** Fax 03/3542-3030. 801 rms and suites. A/C MINIBAR TV TEL. ¥15,000–¥19,000 ($150–$190) single; ¥23,000–¥25,000 ($230–$250) twin or double; ¥29,000–¥34,000 ($290–$340) triple. AE, DC, JCB, MC, V. Station: Shimbashi (5 minutes).

Located on the southern edge of Ginza, with its lobby on the second floor, this hotel offers unexciting but conveniently located guest rooms with tiny bathrooms. Guest rooms with the best views face Tokyo Bay.

Dining/Entertainment: There are four restaurants and bars. The French Lumière specializes in lobsters and steaks, while the Japanese restaurant offers sukiyaki and shabu-shabu, both with good views of Tokyo Bay by day and the lights of Ginza by night.

Facilities: Shopping arcade, beauty shop, barbershop, men's sauna, massage salon, travel agency.

Ginza Nikko Hotel

8-4-21 Ginza, Chuo-ku 104. ☎ **03/3571-4911.** Fax 03/3571-8379. 112 rms. A/C MINIBAR TV TEL. ¥13,000–¥17,800 ($130–$178) single; ¥24,000–¥28,000 ($240–$280) twin; ¥20,000–¥25,000 ($200–$250) double. AE, DC, JCB, MC, V. Station: Shimbashi, Ginza, or Hibiya (5 minutes).

There's nothing fancy or out of the ordinary about this small business hotel, but it's personable, clean, and conveniently located in southern Ginza. In fact, its location on Sotobori Dori can't be beat. Built more than a quarter of a century ago, it's one of the oldest hotels in the area, but has recently been remodeled.

Dining/Entertainment: There's a cafe/restaurant and a bar.

Services: Laundry service, free newspaper.

Mitsui Urban Hotel Ginza

8-6-15 Ginza, Chuo-ku 104. ☎ **03/3572-4131.** Fax 03/3572-4254. 252 rms. A/C TV TEL. ¥12,000–¥17,000 ($120–$170) single; ¥21,000–¥24,500 ($210–$245) double; ¥21,000–¥29,000 ($210–$290) twin. AE, DC, JCB, MC, V. Station: Shimbashi (1 minute).

Because of its location, convenient to Ginza and to the Kasumigaseki and Marunouchi business centers, this attractive hotel caters to both businessmen and tourists. The lobby, on the second floor, has a friendly staff. The guest rooms are small, but bathrooms are larger than in other business hotels. I suggest asking for a room away from the highway overpass beside the hotel.

Dining/Entertainment: There are five restaurants, bars, and lounges. Of these, Munakata is my favorite, a pleasant Japanese restaurant offering reasonably priced mini-kaiseki lunches.

Ramada Renaissance Ginza Tobu Hotel

6-14-10 Ginza, Chuo-ku 104. ☎ **03/3546-0111** or 800/228-2828 in the U.S. Fax 03/3546-8990. 206 rms. A/C MINIBAR TV TEL. ¥19,000–¥24,000 ($190–$240) single; ¥28,000–¥35,000 ($280–$350) double or twin. AE, DC, JCB, MC, V. Station: Ginza (4 minutes) or Higashi-Ginza (1 minute).

This small, reasonably priced, and personable hotel, located on Showa Dori behind the Ginza Matsuzakaya department store, employs a full-time staff of 200, many of whom are Americans. Each room comes equipped with three telephones, bilingual TV with CNN broadcasts and in-house movies, clothesline, massage shower head, and hair dryer. There are also hookups for fax machines. A free *Japan Times* is delivered to your room in the morning.

Dining/Entertainment: The five restaurants and bars include an upscale French restaurant, a Japanese restaurant, and a 24-hour coffee shop.

Services: 24-hour room service.

Facilities: Travel and business center, hairdressing salon.

MODERATE

Ginza Capital Hotel

3-1-5 Tsukiji, Chuo-ku 104. ☎ **03/3543-8211.** Fax 03/3543-7839. 572 rms (all with bath). A/C TV TEL. Main building: ¥9,100 ($91) single; ¥14,800 ($148) twin. Annex: ¥9,500–¥10,500 ($95–$105) single; ¥15,400 ($154) double; ¥15,800 ($158) twin, ¥20,400 ($204) triple. All rates include tax and service charges. AE, DC, JCB, MC, V. Station: Shintomicho (2 minutes).

This hotel and its newer annex, called the New Ginza Capital Hotel, offer a total of 572 rooms within a 10-minute walk of Ginza. A modern and efficient establishment with a friendly staff, it has clean and bright rooms, even though minuscule in size. If being able to look out a window is important, stay away from the annex rooms facing north—their windows have a glazed covering; single rooms in the annex face another building and are dark. Otherwise, annex rooms are a bit more modern. The annex has both a Western and a Japanese restaurant; the main building, a Western one.

TOKYO STATION AREA

VERY EXPENSIVE

Palace Hotel

1-1-1 Marunouchi, Chiyoda-ku 100. ☎ **03/3211-5211,** or 800/44-UTELL in the U.S., 800/223-0888 in the U.S. and Canada. Fax 03/3211-6987. 391 rms. A/C MINIBAR TV TEL. ¥24,000–¥29,000 ($240–$290) single; ¥32,000–¥60,000 ($320–$600) twin; ¥33,000–¥45,000 ($330–$450) double; from ¥100,000 ($1,000) suite. AE, DC, JCB, MC, V. Station: Otemachi (3 minutes).

Because of its proximity to Tokyo's business district, this hotel is a favorite among foreign businessmen; in fact, foreigners account for 65% of its guests. The hotel is across the street from the Imperial Palace and gardens, and its deluxe twin rooms—which are large, face the gardens, and have a balcony—can be highly recommended. Built in 1961, the hotel is small, and repeat guests are rewarded with monogrammed slippers. Renovated in 1993, mauve-toned rooms have well-stocked minibars, marble bathrooms, and large double-paned windows that open; and there are two no-smoking floors.

Dining/Entertainment: Of the hotel's seven restaurants, serving Chinese, Japanese, French, and Italian food, the French-cuisine Crown Restaurant on the 10th floor is the best, offering superb views of the Imperial Palace.

Services: 24-hour room service, free newspaper.

Facilities: Shopping arcade, barbershop, beauty salon, fitness club (located on the 25th floor of the nearby Nomura Bldg., fee ¥3090/$39.90).

EXPENSIVE

Holiday Inn Tokyo

1-13-7 Hatchobori, Chuo-ku 104. ☎ **03/3553-6161.** Fax 03/3553-6040. 119 rms (all with bath). A/C MINIBAR TV TEL. ¥18,150 ($181.50) single; ¥20,350 ($203.50) double. Children under 12 stay free in parents' room. AE, DC, JCB, MC, V. Station: Hatchobori (1 minute).

Located on Shin-Ohashi Dori, this place is similar to familiar Holiday Inns back home. As many as 30% of its guests are Americans, mainly individual travelers. The rooms in this small hotel are fairly large for Tokyo, and come with English-language cable TV and either double or queen-size beds. There's an outdoor swimming pool, free for hotel guests (open from July to September only); baby-sitters are available on request; and a free *Japan Times* is delivered to your room in the morning. There is one Western restaurant, plus a bar. It's about a 20-minute walk to Ginza.

$ Tokyo City Hotel

1-9 Nihombashi Honcho, Chuo-ku 103. ☎ **03/3270-7671.** Fax 03/3270-7671. 266 rms (all with bath). A/C TV TEL. ¥8,800–¥9,100 ($88–$91) single; ¥12,500–¥14,000 ($125–$140) double; ¥13,000–¥14,600 ($130–$146) twin. All rates include tax and service charges. AE, MC, JCB, V. Station: Mitsukoshi-mae (2 minutes).

This is a fine, no-nonsense business hotel offering moderately priced rooms in the middle of the city. A restaurant serves Western food. Although the single rooms are quite small, twins are adequate. You must pay for your room in cash or by credit card at check-in. Price and location are the reasons to stay here.

AKASAKA & TORONOMON

VERY EXPENSIVE

✪ Akasaka Prince Hotel

1-2 Kioi-cho, Chiyoda-ku 102. ☎ **03/3234-1111,** or 800/542-8686, or 800/637-7200 in the U.S. Fax 03/3262-5163. 761 rms. A/C MINIBAR TV TEL. ¥24,000–¥39,000 ($240–$390) single; ¥32,000–¥41,000 ($320–$410) twin; ¥36,000–¥45,000 ($360–$450) double; from ¥95,000 ($950) suite. AE, DC, JCB, MC, V. Free parking. Station: Akasaka-mitsuke (2 minutes).

This 40-story ultramodern white skyscraper caused quite a stir when it opened in 1983, with some Tokyoites complaining it was too cold and sterile. In my opinion, however, the Akasaka Prince is just ahead of its time. Japanese style, after all, has always called for simplicity—and this hotel's design is a projection of simplicity into the world of the 21st century. The lobby is intentionally spacious and empty, lined with almost 12,000 slabs of white marble.

Designed by Kenzo Tange, the hotel's rooms are set on a 45° angle from the center axis of the building's core. This gives each room a corner view, with expansive windows overlooking the city. Rooms are bright—gray, white, or soothing powder blue—with a lot of sunshine, and remind me of a Star Trek stage set. The single rooms are among the nicest in Tokyo, with three windows forming a pleasant alcove around a sofa. Sinks and vanity desks are located away from toilet and bath areas. Request a room overlooking the Akasaka side, and you'll have a view of neon lights down below and Tokyo Tower off in the distance. There's a no-smoking floor.

Dining/Entertainment: There are 13 international restaurants and bars. Le Trianon, the hotel's top Western dining spot, has all the grace, decor, and atmosphere of a fine French restaurant. Top of Akasaka, on the 40th floor, is one of the city's best cocktail lounges with a view (no children allowed).

Services: 24-hour room service, same-day laundry and dry-cleaning service, baby-sitting, free newspaper, no-smoking floor.

Facilities: A fully equipped, excellent business center is open daily with bilingual staff and a spectacular 20th-floor view, travel desk, souvenir shop, florist.

ANA Hotel Tokyo

1-12-33 Akasaka, Minato-ku 107. ☎ **03/3505-1111** or 800/262-4683 in the U.S. and Canada. Fax 03/3505-1155. 876 rms, 27 suites. A/C MINIBAR TV TEL. ¥26,000–¥35,000 ($260–$350) single; ¥34,000–¥38,000 ($340–$380) double or twin; from ¥60,000 ($600) suite. AE, CB, DC, JCB, MC, V. Station: Roppongi, Akasaka, Kamiyacho, Toranomon, or Kokkai Gijido-mae (5 to 10 minutes).

A gleaming white building rising 37 stories above the crossroads of Akasaka, Roppongi, Toranomon, and Kasumigaseki, the ANA Hotel Tokyo has given the Hotel Okura stiff competition since its grand opening in 1986. Its spacious second-floor lobby is of cool, cream-colored marble, with a water fountain serving as a focal point, and the lobby lounge is a favorite among Tokyoites for people-watching.

Rooms are large, with views of Tokyo Bay, Mt. Fuji, or the Imperial Palace. The 34th floor features special executive quarters, which offer the services of a concierge, free continental breakfast, and an evening cocktail hour.

Dining/Entertainment: A dozen restaurants and bars, serving French, Chinese, and Japanese favorites such as kaiseki, shabu-shabu, sushi, and teppanyaki, are available. The Astral Bar on the 37th floor provides live music and fantastic views of the city.

Services: Two free newspapers delivered daily, same-day laundry service.

Facilities: Business center with secretarial services, travel desk, shopping arcade, barbershop and beauty salon, sauna (for men only), outdoor swimming pool (fee: ¥2,000/$20), baby-sitter's room.

Hotel New Otani

4-1 Kioi-cho, Chiyoda-ku 102. ☎ **03/3265-1111,** 800/223-9868 in the U.S., or 800/421-8795 in the U.S. and Canada. Fax 03/3221-2619. 1,612 rms. A/C MINIBAR TV TEL. ¥25,500–¥35,000 ($255–$350) single; ¥27,500–¥44,000 ($275–$440) double or twin. AE, DC, JCB, MC, V. Station: Akasaka-mitsuke (3 minutes) or Yotsuya (5 minutes).

Like a city unto itself, the New Otani is so big that two information desks assist lost souls searching for a particular restaurant or one of the shops in the meandering shopping arcade. If you like quiet, small hotels, this is not for you. The most splendid feature of the hotel is its 400-year-old Japanese garden, which sprawls over 10 acres of ponds, waterfalls, bridges, bamboo groves, and manicured bushes.

The rooms, in the main building or a 40-story tower, are comfortable, offering English-language cable (with CNN) and shoji-like screens on the windows. There are no-smoking floors.

Dining/Entertainment: Some 40 restaurants and bars ply their trade here.

Services: 24-hour room service, free newspaper, same-day laundry service.

Facilities: Shopping arcade with 120 stores, medical offices, post office, tea-ceremony room, business center, chapel with daily services, travel agency, art museum, beauty parlor, barbershop, babysitting, and indoor and outdoor swimming pools, health club, sauna and tennis courts (¥5,150/$51.50 fee charged).

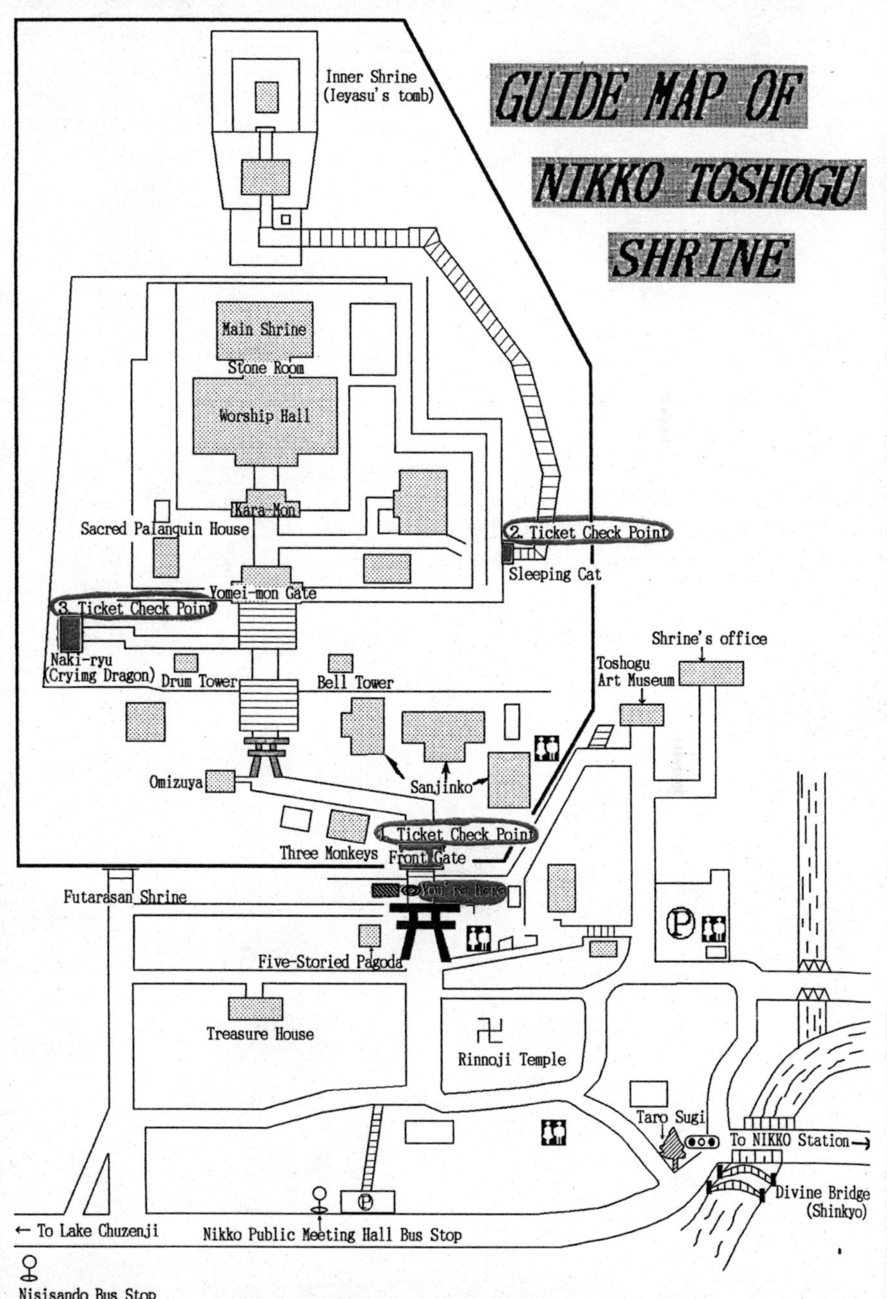
GUIDE MAP OF NIKKO TOSHOGU SHRINE
Inner Shrine
(Ieyasu's tomb)
Main Shrine
Stone Room
Worship Hall
Kara-Mon
Sacred Palanquin House
2. Ticket Check Point
Sleeping Cat
Yomei-mon Gate
3. Ticket Check Point
Naki-ryu
(Cryimg Dragon)
Drum Tower
Bell Tower
Shrine's office
Toshogu
Art Museum
Omizuya
Sanjinko
1. Ticket Check Point
Three Monkeys
Front Gate
You're here
Futarasan Shrine
Five-Storied Pagoda
Treasure House
Rinnoji Temple
Taro Sugi
To NIKKO Station
Divine Bridge
(Shinkyo)
← To Lake Chuzenji
Nikko Public Meeting Hall Bus Stop
Nisisando Bus Stop

Accommodations, Dining & Nightlife In Akasaka

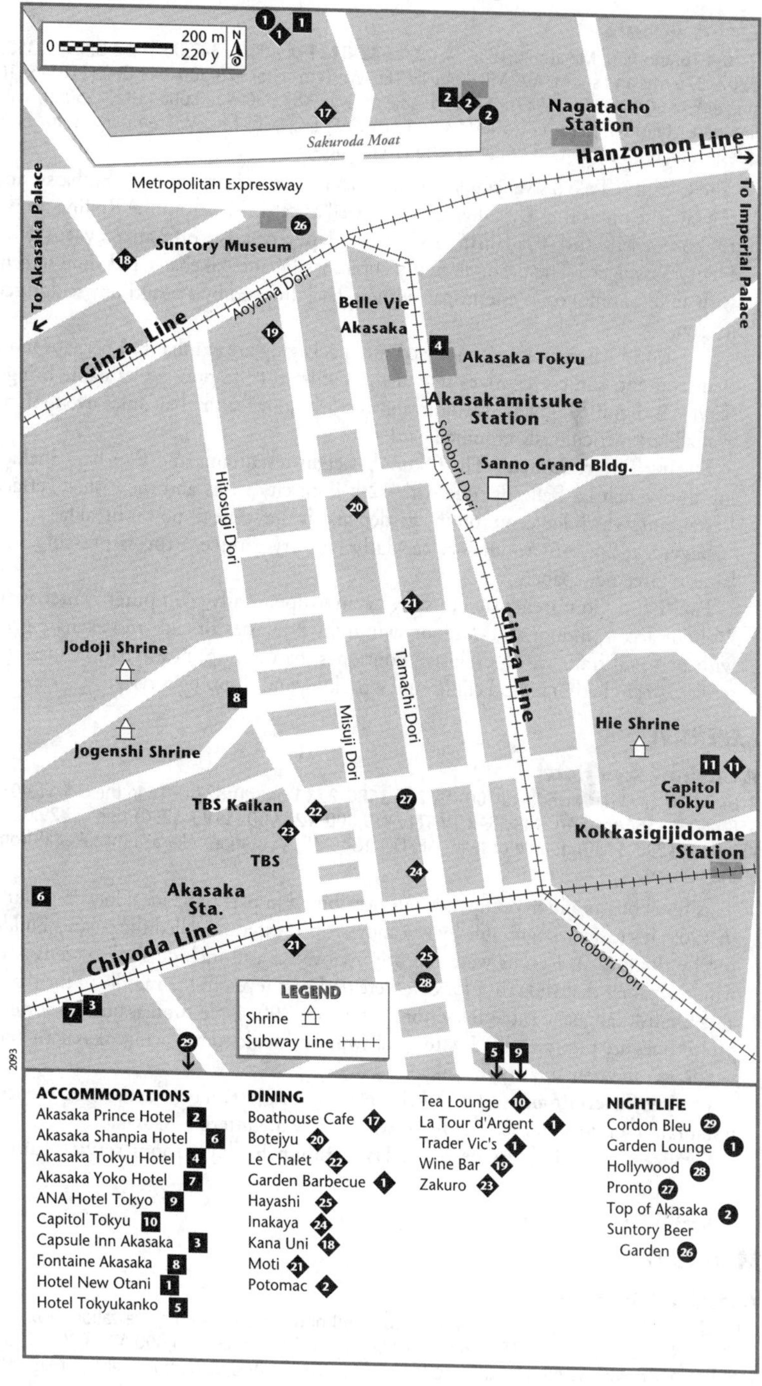

0
200 m
220 y
N
Sakuroda Moat
Nagatacho Station
Hanzomon Line
Metropolitan Expressway
To Akasaka Palace
To Imperial Palace
Suntory Museum
Aoyama Dori
Ginza Line
Belle Vie Akasaka
Akasaka Tokyu
Akasakamitsuke Station
Sotobori Dori
Sanno Grand Bldg.
Hitosugi Dori
Ginza Line
Jodoji Shrine
Jogenshi Shrine
Tamachi Dori
Misuji Dori
Hie Shrine
Capitol Tokyu
Kokkasigijidomae Station
TBS Kaikan
TBS
Akasaka Sta.
Chiyoda Line
Sotobori Dori
LEGEND
Shrine
Subway Line
2093
ACCOMMODATIONS
Akasaka Prince Hotel 2
Akasaka Shanpia Hotel 6
Akasaka Tokyu Hotel 4
Akasaka Yoko Hotel 7
ANA Hotel Tokyo 9
Capitol Tokyu 10
Capsule Inn Akasaka 3
Fontaine Akasaka 8
Hotel New Otani 1
Hotel Tokyukanko 5
DINING
Boathouse Cafe 17
Botejyu 20
Le Chalet 22
Garden Barbecue 1
Hayashi 25
Inakaya 24
Kana Uni 18
Moti 21
Potomac 2
Tea Lounge 10
La Tour d'Argent 1
Trader Vic's 1
Wine Bar 19
Zakuro 23
NIGHTLIFE
Cordon Bleu 29
Garden Lounge 1
Hollywood 28
Pronto 27
Top of Akasaka 2
Suntory Beer Garden 26

✪ Hotel Okura

2-10-4 Toranomon, Minato-ku 105. ☎ **03/3582-0111** or 800/223-6800 in the U.S. Fax 3582-3707. 875 rms and suites. A/C MINIBAR TV TEL. Western style: ¥28,500–¥41,000 ($285–$410) single; ¥37,000–¥79,000 ($370–$790) double or twin; ¥87,000–¥500,000 ($870–$5000) suite; Japanese style: ¥37,000–¥71,500 ($370–$715). AE, DC, JCB, MC, V. Free parking for hotel guests. Station: Toranomon or Kamiyacho (10 minutes).

The Okura is Tokyo's venerable hotel, across the street from the U.S. Embassy, and the favorite of visiting U.S. dignitaries, as well as celebrities from the Rolling Stones to Yo Yo Ma and Vladimir Horowitz. (I personally rode an elevator with Henry Kissinger.) The decor elegantly combines Japanese ikebana and shoji screens with an old-fashioned Western spaciousness, backdropped by a beautifully sculptured garden.

In a world where presentation, face, and packaging are emphasized perhaps more than content, some executives stay at the Okura for the prestige its name brings. Service is dignified, gracious. Rooms on the 5th floor feature balconies overlooking a small but meticulously groomed garden.

Dining/Entertainment: The Okura has eight restaurants and four bars, including the French La Belle Epoque with 12th-floor city views and the casual Terrace Restaurant, which looks out on the garden and is the scene of power breakfasts.

Services: 24-hour room service, daily laundry service, express pressing and laundry, free newspaper.

Facilities: Comprehensive business center open daily, computer center with 24-hour access, indoor and outdoor swimming pool, health club and exercise gym with personal trainers, 41 exclusive boutiques, barbershop, beautyparlor, massage service, steam bath, medical clinic, and a packing and shipping service.

EXPENSIVE

Akasaka Tokyu Hotel

2-14-3 Nagata-cho, Chiyoda-ku 100. ☎ **03/3580-2311** or 800/822-0016 in the U.S. Fax 03/3580-6066. 566 rms. A/C MINIBAR TV TEL. ¥19,000–¥25,000 ($190–$250) single; ¥29,000–¥33,000 ($290–$330) double or twin. AE, DC, JCB, MC, V. Station: Akasaka-mitsuke (in front of the station).

This hotel boasts a high occupancy rate, attributed in part to its ideal location. Built in 1969, it's easily recognizable by its candy-striped exterior (called the pajama building by the locals). Rooms were recently renovated and include shoji screens and window panels that slide shut for complete darkness (even in the middle of the day), and English-language cable television. There are 200 single rooms, but the lower-priced ones are pretty small. Try to get a twin or double room facing Akasaka—the windows can open, a rarity in Tokyo.

Dining/Entertainment: The hotel's five bars and restaurants include the French restaurant Gondola on the 14th floor, with a view of glittering Akasaka.

Services: Laundry service (Monday through Friday), room service (until midnight).

Facilities: Shopping arcade.

MODERATE

Akasaka Yoko Hotel

6-14-12 Akasaka, Minato-ku 107. ☎ **03/3586-4050** or 03/3586-8341 for reservations. Fax 03/3586-5944. 245 rms. A/C TV TEL. ¥8,900–¥9,800 ($89–$98) single; ¥13,000–¥15,000 ($130–$150) twin. AE, MC, V. All rates include tax and service charges. Station: Akasaka (5 minutes, on Akasaka Dori).

In a handy location close to the nightlife of both Roppongi (a 15-minute walk) and Akasaka, this pleasant small business hotel caters primarily to Japanese. For a couple of dollars more in each category, you can get a slightly larger room, which may be worth it if you're claustrophobic. In any case, the bathrooms are barely large enough for even one person. The hotel has a coffee shop, and there are beer- and soda-vending machines.

Hotel Tokyu Kanko

2-21-6 Akasaka, Minato-ku 107. ☎ **03/3582-0451** or 03/3583-4741 for reservations. Fax 03/3583-4023. 48 rms (all with bath). A/C TV TEL. ¥7,300–¥9,800 ($73–$98) single; ¥14,600 ($146) double or twin. AE, DC, JCB, MC, V. Station: Roppongi or Akasaka (10 minutes).

Close to the ANA Hotel, the Tokyu Kanko was built at the time of the 1964 Olympics. It shows its age, being a bit worn around the edges, but it remains popular because of its location. In addition, rooms are larger than in some other business hotels, and bathrooms are tiled, not fitted with the usual plastic walls and fixtures. The cheapest singles, however, have a shower instead of a tub and are a bit drab—they face an inner courtyard and have a glazed window or none at all. If you like the light of day, it may be worth it to splurge for the single with bathtub. The hotel has one coffee shop and a Japanese restaurant.

INEXPENSIVE

$ Asia Center of Japan

8-10-32 Akasaka, Minato-ku 107. ☎ **03/3402-6111.** Fax 03/3402-0738. 172 rms (144 with bath). A/C TV TEL. ¥5,000 ($50) single without bath, ¥6,100–¥7,200 ($61–$72) single with bath; ¥6,600–¥7,400 ($66–$74) twin without bath, ¥10,200–¥12,000 ($102–$120) twin with bath; ¥7,800–¥9,300 ($78–$93) double with bath; ¥10,600 ($106) triple without bath, ¥10,800–¥13,200 ($108–$132) triple with bath. All rates include tax and service charges. No credit cards. Station: Aoyama-Itchome (3 minutes).

A top choice in this category if you're looking for Western-style accommodations in the center of town. However, it's so popular it's often fully booked (reserve six months in advance). Everyone—from businessmen to students to travelers to foreigners teaching English—stays here. (I know one teacher who lived here for years.) Resembling a college dormitory, the Asia Center has rooms with or without private bath, as well as an inexpensive cafeteria and snack bar. Accommodations are basic, no frills, and in the singles you can almost reach out and touch all four walls. Rooms come with the usual bed, desk, heater, and other amenities. The average price of meals served in the cafeteria is ¥600 ($6) for breakfast, ¥850 ($8.50) for lunch, and ¥1,500 ($15) for dinner. It's about a 15-minute walk to Roppongi or Akasaka, where all the night action is.

ROPPONGI & SHIBA

EXPENSIVE

✪ Tokyo Prince Hotel

3-3-1 Shibakoen, Minato-ku 105. ☎ **03/3432-1111.** Fax 03/3434-5551. 484 rms. A/C MINIBAR TV TEL. ¥23,000–¥25,000 ($230–$250) single; ¥24,000–¥35,000 ($240–$350) double or twin; from ¥70,000 ($700) suite. Station: Kamiyacho (5 minutes) or Onarimon (2 minutes), or Hammamatsucho (10 minutes).

Built in 1964 for the Tokyo Olympic Games and set in Shiba Park, the Tokyo Prince is next to Zozoji Temple and Tokyo Tower. The central location makes it possible to walk to Roppongi for nightlife (the walk home is sobering) or to Hibiya or the Tokyo Trade Center on business. Service is that of a small, luxury hotel. While guests

Accommodations, Dining & Nightlife In Roppongi

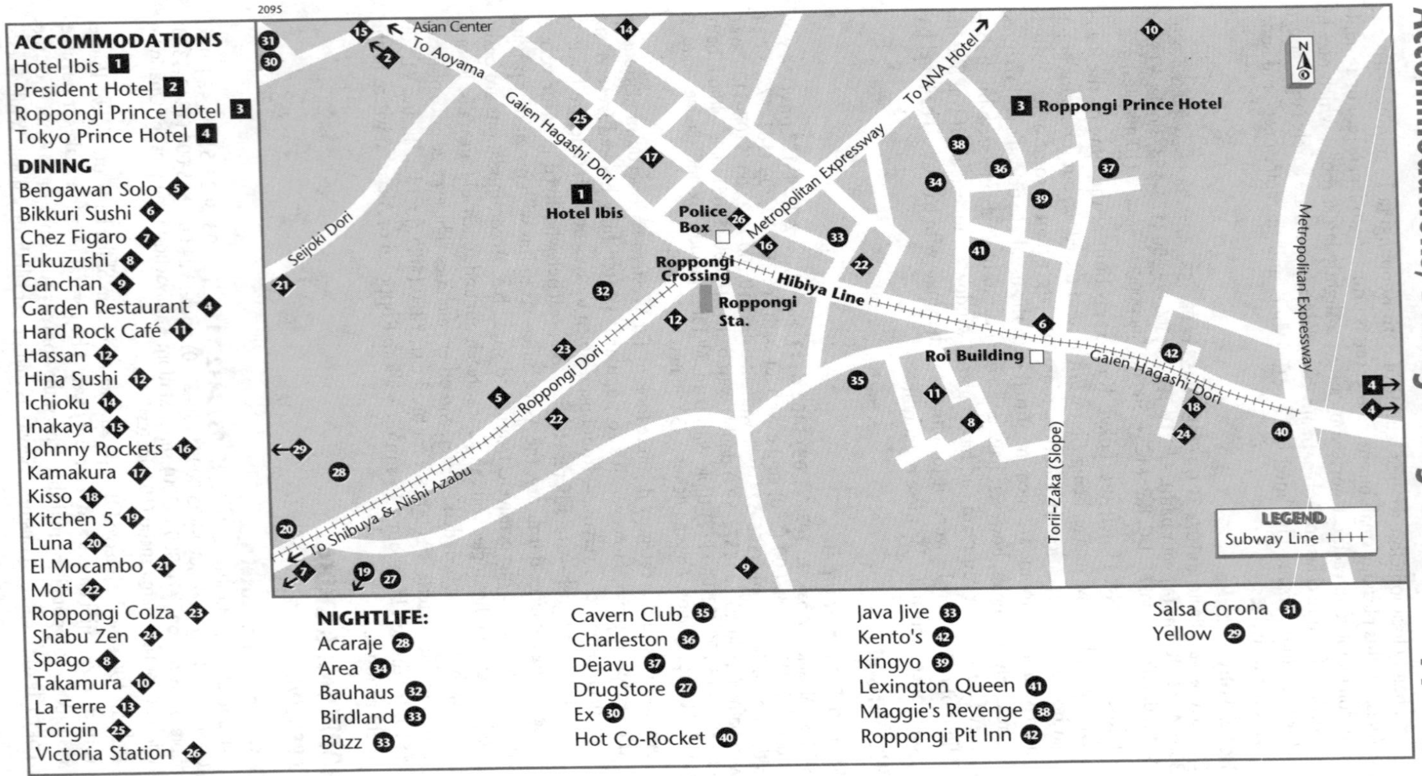

ACCOMMODATIONS
Hotel Ibis 1
President Hotel 2
Roppongi Prince Hotel 3
Tokyo Prince Hotel 4
DINING
Bengawan Solo 5
Bikkuri Sushi 6
Chez Figaro 7
Fukuzushi 8
Ganchan 9
Garden Restaurant 4
Hard Rock Café 11
Hassan 12
Hina Sushi 12
Ichioku 14
Inakaya 15
Johnny Rockets 16
Kamakura 17
Kisso 18
Kitchen 5 19
Luna 20
El Mocambo 21
Moti 22
Roppongi Colza 23
Shabu Zen 24
Spago 8
Takamura 10
La Terre 13
Torigin 25
Victoria Station 26
NIGHTLIFE:
Acaraje 28
Area 34
Bauhaus 32
Birdland 33
Buzz 33
Cavern Club 35
Charleston 36
Dejavu 37
DrugStore 27
Ex 30
Hot Co-Rocket 40
Java Jive 33
Kento's 42
Kingyo 39
Lexington Queen 41
Maggie's Revenge 38
Roppongi Pit Inn 42
Salsa Corona 31
Yellow 29
LEGEND
Subway Line
2095
Asian Center
To Aoyama
Gaien Hagashi Dori
To ANA Hotel
Metropolitan Expressway
Roppongi Prince Hotel
Hotel Ibis
Police Box
Seijoki Dori
Roppongi Crossing
Hibiya Line
Roppongi Sta.
Roppongi Dori
Roi Building
Torii-Zaka (Slope)
To Shibuya & Nishi Azabu

include many foreign business executives, I've seen the Empress and Stevie Wonder here. The Tokyo Prince offers not only no-smoking rooms but a no-smoking lounge with an up-close view of Tokyo Tower. Foreign guests are invited to a cocktail on Thursday nights, where you'll see people of all walks of life and where more than one business partnership has been born. All the spacious, beautifully updated rooms feature view windows that open, two phones, modern litho art, and marble bath areas with nonsteam mirrors. Some rooms are fax/modem ready, ask for one if you plan to use your PC.

Dining/Entertainment: Among the 13 restaurants and lounges are the fine French restaurant Beaux Séjours, the no-smoking lounge Tower View (open to guests only), and Porto, which offers Western-style all-you-can-eat buffets (lunch ¥2,500/$25, dinner ¥4,000/$40) perfect for big appetites.

Services: Same-day laundry service, 24-hour room service, complimentary newspaper.

Facilities: Bilingual executive business center, meeting rooms, outdoor pool in summer (fee: ¥1,000/$10), convenience store, boutiques, and book/magazine shop.

Roppongi Prince Hotel

3-2-7 Roppongi, Minato-ku 106. ☎ **03/3587-1111,** or 800/542-8686 in the U.S. Fax 03/3587-0770. 216 rms. A/C MINIBAR TV TEL. ¥19,500 ($195) single; ¥23,000–¥26,500 ($230–$265) twin or double. AE, DC, JCB, MC, V. Station: Roppongi (10 minutes).

Opened in 1984 (a welcome event in Roppongi, still woefully lacking in hotels), the Roppongi Prince attracts Japanese vacationers aged 20 to 25 and caters to them with a young and cheerful staff, modern designs, and bold colors. The hotel is built around an inner courtyard, which features an outdoor swimming pool with a heated deck—a solar mirror on the roof directs sun rays toward the sunbathers below. Rooms are small but bright and colorful. A good place to be if you want to be close to the action in Roppongi.

Dining/Entertainment: There are Italian, tempura, sushi, and steak restaurants, as well as a coffee shop, bar, and lobby lounge.

Services: Free newspaper.

Facilities: Heated outdoor pool that's open year-round (no fee for guests).

MODERATE

Hotel Ibis

7-14-4 Roppongi, Minato-ku 106. ☎ **03/3403-4411.** Fax 03/3479-0609. 182 rms (all with bath). A/C MINIBAR TV TEL. ¥13,000–¥15,000 ($130–$150) single; ¥16,000–¥19,500 ($160–$195) double; ¥21,500–¥26,000 ($215–$260) twin; ¥27,000 ($270) triple. AE, DC, JCB, MC, V. All rates include tax and service. Station: Roppongi (1 minute).

If you want to stay close to the night action of Roppongi, the Ibis is about as close as you can get. It caters to both businessmen and couples who come to Roppongi's discos and don't make (or want to make) the last subway home. The lobby is on the fifth floor, above which are the guest rooms. Small but comfortable, they feature modern furniture, windows that can be opened, and TV with English-language cable and CNN. On the 13th floor is a branch of the well-known Italian restaurant Sabatini.

HARAJUKU & AOYAMA

MODERATE

National Children's Castle Hotel

5-53-1 Jingumae, Shibuya-ku 150. ☎ **03/3797-5677.** Fax 03/3406-7805. 27 rms (all with bath). A/C TV TEL. ¥6,300 ($63) single; ¥13,000–¥14,000 ($130–$140) twin; from ¥17,400

($174) Japanese-style room. All rates include tax and service charges. AE, DC, JCB, MC, V. Station: Omotesando or Shibuya (10 minutes).

The National Children's Castle or *Kodomo-no-Shiro* is a great place to stay if you're with children. In addition to containing a small hotel on the seventh and eighth floors, this complex boasts a sophisticated indoor/outdoor playground for children, complete with a clinic and restaurants. Hotel guests range from businesspeople to families and young college students. The rooms, mainly twins, are simple, with large windows, but are not child-theme oriented. The most expensive twins, which face toward Shinjuku, have the best views. The hotel's three singles do not have windows, but you can pay extra to stay in a twin. Japanese-style rooms, available for three or more, are a good way for families to experience the traditional Japanese lifestyle. Make reservations at least six months in advance, especially if you plan on being in Tokyo in the summer. The front desk is on the seventh floor. Note that there's an 11pm curfew and check-in isn't until 3pm.

$ President Hotel

2-2-3 Minami Aoyama, Minato-ku 107. ☎ **03/3497-0111.** Fax 03/3401-4816. 210 rms (all with bath). A/C MINIBAR TV TEL. ¥12,000–¥13,000 ($120–$130) single; ¥17,000 ($170) double; ¥17,000–¥21,000 ($170–$210) twin. AE, DC, JCB, MC, V. Station: Aoyama-Itchome (1 minute).

Although a small hotel, the President is one of the best deals in town, offering some of the same conveniences as the larger and more expensive hotels (like room service and TV with CNN), plus a great location between Akasaka, Shinjuku, and Roppongi. Rooms are small but clean and pleasant. The unpretentious lobby has a European atmosphere. The President has two very good restaurants, one Japanese and one French. Foreigners constitute 50% of the clientele.

SHINJUKU

VERY EXPENSIVE

Century Hyatt Tokyo

2-7-2 Nishi-Shinjuku, Shinjuku-ku 160. ☎ **03/3349-0111,** or 800/233-1234 in the U.S. and Canada. Fax 03/3344-5575. 786 rms and suites. A/C MINIBAR TV TEL. ¥30,000–¥38,000 ($300–$380) single; ¥34,000–¥42,000 ($340–$420) double or twin. Discounts for longer stays. AE, DC, JCB, MC, V. Station: Shinjuku (a 10-minute walk, or a free 3-minute shuttle ride).

Located on Shinjuku's west side, this 28-story hotel features an impressive seven-story atrium lobby with three massive chandeliers and an inlaid marble floor. The excellent staff is used to the many foreigners who pass through the hotel's doors. You'll be treated to familiar Hyatt standards.

The refurbished rooms are not only of adequate size but attractive, with English-language cable TV. The bathrooms' bright lights are great for applying makeup. Single rooms do not let in much sunshine. The twin rooms are better, with big windows. The Regency Club—the more expensive, more luxurious floors—offers complimentary breakfast and evening cocktails.

Dining/Entertainment: There are a dozen restaurants and bars, including the well-known Hugo's, with its teppanyaki cuisine; a French restaurant, Chenonceaux; and Japanese and Chinese restaurants. On the 27th floor is Rhapsody, featuring live jazz nightly and a view of the city.

Services: 24-hour room service, same-day laundry service, in-house doctor, free newspaper, free shuttle bus to and from Shinjuku Station (in front of Odakyu Halc Department Store).

Facilities: Indoor swimming pool on the 28th floor (fee: ¥1,500/$15), sauna, business center, shopping arcade, beauty salon, barbershop.

Accommodations, Dining & Nightlife In Shinjuku

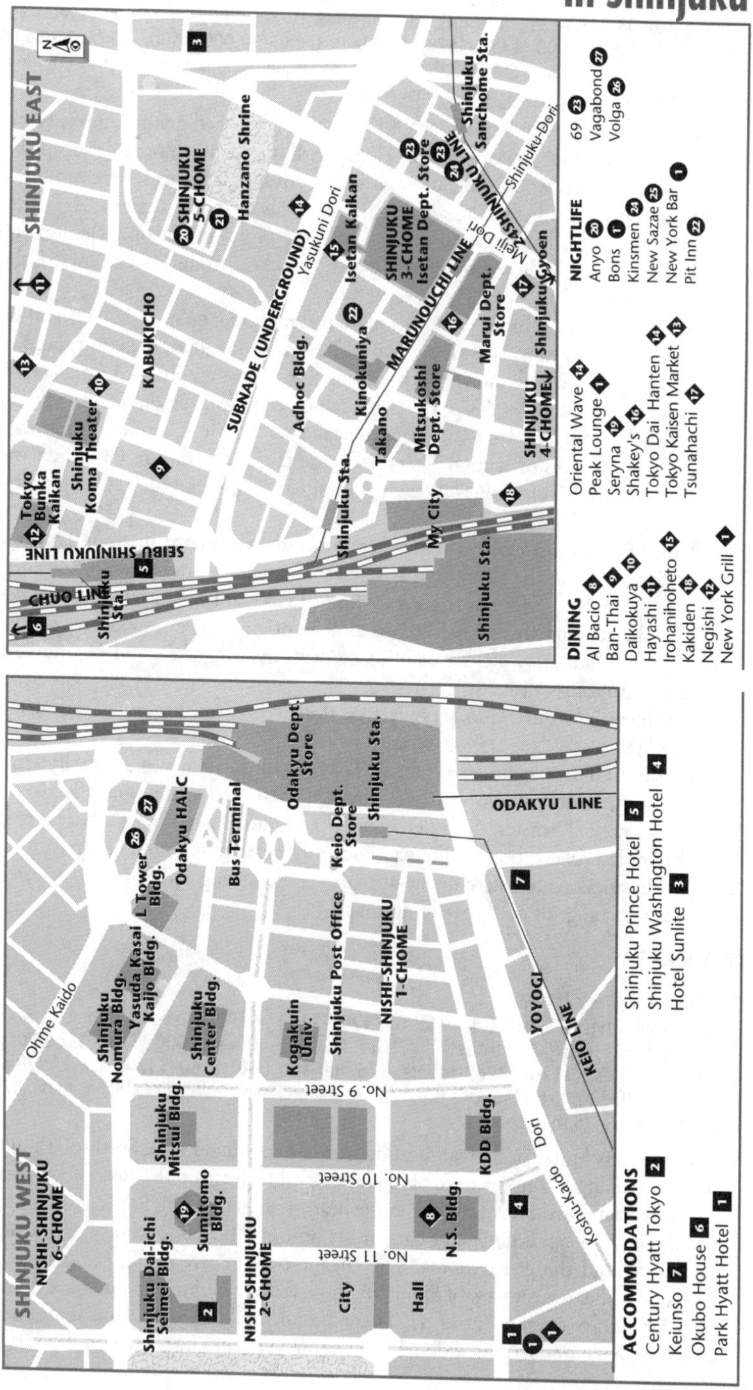

ACCOMMODATIONS
Century Hyatt Tokyo 2
Keiunso 7
Okubo House 6
Park Hyatt Hotel 1
Shinjuku Prince Hotel 5
Shinjuku Washington Hotel 4
Hotel Sunlite 3

DINING
Al Bacio 8
Ban-Thai 9
Daikokuya 10
Hayashi 11
Irohanihoheto 15
Kakiden 18
Negishi 12
New York Grill 1
Oriental Wave 14
Peak Lounge 1
Seryna 19
Shakey's 16
Tokyo Dai Hanten 14
Tokyo Kaisen Market 13
Tsunahachi 17

NIGHTLIFE
Anyo 20
Bons 1
Kinsmen 24
New Sazae 25
New York Bar 1
Pit Inn 22
69 23
Vagabond 27
Volga 26

✪ Park Hyatt Tokyo

3-7-1-2 Nishi-Shinjuku, Shinjuku-ku 163. ☎ **03/5322-1234** or 800/233-1234 in the U.S. and Canada. Fax 03/3532-1288. 178 rms. A/C MINIBAR TV TEL. ¥40,000–¥52,000 ($400–$520) single; ¥45,000–¥57,000 ($450–$570) double or twin; ¥90,000–¥500,000 ($900–$5,000) suites. AE, DC, JCB, MC, V. Station: Shinjuku (a 13-minute walk, or 5-minute free shuttle ride from in front of L-Tower Bldg. subway exit A18).

Located on the 39th to 52nd floors of Kenzo Tange's honed-granite-and-glass sculpture, Shinjuku Park Tower, the Park Hyatt, with its Japanese-taste interiors planned around original art work, is the most gorgeous, advanced, sophisticated, comfortable hotel in Japan and best captures the high-tech, avant-garde design, 21st-century essence of Tokyo. If you can afford it, stay here. Guest-rooms-only elevators offer privacy, and if you do see other guests, they're likely to be personalities, fashion designers, or CEOs.

All rooms average more than 50 square meters (the largest in Tokyo) and offer original art work, expansive views, two dedicated phone lines, data port, fax, voice mail, deep tub, separate shower, walk-in closet, extensive minibar, CD and laser disc players, VCR and wide-screen TV (with cable networks), remote-control curtains, individually controlled air-conditioning, and so on. Sleek modern interiors are warmed by touches of natural fibers, walls are paneled with rare Hokkaido water elm, and hand-woven baskets hide amenities. Lacking for nothing, you're ready to move in.

Dining/Entertainment: The most sophisticated restaurant in all of Tokyo, the New York Grill on the 52nd floor has great food, service, and views, while around the corner the New York Bar is Tokyo's most spectacular live-jazz bar. Kozue is tiered to provide views of Mt Fuji, while you dine on original Japanese cuisine. The Peak Lounge in a four-story atrium bamboo garden serves high tea, and Girandole is a relaxed European-style cafe.

Services: 24-hour room service, free shuttle bus to Shinjuku Station every 10 minutes.

Facilities: The best fitness center in Tokyo, with Jacuzzi, steam and dry saunas, gymnasium, aerobic studio, personal fitness trainers, and game room (fee: ¥1,500/ $15); dramatic 20-meter, 47th-floor pool (free to hotel guests); CD, laser disc and book libraries; bakery; beauty salon; 24-hour parking; airport limousine service; multilingual business center; state-of-the-art video conferencing and function facilities to meet a wide range of needs; wedding chapel.

Moderate

Shinjuku Prince Hotel

1-30-1 Kabuki-cho, Shinjuku-ku 160. ☎ **03/3205-1111** or 800/542-8686 in the U.S. Fax 03/ 3205-1952. 571 rms (all with bath). A/C TV TEL. ¥15,000–¥16,000 ($150–$160) single; ¥17,000–¥32,000 ($170–$320) double; ¥26,000–¥32,000 ($260–$320) twin. Additional person ¥3,000 ($30) extra. AE, DC, JCB, MC, V. Station: Seibu Shinjuku (which is beneath the hotel) or Shinjuku (5 minutes).

This business hotel has a great location, just a five-minute walk north of Shinjuku Station, making it convenient to Shinjuku's nightlife district of Kabuki-cho. A smart-looking streamlined brick building in the heart of Shinjuku, the Prince has shopping arcades and 10 restaurants and bars on its bottom 10 floors, while the rest of its 24 floors hold the guest rooms. The cheapest rooms are small, but all accommodations offer a great view of Shinjuku; those facing Shinjuku Station have double-paned windows to shut out noise. There are no-smoking floors, and some rooms have minibars. Services include 24-hour room service, same-day laundry service, and free English newspapers on request. All in all, a good choice for a moderately priced hotel.

Shinjuku Washington Hotel

3-2-9 Nishi-Shinjuku, Shinjuku-ku 160. ☎ **03/3343-3111.** Fax 03/3342-2575. 1,638 rms (all with bath). A/C MINIBAR TV TEL. ¥11,300 ($113) single; ¥17,000–¥20,000 ($170–$200) double or twin; from ¥30,000 ($300) triple. AE, DC, JCB, MC, V. Station: Shinjuku (10 minutes).

Opened in West Shinjuku in 1984, with an annex added in 1987, this huge white building reminds me of an ocean liner—even the hotel's tiny windows look like portholes. Inside, everything is bright and white, with a lot of open space. The third-floor lobby features a row of machines for automated check-in and checkout, but there are a few humans there to help you with the process. You'll receive a "card key" to activate the electricity. (The annex has its own check-in desk.) There are no bellhops here, no room service. The small guest rooms remind me of ship cabins, but have everything you need. More than 20 bars and restaurants are in the hotel complex, as well as a shopping arcade and a sauna (for men only).

Sunlite Hotel

5-15-8 Shinjuku, Shinjuku-ku 160. ☎ **03/3356-0391.** Fax 03/3356-1223. 197 rms (all with bath). A/C TV TEL. Main building: ¥9,000 ($90) single; ¥15,000 ($150) double; ¥16,000 ($160) twin. Annex: ¥8,600 ($86) single; ¥14,200 ($142) twin. All rates include tax and service charges. AE, JCB, MC, V. Station: Shinjuku (15 minutes) or Shinjuku Sanchome (5 minutes).

In 1985 this business hotel moved across the street from its old location into a spanking-new building, turning the older building into the Hotel Sunlite Annex, with rates slightly lower. Rooms are cheerful and clean, although those in the annex are small (its singles are minuscule). Feelings of claustrophobia are somewhat mitigated by windows that can be opened. The new building's corner twins with windows on two sides are the best. Incidentally, if you like to stay out late, beware. Doors here close at 2am and don't reopen until 5:30am. It's on the east side of Shinjuku Station, on Meiji Dori.

INEXPENSIVE

Okubo House

1-11-32 Hyakunincho, Shinjuku-ku 169. ☎ **03/3361-2348.** 76 beds. ¥3,200 ($32) single; ¥4,300 ($43) double. Dormitory beds ¥1,700 ($17) for men, ¥1,800 ($18) for women. No credit cards. Station: Shin-Okubo (2 minutes).

Judging from the number of old Tokyo hands who stayed here when they first arrived in the city, Okubo House has been around forever. The owners are sometimes gruff; the place is closed during the day from 10am to 4pm and the front doors are locked at 11pm—but it's one of the cheapest places to stay in Tokyo. The private rooms are tiny—accommodating just two or three tatami mats—but they all have windows. The majority of beds here are dormitory style, separate for men and women (as are the public baths). Children are not accepted. Cotton kimonos and Japanese tea are provided, but not meals.

This place is located one station north of Shinjuku Station on the Yamanote Line. To reach it, turn left out of Shin-Okubo's only exit, then turn left again on the first side street, which runs parallel to the train tracks. Okubo House is on this street, with a sign in English.

Tokyo YWCA Sadowara Hostel

3-1-1 Ichigaya Sadowara-cho, Shinjuku-ku 162. ☎ **03/3268-7313.** Fax 03/3268-4452. 21 rms (18 with toilet only, 2 with bath). A/C TEL. (including tax and service) ¥6,180 ($61.80) single with toilet only; ¥12,360 ($123.60) twin with toilet only, ¥14,420 ($144.20) twin with bath. All rates include tax. No credit cards. Station: Ichigaya (Ichigaya exit 7 minutes).

This YWCA is located in a spotless modern building. In addition to women travelers, it also accepts married couples, but only for one of its two twins that have a private bathroom and a kitchenette. All rooms have a sink. For communal use there's an iron and an ironing board, a kitchen, and a refrigerator. The front doors close at midnight.

Tokyo International Youth Hostel

1-1 Kagura-kashi, Shinjuku-ku 162. ☎ **03/3235-1107.** 130 beds. ¥3,000 ($30) per person. Breakfast ¥400 ($4) extra; dinner ¥800 ($8) extra. No credit cards. Station: Iidabashi (west exit 1 minute).

This hostel is definitely the best place to stay in its price range. New, spotlessly clean, and modern, it offers great Tokyo views. No youth-hostel card required; no age limit. The lobby is on the 18th floor of the new Central Plaza Building. All beds are dormitory style, with two, four, or five bunk beds to a room. The rooms are very pleasant, with big windows, and each bed has its own curtain for privacy. If there are vacancies, you can stay longer than the normal three-day maximum. In summer you must reserve about three months in advance. Closed from 10am to 3pm and locked at 10:30pm (lights out). You have free use of a washer and dryer.

MEGURO & SHINAGAWA

EXPENSIVE

✪ Miyako Hotel Tokyo

1-1-50 Shiroganedai, Minato-ku 108. ☎ **03/3447-3111** or 800/336-1136 in the U.S. Fax 03/3447-3133. 498 rms and suites. A/C MINIBAR TV TEL. ¥18,000–¥24,000 ($180–$240) single; ¥25,000–¥38,000 ($250–$380) double or twin. Japanese-style rooms, ¥25,000 ($250) single; ¥30,000 ($300) double. AE, DC, JCB, MC, V. Station: Takanawadai (8 minutes) or free shuttle from Meguro or Shinagawa station.

This affiliate of the famous Miyako Hotel in Kyoto was designed by Minoru Yamasaki, the architect of New York's World Trade Center and Los Angeles' Century Plaza. Japanese account for 70% of the guests. It offers a free shuttle bus to and from Meguro Station and to Shinagawa Station. The lobby overlooks 5½ acres of lush gardens. The guest rooms are large, with huge floor-to-ceiling windows overlooking the hotel's own garden, a famed garden next door, or Tokyo Tower. There are nine sought-after single rooms, all with a semi-double-size bed. This hotel is one of my favorites in Tokyo, for its calm as well as its small-luxury-hotel service. When I didn't have time to go to the post office, the concierge offered to go for me on her lunch hour.

A Note on Japanese Symbols

Many hotels, restaurants, and other establishments in Japan do not have signs giving their names in English letters. As an aid to the reader, the appendix lists the Japanese symbols for all such places described in this guide. Each set of symbols has a number, which corresponds to the number that appears inside an oval next to the establishment's name in the text. Thus, to find the Japanese symbols for, say, the hostel **Shimizu Bekkan** (2), refer to number 2 in the appendix.

Dining/Entertainment: The hotel has nine restaurants, bars, and cocktail lounges. La Clé d'Or, serving continental fare, has a view of the hotel's garden, as does the Yamatoya-Sangen, which offers a variety of Japanese cuisine.

Services: Free newspaper, complimentary shuttle bus, same-day laundry service.

Facilities: Health club with both a huge indoor pool, great for swimming laps, and a sauna (fee: ¥2,000/$20); shopping arcade; barbershop; travel agency; medical clinic; excellent bilingual concierge desk.

MODERATE

✪ Gajoen Kanko Hotel

1-8-1 Shimo-Meguro, Meguro-ku 153. ☎ **03/3491-0111.** Fax 03/3495-2450. 100 rms (all with bath). A/C MINIBAR TV TEL. ¥10,000 ($100) single; ¥17,000–¥21,000 ($170–$210) double or twin; ¥27,000 ($270) family room for three, ¥34,000 ($340) for four. AE, DC, JCB, MC, V. Station: Meguro (west exit 3 minutes).

This older, rather eccentric-looking hotel is one of my favorites in Tokyo. Built in the early 1930s, with a decidedly Asian atmosphere, it boasts wood paneling and Japanese prints on the lobby ceiling and intricately inlaid shell and mother-of-pearl designs in its two old elevators. In its early days it was a hospital; then, after World War II, American army personnel were stationed here for a decade. Over the years the hotel became more and more run-down. In 1986 extensive renovations cleaned up the lobby and guest rooms and added a new wing, and today the hotel caters to a large Chinese clientele. Rooms come in a variety of shapes and sizes, but most have large windows and spacious tiled bathrooms. The best rooms are those on a corner or those facing the backyard, where there are trees. All TVs feature remote control and cable with CNN broadcasts. Facilities include French and Chinese restaurants. A good choice for a romantic.

Miyako Inn Tokyo

3-7-8 Mita, Minato-ku 108. ☎ **03/3454-3111.** Fax 03/3454-3397. 403 rms (all with bath). A/C MINIBAR TV TEL. ¥10,500–¥]13,500 ($105–$135) single; ¥15,000–¥16,000 ($150–$160) double; ¥16,000–¥22,000 ($160–$220) twin. AE, DC, JCB, MC, V. Station: Tamachi, Mita, or Sengakuji (6 minutes).

This combination business-and-city hotel rises 14 stories high in southern Tokyo. Rooms on the top floor have the best views, facing either Tokyo Bay or Tokyo Tower in the distance. Rooms have the usual amenities, and facilities include Japanese, Chinese, and Western restaurants, a bar, and a travel agency. Differences in room rates are reflected in the size of the room and the bed. Service is good, in the Miyako tradition. A reason to stay here is to be in a nontouristy neighborhood.

$ Shinagawa Prince Hotel

4-10-30 Takanawa, Minato-ku 108. ☎ **03/3440-1111** or 800/542-8686 in the U.S. Fax 03/3441-7092. 3,008 rms. A/C TV TEL. Main Tower: ¥8,000–¥9,800 ($80–$98) single. Annex: ¥14,100–¥25,000 ($141–$250) twin; ¥14,600 ($146) double. New Tower: ¥18,000 ($180) single; ¥18,000–¥26,500 ($180–$265) twin; ¥21,000–¥25,500 ($210–$255) double. Station: Shinagawa (1 minute).

With three gleaming white buildings (Main Tower, Annex, and the New Tower) just a minute's walk from the station, the Shinagawa Prince is the largest hotel in Japan and offers numerous facilities: 12 food and beverage outlets, travel desk, convenience shop, shopping arcade, florist, parking, conference rooms, a sports center with 9 indoor tennis courts, 104-lane bowling center, billiards, video games, indoor swimming pool (in summer), outdoor swimming pool, and fitness center (fee charged for most facilities). It caters to Japanese businessmen on weekdays and students on weekends and holidays. The main reasons to stay here are convenience to the station (which has many important lines, including the Shinkansen) and to the airports (both Haneda and Narita), reasonable price for the room quality, and the sporting facilities. It's too big for my taste though.

ASAKUSA & UENO

EXPENSIVE

Asakusa View Hotel

3-17-1 Nishi-Asakusa, Taito-ku 111. ☎ **03/3847-1111.** Fax 03/3842-2117. 341 rms. A/C MINIBAR TV TEL. ¥15,000–¥18,000 ($150–$180) single; ¥21,000–¥23,000 ($210–$230) double; ¥28,000–¥34,000 ($280–$340) twin; ¥34,000 ($340) triple. Japanese-style rooms, from ¥40,000 ($400) for two. AE, DC, JCB, MC, V. Station: Tawaramachi (8 minutes).

This is the only upper-bracket and modern hotel in the Asakusa area, and it looks almost out of place rising among this famous district's older buildings. It's a good place to stay if you want to be in Tokyo's old downtown but don't want to sacrifice any creature comforts. The guest rooms are very pleasant, with sleek contemporary Japanese furnishings and bay windows that let in plenty of sunshine. Rooms facing the front have views of the famous Sensoji Temple. Eight Japanese-style rooms are available, sleeping up to five people.

Dining/Entertainment: Of the six restaurants and bars, Makie is best known, featuring Western cuisine served in the delicate style of Japanese kaiseki. Less formal, but with great city views and a daily lunch buffet, is the Belvedere on the 28th floor.

Services: Free newspaper, darning and stitching service.

Facilities: Indoor swimming pool with a ceiling opened in summer (fee: ¥3,000/ $30), massage, jet bath, shopping arcade, Japanese-style public bath with wooden tubs (fee: ¥1,030/$10.30).

MODERATE

Ryokan Shigetsu

1-31-11 Asakusa, Taito-ku 111. ☎ **03/3843-2345.** Fax 03/3843-2348. 24 rms (all with bath). A/C TV. ¥7,000–¥9,000 ($70–$90) single; ¥13,000–¥17,000 ($130–$170) double. Japanese or western breakfast ¥900 ($9) extra, Japanese dinner ¥2,500 ($25) extra. AE, MC, V. Station: Asakusa (2 minutes).

This half Western/half ryokan accomodation has a great location just off Nakamise Dori, a colorful, shop-lined pedestrian street leading to the famous Sensoji Temple—an area that gives you a feel for the older Japan. A member of the Japanese Inn Group, the ryokan was completely rebuilt in 1995. Japanese breakfast is available, but a Western-style breakfast of eggs, toast, salad, fruit, and coffee can be arranged for the same price.

INEXPENSIVE

Japanese Style

Sakura Ryokan

2-6-2 Iriya, Taito-ku 110. ☎ **03/3876-8118.** Fax 03/3873-9456. 16 rms (6 with bath). A/C TV TEL. ¥5,000 ($50) single without bath, ¥6,000 ($60) single with bath; ¥9,000 ($90) double without bath, ¥10,000 ($100) double with bath; ¥12,000 ($120) triple without bath. Breakfast ¥600 ($6) extra for Western style, ¥700 ($7) extra for Japanese style. AE, MC, V. Station: Iriya (5 minutes).

A member of Japanese Inn and Welcome Inn groups, this modern concrete establishment is located just off the Kappabashi Dori and Kototoi Dori intersection, about a 10-minute walk from Sensoji Temple. The reception area is on the second floor,

Accommodations & Dining In Asakusa

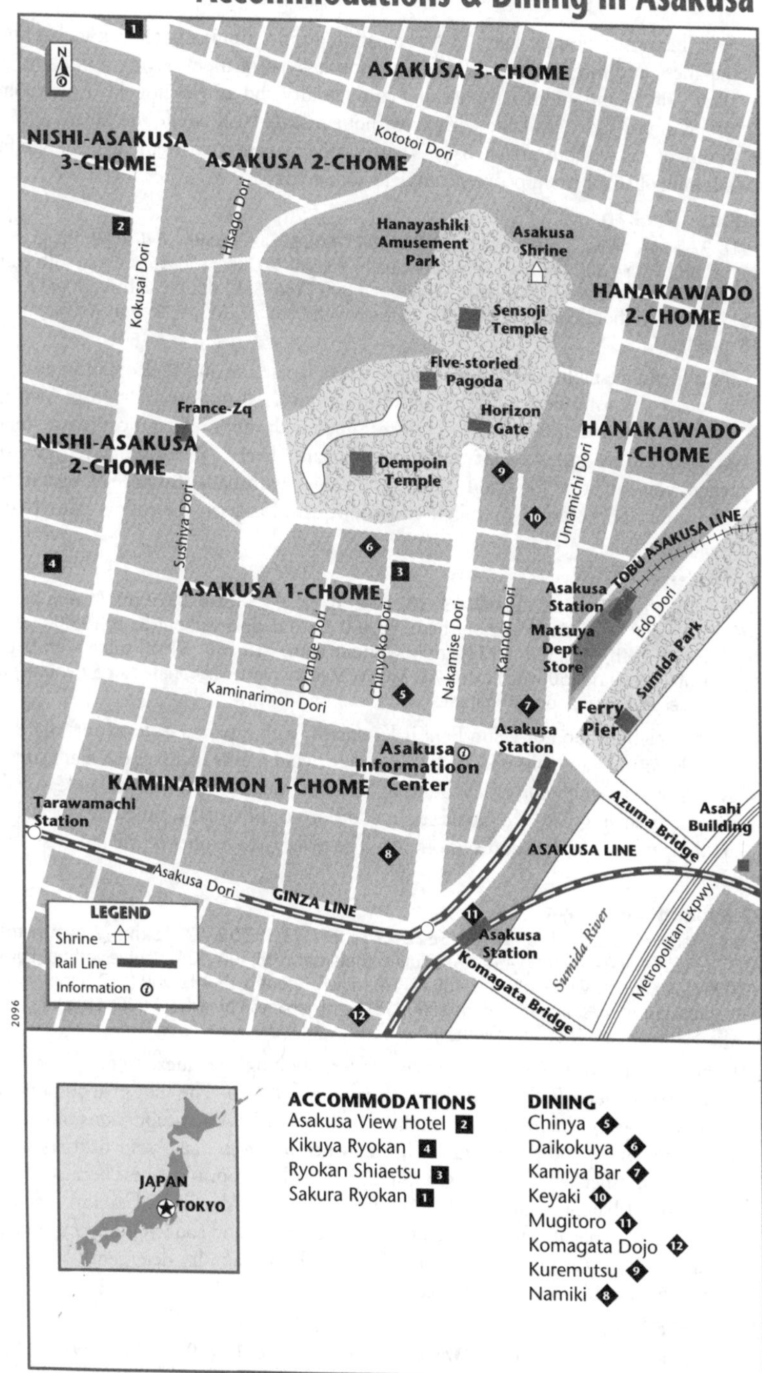

ASAKUSA 3-CHOME
NISHI-ASAKUSA 3-CHOME
ASAKUSA 2-CHOME
Kototoi Dori
Hisago Dori
Kokusai Dori
Hanayashiki Amusement Park
Asakusa Shrine
HANAKAWADO 2-CHOME
Sensoji Temple
Five-storied Pagoda
France-Zq
Horizon Gate
NISHI-ASAKUSA 2-CHOME
Dempoin Temple
HANAKAWADO 1-CHOME
Umamichi Dori
Sushiya Dori
TOBU ASAKUSA LINE
ASAKUSA 1-CHOME
Asakusa Station
Edo Dori
Orange Dori
Chinyoko Dori
Nakamise Dori
Kannon Dori
Matsuya Dept. Store
Sumida Park
Kaminarimon Dori
Ferry Pier
Asakusa Station
Asakusa Informatioon Center
KAMINARIMON 1-CHOME
Tarawamachi Station
Azuma Bridge
Asahi Building
ASAKUSA LINE
Asakusa Dori
GINZA LINE
Asakusa Station
Sumida River
Metropolitan Expwy.
Komagata Bridge
LEGEND
Shrine
Rail Line
Information
2096
JAPAN
TOKYO
ACCOMMODATIONS
Asakusa View Hotel 2
Kikuya Ryokan 4
Ryokan Shiaetsu 3
Sakura Ryokan 1
DINING
Chinya 5
Daikokuya 6
Kamiya Bar 7
Keyaki 10
Mugitoro 11
Komagata Dojo 12
Kuremutsu 9
Namiki 8

and the owner speaks English. A combination business-tourist hotel, Sakura has both Japanese and foreign guests. Rooms are spotless, all of them having a sink and an alarm clock, and guests have use of a coin laundry and an elevator. Half the rooms are Western style, available with or without private bath, while the Japanese-style rooms are all without private bath. There's one Japanese-style room large enough for a family of six or seven people, complete with a terrace.

Kikuya Ryokan

2-18-9 Nishi-Asakusa, Taito-ku 111. ☎ **03/3841-6404.** Fax 03/3841-6404. 10 rms (5 with bath). A/C TV. ¥4,800 ($48) single without bath, ¥5,600–¥6,500 ($56–$65) single with bath; ¥8,200 ($82) double without bath, ¥8,600–¥8,800 ($86–$88) double with bath; ¥11,500 ($115) triple without bath, ¥12,600 ($126) triple with bath. AE, MC, V. Station: Tawaramachi (8 minutes).

This friendly establishment, a member of the Japanese Inn and Welcome Inn groups, is located in a modern redbrick building about a 10-minute walk from Sensoji Temple, just off Kappabashi Dori (a street lined with shops selling those plastic-food displays you see in restaurants throughout Japan). There's a communal refrigerator where you can store food and drinks, and rooms with bath also have refrigerators. The front doors close at midnight and you're asked to leave the rooms from 10am to 5:30pm.

Katsutaro

4-16-8 Ikenohata, Taito-ku 110. ☎ **03/3821-9808.** Fax 03/3821-4789. 7 rms (4 with bath). A/C TV. ¥4,600 ($46) single without bath; ¥8,400 ($84) double without bath, ¥9,000 ($90) double with bath; ¥12,300 ($123) triple without bath, ¥13,200 ($132) triple with bath. Continental breakfast ¥500 ($5) extra. AE, MC, V. Station: Nezu (Ikenohata exit 5 minutes) or Ueno Keisei Skyliner Station (10 minutes).

In the neighborhood of Ueno Park is Katsutaro, with Japanese-style rooms that are quite large and have coin-operated TVs. Try to avoid rooms that face the main street, as these can be quite noisy. The building itself is about 35 years old, and at least half the guests staying here are Japanese. In addition to the usual Japanese tea available at all Japanese inns, free coffee is offered. The place is a member of the Japanese Inn Group.

✪ Ryokan Sawanoya

2-3-11 Yanaka, Taito-ku 110. ☎ **03/3822-2251.** Fax 03/3822-2252. 12 rms (2 with bath). A/C TV TEL. ¥4,500–¥4,800 ($45–$48) single without bath; ¥8,400 ($84) double without bath, ¥9,000 ($90) double with bath; ¥11,400 ($114) triple without bath, ¥12,900 ($129) triple with bath. Breakfast of toast and fried eggs ¥300 ($3) extra; Japanese breakfast ¥900 ($9) extra. AE, V, MC. Station: Nezu (exit 1, 7 minutes).

Although the ryokan itself is relatively modern looking and unexciting, it's located northwest of Ueno Park in a delightful part of old Tokyo. The staff give out a map outlining places of interest, and pamphlets on inexpensive accommodations throughout Japan; and if you pay for the call, the owner will even make your next reservation with another Japanese Inn group inn. Third-floor rooms are best because they have a small balcony; all rooms come with a heater and a sink. Tea and instant coffee are available all day, and facilities include a beer- and soda-vending machine, a coin-operated washing machine and dryer (with free laundry detergent), a refrigerator, and a public bath. Highly recommended.

Yamanaka Ryokan

4-23-1 Ikenohata, Taito-ku 110. ☎ **03/3821-4751.** Fax 03/3821-4770. 13 rms (all with bath). A/C MINIBAR TV TEL. ¥8,000 ($80) single; ¥14,000 ($140) double; ¥21,000 ($210) triple. Breakfast ¥1,000 ($10) extra. No credit cards. Station: Nezu (3 minutes) or JR Ueno Station (20 minutes).

This member of the Welcome Inn group is located in a residential district, in a two-story ferroconcrete building, and is close to Ueno Park attractions. It serves a mixture of Chinese, Western, and Japanese food; dinner costs ¥2,000 ($20).

OTHER NEIGHBORHOODS

VERY EXPENSIVE

✪ Four Seasons Hotel Chinzan-So

2-10-8 Sekiguchi, Bunkyo-ku 112. ☎ **03/3943-2222,** or 800/332-3442 in the U.S., 800/268-6282 in Canada. Fax 03/3943-2300. 286 rms and suites. A/C MINIBAR TV TEL. ¥31,000–¥67,000 ($310–$670) single; ¥33,000–¥67,000 ($330–$670) double or twin; from ¥45,000 ($450) Club Floor double; from ¥60,000 ($600) suite. AE, DC, JCB, MC, V. Station: Edogawabashi (a 2-minute ride), Mejiro (an 8-minute ride), or Ikebukuro (a 10-minute ride).

A bit off the beaten track, the Four Seasons, set in the 17-acre, 100-year-old Chin-zanso Garden, is utterly inviting after a bustling day in Tokyo. The stunning room interiors and public spaces, created by American designer Frank Nicholson, make this, in my opinion, the most beautiful European-style hotel in Japan, yet it's less expensive than other Tokyo hotels in its category. Harmony is achieved by complementary color schemes and garden views from private and public spaces. Overstuffed, elegantly upholstered furnishings are backed by Oriental art, including Japanese woodblock prints.

The smallest room features a king-size bed and is twice the size of most Japanese hotel rooms. All guest rooms offer satellite television, VCRs, a minimum of three telephones, two dedicated lines with modem capacity, facsimile and personal computer outlets, private safes, scales, cotton towels and robes, special shaving/makeup mirrors, and bidet/toilets separated from marble-and-brass bathrooms with exterior showers.

Dining/Entertainment: You have your choice of nine restaurants and bars, including Yang Yuan Zhai (the first overseas outlet of the famous Beijing restaurant Diaoyutai, where heads of state dine) and Bice, featuring hand-picked ingredients and pasta made daily. Le Jardin is a great place for tea.

Services: 24-hour room service, 24-hour laundry, 24-hour multilingual concierge, complimentary shoeshine, your choice of free newspaper (including *USA Today*), complimentary limo service (I love this) to anywhere in Tokyo (weekdays from 8am to 5pm), complimentary in-room fax-machine use, complimentary deluxe bus service to rail and subway stations.

Facilities: Elegant boutiques, amphitheater conference room with simultaneous interpretation facilities and other function rooms for use of between 8 and 700 people, business center, aesthetic salon, and spa (featuring a gorgeous indoor pool, sauna, steam room, Jacuzzi, fitness gym with English-language instruction, and Japanese hot-springs bath) with no spa fee for guests!

EXPENSIVE

✪ The Hilltop Hotel

1-1 Surugadai, Kanda, Chiyoda-ku 101. ☎ **03/3293-2311.** Fax 03/3233-4567. 75 rms. A/C MINIBAR TV TEL. ¥18,000–¥20,000 ($180–$200) single; ¥24,000–¥25,000 ($240–$250) double; ¥26,000 ($260) twin. AE, DC, JCB, MC, V. Station: Ochanomizu or Shin-Ochanomizu (8 minutes) or Jimbocho (5 minutes).

Located, as the name implies, on a hill, this is an old-fashioned, unpretentious hotel with character. Its main building dates back to 1937, with an annex added in the 1970s. Throughout the decades the Hilltop has been a favorite place for writers to stay, including novelist Mishima Yukio. Reportedly beneficial oxygen and negative ions are circulated into the rooms; all I can tell you is I slept like a baby. The double rooms are fairly small, pleasantly homey, and come with cherry-wood furniture (as well as a mahogany desk), fringed lampshades, velvet curtains, a radio, a clock, and old-fashioned heaters with intricate grillwork. This hotel is romantic and intimate; you'll be called by name at the reception desk.

Dining/Entertainment: The hotel's seven restaurants offer steaks, plus Italian, Chinese, and Japanese cuisine. Its best restaurant, the Yamano-ue, serves excellent tempura.

Services: Same-day laundry service.

MODERATE

Fairmont Hotel

2-1-17 Kudan Minami, Chiyoda-ku 102. ☎ **03/3262-1151.** Fax 03/3264-2476. 208 rms (all with bath). A/C MINIBAR TV TEL. ¥11,000–¥21,000 ($110–$210) single; ¥20,000–¥25,000 ($200–$250) double or twin. AE, DC, JCB, MC, V. Station: Kudanshita (10 minutes).

This small hotel is beautifully situated on a quiet street opposite the Imperial Palace moat, which is lined with cherry trees—a real treat when the blossoms burst forth in spring. Guests like the Fairmont because it's an older hotel (built in 1952) and because it's conveniently located, yet away from the hustle and bustle of downtown Tokyo. One of the hotel's restaurants, the Brasserie de la Verdure, has a view of the moat, while the French restaurant, Cerisiers, looks out onto a pleasant small garden with a waterfall. The more expensive rooms are larger and face the palace moat—definitely worth it during cherry-blossom season. All rooms have TV with English-language cable and CNN broadcasts.

Tokyo YMCA Hotel

7 Mitoshiro-cho, Kanda, Chiyoda-ku 101. ☎ **03/3293-1911.** Fax 03/3293-1926. 40 rms (all with bath). A/C TV TEL. ¥11,000 ($110) single; ¥17,000–¥22,000 ($170–$220) twin. YMCA members receive a 10% discount. No credit cards. Station: Shin-Ochanomizu (3 minutes), Ogawamachi (2 minutes), or Awajicho (5 minutes).

Where else but in Tokyo would there be a YMCA as expensive as a moderately priced hotel? However, this place is spanking new, modern, and spotless, with an atmosphere better than most business hotels that fall into this price category. Fully carpeted, it has one Western restaurant, a pharmacy, and a beauty salon, and there's laundry service. Both men and women are accepted, and rooms (which are mostly singles) come with hot water and tea, cotton kimono, and bilingual TV with remote control. Vending machines dispense beer and soft drinks.

Shimizu Bekkan (2)

1-30-29 Hongo, Bunkyo-ku 113. ☎ **03/3812-6285.** 21 rms (2 with bath). A/C MINIBAR TV TEL. ¥7,700 ($77) room without bath or meals, ¥10,000 ($100) room without bath but with breakfast, ¥13,500 ($135) room with dinner and breakfast. Rates are per person and include tax and service. Room with bath ¥1,000 ($10) per person extra. No credit cards. Station: Hongo Sanchome (5 minutes).

A ryokan accepting foreigners, Shimizu Bekkan has a variety of rooms. Several meal options are offered, served in your room, and there are separate public baths for men and women. It's best to take a taxi to get here.

INEXPENSIVE

Ryokan Fuji

6-8-3 Higashi-Koiwa, Edogawa-ku 133. ☎ **03/3657-1062.** Fax 03/3657-1062. 9 rms (all with bath). A/C TV. ¥6,500 ($65) single; ¥12,000 ($120) double; ¥18,000 ($180) triple. No credit cards. Station: JR Koiwa (6 minutes) or Keisei Koiwa (10 minutes).

Family-Friendly Hotels

National Children's Castle Hotel *(see p. 117)* The absolute best place for children, complete with an indoor/outdoor playground and activity rooms for all ages, offering everything from building blocks to computer games.

Sakura Ryokan *(see p. 124)* This modern Japanese-style inn offers a large family room that sleeps up to eight people in traditional Japanese style, on futon laid out on tatami mats.

Holiday Inn Tokyo *(see p. 111)* Children under 12 stay for free, there is an outdoor pool in summer, and baby-sitting services please parents and children alike.

Located in a modern, two-story building in a residential district, this ryokan, a member of the Welcome Inn Group, is a bit out of the way but comes highly recommended by a reader from Belgium. Although the elderly lady who runs the place doesn't speak English, she makes up for it with kindness. Japanese-style meals are served; breakfast is ¥1,000 ($10), and dinner costs ¥2,000 ($20).

Kimi Ryokan

2-36-8 Ikebukuro, Toshima-ku 171. ☎ **03/3971-3766.** 41 rms (none with bath). A/C TEL. ¥5,300 ($53) single; ¥7,000 ($70) double; ¥7,500 ($75) twin. No credit cards. Station: Ikebukuro (west exit 5 minutes).

This place is spotlessly clean, and although it was extensively remodeled in 1986, there are such Japanese touches as sliding screens and traditional Japanese music playing softly in the hallways. Kimi now caters exclusively to foreigners and is so popular there's sometimes a waiting list to get in. The tatami-style guest rooms are cheerful and clean. There are coin-operated heaters and air conditioners, as well as coin-operated TVs (in the twin and double rooms). Facilities include a TV lounge, a soda machine, a pay telephone from which you can make international calls, and free tea available throughout the day. The police station to the right of the subway station has maps that will guide you to Kimi. A great place to stay.

Tokyo Yoyogi Youth Hostel

National Olympic Memorial Youth Center, 3-1 Yoyogi-Kamizono, Shibuya-ku 151. ☎ **03/3467-9163.** 59 beds. ¥2,600 ($26) members; ¥3,200 ($32) nonmembers. MC, V. Station: Sangubashi (5 minutes).

On the west side of Meiji Shrine Outer Garden, in an enclosed complex of buildings surrounded by a fence, this hostel is in Building 14. The whole compound housed American occupation troops after World War II, then accommodated athletes during the 1964 Olympics. It's now devoted to a number of youth activities. No meals are served, but there are cooking facilities. There's a large Japanese-style bath in a neighboring building. The hostel is closed daily from 10am to 5pm, and the front gate closes at 10pm.

YMCA Asia Youth Center

2-5-5 Sarugaku-cho, Chiyoda-ku 101. ☎ **03/3233-0611.** Fax 03/3233-0633. 75 rms (all with bath). A/C TV TEL. ¥7,000 ($70) single; ¥13,000 ($130) twin; ¥16,800 ($168) triple. YMCA member discount ¥500 ($5) per person. All rates include tax. No credit cards. Station: Suidobashi (5 minutes) or Jimbocho (10 minutes).

This modern-looking concrete facility opened in 1980. Both men and women of any age are accepted, and about 30% of the guests are Korean. Rooms are very simple but have all the basics. Japanese or Western breakfasts are ¥1,000 ($10), lunches start at ¥1,000 ($10), and dinners start at ¥1,500 ($15). Facilities include an indoor swimming pool (fee: ¥1,000/$10). There's a midnight curfew.

NARITA AIRPORT

If you find yourself on a stopover at the New Tokyo International Airport in Narita for one or two nights, you may not want to take the one- to two-hour trip to a hotel in Tokyo. There are a number of nearby Western-style hotels that have soundproofed rooms; they also operate free shuttle buses to and from the airport. Reservations can be made at the hotel-information counter in the airport's arrival wing. The telephone prefix for Narita is 0476, which you needn't dial if you're calling from the airport.

If you find yourself with some spare time, be sure to visit Shinshoji Temple, popularly known as Narita-san, which is located close to the train station in downtown Narita. It's a Buddhist temple dedicated to Fudo, god of fire, and is visited by more than 10 million people each year—usually when they have a favor to ask, whether it be good health, a happy marriage, or success in passing a university entrance exam. Behind the temple is a 40-acre Japanese garden with three ponds and many flowering trees and bushes, including wisteria, plum, and cherry.

✪ Radisson International Hotel Narita

650-35 Nanae, Tomisato-mura Inbagun, Chiba. ☎ **0476/93-1234.** Fax 0476/93-4834. 500 rms. A/C TV TEL. ¥15,500 ($155) single; ¥26,500 ($265) double; ¥24,000 ($240) twin. AE, DC, JCB, MC, V. Free 15-minute shuttle service from the airport.

Managed by Radisson hotels (owned by Northwest Airlines) and surrounded by woods and fields, this is probably your best bet at Narita. It offers large comfortable rooms, indoor and outdoor swimming pools, an aerobic center (fee ¥700/$7), and Japanese and Western restaurants. An extensive video library and in-room VCRs help while away the time for the many airline employees who stay here. Personally, I like to spend the night here before I fly out of Tokyo, relaxing and organizing for my next destination. There's free shuttle-bus service daily to Narita-san Temple.

Holiday Inn-Narita

320-1 Tokko, Narita, Chiba. ☎ **0476/32-1234.** Fax 0476/32-0617. 502 rms (all with bath). A/C MINIBAR TV TEL. ¥12,000–¥17,000 ($120–$170) single; ¥20,000–¥30,000 ($200–$300) double; ¥18,000–¥26,000 ($180–$260) twin. AE, DC, JCB, MC, V. Free airport shuttle, every 30 minutes.

This hotel, located just a mile from the airport, is similar to Holiday Inns in the United States. Its pleasantly decorated rooms offer TV with cable and CNN broadcasts. Facilities include an indoor swimming pool, a sauna, gymnasium, tennis court (¥1,500/$15), five restaurants (steaks, plus Japanese, Chinese, and Western cuisine), and a bar-restaurant on the ninth floor with views of the airport.

Narita Airport Rest House

P.O. Box 126, Narita Airport, Chiba. ☎ **0476/32-1212.** Fax 0476/32-1209. 210 rms (all with bath). A/C MINIBAR TV TEL. ¥9,000 ($90) single; ¥12,000 ($120) double; ¥13,000–¥15,000 ($130–$150) twin. AE, DC, JCB, MC, V. Free airport shuttle.

In this square white building located right beside the airport terminal, the rooms are rather sterile but have everything you need, from TV to minibar to alarm clock. Four TV screens in the hotel give the latest information on arrival and departure times for all airlines. There are a Japanese restaurant, a Western restaurant, and a bar in the hotel.

5 Dining

From stand-up noodle shops at train stations to exclusive sushi bars, restaurants in Tokyo number at least 45,000, which gives you some idea of how fond the Japanese are of eating out. In a city where apartments are so small and cramped, entertaining at home is almost unheard of; restaurants serve as places for socializing, meeting friends, and wooing business associates—as well as excuses for drinking a lot of beer, sake, and whiskey. I know people in Tokyo who claim they haven't cooked in years—and they're not millionaires (although they may be bad cooks). They take advantage of one of the best deals in Tokyo—the fixed-price lunch. Called a *teishoku,* and also variously referred to as a *seto ranch, seto coursu,* or simply *coursu,* the fixed-price menu usually includes an appetizer, a main course with several side dishes, coffee or tea, and dessert. Even the most prohibitively expensive Tokyo restaurants often offer set-lunch menus, allowing you to dine in style at very reasonable prices. To keep your costs down, therefore, try eating your biggest meal at lunch. However, because the Japanese tend to order fixed-price meals rather than à la carte, set dinners are also usually available (though not as cheap as set lunches).

Japanese patrons in Tokyo's top restaurants almost never spend their own money because most of them are on expense accounts, without which many of these establishments wouldn't survive. If you're not on an expense account, however, don't despair. The restaurants I've listed in the **expensive** category will allow you to splurge, to experience some of Japan's most exquisite cuisine without having to mortgage your house upon your return home. And don't forget about those set lunches—great bargains by any standard.

So many of Tokyo's good restaurants fall into the **moderate** category, it's tempting simply to eat your way through the city—and the range of cuisine is so great you could eat something different at each meal.

Many of Tokyo's most colorful, noisy, and popular restaurants fall into the **inexpensive** category, frequented by the city's huge working population as they catch a quick lunch or socialize with friends after hours.

No matter what budget you are on, you should at least read the reviews in each category to profit from the set-lunch specials. Remember to check Tokyo's nightlife for more suggestions on inexpensive drinking places serving food. Also remember that a 3% consumption tax will be added to bills totaling less than ¥7,500 ($75). For meals costing ¥7,500 and more, both the 3% consumption tax and a 3% local tax will be added to your bill. In addition, many first-class restaurants, as well as hotel restaurants, will add a 10% to 15% service charge in lieu of accepting tips. Unless otherwise stated, the prices I've given do not include the extra tax and charges.

Note that restaurants that have no signs in English letters are followed by a numbered icon, which is keyed to a list of Japanese symbols in the appendix.

GINZA & HIBIYA

VERY EXPENSIVE

✪ Kamon

Imperial Hotel, 1-1-1 Uchisaiwai-cho. ☎ **03/3504-1111.** Reservations recommended for dinner. Set dinners ¥8,000–¥18,000 ($80–$180); set lunches from ¥3,000 ($30). AE, DC, JCB, MC, V. Daily 11:30am–2:30pm and 5:30–9:30pm. Station: Hibiya (1 minute). TEPPANYAKI.

The interior of Kamon, which means "Gate of Celebration," is like a statement on Tokyo itself—traditionally Japanese, yet ever so high-tech. An excellent place to come for teppanyaki. The steak, seafood, and vegetables grilled before your eyes are mouth-watering good, and service is, of course, Imperial.

✪ L'Osier

8-8-3 Ginza. ☎ **03/3572-2120.** Reservations recommended. Entrees ¥2,600–¥6,500 ($26–$65); main dishes average ¥4,200–¥11,000 ($42–$110); set lunches ¥5,600–¥7,200 ($56–$72). AE, DC, JCB, MC, V. Mon–Sat noon–2:30pm and 5–8:30pm. Station: Ginza (5 minutes). NOUVELLE CLASSIC FRENCH.

A gracious setting, well-trained "garçons," and nouvelle classic cuisine are the attractions of this first-class restaurant, perfect for a romantic meal or to entertain a special guest. The main reason to eat here is Jacques Borie, *chef de cuisine* and decorated with the prestigious Meilleur Ouvrier de France award for his craft. From entrees like *foie gras de canard confit en terrine* to main dishes like *la caillette de pigeon au thym et mignonnette* to petits fours, you will not be disappointed by your meal. Once in the restaurant, you may as well be in France. The restaurant is on the 7th and 8th floors of the Shiseido Parlour Bldg. (the top cosmetics firm); don't be put off by the ground-floor entrance, which is not worthy of the elegance of the restaurant.

Sushiko (3)

6-3-8 Ginza. ☎ **03/3571-1968.** Reservations required. Meals ¥10,000–¥15,000 ($100–$150). No credit cards. Mon–Sat 11:30am–2pm and 5–9:30pm. Closed hols. Station: Ginza or Hibiya (4 minutes). SUSHI.

If you're in pursuit of exclusive sushi in Tokyo, your search will eventually take you here. There's no written menu, and its counter seating is for 11 customers only. Owned by a fourth-generation restaurateur, this establishment doesn't display its fish as in most sushi bars, but rather keeps the fish freshly refrigerated until the moment it meets the swift blade of the expert chefs.

Ten-ichi

6-6-5 Ginza, Namiki Dori. ☎ **03/3571-1949.** Reservations recommended for lunch, required for dinner. Set dinners ¥8,500–¥15,000 ($85–$150); set lunches ¥7,000–¥10,000 ($70–$100). AE, DC, JCB, MC, V. Mon–Sat 11:30am–9:30pm, Sun noon–9pm. Station: Ginza (3 minutes). TEMPURA.

In this restaurant, located on Namiki Dori, in the heart of the Ginza's nightlife, you can sit at a counter to watch the chef prepare your meal. This is the main shop of a 50-year-old restaurant chain that helped the tempura style of cooking gain worldwide recognition by serving important foreign customers. Today Ten-ichi still has one of the best reputations in town for serving the most delicately fried foods.

There are more than 10 Ten-ichi restaurants in Tokyo. Other Ten-ichi restaurants can be found in the Ginza Sony Building at the intersection of Harumi Dori and Sotobori Dori (☎ 03/3571-8373), the Imperial Hotel's Tower basement (☎ 03/3503-1001), Akasaka 3-chome, Misujidori (☎ 03/3583-0107), and both the Shibuya and Ikebukuro Seibu department stores (☎ 03/3496-5277 and 03/3984-1930, respectively).

EXPENSIVE

Benihana of New York

6-3-7 Ginza. ☎ **03/3571-9060.** Reservations recommended. Set meals ¥4,500–¥20,000 ($45–$200); set lunches ¥1,500–¥3,300 ($15–$33). AE, DC, JCB, MC, V. Mon–Sat 11am–10pm; Sun and hols 11am–8pm. Station: Hibiya (5 minutes) or Ginza (10 minutes). TEPPANYAKI.

I'm not sure how to categorize this restaurant. With about 50 Benihana restaurants in the United States, most Americans are familiar with this chain and consider it

Japanese food. However, the restaurant in Tokyo calls itself Benihana of New York, and what's more, all the theatrical bravado and karate-style knife chops are an American tradition and have very little to do with Japanese food-preparation methods. In any case, teppanyaki steak courses are the specialty here (with Kobe beef featured in the more expensive courses), along with side dishes of seafood that might include lobster, squid, shrimp, scallops, and mussels.

Ginza Benkay

7-2-17 Ginza. ☎ **03/3573-7335.** Reservations recommended for dinner. Set dinners ¥7,000–¥20,000 ($70–$200); set lunches ¥1,500–¥4,000 ($15–$40). AE, DC, JCB, MC, V. Mon–Sat 11:30am–2pm and 5–9:30pm (last order). Closed hols. Station: Yurakucho or Hibiya (2 minutes). VARIED JAPANESE.

This pleasant restaurant is a Japan Airlines affiliate and specializes in teppanyaki, sushi, shabu-shabu, lunch boxes, and kaiseki, each served in its own special dining area and available in a variety of price ranges. Coolly decorated with a stone-and-pebble floor, bamboo, wood, and shoji screens, it offers a variety of set meals. Lunch, featuring teppanyaki courses, an assorted plate of sushi, or a small kaiseki lunch box, is the most economical. Dinner courses include teppanyaki, sushi, or kaiseki, and a shabu-shabu course. It's located on the second floor across from the International Arcade on the Ginza side, just a few minutes' walk from the Tourist Information Center.

There's another Ginza Benkay in the basement of the President Hotel in Aoyama (☎ 3402-0246), with the same hours.

Kinsen (4)

4-4-10 Ginza. ☎ **03/3561-8708.** Reservations recommended for lunch, required for dinner. Set dinners ¥8,500–¥10,000 ($85–$100); set lunches ¥2,500–¥7,400 ($25–$74). All prices include tax and service charge. AE, DC, JCB, MC, V. Daily 11:30am–2pm; Mon–Fri 5–9pm; Sat–Sun 5–8pm. Station: Ginza (1 minute). KAISEKI.

A conveniently located, modern kaiseki restaurant in the heart of Ginza, Kinsen is on Harumi Dori, on the fifth floor of the Ginza Kintetsu Building, just across the street from the Jena Bookstore. There's no English menu, but various fixed-price meals are available, so simply choose one to fit your budget. The food is artistically arranged in various bowls and boxes, ranging from elaborate kaiseki dinners and lunch boxes to mini-kaiseki.

MODERATE

Attore

Hotel Seiyo Ginza, 1-11-2 Ginza. ☎ **03/3535-1111.** Pasta ¥1,500–¥3,800 ($15–$38); main dishes ¥2,300–¥4,800 ($23–$48); set lunches ¥1,200 ($12). AE, DC, JCB, MC, V. Daily 11am–10pm. Station: Ginza (5 minutes) or Ginza-Itchome (2 minutes). ITALIAN.

Although the Hotel Seiyo Ginza is one of Tokyo's most expensive and exclusive hotels, this Italian restaurant, located in its basement, serves reasonably priced meals. Modern, cheerful, and pleasant, with an open kitchen separated from the dining hall by a pane of glass, it offers a variety of pasta and main courses—from whole-wheat spaghetti with mushrooms and oven-baked spinach gnocchi with tomato sauce to calamari stuffed with shrimp. If you feel like splurging, there's a second, slightly pricier dining hall, its more elaborate menu including more seafood and meat dishes.

Ginza Daimasu (5)

6-9-6 Ginza. ☎ **03/3571-3584.** Main dishes ¥1,000–¥2,800 ($10–$28); set dinners ¥3,000–¥5,000 ($30–$50); set lunches ¥1,800–¥2,800 ($18–$28). DC, JCB, MC, V. Daily 11:30am–9:30pm. Station: Ginza (2 minutes). VARIED JAPANESE.

This 60-year-old restaurant has a simple, modern decor with Japanese touches. Experienced, kimono-clad waitresses will serve you artfully arranged dishes from the English menu. My *Fukiyose-zen set*—many delicate dishes served in three courses—included beautiful tempura delicacies served in an edible basket and a menu (in Japanese) explaining what I was eating. You'll recognize the restaurant because it's across from the Matsuzakaya department store and has a plastic-food display in the front window. Lunch is served until 3pm.

Kushi Colza (6)

6-4-18 Ginza. ☎ **03/3571-8228.** Reservations recommended. Set dinners ¥3,300–¥5,000 ($33–$50). AE, DC, MC, V. Mon–Fri 5–10pm; Sat–Sun 5–9pm. Station: Hibiya (5 minutes) or Ginza (10 minutes). YAKITORI/KUSHIYAKI.

Kikkoman, a well-known producer of soy sauce, maintains a few restaurants as well, including this one. It serves yakitori and *kushiyaki* (also grilled meats and vegetables on skewers), delicately seasoned with—what else?—Kikkoman soy sauce. Small, pleasant, and with an open counter where you can watch friendly chefs prepare your food. Kushi Colza has an English menu that lists three set dinners, which consist of various skewered filets of beef, fish, eel, or pork, along with an appetizer, salad, soup, and dessert. A la carte selections for skewered specialties average ¥320 to ¥750 ($3.20–$7.50) per skewer. Try the vegetable salad with soy sauce dressing.

✪ **Ohmatsuya** (7)

6-5-8 Ginza. ☎ **03/3571-7053.** Reservations required. Set dinner ¥5,500–¥7,500 ($55–$75). AE, DC, V. Mon–Sat 5–10pm. Station: Ginza (3 minutes). JAPANESE GRILL.

Enter this second-floor restaurant (in the Ail D'Or building), and you're instantly greeted by waitresses clad in traditional countryside clothing and by an old farmhouse atmosphere. Part of the decor was brought from a 17th-century samurai house in northern Japan. Even the style of cooking is traditional, as customers grill their own food over a hibachi. Sake, served in a length of bamboo, is drunk from bamboo cups. Dinner menus, very reasonably priced, include such delicacies as grilled fish, skewered meat, and vegetables. A true find—and easy at that—it's located on Sony Street, the small side street behind the Sony Building.

Rangetsu

3-5-8 Ginza. ☎ **03/3567-1021.** Reservations recommended. Set dinners ¥7,500–¥18,000 ($75–$180); set lunches ¥1,700–¥4,000 ($17–$40). DC, JCB, MC, V. Mon–Sat 11:30am–10pm, Sun and hols 11:30am–9pm. Station: Ginza (3 minutes). SUKIYAKI/SHABU-SHABU/KAISEKI/OBENTO.

This well-known Ginza restaurant has been dishing out sukiyaki, shabu-shabu, traditional lunch boxes, and steaks for more than four decades. It uses only Matsuzaka beef (bought whole and then carved up by the chefs), which ranges from the costlier fine-marbled beef to the cheaper cuts with thick marbling. There are also various crab dishes (including a crab sukiyaki), kaiseki, sirloin steaks, and eel dishes. Especially good deals: the obento lunch boxes, available day and night, and the various set courses of tempura or steak offered for lunch. In the basement is a sake bar, with more than 80 different kinds of sake from all over Japan, which you can also order with your meal. Rangetsu is located on Chuo Dori, across from the Matsuya department store.

Shabusen (8)

Core Bldg. 2F, 5-8-20 Ginza. ☎ **03/3571-1717.** Dishes ¥350–¥1,000 ($3.50–$10); set dinners ¥3,800–¥4,800 ($38–$48); set lunches ¥900–¥2,200 ($9–$22). AE, MC, V. Daily 11am–10pm. Station: Ginza (1 minute). SHABU-SHABU/SUKIYAKI.

Under the management of Zakuro, this is a fun restaurant, where you can cook your own sukiyaki or shabu-shabu in a boiling pot in front of you as you sit at the counter. Orders are shouted back and forth among the staff, service is rapid, and the place is lively. There's an English menu complete with cooking instructions, so it's user-friendly. I had the special shabu-shabu dinner for ¥4,800 ($48), with appetizer, tomato ("super dressing") salad, beef, vegetables, rice porridge, and dessert—it was more than I could eat.

Suehiro (9)

6-11-1 Ginza. ☎ **03/3571-9271.** Reservations required. Set dinners ¥5,000–¥25,000 ($50–$250); set lunches ¥1,500–¥8,000 ($15–$80). AE, DC, JCB, MC, V. Daily 11:30am–10pm. Bay of Ginza, daily 11am–2pm and 5–10:30pm. Station: Ginza (5 minutes). STEAKS/SUKIYAKI.

This successful steak-and-sukiyaki chain, established in 1933 and claiming to be the first restaurant in Tokyo to serve sukiyaki, now boasts 17 stores throughout Japan. Its main branch, located behind Matsuzakaya department store, is in a shiny new building complete with an information counter on the main floor. It offers several floors of dining. Most formal and expensive is the European-style dining hall on the seventh floor, which serves Matsuzaka beefsteaks and teppanyaki. The sixth floor, featuring traditional Japanese decor, specializes in shabu-shabu and sukiyaki. Least expensive is the Bay of Ginza, in the basement, which offers French cuisine; steaks are the main course here. Of the daily specials, the best are the set steak dinners, which start at ¥5,000 ($50) and are available Monday through Wednesday until 7:30pm.

Other conveniently located Suehiro shops are found at 3-16-7 Akasaka (☎ 3585-9855), in the heart of Akasaka, on Hitosugi Dori Street; and 4-1-15 Tsukiji (☎ 3542-3951).

Sushi Sei (10)

8-2-13 Ginza. ☎ **03/3571-2772.** Sushi à la carte ¥100–¥300 ($1–$3); set lunches (basement only) ¥1,000–¥1,500 ($10–$15). AE, DC, JCB, MC, V. Mon–Sat noon–2pm and 5–10:45pm. Closed hols. Station: Hibiya (5 minutes). SUSHI.

One of a dependably good chain of medium-priced sushi bars, serving tender cuts of raw fish, this place is a natural for both novices and appreciative sushi fans. The ground-floor bar serves à la carte only; the basement bar is the place to go if you want one of the three lunch teishoku. The chef will prepare your food and place it on a raised platform on the counter in front of you, which serves as your plate.This restaurant is located near the elevated tracks of the Yamanote Line.

INEXPENSIVE

✪ Atariya (11)

3-5-17 Ginza. ☎ **03/3564-0045.** Yakitori meals ¥1,500–¥2,700 ($15–$27); individual skewers ¥150–¥400 ($1.50–$4). No credit cards. Mon–Sat 5–10pm (last order). Station: Ginza (3 minutes). YAKITORI.

Because it's open only at night and serves yakitori, this is technically a drinking establishment, but it also makes a good choice for inexpensive dining. You have your choice of table or counter seating on the first floor of this yakitori-ya, while up on the second floor you take off your shoes and sit on split-reed mats. The waiters wear colorful twisted headbands. Since meals will include most parts of the chicken, including the liver, gizzard, and skin, you might wish to order à la carte for your favorites. The shop's name means "to be right on target, to score a bull's-eye," and according to its English pamphlet, eating here is certain to bring you good luck. Atariya is located behind the Wako department store (Suzuran Street).

$ Donto (12)

Denki Bldg. basement, 1-7-1 Yurakucho. ☎ **03/3201-3021.** A la carte dishes ¥500–¥8,000 ($5–$80); set dinners ¥3,600–¥7,500 ($36–$75); set lunches ¥800–¥1,500 ($8–$15). AE, DC, JCB, MC, V. Mon–Sat 11am–2pm and 5–9pm. Closed hols. Station: Hibiya (1 minute). NOODLES/TEMPURA/OBENTO/SASHIMI.

Located in Hibiya, across the street from the Tourist Information Center, this is a great place for lunch. Popular with the local working crowd and therefore best avoided between 1 and 2pm, it's pleasantly decorated with shoji screens, wooden floors, and an open kitchen. Choose what you want from the plastic display case, which shows various teishoku and set meals. Everything from noodles, sashimi, and tempura to kaiseki is available. Unfortunately the best deals are daily specials written in Japanese only; ask about them.

$ Farm Grill

Ginza Nine Building 3, 8-5 Ginza. ☎ **03/5568-6156.** Main dishes ¥850–¥2,500 ($8.50–$25); set dinner ¥3,200–¥5,200 ($32–$52); set lunch ¥970 ($9.70). Daily 11am–11pm. AE, MC, V. Station: Shimbashi (exit 1, 4 minutes). CALIFORNIAN.

After all of Tokyo's crammed, tiny restaurants, what strikes you here is space, enough for 260 widely spaced tables. Decor and food were meant to resemble those in a Sonoma County wine restaurant, and they do. Great Farm Grill chicken, penne pasta in a cream sauce, and classic B.L.T.s hit home. Some 65 wines make a respectable cellar. The prices for really good large portions of healthy food are unbelievably low (for Tokyo), and wine by the glass or bottle is inexpensive. Your dining partner's dinner may come 10 minutes after yours.

Munakata

Mitsui Urban Hotel basement, 8-6-15 Ginza. ☎ **03/3574-9356.** Mini-kaiseki lunch ¥2,500 ($25); tempura set meal ¥1,500 ($15); dinners ¥8,000–¥15,000 ($80–$150). AE, DC, JCB, MC, V. Daily 11:30am–9:30pm. Station: Shimbashi (2 minutes) or Hibiya (10 minutes). MINI-KAISEKI/OBENTO/TEMPURA.

Kaiseki is one of the most expensive meals you can have in Japan, but there are some lunch specials here (served until 3:30pm) that make it quite reasonable. This basement restaurant is cozy, with slats of wood and low lighting that give customers a sense of privacy. In addition to mini-kaiseki meals, there are also tempura and various obento lunch boxes, like the Shokado bento for ¥1,300 ($13). A great place for lunch, with an English menu.

TSUKIJI

EXPENSIVE

Tamura (13)

2-12-11 Tsukiji. ☎ **03/3541-2591.** Reservations required for dinner, recommended for lunch. Set dinners from ¥30,000 ($300); set lunches ¥6,000–¥11,000 ($60–$110). AE, DC, JCB, MC, V. Daily noon–3pm (last order 1pm) and 5:30–10pm (last order 7:30pm). Station: Tsukiji (1 minute). KAISEKI.

This modern kaiseki restaurant has a friendly staff of smiling and bowing kimono-clad waitresses and hostesses who make you feel as though they've been waiting all this time just for you. Although the menu is in Japanese only, they'll help you decide what to order; but since there are only set meals, your budget will probably decide for you. Lunch is the most economical time to come, when Tamura is popular with Japanese housewives. You have your choice of either tatami seating or tables and chairs, but the ¥6,500 ($65) lunch is at tables only.

MODERATE

Tentake (14)

6-16-6 Tsukiji. ☎ **03/3541-3881.** Main dishes ¥1,000–¥5,000 ($10–$50); fugu set courses ¥5,900–¥13,500 ($59–$135). No credit cards. Daily noon–10pm. Closed Sun Apr–Sept; first and third Wed Oct–Mar. Station: Tsukiji (7 minutes). FUGU.

People who really know their fugu, or blowfish, will tell you that the only time to eat it is from October through March, when it's fresh. You can eat fugu year-round, however, and a good place to try this Japanese delicacy is Tentake, a place popular with the Tsukiji working crowd. The menu is in Japanese, so if you want suggestions, try the fugu sashimi for ¥2,000 ($20) or the fugu-chiri for ¥3,500 ($35). The latter is a do-it-yourself meal in which you cook raw blowfish, cabbage, dandelion leaves, and tofu in a pot of boiling water in front of you. This is what I had, and it was more than I could eat. There are also fugu dishes that come with a variety of side dishes. Or you can order one of the tempura, eel, or crab dishes. The restaurant, a white-and-black mortar building, is located on Harumi Dori, next to a bridge (from Tsukiji Station, walk in the opposite direction of Ginza).

Before you eat here, be sure you read the description of fugu in "What to Dig Your Chopsticks Into," in Chapter 2.

INEXPENSIVE

Since Tsukiji is where you'll find the nation's largest wholesale fish market, it's not surprising that this area abounds in sushi and seafood restaurants. In addition to the recommendations here, don't neglect the many stalls in and around the market, where you can eat everything from noodles to fresh sashimi.

Edogin (15)

4-5-1 Tsukiji. ☎ **03/3543-4401.** Set dinners ¥1,100–¥10,000 ($11–$100); lunch teishoku ¥1,000 ($10). AE, DC, MC, V. Mon–Sat 11am–9:30pm. Station: Tsukiji (3 minutes). SUSHI.

There are four Edogin sushi restaurants in Tsukiji, all located within walking distance of one another. Since they're close to the famous fish market, you can be assured the fish will be fresh. There's nothing aesthetic about this Edogin—the lights are bright, it's packed with the locals, and it's noisy and busy. It's particularly packed during lunch- and dinnertime because the food is dependably good and plentiful. The menu is in Japanese only, but there's a glass case outside with some of the dishes displayed. As an alternative, look at what the people around you are eating, or if it's lunchtime, order the teishoku served until 2pm. The restaurant is located near the Harumi and Shinohashi Dori intersection, and anyone in the neighborhood will be able to point you in the right direction; look for the building with a string of Japanese lanterns adorning its facade.

✪ Sushi Dai (16)

Tsukiji Fish Market. ☎ **03/3542-1111.** Sushi à la carte ¥200–¥1,000 ($2–$10); sushi seto ¥2,000 ($20). No credit cards. Mon–Sat 5am–2pm. Closed hols. Station: Tsukiji (10 minutes). SUSHI.

Located right in the Tsukiji Fish Market, this restaurant boasts some of the freshest fish in town. The easiest thing to do is order the seto, a set sushi course that usually comes with tuna, eel, shrimp, and other morsels of sushi, along with six rolls of tuna and rice in seaweed *(onigiri)*. Sushi Dai is nestled in a row of barracks housing other restaurants and shops beside the covered market. To find it, cross the bridge that leads to the market grounds, take a right past the various small shops selling knives and fish-related cooking objects, and then your first left. To your right will be the barracks. Sushi Dai is in Building 6 on the third alley. Look for the blue curtains outside its front door.

AKASAKA

VERY EXPENSIVE

Garden Barbecue

New Otani Hotel, 4-1 Kioi-cho, Chiyoda-ku. ☎ **03/3265-1111.** Reservations recommended for dinner. A la carte main dishes ¥1,800–¥9,000 ($18–$90); set dinners ¥8,500–¥17,000 ($85–$170); set lunches ¥4,000–¥6,300 ($40–$63). AE, DC, JCB, MC, V. Daily noon–2pm and 6–9pm. Station: Yotsuya (5 minutes) or Akasakamitsuke (3 minutes). TEPPANYAKI.

Located in the midst of the New Otani Hotel's 400-year-old garden, this teppanyaki restaurant is composed of three glass-enclosed pavilions, all with the same menu of Kobe beef, fish, lobster, and vegetables—cooked on a grill right in front of you. If you order a salad, try the soy-sauce dressing; it's delicious. You will eat surrounded by peaceful views, making this place a good lunchtime choice.

La Tour D'Argent

New Otani Hotel, 4-1 Kioi-cho. ☎ **03/3239-3111.** Reservations required. Appetizers and soups ¥2,500–¥9,200 ($25–$92); main dishes ¥6,200–¥25,000 ($62–$250). AE, CB, DC, JCB, MC, V. Daily 5:30–8:30pm (last reservation accepted). Station: Akasaka-mitsuke (3 minutes) or Yotsuya (5 minutes). CLASSIC FRENCH.

Opened in 1984, La Tour d'Argent is the authentic sister to the one in Paris, which opened back in 1582 and was visited twice by Japan's former emperor Hirohito. Entrance to the Tokyo restaurant is through an impressive hallway with a plush interior and displays of tableware used in the Paris establishment through the centuries. The dining hall looks like a Parisian drawing room, with a heavy curtained elegance. The service is superb, and the food is excellent, though pricey for anyone's pocketbook. The specialty here is duckling—it meets its untimely end at the age of three weeks and is flown to Japan from Brittany. Other dishes on the menu, which changes seasonally, may include sea bass, médaillons of veal in light curry sauce, young pigeon, beef tenderloin, or fricassee of lobster and morels. Diners here are celebrating very special occasions, are on a hefty expensive account, or are jet-setters.

EXPENSIVE

Hayashi (17)

Sanno Kaikan Bldg., 4th floor, 2-14-1 Akasaka. ☎ **03/3582-4078.** Reservations recommended for dinner. Set dinners ¥6,000, ¥8,000, and ¥10,000 ($60, $80, and $100); lunches ¥900 ($9). AE, DC, JCB, MC, V. Mon–Fri 11:30am–2pm and 5:30–11pm; Sat 5:30–11pm. Closed hols. Station: Akasaka (1 minute). JAPANESE GRILL/RICE CASSEROLES.

One of the most delightful old-time restaurants I've been to, this cozy, rustic-looking place serves home-style country cooking and specializes in grilled food, which you prepare yourself over your own square hibachi. Altogether, there are 10 grills in this small restaurant, some of them surrounded by tatami mats and some by wooden stools or chairs. As the evening wears on, the one-room main dining area can get quite smoky, but somehow that just adds to the atmosphere (sorry, couldn't resist saying that). Other nice touches are the big gourds and memorabilia hanging about and the waiters in traditional baggy pants. The ever-present owner of Hayashi, which opened in 1965, believes fire brings people more in touch with their basic feelings. "All mankind loves fire," he said. "For many years man has had a close relationship with fire.

It opens our hearts and makes us relax." Hayashi serves three set menus, which change with the seasons. The ¥6,000 ($60) meal—which will probably end up being closer to ¥8,000 ($80) by the time you add drinks, tax, and service charge—may include such items as sashimi and vegetables, chicken, scallops, and gingko nuts, which you grill yourself. At lunch, only *oyakodomburi* is served: literally, "parent and child," a simple rice dish with egg and chicken on top.

✪ Inakaya (18)

3-12-7 Akasaka. ☎ **03/3586-3054.** Reservations accepted only until 7pm. Average meal ¥10,000 ($100). AE, DC, JCB, MC, V. Dinner only, daily 5–11pm. Station: Akasaka or Akasaka-mitsuke (5 minutes). ROBATAYAKI.

Whenever I'm playing hostess to foreign visitors in Tokyo, I always take them to one of the city's three Inakaya restaurants (the other two are in Roppongi), and they've never been disappointed. The drama of the place alone is worth it. Customers sit at a long counter, on the other side of which are mountains of fresh vegetables, beef, and seafood. And in the middle of all that food, seated in front of a grill, are male cooks—ready to cook whatever you point to, in the style of robatayaki. Orders are yelled out by your waiter and are repeated in unison by all the other waiters, with the result that there's always this excited yelling going on. Sounds strange, I know, but actually it's a lot of fun. Food offerings may include yellowtail, red snapper, sole, king crab legs, giant shrimp, steak, meatballs, gingko nuts, potatoes, eggplant, and asparagus, all piled high in wicker baskets and ready for the grill.

Zakuro (19)

TBS Kaikan Bldg. basement, 5-3-3 Akasaka. ☎ **03/3582-6841.** Reservations recommended. Set dinners ¥5,000–¥16,000 ($50–$160); set lunches ¥1,700–¥2,800 ($17–$28). AE, DC, JCB, MC, V. Daily 11am–9pm (last order). Station: Akasaka (TBS exit 1 minute). SHABU-SHABU/SUKIYAKI/TEPPANYAKI.

Serving Kobe beef, this restaurant offers shabu-shabu, sukiyaki, teppanyaki, tempura, and steaks. For lunch it also offers an obento lunch box, as well as inexpensive sukiyaki. Since Zakuro has an English menu, ordering is no problem. It's popular as a place to take visiting foreign clients.

Moderate

Don't forget to check out the specials at more expensive restaurants, and note that if you don't mind eating in the bar (there are tables, too) **Trader Vic's Boathouse Bar** inside **Trader Vic's** in the New Otani is much less expensive than the main dining room. It has great lunch specials, for example, from appetizers to coffee for ¥1,200 to ¥1,400 ($12 to $14).

Kana Uni

1-1-16 Moto-Akasaka. ☎ **03/3404-4776.** Reservations recommended. Soups and appetizers ¥1,000–¥2,200 ($10–$22); main dishes ¥2,000–¥5,300 ($20–$53). AE, DC, JCB, MC, V. Mon–Sat 6pm–2:30am, Sun 6–11pm. Closed hols. Station: Akasaka-mitsuke (3 minutes). FRENCH.

Not far from Akasaka's nightlife district, this cozy and intimate restaurant/bar is owned and managed by a brother and sister who speak excellent English and who love to have foreign guests. In fact, because the place is a little hard to find, they'll even come and fetch you if you call from Akasaka-mitsuke Station. Open since 1966, Kana Uni features such main dishes as sliced raw tenderloin, steaks, beef stew, grilled fish, sautéed scallops, and poached filet of sole with sea-urchin sauce. There's live jazz nightly, so after dinner, relax with cocktails and enjoy the ambience.

Le Chalet

Shimizu Bldg. basement, 3-14-9 Akasaka. ☎ **03/3584-0080.** Reservations recommended. Appetizers and soups ¥900–¥2,300 ($9–$23); main dishes ¥2,200–¥3,100 ($22–$31); set dinners ¥4,500–¥8,500 ($45–$85); set lunches ¥1,600–¥3,400 ($16–$34). AE, DC, JCB, MC, V. Daily 11:30am–2pm (last order) and 5:30–9pm (last order). Station: Akasaka (1 minute). FRENCH.

A pleasant and modestly priced French restaurant in the heart of Akasaka, Le Chalet has seating for only 30 persons and is decorated in wood paneling, pink, and peach. The ¥4,500 ($45) set dinner includes an hors d'oeuvre, *potage,* fish, a meat dish, dessert, and coffee. The set lunches are a particularly good bargain.

$ Potomac

Akasaka Prince Hotel, 1-2 Kioicho Chiyoda-ku. ☎ **03/3234-1111.** Steak meal $10 (based on daily exchange rate); main dishes ¥1,800–¥3,200 ($18–$32); set dinner ¥3,800 ($38). AE, DC, JCB, MC, V. Open 24 hours daily. Station: Akasakamitsuke (1 minute). STEAK/AMERICAN.

A traditional American coffee shop, Potomac has the best deal in town: steak, vegetables, and bread or rice for $10, based on the daily exchange rate. Everyone, from American businesspeople to Japanese housewives out shopping, eats here.

Tea Lounge

Capitol Tokyu Hotel, 2-10-3 Nagata-cho. ☎ **03/3581-4511.** Reservations recommended Sat–Sun. Lunch buffet ¥3,300 ($33) per person; ¥2,800 ($28) for ladies after 1pm; breakfast buffet ¥2,400 ($24). AE, DC, JCB, MC, V. Mon–Fri 7–10:30am and noon–3pm; Sat–Sun 7am–3pm. Station: Kokkaigijido-mae (exit 5, 1 minute).

Located just off the lobby, with a view of a traditional Japanese garden, the Tea Lounge is casual and pleasant. Seating is on sofas and overstuffed chairs, and this is a perfect setting for a buffet lunch of Japanese and Western fare.

INEXPENSIVE

Don't forget to consider **Hayashi,** on the fourth floor of the Sanno Kaikan Building, 2-14-1 Akasaka, described above as an expensive restaurant. I mention it again here simply because I don't want those of you on a budget to miss it. This is one of the coziest and most delightful restaurants in town. Although dinner is costly, you can enjoy the same atmosphere for much, much less at lunch, when only one dish, *oyakodomburi* (rice with chunks of chicken and omelet on top), is served, with pickled vegetables, clear soup, and tea. Open for lunch Monday through Friday from 11:30am to 2pm.

Boat House Cafe

4-26 Kioicho. ☎ **03/3237-1424.** Burgers ¥300–¥350 ($3–$3.50). No credit cards. Daily 10am–9pm. Closes early when it rains. Station: Akasakamitsuke (2 minutes). HAMBURGER STAND.

Perched on the old imperial moat, where one can rent row boats or feed the ducks, is a hamburger stand offering generous burgers with caramel buns, lettuce, tomato, onion, house sauce, and cheese for a mere $3. Viva la recession in Tokyo! Also a good place to have an inexpensive caffe latte or soft drink. Seating is outside at patio tables on a wooden pier. A great rest stop.

$ Botejyu

3-10-1 Akasaka. ☎ **03/3584-6651.** Dishes ¥1,000–¥4,500 ($10–$45); teishoku ¥750–¥1,250 ($7.50–$12.50). AE, DC, JCB, MC, V. Daily 11am–11pm. Station: Akasaka or Akasaka-mitsuke (5 minutes). OKONOMIYAKI.

This simple second-floor restaurant on Tamachi Dori (above Subway's) specializes in *okonomiyaki,* a Japanese-style pizza/pancake topped with cabbage and a meat such as pork or squid or shrimp. It also serves fried noodles (yakisoba) and its own creation called *tororoyaki,* which is a yam okonomiyaki. Its teishoku, served until 2:30pm, are a great deal and include a main dish such as okonomiyaki, plus rice, soup, and salad.

✪ Moti

3-8-8 Akasaka (☎ **03/3582-3620**) and 2-14-31 Akasaka (☎ **03/3584-6640**). Curries ¥1,100–¥1,500 ($11–$15); tandoori from ¥1,700 ($17); lunch courses ¥950 ($9.50). AE,DC, JCB, MC, V. Daily 11:30am–10pm. Station: Akasaka or Akasaka-mitsuke (5 minutes). INDIAN.

This Indian restaurant is so popular that there are two branches in Akasaka and another two in Roppongi. Moti serves vegetable, mutton, and chicken curries, as well as tandoori. An especially good deal is the set lunch, served until 2:30pm, which gives you a curry, along with Indian bread (*nan*) and tea or coffee.

Winebar

Akasaka Makino Bldg. 3-21-3 Akasaka. ☎ **03/3586-7186.** Main dishes ¥700–¥1,200 ($7–$12); pasta ¥700 ($7); glass of wine from ¥380 ($3.80); bottle of wine ¥2,000–¥3,800 ($20–$38). AE, DC, V. Daily 11:30am–4pm and 5pm–midnight. Station: Akasakamitsuke (4 minutes). WINE/ WESTERN.

Attesting to their popularity, there are seven Winebars in Tokyo. This one in Akasaka offers casual dining on inexpensive veal steak stuffed with mushrooms or meat, and vegetable shish-kabobs as well as a large selection of wines. A daily pasta special is very inexpensive. Popular with Japanese interested in trying different European wines, it's a reasonable place for a meal if you prefer yours with the grape.

ROPPONGI

Because Roppongi is such a popular nighttime hangout for young Tokyoites, as well as for foreigners, it boasts a large number of both Japanese and Western restaurants. To find the location of any of the Roppongi addresses below, stop by the tiny police station on Roppongi Crossing (Roppongi's main intersection of Roppongi Dori and Gaien-Higashi Dori), where you'll find a map of the area. If you still don't know where to go, ask one of the policemen.

Adjacent to Roppongi is another popular nighttime area—Nishi-Azabu. Once a residential neighborhood, Nishi-Azabu changed its character when it began to absorb the overflow of Roppongi. It has restaurants and nightclubs; many of the restaurants offer a selection of foreign cuisines.

VERY EXPENSIVE

Takamura (20)

3-4-27 Roppongi. ☎ **03/3585-6600.** Reservations required (for lunch, the day before at the latest). Set dinners ¥15,000–¥20,000 ($150–$200); set lunches ¥10,000 ($100). AE, DC, JCB, MC, V. Tues–Sat noon–3pm and Mon–Sat 5–10:30pm (last order 8pm). Station: Roppongi (5 minutes). KAISEKI.

Takamura is a must for everyone who can afford it. Located on the edge of the hot spot that is Roppongi, this wonderful 45-year-old house is like a peaceful oasis that time forgot. Each of its eight rooms is different, with windows looking out onto miniature gardens with bamboo and charcoal hearths built into the floor. Takamura has a very Japanese feeling, expanding proportionately with the arrival of your meal—seasonal kaiseki food arranged so artfully you almost hate to destroy it. Your pleasure increases, however, as you savor the various textures and flavors of the food. Specialties here may include quail, sparrow, or duck, grilled on the hearth in your own private tatami room. Seating, by the way, is on the floor, as it is in most traditional Japanese restaurants. The price of dinner here usually averages about ¥25,000 to ¥30,000 ($250 to $300) by the time you add drinks, tax, and service charge. Dinner is for parties of four or more, while lunch is available only toparties of two or more, and you must make reservations at least a day in advance. There are two entrances to Takamura, marked by wooden gates complete with little roofs. The sign on the restaurant is in Japanese only, but look for the credit-card signs.Taxi drivers should have no trouble finding it.

EXPENSIVE

Fukuzushi (21)

5-7-8 Roppongi. ☎ **03/3402-4116.** Reservations recommended, especially for dinner. Set dinners ¥6,000–¥10,000 ($60–$100); set lunches ¥2,500 ($25). AE, DC, JCB, MC, V. Mon–Sat 11:30am–2pm and 5:30–11pm; Sun 5:30–11pm. Closed hols. Station: Roppongi (4 minutes). SUSHI.

One of the classiest sushi bars in town, tucked underneath Spago restaurant (behind the Roi Building in Roppongi), this place has an entrance through a small courtyard, and an interior of red and black. Some people swear it has the best sushi in Tokyo, although with 7,000 sushi bars in the city, I'd be hard-pressed to say which one is tops. Certainly, you can't go wrong here. The English menu opens up like a fan and offers a variety of choices of sashimi and *nigiri-zushi.* Most dinners average about ¥10,000 ($100), but if you're careful about your drinks and the amount you order, you can eat for less.

Kisso

Axis Bldg., 5-17-1 Roppongi. ☎ **03/3582-4191.** Reservations recommended for dinner. Set dinners ¥8,000–¥13,000 ($80–$130); set lunches ¥1,200–¥5,000 ($12–$50). AE, DC, JCB, MC, V. Mon–Sat 11:30am–2pm and 5:30–9pm (last order). Closed hols. Station: Roppongi (5 minutes). KAISEKI.

This thoroughly modern establishment sells Japanese gourmet cookware, including expensive ceramics, utensils, and lacquerware of contemporary design, in its shop up on the third floor. The restaurant, located in the basement of this interesting building filled with shops dedicated to the best in interior design, is simple but elegant, with heavy tables, sprigs of flowers, and soft lighting. The food is kaiseki and comes only in set meals, served (as you might guess) in/on beautifully lacquered bowls/trays, as well as on ceramic plates. I love eating here because to me Kisso represents all the best that is modern Japan—understated elegance, a successful marriage between the contemporary and the traditional. There should be more places like this in Tokyo. From Roppongi Station, walk toward Tokyo Tower on Gaien-Higashi Dori; the Axis Building will be on your right.

Spago

5-7-8 Roppongi. ☎ **03/3423-4025.** Reservations required. Pizza and pasta ¥1,900–¥2,000 ($19–$20); main dishes ¥2,900–¥5,700 ($29–$57). AE, DC, JCB, MC, V. Mon–Fri 11:30am–2pm and 4–10pm; Sat, Sun, and hols 6–9:30pm. Station: Roppongi (4 minutes). CALIFORNIAN.

Spago serves Californian cuisine created by its owner, Wolfgang Puck, an Austrian-born chef who has a similar restaurant in Los Angeles. The atmosphere here is bright, airy, and cheerful—very Californian—with huge bouquets of flowers, potted palms, ferns, white walls, and a colorful mural. The menu changes every three months to reflect what's in season, but examples of what has been offered in the past include spicy fettuccine with grilled shrimp and fresh basil; sliced breast of duck with Japanese oba leaves and plum-wine sauce; angel-hair noodles with goat cheese, broccoli, and thyme; grilled spicy chicken with garlic and Italian parsley; and roasted baby lamb with a cabernet, mustard, and rosemary sauce. If you order pizza, it will come not with tomato sauce but with olive oil, making it much lighter, so the emphasis is on the toppings. Needless to say, the main dishes are always imaginative, and the service is great. Dining here is a pleasure, and as you might expect, Spago has the largest selection of California wines in town. For dessert, try the restaurant's homemade ice cream. An average dinner check, including wine, tax, and service, is about ¥10,000 ($100).

Moderate

Chez Figaro

4-4-1 Nishi Azabu. ☎ **03/3400-8718.** Reservations recommended. Main dishes ¥4,500–¥5,000 ($45–$50); set dinners from ¥5,000 ($50); set lunches ¥2,500–¥3,500 ($25–$35). AE, DC, JCB, MC, V. Daily noon–2pm and 6–9pm (last order). Station: Hiroo (exit 3, 7 minutes); Roppongi (15 minutes). TRADITIONAL FRENCH.

Chez Figaro has been serving traditional French cooking since 1969 and is still popular with both foreigners and Japanese. A small and cozy place, it offers such specialties as homemade pâté, escargots, saffron-flavored fish soup, stuffed quail with grapes, steak, and young duckling with orange sauce. To reach Chez Figaro from Hiroo, take exit 3 and walk straight towards Nishi-Azabu Crossing; it's on your left.

Garden Restaurant

Tokyo Prince Hotel, 3-3-1 Shibakoen. ☎ **03/3432-1111.** Main dishes ¥500–¥1,400 ($5–$14); set meal ¥5,000 ($50); all-you-can-drink ¥2,500 ($25); set meal, plus all-you-can-drink ¥6,500 ($65). AE, DC, JCB, MC, V. May–June daily 5:30–8pm; July–mid-Sept daily 5:30–9pm. Closed mid-Sept–April. Station: Kamiyacho (5 minutes) or Onarimon (2 minutes) or Hammamatsucho (10 minutes). TEPPANYAKI.

In a lovely garden setting, this lively beer garden offers teppanyaki steak sets (rib loin steak, lamb chop, lobster, cuttlefish, vegetables, noodles, salad, and fruits). If you enjoy drinking, the all-you-can-drink (sake, whiskey, draft beer, and soft drinks) plus tenpanyaki set is a great deal. It's definitely possible to drink up the Garden's profits, and that being the general idea, there's a very relaxed, fun atmosphere. A great chance to see the Japanese unwind.

Hassan (22)

Denki Bldg. basement, 6-1-20 Roppongi. ☎ **03/3403-8333.** Reservations suggested for dinner. Set dinners ¥3,900–¥5,900 ($39–$59); set lunches ¥2,700–¥6,300 ($27–$63). AE, DC, JCB, MC, V. Daily 11:45am–2:30pm and 4:30–11pm (last order). Station: Roppongi (1 minute). SHABU-SHABU.

This modern basement restaurant offers shabu-shabu with various options listed on its English menu. Seating is at tables, waitresses wear kimonos, and *koto* (Japanese zither) music plays in the background. If you take the road toward Shibuya from Roppongi Crossing, Hassan will soon be on your left. In a separate section of the same restaurant is Hina Sushi, below.

Hina Sushi

Denki Bldg. basement, 6-1-20 Roppongi. ☎ **03/3403-8333.** Reservations suggested for dinner. All-you-can-eat sushi for 90 minutes ¥4,300 ($43), for 120 minutes ¥4,800 ($48). AE, DC, JCB, MC, V. Mon–Fri 11:45am–2:30pm and 4:30–11pm (last order); Sat–Sun, hols 11:45am–9:30pm (last order). Station: Roppongi (1 minute). SUSHI.

Never get enough sushi? This place is for you, with two all-you-can-eat sushi formulas to choose from: 90 minutes for ¥4,300 ($43) or 120 minutes ¥4,800 ($48). The

120-minute formula includes your choice of any sushi, while the 90-minute formula restricts more costly ingredients like *uni* (sea urchin) and *ikura* (roe eggs). Seating is at a sushi counter, and it's the same Japanese-music-and-kimono atmosphere as Hassan, above. Serious sushi lovers, you've found your paradise.

✪ Kitchen Five

4-2-15 Nishi-Azabu. ☎ **03/3409-8835.** Dishes ¥950–¥2,200 ($9.50–$22). No credit cards. Tues–Sat 6–9:45pm (last order). Closed hols and late July–early Sept. Station: Roppongi or Hiroo (15 minutes). MEDITERRANEAN/ETHNIC.

If it's true that cooking with love is the best spice, then perhaps that's why Yuko Kobayashi's 11-year-old, 16-seat restaurant is so popular (get there before 7pm or after 9:30pm to get a seat). She goes to market every morning to fetch ingredients for such dishes as *coxinhas de galinha,* stuffed eggplant, *fritata de verdure,* moussaka, and *tajin.* Every summer Kobayashi goes off to search for recipes in Sicily, South America, or northern Africa. The love for what she does shines in her black eyes as she cooks, serves, and walks you through the menu of daily dishes displayed. Whenever I'm in Tokyo, I head straight for Kitchen Five. Note that though you can eat here quite cheaply, the food is so delicious, you may be tempted to order quite a lot. When you add wine to a number of dishes, your bill will add up. From the Nishi-Azabu crossing, head toward Hiroo and turn right opposite the gas station. Highly recommended.

El Mocambo

1-4-38 Nishi-Azabu, Minatoku. ☎ **03/5410-0468.** Dishes ¥500–¥2,500 ($5–$25). AE, JCB, MC, V. Mon–Thurs 6pm–midnight; Fri–Sat 6pm–2am. Station: Roppongi (15 minutes). LATIN AMERICAN.

South American music (live on Tuesday with a ¥1,000 ($10) cover charge), the staff, and the menu make this a haven for south-of-the-border aficionados. Although the restaurant is in the second basement, it has high windows that look out on a central courtyard; the Aztec modern decor includes ceiling fans and interesting art. Try the Peruvian pork specialty cooked with sweet potato (¥1,580/$15.80) or the tacos that you make at your table with fresh flour tortillas and a filling of your choice, such as *bistec con cebollitas, cecina de puerco,* or *chorizo,* each for ¥500 ($5). Drinks include beers from Peru, Mexico, and Panama for ¥650 ($6.50); the house specialty, *caipirinha* (a Brazilian fresh-fruit and rum cocktail), is ¥1,000 ($10). El Mocambo is down Seijoki Dori, across from Stars and Stripes.

Roppongi Colza

Clover Bldg., 7-15-10 Roppongi. ☎ **03/3405-5631.** Reservations recommended for dinner. Main dishes ¥1,000–¥11,000 ($10–$110); set dinners ¥6,900–¥15,000 ($69–$150); set lunches ¥1,200–¥4,000 ($12–$40). AE, DC, JCB, MC, V. Mon–Sat 11:30am–2pm and 5–9:30pm, Sun and hols noon–3pm and 5–8:30pm. Station: Roppongi (1 minute). TEPPANYAKI/GRILLED SEAFOOD.

Another Kikkoman restaurant, this locale specializes in teppanyaki steaks and seafood, flavored with Kikkoman condiments. Set courses include various cuts of Matsuzaka beef; seafood, such as scallops, scampi, sole, or turbot; side dishes; and dessert.

Shabu Zen (23)

5-17-16 Roppongi. ☎ **03/3585-5388.** Reservations recommended. Shabu-shabu and sukiyaki ¥3,300–¥10,000 ($33–$100). AE, DC, JCB, MC, V. Mon–Sat 5–10:30pm, Sun and hols 5–10pm. Station: Roppongi (5 minutes). SHABU-SHABU/SUKIYAKI.

This restaurant has both an English-speaking staff and a menu in English (along with color illustrations). For ¥4,300 ($43) per person, you can eat all the shabu-shabu or sukiyaki you want. The shabu-shabu menu includes an unlimited amount of meat and vegetables, plus noodles and rice. Shabu Zen is located behind the Axis Building. There's also a "Weekend and Horyday [*sic*]" menu for ¥3,000 to ¥5,000 ($30 to $50).

La Terre

1-9-20 Azabu-Dai, Minatoku. ☎ **03/3583-9682.** Reservations recommended. Main dishes ¥2,800–¥4,200 ($28–$42); set dinners ¥6,000–¥10,000 ($60–$100); set lunches ¥2,000–¥4,000 ($20–$40). AE, DC, JCB, V. Lunch Mon–Sat 11:30am–2pm (last order) and 6–8:30pm (last order). Closed hols. Station: Kamiyacho (3 minutes). NOUVELLE FRENCH.

The service is adequate but far from friendly (if you're not a regular) at this hidden-away French bistro with outdoor seating. To avoid the 10% service charge added to your bill at night, go for lunch. The basic lunch for ¥2,500 ($25) includes *potage du jour* (pumpkin soup), *canard au poivre vert,* baskets of fresh French bread and butter, *gâteau,* and tea. For lunch under a huge cherry tree, reserve in advance during cherry season. To get here, from Kamiyacho Station, walk toward Tokyo Tower, then turn right at the Reiyukai Temple and go up the stairs; it's on your left.

Victoria Station

4-9-2 Roppongi. ☎ **03/3479-4601.** Reservations recommended. Main dishes ¥1,500–¥2,500 ($15–$25); set dinners ¥3,000–¥4,600 ($30–$46); set lunches ¥800–¥2,000 ($8–$20). AE, DC, JCB, MC, V. Mon–Sat 11am–midnight, Sun and hols 11am–11pm. Station: Roppongi. STEAKS/HAMBURGERS.

If you're hungering for American steaks, salads, and soups, Victoria Station may be the closest you can come. It specializes in roast prime beef and steaks and has one of the best salad bars in town. Hashed beef plus rice and a trip to the salad bar at lunch costs just ¥1,280 ($12.80). If you're interested mainly in beverages or lighter dishes, there's a cocktail bar upstairs with its own menu. Victoria Station is located close to Roppongi Crossing, almost catercorner from the Almond Coffee Shop.

INEXPENSIVE

Bengawan Solo

7-18-13 Roppongi. ☎ **03/3408-5698.** Main dishes ¥950–¥1,800 ($9.50–$18); set lunch ¥800–¥1,100 ($8–$11); set dinners ¥3,500–¥9,500 ($35–$95). AE, JCB, MC, V. Daily 11:30am–3pm and 5–11pm (last order 9:45pm). Station: Roppongi (C2 exit, 2 minutes). JAVANESE.

Friendly Indonesian waiters and decor add to the spicy goodness of Bengawan's traditional Indonesian food. There are lots of healthy vegetarian choices like tempe (Indonesian tofu) and gado-gado salad (with peanut sauce). This is one of the first ethnic restaurants to open in Tokyo (1954), and you're likely to find some old-Tokyo-hands dining here. Perennial favorites are beef in hot sauce and shrimp in coconut cream.

Bikkuri Sushi

3-14-9 Roppongi. ☎ **03/3403-1489.** Dishes ¥130–¥500 ($1.30–$5). No credit cards. Daily 11am–5am. Station: Roppongi (3 minutes). SUSHI.

In this establishment, plates of sushi move along a conveyor belt past customers seated at the counter. They simply help themselves to whichever plates strike their fancy; this makes dining a cinch, since it's not necessary to know the name of anything. The white plates of sushi are all priced at ¥130 ($1.30), while the colored dishes run ¥250 ($2.50) and ¥500 ($5). Your bill is tallied according to the number of plates you've taken. One of the cheapest places to eat in this popular nightlife district, it's located on the road leading to Tokyo Tower, on the left-hand side of the road across the street from the Roi Building.

Ganchan (24)
6-8-23 Roppongi. ☎ **03/3478-0092.** Yakitori skewers ¥200–¥300 ($2–$3); yakitori set course ¥2,500 ($25). JCB, V. Mon–Fri 6pm–2am; Sat, Sun, and hols 6pm–midnight. Station: Roppongi (7 minutes). YAKITORI.

This is one of my favorite yakitori-ya, and many a night I've spent here. Small and intimate, it's owned by a friendly and entertaining man who can't speak English worth a darn but keeps trying with the help of a worn-out Japanese-English dictionary he keeps behind the counter. He also keeps an eclectic cassette collection—I never know whether to expect Japanese pop tunes or mellower Simon and Garfunkel. Seating is along just one counter, with room for only a dozen or so people. Though there's an English menu, it's easiest to order the yakitori *seto,* a set course that comes with salad and soup and eight skewers of such items as chicken, beef, meatballs, green peppers, and asparagus with rolled bacon.

To reach this place, take the small street going downhill on the left side of the Almond Coffee Shop; Ganchan is at the bottom of the hill on the right—look for the big white paper lantern.

Hard Rock Cafe
5-4-20 Roppongi. ☎ **03/3408-7018.** Main dishes ¥1,280–¥3,900 ($12.80–$39). AE, DC, JCB, MC, V. Mon–Thurs 11:30am–2am, Fri–Sat 11:30am–4am, Sun and hols 11:30am–11:30pm. Station: Roppongi (3 minutes). AMERICAN.

If you have disgruntled teenagers in tow, bring them to this world-famous hamburger joint dedicated to rock and roll to ogle the memorabilia on the walls, chow down on a burger, and look over the T-shirts for sale. In addition to hamburgers, the menu includes salads, sandwiches, steak, barbecued pork ribs, and fajitas. The music, by the way, is loud. From Roppongi Station, walk toward Tokyo Tower and take a right at McDonald's.

✪ Ichioku (25)
4-4-5 Roppongi. ☎ **03/3405-9891.** ¥700–¥1,400 ($7–$14). No credit cards. Mon–Sat 5pm–1am; Sun and hols 5–11pm. Station: Roppongi (4 minutes). JAPANESE ORIGINALS.

One of my favorite restaurants in Tokyo for casual dining, Ichioku opened in the early 1970s. It's a tiny, cozy place with only eight tables, and you fill out your order yourself from the menu in English, complete with pictures, glued onto your table underneath clear glass. The food can best be called Japanese nouvelle cooking, with original creations offered at very reasonable prices. There's tuna and ginger sauté, mushroom sauté, shrimp spring rolls, asparagus salad, fried potatoes, and a dish of crumbled radish and tiny fish. I recommend the tofu steak (fried tofu and flakes of dried fish), as well as the cheese *gyoza* (a fried pork dumpling with cheese melted on it). The restaurant is tucked away on a side street; look for the Rastafarian colors and a yin/yang sign.

✪ Johnny Rockets
3-11-10 Roppongi. ☎ **03/3423-1955.** ¥400–¥1,200 ($4–$12); fixed-price lunch ¥700–¥1,000 ($7–$10). Sun–Thur 11am–11pm; Fri and Sat 11am–5am. Station: Roppongi. HAMBURGERS.

Quite simply, the best burgers in town. At ¥1,000 ($10) they're also a bit steep; however, they're so huge they'll definitely hit the spot. Perched on the second floor of a building on Roppongi Crossing, Johnny Rockets is decorated like an American '50s diner, and when certain songs come on the jukebox, the waitresses all stop to sing and dance in unison, just like in the movies. Seating is on a first-come, first-served basis at the counters, and smoking is not allowed. Other goodies on the menu include sandwiches, fries (including fries topped with chili), malts, shakes, floats, and pie à la mode. From 11am to 4pm daily, a fixed-price lunch offers a hamburger or sandwich, fries, and a drink (unlimited refills).

Kamakura

4-10-11 Roppongi. ☎ **03/3405-4377.** Yakitori skewers ¥170–¥300 ($1.70–$3); set dinners ¥2,300–¥7,000 ($23–$70). AE, DC, JCB, MC, V. Mon–Sat 6–11pm. Station: Roppongi (2 minutes). YAKITORI.

Much more refined than most yakitori-ya, this establishment is decorated with paper lanterns and sprigs of fake but cheerful spring blossoms, with traditional kotomusic playing softly in the background. The English menu lists yakitori set courses, and à la carte sticks include those with shrimp, meatballs, squid, eggplant, and mushrooms. Kamakura is located across from the Ibis Hotel, down a side street.

Luna

1-11-10 Nishi-Azabu, Minatoku. ☎ **03/3403-1318.** Pasta, pizza, and main dishes ¥880–¥1,600 ($8.80–$16); set lunch ¥700–¥850 ($7–$8.50). AE, JCB, MC, V. Mon–Sat 11:30am–5am, Sun 5pm–5am (last order 40 minutes before closing). Station: Roppongi (10 minutes). ITALIAN.

An English menu and *gaijin* (foreign) staff welcome you in this small cafe. The eggplant-and-spinach spaghetti (¥980/$9.80) and the parmigiano (¥1,200/$12)—a dish of spinach, rice, and cheese ladled out of a huge half of round cheese crust—are recommended. You can have dinner for two with wine for ¥5,000 ($50). From Roppongi Station, walk toward Shibuya; Luna is on the last street on the right before the Nishi-Azabu crossing.

✪ Moti

6-2-35 Roppongi. ☎ **03/3479-1939.** Curries ¥1,100–¥1,800 ($11–$18); tandoori from ¥1,700 ($17); set lunches ¥950 ($9.50). AE, DC, JCB, MC, V. Mon–Sat 11:30am–10pm (last order); Sun noon–10pm. Station: Roppongi (three minutes). INDIAN.

This is my favorite Indian restaurant in town. Dishes include vegetable curries, chicken and mutton curries (I usually opt for the sag mutton—lamb with spinach), and tandoori chicken. Set lunches, served until 2:30pm, offer a choice of vegetable, chicken, or mutton curry, along with Indian bread (nan) and tea or coffee. Moti is on the left side of the street as you walk from Roppongi Crossing toward Shibuya.

There are other Moti restaurants, two in Akasaka—on the second floor of the Akasaka Floral Plaza, 3-8-8 Akasaka (☎ 03/3582-3620); and on the third floor of the Kinpa Building, 2-14-31 Akasaka (☎ 03/3584-6640). A second Roppongi location is Moti Darbar, on the third floor of the Roppongi Plaza Building, 3-12-6 Roppongi (☎ 03/5410-6871).

Torigin (26)

4-12-6 Roppongi. ☎ **03/3403-5829.** Yakitori skewers ¥140–¥250 ($1.40–$2.50); kamameshi ¥800–¥900 ($8–$9). No credit cards. Mon–Sat 11:30am–3pm and 5–11pm. Station: Roppongi (2 minutes). YAKITORI/RICE CASSEROLES.

Part of a chain of yakitori establishments, this no-frills place is typical of the smaller Japanese restaurants all over the country patronized by the country's salarymen, who stop off for a drink and bite to eat before boarding the commuter trains for home. An English menu includes skewers of grilled chicken, gingko nuts, green peppers, quail eggs, and asparagus with rolled bacon, as well as various *kamameshi* (rice casseroles cooked and served in their own little pots and topped with chicken, bamboo shoots, mushrooms, crab, salmon, or shrimp).

HARAJUKU & AOYAMA

EXPENSIVE

L'Orangerie de Paris

Hanae Mori Bldg., 5th floor, 3-6-1 Kita-Aoyama, Minato-ku. ☎ **03/3407-7461.** Reservations required for dinner and Sunday brunch. Main dishes ¥3,000–¥8,000 ($30–$80); set dinners ¥8,000 ($80); set lunch and Sunday brunch ¥4,000 ($40). AE, DC, JCB, MC, V. Daily 11:30am–2:30pm; Mon–Sat 5:30–10pm (last order 9:30pm). Station: Omotesando. NOUVELLE FRENCH.

This well-known Tokyo branch, the sibling of the Parisian restaurant of the same name, is located in chic Omotesando, on the 5th floor of fashion designer Hanae Mori's building (designed by Kenzo Tange). Check out Mori's front shop windows—they're always interesting. The menu changes often but always offers set lunches and dinners. The very popular Sunday brunch seems to attract half the foreign population in Tokyo.

Sabatini

Suncrest Bldg., 2-13-5 Kita-Aoyama. ☎ **03/3402-3812.** Reservations recommended for dinner. Pasta ¥1,800–¥3,400 ($18–$34); main dishes ¥3,000–¥7,600 ($30–$76); set lunch ¥5,000 ($50); set dinner ¥15,000 ($150). AE, DC, JCB, MC, V. Daily 11:30am–2:30pm and 5:30–11pm. Station: Gaienmae (2 minutes). ITALIAN.

The three Italian brothers who own Sabatini have had a restaurant in Rome for more than 30 years. They take turns overseeing the Tokyo restaurants, so one of them is always here. This restaurant, with its Italian furniture and tableware and strolling musicians, seems as if it has been moved intact from the Old World. In fact, the only thing to remind you you're in Tokyo are the Japanese waiters. The menu includes soups, spaghetti, seafood, veal, steak, lamb, and a variety of vegetables. You can do it cheaper at lunch with the set menu, which gives you a choice of soup or pasta, fish or meat, and salad and coffee. There's also brunch on Saturday and Sunday; though a bit pricey (¥6,200/$62), it's quite delicious. Sabatini is located on Aoyama Dori.

MODERATE

✪ El Castellano

2-9-11 Shibuya. ☎ **03/3407-7197.** Reservations recommended. Main dishes ¥2,100–¥2,700 ($21–$27); paella for two ¥3,800 ($38). No credit cards. Daily 6–11pm. Station: Omotesando or Shibuya (10 minutes). CASTILIAN.

Señor Vicente Garcia is El Castellano and a true host; you can leave Tokyo and return four years later—he still remembers who you are. And we, his faithful clients, how can we forget his smiling face? The only time you'll see him frown is over a game of chess going on in the corner with a South American diplomat. The walls are covered in signatures of happy customers, some of whom (having drunk a little too much red wine) may be dancing on the tables to flamenco music. In short we feel at home. The custom is to let Sr. Garcia order for you (although not de rigeur); he'll choose the best appetizer (tortilla or *gambas,* perhaps) and, of course, paella, the best this side of Sevilla. Though you can eat for less, expect to spend ¥5,000 ($50) per person for dinner with wine. It's located on the second floor across Aoyama Dori from National Children's Castle (not a big sign, so look).

$ Flo

4-3-3 Jingumae. ☎ **03/5474-0611.** Main dishes ¥2,200–¥3,800 ($22–$38); set dinners ¥5,000–¥6,000 ($50–$60); set lunch ¥1,700 ($17); lunch buffet ¥1,600 ($16). Daily 11:30am–3pm and 5–11:30pm; lunch buffet Mon–Fri (except hols) 10am–5pm. Station: Omotesando (4 minutes). FRENCH BISTRO.

French restaurateurs have opened this beautiful bistro with authentic staff and food. Lunch may be *potage crème de Saint-Jacques* and *confit de canard* with roasted new potatoes in bacon-and-mushroom sauce. Of course, all the typical and irresistible French desserts—from *mille feuilles* to crème brûlée—are offered. But perhaps most tempting is the upstairs all-you-can-eat buffet (one of the best I've seen in Tokyo), which boasts appetizers to desserts. Clientele are French businessmen to Japanese housewives, and why not? You can't go wrong here if you're hungry for French bistro food.

Lunchan

1-2-5 Shibuya. ☎ **03/5466-1398.** Reservations required for Sun brunch. Main dishes ¥1,600–¥2,800 ($16–$28); set lunches ¥1,200–¥2,800 ($12–$28); Sunday brunch ¥2,500 ($25). AE, DC, JCB, MC, V. Daily 11am–11pm; brunch Sun 11am–3pm. Station: Omotesando or Shibuya (10 minutes). AMERICAN.

American chef David Chiddo created original recipes for this contemporary, open, and airy mauve-and-teal bistro. Choose from among such dishes as pizza al forno, herb roast chicken, or Thai-style spicy shrimp sauté. A wide selection of lunch specials are offered, including sandwiches with all the trimmings. Sunday brunch features breakfast treats like eggs benedict. Easy to find, Lunchan—a combination of the words "lunch" and "chan," a Japanese title used for children or close friends and relatives—is across the side street from the National Children's Castle.

Sabatini Pizzeria Romana

Suncrest Bldg., 2-13-5 Kita-Aoyama. ☎ **03/3402-2027.** Pasta and pizza ¥1,300–¥1,750 ($13–$17.50); main dishes ¥2,700–¥4,000 ($27–$40); set lunches ¥2,300–¥3,800 ($23–$38). AE, DC, JCB, MC, V. Daily 11:30am–2:30pm and 5:30–11pm. Station: Gaienmae (1 minute). ITALIAN.

This restaurant, opened in 1984 and owned by three brothers from Rome who operate an expensive Italian restaurant (also located in the Suncrest Building), offers the closest thing to real Italian pizza in town. Many ingredients are flown in from Italy, including olive oil, huge slabs of Parmesan and other cheeses, as well as the restaurant's large wine selection; they've even shipped in a pasta machine. In addition to pizzas, the place also serves spaghetti, lasagne, fettuccine, and meat dishes. All you need order, however, is pizza. The pizzeria is at the intersection of Aoyama Dori and Killer Dori.

Selan

2-1-19 Kita-Aoyama. ☎ **03/3478-2200.** Reservations recommended. Main dishes ¥2,000–¥3,500 ($20–$35); set dinners ¥3,800–¥6,000 ($38–$60); set lunch ¥1,900–¥3,800 ($19–$38). AE, DC, JCB, MC, V. Daily 11:30am–2:30pm and 6–9:30pm. Station: Gaienmae or Aoyama-Itchome (5 minutes). NOUVELLE JAPONAISE.

It looks like a French restaurant, with its sidewalk seating and pink, chandeliered interior, and the menu offers such fare as steaks, chicken, fish, lobster, and duck. However, the food is cooked using Japanese ingredients and thus may be classified as "nouvelle japonaise" cuisine. In any case, it's a successful marriage between French and Japanese cooking, with such innovative dishes as flounder stuffed with chopped shrimp and calamari and topped with sea urchin and vegetables, and seared bonito salad with soy sauce, garlic, and oil dressing. Little wonder that this is fast becoming one of Tokyo's most popular mealtime retreats. Large windows overlook a pleasant tree-lined street, especially beautiful in autumn when the leaves are yellow. Head upstairs for a meal; if the weather is fine and all you want is a coffee, try to get one of the ground-floor cafe's outdoor tables.

INEXPENSIVE

El Amigo

4-30-2 Jingumae. ☎ **03/3405-9996.** Dishes ¥600–¥1,000 ($6–$10). No credit cards. Mon–Fri 5:30pm–midnight; Sat–Sun 5pm–midnight. Station: Meiji-Jingumae (1 minute). MEXICAN.

One of the cheapest Mexican restaurants in town, they cut corners, using cabbage instead of lettuce, but otherwise it's the usual tacos and enchiladas, margaritas, and Mexican beer—a lot of people come here just for those margaritas. Often crowded, there's an outdoor patio of sorts, below street level. It's located near the Omotesando Dori and Meiji Dori intersection, on a side street beside Wendy's.

Bamboo Sandwich House

5-8-8 Jingumae. ☎ **03/3406-1828.** Sandwiches ¥450–¥800 ($4.50–$8). No credit cards. Daily 11am–9pm. Station: Omotesando (5 minutes), Meiji-Jingumae, or Harajuku. SANDWICHES.

Located off Omotesando on a side street, this place offers more than 20 sandwich fillings, and you have your choice of white or rye bread. What's more, it's probably the only place in town to offer a bottomless cup of coffee for a mere ¥220 ($2.20), a price that hasn't changed in a dozen years. This is a good place for a coffee break in a cheerful setting, and it even has outdoor seating.

Café Des Près

3-5-28, Kita-Aoyama. ☎ **03/5411-3721.** Coffee ¥620 ($6.20); glass of wine ¥820 ($8.20); sandwiches ¥800–¥1,000 ($8–$10). Mon–Thur 8am–midnight; Sat–Sun and hols 8am–4pm. Station: Omotesando (2 minutes). CAFE.

Close to the Omotesando intersection, Café des Près has a Parisian atmosphere, with cafe tables and wicker chairs and an open-to-the-sidewalk front. In addition to cappuccino or beer, you can have Parisian favorites like *croque monsieur* and croissant and other bistro fare. It's chiefly a beautiful-people-watching spot and, as such, good for a break in sightseeing.

Genrokusushi (27)

5-8-5 Jingumae. ☎ **03/3498-3968.** Sushi ¥120 and ¥240 ($1.20 and $2.40) each. No credit cards. Daily 11am–9pm. Station: Meiji-Jingumae (2 minutes) or Omotesando (5 minutes). SUSHI.

This is another one of those fast-food sushi bars where plates of food are conducted along the counter on a conveyor belt. Customers help themselves to whatever strikes their fancy. To figure your bill, the cashier simply counts the number of plates you took from the conveyor belt. There are also take-out sushi boxes starting at ¥400 ($4), which you might want to eat in nearby Yoyogi Park. Genrokusushi is on Omotesando Dori, close to the Oriental Bazaar.

Harvester

1-13-13 Jingumae. ☎ **03/3478-1031.** Main dishes ¥650 ($6.50); salads and sandwiches ¥230–¥500 ($2.30–$5). No credit cards. Daily 8am–11pm. Station: Harajuku or Meiji-Jingumae (1 minute). ROAST CHICKEN.

Light and airy, with open seating on Omotesando Dori, this cafeteria-style cafe specializes in roasted chicken at reasonable prices. There are also pita bread sandwiches and coffee for only ¥300 ($3). An inexpensive stop for real food and people watching. It's at the Meijijingu end of Omotesando Dori.

✪ Mominoki House

2-18-5 Jingumae. ☎ **03/3405-9144.** Dishes ¥1,000–¥2,000 ($10–$20); set lunches ¥850–¥1,500 ($8.50–$15). No credit cards. Mon–Sat 11am–10pm (last order), hols 3–10pm. Station: Harajuku or Meiji-Jingumae (15 minutes). NOUVELLE JAPANESE/MACROBIOTIC.

Mominoki House dishes could be described as French, except they're the creations of a chef who uses lots of soy sauce, ginger, Japanese vegetables, and macrobiotic foods. This alternative restaurant, in a category by itself, features hanging plants and split-level dining, allowing for more privacy than one would think possible in such a tiny place. Its recorded jazz collection is extensive, and on weekends there's live music. Dishes may include the likes of tofu steak, duck, sole, escargots, eggplant gratin (delicious), salads, and homemade sorbet. An especially good deal is the daily lunch special, featuring brown rice, miso soup, salad, fish or another main dish, and a glass of wine. There's an English menu, but daily specials are written on the blackboard, in Japanese only. The chef speaks English, so if in doubt ask him what he recommends. You're best off taking a taxi from either the Harajuku or the Meiji-Jingumae Station.

SHINJUKU

VERY EXPENSIVE

Kakiden (28)

3-37-11 Shinjuku. ☎ **03/3352-5121.** Reservations recommended for lunch, required for dinner. Set dinners ¥10,000–¥15,000 ($100–$150); set lunches ¥4,000 ($40). AE, DC, JCB, MC, V. Daily 11am–9pm (last order). Station: Shinjuku (east exit, 1 minute). KAISEKI.

Although located on the eighth floor of a rather uninspiring building on the east side of Shinjuku Station, next to My City shopping complex, Kakiden has a relaxing teahouse atmosphere, with low chairs, shoji screens, bamboo trees, and soothing traditional Japanese music playing softly in the background. Sibling restaurant to one in Kyoto, founded more than 260 years ago as a catering service for the elite, this kaiseki restaurant serves set meals that change with the seasons, according to what's fresh and available. The menu is in Japanese only, so simply pick a meal to fit your budget. Some of the more common dishes here will include fish, vegetables, eggs, sashimi, shrimp, and mushrooms, but don't worry if you can't identify everything. I've found that even the Japanese don't always know what they're eating. The set lunch is available until 3pm.

✪ New York Grill

Park Hyatt Hotel, 3-7-1-2 Nishi-Shinjuku. ☎ **03/5322-1234.** Reservations recommended. Main dishes ¥2,700–¥7,500 ($27–$75); set lunch ¥4,200 ($42); set dinners ¥10,000–¥15,000 ($100–$150); brunch ¥5,800 ($58). AE, DC, JCB, MC, V. Daily 11:30am–2:30pm and 5:30–10:30pm. Station: Shinjuku (a 13-minute walk, or 5-minute free shuttle ride from in front of L-Tower Bldg. subway exit A18).

On the 52nd floor, in the midst of Shinjuku's highrise district, surrounded on four sides by glass, art work by Valerio Adami, live jazz music, a 1,700-bottle wine cellar (featuring California wines), the New York Grill is simply the most sophisticated place to dine in all of Japan. But the restaurant doesn't rely on dramatic setting alone. Chef Angela Loftus creates generous portions of delectable roast duck, grilled salmon, and New Zealand rack of lamb in an open kitchen. Manager Brian Marcus, dedicated to service, keeps a close eye on his waiters. Who dines here? Why everybody, including Park Hyatt guests like Sting. Although this is in the very-expensive category, the appetizer plate (¥5,000/$50), with a selection of delicacies like smoked salmon pizza with red onions, cream cheese, chives, and caviar, or the Mediterranean platter (¥4,000/$40), with pita, hummus, tabbouleh, lentil salad, baba ghanouj, tomato, and feta, are each enough for two people. I wouldn't miss it.

Seryna
Shinjuku Sumitomo Bldg., 52nd floor, 2-6-1 Nishi-Shinjuku. ☎ **03/3344-6761.** Reservations recommended for dinner. Main dishes ¥6,500–¥12,000 ($65–$120); set dinners ¥10,000–¥20,000 ($100–$200); set lunches ¥1,800–¥5,500 ($18–$55). AE, DC, JCB, MC, V. Daily 11:30am–9:30pm. Station: Shinjuku (west exit, 7 minutes). SHABU-SHABU/SUKIYAKI/TEPPANYAKI.

Perched high above Shinjuku in one of the city's best-known skyscrapers, and offering city views, Seryna serves Kobe steaks, shabu-shabu, sukiyaki, and teppanyaki. There's an English menu, and lunches are especially reasonable, making it a good stopping-off place if you're exploring the west side of Shinjuku.

Moderate

✪ Ban-Thai
1-23-14 Kabuki-cho. ☎ **03/3207-0068.** Main dishes ¥1,100–¥1,900 ($11–$19); set lunches ¥750–¥850 ($7.50–$8.50); set dinner ¥3,000 ($30). AE, JCB, MC, V. Mon–Fri 11:30am–3pm and 5–11pm; Sat–Sun and hols 11:30am–11pm. Station: Shinjuku (7 minutes). THAI.

The Thai staff here prepares and serves excellent and authentic Thai dishes, with 90 mouth-watering items listed on the menu. My favorites are the cold and spicy meat salad, the chicken soup with coconut and lemon grass, and the pat Thai (Thai fried rice). Live Thai music from 5pm. Ban-Thai stands in the seediest part of Kabuki-cho (don't worry, the interior is nicer than the exterior), on a neon-lit pedestrian street connecting the Koma Building with Yasukuni Dori. Located on the third floor, it's a bit difficult to find, so look for the numbers of the address on the building.

To get here from Shinjuku Station, take exit 3 and you'll come out at the small pedestrian street with a red neon archway; Ban-Thai is halfway down on your left. Note that if you make a reservation there's a ¥300 ($3) per-person table charge; also, portions are not large, so if you order several portions and add beers, your tab can become quite high.

Tokyo Dai Hanten
Oriental Wave Bldg. 3F, 5-17-13 Shinjuku. ☎ **03/3202-0121.** Reservations recommended. Main dishes ¥2,000–¥5,500 ($20–$55); dim sum ¥600 ($6). AE, DC, JCB, MC, V. Daily 11am–10pm. Station: Shinjuku Sanchome (2 minutes). CHINESE.

Tokyo Dai Hanten, on the third floor of the Oriental Wave Building, is a branch of an established Chinese restaurant in Shinjuku, with six floors for dining (the fourth through eighth floors are for banquets). With an English menu and *gaijin* (foreign) waiters, you'll have no trouble dining here on braised whole fish or rolled fried prawns. Sample the dim sum wagon for such delicacies as sweet beans and deep-fried pork dumplings. Of course you'll eat better if you're in a group.

Tokyo Kaisen Market
2-36-1 Kabukicho, Shinjuku. ☎ **03/5273-8301.** Reservations recommended. Appetizers and soups ¥700–¥2,800 ($7–$28); main dishes ¥1,000–¥6,000 ($10–$60); set dinners ¥5,500–¥7,000 ($55–$70). AE, DC, JCB, MC, V. Mon–Fri 5pm–midnight, Sat–Sun and hols noon–midnight. Station: Shinjuku (5 minutes). SEAFOOD/ASIAN.

The ground floor of this multilevel, open-beam, warehouse-style restaurant is a real fish market, with tanks and white tiles. Catch your dinner and they'll cook it any way you like for ¥800 ($8). It's also a drinking establishment; if you come without a reservation after 7pm, you'll find yourself having a beer or cocktail and waiting in the high-tech bar. Try a selection of sashimi (*moriawase*), Chinese-style lobster, or a vegetarian delight, five kinds of tofu for two. Also, the deep-fried salmon in sweet-and-sour sauce is not to be missed. There's an English menu, but daily fresh specials are on the blackboard in Japanese, so ask for a translation.

Tsunahachi (29)

3-31-8 Shinjuku. ☎ **03/3352-1012.** Reservations recommended. Tempura à la carte ¥350–¥1,000 ($3.50–$10); teishoku ¥1,200–¥2,000 ($12–$20). AE, JCB, V. Daily 11am–10pm. Station: Shinjuku (east exit, 5 minutes). TEMPURA.

A restaurant serving tempura, Tsunahachi first opened in 1923. Now there are more than 40 branch restaurants in Japan, including three in Shinjuku Station alone, and others in Ginza and Akasaka. Hours may vary, but most shops are open daily from 11:30am to 10pm. This main shop, on the east side of Shinjuku, is one of the largest, and its least expensive set meal includes deep-fried shrimp, three kinds of fish, a vegetable, and a shrimp ball.

INEXPENSIVE

Al Bacio

N.S. Building, 2-4-1 Nishi-Shinjuku. ☎ **03/3348-1393.** Anitpasti ¥750–¥1,400 ($7.50–$14); main dishes ¥1,300–¥2,300 ($13–$23); pastas ¥1,000–¥1,600 ($10–$16). No credit cards. Daily 11:30am–2pm and 5–9:30pm. Station: Shinjuku (west exit, 8 minutes). ITALIAN.

A "buona sera" greeting, Italian contemporary music, and a city view is what you get at this casual but tableclothed restaurant. Pasta portions are large enough to serve two. A large blackboard at the door lists daily specials. Featured is fish—baked, grilled, or in papillote. This is a good place to come for an inexpensive European fish dinner if you want to experience a west Shinjuku highrise.

Café Oriental Wave

5-17-13 Shinjuku. ☎ **03/3203-2881.** Tea, coffee, or desserts ¥500–¥1,000 ($5–$10). No credit cards. Daily 11am–11pm. Station: Shinjuku-sanchome (5 minutes) or Shinjuku (7 minutes). COFFEE SHOP.

Café Oriental Wave is in a building of Oriental-style dining, with Rajini and Tokyo Dai Hanten (listed above) upstairs. The interior feels colonial, with green silk moiré and high-backed sofas; you'll be served from ultimate-design sugar bowls and teapots. Right on Yasukuni Dori, near the small street leading to Hanazono Jinja (shrine), the café is a great place for watching people go by.

$ Irohanihoheto (30)

3-15-15 Shinjuku. ☎ **03/3359-1682.** Yakitori ¥300–¥450 ($3–$4.50) per skewer; set meals ¥2,800–¥3,800 ($28–$38). No credit cards. Sun–Thurs 5–11:30pm, Fri–Sat 5pm–4am. Station: Shinjuku Sanchome (5 minutes) or Shinjuku (10 minutes). YAKITORI/VARIED.

Irohanihoheto is a chain of drinking establishments with a menu so varied, extensive, and cheap that most people eat here as well. Extremely popular with university students, it bills itself as an "Antique Pub," the meaning of which becomes even more elusive once you're inside. The main hall looks imitation barn to me, with rafters, hurricane lamps, and glass lanterns everywhere. A second room is more traditional Japanese, with tatami seating and folkcrafts hanging about. People don't come here for the decor, however, but because of the prices. The menu of Japanese and Western food is in Japanese only, but there are pictures. It includes yakitori, fried noodles, potato salad, sashimi, grilled meatballs, *nikujaga* (potato and meat stew, one of my favorites), and dozens of other dishes. This restaurant with the impossible name is located on Shinjuku's east side, on Yasukuni Dori, on the sixth floor of a building next to Isetan Kaikan.

Negishi (31)

2-45-2 Kabuki-cho. ☎ **03/3232-8020.** Main dishes ¥550–¥800 ($5.50–$8); lunch teishoku ¥850–¥1,200 ($8.50–$12); set dinner ¥1,290 ($12.90). No credit cards. Daily 11am–3pm and 5pm–midnight. Station: Shinjuku or Seibu Shinjuku (3 minutes). JAPANESE GRILLED OX TONGUE/OX-TAIL SOUP/BOILED WHEAT WITH YAM.

It would be easy to overlook Negishi, a tiny hole-in-the-wall with just a counter and a few tables, located near America Boulevard, on a tiny side street beside Green Plaza. It would be a shame, however, to miss its healthful, low-calorie foods. It specializes in Japanese stews, ox-tail soup, and *mugi-toro* (boiled wheat with grated yam). You might also want to try *tan-yaki*, grilled ox tongue, which is low in calories and fat but rich in protein.

The Peak Lounge

Park Hyatt Hotel, 3-7-1-2 Nishi-Shinjuku. ☎ **03/5322-1234.** High tea set ¥2,500 ($25); sandwiches ¥1,500 ($15); teas and coffees ¥1,100–¥1,400 ($11–$14). AE, DC, JCB, MC, V. Mon–Fri 11:00am–10:30pm; Sat–Sun 10am–10:30pm; high tea daily 2–5pm. Station: Shinjuku, (a 13-minute walk, or 5-minute free shuttle ride from in front of L-Tower Bldg., subway exit A18).

The Peak Lounge, on the 41st floor in an atrium, offers seating amidst seven-meter-high bamboo, lots of light, and fantastic views of the Kanto Plain and Mt. Fuji (if it's clear). For those days when a light, early dinner will do (or a late lunch?), this is the perfect setting in which to take high tea, complete with salmon and cream cheese, bone ham, cucumber, egg and mustard cress sandwiches, fresh scones, pastries, and tea.

Shakey's

3-30-11 Shinjuku. ☎ **03/3341-0322.** All-you-can-eat pizza lunch ¥600 ($6). No credit cards. Daily 11am–2pm. Station: Shinjuku Sanchome (1 minute). PIZZA.

If you want to gorge yourself on pizza, the best deal is at one of the 20 or so Shakey's around town, offering great all-you-can-eat pizza, spaghetti, and fried potatoes for lunch every day from 11am to 2pm. The Shakey's in Shinjuku is across the street from the Isetan department store on Shinjuku Dori.

MEGURO & SHINAGAWA

EXPENSIVE

Yamatoya Sangen

Miyako Hotel, 1-1-50 Shiroganedai. ☎ **03/3445-0058.** Set dinners ¥7,800–¥13,000 ($78–$130); set lunches ¥2,500–¥12,000 ($25–$120). AE, DC, JCB, MC, V. Daily 11:30am–2pm and 5–9:30pm. VARIED JAPANESE.

Although Japanese restaurants usually specialize in only one type of cooking, this hotel restaurant serves a variety of foods, from shabu-shabu, tempura, kaiseki, and sushi to eel. Each cuisine is given appropriate care, however. If you've been intimidated by the thought of eel, this is a good place to try it for the first time. The restaurant overlooks the hotel's Japanese garden and is simply decorated with shoji screens and slats of wood.

INEXPENSIVE

Tonki (32)

1-1-2 Shimo Meguro, Meguro-ku. ☎ **03/3491-9928.** Set meal ¥1,500 ($15). JCB, V. Wed–Mon 4–11pm (last order 10:30pm). Closed third Mon of each month. Station: Meguro (west exit, 1 minute). TONKATSU.

This is probably the best-known *tonkatsu* (pork cutlet) restaurant in town, and you'll probably have to wait for a seat at the counter. A man will ask whether you want the *hirekatsu* (a filet cut of lean pork) or the *rosukatsu* (loin cut). If you're uncertain, he'll hold up the two slabs of meat and you just point to one. No matter which you pick, ask for the teishoku, the set meal, featuring soup, rice, cabbage, pickled vegetable, and tea. The man will scribble your order down on a piece of paper and put it with all the other scraps of paper, miraculously keeping track of not only which order belongs to whom but also which customers have been waiting for a seat the longest. The open kitchen behind the counter takes up most of the space in the restaurant, and as you eat you can watch the dozen or so cooks scrambling to turn out orders. Never a dull moment. You can get free refills of tea and cabbage. Tonki is on the west side of the station, down the street with Sanwa bank; take the next left. It has blue curtains over its sliding glass doors. A Tonki annex (☎ 03/3443-1577) is on the east side of the station, across the street, on the 2nd floor.

ASAKUSA

EXPENSIVE

Mugitoro (33)

2-2-4 Kaminarimon. ☎ **03/3842-1066.** Reservations recommended. Set dinners ¥6,000–¥13,000 ($60–$130); set lunch ¥3,500 ($35). AE, DC, JCB, MC, V. Daily 11:30am–8:30pm (last order). Station: Asakusa (2 minutes). YAMS.

Founded about 60 years ago but now housed in a new building, this restaurant specializes in *tororo-imo* (yam). Popular as a health food, yams are featured in almost all the dishes; the menu changes monthly. If you're walking here from Sensoji Temple, walk south on Edo Dori (with your back to Kaminarimon Gate) until you reach the first big intersection. Komagatabashi Bridge will be to your left, and Mugitoro is right beside the bridge and a tiny playground. Look for the big white lanterns hanging outside.

Kuremutsu (34)

2-2-13 Asakusa. ☎ **03/3842-0906.** Reservations required. Set meals from ¥8,000 ($80); kaiseki meals from ¥9,000 ($90). No credit cards. Fri–Wed 4–10pm. Station: Asakusa (5 minutes). KAISEKI/JAPANESE GRILL.

Located just southeast of Sensoji Temple, Kuremutsu is actually a tiny house tucked behind an inviting courtyard with a willow tree, a millstone covered with moss, and an entrance invitingly lit with lanterns. Inside, it's like a farmhouse in the countryside, filled with farm implements, old chests, masks, cast-iron tea kettles, hibachi, and other odds and ends. Traditionally dressed to match the mood, waitresses will bring you fresh grilled fish, the restaurant's specialty, as well as platters of assorted sashimi and kaiseki. The menu is in Japanese only, and since only cash is accepted, make sure you know what you've ordered.

MODERATE

Komagata Dojo (35)

1-7-12 Komagata, Taito-ku. ☎ **03/3842-4001.** Reservations recommended for dinner. Dishes ¥300–¥1,500 ($3–$15); set dinners ¥2,000–¥6,000 ($20–$60); teishoku ¥3,600 ($36). DC, JCB, MC, V. Daily 11am–9pm. Station: Asakusa (3 minutes). DOJO.

Following a tradition spanning more than 185 years, this old-style dining hall specializes in *dojo,* a tiny sardinelike river fish that translates as a "loach." It's served in a variety of styles, from grilled to stewed. Teishoku are available throughout the day. The dining area is simply one large room of tatami mats, with ground-level boards serving as tables and waitresses in traditional dress moving quietly about. To reach the restaurant, walk south on Edo Dori (away from Kaminarimon Gate and Sensoji Temple). The restaurant—a large, old-fashioned house on a corner, with blue curtains at its door—is on the right side of the street, about a five-minute walk from Kaminarimon Gate, past the Bank of Tokyo.

INEXPENSIVE

Chinya (36)

1-3-4 Asakusa. ☎ **03/3841-0010.** ¥2,900–¥6,000 ($29–$60). DC, JCB, MC, V. Thurs–Tues 11:30am–9:15pm. Station: Asakusa (1 minute). SHABU-SHABU/SUKIYAKI.

Established in 1880, Chinya is an old sukiyaki restaurant with a new home in a seven-story building, located to the left of the Kaminarimon Gate if you stand facing the famous Asakusa Kannon Temple (look for the sukiyaki sign). The entrance to this place is open-fronted. To the left of this main entrance is another entrance, leading to the basement, where you'll find a small, one-room casual eatery offering inexpensive plates of sukiyaki and shabu-shabu. Seating is around a counter, where you can watch the cooks at work. If you feel like a more relaxed meal, the main restaurant upstairs offers a very good shabu-shabu or sukiyaki set lunch for ¥2,500 ($25), available until 3pm and including soup and side dishes.

Daikokuya (37)

1-38-10 Asakusa. ☎ **03/3844-1111.** ¥1,450–¥1,700 ($14.50–$17). No credit cards. Thurs–Tues 11am–8:30pm. Station: Asakusa (5 minutes). TEMPURA.

This simple tempura restaurant has been popular with the locals since 1887, and though it does not offer the most refined tempura, it has atmosphere. The specialty is *ebi tendon* (prawn tempura on a bowl of rice), but you might try the tempura *ebi* (shrimp), *kisu* (smelt), or *kaki* (oysters). Daikokuya is off Nakamise Dori, to the west. To reach it, take the small street that passes by the south side of Dempoin Temple (also spelled Demboin); the restaurant is at the first intersection, a white corner building with a Japanese-style tiled roof and sliding front door. They have an annex around the corner for the overflow.

Kamiya Bar

1-1-1 Asakusa. ☎ **03/3841-5400.** ¥250–¥1,400 ($2.50–$14). No credit cards. Wed–Mon 11:30am–9:30pm (last order). Station: Asakusa (1 minute). JAPANESE/WESTERN.

This inexpensive eatery, established in 1880 as the first Western bar in Japan, serves both Japanese and Western fare on its three floors. The first and second floors offer Western food, including fried chicken, smoked salmon, spaghetti, fried shrimp, and hamburger steak, while the third floor serves Japanese food ranging from udon noodles and yakitori to tempura and sashimi. I personally prefer the third floor, for both its food and its atmosphere. Although the menus are in Japanese only, there are extensive plastic-food display cases. In any case, this is a very casual restaurant, very much a place for the locals. It can be quite noisy and crowded. A plain brown-tiled building, Kamiya Bar is located almost on top of the Asakusa subway station, not far from Kaminarimon Gate.

Keyaki (38)

1-34-5 Asakusa. ☎ **03/3844-9012.** A la carte dishes ¥550–¥9,000 ($5.50–$90); lunch teishoku ¥1,200–¥1,800 ($12–$18). No credit cards. Tues–Sun 11:30am–2pm and 5–10pm. Station: Asakusa (3 minutes). EEL.

This eel restaurant is on the second street parallel to and east of Nakamise Dori—look for the brown flag with an eel on it and for the fish tank just inside the front door. A small place, with just a counter, a couple of tables, and an adjoining tatami room, Keyaki offers an eel set-lunch course (*unagi seto*), as well as tempura or sashimi courses. Try the house specialty, a sake called *ginjo-shu.*

✪ Namiki (39)

2-11-9 Kaminarimon. ☎ **03/3841-1340.** ¥600–¥1,500 ($6–$15). No credit cards. Fri–Wed 11:30am–7:30pm. Station: Asakusa (3 minutes). NOODLES.

Asakusa's best-known noodle shop offers plain noodles in cold or hot broth, as well as more substantial tempura and noodles—on an English menu. Seating is at tables or on tatami mats, but since it's small you won't be able to linger if people are waiting. To reach the restaurant, take the road that leads south and away from Asakusa Kannon Temple and Kaminarimon Gate. Namiki is a brown building on the right side of the street, with some bamboo trees by the front door.

UENO

EXPENSIVE

Izu'ei (40)

2-12-22 Ueno. ☎ **03/3831-0954.** Reservations recommended. Main dishes ¥1,500–¥3,000 ($15–$30); set meals ¥2,000–¥20,000 ($20–$200). AE, DC, JCB, MC, V. Daily 11am–9:30pm. Station: JR Ueno Station (3 minutes). EEL.

Put aside all your prejudices about eels and head for this modern, yet traditionally decorated restaurant with a 260-year history dating back to the Edo Period. Since eels are grilled over charcoal, the Japanese place a lot of stock in the quality of the charcoal used, and this place boasts its own furnace in the mountains of Wakayama Prefecture, which produces the best charcoal in Japan. *Unagi donburi* (rice with strips of eel on top), tempura, and sushi are available. Izu'ei is across the street from Shinobazu Pond and the Shitamachi Museum.

INEXPENSIVE

Maharaja

Nagafuji Bldg. Annex, 3rd floor, 4-9-6 Ueno. ☎ **03/3835-0818.** Main dishes ¥1,100–¥1,900 ($11–$19); set meals ¥1,150–¥2,200 ($11.50–$22); weekday set lunch ¥1,000 ($10); Sat–Sun buffet ¥1,300 ($13). No credit cards. Daily 11am–9:30pm. Station: JR Ueno (2 minutes). INDIAN.

This spotless modern restaurant offers curries and tandoori at inexpensive prices. If you are in Ueno on Saturday or Sunday, take advantage of the all-you-can-eat buffet served from 11am to 3pm. Decorated in peach and pink, with etched mirrors and lots of brass, Maharaja is located in a modern building situated between busy Chuo Dori and the Ameyokocho shopping street.

SHIBUYA & DAIKANYAMA

MODERATE

Deux Maggots

Bunkamura, 2-24-1 Dogenzaka. ☎ **03/3477-9124.** Main dishes ¥1,000–¥3,000 ($10–$30); sandwiches ¥800–¥1,200 ($8–$12); set lunches ¥1,300–¥3,500 ($13–$35); set dinners ¥3,500–¥7,000 ($35–$70). AE, DC, JCB, MC, V. Daily 11am–10:30pm. Station: Shibuya (5 minutes). FRENCH BISTRO.

Rich wood paneling, people-watching windows, a bridge from which one looks down on the diners two floors below, and terrace seating make this a sophisticated stop for lunch or coffee. A joint venture with the Parisian Les Deux Maggots (literati hangout since 1885), dine here on *paupiette de langoustine* or something less serious like *croque monsieur.* In the sleek Bunkamura complex, Japan's largest cultural center, it's the best escape from Shibuya's teeny-bopper scene and crowds.

Tableaux

Sunroser Daikanyama Bldg., 11-6 Sarugaku-cho. ☎ **03/5489-2201.** Main dishes ¥1,300–¥4,800 ($13–$48); set lunches ¥1,200–¥3,200 ($12–$32). AE, DC, JCB, MC, V. Mon–Sat 11:30am–2pm; Sun 11:30am–2:30pm; Sun–Thurs 5:30–10:30pm; Fri–Sat 5:30–11pm; tea lounge Mon–Fri 2–5:30pm. Station: Daikanyama (5 minutes). INTERNATIONAL.

Designer Margaret O'Brien created a rich Russian-tearoom atmosphere, using bead-fringed curtains, gilt mirrors, chandeliers, stars and moons, animal-skin, velvet upholstery, and deep colors. The food is excellent and reasonable despite the avant-garde setting and clientele. For the health-conscious, there's a large selection of vegetarian dishes and fish or charcoal-grilled free-range chicken. For the rest, order zuwai crab pancakes with whipped cream cheese, chives, and Beluga caviar or sautéed foie gras. An English menu and an American manager make ordering easy and service assured. After dining, try the coffee/tea and cake set for ¥500 ($5). Your selection of herb and black teas will be ceremoniously offered from a cigar box. You might want to come just for tea and enjoy the interior design.

INEXPENSIVE

$ Irohanihoheto (30)

1-19-3 Jinnan, Shibuya-ku. ☎ **03/3476-1682.** ¥350–¥980 ($3.50–$9.80). No credit cards. Sun–Thur 5pm–2am; Fri–Sat 5pm–4am. Station: Shibuya (10 minutes). YAKITORI/VARIED.

This boisterous drinking establishment offers inexpensive dining and is extremely popular with university students; if you get here after 7pm, you may have to wait for a place to sit. The extensive menu of both Japanese and Western food is in Japanese, but with pictures, and features *nikujaga* (potato-and-meat stew), fried tofu, *oden* (a tofu, fishcake, and vegetable stew), yakitori, fried noodles, potato salad, sashimi, and much more. Near the Parco I and II department stores, the restaurant is a little hard to find. Once you get to Parco, you'll probably have to ask someone on the street (it's in the basement of a modern building).

Laura Ashley

Tokyu Honten, 2-24-1 Dogenzaka, Shibuya-ku. ☎ **03/3477-3111.** Tea and coffee ¥700 ($7); high tea ¥1,500 ($15); sandwiches ¥600–¥1,200 ($6–$12). Wed–Mon 10am–6:30pm. Station: Shibuya (5 minutes). TEA.

Laura Ashley–clad pinafored waitresses and Laura Ashley tablecloths and dishes set the mood for this tearoom. You can order scones and cakes with your tea or coffee, or you can go all out for the high tea served with sandwiches, cakes, and scones. Laura Ashley is on the fourth floor of the main Tokyu department store, which is next to Bunkamura—literally "culture village," a complex of museum, theaters, bookstore, and shops, worth a stroll.

The Prime

2-29-5 Dogenzaka. ☎ **03/3770-0111.** ¥500–¥1,000 ($5–$10); set lunches ¥500–¥1,200 ($5–$12). No credit cards. Daily 11:30am–10pm. Station: Shibuya (3 minutes). INTERNATIONAL.

If you're in Shibuya, it's worth checking out the Prime on Dogenzaka. It's filled with restaurants and amusements. The second floor is a large cafeteria, with various counters offering dishes from around the world, ranging from bagels and sandwiches to Indian curries, Chinese food, sushi, salads, and pastas. The advantage is seeing what you're ordering. In the basement is a noisy pachinko parlor with the unlikely name Orchestra. Who's conducting?

Red Thunder Cafe

24-1 Sarugaku-cho. ☎ **03/3462-4750.** Main dishes ¥800–¥1,600 ($8–$16); set meals ¥1,200–¥2,000 ($12–$20). AE, JCB, MC, V. Daily noon–4am. Station: Daikonyama (5 minutes). TEX-MEX/NATIVE AMERICAN.

Rough wood, horse blankets, and other Wild West trappings, plus Harleys parked in front, create this biker-cum-Southwest cafe/saloon featuring faux mud walls. The roof rolls back to create outdoor seating. Appetizers from nachos to chili con carne go down well with beer or magaritas. The huge Mexican hamburger steak and the Navajo fry bread are popular.

Shizenkan II

3-9-2 Shibuya. ☎ **03/3486-0281.** Set meals ¥750–¥1,500 ($7.50–$15). MC, V. Open Mon–Sat 11am–8pm. Station: Shibuya (2 minutes). VEGETARIAN.

Although the decor is uninteresting (half health food store/half seating at big communal tables), healthy inexpensive meals are served here. Food displays outside show sample menus. The monk's set (*Rokukaku ryori*) has a selection of different vegetarian dishes and includes brown rice, soup, coffee, and cake. A good place for a quiet meal.

OTHER NEIGHBORHOODS

MODERATE

Hanezawa Beer Garden

3-12-15 Hiroo, Shibuya-ku. ☎ **03/3400-6500.** Reservations required. Main dishes ¥5,000–¥6,000 ($50–$60). No credit cards. Daily 5–9pm. Closed Oct–Mar. Station: Ebisu, Omotesando, or Shibuya; then take a taxi. JAPANESE BARBECUE.

This is a lovely place to go for a meal and drinks. An outdoor garden spread under trees and paper lanterns, it looks traditionally Japanese and serves sukiyaki, shabu-shabu, Mongolian barbecue (cooked at your table), and a variety of snacks and other dishes. Note that if you want shabu-shabu or sukiyaki, however, you should notify the restaurant the day before. A mug of foaming beer starts at ¥500 ($5).

✪ Kandagawa (41)

2-5-11 Soto, Kanda. ☎ **03/3251-5031.** Reservations required. Main dishes ¥2,300–¥3,500 ($23–$35). MC. Mon–Sat 11:30am–2pm and 5–7pm. Closed national hols. Station: Akihabara (5 minutes). EEL.

Dining in this beautiful, old-fashioned, traditional Japanese restaurant, famous for its eel dishes since the Edo Period, is unforgettable. A Japanese-style wooden house, hidden behind a wooden gate, it offers seven private tatami rooms, as well as a larger tatami dining room. The menu, in Japanese only, offers side dishes of soup, rice, and Japanese pickles, and such main dishes as *kabayaki* (broiled and basted eel); *unaju* (broiled eel on rice with a sweet sauce); *shiroyaki* ("white" eel, broiled without soy sauce or oil); and *umaki* (eel wrapped in an omelet). There's also grilled eel's liver, plus sashimi. Expect to spend a minimum of ¥7,500 ($75) per person, including drinks, appetizers, tax, and service. Since no one here speaks English, it's best to have a Japanese make your reservation, at which time you must order the dishes you'd like to be served.

INEXPENSIVE

✪ Nomi no Ichi

2-17-8 Ebisu, Shibuya-ku. ☎ **03/5420-3691.** Set lunch ¥1,000 ($10); set dinner ¥2,900 ($29); French wines ¥3,300–¥7,500 ($33–$75). AE, DC, MC, V. Mon–Thur 11:30am–2pm and 6–11pm; Sat and hols 6–11pm. Station: Hiroo or Ebisu (10 minutes). TRADITIONAL FRENCH.

Nomi no Ichi (or *Marché aux Puces*) got its name from the deco-style furnishings bought at flea markets, but there the resemblance to anything discount ends. Simply put, this is the best French restaurant in terms of quality to price in Japan. Mr. Kondo, owner, chef, and former French resident, entices French customers (70% of the clientele) with classic French *salade foie gras, côtes d'agneaux au thym,* and *confit de canard* at unbelievably low (for Japan) prices. Lunch includes soup, appetizer, and fish or meat, while dinner includes an appetizer, main course, desserts or *fromage,* and café. As in France, linger at your table (perhaps over mouthwatering desserts) as long as you like.

Yabu-Soba (42)

2-10 Awajicho, Kanda. ☎ **03/3251-0287.** ¥600–¥1,500 ($6–$15). No credit cards. Tues–Sun 11:30am–7pm. Station: Awajicho (5 minutes) or Akihabara (10 minutes). NOODLES.

Soba (noodle) shops are among the least expensive restaurants in Japan, and this is one of Tokyo's most famous noodle places, established in 1880. Surrounded by a wooden gate and with a small bamboo-and-rock garden, the house features shoji screens, a wooden ceiling, and a dining area with tatami mats and tables. It is filled with middle-aged businessmen and housewives, so if you come during lunchtime you may have to wait for a seat. There's a menu in English, featuring noodles with shredded yam, topped with crispy shrimp tempura or served with grilled eel. Listen to the woman sitting at a small counter by the kitchen—she sings out orders to the chef, as well as hellos and good-byes to customers. Yabu-Soba is located between Awajicho and Akihabara stations, near Sotobori Dori and Yasukuni Dori.

What to See & Do in Tokyo

5

Tokyo hasn't fared very well over the centuries. Fires and earthquakes have taken their toll, old buildings have been torn down in the zeal of modernization, and World War II left most of the city in ruins. The Tokyo of today has very little remaining of historical significance. Save your historical sightseeing for places like Kyoto, Nikko, and Kamakura, and consider Tokyo your introduction to Japan's economic miracle, the showcase of the nation's accomplishments in the arts, technology, fashion, and design. It's the best place in the world for taking in Japan's performing arts, such as Kabuki, and such diverse activities as the tea ceremony and flower arranging. Tokyo also has more museums than any other city in Japan, as well as a wide range of other attractions—from parks to temples. Go shopping, explore mammoth department stores, experiment with restaurants, visit museums, walk around the city's various neighborhoods, and take advantage of its glittering nightlife. There are plenty of things to do in Tokyo. I can't imagine being bored even for a minute.

SUGGESTED ITINERARIES

Two things to remember in planning your sightseeing itinerary are that the city is huge and that it takes time to get from one end to the other. Plan your days so you cover it neighborhood by neighborhood, coordinating sightseeing with dinner and evening plans. To help you get the most out of your stay, the suggested itineraries below will guide you to the most important attractions. Note, however, that some attractions are closed one day of the week, so plan your days accordingly.

IF YOU HAVE 1 DAY Start by getting up in the wee hours of the morning (if you've just flown in from North America, you'll be suffering from jet lag anyway and will find yourself wide awake by 5am) and head for the Tsukiji Fish Market, Japan's largest wholesale fish market (closed Sunday and holidays). Be brave and try a breakfast of the freshest sushi you'll ever have. By 9am you should be on the Hibiya Line on your way to Ueno, where you should race to the Tokyo National Museum, the country's largest and most important museum (closed Monday). From there you should head to Asakusa for lunch in one of the area's traditional Japanese restaurants, followed by a walk on Nakamise Dori (good for souvenirs) to Sensoji

Temple. In the afternoon you might want to go to Ginza for some shopping, followed by dinner in a restaurant of your choice. Drop by a yakitori-ya, a typical Japanese watering hole, for a beer and a snack. You might be exhausted by the end of the day, but you'll have seen some of the city's highlights.

IF YOU HAVE 2 DAYS Because two days still isn't much time, on the first day get up early and go to Tsukiji Fish Market to eat sushi for breakfast. Next, head for the nearby Hama Rikyu Garden, which opens at 9am (closed Monday). It's about a 20-minute walk from Tsukiji, or a short taxi ride away. After touring the garden, board the ferry that departs from inside the grounds for a trip up the Sumida River to Asakusa, where you can visit Sensoji Temple and shop along Nakamise Dori, followed by lunch in a traditional Japanese restaurant. In early afternoon, head to Hibiya for a glimpse of the Imperial Palace (closed to the public), followed by a stroll through Ginza and some shopping. If there's a performance, drop by the Kabukiza theater for part of a Kabuki play. Have dinner at a Ginza restaurant or at a yakitori-ya.

On the second day, head for Ueno, where you should walk through Ueno Park to the Tokyo National Museum. For lunch, board the Yamanote Line and go to Shinjuku Station, where, on the west side, there are a number of skyscrapers with top-floor restaurants that offer panoramic views of the city. After lunch, reboard the Yamanote Line and go two stations south to Harajuku, where you can visit Meiji Jingu Shrine, Tokyo's most famous Shinto shrine; the Ota Memorial Museum of Art, with its collection of woodblock prints; and the Oriental Bazaar, a great shop for souvenirs. Devote the rest of your afternoon to shopping, visiting more museums, or other attractions. Spend the evening in one of Tokyo's famous nightlife districts, such as Shinjuku or Roppongi.

IF YOU HAVE 3 DAYS Spend the first two days as outlined above, and on the third day head for Kamakura, one of Japan's most important historical sites. Located an hour south of Tokyo by train, Kamakura served as the capital back in the 1100s and is packed with temples and shrines.

IF YOU HAVE 4 DAYS OR MORE Consider yourself lucky. Spend the first three days as outlined above. Devote the fourth day to pursuing your own interests, such as a trip to one of Tokyo's numerous specialty museums or a sumo stable, an appointment with an acupuncturist, shopping, or following one of the recommended walking tours in this chapter. This may be the evening to spend in wild partying, staying out until the first subways start running at 5am.

On the fifth day, you might visit Nikko, approximately two hours north of Tokyo, to see the sumptuous mausoleum of Tokugawa Ieyasu, the shogun who succeeded in unifying Japan in the 1600s or you might consider a two-day trip to Hakone, famous for its open-air sculpture museum. Hakone also has some of the best old-fashioned Japanese inns near Tokyo, and if the weather is clear, it also offers great views of Mt. Fuji. See chapter 6 for more excursions.

1 The Top Attractions

The Imperial Palace

The Imperial Palace, where Japan's imperial family lives, can be considered the heart of Tokyo. Built on the very spot where Edo Castle used to stand during the days of the Tokugawa shogunate, it became the imperial home at its completion in 1888. The original structure was destroyed during air raids in 1945, and the palace was rebuilt in 1968. Except on New Year's Day and on the Emperor's Birthday (December 23), when the grounds are open to the public, the palace remains off-limits to

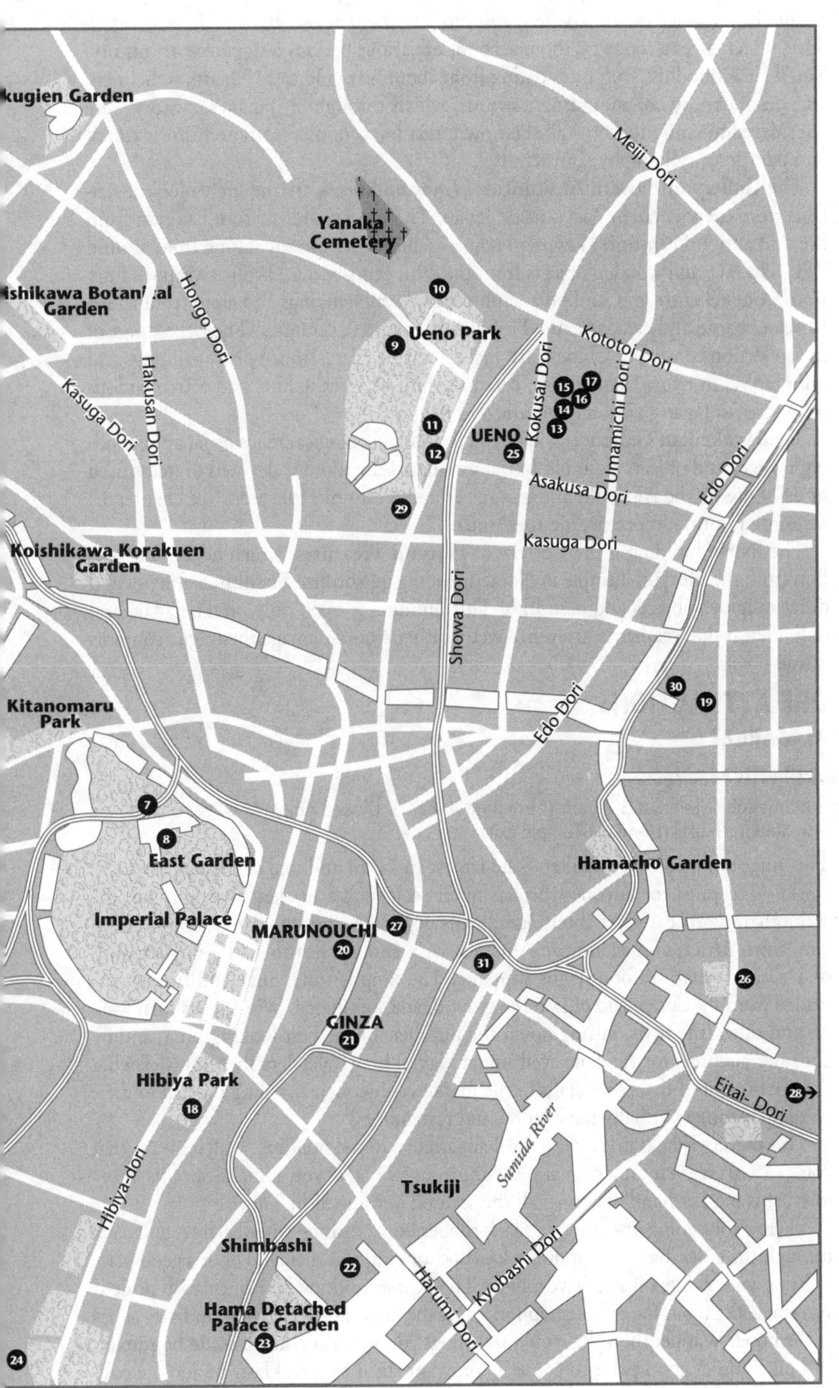
kugien Garden
Yanaka Cemetery
ishikawa Botani al Garden
Hongo Dori
Meiji Dori
Ueno Park
Kototoi Dori
Kasuga Dori
Hakusan Dori
Kokusai Dori
Umamichi Dori
UENO
Asakusa Dori
Edo Dori
Kasuga Dori
Koishikawa Korakuen Garden
Showa Dori
Kitanomaru Park
Edo Dori
East Garden
Hamacho Garden
Imperial Palace
MARUNOUCHI
GINZA
Hibiya Park
Eitai- Dori
Sumida River
Tsukiji
Hibiya-dori
Shimbashi
Kyobashi Dori
Harumi Dori
Hama Detached Palace Garden
7
8
9
10
11
12
13
14
15
16
17
18
19
20
21
22
23
24
25
26
27
28
29
30
31

inside the entrance is a desk where you can buy the *Tokyo National Museum Handbook,* which gives a room-by-room account of various periods in Japanese art history. You'll view Buddhist sculptures dating from about A.D. 538 to 1192; armor, helmets, and decorative sword mountings; swords, which throughout Japanese history were considered to embody spirits all their own; textiles; ceramics from prehistoric times; and paintings, calligraphy, and scrolls.

The **Gallery of Eastern Antiquities** (*Toyokan*) houses art and archeological artifacts from everywhere in Asia outside Japan. There are Buddhas from Pakistan from the 2nd and 3rd centuries; Egyptian relics, including a mummy dating from around 751–656 B.C. and wooden objects from the 20th century B.C.; bronze weapons from Iran; stone reliefs from Cambodia; embroidered wall hangings and cloth from India; Korean bronze and celadon; and Thai and Vietnamese ceramics. The largest part of the collection consists of Chinese art, including jade, glass, stone reliefs, paintings and calligraphy, mirrors, lacquerware, ceramics, and bronzes. China had a tremendous influence on Japan's art, architecture, and religion.

The **Hyokeikan Gallery** is where you'll find archeological relics of Japan, including pottery and objects from old burial mounds. One room is devoted to items used in daily life by the Ainu, the indigenous ethnic group of Hokkaido (see chapter 12 for more information regarding the Ainu).

The fourth building is the **Gallery of Horyuji Treasures,** which houses a collection from the Horyuji Temple in Nara, including gilt-bronze Buddhist statuettes and other religious objects and paintings. This building is open only on Thursday, and only then if the weather is dry, since wet weather would damage the fragile contents inside.

MORE ATTRACTIONS

FISH MARKET

Tsukiji Fish Market

Free admission. Mon–Sat 3–10am (best time 4–8am). Closed hols, New Year's, and Aug 15–16. Station: Tsukiji (Honganji Temple exit).

This huge wholesale fish market—the largest in Japan and one of the largest in the world—is a must for anyone who has never seen such a market in action, and the action here starts early. At about 3am, boats begin arriving from the seas around Japan, from Africa, and even from America, with enough fish to satisfy the demands of a nation where seafood reigns supreme. The king is tuna, huge and frozen, unloaded from the docks, laid out on the ground, and numbered. Wholesalers then walk up and down the rows, jotting down the numbers of the best-looking tuna, and by 6am the auctions for tuna are well under way. The wholesalers then transfer what they've bought to their own stalls in the market, subsequently selling the fish to their regular customers, usually retail stores and restaurants.

This market is held in a cavernous, hangarlike covered building, which means that you can visit it even on a dismal rainy morning. To give you some idea of its enormity, this market handles almost all the seafood consumed in Tokyo.

There's a lot going on—men in black rubber boots rushing wheelbarrows and carts through the aisles, hawkers shouting, knives chopping and slicing. This is a good place to bring your camera if you have a flash: The people working here burst with pride if you single them out for a photograph. Because the floors are wet, leave your fancy shoes at the hotel. Wander the aisles, you'll see things you wouldn't dream could be edible.

This is also a good place to come if you want sushi for breakfast. Beside the covered market are rows of barracklike buildings divided into sushi restaurants and shops

Frommer's Favorite Tokyo Experiences

A Stroll Through Sensoji Temple. More than any other place in Tokyo, Sensoji Temple and the surrounding Asakusa convey a feeling of old Tokyo. Nakamise Dori, the pedestrian lane leading to the temple, is lined with shops selling souvenirs and traditional Japanese goods.

An Evening in a Yakitori-ya. There's no better place to observe Tokyo's army of office workers at play than at a yakitori-ya, a drinking establishment that serves skewered foods and bar snacks. Fun, noisy, and boisterous.

A Kabuki Play at the Kabukiza Theater. Kabuki has served as the most popular form of entertainment for the masses since the Edo Period. Watch the audience as they yell their approval; watch the stage for its gorgeous costumes, stunning stage settings, and easy-to-understand dramas of love, duty, and revenge.

Sunday in Harajuku. Start with a Sunday brunch; then stroll the promenade of Omotesando Dori to the Olympic stadiums, where young musicians, dancers, and performers entertain the crowds. Shop the area's boutiques; relax at a sidewalk cafe.

A Day of Sumo. Nothing beats watching huge sumo wrestlers, most weighing well over 200 pounds, throw each other around. Matches are held in Tokyo in January, May, and September. Great fun and not to be missed.

Department Store Shopping. Tokyo's department stores are huge, spotless, and filled with merchandise you never knew existed. Tobu in Ikebukuro is the city's largest, a virtual city in itself. The greatest concentration is in Shibuya. Be the first to enter in the morning and you can see all the employees lined up to bow to incoming customers.

A Spin Through Kabuki-cho. Shinjuku's Kabuki-cho has the craziest nightlife in all of Tokyo, with countless strip joints, pornography shops, restaurants, bars, and the greatest concentration of neon you're likely to see anywhere. A fascinating place for an evening's stroll.

Clubs in Roppongi. You can dance and party the night away in the madness that's Roppongi; most revelers party till dawn.

related to the fish trade. Sushi Dai, for example, offers a *seto* for ¥2,000 ($20); it's open every day except Sunday and holidays from 5am to 2pm.

As you walk the distance between the Tsukiji subway station and the fish market, you'll find yourself in a delightful district of tiny retail shops and stalls where you can buy the freshest seafood in town, plus dried fish and fish products, seaweed, vegetables, and cooking utensils. In this area and beside the market are stalls selling cheap sushi, noodles, and fish, catering mainly to buyers and sellers at the market who come for a quick breakfast.

There are also a lot of pottery shops and stores that sell plastic and lacquered trays, bowls, and cups. Although they usually sell in great quantities to restaurant owners, shopkeepers will usually sell to the casual tourist as well.

PARKS & GARDENS

Although Japan's most famous gardens are not in Tokyo, the first three places listed below use principles of Japanese landscaping and give visitors an idea of the scope and style of these gardens. The fourth listing, Ueno Park, is Tokyo's largest park and contains a number of museums and attractions, making it one of the city's most visited places.

Hama Rikyu Garden

1-1 Hamarikyuteien, Chuo-ku. ☎ **03/3541-0200.** Admission ¥300 ($3). Tues–Sun 9am–4:30pm. Station: Shimbashi (10 minutes).

Considered by some to be the best garden in Tokyo, this was once the site of a villa of a former feudal lord where the Tokugawa shoguns practiced falconry. In 1871 possession of the garden passed to the imperial family, and it was opened to the public after World War II. Come here to see how the upper classes enjoyed themselves during the Edo Period. Surrounded by water on three sides, the garden contains an inner tidal pool, spanned by three bridges draped with wisteria. There are also other ponds, a promenade along the river lined with pine trees, moon-viewing pavilions, and teahouses. From a boarding pier inside the garden's grounds, ferries depart for Asakusa every hour or so between 10am (10:15am on weekends and holidays) and 4:05pm; the fare is ¥560 ($5.60) one-way.

East Garden

1-1 Chiyoda, Chiyoda-ku. ☎ **03/3213-1111.** Free admission. Tues–Thurs and Sat–Sun 9am–4pm (enter by 3pm). Station: Otemachi, Takebashi, or Nijubashi-mae.

The 53 acres of the formal *Higashi Gyoen* were once part of Edo Castle, of which a stone foundation still remains. A pleasant and peaceful oasis right in the heart of the city, the garden contains sculpted bushes and a pond framed with wisteria. It's east of the Imperial Palace.

Shinjuku Gyoen

11 Naitocho, Shinjuku-ku. ☎ **03/3350-0151.** Admission ¥200 ($2). Tues–Sun 9am–4:30pm (enter by 4pm). Station: Shinjuku Gyoen-mae (2 minutes).

Formerly the private estate of a feudal lord and then of the imperial family, this is a wonderful park for strolling because of the variety of its planted gardens—styles ranging from French and English to Japanese traditional. It amazes me every time I go there. The park's 144 acres make it one of the city's largest, and each bend in the pathway brings something completely different: Ponds and sculpted bushes give way to a promenade lined with sycamores, which opens up into a rose garden. Cherry blossoms, azaleas, chrysanthemums, and other flowers provide splashes of color from spring through autumn. A greenhouse is filled with tropical plants.

Ueno Park

Taito-ku. Free admission to Ueno Park; separate admissions to each of its attractions. Ueno Park, daily 24 hours. Station: Ueno (1 minute).

Ueno Park and its many attractions—on the northeast edge of the Yamanote Line—constitute one of the most popular places in Tokyo for Japanese families on a day's outing. Opened in 1873, it was the city's first public park and the first place in Japan to see the establishment of a museum and a zoo. Today, it's one of the largest parks in Tokyo and a cultural mecca with a number of museums, including the prestigious **Tokyo National Museum** and the delightful **Shitamachi Museum,** with its displays of old Tokyo; **Ueno Zoo;** and **Shinobazu Pond,** a bird sanctuary.

A landmark in the park is a **statue of Takamori Saigo,** a samurai born in 1827 near Kagoshima on Kyushu Island. After helping restore the emperor to power after the downfall of the Tokugawa shogunate, Saigo subsequently became disenchanted with the Meiji regime when rights enjoyed by the military class were suddenly rescinded. He led a revolt that failed, and ended up taking his own life in ritualistic suicide. The statue, erected in 1898, became the center of controversy when

Gen. Douglas MacArthur, leader of the occupation forces in Japan after World War II, demanded that the statue be removed because of its ties to nationalism. The Japanese people protested in a large public outcry, and MacArthur finally relented. Today, the statue is one of the best known in Tokyo.

Another well-known landmark in Ueno Park is **Toshogu Shrine.** Erected in 1651, it is dedicated to Tokugawa Ieyasu, founder of the Tokugawa shogunate. Stop here to pay respects to the man who made Edo (present-day Tokyo) the seat of his government and thus elevated the small village to the most important city in the country. The pathway to the shrine is lined with massive stone lanterns that were donated by various feudal lords.

The busiest time of the year at Ueno Park is in April, during the cherry-blossom season, and people come here en masse to celebrate the birth of the new season. It's not the spiritual communion with nature that you might think, however. In the daytime on a weekday, Ueno Park may be peaceful and sane enough, but on the weekends and in the evenings during cherry-blossom season, havoc prevails as office workers break out of their winter shells. Whole companies of workers converge on Ueno Park to sit under the cherry trees on plastic or cardboard, where they drink sake and beer and get drunk and rowdy. The worst offenders are those who sing loudly into microphones, accompanied by cassettes playing the appropriate instrumental music to each song; this is a popular entertainment called karaoke, also found in special clubs devoted to it. At any rate, visiting Ueno Park during cherry-blossom season is an experience no one should miss. More than likely you'll be invited to join one of the large groups—by all means do.

OBSERVATION PLATFORM

Observatory

In the Sunshine City Bldg., 3-1-1 Higashi Ikebukuro. ☎ **03/3989-3331.** Admission ¥620 ($6.20), ¥310 ($3.10) children. Daily 10am–8:30pm. Station: Ikebukuro (5 minutes).

At the northern end of Tokyo is the 60-story Sunshine City Building. On the top floor is an observatory. A special elevator—reputedly the world's fastest—whisks you there in 35 seconds. If you want to forgo the price of the observatory and the fast elevator, take one of the regular elevators to the 59th floor, where you can relax over a cup of coffee at Le Trianon Lounge, open Monday through Saturday from 11:30am to midnight; Sunday from 11:30am to 11pm.

Tokyo Metropolitan Government Office (TMG)

2-8-1 Nishi-Shinjuku. ☎ **03/5321-1111.** Free admission. Tues–Sun 9:30am–5pm. Closed Tues when Mon is a hol, and Dec 29–Jan 3. Station: Shinjuku (10 minutes).

One of the purposes of the TMG is "a new face to symbolize Tokyo as a world metropolis." This shiny, new, architecturally interesting complex of three buildings (TMG No. 1, TMG No. 2, and the Assembly Building) succeeds. The observatories are located at a height of 202 meters (656.5 feet) on the 45th floors of both the north and south towers of the TMG No. 1 Building (height: 790 feet), with access from the first floor when ascending. When descending, you're requested to get off at the second floor. On the second floor are two history corners; the explanations are in Japanese only, but the videos and photos are self-explanatory and provide invaluable glimpses into how the city was. The Observatory is a large round room, making for a 360° view. A cafe in the center serves coffee, ice cream, toast, and cheesecake, all under ¥350 ($3.50). Of course, there's a souvenir shop, offering soap, perfume, postcards, and drinking glasses, among other items—all with Tokyo themes. Pick up a bilingual guide to the Observatory at the information desk on the first or second floor.

Tokyo Tower

4-2 Shiba Koen, Minato-ku. ☎ **03/3433-5111.** Admission to main observatory (493 feet high), ¥820 ($8.20) adults and ¥450 ($4.50) children 4–11; top observatory (820 feet high), ¥1,420 ($14.20) adults and ¥950 ($9.50) children 4–11. Apr–Oct, daily 9am–8pm; Nov–Mar, daily 9am–7pm. Station: Onarimon or Kamiyacho (5 minutes).

Japan's most famous observation tower, Tokyo Tower was built in 1958 and modeled after the Eiffel Tower in Paris. Lit up at night, this 1,089-foot tower is a familiar landmark in the city's landscape but has lost its popularity over the decades, with the construction of Tokyo's skyscrapers. The best time of year to go up is supposedly during Golden Week, at the beginning of May. With many Tokyoites gone from the city and most factories and businesses closed down, the air is thought to be the cleanest and clearest at this time, affording views of the far reaches of the city—and exactly how far this city stretches will amaze you.

MUSEUMS

Note that most museums are closed on Monday and the first three days of the New Year. If Monday happens to be a national holiday, however, most museums will remain open but will close Tuesday instead. Call beforehand to avoid disappointment. Remember, too, that you must enter museums at least 30 minutes before closing time. For a listing of current special exhibitions, consult the *Tokyo Journal*, published monthly.

Museums of the Arts

Goto Museum of Art

3-9-25 Kaminoge, Setagaya-ku. ☎ **03/3703-0661.** Admission ¥700 ($7) and up adults, ¥500 ($5) children. Tues–Sun 9:30am–4:30pm (enter by 4pm). Closed during exhibit changes. Station: Kaminoge on the Toyoko Line.

The *Goto Bijutsukan* houses fine arts and crafts of ancient Japan, China, and other Asian countries, including calligraphy, paintings, ceramics, and lacquerware. Surrounding the museum is a garden with a teahouse.

Hara Museum of Contemporary Art

4-7-25 Kita-Shinagawa, Shinagawa-ku. ☎ **03/3445-0651.** Admission ¥700 ($7) adults, ¥500 ($5) students and children. Tues, Thurs–Sun 10am–5pm; Wed 10am–8pm. Station: Shinagawa; then take a taxi.

Devoted to contemporary international and Japanese art, *Hara Bijutsukan* is housed in a Bauhaus-style art deco former Hara family home. The building itself is worth the trip. Featuring paintings and sculptures mainly from the 1950s and 1960s by Japanese and foreign artists, it also holds regular exhibitions for rising young artists.

National Museum of Modern Art

Kitanomaru Koen Park, Chiyoda-ku. ☎ **03/3214-2561.** Admission ¥900 ($9) adults, ¥500 ($5) students, ¥200 ($2) children; more for special exhibits. Tues–Thurs and Sat–Sun 10am–5pm; Fri 10am–7pm. Station: Takebashi (5 minutes).

The *Tokyo Kokuritsu Kindai Bijutsukan* displays modern Japanese art, including paintings, sculptures, prints, watercolors, and drawings, dating from the Meiji Period onward. This is the largest collection of modern Japanese art housed under one roof. A few Western artists are also represented. Note however, that contemporary art is now shown at the Museum of Contemporary Art, Tokyo (see below).

National Museum of Western Art

Ueno Park, Taito-ku. ☎ **03/3828-5131.** Admission ¥400 ($4) adults, ¥130 ($1.30) students, ¥70 (70¢) children. Tues–Sun 9:30am–5pm. Station: Ueno (5 minutes).

With a main building designed by Le Corbusier, the *Kokuritsu Seiyo Bijutsukan* features Western art, with a concentration on French impressionism. Artists include Renoir, Monet, Sisley, Manet, Degas, and Cézanne, as well as El Greco, Goya, and Delacroix. The museum is also famous for its 50-odd sculptures by Rodin, the third-largest Rodin collection in the world.

Nezu Art Museum

6-5-36 Minami Aoyama, Minato-ku. ☎ **03/3400-2536.** Admission ¥1,000 ($10) adults, ¥700 ($7) students and children. Tues–Sun 9:30am–4:30pm. Closed days following hols, during exhibit changes, and Aug. Station: Omotesando (10 minutes).

The *Nezu Bijutsukan* houses a fine collection of Asian art, including Chinese bronzes, Japanese calligraphy, Korean ceramics, and other artwork. The museum is surrounded by a delightful small garden with several teahouses and a small restaurant.

Museum of Contempory Art, Tokyo

4-1-1 Miyoshi, Koto-ku. ☎ **03/5245-4111.** Admission ¥1,200 ($12) adults, ¥600 ($6) students. Tues–Thur and Sat–Sun 10am–6pm; Fri 10am–9pm. Station: Kiba, on the Tozai Line (15 minutes).

The newly opened MOT (pronounced *Motta,* and for some reason not known as MOCA Tokyo, as one might expect) is inconveniently located, and the hangarlike space (7,000 sq. meters) is too vast. Still it's about time Tokyo had a contemporary showplace, and if you are a fan of the avant-garde, you'll want to come here. You are best off taking a taxi from the station.

Ota Memorial Museum of Art

1-10-10 Jingumae, Shibuya-ku. ☎ **03/3403-0880.** Admission ¥500–¥800 ($5–$8) adults, ¥400–¥600 ($4–$6) students and children. Tues–Sun 10:30am–5:30pm (enter by 5pm). Closed from the 27th to the end of each month. Station: Harajuku or Meiji-Jingumae (2 minutes).

The *Ota Kinen Bijutsukan* is a great museum featuring the private ukiyo-e (woodblock print) collection of the late Ota Seizo, who early in life recognized the importance of ukiyo-e as an art form and dedicated his life to its preservation. Exhibitions of the museum's 12,000 prints are changed monthly, with descriptions of the displays in English. The museum itself is small but delightful, with such traditional touches as bamboo screens, stone pathways, and even a small tearoom that sells Japanese sweets.

Suntory Museum of Art

On the 11th floor of the Suntory Bldg., 1-2-3 Moto-Akasaka, Minato-ku. ☎ **03/3470-1073.** Admission ¥500–¥1,000 ($5–$10) adults, ¥500–¥600 ($5–$6) students, ¥200–¥300 ($2–$3) children. Tues–Thurs and Sat–Sun 10am–5pm, Fri 10am–7pm. Closed during exhibit changes. Station: Akasaka-mitsuke (1 minute).

Exhibitions at the *Suntory Bijutsukan* change regularly and may feature ceramics, screens, glass objects, lacquerware, paintings, or prints, on loan from other museums and collections from around the world. It is funded by the whiskey and beer giant, Suntory.

Tokyo Metropolitan Art Museum

Ueno Park, Taito-ku. ☎ **03/3823-6921.** Admission ¥500–¥800 ($5–$8) per person, depending on the exhibit. Tues–Sun 9am–5pm (enter by 4pm). Closed during exhibit changes. Station: Ueno (6 minutes).

The *Tokyo-To Bijutsukan* features modern Japanese works, mainly by 20th-century artists, with temporary exhibitions.

Specialized Museums

✪ Crafts Gallery

Kitanomaru Koen Park, Chiyoda-ku. ☎ **03/3211-7781.** Admission ¥400–¥800 ($4–$8) adults, ¥130–¥250 ($1.30–$2.50) students, ¥70 (70¢) children; price depends on the exhibit. Tues–Sun 10am–5pm. Station: Takebashi (10 minutes).

Housed in a Gothic-style brick building constructed in 1910 as headquarters of the Imperial Guard, the *Bijutsukan Kogeikan* collects contemporary crafts, including lacquerware, ceramics, textiles, bamboo works, and dolls, which it shows in rotating exhibitions.

Daimyo Clock Museum

2-1-27 Yanaka, Taito-ku. ☎ **03/3821-6913.** Admission ¥300 ($3) adults, ¥200 ($2) students, ¥100 ($1) children 6–11. Tues–Sun 10am–4pm. Closed Dec 25–Jan 15 and July–Sept. Station: Nezu (10 minutes).

The *Daimyo Tokei Hakubutsukan* displays about 50 clocks drawn from its extensive collection of Edo Period timepieces. Displays change annually.

Fukugawa Edo Museum

1-3-28 Shirakawa, Koto-ku. ☎ **03/3630-8625.** Admission ¥300 ($3) adults, ¥50 (50¢) children 6–11. Daily 10am–4:30pm. Station: Monzen-Nakacho or Morishita; then a 15-minute walk or bus no. 33 toward Kiyosumi Garden to the Kiyosumi Teien-mae bus stop.

The *Fukagawa Edo Shiryokan* reproduces a 19th-century neighborhood in Fukagawa, a prosperous community on the east bank of the Sumida River during the Edo Period. The hangarlike interior of this delightful museum contains 11 houses, vegetable and rice shops, a fish store, two inns, and tenement homes. There are lots of small touches and flourishes to make the community seem real and believable—a cat sleeping on a roof, a snail crawling up a fence, a dog relieving itself on a pole, and sounds of birds, a vendor shouting his wares, horses' hooves clattering, and a dog barking. Of Tokyo's museums, this one would probably be the preferred choice of children.

Hatakeyama Memorial Museum

2-20-12 Shiroganedai Minato-ku. ☎ **03/3447-5787.** Admission ¥500 ($5) adults, ¥350 ($3.50) students and children 6–11. Apr–Sept, Tues–Sun 10am–5pm; Oct–Mar, Tues–Sun 10am–4:30pm. Closed first week in Jan, and third and fourth weeks in Mar, June, Sept, and Dec. Station: Takanawadai (6 minutes).

The *Hatakeyama Kinenkan* emphasizes tea-ceremony ceramics and other objects, but it also has paintings, calligraphy, sculptures, and lacquerware from ancient Japan and China.

Furniture Museum

JIC Bldg., 3-10 Harumi, Chuo-ku. ☎ **03/3533-0098.** Admission ¥400 ($4) adults, ¥200 ($2) children. Thurs–Tues 10am–4:30pm. Closed hols. Station: Ginza or Tsukiji; then take a taxi.

Traditional Japanese furniture, as well as some antique European furniture, is preserved and displayed in the *Kagu No Hakubutsukan.*

Paper Museum

1-1-8 Horifune, Kita-ku. ☎ **03/3911-3545.** Admission ¥200 ($2) adults, ¥100 ($1) children. Tues–Sun 9:30am–4:30pm. Closed hols. Station: Oji, across from the south exit.

For enthusiasts of traditional handmade Japanese paper, the *Kami No Hakubutsukan* displays products and utensils used in its creation.

National Science Museum

Ueno Park, Taito-ku. ☎ **03/3822-0111.** Admission ¥400 ($4) adults, ¥70 (70¢) children. Tues–Sun 9am–4:30pm. Station: Ueno (5 minutes).

The *Kokuritsu Kagaku Hakubutsukan* is a sprawling complex covering everything from the evolution of life to electronics in Japan, aircraft, and automobiles. Unfortunately, not all displays are in English, but the museum is worth visiting for its exhibits relating to Japan, including its displays on the origin and development of the Japanese people, examples of Japanese architecture (no nails were used to join heavy wooden beams), the process of making Japanese lacquerware and paper, a "Zero" fighter plane from World War II, and an excellent collection of antique Japanese clocks.

Japan Folk Crafts Museum

4-3-33 Komaba, Meguro-ku. ☎ **03/3467-4527.** Admission ¥1,000 ($10) adults, ¥500 ($5) students, ¥200 ($2) children 6–11. Tues–Sun 10am–5pm. Station: Komaba-Todaimae, on Keio-Inokashira Line (5 minutes).

The *Nippon Mingeikan* displays folk art gathered from around Japan, including furniture, pottery, and textiles, much of it dating from the Edo and Meiji eras. Crafts from other Asian (as well as from European) countries are also on display in this special museum.

Shitamachi Museum

Ueno Park, Taito-ku. ☎ **03/3823-7451.** Admission ¥200 ($2) adults, ¥100 ($1) children. Tues–Sun 9:30am–4:30pm. Station: Ueno (3 minutes).

Shitamachi means "downtown" and refers to the area of Tokyo in which commoners used to live, mainly around Ueno and Asakusa. There's very little left of old downtown Tokyo; and with that in mind, the *Shitamachi Fuzoku Shiryokan* seeks to preserve for future generations a way of life that was virtually wiped out by the great earthquake of 1923 and then by World War II. There are shops set up as they may have looked back then, including a merchant's shop and a candy shop, as well as one of the Shitamachi tenements common at the turn of the century. Long, narrow buildings with one roof over a series of dwelling units separated by thin wooden walls, these were the homes of the poorer people, confined to the narrow back alleys. Everyone knew everyone else's business; few secrets could be kept in such crowded conditions. The alleyways served as communal living rooms. Children played in them, and families sat outside to catch whatever breeze there might be. The museum also displays relics relating to the life of these people, including utensils, toys, costumes, and tools, most of which are not behind glass but are simply lying around so that you can pick them up and examine them more closely. The museum's collections were all donated by individuals, many living in Shitamachi.

Sugino Costume Museum

4-6-19 Osaki, Shinagawa-ku. ☎ **03/3491-8151.** Admission ¥200 ($2) adults, ¥100 ($1) children. Mon–Sat 10am–4pm. Closed hols and Aug. Station: Meguro (7 minutes).

Clothing of Western Europe from around the 18th century, as well as that worn in Japan and other Asian countries, is displayed at the *Sugino Gakuen Isho Hakubutsukan.* Included are kimono, samurai outfits, and costumes worn in Noh dramas and the comic kyogen plays that accompany them.

Sumo Museum

1-3-28 Yokoama, Sumida-ku. ☎ **03/3622-0366.** Free admission, but during tournaments you must have sumo tickets to enter the stadium. Mon–Fri 9:30am–4:30pm. Closed hols. Station: Ryogoku (1 minute).

Located in the Kokugikan sumo stadium, the *Sumo Hakubutskan* shows the history of sumo since the 18th century, with portraits and mementos of past grand champions.

Drum Museum

2-1-1 Nishi-Asakusa, Taito-ku. ☎ **03/3842-5622.** Admission ¥300 ($3) adults, ¥150 ($1.50) children. Wed–Sun 10am–5pm. Closed hols. Station: Tawaramachi (2 minutes) or Asakusa (5 minutes).

Taikokan, a rather new museum, houses traditional Japanese drums, including those used in festivals throughout the country, as well as drums from around the world. With the exception of some of the rare, older pieces, many of the drums can be touched and played, making this a good bet with children. There are also videos of drumming from Japan and around the world.

Kite Museum

Taimeiken Bldg., 5th floor, 1-12-10 Nihombashi, Chuo-ku. ☎ **03/3275-2704.** Admission ¥200 ($2) adults, ¥100 ($1) children. Mon–Sat 11am–5pm. Closed hols. Station: Nihombashi (3 minutes).

Kites from Japan and countries around the world are displayed here at the *Tako No Hakubutsukan.*

Tepco Electric Energy Museum

1-12-10 Jinnan, Shibuya-ku. ☎ **03/3477-1191.** Free admission. Thurs–Tues 10:30am–6:30pm. Station: Shibuya (5 minutes).

If you have children with you, or you are interested in electricity, drop by Tokyo Electric Power Company's (TEPCO) public-service facility. Established to teach urban dwellers how electricity is generated, supplied, and consumed, it offers four floors of displays, including a model of a nuclear reactor and a "house of the future," equipped with the latest appliances and technology. TEPCO, 40% of whose power supply is nuclear, operates 11 nuclear power plants to supply Tokyo and vicinity. An English-language pamphlet describes the displays. Hands-on exhibits and 1,000 illustrated books in 50 languages make it fun for young people.

Sword Museum

4-25-10 Yoyogi, Sumida-ku. ☎ **03/3379-1386.** Admission ¥515 ($5.15) adults, free for children under 12. Tues–Sun 9am–4pm. Station: Sangubashi, on the Odakyu Line.

The *Token Hakubutsukan* pays tribute to Japanese swords, with more than 6,000 in its collection. Considered by the Japanese to embody spirits all their own, Japanese swords rank as an art form of the highest degree, and in feudal Japan swordmakers were respected masters.

Tokyo Metropolitan Edo-Tokyo Museum

1-4-1 Yokoami, Sumida-ku. ☎ **03/3626-8000.** Admission ¥500 ($5) adults, ¥250 ($2.50) students through high school. Tues–Wed and Sat–Sun 10am–6pm, Thur–Fri 10am–9pm. Station: Ryogoku on the JR Sobu Line (3 minutes).

Located in the heart of Shitamachi (downtown), in a very modern-looking kura (rice granary) with an outside elevator, this new museum (opened in 1993) is the city government's ambitious attempt to present the history, art, and scientific achievements of Tokyo from its beginnings to the present. Enter the museum by crossing over a replica of Nihonbashi Bridge; on opposite sides are the Edo and Tokyo Zones. Edo, the old name for Tokyo, was the capital of the shoguns from 1603 until 1868. Here the life of shoguns, merchants, and craftspeople is displayed. On the Tokyo side, the rapid advances after the Meiji Restoration, the Great Kanto Earthquake, and the bombing raids of World War II are presented. The museum is not limited to display cases—entire reconstructed buildings, scaled-down dioramas, and video presentations are offered. The museum has collected more than 170,000 items (43% were donated by Tokyo residents themselves), but some 90% of the permanent collection cannot be displayed because of a "lack of space," despite the seven floors. There's a video library in the basement that includes 26 English videos on topics from folklore to fine arts. You can rent a cordless headset from the ticket vendor for a ¥3,000 ($30) refundable deposit for narration in English.

A Museum Nearby

National Museum of Japanese History

117 Jonai-cho, Sakura, Chiba Prefecture. ☎ **043/486-0120.** Admission ¥400 ($4) adults, ¥250 ($2.50) high school and college students, ¥110 ($1.10) children. Tues–Sun 9:30am–4:30pm. Station: Keisei Sakura on the Keisei Line (15 minutes), or Sakura on the JR Sobu Line (a 15-minute bus ride).

Although it's 70 minutes outside Tokyo, the Rekihaku is worth a visit if you have extended time in Tokyo. It's located in the beautiful Sakura Castle Park, where the home of Lord Hotta, an important shogun, once stood. The museum is divided into four galleries, covering the Paleolithic era to the Nara Period; the Heian Period to the Azuchi-Momoyama Period; the Edo Period; and traditional popular culture, including Awa puppet heads and fishing gear. In the special-exhibit galleries are displayed one-tenth-scale models of structures designated "national treasures" or "important cultural assets."

ESPECIALLY FOR CHILDREN

Fujita Venté

Fujita Headquarters Building, 4-6-15 Sendagaya, Shibuya-ku. ☎ **043/3796-2486.** Free admission. Fri–Wed 10am–6pm. Closed Aug 13–17. Station: JR Yoyogi or Sendagaya (5 minutes).

Interactive exhibitions are the big draw here for children and the young at heart. Designed to showcase the large construction company Fujita, events (like an antique tin toy exhibit), lectures, and films are also put on. High-tech amusement rides incorporating Fujita technology are also featured.

Hanayashiki

2-28-1 Asakusa, Taito-ku. ☎ **043/3842-8780.** Admission ¥800 ($8) adults, ¥400 ($4) children. Wed–Mon 10am–6pm (5pm in winter). Station: Asakusa (7 minutes).

Japan's oldest amusement park is located northwest of the famous Sensoji Temple in Asakusa. Small by today's standards, it offers a small roller coaster and diversions that would appeal to younger children.

Hibiya City Ice Skating Rink

Hibiya Kokusai Bldg., 2-2-3 Uchisaiwaicho. ☎ **043/3595-0295.** Admission ¥600 ($6); skate rental ¥600 ($6). Mon–Fri 3–8pm, Sat–Sun 11am–7pm. Closed first Mon in March to Christmas. Station: Uchisaiwaicho (in front of the station) or Hibiya (5 minutes).

This has to be one of the best deals in Tokyo, since it's inexpensive, fun for the whole family, and right in the center of town (practically across from the Imperial Hotel). Lessons are available.

International Aquarium

World Import Mart Bldg., 10th floor, Sunshine City, 3-1-3 Higashi Ikebukuro. ☎ **043/3989-3466.** Admission ¥1,600 ($16) adults, ¥800 ($8) children 4–12 (under 4 free). Mon–Sat 10am–6pm, Sun 10am–6:30pm. Station: Higashi Ikebukuro (5 minutes) or Ikebukuro (8 minutes).

Claiming to be the world's highest aquarium, this 20-year-old attraction is in the Sunshine City complex in Ikebukuro. It's home to more than 40,000 fish and animals of 985 types, including dolphins, octopuses, eels, piranhas, sea horses, sea otters, seals, giant crabs, and rare species of fish. There are several shows, including performances by the sea lions, but this may be the only place on earth that has a fish performance, the "fish circus," featuring an electric eel (which gives off an electric charge) and an archer fish.

National Children's Castle

5-53-1 Jinguemae, Shibuya-ku. ☎ **03/3797-5666.** Admission ¥500 ($5) adults, ¥400 ($4) children 3–17 (free for children under 3). Tues–Fri 12:30–5:30pm, Sat–Sun and hols 10am–5:30pm. Station: Omotesando (exit B2, 7 minutes).

If you have children, you'll want to bring them to *Kodomo No Shiro.* Conceived by the Ministry of Health and Welfare to commemorate the International Year of the Child in 1979, the Children's Castle opened in 1985, its activity rooms designed to appeal to children of all ages. A video library offers videos on everything from fairy tales and Golden Book series to "Sesame Street" and even rock videos. There's a list of videos in English from which to choose, and viewing is in your own private cubicle. A Play Hall features building blocks, a jungle gym, table tennis and football for older kids, a large dollhouse, and computer games. Children can make their own creations in a supervised art room, and on the roof is a playground.

Tokyo Disneyland

1-1 Maihama, Urayasu-shi, Chiba Prefecture. ☎ **0473/54-0001.** Disneyland Passport, including entrance to and use of all attractions: ¥4,800 ($48) adults, ¥4,400 ($44) junior high and high school students, ¥3,300 ($33) children 4–11 (under 4 free). Starlight admission after 5pm during extended hours, ¥3,800 ($38) adults, ¥3,500 ($35) juniors, ¥2,300 ($23) children. Mon–Fri 9 or 10am–8 or 9pm, Sat–Sun 9am–10pm, with slightly shorter hours in winter. Schedule is subject to change, so call in advance. Shuttle buses run at 10-minute intervals from Tokyo Station directly to Disneyland's front gate in 35 minutes. The bus stop is behind the Tekko Building on the Yaesu-guchi side of Tokyo Station. One-way fare: ¥600 ($6) adults, ¥300 ($3) children. You can also take JR Keiyo Line from Tokyo Station to Maihama Station, from which park is a few minutes' walk.

Some people's vacation goal is to "do" all the Disney parks in the world. If you have similar goals (or if your children's vote wins), you will want to visit Tokyo Disneyland. Virtually a carbon copy of the back-home version, you can find the Jungle Cruise, Pirates of the Caribbean, Haunted Mansion, and Space Mountain. The hottest attraction is the new Fantillusion, a spectacular parade of thousands of lights using state-of-the-art fiber optics, light-emitting costumes, and electro-luminescence techniques. Scheduled to open in April 1996 is Toontown, a new themed land (there are six others), featuring Disney characters at home, work, and play and the chance to interact with Mickey Mouse and other Disney friends. Tickets for Tokyo Disneyland can be purchased in advance at the Tokyo Disneyland Ticket Center, located near Yurakucho subway station, and at major travel agencies.

Ueno Zoo

Ueno Park, Taito-ku. ☎ **03/3828-5171.** Admission ¥500 ($5) adults, ¥200 ($2) children 12–14, free for children under 12 and senior citizens. Tues–Sun 9:30am–4:30pm. Closed some hols. Station: Ueno (5 minutes).

Opened back in 1882, the Ueno Zoo is small but very popular with Japanese families. The main attractions are two giant pandas that were donated by the Chinese government. These two celebrities are so popular, in fact, that there are always long lines to their cages on weekends, and there are all kinds of souvenirs you can buy with pandas on them. The zoo also has an aquarium, plus a large aviary filled with tropical plants that you can walk through.

Yoyogi Koen

2-1 Yoyogi-Kamizono-cho, Shibuya-ku. ☎ **03/3469-6081.** Free admission. Daily sunrise–sunset. Station: Harajuku or Meiji-Jingumae (2 minutes).

A great park for flying kites (on sale at one of the concessions), feeding the ducks in the pond, and picnicking. Near the west end are tricycles and bikes available free of charge, daily from 9am to 4pm, and an open area for riding. Adjacent to the shrine, with its famous iris garden, the park is perfect for long walks. (Don't try to take your stroller on the gravel paths inside the shrine.)

WALKING TOUR 1
Asakusa

Start: Hinode Pier, near Hamamatsucho Station.
Finish: Kappabashi Dori.
Time: Allow approximately three hours, including the boat ride.
Best Times: Tuesday through Friday, when the crowds aren't as big.
Worst Times: Monday (when some attractions are closed) and Sunday (when shops on Kappabashi Dori are closed).

Asakusa is the heart of old downtown Tokyo, where the merchants settled when the Tokugawas made Edo the seat of their shogunate government. In those days, merchants were considered quite low on the social ladder and were restricted regarding where they could live and even what they could wear. Gradually, however, the merchants became wealthy, and whole new forms of popular entertainment arose to occupy their time. Theaters for Kabuki and Bunraku were built and flourished in Asakusa. Ukiyo-e (woodblock prints) became the latest artistic rage, with scenes depicting beauties and Kabuki stars, as well as daily life in Edo. To the north of Asakusa was Yoshiwara, the most famous geisha and pleasure district in the city. Unfortunately, Asakusa has not escaped the modernization that swept through Japan over the past century, but more than anywhere else in Tokyo it still retains the charm of old downtown Edo and a festive atmosphere, crowded with stalls and with people visiting its most famous attraction, Sensoji Temple. For Japanese, visiting Asakusa evokes feelings of nostalgia. For tourists, it provides a glimpse of the way things were.

The most dramatic way to arrive in Asakusa is by boat, just as people used to arrive in the olden days (if you want to forgo the boat ride, take the subway to Asakusa Station and start from there). Start this tour, therefore, by boarding a ferry at:

1. **Hinode Pier** (closest subway station: Hamamatsucho). The boat makes its way along the Sumida River, just as in past centuries boats carried wealthy townsmen to the pleasure district of Yoshiwara. Although much of what you see along the river today is only concrete embankments, I recommend the trip because it affords a different perspective of Tokyo—barges making their way down the river, highrise apartment buildings (with laundry fluttering from balconies), warehouses, and superhighways. The boat passes under approximately a dozen bridges during the 40-minute trip, each bridge completely different. Ferryboats ply the waters between Asakusa and Hamamatsucho about every half hour or hour, starting at 10:25am, but because schedules change it's best to call ahead (☎ 03/3841-9178 or 03/3457-7830). Cost of the ferry one-way is ¥560 ($5.60). The first stop on the ferry is at:
2. **Hama Rikyu Garden,** where more passengers are picked up. If you're interested in seeing the garden, considered by many to be Tokyo's finest, you can start your

tour here; but you must first pay the ¥300 ($3) admission. (See "Park & Gardens," above, for more details on the garden.)

Upon arrival in Asakusa, walk from the boat pier a couple of blocks inland, where you'll soon see the colorful Kaminarimon Gate. Across the street from this gate is the:

3. **Asakusa Information Center,** 2-18-9 Kaminarimon (☎ 03/3842-5566). Open daily from 9:30am to 8pm, it's staffed by English-speaking volunteers 10am to 5pm. Stop here to pick up a map of the area and to ask directions to restaurants and other sights you might be interested in visiting. In addition, note that huge Seiko clock on the center's facade—a mechanical music clock, with performances every hour on the hour from 10am to 7pm. Then it's time to head across the street, to the:
4. **Kaminarimon Gate,** unmistakable with its bright red colors and a huge lantern hanging in the middle. Those statues inside the gate are the gods of thunder and of rain, ready to protect the deity enshrined in the temple. Once past the gate, you'll find yourself immediately on a pedestrian lane called:
5. **Nakamise Dori,** which leads straight to the temple. This lane is lined with stalls selling fabrics, shoes, toys, Japanese crackers (called *sembei*), trinkets, bags, umbrellas, Japanese dolls, clothes, fans, masks, and traditional Japanese accessories, such as brightly decorated straight hairpins, black hairpieces, and wooden combs. It's a great place for souvenir and gift shopping.

TAKE A BREAK If you're hungry for lunch, there are a number of possibilities in the neighborhood. **Chinya,** 1-3-4 Asakusa, located near Kaminarimon Gate, has been serving sukiyaki since 1880. Nearby is **Namiki,** 2-11-9 Kaminarimon, Asakusa's best-known noodle shop. (See chapter 4 for more details on both these places.)

At the end of Nakamise Dori, as you head toward the temple, is another gate, which opens on a square filled with pigeons and a large:

6. **Incense burner,** where worshippers "wash" themselves to ward off or help against illness. If, for example, you have a sore throat, be sure to rub some of the smoke over your throat for good measure. But the dominating building of the square is:
7. **Sensoji Temple,** Tokyo's oldest temple. Founded in the 7th century, Sensoji Temple is dedicated to Kannon, the Buddhist goddess of mercy, and is therefore popularly called the Asakusa Kannon Temple. According to legend, the temple was founded after two fishermen pulled up a golden statue of Kannon from the sea. The sacred statue is still housed in the temple, carefully preserved inside three boxes, and even though it's never on display and the public has never seen it, people still flock to the temple to pay their respects. Within the temple is a counter where you can buy your fortune by putting ¥100 ($1) into a wooden box and extracting one of the long wooden sticks inside. The stick will have a number on it, which corresponds to one of the numbers on a set of drawers. Take out the fortune from the drawer that has your number. Although it's written in Japanese only, you can take it to the counter on the left, where you can ask for a translation (if the counter is unoccupied, you can also ask at the Asakusa Information Center). If you don't like your fortune, you can negate it by tying it to one of the wires provided or to the twig of a tree.

On the right side of the temple is a shrine, the:

8. **Asakusa Jinja Shrine,** built in commemoration of the two fishermen who found the statue of Kannon. Northwest of Sensoji Temple is:

Walking Tour—Asakusa

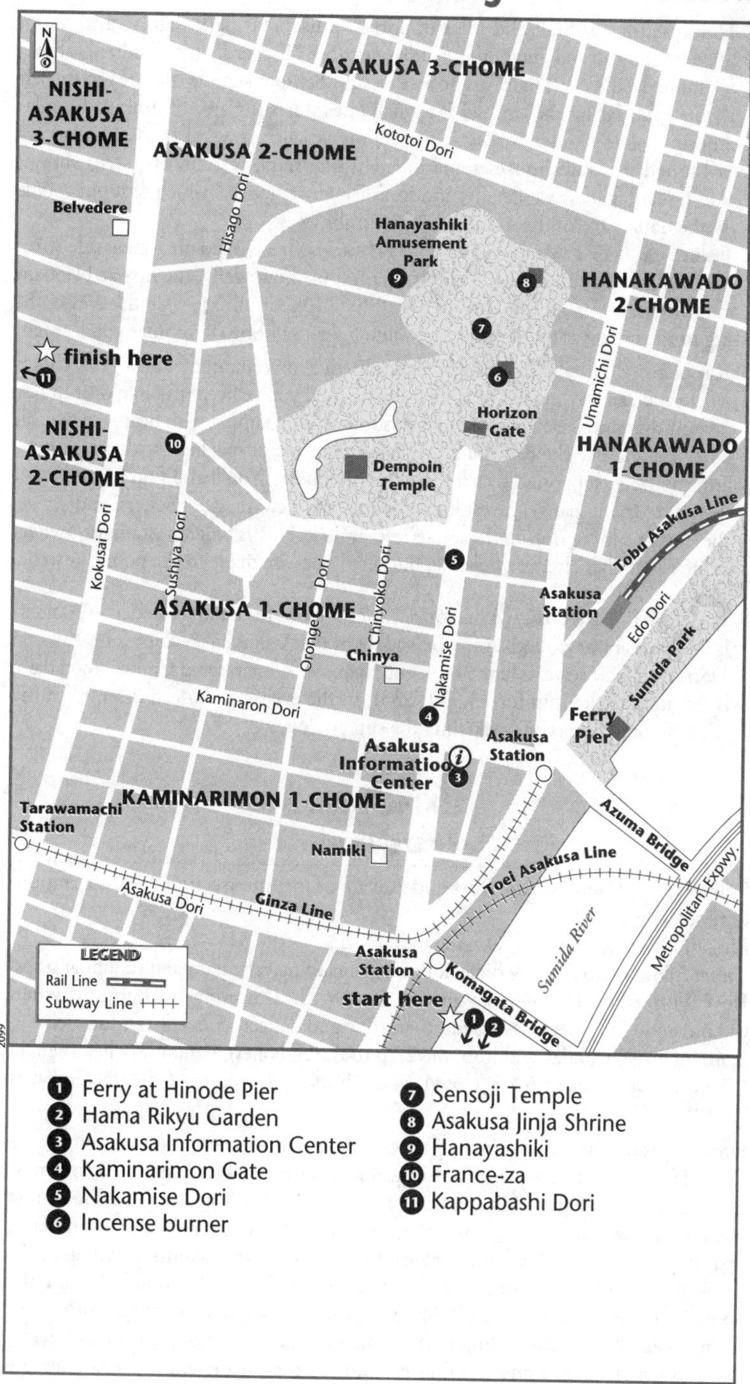

N
ASAKUSA 3-CHOME
NISHI-ASAKUSA 3-CHOME
ASAKUSA 2-CHOME
Kototoi Dori
Hisago Dori
Belvedere
Hanayashiki Amusement Park
HANAKAWADO 2-CHOME
Umamichi Dori
finish here
Horizon Gate
NISHI-ASAKUSA 2-CHOME
Dempoin Temple
HANAKAWADO 1-CHOME
Tobu Asakusa Line
Kokusai Dori
Sushiya Dori
Oronge Dori
Chinyoko Dori
Nakamise Dori
Asakusa Station
ASAKUSA 1-CHOME
Edo Dori
Chinya
Sumida Park
Kaminaron Dori
Ferry Pier
Asakusa Informatioo Center
Asakusa Station
KAMINARIMON 1-CHOME
Tarawamachi Station
Azuma Bridge
Namiki
Toei Asakusa Line
Metropolitan Expwy.
Asakusa Dori
Ginza Line
Sumida River
LEGEND
Rail Line
Subway Line
Asakusa Station
Komagata Bridge
start here
2099
1 Ferry at Hinode Pier
2 Hama Rikyu Garden
3 Asakusa Information Center
4 Kaminarimon Gate
5 Nakamise Dori
6 Incense burner
7 Sensoji Temple
8 Asakusa Jinja Shrine
9 Hanayashiki
10 France-za
11 Kappabashi Dori

9. **Hanayashiki,** a small and kind of corny amusement park that opened about 40 years ago and still draws in the little ones. (See "Especially for Children," above, for more details.) But most of the area west of Sensoji Temple (the area to the left if you stand facing the temple) is a small but interesting area of Asakusa popular among Tokyo's older working class. This is where several of Asakusa's old-fashioned pleasure houses remain, including bars, restaurants, strip shows, traditional Japanese vaudeville, and so-called "love hotels," which rent out rooms by the hour. One of the most famous strip shows is:
10. **France-za,** 1-43-12 Asakusa (☎ 03/3841-6631). It's located on a small side street that leads west from Sensoji Temple. With four shows daily, the first at 11:30am and the last at 6:30pm, it charges a ¥4,000 ($40) entrance fee—and leaves nothing to the imagination. If you keep walking west, within 10 minutes you'll reach:
11. **Kappabashi Dori,** Tokyo's wholesale district for restaurant items. Yes, this is where you can buy models of all that plastic food you've been drooling over in restaurant displays. Ice cream, pizza, fish, sushi, mugs foaming with beer—they're all here, looking like the real thing. My favorite is one of spaghetti with a fork hovering above it, supported by a few strands of noodles. You'll also find kitchenware, including frying pans, knives, lunch boxes, lacquerware, rice cookers, and *noren,* the curtains hung outside Japanese restaurants. This is where restaurant owners come to purchase items wholesale, but retail sales are made to the public as well.

TAKE A BREAK A great place for lunch or for ending the day in Asakusa is 28 floors above ground, at the **Belvedere** in the Asakusa View Hotel, on Kokusai Dori Avenue. It serves a lunch buffet of Japanese, Western, and Chinese food daily from noon to 2:30pm for ¥3,300 ($33); in the evening, you can listen to music while sipping drinks and watching the sun go down.

WALKING TOUR 2
Harajuku

Start: At the Omotesando Dori and Aoyama Dori intersection (nearest station: Omotesando).
Finish: Olympic stadiums, Omotesando Dori.
Time: Allow approximately three hours, not including restaurant and shopping stops.
Best Time: Sunday, when you can start with a Sunday brunch and when Omotesando Dori becomes a pedestrian zone and dancers converge on the scene.
Worst Times: Monday and from the 27th to the end of every month (when the Ota Memorial Museum of Art is closed) and Thursday (when the Oriental Bazaar is closed).

Harajuku is one of my favorite neighborhoods in Tokyo. Sure, I'm too old to really fit in. If you're over 25, you're apt to feel ancient here, since this is Tokyo's most popular and trendy place for Japanese high school and college students. The young come here to see and be seen, and there are Japanese punks, girls dressed in black, and young couples in their fashionable best. But I like Harajuku for its vibrancy, its sidewalk cafes, its street hawkers, and its fashionable clothing boutiques. It's also the home of Tokyo's most important Shinto shrine, as well as a woodblock-print museum, an excellent souvenir shop of traditional Japanese items, and a park with wide-open spaces. Formerly the training grounds of the Japanese army and later the

Walking Tour — Harajuku

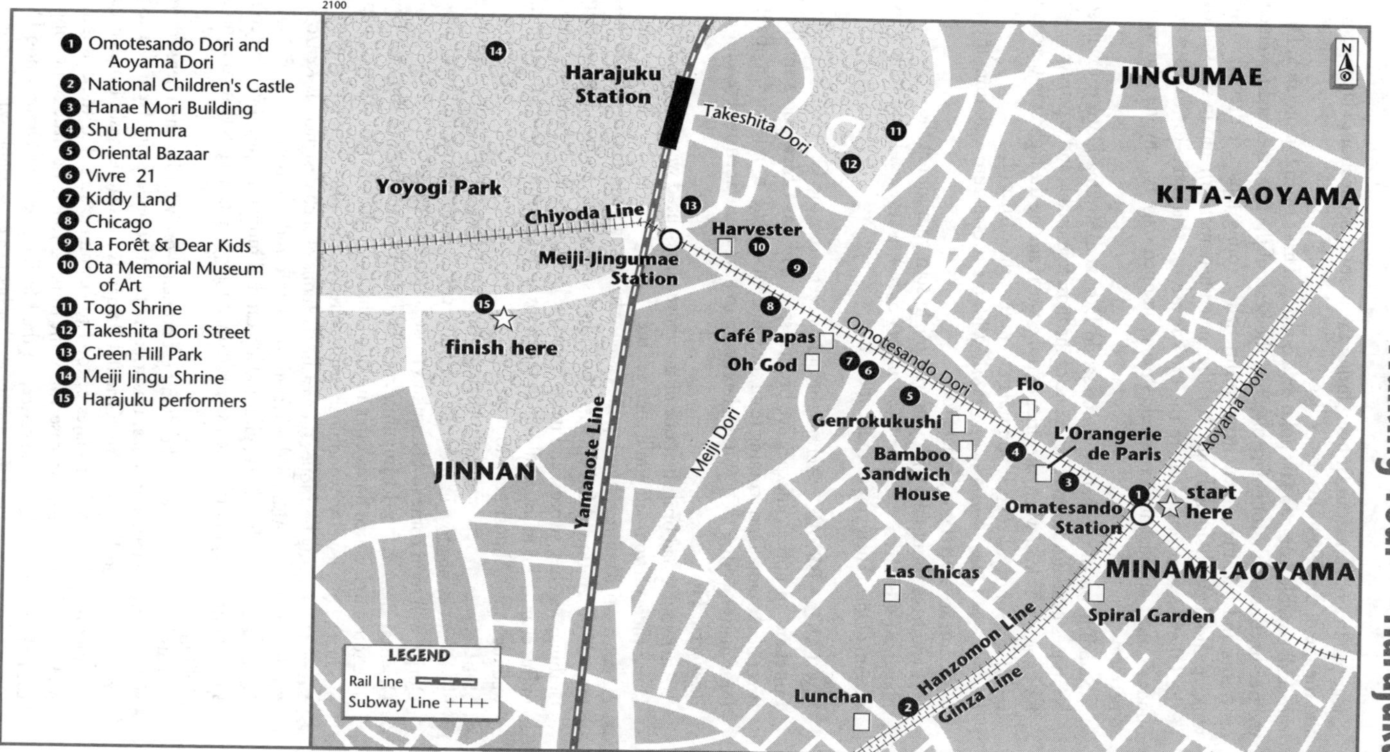

residential area of American families during the postwar occupation, Harajuku was also the site of the 1964 Olympic Village.

If at all possible, come to Harajuku on a Sunday. That's when Omotesando Dori, the tree-lined main thoroughfare bisecting the heart of the area, is closed to vehicular traffic and becomes a pedestrian promenade. Young Japanese dressed to kill walk up and down holding hands (a rather new phenomenon), and in the shadow of the Olympic stadiums, where the crowds are the thickest—for that's where Sunday's most unusual attraction takes place, an open stage for anyone who wants to perform.

Standing on the corner of Omotesando Dori and Aoyama Dori, you will see boutiques in all directions. This is one of the most fashionable and expensive neighborhoods in Tokyo, where the price of real estate is among the highest in the country. If it's Sunday, I suggest you start this tour at the corner of:

1. **Omotesando Dori and Aoyama Dori,** Within a two-minute walk from this intersection are several good places for:

   If you have youngsters with you, you might start your tour at the:

2. **National Children's Castle** (*Kodomo no Shiro*), a seven-minute walk down Aoyama Dori. Then you can take them to:

TAKE A BREAK Across the side street from the Children's Castle is **Lunchan,** an upbeat, inexpensive brunch spot. Try **Las Chicas,** on a small side street off Aoyama Dori (coming from the Children's Castle, turn left at City Bank), for something ethnic. Or you might choose to have an inexpensive French bistro *déjeuner* at **Flo.**

After you've had brunch at one of the above places, head west on Omotesando Dori, where on your left you'll soon see the:

3. **Hanae Mori Building,** housing the fashions by this famous designer. In the basement is the Antique Market, with individual stallkeepers selling china, jewelry, clothing, watches, swords, and items from the 1930s. (See the "Shopping" section in this chapter for more details on all the shops and department stores listed in this walking tour.) Almost next door is:
4. **Shu Uemura.** A very successful chain of makeup products, it features cosmetics, blush, and eyeshadow in incredible rainbow colors. Continuing on Omotesando Dori, you'll soon come to Harajuku's most famous store, the:
5. **Oriental Bazaar,** 5-9-13 Jingumae, one of Tokyo's best places to shop for Japanese souvenirs. Three floors offer antique chinaware, old kimono, Japanese paper products, fans, jewelry, woodblock prints, screens, and more. Not far away is:
6. **Vivre 21,** boasting boutiques showcasing fashions of such designers as Kenzo and Kazuya Hirayama. Also on the left side of Omotesando Dori is:
7. **Kiddy Land,** which sells gag gifts and a great deal more than just toys. You could spend hours here, but it's often so packed with giggling teenagers that you end up rushing out.

This is for those of you who didn't eat brunch—ready for lunch? There are several inexpensive restaurants near this stretch of Omotesando Dori. **Genrokusushi,** on Omotesando Dori near the Oriental Bazaar, is a fast-food sushi bar that uses a conveyor belt to deliver plates of food to customers seated at the counter. It also sells take-out sushi, in case you want to pack yourself a little something to eat later in Yoyogi Park. **Harvester**, on the Meijijingu end of Omotesando Dori, serves roasted chicken and inexpensive sandwiches in a great people-watching setting.

Closest to the Meiji-Omotesando Dori intersection is the **Café de Rope,** 6-1-8 Jingumae, the oldest outdoor cafe in Harajuku.

The first big intersection you come to on Omotesando Dori is Meiji Dori. This crossroad is the heart of Harajuku. If you cross Meiji Dori, you'll arrive almost immediately at a shop with the unlikely name of:

8. **Chicago,** which nonetheless stocks hundreds of used and new kimono and yukata in a corner of its basement. On the corner of the Omotesando and Meiji Dori intersection is:
9. **La Forêt,** a building filled with trendy shoe and clothing boutiques. The less expensive boutiques tend to be on lower floors, more exclusive boutiques higher up. Next to La Forêt is Dear Kids La Forêt, an entire department store dedicated to children. Kids will love to wander the four floors of ultra-cute clothing, kid-in-mind restaurants, a just-for-kids hair salon and gallery. Behind La Forêt is one of my favorite museums, the:
10. **Ota Memorial Museum of Art,** 1-10-10 Jingumae. It features the private ukiyo-e (woodblock prints) collection of the late Ota Seizo. Exhibitions of the museum's 12,000 prints are changed monthly. (See "Museums," above, for more details.)

Return to Meiji Dori and continue north. If it's the first or fourth Sunday of the month, you might want to go on walking a few minutes until on your left you see:

11. **Togo Shrine.** A flea market is held on the grounds of the shrine on the first and fourth Sunday of the month, when everything from old chests, dolls, and inkwells to kitchen utensils and kimono are for sale, spread out on a sidewalk that meanders under trees to the shrine. Beginning early in the morning, the market usually goes on until about 3pm.

Otherwise, turn left off Meiji Dori onto the first side street past Dear Kids La Forêt, a pedestrians-only street called:

12. **Takeshita Dori.** Lined nonstop with stores, this narrow street is usually packed with young people—mostly Japanese teenagers who've come in from the countryside to hunt for bargains in shops with doors flung open wide to the crowds. You'll pass record shops, shoe stores, and coffee shops—it's all there.

At the top end of Takeshita Dori, where you'll see Harajuku Station, turn left. Soon, across from the station, you'll see a small enclosed area called:

13. **Green Hill Park,** where young vendors set up stalls of clothing and accessories. You can find bargains here, although some of the leather-studded items might be too bizarre for the folks back home. Just past the station, turn right and walk over the bridge above the tracks, where you'll then find yourself at the entrance of:
14. **Meiji Jingu Shrine.** The most venerable shrine in Tokyo, Meiji Jingu Shrine opened in 1920, dedicated to Emperor and Empress Meiji. (See "The Top Attractions," above, for more details.) On the way to the shrine you can stop off at the Iris Garden, spectacular for its irises in late June. A stream meanders through the garden, and if you follow it to its source, you'll find a spring where you can drink the cold water. North of the shrine complex is the Treasure Museum, with the garments and personal effects of Emperor and Empress Meiji.

Retrace your steps back to the entrance of the shrine, turn right, and you'll see a mass of people on the wide boulevard, which is closed to traffic on Sunday. Here, from about noon to 5pm, are the:

15. **Harajuku performers.** In what is Tokyo's best free show, everyone—from rock 'n' rollers and break dancers to roller skaters, rock bands, and pantomime artists—converges on Omotesando Dori, in the shadow of the Olympic stadiums, to do his or her thing on the street. It all started in the 1970s, when a group of kids got together and began dancing to music they brought with them on portable cassette players. Gradually, the number of young dancers grew, until by the mid-1980s there were as many as several hundred teenagers dancing in the street, dressed

either in styles of the 1950s or in colorful circuslike clothing. Although today the number of dancers has dwindled, a few diehards are still here. Like most undertakings in Japan, this is group participation, with each group having its own cassette player, music, leader, and costumes. Individual dancing is out, and if by chance you simply joined in, the other dancers would regard you with astonishment and consider you slightly weird. The fun consists in simply wandering about, observing group after group. You might also come across a roller-skating club putting on stunts, young boys performing on trick bicycles, a pantomimist, and, in recent years, lots of rock bands. In this carnival-like atmosphere, there are also stalls selling everything from fried noodles to roasted corn on the cob to a kind of Japanese omelet.

After you've visited Meiji Jingu Shrine, seen the Sunday dancers of Harajuku, and fought your way through the crowds, you're probably ready to imbibe a drink or two. Although Tokyo doesn't have many sidewalk cafes, Harajuku is blessed with several:

TAKE A BREAK Located on the fifth floor of the Hanae Mori Building on Omotesando Dori, **L'Orangerie de Paris** is the most expensive and exclusive brunch spot, attracting the foreign expatriate population. **Spiral Garden,** on Aoyama Dori, is slightly cheaper and more casual. Be sure to make reservations beforehand, since these places are popular. (See chapter 4 for details on the restaurants in this walking tour.)

2 Organized Tours

There are several group tours of Tokyo and its environs, offered by the **Japan Travel Bureau (JTB)** (☎ 03/3276-7777) and such tour companies as the **Japan Gray Line** (☎ 03/3433-5745 and 03/3436-6881), with bookings easily made at most tourist hotels. Day tours may include Tokyo Tower, the Imperial Palace district, Asakusa Sensoji Temple, Meiji Jingu Shrine, and Ginza. There are a number of organized evening tours that take in such activities as Kabuki. If your time is limited, you might be interested in one or more of these day and evening tours, although be warned they are very tourist-oriented. Prices range from about ¥3,500 ($35) for a morning tour to about ¥12,800 ($128) for a night tour, which includes dinner and Kabuki.

One tour you might consider joining because you can't do it on your own is the **Industrial Tokyo tour,** offered by JTB once a week on Thursdays. Plants toured may include Isuzu Motors, Toshiba Science Center, and Kirin Brewery. The price of this tour is ¥9,400 ($94), including lunch.

3 Cultural Experiences

IKEBANA Instruction in ikebana, or flower arranging, is available at a number of schools in Tokyo. Information can be obtained from **Ikebana International,** Ochanomizu Square Building, 1-6 Surugadai, Kanda (☎ 03/3293-8188). Otherwise, one school particularly good for foreigners is the **Ichiyo School Nakano,** 4-17-5 Nakano (☎ 03/3388-0141); it provides instruction in English at various sites around Tokyo and will give certifications. A series of nine lessons costs ¥36,000 ($360). Other well-known schools include the **Sogetsuryu Ikebana School,** 7-2-21 Akasaka (☎ 03/3408-1126; closest station: Aoyama-Itchome), with instructions in English on Monday and Friday at 10am and noon for about ¥3,500 ($35), including materials, but cost depends upon how many classes you take; and the **Ohararyu Ikebana School,** 5-7-17 Minami Aoyama (☎ 03/3499-1200; closest station: Omotesando), where you can join in lessons Monday through Friday from 10am for ¥3,500 ($35) per lesson, including materials. Appointments should be made in advance.

If you wish to see ikebana, ask at the **Tourist Information Office** whether there are any special exhibitions. Department stores sometimes have special ikebana exhibitions in their galleries. Another place to look is **Yasukuni Shrine,** located on Yasukuni Dori, northwest of the Imperial Palace (closest station: Ichigaya or Kudanshita). Although dedicated to Japanese war dead, the shrine also has ongoing exhibitions of ikebana on its grounds.

TEA CEREMONY Several first-class hotels in Tokyo hold tea ceremonies with instruction in English. Since they are often booked by groups, be sure to call in advance to see whether you can participate. **Seisei-an,** on the seventh floor of the Hotel New Otani, 4-1 Kioi-cho, Chiyoda-ku (☎ 03/3265-1111, ext. 2443; closest station: Yotsuya or Akasaka-mitsuke), holds a 30-minute instruction on Thursday through Saturday from 11am to 4pm. The cost is ¥1,030 ($10.30). **Chosho-an,** on the seventh floor of the Hotel Okura, 2-10-4 Toranomon, Minato-ku (☎ 03/3582-0111; closest station: Toranomon), gives instruction anytime between 11am and noon and between 1 and 5pm. The cost is ¥1,000 ($10). At **Toko-an,** on the fourth floor of the Imperial Hotel, 1-1-1 Uchisaiwaicho, Chiyoda-ku (☎ 03/3504-1111; closest station: Hibiya), instruction is from 10am to noon and 1pm to 4pm, daily except Sunday and holidays. Reservations are required. The cost is ¥1,100 ($11).

ACUPUNCTURE & JAPANESE MASSAGE Although most Westerners have heard about acupuncture, they may not be familiar with *shiatsu* (Japanese pressure-point massage). Many first-class hotels in Japan offer shiatsu, as do the two clinics listed below.

There are acupuncture clinics everywhere in Tokyo, and the staff of your hotel may be able to tell you of the one nearest you. If you want a specific recommendation, try **Kojimachi Rebirth,** on the second floor of the Kur House Building, 4-2-12 Kojimachi, Chiyoda-ku (☎ 03/3262-7561). Hours here are 9:30am to 9pm Monday through Friday and until 8pm Saturday; closed holidays. First-time fee is ¥7,500 ($75) for shiatsu massage and ¥5,000 ($50) for acupunture.

Similarly, in Shinjuku there's the **Seibu Shinjuku Ekimae Clinic,** located above a pharmacy on the fourth floor of the Chiyoda Building, 2-45-6 Kabuki-cho (☎ 03/3209-9217; closest station: Seibu Shinjuku), across the street from a group of shops called American Blvd. Open Monday through Saturday from 9am to 1pm (closed holidays), it offers treatments in acupuncture, shiatsu, and moxibustion (small cones of wormwood, used on specific points for heat stimulation). A doctor trained in Western medicine is also in residence. A treatment of both acupuncture and shiatsu is ¥5,000 ($50). You can also have a shiatsu massage at Asakusa Kannon Onsen (see below).

PUBLIC BATHS If you won't have another opportunity to visit a communal bath in Japan, I suggest that you go at least once to a neighborhood *sento* (public bath). Altogether, Tokyo has an estimated 2,000 sento, which may sound like a lot but is nothing compared to the 20,000 the city used to have. Easily recognizable by a tall chimney and shoe lockers just inside the door, a sento sells about anything you might need at the bathhouse—soap, shampoo, towels, and even underwear.

Since there are so many public baths spread throughout the city, it's best simply to go to the one most convenient to you. If you prefer a suggestion, however, the **Azabu Juban Onsen,** 1-5 Azabu Juban, Minato-ku (☎ 03/3404-2610; closest station: Roppongi), is the one I used to go to when I lived for a while in an apartment without a tub or shower (in those days it cost one-third what it now does now). Closed on Tuesday but open the rest of the week from 11am to 9pm, it has brownish water that actually comes from a hot spring. Admission here is ¥1,200 ($12).

The **Asakusa Kannon Onsen,** 2-7-26 Asakusa, Taito-ku (☎ 03/3844-4141), is located just west of Sensoji Temple. This one, opened in 1957, also boasts water from a hot spring and has the atmosphere of a real neighborhood bath. It's open Friday through Wednesday from 6:30am to 6pm (closed Friday if Thursday is a holiday). The fee is only ¥600 ($6). A shiatsu massage here is ¥4,000 ($40).

Although it's far from Tokyo, about 1½ hours by train from Shinjuku Station, you may wish to visit **Kappa Tengoku** (43) just for the experience of open-air bathing (☎ 03/0460-6121). Located on a hill directly behind Yumoto Station in the heart of Hakone, this is the closest open-air bath to Tokyo. It's open daily from 10am to 10pm, and admission is ¥500 ($5).

ZAZEN Sitting meditation is occasionally offered with instruction in English by a few temples in the Tokyo vicinity. **Eiheiji Temple,** 2-21-34 Nishi-Azabu, Minato-ku (☎ 03/3400-5232), holds a zazen every Monday from 7 to 9pm, charging ¥100 ($1). Instruction here, however, is in Japanese only. The station is Roppongi, from which it's a 10-minute walk. For more information, contact the Tourist Information Center.

4 Spectator Sports

For information on current sporting events taking place in Tokyo, ranging from kick boxing and pro wrestling to soccer, table tennis, and golf classics, check the monthly magazine *Tokyo Journal.*

BASEBALL The Japanese are so crazy about baseball, you'd think they invented the game. Even the annual high school playoffs keep everyone glued to their TV sets. In Tokyo, the home teams are the **Yomiuri Giants** and the **Nippon Ham Fighters,** both of which play at the Tokyo Dome (☎ 03/3811-2111; closest station: Suidobashi); and the **Yakult Swallows,** which play at Jingu Stadium (closest station: Gaienmae). Other teams playing in the vicinity of Tokyo are the Chiba Lotte Marines, the Seibu Lions, and the Yokohama Bay Stars. Advance tickets go on sale on Friday, two weeks prior to a game, and can be purchased at the stadium or, for Tokyo teams, at any Playguide office.

MARTIAL ARTS If you're interested in the martial arts, including kendo and aikido, stop by the Tourist Information Center for its list of schools which allow you to watch practice. If you're interested, you can also join on a monthly basis for instruction.

Otherwise, contact the various federations directly: **Aikido World Headquarters** (☎ 03/3203-9236); the **All-Japan Judo Federation** (☎ 03/3818-4199); the **Japan Karate-do Federation** (☎ 03/3503-6637); and the **All Japan Kendo Federation** (☎ 03/3211-5804). All have member schools in Tokyo. Telephone to make an appointment.

SUMO Sumo matches are held in Tokyo at the **Kokugikan,** 1-3-28 Yokoami, Sumida-ku (☎ 03/3623-5111; closest station: Ryogoku), a sumo stadium completed in 1985. Matches are held in January, May, and September for 15 consecutive days, beginning at around 10am and lasting until 6pm; the top wrestlers compete after 4pm. The best seats are ringside box seats, but they're bought out by companies and by friends and families of sumo wrestlers. Usually available are balcony seats, which can be purchased at any Playguide (a ticket outlet in Tokyo, with counters throughout the city) or at the Kokugikan ticket office beginning at 9am every morning of the tournament. Prices range from about ¥1,500 to ¥10,500 ($15 to $105). Sumo matches are broadcast on the NHK channel of Japanese television.

If no tournament is going on, you might want to visit a sumo stable to watch the wrestlers train. There are more than 30 stables in Tokyo, many of which are located in Ryogoku, close to the sumo stadium. Call first to make an appointment and to make sure the wrestlers are in town. Stables include **Dewanoumi Beya,** 2-3-15 Ryogoku, Sumida-ku (☎ 03/3631-0090); **Izutsu Beya,** 2-2-7 Ryogoku, Sumida-ku (☎ 03/3633-8920); and **Kasugano Beya,** 1-7-11 Ryogoku, Sumida-ku (☎ 03/3631-1871). The Tourist Information Center has a list of other stables as well.

5 Shopping

One of the delights of being in Japan is the shopping, but it's not only the tourists who go crazy. The Japanese themselves are avid shoppers, and it won't take you long to become as convinced as I am that shopping is the number one pastime in Tokyo. Women, men, couples, and even whole families go on buying expeditions in their free time, making Sunday the most crowded shopping day of the week.

THE SHOPPING SCENE

Traditional Japanese crafts and souvenirs that make good buys include woodblock prints (ukiyo-e), toys and kites, bamboo window blinds, Japanese dolls, carp banners, swords, lacquerware, ikebana accessories, ceramics, fans, masks, knives and scissors, sake, and silk and cotton kimono. Also popular are products made of Japanese paper (*washi*), such as umbrellas, lanterns, boxes, wallets, and stationery. Japan is famous for its workmanship in electronic products, but because of the present exchange rate, you can probably find these products just as cheaply, or even more cheaply, in the United States. If you think you want to shop for electronic products, therefore, it pays to do some comparison shopping before you leave home so that you know what the prices are.

Remember that a 3% consumption tax will be added on to the price marked, but all major department stores in Tokyo will refund the tax on purchases amounting to more than ¥10,000 ($100). Ask at the store's information counter (usually located near the main entrance) for the special form to be filled out by the sales clerks and for the location of the refund counter. Be sure to bring your passport.

SALES Department stores have sales throughout the year, during which you can pick up bargains on everything from electronic goods and men's suits to golf clubs, toys, kitchenware, food, and lingerie. There are even sales for used wedding kimono. The most popular—and crowded—sales are for designer clothing, usually held twice a year, in July and December or January. In fact, most people I know who live in Tokyo buy their Japanese designer clothing only during these sales. You can pick up fantastic clothing at cut-rate prices—but be prepared for the crowds. To find out about current sales, check the ***Tokyo Journal,*** the monthly guide to what's going on in Tokyo.

Items on sale in department stores are usually found on one of the top floors, with sometimes an entire floor devoted to the sale. Whenever I go to a department store, I can't resist riding the up escalators until I finally reach the bargain floor. I've come upon sales I never knew existed and ended up buying things I never really needed. The *Tokyo Journal* also lists the various exhibitions being held at department store art galleries.

SHIPPING IT HOME Many first-class hotels in Tokyo provide a packing and shipping service. In addition, most large department stores, as well as tourist shops such as the Oriental Bazaar and antiques shops, will ship your purchases overseas.

If you wish to ship packages yourself, the easiest method is to go to a post office and purchase an easy-to-assemble cardboard box, available in three sizes (along with the necessary tape and string). Packages mailed abroad cannot weigh more than 20 kilograms (about 44 pounds), and keep in mind that only the larger international post offices accept packages to be mailed overseas. Remember, too, that mailing packages from Japan is expensive. Ask your hotel concierge for the closest international post office.

BEST BUYS Tokyo is the country's showcase for everything from the latest in camera or stereo equipment to original woodblock prints. You don't have to spend a fortune shopping, either. You can pick up handmade Japanese paper products or other souvenirs, for example, for a fraction of what they would cost in import shops in the United States. In Harajuku it's possible to buy a fully lined dress of the latest fashionable craze for $50, and I can't even count the number of pairs of shoes I've bought in Tokyo for a mere $30. Used cameras can be picked up for a song, reproductions of famous woodblock prints make great inexpensive gifts, and many items—from pearls to electronic video and audio equipment—can be bought tax free.

Another enjoyable aspect of shopping in Tokyo is that specific areas are often devoted to certain products, sold wholesale but also available to the individual shopper. Kappabashi Dori, for example, is where you'll find shops specializing in plastic-food replicas and kitchenware, while Kanda is known for its bookstores. Akihabara is packed with stores selling the latest in electronics. Ginza is the chic address for clothing boutiques, as well as art galleries. Shibuya has more than a dozen department stores, while Harajuku and Daikanyama are the places to go for youthful, fun, and inexpensive fashions.

SHOPPING A TO Z

ANTIQUES & CURIOS

In addition to the listings here, look for antiques in the Oriental Bazaar and flea markets. On Koto Dori, the street that makes a T with Aoyama Dori at Kinokuniya (the international market), there are some very serious antiques shops. You may see only a vase in the window or a single scroll; these are for the serious connoisseur.

Antique Market

Hanae Mori Bldg. basement, Omotesando Dori, 3-6-1 Kita-Aoyama, Minato-ku. ☎ **03/3406-1021.**

Individual stall holders here sell china, jewelry, clothing, swords, watches, woodblock prints, and 1930s kitsch; and prices are high. Open daily from 11am to 8pm.

✪ Kurofune

7-7-4 Roppongi. ☎ **03/3479-1552.**

Located in a large house in Roppongi, Kurofune specializes in original (un-refinished) Japanese antique furniture. This is the largest shop offering mid- to top-quality furniture; there are some very good things here. Kurofune is a favorite place to visit, even if I can't buy—there are so many beautiful things to see. The stock also includes fabrics, prints, maps, and folk art. Owned by American John Adair, who has lived in Japan more than 20 years, he knows his trade and will share his knowledge. Fax him (03/3479-0719) for a map to get there. Open Monday through Saturday from 10am to 6pm.

Mayuyama

2-5-9 Kyobashi, Chuo-ku. ☎ **03/3561-5146.**

One of the best-known names in fine antiques, this shop was first established in 1905 and is one of Tokyo's oldest and most exclusive antiques shops. Housed in a distinguished-looking stone building between Kyobashi and Takaracho, within walking distance of Tokyo Station, Mayuyama deals in ceramics and pottery, scrolls and screens from Japan, China, and Korea—at expectedly high prices. Open Monday through Saturday from 10am to 6pm; closed national holidays.

Tokyo Antique Hall

3-9-5 Minami Ikebukuro. ☎ **03/3982-3433** or 3980-8228.

The *Komingu Kottokan* is one of the best places for one-stop bric-a-brac hunting since there are some 35 dealers' stalls. Although most articles are marked, it's okay to try bargaining. You could spend hours here, looking over furniture, ceramics, woodblock prints, jewelry, lacquerware, swords, china, hair combs, Japanese army memorabilia, kimono and fabrics, scrolls and screens, samurai gear, clocks, watches, dolls, and other items too numerous to list. Antiques are both Japanese and Western, and dealers here work the flea markets across the country, so many are not open during the flea markets. From Ikebukuro station walk 10 minutes, take a right out of the station's east side, walking south on Meiji Dori; the shop will be on your left. Open Friday through Wednesday from 11am to 7pm (try to get here before 5pm because some stalls close down early if business is slow).

Arcades & Tax-Free Shops

Shopping arcades are found in several of Tokyo's first-class hotels. While they don't offer the excitement and challenge of going out and rubbing elbows with the natives, they are convenient, sales clerks speak English, and you can be assured of top-quality merchandise. The **Imperial Hotel Arcade** is one of the best, with shops selling pearls, woodblock prints, toys, antiques, and expensive name-brand clothing like Hanae Mori. The Okura and New Otani Hotels also have extensive shopping arcades.

Underground shopping arcades are found around several of Tokyo's train and subway stations, the biggest of which are at Tokyo and Shinjuku stations. Serving commuters on their way home, they often have great sales and bargains on clothing, accessories, and electronics. In Ikebukuro, the city's tallest skyscraper, Sunshine City, contains more than 200 shops, including the **World Import Mart,** selling different foods and goods from 50 countries.

Other good places to shop if you're short of time are duty-free stores. To qualify, you must present your passport, whereupon you'll be issued a piece of paper that you surrender at the Customs desk when departing Japan (the Customs desk at the Narita airport is well marked, so you can't miss it). At that time you may also be requested to show the product to Customs officials.

The best-known tax-free arcade is the **International Arcade,** 1-7-23 Uchisaiwaicho, Chiyoda-ku (☎ 03/3571-1528), located close to the Imperial Hotel (in Hibiya), under the train tracks. Stores here are open daily from 10am to 6:30pm and include merchandise from pearls and cameras to kimono, china, woodblock prints, and electronics.

The **Narita airport's duty-free shops** are also good places to shop for alcoholic products, such as sake or whiskey, but prices are not necessarily cheaper.

Books

Yasukuni Dori in Jimbocho-Kanda is a street lined with bookstores, which no bibliophile should pass up. In this mecca for both new and used books, there are more than 50 shops, several of which deal in books written in English. In general English-language books will be more expensive in Japan than at home.

Kinokuniya

3-17-7 Shinjuku. ☎ **03/3354-0131.**

Located on Shinjuku Station's east side on Shinjuku Dori, Kunokuniya's sixth floor offers a wide selection of books and magazines in English, including dictionaries and textbooks for students of Japanese. Open daily from 10am to 8pm. Closed some Wednesdays.

Kitazawa

2-5 Jimbocho. ☎ **03/3263-0011.**

This place has an overwhelming selection of books on Japan, including those most recently published. It also has old and rare books. Open Monday through Saturday from 10am to 6pm.

Ohya Shobo

1-1 Jimbocho. ☎ **03/3291-0062.**

This shop in Kanda claims to have the largest stock of old Japanese illustrated books, woodblock prints, and maps in the world. Open Monday through Saturday from 10:30am to 6:30pm; closed holidays.

✪ Tower Records and Books

1-22-14 Jinan, Shibuya-ku. ☎ **03/3496-3661.**

My friends in Tokyo don't shop anywhere else for their books and magazines now that Tower has opened. Why? Prices are much lower than elsewhere, with magazines about half-price. While other stores haven't passed the high-yen import advantage on to customers, Tower has. The seventh floor has a good selection of English-language books, as well as magazines and newspapers from around the world. It's open daily 10am to 10pm, but closed the last Wednesday of the month. There are Tower Records in West Shinjuku (☎ 03/3340-3851), East Shinjuku (☎ 03/5379-4101), and Ikebukuro (☎ 03/3983-2010), as well as all over Japan.

Tuttle Book Shop

1-3 Jimbocho. ☎ **03/3291-7072.**

This shop, the Tokyo branch of a Vermont firm, has a wide selection of books on Japan and the Far East written in English, as well as Japanese-language books. Open Monday through Friday from 10:30am to 6:30pm, and on Saturday and national holidays from 11am to 6pm.

Cameras & Film

You can purchase cameras at many duty-free shops, including those in Akihabara, but if you're really serious about photographic equipment or want to stock up on film, make a trip to a shop dealing specifically in cameras. If purchasing a new camera is too formidable an expense, consider buying a used camera. New models come out so frequently in Japan that older models can be grabbed up for next to nothing.

Camera No Kimura

1-18-8 Nishi Ikebukuro. ☎ **03/3981-8437.**

This store, west of Ikebukuro Station, has a good selection of used cameras. Open Monday to Saturday from 8am to 8pm, and on Sunday and holidays from 10am to 7pm.

East West Sigma

3-2-6 Nishi-Azabu, Minato-ku. ☎ **03/3497-3931.**

Where professionals bring their film for processing, Kodak color slides can be processed within 24 hours and Ektachrome in 2 hours. It's located on Terebi Asahi Dori, the first major left if you're walking towards Shibuya from Roppongi Crossing on Roppongi Dori. Open Monday through Friday from 9am to 7pm and Saturday from 9am to 5pm. Closed holidays and the second and fourth Saturday of the month.

Matsuzakya Camera

1-27-34 Takanawa, Minato-ku. ☎ **03/3443-1311.**

Used Japanese and foreign cameras are sold at this shop, a 15-minute walk from Shinagawa Station. Open Monday to Saturday from 10am to 7pm, and on Sunday and holidays from 10am to 6pm.

Yodobashi Camera

1-11-1 Nishi Shinjuku. ☎ **03/3346-1010.**

Shinjuku is the photographic equipment center for Tokyo, and this store one block west of the station is the biggest in the area. It ranks as one of the largest discount camera shops in the world, with around 30,000 items in stock, and reputedly sells approximately 500 to 600 cameras daily. In addition to cameras, it also has watches, calculators, typewriters, and cassette players. Its duty-free section is on the second floor, and even though prices are marked, you can bargain here. Come here to stock up on film. Open daily from 9:30am to 9pm.

Crafts & Traditional Japanese Products

If you want to shop for traditional Japanese folk crafts, a number of stores in Tokyo offer such items as fans, paper products, chinaware, lacquerware, kimono, and bamboo products. In addition to the shops listed below, remember that department stores have crafts sections boasting wide selections of everything from kitchenware to lacquerware to kimono. Also, Nakamise Dori, a pedestrian lane leading to Sensoji Temple in Asakusa, is packed with stalls selling everything from wooden *geta* shoes to hairpins worn by geisha.

Beniya Folkscraft Shop

2-16-8 Shibuya. ☎ **03/3400-8084.**

On four narrow floors here, artisanal goods from all over Japan at prices ranging from inexpensive to dear are offered. Items for sale include rattan, bamboo, ceramics, baskets, dishes, jewelry, lacquerware, place mats, napkins, noren, glassware, and bolts of dyed Japanese Yuzen cloth. In the basement there's a coffee shop and on the fifth floor there's a folk- and industrial-crafts gallery. Rental galleries are above. No credit cards accepted. Open Friday to Wednesday from 10am to 7pm.

Bingoya

10-6 Wakamatsucho. ☎ **03/3202-8778.**

Folk art and crafts are sold on six floors of this small building, including traditional toys such as tops and dolls, handmade paper products, baskets, straw boots, items made from cherry bark, chopsticks, pottery, glassware, lacquerware, and fabrics from all over Japan. Station: Akebonobashi (15 minutes) or Shinjuku (west exit, then bus no. 74 or 76 to the Kawada-cho bus stop). Open Tuesday to Sunday from 10am to 7pm.

Hakusuke (44)

2-2-14 Asakusa. ☎ **03/3841-7058.**

For traditional Japanese cosmetics (*keisho hin*), come to Hakushite, a 200-year-old, family-owned shop. I was recently waited on by a 78-year-old woman whose face advertises the virtues of the products she sells. Once upon a time, when white teeth were thought ugly, this shop stocked teeth blackener, but today you can pick up *kombu no funori* (a seaweed hair treatment), *tsubaki* (camelia) oil for healthy hair, or *uguisu no kona* (nightingale droppings) for soft, smooth skin—mix it with a little soap to wash your face (a 3-month treatment is ¥1,000/$10). Customers, now as before, are geisha and kabuki actors, as makeup for these roles is stocked. You'll also find hairpins for fancy Japanese hairdos. It's one street east of Nakamise Dori, very near Denpoin. Open Wednesday to Monday 11am to 5pm.

Japan Traditional Craft Center

Plaza 246 Bldg., 3-1-1 Minami Aoyama. ☎ **03/3403-2460.**

Located on the corner of Gaien-nishi Dori and Aoyama Dori (above a Häagen-Dazs), the *Zenkoku Dentoteki Kogeihin Senta* is worth a trip even if you can't afford to buy anything. Established to publicize and distribute information on Japanese crafts, it's a great introduction to both traditional and contemporary Japanese design. In addition to its permanent exhibition, it sells various crafts from all over Japan on a rotating basis, so there are always new items on hand. Crafts for sale usually include lacquerware, ceramics, fabrics, paper products, bamboo items, dolls, writing brushes, metalwork, and more. Prices are high, but rightfully so. There's also a small shop on the first floor. Open Friday to Wednesday from 10am to 6pm.

Kokkusai Kanko Kaikan

1-8-3 Marunouchi, Chiyoda-ku, and on the 9th floor of the Daimaru department store (same address). ☎ **03/3215-1181.**

What finds these two places are! Located right beside each other, practically on top of Tokyo Station, they contain tourism promotional offices for every prefecture in Japan—each of which also sells its own special goods and products. Altogether, there are 49 of these little shops, spread along the first through fourth floors of the Kokusai Kanko Kaikan Building and on the ninth floor of the Daimaru department store. You won't find such a varied collection anywhere else in Japan; and prices are very reasonable, cheaper than at department stores. What's more, no one shops here. You don't have time to go to Okayama to buy its famous Bizen pottery? You forgot to buy your clay *ningyo* doll while in Fukuoka? You can find those here, as well as toys, lacquerware, pottery, glassware, paper products, sake, *kokeshi* dolls, bamboo ware, pearls, china, and everything else Japan makes. Open Monday through Friday from 9am to 5pm.

✪ Oriental Bazaar

5-9-13 Jingumae. ☎ **03/3400-3933.**

This is Tokyo's best-known and largest souvenir/crafts shop, selling products at reasonable prices. It's located on Omotesando Dori in Harajuku, easily distinguished by its Asian-looking facade of orange and green. It offers three floors of souvenir and gift items, including cotton yukata, polyester and silk kimono (new and used), woodblock prints, paper products, fans, Japanese swords, lamps and vases, Imari chinaware, sake sets, Japanese dolls, and pearls. This store will also ship things home for you. Open Friday to Wednesday from 9:30am to 6:30pm.

Department Stores

Japanese department stores are institutions in themselves. Usually enormous, well-designed, and chock-full of merchandise, they have about everything you can imagine, including museums and art galleries, pet stores, rooftop playgrounds or greenhouses, travel agencies, restaurants, grocery markets, and flower shops.

You could easily spend a whole day in a department store, eating, attending cultural exhibitions, planning your next vacation, and exploring the various departments. Microcosms of Japanese society, these department stores reflect the affluence of modern Japan, offering everything from wedding kimono to fashions by the world's top designers. And one of the most wonderful aspects of the Japanese department store is its courteous service.

If you arrive at a store as its doors open, at 10am, you will witness a daily rite: Lined up at the entrance, the entire staff will bow in welcome. Some Japanese shoppers arrive just before opening time so as not to miss this favorite ritual. Sales clerks are everywhere, ready to help you. In many cases you don't even have to go to the cash register once you've made your choice. Just hand over the product, along with your money, to the sales clerk, who will return with your change, your purchase neatly wrapped, and an "*arigatoo gozaimashita*" (thank you very much). A day spent in a Japanese department store could spoil you for the rest of your life.

Department stores are convenient places to shop for traditional Japanese items, including lacquerware, china and kitchenware, trays, gift items, toys, furniture, sporting goods, shoes, cosmetics, jewelry, clothing, sweets, lingerie, belts, hats, and household goods. The basement is usually devoted to foodstuffs: fresh fish, produce, and pre-prepared snacks and dinners. There are often free samples of food. If you're feeling slightly hungry, therefore, walking through the food department could do nicely for a snack. Many department stores include boutiques of such famous Japanese and international fashion designers as Issey Miyake, Rei Kawakubo (creator of Comme des Garçons), Hanae Mori, Christian Dior, Calvin Klein, and Brooks Brothers, as well as a department devoted to the kimono. To find out what's where, stop by the store's front entrance and ask for floor-by-floor guides in English.

Hours are generally 10am to 7pm, and since department stores close on different days of the week, you can always find several that are open, even on Sunday and holidays (which are major shopping days in Japan). All major credit and charge cards are accepted.

In Ginza & Nihombashi

Hankyu

2-5-1 Yurakucho. ☎ **03/3575-2233.**

A department store located in Yurakucho between the Hibiya and Ginza subway stations, this relative newcomer to the area has the usual food, clothing, and household goods departments. Open Friday to Wednesday from 10am to 7pm.

Matsuya

3-6-1 Ginza. ☎ **03/3567-1211.**

In the opposite direction from Ginza 4-chome Crossing, on Chuo Dori Avenue, this is one of my favorite department stores in Tokyo. It has a good selection of Japanese folkcraft items, kitchenware, and beautifully designed contemporary household goods, in addition to the usual clothes and accessories. If I were buying a wedding gift, this is one of the first places I'd look. Open Wednesday to Monday from 10am to 7pm.

Matsuzakaya

6-10-1 Ginza. ☎ **03/3572-1111.**

Located one block from Ginza 4-chome Crossing on Chuo Dori in the direction of Shimbashi, this is an older, more established mart, and was the first department store in Japan that did not require customers to take off their shoes at the entrance. Established more than 300 years ago, it appeals to Tokyo's older generation. Open Thursday to Tuesday from 10am to 7pm.

Mitsukoshi

1-4-1 Nihombashi Muromachi. ☎ **03/3241-3311.**

In Nihombashi, this is one of Japan's oldest department stores. First opened as a kimono shop back in the 1600s, today it has many name-brand boutiques, including Givenchy, Dunhill, Chanel, Hanae Mori, Oscar de la Renta, Christian Dior, and Tiffany. Its kimono, by the way, are still hot items. The building itself is old, stately, and attractive, making shopping here a pleasure. To reach it, use Mitsukoshimae Station, which means "in front of Mitsukoshi." Open Tuesday to Sunday from 10am to 7pm.

Another branch, located right on Ginza 4-chome Crossing (☎ 03/3562-1111), is popular with young shoppers. Open Monday to Friday from 10am to 5:30pm and on Saturday from 10am to 6pm.

Printemps

3-2-1 Ginza. ☎ **03/3567-0077.**

This store, a branch of Paris's fashionable Au Printemps, is a relative newcomer on the Ginza scene. A fun, young store with announcements in both French and Japanese, it's very popular with Tokyo's young generation. Open Thursday to Tuesday from 10am to 7pm.

Seibu

2-5-1 Yurakucho. ☎ **03/3286-0111.**

Located in Yurakucho between the Hibiya and Ginza subway stations, this store consists of two buildings, one selling clothing and accessories, the other specializing in interior design and kitchenware. Open Thursday to Tuesday from 10am to 7pm.

Takashimaya

2-4-1 Nihombashi. ☎ **03/3211-4111.**

This department store, located near Nihombashi Station, provides stiff competition for the above-listed Mitsukoshi, with a history just as long. It also has boutiques by such famous designers as Chanel, Laroche, Dunhill, Céline, Lanvin, Louis Vuitton, Gucci, Christian Dior, Issey Miyake, and Kenzo. Open Thursday to Tuesday from 10am to 7pm.

Wako

4-5-11 Ginza. ☎ **03/3562-2111.**

On the corner of Ginza 4-chome Crossing, this is one of the few buildings in the area to have survived World War II. Its distinctive clock tower and innovative window displays are Ginza landmarks. Wako specializes in imported fashions, luxury items, and Seiko timepieces. Certainly one of the classiest stores around, with prices to match. Open Monday to Thursday from 10am to 5:30pm and on Friday and Saturday from 10am to 6pm; closed holidays.

In Ikebukuro

Seibu

1-28-1 Minami Ikebukuro. ☎ **03/3981-0111**.

Seibu, though not the largest department store, has 47 entrances, thousands of sales clerks, 63 restaurants, 12 floors, 31 elevators, and an average 170,000 shoppers a day. Two basement floors are devoted to foodstuffs—you can buy everything from taco shells to octopus to seaweed. Dishes are set out so that you can nibble and sample the food as you move along, and hawkers yelling out their wares give the place a marketlike atmosphere. Fast-food counters sell salads, grilled eel, chicken, sushi, and other ready-to-eat dishes. The rest of the floors offer clothing, furniture, art galleries, kitchenware, and a thousand other things, and many of the best Japanese and Western designers have boutiques here. Open Wednesday through Monday from 10am to 8pm.

Tobu/Metropolitan Plaza

1-1-25 Nishi-Ikebukuro. ☎ **03/3981-2211** (information in English).

Reopened and expanded in 1993 to 83,000 square meters, Tobu's Ikebukuro store is now Japan's largest. As many as 180,000 customers pass through its doors daily, served by nearly 3,000 clerks. Tobu has tripled its basement food floor to 254 shops, since food sales make up 15% to 20% of total department-store sales. Yearly sales come to a whopping ¥180 billion ($1.8 billion). Adjoining Metropolitan Plaza houses the Tobu Museum of Art, 130 specialized boutiques, 25 restaurants, a sports club, and parking facilities. Open Thursday to Tuesday from 10am to 7pm.

In Shibuya

In recent years, Shibuya has emerged as a shopping mecca for the fashionable young, and so many stores have opened in the last few years that there's a bona fide store war going on. Tokyu and Seibu are the two big names, both of which keep opening more and more shops around Shibuya Station. In addition to the big stores here, check the "Fashions" section for Shibuya's fashion department stores.

Seibu

21-1 Udagawacho. ☎ **03/3462-0111.**

Similar to the main store in Ikebukuro, it carries everything from accessories and art to stationery and wine. Designer boutiques here include Comme des Garçons, Giorgio Armani, Issey Miyake, Jun Ashida, Kenzo, and Yohji Yamamoto. Other Seibu stores include Loft (with items for the home and hobbyist, a stiff competitor of Tokyu Hands), Parco, and Seed (the last two are fashion stores, described below). Open Thursday to Tuesday from 10am to 7pm.

Tokyu

2-24-1 Dogenzaka. ☎ **03/3477-3111.**

A more conservative department store, Tokyu appeals to a 30s-and-up group. Tokyu's adjacent ultramodern Bunkamura complex is the largest cultural center in Japan and worth a visit. It contains a museum, theaters (the Tokyo Film Festival is held here), a bookstore, and cafes. Other Tokyu-affiliated stores include a smaller shop right above Shibuya Station, Tokyu Hands (everything imaginable for the hobbyist and the home), and the three One Oh Nine shops (filled with clothing boutiques, housewares, the latest music, and even a Body Shop). Open Wednesday to Monday from 10am to 7:30pm.

In Shinjuku

Isetan

3-14-1 Shinjuku. ☎ **03/3352-1111.**

Isetan is a favorite among foreigners living in Tokyo. It has a good line of conservative clothing appropriate for working situations, as well as contemporary and fashionable styles, including designer clothes (Issey Miyake, Kansai, and Yohji Yamamoto). It also has a great kimono section and a foreign-customer service counter. It's located about a five-minute walk west of Shinjuku Station on Shinjuku Dori. Open Thursday to Tuesday from 10am to 7:30pm.

Keio

1-1-4 Nishi Shinjuku. ☎ **03/3342-2111.**

Another department store right over the station is Keio, which specializes in everyday products for the hordes of commuters passing through. Open Friday to Wednesday from 10am to 7pm.

Odakyu

1-1-3 Nishi Shinjuku. ☎ **03/3342-1111.**

Odakyu is hard to miss, since it's located right above Shinjuku Station. Its merchandise is fairly middle-of-the-road. Open Wednesday to Monday from 10am to 7pm.

Dolls

Asakusabashi is the place to go for dolls, with several stores lining Edo Dori. These two stores are among the best known.

Kyugetsu

1-20-4 Yanagibashi, Taito-ku. ☎ **03/3861-5511.**

This is one of the biggest doll shops in Japan, located in front of Asakusabashi Station. It sells Japanese dolls ranging from elegant creatures with porcelain faces, delicate coiffures, and silk kimono to wooden dolls called *kokeshi.* Open daily from 9am to 6pm (until 5pm on Sunday).

Yoshitoku Dolls

1-9-14 Asakusabashi, Taito-ku. ☎ **03/3863-4419.**

Yoshitoku Dolls has had a shop at this location since 1711. One of the largest shops in the area, it sells a variety of Japanese dolls, including *Hakata* (fired-clay painted dolls representing traditional characters) and kokeshi, as well as kimono-clad babies, Kabuki figures, masks, souvenirs, and some antiques. Open daily from 9:30am to 5pm; closed national holidays.

Electronics

The largest concentration of electronics and electrical-appliance shops in Japan is in an area of Tokyo called Akihabara. Although you can find good deals on video and audio equipment elsewhere, Akihabara is special simply for its sheer volume. With more than 600 multilevel stores, shops, and stalls, Akihabara accounts for one-tenth of the nation's electronics and electrical-appliance sales. An estimated 50,000 shoppers come here on a weekday, 100,000 per day on a weekend. It may surprise you to learn that 80% of Japan's consumer electronics market is domestic.

Even if you don't buy anything, it's great fun walking around (and if you do intend to buy something, make sure you know what it would cost back home—with the present exchange rate, there are few bargains in Japanese electronics products, but you may be able to pick up something unavailable back home). Most of the stores and stalls are open-fronted, many of them are painted neon green and pink, and inside, lights are flashing, fans are blowing, was hing machines are shaking and shimmying, stereos are blasting. Salesmen yell out their wares, trying to get customers to look at their rice cookers, computers, video equipment, cassette players, TVs, calculators, and watches. This is the best place to go to see the latest models of everything electronic, an educational experience in itself.

If you purchase anything, make sure that it's made for export—that is, instructions in English, an international warranty, and the product has the correct electrical connectors.

Simply look for signs saying DUTY FREE. Good buys in Akihabara include cassette players, stereo equipment and CD players, watches, calculators, video equipment, and portable electronic typewriters. Be sure to bargain, and don't buy at the first place you go to. One woman I know who was looking for a portable cassette player bought it at the third shop she went to for ¥4,000 ($40) less than what was quoted to her at the first shop. All the larger shops in Akihabara have duty-free floors where the products are designed for export. Some of the largest shops are **Yamagiwa,** 3-13-10 Soto-Kanda (☎ 03/3253-2111); **Laox,** 1-2-9 Soto-Kanda (☎ 03/3253-7111); and **Hirose Musen,** 1-10-5 Soto Kanda (☎ 03/3255-2211). If you're serious about buying anything, comparison-shop at these stores first.

The easiest way to get to Akihabara is via the Yamanote Line or the Keihin Tohoku Line to the JR Akihabara Station. You can also take the Hibiya subway line to Akihabara Station, but it's farther to walk. Most shops are open daily from about 10am to 7pm.

Another place to look for electric and electronic equipment is the **Nishi-Ginza Electric Center,** 2-1-1 Yurakucho (☎ 03/3503-4481; closest station: Yurakucho or Hibiya). It's located in Ginza, next to the International Arcade and under the train tracks. Shops here sell radios, cassette players, calculators, CD players, and other electrical and electronic gadgets duty free. It's open Tuesday through Saturday from 10am to 7pm, and on Sunday and holidays from 10am to 6pm.

FASHIONS

Fashion department stores are multistoried buildings filled with concessions of various designers and labels. The stores below are some of the largest.

For Children

Dear Kids La Forêt

1-8-10 Jingumae. ☎ **03/3475-0411.**

The best thing that ever happened to kids is Dear Kids La Forêt, with kids clothing by Sesame, Mini Batsu, Sonia Rykiel, N.Y. Kids, and others. Check out Shirley Temple on the ground floor for heartbreaking lace, eyelet, and velveteen magic fashions. Zusso is a hair salon just for kids, with cartoons on TV at kid-friendly haircutting stations (haircuts ¥3,800/$38, walk-ins OK; open 10am to 6pm daily). Milky Way, with its astrological/star theme, is a whimsical place to dine (open daily 11am to 8pm) on the fourth floor. There's also an Earth Kids Gallery and print shop. Open 10am to 7pm daily.

For Men & Women

La Forêt

1-11-6 Jingumae. ☎ **03/3475-0411.**

Near Harajuku's main intersection of Omotesando Dori and Meiji Dori, it's not only the largest store in Harajuku, it's also one of the most fashionable. Young designers like Masaki Matsushima and Maruyama Kei are here, as well as names like Plantation by Issey Miyake. Although some of the boutiques are expensive, reasonably priced fashions are in the basement and on the fourth floor. Open daily from 11am to 8pm.

Parco

15-1 Udagawacho. ☎ **03/3464-5111.**

A division of Seibu, Parco is divided into three buildings called Parco 1, 2, and 3. Parco 1 and 2 are filled with designer boutiques for men and women, including such avant-garde Japanese designers and designs as Yohji Yamamoto, Nicole, Comme des Garçons, and Issey Miyake, while Parco 3 is devoted to household goods and interiors. Parco has two sales a year that you shouldn't miss if you're here—one in January and one in July. Open daily from 10am to 8:30pm.

Seed

21-1 Udagawacho. ☎ **03/3462-0111.**

One of Seibu's newer ventures in the store wars of Shibuya, Seed consists of eight floors devoted to the newest of the new in design talent. There will be a lot of names you're probably not familiar with, along with such notables as Paul Smith, Katharine Hamnett, Takeo Kikuchi, and Jean Paul Gaultier. Open Thursday to Tuesday from 11am to 8pm.

Vivre 21

5-10-1 Jingumae. ☎ **03/3498-2221.**

Not far from La Forêt is Vivre, a sleek white building filled with fashionable boutiques selling designer clothing and jewelry. Nicole, Montana, Thierry Mugler, Jean Paul Gaultier, and Junko Shimada are just a few of the concessions here. In the basement is a shop selling kitchenware, plus a cafe. Open daily from 11am to 8pm.

Designer Boutiques

The block between Omotesando Crossing and the Nezu Museum has become the Rodeo Drive of Japan, the showcase of top designers. Even if you can't buy here (steep prices for most pocketbooks), a stroll is de rigeur for clothes hounds and those interested in design. The classy boutiques listed here are all on this street.

Comme des Garçons

5-2-1 Minami. ☎ **03/3406-3951.**

Located on the right side of the boutique-lined street is Rei Kawakubo's showcase store of both men's and women's designs. The boutique's daring black-and-white windows and clothes to die for make this a wonderful stop, even if you can't afford the price tags (probably nothing less than ¥50,000/$500). Open daily from 11am to 8pm.

Issey Miyake

3-18-11 Minami-Aoyama. ☎ **03/3423-1407.**

Across the street from Comme des Garçons (above), in a modern design building with an entranceway suggestive of an anatomical body part, there are two floors of cool, spacious displays of Miyake's interestingly structured designs. One half of the building is dedicated to men's and one half to women's clothing, accessories, and footwear. Another part of the building is devoted to scents. Ignore the stuck-up clerks and enjoy the clothing. Issey Miyake's Permanente (☎ 03/3499-6476) collection of classics is farther down the street (toward the Nezu Museum), on the opposite side in the From-1st Bldg. Open 11am to 8pm daily.

Yohji Yamamoto

5-3-6 Minami-Aoyama. ☎ **03/3409-6006.**

Clothes sparingly hung, flaunting the interior space, Yohji Yamamoto's unique designs are displayed here. Making a name for himself in Paris as well as Japan, Yamamoto's popularity is based on the classic wearability of his clothes. Open daily from 11am to 8pm.

Discount Fashions

Recently a number of overruns and discount shops, as well as secondhand consignment shops have opened up near Ebisu Station and in the direction of Hiroo. They are difficult to find, so I suggest that serious shoppers ask at the koban (police box) at Ebisu Station or take a cab. Prices here will be half what you'd pay in a designer boutique for this season's or last year's men's and women's fashions. Secondhand clothes have little or no wear. **Garret,** at 4-9-13 Ebisu (1 minute from the south east exit of the JR Ebisu Station), is where a men's current-season Comme des Garçons Homme suit can be had for ¥57,000 ($570). It's open daily from 11am to 9pm. Next door to Garret is **Norma Jean,** which carries mostly Western designers' new factory overstock with prices from ¥2,500 to ¥25,000 ($25 to $250). It's open Wednesday to Monday from 1pm to 8pm. **One Fifth** at 1-26-15 Ebisu (☎ 03/3442-1366) and **Chocolate Soup** at 2-6-29 Ebisu (☎ 03/3442-1447) are near each other, run by the same company and open 11am to 8pm daily. Pick up, for example, an Issey Miyake pleated top for ¥8,800 ($88) at One Fifth and a Katharine Hamnett wool dress for ¥17,800 ($178) at Chocolate Soup. **Ultra Queen** is nearby at 2-6-32 Ebisu (☎ 03/3449-9531) and has an amusing mix of used clothes, designer clothes, and originals using recycled clothes. It's open daily from 11am to 8pm. **Petite Vogue,** closer to Hiroo Station at 2-25-18 Ebisu (☎ 03/3444-6892) has consignment clothing.

Harajuku has the oldest used-clothing shops, including **Chicago's** on Omotesando Dori, but they offer mostly U.S. nostalgia at 10 times U.S. thrift-store prices. Trendy Daikanyama, one stop beyond Shibuya on the Toyoko Line and a good place for a stroll, has **Circus** (23-5 Daikonyama, across the lane from the Red Thunder Café, ☎ 03/3770-3977), with its used designer fashions (Romeo Gigli, Katharine Hamnett) for a fraction of the original costs (open noon to 8pm). And **Antiquelosium** (20-23 Daikanyama, ☎ 03/3461-5295) has real antique clothing to handpicked stylish 40's dresses (open Tuesday to Sunday from 1pm to 7pm).

Flea Markets

Flea markets, of course, are good opportunities to shop for antiques as well as for delightful junk. Don't expect to find any good buys in furniture, but you can pick up secondhand kimono, kitchenware, small chests, dolls, household items, and odds and ends. The markets usually begin as early as 6am and last until 4pm or so, but go early if you want to pick up bargains. Bargaining is expected. There are flea markets every weekend in Tokyo.

In addition to the regularly scheduled ones listed here, there are markets held occasionally at various other places in Tokyo, especially in summer. Check the *Tokyo Journal* for a list of the month's markets.

Togo Shrine, described in the Harajuku Walking Tour (above), has a flea market for antiques on the first and fourth Sundays of the month. Since it's held outside, it's canceled if it rains. It's good for used kimono, furniture, and curios. Open from 4am to 3pm.

Nogi Shrine (near Nogizaka Station) has an antiques flea market the second Sunday of the month dawn to dusk; this is also canceled when it rains.

In Roppongi, the steps of the **Roi Building** become a market as dealers lay out their wares on the fourth Thursday and Friday of every month from 7am to 6pm. Items here are generally small, since space is limited.

Although held irregularly (once or twice a month on a Sunday, from 10am to 4pm), the **Yoyogi Park** flea market is the place to go for secondhand goods. Only used items may be sold, and since there aren't many outlets for such goods in Japan, it resembles a huge American yard sale. Since anyone can buy space here, vendors range from foreigners moving away from Japan who are eager to get rid of what they've accumulated to Japanese families selling unwanted junk. It's held near Yoyogi Park and NHK Hall.

Finally, the closest thing Tokyo has to a permanent flea market is **Ameya Yokocho,** also referred to as Ameyokocho or Ameyacho. Located near Ueno Park, it's a narrow shopping street along the elevated tracks of the Yamanote Line between Ueno and Okachimachi Stations. Originally a wholesale market for candy and snacks and later a black market in U.S. Army goods after World War II, Ameya Yokocho today consists of approximately 400 stalls selling discounted items including everything from fish and vegetables to handbags and clothes. Early evening is the most crowded time, as workers rush through on their way home and hawkers shout out their wares. The scene retains something of the shitamachi spirit of old Tokyo. Although housewives have been coming here for years, in more recent times young Japanese have also discovered it as a good bargain spot for fashions and accessories. Some shops close on Wednesday, but otherwise hours here are from about 10am to 7pm. Don't even think of coming here on a holiday—it's a standstill pedestrian traffic jam.

Flower-Arranging & Tea-Ceremony Accessories

In addition to this shop, other good places to look for these traditional wares are department stores. The Japan Traditional Craft Center, described above under "Crafts & Traditional Japanese Products," usually has beautiful bamboo vases and other accessories for flower arranging.

Tsutaya

5-10-5 Minami Aoyama, Minato-ku. ☎ **03/3400-3815.**

Tsutaya has everything you might need for ikebana (flower arranging) or the Japanese tea ceremony, including vases of unusual shapes and sizes and tea whisks. Open from 9am to 6:30pm; closed the first and fourth Sundays and the second and third Fridays of each month.

Interior Design

The department stores listed above have furniture and interior design sections, and Ikebukuro's **Seibu** (see above) has an especially well-known and popular department. My favorite is the Design Collection on the seventh floor of Ginza's **Matsuya** (see above), which displays items from around the world selected by the Japan Design Committee as examples of fine design. Included may be such goods as the Alessi teapot from Italy, Braun razors and clocks, and Porsche sunglasses.

A very good place for studying the latest in contemporary Japanese interior design is the **Axis Building,** 5-17-1 Roppongi (closest station: Roppongi). There are some two dozen shops here, most devoted to high-tech interior design. The majority of the products are Japanese, but there are also selected goods from the United States and Europe. Shops feature various aspects of contemporary design, from sleek and unusual lighting fixtures to textiles and linens, clocks, kitchenware, office accessories, and lacquered furniture. Don't neglect the shops in the basement. Hours vary for each shop, but most are open from 11am to 7pm; closed on Sunday and holidays. The Axis Building is on your right as you walk on Gaien-Higashi Dori in the direction of Tokyo Tower.

One of the big department-store chains, Marui, has opened **In the Room,** a nine-floor building of interior goods located at 1-21-3 Jinnan, Shibuya-ku (☎ 03/3464-0101). Part of the surge in department stores in Shibuya and the wave of interest in home furnishings as the fashion sales fell off, In the Room is filled with a variety of goods, from cute teddy bears to serious functional furniture. In the Room is open Thursday through Tuesday from 11am to 8pm.

Kimono

The Oriental Bazaar, described earlier under "Crafts & Traditional Japanese Products," has a good selection of new and used kimono, including elaborate wedding kimono. In addition, department stores sell kimono, notably Takashimaya and Mitsukoshi in Nihombashi and Isetan in Shinjuku. They have sales on rental wedding kimono at least once a year (check the *Tokyo Journal*). Flea markets are also good for used kimono and yukata.

Chicago

6-31-21 Jingumae. ☎ **03/3409-5017.**

The place to go for used kimono. Located on Omotesando Dori in Harajuku, it stocks hundreds of used kimono and cotton yukata in the very back of the shop, past the 1950s clothing. There are many used kimono in the price range of ¥1,500 to ¥5,000 ($15 to $50). Open daily from 11am to 8pm.

Hayashi Kimono

International Arcade, 2-1-1 Yurakucho. ☎ **03/3501-4012.**

Established in 1913, Hayashi Kimono sells silk and polyester kimono, including wedding kimono and the short *happi-coat.* It also sells cotton yukata, men's and children's kimono, and *obi,* the sash worn around a kimono. If you're buying a gift for someone back home, this is the best place to start. Hayashi Kimono has two concessions in the International Arcade. Open daily from 10am to 7pm; closes at 6pm on Sunday.

Kitchenware & Tableware

In addition to the department stores listed above, there are two areas in Tokyo with a number of shops filled with items related to cooking and serving. In Tsukiji, along the streets stretching between Tsukiji Station and Tsukiji Fish Market, are shops selling pottery, serving trays, bowls, dishes, wonderful fish knives, and lunch boxes.

The second place to look is Kappabashi Dori near the Tawaramachi subway station, Japan's largest wholesale area for cookware. There are approximately 150 specialty stores selling cookware here, including sukiyaki pots, woks, lunch boxes, pots and pans, aprons, knives, china, lacquerware, rice cookers, and disposable wooden chopsticks. Although stores in Tsukiji and Kappabashi are wholesalers selling mainly to restaurants, you're welcome to browse and purchase as well. Stores in both areas are closed on Sunday.

Paper Products

Kurodaya

1-2-5 Asakusa. ☎ **03/3844-7511.**

If you're visiting Asakusa, you might want to stop in at this shop, located right beside Kaminarimon Gate. First opened back in 1856, it sells traditional Japanese papers, kites, papier-mâché masks, boxes, and other products made of paper. Open Tuesday to Sunday from 11am to 7pm.

Washikobo

1-8-10 Nishi Azabu, Minato-ku. ☎ **03/3405-1841.**

Washikobo is about seven minutes on foot from the station, on the right side of the street as you walk toward Shibuya. This store deals almost exclusively in handmade Japanese paper and handcrafts from various parts of Japan. It sells paper and cardboard boxes, paper wallets, notebooks, paper lamps, toys, and sheets of beautifully crafted paper. Open Monday to Saturday from 10am to 6pm; closed national holidays.

Pearls

Asahi Shoten

Imperial Hotel Arcade, 1-1-1 Uchisaiwaicho. ☎ **03/3503-2528.**

This pearl shop in the Imperial Hotel Arcade has a good selection in the modest-to-moderate price range. Open daily from 9am to 7pm.

K. Uyeda Pearl Shop

Imperial Hotel Arcade, 1-1-1 Uchisaiwaicho. ☎ **03/3503-2587.**

In business since 1884, this shop has a wide selection of pearls in many different price ranges. Open Monday through Saturday from 10am to 7pm, and on Sunday and holidays from 10am to 6pm.

Mikimoto

4-5-5 Ginza. ☎ **03/3535-4611.**

The first really good cultured pearl was produced back in 1913 by a Japanese man named Mikimoto Koichi. Today, Mikimoto is one of the most famous names in the world of cultured pearls. The main shop is not far from Ginza 4-chome Crossing. Open Thursday to Tuesday from 10:30am to 7pm.

Mikimoto has a branch shop at the Imperial Hotel Arcade, Uchisaiwaicho (☎ 03/3591-5001), open Monday to Saturday from 10am to 7pm.

Records, Cassettes & Compact Discs

✪ Tower Records

1-22-14 Jinan, Shibuya-ku. ☎ **03/3496-3661.**

From classical to new releases and Japanese pop to games and CD roms, it's all here in six floors of music to choose from. The basement houses a cafe; the seventh floor, imported books and magazines; and the eighth floor is an event space. Its open daily 10am to 10pm, but closed the last Wednesday of the month. There are Tower Records in West Shinjuku (☎ 3340-3851), East Shinjuku (☎ 5379-4101), and Ikebukuro (☎ 3983-2010).

Virgin Megastore

Marui 101 Bldg. basement, 3-30-16 Shinjuku. ☎ **03/3353-0056.**

Located on Shinjuku Dori, Virgin stocks 150,000 CD titles and 15,000 videos, and what's more, offers 50 listening stations. Open daily from 10:30am to 7:30pm; closed the second and fourth Wednesdays of each month.

Wave

6-2-27 Roppongi. ☎ **03/3408-0111.**

This innovative store, a branch of Seibu, has a computerized record-reference system and a comprehensive selection of records, cassettes, CDs, and videos. On the first floor are headphones to help you select from 200 of the top hits. In the basement is Ciné Vivant, a minitheater that shows foreign films four or five times daily. Open Monday to Saturday from 11am to 10pm and on Sunday from 11am to 8pm; closed the first and third Wednesdays of each month. Wave is three minutes on foot from Roppongi station, on the left side of Roppongi Dori as you walk in the direction of Shibuya.

If you're in Ikebukuro, there's a second Wave outlet located at 1-19-6 Minami-Ikebukuro (☎ 3980-1111), across from the Seibu department store. Open Wednesday to Monday from 10am to 7pm. Take Ikebukuro Station's east exit, turn right and walk south on Meiji Dori.

SAKE

✪ Nihonshu Center

5-9-1 Ginza. ☎ **03/3575-0656.**

This is a good place to go to learn more about sake, and you can sample five different kinds of the brew for ¥300 ($3)—and you get to keep the sake cup. A great deal! The center sells sake from regions throughout Japan. It's located on Harumi Dori, not far from Ginza 4-chome Crossing, in the direction of Higashi Ginza, on the right side of the street (look for a sign that says SAKESPO 101). Open Friday to Wednesday from 10:30am to 6:30pm; closed holidays.

SOUVENIRS

The best places to look for souvenir items are the Oriental Bazaar, listed above in "Crafts & Traditional Japanese Products," and the pedestrian shopping lane called Nakamise Dori, described in the Asakusa Walking Tour. In addition, the International Arcade, described in the Ginza Walking Tour, is full of shops selling kimono, china, woodblock prints, pearls, and other Japanese products.

SWORDS

Other places to look for swords include the Oriental Bazaar, the Tokyo Antique Hall, and the Antique Market in the basement of the Hanae Mori Building in Omotesando.

Japan Sword

3-8-1 Toranomon. ☎ **03/3434-4321.**

This is the best-known sword shop in Tokyo, also dealing in sword accessories, sword guards, and kitchen cutlery. Coming here to see its displays is like visiting a museum. It is closest to Kamiyacho Station. Open Monday to Friday from 9:30am to 6pm and on Saturday from 9:30am to 5pm; closed holidays.

WOODBLOCK PRINTS

In addition to the store listed below, other good places for woodblock prints, including original antiques and reproductions, are the Oriental Bazaar and the Antique Market in the basement of the Hanae Mori Building, both on Omotesando Dori in Harajuku.

Sakai Kokodo Gallery

1-2-14 Yurakucho. ☎ **03/3591-4678.**

This gallery across from the Imperial Hotel claims to be the oldest woodblock print shop in Japan. The first shop was opened back in 1870 in the Kanda area of Tokyo by the present owner's great-grandfather, and altogether four generations of the Sakai family have tended the store. This is a great place for original prints, as well as for reproductions of such great masters as Hiroshige. (If you're really a woodblock print fan, you'll want to visit the Sakai family's excellent museum in the small town of Matsumoto in the Japan Alps.) Open daily from 11am to noon and 1pm to 6pm.

6 Tokyo After Dark

By day, Tokyo is arguably one of the least attractive cities in the world. A congested mass of concrete, it has too many unimaginative buildings, too many cars and people, and not enough trees and greenery.

Come dusk, however, Tokyo comes into its own. The drabness fades, and the city blossoms into a profusion of giant neon lights and paper lanterns, and its streets fill with millions of overworked Japanese out to have a good time. If you ask me, Tokyo at night is unequivocally one of the craziest cities in the world. It's a city that never gives up and never seems to sleep. The entertainment district of Roppongi, for example, is as crowded at 3am as it is at 3pm. Many establishments stay open until the first subways start running after 5am. Whether it's jazz, reggae, gay bars, sex shows, discos, mania, or madness that you're searching for, Tokyo has it all.

To understand Tokyo's nightlife, you first have to know that there is no one center of nighttime activity. Rather, there are many nightspots spread throughout the city, each with its own atmosphere, price range, and clientele. Most famous are probably Ginza, Akasaka, Shinjuku, and Roppongi. Before visiting any of the locales suggested in this guide, be sure to walk around and absorb the atmosphere. The streets will be crowded, the neon lights will be overwhelming, and you never know what you might discover on your own.

Although there are many bars, discos, and restaurants packed with young Japanese men and women, nightlife in Japan is still pretty much a man's domain, just as it has been for centuries. At the high end of this domain are the geisha bars, where highly trained women entertain by playing traditional Japanese instruments, singing, and holding witty conversations—and nothing more risqué than that. Generally speaking, such places are outrageously expensive and closed to outsiders. As a foreigner, you'll have little opportunity to visit a geisha bar unless you're invited by a business associate, in which case you should consider yourself extremely fortunate.

More common than geisha bars, and generally not quite as expensive, are the so-called hostess bars, many of which are located in Ginza and Akasaka. A woman will sit at your table, talk to you, pour your drinks, listen to your problems, and boost your ego. You buy her drinks as well, which is one reason the tab can be so high. Hostess bars in various forms have been a part of Japanese society for centuries. Most foreigners will probably find the cost of visiting a hostess bar not worth the price, as the hostesses usually speak only Japanese, but such places provide Japanese males with sympathetic ears and the chance to escape the world of both work and family. Men usually have their favorite hostess bar, often a small place with just enough room for regular customers. In the more exclusive hostess bars, only those with an introduction are allowed entrance. And in almost all cases, Japanese companies are picking up the tab.

The most popular nightlife establishments are drinking locales, where the vast majority of Japan's office workers, college students, and expatriates go for an evening out. These places include Western-style bars, as well as Japanese-style watering holes, called *nomi-ya*. Yakitori-ya, restaurant-bars that serve yakitori and other snacks, are included in this group.

At the low end of the spectrum are Tokyo's topless bars, sex shows, massage parlors, and pornography shops, with the largest concentration of such places in Shinjuku.

In addition to the establishments listed here, be sure to check the Japanese restaurants listed in the inexpensive category for a relatively inexpensive night out on the town. Many places serve as both eateries and watering holes, especially those that dish out skewers of yakitori.

And finally, one more thing you should be aware of is the "table charge" that many bars and cocktail lounges charge their customers. Included in the table charge is usually a small appetizer—maybe nuts, chips, or a vegetable. At any rate, the charge is usually between ¥300 and ¥500 ($3 and $5) per person. Some establishments levy a table charge only after a certain time in the evening; others may add it only if you don't order food from the menu. If you're not sure and it matters to you, be sure to ask before ordering anything. Some locales call it an *otsumami,* or snack charge. Remember, too, that a 3% consumption tax will be added to your bill. Some establishments, especially nightclubs, hostess bars, and some dance clubs, will also add a 10% to 20% service charge.

To find out what's happening in the entertainment scene (contemporary and traditional music and theater, exhibitions in museums and galleries, films, and special events), you will find the best publication to be the *Tokyo Journal.* Published monthly and available for ¥600 ($6) at foreign-language bookstores, restaurants, and bars, it also has articles of interest to foreigners in Japan.

To secure tickets, you can always go to the theater or hall itself. However, if you're staying in one of the upper-class hotels, the concierge or guest-relations manager will usually obtain tickets for you. Otherwise, a much easier way to secure tickets is through one of several ticket services available. **Ticket PIA** is probably your best bet, as it has an English-language service. Ticket services include **Ticket PIA** (☎ 03/5237-9990), **Ticket Saison** (☎ 03/3286-5482), and **CN Playguide** (☎ 03/5802-9999).

PERFORMING ARTS

KABUKI Among the several theaters in Tokyo with regular showings of Kabuki, **Kabukiza,** 4-12-15 Ginza (☎ 03/541-3131, or 03/5565-6000 for reservations; located above the Higashi-Ginza subway station), is the best known. This theater has about eight or nine Kabuki productions a year, each of which runs 25 days (there are no shows in August). Usually, there are two different programs being shown; matinees run from about 11 or 11:30am to 4pm, and evening performances run from about 4:30 or 5pm to about 9pm. It's considered perfectly okay to come for only part of a performance. In addition to English programs explaining the plot, which cost ¥1,000 ($10), there are English earphones for rent (¥600/$6, plus a ¥1,000/$10 refundable deposit) providing a running commentary on the story, music, actors, stage properties, and other aspects of Kabuki. Obviously, buying a program or renting earphones will add immensely to your enjoyment of the play.

Tickets generally range from about ¥2,500 to ¥16,000 ($25 to $160), depending on the program and the seat location. Advance tickets can be purchased at the Advance Ticket Office, to the right side of Kabukiza's main entrance, from 10am to 6pm. Otherwise, tickets for each day's performance are placed on sale one hour before the start of each matinee and evening performance.

If you want to come for only part of a performance (say, for an hour or so), you can do so for as little as ¥700 to ¥1,000 ($7 to $10) for seats on the fourth floor, on a first-come, first-served basis. No earphones are available, but you can still buy a program.

If you're in Tokyo in August, when there are no Kabuki performances at Kabukiza, you can usually see Kabuki at the **National Theater of Japan** or *Kokuritsu Gekijo* (☎ 03/3265-7411) 4-1 Hayabusacho, Chiyoda-ku (Subway: Hanzomon, Kojimachi, or Nagatacho). Kabuki is scheduled here throughout the year except during May, September, and December, when Bunraku is being staged instead. Ticket prices range from about ¥1,500 to ¥9,000 ($15 to $90).

NOH Noh performances are given at a number of locations in Tokyo, with tickets generally ranging from ¥2,000 to ¥5,000 ($20 to $50). Performances are usually in the early afternoon, at 1pm, or in the late afternoon, at 5 or 6:30pm; but check the *Tokyo Journal* for exact times. Following is a list of several Noh theaters, of which the National Noh Theater is the most famous:

Hosho Nohgakudo (☎ 03/3811-5753) 1-5-9 Hongo, Bunkyo-ku. Station: Suidobashi (5 minutes).
Kanze Nohgakudo (☎ 03/3469-5241) 1-16-4 Shoto, Shibuya-ku. Station: Shibuya (15 minutes).
Kita Nohgakudo (☎ 03/3491-7773) 4-6-9 Kami-Osaki, Shinagawa-ku. Station: JR Meguro (15 minutes toward Gajoen).
National Noh Theater or *Kokuritsu Nohgakudo* (☎ 03/3423-1331) 4-18-1 Sendagaya, Shibuya-ku. Station: Sendagaya.
Tessenkai Butai (☎ 03/3401-2285) 4-21-29 Minami Aoyama, Minato-ku. Subway: Omotesando exit A4.
Umewaka Nohgakudo (☎ 03/3363-7748) 2-6-14 Higashi-Nakano, Nakano-ku. Subway: Nakano Sakaue.
Yarai Nohgakudo (☎ 03/3268-7311) 60 Yaraicho, Shinjuku-ku (located up the hill from the Yarai exit of Kagurazaka Station on the Tozai subway line).

BUNRAKU Some three Bunraku performances a year, in May, September, and December, are staged at **The National Theater of Japan** or *Kokuritsu Gekijo* (☎ 03/3265-7411), 4-1 Hayabusacho, Chiyoda-ku (Station: Hanzomon, Kojimachi, or Nagatacho). There are usually two performances daily, with tickets costing ¥4,000 to ¥4,800 ($40 to $48). Earphones with English explanations are available for ¥650 ($6.50).

WESTERN CLASSICAL MUSIC Among the best known orchestras in Tokyo are the **Tokyo Philharmonic Orchestra** (☎ 03/3256-9696), the **Japan Philharmonic Orchestra** (☎ 03/3234-5991), the **Tokyo Prefectural Orchestra** (☎ 03/3822-0727), and the **NHK Philharmonic Orchestra** (☎ 03/3465-1780). They play in various theaters in Tokyo, with the majority of performances in either Suntory Hall or NHK Hall. Since the schedule varies, it's best to call the orchestra directly or check with the *Tokyo Journal* to see whether there's a current performance. Also check to see if there's a performance by the famed **Tokyo String Quartet.**

Major Concert & Performance Halls

Bunkamura (☎ 03/3477-3244) 2-24-1 Dogenzaka Shibuya-ku. (Station: Shibuya). Bunkamura includes Orchard Hall and Theater Cocoon.

Kabukiza (☎ 03/3541-3131) 4-12-15 Ginza. (Subway: Higashi-Ginza).

Nakano Sun Plaza (☎ 03/3388-1151) 4-1-1 Nakano, Nakano-Ku. (Station: Nakano).

National Theater of Japan or *Kokuritsu Gekijo* (☎ 03/3265-7411) 4-1 Hayabusacho, Chiyoda-ku. (Subway: Hanzomon, Kojimachi, or Nagatacho).

NHK Hall (☎ 03/3465-1751) 2-2-1 Jinnan, Shibuya-ku. (Station: Harajuku or Shibuya).

Sunshine Gekijo Theater (☎ 03/3987-5281) Sunshine City Bunka Kaikan, 3-1-4 Higashi Ikebukuro. (Station: Higashi Ikebukuro).

Suntory Hall (☎ 03/3505-1001) Ark Hills, 1-13-1 Akasaka. (Subway: Akasaka, Toranomon, or Roppongi).

Tokyo Bunka Kaikan (☎ 03/3828-2111) Ueno Park (Station: Ueno, Koen exit).

DANCE There is a steady stream of dance companies performing in the capital, including Japanese and foreign ballet companies and modern dance groups. One of the best-known forms of modern Japanese dance is Butoh: it features performers who create their own highly individualistic interpretations. Unfortunately, Butoh is more popular abroad than it is in Japan. To see what's being performed where, check the *Tokyo Journal*.

TAKARZUKA KAGEKIDAN This world-famous, all-female troupe stages elaborate musical revues, with dancing, singing, and gorgeous costumes. The first Takarazuka troupe, formed in 1912 at a resort near Osaka, gained instant notoriety because all its performers were women, in contrast to the all-male Kabuki. When I went to see this troupe perform, I was surprised to find that the audience consisted almost exclusively of women.

Performances are held generally in March, April, July, August, November, December, and sometimes in June in Tokyo at **Tokyo Takarazuka Gekijo** (☎ 03/3591-1711, 03/3201-7777 for reservations), 1-1-3 Yurakucho. Occasionally a performance is held in the Kabukiza theater in Higashi-Ginza. Inquire at the Tourist Information Center for more information. Tickets generally range from about ¥1,200 to ¥5,000 ($12 to $50).

THE CLUB & MUSIC SCENE

ENTERTAINMENT DISTRICTS

Ginza is a chic and expensive shopping area by day, but at night transforms itself into a dazzling entertainment district of restaurants, bars, and first-grade hostess bars. It's the most sophisticated of Tokyo's nightlife districts and also one of the most expensive, so you have to exercise great caution in choosing a place in which to settle down for the evening; otherwise, you might be paying for the experience for a long time to come. Ginza clubs, notorious for being ridiculously expensive, are supported solely by business executives out on expense accounts. Remember that hardly any of the Japanese businessmen you see out carousing in Ginza's expensive hostess bars are paying for it out of their own pockets. The cost is simply too prohibitive, with bills running from $100 to $500 per person. Since I'm not wealthy, I personally prefer Shinjuku and Roppongi to Ginza for nighttime entertainment. However, because Ginza does have some fabulous restaurants, I am including some suggestions of things to do in the area if you happen to find yourself here after dinner. Remember, the cheapest way to absorb the atmosphere in Ginza is simply to wander about, particularly around Namiki Dori.

Not quite as sophisticated as Ginza, **Akasaka** nonetheless has its share of exclusive geisha and hostess bars, hidden away behind forbidding walls and exquisite front courtyards. More accessible are the many drinking bars, cabarets, restaurants, and inexpensive holes-in-the-wall. Popular with both executive tycoons and ordinary office workers, as well as foreigners staying in one of Akasaka's many hotels, this district stretches from the Akasaka-mitsuke subway station along three narrow streets, called Hitotsugui, Misuji, and Tamachi, all the way to the Akasaka subway station and beyond. For orientation purposes, stop by the koban (police box) at the huge intersection of Aoyama Dori and Sotobori Dori at Akasaka-mitsuke Station.

Northeast of **Shinjuku** Station is an area called **Kabuki-cho,** which undoubtedly has the craziest nightlife in all of Tokyo. A world of its own, it's sleazy, chaotic, crowded, vibrant, and fairly safe—block after block of strip joints, massage parlors, pornography shops, peep shows, bars, restaurants, and lots of drunk Japanese men. I wouldn't be surprised to hear that (with the possible exception of Munich's Oktoberfest) there are more drunk people per square meter in Shinjuku than anywhere else in the world. Shinjuku's primary night hot spot has nothing to do with Kabuki. Apparently at one time there was a plan to bring some culture to the area by introducing a Kabuki theater; the plan never materialized, but the name stuck. Although Kabuki-cho has always been the domain of salarymen out on the town, in recent years young Japanese, including college-age men and women, have claimed parts of it as their own, with the result that there are a few inexpensive drinking establishments well worth the visit.

To the east of Kabuki-cho is a smaller district called **Goruden Gai,** which is "Golden Guy" mispronounced. It's a neighborhood of tiny alleyways leading past even tinier bars, each consisting of just a counter and a few chairs. Closed to outsiders, these bars cater to regular customers. On hot summer evenings the *mama-san* of these bars sit outside on stools and fan themselves, soft red lights melting out of the open doorways. Things aren't as they appear, however. These aren't brothels—they're simply bars, and the "mama"-san are as likely to be men as women. Unfortunately, Goruden Gai sits on such expensive land that many of the bar owners are being forced to sell their shops. Some of them are already boarded up, awaiting land developers who are itching to build a highrise. It's a shame, because this tiny neighborhood is one of the most fascinating in all of Tokyo.

Even farther east is **Shinjuku 2-chome,** officially recognized as the gay-bar district of Shinjuku. It's here that I was once taken to a host bar featuring young men in crotchless pants. Strangely enough, the clientele included both gay men and groups of young, giggling office girls. The place has since closed down, but Shinjuku is riddled with places bordering on the absurd.

The best thing to do in Shinjuku is simply to walk about. In the glow of neon light, you'll pass everything from smoke-filled restaurants to hawkers trying to get you to step inside so they can part you from your money. If you're looking for strip joints, topless or bottomless coffee shops, peep shows, or pornography shops, I leave you to your own devices, but you certainly won't have any problems finding them. In Kabuki-cho alone, there are an estimated 200 sex businesses in operation, including bathhouses where women are available for sex, usually at a cost of around ¥30,000 ($300). Although prostitution is illegal in Japan, everyone seems to ignore what goes on behind closed doors.

A word of warning for women traveling by themselves—forgo the experience of Shinjuku. Although you're relatively safe here, with so many people milling about, you won't feel comfortable with so many inebriated fellows stumbling around. If there are two of you, however, you'll be okay. I took my mother to Kabuki-cho for a spin around the neon, and we escaped relatively unscathed.

Besides walking around and dining in Shinjuku (see chapter 4), you can also hear music and visit inexpensive drinking establishments. Although most of the night action in Shinjuku is east of the station, the west side also has an area of inexpensive restaurants and bars.

Roppongi is the most fashionable and hip place to hang out for Tokyo's younger crowd. It's also a favorite with Tokyo's foreign community, including the many models in the city, businessmen, and English teachers. With more discos than any other place in town, Roppongi also has more than its fair share of jazz houses, restaurants, expatriate bars, and pubs. Some Tokyoites complain that Roppongi is too crowded, too trendy, and too commercialized (and has too many foreigners), but for the casual visitor I think Roppongi offers an excellent opportunity to view what's new and hot in the capital city.

For orientation purposes, the center of Roppongi is Roppongi Crossing (the intersection of Roppongi Dori and Gaien-Higashi Dori), at the corner of which sits the garishly pink Almond Coffee Shop. The coffee shop itself has mediocre coffee and desserts at terribly inflated prices, but the sidewalk in front of the store is the number one meeting spot in Roppongi. If you're going to meet a friend in Roppongi, this is probably where it will be.

If you need directions, there's a conveniently located koban (police box) catercorner from the Almond Coffee Shop and next to the Mitsubishi Bank. It has a big map of the Roppongi area, showing the address system, and someone is always there.

Recently, Roppongi has spread over into neighboring **Nishi-Azabu,** with restaurants and nightclubs popping up. The center of Nishi-Azabu is the next big crossroads, Nishi-Azabu Crossing, down the expressway avenue toward Shibuya from Roppongi.

One of the most popular districts for young Japanese by day, **Harajuku** doesn't have much of a nightlife district because of the city zoning laws. There are a few places scattered through the area, however, that are good alternatives if you don't like the crowds or the commercialism of Tokyo's more famous nightlife districts.

NIGHTCLUBS & HOSTESS BARS

Club Maiko

Aster Plaza Bldg., Suzuran Dori., 7-7-6 Ginza. ☎ **03/3574-7745.** Cover ¥8,000 ($80); special package deal for foreigners, including entrance and show charge, snacks, and free drinks. Station: Ginza (3 minutes).

If you're interested in visiting a hostess bar, one in Ginza that's receptive to foreigners and not prohibitively expensive is this club, located in a modern building in the heart of the area. The hostesses here are geisha and *maiko,* who are young women still training to be geisha. At this small bar, consisting of a few tables and a long counter, the women put on dancing shows and in between performances sit and talk with customers. With its traditional music and atmosphere, this may be the closest you'll get to Japan's geisha bars. Performances are given by the geisha four times nightly. Hostess drinks run ¥1,000 ($10). Open Monday to Saturday from 6pm to midnight; closed holidays.

Cordon Bleu

6-6-4 Akasaka. ☎ **03/3582-7800** or 3585-6980. Dinner and drinks, including show ¥12,000 ($120) or ¥150 ($150); show only ¥4,000 ($40), plus ¥1,000 ($10) drink minimum; 10% service charge and tax. Station: Akasaka (5 minutes).

Small and intimate, this well-known 150-seat nightclub in Akasaka features topless Japanese and foreign dancers, and former guests have included boxer Muhammad Ali and the late John Lennon. Two different dinner plans are offered, or you can choose to pay for the show only, but then there's a minimum drink charge. Open daily from 6pm, with shows at 7:30 and 10pm.

✪ Kingyo

3-14-17 Roppongi. ☎ **03/3478-3000.** Cover ¥4,000 ($40). Reservations advisable for the two shows at 7:30 and 10pm, and the extra show at 1:30am on Fri and Sat.

Near the Roppongi cemetery, you can't miss this drag cabaret—it has an obvious phallic sign outside. Inside, red counters, and chairs and walls lit in dim rosy pink, suggest a warm dark place, and mirrors shaped like genitalia complete the theme. Tables are smack up against the stage where between shows hostesses sit and charm customers. Because the show is high-energy, technically sophisticated, and fast-paced, and features elaborate costume changes, it's very enjoyable. Just try to guess which of the lovely dancers is female (there were two when I was there)—it's practically impossible. Clients range from housewives to gay couples to bosses who bring their O.L. (Tokyo slang for office lady) to embarrass them. Open daily.

LIVE-MUSIC HOUSES

Bau Haus

Wada Bldg., 6th floor, 7-15-9 Roppongi. ☎ **03/3403-0092.** Cover ¥1,300 ($13), one drink minimum, plus 20% service charge. Station: Roppongi (3 minutes).

This small club reminds me of somebody's 1960s garage, with the addition of low velveteen sofas. It's owned and operated by the house band, who serve the regular clientele, mostly foreigners, between sets! The band plays rock and roll, led by singer Kay-chan, a kind of Japanese David Bowie, who puts on quite a show—a bit raunchy in places. Kind of like a weird hostess club, he'll come and sit at your table between sets if you ask him. Bau Haus is located on the second street on your right as you descend toward Nishi-Azabu from the Roppongi crossing. Open Monday to Saturday from 8pm to 1am.

Birdland

Square Bldg., 3-10-3 Roppongi. ☎ **03/3478-3456.** Cover ¥1,500 ($15), plus ¥1,500 ($15) drink minimum, and 10% service charge. Station: Roppongi (2 minutes).

Down to earth and featuring good jazz, Birdland is a welcome refuge from Roppongi's madding crowd. It's located in the basement of the Square Building, well known for its discos on the upper floors. Small and cozy, with candles and soft lighting, this jazz house features live music performed by Japanese musicians every day of the week. Open Sunday to Thursday from 6pm to midnight and on Friday and Saturday from 6pm to 1am.

Blue Note

5-13-3 Minami Aoyama. ☎ **03/3407-5781.** Cover ¥7,000–¥13,000 ($70–$130), including one drink. Station: Omotesando (7 minutes).

One of the newest—and most expensive—nightclubs to open in Tokyo in recent years, this sophisticated jazz club is cousin to the famous Blue Note in New York and, with its blue interior, is almost an exact replica. It manages to draw top-notch jazz musicians: Oscar Peterson, Sarah Vaughan, Tony Bennett, Betty Carter, Lou Rawls, Sergio Mendes, and the Milt Jackson Quartet have all performed here. Open Monday to Saturday from 6pm to 1am, with shows at 7:30 and 10pm.

Cavern Club

5-3-2 Roppongi. ☎ **03/3405-5207.** Cover ¥1,300 ($13), music charge, one drink minimum, plus a 20% service charge. Station: Roppongi (4 minutes).

If you know your Beatles history, you'll know Cavern is the name of the Liverpool club where the Beatles got a start. The Tokyo club features house bands performing Beatles music exclusively, and very convincingly at that. Decorated with photos and memorabilia of the famous four, and extremely popular with both Japanese and foreigners, it's packed on weekends—with long waiting lines. Reservations are taken, but are good for only one show—then you have to leave. Open Monday to Saturday from 6pm to 2:30am and on Sunday and holidays from 6pm to midnight.

Crocodile

6-18-8 Jingumae. ☎ **03/3499-5205.** Cover ¥2,000–¥3,000 ($20–$30). Station: Meiji-Jingumae (10 minutes).

Located on Meiji Dori between Harajuku and Shibuya, this establishment is popular with the young and describes itself as a casual rock 'n' roll club, with live bands ranging from rock and blues to jazz-fusion, reggae, country, and experimental. It has an interesting interior and a good atmosphere; and the clientele ranges from Japanese with bleached-blond hair and earrings to English-language teachers, depending on the music. Open daily from 6pm to 2am, with live music from 8 to 9:30pm.

✪ New York Bar

Park Hyatt Hotel, 52nd floor, 3-7-1-2 Nishi-Shinjuku. ☎ **03/5322-1234.** Cover ¥1,500 ($15) (no charge if you dine in the adjacent New York Grill). Station: Shinjuku (13 minutes on foot or free shuttle from in front of the L-Tower building, exit A 18).

With views of West Shinjuku, Manhattan jazz, and ambience, this is the most sophisticated place to hear live jazz in Tokyo. There is bar and table seating under a vibrant, New York–theme painting by Valerio Adami. Drinks start at ¥1,000 ($10). An extensive wine list features California wines. Open daily from 5:30pm.

Piga Piga

Nanshin Bldg., 1-8-16 Ebisu Minami. ☎ **03/3715-3431.** Cover ¥2,500 ($25) Mon–Thurs; ¥3,000 ($30) Sat–Sun, and hol eves; plus ¥3,000 ($30) drinks/snack minimum. Station: JR Ebisu (2 minutes; out of the main west exit turn left down the second street away from and parallel to the tracks).

Though pricey, Piga Piga offers great music with live African bands from Tanzania, Zaire, and Kenya—the real thing. You have to buy 12 tickets (*piga*) at the door for ¥3,000 ($30), which you spend on food and drink. The decor is African, as are the beer and cocktails and the food. There are five sets a night, but you sometimes have to stand in line to get in. Open Monday to Saturday from 6pm to 1am.

Roppongi Pit Inn

3-17-7 Roppongi. ☎ **03/3585-1063.** Cover ¥3,000 ($30) and up, depending upon the group. Station: Roppongi (7 minutes down Gaien-Higashi Dori toward Tokyo Tower).

Another well-known music house, this is a no-frills basement establishment catering to a younger crowd and boasting some of the finest in native and imported fusion and jazz rock. Open daily from 6:30pm, with shows about 7:30 and 9pm.

Shinjuku Pit Inn

3-16-4 Shinjuku. ☎ **03/3354-2024.** Cover (including one drink) from ¥1,300 ($13) for the 2:30pm show, from ¥3,000 ($30) for the evening shows. Station: Shinjuku Sanchome (1 minute).

This is one of Tokyo's most famous jazz, fusion, and blues clubs, and features both Japanese and foreign musicians. An institution for more than 20 years, this basement locale near the Isetan department store, with exposed pipes and bare concrete walls, places more emphasis on good music than on atmosphere. Since only a few snacks (such as potato chips and sandwiches) are available, eat before you come. There are three programs daily—at 2:30, 7:30, and 9:30pm—making it a great place to stop for a bit of music in the middle of the day.

DANCE CLUBS & DISCOS

Roppongi is disco heaven, with approximately two dozen establishments clustered in the vicinity. Since the set cover charge often includes drinks and food, they can be the cheapest way to spend an evening. If you prefer to dance to live music, Roppongi has plenty of dance clubs as well. Keep in mind, however, prices are often higher for men than for women, and are also slightly higher on weekends. Although discos are required by law to close at midnight, many of them ignore the decree and simply stay open until dawn. Roppongi has spread over into neighboring Nishi-Azabu, with restaurants and nightclubs popping up. The center of Nishi-Azabu is the next big crossroads, Nishi-Azabu Crossing, down the expressway avenue toward Shibuya from Roppongi.

Area

Nittaku Bldg., 3-8-15 Roppongi. ☎ **03/3479-3721.** Cover (including unlimited drinks and food, except beer): ¥4,000 ($40) for women; ¥4,500 ($45) for men. Station: Roppongi (3 minutes).

Area has a spaciousness that belies the fact that it's actually in the basement of the Nittaku Building. This is one of the best discos for dancing and observing—there are elevated blocks for the nerviest of the dancers, who like showing off what they can do. The lighting is good, curtains lower and rise on the dance floor, and the ceiling is mirrored. All in all, this place somehow seems a bit wilder than most, and it's popular mainly with young Japanese women. Open Tuesday to Saturday from 6pm to midnight (but really until about 2am).

Buzz

Square Bldg., 3-10-3 Roppongi. ☎ **03/3470-6391.** Cover (including tickets good for five drinks): ¥3,000 ($30) for women, ¥4,000 ($40) for men. Station: Roppongi (3 minutes).

Buzz is one of several discos in this building. Using the catchwords "Video & Dance," the gimmick here is the presence of screens that show rock videos, allowing you to dance while watching your favorite performer. For some reason, it's decorated "like a New York rooftop," whatever that is, complete with clouds painted on the walls and—get this—giant flies hanging from the ceiling. Although the "official" closing time is midnight, Buzz actually stays open much later. Open daily from 6pm to sometimes 5am.

Hot Co-Rocket

5-18-2 Roppongi. ☎ **03/3583-9409.** Cover (including two drinks): ¥2,000 ($20) Mon–Thur, ¥3,000 ($30) Fri–Sat. Station: Roppongi (7 minutes).

If you like your music loud, you won't be disappointed at this club, located across from the Porsche dealership as you walk from Roppongi Crossing toward Tokyo Tower. Live reggae bands regale the crowds here, and there's a tiny dance floor. Sunday night features disco music only. Open Monday to Thursday from 7pm to 3am and on Friday and Saturday until 5am.

Java Jive

Square Bldg., 3-10-3 Roppongi. ☎ **03/3478-0088.** Cover (including 10 tickets for food or drinks): ¥3,000 ($30) for women, ¥4,000 ($40) for men. Station: Roppongi (3 minutes).

Of the discos in the Square Building, the current favorite remains the immensely popular (and very crowded) Java Jive—a two-level establishment, with loose-limbed Jamaican cutouts dancing in silhouette along the wall (I think you'll have to see this for yourself to understand what I mean). Tropical palms and the flicker of electric candles add to the atmosphere—the dance floor even used to be sand, but it was covered over when it proved too difficult to writhe upon. A live reggae and salsa band is featured every night except Sunday—disco night. (This place is so cavernous and crowded, however, that friends who have been here swear they never even realized there was a live band, though that was probably due to the condition they were in.) Most drinks take two or three tickets, but not beer, which must be bought from vending machines. Open daily from 6pm to midnight officially, until 4am or later unofficially.

Kento's

Daini Bldg., 5-3-1 Roppongi. ☎ **03/3401-5755.** Cover ¥1,300 ($13), plus 20% service and one drink minimum. Station: Roppongi (4 minutes).

Kento's was one of the first establishments to open when the wave of 1950s nostalgia hit Japan in the 1980s, and has even been credited with creating the craze. This is the place to come to if you feel like dancing and twisting the night away to tunes of the '50s and '60s, played by live bands. It's decorated with posters of such stars as Elvis and Connie Francis, has waiters with slicked-back hair, and even the microphones are decades old. Although there's hardly room to dance, that doesn't stop the largely over-30 Japanese audience from doing a kind of rock 'n' roll twist in the aisles. If you get hungry, you can order such snacks as chicken, pizza, spaghetti, sausage, salads, and a rather peculiar treat consisting of butter raisins. There are now other Kento's dance clubs all over Japan, including one in Ginza at 6-7-12 Ginza (☎ 03/3572-9161). Both places are open Monday to Saturday from 6pm to 2:30am, and on Sunday and holidays from 6pm to midnight.

Lexington Queen

Daisan Goto Bldg., 3-13-14 Roppongi. ☎ **03/3401-1661.** Cover (including 12 tickets for food—including sushi—and drinks): ¥3,000 ($30) for women, ¥4,000 ($40) for men. Station: Roppongi (3 minutes).

Opened in 1980, Lexington Queen is an old-timer in the crazy world of discos, having been the reigning queen for more than a decade. The list of its guests reads like a *Who's Who* of foreign movie and rock stars who have visited Tokyo—Stevie Wonder, Rod Stewart, Liza Minnelli, Sheena Easton, Joe Cocker, Dustin Hoffman, John Denver, Jacqueline Bisset, Spandau Ballet, and Jennifer Beals, to name a few. One night when I was there, Duran Duran walked in. Popular with foreign models working in Tokyo, Lexington Queen is managed by Bill Hersey, who, appropriately enough, writes a gossip column for the *Weekender*. This is evidently the best place to be on Halloween and New Year's if you can stand the crowds. Note, however, that men unaccompanied by women are not allowed entrance. Open daily from 6pm to midnight officially, until 2 or 3am unofficially.

Yellow

1-10-11 Nishi-Azabu. ☎ **03/3479-0690.** Cover (including one or two drinks) from ¥4,000 ($40), depending on the DJ and the event. Station: Roppongi (10 minutes, head toward the Nishi-Azabu crossroads and take the third-to-last right before the crossing; it's in the second block on the right).

Closed on and off by the "boys in blue," this is a true underground disco, with a spacious basement area and atmosphere. It stages offbeat artsy events, such as *butoh* performances. Some nights are gay nights, others X-stasy. Guest DJs from abroad make appearances, playing a variety of music from reggae to hip-hop and techno. Only the in-the-know are supposed to go here, so there's no sign whatsoever, just a blank, yellow neon square. It's busiest from 2 to 4am. Open Monday to Saturday from 9pm to midnight officially, until 4am unofficially; usually closed Sunday, and sometimes Tuesday, but not always—call before you go to find out if it's open.

THE BAR SCENE

GINZA

Henry Africa

7-2-17 Ginza. ☎ **03/3573-4563.** Station: Hibiya or Yurakucho, across from the Yamanote Line elevated tracks, entrance around the corner, past the tobacco shop.

This is one of several Henry Africa pubs in Tokyo. Decorated in the theme of an African hunt, with potted plants, Tiffany-style lampshades, and a wood-plank floor, it's a comfortable place for a drink where visitors will feel right at home. Beer starts at ¥700 ($7). Open Monday to Saturday from 10am to 11:30pm, and on Sunday and holidays from 3:30 to 10:30pm.

Lupin (45)

5-5-11 Ginza. ☎ **03/3571-0750.** Station: Ginza (2 minutes).

If you're looking for a quiet place for a drink, you can't find a more subdued place than Lupin, located in a tiny alley behind Ketel, a German restaurant. This tiny basement bar first opened back in 1928 and has changed little over the decades. Featuring a long wooden bar and wooden booths and cabinets, it's so quiet here you can hear yourself think. As though the world of jukeboxes and stereos has passed Lupin by, no music is ever played here, making it a good place to come if you want to talk. A large bottle of beer starts at ¥800 ($8); mixed drinks start at ¥1,000 ($10). Open Monday to Saturday from 5 to 11pm.

Old Imperial

Imperial Hotel, 1-1-1 Uchisaiwaicho. ☎ **03/3504-1111.** Station: Hibiya.

A lovely spot for a sophisticated, quiet, and comfortable drink at intimate tables or (nice if your alone) the bar under original 1923 Frank Llyod Wright deco-style murals. Count on getting your drink just as you want.

Sapporo Lion

7-9-20 Ginza. ☎ **03/3571-2590.** Station: Ginza (3 minutes).

Sapporo beer is the lure of this small beer hall with its mock Gothic ceiling, located on Chuo Dori not far from the Matsuzakaya department store. The English-language menu lists snacks ranging from yakitori to salads, spaghetti, and shrimp with chili sauce. Beer starts at ¥490 ($4.90). Open daily from 11:30am to 11pm.

$ Pronto Pronto

8-6-25 Ginza. ☎ **03/3571-7864.** Station: Ginza (3 minutes).

Tokyo is filled with so-called "cafebars," which are combination coffee shops and bars popular with young Japanese women and couples. This cafebar in Ginza is easy to find because it's on Namiki Dori. It serves as a neighborhood coffee shop until 5pm, with a cup of coffee going for a mere ¥160 ($1.60). From 5:30pm it's a bar, with beer starting at ¥430 ($4.30). Shots are its specialty, costing only ¥380 ($3.80) a glass. Open Monday to Saturday from 8am to 11pm and on Sunday from 8am to 9:30pm.

$ Yagura Chaya (46)

Riccar Bldg. basement, 6-2-1 Ginza. ☎ **03/3571-3494.** Station: Ginza or Hibiya.

If you're looking for a boisterous drinking atmosphere, I recommend this Japanese-style yakitori-ya in the Riccar Building, not far from the Imperial Hotel. Look for a traditional-looking restaurant, with lockers just inside the door where you're supposed to deposit your shoes. Popular with businessmen, couples, and large groups, it's decorated with antiques and traditional crafts. It offers a large menu (in Japanese only), including sashimi, yakitori, fish, oden, and pizza. Beer starts at ¥550 ($5.50); sake, at ¥880 ($8.80). Open daily from 5pm to midnight.

AKASAKA

Garden Lounge

Hotel New Otani, 4-1 Kioi-cho. ☎ **03/3265-1111.** Cover ¥300 ($3) Mon–Fri, ¥600 ($6) Sat. Station: Akasaka-mitsuke.

If you'd rather rest your eyes on a Japanese landscape garden than on neon lights, try the Garden Lounge, which looks out over a 400-year-old garden complete with waterfall, pond, bridges, and manicured bushes. Cocktails, which begin at ¥1,000 ($10), are served every evening, and there's live-music entertainment nightly except Sunday. Open daily from 6 to 10pm.

Hollywood

2-14-5 Akasaka. ☎ **03/5583-1108.** Station: Akasaka (3 minutes).

With a theme of Hollywood stars, this bar in the transformed Mikado Theatre building offers original cocktails (¥1,000/$10) named after Hollywood luminaries, beer (¥700/$7), and, in the afternoon, coffee (¥500/$5). A sophisticated setting with a bar and a few tables, it overlooks the Garden Restaurant, a slick open space using wood squares and cement slabs in natural forms, serving Chinese food.

Pronto

3-12-1 Akasaka. ☎ **03/3582-3717.** Station: Akasaka or Akasaka-mitsuke (located on Tamachi Dori).

Pronto serves as an inexpensive coffeehouse by day and a bar by night, and offers cups of coffee for only ¥160 ($1.60). A friendly, English-speaking owner is a plus. Beer starts at ¥430 ($4.30) and cocktails, at ¥380 ($3.80), while snacks like dim sum or corn chips and salsa are ¥480 ($4.80). Open Monday to Saturday from 7:30am to 5pm as a coffeehouse and from 5:30pm to 11pm as a bar (closed holidays).

Top of Akasaka

Akasaka Prince Hotel, 40th floor, 1-2 Kioi-cho. ☎ **03/3234-1111.** Station: Akasaka-mitsuke.

Whenever I go to Akasaka, I like to start out the evening with a quiet drink at this fancy and romantic cocktail lounge. With the city of Tokyo as a dramatic backdrop, I can watch the day fade into darkness as millions of lights and neon signs twinkle in the distance. Note that no children are allowed. Cocktails average ¥1,300 ($13). Daily 5pm to 2am.

SHINJUKU

Anyo (47)

1-1-8 Kabuki-cho. ☎ **03/3209-7253.** Station: Shinjuku Sanchome (10 minutes).

This tiny bar, with room for only a dozen or so people, is typical of a multitude of miniature establishments that line the alleyways of Goruden Gai, a unique nightlife neighborhood east of Kabuki-cho. However, unlike most of the establishments here, it welcomes foreigners and is run by a very friendly woman who speaks some English. In business for more than 20 years, it attracts a regular clientele that ranges from businessmen to those in the advertising industry. This place is a true find for the opportunity it affords of a different view of Japanese life, but prices can add up. There's a ¥500 ($5) table charge per person. Beer ranges from ¥500 to ¥800 ($5 to $8). Open Monday to Saturday from 7pm to 2am; closed holidays and in mid-August.

Bon's

1-1-10 Kabuki-cho. ☎ **03/3209-6334.** Station: Shinjuku Sanchome (10 minutes).

This is another accessible place if you feel like having a drink in Shinjuku's Goruden Gai, a warren of tiny alleyways and even tinier bars. Bon's is on its very eastern edge, near Hanazono Shrine. Larger than most of the bars here, the establishment caters to a 30-ish Japanese clientele and boasts a Mickey Mouse collection behind a glass case. Note that there's a table charge of ¥600 ($6); beer starts at ¥600 ($6). Open Monday to Saturday from 7pm to 5am, and on Sunday and holidays 7pm to 3am.

✪ Vagabond

1-4-20 Nishi Shinjuku. ☎ **03/3348-9109.** Station: Shinjuku (2 minutes).

Although most of the night action in Shinjuku is east of the station, the west side also has an area of inexpensive restaurants and bars. This second-floor establishment (in the second alley behind Odakyu Halc) is owned by the effervescent Mr. Matsuoka, who can be found either here or over at nearby Volga (described below). Vagabond features a jazz pianist nightly, beginning at 7:30pm. Although there's no music charge per se, there is an obligatory snack charge of ¥500 ($5) for the bowl of chips automatically brought to your table. Small and cozy, this place is popular with foreigners who live close to Shinjuku Station and with Japanese who want to rub elbows with foreigners. Its Guinness brings in customers from the United Kingdom. Beer starts at ¥400 ($4). The only drawback is its one bathroom, but as one customer pointed out, the queue is a good place to meet people. Open daily from 5:30 to 11:30pm (closes Sunday at 10:30pm).

✪ Volga (48)

1-4 Nishi Shinjuku. ☎ **03/3342-4996.** Station: Shinjuku.

Located right down the street from Vagabond, described above, Volga is a yakitori-ya housed in an ivy-covered two-story brick building. It has an open grill facing the street and a smoky and packed drinking hall typical of older establishments across the country. Rooms are tiny and simply decorated with wooden tables and benches, and the clientele is middle-aged. Very Japanese. Skewers of yakitori start at ¥100 ($1). A huge bottle of beer (enough for two to share) is ¥700 ($7). Open Monday to Saturday from 5:30 to 10:30pm; closed holidays.

SHINJUKU 2-CHOME

These establishments are located east of Kabuki-cho and Goruden Gai in an area known as 2-chome, which has a mixture of gay and straight bars. The nearest subway station is Shinjuku Sanchome, but if you're walking from Kabuki-cho, walk east on Yasukuni Dori until you come to a large intersection where you can see a large building called Bygs. These establishments are located on a small street behind Bygs.

Kinsmen

2-18-5 Shinjuku. ☎ **03/3354-4949.**

This gay bar, located in the building next to 69 (see below), up on the second floor, welcomes customers of all persuasions and is a good place to come if you want to hear yourself talk. It's a pleasant oasis in 2-chome, small and civilized, with a huge flower arrangement dominating the center of the room. Beer prices start at a low ¥600 ($6), and there's no table charge. Open daily from 9pm to 5am.

New Sazae

Ishikawa Bldg., 2nd floor, 2-18-5 Shinjuku. ☎ **03/3354-1745.**

After 69 closes, many who refuse to call it quits migrate around the corner to New Sazae. The place is a dive, and the crowd is a bit rowdy, but if you get this far you're probably where you belong. The first drink costs ¥1,000 ($10), following drinks ¥700 ($7). Open daily 10pm to 6am (5am on weekdays).

69

Daini Seiko Bldg. basement, 2-18-5 Shinjuku.

An undisputed old-timer, beginning first as a gay bar in this heart of the gay district, 69 is now mainly heterosexual. This is the place people gravitate to after an evening in Shinjuku, moving on from here to other nearby bars. Playing primarily reggae music, this dive is tiny, and often so packed it reminds me of the Yamanote Line during rush hour. It usually has a healthy mix of both foreigners and Japanese, with an atmosphere unlike that of any other place in Tokyo. The first drink costs ¥1,000 ($10), following drinks ¥600 ($6). Open Friday to Wednesday from 8:30pm to midnight.

Roppongi

✪ Acarajé

1-8-19 Nishi-Azabu. ☎ **03/3401-0973.** Station: Roppongi (7 minutes).

This tiny Brazilian bar is a friendly place, filled with regulars and with an atmosphere more like that of a private party. Highly recommended, it gets crowded—I once planned to meet someone here, and we both swore we were there at the same time, but we never saw each other. Beer and cocktails start at ¥800 ($8), and Brazilian food is good and inexpensive. It's behind Roppongi Dori on the right side, going toward Shibuya. A second bar, Acarajé Tropicana (03/3477-4690), is just off Roppongi Dori farther down and has more room for dancing to Brazilian sounds. It's open from 6pm to 2am Monday to Saturday.

Charleston

3-8-11 Roppongi. ☎ **03/3402-0372.** Station: Roppongi (3 minutes).

Charleston started out (20 years ago) as a hip, all-night party place for foreign models, businessmen, and Far East travelers (you had to be non-Japanese to enter in those heady days). It's now a pizzeria/bar/cafe with an open front and a clientele and corresponding atmosphere different each time I come here. Sometimes it's filled with U.S. military men on leave, sometimes with foreign businessmen dressed in suits, and sometimes with characters who must have dragged themselves up from the deep refusing to let die one of Roppongi's oldest establishments. It's across from the graveyard. Beer is ¥650 ($6.50), cocktails from ¥850 ($8.50). Open daily from 5pm to 6am.

Drugstore

Wall Bldg., 4-2-4 Nishi-Azabu. ☎ **03/3409-8222.** Station: Roppongi (15 minutes).

Drugstore is a contemporary bar on the first and second floors of the Wall, an entertainment building with J Men's (male striptease) downstairs and a romantic Italian restaurant, Cibrero, upstairs. Its attractions are contemporary sounds, a sculpture by designer Nigel Coates behind the bar, outdoor seating, and wide-open doors—a blessing for nonsmokers. Managed by and popular with *gaijin* (foreigners), it's packed out to the sidewalks late at night, where some sit on Harleys and talk over beer (¥800/ $8). Drugstore is on Gaien Nishi Dori; walking from Roppongi, turn left at the Nishi-Azabu crossroads. Open Sunday to Thursday from 7pm to midnight, and until 5am on Friday and Saturday.

Ex

7-7-6 Roppongi. ☎ **03/3408-5487.** Station: Roppongi (5 minutes).

Located on the diagonal street across from the former Defense Agency as you walk on Gaien-Higashi Dori toward Nogizaka, Ex, whose name, appropriately enough, means "bottoms up," is a bit of old Germany right in the heart of Tokyo. It's primarily a beer-drinking establishment, but owner Horst serves hearty helpings of German food. There's no menu, so you just have to ask Horst what's cooking, but common dishes are schnitzel, various kinds of wurst, boiled ribs of pork, sauerkraut, and fried potatoes. Ex is a tiny place, just a half-circle of a bar with enough seating for 15 people, but it's usually packed with German businessmen and expatriates who don't mind standing to drink their favorite brand of German beer. Eating is usually done good-naturedly in shifts. Hanging from the ceiling and on the walls are such German paraphernalia as beer mugs, soccer pennants, and photos of German celebrities who have visited Ex. Beer here starts at ¥700 ($7). Open Monday to Saturday from 5pm to 2am.

Pachinko Parlors

Brightly lit and garish, pachinko parlors are packed with upright pinball-like machines, with row upon row of Japanese businessmen, housewives, and students sitting intently immobile in front of them. Popular since the '50s, pachinko is a game in which ball bearings are flung into a machine, one after the other. Humans control the strength with which the ball is released, but otherwise there's very little to do. Some players even wedge a match stick under the control and just watch the machine with folded arms. Points are amassed according to which holes the ball bearings fall into. Just ¥100 ($1) gives you 25 ball bearings, which don't last for long. If you're good at it, you win ball bearings back, which you can subsequently trade in for food, cigarettes, watches, calculators, and the like.

It's illegal to win money in Japan, but outside many pachinko parlors and along back alleyways, there are slots where you can trade in the watches, calculators, and other prizes for cash. You never see who hands you your cash, and they never see who's handing over the goods. Police, meanwhile, just look the other way.

Pachinko parlors, mostly run by Koreans, compete in an ever-escalating war of themes, lights, and noise. Step inside one, you'll wonder how anyone could possibly think; the noise level of thousands of ball bearings clanking is awesome. Perhaps that's the answer to its popularity: you can't think, making it a getaway pastime. Some people seem to be addicted to the mesmerizing game, and newspaper articles talk of errant husbands who never come home anymore, while pychologists analyze its popularity. At any rate, every hamlet now seems to have a pachinko parlor, and there are probably more pachinko parlors in major cities, like Tokyo, than streetlights.

Maggie's Revenge

3-8-12 Roppongi. ☎ **03/3479-1096.** Cover ¥800 ($8) Mon–Thur and ¥1,000 ($10) Fri–Sat. Station: Roppongi (4 minutes).

Another expatriate bar that's popular also with the Japanese, Maggie's has live music every night, provided usually by a guitar or a piano soloist. Sometimes the music's good, sometimes not—you take your chances. Beers start at ¥600 ($6) and cocktails at ¥800 ($8); there's also a good selection of liqueurs, brandies, and champagnes. Open daily from 6:30pm to 3am.

Salsa Corona

7-7-4 Roppongi. ☎ **03/3746-0244.** Station: Roppongi (5 minutes).

Part of the Latin American music fad in Tokyo, this faux-Spanish-tile-and-adobe-walled basement bar is adorned with Latin record album covers and posters. Everyone's dancing, although there's no real dance floor. Corona beers and various cocktails cost ¥1,000 ($10), and the food—feijoada, empanadas, nachos—runs about the same. Its located near Ex (above). Open daily from 6pm to 5am.

Harajuku & Aoyama

Oh God

6-7-18 Jingumae. ☎ **03/3406-3206.** Station: Meiji-Jingumae (5 minutes up Omotesando Dori behind the Café de Rope).

If you find yourself in Harajuku after nightfall, this mellow, dimly lit bar features a mural of a city at sunset and shows free foreign films every night beginning at 6pm

(9pm on weekdays). I've seen everything from James Bond to Fassbinder to grade-B movies here. There are also two pool tables. Beer starts at ¥650 ($6.50), cocktails at ¥750 ($7.50). Open daily from 6pm to 6am.

EBISU

Bodeguita

1-7-3 Ebisu Minami, Shibuya-ku. ☎ **03/3715-7721.** Station: Ebisu (2 minutes).

Out of the station's main west-side entrance, go one block left on the second street away from and parallel to the tracks to Bodeguita, a very small, crowded Cuban club. Despite the space, regulars are dancing to Latin music videos, while others are enjoying *arroz saltado* (rice, fried potatoes, and meat) or *arroz con frijoles* (the classic rice and beans). The food, which costs ¥900 to ¥1,200 ($9 to $12), is delicious, and portions are generous. Wash it down with beer (Tecate) at ¥700 ($7) or cocktails for ¥700 to ¥1,300 ($7 to $13). At this family-run place, a single woman will feel welcome. Open Monday to Saturday from 6pm to midnight.

FILMS

Going to the movies is an expensive pastime in Tokyo, with admission averaging about ¥1,800 ($18) for adults, ¥1,400 ($14) for university students, ¥1,300 ($13) for junior and senior high school pupils, and ¥1,000 ($10) for children and senior citizens (past 60). As perhaps an admission that prices are high, some theaters accept credit cards. If you want to see one of Hollywood's latest releases (which usually take a few months to reach Japan), you may also have to contend with long lines and huge crowds. To see what's on where, check the *Tokyo Journal*, published monthly and sold in bookstores for ¥600 ($6), which lists more than 100 cinemas. Note that theaters in Tokyo close early, with the last showing usually around 7pm. Movies are shown in the original language, with Japanese subtitles.

One of my favorite theaters is **Ciné Vivant** (☎ 03/3403-6061), located in the Wave Building, 6-2-27 Roppongi. It specializes in European films, mostly new works, with about four or five showings daily, starting at 12:40pm, and with the same admission prices given above.

Another good place to see films—albeit mostly of the B-grade variety, but sometimes classics—is at **Oh God** (listed above). A bar, it charges no admission, though beer starts at a high ¥650 ($6.50). Movies, which generally start at 9pm on weekdays and 6pm on weekends, are shown throughout the evening, with the last movie beginning at 3am. I've seen everything from sci-fi horror flicks to James Bond and Fassbinder here. Call to see what's playing.

If you're interested in seeing Japanese classics, your best bets are movies shown on Saturday and Sunday at the **National Museum of Modern Art,** in Kitanomaru Koen Park (Station: Takebashi). Movies include both Japanese and foreign films (some with English subtitles), and programs change often; call the **National Film Center** (a branch of the museum) to see what's playing (☎ 03/3561-0823) and to check the times. Admission to the movies is ¥400 ($4).

6 Easy Excursions from Tokyo

If your stay in Tokyo is long enough, you should consider taking excursions to some of the sights in the vicinity. Kamakura and Nikko, for example, rank as two of the most important historical sites in Japan, while the Fuji-Hakone-Izu National Park serves as a huge recreational playground for the residents of Tokyo. Mashiko, a pottery village, can be visited on its own, or it can be seen in combination with Nikko. Kawasaki and Yokohama have a few worthwhile museums and attractions that warrant visits.

Before departing Tokyo, stop by the Tourist Information Center (TIC) for a color brochure called "Side Trips from Tokyo," which carries information on Kamakura, Nikko, Hakone, and the Mt. Fuji area. The TIC also has a map of Tokyo's vicinity, as well as pamphlets on individual destinations. "Hakone and Kamakura," for example, includes a map of Kamakura and how to get to some of the village's most important sights by bus.

1 Kamakura

30 miles S of Tokyo

If you take only one day trip outside Tokyo, it should be to Kamakura, especially if you're unable to include the ancient capitals of Kyoto and Nara in your travels. Kamakura is a delightful hamlet with no fewer than 65 Buddhist temples and 19 Shinto shrines spread throughout the village and the surrounding wooded hills. Most of these were built centuries ago, when a warrior named Yoritomo Minamoto seized political power and established his shogunate government in Kamakura back in 1192. Wanting to set up his seat of government as far away as possible from what he considered to be the corrupt imperial court in Kyoto, Yoritomo selected Kamakura because it was easy to defend. The village is enclosed on three sides by wooded hills and on the fourth by the sea, a setting that lends a dramatic background to its many temples and shrines.

Although Kamakura remained the military and political center of the nation for a century and a half, the Minamoto clan was in power for only a short time. After Yoritomo's death, both of his sons were assassinated, one after the other, after taking up military rule. Power then passed to the family of Yoritomo's widow, the Hojo family, who ruled until 1333, when the emperor in Kyoto sent troops to

Easy Excursions From Tokyo

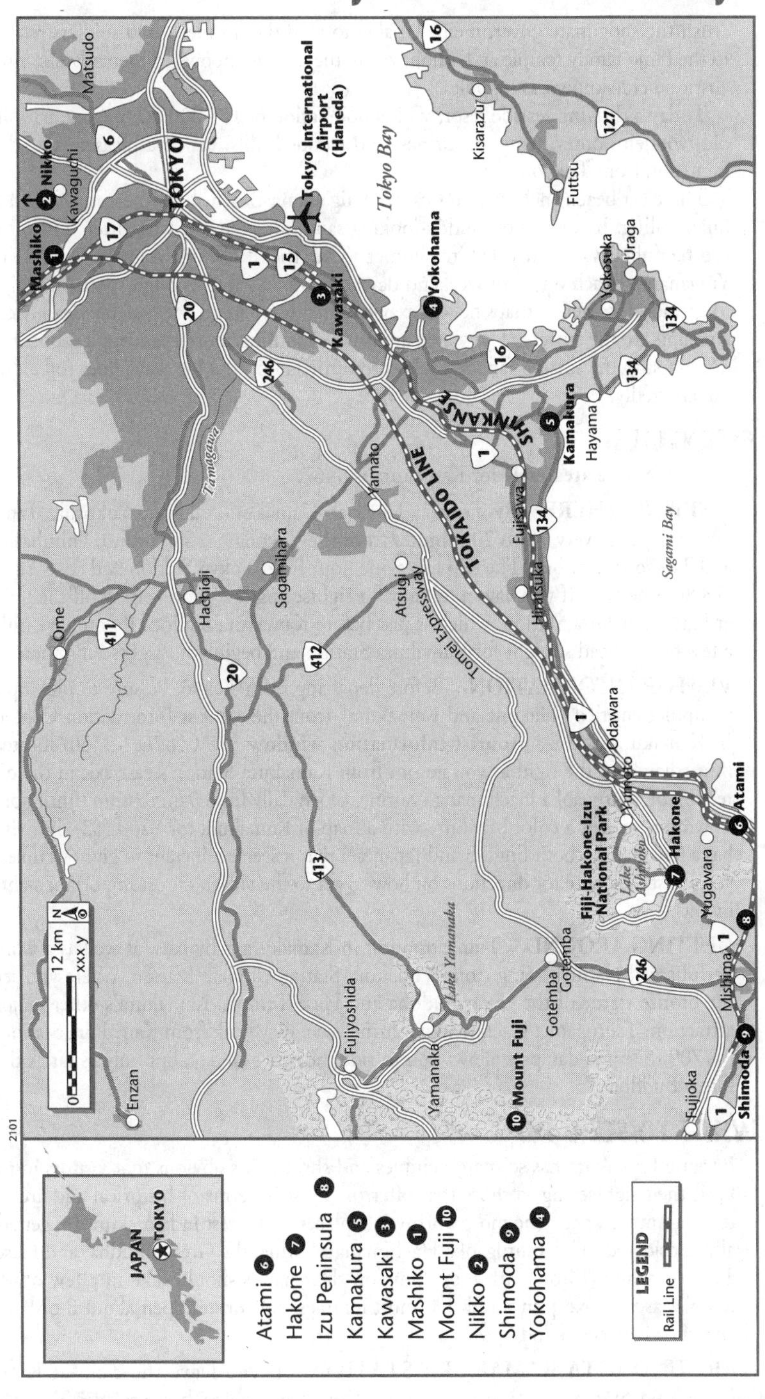

crush the shogunate government. Unable to stop the invaders, 800 soldiers retired to the Hojo family temple at Toshoji, where they all disemboweled themselves in ritualistic suicide known as seppuku.

Today a thriving seaside resort with a population of 175,000, Kamakura, with its old wooden homes, temples, shrines, and wooded hills, makes a pleasant one-day excursion from Tokyo.

There's a beach in Kamakura called Yuigahama Beach, but I personally find it unappealing. It consists of muddy-looking sand, often strewn with litter, and yet it can be unbelievably crowded in summer. (One friend of mine told me he came to Yuigahama Beach on a hot weekend day and couldn't find enough space on which to spread his towel. Perhaps he was exaggerating, but you get the general idea.) Most amusing are the surfers. The waves are usually nothing more than ripples, but that doesn't stop the surfing fanatics, who promptly fall off if a big wave does roll along unexpectedly.

ESSENTIALS

The **telephone area code** for Kamakura is 0467.

GETTING THERE **By Train** To reach Kamakura, take the Yokosuka Line, which departs every 10 to 20 minutes from the Yokohama, Shinagawa, Shimbashi, and Tokyo JR stations. The trip takes one hour from Tokyo Station and costs ¥880 ($8.80) one-way. If you have a full day for sightseeing, I suggest getting off the train at Kita-Kamakura Station, which is just before Kamakura Station. If you have only a few hours, head straight for Kamakura Station and begin your sightseeing there.

VISITOR INFORMATION Before departing from Tokyo, be sure to pick up a pamphlet entitled "Hakone and Kamakura" from the Tourist Information Center. In Kamakura, there's a **tourist information window** (☎ 0467/22-3350) located immediately to the right as you go out from Kamakura Station's east exit in the direction of Tsurugaoka Hachimangu Shrine. Open daily from 9am to 6pm (until 5pm in winter), it sells a color brochure with a map of Kamakura for ¥200 ($2), but also has a free map (in both English and Japanese) that it seems reluctant to give out unless you insist. Ask here for directions on how to get to the village's most important sights by bus.

GETTING AROUND Transportation in Kamakura is by **bus,** as well as a wonderful small **train** running from Kamakura Station to Hase Station, where you see the bronze statue of the Great Buddha and Hase Temple. Kamakura's other major attraction, Tsurugaoka Hachimangu Shrine, is an easy walk from Kamakura Station. A ¥700 ($7) one-day pass allows you to ride the buses all day, but only as far as the Great Buddha.

WHAT TO SEE & DO

Because Kamakura has so many temples and shrines, it's obvious that visitors must limit their sightseeing to those that offer the most in terms of historical and architectural importance. The most worthwhile places of interest in kamakura are generally considered to be Tsurugaoka Hachimangu Shrine, the Great Buddha, and Hase Temple, while visitors with more time on their hands should take in a few other temples as well. Keep in mind that most temples and shrines open about 8 or 9am and close between 4 and 5pm.

AROUND KITA-KAMAKURA STATION If you leave the train at Kita-Kamakura Station, within a minute's walk you can reach **Engakuji Temple**

Kamakura

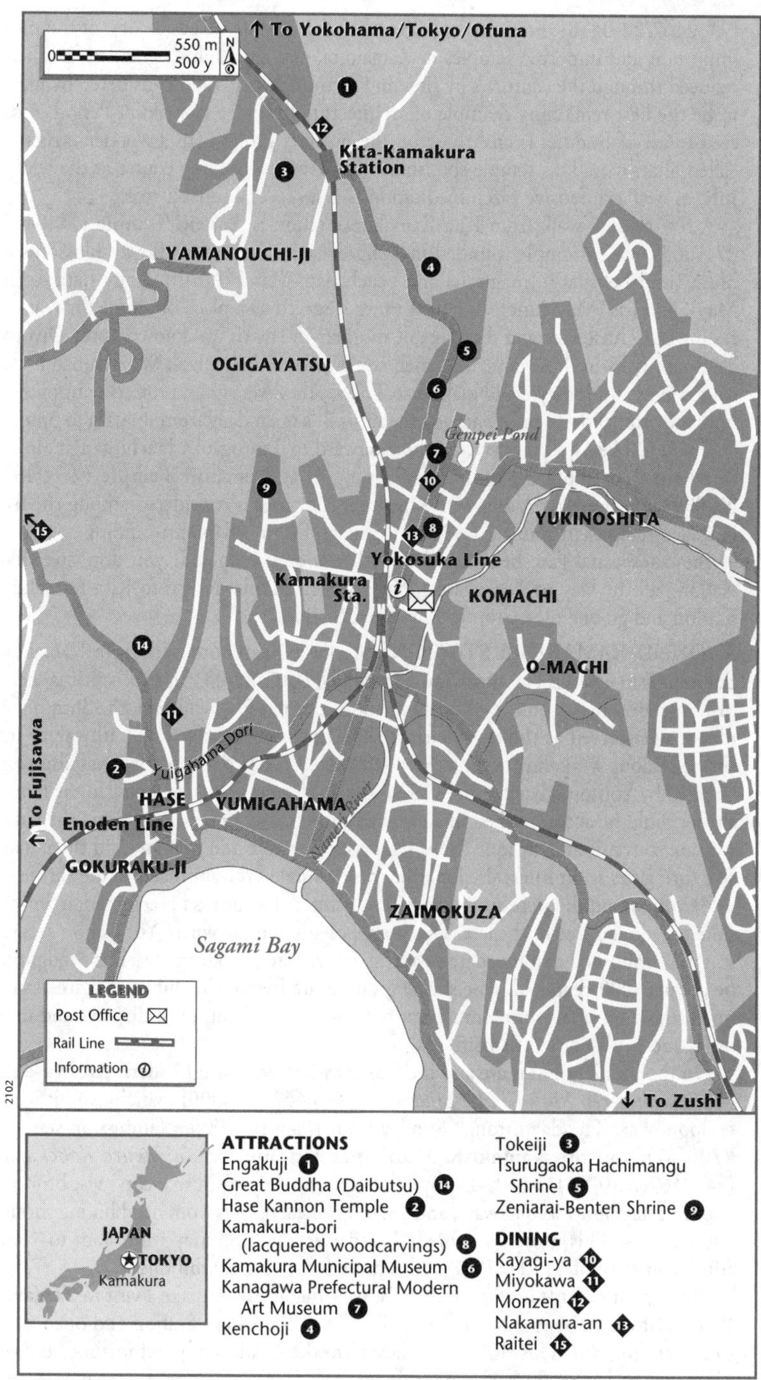

↑ To Yokohama/Tokyo/Ofuna
550 m
500 y
N
0
Kita-Kamakura Station
YAMANOUCHI-JI
OGIGAYATSU
Gempei Pond
YUKINOSHITA
Yokosuka Line
Kamakura Sta.
KOMACHI
O-MACHI
Yuigahama Dori
HASE
YUMIGAHAMA
Nameri River
Enoden Line
GOKURAKU-JI
↑ To Fujisawa
ZAIMOKUZA
Sagami Bay
LEGEND
Post Office
Rail Line
Information
↓ To Zushi
2102
JAPAN
TOKYO
Kamakura
ATTRACTIONS
Engakuji 1
Great Buddha (Daibutsu) 14
Hase Kannon Temple 2
Kamakura-bori (lacquered woodcarvings) 8
Kamakura Municipal Museum 6
Kanagawa Prefectural Modern Art Museum 7
Kenchoji 4
Tokeiji 3
Tsurugaoka Hachimangu Shrine 5
Zeniarai-Benten Shrine 9
DINING
Kayagi-ya 10
Miyokawa 11
Monzen 12
Nakamura-an 13
Raitei 15

(☎ 0467/22-0478). Founded in 1282, this Zen temple was once one of the most important and imposing temples in Kamakura, and although its grandeur has been reduced through the centuries by fires and earthquakes, it's still considered by many to be the best remaining example of architecture from the Kamakura Period. A sacred tooth of Buddha is enshrined on the precinct grounds in a wooden structure called Shari-den. This temple sponsors a five-day Zen training course at the end of July, as well as intensive zazen meditation courses several times a year.

A five-minute walk from Kita-Kamakura Station is **Tokeiji Temple** (☎ 0467/22-1663), a Zen temple founded in 1285. Visited now for its flower blossoms of plum (mid-February), magnolia and peach (late March/April), peony (late April/May), and iris (May/June), in feudal times it served as a place of refuge for women fleeing cruel husbands and disagreeable mothers-in-law (it was known as the Divorce Temple). Back in those days, only men could divorce their wives. Women had no legal recourse, but if they could make it to Tokeiji, they were given protection from their husbands and allowed to live among the nuns. It's open daily from 8:30am to 5pm.

If you feel like walking, you can hike onward to Tsurugaoka Hachimangu Shrine (see below) in about 30 minutes, stopping in at **Kenchoji Temple** (☎ 0467/22-0981) on the way. Along with Engakuji, Kenchoji is considered among the five best Zen temples in Kamakura. Note the magnificent cedars surrounding it, as well as the ceremonial gate held together with wooden wedges. If you don't feel like walking all the way to Tsurugaoka Hachimangu Shrine, return to Kita-Kamakura Station and go one more stop to Kamakura Station.

AROUND KAMAKURA STATION About a 10-minute walk from Kamakura Station, **Tsurugaoka Hachimangu Shrine** (☎ 0467/22-0315) is the spiritual heart of Kamakura. It was built by Yoritomo and dedicated to Hachiman, the Shinto god of war who served as the clan deity of the Minamoto family. The pathway to the shrine is along Wakamiya Oji, a cherry-tree-lined pedestrian lane that was also constructed by Yoritomo back in the 1190s, so that his oldest son's first visit to the family shrine could be accomplished in style with an elaborate procession. Along the pathway are souvenir and antique shops selling lacquerware and folk art, and three massive torii gates set at intervals along the route to signal the approach to the shrine.

As you ascend the steps to the vermilion-painted Tsurugaoka Hachimangu Shrine, note the gingko tree to the left. This is supposedly the site where Yoritomo's second son was ambushed and murdered back in 1219. The gingko tree itself is thought to be about 1,000 years old. The shrine grounds are free to the public and are always open (there's a small shrine museum, but with only a handful of displays and only in Japanese, it's not worth visiting).

On the shrine grounds are also the **Kanagawa Prefectural Modern Art Museum** or *Kanagawa-ken Ritsu-Kindai Bijutsukan* (☎ 0467/22-5000), which exhibits contemporary art Tuesday through Sunday from 10am to 4:00pm (admission starts at ¥700/$7), and the **Kamakura Municipal Museum** or *Kamakura Kohokukan* (☎ 0467/22-0753), which displays a collection of scrolls, urns, carvings, bronzes, swords, calligraphy, lacquerware, and other historical objects from neighboring shrines and temples. This museum is open Tuesday through Sunday from 9am to 4pm; admission starts at ¥150 ($1.50) and is more for special exhibitions.

Although it's a little bit far out of the way, it might pay to make a visit to **Zeniarai-Benten Shrine,** about a 20-minute walk west of Kamakura Station and open daily from 8am to 5pm. This shrine is dedicated to the goddess of good fortune, and on Asian zodiac days of the snake, worshippers believe that if you take your money and wash it in spring water in a small cave on the shrine grounds, your money will double or triple itself later on. Of course, this being modern Japan, don't be surprised if you see a bit of ingenuity. My Japanese landlady told me that when she visited the shrine she didn't have much cash on her, so she washed something she thought would be equally as good—her plastic credit card. As a shrine dedicated to the goddess of fortune, it's fitting that admission here is free.

AROUND HASE STATION To get to the attractions around Hase Station, you can go by bus, which departs from in front of Kamakura Station, or you can go by the Enoden train line, on a tiny train that putt-putts its way seemingly through backyards on its way from Kamakura Station to Hase and beyond (to Enoshima and Fujisawa). Since there's only one track, trains have to take turns going in either direction. I would suggest taking the bus from Kamakura Station directly to the Great Buddha, walking to Hase Shrine, and then taking the Enoden train back to Kamakura Station.

Probably Kamakura's most famous attraction is the **Great Buddha** (☎ 0467/22-0703), called the Daibutsu in Japanese. Thirty-seven feet high and weighing 93 tons, it's the second-largest bronze image in Japan. The largest Buddha is in Nara, but in my opinion the Kamakura Daibutsu is much more impressive. For one thing, whereas the Nara Buddha sits enclosed in a wooden structure that reduces the effectiveness of its size, the Kamakura Buddha sits outside against a dramatic backdrop of wooded hills. Cast in 1252, the Kamakura Buddha was indeed once housed in a temple, but a huge tidal wave destroyed the wooden structure and the statue has sat under sun, snow, and stars ever since. I also prefer the face of the Kamakura Buddha. I find it more inspiring and divine, as though with its half-closed eyes and calm, serene face it's somehow above the worries of the world—wars, natural disasters, other calamities, and sorrow. It's as though it represents the plane above human suffering, the point at which birth and death, joy and sadness merge and become one and the same. If you want, you can go inside the statue—it's hollow. The Daibutsu is open daily from 7am to 6pm, closing at 5:30pm in winter. Admission is ¥200 ($2), and your entry ticket is a nice souvenir.

Nearby, **Hase Temple** or *Hasedera* (☎ 0467/22-6300), constructed on a hill with a sweeping view of the sea, is the home of an 11-headed gilt statue of Kannon, the goddess of mercy. More than 30 feet high and the tallest wooden image in Japan, it was made from a single piece of camphorwood back in the 8th century. The legend surrounding this Kannon is quite remarkable. Supposedly two wooden images were made from the wood of a huge camphor tree. One of the images was kept in Hase, not far from Nara, while the second image, if you can imagine, was given a short ceremony and then duly tossed into the sea to find a home of its own. The image drifted 300 miles eastward and washed up on shore, but was thrown back in again because all who touched it became ill or incurred bad luck. Finally, the image reached Kamakura, where it gave the people no trouble. This was interpreted as a sign that the image was content with its surroundings, and Hase Temple was erected at its present site. Another statue housed here is one of Amida, a Buddha who promised rebirth in the Pure Land to the West to all who chanted his name. It was created by orders of Yoritomo Minamoto upon his 42nd birthday, considered an unlucky year for men.

As you climb up the steps to Hase Temple and its Kannon, you'll encounter statues of a different sort. All around you will be likenesses of Jizo, the guardian deity of children. Although parents originally came to Hase Temple to set up statues to represent their children in hopes the deity would protect and watch over them, through the years the purpose of the Jizo statues has changed. Now they represent miscarried, stillborn, or, most frequently, aborted children. More than 50,000 Jizo statues have been offered here since the war, but the thousand or so you see now remain only a year before being burned or buried to make way for others. Some of the statues, which can be purchased on the temple grounds for ¥2,000 to ¥50,000 ($20 to $500), are fitted with hand-knitted caps and sweaters. The effect is quite chilling.

Admission to Hase Temple, which is open daily from 9am to 5pm (until 4:30pm in winter), is ¥200 ($2).

DINING

MODERATE

Miyokawa (49)

1-16-17 Hase. ☎ **0467/25-5556.** Reservations recommended. Mini-kaiseki ¥5,500–¥10,000 ($55–$100); obento ¥2,300–¥5,000 ($23–$50); Japanese steak set meal ¥3,500 ($35). MC, V. Daily 11am–9pm. Station: Hase (5 minutes). MINI-KAISEKI/OBENTO.

This modern restaurant, located on the main road that leads from Hase Station to the Great Buddha and about a five-minute walk from each, specializes in kaiseki, including beautifully prepared mini-kaiseki set meals that change with the seasons. It also offers an obento lunch box, the least expensive of which is served in a container shaped like a gourd, as well as a set meal featuring steak prepared Japanese style.

Monzen (50)

Yamanouchi 407. ☎ **0467/25-1121.** Obento teishoku ¥3,000–¥5,000 ($30–$50); vegetarian set courses from ¥4,000 ($40); kaiseki from ¥6,000 ($60). AE, DC, JCB, MC, V. Mon–Fri 11am–3pm and 5–9pm, Sat–Sun 11am–9pm (last order 7:30pm). Station: Kita-Kamakura (1 minute). KAISEKI/OBENTO/VEGETARIAN.

This modern-looking kaiseki restaurant is located just across the tracks from Engakuji Temple in Kita-Kamakura. The main dining hall is on the second floor, and seating is on tatami mats at low tables. Although there's no English menu, there are pictures of various meals available, including kaiseki, obento teishoku, and *shojin-ryoori,* vegetarian set courses commonly served at Buddhist temples.

INEXPENSIVE

In addition to the suggestions here, there's a pavilion at Hase Temple, described above, which serves oden, noodles, beer and soft drinks, with indoor and outdoor seating. There's a great view from here, making it a good place for a snack on a fine day.

Kayagi-ya (51)

2-11-16 Komachi. ☎ **0467/22-1460.** Dishes ¥1,200–¥2,000 ($12–$20); teishoku ¥2,500 ($25). No credit cards. Sat–Thurs noon–6pm. Station: Kamakura (5 minutes). EEL.

Closer to Kamakura Station, this modest, older-looking restaurant serves several different kinds of inexpensive eel dishes, my favorite of which is the *unagi donburi* (eel served on top of rice). The place is located on Wakamiya Oji Avenue (on the left side if you're walking from the station to Tsurugaoka Hachimangu Shrine), next to a lumberyard.

Nakamura-an (52)

1-7-6 Komachi. ☎ **0467/25-3500.** Noodles ¥600–¥1,600 ($6–$16). No credit cards. Fri–Wed noon–6pm. Station: Kamakura (3 minutes). NOODLES.

This noodle restaurant, between Kamakura Station and Hachimangu Shrine, is located on a side street off Wakamiya Oji Avenue. It's easy to spot because of the front window, where you can watch noodles being made. There's also a front-window display of plastic food, so it's easy to make your selection. I can never resist ordering the tempura soba.

Raitei (53)

Takasago. ☎ **0467/32-5656.** Reservations required for kaiseki. Noodles ¥850–¥2,500 ($8.50–$25); obento lunch boxes ¥3,500–¥4,500 ($35–$45). AE, DC. Daily 11am–sundown (about 6:30pm in summer). Bus: 4 or 6 from platform 2 to Takasago stop. NOODLES/OBENTO.

This is the absolute winner for a meal in Kamakura, and visiting Raitei is as much fun as visiting the city's temples and shrines. It's situated on the edge of Kamakura, surrounded by verdant countryside, and the wonder is that it serves inexpensive soba (Japanese noodles), as well as priestly feasts of kaiseki (which you must reserve in advance, with prices beginning at ¥6,000/$60). Upon entering the front gate, you must pay an entry fee of ¥500 ($5), which counts toward the price of your meal at the restaurant. If you're here for soba or one of the obento lunch boxes, go down the stone steps to the back entry of the restaurant, where you'll be given an English menu with such offerings as noodles with chicken, mountain vegetables, tempura, and more. The pottery used comes from the restaurant's own specially made kiln. When you've finished your meal, be sure to walk the path circling through the garden past a bamboo grove, stone images, and a miniature shrine. The stroll takes about 20 minutes, unless you stop for a beer at the refreshment house, which has outdoor seating and a view of the countryside.

2 Nikko

90 miles N of Tokyo

Since the publication of James Clavell's novel *Shogun,* many people have become familiar with Tokugawa Ieyasu, the real-life powerful shogun of the 1600s on whom Clavell's fictional shogun was based. Quashing all rebellions and unifying Japan under his leadership, Tokugawa built such a military stronghold that his heirs continued to rule Japan for the next 250 years without serious challenge.

If you'd like to join the millions of Japanese who through the centuries have paid homage to this great man, travel 90 miles north of Tokyo to Nikko, where a mausoleum was constructed in his honor in the 17th century and where his remains were laid to rest. *Nikko* means "sunlight," an apt description of the way the sun's rays play upon this sumptuous mausoleum of wood and gold leaf. Surrounding it are thousands of cedar trees in a 200,000-acre national park, home also to a temple, a shrine, and another mausoleum. A trip to Nikko can be combined with a visit to Lake Chuzenji, a jewel of a lake about an hour's bus ride from the mausoleum.

ESSENTIALS

The **telephone area code** for Nikko is 0288.

GETTING THERE **By Train** The easiest, fastest, and most luxurious way to get to Nikko is on the Tobu Line's limited express (reservations necessary), which departs from Asakusa Station and costs ¥2,530 ($25.30) one-way for the 1 1/2-hour trip. Slower trains for ¥1,270 ($12.70) one-way take 2 hours and 10 minutes. Trains depart every hour or less. If you have a Japan Rail Pass, take the shinkansen from Ueno to Utsunomiya (50 minutes) and change there for Nikko (45 minutes). The Tobu and JR stations in Nikko are located almost side by side in the village's downtown area. Tobu (☎ 0288/3281-6622) also runs day tours, which include transportation to and from Tokyo, sightseeing in Nikko, and lunch for ¥20,000 ($200).

VISITOR INFORMATION Before leaving Tokyo, pick up a leaflet called "Nikko" from the Tourist Information Center (TIC). It gives the train schedule for both the Tobu Line, which departs from Asakusa Station, and JR trains that depart from Ueno Station. The TIC also has some color brochures with maps of the Nikko area.

The **Nikko Tobu Station tourist information counter** (☎ 0288/53-4511) is staffed by a friendly lady who speaks just enough English to give you a map, answer basic questions, and point you in the right direction. It's open daily 9am to noon and 1 to 5pm. You can also make hotel and ryokan reservations here and buy one-way bus tickets onward to Lake Chuzenji for ¥1,100 ($11) at a nearby counter.

The **Nikko Information Center** (☎ 0288/54-2496), located on the main road leading to Toshogu Shrine, has English-speaking staff (who seem put out to answer questions) and lots of information in English about Nikko, including information on public hot springs, in case you are on a day trip. It's open daily from 8:30am to 5pm.

GETTING AROUND You can **walk** from the Nikko train stations to Toshogu Shrine in less than half an hour. From Tobu Station simply walk straight out the main exit, pass the bus stands, and then turn right. There are signs pointing the way in English. Keep walking on this main road (you'll pass the Nikko Information Center about halfway down, on the left side) until you come to a T intersection with a vermilion-colored bridge spanning a river (about a 15-minute walk from the train stations). The stone steps opposite lead up the hill into the woods and to the mausoleum. You can also get to the T intersection by **bus,** getting off at the Shinkyo bus stop.

If you're heading to Chuzenji, buses depart from in front of Tobu Station, with a stop at the Shinkyo bus stop near the mausoleum. You can therefore visit the historical sights in Nikko before boarding the bus and continuing onto Chuzenji.

WHAT TO SEE & DO

Tokugawa Ieyasu's mausoleum is on the edge of town, which you can reach on foot in about half an hour or by bus from either the Tobu or JR Station in about 10 minutes. The first indication that you're nearing Tokugawa's mausoleum, which is called Toshogu Shrine, is the vermilion-painted **Sacred Bridge** (*Shinkyo*), arching over the rushing Daiyagawa River. It was built in 1636, and for more than three centuries only shoguns and their emissaries were allowed to cross it. Even today, mortal souls like us are prevented from completely crossing it because of a barrier at one end.

Across the road from the bridge are some steps leading into a forest of cedar, where after a five-minute walk you'll see a statue of a priest named Shodo, who founded Nikko 1,200 years ago, and the first major temple, **Rinnoji Temple.** You can buy a combination ticket here for ¥900 ($9), which allows entry to Rinnoji Temple, Toshogu Shrine, neighboring Futarasan Shrine, and another Tokugawa mausoleum. Once at Toshogu Shrine, you'll have to pay an extra ¥500 ($5) to see Ieyasu's tomb. A combination ticket is also sold at the entry to Toshogu Shrine, but at a price of ¥1,250 ($12.50), which also includes admission to the inner recesses of the mausoleum.

At Rinnoji, visit the **Sanbutsudo Hall,** which contains three wooden images of Buddha plated with gold leaf. One of the best things to see at Rinnoji Temple, however, is its **Shoyo-en Garden,** which requires a separate ¥300 ($3) admission and is located opposite the Sanbutsudo Hall. Completed in 1815 and typical of Japanese landscaped gardens of the Edo Period, this strolling garden provides a different vista with each turn of the path, making it seem much larger than it actually is. The garden's English-language pamphlet says that Ulysses S. Grant visited here in 1879, two years after leaving the U.S. presidency.

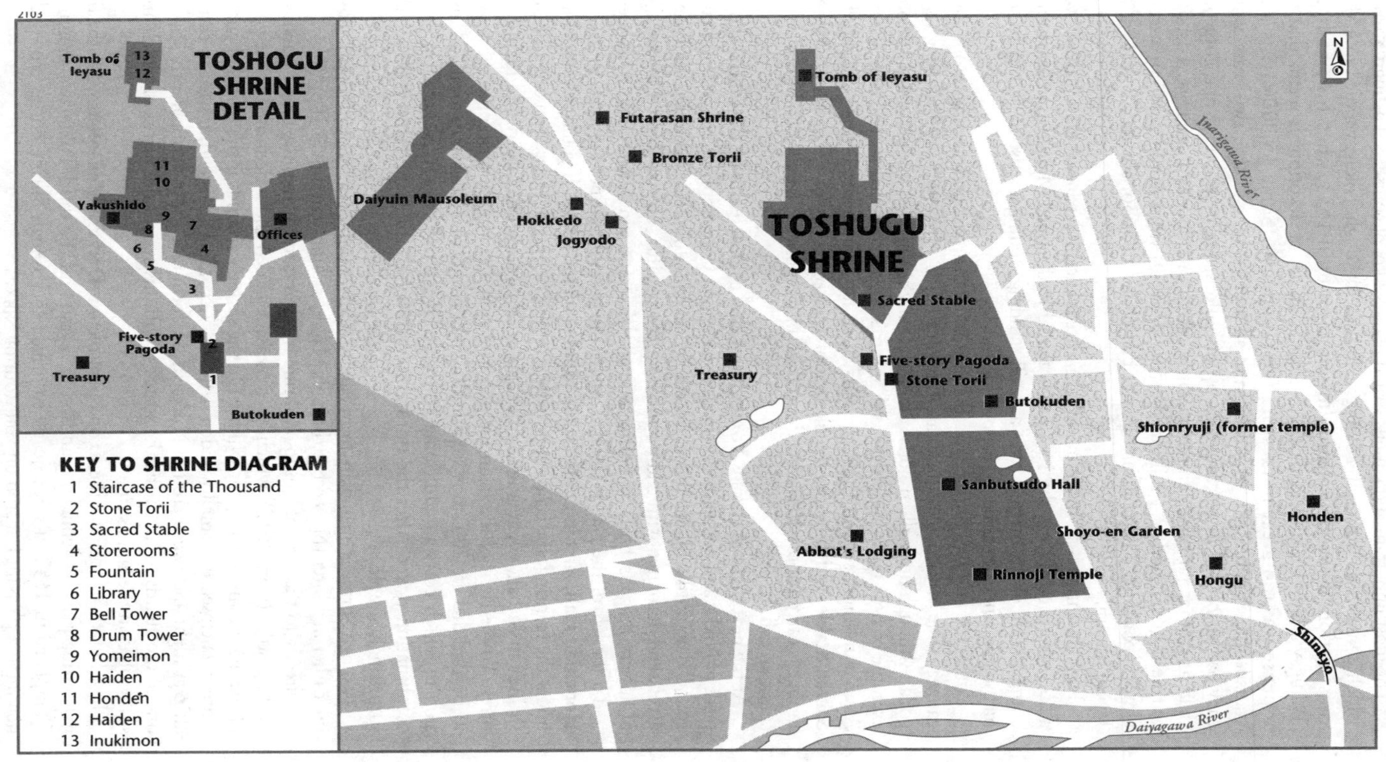

Inarigawa River
Tomb of Ieyasu
TOSHUGU SHRINE
Sacred Stable
Five-story Pagoda
Stone Torii
Butokuden
Futarasan Shrine
Bronze Torii
Treasury
Daiyuin Mausoleum
Hokkedo
Jogyodo
Sanbutsudo Hall
Rinnoji Temple
Abbot's Lodging
Shoyo-en Garden
Shionryuji (former temple)
Hongu
Honden
Shinkyo
Daiyagawa River
TOSHOGU SHRINE DETAIL
Tomb of Ieyasu
Yakushido
Offices
Five-story Pagoda
Treasury
Butokuden
KEY TO SHRINE DIAGRAM
1 Staircase of the Thousand
2 Stone Torii
3 Sacred Stable
4 Storerooms
5 Fountain
6 Library
7 Bell Tower
8 Drum Tower
9 Yomeimon
10 Haiden
11 Honden
12 Haiden
13 Inukimon

The most important and famous structure in Nikko, of course, is **Toshogu Shrine,** which contains the tomb of Tokugawa Ieyasu. Although Tokugawa died in 1616, construction of the mausoleum did not begin until 1634, when his grandson, Tokugawa Iemitsu, undertook the project as an act of devotion. It seems that no expense was too great in creating the monument. Some 15,000 artists and craftspeople were brought to Nikko from all over Japan, and after two years' work they had succeeded in erecting a group of buildings more elaborate and gorgeous than any other Japanese temple or shrine. Rich in colors and carvings, Toshogu Shrine is gilded with 2.4 million sheets of gold leaf (that would cover an area of almost six acres). The mausoleum was completed in 1636, almost 20 years after Ieyasu's death.

Toshogu Shrine is set in a grove of magnificent ancient Japanese cedars planted over a 20-year period during the 1600s by a feudal lord named Matsudaira Masatsuna. Some 13,000 of the original trees are still standing, adding a sense of dignity to the mausoleum and the shrine, and appearing timeless.

You enter Toshogu Shrine via a flight of stairs that pass under a huge stone torii gateway, one of the largest in Japan. On your left is a five-story, 115-foot-high pagoda. Although normally pagodas are found only at temples, this pagoda is just one example of how both Buddhism and Shintoism are combined at Toshogu Shrine. After climbing a second flight of stairs, turn left, where you'll presently see the **Sacred Stable,** which houses the likeness of a sacred white horse. Look for the three monkeys carved above the stable door, fixed in the pose of "see no evil, hear no evil, speak no evil."

At the next flight of stairs is **Yomeimon Gate,** considered to be the central showpiece of Nikko and popularly known as the Twilight Gate, implying that it could take you all day (until twilight) to see everything carved onto it. Painted in red, blue, and green, and decorated with gilding and lacquerwork, this gate has about 400 carvings of flowers, dragons, birds, and other animals. It's almost too much to take in at once.

To the left of the gate is the hall where the portable shrines are kept, as well as **Honchido Hall,** famous for its dragon painting on the ceiling. If you clap your hands under the painting, the echo supposedly resembles a dragon's roar. You can visit the shrine's main hall, where guides will explain (in Japanese) its history and main features. To the right of the main hall is a gate with a carving of a sleeping cat above it. Beyond that are 200 stone steps leading past cedars to Tokugawa's tomb, admission to which costs an additional ¥500 ($5) if it's not already included in your combination ticket. After the riotous colors of the shrine, the tomb itself seems surprisingly simple.

Toshogu Shrine is open daily from 8am to 5pm (you must enter by 4:30pm), closing earlier in winter (November through March) at 4pm (enter by 3:30pm).

Directly to the west of Toshogu Shrine is **Futarasan Shrine,** the oldest building in the district (from 1617), which has a pleasant garden and is dedicated to the gods of the mountains surrounding Nikko. On the shrine's grounds is the so-called ghost lantern, enclosed in a small wooden structure. According to legend, it used to come alive at night and sweep around Nikko in the form of a ghost. It apparently scared one of the guards so much that he struck it with his sword, the marks of which are still visible on the lamp's rim.

Past Futarasan Shrine is the second mausoleum, **Daiyuin Mausoleum.** It's the final resting place of Iemitsu, grandson of Ieyasu and the third Tokugawa shogun. Completed in 1653, it's not nearly so ornate as Toshogu Shrine nor as crowded, making it a pleasant last stop on your tour of Nikko.

After touring Nikko's shrines, you can catch a bus not far from the vermilion-painted bridge for **Lake Chuzenji** (you can also board it in front of the JR or Tobu Station). The ride costs ¥1,100 ($11) one way and takes about 50 minutes, winding higher and higher along hairpin roads. The view is breathtaking—I've even seen bands of monkeys along the side of the road. On the shores of Lake Chuzenji are many ryokan, souvenir stores, and coffee shops, making it a popular holiday resort. Things to do include visiting Tachiki Kannon Temple, beside the lake; going on an hour-long boat cruise; and visiting nearby Kegon Falls, a 300-foot waterfall.

ACCOMMODATIONS

Most ryokan are strung along the shores of Lake Chuzenji at a resort called Chuzenji Onsen. Keep in mind, however, that the majority of them are closed during the winter months and are open only from about mid-April to mid-November. If you want to stay in one of these ryokan, it's best to reserve a room in advance, which you can do at a travel agency. You can also make a reservation upon arrival at Nikko at the accommodation-reservation window inside Nikko Tobu Station (☎ 0288/54-0864); they'll charge a ¥200 to ¥500 ($2 to $5) fee but will take care of all arrangements for you. Ryokan owners in this area don't speak English and aren't likely to take you in if you simply show up at their door (I've done it this way, but I had to try several places before I finally found a sympathetic manager). If it's peak season, you should definitely reserve a room at a travel agency before leaving Tokyo. Most ryokan start at ¥10,000 ($100) per person, including two meals; rates rise to as much as ¥25,000 ($250) per person during peak season. There's little difference in what they offer: basically a tatami room, coin-operated TV, hot tea, breakfast and dinner served in your room, and a cotton kimono. Be sure to specify whether you want a lakeside view.

EXPENSIVE

Nikko Kanaya Hotel

1300 Kami-Hatsuishi, Nikko City, Tochigi Prefecture 321-14. ☎ **0288/54-0001.** Fax 0288/53-2487. 81 rms (65 with bath). MINIBAR TV TEL. ¥8,000 ($80) single with toilet only, ¥10,000 ($100) single with shower and toilet, ¥11,000–¥35,000 ($110–$350) single with bath; ¥10,000 ($100) twin with toilet only, ¥12,000 ($120) twin with shower and toilet, ¥13,000–¥40,000 ($130–$400) twin with bath. ¥3,000 ($30) extra on Sat and evening before national hols; ¥5,000–¥10,000 ($50–$100) extra during peak season. AE, DC, JCB, MC, V. Bus: From Nikko stations to the Shinkyo stop, a 5-minute ride. On foot: 15 minutes.

A distinguished-looking old-fashioned place secluded on a hill above the red Sacred Bridge, this is the most famous hotel in Nikko, combining the rustic heartiness of a European country lodge with elements of old Japan. First established in 1873, it has played host to a number of VIPs—Charles Lindbergh, Indira Gandhi, Helen Keller, Eleanor Roosevelt, David Rockefeller, Shirley MacLaine, and Albert Einstein, to name a few.

All rooms are Western-style twins and doubles, the differences in their prices based on room size, view, and facilities. Rooms are rather old-fashioned but cozy, and do not have air-conditioning, since the high altitude of Nikko rarely warrants it.

Dining/Entertainment: The hotel has a small Japanese restaurant serving shabu-shabu; a wonderful dining hall, serving Western food; and an inexpensive coffee shop with a nice view.

Facilities: Souvenir shops, small outdoor heated swimming pool (in summer), outdoor skating rink (in winter), Japanese garden.

Chuzenji Kanaya Hotel

2482 Chugushi, Nikko City, Tochigi Prefecture 321-16. ☎ **0288/51-0001.** Fax 0288/51-0011. 60 rms (all with bath). A/C MINIBAR TV TEL. ¥20,000–¥68,000 ($200–$680) per person, including two meals. Plus ¥10,000 ($100) in high season. AE, DC, JCB, MC, V. Bus: From Nikko to Lake Chuzenji, a 50-minute ride.

This is a wonderful, luxurious getaway, built in a comfortable and environment-matching mixture of Japanese and Canadian woods styles. The lobby sports a huge fireplace (more expensive rooms have a little one), and rooms are elegant. There's a hot springs overlooking the lake, and fishing, swimming, boating, and golfing facilities make this a sporting paradise. The Yukon Coffee House, the Boathouse restaurant (serving Japanese and Western cuisine), and a bar complete the facilities.

INEXPENSIVE

✪ Hatori-An

8-28 Takumi-cho, Nikko 321-14. ☎ **0288/53-5828.** Fax 0288/53-3883. 11 rms (all with bath). TV TEL. ¥5,200–¥6,200 ($52–$62) single; ¥10,400–¥12,400 ($104–$124) double. AE, MC, V. Bus: From Nikko stations to the Sogo Kaikan-mae stop, a 7-minute ride; then a 9-minute walk.

Owned by the friendly family who runs Turtles Inn, this is my favorite place to stay in Nikko. One dip in the hot-springs bath that overlooks the river will tell you why. At night you are lulled to sleep by the rush of the river waters. A plentiful breakfast costs ¥1,000 ($10) in the pleasant living area/dining room; take your dinner at Turtle Inn (see below). Use the refrigerator to store your own food and drink; buy a pizza from the freezer and microwave it yourself. Lowest room rates listed (for both inns) are for weekdays and highest for weekends and peak season.

Nikko Youth Hostel

2854 Tokorono, Nikko City, Tochigi Prefecture 321-14. ☎ **0288/54-1013.** 48 beds. ¥3,000 ($30). Breakfast ¥460 ($4.60) extra; dinner ¥720 ($7.20) extra. No credit cards. Station: Nikko (25 minutes).

Located north across the river in quiet surroundings, this hostel accepts both Japan Youth Hostel Association (JYHA) members and nonmembers. Sleeping is in bunk beds, with four to eight people to a room. There's a coin-operated laundry.

Turtle Inn

2-16 Takumi-cho, Nikko, 321-14. ☎ **0288/53-3168.** Fax 0288/53-3883. 11 rms (3 with bath). TV. ¥4,000–¥5,000 ($40–$50) single without bath, ¥4,800–¥5,800 ($48–$58) single with bath; ¥8,000–¥10,000 ($80–$100) double without bath, ¥9,600–¥11,600 ($96–$116) double with bath; ¥12,000–¥15,000 ($120–$150) triple without bath. AE, MC, V. Bus: From Nikko stations to the Sogo Kaikan-mae stop, a 7-minute ride; then a 5-minute walk.

A member of the Japanese Inn Group, this pension is not as picturesque as St. Bois, described below, but it's closer to Toshogu Shrine and is run by the very friendly Fukuda family. Mr. Fukuda speaks English and is very helpful in planning a sightseeing itinerary for the area. In this new two-story house on a quiet side street beside the Daiyagawa River, rooms are bright and cheerful, in both Japanese and Western styles, though the three tatami rooms are without bath. Excellent Western dinners (with Japanese touches) for ¥2,000 ($20) and Western breakfasts for ¥800 to ¥1,000 ($8 to $10) are available if you order them in advance. Highly recommended.

St. Bois

1560 Tokorono, Nikko City, Tochigi Prefecture 321-14. ☎ **0288/53-0082.** Fax 0288/53-3399. 11 rms (4 with bath). TV. ¥5,000 ($50) single without bath, ¥5,500 ($55) single with bath; ¥9,000 ($90) double without bath, ¥10,000 ($100) double with bath; ¥12,900 ($129) triple without bath. AE, V. Station: Nikko (15 minutes).

Another member of the Japanese Inn Group, this country-style lodge, located atop a hill and nestled among pine trees on the edge of Nikko, is a 30-minute walk from

Toshogu Shrine. It's very peaceful here. Unfortunately the last time I was here, the manager was rather surly (perhaps she'd gotten up on the wrong side of the futon). A Western-style breakfast is available for ¥800 ($8) if you order the night before, and dinner is available for ¥2,700 ($27) if you order it by 3pm.

DINING

MODERATE

Main Dining Hall

Nikko Kanaya Hotel, 1300 Kami-Hatsuishi. ☎ **0288/54-0001.** Reservations recommended during peak season. Main dishes ¥2,500–¥8,000 ($25–$80); set lunches ¥3,500 ($35). AE, DC, JCB, MC, V. Daily noon–3pm and 6–7:30pm. WESTERN.

Even if you don't spend the night here, you might want to come for a meal in the hotel's quaint dining hall, one of the best places in town for lunch. Since it's beside the Sacred Bridge, only a 10-minute walk from Toshogu Shrine, you can easily combine it with your sightseeing tour of Nikko. I suggest Nikko's specialty, locally caught rainbow trout, available in three different styles of cooking. I had mine cooked Kanaya style, covered with soy sauce, sugar, and sake, grilled and served whole. The best bargain is the set lunch, available until 3pm, which comes with soup, salad, and main dish.

Masudaya

439 Ichiyamachi. ☎ **0288/54-2151.** Reservations recommended for private rooms. Set meals ¥3,980 ($39.80) and ¥5,300 ($53). No credit cards. Fri–Wed 11am–2pm (open Thurs if a hol). Station: Nikko (5 minutes). LOCAL JAPANESE SPECIALTIES.

Only two fixed-price meals are served at this Japanese-style, traditional restaurant, both featuring a local specialty, *yuba.* Made from soybeans, yuba could be eaten only by priests and members of the imperial family until about 100 years ago. Now you can enjoy it, too, along with such side dishes as rice, sashimi, soup, fried fish, and vegetables. Dining is either in a common dining hall with chairs or, for the more expensive meals, in private tatami rooms, for which you should make a reservation. Masudaya is on the left side of the main street leading to Toshogu Shrine.

INEXPENSIVE

Gyoza House

257 Matsubara-cho. ☎ **0288/53-0494.** Main dishes ¥400–¥800 ($4–$8). No credit cards. Summer, daily 11am–8pm. Winter, daily 11am–7pm. Station: Nikko (2 minutes). GYOZA.

On the main street leading to Toshogu Shrine, a red awning and a bright green facade signal the existence of this simple restaurant, which offers gyoza (Chinese dumplings) and ramen (noodle-and-vegetable soup). Gyoza House has an English menu and pictures, listing such unique dishes as curry gyoza, shoyu gyoza (in a soup broth), and spicy ramen. It also offers an obento, for takeout only—which you could eat on the grounds of Toshogu Shrine.

3 Mashiko

62 miles N of Tokyo

Mashiko is a small village known throughout Japan for its *Mashiko-yaki,* distinctive, heavy, country-style pottery. A visit to Mashiko is usually combined with an overnight trip to Nikko, since both are not far from the town of Utsunomiya, north of Tokyo. Since the major attraction in Mashiko is its pottery shops and kilns, and there's little in the way of restaurants and accommodations, I suggest coming here just for the day, returning to Tokyo or traveling on to Nikko before nightfall.

Mashiko gained fame back in 1930, when the late Hamada Shoji, designated a "living national treasure," built a kiln in this tiny village and introduced Mashiko ware throughout Japan. Other potters have since taken up his technique, producing ceramics for everyday use, including plates, cups, vases, and tableware. Altogether, there are about 50 pottery shops in Mashiko, along with a number of kilns, where you can simply wander in, watch the craftspeople at work, and even try your own hand at throwing or glazing a pot.

ESSENTIALS

The **telephone area code** for Mashiko is 0285.

GETTING THERE **By Train** The easiest, fastest way is to take the shinkansen from Ueno to Utsunomiya (50 minutes) and transfer to a bus for a 40-minute ride to Mashiko. From Utsunomiya Station's main exit, walk straight away from the police station (on the left as you exit the station) one block (don't count the street that runs in front of the station). The bus stop for Mashiko is to your left on this street, which runs to the Miano Hashi (bridge). But not all buses go to Mashiko, so you have to ask the bus driver. Another way to reach Mashiko—by three-hour train ride—is to take the Tohoku Line from Ueno to Oyama, change there to the Mito Line for Shimodate, and change for Mohka where you change for Mashiko.

WHAT TO SEE & DO

The whole process of making pottery can be seen at the 130-year-old **Tsukamoto Pottery** (☎ 0285/72-3223), and visitors can try their hand at kneading clay, turning the potter's wheel, or hand-molding a pot. It's open Friday through Wednesday from 9:30am to noon and 1:30 to 5pm, but you must make a reservation at least one month in advance for weekends and one day ahead for weekdays. There's no admission fee, but potting costs ¥1,030 ($10.30), plus the price of materials (¥720 to ¥1,440/$7.20 to $14.40). But it takes two months to obtain your work of art (if you have it fired), and they ship only within Japan.

At the **Mashiko Reference Collection Museum** or *Mashiko Sankokan* (☎ 0285/72-5300), open from 9:30am to 4:30pm every day except Monday, New Year's, and the month of February, you can see works by Hamada, as well as a collection of Eastern and Western glass, ceramics, fabrics, furniture, and paintings, including pieces by Bernard Leach and Kanjiro Kawai. Charging an admission of ¥800 ($8) for adults (half price for children), the museum is housed in several thatch-roofed structures, which served as Hamada's workshop. His kilns are still there, built along a sloping hill and once heated with wood.

The main reason people come to Mashiko is to shop. There are more than a dozen shops along the main road of Mashiko, offering a wide variety of pottery produced by the town's potters. Simply wander in and out—you're sure to find something that pleases you. By the way, **Hiroshi Higeta** (☎ 0285/72-3162) has an indigo-dying cottage industry and shop selling his wares along the main road, which makes for an interesting visit.

4 Yokohama

20 miles S of Tokyo

There are few attractions in Yokohama to warrant a visit by the short-term traveler to Japan. However, if you find yourself in Tokyo for an extended period, Yokohama is a pleasant and easy destination for an afternoon or one-day excursion.

A rather new city in Japan's history books, Yokohama was nothing more than a tiny fishing village when Commodore Perry arrived in the mid-1800s and demanded that Japan open its doors to trade. Nevertheless, the village was selected by the shogun as one of several ports to be opened for international trade, and in 1859 the first foreign settlers arrived. To accommodate them, Yokohama was divided into two parts—Outside the Barrier (Kangai) and Inside the Barrier (Kannai). A canal was dug between the two, and the foreigners were placed in Kannai, ostensibly to protect them from irate samurai, who were disgruntled with these foreign intruders and might have tried to assassinate them. It's probably not too far-fetched to assume, however, that this separation between foreigner and Japanese was also meant to isolate the strangers. After all, following more than two centuries of isolation from the rest of the world, the Japanese were bound to be at least a little cautious about foreigners and their habits. But as Japan entered the Meiji Period in full swing, relations relaxed and the foreigners moved to a nearby hill known as the Bluff.

Even so, throughout the 19th century the foreigners in Yokohama continued to be a source of great curiosity for the Japanese, who came from as far away as Tokyo to look at them and to see the Western goods that were being imported. Serving as the capital city's port, Yokohama grew by leaps and bounds, becoming so important that the first railroad in Japan linked Tokyo with Yokohama, reducing the 10-hour journey by foot to less than an hour.

Today, Yokohama is still an important international port and still supports a large international community, with many foreigners continuing to reside on the Bluff. Yokohama also has a large Chinese population, descendants of immigrants who moved here shortly after Japan opened itself to trade. With a population of almost three million, Yokohama is Japan's second-largest city.

ESSENTIALS

The **telephone area code** for Yokohama is 045.

GETTING THERE **By Train** Yokohama is easily reached by train from Tokyo, Shimbashi, Shinagawa, and Yurakucho stations via the JR Keihin-Tohoku Line and from Shibuya Station via the Tokyu-Tokyoko Line. It takes about 40 minutes to reach Yokohama Station from Tokyo Station and about 30 minutes from Shinagawa. If you want to go directly to Kannai Station in the old part of Yokohama, where most of its attractions are centered, the Keihin-Tohoku Line from Tokyo Station, with stops in Yurakucho, Shimbashi, Shinagawa, and Yokohama Stations, reaches Kannai Station in about 45 minutes. Kannai Station is connected to Yokohama Station by subway, train, bus, and even boat.

In addition to the two train lines above, you can also take the Yokosuka Line, which departs from Tokyo, Shinagawa, and Shimbashi stations. Note, however, that it stops only at Yokohama Station.

VISITOR INFORMATION The **Yokohama Municipal Tourist Association** is located in the Sangyo Boeki Center, 2 Yamashita-cho, Naka-ku (☎ 045/641-5824), close to the harbor and an easy walk from Kannai Station. This tourist office is one of the best and most efficient I've come across in Japan, and its English-language map is excellent. The staff speaks English, can give you all kinds of brochures on the city, and can also arrange for you to visit with a Japanese family under Yokohama's **Home Visit System.** Be sure to call to set up the appointment at least a day in advance of your intended visit. The tourist office is open daily from 10am to 6pm.

Next door to the city tourist office, in the Silk Center, is the **Kanagawa Prefectural Tourist Office** (☎ 045/681-0007), where you can also obtain information on

Hakone and Kamakura, since they're both in Kanagawa Prefecture. It's open Monday through Friday from 9am to 5pm and on Saturday from 9am to noon.

GETTING AROUND Both the Japan Railways **Keihin-Tohoku Line** and the **Tokyu-Toyoko Line** pass through Yokohama Station and continue on to Sakuragicho and Kannai stations, convenient to most of Yokohama's attractions. Another way to get from Yokohama Station to Kannai is by **shuttle boat.** The boats depart from the Sogo department store, across the street from Yokohama Station's east exit. Called the Sea Bass, they deposit passengers at Yamashita Park, described later in this chapter. Boats leave about three times an hour and afford a view of the city from the water. The fare is ¥500 ($5), considerably cheaper than the harbor cruises offered. The **Blue Line** is a double-decker bus, which stops at most of the tourist attractions. The fare is ¥270 ($2.70), and there are explanations in English.

WHAT TO SEE & DO

AROUND YOKOHAMA STATION The biggest attraction here is **Sogo,** 2-18-1 Takashima (☎ 045/465-2111), Japan's second-largest department store. It employs 5,000 sales clerks, who serve as many as 150,000 customers a day—a number that can swell to double that on a weekend. Check out the Sogo Art Museum on the 6th floor; for branches of famous restaurants in Japan, go to the 10th floor. Sogo is open Wednesday through Monday from 10:30am to 7:30pm; its restaurants stay open until 10pm.

Also in Sogo is the **Hiraki Ukiyoe Museum** or *Hiraki Ukiyoe Bijitsukan,* a delightful museum devoted exclusively to woodblock prints. It has an impressive collection of some 8,000 prints; exhibitions change every month. Open Wednesday through Monday from 10am to 7pm. Entrance fees are ¥500 ($5) for adults. Outside the museum a shop selling cards, scarves, coasters, and prints with Ukiyoe themes is a good place for souvenirs.

From Sogo, you can take the Sea Bass shuttle boat, described above, to Kannai.

AROUND KANNAI STATION Your first stop in Kannai should be the **Silk Center,** in which you'll find both the prefectural tourist office and the **Silk Museum,** 1 Yamashita-cho, Naka-ku (☎ 045/641-0841). For many years after Japan opened its doors, silk was its major export, and most of it was shipped to the rest of the world from Yokohama, the nation's largest raw-silk market. In tribute to the role silk has played in Yokohama's history, this museum has displays showing the metamorphosis of the silkworm and how silk is obtained from cocoons; it also has exhibits of various kinds of silk fabrics, as well as gorgeous kimono. The Silk Museum is open Tuesday through Sunday from 9am to 4:30pm; admission is ¥300 ($3) for everyone age 12 and over, ¥100 ($1) for children 6 to 11 (children under 6 free).

Just a few minutes' walk from the Silk Center is **Yamashita Park,** laid out after the huge earthquake in 1923, which destroyed much of Tokyo and Yokohama. Japan's first seaside park, Yamashita Park is a pleasant place for a stroll along the waterfront, where you have a view of the city's mighty harbor. This is also where

Impressions

Yokohama does not improve on further acquaintance. It has a dead-alive look. It has irregularity without picturesqueness, and the gray sky, gray sea, gray houses, and gray roofs look harmoniously dull.

—Isabella Bird, *Unbeaten Tracks in Japan,* 1880

you'll arrive if you've come to Kannai by the Sea Bass shuttle boat. At one end of the park is the 348-foot-high **Marine Tower,** with an observation platform that provides an excellent view of the city, port, and sometimes even Mt. Fuji. It's open daily from 10am to 9pm (to 7pm in winter) and charges admission of ¥700 ($7) for everyone age 12 and over, ¥350 ($3.50) for children 6 to 11 (children under 6 free). Moored at a pier off the park is the *Hikawa Maru,* a transoceanic liner built in 1930. Its maiden voyage was to Seattle, after which it crossed the Pacific 238 times until it was retired in 1960. Today, it houses a restaurant and beer garden, but the admission fee of ¥800/$8 (half price for children) may deter you from wishing to dine here. Near here is a favorite of mine, the **Doll Museum,** which houses 7,800 dolls from 130 countries around the world, including of course Japanese *hina* (elaborate dolls representing the empress and emperor used for the March Hina festival) and *kokeshi* (simple wooden dolls). It's open from 9:30am to 5pm Tuesday to Sunday.

From Yamashita Park, you can also take a sightseeing tour by boat of **Yokohama harbor**—a tour that, according to the boat company's English brochure, "will fill up your complete satisfactions." Conducted in Japanese only, there's a 40-minute cruise daily at 3:40pm, which costs ¥900 ($9) and a 60-minute cruise at 10:30am daily, costing ¥1,200 ($12). Four daily 90-minute cruises cost ¥2,000 ($20) each. Price reductions are available for children.

Just a minute's walk from the Silk Center is the **Yokohama Archives of History** (☎ 045/201-2100) at 3 Nippon O-dori, with exhibits and pictures relating to the opening of Japan to foreigners and the establishment of Yokohama as an international port. A very small museum, the *Yokohama Kaiko Shiryokan* can be toured quickly just to get an idea of early Yokohama. Open Tuesday through Sunday from 9:30am to 5pm; closed on days following public holidays. The entrance fee is ¥200 ($2) for adults, half price for children.

AROUND SAKURAGICHO STATION If you're really a museum buff, you should wander over to the **Kanagawa Prefectural Museum** (☎ 045/201-0926) at 5-60 Minaminaka-dori, a 7-minute walk from Sakuragicho Station, or about a 20-minute walk from the Silk Center. In a Western-style building constructed in 1904 to house the nation's first modern foreign-exchange bank, the *Kanagawa Kenritsu Hakubutsukan* exhibits items related to natural science, archeology, history, and folklore in Kanagawa Prefecture. Yokohama, incidentally, is Kanagawa Prefecture's chief town. Included in the collection are rooms of a traditional Japanese farmhouse, tools for farming and silk production, and models of both Perry's ships and of Japan's first train, which ran between Tokyo and Yokohama. The museum is open Tuesday through Sunday from 9am to 5pm, and the entrance fee is ¥300 ($3).

Also near Sakuragicho Station is the **Yokohama Museum of Art** (☎ 045/221-0300) at 3-4-1 Minatomirai. With an emphasis on works by Western and Japanese artists since the 1850s, the museum's ambitious goal is to collect and display art reflecting the mutual influence between the modern art of Europe and that of Japan since the opening of Yokohama's port in 1859. Designed by Kenzo Tange and Urtec Inc., *Yokohama Bijutsukan* houses exhibits from its permanent collection—these are changed several times a year—as well as special exhibits on loan from other museums. Thus, no matter how many times you visit the museum, there's always something new to see. Hours here are 10am to 6pm, Friday through Wednesday. Admission is ¥500 ($5) and up, depending on the exhibition.

MORE SIGHTS As you gaze out over the harbor from Yamashita Park, you can see one of Yokohama's newest sights, the **Yokohama Bay Bridge.** Designed to ease congestion, it also features a 1,000-foot pedestrian walkway on the underbelly of the bridge, which extends to an observation deck, offering views of the harbor. Called the **Sky Walk,** it charges an admission of ¥600 ($6) and is open daily from 9am to 9pm April to October and from 10am to 6pm November to March. To reach the Sky Walk, which is on the opposite side of the harbor from Yamashita Park, take bus 109 from Sakuragicho Station's platform 6 and get off at the last stop.

In my opinion, **Sankei-en Garden** is the best reason for visiting Yokohama. Although not itself old, this lovely park contains a number of historical old buildings that were brought here from other parts of Japan, all situated around streams and ponds. Divided into an Inner Garden and an Outer Garden, the park was laid out back in 1906 by Tomitaro Hara, a local millionaire who made his fortune exporting silk. As you wander along the gently winding pathways, you'll see a villa built in 1649 by the Tokugawa Shogunate clan, tea arbors, a 500-year-old pagoda, and a farmhouse built in 1650 without the use of nails. No matter what the season, the views here are beautiful.

The easiest way to reach Sankei-en Garden is by bus no. 8, which departs from Yokohama Station and winds its way through Kannai and past Chinatown before reaching the Sankei-en-mae bus stop. It's therefore easy to combine Sankei-en and Kannai in a day's sightseeing tour. In fact, you may want to come first to Sankei-en Garden and then take the bus back to Kannai, ending up in Chinatown for dinner. Sankei-en is open daily from 9am to 4:30pm (enter by 4pm), and admission is ¥300 ($3) for the Outer Garden, another ¥300 ($3) for the Inner Garden.

DINING

CHUKAGAI Chinatown, in Yamashita-cho, Naka-ku, consists of one main street and dozens of offshoots, with restaurant after restaurant serving Chinese food, primarily Cantonese. Most of the restaurants have plastic-food displays or pictures of their menu, so let your budget be your guide. Many also have English menus. Most dishes run ¥800 to ¥3,000 ($8 to $30), and set lunches go for ¥800 to ¥900 ($8 to $9). Larger restaurants accept credit cards; those that do display them on the front door. Most Chinatown restaurants are open from 11am to 7:30pm; some close Tuesday or Wednesday, but there are always restaurants open. Among the larger, better-known ones are **Manchinro** and **Heichinro,** both of which serve Cantonese food; **Saika,** which specializes in dim sum; and **Kaseiro** and **Peking Hanten,** both of which serve Pekinese food.

Chinatown is about a 15-minute walk from Kannai Station or a 10-minute walk from Ishikawacho Station. For more information call the Chinatown Information Office (☎ 045/662-1252).

SOGO DEPARTMENT STORE Japan's second-largest department store, Sogo is located at 2-18-1 Takashima, in Nishi-ku (☎ 045/465-2111; Yokohama Station, east exit). There are approximately 40 restaurants and coffee shops here, the best of which are on the 10th floor, called Gourmet Ten. It features branches of many famous restaurants, including **Tenichi,** which serves tempura; **Shisen,** a Chinese restaurant; **Chikuyotei,** a famous eel restaurant; and **Sabatini,** an Italian restaurant from Rome, with a branch also in Tokyo. Other restaurants serve udon noodles, Kyoto specialties, kaiseki, shabu-shabu, sukiyaki, sushi, and Kobe beef. Since all restaurants have plastic-food display cases outside their doors, ordering is easy. Most dishes run ¥650 to ¥1,500 ($6.50 to $15), and set meals go for ¥1,500 to ¥7,500 ($15 to $75). Some restaurants accept credit cards; those that do display them on the door. The store restaurants are open Wednesday through Monday from 11am to 10pm.

5 Mount Fuji

62 miles SW of Tokyo

Mt. Fuji, affectionately called "Fuji-san" by the Japanese, has been revered as sacred since ancient times. Throughout the centuries Japanese poets have written about it, painters have painted it, pilgrims have flocked to it, and more than a few people have died on it. Without a doubt this mountain has been photographed more than anything else in Japan.

Visible on a clear day from as far as 100 miles away, Mt. Fuji is stunningly impressive. At 12,388 feet it towers far above anything else around it, a symmetrical cone of almost perfect proportions. Mt. Fuji is majestic, grand, and awe-inspiring. To the Japanese it symbolizes the very spirit of their country. Unfortunately, Fuji-san is almost always cloaked in clouds. If you catch a glimpse of this mighty mountain (which you can do from the bullet train between Tokyo and Nagoga), consider yourself extremely lucky.

ESSENTIALS

The **telephone area code** for Mt. Fuji is 0555.

GETTING THERE **By Train and Bus** Most climbs to the top of Mt. Fuji start at Go-go-me, or the Fifth Stage, on either the Kawaguchiko Trail or the Gotemba Trail, though there are others. The Kawaguchiko Trail winds from Kawaguchiko Station to the summit; the Gotemba Trail, from Gotemba Station to Fuji's top. Direct bus service is available to Go-go-me from Hammatsucho or Shinjuku in Tokyo. There are some 15 buses a day from mid-July to the end of August, with less frequent service April through mid-July and September through October. The one-way fare from Hamatsucho to Go-go-me is ¥2,800 ($28); the ride takes about 3 hours. From Shinjuku the one-way fare is ¥2,600 ($26), and the trip takes about 2¹/₂ hours. Reservations are necessary through Fuji Kyuko Railway (☎ 0555/3374-2221) or a travel agent. If you want to use your Japan Rail Pass, you can leave from Tokyo's Shinjuku Station via the JR Chuo Line to Otsuki, where you change to the Fuji Kyuko Line for Kawaguchiko. The trip takes about 2 hours. From Kawaguchiko Station, you can take a 55-minute bus ride for ¥1,610 ($16.10) to Go-go-me; it runs April through November 23. Bus service is suspended in winter when Mt. Fuji is blanketed in snow and is considered too dangerous for the novice climber. Check with Fuji Kyuko Railway (☎ 0555/3374-2221) for schedules.

VISITOR INFORMATION More information regarding train and bus schedules can be obtained from the Tokyo Tourist Information Center in leaflets called "Mt. Fuji and Fuji Five Lakes" and "Climbing Mt. Fuji."

CLIMBING MOUNT FUJI

Mt. Fuji is part of a larger national park called Fuji-Hakone-Izu National Park. Of the handful of trails leading to the top, the most popular ones for Tokyoites are the Kawaguchiko Trail for the ascent and the Subashiri Trail for the descent. All trails are divided into 10 different stages, with the Fifth Stage located about 8,250 feet up. It takes about five hours to reach the summit and three hours for the descent.

Because of snow and inclement weather from fall through late spring, the best time to make an ascent is during the "official" climbing season, from July 1 to August 31. It's also the most crowded time of the year. Consider the fact that there are approximately 120 million Japanese, most of whom wouldn't dream of climbing the mountain outside the "official" two months it's open, and you begin to get the picture.

More specifically, about 400,000 people climb Fuji-san every year, mostly in July and August and mostly on weekends. In other words, if you plan on climbing Mt. Fuji on a Saturday or a Sunday in summer, go to the end of the line, please.

Don't be disappointed when your bus deposits you at Kawaguchiko Fifth Stage, where you'll be bombarded with an overflow of souvenir shops, restaurants, and busloads of tourists. Most of these tourists aren't climbing to the top, and as soon as you get past them and the blaring loudspeakers, you'll find yourself on a steep rocky path, surrounded only by scrub brush and with hikers on the path below and above you. After a couple of hours, you'll probably find yourself above the roily clouds, which stretch in all directions. It will be as if you were on an island, barren and rocky, in the middle of an ocean.

You needn't have had climbing experience to ascend Mt. Fuji, but you do need stamina and a good pair of walking shoes. It's possible to do it in tennis shoes, but if the rocks are wet they can get awfully slippery. You should also bring a light plastic raincoat (which you can buy at souvenir shops at the Fifth Stage), a sun hat, and a sweater for the evening. It gets very chilly on Mt. Fuji at night.

As for sleeping, there are about 25 mountain huts along the Kawaguchiko Trail above the Fifth Stage, but they're very primitive, providing only a futon and toilet facilities. The cost without meals is ¥4,000 ($40) per person, and with meals it's ¥6,000 ($60) per person. When I stayed in one of these huts, dinner consisted of dried fish, rice, bean-paste soup, and pickled vegetables; breakfast was exactly the same.

The usual procedure for climbing Mt. Fuji is to start out in early afternoon, spend the night near the summit, get up early in the morning to watch the sun rise, and then climb the rest of the way to the top, where there's a one-hour hiking trail that circles the crater. Hikers then begin the descent, reaching the Fifth Stage about noon.

In recent years, however, a new trend has started in which climbers arrive at the Fifth Stage late in the evening and then climb to the top through the night with the aid of flashlights. After watching the sun rise, they then make their descent. That way, they don't have to spend the night in one of the huts.

Climbing Mt. Fuji is definitely a unique experience, but there is a saying in Japan: "Everyone should climb Mt. Fuji once; only a fool would climb it twice."

6 Hakone

60 miles SW of Tokyo

As part of the Fuji-Hakone-Izu National Park, Hakone is one of the closest and most popular resorts for residents of Tokyo. Blessed with beautiful scenery, Hakone has about everything a vacationer could wish for—hot-spring resorts, mountains, lakes, breathtaking views of Mt. Fuji, and interesting historical sites. You can tour Hakone as a day trip, but adding an overnight stay near Lake Ashi, or in the mountains, where you can soak in the water of hot springs, is much more pleasant. If you plan to return to Tokyo, I suggest leaving your luggage in storage at your Tokyo hotel and traveling to Hakone with only an overnight bag.

ESSENTIALS

The **telephone area code** for Hakone is 0460.

GETTING THERE **By Train** Getting to Hakone is half the fun! Start out by train from Tokyo, then switch to a small two-car train that zigzags up the mountain, change to a cable car and then a smaller ropeway, and end your trip with a boat ride across Lake Ashi, stopping off to see major attractions along the way. From Lake Ashi (from either Togendai or Hakone-machi), you can then board a bus bound for Odawara Station (an hour's ride), where you can then take the train back to Tokyo. From Togendai, there are also buses that go directly to Shinjuku Station.

By Bus Odakyu buses depart every hour from Shinjuku Station's west exit bound for Togendai on Lake Ashi. The trip takes 2 hours and 10 minutes. Reservations are recommended. Call Odakyu at 03/3481-0103.

VISITOR INFORMATION Before leaving Tokyo, pick up the "Hakone and Kamakura" leaflet available from the Tourist Information Office. It lists the time schedules for the extensive network of trains, buses, cable cars, and pleasure boats throughout the Hakone area.

GETTING AROUND The most economical way to see Hakone is via the **Hakone Free Pass,** which, despite its name, isn't free but does give you a round-trip ticket from Shinjuku Station to Odawara or Hakone Yumoto in Hakone and includes almost all other modes of transportation in Hakone (see "Getting There," above). The pass avoids the hassle of having to buy individual tickets and also provides discounts on several of Hakone's attractions. Valid for four days, it costs ¥5,400 ($54), from Shinjuku. There is an Odakyu Romance Car surcharge of ¥800 ($8). The Romance Car travels from Shinjuku all the way to Hakone Yumoto Station in about 1½ hours; the slower train travels from Shinjuku only as far as Odawara in the same amount of time. If you have a Japan Rail Pass, you should take the Shinkansen bullet train from Tokyo Station to Odawara (not all bullet trains stop there, so make sure yours does). From there, you can travel on the private railways, cable cars, buses, and boats for the ¥4,050 ($40.50) Hakone Free Pass, also valid for four days. All passes can be purchased at any station of the Odakyu Railway, including Shinjuku Station.

WHAT TO SEE & DO

If you plan on spending only a day in Hakone, you should leave Tokyo very early in the morning. If you're spending the night—and I strongly urge that you do—you can arrange your itinerary in a more leisurely fashion and devote more time to Hakone's attractions. You may wish to travel only as far as your hotel the first day, stopping at sights along the way and in the vicinity. The next day you could continue with the rest of the circuit through Hakone. If you want to do most of your sightseeing the first day, you can travel all the way to Lake Ashi and from there take a bus to all accommodations recommended below.

THE TRAIN TRIP Regardless of whether you travel via Shinkansen, the Odakyu Romance Car, or the ordinary Odakyu express, you'll end up at either Odawara Station, considered the gateway to Hakone, or Hakone Yumoto Station. At either station, you can transfer to the **Hakone Tozan Railway,** a small two-car train that winds its way through forests and over streams as it travels upward to Gora, making several switchbacks along the way. The entire trip from Hakone Yumoto Station to Gora takes only 45 minutes, but it's a beautiful ride, on a narrow track through the mountains. The train makes about a dozen stops before reaching Gora, including Tonosawa and Miyanoshita, two hot-spring spa resorts with a number of old ryokan and hotels (refer to my food and lodging recommendations). Some of these ryokan date back several centuries, from the days when they were on the main thoroughfare to Tokyo, the old Tokaido Highway. Miyanoshita is also the best place for lunch.

As for things to do along the way, you can begin your trip with some open-air bathing at the public baths behind Hakone Yumoto Station, called **Kappa Tengoku** (43) (☎ 0460/5-6121). Probably the closest outdoor baths in the vicinity of Tokyo, they're open from 10am to 10pm and charge ¥700 ($7) admission for those over 6, and ¥400 ($4) for 2- to 6-year-olds. From Hakone Yumoto Station, take a right and go under the train tracks, and then take an immediate right again. Walk uphill and follow the sign (in kanji only) up the steps to what looks like a house. The baths are in the woods behind the house.

The most important stop on the Hakone Tozan Railway is the next-to-the-last stop, Chokoku-no-Mori, where you'll find the famous **Hakone Open-Air Museum** (☎ 0460/2-1161), with more than 100 sculptures by artists from around the world, including Rodin, Henry Moore, Imoto Atusushi, and Yodoi Toshio. Using nature itself as a dramatic backdrop, this museum spreads through glens and gardens and over ponds. There's also an indoor exhibit of paintings and sculptures, including a collection of Picasso's works. You'll want to spend at least a couple of hours here. Open daily from 9am to 5pm (until 4pm in winter), the museum charges ¥1,500 ($15) for those 12 and over, ¥800 ($8) for children 6 to 11 (children under 6, free).

BY CABLE CAR & ROPEWAY From Gora you can travel by cable car, which leaves every 15 minutes and arrives 9 minutes later at the end station of Sounzan, making several stops along the way. One of the stops is Koen-Kami, which is only a minute away from the **Hakone Art Museum** (☎ 0460/2-2623). Open Friday through Wednesday from 9am to 4:30pm (until 4pm in winter), the *Hakone Bijutsukan* displays Japanese pottery and ceramics from the Jomon Period (around 4000 B.C.) to the Edo Period. Included are water jars, terra-cotta vessels taken from burial grounds dating from before the 7th century, Bizen ware from Okayama, and 17th-century Imari ware. A lovely Japanese landscape garden of moss and bamboo is on the museum grounds. Admission is ¥800 ($8) and ¥500 ($5) for students.

From Sounzan you board a small ropeway for a long haul down the mountain to Togendai, which lies beside Lake Ashi, known as Lake Ashinoko in Japanese. Before reaching Togendai, however, get off at the first intermediary station, Owakudani, the ropeway's highest point. Here you can take a 30-minute hike along a nature path through Owakudani, which means "Great Boiling Valley." Sulfurous steam escapes from fissures in the rock, testimony to volcanic activity still present here. In Owakudani you'll also find the **Natural Science Museum** (☎ 0460/4-9149), with displays on the fauna, flora, geology, and volcanic origins of Hakone. It's open from 9am to 5:30pm (until 4:30pm in winter) and charges an admission of ¥400 ($4) for those 12 and over, ¥250 ($2.50) for children. Before starting back down on the ropeway, stop off for a drink at the second floor of the ropeway station, where you have fantastic views of Hakone and of Mt. Fuji if it's not covered by clouds.

LAKE ASHI From Togendai you can take a pleasure boat across Lake Ashi, also referred to as "Lake Hakone" in English brochures. Believe it or not, one of the boats crossing the lake is a replica of a centuries-old man-of-war. It takes about half an hour to cross the lake to Hakone-machi (also called simply Hakone; *machi* means city) and Moto-Hakone, two resort towns right next to each other on the southern edge of the lake. This end of the lake affords the best view of Mt. Fuji, a view often depicted in tourist publications.

In Hakone-machi you should visit the **Hakone Checkpoint,** a reconstructed guardhouse. Originally built in 1618, *Hakone Sekisho* served as a checkpoint on the famous **Tokaido Highway,** which connected Edo (present Tokyo) with Kyoto. In feudal days, local lords, called *daimyo,* were required to spend alternate years in Edo, and their wives were kept on in Edo as hostages so that the lords wouldn't plan rebellions while in their homelands. This was one of the points along the highway where travelers were checked. Although it was possible to sneak around it, violators who were caught were promptly executed. The checkpoint is open daily from

8:30am to 4:30pm (until 4pm in winter), and admission is ¥200 ($2) for adults and ¥100 ($1) for children.

Not far from the checkpoint is the **Hakone Detached Palace Garden,** which lies on a small promontory on Lake Ashi. Originally part of an imperial villa built in 1887, the garden is open free to the public. It not only offers a fine view of the lake but also displays historical materials relating to the old Tokaido Highway, including weapons, armor, palanquins, and items from life during the Edo Period. For more information on either the Hakone Checkpoint or the Detached Palace Garden, call the Hakone Town Office (☎ 0460/5-7111).

Between Hakone-machi and Moto-Hakone is part of the Tokaido Highway itself. Lined with ancient and mighty cedars, 1 1/4 miles of the old highway follow the curve of Lake Ashi and make a pleasant stroll (unfortunately, a road of the 20th century has been built right beside the original one). In Moto-Hakone is **Hakone Shrine,** revered by samurai until the Meiji Restoration in 1868. Especially picturesque is its red torii gate, standing in the water.

ACCOMMODATIONS

Japan's ryokan sprang into existence to accommodate the stately processions of daimyo and shogun as they traversed the roads between Edo and the rest of Japan. Many of these ryokan were built along the Tokaido Highway, and some of the oldest are found in Hakone.

EXPENSIVE

✪ The Fujiya Hotel

359 Miyanoshita, Hakone-machi, Ashigarashimo-gun 250-04. ☎ **0460/2-2211.** Fax 0460/2-2210. 146 rms (all with bath). A/C MINIBAR TV TEL. $118–$119 single or double special foreigners' rate; ¥20,000–¥45,000 ($200–$450) single or double; ¥50,000–¥100,000 ($500–$1,000) suite (higher rates are for weekends and peak season). AE, DC, JCB, MC, V. Station: Miyanoshita, Hakone Tozan Railway (5 minutes).

Established in 1878, it's the grandest, most majestic old hotel in Hakone and one of the oldest Western-style hotels in Japan. It's a lovely establishment, with such Asian touches as a Japanese-style roof, lots of windows, and wooden corridors. It consists of five separate buildings, all different and added on at various times in the hotel's 118-year history. One is shaped like a pagoda, while another has turrets and a roof shaped like that of a Japanese temple. The old-fashioned rooms have high ceilings and wooden furniture. In the back of the hotel are a garden with a waterfall and a pond full of carp. There's an outdoor swimming pool, as well as an indoor thermal pool fed by water from a hot spring. The hotel even has its own greenhouse. The accommodating front-desk personnel speak very good English. Even if you don't stay here, do come for a meal or tea. Room rates are based on room quality and season, with the highest rate for a deluxe room on a weekend in peak season. The special rate for foreign visitors is based upon the age of the hotel (in 1996 the rate is $118) and is not available on Saturdays. It also includes a 10% discount on breakfast and dinner.

Dining/Entertainment: The Fujiya's main dining hall, dating from 1930, is perhaps the best place for a meal in Hakone. It offers a variety of Western dishes, from spaghetti and sandwiches for lunch to trout or steaks for dinner. It's an experience I wouldn't miss. Afternoon high tea with scones and cinnamon toast is served in the charming tea lounge for ¥1,000 ($10).

Services: Free newspaper, free shoeshine kit, massage, mah-jongg, free parking.

Facilities: Shopping arcade, indoor and outdoor swimming pools, hot-spring baths, pleasant garden, greenhouse, golf course.

Hakone Prince Hotel

144 Moto-Hakone, Hakone-machi, Ashigarashimo-gun 250-05. ☎ **0460/3-7111.** Fax 0460/3-7616. 296 rms (all with bath). MINIBAR TV TEL. Ryuguden complex, ¥30,000–¥32,000 ($300–$320) per person, including two meals, tax, and service charge (extra charge during peak season). Western-style hotel, ¥30,000–¥42,000 ($300–$420) double. Western-style cabins, ¥42,000 ($420) for up to four people. Add ¥10,000 ($100) during peak season. AE, DC, JCB, MC, V. Bus: From Odawara Station or Hakone Yumoto Station to the Hakone-en stop (last stop).

This luxurious hotel is situated on secluded property right on Lake Ashi. The various types of rooms available here are in several differently styled complexes that sprawl over the well-tended grounds.

The **Ryuguden** (54) complex with its Japanese-style tatami rooms resembles an Asian palace. It's a grand structure, built in 1936, with iron lanterns hanging from its upturned wooden eaves and sculptured bushes gracing its manicured lawns. Prices vary according to the room and the meals ordered.

Not far from the Ryuguden complex is the Hakone Prince's Western-style hotel, designed by Japanese architect Togo Murano in a circular shape so that each room has a different panoramic view, complete with balcony.

And finally, you can also stay in one of the individual pine log cabins (the wood imported from Finland), spread underneath the trees in a kind of village and sleeping up to four people each.

Dining/Entertainment: There are two restaurants serving Japanese, Western, and Chinese food; one bar; and a coffee shop.

Services: Free newspaper (not available in cabins).

Facilities: Gardens, tennis courts (with night lighting), public baths (overlooking the lake), outdoor pool, ice-skating rink (winter only), and arboretum.

Ichinoyu (55)

90 Tonosawa, Hakone-machi, Ashigarashimo-gun 250-03. ☎ **0460/5-5331.** Fax 0460/5-5335. 21 rms (11 with bath). A/C MINIBAR TV TEL. ¥9,800–¥14,800 ($98–$148) Sunday through Friday; ¥3,000 ($30) extra Saturday and holidays. All rates per person, including two meals. AE, DC, JCB, MC, V. Station: Tonosawa, Hakone Tozan Railway (6 minutes).

Ichinoyu, first opened more than 360 years ago, is now in its 15th generation of owners. It claims to be the oldest ryokan in the area and was once honored by the visit of a shogun. Located near Tonosawa Station (on the Hakone Tozan Line), this delightful, rambling wooden building stands on a tree-shaded winding road that follows the track of the old Tokaido Highway. On one side of the ryokan is a roaring river.

The oldest rooms here date from the Meiji Period, more than 100 years ago. The two rooms I like the most are called Seseragi and Matsu (rooms are usually named in ryokan). Old-fashioned, they face the river and consist mainly of seasoned and weathered wood. Old artwork, wall hangings, and paintings decorate the ryokan, and some of the rooms have old wooden bathtubs. Both the communal tubs and the tubs in the rooms have hot water supplied from a natural spring.

Naraya

162 Miyanoshita, Hakone-machi, Ashigarashimo-gun 250-04. ☎ **0460/2-2411.** Fax 0460/7-6231. 20 rms (19 with bath). MINIBAR TV TEL. ¥28,000–¥60,000 ($280–$600) per person. All rates include two meals and service charge. AE, DC, V. Station: Miyanoshita, Hakone Tozan Railway (5 minutes).

Across the street from the Fujiya Hotel is Naraya, an elegant traditional Japanese inn with tiled roof, wooden walls, shoji screens, and hot-spring baths. Although the inn's history stretches back several hundred years, the present building is about a century old. The tatami rooms here have inspiring views of a large landscape garden and mountains beyond. This is a great place to relax and revel in nature's beauty, and the meals served are worth the price of staying here.

INEXPENSIVE

Fuji-Hakone Guest House

912 Sengokuhara, Hakone, Kanagawa 250-06. ☎ **0460/4-6577.** Fax 0460/4-6578. 12 rms (none with bath). ¥5,000–¥6,000 ($50–$60) single; ¥10,000–¥12,000 ($100–$120) twin; ¥14,000–¥16,000 ($140–$160) triple. Plus ¥150 ($1.50) local tax per person. Peak season and weekends ¥1,000–¥2,000 ($10–$20) extra. Western breakfast ¥800 ($8) extra. AE, MC, V. Bus: Hakone Tozan Bus (included in the Hakone Free Pass) from Togendai (10 minutes) or from Odawara Station (45 minutes) to the (announced in English) Senkyoro-mae stop.

Although it's a bit isolated, this Japanese Inn group member offers inexpensive lodging in tatami rooms. Kept spotlessly clean, this modern house in tranquil surroundings set back from a tree-shaded road is run by a man who speaks very good English. Some of the rooms face the Hakone mountain range. Facilities include a public hot-spring bath, coin-operated laundry and dryer, a large lounge area with bilingual TV, and a communal refrigerator. The family running the guesthouse prefer guests stay at least two nights. Unless you want a Japanese room, it's more reasonable to stay at the Fujiya Hotel with its special foreigner's rate.

DINING

Main Dining Room

In the Fujiya Hotel, 359 Miyanoshita. ☎ **0460/2-2211.** Set dinners ¥5,800–¥15,000 ($58–$150); set lunches ¥4,000–¥6,000 ($40–$60). AE, DC, JCB, MC, V. Daily noon–3pm and 6–8:30pm. Station: Miyanoshita, on the Hakone Tozan Railway (5 minutes). WESTERN.

The Fujiya Hotel, Hakone's grandest hotel and conveniently located near a stop on the two-car Hakone Tozan Railway, is the most memorable place for a meal. The main dining hall, dating from 1930, is very bright and cheerful, with a high, intricately detailed ceiling, large windows with Japanese screens, a wooden floor, and white tablecloths. The views are nice, and the service is attentive. For lunch you can have such dishes as pilaf, spaghetti, sandwiches, chicken, rainbow trout, and hamburger steak, while the more expensive dinner menu includes steaks, fish, grilled chicken, and stews. Good food in an impressive setting.

7 The Izu Peninsula

Whenever Tokyoites want to spend a few days at a hot-spring spa on the seashore, they head for the Izu Peninsula. Jutting out into the Pacific Ocean, Izu boasts some fine beaches, verdant and lush countryside, and a dramatic coastline marked in spots by high cliffs and tumbling surf. However, even though the scenery is at times breathtaking, there's little of historical interest to lure the short-term visitor to Japan; make sure you've seen both Kamakura and Nikko before you consider coming here. Keep in mind also that Izu's resorts are terribly crowded during the summer vacation period, from mid-July to the end of August.

But the best way to enjoy Izu is to drive, making this one of the few times when it may be worthwhile to rent your own car. There's a road that hugs the coast all the way around the peninsula, which you can drive easily in a day. If you're traveling by public transportation, an interesting route is to take the Shinkansen bullet train to Atami, travel by limited express to Shimoda, take the bus from Shimoda to

Dogashima, and from there take a boat to Numazu, where you can catch a train back to Tokyo. Before leaving Tokyo, be sure to pick up the leaflet "The Izu Peninsula" at the Tourist Information Center.

If you're traveling during the peak summer season, you should make reservations at least several months in advance. Otherwise, there are hotel, ryokan, and minshuku reservation offices in all of Izu's resort towns which will arrange accommodations for you, but be aware that if a place has a room still open at the last minute in August, there's probably a reason for it—poor location, poor service, or unimaginative decor. I took my chances one August and arrived in Atami without prior arrangements. The "ryokan" arranged by the accommodations office at the Atami train station was the worst I've ever stayed in. It pays to plan ahead. Below are recommended accommodations in Atami, Shimoda, and Dogashima, three towns that provide a good overview of what the peninsula has to offer.

ATAMI

30 miles SW of Tokyo

Atami means "hot sea." Legend has it that a long time ago there was a hot geyser spewing forth in the sea, killing a lot of fish and marine life. The concerned fishermen asked a Buddhist monk to intervene on their behalf and to pray for a solution to the problem. The prayers paid off when the geyser moved itself to the beach. Not only was the marine life spared, but Atami was blessed with hot-spring water the townspeople could henceforth bathe in.

Today, Atami—with a population of more than 50,000—is a conglomeration of hotels, ryokan, restaurants, pachinko parlors, souvenir shops, and a sizable red-light district. The city itself is not very interesting, but it's the most easily accessible hot-spring resort from Tokyo and has a wonderful art museum. In fact, the art museum is so famous that Tokyoites will come to Atami on a day trip just to see it.

ESSENTIALS

The **telephone area code** for Atami is 0557.

GETTING THERE **By Train** From Tokyo Station it's one hour by Shinkansen bullet train (since not all bullet trains stop in Atami, make sure yours does).

VISITOR INFORMATION The **Atami Tourist Information Office** is located to the left as you exit the train station (☎ 0557/81-6002) and is open daily from 10am to 6pm. No English is spoken, but English literature and a map are available. Buy your MOA tickets here for ¥200 ($2) less than at the museum.

WHAT TO SEE & DO

Be sure to see the **MOA Art Museum** (☎ 0557/84-2511), located on top of a hill a short bus ride away from Atami Station. Housed in a modern building at the headquarters of the Church of World Messianity, this museum includes woodblock prints, ceramics, lacquerware, and artwork from the collection of Mokichi Okada, leader of this relatively new religion in Japan. The place is open Friday through Wednesday from 9:30am to 5pm (you must enter by 4:30pm), and admission is ¥1,500 ($15) for adults, ¥1,000 ($10) for students, and ¥700 ($7) for children, but remember you can prepay your tickets for ¥200 ($2) less each at the station's tourist information counter. To reach MOA take the bus from platform 4 to the last stop; one-way fare is ¥150 ($1.50).

ACCOMMODATIONS

Hotel New Akao (56)

1993-250 Atami, Atami City 413. ☎ **0557/82-5151.** Fax 0557/83-0831. 350 rms (all with bath). A/C MINIBAR TV TEL. ¥22,500–¥25,000 ($225–$250) per person Sun–Fri, plus ¥2,000 ($20) on Sat. All rates include two meals and service charge. AE, DC, JCB, MC, V. Directions: Hotel shuttle bus, 10 minutes from Atami Station, with departures once an hour.

This large pleasure hotel is one of the most conspicuous resort hotels on the Izu Peninsula, hemmed in on one side by cliffs and on the other by the blue sea. Rooms in both Japanese and Western style are available, simply but tastefully done, all with large windows facing the water and a private bath. Obviously, what you're paying for here is use of the facilities rather than luxurious rooms. My only complaint about this hotel is that it's so popular and crowded during peak season that the front desk seems too busy to be very accommodating.

Dining/Entertainment: This hotel has about everything most Japanese want in a vacation, including a fancy dining hall affording an unusual view of surf crashing into cliffs, and karaoke.

Facilities: Swimming pool, roped-off area in the sea for swimming, large hot-spring public bath, *rotenburo* or outdoor hot-spring bath, outdoor garden complete with arbors and Corinthian pillars, small miniature golf area.

Kiunkaku (57)

4-2 Showacho, Atami City 413. ☎ **0557/81-3623.** Fax 0557/81-9795. 25 rms (20 with bath). A/C MINIBAR TV TEL. ¥30,000–¥80,000 ($300–$800) per person. All rates include two meals and service charge. Directions: Take a taxi from Atami Station, an 8-minute ride.

One of Atami's oldest ryokan, Kiunkaku has a beautiful garden with a meandering stream, manicured bushes, and stunted pine trees. It has one of the most pleasant coffee shops I've seen in a ryokan, and facilities include hot-spring baths and an outdoor pool. Although rooms encircle the garden, they are artfully concealed from one another and give optimum privacy through the clever use of bushes and mounds. There are various styles of rooms available: The most expensive are those with the best view, the most space, and the best meals. Tamahime, for example, the ryokan's one Western-style room, has changed little over the decades. It sports stained-glass windows, a paneled ceiling, a fireplace (no longer used), a monstrous old dresser, and cozy furniture—plus a good view of the garden. But at ¥75,000 ($750), it's out of my range.

New Fujiya Hotel

1-16 Ginza-cho, Atami City 413. ☎ **0557/81-0111.** Fax 0557/81-8052. 350 rms (all with bath). A/C MINIBAR TV TEL. With two meals, ¥21,000 ($210) per person. Without meals (only on weekdays), ¥24,200 ($242) twin. AE, DC, JCB, MC, V. Directions: Take a taxi from Atami Station (5 minutes).

Built just before the 1964 Summer Olympics, but since renovated,the staff here is friendly, efficient, and used to foreigners. Although the New Fujiya is located a few blocks inland, its top-floor rooms have partial views of the water. The cheapest rooms are those that face an inside courtyard. Both Japanese- and Western-style rooms are available.

Dining/Entertainment: In addition to a coffee shop and three restaurants, there's a nightclub—usually with performances by rather scantily clad women.

Facilities: Indoor pool, video-game corner, hot-spring public bath and sauna, outdoor hot-spring spa.

Dining

Kyotei (58)

2-11 Tahara Honcho. ☎ **0557/82-0066.** Set meals ¥1,800–¥2,600 ($18–$26). No credit cards. Open Fri–Wed noon–3pm and 5:30–9pm. SUSHI.

For excellent sushi try a set meal here of nigiri or chiraishi for lunch. To get here, walk down the second covered shopping arcade away from and on the right-hand side of the station; when the shopping arcade ends, Kyotei is catercorner across the street. Small wooden boats grace its window.

SHIMODA

112 miles SW of Tokyo

Located on the southeast end of the Izu Peninsula, Shimoda is famous as the site where Commodore Perry set anchor in 1854 to force Japan to open its doors to trade. Shimoda is also where the first American diplomatic representative, Townsend Harris, lived before setting up permanent residence in Yokohama.

Essentials

The **telephone area code** for Shimoda is 0558.

GETTING THERE **By Train** From Tokyo's Shinjuku, Ikebukuro, or Tokyo Station take the Izu Superview Odoriko direct to Shimoda Izukyu Station. Your rail pass works as far as Ito from where you must pay (¥1,440 to ¥1,850/$14.40 to $18.50, depending on the train), but not transfer.

VISITOR INFORMATION The **Shimoda Tourist Office,** located to the right out of the wicket and behind the taxi station, is open daily from 9am to 5pm (☎ 0558/22-1531). They have a map of Shimoda, don't speak English, and gave me the wrong bus number to Haji. So for transportation info check at the transportation information counter just outside the ticket wicket.

What to See & Do

Ryosenji Temple, located about a 15-minute walk from Shimoda Station, is where Perry and representatives of the Tokugawa shogunate government signed the treaty to open up Japan. Strangely enough, the temple also houses a small museum of erotica. Open 8:30am to 5pm, it charges ¥500 ($5) admission.

Hofukuji Temple, about a five-minute walk from Shimoda Station, is dedicated to Tojin Okichi, the mistress of Townsend Harris while he lived in Shimoda. Although today no one is exactly certain how it came about that she was chosen, we do know that she ended her life by drowning herself after he left. This temple contains both her tomb and her personal artifacts. Open 8am to 5pm, it charges ¥300 ($3) admission.

About 20 minutes south of Shimoda by bus is **Yumigahama Beach,** considered by many to be the best public beach in Izu. If you're on a budget, head for **Sotoura,** a small bay on the edge of Shimoda with about 60 minshuku and pensions. It has its own small beach and is popular with young people and families.

Accommodations & Dining

✪ Haji (59)

708 Sotoura-Kaigan, Shimoda City. ☎ **0558/22-2597.** Fax 0558/23-1064. 7 rms (4 with toilet only). A/C TV. ¥7,000 ($70) per person. All rates include two meals. No credit cards. Directions: A 10-minute ride from Shimoda Station on bus 7 to Sotouraguchi stop or a 5-minute taxi ride.

Haji is a small, spotlessly clean, and simple minshuku. The owner speaks English and is happy to see foreign guests. Located in a part of Shimoda called Sotoura, which boasts its own beach and is popular with vacationing families, the minshuku is 200 meters from the beach. The food served in the pleasant communal dining room is good and plentiful. While you must make your reservation three months in advance for the summer, I stayed here on a June weekday and was the only guest. I couldn't imagine a more relaxing, quiet getaway.

Shimoda Tokyu Hotel

5-12-1 Shimoda-shi 415. ☎ **0558/22-2411.** Fax 0558/22-4970. 117 rms (all with bath). A/C MINIBAR TV TEL. Peak season, ¥37,500 ($375) double or twin; ¥38,500–¥46,000 ($385–$460) tatami room for two. Off-season, ¥25,000 ($250) double; ¥20,500–¥26,000 ($205–$260) tatami room for two people. AE, DC, JCB, MC, V. Directions: Take a taxi (10 minutes).

This large, white hotel occupies the top of a hill not far from the sea. Most of its rooms are Western style; it also has 10 Japanese-style tatami rooms. Probably the best thing about the hotel is its outdoor bathing possibilities on a small white-sand beach.

Dining/Entertainment: In addition to Western and Japanese dining facilities, from mid-July through August, there's an outdoor barbecue.

Services: Free newspaper.

Facilities: Hot-spring spa, outdoor swimming pool, sea-bathing area.

DOGASHIMA

112 miles SW of Tokyo

With its fishing boats, tiny lanes and back alleyways, sandy beach, clear water, and rock formations jutting out of the sea, Dogashima is one of my favorite villages on Izu's less developed west side. There's not much to do here except relax, swim, and walk around—which may be exactly what you're looking for.

ESSENTIALS

The **telephone area code** for Dogashima is 0558.

GETTING THERE **By Bus** From Shimoda, it takes one hour to reach Dogashima by bus. The bus leaves from platform 2, but check to make sure.

By Boat There are boats from Numazu to Dogashima.

VISITOR INFORMATION The **tourist office** (☎ 0558/52-1268) is located across the street from the bus terminal in a tiny one-room building not far from the boat pier. It's open in July and August, daily from 8:30am to 5pm (sometimes closed Sunday); September to June, Monday through Friday from 8:30am to 5pm and on Saturday from 8:30am to noon (closed national holidays).

ACCOMMODATIONS

Ginsuiso (60)

2977-1 Nishina, Nishi-Izu-cho. ☎ **0558/52-2211.** Fax 0558/52-1210. 90 rms (all with bath). A/C MINIBAR TV TEL. Summer, ¥40,000 ($400) per person. Off-season, ¥26,000 ($260) per person. All rates include two meals. AE, DC, JCB, MC, V. Directions: Take a taxi (5 minutes).

The excellent service at Dogashima's most exclusive luxury-resort ryokan begins as soon as you arrive, with staff personnel at the door to greet you. This stunningly white hotel sprawls along a cliff over the sea and has its own private beach and outdoor swimming pool. All the rooms come with views of the sea. Because it's popular with large Japanese tour groups, you should book well in advance, particularly in summer.

Dining/Entertainment: In addition to a lounge, there's a cabaret show beginning nightly at 9:30pm.

Services: Free newspaper.

Facilities: Outdoor swimming pool, private beach.

Kaikomaru (61)

Nishi-Izu-cho, Sawada. ☎ **0558/52-1054.** Fax 0558/52-2546. 8 rms (none with bath). A/C TV. ¥7,000 ($70) per person. All rates include two meals. No credit cards. Directions: A 7-minute walk from the Dogashima bus stop.

At this tiny family-run minshuku with tatami rooms on Dogashima's main road, no one speaks English. But the family, which seems to include everyone from children to grandparents, is friendly if a bit shy. If you don't mind that, you'll like this place. Use of the hot-spring bath costs ¥200 ($2) extra.

7

Kyoto

If you go to only one place in all of Japan, Kyoto should be it. As the only major Japanese city spared bombing attacks during World War II, Kyoto is charming and captivating. As you walk its narrow streets and along its tiny canals, you will be struck with images of yesterday. Old women in kimono bend over their "garden," which may consist of only a couple of gnarled bonsai beside their front door. An open-fronted shop reveals a man making tatami mats, the musty smell of the rice mats reminiscent of earth itself. Perhaps you'll see a geisha shuffling to her evening appointment in Gion, a small enclave of solemn brown wooden houses where the sounds of laughter and traditional Japanese music escape through shoji screens. Nijo Castle is still here, built by the Tokugawas and famous for its creaking floorboards, designed to warn of enemy intruders. The famous Ryoanji rock garden is here, a Zen garden of pebbles and stones. There is a pleasant stroll from Koyomizu Temple to Heian Shrine, with tea gardens, pottery shops, and temples along the way. In the evening in the summertime, couples sit along the banks of the Kamo River, which cuts through the heart of the city.

1 Kyoto Past & Present

KYOTO TODAY

As your Shinkansen bullet train glides into Kyoto Station your first reaction is likely to be one of great disappointment. There's Kyoto Tower looming in the foreground, looking like some misplaced spaceship. Modern buildings and hotels surround you on all sides, making Kyoto look like just any other Japanese town.

But nestled in between all those buildings are an incredible 1,700 Buddhist temples and 300 Shinto shrines, narrow alleyways and willow-lined canals, gardens of rock and moss, and enough history to fill many volumes. If you stay here long enough, you'll grow to understand why I consider Kyoto Japan's most romantic city.

Kyoto has always led a rather fragile existence, as a look at any of its temples and shrines will tell you. Made of wood, they have been rebuilt countless times, destroyed through the years by man, fire, and earthquake. As a product of the past and the present, Kyoto is a synthesis of all that is Japan in the 20th century. No one who comes to this country should miss the wealth of experience this ancient capital has to offer.

What's Special About Kyoto

Temples and Shrines

- 1,700 Buddhist temples, including Kiyomizu Temple, Nanzenji Temple, Ginkakuji (Silver Pavilion), and Kinkakuji (Gold Pavilion).
- 300 Shinto shrines, including Heian Shrine.

Palaces, Castles, and Villas

- Kyoto Imperial Palace, home of the imperial family for more than 500 years.
- Nijo Castle, home of the Tokugawa shogun and considered the quintessence of Momoyama architecture.
- Katsura Imperial Villa and Shugakuin Imperial Villa, two of Japan's most famous villas, both with renowned gardens.

Gardens

- Heian Shrine Garden, typical of gardens constructed during the Meiji Period.
- Nijo Castle Garden, designed by famous gardener Kobori Enshu.
- Saihoji, famous for its moss garden.
- Gardens of Katsura and Shugakuin imperial villas.
- Ryoanji Temple, with the most famous Zen rock garden in Japan.

Japanese-style Accommodations

- Ryokan in all price categories, making this one of the best cities in Japan to experience living as the Japanese do.
- The opportunity to spend the night at a temple or shrine.

Cuisine

- Kyo-ryoori, Kyoto cuisine with regional specialties.
- Kyo-kaiseki, a variation of kaiseki that includes regional specialties.
- Vegetarian tofu dishes, served at Buddhist temples and surrounding restaurants.

Shopping

- A mecca for shoppers looking for traditional crafts.

A LOOK AT THE PAST

Kyoto served as Japan's capital for more than 1,000 years, from 794 to the Meiji Restoration in 1868. It was laid out in a grid pattern borrowed from the Chinese, with streets running north, south, east, and west. Its first few hundred years, from about 800 to the 12th century, were perhaps its grandest, a time when culture blossomed and the court nobility led luxurious and splendid lives. If you have any fantasies about old Japan, perhaps they fit into the Heian Period. There were poetry-composing parties and moon-gazing events. Buddhism flourished and temples were built. A number of learning institutions were set up for the sons and daughters of aristocratic families, and scholars were versed in both Japanese and Chinese.

Toward the end of the Heian Period, however, military clans began clashing for power, resulting in a series of civil wars that eventually pushed Japan into the feudal era of military government that lasted nearly 680 years—until 1868. The first shogun to rise to power was Yoritomo Minamoto, who set up his shogunate government in Kamakura. With the downfall of the Kamakura government in 1336, however, Kyoto once again became the seat of power for the country. The beginning of this era, known as the Muromachi and Azuchi-Momoyama Periods, was marked by extravagant prosperity and luxury, expressed in such splendid villas as Kyoto's Gold

Pavilion and Silver Pavilion. Lacquerware, landscape paintings, and the art of metal engraving came into their own. Zen Buddhism was the rage. And despite the civil wars that rocked the nation in the 15th and 16th centuries and destroyed much of Kyoto, culture flourished. During these turbulent times Noh drama, the tea ceremony, flower arranging, and landscape gardening gradually took form.

Emerging as victor in the civil wars, Tokugawa Ieyasu established himself as shogun and set up his military rule in Edo (present Tokyo), far to the east. For the next 250 years Kyoto remained the capital in name only, and in 1868 (which marked the downfall of the Tokugawa shogunate and the restoration of the emperor to power), the capital was officially moved from Kyoto to Tokyo. Thus Tokyo mushroomed into the concrete megalopolis it is today. Kyoto, with a population of about 1 1/2 million people, remains very much a city of the past.

2 Orientation

ARRIVING

BY PLANE If you're arriving in Japan at Kansai International Airport (Osaka), the Haruka Limited Express train has a direct service every 30 minutes to Kyoto Station. The trip takes 75 minutes and costs ¥3,430 ($34.30), or you can ride it free with your JR railpass. It operates daily from 6:15am to 8:16pm.The JR Kanku Kaisoku departs every 30 minutes from Kansai airport and arrives in Kyoto 90 minutes later with a change at Osaka station. The cost is ¥1,800 ($18), or free for railpass holders.

BY TRAIN One of the major stops on the Shinkansen bullet train, Kyoto is less than three hours away from Tokyo and only 20 minutes from Shin-Osaka Station in Osaka. There are also local commuter lines that connect Kyoto directly with Osaka Station and Sannomiya and Motomachi stations in Kobe. For information on train schedules, drop by the **Travel Information Service (TIS)** at Kyoto Station or call 075/371-0036 between 10am and 7pm.

BY BUS There's a **night bus** that departs Tokyo Station every evening for Kyoto, arriving the next morning. The fare is ¥8,030 ($80.30) one-way.

VISITOR INFORMATION

The **Tourist Information Center (TIC)** is about a minute's walk from Kyoto Station's north side (take the Karasuma Central Exit out of Kyoto Station). It's located on the ground floor of the Kyoto Tower Building, Higashi-Shiokojicho, Shimogyo-ku (☎ 075/371-5649), with the entrance around the corner on Karasuma Dori. Open Monday through Friday from 9am to 5pm and on Saturday from 9am to noon, it has a staff that speaks excellent English and can help you with all your questions regarding Kyoto. The TIC distributes a great city map in English and has brochures and leaflets not only on Kyoto but on other destinations in Japan as well. Be sure to pick up the leaflet "Walking Tour Courses in Kyoto."

Keep in mind, however, that the TIC is closed on Sunday, Saturday afternoon, and weekdays after 5pm, so plan your arrival accordingly. Otherwise, there's the local **Kyoto City Information Office,** also located on the station's north side. Some clerks here speak English, and you can get directions to your hotel. It's open daily from 9am to 5pm. You can also call the **Japan Travel-Phone.** For any questions you might have regarding Western Japan, call 0088/222-4800; for Eastern Japan call 0088/22-2800, daily between 9am and 5pm.

TOURIST PUBLICATIONS In addition to the brochures and leaflets distributed by the TIC, a monthly tabloid distributed free at hotels and restaurants is the *Kyoto*

Visitor's Guide, which contains maps, a calendar of events, and information on sightseeing and shopping. In addition, a monthly English magazine called *Kansai Time Out* carries information and articles on Kyoto, Osaka, and Nara. It's available in Kyoto at both the Maruzen and Izumiya bookstores for ¥300 ($3).

CITY LAYOUT

Most of Kyoto's attractions and hotels are north of Kyoto Station. The largest concentration of restaurants, shops, bars, and nightlife activity spreads in a radius from the Kawaramachi-Shijo Dori intersection and includes a narrow street called Pontocho and the geisha district of Gion. Temples are sprinkled throughout Kyoto.

FINDING AN ADDRESS Kyoto's address system is actually quite simple once you understand what the directions mean. Many of its streets are named. Those north of Kyoto Station that run east-west are numbered; for example, the *shi* of Shijo Dori Avenue means "four." *Agaru* means "to the north," *sagaru* means "to the south," *nishi-iru* means "to the west," and *higashi-iru* means "to the east." Thus an address that reads Shijo-agaru means "north of Shijo Dori (or Fourth) Avenue." In addition, many addresses indicate which cross streets a building is near. Therefore, the address for the Hotel Gimmond, which is Takakura Oike Dori, means that the hotel is near the intersection of Takakura Dori and Oike Dori. Complete addresses include the ward, or *ku,* such as Higashiyama-ku.

NEIGHBORHOODS IN BRIEF

Shimogyo-ku The ward that stretches from Kyoto Station north to Shijo Dori Avenue, catering to tourists with its cluster of hotels and to commuters with its shops and restaurants.

Nakagyo-ku The central part of Kyoto west of the Kamo River and embracing Kyoto's main shopping and nightlife districts, with most of the action on Kawaramachi and Shijo Dori Avenues. In addition to its many shopping arcades, restaurants, and bars, Nakagyo-ku also has a number of exclusive ryokan, tucked away in delightful neighborhoods typical of old Kyoto. Home also of Nijo Castle, Nakagyo-ku is one of the most desirable places to stay in terms of convenience and atmosphere.

Higashiyama-ku East of the Kamo River, this ward in eastern Kyoto boasts a number of the city's most famous temples and shrines, as well as a number of restaurants specializing in Kyoto cuisine and Buddhist vegetarian dishes. It's a great area for walking and boasts several ryokan as well.

Gion Kyoto's geisha entertainment district, where customers are entertained in traditional wooden geisha houses. These houses are not open to the public, but the area makes for a fascinating stroll.

Pontocho Kyoto's most famous street for nightlife, a narrow lane that parallels the Kamo River's west bank not far from the Kawaramachi-Shijo Dori intersection. It's lined with exclusive hostess clubs, bars, and restaurants that boast outdoor verandas that extend over the Kamo River.

3 Getting Around

BY PUBLIC TRANSPORTATION Kyoto has both a subway and a bus network. All directions are from Kyoto Station, unless otherwise indicated. Numbers in parentheses after stations and bus stops refer to the time it takes to reach your destination on foot.

By Subway There's only one subway line in Kyoto, which is useful only for going to the Imperial Palace. It runs from Kitayama in the north through Kitaoji and Kyoto Station to Takeda in the south. Fares range from ¥180 ($1.80) for the shortest distance to ¥270 ($2.70) from end to end, with service from 5:30am to about 11:20pm.

By Bus The easiest way to get around Kyoto is by bus. The city map given out by the TIC shows major bus routes. Some of the buses travel in a loop around the city, while others go back and forth between two destinations. At any rate, get on at the back of the bus. If the bus is traveling a long distance out to the suburbs, there will be a ticket machine right beside the back door—take the ticket and hold on to it. It has a number on it and will tell the bus driver when you got on and how much you owe. You can see for yourself how much you owe by looking for your number on a panel at the front of the bus. Unsurprisingly, your fare rises the longer you stay on the bus. If you're on a loop bus, however, the fare is the same no matter how long you stay on—¥200 ($2)—and you pay when you get off. Exact fare is required, which you drop into the machine next to the driver. There's also a change machine for ¥100 and ¥1,000 bills. There are no transfer tickets, so you have to pay separately for each ride. For convenience, you may wish to purchase a booklet of five ¥200 ($2) bus tickets plus a ¥100 ($1) ticket (called *kaisuken*) for ¥1,000 ($10), available from bus drivers.

BY TAXI Taxis in Kyoto come in two different sizes, with correspondingly different fares. Small ones are ¥580 ($5.80) for the first 2 kilometers (1 1/4 miles) and large ones are ¥590 ($5.90). Taxis can be waved down, or, in the city center, boarded at marked taxi stands or at hotels. MK Taxi (☎ 075/721-2237) offers individualized guided tours in English.

BY CAR See "Getting Around" in chapter 3.

Driving Rules Because Kyoto is laid out in a grid pattern, driving by car is not as difficult as in many Japanese cities. However, with traffic often congested, it ends up being a slow way to get around the city. In addition, there are many one-way streets, particularly in the center of the city. Parking is another headache. You're best off walking and using Kyoto's public transportation.

Rentals There are many car-rental agencies in Kyoto. Among them are: **Mazda Rent-A-Car,** Kawaramachi-Nishi-Iru, Gojo-dori, Shimogyo-ku (☎ 075/681-7779); **Nippon Rent-A-Car,** Higashi-Kujo Muromachi (☎ 075/671-0919); **Nissan Rent-A-Car,** Higashi-iru Nishinotoin Shiokoji, Shimogyo-ku (☎ 075/351-4423); and **Toyota Rent-A-Lease** (☎ 075/365-0100).

Parking As in the rest of Japan, parking is a problem in Kyoto, especially because many streets are too narrow to accommodate both parking and traffic. There are several parking garages around Kyoto Station, as well as parking lots in Nakagyo-ku. Major hotels also offer parking.

BY BICYCLE A popular way to get around Kyoto is by rental bike, made easy because there are few hills and most streets are named. **Rental Pia Service,** located across the street from Kyoto Station's south exit (☎ 075/672-3445), rents bicycles for ¥1,100 ($11) a day in March, April, and August through November, but charges ¥200 ($2) less off-season.

FAST FACTS: Kyoto

American Express There is an office at Kawaramachi Sanjo-Sagaru (☎ 075/22-3677). It's open Thursday through Tuesday from 10am to 6pm.

Area Code The telephone area code for Kyoto is 075.

Baby-sitters Your best bet is to inquire at your hotel. Major hotels can usually arrange a sitter and the Miyako's Little Mate Babysitting Room is a safe place to leave young ones even if you are not a hotel guest (¥4,500 to ¥5,000/$45 to $50 for two hours).

Bookstores There are two conveniently located stores selling books in English. *Maruzen,* Kawaramachi Takoyakushi-agaru, Nakagyo-ku (☎ 075/241-2161), part of a national bookstore chain, stocks novels as well as books on Japan. Located north of the Kawaramachi-Shijo Dori intersection, it's open Monday, Tuesday, and Thursday through Saturday from 10am to 7pm and on Sunday and holidays from 10am to 6:30pm. The *Izumiya Book Center* is in the Avanti department store just south of Kyoto Station (☎ 075/682-5031). It's open Friday through Wednesday from 10am to 8pm.

Business Hours **Banks** are open Monday through Friday from 9am to 3pm. An establishment with longer hours is the High Touch Plaza of the Kyoto Shinkin Bank, located on Shijo Dori Avenue, Yanagino-banba, Shimogyo-ku (☎ 075/255-3646). It's open Thursday through Tuesday from 10am to 5pm, including holidays. Department **stores** in Kyoto stay open from 10am to 7pm, while smaller shops in the downtown area remain open from about 10am to 8pm.

Car Rentals See "Getting Around," earlier in this chapter.

Climate See "When to Go," in chapter 3.

Currency See "Money," in chapter 3.

Currency Exchange In addition to banks, another place to exchange money is at the large department stores like Takashimaya, Daimaru, and Kintetsu. If you need to cash a traveler's check outside these hours and your hotel doesn't have the facilities to do so, both the Grand and New Miyako Hotels will cash traveler's checks even if you aren't a hotel guest.

Credit cards are accepted by most major establishments. If you need to use your credit card to obtain a cash advance, Nanto Bank (☎ 075/223-2200) on the southwest corner of Karasuma Oike handles MasterCard advances; and Sumitomo Bank has two locations for VISA—Karasuma Sanjo-agaru, Nakagyo-ku (☎ 075/221-2111), and Shijo Kawaramachi-nishi, Shimogyo-ku (☎ 075/223-2821).

Dentist The *Tourist Information Center (TIC)* (☎ 075/371-5649) has a list of approximately half a dozen dentists who speak English.

Doctor The *TIC* (☎ 075/371-5649) has a list of approximately a dozen doctors who speak English. If the TIC is closed or you'd rather talk to a doctor directly, *Dr. Sakabe,* Gokomachi, Nijo-sagaru, Nakagyo-ku (☎ 075/231-1624), is an internist who speaks excellent English, and he can refer you to other doctors as well.

Drugstores Drugstores, called *kusuri-ya* in Japanese, are open the usual business hours and are found throughout the city. For aspirin and other minor needs, there are convenience stores open late into the night.

Electricity In both Kyoto and Nara it's 100 volts, 60 cycles, almost the same as in the United States (110 volts, 60 cycles).

Emergencies The same all over Japan, the national emergency telephone numbers are 110 for police and 119 for calling an ambulance or for reporting a fire.

Film See "Photographic Needs," below.

Hairdressers and Barbers Several hotels in Kyoto have both beauty salons and barbershops where you're most likely to find someone who speaks English.

Consult the hotel section for hotels with such facilities. Department stores also have beauty salons.

Holidays See "When to Go," in chapter 3.

Hospitals Most hospitals are not equipped to handle emergencies 24 hours a day, but a system has been set up in which hospitals handle emergencies on a rotating basis. If you go by ambulance, it must take you to one of these. The *Kyoto Second Red Cross Hospital (Daini Sekijuji Byoin),* Marutamachi-sagaru, Kamanza Dori, Kamikyo-ku (☎ 075/231-5171), is staffed 24 hours a day, but referral by a doctor who knows your problem is expected. English is spoken at *Japan Baptist Hospital (Nihon Baputesuto Byoin),* 47 Yamanomoto-cho, Kitashirakawa, Sa-kyo-ku (☎ 075/781-5191). Other hospitals in Kyoto include the *Kyoto University Hospital (Kyoto Daigaku Byoin),* Shogoin Kawahara-cho, Sakyo-ku (☎ 075/751-3111), and the *Kyoto Municipal Hospital (Kyoto Shiritsu Byoin),* Gojo Dori Onmae, Nakagyo-ku (☎ 075/311-5311).

Information See "Information & Entry Requirements," in chapter 3.

Laundry and Dry Cleaning Most hotels provide laundry and dry cleaning services, but usually not on Sunday and holidays. Since self-service laundries are common in Japan, ask at your hotel for the location of the nearest one.

Lost Property If you left something on the Shinkansen bullet train, call 075/691-1000 to see whether it has been found. Items lost at Kyoto Station are turned in to the lost-and-found office (☎ 075/371-0134). If you lost something along a street or outside, contact the Shichijo Police Station (☎ 075/371-2111). Taxi Kyodo Center (☎ 075/672-1110) handles lost and found for all taxi companies. If you are still having problems, the TIC suggests you visit their office.

Luggage Storage/Lockers Kyoto Station has lockers for storing luggage beginning at ¥200 ($2) for 24 hours.

Newspapers and Magazines The *Japan Times, International Herald Tribune,* and other newspapers published in Tokyo are available in Kyoto. In addition, *Kansai Time Out,* with information on the arts and entertainment in Kyoto, Osaka, and Kobe, is sold in bookstores.

Photographic Needs There are many camera and film shops in Nakagyo-ku, especially on Shijo and Kawaramachi Dori avenues and in the covered shopping arcades. Department stores also sell film.

Police See "Emergencies," above.

Post Office The *Kyoto Central Post Office* is located just west of Kyoto Station at 843-12 Higashi-shiokoji-cho, Shimogyo-ku (☎ 075/365-2471). It's open Monday through Friday from 9am to 7pm, on Saturday from 9am to 5pm, and on Sunday and holidays from 9am to 12:30pm. You can mail packages bound for international destinations here. You can also have your own mail delivered Post Restante here, but you have to pick it up within one month if it's international mail and within 10 days if it's domestic.

Prefecture Kyoto city is the capital of Kyoto Prefecture.

Restrooms Hotel lobbies, fast-food chains, coffee shops, subway stations, and Kyoto Station are the best places to look for restrooms.

Safety Kyoto, like Tokyo and other cities in Japan, is generally safe. Yet there are precautions you should take whenever you're traveling in an unfamiliar city or country. Stay alert and be aware of your immediate surroundings. Wear a money belt and keep a close eye on your possessions. Be especially careful with cameras, purses, and wallets—all favorite targets of thieves and pickpockets. Be doubly alert when walking along dark streets and in public parks after dark (in fact, if you're alone, it would be wiser to stay out of parks after dark). Every society, even one as relatively safe as Japan's, has its criminals. It's your responsibility to exercise caution at all times, even in the most heavily touristed areas.

Shoe Repairs Department stores have shoe-repair counters.

Taxes For information on taxes applied to goods, and to hotel and restaurant bills, see "Fast Facts: Japan," in chapter 3.

Taxis See "Getting Around," earlier this chapter.

Television Major hotels in Kyoto have cable TV, called ACTV, available on channel 5. English-language programs are available throughout the day, including CNN broadcasts and information on local sightseeing.

4 Accommodations

There are many types of accommodations available in Kyoto, from exclusive Japanese inns to business hotels to rock-bottom dormitorylike lodgings. If you've never stayed in a ryokan, Kyoto is probably the best place to do so. With the possible exception of some hot-spring resorts, Kyoto has more choices of ryokan in all price categories than any other city in Japan. Small, usually made of wood, and often situated in delightfully quaint neighborhoods, these ryokan can enrich your stay in Kyoto by putting you in direct touch with the city's traditional past. Remember that in upper- and medium-priced ryokan the room charge is per person, and though the prices may seem prohibitive at first glance, they include two meals and service charge. The meals are feasts, not unlike kaiseki meals you'd receive at a top restaurant. Ryokan in the budget category, on the other hand, usually do not serve meals unless stated otherwise, and they often charge per room rather than per person.

But even if you decide to stay in a hotel, Kyoto has excellent choices in all price ranges (many hotels also have Japanese-style rooms available). Whichever type of accommodation you select, make reservations in advance. Kyoto is a favorite holiday destination for the Japanese, receiving as many as 10 million visitors each year.

Remember rooms costing ¥15,000 ($150) and more have a 6% tax added to the bill. For rooms costing less than ¥15,000, a 3% tax will be added. In addition, upper-range hotels will add a 10% to 15% service charge.

Because Kyoto is relatively small and is served by such a good bus system, no matter where you stay you won't be too far away from the heart of the city. Most hotels and ryokan, however, are concentrated around Kyoto Station (Shimogyo-ku ward) in central Kyoto, not far from the Kawaramachi-Shijo Dori intersection (Nakagyo-ku ward), and east of the Kamo River (called Higashiyama-ku and Sakyo-ku wards).

AROUND KYOTO STATION

EXPENSIVE

Kyoto Grand Hotel •

Horikawa-Shiokoji, Shimogyo-ku, Kyoto 600. ☎ **075/341-2311.** Fax 075/341-3073. 506 rms. A/C MINIBAR TV TEL. ¥12,000–¥17,000 ($120-$170) single; ¥18,000–¥27,000 ($180–$270) twin; ¥21,000–¥28,000 ($210–$280) double; ¥35,000 ($350) quad. Japanese-style rooms: ¥30,000 ($300) single or double. AE, DC, JCB, MC, V. Transportation: Free hotel shuttle bus every 15 minutes from 8am to 9pm, Kyoto Station's Hachijo Guchi exit; otherwise, a 10-minute walk from Kyoto Station.

Built in 1969 just before the Osaka Expo, this has been one of Kyoto's grand hotels ever since. The building's flat roof and railed ledges resemble traditional Japanese architecture, while the inside is a successful blend of traditional and modern. The rooms, for example, have shoji screens and fresh-flower arrangements, yet come with remote-control bilingual TV (with CNN), soundproof windows, clock, radio, and other modern conveniences. The lobby and rooms were being redone in 1993 when I visited. There's an English-language guest-relations coordinator, and the hotel also issues its own maps and sightseeing information on Kyoto in English.

Dining/Entertainment: Eight superb restaurants are popular with Kyoto's residents, including the city's only revolving restaurant and Gourmand Tachibana, where French food is served kaiseki style.

Services: Free shuttle bus to Kyoto Station, free English-language newspaper, same-day laundry service, baby-sitting.

Facilities: Indoor swimming pool (fee: ¥2,000/$20), sauna (men only), Jacuzzi (women only), beauty salon, bakery, and barber, souvenir, and clothing and accessories shops.

MODERATE

Hotel New Hankyu Kyoto

Shiokoji-dori, Shimogyo-ku, Kyoto 600. ☎ **075/343-5300.** Fax 075/343-5324. 319 rms. A/C MINIBAR TV TEL. ¥12,000–¥13,500 ($120–$135) single; ¥17,000–¥23,000 ($170–$230) twin; ¥21,000–¥23,000 ($210–$230) double; Japanese-style rooms, ¥44,000 ($440) for four people. AE, DC, JCB, MC, V. Directions: Walk from Kyoto Station's north side (Karasuma Central exit) about 1 minute.

Across the street from Kyoto Station's north side, this is one of the better hotels in this category. About 10% of its guests are foreigners, and of particular help to visitors is its information desk in the lobby, where the English-speaking staff can answer any questions you might have regarding your stay in Kyoto. The front-desk staff is very efficient and polite. Restaurants include a steakhouse and a Chinese restaurant, as well as a branch of the famous Minokichi Restaurant. The more expensive twins face the station and have soundproof windows; the doubles all face toward the back of the hotel, which delivers a free English-language newspaper to its guests.

Kyoto Century Hotel

680 Higashishiokoji-cho, Shiokoji-sagaru, Higashinotoin-dori, Shimogyo-ku, Kyoto 600. ☎ **075/351-0111.** Fax 075/343-3721. 243 rms. A/C MINIBAR TV TEL. ¥14,000–¥25,000 ($140–$250) single; ¥18,000–¥27,000 ($180–$270) double; ¥22,000–¥27,000 ($220–$270) twin. AE, DC, JCB, MC, V. Directions: Walk east of Kyoto Station, less than 2 minutes.

Located just east of Kyoto Station, this brick hotel features a four-story atrium lobby, five restaurants and bars, and an outside swimming pool (fee: ¥2,000/$20). All rooms include TV (with CNN broadcasts) and minibar. Ask for a room facing east toward Higashiyama-ku. Although the view is nothing special, it's a lot better than the view toward the west, which looks squarely at the rooms of a neighboring hotel. Services

Kyoto Accommodations

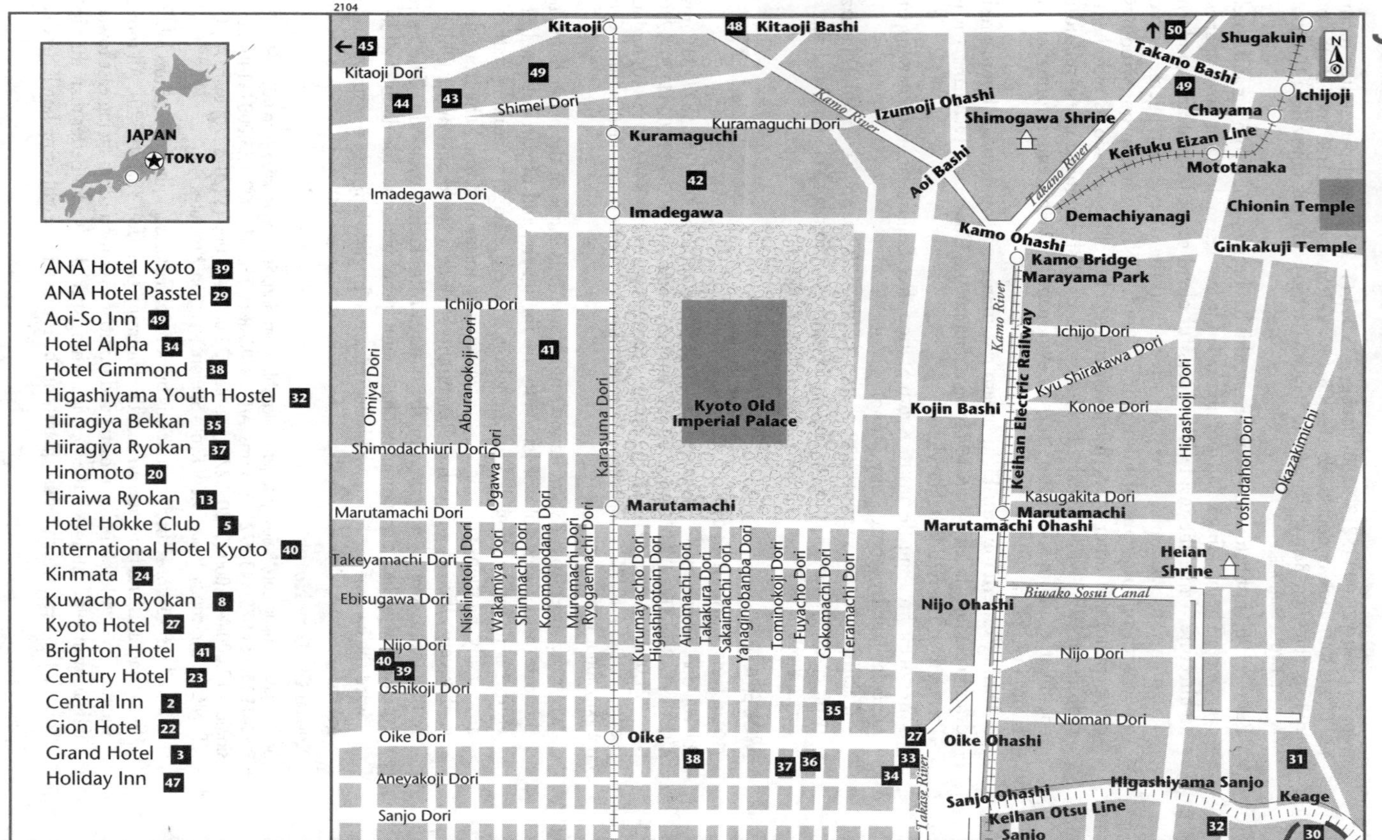

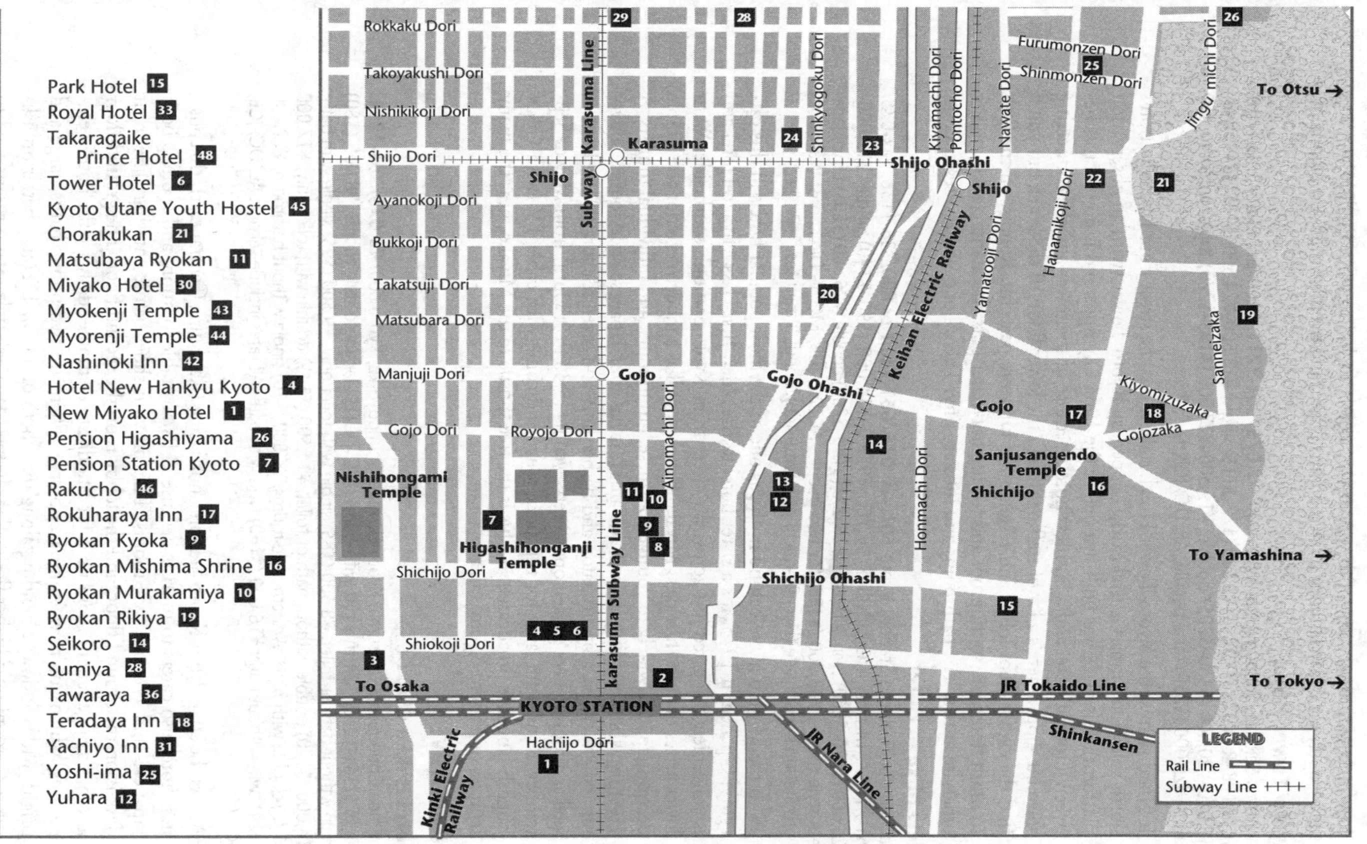
Park Hotel 15
Royal Hotel 33
Takaragaike Prince Hotel 48
Tower Hotel 6
Kyoto Utane Youth Hostel 45
Chorakukan 21
Matsubaya Ryokan 11
Miyako Hotel 30
Myokenji Temple 43
Myorenji Temple 44
Nashinoki Inn 42
Hotel New Hankyu Kyoto 4
New Miyako Hotel 1
Pension Higashiyama 26
Pension Station Kyoto 7
Rakucho 46
Rokuharaya Inn 17
Ryokan Kyoka 9
Ryokan Mishima Shrine 16
Ryokan Murakamiya 10
Ryokan Rikiya 19
Seikoro 14
Sumiya 28
Tawaraya 36
Teradaya Inn 18
Yachiyo Inn 31
Yoshi-ima 25
Yuhara 12
Rokkaku Dori
Takoyakushi Dori
Nishikikoji Dori
Shijo Dori
Ayanokoji Dori
Bukkoji Dori
Takatsuji Dori
Matsubara Dori
Manjuji Dori
Gojo Dori
Royojo Dori
Ainomachi Dori
Shichijo Dori
Shiokoji Dori
Hachijo Dori
Karasuma Line
Subway
Karasuma
Shijo
Gojo
Karasuma Subway Line
Shinkyogoku Dori
Kiyamachi Dori
Pontocho Dori
Nawate Dori
Furumonzen Dori
Shinmonzen Dori
Jingu michi Dori
Shijo Ohashi
Shijo
Keihan Electric Railway
Yamatooji Dori
Hanamikoji Dori
Sanneizaka
Kiyomizuzaka
Gojozaka
Gojo Ohashi
Gojo
Honmachi Dori
Sanjusangendo Temple
Shichijo
Shichijo Ohashi
Nishihongami Temple
Higashihonganji Temple
To Otsu →
To Yamashina →
To Tokyo →
To Osaka
KYOTO STATION
JR Tokaido Line
JR Nara Line
Shinkansen
Kinki Electric Railway
LEGEND
Rail Line
Subway Line

here include those at some of the upper-class hotels, including a free English-language newspaper, same-day laundry service, room service, and overnight film development.

Kyoto Tower Hotel

Karasuma Shichijo, Shimogyo-ku, Kyoto 600. ☎ **075/361-3211.** Fax 075/343-5645. 164 rms. A/C MINIBAR TV TEL. ¥7,700–¥11,500 ($77–$115) single; ¥13,500–¥24,500 ($135–$245) twin; ¥15,000–¥20,500 ($150–$205) double; ¥19,500–¥27,000 ($195–$270) triple; Japanese-style rooms, ¥25,000 ($250) for 2 people. AE, DC, JCB, MC, V.

It's hard to miss the Kyoto Tower Hotel, right across the street from Kyoto Station's north side (Karasuma Central exit). Topped by Kyoto Tower (with an observation platform), this place was built just before the 1964 Olympics and is now a cross between a tourist hotel and a business hotel. Because of the tower and the connecting souvenir shops, there's a lot of traffic through the lower floors of the hotel, but you'll find the eighth-floor lobby and restaurant a bit more peaceful. Rooms, on the fifth to ninth floors, are soundproof and feature hot-water pots and alarm clocks, among other amenities. The bathrooms and tubs are tiny. There's one Western restaurant.

New Miyako Hotel

Hachijo-guchi, Kyoto Station, Kyoto 601. ☎ **075/661-7111** or 800/336-1136. Fax 075/661-7135. 714 rms. A/C MINIBAR TV TEL. ¥9,000–¥14,000 ($90–$140) single; ¥17,000–¥26,000 ($170–$260) twin, ¥19,000–¥26,000 ($190–$260) double, ¥26,500 ($265) triple; Japanese-style rooms, ¥38,000 ($380) for two people. AE, DC, JCB, MC, V. Directions: Walk from Kyoto Station's south side (Hachijo-guchi exit, west side), about 3 minutes.

With the Miyako name behind it, this is one of the most popular hotels in this category. Opened in 1975, it's a sister hotel to the older, first-class Miyako Hotel and is conveniently located just across the street from Kyoto Station's south side. With lower prices than the first-class Miyako Hotel, as well as a modern exterior and simple decor, it appeals widely to younger Japanese, group tours, and individual tourists. A 10-story white building shaped like an H, it has four Japanese-style rooms, souvenir and gift shops, a beauty salon and barbershop, and seven restaurants and bars, as well as a rooftop beer garden open every evening (5:30 to 9:30pm) from May to September. Rooms are large for this price range and come with cable TV (with CNN English-language broadcasts). A plus is the free shuttle to the Miyako, near the many temples of Eastern Kyoto.

INEXPENSIVE

Hotel Hokke Club (62)

Shomen Chuoguchi, Karasuma, Kyoto-Eki-mae, Shimogyo-ku, Kyoto 600. ☎ **075/361-1251.** Fax 075/361-1255. 134 rms (50 with bath). A/C TV TEL. Japanese-style rooms, ¥8,000 ($80) single wthout bath or toilet, ¥8,500 ($85) single with toilet only, ¥9,500 ($95) single with bath; ¥14,000 ($140) double without bath or toilet, ¥14,500 ($145) double with toilet only, ¥17,000 ($170) double with bath. Western-style rooms, ¥7,000 ($70) single without bathroom; ¥12,400 ($124) twin without bath; ¥16,000 ($160) twin with bath. All rates include service. AE, DC, JCB, MC, V.

Across the street from Kyoto Station's north side (Karasuma Central exit), this business hotel also caters to tourists because of its favorable location, and it offers both Japanese- and Western-style rooms. Take off your shoes before entering. The front desk is on the ground floor, and the lobby is on the second floor. The ground floor also has a large tatami room used for Buddhist ceremonies daily by the hotel's employees, which you're welcome to observe. There are two public baths, large and bright, with windows extending along the length of one wall. You're better off asking for a room on a higher floor. The cheapest Japanese-style tatami rooms tend to be rather small and have tiny windows, and all rooms are very simple, though some have a stocked refrigerator.

Kuwacho Ryokan

Higashi-Honganji-mae, Shimogyo-ku, Kyoto 600. ☎ **075/371-3191.** 14 rms (all with bath). A/C TV TEL. ¥5,800 ($58) single; ¥9,500 ($95) twin; ¥13,500 ($135) triple. All rates include service. No credit cards. Directions: Walk north of Kyoto Station, about 5 minutes.

Despite its name, this place offers both Western- and Japanese-style rooms and is very conveniently located just north of Kyoto Station and east of Higashi Honganji Temple. A modern concrete three-story building (no elevator), it offers rooms with coin-operated TV, a safe for valuables, and cotton kimono, among other amenities. Rooms facing the front even have a small balcony. I prefer the Japanese-style rooms (somehow, bare rooms are more becoming to tatami than to Western-style rooms). No meals are served.

Pension Station Kyoto

Shichijo-agaru, Shinmachi, Shimogyo-ku, Kyoto 600. ☎ **075/882-6200.** Fax 075/862-0820. 16 rms (2 with bath). A/C TV. ¥4,500 ($45) single without bath; ¥8,500 ($85) double without bath, ¥10,000 ($100) double with bath; ¥12,000 ($120) triple without bath, ¥13,500 ($135) triple with bath. AE, MC, V. Directions: Walk from Kyoto Station, about 7 minutes.

A member of the Japanese Inn Group, this pension offers Japanese-style and Western-style rooms; two of the latter sleep two or three people and have a private bathroom. Located just west of Higashi Honganji Temple, the place gets a bit carried away in its use of fake flowers as decoration, but is nevertheless cheerful and spotlessly clean. Rooms come with coin-operated TV and heater, among other amenities, and there's a coin-operated laundry. Western breakfasts are available for ¥800 ($8), while Japanese dinners cost ¥2,000 ($20).

Hinomoto

375 Kotakecho, Matsubara-agaru, Kawaramachi Dori, Shimogyo-ku, Kyoto 600. ☎ **075/351-4563.** Fax 075/351-3932. 6 rms (none with bath). A/C TV TEL. ¥3,500–¥4,500 ($35–$45) single; ¥7,000–¥8,000 ($70–$80) double; ¥10,500 ($105) triple. Western breakfast ¥300 ($3) extra; Japanese breakfast ¥1,000 ($10) extra. AE, MC, V. Bus: To Matsubara.

This ryokan is located a bit far from Kyoto Station (about a 30-minute walk north) but is convenient if you want to stay closer to the action around the Kawaramachi-Shijo Dori intersection. A two-story home, it has a front facade of brick, but the rest is of wood. Although the couple running this ryokan do not speak much English, they welcome foreigners, and many French stay here. Rooms are pleasant, the location is quiet and convenient, and the public bath is made of wood. As you enter, a dog (made of stone) will bark to announce your arrival.

✪ Hiraiwa Ryokan

314 Hayao-cho, Kaminoguchi-agaru, Ninomiyacho-dori, Shimogyo-ku, Kyoto 600. ☎ **075/351-6748.** Fax 075/351-6969. 21 rms (none with bath). A/C TV. ¥4,000-¥5,000 ($40-$50) single; ¥7,500–¥8,500 ($75–$85) double; ¥11,500 ($115) triple. Western breakfast ¥300–¥700 ($3–$7) extra; Japanese breakfast ¥1,000 ($10) extra. AE, MC, V. Bus: To Kawaramachi Shomen.

This inexpensive ryokan is one of the best-known and oldest members of the Japanese Inn Group, and several feature stories have been published about it and the couple in charge. They speak almost no English and yet have been welcoming foreigners from all over the world for many years. Spread through the main building and a new annex, the guest rooms are spotless and come with towel and cotton kimono. Facilities include coin-operated washer and dryer, and there are even heated toilet seats. Breakfasts are communal affairs around the kitchen table. There are showers and a small public bath, but better still is the neighborhood public bath just around the corner, which charges ¥300 ($3). This ryokan is about a 15-minute walk from Kyoto Station, and it locks its front doors at 11pm.

✪ Matsubaya Ryokan

Nishi-iru, Higashinotouin, Kamijuzuyamachi Dori, Shimogyo-ku, Kyoto 600. ☎ **075/351-3727** or 351-4268. Fax 075/351-3505. 11 rms (none with bath). A/C TV TEL. ¥4,500 ($45) single; ¥9,000 ($90) double; ¥12,600 ($126) triple. Japanese breakfast ¥1,000 ($10) extra; Japanese dinner ¥3,500 ($35) extra. AE, MC, V. Directions: Walk north of Kyoto Station, about 8 minutes.

Located just east of Higashi Honganji Temple and a member of the Japanese Inn Group, this traditional ryokan opened in 1885 is a great choice in this category. It's owned and managed by the friendly and irrepressibly energetic Mrs. Hayashi, representing the fifth generation of innkeepers. She'll talk on and on to you in Japanese, even if you don't understand, making you wish you did. Her best rooms have wooden balconies facing a miniature inner courtyard. Another good choice: the rooms facing a tiny enclosed garden. Reservations require a deposit equal to one night's lodging, payable by cashier's or traveler's check, international money order, or credit card. Towels and cotton kimono are provided, and rooms have coin-operated TV. Facilities include two public baths and a coin-operated laundry. Highly recommended. Please return by 11pm, and when faxing, please be respectful of the time difference—Mrs. Hayashi isn't getting any younger, and she's been so kind to so many travelers.

Ryokan Kyoka

Higashi-iru, Higashinotouin, Shimojuzuyamachi-dori, Shimogyo-ku, Kyoto 600. ☎ **075/371-2709.** Fax 075/351-2709. 10 rms (none with bath). A/C TV. Japanese-style rooms, ¥4,000–¥4,500 ($40–$45) per person. Western breakfast ¥350–¥700 ($3.50–$7) extra; Japanese breakfast ¥1,000–¥1,500 ($10–$15) extra; Japanese dinner ¥3,000–¥5,000 ($30–$50) extra. AE, V. Directions: Walk north 8 minutes.

This simple ryokan, located east of Higashi Honganji Temple, offers 10 tatami rooms with coin-operated TV. Facilities include a coin laundry, and there are bikes for rent (¥500/$5 a day). A member of the Japanese Inn Group, this is one of the few places to offer such an elaborate dinner.

Ryokan Murakamiya

270 Sasaya-cho, Shichijo-agaru, Higashi-notouin-dori, Shimogyo-ku, Kyoto 600. ☎ **075/371-1260.** Fax 075/371-7161. 8 rms (none with bath). A/C TV. ¥4,000–¥4,400 ($40–$44) per person. Japanese breakfast ¥1,000 ($10) extra. AE, MC, V. Directions: Walk northeast, 7 minutes.

Not far from the Matsubaya (see above), this small and clean ryokan offers nicely decorated rooms—some with old-style ceilings and woodwork—in a 50-year-old traditional wooden building. The owner is friendly and accommodating and does her best to communicate, even though her English is limited. There's a coin-operated laundry, and a Japanese breakfast is available if you order it the night before. A member of the Japanese Inn Group, the ryokan locks its front door at 11pm.

✪ Yuhara

Shomen-agaru, Kiyamachi Dori, Shimogyo-ku, Kyoto 600. ☎ **075/371-9583.** Fax 075/371-9583. 9 rms (none with bath). A/C TV. ¥4,000 ($40) per person. No credit cards. Bus: To Kawaramachi Shomen.

This small ryokan has been welcoming guests from all over the world for some 40 years. Pleasantly located beside the tree-lined narrow Takasegawa canal in a quiet residential area a 10-minute walk from Kyoto Station, it's run by an enthusiastic woman who speaks some English. There are nice touches everywhere, from the shoji screens and artwork in the rooms to the plants and bamboo decorations in the hallways. One of the rooms is Western style, and three have their own sink. The largest room looks out onto a miniature courtyard.

CENTRAL KYOTO

EXPENSIVE

ANA Hotel Kyoto

Nijojo-mae, Horikawa Dori, Nakagyo-ku, Kyoto 604. ☎ **075/231-1155** or 800/ANA HOTELS in the U.S. and Canada. Fax 075/231-5333. 303 rms. A/C MINIBAR TV TEL. ¥11,000–¥16,000 ($110–$160) single; ¥19,000–¥26,000 ($190–$260) twin; ¥22,000–¥24,000 ($220–$240) double. AE, DC, JCB, MC, V. Bus: To Nijojo-mae.

Located just across the street from Nijo Castle, some rooms have views of the castle grounds. This property has one of the most stunning lobbies in town, complete with a glass wall overlooking an impressive waterfall and tiny landscape garden. Rooms are attractive and comfortable, with well-crafted furniture reflecting Asian design and with lots of space in the bathrooms for spreading out cosmetics and toiletries. None of the singles face the castle; twin and double rooms that do so start at ¥24,000 ($240).

Dining/Entertainment: First-rate restaurants serve Japanese, Chinese, and Western cuisine. Nijo is a French restaurant that serves both traditional cuisine and French kaiseki meals, and Unkai is ANA's signature Japanese restaurant.

Services: Free English-language newspaper twice a day, same-day laundry service.

Facilities: Indoor swimming pool and sauna (fee: ¥3,000/$30), beauty salon, shopping arcade.

✪ Hiiragiya Ryokan

Anekoji-agaru, Fuyacho, Nakagyo-ku, Kyoto 604. ☎ **075/221-1136.** Fax 075/221-1139. 33 rms (3 with toilet only, 28 with bath and toilet). A/C TV TEL. ¥25,000 ($250) per person in a room without bath or toilet, ¥30,000–¥100,000 ($300–$1,000) per person in a room with bath and toilet. AE, DC, JCB, MC, V. All rates include two meals and service charge. Taxi: 10 minutes.

As fine an example of a traditional inn as you'll find in Japan, this exquisite ryokan opened in 1818 as a seafood merchant's shop and was converted into an inn in 1861 to cater to visiting merchants. Under the same family ownership for six generations, it offers the ultimate in Japanese-style living, with a very accommodating staff that is helpful in initiating foreigners unfamiliar with Japan to the joys of the traditional inn. Located on the corner of Fuyacho and Oike streets in the heart of old Kyoto, the ryokan lies hidden behind walls of wood and earth-toned yellow mortar, topped by a traditional tiled roof. Entry is through a stone courtyard, with the rest of the ryokan making artful use of wood, bamboo, screens, and stones in creating a haven of simple design.

The best room in the house is no. 30, with magnificent views of the garden; at ¥100,000 ($1,000) per person (¥90,000/$900 off-season), however, it's probably a bit out of range for most of us. The next most expensive room is the one I find the most beautiful, a corner room with antiques and plenty of sunshine, going for ¥60,000 ($600) per person. All accommodations are decorated with art and antiques. Even the remote controls for the lights and curtains are artfully concealed in specially made lacquered boxes shaped like gourds (invented by the present owner's grandfather). Western-style breakfasts are available upon request. Guests who have stayed here include princes of the Japanese royal family, former prime minister Tojo, Charlie Chaplin, and designer Pierre Cardin. The three public baths and the tubs in the guest rooms—all handmade—are of Chinese pine, soft to the touch.

✪ Kinmata (63)

407 Gokomachi, Shijo-agaru, Nakagyo-ku, Kyoto 604. ☎ **075/221-1039.** Fax 075/231-7632. 7 rms (none with bath, 2 with toilet only). A/C TV TEL. From ¥15,000 ($150) per person, including breakfast; ¥25,000–¥35,000 ($250–$350) per person, including two meals. All rates include service charge. AE, DC, JCB, MC, V. Bus: To Shijokawaramachi.

First opened in the early 1800s, this is a beautiful traditional wooden inn in the heart of Kyoto. Its earliest customers were medicine peddlers, and in the hallway hangs an old sign announcing the house rules of past centuries—no gambling, no prostitution, no mah-jongg, and no noisy parties. The present owner represents the seventh generation of innkeepers here and is renowned as a chef, preparing kaiseki meals for his guests. Even if you don't stay here, you can come just for a meal (lunch ¥6,000/ $60 and up). With only six rooms, Kinmata is exquisite inside and out, complete with an inner courtyard and peaceful garden. The public bath is of cypress. The place is located just north of Shijo Avenue on Gokomachi Street.

Kyoto Hotel

Kawaramachi-Oike, Nakagyo-ku, Kyoto 604. ☎ **075/223-2333.** Fax 075/254-2529. 322 rms. A/C MINIBAR TV TEL. ¥16,000–¥18,000 ($160–$180) single; ¥31,000–¥45,000 ($310–$450) double; ¥25,000–¥50,000 ($250–$450) twin; ¥50,000 ($500) quad; ¥80,000–¥100,000 ($800–$1,000) suites. AE, DC, JCB, MC, V. Subway: Oike Station (3 minutes).

Originally opened in 1888, the Kyoto Hotel was completely rebuilt and reopened in 1994. The spacious lobby was designed after the original 1920's ballroom. The design of the common areas successfully blends Japanese and Western, old and new. Rooms built around a central atrium have every convenience, views, and such amenities as satellite TV and fax lines. The latest technology in safety equipment and design were used throughout. A special effort to be hospitable (their motto is Service with a Smile), an English-speaking staff, a convenient location in the heart of Kyoto, history, and luxury make this an excellent choice for the visitor.

Dining/Entertainment: Nine food and beverage outlets include an English-style bar, Chinese and Japanese cuisine, plus dining with a view (Pictoresque).

Services: Free newspaper, free parking.

Facilities: Beauty salon and barber shop; florist; boutiques; souvenir shop; baby-sitting room; and indoor pool, Jacuzzi, and sauna (fee: ¥2,000/$20).

Kyoto Brighton Hotel

Nakadachiuri, Shinmachi-dori, Kamigyo-ku, Kyoto 602. ☎ **075/441-4411.** Fax 075/431-2360. 183 rms. A/C MINIBAR TV TEL. ¥21,000–¥34,000 ($210–$340) single; ¥28,000–¥39,000 ($280–$390) double; ¥30,000–¥38,000 ($300–$380) twin. AE, DC, JCB, MC, V. Subway: Imadegawa Station (8 minutes).

Near the Imperial Palace and named after England's seashore resort to evoke a sense of light, airy brightness, the Brighton Hotel flaunts space with a huge, six-story atrium rising above the lobby and glass-enclosed elevators. With space at such a premium in Japan, the air in this atrium is a statement of luxury. The corridors to all rooms ring the atrium and are well lit, so even women traveling alone should feel very safe here. Accommodations are large, the more expensive rooms containing a couch and lounging area are separated from the bedroom by a partition. There are no single rooms; rather, people traveling alone can stay in double or twin-bedded rooms at lower rates. Needless to say, service is superb. Even though this hotel is a bit far from the action, many guests stay here for precisely that reason.

Dining/Entertainment: There are seven restaurants serving French, Japanese, and Cantonese food, including Kyoto-style kaiseki.

Services: Free English-language newspaper twice a day, same-day laundry service.

Facilities: Outdoor swimming pool open only in July and August (fee: ¥4,000/ $40), beauty salon, souvenir shop.

Family-Friendly Hotels

Kyoto Holiday Inn *(see p. 273)* Children under 12 stay free in their parents' room at this hotel, which boasts indoor and outdoor pools (the outdoor pool is free to hotel guests), tennis courts, an indoor ice-skating rink, a bowling alley, and a mall with many children's favorite restaurant, McDonald's.

The Miyako *(see p. 269)* The hotel's "Little Mate Babysitting" room is available for quick nappy changes or as a place to take a break with your baby or to leave your little ones with a great bilingual staff. Lots of toys and attention in a safe environment mean that both parents and youngsters will be pleased.

Kyoto Royal Hotel

Sanjo-agaru Kawaramachi, Nakagyo-ku, Kyoto 604. ☎ **075/223-1234.** Fax 075/223-1702. 331 rms. A/C MINIBAR TV TEL. ¥10,000–¥13,500 ($100–$135) single; ¥18,000–¥20,000 ($180–$200) double; ¥22,000–¥24,000 ($220–$240) twin; ¥34,000 ($340) quad. AE, DC, JCB, MC, V. Bus: To Kawaramachi-Sanjo.

In the heart of Kyoto on Kawaramachi Dori, this typical tourist hotel has a friendly staff and tries to achieve a top-class atmosphere, but the Royal doesn't offer the facilities of Kyoto's other top hotels. Still, it has a convenient location, plus an information desk to help guests with local sightseeing. The rooms are comfortable and bright. Note that most single rooms and some doubles face an inner courtyard, which cuts down on noise but also on sunshine.

Dining/Entertainment: Seven restaurants and bars, including restaurants serving Szechuan (Chinese) and Kyo-ryoori cuisine. A French restaurant on the 10th floor offers panoramic views of the city and surrounding hills.

Facilities: Gift shop.

✪ Sumiya

Sanjo-sagaru, Fuyacho, Nakagyo-ku, Kyoto 604. ☎ **075/221-2188.** Fax 075/221-2267. 25 rms (all with bath). A/C MINIBAR TV TEL. ¥25,000–¥50,000 ($250–$500) per person. All rates include two meals and service charge. AE, DC, JCB, MC, V. Taxi: 10 minutes.

Another traditional Japanese inn located on Fuyacho Dori, this one offers excellent service amid simple yet elegant surroundings. Some rooms have wonderful views of tiny private gardens, with outdoor benches or platforms for sitting. Western breakfasts are available, and meals feature Kyoto kaiseki cuisine. Not far from the other ryokan listed here, Sumiya has a great location in a typical Kyoto neighborhood, and yet is less than a 10-minute walk from downtown Kyoto.

Tawaraya

Oike-Sagaru, Fuyacho, Nakagyo-ku, Kyoto 604. ☎ **075/211-5566.** Fax 075/211-2204. 18 rms (all with bath). A/C TV TEL. ¥35,000–¥90,000 ($350–$900) per person double, including two meals. AE, DC, JCB, V. Taxi: 10 minutes.

Across the street from the Hiiragiya is another distinguished, venerable old inn, which has been owned and operated by the same family since it opened in the first decade of the 1700s. The present owner is Mrs. Toshi Okazaki Sato, who represents the 11th generation of innkeepers. Unfortunately, fire consumed the original building, so the oldest part of the ryokan now dates back only 175 years. This inn has had an impressive list of former guests, including the king of Sweden, former Canadian prime minister Pierre Trudeau, Leonard Bernstein, and Barbra Streisand. Saul Bellow wrote in the ryokan's guest book, "I found here what I had hoped to find in Japan—the human scale, tranquility, and beauty." With refined taste reigning supreme, each room here is different and exquisitely appointed. Some, for example, have glass sliding doors opening onto a mossy garden of bamboo, stone lanterns, and manicured bushes, with cushions on a wooden veranda from which you can soak in the peacefulness.

MODERATE

ANA Hotel Passtel

Higashino-toin, Sanjo-sagaru, Nakagyo-ku, Kyoto 604. ☎ **075/213-0111.** Fax 075/211-7963. 118 rms. A/C MINIBAR TV TEL. ¥8,000–¥9,900 ($80–$99) single; ¥18,000–¥22,000 ($180–$220) twin; ¥12,000 ($120) double. AE, DC, JCB, MC, V. Subway: Oike Station (2 minutes).

Located near the Museum of Kyoto in the heart of old Kyoto, this pleasant and modern hotel features a large ikebana flower arrangement in its marble lobby. Although it calls itself a tourist hotel, I consider it a business hotel, since 85 of its 118 rooms are singles. Rooms are of adequate size, but note that doubles have only semi-double-size beds.

Hotel Alpha

Kawaramachi, Sango-agaru, Nakagyo-ku, Kyoto 604. ☎ **075/241-2000.** Fax 075/211-0533. 119 rms. A/C MINIBAR TV TEL. ¥8,200–¥8,800 ($82–$88) single; ¥15,500 ($155) double; ¥14,300–¥17,500 ($143–$175) twin; Japanese-style rooms, ¥24,000–¥29,000 ($240–$290)for two people. All rates include tax and service charge. AE, DC, JCB, MC, V. Bus: To Kawaramachi-Sanjo.

This small and pleasant brick business hotel, which opened in 1982, has a great location just off Kawaramachi Dori not far from where it meets Sanjo Dori. Its entrance is on a side street called Anekoji Dori. Semi-double-size beds are in almost all the rooms. Since the cheapest singles face an inner courtyard and are fairly dark, it may be worthwhile to dish out the extra yen for a brighter room. A few Japanese-style rooms are available. The hotel's one restaurant serves Kyoto cuisine.

Hiiragiya Bekkan

Gokomachi, Nijo Dori, Nakagyo-ku, Kyoto 604. ☎ **075/231-0151.** Fax 075/231-0153. 14 rms (10 with toilet only). A/C TV TEL. ¥14,000–¥25,000 ($140–$250) per person. All rates include two meals. AE, DC, JCB, MC, V. Taxi: 10 minutes.

Under the same management as the exclusive Hiiragiya Ryokan, this is a very good choice among Kyoto's medium-priced Japanese inns. Run by a friendly, accommodating staff, this small ryokan has a warm and homey feel to it. Opened in 1961, it's relatively new by ryokan standards but manages to transmit a traditional atmosphere, as most of the rooms open onto a small garden. The management prefers guests take meals here, but if you are staying a few days, ask about a simple room charge (10% less).

Hotel Gimmond

Takakura Oike Dori, Nakagyo-ku, Kyoto 604. ☎ **075/221-4111.** Fax 075/221-8250. 140 rms. A/C MINIBAR TV TEL. ¥8,500–¥9,500 ($85–$95) single; ¥14,500 ($145) double; ¥15,000–¥20,500 ($150–$205) twin. AE, DC, JCB, MC, V. Subway: Oike Station (3 minutes).

Situated on Oike Dori, this smaller hotel calls itself a tourist hotel, although its rooms resemble those of a business hotel, being rather plain and bare but equipped with alarm clock and TV with pay video. All rooms are soundproof, but I still think those that face away from Oike Dori are quieter. There's one restaurant serving Western food, plus one lounge.

Kyoto International Hotel

Nijo-mae, Horikawa Dori, Nakagyo-ku, Kyoto 604. ☎ **075/222-1111.** Fax 075/231-9381. 280 rms. A/C MINIBAR TV TEL. ¥9,000–¥15,000 ($90–$150) single; ¥23,000 ($230) double; ¥16,000–¥25,000 ($160–$250) twin; ¥23,000 ($230) Japanese style for two. AE, DC, JCB, MC, V. Bus: To Nijojo-mae.

Opened more than 30 years ago in time for the 1964 Olympics, but since renovated, *Kyoto Kokusai* hotel is located across from Nijo Castle. Despite its name, approximately 80% of its guests are Japanese. Its lobby overlooks a pleasant, lush garden, and facilities include four restaurants, two bars, and a shopping arcade. In summer it has a beer garden open from 6 to 9pm. Rooms are decorated with traditional shoji screens, yet have modern conveniences, including a toilet that sprays water at the push of a button (the Japanese version of the bidet). The higher-priced twins and doubles face the castle, but none of the singles do.

INEXPENSIVE

$ Kyoto Central Inn

Shijo Kawaramachi, Nishi-iru, Shimogyo-ku, Kyoto 600. ☎ **075/211-1666.** Fax 075/241-2765. 150 rms (all with bath). A/C TV TEL. ¥7,000–¥9,000 ($70–$90) single; ¥11,000–¥13,000 ($110–$130) double or twin. AE, DC, JCB, MC, V. Bus: To Shijo-Kawaramachi.

As the name implies, this inn is centrally located in the heart of the city, near the intersection of Shijo and Kawaramachi streets. Although it's a business hotel, because it occupies one of the best spots in town, about 50% of its guests are tourists. Rooms are small but adequate. The hotel's coffee shop serves American breakfasts.

EASTERN KYOTO

EXPENSIVE

Kyoto Park Hotel

644-2 Mawarimachi, Sanjusangendo, Higashiyama-ku, Kyoto 605. ☎ **075/525-3111.** Fax 075/553-1101. 268 rms. A/C MINIBAR TV TEL. ¥8,000–¥10,000 ($80–$100) single; ¥17,000–¥40,000 ($170–$400) twin; ¥19,000 ($190) double. Sat add ¥1,000 ($10). AE, DC, JCB, MC, V. Bus: To Sanjusangendo-mae.

Located across the street from the National Museum, this hotel is a good starting point for strolls through eastern Kyoto, including the pleasant walk from nearby Kiyomizu Temple to Heian Shrine. With its stained-glass windows, plants, and statues, it's reminiscent of a European hotel, with grounds that include both a rock garden and a garden containing a waterfall, cliff, and pond. Flowered wallpaper brightens up the rooms, and especially nice are the more expensive twin rooms on the fifth floor, each with a balcony overlooking the garden.

Dining/Entertainment: On the premises are French, Chinese, and Japanese restaurants; a sushi bar; a coffee shop; a lobby lounge; and a bar.

Facilities: Shopping arcade, beauty parlor, florist, photo studio.

✪ The Miyako

Sanjo Keage, Higashiyama-ku, Kyoto 605. ☎ **075/771-7111,** or 800/336-1136 in the U.S. and Canada. Fax 075/751-2490. 528 rms. A/C MINIBAR TV TEL. ¥15,000–¥43,000 ($150–$430) single; ¥21,000–¥48,000 ($210–$480) double/twin; ¥43,000–¥48,000 ($430–$480) double/twin on Sky Floors; ¥30,000–¥100,000 ($300–$1,000) double in the Japanese annex. AE, DC, JCB, MC, V. Free parking. Free shuttle bus every 30 minutes from Kyoto Station or Keihan Sanjo Station.

If you're looking for an older, more established hotel with a history, one of the best known in Japan, I'd recommend staying here. The Miyako, one of the "Leading Hotels of the World," is close to some of Kyoto's most famous temples and attractions, and spreads over more than 16 acres on top of a hill at the northeastern end of the city, commanding a good view of the surrounding hills. First opened back in 1890, it has boasted a guest list that reads like a *Who's Who* of visitors to Japan—Queen Elizabeth II, Prince Charles and Princess Diana, Anwar El-Sadat, Edward Kennedy, Gerald Ford, and Ronald Reagan, to name just a few. In fact, the Miyako Hotel is so well known around the world, half its guests are foreigners. It offers good value for what you pay.

Its Western-style rooms come in a variety of decors and price ranges, but all are cozy, comfortable, and large. The 10th and 11th floors of a wing added in 1992 are "Sky Floors," where you can check in directly; the helpful, bilingual Sky Desk staff is available from 7am to 10pm to take care of your every whim. Complimentary breakfast, tea, and cocktails are served in a private lounge with a great view. Also, 20 Japanese-style rooms are available in two annexes (connected to the main hotel by a covered passageway), which manage to maintain the atmosphere of a traditional ryokan with views of a Japanese garden.

Dining/Entertainment: Among the 13 restaurants, cafes, and bars you'll find a variety of cuisines—Japanese, Chinese, continental, and Danish.

Services: Free English-language newspaper twice a day, same-day laundry service, baby-sitting.

Facilities: Japanese garden, shopping arcade, beauty salon, barbershop, indoor and outdoor swimming pools, (free to hotel guests), fitness club, Jacuzzi, saunas, tennis courts, birdwatching and nature path, florist, tea ceremony (fee ¥1,133/$11.33), and sun deck.

✪ Seikoro

Gojo-sagaru, Tonyamachi, Higashiyama-ku, Kyoto 605. ☎ **075/561-0771.** Fax 075/541-5481. 23 rms (all with bath). A/C TV TEL. ¥25,000–¥60,000 ($250–$600) per person double, with two meals and service; less 30% for room without meals. AE, DC, JCB, MC, V. Bus: To Kawaramachi Gojo. Keihan Electric Railway: Gojo Station.

Established in 1831, the present ryokan dates from about a century ago. After passing through a traditional front gate and small courtyard, you'll find yourself in a cozy parlor replete with an eclectic mixture of both Japanese and Western antiques, including an old grandfather clock. The rooms, also decorated in antiques, are very homey and comfortable; some overlook a garden. Rooms in an annex built just before the 1964 Olympics are high enough that you can see over the surrounding rooftops, but I always prefer rooms in the oldest buildings. The owner, who speaks good English, doesn't mind if you take your meals elsewhere, especially if you're going to be here for a while. Seikoro is located just a few minutes' walk east of the Kamo River.

Yachiyo Inn

34 Nanzenji-Fukujicho, Sakyo-ku, Kyoto 606. ☎ **075/771-4148.** Fax 075/771-4140. 25 rms (20 with bath). A/C TV TEL. From ¥15,000 ($150) per person, double occupancy. All rates include two meals and service charge. 30% less without meals. AE, DC, JCB, MC, V. Bus: To Hoshoji-mae.

Situated on the approach to Nanzenji Temple, this inn has a large foreign clientele. Formerly a villa (it became a ryokan after World War II), the building is about 100 years old but has been remodeled so that it seems almost new. All accommodations on the ground floor open onto a small garden; less expensive ones are located on the second floor. There are wooden bathtubs in most rooms, along with showers and Western toilets. Rooms also boast transom carvings and ikebana flower arrangements. This ryokan doesn't mind if you prefer to take your meals elsewhere. If you're staying in Kyoto for a few days, you might want first to take breakfast and dinner at the ryokan and then later start going out to Kyoto's many restaurants.

MODERATE

Kyoto Gion Hotel

555 Gion, Higashiyama-ku, Kyoto 605. ☎ **075/551-2111.** Fax 075/551-2200. 135 rms. A/C MINIBAR TV TEL. ¥9,800–¥10,000 ($98–$100) single; ¥16,000–¥16,500 ($160–$165) twin; ¥18,500 ($185) triple. AE, DC, JCB, MC, V. Bus: To Gion.

This is an older, simple hotel with no extra frills but a great location on Shijo Dori in the heart of Gion near Yanaka Shrine. Within easy walking distance of shops, nightlife, and the many sights in Higashiyama-ku, it has a Western and a Japanese restaurant, a bar, and during the summer months, a rooftop beer garden. The lobby and front desk are up on the second floor. Rooms are simple, with ceiling-to-floor windows.

Japanese Style

Ryokan Rikiya (64)

Ryozen Kannon-mae, Higashiyama-ku, Kyoto 605. ☎ **075/561-2814.** 10 rms (2 with bath). A/C MINIBAR TV TEL. Room only, ¥8,000 ($80) per person without bath, ¥10,000 ($100) per person with bath. Room and two meals, ¥20,500 ($205) per person with bath. AE, DC, JCB, MC, V. Bus: To Yasui.

Ryokan Rikiya is located in front of Ryozen Kannon, between Kiyomizu Temple and Maruyama Park. This is a quiet family-run ryokan in a modern building. The best room is named Daiyu, has its own bathroom, and faces toward the front courtyard. This ryokan doesn't mind if you take your meals elsewhere.

Yoshi-ima

Hanimikoji-Nishi, Shinmonzen Dori, Gion, Higashiyama-ku, Kyoto 605. ☎ **075/561-2620.** Fax 075/541-6493. 20 rms (18 with bath). A/C TV TEL. ¥18,000–¥30,000 ($180–$300) per person. All rates include two meals and service charge. AE, DC, MC, V. Taxi: 10 minutes.

One of the best things about this ryokan is its location on Shinmonzen shopping street, in a quaint neighborhood of small wooden homes and antiques shops within easy walking distance of Gion and the Kawaramachi district. Much of the ryokan is relatively new and modern, although there are a few older rooms available in a wooden building for the same price. The best room has a view of the garden. Most of the guests here are booked through the Japan Travel Bureau, including foreigners. In fact, sometimes the whole ryokan is filled with foreigners only.

INEXPENSIVE

✪ Ladies' Hotel Chorakukan

Maruyama Park, Higashiyama-ku, Kyoto 605. ☎ **075/561-0001.** Fax 075/561-0006. 21 rms (all with toilet only). A/C TV TEL. ¥5,000 ($50) single; ¥9,000 ($90) double. No credit cards. Bus: To Yasaka (7 minutes).

This small, eccentric-looking hotel is *for women only* and has a pleasant location on the edge of Maruyama Park. An imposing Western-style building constructed just after the turn of the century, it has modified its interior so much through the decades, mixing the grand with the gaudy, that the atmosphere is comically bizarre. The lobby, for example, has a chandelier and a high gilded ceiling, but the rest of the room sports plastic moldings and decorations. Each guest room is slightly different, and there are two Japanese-style rooms. A hotel with personality, it would make a great set for a comedy. Highly recommended.

Pension Higashiyama

Sanjo-sagaru, Shirakawa-suji, Higashiyama-ku, Kyoto 605. ☎ **075/882-1181.** Fax 075/862-0820. 13 rms (3 with bath). A/C TV. ¥4,500 ($45) single without bath; ¥8,500 ($85) double without bath, ¥10,500 ($105) double with bath; ¥12,500 ($125) triple without bath, ¥13,500 ($135) triple with bath. AE, MC, V. Bus: To Chion-in-mae.

Opened in 1985, this clean, cheerful establishment on a small street on the bank of the Shirakawa River is not far from the Miyako Hotel on Kyoto's east side. Its rooms, some of which overlook the willow-lined stream, are mainly Western style, with flowered wallpaper and quilts on the bed, but three Japanese-style tatami rooms are also available. Rooms come with coin-operated TV, and there's a coin-operated laundry on the premises. The front doors are locked at 11:30pm. Pension Higashiyama is under the same management as Pension Station Kyoto and has the same fax number, so be sure to specify which pension you wish to reserve a room in.

Rokuharaya Inn (65)

147 Takemuracho Rokuhara, Higashiyama-ku, Kyoto 605. ☎ **075/531-2776.** Fax 075/531-8261. 6 rms (none with bath). A/C TV. ¥4,500 ($45) single; ¥5,000–¥5,500 ($50–$55) per person. Breakfast ¥1,000 ($10) extra; dinner ¥3,000 ($30) extra. AE, MC, V. Bus: To Gojozaka.

This inexpensive ryokan, located on a small residential street typical of Kyoto, offers just the basics. In my opinion the best rooms are on the second floor of this two-story, wooden building. More foreigners stay here than Japanese. Each room has a coin-operated TV but not much more—just your average Japanese tatami room. There's a coin-operated laundry.

Ryokan Mishima Shrine

Umamachi-dori, Higashioji Higashi-iru, Higashiyama-ku, Kyoto 605. ☎ **075/551-0033.** Fax 075/531-9768. 7 rms (all with toilet only). A/C TV. ¥4,500 ($45) single; ¥8,000 ($80) double; ¥12,000 ($120) triple. AE, MC, V. Bus: To Higashiyama-Umamachi.

This ryokan, a member of the Japanese Inn Group, is located on the grounds of Mishima Shrine, a small Shinto shrine visited by women who desire children and by women already pregnant who wish to ensure a safe delivery. You can have your picture taken in traditional shrine garb, free if you have your own camera and ¥240 ($2.40) if you have it taken with the shrine's Polaroid. Although the shrine was founded about 150 years ago, the Japanese-style rooms are located in a new building that opened in the mid-1980s. Spotless and simple, the ryokan caters largely to foreigners in the summer and to Japanese in the winter. Cotton kimono and towels are provided, and rooms have coin-operated TVs as well as private toilets. Facilities include four public baths and a coin-operated washing machine. No meals are served. The family running this place speaks some English.

Teradaya Inn

583 Higashi Rokuchome, Gojobashi, Higashiyama-ku, Kyoto 605. ☎ **075/561-3821.** Fax 075/531-8261. 4 rms (none with bath). A/C TV. ¥6,000 ($60) per person. Breakfast ¥1,000 ($10) extra; dinner ¥3,000 ($30) extra. AE, MC, V. Bus: To Gojozaka.

Under the same ownership as the Rokuharaya Inn (above) and therefore with the same fax number, this concrete inn is located just off the sloping approach to Kiyomizu Temple in eastern Kyoto, about halfway up (look for the large sign in English). Yukata are provided, and TVs and air conditioners are coin operated. Rooms on the second floor are the brightest. Facilities include a public bath and a coin-operated laundry.

NORTHERN KYOTO

EXPENSIVE

✪ Kyoto Takaragaike Prince Hotel

Takaragaike, Sakyo-ku, Kyoto 606. ☎ **075/712-1111** or 800/228-3000 in the U.S. and Canada. Fax 075/712-7677. 322 rms. A/C MINIBAR TV TEL. ¥31,000–¥37,000 ($310–$370) single, double, or twin; ¥70,000–¥200,000 ($700–$2,000) suite. AE, DC, JCB, MC, V. Taxi: 30 minutes.

Although a bit inconveniently located on the northern fringes of the city, this hotel is useful for those attending conferences in the Kyoto International Conference Hall across the street. Another advantage is nearby Takaragaike Park, complete with jogging paths, pond, botanical garden, and wood-covered hills. If you want the benefits of being in the countryside but don't want to give up the comforts of a first-class hotel, this may be the place for you.

Designed by the famous architect Togo Murano, this imposing circular hotel has the unmistakable touches of a Prince Hotel, including its excellent service, cheerful staff, and its bright color schemes of white, pink, and purple. The rooms are positively palatial, with a sink and vanity area separated from the bathroom. Upon arrival at the hotel, you will be treated to a complimentary tea and sweet, brought to your room by a kimono-clad hostess. Should you have any questions regarding the hotel or Kyoto during your stay, there's a guest-relations officer on duty to help arrange everything—from reserving train tickets to arranging picnics in the park.

Dining/Entertainment: Beaux Séjours, under the direction of a French chef, is the hotel's signature restaurant. Other restaurants serve Japanese food, including sushi and tempura, and Chinese cuisine from Peking. There are also a coffee shop and a bar.

Services: Complimentary green tea upon arrival, free English-language newspapers twice a day, same-day laundry service, baby-sitting, free shuttle bus to Kyoto Station.

Facilities: Business center, beauty salon, souvenir shop.

MODERATE

Kyoto Holiday Inn

36 Nishihiraki-cho, Takano, Sakyo-ku, Kyoto 606. ☎ **075/721-3131.** Fax 075/781-6178. 267 rms. A/C MINIBAR TV TEL. ¥10,000 ($100) single; ¥14,000–¥17,000 ($140–$170) double; ¥18,500–¥22,500 ($185–$225) twin. Children under 12 stay free in parents' room. AE, DC, JCB, MC, V. Free parking. Bus: To Takano.

Although it's rather inconveniently located in the northeast corner of Kyoto, far from most of the city's sights, this inn provides facilities normally found only at resort hotels, including indoor and outdoor swimming pools (outdoor pool free to hotel guests; indoor pool, ¥2,000/$20), tennis courts, an indoor ice-skating rink, a sauna and gym, a golf-driving range, and a 100-lane bowling alley. A shopping and restaurant mall features a dozen different restaurants and a rooftop beer garden (open from 5 to 9pm in the summer). A number of different kinds of rooms are available, and all beds, even those in twin rooms, are of double size. The hotel maintains a shuttle-bus service to Kyoto Station.

INEXPENSIVE

$ Aoi-So Inn

16-8 Nakamizocho, Koyama, Kita-ku, Kyoto 603. ☎ and fax **075/431-0788.** 20 rms. None with bath. ¥2,800 ($28) per person. No credit cards. Station: Kuramaguchi (3 minutes from exit 2, turn left at Kuramaguchi Hospital.).

Located in a quiet Japanese house with tatami rooms and a garden, Aoi-So Inn offers reasonable accommodation to foreigners. The owner, Asai-san, speaks some English. Discount offered for longer stays. It is conveniently located near the Old Imperial Palace.

Higashiyama Youth Hostel

Shirakawabashi, Sanjo-dori, Higashiyama-ku, Kyoto 605. ☎ **075/761-8135.** 130 beds. A/C. ¥4,000 ($40) for Japanese, ¥3,800 ($38) non-Japanese. All rates include breakfast and dinner. No credit cards. Bus: To Higashiyama-Sanjo.

Of the several youth hostels in and around the Kyoto area, this is the most convenient and the closest to Kyoto Station. The modern concrete building has bunk beds, and guests are required to take breakfast and dinner here. Be sure to call in advance, since this place is sometimes booked full with school groups. English is spoken. There's a 10:30pm curfew.

Kyoto Utane Youth Hostel

29 Nakayama-cho, Uzumasa, Ukyo-ku, Kyoto 616. ☎ **075/462-2288.** Fax 075/462-2289. 168 beds. A/C. ¥2,650 ($26.50) per person, ¥3,850 ($38.50) per person with two meals. JCB, MC, V. Bus: To the Youth Hostel-mae stop.

Located in the northwestern part of the city near Ryoanji Temple, which is famous for its Zen rock garden, this youth hostel is a modern, concrete structure offering bunk-bed accommodation. Facilities include a coin-operated laundry, bicycles for rent, tennis courts, and kitchen facilities. Breakfast features all the bread you can eat.

Myokenji Temple (66)

Teranouchi Horikawa, Kamigyo-ku, Kyoto 602. ☎ **075/414-0808** or 431-6828. 50 beds. ¥5,000 ($50) per person. All rates include breakfast. No credit cards. Bus: To Teranouchi.

If you want to stay in a Buddhist temple and don't mind sharing a room, both Myokenji and Myorenji (below) have simple accommodations on their temple grounds. Myokenji, in a pleasant, quiet residential area in northern Kyoto, offers traditional tatami rooms surrounded by moss-covered gardens and bamboo. It's secluded and in a world of its own, almost as if it were out in the country instead of in a bustling city. Since most temples offering accommodations cater largely to groups, you should make a reservation here at least several weeks in advance. Most rooms are large, sleeping as many people as will fit into them; but if no group is booked, you're likely to have the place to yourself. As in all Buddhist temples, the breakfast served here is vegetarian.

Myorenji Temple (67)

Teranouchi Horikawa, Kamigyo-ku, Kyoto 602. ☎ **075/451-3527.** 20 beds. ¥4,000 ($40) per person. All rates include breakfast and ticket for neighborhood public bath. No credit cards. Bus: To Teranouchi.

Not far from the above temple is Myorenji, founded more than 650 years ago and now run by a jolly woman named Chizuko-san, who speaks a little English. Since she manages this place virtually single-handedly, she prefers guests who stay two or three days and requests them to make reservations at least a week (and preferably a month) in advance. The temple buildings, about 200 years old, offer rooms with a view of gardens, including a rock garden with raked pebbles. Sleeping is on futon spread out in large rooms, and again it's possible that you'll have a room to yourself if no groups happen to be staying here. Since there are no bathing facilities on the temple grounds, guests are given a ticket to use the neighborhood bath. If you're interested in attending services, they're held every morning at 6:30am.

Nashinoki Inn

Agaru Imadegawa Nashinoki Street, Kamikyo-ku, Kyoto 602. ☎ **075/241-1543.** 7 rms (none with bath). A/C TV. ¥5,000 ($50) single; ¥8,000 ($80) double; ¥13,000 ($130) triple. Japanese or Western breakfast ¥900 ($9) extra. No credit cards. Subway: Imadegawa Station (13 minutes).

In a quiet, peaceful neighborhood north of the Kyoto Imperial Palace, this ryokan is run by a warm and friendly older couple who speak some English. Staying here is like living with a Japanese family, since the home looks very lived in and is filled with the personal belongings of a lifetime. Some of the tatami rooms, which feature such touches as vases, Japanese dolls, and pictures, are quite large and adequate for families. Breakfast is served in your room.

Rakucho

67 Higashihangi-cho, Shimogamo, Sakyo-ku, Kyoto 606. ☎ **075/721-2174.** Fax 075/791-7202. 8 rms (none with bath). A/C TV. ¥4,500–¥5,000 ($45–50) single; ¥7,500–¥8,000 ($75–$80) double; ¥10,500–¥11,000 ($105–$110) triple. AE, MC, V. Subway: Kitaoji Station (10 minutes). Bus: To Furitsu-Daigakumae (3 minutes).

In northern Kyoto, this ryokan is not as conveniently situated as most of the other inns listed above, but all the rooms here are pleasant and clean, with heating and a view of a small, peaceful garden; some rooms also have a refrigerator. Entrance to the ryokan is through a well-tended tiny courtyard filled with plants. A member of the Japanese Inn Group, the place offers a coin-operated laundry.

5 Dining

Kyoto's specialties include vegetarian dishes, which were created to serve the needs of Buddhist priests and pilgrims making the rounds of Kyoto's many temples. Called *shojin ryoori,* these vegetarian set meals include tofu simmered in a pot at your table (*yudofu*) and an array of local vegetables. Kyoto is also known for its kaiseki (Kyo-kaiseki), originally conceived as a meal to be taken during the tea ceremony but eventually becoming an elaborate feast enjoyed by the capital's nobility. Today, Kyoto abounds in restaurants serving both vegetarian tofu dishes and kaiseki meals fit for an emperor. A restaurant advertising that it serves Kyo-ryoori offers a variety of Kyoto cuisine.

Most of Kyoto's traditional Japanese restaurants are located in the heart of the city, in Nakagyo-ku, spreading to the east in areas called Higashiyama-ku and Sakyo-ku. Choices in fast food and reasonably priced set meals abound in restaurants around Kyoto Station, which cater to tourists, commuters, and shoppers. I have divided Kyoto's restaurants according to district, adding some Western-style restaurants as well.

AROUND KYOTO STATION

In addition to the restaurants listed here, a good place for inexpensive dining is the **Kintetsu Mall,** located on the west side of Kyoto Station (under the tracks) and offering two dozen restaurants serving a wide variety of inexpensive meals.

EXPENSIVE

Minokichi

Hotel New Hankyu Kyoto, Shiokoji Dori. ☎ **075/343-5300.** Reservations recommended. Kyo-kaiseki ¥6,500–¥12,000 ($65–$120); Kyo-ryoori ¥5,000–¥6,000 ($50–$60); set lunches ¥2,000–¥3,500 ($20–$35). AE, DC, JCB, MC, V. Daily 11:30am–9pm (last order). Directions: 1 minute north. KYO-KAISEKI/KYO-RYOORI.

A branch of the famous Minokichi restaurant first established in Kyoto more than 260 years ago, this establishment is designed to resemble a lane in a typical traditional Japanese village, with waitresses in kimono and Japanese music playing in the background to help set the mood. The menu includes Kyoto-style kaiseki cuisine and typical Kyoto dishes, as well as such Japanese favorites as obento lunch boxes and eel. Set lunches, served daily until 4pm, are especially good bargains, offering everything from eel to mini-kaiseki.

INEXPENSIVE

Gio Giono

Renaissance Bldg., 849 Higashi Shiokojicho. ☎ **075/365-0202.** Pasta and pizza ¥900–¥1,300 ($9–$13); meat dishes ¥1,200–¥1,500 ($12–$15); set dinners ¥3,000–¥5,000 ($30–$50); set lunches ¥900–¥2,500 ($9–$25). AE, DC, JCB, MC, V. Daily 11:30am–2:30pm and 5:30–10pm. Directions: Walk 1 minute northeast on Shiokoji Dori. ITALIAN.

Next to Kyoto Station is the Renaissance Building, which features several restaurants, including a coffee shop, a Chinese restaurant, and a beer hall. Best for a meal, however, is Gio Giono, an informal Italian restaurant serving pizza, pasta, and such main dishes as grilled pork ribs, sautéed scallops, and veal cutlet. There's an English-language dinner menu. An especially good deal is the ¥900 ($9) set lunch, available until 2:30pm and offering a choice of daily pasta, pasta salad, or risotto, as well as serve-yourself antipasto and salad, soup, and coffee.

✪ Izusen (68)

On the second floor of the Surugaiya Bldg., Karasuma Shichijo Dori-sagaru. ☎ **075/343-4211.** Set meals ¥1,800–¥5,300 ($18–$53). No credit cards. Fri–Wed 11am–8pm. Directions: Walk 1 minute to the building just north of the Tourist Information Center, on Karasuma Dori. KYO-RYOORI/VEGETARIAN.

Although the decor is simple, the food in this restaurant is great and beautifully presented, featuring local Kyoto and vegetarian dishes. There's an English menu, and seating is either at tables or on tatami mats. There is a variety of fixed-price meals from which to choose, offering soup, appetizer, rice, a main dish, and side dishes. A vegetarian meal for ¥1,800 ($18), for example, is a light meal usually served at a tea ceremony. I usually opt for the Hana course, which costs ¥2,700 ($27) and features Kyoto cuisine, including tempura, sashimi, various vegetables, broiled fish, rice, and soup. This is one of my favorite restaurants in Kyoto.

Mimosa

Grand Hotel, Horikawa-Shiokoji. ☎ **075/341-2311.** Reservations recommended. All-you-can-eat buffet ¥1,800 ($18) at breakfast, ¥2,500 ($25) at lunch, ¥3,800 ($38) at dinner. Prices include service and tax. AE, DC, JCB, MC, V. Daily 6:30–10am, 11:30am–2:30pm, and 5:30–8:30pm. Transportation: Free hotel shuttle bus (from 8am to 9pm) from Kyoto Station's Hachijo Guchi exit; or a 10-minute walk. VARIED.

Mimosa, with its elegant central atrium and light/dark color scheme, offers an airy setting for all-you-can-eat buffets, which have become so popular that now reservations are recommended. The breakfast buffet offers a great salad and fruit bar as well as traditional breakfast foods, while lunch and dinner buffets range from appetizers, soups, and salads to curry, rice, pastas, fish, and meats. For those traveling with little ones, children 3 to 6 are charged only ¥1,000 ($10) for breakfast, ¥1,250 ($12.50) for lunch, and ¥2,200 ($22) for dinner, while those under 3 eat free. Finicky eaters are sure to find something to please them.

A Note on Japanese Symbols

Many hotels, restaurants, and other establishments in Japan do not have signs giving their name in English letters. As an aid to the reader, Appendix C lists the Japanese symbols for all such places described in this guide. Each set of symbols has a number, which corresponds to the number that appears inside an oval next to the establishment's boldfaced name in the text. Thus, to find the Japanese symbols for, say, **Izusen** (68), refer to the number 68 in the appendix.

CENTRAL KYOTO

The heart of Kyoto's shopping, dining, and nightlife district is in Nakagyo-ku, especially on Kawaramachi and Shijo Dori and in the many side streets.

EXPENSIVE

Manyoken

Fuyacho Shijo. ☎ **075/221-1022.** Reservations recommended. Main dishes ¥4,000–¥12,000 ($40–$120); set dinners ¥10,000–¥20,000 ($100–$200); set lunches ¥7,500 ($75). AE, DC, JCB, MC, V. Wed–Mon 11:30am–3pm and 5–8:30pm (last order). Bus: To Shijo-Fuyacho. FRENCH.

Located on Shijo Dori, Manyoken is one of Kyoto's best-known restaurants, with more than 80 years of experience serving French cuisine. With its chandeliers, fresh roses, white tablecloths, and drawing-room atmosphere, this elegant restaurant serves a set lunch and set dinners, all of which change monthly. A la carte selections include steak, lobster, fish, and chicken. Although the menu changes often, a typical meal here may start out with escargots in bourguignon sauce, followed by onion soup, sirloin steak cooked with a special house sauce, and then baked Alaska or soufflé in Curaçao or chocolate.

Top of Kyoto

Kyoto Grand Hotel, Horikawa Shiokoji. ☎ **075/341-2311.** Reservations recommended. Daily from 11:30am to 11pm. Set lunches from ¥2,500 ($25); set dinners from ¥6,000 ($60); Sun brunch buffet ¥3,500 ($35). AE, DC, MC, V. Daily 11:30am–2pm and 5–11pm (brunch until 2:30pm Sunday). Directions: Free shuttle. FRENCH.

Kyoto's only revolving restaurant offers excellent views over the tops of Kyoto's temples to the mountains surrounding the city. In an Italian marble decor, lobster with sweetbreads and caviar, smoked Norwegian salmon with papaya, rack of lamb, and steaks are offered. My French companion was favorably impressed with the cuisine. Adjoining the restaurant is a comfortable cocktail lounge, where you can relax with a drink after dinner.

✪ Misogi-gawa (69)

Sanjo-sagaru, Pontocho. ☎ **075/221-2270.** Reservations required. Main dishes ¥3,000–¥5,000 ($30–$50); set dinners ¥12,000–¥25,000 ($120–$250). AE, DC, JCB, MC, V. Tues–Sun 4:30–9pm. Bus: To Sanjo-Kawaramachi. FRENCH KAISEKI.

Serving nouvelle French cuisine that utilizes the best of Japanese style and ingredients in what could be called French kaiseki, this lovely and exclusive restaurant stands on a narrow street called Pontocho, which parallels the Kamo River and is one of Kyoto's most famous nightlife districts. Located in a century-old renovated wooden building that once belonged to a geisha who used it as her entertainment house, Misogi-Gawa successfully blends the two cuisines into dishes artfully prepared and served on Japanese tableware. In fact, part of the delight of eating here lies in receiving the various courses of the fixed-price meals, each one exquisitely arranged as though a work of art. Dining is either at a counter or in private tatami rooms, and you have a choice of eating with either chopsticks or knife and fork. The menu (written in French and changing regularly) includes lobster, sole, scallops, and various beef dishes.

Misono

Petit Monde Bldg., 5th floor, Takoyakushi, Kawaramachi. ☎ **075/255-2981.** Main dishes ¥1,000–¥15,000 ($10–$150); set dinners ¥9,000–¥16,000 ($90–$160); set lunches ¥2,000–¥7,500 ($20–$75). AE, DC, MC, V. Daily 11:30am–10pm. Directions: Walk 2 minutes up Kawaramachi Dori from Shijo Station. TEPPANYAKI.

Misono is a branch of the famous Kobe restaurant, which claims to have invented teppanyaki. You can bet with a reputation like that it will live up to its good name.

Your waiter will prepare your meal in front of you (though with less fanfare than in other teppanyaki places) in a comfortable, dark wood–wainscoted room with a city view. I had the So course for ¥12,000 ($120); it included 200 grams of Kobe steak, salad, smoked tongue, clams, scallops, vegetables, and fruit. The restaurant has a menu in English.

Tempura Yoshikawa

Tominokoji Dori, Oike-sagaru. ☎ **075/221-5544.** Reservations required. Tempura set dinners ¥6,000–¥20,000 ($60–$200); tempura set lunches ¥2,000–¥10,000 ($20–$100). AE, DC, JCB, MC, V. Daily 11am–2pm and 5–8:30pm (last order). Subway: Oike Station (7 minutes). TEMPURA.

If you're hungering for tempura, this restaurant near Oike Avenue with its sign in English is easy to find. Located in an old-fashioned part of Kyoto that boasts a number of expensive ryokan, it's a tiny, intimate place with a traditional atmosphere, and the counter seats only 12. Meals in tatami rooms are more expensive. Kaiseki meals here start at ¥20,000 ($200) and are served in a private tatami room.

Unkai

ANA Hotel Kyoto, Nijojo-mae, Horikawa Dori Avenue. ☎ **075/231-1155.** Shabu-shabu ¥9,000 ($90); vegetarian set meals ¥6,000 ($60); kaiseki ¥10,000–¥20,000 ($100–$200); set lunches ¥4,000 ($40). AE, DC, JCB, MC, V. Daily 11:30am–2:30pm and 5–10pm. Bus: To Nijojo-mae. KAISEKI/SHABU-SHABU/VEGETARIAN.

In a convenient location across from the main entrance of Nijo Castle, this restaurant has a modern and refined decor, ceiling-to-floor windows, kimono-clad waitresses, and an English menu. The varied menu includes shabu-shabu, kaiseki, tempura, and *shojin* (a vegetarian set meal typical of Kyoto).

MODERATE

Ashoka

Kikusui Bldg., 3rd floor, Teramachi Dori. ☎ **075/241-1318.** Main dishes ¥1,300–¥1,800 ($13–$18); set dinners ¥2,500–¥5,800 ($25–$58); set lunches ¥1,300 ($13). AE, DC, JCB, MC, V. Daily 11:30am–2:30pm and 5–9pm (until 8pm Sun). Closed second Tues of the month. Bus: To Shijo-Kawaramachi intersection (3 minutes). INDIAN.

One of Kyoto's most popular Indian restaurants, Ashoka serves vegetarian and meat curries, including mutton, chicken, fish, vegetable, and shrimp selections. I started my meal here with mulligatawny Madrasi, a South Indian soup, and followed with Indian bread stuffed with minced meat along with mutton *sagwala* (mutton and spinach). Ashoka is located just north of Shijo Dori at the beginning of the Teramachi covered shopping arcade.

Izumoya (70)

Shijo-agaru, Pontocho. ☎ **075/211-2501.** Reservations recommended, especially for kaiseki. Obento ¥2,800–¥4,800 ($28–$48); shabu-shabu or sukiyaki from ¥3,200 ($32); kaiseki ¥6,000–¥10,000 ($60–$100). AE, DC, JCB, MC, V. Thurs–Tues noon–9pm (last order). Bus: To Shijo-Kawaramachi intersection. KAISEKI/SHABU-SHABU/TEMPURA/EEL.

It's easy to find this restaurant, a many-storied place on Shijo Dori right beside the bridge spanning the Kamo River. The backside of the restaurant faces the river, and in the summer a wooden veranda is constructed on stilts over the water (open from 6 to 10pm). Popular with tourists and groups, Izumoya serves a wide variety of dishes on its various floors, including shabu-shabu and set meals of tempura, sashimi, eel, and other Japanese dishes. Only kaiseki meals are served on the outdoor veranda and by reservation only. Although the menu is in Japanese only, there's a large display of plastic food at the front door.

Family-Friendly Restaurants

Capricciosa *(see p. 282)* Inexpensive dining on pasta and pizza and enormous portions make this restaurant popular with families.

Gio Giono *(see p. 276)* A casual Italian restaurant serving pizza and spaghetti, conveniently located near Kyoto Station.

Knuckles New York Eatery *(see p. 288)* New York deli–style sandwiches and authentic, healthy food are featured in this Western-style restaurant.

Mimosa *(see p. 276)* Offering all-you-can-eat buffets with reduced prices for children 3 to 6 and free for kids under 3, Mimosa is sure to please parents with its prices and children with its wide selection.

Kyoshiki

Fuyacho Dori, Sanjo-agaru. ☎ **075/221-4866.** Set meals ¥3,000–¥8,500 ($30–$85). AE, DC, JCB. Daily 11:40am–8:00pm (last order). Bus: To the Kawaramachi-Sanjo stop (5 minutes). KAISEKI/KYO-RYOORI.

This reasonably priced kaiseki restaurant, just north of Sanjo Dori on Fuyacho Dori, was converted from a private home about 20 years ago. I recommend the Hisago fixed-price meal for ¥3,000 ($30) offered on the English-language menu, which is a variety of seasonal food served in individual dishes that stack neatly on top of one another to form a gourd; you take the bowls apart to eat. The atmosphere here is relaxed and comfortable. On Wednesday free tea and sweets are served with lunch until 4pm.

Tagoto (71)

Shijo-Kawaramachi, Nishi-iru, Kitagawa. ☎ **075/221-1811.** Reservations not required for the second floor. Obento and set meals ¥3,000–¥3,800 ($30–$38); Kyo-ryoori ¥6,000–¥10,000 ($60–$100). AE, DC, JCB, MC, V. Daily 11am–9pm. Bus: To the Shijo-Kawaramachi intersection. KYO-RYOORI/KAISEKI/OBENTO.

Nestled in an inner courtyard off busy Shijo Dori and offering a peaceful retreat in the heart of downtown Kyoto, this restaurant has been serving a variety of Japanese food at moderate prices since 1868. Its entrance is near the Kyoto Central Inn (look for a tiny door with a white sign; step through it and follow the passageway to the back courtyard). The menu includes Kyo-ryoori set meals, tempura, eel dishes, obento lunch boxes, seasonal kaiseki courses, and sashimi. Inexpensive noodles and set lunches for less than ¥1,000 ($10) are served until 2pm.

INEXPENSIVE

Beer Market Ichiba Coji

Withyou Bldg., Teramachi. ☎ **075/252-2008.** Main dishes ¥600–¥1,500 ($6–$15); set meals ¥2,500–¥3,500 ($25–$35). AE, DC, JCB, MC, V. Daily 11:30am–10:15pm (last order). Bus: To Shijo-Kawaramachi. CHINESE/PAO/ASIAN.

It's difficult to classify this place, which calls itself a "Kyoto mini-brewery," serving its own original beer and claiming to have more beer on tap than any other establishment in Kyoto. But it is certainly much more than that. Visually it's the most interesting and exciting new-age restaurant I've seen in Kyoto, reminding me of high-tech establishments in Tokyo. Ichiba Coji features bare concrete walls, white pebbles on the floor, black furniture, and an elevated dining platform above a running stream. The waitresses and cooks are all decked out in Asian baggy pants, and the food is eclectic, although I guess it's more Chinese than anything else. The specialty of the

Kyoto Dining & Attractions

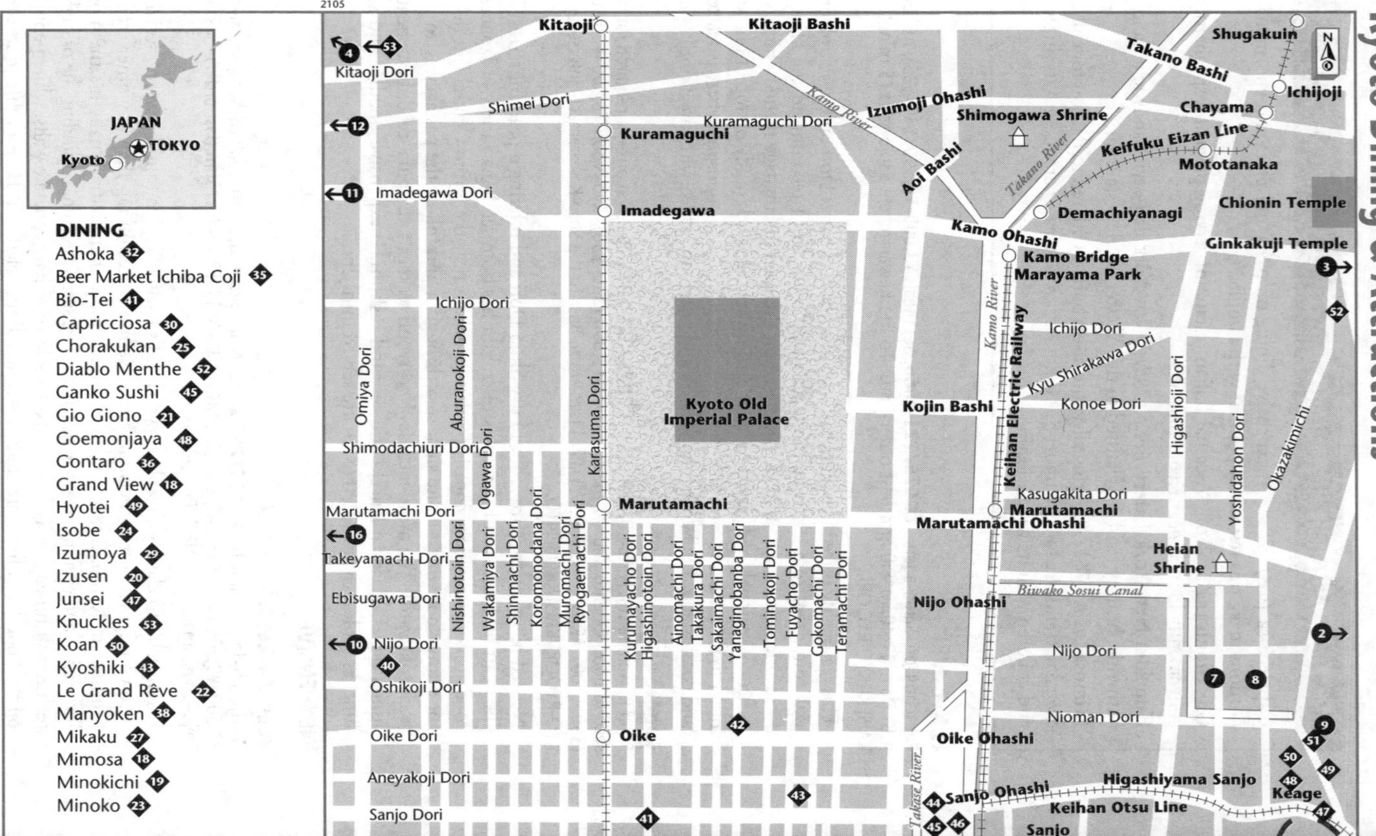

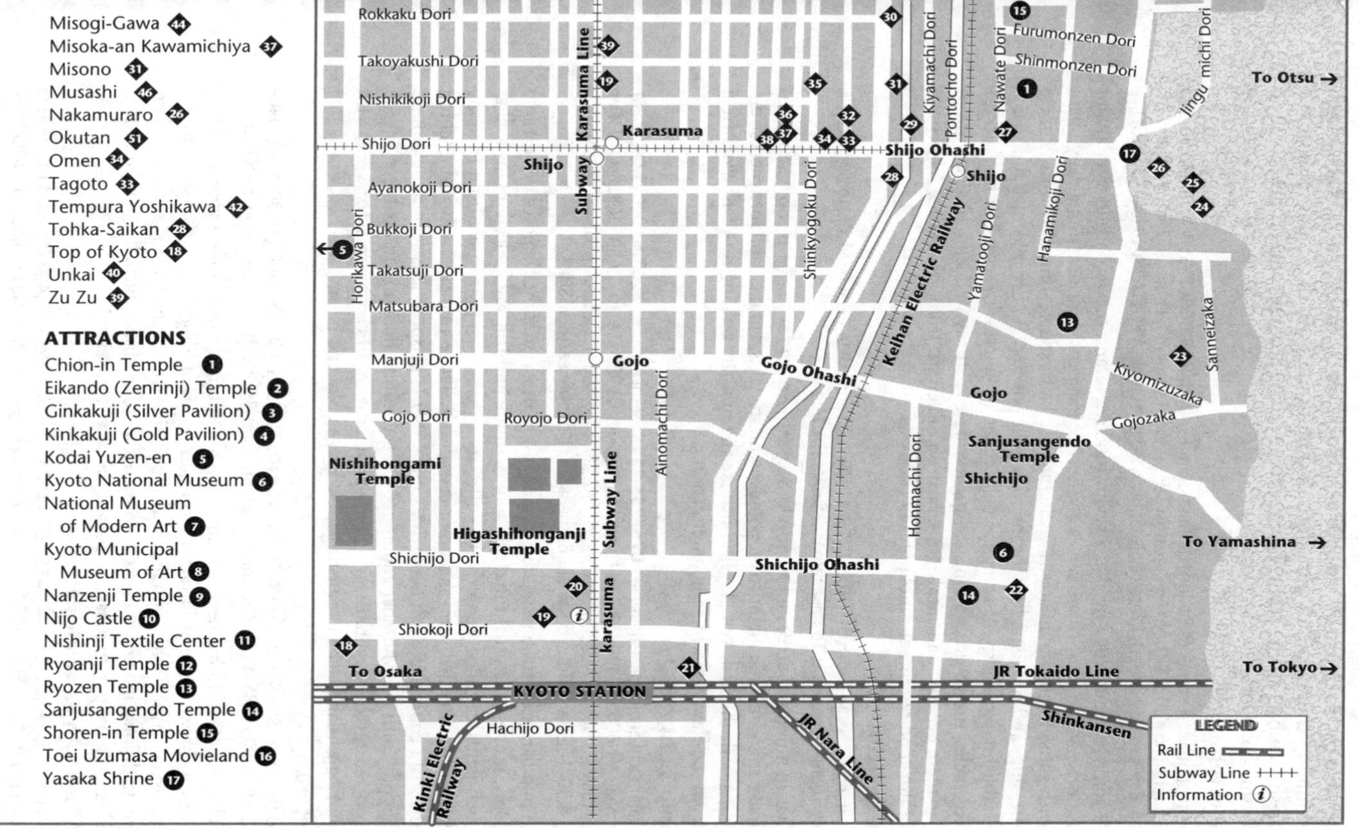
Misogi-Gawa 44
Misoka-an Kawamichiya 37
Misono 31
Musashi 46
Nakamuraro 26
Okutan 51
Omen 34
Tagoto 33
Tempura Yoshikawa 42
Tohka-Saikan 28
Top of Kyoto 18
Unkai 40
Zu Zu 39
ATTRACTIONS
Chion-in Temple 1
Eikando (Zenrinji) Temple 2
Ginkakuji (Silver Pavilion) 3
Kinkakuji (Gold Pavilion) 4
Kodai Yuzen-en 5
Kyoto National Museum 6
National Museum of Modern Art 7
Kyoto Municipal Museum of Art 8
Nanzenji Temple 9
Nijo Castle 10
Nishinji Textile Center 11
Ryoanji Temple 12
Ryozen Temple 13
Sanjusangendo Temple 14
Shoren-in Temple 15
Toei Uzumasa Movieland 16
Yasaka Shrine 17
Rokkaku Dori
Takoyakushi Dori
Nishikikoji Dori
Shijo Dori
Ayanokoji Dori
Bukkoji Dori
Takatsuji Dori
Matsubara Dori
Manjuji Dori
Gojo Dori
Royojo Dori
Horikawa Dori
Karasuma Line
Subway
Karasuma
Shijo
Gojo
Subway Line
karasuma
Ainomachi Dori
Shinkyogoku Dori
Kiyamachi Dori
Pontocho Dori
Nawate Dori
Furumonzen Dori
Shinmonzen Dori
Jingu michi Dori
Shijo Ohashi
Keihan Electric Railway
Yamatooji Dori
Hanamikoji Dori
Sanneizaka
Kiyomizuzaka
Gojozaka
Gojo Ohashi
Gojo
Sanjusangendo Temple
Shichijo
Honmachi Dori
Shichijo Ohashi
Nishihongami Temple
Higashihonganji Temple
Shichijo Dori
Shiokoji Dori
Hachijo Dori
To Osaka
KYOTO STATION
Kinki Electric Railway
JR Nara Line
JR Tokaido Line
Shinkansen
To Otsu →
To Yamashina →
To Tokyo →
LEGEND
Rail Line
Subway Line
Information

house is pao food, morsels wrapped in lettuce leaves; for fillings you can choose from shrimp in chili sauce, dry curry pilaf, and much more. All the food is seasonal and fresh. Ichiba Coji is in the Teramachi covered shopping arcade, just north of Nishikikoji Dori.

$ Bio-Tei (72)

On the southwest corner of Sanjo-Higashinotouin. ☎ **075/255-0086.** ¥350–¥700 ($3.50–$7); lunch teishoku ¥800 ($8). No credit cards. Tues noon–1pm, Wed–Fri noon–2pm, Wed and Fri–Sat 5–8:30pm (last order). Closed hols. Subway: Oike Station. VEGETARIAN/HEALTH FOOD.

If you're yearning for a meal in a health-food restaurant, this second-floor restaurant near the Museum of Kyoto serves a variety of inexpensive dishes from a daily menu with some English translations, including rice balls, soups, tofu salad with Chinese dressing, and fermented soy beans with yam powder. A very informal and casual establishment, it also offers a great daily teishoku lunch with several dishes, pickled vegetables, brown rice, and miso soup. Seating is at sturdy wooden tables hewn from Japanese cypress, and meals are served on tableware from local kilns. As befits a health-food restaurant, smoking is not allowed.

$ Capricciosa

Kawaramachi Sanjo Sagaru. ☎ **075/255-3717.** Pizza and pasta ¥1,500 ($15). No credit cards. Daily 10am–11pm. Bus: To Kawaramachi Sanjo. ITALIAN.

Italian music and decor and plentiful, inexpensive pasta (one order is enough for two) make this casual restaurant chain popular with students, families, and foreigners struggling with the high yen. To find it, take the first left walking down Kawaramachi from the Kawaramachi Sanjo intersection.

Ganko Sushi (73)

Kawaramachi-Sanjo, Higashi-iru. ☎ **075/255-1128.** Sushi à la carte ¥260–¥2,000 ($2.60–$20); set meals ¥1,600–¥2,400 ($16–$24); set lunches ¥680–¥980 ($6.80–$9.80). JCB, MC, V. First floor daily 11:30am–10:30pm, second floor daily 4–10:30pm, basement daily 11:30am–2pm and 4:30–10:30pm. Bus: To Kawaramachi-Sanjo (1 minute east). SUSHI.

A popular, lively sushi restaurant located just to the west of the Kamo River on Sanjo Dori, it offers the usual tuna, eel, bonito, squid, and fish sushi selections, as well as such items as grilled yakitori and kushikatsu, shabu-shabu, tempura, tofu (ranging from fried to grilled), and shrimp or crab dishes. There's a menu in English. Behind the sushi counter is a fish tank with some rather large specimens swimming around happily until their number comes up. On the second floor and in the basement are two robatayaki restaurants, which are popular with office workers after work, with an English-language menu listing grilled vegetables and meats.

Gontaro (74)

Fuyacho Dori, Shijo-agaru. ☎ **075/221-5810.** Noodles ¥680–¥1,400 ($6.80–$14); nabe ¥3,500–¥5,000 ($35–$50). JCB. Thurs–Tues 11:30am–10pm. Bus: To Shijo Dori. NOODLES.

This noodle shop has been serving its own handmade noodles for a mere 70 years. It's on the west side of Fuyacho Dori, just north of Shijo Dori; look for a tiny recessed courtyard, white curtains, and a lone pine tree. A small place, with a modern yet traditional interior, it offers various noodle (soba) dishes, including tempura soba, chicken soba, potato soba, and soba sushi, as well as nabe.

✪ Misoka-An Kawamichiya

Fuyacho Dori, Sanjo-agaru. ☎ **075/221-2525.** Noodles ¥550–¥1,400 ($5.50–$14); *Hokoro* ¥3,800 ($38). AE, V. Fri–Wed 11am–8pm. Bus: To Kawaramachi-Sanjo (5 minutes). NOODLES.

Charming and delightful, with a central courtyard and cubbyhole rooms, this tiny noodle shop is about 300 years old—and makes a great place for an inexpensive meal in the heart of traditional Kyoto. On Fuyacho Dori, just north of Sanjo Dori, it offers plain buckwheat noodles, as well as noodles with such adornments as tempura and chicken and onions. Its specialty is a one-pot noodle dish called *Hokoro,* which includes chicken, tofu, mushrooms, and vegetables and is enough for two. There's a menu in English.

$ Musashi (75)

Kawaramachi-Sanjo agaru. ☎ **075/222-0634.** ¥140–¥290 ($1.40–$2.90) per plate. No credit cards. Daily 11am–9:40pm. Bus: To Kawaramachi-Sanjo. SUSHI.

For a cheap meal of raw fish, this restaurant can't be beat. With a convenient location on the northwest corner of the Kawaramachi-Sanjo intersection, it offers morsels of sushi via a conveyor belt that moves along the counter. Simply reach out and take whatever strikes your fancy. Plates of tuna, octopus, sweet shrimp, eel, crab salad, and more are offered. Take-out sushi is also available from the front counter.

Omen (76)

Gokomachi Dori Shijo Agaru. ☎ **075/255-2125.** Main dishes ¥450–¥1,200 ($4.50–$12); set meals ¥1,250–¥2,300 ($12.50–$23). No credit cards. Fri–Wed 11am–10pm. Subway: Karasuma (1 minute). UDON.

Vegetable udon is primarily served here, and the house's traditional style is to serve the wheat noodles in a flat wooden bowl, the sauce in a pottery bowl, and the vegetables delicately arranged (sushi style) on a handmade platter, and a bowl of sesame seeds alongside. You dip and mix yourself, unlike in other udon shops where it all arrives like a stew swimming in one bowl. Casual atmosphere and healthy food at reasonable prices make this restaurant popular. A branch is near Ginkakuji (☎ 771-8994), one at Sanjo (☎ 255-2161), and one in New York.

Tohkasaikan

Nishizume, Shijo Ohashi. ☎ **075/221-1147.** Main dishes ¥1,000–¥2,700 ($10–$27); set meals ¥5,000–¥8,000 ($50–$80). AE, DC, JCB, MC, V. Daily 11:30am–9:30pm (last order). Bus: To Shijo-Kawaramachi. BEIJING CHINESE.

This Beijing-style Chinese restaurant, on Shijo Dori just west of the bridge spanning the Kamo River, is in a large, yellow stone building (it started out as a Western restaurant). It features an ancient elevator, lots of wood paneling, high ceilings, and old-fashioned decor. From June to mid-September you can sit outside on a wooden veranda (supported by stilts) over the Kamo River. If it's winter or raining, consider sitting in the fifth-floor dining room, which has nice views of the city. The best views, however, are from the rooftop garden, open during the summer, where you can order mugs of beer and dine on dishes from the extensive English-language menu, including sweet-and-sour pork, cooked shrimp with arrowroot, and chicken and green pepper. The service tends to be slow, and I've had better Chinese food, but the atmosphere is great and reminiscent of another era. The place is popular with families.

Zu Zu (77)

Takoyakushi-agaru, Pontocho. ☎ **075/231-0736.** ¥350–¥800 ($3.50–$8). AE, MC, V. Daily 6pm–midnight (last order). Bus: To Shijo-Kawaramachi (5 minutes). VARIED.

Staffed by friendly young Japanese, this small and informal restaurant/bar is on Pontocho, just north of the playground that splits the narrow pedestrian lane in half. It's on the inland side of the street—keep your eyes peeled for a white-stucco-and-stone facade and a menu in English. Eclectic mixes of Japanese, Chinese, and French food include rack of roast sparerib, chicken steak, scallops in butter sauce, and what the staff calls "garlic food."

EASTERN KYOTO

In addition to the restaurants discussed below, there are a lot of informal and inexpensive locales in and near Kiyomizu Temple, so you shouldn't have any problems finding a place to eat. If the weather is fine, you might wish to stop for noodles and a beer on the Kiyomizu Temple grounds, where you'll find several tatami-mat pavilions.

EXPENSIVE

Grand View

Miyako Hotel, Sanjo Keage. ☎ **075/771-7111.** Reservations recommended for a window seat. Set lunches ¥2,500–¥4,000 ($25–$40); set dinners ¥5,500–¥10,000 ($55–$100). AE, DC, JCB, MC, V. Daily 11:30am–2pm and 5–10pm. Directions: Free shuttle. FRENCH CROSSOVER.

With a view as grand as its name, a seasonal menu, chefs and sommelier trained in France, and the famous Miyako service, this restaurant is a fine place for a romantic meal in an elegant dining room of mauve and gold. The food prepared French style uses Asian ingredients and touches. Menu selections range from an appetizer of goose liver on sautéed bean curd mixed with yams and scallops to mashed Chinese yams wrapped with bread and roasted Canadian lobster. Even though only set menus are offered, one chooses from a variety of appetizers and main courses. The wine list includes French, Californian, German, and Italian wines.

✪ Hyotei (78)

Kusakawa-cho 35, Nanzenji. ☎ **075/771-4116.** Reservations required for kaiseki, recommended for obento. Kaiseki lunches from ¥18,000 ($180), dinners from ¥20,000 ($200); obento lunch boxes from ¥4,500 ($45); breakfast from ¥4,000 ($40). AE, DC, JCB, MC, V. Daily 8am–7pm. Closed the second and fourth Tues of month. Bus: To Nanzenji. KAISEKI/OBENTO.

East of Shirakawa Dori on the main road leading to Nanzenji Temple (look for a plain facade hidden behind a bamboo fence, with a sign shaped like a gourd), this three-centuries-old restaurant first opened its doors to serve pilgrims and visitors on their way to Nanzenji Temple.

Today it consists of two parts, one offering expensive kaiseki meals and the other offering seasonal obento lunch boxes. The kaiseki meals are served in separate tiny houses situated around a beautiful garden with a pond, maple trees, and bushes. The oldest house, which resembles a small teahouse, is more than 300 years old. Seating is on cushions on a tatami floor in your own private room, and your food is brought to you by kimono-clad women. The other part of the restaurant serves obento lunch boxes; the menu depends on the season, and seating here is at tables and chairs.

Mikaku (79)

Nawate Dori, Shijo-agaru, Gion. ☎ **075/525-1129.** Reservations recommended. Steak and shabu-shabu meals ¥5,000–¥15,000 ($50-$150); set lunches ¥4,500 ($45). AE, DC, JCB, MC, V. Mon–Sat noon–2:30pm and 5–9:30pm (last order). Bus: To Shijo Keihan-mae. JAPANESE STEAKHOUSE.

Established about 50 years ago by the present owner's grandfather, this restaurant in the heart of Gion is located in a 100-year-old building which was once a private home. The house specialty is an *aburayaki* meal, which consists of beef filet cooked with various vegetables and seasoned with soy sauce and wine. Sukiyaki, *mizudaki* (similar to shabu-shabu but stronger in taste), and teppanyaki are also served. If you order sukiyaki or mizudaki, you'll sit in your own private tatami room on the second floor. If you order teppanyaki, you'll sit at a counter where the chef (the first women teppanyaki chefs I've seen) will prepare your food in front of you on a hot griddle. Outside the window is a pleasant view of a canal. There's an English-language menu.

Minokichi of Kyoto

Sanjo-agaru, Dobutsuen-mae Street. ☎ **075/771-4185.** Reservations recommended for dinner and kaiseki orders. Kyo-kaiseki ¥15,000–¥30,000 ($150–$300); set dinners from ¥20,000 ($200); set lunches ¥15,000 ($150). AE, DC, JCB, MC, V. All rates include tax and service. Daily 11:30am–7:30pm (last order). Bus: To Jingumichi stop (3 minutes). KYO-KAISEKI.

One of Kyoto's best-known restaurants, Minokichi of Kyoto was first established more than 260 years ago and now has several branches in Japan, including a handful in Kyoto, Osaka, and Tokyo. This flagship restaurant consists of various dining venues in several buildings, the most enjoyable of which is tatami seating in the oldest building, with an open square hearth and views of a graceful bamboo garden. The specialty of the restaurant is Kyoto kaiseki, reflecting the gourmet dining style of the upper classes during the Heian Period more than 800 years ago. Emphasis is on the appearance of the food, with great care given to the selection and preparation of seasonal ingredients. Although the dishes themselves change, a kaiseki meal here always consists of eight items: appetizer, raw fish, soup, food cooked in delicate broth, steamed food, broiled food, deep-fried food, and vinegared food.

✪ Minoko (80)

480 Kiyoi-cho, Shimogawara-dori, Gion. ☎ **075/561-0328.** Reservations recommended for lunch, required for dinner. Kaiseki ¥13,000 ($130); mini-kaiseki lunch ¥10,000 ($100); obento lunch box ¥5,000 ($50). DC, MC, V. Daily 11:30am–11pm (last order 8pm). Closed second and fourth Wed of each month. Bus: To Yasaka Shrine/Gion. KAISEKI/OBENTO.

Formerly a villa, Minoko is an enclave of traditional Japan, with a simple, austere exterior and an interior of winding wooden corridors, tatami rooms, and a garden. Opened about 70 years ago by the present owner's father, Minoko does its best to retain the spirit of the tea ceremony. For lunch, for example, you can order an informal obento lunch box called *chabako-bento,* named after the lacquered box it's served in, which is traditionally used to carry tea utensils to outdoor tea ceremonies. It's served from 11:30am to 2:30pm. For lunch you can also order the *hiru-kaiseki,* a mini-kaiseki set meal. Lunch is served communally in a large tatami room with a view of a beautiful tea garden. If you come here for dinner, which features kaiseki, you'll eat in your own private tatami room. Elaborate kaiseki dinners include a special kind of kaiseki called *cha-kaiseki,* usually served at tea-ceremony gatherings. Minoko is just a couple of minutes' walk south of Yasaka Shrine.

MODERATE

Isobe (81)

In Maruyama Park, Ikenohata. ☎ **075/561-2216.** Set meals ¥2,800–¥14,000 ($28–$140). AE, DC, JCB, MC, V. Daily 11am–10pm. Bus: To Gion stop (10 minutes). VARIED JAPANESE.

A convenient place to stop for lunch if you're walking from Kiyomizu Temple to Heian Shrine, this restaurant is on the southeastern edge of Maruyama Park (if you're walking from Kiyomizu, take a right at the entrance to the park) and is easily recognized by its outdoor red umbrella (the logo also used for its sign). The same menu is available day and night and includes an obento, shabu-shabu, a tempura set meal for ¥3,300 ($33), and kaiseki. This modern, pleasant restaurant offers a nice view of the park from its dining room.

Junsei

60 Kusakawa-cho, Nanzenji. ☎ **075/761-2311.** Reservations required only for kaiseki. Tofu set meals ¥3,000–¥4,000 ($30–$40); kaiseki set meals ¥10,000–¥20,000 ($100–$200). AE, DC, JCB, MC, V. Daily 11am–7:30pm (last order). Bus: To Hosho Jicho. TOFU/KAISEKI/ OBENTO.

Located on the road to Nanzenji Temple, this restaurant specializing in tofu dishes opened in 1961, but the grounds and garden were originally part of a private institution established in the 1830s, during the shogun era. Although Junsei is popular with tour groups and is tourist-oriented, the food is good and an English-language menu makes ordering easy. There are several buildings spread throughout the grounds, and what you eat determines where you go—as soon as you arrive, you'll be given a menu and asked what you want to eat. I chose a *yudofu* (tofu) set meal and was directed to an older building filled with antiques and tatami mats. My meal came with vegetable tempura and various tofu dishes, including fried tofu on a stick and tofu boiled in a pot at my table. Other set meals include kaiseki (by reservation only) and shabu-shabu or sukiyaki. After your meal, be sure to take a stroll through the garden.

Le Grand Reve

Kyoto Park Hotel, Shichijo Dori. ☎ **075/525-3111.** Main dishes ¥1,500–¥2,500 ($15–$25); set dinners ¥6,000–¥10,000 ($60–$100); set lunches ¥2,800–¥5,000 ($28–$50). Daily 11am–3pm and 5–9pm (last order). Bus: To Sanjusangendo-mae. FRENCH/FRENCH KAISEKI.

There aren't many restaurants in this vicinity, making this a good place to go for lunch or dinner if you're visiting Sanjusangendo Hall or the Kyoto National Museum. Located on Shichijo Dori in the Park Hotel, this formal dining hall is small and intimate, overlooking a beautiful garden with a waterfall and pond. For lunch it serves a French kaiseki meal, which is French food prepared with the imagination of kaiseki and eaten with chopsticks. The menu changes with the seasons, but past main dishes have included sautéed chicken and grilled duck with lemon-and-honey sauce.

✪ Okutan (82)

86-30 Fukuchi-cho, Nanzenji. ☎ **075/771-8709.** Reservations recommended. Yudofu set meal ¥3,000 ($30); à la carte dishes ¥450–¥1,000 ($4.50–$10). No credit cards. Fri–Wed 10:30am–6pm (last order). Bus: To Eikando-mae stop. TOFU/VEGETARIAN.

This is one of the oldest, most authentic, and most delightful tofu restaurants in Kyoto, located just north of Nanzenji Temple's main gate (called the San Mon Gate). Founded about 350 years ago as a vegetarian restaurant serving Zen dishes to Buddhist monks, this wooden place with a thatched roof serves just one thing, a tofu set meal (yudofu), with the finishing touches provided by a pond, a garden, and peacefulness. Okutan is very simple and rustic, with seating either in tatami rooms or outdoors on cushioned platforms. Women dressed in traditional rural clothing bring your food. The tofu set meal includes boiled tofu, fried tofu, vegetable tempura, yam soup, and pickled vegetables. If you're still hungry, you can order some of the above items à la carte. This restaurant is especially delightful in fine weather. Highly recommended.

Inexpensive

Chorakukan (83)

Maruyama Park. ☎ **075/561-0001.** Main dishes ¥900–¥6,000 ($9–$60); set lunch ¥1,400 ($14). No credit cards. Daily 11am–7:30pm. Bus: to Gion/Yasaka Shrine (5 minutes). WESTERN.

There aren't many Western restaurants in eastern Kyoto, but if you're walking from Kiyomizu Temple to Heian Shrine, this informal establishment is tucked away in the southwest corner of Maruyama Park, in a large stone-and-brick Western-style building dating from the Meiji Period, with a huge stone lantern in its driveway. The building features elaborate woodwork and marble, but while the inexpensive Western restaurant downstairs is nothing fancy, it's restful; classical music plays in the background, and there's a view of some maple trees. The dishes include fried shrimp, grilled chicken with bacon, spaghetti, curry, and sandwiches. There are also lunch specials served from 11am to 3pm, when you have your choice of either a Western-style lunch or a Japanese-style box lunch. After lunch you may wish to retire to the building's coffee shop, a beautiful room reminiscent of European coffee shops.

Diabolo Menthe

Shirakawa Dori Higashi, Ginkakuji sagaru. ☎ **075/751-2887.** Set lunch ¥700–¥900 ($7–$9); main dishes ¥700 ($7). No credit cards. Fri–Wed 11am–7pm. Bus: To Ginkakuji. WESTERN.

Located one block east of Shirakawa Dori and south of Ginkakkuji-michi, this is a casual cafe serving pasta, salads, and hamburgers. The inexpensive lunch of the day is worth checking out. Just stopping for coffee? It goes for ¥350 ($3.50). Arty locals and foreign locals hang out here.

Goemonjaya (84)

67 Kukasawa-cho, Nanzenji. ☎ **075/751-9638.** ¥700–¥2,500 ($7–$25). No credit cards. Daily 11am–7:30pm (last order). Closed first and third Tues of each month. Bus: To Hosho Jicho. TOFU/TEMPURA/NOODLES.

An inexpensive restaurant serving tofu dishes, tempura, and noodles, Goemonjaya is across the street from Yachiyo Ryokan on the road leading to Nanzenji Temple. Look for its red lantern beside the road and for a display case of plastic food. This typical Japanese restaurant with tatami seating is back off the main road, past a red umbrella (summer only), a small garden, and a waterfall and pond (filled with carp).

Koan (85)

Shotekiin Temple, Fukuchi-cho, Nanzenji. ☎ **075/771-2781.** Set meals ¥3,000–¥5,000 ($30–$50); vegetarian dishes ¥300–¥1,000 ($3–$10). No credit cards. Thurs–Tues 11am–4:30pm. Bus: To Eikando-mae. TOFU/VEGETARIAN.

Situated just north of Nanzenji Temple, Koan is a simple restaurant on the grounds of a small temple, beside a large wooden gate that straddles the road. It offers vegetarian and tofu dishes characteristic of Zen temple meals usually served to monks, which you can eat in an open-air pavilion in the shade of a small and peaceful courtyard. There is a menu in English.

✪ Nakamuraro (86)

Yasaka-jinja-uchi, Gion. ☎ **075/561-0016.** Tofu dengaku obento ¥3,500 ($35); three sticks of tofu dengaku ¥600 ($6). No credit cards. Daily 11:30am–6pm for tofu obento, to 7pm for kaiseki. Closed last Thurs of each month. Bus: To Yasaka Shrine/Gion. TOFU/KAISEKI.

Opened 400 years ago to serve worshippers on their way to Yasaka Shrine, this tiny one-room teahouse is said to be the oldest restaurant in Japan. (It is now in its 12th generation of restaurateurs.) Located at the south entrance to Yasaka Shrine, right next to the stone torii gate, it has an open facade in summer and specializes in *tofu dengaku,* skewers of tofu smothered in miso sauce. Best is the *tofu dengaku obento.* If you simply want to try the restaurant's specialty but don't want to eat a complete meal, you can order three sticks of tofu dengaku. Beside the teahouse is a handsome wooden restaurant, added in the 19th century, where more expensive meals are served in lovely rooms overlooking a magnificent garden. In the evenings, kaiseki meals are served.

NORTHERN KYOTO

Knuckles New York Eatery

Kitaoji Senbon Higashi-iru. ☎ **075/441-5849.** Main ¥650–¥1,200 ($6.50–$12); sandwiches ¥1,000 ($10); set lunch ¥850 ($8.50). AE, MC, V. Tues–Sun 11am–10pm. Bus: 5 to Funaokayama. AMERICAN.

This is a haven for visitors to Daitokuji Temple and other sights in northern Kyoto, where you can have a real Reuben, pastrami, or grilled cheese sandwich. Or how about a Knuckle salad with tomato, lettuce, sprouts, avocado, cheese, and potato? The lunch specials served until 2:30pm are a great deal. Or take a break here for a drink—herb teas (¥400/$4), beer, and cocktails (¥600 to ¥700/$6 to $7), or margaritas by the pitcher (¥3,000/$30). And don't forget the New York cheesecake.

6 Attractions

Because Kyoto has 1,700 Buddhist temples, 300 Shinto shrines, and numerous gardens, museums, and other worthwhile sights, it's obvious that you must carefully plan your itinerary. Even the most avid sightseer can become jaded after days of visiting yet another temple or shrine—and after a while, how much can your memory retain? Be sure to temper your visits to cultural and historical sights with time spent simply walking around. Kyoto is a city best seen on your own two feet, exploring small alleyways and curio shops, pausing to soak in the beauty of its carefully landscaped gardens. If you spend your days in Kyoto racing around in a taxi or a bus from one temple to another, the essence of this ancient capital and its charm may literally pass you by.

SUGGESTED ITINERARIES

IF YOU HAVE 1 DAY If you have only a single day to spend in Kyoto, spend it in eastern Kyoto, including the stroll from Kiyomizu Temple to Heian Shrine, topping it off with a visit to the Silver Pavilion, and, if time permits, a short stop at the Kyoto Handicraft Center for some shopping. In the evening, visit Gion Corner, with its cultural demonstrations, topped with a stroll through Gion—and then start planning for your next trip back to Kyoto.

IF YOU HAVE 2 DAYS Spend the first day in eastern Kyoto, as outlined above. On the second day, visit Nijo Castle in central Kyoto; and Ryoanji Temple, with its famous rock garden; and the Golden Pavilion in northwestern Kyoto. End the day shopping in the Shijo-Kawaramachi shopping district. Eat dinner at a restaurant serving Kyoto cuisine, followed by a stroll down Pontocho. Such a two-day tour would present you a well-rounded view of Kyoto by giving you the chance to see temples, a shrine, gardens, and a former shogun's palace.

IF YOU HAVE 3 DAYS Spend the first two days in and around Kyoto, as outlined above. On the third day, head for Nara, Japan's ancient capital, and its many temples and historical attractions. If it's summer, spend the evening in Arashiyama, where you can board a wooden boat and observe cormorant fishing.

IF YOU HAVE 5 DAYS OR MORE Spend the first two days in eastern Kyoto, including the two strolls described later in this section. On the third day, add Nijo Castle, Ryoanji Temple, and the Golden Pavilion, as outlined in "If You Have Two Days," above. Spend the fourth day in Nara. On the fifth day, visit the Katsura Imperial Villa, Saihoji Moss Temple, or one of the other recommended destinations in the environs of Kyoto. An alternative is to visit those museums you haven't had time for, shop, or pursue your own interests.

THE TOP ATTRACTIONS

Before setting out on your walking tours (see below), be sure to stop by the Kyoto Tourist Information Center (TIC), located across from the Kyoto Station in the Kyoto Tower Building, Higashi-Shiokojicho, Shimogyo-ku (☎ 075/371-5649), to pick up a leaflet called "Walking Tour Courses in Kyoto." It contains four maps for strolling tours of Kyoto, including the walk from Kiyomizu Temple to Heian Shrine and on to the Silver Pavilion, which I've outlined below in more detail. The TIC also has city maps and a colorful brochure listing Kyoto's most important sites.

Keep in mind, too, that you must enter Kyoto's museums, shrines, and temples at least a half hour before closing time.

EASTERN KYOTO

The eastern part of Kyoto, embracing the area of Higashiyama-ku, with its Kiyomizu Temple, and stretching up all the way to the Silver Pavilion (Ginkakuji Temple), is probably the richest in terms of culture and charm. Although the walking-tour leaflet distributed by the TIC claims that you can walk from Kiyomizu Temple to Heian Shrine in 50 minutes, I don't see how it would be possible unless you ran the whole way. I've walked this route at least six times and it's always taken me the better part of a day—perhaps I'm slow, but it's a pace that I've found does justice to this wonderful area of Kyoto.

The two strolls I've listed below, one through Higashiyama-ku and the other so-called Philosophers' Stroll, are logical continuations of each other. If you don't finish Higashiyama-ku in one day, therefore, you could start where you left off on the following day and then continue on with the Philosophers' Stroll. In any case, since eastern Kyoto has some of the city's most traditional and beautiful restaurants, be sure to read through the dining section to decide beforehand where you might want to eat lunch or dinner. The majority of the traditional restaurants are in the vicinity of Nanzenji Temple. If you'd like to try a tea ceremony, the Miyako (☎ 075/771-7111) has instruction in English, a pamphlet on *chado* (the way of tea), and a nice tea utensils shop. Because of the hotel's location, you could start your sightseeing day or end it with that tea ceremony. No reservations are necessary (though if you're limited on time, its better to make one), and the cost is ¥1,133 ($11.33) for the one-hour ceremony.

NORTHWESTERN KYOTO

The inspiration for the Silver Pavilion (see Walking Tours, below) was **Kinkakuji,** the Gold Pavilion (☎ 075/461-0013), which you can reach by taking bus 205 from Kyoto Station (platform B3) to the Kinkakuji-michi stop. One of Kyoto's best-known attractions, it was constructed in the 1390s as a retirement villa for Shogun Ashikaga Yoshimitsu and features a three-story pavilion covered in gold leaf and topped with a bronze phoenix on its roof. Apparently, the retired shogun lived in shameless luxury while the rest of the nation suffered from famine, earthquakes, and plague. If you come here on a clear day, the Gold Pavilion shimmers against a blue sky, its reflection captured in the waters of a calm pond. However, this pavilion is not the original. In 1950 a disturbed student monk burned Kinkakuji to the ground, a story told by author Mishima Yukio in his famous novel *The Temple of the Golden Pavilion.* The temple was rebuilt in 1955. Be sure to explore the surrounding park, with its moss-covered grounds and teahouses. It's open daily from 9am to 5:30pm (from October to March until 5pm). Admission is ¥400 ($4).

About a half-hour walk southwest of the Gold Pavilion is **Ryoanji Temple** (☎ 075/462-2216), with what is probably the most famous Zen rock garden in all of Japan. Fifteen rocks set in waves of raked white pebbles are surrounded on three sides by a wall and on the fourth by a wooden veranda. Sit down here and contemplate what the artist was trying to communicate. The interpretation of the rocks is up to the individual (to my mind they look like mountains rising up from the sea). My only objection to this peaceful place is that, unfortunately, it's usually not peaceful—a loudspeaker extols the virtue of the garden, destroying any chance for peaceful meditation. If you get here early enough, you may be able to escape both the crowds and the noise. After visiting the rock garden, be sure to take a walk around the 1,000-year-old pond. At one corner is a beautiful little restaurant with tatami rooms and screens, where you can eat yudofu (boiled tofu with vegetables) for ¥1,700 ($17) or drink a beer and enjoy the view. Note that if you order only a beer, which costs ¥550 ($5.50), an extra ¥300 ($3) will be added to the bill. The view, however, is well worth it. Ryoanji is open daily from 8am to 5pm in summer, to 4:30pm in winter. Admission is ¥400 ($4).

Ready for some fun? How about going to the **Toei Uzumasa Eiga Mura** (Toei Uzumasa Movieland), 10 Higashihachigaokacho Uzumasa Ukyo-ku (☎ 075/881-7716), where many of Japan's samurai flicks are made? Open daily from 9am to 5pm (9:30am to 4pm December through February) and closed December 21 to January 1, it charges an admission of ¥2,000 ($20) for adults and ¥900 ($9) for children. Resembling an amusement park more than a movie studio, it has both outdoor and indoor sets, and if you're lucky you'll see a movie in the making. Reconstructed houses re-create the mood, setting, and atmosphere of feudal Japan, while indoor museums show miniature castles, houses, and items from the history of Japanese film. Who knows, you may even see a famous star walking around dressed in samurai garb. You can also have a photo taken of yourself decked out in a kimono or samurai gear. Since Movieland is clearly a commercial venture, come here only if you have a lot of time, are sick of temples, or have youngsters in tow. To reach it, take bus 71, 72, or 73 to the Uzumasa Koryoji stop.

Central Kyoto

Much of central Kyoto has been taken over by the 20th century, but there are a few interesting sites worth investigating. **Kyoto Imperial Palace** (☎ 075/221-1215), near the Imadegawa subway station, is where the imperial family lived from 1331 until 1868, when they moved to Tokyo. The palace was destroyed several times by fire, and the present buildings date from 1855. Modestly furnished, with delicate decorations, the palace shows the restful designs of the peaceful Heian Period. The gardens are graceful. Permission to visit the palace must be obtained in advance from the Imperial Household Agency Office (☎ 075/211-1215) on the Imperial Palace grounds near the Inui Gomon Gate. It's open Monday through Friday from 8:45am to noon and 1 to 4pm (closed on national holidays and December 25 to January 4). Foreign visitors may apply in person, one day in advance or on the same day, by arriving before 9:40am for the 10am English-language tour or before 1:40pm for the 2pm tour, also in English. For the tours on the third Saturday of every month and every Saturday of April, May, October, and November, apply one day in advance. You have to be over 20 years of age (or be accompanied by an adult) and have no more than four people in your party to apply. Be sure to bring your passport. The tours are free but are conducted quickly, leaving little time for dawdling or taking photographs.

Whereas the Imperial Palace is where the royal family resided, **Nijo Castle,** Horikawa Dori (☎ 075/341-0096), is where the Tokugawa shogun stayed whenever he left Edo and visited Kyoto. It was built by the first Tokugawa shogun, Ieyasu, and is considered the quintessence of Momoyama architecture, with delicate transom wood carvings and paintings on sliding doors. The castle has 33 rooms, some 800 tatami mats, and an understated elegance, especially when compared to the castles being built in Europe at the same time. All the sliding doors on the outside walls of the castle can be removed in summer, breezes to sweep through the building. Typical for Japan at the time, rooms were unfurnished, the mattresses stored in closets.

To protect the shogun from real or imagined enemies, the castle was protected by a moat and stone walls. How deep the shogun's paranoia ran, however, is apparent by the installation of the so-called nightingale floor inside the castle itself. Corridors were fitted with floorboards that squeaked when trod upon, and there were hidden alcoves for bodyguards.

Outside the castle is a garden famous in its own right, designed by the renowned gardener Kobori Enshu. The original grounds of the castle, however, were without trees—supposedly because the falling of leaves in autumn reminded the shogun and his tough samurai of life's transitory nature, making them terribly sad. Incidentally, I prefer Nijo Castle to the Imperial Palace because you can explore its interior on your own.

Nijo Castle is open daily from 8:45am to 4pm; the garden remains open until 5pm. The ¥500 ($5) admission covers both the castle and the garden.

A newer attraction in central Kyoto is the **Museum of Kyoto,** Sanjo-Takakura (☎ 075/222-0888), which opened in 1988. Through video displays, slides, and even holograms, the *Kyoto Bunka Hakubutsukan* attempts to present the 1,200 years of Kyoto's history. Exhibited are prehistoric relics, glassware, fans, crafts, and artwork. The third-floor exhibition hall displays the works of contemporary artists and craftspeople. My only complaint is that explanations are in Japanese only—if enough people complain, maybe this will be corrected. Be sure to check out the holographic display of workers constructing the vermilion-colored shrine. A special feature of the museum is its film library, containing hundreds of Japanese classics, from silent movies to those filmed up to 20 years ago (the Japanese movie industry was based in Kyoto for decades). Movies are shown twice daily (at last check, at 2 and 6:15pm, but you'd be wise to confirm the time), and admission is included in the museum entry fee. The museum is open daily from 10am to 8:30pm, closed the third Wednesday of the month. Admission is ¥500 ($5), and it's a three-minute walk from the Oike subway station.

About a mile north of Nijo Castle is the **Nishijin Textile Center** or *Nishijin-Ori Kaikan* (☎ 451-9231), dedicated to the weavers who for centuries produced elegant textiles for the imperial family and the nobility. The history of Nishijin textiles began with the history of Kyoto itself back in 794, and by the Edo Period there were an estimated 5,000 weaving factories. The museum regularly holds weaving demonstrations, historical displays, and kimono shows. Admission to the hall itself is free; the kimono show costs ¥360 ($3.60). Hours for the textile hall are 9am to 5pm daily, and it's located on Horikawa Dori, Imadegawa-minamiiru, Kamigyo-ku, about a seven-minute walk from the Imadegawa subway station.

If you're interested in learning more about the Kyo-Yuzen method for dyeing silk for kimono, visit **Kodai Yuzen-en** (☎ 075/811-8101), a couple of minutes' walk northwest of the Horikawa Dori and Gojo Street intersection. It has displays and demonstrations showing the 300-year history of Yuzen dyeing, plus a shop where

Frommer's Favorite Kyoto Experiences

A Night in a Ryokan. Kyoto is one of the best places in Japan to experience the traditional inn, where guests sleep on futon in a tatami room and are treated to elaborate Japanese meals.

A Tofu Vegetarian Meal in a Garden Setting. *Shojin ryoori,* vegetarian meals served at Buddhist temples, are one of Kyoto's specialties. They're served at a number of rustic restaurants with outdoor seating in a garden.

A Visit to a Japanese Garden. Kyoto has a wide range of traditional gardens, from Zen rock gardens once used by priests for meditation to miniature landscape gardens that once belonged to the ruling classes.

A Stroll Through Eastern Kyoto. Temples, shrines, gardens, shops, and traditional neighborhoods are highlights of a day spent walking through this historic part of Kyoto.

Nishi-Koji Dori. This fish-and-produce market right in the heart of the city puts visitors in direct contact with Kyoto's residents, as both housewives and restaurant owners buy their day's food, just as their ancestors did for more than 300 years.

Shopping for Traditional Crafts. Passed down from generation to generation, traditional arts and crafts thrive in Kyoto, with small specialty shops selling everything from fans to wooden combs.

A Visit to Gion. Kyoto's traditional pleasure quarter, where geisha entertain businessmen on expense accounts, is fascinating for its austere architecture, hushed atmosphere, and the sight of geishas hurrying to their evening appointments.

Cormorant Fishing. There's no more romantic way to spend a summer's evening than drifting down the river in a wooden boat decorated with paper lanterns, watching men at work fishing with the help of cormorants.

An Evening's Stroll Through Pontocho. A small, narrow pedestrian lane, Pontocho is lined with hostess bars, restaurants, and drinking establishments. End the evening seated on the banks of the nearby Kamo River, a popular spot for Kyoto's young couples.

Yuzen goods are sold. It's open daily from 9am to 5pm and charges a ¥500 ($5) admission. To reach it, take bus 9 or 28 from Kyoto Station to the Horikawa-Matsubara stop.

If you've never been to a market in Japan, you'll probably want to take a stroll down **Nishiki-Koji Dori,** a fish-and-produce market right in the heart of town. A covered pedestrian lane stretching west from Teramachi Dori (and just north of Shijo Dori), Nishiki-Koji has been Kyoto's principal food market for more than three centuries. This is where the city's finest restaurants and inns buy their food, and you'll find open-fronted shops and stalls selling seasonal vegetables, fish, beans, seaweed, pickled vegetables, and more. Shops are open from the early-morning hours until about 7 or 8pm; many close on either Wednesday or Sunday.

Around Kyoto Station

Just north of Kyoto Station are two massive temple compounds, **Nishi-Honganji** and **Higashi-Honganji.** They were once joined as one huge religious center called Honganji, but split after a disagreement several centuries ago. Higashi-Honganji is Kyoto's largest wooden structure, while Nishi-Honganji is the older temple and represents an outstanding example of Buddhist architecture. Only parts of both temples are open to the public; however, you can phone (☎ 075/371-5181 in Japanese only) for an appointment to visit.

North of these two temples, on Horikawa Dori, is the **Costume Museum,** on the fifth floor of the Izutsu Building, Shinhanaya-cho kado (☎ 075/351-8388). Though small, it includes traditional Japanese clothing, ranging from hunting outfits worn during the Kamakura Period to ceremonial court dress, including elaborate kimono. About a 20-minute hike from Kyoto Station, it's open Monday through Saturday from 9am to 5pm; admission is ¥300 ($3).

NEARBY ATTRACTIONS

If this is your first visit to Kyoto and you're here only a short while, you should concentrate on the sightseeing sites in Kyoto itself. If, however, this is your second trip to Kyoto or you're here for an extended period of time, there are a number of worthwhile attractions in the region surrounding Kyoto.

Note: The Katsura Imperial Villa, Shugakuin Imperial Villa, and Saihoji (popularly called the Moss Temple) all require advance permission to visit. To see the Katsura Imperial Villa or Shugakuin Imperial Villa, you follow the same procedure as for the Kyoto Imperial Palace—that is, you must apply for permission in person at the Imperial Household Agency Office the day of (only in the off-season) or before (at least a week, to be sure) the tour (see the information on the imperial palace, above, for the agency's location, office hours, and other requirements). Unfortunately those under age 20 may not visit Katsura or Shugakuin. Tours are conducted in Japanese only, but an English-language video is shown. The time of your tour will be designated when you apply.

KATSURA IMPERIAL VILLA Located about a 15-minute walk from Katsura Station on the Hankyu railway line or a 30-minute bus ride from Kyoto Station (take bus 33 to the Katsura Rikyu Mae stop), the Katsura Imperial Villa is considered the jewel of traditional Japanese architecture and landscape gardening. It was built between 1620 and 1624 by Prince Toshihito, brother of the emperor, and construction was continued by Toshihito's son. The garden, markedly influenced by Kobori Enshu, Japan's most famous garden designer, is a "stroll garden" in which each turn of the path brings an entirely new view.

The first thing you notice upon entering Katsura is its simplicity—the buildings were all made of natural materials, and careful attention was paid to the slopes of the roofs and to the grain, texture, and color of the various woods used. A pavilion for viewing the moon, a hall for imperial visits, a teahouse, and other buildings are situated around a pond, and as you walk along the pathway you are treated to views that literally change with each step you take. Islets, stone lanterns, various scenes (representing the seashore, mountains, and hamlets), manicured trees, and bridges of stone, earth, or wood that arch gracefully over the water—everything is perfectly balanced. No matter where you stand, the view is complete and in harmony. Every detail was carefully planned, down to the stones used in the pathways, the way the trees twist, and how scenes are reflected in the water. Little wonder that the Katsura Imperial Villa has influenced architecture not only in Japan but around the world.

SHUGAKUIN IMPERIAL VILLA Located about a 15-minute walk from the Shugakuin Rikyu Michi bus stop (take bus 5 from Kyoto Station), the Shugakuin Imperial Villa was built in the mid-1600s for Emperor Go-Mizunoo, who became a monk after his abdication. Its stroll garden, among Kyoto's largest, is divided into three levels. The upper garden, with its lake, islands, and waterfalls, is the most extensive of the three and uses the principle known as "borrowed landscape," in which the surrounding landscape is incorporated into the overall garden design. The gardens are more spacious than most Japanese-style gardens, and the view of the surrounding countryside is grand.

SAIHOJI Popularly known as Kokedera, the Moss Temple, Saihoji is famous for its velvety-green moss garden spread underneath the trees. Altogether, there are more than 40 different varieties of moss throughout the grounds, giving off an iridescent and mysterious glow that's at its best just after a rain. Because the monks are afraid that huge numbers of visitors would trample the moss to death, prior permission is needed to visit Saihoji, which you can obtain by writing to the temple at least 10 days in advance. The address is Saihoji Temple, Matsuo Kamigaya-cho, Nishikyo-ku, Kyoto (☎ 075/391-3631), and you should give your name, address, age, occupation, and the date you'd like to visit (plus second and third choices). Include a self-addressed return envelope and International Reply Coupons for return postage. (If you are in Japan, you should send a double postcard or *ofuku hagaki.*) The cost of a temple visit, which includes Sutra writing demonstrations, is an offering of at least ¥3,000 ($30) and can be paid when you pick up your ticket. To reach Saihoji, take bus 73 from Kyoto Station to the Kokedera stop.

ENRYAKUJI TEMPLE Along with Mt. Koya, south of Osaka, Enryakuji Temple (☎ 0775/78-0551) is one of the most important centers of Buddhism in Japan. Located atop Mt. Hiei, Enryakuji Temple was founded back in 788 at the order of Emperor Kammu to ward off evil spirits that might come from the northeast. At one time, Enryakuji Temple consisted of as many as 3,000 buildings and maintained an army of warrior monks that made raids on rival temples. Because of the temple's political and military power, an army organized by Nobunaga Oda attacked Enryakuji and destroyed it in 1571. Although some of the temple was subsequently rebuilt, it never again reached its former powerful position. However, there are a number of fine buildings spread out under large cedar trees in a peaceful atmosphere. Open daily, in summer from 8:30am to 4:30pm and in winter from 9am to 4pm, it charges a ¥500 ($5) admission. To reach it, take bus 16 or 17 or the Keihan Electric Railway to Demachiyanagi Station and transfer there to the Eisan Electric Railway Line bound for Yase-yuen, the last stop. There you'll find the Keifuku Cable Car, followed by the Hieizan Ropeway, which will take you to the top. The entire trip takes approximately an hour.

BYODOIN TEMPLE Located in the town of Uji, about 11 miles southeast of Kyoto, Byodoin Temple (☎ 0774/21-2861) is a good example of temple architecture of the Heian Period. Originally a villa, it was converted into a temple in 1053. Most famous is the main hall, known as the Phoenix Hall, the only original building remaining. It has three wings, creating an image of the mythical bird of China, the phoenix, and on the gable ends are two bronze phoenixes. On the temple grounds is one of the most famous bells in Japan, as well as a monument to Yorimasa Minamoto, who took his own life here after being defeated by the rival Taira clan. Byodoin is located about a 10-minute walk from the Uji JR Station (there's a map of the town in front of the station). Admission is ¥400 ($4), and though the grounds of the temple are open daily from 8:30am to 5pm, note that the Phoenix Hall is open from 9am to 5pm.

FUSHIMI-INARI SHRINE Just a minute's walk from the JR Inari Station, Fushimi-Inari Shrine has long been popular with merchants, who come here to pray for success and prosperity. One of Japan's most celebrated Shinto shrines, it was founded back in 711 and is dedicated to the goddess of rice. The $2^1/_2$-mile-long pathway behind the shrine is lined with more than 10,000 red torii gates, presented by worshippers throughout the ages, and there are also stone foxes, which are considered messengers of the gods. It's a glorious walk as you wind through the woods and then gradually climb a hill, from where you have a good view of Kyoto. At several places along the path are small shops where you can sit down for a bowl of noodles or other refreshment. Admission is free, and the expansive grounds never close.

Note: Both Byodoin Temple and Fushimi-Inari Shrine are on the same JR line that continues to Nara. If you plan on spending the night in Nara, you could easily take in these two attractions on the way.

CORMORANT FISHING IN ARASHIYAMA If you're lucky enough to be in Kyoto during July and August, I highly recommend that you spend one evening on the Oi River, drifting in a wooden boat and watching men fishing with trained cormorants (seabirds). Cormorant fishing is held in Arashiyama every evening (except when there's a full moon or during and after a heavy rain) from July 1 to August 31. You should reach Arashiyama before 7pm, and for a fee of ¥1,500 ($15) you can board a narrow wooden boat gaily decorated with paper lanterns. Along with dozens of others, your boatman will pole you down the river so that you can see the fishing boats lit by blazing torches. The cormorants, with rings around their necks so that they don't swallow the fish they catch, dive under the water for ayu, a small river fish. Water taxis ply the river offering snacks and beer. I find the whole experience of watching the cormorants, and of being a part of the flotilla of wooden boats and paper lanterns, terribly romantic. It's a lovely way to spend a warm summer's evening.

You can reach Arashiyama by bus 71, 72, or 73 from Kyoto Station to the Arashiyama stop, followed by a one-minute walk; or by taking the JR Sagano Line from Kyoto Station to Saga Station, from which it's a 15-minute walk.

A MAZE Just trying to find your way around Japan's big cities can be challenging enough, but if you enjoy frustration at every turn, visit the **Kyoto Daigo Granmaze** (☎ 075/621-2207), a specially constructed maze for humans. Opened in 1985, the Kyoto Granmaze was the start of the maze craze that has since spread to other parts of Japan. Covering an area about half the size of a football field, this maze features wooden walls about 6½ feet tall, with lookout towers posted every so often to let you survey your position.

Although the record time for finding one's way out is eight minutes, it takes most people about an hour. If you take longer, don't feel bad—one person wandered around for four hours and 34 minutes before reaching the finish line. To get to the Granmaze, take the Keihan Uji Line to Rokujizo Station, from which it's about a seven-minute walk north of the station (make sure you have the right line—otherwise you might well end up in Osaka, with more frustration than you bargained for). The Granmaze opens daily at 9am, and lost souls are flushed out at sunset. Admission is ¥700 ($7).

ESPECIALLY FOR CHILDREN

There are several attractions listed above that would appeal to children. When they need to run and play, take them to **Maruyama Park,** described below in my first Walking Tour. An alternative is the **Philosophers' Stroll,** a one-mile walk along a tree-lined canal; see my second Walking Tour. The **Toei Uzumasa Eiga Mura** (Movieland) in northwestern Kyoto, where samurai flicks are filmed, is Japan's answer to Hollywood's MGM Studios. Your youngsters will be able to wander through a mock feudal village and see people dressed in period costumes. For teenagers, cormorant fishing in Arashiyama may be a fun way to spend an evening. The Rapids

Shooting Tour (see "Organized Tours," below) provides a different kind of river excitement.

ORGANIZED TOURS

Although I believe being herded around Kyoto's temples in a large group can never compete with the experience of wandering around at your own leisure, you may find yourself so short of time you feel compelled to join an organized tour. Both morning and afternoon tours are offered by the **Japan Travel Bureau** (☎ 075/341-1413) and the **Kintetsu Gray Line** (☎ 075/691-0903). Sites visited may include the Imperial Palace, Nijo Castle, the Golden Pavilion, Heian Shrine, Sanjusangendo Hall, and Kiyomizu Temple. Three-hour tours cost about ¥5,000 ($50) for adults and ¥4,000 ($40) for children.

For those who want a more personalized tour, **student guides** from Kyoto, Doshisha, and Kyoto Women's Universities are available through the **Tourist Information Center (TIC),** Kyoto Tower Building, Higashi-Shiokojicho, Shimogyo-ku (☎ 075/371-5649). (Students are happy to act as voluntary guides because they can practice their English.) You must apply at the TIC one or two days in advance, and you're expected to pay for the student's transportation, entrance fees to shrines and temples, and lunch.

Another tour that you may consider joining is the **Rapids Shooting Tour** (☎ 07712/2-5846). March through November, flat-bottomed wooden boats depart from Kameoka seven times daily, with fewer departures in heated boats during the winter months. The trip lasts about two hours and covers approximately 10 miles of the Hozu River, ending in Arashiyama. The rapids are not dangerous (in fact, most of them are nothing more than small riffles), and the trip is a very pleasant and relaxing way to see something of the surrounding countryside of wooded hills and a winding gorge. The cost of the trip is ¥3,700 ($37) for adults and ¥2,000 ($20) for children. To reach Kameoka, take the San'in JR Line from Kyoto Station to Kameoka Station, from which it's an eight-minute walk. For more information on the tour or how to get to Kameoka, contact the TIC.

WALKING TOUR 1
Higashiyama-ku

Start: Sanjusangendo Hall, Shichijo Dori.
Finish: Kyoto Handicraft Center, Kumano Jinja Higashi.
Time: Allow approximately six hours, including stops for shopping and museums.
Best Times: Weekdays, when temples and shops aren't as crowded.
Worst Times: Monday, when museums are closed.

A stroll through Higashiyama-ku will take you to Kiyomizu Temple and Heian Shrine, two of Kyoto's most famous attractions, as well as through some of Kyoto's most charming neighborhoods en route. To reach Sanjusangendo Hall, located just south of Shichijo Dori, a block or so east of the Kamo River, walk 20 minutes from Kyoto Station or take bus 206 to the Sanjusangendo-mae stop.

1. **Sanjusangendo Hall** is the name popularly given to Rengeoin Temple (☎ 075/525-0033). The hall is only some 50 feet wide, but it stretches almost 400 feet—and it's filled with more than 1,000 images of the thousand-handed Kannon. There are row upon row of these gold figures glowing in the dark hall, and in the middle is a large seated figure of Kannon, flanked by her 28 disciples. The large Kannon was carved in 1254 by Tankei, a famous sculptor from the Kamakura

Walking Tour—Higashiyama-ku

Period, and the hall itself dates from 1266. At the back of the hall is a 130-yard-long archery range, where a competition is held every January 15. Sanjusangendo is open daily, from 8am to 5pm (enter by 4:30pm) in summer and 8am to 4pm (enter by 3:30pm) in winter. Admission is ¥500 ($5).

Across the street and to the northeast of Sanjusangendo Hall is the:

2. **Kyoto National Museum** (*Kokuritsu Hakubutsukan*), 527 Chaya machi (☎ 075/541-1151). Established in the latter half of the last century as a repository for art objects and treasures that belonged to both Kyoto's temples and individuals, it displays historical items, artwork, and handcrafts, including a great collection of ceramics, Japanese paintings, calligraphy, lacquerware, textiles, and sculptures. Admission is ¥400 ($4), and the museum is open Tuesday through Sunday from 9am to 4pm.

TAKE A BREAK Just past the National Museum is the Park Hotel, where you'll find the delightful **Le Grand Rêve,** a restaurant with views of a beautiful garden and serving French kaiseki—that is, served in courses and eaten with chopsticks. (See "Dining," earlier in this chapter, for more details.)

Just beyond the Park Hotel is Higashioji Dori, where you should take a left and walk 5 minutes or so until you come to the big intersection with the overpass to Gojo Dori, turn left at the first street to reach:

3. **Kawai Kanjiro Memorial House** (☎ 075/561-3585), the home and studio of the well-known and internationally decorated potter Kawai Kanjiro. A supporter of Japanese crafts, this versatile man made much of the furniture and furnishings in his former home, now a delightful museum. Admission is ¥700 ($7). Go back to Gojo Dori and take a right onto the diagonal road leading uphill across the street called:
4. **Gojo-zaka.** It's lined with pottery shops, but don't go crazy shopping yet—there are many more shops to come. At the top of Gojo-zaka are stairs leading to:
5. **Kiyomizu Temple** (☎ 075/551-1234). First founded in 798 and rebuilt in 1633 by the third Tokugawa shogun, Iemitsu, the temple occupies an exalted spot. The main hall is built over a cliff and features a large wooden veranda supported by 139 pillars, each 49 feet high. The magnificence of the height and view is so well known to the Japanese that the idiom "jumping from the veranda of Kiyomizu Temple" means that they're about to undertake some particularly bold or daring adventure. To appreciate the grandeur of the main hall with its pillars and dark wood, walk to the three-story pagoda, which affords the best view of the main hall, built without the use of a single nail. From the pagoda, descend the steps to Otowa Fall, where you'll see Japanese lined up to drink from the refreshing spring water. The temple is open daily from 8am to 6pm and charges ¥300 ($3) admission.

TAKE A BREAK On the grounds of Kiyomizu Temple, just beside Otowa Fall, is **an open-air pavilion** where you can sit on tatami and enjoy noodles and a beer or shaved ice colored with various flavors. This is a great place to stop (and now you know why this walk takes me all day). If you're lucky to be here in fall, the fiery reds of the maple trees will set the countryside around you on fire. These pavilions are open Friday through Wednesday from 9am to 5pm.

Before departing Kiyomizu Temple, be sure to make a stop at:

6. **Jishu Shrine** (☎ 075/541-2097), regarded as a dwelling place of the deity in charge of love and a good match. This vermilion-colored Shinto shrine (free admission) is easy to spot, located as it is behind and to the left of Kiyomizu's main

temple hall. There's an English-language pamphlet that gives the history of the shrine, and throughout the grounds are signs and descriptions in English telling about its various parts; for once you're not left in the dark as to the purpose of the various statues and memorials and what the Japanese are doing as they make their rounds. Very enriching. You can buy various good-luck charms for everything from a happy marriage to easy delivery of a child to success in passing an examination. On the shrine's grounds are two stones placed about 30 feet apart—if you're able to walk from one stone to the other with your eyes closed, you're supposedly guaranteed success in your love life. It sure doesn't hurt to try.

From Kiyomizu Temple, take the road leading downhill directly in front of the temple's main gate, where you'll find shop after shop selling sweets, pottery, fans, ties, hats, souvenirs, and curios. It's okay to go crazy shopping here, but remember, you're going to have to carry whatever you buy. After passing a couple of small shrines nestled in among the shops, you'll come to a split in the road and a shrine on the right shaded by trees in front. Just beside this shrine are steps leading downhill to the right to a place called:

7. **Sannenzaka Slope.** It leads past lovely antiques and curio shops and winds through neighborhoods of wooden buildings reminiscent of old Kyoto. Eventually you'll come to:
8. **Ryozen Kannon Temple,** with its huge white statue dedicated to Japan's unknown soldiers who died in World War II. Past Ryozen Kannon Temple and just before the street ends at a pagoda with a crane on top, keep your eyes peeled for a teahouse on your right.

TAKE A BREAK The **Kodaiji Rakusho Tea Room** (87) (☎ 075/561-6892) at 517 Washiochiyo is a lovely place, one of my favorite tearooms in Kyoto. It has a 100-year-old miniature garden, which you can glimpse from the street through a gate and which contains a pond with some of the largest carp I've ever seen, some of which are 20 years old and winners of those many medals displayed in the back room. In summer, stop for *somen* (finely spun cold noodles), tea, or traditional desserts, and refresh yourself with views of the small but beautiful garden. Open from 9:30am to 5:30pm; closed one day a week, but not on a fixed day.

Continuing on your stroll, take a right at the pagoda and then an immediate left, which marks the beginning of:

9. **Maruyama Park.** This is one of Kyoto's most popular city parks, filled with ponds, pigeons, and gardens. In spring, this is one of the most popular spots for the viewing of cherry blossoms. Beside Maruyama Park is:
10. **Yasaka Shrine,** also known as **Gion Shrine** for its proximity to the Gion district. Its present buildings date from 1654, and its stone torii on the south side are considered among the largest in Japan. Admission here is free.

TAKE A BREAK If you need a meal more substantial than the open-air pavilions at Kiyomizu or the teahouse were able to provide, good choices for Japanese food are **Nakamuraro,** a 400-year-old teahouse located next to Yasaka Shrine's stone torii and serving skewers of grilled tofu, and **Isobe,** located on the southern edge of Maruyama Park and offering obento lunch boxes, tempura, shabu-shabu, and an assortment of Japanese cuisine. For Western food, there's the **Chorakukan,** located in a Meiji-era building at the southwest corner of Maruyama Park. (See "Dining," earlier in this chapter, for more details on all three establishments.)

After taking your time strolling through Maruyama Park, you'll come to:

11. Chion-in Temple (☎ 075/531-2111), founded in 1234 as a center of the Jodo sect of Buddhism. Famous for its enormous gate, rising almost 80 feet, the temple also has Japan's largest bell, weighing 74 tons. Entrance to the temple precincts is free; if you wish to visit its treasure hall, the admission is ¥400 ($4). It's open daily from 9am to 4pm. Just north of Chion-in is:

12. Shoren-in Temple (☎ 075/561-2345), built as a villa for the abbots of a Buddhist sect. The present buildings date from 1895. The temple has an impressive 15th-century garden, considered one of the best in Kyoto. Open daily from 9am to 5pm (last entry at 4:30pm), it charges an admission of ¥400 ($4).

From Shoren-in Temple, continue walking north on Jingumichi Dori Avenue, passing Sanjo and Niomon Dori (you'll know you're on the right track when you spot the vermilion-colored torii gate straddling a street busy with traffic). You'll soon come to several museums you might want to stop in on, among them the:

13. Kyoto Municipal Museum of Art or *Kyoto-shi Bijitsukan* (☎ 075/771-4107), which is the city's repository for local art, while the:

14. National Museum of Modern Art or *Kyoto Kokuritsu Kindai Bijutsukan* (☎ 075/761-4111) offers changing exhibitions of modern art. It's open Tuesday through Sunday from 9:30am to 5pm (to 8pm on Friday). My favorite, however, is the:

15. Kyoto Municipal Museum of Traditional Industry (*Kyoto-shi Dento Sangyo Kaikan*) (☎ 075/761-3421). Crafts displayed and sold here range from pottery to lacquerware to textiles, bamboo products, damascene jewelry, knives, and dolls. Prices are high, but so is the quality. There are also frequent demonstrations by local artists. Unfortunately, the museum was closed for several years for remodeling but was due to open in 1996, so check with the Tourist Information Center.

Directly north of the museums is:

16. Heian Shrine. If orange and green are your favorite colors, you're going to love this shrine, one of Kyoto's most famous. Although it was built as late as 1895, in commemoration of the 1,100th anniversary of the founding of Kyoto, Heian Shrine is a replica of the first imperial palace, built in Kyoto in 794, giving you some idea of the architecture back then. The most important thing to see here, however, is the garden, the entrance to which is on your left as you face the main hall. Admission is ¥500 ($5), and daily hours are 8:30am to 5:30pm (to 4:30pm in winter). Typical of gardens constructed during the Meiji Era, it's famous for its weeping cherry trees in spring, its irises and water lilies in summer, and its changing maple leaves in fall.

After visiting Heian Shrine, you may want to stop off to do some shopping at the:

17. Kyoto Handicraft Center (☎ 075/761-5080), located behind the shrine on its north side, open daily from 10am to 6pm (to 5:30pm December through February). It's the best place in Kyoto for one-stop shopping for souvenirs of Japan, including pearls, kimono and yukata, fans, paper products, and more. (See "Shopping," later in this chapter, for complete information.)

WALKING TOUR 2
Philosophers' Stroll

Start: Nanzenji Temple.
Finish: Ginkakuji, the Silver Pavilion.
Time: Allow approximately three hours, including stops along the way.
Best Times: Early on weekdays, when it isn't as crowded.
Worst Times: There are no bad times for this stroll.

Walking Tour—Philosophers' Stroll

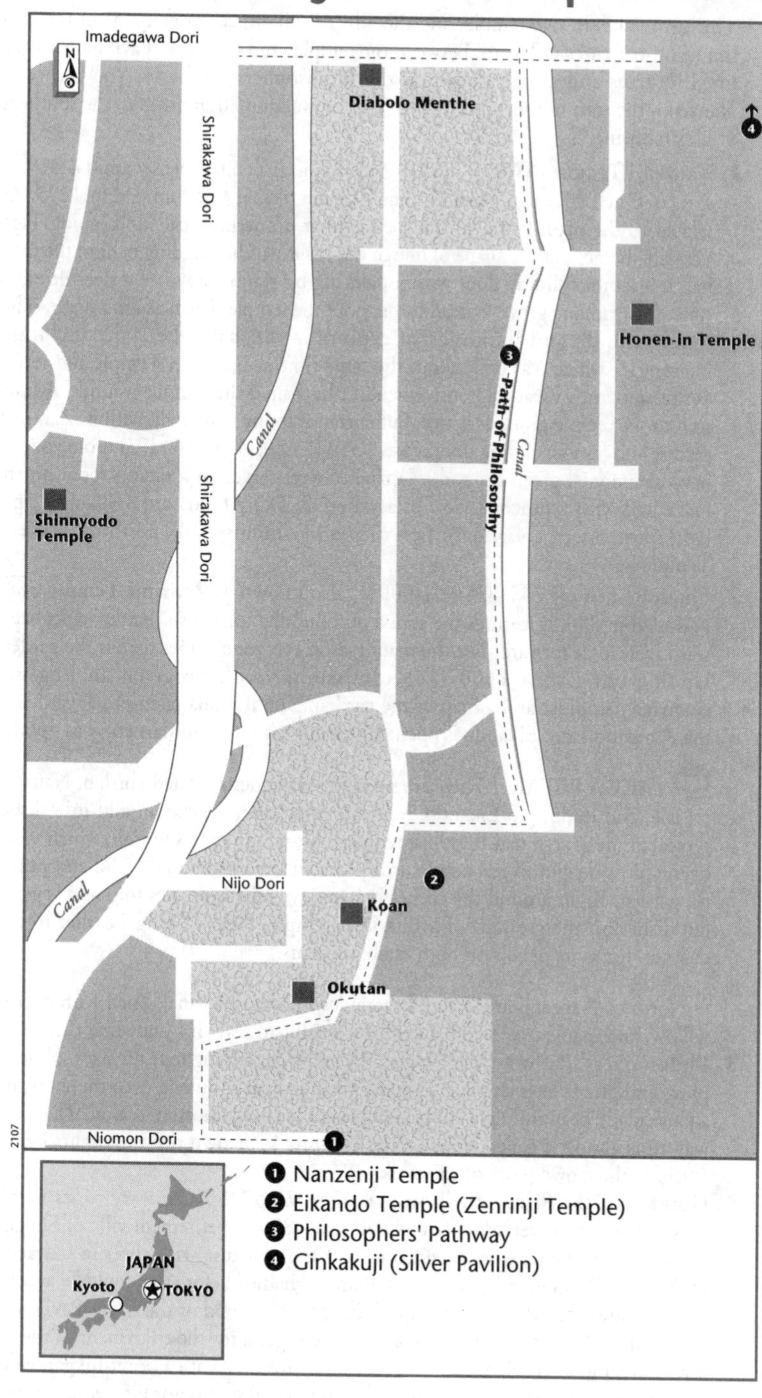

This stroll takes in two temples and the Silver Pavilion, considered one of the most beautiful structures in Kyoto. Between the temples and the Silver Pavilion is a canal lined by trees and a path known as the Philosophers' Pathway. You can reach Nanzenji, the start of this tour, by bus 5, or by walking 20 minutes to the southeast of Heian Shrine.

1. **Nanzenji Temple** (☎ 075/771-0365) is a Rinzai Zen temple set amid a grove of spruce. One of Kyoto's most famous Zen temples, it was founded in 1293. Attached to the main hall is a Zen rock garden, sometimes called "Leaping Tiger Garden" because of the shape of one of the rocks. In the building behind the main hall is a famous sliding door with a painting by Kano Tanyu of a tiger drinking water in a bamboo grove. Spread throughout the temple precincts are a dozen other lesser temples and buildings to explore if you have the time, including Nanzen-in, which was built about the same time as Nanzenji Temple and served as the emperor's vacation house whenever he visited the temple grounds. Admission to the temple grounds is free, but entrance to the main hall, with its Zen rock garden and famous sliding door, costs ¥350 ($3.50). For ¥300 ($3) more you can have ceremonial green tea and a Japanese sweet served in a tatami room off the main hall with a peaceful view of a waterfall. Daily hours are 8:30am to 5pm (you must enter by 4:30pm). Less than a five-minute walk north of Nanzenji Temple is:
2. **Eikando Temple** (☎ 075/761-0007), also known as **Zenrinji Temple** (88) Founded in 856, it features the statue of a Buddha turned so that he looks backward instead of forward, but the main reason everyone comes here is the garden. Upon paying your ¥400 ($4) admission, you'll be given an English-language pamphlet and a map of the garden. The Buddha facing backward is in the Amidado Hall. Eikando is open daily from 9am to 5pm (last entry at 4pm).

TAKE A BREAK There are two great restaurants located north of Nanzenji on the road leading to Eikando, both of which offer vegetarian and tofu dishes typical of meals served at Buddhist temples. Most famous is **Okutan,** which is one of the most delightful restaurants in Kyoto, with views of a beautiful and peaceful garden. Right around the corner is **Koan,** which also serves tofu and vegetarian dishes on the grounds of a Buddhist temple. (See "Dining," earlier in this chapter, for more details on both establishments.)

North of Nanzenji and Eikando temples is a narrow canal, lined with cherry, willow, and maple trees and flanked by a small pathway. It's known as the:

3. **Philosophers' Pathway,** referring to the fact that, throughout the ages, philosophers and priests have strolled along the tranquil canal thinking deep thoughts. It's a particularly beautiful sight in spring during the cherry-blossom season. The pathway runs almost a mile, allowing you to think your own deep thoughts before reaching the crown jewel of this walk:
4. **Ginkakuji, the Silver Pavilion** (☎ 075/771-5725). Contrary to its name, however, it isn't silver at all. It was built in 1482 as a retirement villa of Shogun Ashikaga Yoshimasa, who intended to coat the structure with silver in imitation of the Gold Pavilion built by his grandfather. He died before this could be accomplished, however, which is just as well because the wood of the Silver Pavilion is beautiful just as it is. The whole complex is designed for the enjoyment of the tea ceremony, moon viewing, and other aesthetic pursuits, with a beautiful garden of sand, rocks, and moss. One Kyoto resident told me that this was his favorite temple in the whole city (the residence became a temple after Ashikaga's death). At any

rate, you can easily imagine the splendor, formality, and grandeur of the life of Japan's upper class as you wander the grounds. Admission is ¥400 ($4), and daily hours are 9am to 5pm (to 4:30pm in winter).

TAKE A BREAK If strolling and thinking made you hungry and thirsty, head for **Diabolo Menthe** located a block east of Shirakawa Dori and to the south of Ginkakuji-michi. (See "Dining," earlier in this chapter, for more details.)

7 Shopping

As the nation's capital for more than 1,000 years, Kyoto became home to a number of crafts and exquisite art forms that catered to the elaborate tastes of the imperial court and the upper classes. Today, you can shop for everything from Noh masks to silk to cloisonné and lacquerware in Kyoto.

THE SHOPPING SCENE

There are a number of tiny specialty shops in Kyoto, the majority situated in Gion, along Shijo Dori, and in the area of Kawaramachi Dori. The square formed by **Kawaramachi Dori, Shijo Dori, Sanjo Dori,** and **Teramachi Dori,** for example, includes a covered shopping arcade and specialized shops selling lacquerware, combs and hairpins, knives and swords, tea and tea-ceremony implements, and more. If you're looking for antiques, woodblock prints, and art galleries, head toward **Shinmonzen Street** in Gion, which parallels Shijo Dori to the north on the east side of the Kamo River. Pottery shops are found in abundance on the roads leading to Kiyomizu Temple in Higashiyama-ku.

For clothing, accessories, and modern goods, Kyoto's many department stores are good bets and are conveniently located near Kyoto Station or in the heart of Nakagyo-ku near the Shijo-Kawaramachi intersection. In addition, there's a huge underground shopping mall called **Porta** that radiates from the Karasuma (north) side of Kyoto Station, with boutiques selling everything from clothing and shoes to stationery.

SHOPPING A TO Z

CRAFTS & SPECIALTY SHOPS

Aritsugu

Nishiki-Koji Dori, Gokomachi Nishi-iru, Nakagyo-ku. ☎ **075/221-1091.**

The fact that this family-owned business is located near the Nishiki-Koji market is appropriate, since it sells hand-wrought knives and other handmade cooking implements, including sushi knives, bamboo steamers, pots, pans, and cookware used in the preparation of traditional Kyoto cuisine. In business for 400 years, the shop counts the city's top chefs among its customers. Open Monday through Saturday from 9am to 5:30pm. It's at the east end of Nishiki-Koji Dori, a block north of Shijo Dori.

Gado

27 Miyashiki-cho, Hirano. ☎ **075/464-1655.**

This shop is conveniently located near the Golden Pavilion on the way to Ryoan-ji; you may want to stop in to browse. The gallery offers original woodblock prints for sale and shows a video on woodblock prints. Open daily from 9am to 6pm (Sunday from 10am).

Kasagen

284 Gion-machi, Kitagawa. ☎ **075/561-2832.**

Kasagen has been making traditional umbrellas (*bangasa*) since 1861. They are more expensive than elsewhere but of high quality, made to last a lifetime. Open daily 9:30am to 9pm.

Kikuya

Manjuji Dori, Sakaimachi, Higashi-iru. ☎ **075/351-0033.**

Kikuya has a good selection of used kimono, haori, geta, and kimono accessories for both adults and children. Although they are not antiques as Kikuya advertises, but simply secondhand, the goods here are beautiful and timeless. Also everything is in good condition (Japanese wear kimono only for special occasions), but be sure to look thoroughly for any spots, etc. Prices seem high to me (being an old-Japan-hand, I remember buying kimono by the bale); expect to pay ¥3,000 ($30) for a silk haori or child's kimono. No credit cards are accepted. Open Monday through Saturday 9am to 7pm. Station: Gojo (five minutes).

✪ Kyoto Craft Center

275 Gion, Kitagawa, Higashiyama-ku. ☎ **075/561-9660.**

Whereas the Kyoto Handicraft Center, described below, is good for souvenirs and inexpensive gifts for the folks back home, this crafts center features beautifully designed and crafted items by local and famous artisans. Located on Shijo Dori east of the Kamo River in the heart of Gion (bus to Ishidanshita), the Kyoto Craft Center devotes its two floors to a wide range of products, including jewelry, scarves, pottery, glass, fans, damascene, baskets, and much more. This is the place to shop for wedding gifts or something very special for yourself, and since the products are continually changing, there's always something new. Open Thursday to Tuesday from 10am to 6pm.

Kyoto Handicraft Center

Kumano Jinja Higashi, Sakyo-ku. ☎ **075/761-5080.**

For one-stop shopping, your best bet is this huge crafts center, just north of Heian Shrine on Marutamachi Dori (bus to Kumano-jinja-mae). Seven floors of merchandise contain almost everything Japanese imaginable—pearls, lacquerware, dolls, kimono, woodblock prints, pottery, cameras, cassette players, items made of Japanese paper, swords, lanterns, silk and textile goods, painted scrolls, and music boxes. And that's just for starters. You can even buy the socks to be worn with geta wooden shoes and the obi sashes to be worn with the kimono. You can easily spend an hour or two here wandering around, and there are also demonstrations showing artisans at work on various crafts, including hand-weaving, woodblock printing, and the production of damascene. Open daily from 10am to 6pm; closed December 31 through January 3.

Kyoto Municipal Museum of Traditional Industry

9-2 Seishoji-cho, Okazaki, Sakyo-ku. ☎ **075/761-3421.**

Described earlier under the walking tour of eastern Kyoto, the Kyoto-Shi Dento Sangyo Kaikan is due to reopen in 1996. Check with the TIC.

Jusan-Ya

Otabi-cho, Shijo Dori, Shinkyogoku Higashi-iru, Shimogyo-ku. ☎ **075/221-2008.**

Handcrafted boxwood hair combs and ornamental hairpins, made by a fifth generation of comb makers, are on display at this shop in central Kyoto on Shijo Dori, west of Kawaramachi Dori. Open daily from 10am to 9pm.

Miyawaki Baisen-An

102 Tominokoji-nishi, Rokkaku-dori, Nakagyo-ku. ☎ **075/221-0181.**

This elegant shop on Rokkaku-dori, just west of Tominokoji, has specialized in handmade fans since 1823, especially fans characteristic of Kyoto. English is spoken, and prices start at ¥2,300 ($23). Open daily from 9am to 5pm (until 6pm in summer).

Sawakichi Stone Store

551 Gojozaka, Higashiyama-ku. ☎ **075/561-2802.**

If you want to decorate your garden back home with a Japanese stone lantern, drop by this store located on a large intersection just west of the approach leading to Kiyomizu Temple. It offers a variety of styles and sizes in stone lanterns. Open daily from 9am to 6pm. (Bus: to Gojozaka).

Tanakaya (89)

Shijo Dori, Yanaginobanba-higashi. ☎ **075/221-1959.**

If you're interested in Japanese dolls, this is a good place to browse for Kyoto-style dolls, Noh masks, and inexpensive miniature animals. The shopkeepers speak English. It's on Shijo Dori, just east of Yanaginobanba. Open Thursday to Tuesday from 10am to 6pm.

Yamato Mingei-Ten

Kawaramachi Dori, Takoyakushi-agaru, Nakagyo-ku. ☎ **075/221-2641.**

This shop on Kawaramachi Dori, next to Maruzen bookstore, has been selling folkcrafts and folk art from all over Japan for more than four decades, including ceramics, glassware, lacquerware, textiles, paper products, baskets, and other handcrafted items. Open Wednesday to Monday from 10am to 8:30pm.

Zohiko Lacquerware

Okazaki Park near Heian Shrine. ☎ **075/752-7777.**

This store carries on the tradition of Kyoto lacquerware, which has been produced in the ancient capital for 1,000 years. The showroom offers various lacquer products for sale. Open Monday to Saturday from 9am to 5:30pm; closed national holidays.

DEPARTMENT STORES

Department stores are good places to shop for Japanese items and souvenirs, including pottery, lacquerware, and kimono. Since department stores are closed different days of the week, you'll always find several open.

Daimaru

Shijo Dori. ☎ **075/211-8111.**

Located farther west than two of the stores listed below, this smaller store sells everything from clothing and food to electronic goods. There's a foreign-exchange and information counter on the first floor. Open Thursday to Tuesday from 10am to 7pm.

Hankyu

Southeast corner of the Shijo and Kawaramachi intersection. ☎ **075/223-2288.**

Just across the street from the Takashimaya department store (see below), Hankyu offers seven floors of fashion, housewares, and food. The top two floors are devoted to restaurants, offering a variety of food at reasonable prices. Open Wednesday to Monday from 10am to 7:30pm.

Kinetsu

Karasuma, Shichijo-sagaru, Shimogyo-ku. **075/361-1111.**

Located across the street from Kyoto Station's north exit, this is a convenient store for all those necessities, from film to toiletries and food. Its foreign-exchange service on the first floor is a good place to exchange money after the banks close. Open Friday to Wednesday from 10am to 7pm. Restaurants on the seventh and eighth floors are open from 11am to 10pm.

Takashimaya

Southwest corner of the Shijo and Kawaramachi intersection. **075/221-8811.**

In the heart of Kyoto, Takashimaya is one of Japan's oldest and most respected department stores. It has a good selection of traditional crafts. Open Thursday through Tuesday from 10am to 7pm.

A Flea Market

On the first Sunday of each month a flea market is held at **Toji Temple,** located about a 15-minute walk southwest of Kyoto Station. Japan's largest monthly market, it's also one of the oldest, with a history stretching back more than 700 years. The market began in the 1200s as pilgrims began flocking to Toji Temple to pay their respects to Kobo Daishi, who founded the Shingon sect of Buddhism. Today, Toji Temple is still a center for the Shingon sect, and its monthly market is a colorful affair with booths selling antiques, old kimono, and other items. Worshippers come to pray before a statue of Kobo Daishi and to have their wishes written on wooden slats by temple calligraphers. Even if you don't buy anything, the festive atmosphere of the market and booths makes a trip here a memorable experience.

8 Kyoto After Dark

Nothing beats spending a fine summer's evening strolling the streets of Kyoto. From the geisha district of Gion to the bars and restaurants lining the narrow street of Pontocho, Kyoto at night is a city utterly charming and romantic. Begin your evening with a walk along the banks of the Kamo River—it's a favorite place for young couples in love. In the summer, restaurants along the river stretching north and south of Shijo Dori erect outdoor wooden platforms on stilts over the water. Illuminated with paper lanterns, they look like images from Kyoto's past.

Gion is located in Higashiyama-ku on the east side of the Kamo River, about a five-minute walk from the Shijo-Kawaramachi intersection. To reach it, walk west on Shijo, and then take a right on Hanamikoji Dori. A good time to take a walk is around dusk, when geishas are on their way to work.

Pontocho is a narrow street that parallels the Kamo River's west bank and stretches north from Shijo Dori to Sanjo Dori. Riddled with geisha houses, hostess bars, restaurants, and bars that fill every nook and cranny, Pontocho makes for a fascinating walk as you watch groups of Japanese enjoying themselves.

Although many of these restaurants lining the river have outdoor verandas in summer, I was able to include only a couple of them in this book, which you'll find listed in the "Dining" section of this chapter. Unfortunately, most of the restaurants in Pontocho are unreceptive to foreigners, and I was turned away from establishment after establishment with the excuse that the place was full—even when I could see that it was not. The Kyoto Tourist Information Center (TIC) informed me they don't recommend Pontocho to foreigners simply because of the cold reception. However, I think it's worth walking through Pontocho because the area is so interesting and so Japanese. Although most of the bars and clubs are virtually impossible to enter without an introduction, you might want to come here for a meal at one of the restaurants recommended in this book. And if you're feeling adventurous and are determined to find seating under the paper lanterns on one of the open verandas, maybe you'll be lucky.

Gion

A small neighborhood in the ancient capital of Kyoto, Gion is an area of plain wooden buildings devoid of flashing neon signs. In fact, as the geisha entertainment district of the city, there's something almost austere and solemn about Gion, as though its raison d'être were infinitely more important and sacred than mere entertainment. Gion is a shrine to Kyoto's past, an era when geishas numbered thousands in the city.

As you stroll the narrow streets of Gion, perhaps you'll see a geisha or maiko (a young woman training to be a geisha) clattering in her high wooden shoes on her way to her evening appointment. She will be dressed in a brilliant kimono, her face a chalky white, and her hair adorned with hairpins and ornaments. From geisha houses, music and laughter lilt out from behind paper screens, all the more inviting because you cannot enter. Not even the Japanese will venture inside without proper introductions.

Today there are only a mere couple of hundred geisha. After all, in today's high-tech world, few women are willing to undergo the years of rigorous training to learn how to conduct the tea ceremony, to play the samisen (a three-stringed musical instrument), or to perform ancient court dances. And contrary to popular Western misconceptions, geishas are not prostitutes. Rather, they are trained experts in conversation and coquettishness whose primary role is to make men feel like kings while in the soothing enclave of the geisha house.

Another good place to look is Kiyamachi, a small street that parallels Pontocho to the west and runs beside a small canal.

THE ENTERTAINMENT SCENE To find out what's being performed where in Kyoto, purchase the monthly magazine called *Kansai Time Out,* available in Kyoto at both the Maruzen and Izumiya bookstores and costing ¥300 ($3). Although major concerts are infrequent in Kyoto (they're usually held in nearby Osaka), the magazine is the best source for finding out what's going on in the classical and modern music scene.

A monthly tabloid distributed free at hotels and restaurants, the *Kyoto Visitor's Guide,* contains maps, a calendar of events and performances for the month, and information on sightseeing and shopping.

Finally, don't forget the TIC itself, which has information on Noh performances; Kabuki drama, which is staged in Kyoto several times a year; and such special events as court music that may be taking place at one of the city's shrines.

TRADITIONAL CULTURAL PROGRAMS

Gion Corner

Yasaka Hall, Hanamikoji Dori, Shijo-sagaru. ☎ **075/561-1119.** Tickets ¥2,500 ($25). Tickets are available at most hotels, travel agencies, and at Gion Corner itself.

After strolling around Gion, visit Gion Corner, located on Hanamikoji Dori south of Shijo Dori. Special variety programs are held every night from March 1 to November 29, with demonstrations of the tea ceremony, flower arrangement, *koto* (Japanese harp) music, *gagaku* (ancient court music and dance), *kyogen* (Noh comic play), *kyomai* (Kyoto-style dance, performed by maiko), and *bunraku* (puppetry). This is an excellent way to see a variety of ancient Japanese entertainment in a short period of time. There are two shows nightly, at 7:40 and again at 8:40pm. Reservations are not necessary, but get there early, since the 250 seats are on a first-come, first-served basis.

THE CLUB & LIVE MUSIC SCENE

ROCK

AG History

Imagium Bldg., Shijo Dori, Kobashi-nishi-iru. **075/223-2911.** Cover ¥1,700 ($17) plus one-food, one-drink minimum.

Imagium is a multi-entertainment building just north of Shijo and west of Kiyamachi in the nightlife district. On the fifth floor is AG History, a '50s music live house with '50s-garbed staff and zoot-suited bands. A fun place with a lot of kitch, it's crowded not with baby boomers but with kids who weren't even born yet way back then in the rocking '50s. Beer and snacks (pizza, fried potatoes) go for ¥700 ($7). Open Monday to Thursday from 6pm to 1am, Friday and Saturday until 2am, and Sunday until midnight.

Kyoto Cavern Club and Kento's

Hitotsume-nishi-iru, Hanamikoji Dori, Shijo-sagaru. ☎ **075/551-1369** (Cavern Club), 075/551-2777 (Kento's). Separate cover ¥1,300 ($13), plus 20% service and one-drink, one-dish minimum (each from ¥500/$5) per person.

Located in the heart of Gion, this is the Kyoto branch of two popular Tokyo entertainment clubs, under the same ownership. The Cavern Club, as its name implies, features a house band playing exclusively Beatles songs. Kento's is where enthusiasts of yesterday come to hear oldies but goldies of the '50s and '60s. The clubs are located just off Hanamikoji, in a plain building in keeping with Gion's atmosphere. Cavern Club is open Monday through Thursday from 6:30pm to 12:30am, on Friday from 6pm to 1am, and on Saturday from 6pm to 2am; Kento's is open Monday to Saturday from 6:30pm to 2am and on Sunday from 6:30pm to midnight.

Taku Taku (90)

Tominokoji-Bukkoji. ☎ **075/351-1321.** Cover ¥1,600 ($16), including one drink; ¥6,000 ($60) English or U.S. bands.

If you want to hear live music, head for this old sake warehouse with a plain decor. Featuring heavy metal, rock, soul, blues, reggae, jazz, and punk rock, it caters mainly to Kyoto's college students. To find Taku Taku, walk south from Shijo Dori on Tominokoji Dori for about three minutes. It's just past the red-and-white spiral of a barbershop, on the right-hand side of the street behind a small parking lot. Listen for the music. Beer runs ¥500 ($5). Open daily from 6 to 11pm, with live music usually from 7 to 9pm.

JAZZ

Jing Jang

Imagium Bldg., Shijo Dori, Kobashi-nishi-iru. ☎ **075/223-2911.**

Imagium (see AG History above), which offers eight floors of eating, drinking, and dancing, is the glitziest thing to hit Kyoto in some time and looks as if it had been imported straight out of Tokyo—and Kyoto purists grumble that Tokyo is exactly where it belongs. On the third floor is Jing Jang, a dinner club with a sophisticated setting, waitresses in cross-over kimono cloth skirts and shirts, and a variety of jazzy sounds from black contemporary to classic jazz. It features shabu-shabu, with all-you-can-eat formulas (¥3,600 to ¥4,600/$36 to $46) and all-you-can-drink (an additional ¥1,000/$10)—well, at least all you can for 1 1/2 hours.

Rag

Empire Bldg., 5th floor, Kiyamachi Dori, Sanjo Agaru. ☎ **075/241-0446.** Live music cover from ¥1,500 ($15), depending upon the band, plus one-dish, one-drink (each from ¥500/$5) minimum per person.

The crowd here depends on the group, with West Montgomery–style bands drawing an older, more quiet crowd, while rock groups can attract a young and rowdy bunch. So you have to check out who's playing. After live hours (6 to 11pm), the view from the bar is pleasant and it's a good place for a drink. Open daily from 6pm to 4:30am.

THE BAR SCENE

YAKITORI-YA

$ Irohanihoheto (30)

Aqua Bldg., 5th floor, Sanjo-sagaru, Yamato-oji Dori, Higashiyama-ku. ☎ **075/541-1683.**

A popular place among Kyoto's college crowd, Irohanihoheto is located on Yamato-oji Dori on the fifth floor of a white-tiled building just south of Sanjo-Keihan Station. One of a chain of drinking establishments with headquarters in Hokkaido, Irohanihoheto is known for its rustic decor, which always includes heavy wooden beams held together with ropes to give it a country atmosphere, shoji screens, and crafts hanging down from the ceiling. It's also known for its low prices. The extensive Japanese menu with pictures includes yakitori, gyoza, soba noodles, sashimi, salads, and vegetables, with most items costing less than ¥400 ($4). Draft beer starts at ¥380 ($3.80). Open daily from 5:30pm to 3:30am (to 5am on Saturday).

Suishin Honten (91)

Pontocho, Sanjo Dori-sagaru. ☎ **075/221-8596.**

This inexpensive yakitori-ya, part of a chain of Suishin yakitori restaurants, is very popular with young Japanese. It's on the west side of Pontocho, just south of Sanjo Dori Avenue. Look for a big white sign, red curtains hanging outside the front door, and a large display case of plastic food. The menu includes two skewers of yakitori (¥250/$2.50), five kinds of katsuyaki (¥450/$4.50), and assorted sushi (¥580/$5.80). This is a good place to stop off for a beer; small mugs of beer cost ¥450 ($4.50). Be sure to remove your shoes at the entryway and place them in one of the lockers provided. Open daily from 4:30 to 11:30pm (until midnight on Saturday).

BARS

Bar Isn't It

Karamachi Sanjo Sagaru. ☎ **075/221-5399.** Live music cover ¥500 ($5) Thurs–Fri.

Springing up all over Kansai and soon to be in Tokyo is a chain of Bar Isn't Its, offering for ¥500 ($5) all food and drink self-service, contemporary music, and snotty, we-are-so-cool-we-work-in-Japan *gaijin* (foreign) management. Still, it's cheap, and this is where all the foreigners are, and as such, a good place to meet them. Vending machines dispense beer, and you can win a free beer by putting your empty in a kind of slot machine. Yes, it's a pick-up place, but if you're not a Japanese girl, forget it; no one is interested in you. The decor is interesting art work by student artists and open plumbing, basement modern. Thursdays and Saturdays there's live music, and Saturdays a live DJ plays rock to hiphop to reggae. Open daily from 6pm to 2am–5am.

Louisiana Mama

Rekusu Bldg., Shioya-machi, Takoyakusi-kudaru, Kawaramachi Dori. ☎ **075/252-2199.** Live music cover ¥500 ($5) Thurs–Fri.

Owned by the same company as Bar Isn't It, Louisiana Mama is completely different. Again, all food (pizza, hot dogs, and gumbo) and drinks are ¥500 ($5), but here the small, green weathered-wood–wainscoted interior, a large Louisisana cafe mural, a fireplace, bar seating, service, and music one can talk over make for a more intimate setting. The manager, Danyelle, makes everyone feel at home and has a friendly, open smile and handshake. A single woman would feel comfortable coming here alone. It's popular with foreigners (businesspeople to French teachers) and Japanese alike. Walking up from Kawaramachi Shijo intersection, it's on the right side of the alley, the third street on the right; it is hard to find because the sign is tiny. Don't give up; it's worth finding. Thursdays and Saturdays there's live music, and Saturdays a live DJ; otherwise Danyelle plays jazz to Madonna. Open daily 6pm to 5am.

Pig & Whistle

Shobi Bldg., 2nd floor, 115 Ohashi-cho, Ohashi, Higashi Iru, Sanjo Dori. ☎ **075/213-6911.**

Packed with local foreigners "networking," the Pig & Whistle is a traditional English pub where you can play darts, stand at the bar, or sit at a table with your mum. Check out the bulletin board for apartments to rent, exchanges, and other such information. The pub boasts 120 varieties of scotch and bourbon, with cocktails or beer costing ¥450 to ¥750 ($4.50 to $7.50). Of course, you can have fish and chips for ¥700 ($7) or a variety of such other dishes. Noisy and fun. Open daily from 5pm to midnight (until 1am Friday and Saturday).

Rub A Dub

Sanjo-sagaru, Kiyamachi. ☎ **075/256-3122.**

If you like reggae, one more bar worth mentioning is this tiny basement establishment, unpretentious and primitive. In fact, this could be the only bar in the world that *tries* to imitate the poverty of Jamaica, with a corrugated tin wall and a thatched roof over the bar. The music isn't live, but prices are low. It's on Kiyamachi Street, a couple of shops south of Sanjo Dori Avenue, below a drugstore. Beer and cocktails are ¥600 ($6). Open daily 6pm to 2am (until 3 or 4 am Friday and Saturday).

CAFES

François Salon de Thé

Shijo Kobashi Nishizume-Minami. ☎ **075/351-4042.**

If evening entertainment to you means a cup of coffee or tea or a drink in quiet surroundings, this is the place for you. Located on a small street running along the west side of a tiny canal just a minute's walk southwest of the Shijo Avenue Bridge, which spans the Kamo River, the François Salon de Thé is more than 60 years old. Its facade resembles a miniature castle, while the small interior has an atmosphere similar to that of an old Viennese coffeehouse. A domed ceiling, dark-wood paneling, stained-glass windows, heavy red-cushioned chairs, and classical music make drinking a cup of coffee here a pleasant and relaxing experience—and a good place to escape the crowds. Tea and coffee start at ¥500 ($5); beer is ¥550 ($5.50). Open daily 10am to 10pm.

Karafuneya

Sanjo-sagaru, Pontocho. ☎ **075/255-1414.**

If you yearn to sit under the stars on one of the verandas overlooking the Kamo River, this coffee shop is Pontocho's most accessible establishment. Unfortunately, the veranda is open only in summer, and there's an order minimum. Still, it's a small price to pay for the chance to relax outdoors, and what I like most about this place is its location right beside a small fall in the river, which produces a roar loud enough to obliterate all traffic noises. Open daily from noon to 3:30am (until 5:30am Saturday and Sunday).

BEER GARDENS

ANA Hotel Kyoto

Nijo-Castle-Mae, Horikawa Dori, Nakagyo-ku. ☎ **075/231-1155.**

A good place to top off a late-afternoon visit to Nijo Castle is this rooftop beer garden on the ANA Hotel, located on Horikawa Dori and offering a view of the castle. Beer starts at ¥600 ($6). Open from the end of June to August, daily from 6 to 9pm.

New Miyako Hotel

Hachijo-guchi, Kyoto Station. ☎ **075/661-7111.**

A good place for a beer if you're in the vicinity of Kyoto Station is this rooftop beer garden at the New Miyako Hotel. Beer starts at ¥600 ($6). Open May to August, daily from 5:30 to 9:30pm.

9 An Excursion to Nara

In the beginnings of Japanese history, the nation's capital was moved to a new site each time a new emperor came to the throne. In 710, however, the first permanent Japanese capital was set up at Nara. Not that it turned out to be so permanent—after only 74 years the capital was moved first to Nagaoka and shortly thereafter to Kyoto, where it remained for more than 1,000 years. What's important about those 74 years is that they witnessed the birth of Japan's arts, crafts, and literature, as Nara imported everything from religion to art and architecture from China. Even the city itself, laid out in a rectangular grid pattern, was modeled after Chinese concepts. It was during the Nara Period that Japan's first historical account, first mythological chronicle, and first poetry anthology (with 4,173 poems) were written. Buddhism flourished, and Nara grew as the political and cultural center of the land.

The Japanese flock here because it gives them the feeling they're communing with ancestors. Foreigners come here because Nara offers them a glimpse of a Japan that was. Remarkably enough, many of Nara's buildings and temples remain intact, and long ago someone had enough foresight to enclose many of these historical structures in the quiet and peaceful confines of a large and spacious park. Although most visitors come to Nara on only a day trip from Kyoto, there's more than enough here to occupy two full days. For that reason, I've included some recommendations in accommodations. If you stay here overnight, be sure to take advantage of an evening or early-evening stroll through Nara Park.

ESSENTIALS

The **telephone area code** for Nara is 0742.

GETTING THERE Nara, 26 miles south of Kyoto, is easily reached in about 33 minutes from Kyoto Station on the *Kintetsu Limited Express* of Kinki Nippon Railways, which whisks you directly to Nara Kintetsu Station. If you have a Japan Rail Pass, you can take the slower JR train from Kyoto Station to Nara JR Station in about an hour. You can also reach Nara from Osaka in about 30 to 50 minutes, depending on the train and the station from which you leave.

VISITOR INFORMATION Pick up brochures and information on Nara before leaving Kyoto at the Tourist Information Center. The Kyoto map distributed there also has a map of Nara on the reverse side. Be sure also to pick up the leaflet "Walking Tour Courses in Nara."

In Nara itself, there are **tourist information offices** at both JR Station (☎ 0742/22-9821), open daily from 9am to 5pm, and Kintetsu Station (☎ 0742/24-4858), open daily from 9am to 5pm. Both have good brochures and maps, with useful information on how to get around Nara by bus. For more detailed information on Nara, visit the **Nara City Tourist Center,** 23-4 Kamisanjo (☎ 0742/22-3900), located in the heart of the city on Sanjo Dori, about a five-minute walk from both train stations. It's open daily from 9am to 9pm. Finally, there's a fourth **tourist office,** located at Sarusawa-ike Pond, not far from Nara's many tourist attractions. It's open daily from 9am to 5pm.

If you'd like your own personal guide of Nara, volunteer **Goodwill Guides** will be glad to show you the sights in exchange for the chance to practice their English. One guide each is posted at both the JR and Kintetsu station tourist offices and is available to the first tourists who show up any day except Sunday. If you'd like to reserve a guide in advance, call 0742/45-0221 the day before to arrange a time. Student guides, who can be friendlier, are also available. Telephone 0742/26-4753 for information and to set up an appointment.

To find out about festivals and exhibitions in Nara, call 0742/27-1313 for a two-minute taped recording in English.

GETTING AROUND Nara's Kintetsu and JR stations are about a 10-minute walk from each other. Most of Nara's sites are to the east of the two stations, within easy **walking** distance. To visit the areas of Horyuji and Nishinokyo, take a **bus,** no. 52, from either the JR station or Kintetsu station. It has announcements of its stops recorded in English. Other buses bound for the Horyuji and Nishinokyo temple areas (such as nos. 97, 98, and 60; the last is fastest) are indicated in the brochure of Nara available at the Nara tourist offices.

WHAT TO SEE & DO

The best way to enjoy Nara is to arrive early in the morning before the first tour buses start pulling in. If you don't have much time, the most important sites to see are Todaiji Temple, Kasuga Shrine, and Kofukuji Temple, which you can see in about two or three hours. If you have more time, add Horyuji Temple.

Around Nara Park

With its ponds, grassy lawns, trees, and temples, Nara Park covers about 1,300 acres and is home to more than 1,000 deer, which roam freely through the park. As you walk east from either the JR or the Kintetsu train station, the first temple you reach is **Kofukuji Temple** (☎ 0742/22-7755), founded in 710 as the family temple of the Fujiwaras, the second most powerful clan after the imperial family. At one time as many as 175 buildings were erected on the Kofukuji Temple grounds, but through centuries of civil wars and fires most of the structures were destroyed. Only a handful of buildings still remain, but even these were rebuilt after the 13th century. The five-story pagoda, first erected in 730, was burned down five times. The present pagoda dates from 1426 and is an exact replica of the original; at 164 feet tall, it's the second-tallest pagoda in Japan (the tallest is at Toji Temple in Kyoto). The temple's **Treasure House,** charging an admission of ¥500 ($5) and open daily from 9am to 5pm, displays many statues and works of art originally contained in the temple's buildings, the most famous of which is a statue of Ashura carved in the 8th century.

To the east of Kofukuji is the **Nara National Museum** or *Nara Kokuritsu Hakubutsukan* (☎ 0742/22-7771), which houses invaluable Buddhist art and archeological relics. Many statues and other items originally contained in Nara's many temples are now housed here, including sculptures, paintings, calligraphy, and

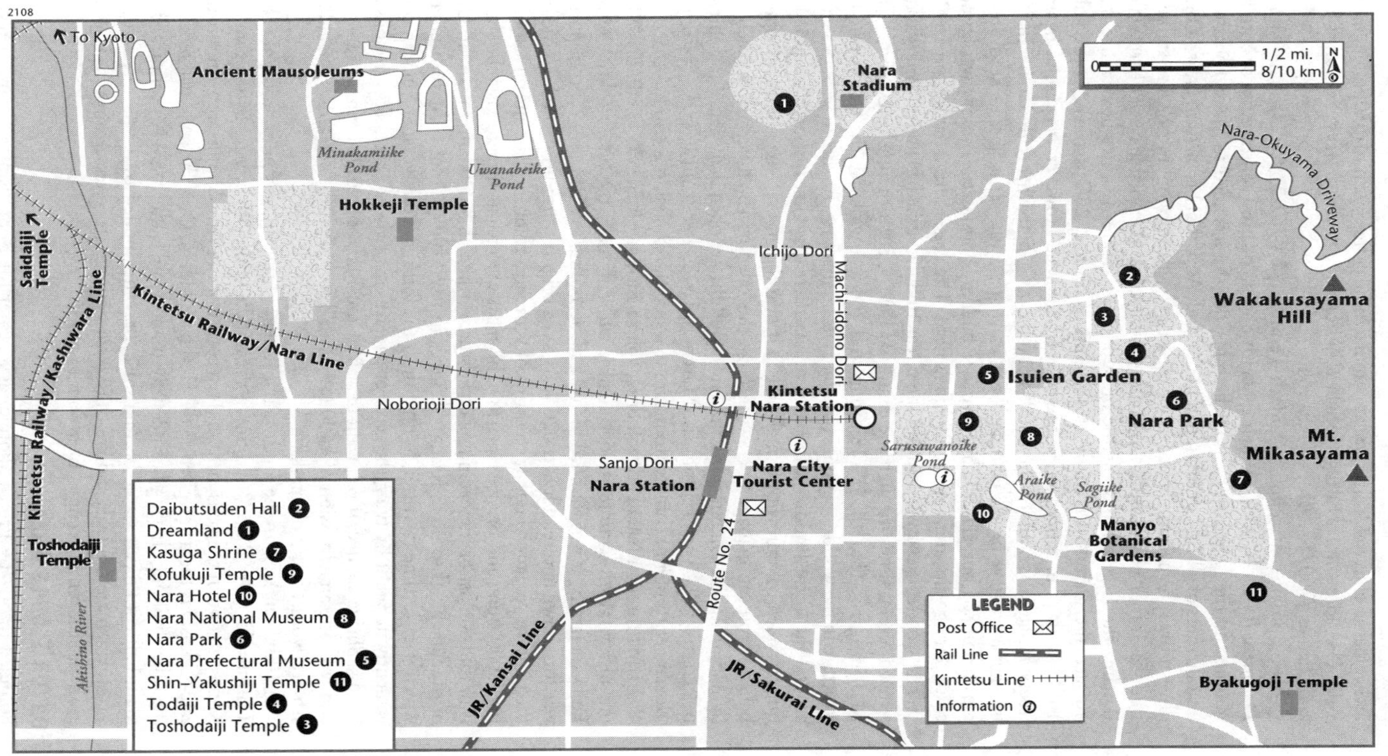
2108
To Kyoto
Ancient Mausoleums
Nara Stadium
1/2 mi.
8/10 km
N
Minakamiike Pond
Uwanabeike Pond
Hokkeji Temple
Nara-Okuyama Driveway
Saidaiji Temple
Ichijo Dori
Machi-idono Dori
Kintetsu Railway/Kashiwara Line
Kintetsu Railway/Nara Line
Wakakusayama Hill
Isuien Garden
Kintetsu Nara Station
Nobarioji Dori
Nara Park
Mt. Mikasayama
Sarusawanoike Pond
Sanjo Dori
Nara Station
Nara City Tourist Center
Araike Pond
Sagiike Pond
Manyo Botanical Gardens
Toshodaiji Temple
Route No. 24
Akishino River
JR/Kansai Line
JR/Sakurai Line
Byakugoji Temple
Daibutsuden Hall 2
Dreamland 1
Kasuga Shrine 7
Kofukuji Temple 9
Nara Hotel 10
Nara National Museum 8
Nara Park 6
Nara Prefectural Museum 5
Shin–Yakushiji Temple 11
Todaiji Temple 4
Toshodaiji Temple 3
LEGEND
Post Office
Rail Line
Kintetsu Line
Information

archeological objects. Open Tuesday through Sunday from 9am to 4:30pm, it charges ¥400 ($4) admission. During special exhibitions, the museum stays open until 5pm and charges ¥760 ($7.60) for admission.

Nara's premier attraction is **Todaiji Temple** (☎ 0742/22-5511), along with its **Daibutsu** (Great Buddha). When Emperor Shomu ordered construction of both the temple and the Daibutsu back in the mid-700s, he intended to make Todaiji the headquarters of all Buddhist temples in the land. As part of his plans to create a Buddhist utopia, he commissioned work on an overwhelmingly huge bronze statue of Buddha. It took eight castings to finally complete this remarkable work of art, which remains the largest bronze statue of Buddha in Japan. At a height of more than 50 feet, the Daibutsu is made of 437 tons of bronze, 286 pounds of pure gold, 165 pounds of mercury, and 7 tons of vegetable wax. However, because of Japan's frequent natural calamities, the Buddha of today isn't quite what it used to be. In 855, in what must have been a whopper of an earthquake, the statue lost its head. It was repaired in 861 but, alas, the huge wooden building housing the Buddha was burned twice during wars, melting the Buddha's head. The present head dates from 1692.

The wooden structure housing the Great Buddha, called Daibutsuden, was destroyed several times through the centuries; the present structure dates from 1709. Measuring 161 feet tall, 187 feet long, and 164 feet wide, it's the largest wooden structure in the world—but only two-thirds its original size. Be sure to walk in a circle around the Great Buddha to see it from all different angles. Behind the statue is a huge wooden column with a small hole in it near the ground. According to popular belief, if you can manage to crawl through this opening you'll be sure to reach enlightenment. The Daibutsuden and Great Buddha are open daily: April to September from 7:30am to 5:30pm, in March and October from 8am to 5pm, and November through February from 8am to 4:30pm. Admission is ¥400 ($4).

A stroll through Nara Park will bring you to **Kasuga Shrine** (☎ 0742/22-7788), one of my favorite Shinto shrines in all Japan. Originally the tutelary shrine of the Fujiwara family, it was founded in 768 and, according to Shinto concepts of purity, was torn down and rebuilt every 20 years in its original form until 1863. Nestled in the midst of verdant woods, it's a shrine of vermilion-colored pillars and an astounding 3,000 stone and bronze lanterns. The most spectacular time to visit the shrine is in mid-August or the beginning of February, when all 3,000 lanterns are lit. One of the fun things to do at Kasuga Shrine is to pay ¥100 ($1) for a slip of paper on which your fortune is written in English. If the fortune is unfavorable, you can conveniently negate it by tying the piece of paper to the twig of a tree. The grounds of Kasuga Shrine are free. If you want to visit its museum, open daily from 9am to 4pm and charging an admission of ¥400 ($4), you'll see the shrine's treasures, including armor, swords, and Noh masks.

A 10-minute walk to the southwest of Kasuga Shrine brings you to **Shin-Yakushiji Temple** (☎ 0742/22-3736), built in the middle of the 8th century by the Empress Komyo to obtain the gods' help in the recovery of Emperor Shomu from an eye disease (Yakushi is the name given to the Healing Buddha). Only the main hall remains, the other buildings having been destroyed and rebuilt after the 13th century. The main hall contains a statue of Yakushi-nyorai surrounded by 12 pottery figures, 11 of which are originals and are considered national treasures. Admission is ¥400 ($4), and the temple is open from 9am to 5pm.

Horyuji Temple Area

Founded in 607 by Prince Shotoku as a center for Buddhism in Japan, **Horyuji Temple** (☎ 0745/75-2555) is one of Japan's most significant gems in terms of both architecture and art. It was from here that Buddhism blossomed and spread throughout the land. Today, about 45 buildings remain, some of them dating from the end of the 7th century and comprising what are probably the oldest wooden structures in the world. At the western end of the grounds is the two-story, 58-foot-high **Golden Hall** or *Kondo*, which is considered the oldest building at Horyuji Temple. Next to the main hall is a five-story pagoda, which dates from the foundation of the temple. It contains four scenes from the life of Buddha, including Buddha's cremation and entry into Nirvana. The **Great Treasure House** or *Daihozoden*, a concrete building constructed in 1941, contains temple treasure, including statues and other works of art from the 7th and 8th centuries. On the eastern precincts of Horyuji Temple is an octagonal building built in 739 called **Yumedono Hall,** or the **Hall of Dreams.** Supposedly Prince Shotoku used this building for quiet meditation.

Admission to Horyuji Temple, the Treasure House, and the Hall of Dreams is ¥1,000 ($10). The grounds are open daily from 8am to 5pm (from November 20 to March 10, it closes at 4:30pm).

East of Yumedono is **Chuguji Temple,** a nunnery built for members of the imperial family. It contains two outstanding works of art. The wooden statue of Miroku-bosatsu, dating from the 7th century, is noted for the serene and compassionate expression on its face. The Tenjukoku Mandala, the oldest piece of embroidery in Japan, was originally 16 feet long and created by Shotoku's widow and her female companions, with scenes depicting life of the times. Only a replica of the fragile embroidery is now on display. Admission here is ¥300 ($3).

NISHINOKYO AREA

If you still have time to spend in Nara, it's worth making a trip to the vicinity of Nishinokyo Station to visit two more temples. **Toshodaiji Temple** (☎ 33-7900) was founded in 759 by Ganjin, a high priest from China who was invited to Japan by the emperor to help spread Buddhism. Ganjin's initial attempts to reach Japan were thwarted by pirate attacks, storms, and five shipwrecks. During one of these voyages, Ganjin lost his sight through disease. He finally reached Japan in 754 at the age of 66 and set to work constructing this magnificent temple. Its main hall and lecture hall still stand and are both national treasures. The main hall contains various statues and its front pillars are thought to resemble Greek architecture, the concept of which may have been brought to Japan via the Silk Road. Also on the temple's grounds is Ganjin's tomb. Admission is ¥300 ($3). Daily hours are 8:30am to 4:30pm.

About 800 yards south of Toshodaiji is **Yakushiji Temple** (☎ 33-6001), which contains more Buddhist statues. It was erected by Emperor Tenmu in hopes that his wife would recover from illness—and must have worked because she ended up succeeding him to the throne. Its three-story pagoda, the only original structure remaining, is believed to date from 698 and looks as if it has six stories because of the intermediate roofs. Admission to its treasure hall is ¥400 ($4). Open daily from 8:30am to 5pm.

ACCOMMODATIONS

Furuichi (92)

Higashitera Hayashimachi, Nara 630. ☎ **0742/22-2440.** Fax 0742/23-7807. 14 rms (4 with bath). A/C TV TEL. ¥4,500 ($45) per person without bath; ¥6,000 ($60) per person with bath. Including two meals, ¥8,000 ($80) per person. MC, V. Directions: 10 minutes from Kintetsu Nara, 15 minutes from JR Nara.

This budget accommodation looks modern and unexciting from the outside, but its Japanese-style rooms are very pleasant, with traditional shoji screens and seating space beside the windows. Some rooms have a bathroom, and all have a sink. Furuichi is located close to Sarusaw-ike Pond and Nara's many attractions. The only drawback is that no one here speaks English.

Kikusuiro (93)

1130 Takahata-cho Bodaimachi, Nara 630. ☎ **0742/23-2001.** 14 rms (8 with bath). A/C TV TEL. ¥33,000 ($330) per person without bath, ¥41,000–¥65,000 ($410–$650) per person with bath. All rates include two meals and service charge. No credit cards. Directions: 10 minutes from Kintetsu Nara, 15 minutes from JR Nara.

If you want to stay in a Japanese-style ryokan, you can't find a more beautiful example than this lovely 120-year-old inn, located not far from Nara Park. An imposing structure with an ornate Japanese-style roof and surrounded by a white wall, it makes artful use of various woods to create pleasing forms of decoration in its tatami rooms, including delicately carved transoms. Rooms, some of which face Ara-ike Pond, are outfitted with scrolls and antiques and are connected to one another with rambling wooden corridors; some rooms have minibars. There is also a beautiful garden.

Adjacent to the ryokan are both Western- and Japanese-style restaurants. The Japanese restaurant is new and decorated with bamboo and paper lanterns. Open daily from 11am to 8:30pm, it features sukiyaki or shabu-shabu, obento mini-kaiseki, and kaiseki.

Nara Hotel

Nara-Koennai, Nara 630. ☎ **0742/26-3300.** Fax 0742/23-5252. 132 rms (all with bath). A/C MINIBAR TV TEL. ¥12,000 ($120) single; ¥21,000–¥50,000 ($210–$500) twin; ¥22,000–¥23,000 ($220–$230) double. AE, DC, JCB, MC, V. Taxi: 10 minutes.

One of the most famous places to stay in Nara, the Nara Hotel was built in 1909 and sits like a palace on top of a hill overlooking several ponds. Near Nara Park, and similar to Japan's other hotels built decades ago to accommodate the foreigners who poured into the country following the Meiji Restoration, it is constructed as a Western-style hotel but has many Japanese features—a Japanese-style roof, wooden eaves, the use of fine woods throughout. The Japanese imperial family has stayed here. You have your choice of staying in the old section of the hotel, with its high ceilings and comfortable old-fashioned decor, or in the new addition, which opened in 1984 and offers pleasant and modern rooms with verandas. I personally prefer the older rooms—they're also less expensive than those in the new wing. Facilities include a souvenir shop and two restaurants serving Western food, including a beautiful main dining hall, Mikasa, serving fixed-price dinners for ¥4,000–¥8,000 ($40–$80) as well as lunches and afternoon tea.

Seikan-so

29 Higashi-Kitsuji-cho, Nara 630. ☎ **0742/22-2670.** Fax 0742/22-2670. 13 rms (none with bath). A/C TV. ¥3,800 ($38) per person. AE, MC, V. Directions: Walk 15 minutes from Kintetsu Nara, or 25 from JR Nara.

This is a lovely inexpensive Japanese-style accommodation. In fact, it's one of the most beautiful ryokan in the Japanese Inn Group that I've seen. Located in a quiet neighborhood, it dates from 1916 and is owned by a friendly young couple who speak English. The ryokan, a traditional Japanese building, wraps itself around an inner garden complete with azalea bushes and manicured trees. Some rooms face the garden—request one of these when making your reservation. A Japanese or Western breakfast is available.

DINING

Harishin (94)

15 Nakashinya-cho. ☎ **0742/22-2669.** Obento ¥2,700 ($27). JCB, MC, V. Tues–Sun 11:30am–3pm (last order). If Mon is a national holiday, it remains open and closes on Tues instead. Directions: Walk five minutes south of Sarusawa-ike Pond, on the road that leads south from the east edge of the pond (stop at the tourist office for directions). OBENTO.

Many tourists never see this lovely part of old Nara, near Gangoji Temple. The restaurant itself is a 200-year-old house of ocher-colored walls and a wood-slat facade, and dining is on tatami with a view of a garden. Only one thing is served—an obento changing with the season. On my last visit, my meal included an appetizer of pumpkin gelatin, strawberry wine, soup, vegetables, and various exquisitely prepared dishes.

Yugayama (95)

1071 Takabatake-cho. ☎ **0742/22-3834.** Main dishes ¥400–¥2,000 ($4–$20); set dinners ¥3,500–¥7,000 ($35–$70); set lunch ¥1,000 ($10). AE, DC, JCB, MC, V. Mon–Sat 11am–10pm (last order), Sun 11am-9pm (last order). Directions: 5 minutes south of Nara Park. HOKKAIDO SPECIALTIES.

Across from the main entrance to the Nara Hotel, Yugayama features Hokkaido cuisine and decor (large, dark-wood-carved bears and Ainu designs). You can sit at the counter, on tatami at tables with wells underneath for your legs, or at conventional tables. The food is offered in several styles: *nabe* (stewed), *shashimi* (raw), *kushiyaki* (roasted on skewers), and *ishiyaki* (cooked on a stone). Along with corn and potatoes, there's lots of fresh seafood. We had Hokai-ishiyaki for ¥4,000 ($40) per person; it consisted of shrimp, crab, scallops, salmon, squid, bell peppers, eggplant, two kinds of mushrooms, potato, cabbage, and onions. Our food was brought to us uncooked on a huge platter by kimono-clad waitresses, and we grilled it ourselves on a hot stone. *Seiromushi* is a favored rice-based lunch special. This place is popular with the tour buses, so eat early or late to avoid the crowds. Highly recommended.

8 The Japan Alps

Lying in the central part of Honshu, the Japan Alps consist of several volcanic mountain ranges. With the exception of Japan's tallest mountain, Mt. Fuji, all of Japan's loftiest mountains are in these ranges, making the Japan Alps a popular destination for hikers and nature-lovers. Some of the villages nestled in the mountains remain relatively unchanged, giving visitors the unique opportunity to see how mountain people have lived through the centuries.

SEEING THE JAPAN ALPS

Because towns and villages in this region are spread out—with lots of mountains in between—the traveling isn't as fast in this part of the country as on Honshu's broad plains. If you're coming from Tokyo, your best strategy is to start with a direct train from Shinjuku Station to Matsumoto. From there, take the Chuo Honsen Line early in the morning to Nakatsugawa, where you can then board a bus for Magome and spend the day hiking to Tsumago. By late afternoon, you should be back on the Chuo Honsen Line bound for Nagoya, where you then change trains for Takayama, reaching it in time for dinner. Takayama is the best starting-out point for bus rides to Ogimachi (in Shirakawa-go). There are two buses a day to make the 2½-hour trip, with a change in Makiro. From Ogimachi, buses depart for Nagoya and Kanazawa (though not direct). There is a bus (again, not direct) between Matsumoto and Takayama, but it operates only in summer (because of heavy snowfall) and isn't very convenient.

1 Takayama

330 miles NW of Tokyo, 103 miles NE of Nagoya

Located in the Hida Mountains of the Japan Alps, Takayama is surrounded by 10,000-foot peaks, making the train ride here breathtaking. The village, situated on a wide plateau, was founded back in the 16th century by Lord Kanamori, who selected the site because of the impregnable position afforded by the surrounding Hida Mountains. Modeled after Kyoto but also with strong ties to Edo (the former name of Tokyo), Takayama borrowed from both cultural centers in developing its own architecture, food, and crafts, much of them still preserved today because of its centuries of remote isolation in the Japan Alps.

What's Special About the Japan Alps?

Natural Spectacles

- Some of the highest mountains in Japan.
- Good hiking trails through beautiful countryside, including the hike between Magome and Tsumago; for more serious hikers, trails leading out of Kamikochi.
- Breathtaking train rides.

Great Towns and Villages

- Takayama, with its preserved merchants' homes, its museums, and its unique food and architecture.
- Shirakawa-go, nestled in a valley hemmed in by mountains, with more than 150 thatched farmhouses, barns, and sheds set in the midst of paddies.
- Matsumoto, a castle town.
- Magome and Tsumago, two old post towns linked by a five-mile pathway.

Architectural Highlights

- Merchants' homes in Takayama, built in the 18th century and typical of classical design of the region.
- Thatched farmhouses, most more than 200 years old and some of them converted to minshuku accommodations.
- Matsumoto Castle, built in 1504 and possessing the oldest existing keep in Japan.

Regional Food and Cuisine

- *Hoba miso,* a Takayama specialty served at breakfast, consisting of soybean paste mixed with scallions and other ingredients, and cooked on a magnolia leaf at your table.
- Rice sake of Shirakawa-go, famous for its milky color, potency, and thickness (provided by rice kernels).
- *Sansai,* fresh mountain vegetables.

The heart of Takayama is delightful, with homes of classical design typical of 18th-century Hida. The streets of the old town are narrow and clean, flanked on both sides by tiny canals of running water. Rising up from the canals are one- and two-story homes and shops of gleaming dark wood with overhanging roofs. Latticed windows and slats of wood play games of light and shadow in the white of the sunshine. In open shop doors, strips of blue cloth flutter in the breeze. As you walk down the streets, you'll notice huge cedar balls hanging from the eaves in front of several shops, indicating a sake factory. Altogether, there are eight sake factories in Takayama, most of them small affairs. Go inside, sample the sake, and watch men stirring rice in large vats. Takayama is a town that invites exploration.

ESSENTIALS

The **telephone area code** for Takayama, lying in the northern part of Gifu Prefecture, is 0577.

GETTING THERE By Train The easiest way to get here is by direct train from Nagoya, with about eight departures daily for the $2^1/_2$-hour trip. There is also a direct train from Osaka via Kyoto, which takes 5 hours.

VISITOR INFORMATION The local **tourist office** (☎ 0577/32-5328) is located in a wooden booth on the east side of Takayama Station. You can pick up an English brochure and a map of the town. The office is open daily from 8:30am to 6:30pm (to 5pm in winter).

GETTING AROUND Most of Takayama's attractions lie to the east of the train station and are easily reached **on foot.** An alternative is to rent a **bicycle** from one of the many rental shops ringing the station; the cost averages ¥300 ($3) per hour or ¥1,300 ($13) for the whole day.

WHAT TO SEE & DO

Takayama's main attraction is its old merchants' houses, which are clustered together in the old town on narrow streets called Sannomachi and Ninomachi. Be sure to allow time for just wandering around. Shops in the area sell Takayama's specialties, including sake, yew wood carvings, and a unique lacquerware called *shunkei-nuri.* Almost all the attractions listed below are closed during the New Year's holidays.

Hida Minzoku Mura Folk Village

☎ **0577/33-4714.** Entrance to all museums and to the folk village ¥700 ($7). Daily 8:30am–5pm. Directions: To reach Hida Minzoku Mura Folk Village, take bus departing from platform 2 in front of Takayama Station to the last stop. Otherwise, it's about a 30-minute walk from the train station.

Popularly called *Hida no Sato,* the Hida Minzoku Mura Folk Village is an open-air museum of more than 30 old thatched farmhouses, showing how farmers and artisans used to live in the Hida Mountain region. The whole village is picturesque, with swans swimming in the central pond, green moss growing on the thatched roofs, and flowers blooming in season. Some of the houses have *gassho-zukuri*-style roofs, built steeply to withstand the heavy snowfalls. The tops of the roofs are said to resemble hands joined in prayer. There are shingle-roofed homes, houses with earthen floors, a woodcutter's hut, a grain storehouse, and a house in which the second floor was used as a silkworm nursery. All the structures, which range in age from 100 to 500 years, are open to the public and are filled with utensils, tools, and furniture used in daily life. On display, for example, are old spindles and looms, utensils for cooking and dining, instruments used in the silk industry, farm tools, sleds, and straw boots and capes worn to fend off wet snow.

Workshops have been set up in one corner of the village grounds to demonstrate textile dyeing and weaving, lacquerwork, and wood sculpture. Within walking distance of the folk village is the **Hida Folklore Museum** or *Hida Minzoku-kan,* with more displays on life in the Hida region. Next to the folklore museum is the **Museum of Mountain Life,** with displays on the history of mountaineering in the Japan Alps and regional flora and fauna.

Merchants' Houses

North end of Shimo-Ninomachi Street. Yoshijima-ke ¥300 ($3); Kusakabe Mingeikan ¥500 ($5). Summer, both houses, daily 9am–5pm. Winter (Dec–Feb), Yoshijima-ke, Wed–Mon 9am–4:30pm; Kusakabe Mingeikan, daily 9am–4:30pm.

Located side by side, **Yoshijima-ke** or Yoshijima House (☎ 0577/32-0038) and **Kusakabe Mingeikan** (☎ 0577/32-0072) are two merchants' mansions that once belonged to two of the richest families in Takayama. Of the two, the Yoshijima House is my favorite. With its exposed attic, heavy crossbeams, sunken fireplace, and sliding doors, it's a masterpiece of geometric design. It was built in 1907 as both the home and factory of the Yoshijima family, well-to-do brewers of sake in Takayama. Notice how the beams and wood of the home gleam, a state attained through decades of polishing as each generation of women did their share in bringing the wood to a luster. Yoshijima-ke is also famous for its lattices, typical of Takayama yet showing an elegance influenced by Kyoto.

Not quite as rustic, the Kusakabe Mingeikan merchant house is more refined and imposing, built in 1879 for a merchant dealing in silk, lamp oil, and finance. Its architectural style is considered unique to Hida, and on display are items handed down through the generations, arranged just as they would have been in the 18th and 19th centuries.

More Museums

Fuji Folk Craft Museum

69 Kamisanno-machi. ☎ **0577/32-0108.** Admission ¥300 ($3). Daily 9am–5pm.

Just down the street from the Hida Folk Archeological Museum (below) on Sannomachi Street, a 10-minute walk from the train station, is *Fuji Bijutsu Mingei-Kan*, which contains a varied collection of furniture, clothing, combs, dolls, pottery, and lacquerware, most dating from the Edo Period. Included are some beautiful *tansu* (chests), smoking utensils, belt pouches with netsuke, swords, paper-covered lamps, farming tools, and spinning wheels. Many items are identified in English, and the entrance gate was once the outer gate of Takayama Castle, which is no longer in existence. A very worthwhile museum.

Hida Folk Archeological Museum

82 Kamisanno-machi. ☎ **0577/32-1980.** Admission ¥350 ($3.50). Summer, daily 8am–6pm; winter, daily 9am–5pm.

Hida Minzoku Kokokan, an interesting old house in the heart of Takayama on Sannomachi Street, about a 10-minute walk from the train station, once belonged to a doctor and contains several trick devices, including secret passageways and a hanging ceiling. Imagine inviting an enemy to your home, offering him the best room in the house, and then sneaking upstairs to chop the rope that holds up the suspended ceiling. The ceiling plunges down with a loud thud, neatly crushing your enemy to death. Rather dramatic, don't you think? And of course, very effective. Back in the old days of Japan's continuing civil wars, trickery was sometimes the only way to survive the constant power struggles. This museum also has a collection of earthenware and folk tools.

Historical Government House

1-5 Hachi-ken-machi. ☎ **0577/32-0643.** Admission ¥360 ($3.60). Apr–Oct, daily 8:45am–5pm; Nov–Mar, daily 8:45am–4:30pm.

Once a manor house for administrators in Takayama, *Takayama Jinya* is the only building of its kind in Japan. Constructed like a miniature castle, with an outer wall and imposing entrance gate, it contains a rice granary (rice was collected as a tax), chambers and courts, and historical records. An English-language pamphlet describing the history of the building and its purpose is available. The structure is a 10-minute walk from the train station.

✪ Inro Museum

1-98 Ojin-machi. ☎ **0577/32-8500.** Admission ¥500 ($5). Daily 8:30am–5pm. Closed Dec–Mar.

If you're at all an enthusiast of the tiny yet intriguing *inro*, a small portable medicine case, you must not miss the *Inro Bijitsukan*. It displays Japan's largest collection of 18th-century inro and *netsuke*, a toggle or counterweight used to hang inro (as well as purses and tobacco pouches) from kimono sashes. Over 300 rare inro and netsuke, delicately carved from boxwood, ivory, ceramic, or lacquerware, are on display, as well as dolls, screens, and kimono from the Edo Period (1603–1867). The inro are displayed with their original and thematically matching netsuke intact. The museum is located in a beautiful *kura,* or storehouse, just off Omotesando Dori, not far from Yoshijima-ke.

Lacquerware Museum

1-88 Kanda-cho. ☎ **0577/32-3373.** Admission ¥300 ($3). Summer, daily 8:30am–5:30pm; winter, daily 9am–5pm.

Hida Takayama Shunkei Kaikan displays Takayama lacquerware known for its transparency, which shows off the wood grain. Refined of taste like the ancient capital from which it came (Kyoto), it is admired all over Japan. The museum displays some 1,000 items, from furniture to boxes, dating from the 17th century to the present. One exhibit explains the multistage production technique and tools of the craft. A great museum shop has pretty buys from ¥200 ($2) for souvenirs to ¥100,000 ($1,000) for the serious investor. It's located a 10-minute walk from the train station, not far from, and on the west side of, Yayoi Bashi (bridge).

Lion Dance Ceremony Exhibition Hall

53-1 Sakura-machi. ☎ **0577/32-0881.** Admission ¥600 ($6). Daily 8:30am–5pm.

More than 800 lion masks, used in Japanese festivals around the country, are on display here at the *Kyodo Gangu-Kan,* including those of the Hida region. There are video presentations of local folk dances, as well as demonstrations of marionettes used in Takayama's two festival parades. The hall is just a minute's walk from Takayama Festival Floats Exhibition Hall, below.

Takayama Festival Floats Exhibition Hall

178 Sakura-machi. ☎ **0577/32-5100.** Admission ¥800 ($8). Mar–Nov, daily 8:30am–5pm; Dec–Feb, daily 9am–4:30pm.

Not far from the merchants' houses is *Takayama Yatai Kaikan,* located in the precincts of Sakurayama Hachimangu Shrine, about a 5-minute walk from the old town or a 15-minute walk from the train station. Here you can see some of the huge, elaborate floats used for Takayama's famous parade in its autumn festival. Most of them date from the 17th century and were built by famous craftspeople of the village. Special features include marionettes, which are made to dance through the streets during festival time. The hall also contains Japan's largest portable shrine. Included in the admission price is a visit to *Sakurayama Nikko Kan,* which houses a miniature replica of the Nikko Toshogu shrine in Nikko, Japan.

Toy Museum

33-2 Kami-Ichi-no-machi. ☎ **0577/32-1183.** Admission ¥250 ($2.50). Daily 8:30am–5pm.

A 10-minute walk from the train station, *Kyodo Gangu-Kan* houses a collection of dolls and folk toys from around the country, dating from the 17th century to today.

ACCOMMODATIONS

There are by far more minshuku and ryokan in Takayama than hotels, making it the perfect place to stay in a traditional Japanese inn. In fact, staying in a tatami room and sleeping on a futon is the best way to immerse yourself in the life of this small community.

And the best news is that there are places to fit all budgets. All rates below for ryokan and minshuku follow the Japanese system in that they are on a per-person basis and include breakfast, dinner, and service charges. Tax is extra. You should be aware that in peak season (August and during festival times in April and October), prices will be higher, generally between 10% and 20% more.

Directions given are from Takayama Station.

RYOKAN

Asunaro (96)

2-96-2 Hatsuda-cho, Takayama 506. ☎ **0577/33-5551.** 20 rms (12 with bath). A/C MINIBAR TV TEL. ¥12,000–¥35,000 ($120–$350) per person. Peak season from ¥20,000 ($200) per person. All rates include breakfast, dinner, and service. AE, DC, JCB, MC, V. Directions: Walk about 5 minutes northeast.

This modern ryokan, recently renovated with traditional fixtures from old buildings, offers fairly standard tatami rooms, all with their own toilet and most with bath as well. The higher rates during peak season are due in part, the management says, to more elaborate meals.

Hida Gasshoen (97)

3-829 Nishinoishiki-cho, Takayama 506. ☎ **0577/33-4531.** 24 rms (5 with bath). A/C MINIBAR TV TEL. ¥8,000 ($80) per person without bath, ¥9,000–¥13,000 ($90–$130) per person with bath. Rates ¥1,000 ($10) higher on Sat and July 20–Aug. All rates incude breakfast, dinner, and service. No credit cards. Directions: Walk 10 minutes.

Another ryokan close to the Folk Village, Hida Gasshoen is secluded on a hillside, and its approach has one of the most impressive stone walls I've ever seen—massive boulders, some of which measure 10 feet high, all neatly piled on top of one another. The main building, housing most of the guest rooms, was built in 1980 and was designed to resemble an old *gassho-zukuri* farmhouse. Meals are served in a genuine 200-year-old thatched farmhouse. Rooms in a separate ancient house have their own private bath and toilet, and one of the five rooms with bath is a combination room, with both a bed and tatami.

Kinkikan (98)

48 Asahimachi, Takayama 506. ☎ **0577/32-3131.** 14 rms (10 with bath). A/C MINIBAR TV TEL. ¥15,000–¥25,000 ($150–$250) per person. All rates include breakfast, dinner, and service. AE, JCB, V. Directions: Walk 6 minutes.

Kinkikan is right in the center of old Takayama, set back from a small side street and surrounded by a wall. Dating from the Edo Period and once owned by Lord Kanamori, it later served as a restaurant and today is still famous for its meals. The small lobby, full of furniture made of *shunkei-nuri* lacquerware crafted in Takayama, opens onto a delightful 300-year-old garden, just the kind of place that invites relaxation. Most of the guest rooms were built about a decade ago, each one utilizing Japanese craftsmanship in its own distinctive interior design. One room, for example, has shoji screens and wall trimmings in shunkei-nuri lacquer, while another room is decorated with the wood of local trees. Three rooms on the ground floor have peaceful views of the garden. All rooms have private toilet, and most have private bath as well. As with all ryokan, however, there's a public bath for communal bathing; this one was built about seven years ago.

Ryokan Hishuya (99)

1-464 Kami-Okamoto-cho, Takayama 506. ☎ **0577/33-4001.** Fax 0577/34-5065. 14 rms (all with bath). A/C MINIBAR TV TEL. ¥15,000–¥25,000 ($150–$250) per person. All rates include breakfast, dinner, and service. AE, DC, JCB, V. Bus: From platform 2 to the last stop.

Built a little more than a decade ago and possessing all the grace and charm you'd expect from a first-class ryokan, this place is just a minute's walk from the Hida Minzoku Mura Folk Village on the quiet outskirts of town. Its rooms have views of either the garden surrounding the ryokan or the distant mountain peaks. Five rooms have their own wooden bathtub and are more expensive; the other rooms all have the smaller unit bathroom typically found in a business hotel. Dinner is served individually in the guest rooms, while breakfast is served in a communal dining hall. If you request it in advance, you can get a Western breakfast of scrambled eggs, toast, ham, coffee, and juice. If requested in advance, shabu-shabu is served to guests who stay a second night.

Seiryu (100)

6 Hanakawa-cho, Takayama 506. ☎ **0577/32-0448.** Fax 0577/35-2345. 24 rms (all with bath). A/C MINIBAR TV TEL. ¥10,000–¥25,000 ($100–$250) per person, depending on day of week and season. All rates include breakfast, dinner, and service. AE, JCB, MC, V. Directions: Walk 6 minutes.

Down the street from Kinkikan (described above) is this modern ryokan. Two rooms combine beds with a separate tatami section, making them good choices if you want the feel of living on tatami but prefer the comforts of a bed. Although dinner is served in your own room, breakfast is served in a tatami dining hall, with each person receiving his or her own little tray. For a Western breakfast, request it the day before.

MINSHUKU

Hachibei (101)

1-389 Kami-Okamoto-cho. ☎ **0577/33-0573.** Fax 0577/35-2389. 32 rms (none with bath). A/C TV TEL. ¥7,000 ($70) per person. All rates include breakfast, dinner, and service. V. Transportation: Hachibei has its own shuttle bus and will pick you up if you call from the station.

A few minutes' walk from the Hida Minzoku Mura Folk Village, this minshuku is a big old house with a new addition. It has a pleasant open hearth where guests can sit and socialize in the evening. Most of those staying here are young Japanese. The public baths are large and in the new wing look out on a tiny garden. The front garden features a red arched bridge, koi pond, and marble table and seats.

✪ Minshuku Sosuke

1-64 Okamoto, Takayama 506. ☎ **0577/32-0818.** 13 rms (none with bath). A/C TV. ¥7,500–¥10,000 ($75–$100) per person. All rates include breakfast, dinner, and service. No credit cards. Directions: Walk 8 minutes southwest.

The entryway of this delightful minshuku across from the Green Hotel resembles those of farmhouses on display at the Folk Village, filled with country knickknacks and exuding a warm and friendly atmosphere. There's an old open-hearth fireplace, called an *irori,* in the communal room to the left as you enter—if it's chilly you'll be invited to sit down and warm yourself. The couple running this minshuku are outgoing and friendly. The cuisine served includes local specialties and is plentiful and delicious. Mealtimes are especially fun. Everyone is seated around one long table, where each person introduces himself or herself. Since most of the guests are Japanese, this is a good opportunity to learn about other parts of the country. Although the building housing the minshuku is 160 years old, the inside has been remodeled, and all the rooms are spotlessly clean. Children are warmly welcomed.

Yamakyu

58 Tenshoji, Takayama 506. ☎ **0577/32-3756.** Fax 0577/35-2350. 28 rms (none with bath). A/C TV TEL. ¥7,000 ($70) per person. All rates include breakfast, dinner, and service. No credit cards. Taxi: 5 minutes.

Yamakyu has a deserved reputation for serving the best meals in town in its price range. Although it's located a bit far from the station—about a 20-minute walk or a 5-minute taxi ride—it's only a 10-minute walk to the old part of town. As with most minshuku, the Japanese-style rooms are without private bathroom, but the public baths are large and pleasant. Display cases line the corridors, showing off a collection of glass bowls, vases, clocks, and lamps.

Hotels

Four Seasons

1-1 Kanda-cho, Takayama 506. ☎ **0577/36-0088.** Fax 0577/36-0080. 46 rms (all with bath). AC MINIBAR TV TEL. ¥12,436–¥13,596 ($124.36–$135.96). All prices include tax and service. AE, MC, V. Directions: Walk 8 minutes from the station on Kokubunji Street and turn left for the Lacquerware Museum.

Although this modern-looking building is unfortunately out of place in Takayama, the hotel is an excellent choice in terms of quality of rooms for price. Some rooms have wooden floors (important for the allergy conscious), and all have views. Free tea and ¥250 ($2.50) coffee are offered all day in the pleasant lobby, and a large Japanese bath with Jacuzzi overlooking a small garden is a plus. Vending machines dispense beer and soda. A restaurant serves Japanese food and becomes an inexpensive izakaya in the evening. (By the way, no it is not part of the famous top-notch Four Seasons Hotels.)

Takayama Green Hotel

2-180 Nishinoishiki-cho, Takayama 506. ☎ **0577/33-5500.** With breakfast and dinner, ¥18,000 ($180) per person double or twin with bath; ¥12,000 ($120) per person triple with bath. In peak seasons and Sat–Sun ¥2,000–¥4,000 ($20–$40) per person extra. AE, DC, JCB, MC, V. Directions: Walk 8 minutes southwest.

The largest hotel in town, this is the place to stay if you like all the conveniences in one building—restaurants, bar, beer garden (open summers only), shopping, beauty and barber salons, bike rentals, tennis courts, public bath, tea lounge, and sushi bar. The hotel has only five singles, all without bath. There are both Japanese- and Western-style rooms. A new annex was under construction as I prepared this edition, and as a consequence, information may change and prices may go up.

A Youth Hostel

Youth Hostel Tenshoji Temple

83 Tenshoji-machi, Takayama 506. ☎ **0577/32-6345.** 150 beds. ¥3,800 ($38) for JYHA members, ¥4,300 ($43) for nonmembers. Without meals ¥2,600 ($26). Private room ¥1,000 ($10) extra. All rates include breakfast, dinner, and service. No credit cards. Directions: Walk 20 minutes east of Takayama Station.

This youth hostel is located in a temple, a good hike from the station. Unfortunately, there's no bus to the hostel. Guests sleep on futon in tatami rooms. The woman running the hostel told me that for family reasons she may not go on serving meals.

Dining

Takayama has some local specialties that you should try while you're here. The best known is *hoba miso,* which is soybean paste mixed with dried scallions, ginger, and mushrooms and cooked on a dry magnolia leaf at your table above a small clay burner. *Sansai* are mountain vegetables, including edible ferns and other wild plants, and *ayu* is river fish, grilled with soy sauce or salt.

Expensive

Kakusho (102)

2-98 Babacho. ☎ **0577/32-0174.** Reservations required. Set meal ¥10,000 ($100); obento ¥5,500 ($55). Tax and service charge extra. No credit cards. Daily 11:30am, 1:30pm, 5:30pm, and 7pm. Closed sometimes Wed, sometimes Thurs. VEGETARIAN.

For the big splurge, you should dine at Kakusho, which offers local vegetarian fare called *shojin-ryoori,* typically served at Buddhist temples. Situated on the slope of a hill in the eastern part of the city, a few minutes' walk from old town, this 250-year-old building with heavy wooden beams and ocher-colored walls is surrounded by a mossy garden and a clay wall. You must make a reservation (it is not even open for dinner unless it's reserved) to dine here, and there's only one meal, *tenshin obento,* served in private tiny tatami rooms in a separate old building in the back with a view of the mossy garden. This place is worth the price of the various mountain vegetables, mushrooms, nuts, and tofu you'll be served.

MODERATE

Bandai Kado Mise (103)

50 Hanakawa-cho. ☎ **0577/33-5166.** Set meals ¥1,100–¥4,300 ($11–$43); mountain vegetable teishoku ¥2,100 ($21). No credit cards. Thurs–Tues 11am–3pm and 5–8pm. LOCAL SPECIALTIES.

If Suzuya, described below, is closed or crowded, try this nearby restaurant called Bandai Kado Mise, located across the street and a few shops down, a five-minute walk from the station, near Kokubunji Street. It doesn't have an English menu, so the easiest thing to do is to order one of the obento box meals or the mountain vegetable teishoku. Tempura or Hida beef teishoku are also available.

Sara (104)

Kamisanno-machi. ☎ **0577/35-0174.** Reservations recommended. Set dinners ¥5,000–¥10,000 ($50–$100); set lunches ¥1,000–¥3,500 ($10–$35). No credit cards. Lunch 11:30am–2:30pm; dinner 5:30–7:30pm. Closed sometimes Wed, sometimes Thurs. VEGETARIAN/FISH.

Owned by the same family that runs Kakusho (see above), Sara, in a modern Japanese setting, serves vegetarian cuisine at lower prices. For lunch, it offers either soba set meals or shojin ryori obento. In the evening, there are vegetarian or fish meals. Seating is on tatami mats upstairs or on pillows at a low counter, where the servers are in a well below, backed by a small window garden. Notice the handmade paper shoji screens. Sara closes on the same days as Kakusho, which can be erratic—reservations are a good idea. Sara is a 10-minute walk from the station, around the corner from the Fuji Folk Craft Museum and across from a forge and candle maker.

Suzuya (105)

24 Hanakawa-cho. ☎ **0577/32-2484.** Reservations recommended. Set meals ¥1,100–¥3,100 ($11–$31). AE, V. Wed–Mon 11am–3pm and 5–7:30pm. LOCAL SPECIALTIES.

This place, which specializes in Takayama cuisine, is easy to recognize by the curtains with bells hanging above the front door and the cedar ball hanging from the eaves. Inside, it's darkly lit, with shoji screens covering the windows, wooden beams above, and traditional Takayama country decor. This place is so popular that if you come for lunch between noon and 1pm, you'll probably have to wait for a table. There's an English-language menu, with such local specialties as mountain vegetables, hoba miso, ayu river fish, Takayama-style buckwheat noodles, Hida beef, and *tobanyaki,* which is a stew of leeks, Japanese green peppers, mushrooms, and various chicken parts (including liver, gizzard, skin, and meat), which you cook at your table in your own personal cooker. Also cooked at your table is the *sansai-misonabe,* a stew with Chinese cabbage, chicken, and various mountain vegetables flavored with miso. This place, a five-minute walk from Takayama Station, is highly recommended.

INEXPENSIVE

Ichoo

1-9612 Sowacho. ☎ **0577/33-8913.** Set lunches ¥800–¥1,500 ($8–$15). No credit cards. Tues–Sun 9am–10pm. PIZZA/SANDWICHES.

If you're staying in a ryokan or a minshuku and hunger for something different from what you had for breakfast and dinner, maybe homemade pizza will hit the spot. This small coffee shop is located on the left side, going up Kokubunji Dori, just after the Hida Kokubunji (shrine) and before the taxi stand, about halfway between the station and the river. Look for a white wooden door. Pizzas are large, with a generous amount of cheese. If they don't have any pizzas (it happens), try the sandwiches—they're good.

Jizakaya (106)

Suehiro Nibangai. ☎ **0577/34-5001.** ¥600–¥1,800 ($6–$18). No credit cards. Fri–Wed 5pm–1am. VARIED JAPANESE.

Technically a drinking place because of the dozen different varieties of sake it sells, Jizakaya also serves a wide variety of Japanese food, including tofu, steak, noodles, and river fish. A large room with tatami and low tables, this place has a convivial drinking-hall atmosphere. The menu is in Japanese only, but you can easily see what others are ordering. *Motsu-nabe,* a beef-liver stew, is a specialty offered for ¥900 ($9). Jizakaya is a five-minute walk east of Takayama Station, to the left off Kokubunji Dori and across from a park.

Kofune (107)

6-6 Hanasato-cho. ☎ **0577/32-2106.** Dishes ¥550–¥2,200 ($5.50–$22). No credit cards. Thurs–Tues 10:30am–3pm and 5–8pm. Directions: Exit the train station and walk 2 minutes toward the river; the noodle shop will be on your left. SOBA/UDON.

If you're looking for an inexpensive meal, this homey, pleasant noodle shop is just a few minutes' walk from the station. It has an English menu with photos, offering such dishes as noodles served plain or with river fish, tempura, or mountain vegetables. The tempura soba or udon teishoku (set meal) includes tempura, river fish, and grilled mountain vegetables.

2 Shirakawa-go

With its thatch-roofed farmhouses, rice paddies trimmed with flowerbeds, roaring river, and pine-covered mountains rising on all sides, Shirakawa-go is one of the most picturesque regions in Japan. Sure, it has its share of tour buses, especially in May, August, and October, but because of its rather remote location and because it's accessible only by bus, Shirakawa-go still remains off the beaten path for most tourists in Japan. A visit to this rural region could well be the highlight of your trip.

Stretching almost 5 miles beside the Shokawa River and squeezed to a width of only 1.8 miles between towering mountains, Shirakawa-go is a tiny region with a population of 1,900 living in several small communities. Because Shirakawa-go is hemmed in by mountains, land for growing rice and other crops has always been scarce and valuable. As a result, farmhouses were built large enough to hold extended families, sometimes with as many as several dozen family members living under one roof. Because there was not enough land available for young couples to marry and build houses of their own, only the oldest son was allowed to marry. The other children were required to spend their lives living with their parents and helping with the farming. But even though younger children were not allowed to marry, a man was allowed to choose a young woman, visit her in her parents' home, and father her children. The children then remained with the mother's family, becoming valuable members of the labor force.

Before the roads came to Shirakawa-go, winter always meant complete isolation, as snow six feet deep blanketed the entire region. Open-hearth fireplaces (irori) were commonplace in the middle of the communal room. They were used both for cooking and for warmth, and because there were no chimneys, smoke simply rose into the levels above. So the family lived on the ground floor, with the upper floors used for silk cultivation and storage of utensils. Because of the heavy snowfall, roofs were constructed at steep angles, known as gassho-zukuri in reference to the fact that the tops of the roofs look like hands joined in prayer.

Today, there are about 190 thatched farmhouses, barns, and sheds in Shirakawa-go, most of them built about 200 to 300 years ago. The thatched roofs are about two feet thick and last about 50 years. The old roofs are replaced in Shirakawa-go every April, when one to four roofs are replaced on successive weekends. The whole process involves about 200 people, who can replace one roof in a couple of days.

The most important village for visitors is **Ogimachi,** with its 600 residents. It has minshuku and a couple of museums, including an open-air museum of old thatched farmhouses depicting how life used to be in the region before roads opened it up to the rest of the world.

ESSENTIALS

Ogimachi lies in Gifu Prefecture, 347 miles northwest of Tokyo. The **telephone area code** for Ogimachi is 05769.

GETTING THERE The most common way of reaching Ogimachi is **by bus** from Takayama, with a change of buses in Makido. The entire trip takes about three hours along winding mountain roads and costs ¥3,100 ($31) one-way. If you have a JR Rail Pass, however, you can use it between Makido and Ogimachi, in which case you'll need to buy a ticket only for the stretch between Takayama and Makido, which costs ¥1,800 ($18). Buses run throughout the year, with about three departures from Takayama daily, depending on the season. You can also reach Ogimachi by JR Tokai bus from Nagoya, costing ¥4,400 ($44) one-way. From Kanazawa, Meitetsu buses depart for Ogimachi between July and November and cost ¥2,300 ($23) one-way.

VISITOR INFORMATION There's a **tourist office** (☎ 05769/6-1751 or 6-1013) located in a small square in the center of the town. You can reserve a room in a minshuku here if you haven't already done so, as well as pick up a pamphlet in English. If you want to make the tourist office your very first stop upon arrival in Shirakawa-go, get off at the bus stop called Gassho-Shuraku. The tourist office is about a minute's walk away and is open Thursday through Tuesday from 8:30am to 5pm.

GETTING AROUND Your own two feet can do it best. You can **walk** from one end of the village to the other in about 10 minutes. You can also rent a **bicycle** at Tezuka for ¥510 ($5.10) per hour, with lower half- and full-day rates.

SPECIAL EVENTS The **Doburoku Matsuri Festival** is held at Shirakawa-go from October 14 through 19 every year.

WHAT TO SEE & DO

To see how rural people lived in past centuries in the Japan Alps, you should visit the **Shirakawa-go Gassho Zukuri Minkaen,** an open-air museum with 25 gassho-zukuri houses and sheds filled with implements and tools. In some of the buildings, artisans are engaged in woodworking, pottery, basket weaving, and toy making. All the buildings are open to the public, and you are allowed to wander at will. It is located about a five-minute walk from Ogimachi, along a footpath that takes you over a suspension bridge and through a narrow tunnel. Hours are 8:30am to 5pm most of the year; in the winter, from December through March, they are 9am to 4pm, while in August they are 8am to 6pm. The entrance fee is ¥700 ($7) for visitors 12 and over, half price for children 6 to 11, and free for children under 6.

Next to Gassho Zukuri Minkaen is a soba restaurant and crafts center, **Soba Dojo** (Buckwheat Noodle Center), which opened in 1993 in a beautiful all-*hinoki* (cedar)-wood gassho-zukuri. Here you can learn how to make soba from buckwheat flour. For ¥1,800 ($18), you can make 280 grams of soba, which you then can eat on the premises or take home with you to feed to a party of six. Reservations are required in advance; contact the Shirakawa Village Office at 517 Hatogaya, Shirakawa, Ohno, Gifu 501-56 (☎ 05769/6-1311). Soba is made on low wooden tables; you sit on cushions and are provided with an apron. To dine on your creation, you retire to a tatami.

In addition to the open-air museum, there are several other old farmhouses in Ogimachi open to the public. **Seikatsu Shiryokan** (108) (☎ 05769/6-1818), open April through November, daily from 8am to 5pm, displays farm implements and folkcrafts, including cooking utensils, lacquerware, household items, and clothing. The upstairs is crammed with all kinds of farming tools and items used in everyday life, including mountain backpacks, hatchets, handmade skis, saddles, and implements for silk cultivation. Charging an admission of ¥200 ($2), half price for children, Seikatsu Shiryokan is located on the southern edge of town, past the Juemon minshuku (described in "Accomodations," below). **Myozenji** (109) (☎ 05769/6-1009) is a 170-year-old house with farm equipment, straw raincoats, palanquins, and other relics on display. You can walk around upstairs and inspect how the roof looks from the inside. If a fire is burning in the downstairs irori, you can also see how smoky the upstairs can get. Attached to the house is the main hall of Myozenji Temple, which is more than two centuries old. Hours here are generally from 7:30am to 5pm (8am to 5pm in winter), and admission is ¥200 ($2). Myozenji is located in the heart of Ogimachi.

Not far from Myozenji is a relatively new museum, **Doburoku Matsuri no Yakata** (110) (☎ 05769/6-1655), erected in honor of the Doburoku Matsuri Festival, held in Shirakawa-go every year from October 14 to 19. Centering on a locally produced and potent sake, the festival is held just outside the museum's grounds at Hachimanjinja Shrine. The ¥800 ($8) entrance fee allows you to see some of the costumes worn during the festival and to try some of the festive sake. The highlight of the museum, however, is the hour-long video that shows the festival activities, including dances, parades, and plenty of drinking. Although the video is rather corny in parts, it's probably the next best thing to being at the festival itself. The museum is open daily from 8:30am to 4:30pm (closed in winter).

And finally, for an overview of the entire village, walk along the gently sloping road that leads from the north of Ogimachi to the **Ogimachi Viewing Point.** There's a restaurant up here, but in my opinion the best thing to do is bring your own snack and walk to the hill's westernmost point (that is, toward the river, where there are some secluded benches). From here you have a marvelous view of the whole valley.

ACCOMMODATIONS

Because huge extended families living under one roof are a thing of the past, many residents of Ogimachi have turned their gassho-zukuri homes into minshuku. There are more than two dozen minshuku in Ogimachi, giving visitors the unique chance to stay in a thatched farmhouse with a family that might consist of grandparents, parents, and children. English is limited to the basics of "bath," "breakfast," and "dinner," but smiles go a long way. Most likely the family will drag out their family album with its pictures of winter snowfall and the momentous occasion when their thatched roof was repaired.

All minshuku charge approximately ¥6,800 to ¥10,000 ($68 to $100) per person, including two meals. Tax and a heating charge of ¥300 ($3) are extra. Most of them are fairly small affairs, with about five to nine rooms open to guests. Rooms are basic, without bath or toilet, and you're expected to roll out your own futon. Staying in any of the minshuku listed here will be a memorable experience; all of them have thatched roofs, and rates include breakfast and dinner, but none accept credit cards or have private baths.

Juemon (111)

Shirakawa, Mura, Ogimachi, Ono-gun, Gifu. ☎ **05769/6-1053.** 10 rms. ¥8,000 ($80) per person.

Located on the southern edge of Ogimachi, near the Doburoku Matsuri-no-kan bus stop, this minshuku features an irori in the dining room and recently remodeled bathroom facilities. Juemon is a favorite place for foreigners traveling in Japan; the outgoing woman who runs this place is quite a character.

Magoemon (112)

Shirakawa, Mura, Ogimachi, Ono-gun, Gifu. ☎ **05769/6-1167.** 6 rms. ¥6,800–¥7,000 ($68–$70).

Magoemon stands by the suspension bridge on the way to the open-air museum, a few minutes' walk from the bus stop toward the river. Two rooms overlook the Shokawa river. About 200 years old, this minshuku features a cozy living room with open-hearth irori, a wooden communal bathtub, and Western-style flush toilets.

Nodaniya (113)

Shirakawa, Mura, Ogimachi, Ono-gun, Gifu. ☎ **05769/6-1011.** 5 rms. ¥6,800 ($68) per person.

Life in this minshuku, across from Hachiman-jinja, centers around the irori, where you'll dine. I had some of the best food I've ever had in a minshuku. The family is very friendly; the owners went out of their way to help me do my laundry and tempt my daughter with children's favorite foods.

Otaya (114)

Shirakawa, Mura, Ogimachi, Ono-gun, Gifu. ☎ **05769/6-1425.** 5 rms. ¥6,800 ($68) per person.

Otaya is located less than a five-minute walk from the bus stop on the northern edge of the village, giving it a little more privacy. A couple of the rooms face a small river that cuts deep into a ravine. A pond outside the front door contains the fish you'll have for dinner.

Yosobe (115)

Shirakawa, Mura, Ogimachi, Ono-gun, Gifu. ☎ **05769/6-1172.** 4 rms. ¥6,800 ($68) per person.

Yosobe, a small minshuku a few minutes' walk from the bus stop, near the tourist office, has a communal dining area that's small and friendly, with an irori in the middle of the room. The rooms facing the front of the house open onto wooden verandas, polished smooth by years of wear. In case it matters, the toilets here are nonflush, in the Japanese style.

DINING

Since all minshuku and ryokan serve breakfast and dinner, you'll need only a lunch venue.

Gassho

Shirakawa-go Gassho Zukuri Minkaen. ☎ **05769/6-1419.** ¥600–¥1,500 ($6–$15). No credit cards. Daily 8:30am–5pm. Closed Dec–Mar. NOODLES/OBENTO/LOCAL SPECIALTIES.

If you're visiting the open-air museum and want a quick lunch or snack, next to the museum's entrance you'll find two thatch-roofed establishments that combine modern restaurants with souvenir shops. Simple places, they offer noodles, obento lunch boxes, and sansai or hoba miso teishoku. Gassho offers a teishoku for ¥1,500 ($15), with mountain vegetables.

Irori (116)

☎ **05769/6-1737.** ¥450–¥1,600 ($4.50–$16). No credit cards. Summer, Wed–Mon 8:30am–11pm. Winter, Wed–Mon 10am–11pm. LOCAL SPECIALTIES.

This place, on Ogimachi's main road, a few minutes' walk from the tourist office, is easy to spot because of a huge block of gnarled wood beside its front door. The inside of this gassho-zukuri house is appropriately rustic and even has an irori where you can fry your own fish on a skewer. The menu, in Japanese only, includes fresh river fish (*ayu*), wild mountain vegetables called *sansai, hoba miso* (soybean paste cooked on a magnolia leaf over a small clay pot), *yakisoba* (fried noodles), and *sansai-soba* (mountain vegetables and noodles). I opted for the *yakidofu teishoku* set meal, which consists of fried tofu covered with fish flakes, vegetables, rice, and soup. You might also want to come here for a nightcap. Beer starts at ¥500 ($5) and sake at ¥400 ($4).

Kitanosho (117)

☎ **05769/6-1506.** Noodles ¥600 ($6); teishoku ¥1,100–¥1,600 ($11–$16). No credit cards. Daily 10am–5pm. Closed Dec–Mar. Directions: Walk to the southern edge of Ogimachi (about a 10-minute walk from tourist office); it's on the right side, across from Juemon minshuku. LOCAL SPECIALTIES.

Another large thatched farmhouse that has been turned into a restaurant, this one is on the other side of town. It also has an irori, in the middle of a large tatami room. From the dining hall you can look out over the Shokawa River. When you finish your meal, climb the steep stairs to have a look at the second floor, where the heavy wooden beams are held together with just rope. Dishes include river fish, *sansai udon* (noodles and mountain vegetables), curry rice, hoba miso, and *oyakodon* (chicken and egg on rice). The menu is in English with photos. You can order complete meals: the *sansai teishoku* for ¥1,100 ($11) or the *iwana teishoku* (river fish) for ¥1,600 ($16).

3 Matsumoto

146 miles NW of Tokyo

Located in the middle of a wide basin about 660 feet above sea level and surrounded on all sides by mountain ranges, Matsumoto boasts a fine feudal castle with the oldest existing donjon (keep) in Japan, as well as an outstanding woodblock-print museum. Although the city itself (pop. 200,000) is modern, with little remaining from its castle days, I find the town pleasant, the air fresh, and its people among the nicest I've encountered in Japan. Most travelers pass through Matsumoto on their way to more remote regions of the Japan Alps. Encircled with towering peaks, sparkling mountain lakes, and colorful wild flowers, Matsumoto serves as the gateway to hiking trails in the Japan Alps and in nearby Chubu Sangoku National Park.

ESSENTIALS

The **telephone area code** for Matsumoto, lying in Nagano Prefecture, is 0263.

GETTING THERE **By Train** There's a direct JR line to Matsumoto from Tokyo's Shinjuku Station. The *Limited Express Azusa* reaches Matsumoto in about $2^1/_2$ hours, while the *Express Alps* takes a bit longer, about 5 hours. The Azusa costs

¥6,080 ($60.80) and the Alps ¥5,050 ($50.50). There's also a direct train from Nagoya, which takes about 2¼ hours.

By Bus From Tokyo's Shinjuku Station, the bus takes about 3¼ hours at a cost of ¥3,400 ($34); from Nagoya, 3½ hours at a cost of ¥3,400 ($34); from Osaka, 5½ hours at a cost of ¥5,600 ($56).

VISITOR INFORMATION Before departing from Tokyo, be sure to pick up a sheet called "Matsumoto and Kamikochi" at the Tourist Information Center. It gives the latest train schedules, as well as information on sights in and around Matsumoto. It also recommends hiking trips (lasting two to four hours) from Kamikochi, a small village that you can reach in a little more than two hours via train and bus from Matsumoto.

In Matsumoto itself, the **tourist information window** is on the east side of Matsumoto Station (☎ 0263/32-2814). Open daily from 9:30am to 8pm in summer (9am to 6pm in winter), it has a good pamphlet with a map of the city (destinations are written in English). Its excellent English-speaking staff will also help with accommodations.

GETTING AROUND You can **walk** to Matsumoto Castle, just a mile northeast of the station. If you want to visit the other sights, however, you'll have to go by **bus** or **taxi.**

WHAT TO SEE & DO

Originally built in 1504, when Japan was in the throes of continuing bloody civil wars, **Matsumoto Castle** (☎ 0263/32-2902) is a fine specimen of a feudal castle, with the oldest existing donjon in the country. Surrounded by a willow-lined moat with ducks and white swans, the outside walls of the donjon are black, earning the place the nickname of Karasu-jo, or Crow Castle. It's a rather small castle, dark and empty inside. Take your shoes off at the entrance and walk in stocking feet over worn wooden floors and up steep and narrow steps until you finally reach the sixth floor, from which you have a nice view of the city. The castle grounds are open daily from 8:30am to 5pm. An entrance fee of ¥500 ($5) includes admission to the **Japan Folklore Museum,** located next to the castle. A rather eclectic museum, it has displays relating to archeology, history, and the surrounding region, including armor, an ornate palanquin, clothing, farming equipment, butterflies from around the world, insects, animals of the Japan Alps, and a wonderful collection of old clocks from Japan and other nations.

The **Japan Ukiyo-e Museum,** 2206-1 Koshiba, Shimadachi (☎ 0263/47-4440), is one of the best museums of woodblock prints in Japan. It houses the ukiyo-e collection of Tokichi Sakai, which contains more than 100,000 prints, including representative masterpieces of all known ukiyo-e artists. It's believed to be the largest collection of its kind in the world. The exhibition changes every two months. A 10-minute slide show with explanations in English introduces the current exhibition, and a pamphlet in English describes the history of the collection and how woodblock prints are made. The museum is open Tuesday through Sunday from 10am to 5pm and charges ¥800 ($8) admission. From the Matsumoto JR Station platform 7, take the Kamikoshi Line 10 minutes to Oniwa Station (¥170/$1.70; JR Rail Pass not accepted) and then walk 15 minutes. If that's too complicated, the ¥1,200 ($12) taxi ride is well worth it.

One more museum worth visiting if you have time is the **Matsumoto Folkcraft Museum** or *Matsumoto Mingei-kan* (118) (☎ 0263/33-1569), located about 15 minutes by bus or taxi from Matsumoto Station (if you're going by bus, take the platform 1 bus and get out at the Shimoganai Mingeikan Guchi stop). Open Tuesday through Sunday from 9am to 5pm, it contains products of wood, glass, bamboo, and porcelain from Japan and foreign countries. Particularly beautiful are its wooden chests. Admission is ¥200 ($2).

If perchance you studied violin when you were young, maybe you were one of the countless children around the world who learned by the well-known Suzuki Method. In Matsumoto is the famous **Suzuki Shin-ichi Talent Education Institute,** where young and old alike from around the world come to study violin, piano, cello, and flute. Dr. Suzuki, founder of the method, is now in his late 90s but is still actively involved in the daily lessons. Group and private lessons for both pupils and teachers of the Suzuki Method are held throughout the week; guests are welcome to watch, but you must make advance reservations. There are also periodic concerts given by graduating musicians of the institute. For more information and to make reservations, call the institute anytime between 9am and 5pm Monday through Saturday (☎ 0263/32-7171). Dr. Suzuki's group lesson is generally held from 9 to 11am, but it would be wise to check the time beforehand.

Commemorating another famous Matsumoto musician is the **Saito Kinen Festival** in early September, with director Seiji Ozawa and such international big names as Jessye Norman participating. Saito Kinen was an early prominent conductor of Western music and influenced other musicians, Ozawa among them. If you're in Matsumoto in September, get details from the tourist office (☎ 0263/32-2814).

If you're traveling with youngsters, you might want to take a trip to **Alps Park,** located on one of Matsumoto's surrounding wooded hills, where you'll find the Alps Dream Coaster. I don't know who thinks up these names, but this one is a toboggan run and doesn't allow much time for dreaming. The race down the hill and around curves takes only a few minutes, during which time you swear you're going to fly off course. Closed in the winter, it's open the rest of the year from 9am to 5pm, and one trip down costs ¥300 ($3) for those 12 and older; ¥200 ($2) for children 6 to 11; free for kids under 6. To reach Alps Park, take the bus from Matsumoto Station bound for Alps Koen; the trip takes about 25 minutes. Since there are only five buses daily, ask for the timetable at the tourist office. A restaurant and hiking trails are located in the park.

ACCOMMODATIONS

Because Matsumoto is popular primarily with hikers used to roughing it along nature trails, the facilities available are geared mainly toward convenience. However, to accommodate the Saito Kinen Festival and an increasing number of foreign tourists, a luxury-style hotel has been built. Directions are from Matsumoto Station.

EXPENSIVE

Buena Vista

1-2-1 Honjo, Matsumoto 390. ☎ **0263/37-0111.** Fax 0263/28-3325. 200 rms (all with bath). A/C MINIBAR TV TEL. ¥8,000–¥11,000 ($80–$110) single; ¥15,000–¥27,000 ($150–$270) twin; from ¥60,000 ($600) suite. AE, DC, JCB, MC, V. Directions: Walk 5 minutes.

Matsumoto's newest and fanciest hotel, the Buena Vista is a white gleaming structure built to blend with the city by, among other things, repeating the region's sloped-roof designs. In the modern interior there are Japanese lithographs and international artworks. Built to accommodate conferences and festivals, this is where performers, such as Jessye Norman, stay during the Saito Kinen Festival. International bell captains are at your service to help you in English.

Rooms in restful colors have semi-double, quilt-covered beds and larger-than-usual tiled baths, plus CNN. The more expensive corner twins are larger and have a separate sink area, with a handy velveteen vanity stool. Unfortunately, there are no doubles. Higher room rates are for peak season; the winter ¥8,000 single is a great bargain.

Dining/Entertainment: Five restaurants serve continental, Chinese, Japanese, and coffeehouse fare. There are two bars and one disco.

Services: Same-day laundry.

Facilities: Conference hall with six-language interpreting facility, business center, gift shop with a good selection of Nagano Prefecture crafts, newsstand, beauty salon, florist.

MODERATE

Hotel New Station

1-1-11 Chuo, Matsumoto 390. ☎ **0263/35-3850.** Fax 0263/35-3851. 103 rms (all with bath). A/C TV TEL. ¥6,700–¥7,200 ($67–$72) single; ¥11,200 ($112) double; ¥11,200–¥14,200 ($112–$142) twin. All rates include tax and service. AE, DC, JCB, MC, V. Directions: Walk 1 minute.

This business hotel offers a very pleasant and good-size single with a comforter and large desk. All rooms come with coin-operated TV. The front-desk personnel are very helpful and accommodating, but not much English was spoken here during my last visit. Doubles have semi-double beds. A restaurant turns into a lounge at night.

Matsumoto Tokyu Inn

1-3-21 Fukashi, Matsumoto 390. ☎ **0263/36-0109.** Fax 0263/36-0883. 160 rms (all with bath). A/C MINIBAR TV TEL. ¥9,000 ($90) single; ¥16,600 ($166) double or twin; ¥26,600 ($266) deluxe twin. AE, DC, JCB, MC, V. All rates include service. Directions: Across from the station.

The Matsumoto Tokyu Inn is a practical, clean, convenient, and pleasant business hotel. Four kinds of rooms are offered: a nicely decorated single with semi-double-size bed; a double-bedded room; a twin; and a deluxe twin with sofa, chairs, and a separate vanity area with its own sink. Facilities include the Shangri-La restaurant, serving Western and Japanese dinners, a bar/lounge, and vending machines on the eighth floor. As a service to the forgetful, rugs in the elevator tell what day of the week it is (they are changed daily).

INEXPENSIVE

Enjyoh Bekkan

110 Utsukushigahara-onsen, Satoyamabe-ku, Matsumoto 390. ☎ **0263/33-7233.** Fax 0263/36-2084. 19 rms (8 with bath). TV. ¥4,800 ($48) single without bath, ¥5,800 ($58) single with bath; ¥9,000 ($90) twin without bath, ¥10,300 ($103) twin with bath; ¥12,500 ($125) triple without bath, ¥14,700 ($147) triple with bath. Breakfast ¥800 ($8) extra; Japanese-style dinner ¥4,500 ($45) extra. AE, MC, V. Bus: 20 minutes to Utsukushigahara-onsen Bus Terminal.

Although it's a bit far from the center of Matsumoto, this simple ryokan is a member of the Japanese Inn Group and offers simple and clean tatami rooms. What's more, it's located near a hot spring and offers hot-spring bathing 24 hours a day.

$ Hotel Ikyu (119)

1-11-13 Honjo, Matsumoto 390. ☎ **0263/35-8528.** Fax 0263/35-9500. 19 rms (all with toilet only). A/C MINIBAR TV TEL. ¥4,500 ($45) per person without meals, ¥7,000 ($70) per person including breakfast and dinner. No credit cards. Directions: Walk 8 minutes.

A bit on the old side but very reasonably priced and run by friendly people, the Hotel Ikyu is popular with young Japanese. Fourteen tatami rooms and five Western-style rooms are available, all with heater, stocked fridge, hot-water pot for tea, and coin-operated TV, among other amenities. There are lots of windows in this place and added touches like plants in the stairwell. Meals are served in a small dining hall adjoining the hotel.

Matsumoto Tourist Hotel

2-4-24 Fukashi, Matsumoto 390. ☎ **0263/33-9000.** 104 rms (66 with bath). A/C TV TEL. ¥5,200 ($52) single without bath, ¥5,900–¥7,500 ($59–$75) single with bath; ¥11,500 ($115) double or twin with bath. Japanese-style tatami rooms without private bath, ¥5,500 ($55) for one person, ¥9,300 ($93) for two people, ¥12,000 ($120) for three. AE, DC, JCB, MC, V. Directions: Walk 6 minutes.

This business hotel has one restaurant serving both Western breakfast and Japanese food, a public bath, and a vending area. Its staff is very friendly, but again, no one speaks much English. All rooms are simple and some have a refrigerator. Stay here if you prefer a Western-style hotel.

Suminoe (120)

3-2-10 Fukachi Matsumoto 390. ☎ **0263/32-0415.** 10 rms (none with bath). TV. ¥3,000 per person. No credit cards. Directions: Walk 8 minutes.

Ok, so it's just the basics, a bare tatami room, but it's inexpensive, and there's heating and a communal shower and bath. The man who runs it is friendly enough and collects mountain rocks. To reach Suminoe, turn right out of the station, left at Fujitsu Plaza, then keep going straight until the street turns into a small lane alongside a stream. When the stream is on your right side, look left for Suminoe in a white building. Suminoe is on the tourist information center map, but it's misplaced.

DINING

Hanakurabe

Buena Vista Hotel, 1-2-1 Honjo. ☎ **0263/37-0111.** Main dishes ¥1,000–¥3,500 ($10–$35); set lunches ¥900–¥4,000 ($9–$40); set dinners ¥3,500–¥6,000 ($35–$60). All rates include tax and service. AE, DC, JCB, MC, V. Daily 11:30am–10pm. SUSHI/TEPPANYAKI/KAISEKI.

Hanakurabe is a good choice to try out various Japanese cuisines. You can either sit at counters to watch sushi or teppanyaki prepared or dine at tables or in private tatami rooms with sunken *kotatsu* (in this case, heated floorboards in a well under the table) to warm your feet. Graceful in their kimono, the waitresses are very attentive. I had the Gozen set meal for ¥2,500 ($25); it consisted of seaweed, pickles, soup, rice, dessert, and tea.

Kajika (121)

1-2-21 Fukashi. ☎ **0263/35-7632** or 36-7716. Reservations recommended for tatami rooms. Kaiseki ¥6,000–¥15,000 ($60–$150); lunch teishoku ¥1,000–¥3,000 ($10–$30). AE, DC, JCB, MC, V. Mon–Sat 11:30am–2pm and 5–10pm. Closed hols. Directions: In the Cosmo Building behind the bus terminal. KAISEKI/VARIED JAPANESE.

Kajika, a modern Japanese restaurant, is decorated in stained dark wood and cool white walls. The lunch menu is quite reasonable, with various kinds of teishoku available, ranging from the ubiquitous obento lunch box to sashimi, tempura, and soba set meals. At dinnertime, only kaiseki and set dinners are served.

Naja

4-3-20 Ote. ☎ **0263/36-9096.** Main dishes ¥450–¥800 ($4.50–$8); set meals ¥800 ($8). No credit cards. Mon–Sat 11:30am–11pm. Directions: Walk 10 minutes. VEGETARIAN.

If you're a vegetarian or a fan of natural foods, head for Naja. A tiny place with only three tables, it looks and sounds as if it had been transported from a commune in the woods of California—a plain wooden decor and music from the '60s playing in the background. Its English menu lists a daily brown-rice set meal, as well as such offerings as soybean curry with yogurt, noodles, tofu steak, and brown-rice porridge. On a tiny alley, walk straight away from the station on Ekimae street, turn left at the post office street, cross the bridge, turn right in front of the police box, and after you pass the next bridge, left at the alleyway which has a white coffee shop on the corner.

Shikimi (122)

1-5-5 Chuo. ☎ **0263/35-3279.** Unagi donburi (eel on rice) ¥1,600 ($16); platters of assorted sushi (moriawase) ¥1,600–¥3,300 ($16–$33). No credit cards. Mon–Wed, Fri 11:45am–3pm and 4:30–9:30pm; Sat–Sun 11:45am–9pm. Directions: Walk 4 minutes. EEL/SUSHI.

For inexpensive Japanese fare close to Matsumoto Station, try Shikimi, which specializes in eel and sushi. An atmosphere of old Japan is evoked with its traditional tiled roof and its cast-iron lanterns hanging from outside eaves. The inside is a successful blend of the old and new, tastefully decorated with wooden sliding doors, small tatami rooms, a wooden counter, and paper lanterns. I recommend the *unagi donburi* (strips of eel on rice), which comes with soup and pickled vegetables. If sushi is more to your liking, try one of Shikimi's platters of assorted sushi, called *moriawase,* available in three different sizes.

Taiman

4-2-4 Ote. ☎ **0263/32-0882.** Reservations recommended. Main dishes ¥3,000–¥9,000 ($30–$90); set meals ¥5,000–¥18,000 ($50–$180). AE, DC, JCB, MC, V. Thurs–Tues 11:30am–2pm and 5–9pm (last order 8pm). Directions: Walk 10 minutes. FRENCH.

If you feel like treating yourself to a wonderful French meal in rustic yet elegant surroundings not far from Matsumoto Castle, this is an excellent choice. The inside of this ivy-covered building has heavy wooden beams, high ceilings, fresh flowers on the tables, and elaborate cutlery. Set dinners with changing menus are available, as well as less expensive fixed-price meals of either sole or stewed beef, which are always on the menu and come with soup and dessert. A la carte dishes include roast lamb. My luncheon for ¥5,000 ($50), which included bread or rice, started with an hors-d'oeuvre plate of marinated squid, lox, cream cheese, capers, and grated onion. The next course was crab gratin, cooked in a cheese-and-tomato base, resembling lasagne. The main dish was sautéed pork wrapped in bacon and topped with cheese. Also included in the price were salad, dessert, and coffee.

4 Magome & Tsumago

Approximately 61 miles E of Nagoya, 55 miles SW of Matsumoto

If you're traveling between Nagoya and Matsumoto, you'll most likely pass through the Kiso Valley in the mountainous Nagano Prefecture. Surrounded by the towering Japan Alps, the deep valley formed by the Kiso River has always served as a natural passageway through the hills. In fact, it was one of the two official roads that linked Kyoto with Edo (present-day Tokyo) back in the days of the Tokugawa shogunate (the other route was the Tokaido Highway, which passes through Hakone). Known as the Nakasendo Highway, it was the route of traveling daimyo (feudal lords) and entourages of samurai retainers journeying between Japan's two most important towns. To serve their needs, 11 post towns sprang up along the Nakasendo Highway. Back then, it took three days to travel through the valley.

Of the old post towns, Magome and Tsumago are two that still survive, with many of the old buildings left intact. A five-mile pathway skirting the Kiso River links the two villages, providing hikers with the experience of what it must have been like to travel the Nakasendo Highway back in the Edo Period. Visits to the picturesque villages, as well as the hike, can easily be accomplished in a one-day excursion from Nagoya or Matsumoto.

ESSENTIALS

The **telephone area code** for both Magome and Tsumago, lying in Nagano Prefecture, is 0264.

GETTING THERE **By Train & Bus** Since neither Magome nor Tsumago is directly on a train line, you'll have to make the final journey by bus. To reach Magome, take the Chuo Honsen Line (which connects Nagoya and Matsumoto) to Nakatsugawa Station, from which it's a 35-minute bus ride to Magome. Nakatsugawa Station is 1 hour from Nagoya and about 1¼ hours from Matsumoto. Tsumago is only a 7-minute bus ride from Nagiso Station (¥270/$2.70), which is also on the Chuo Honsen Line. Note that not all trains stop in Nagiso or Nakatsugawa, so make certain your train stops where you want to go. Note also that buses are not very frequent, so you might want to inquire about bus schedules beforehand (because it's in the same prefecture, the Matsumoto Station tourist office has information on bus schedules). If you can't walk the distance between Magome and Tsumago, there's also a bus that travels between the two villages. You could walk around Tsumago and then take a bus. In any case, you are better off starting in Tsumago, as walking the other direction is mostly uphill.

If you have luggage, you might be interested in knowing that a **luggage-transfer service** between Magome and Tsumago is available daily from July 20 through August, and on Saturday, Sunday, and national holidays from April 15 to September 20. Luggage is accepted at either town's tourist office no later than 9am for morning delivery and no later than 1pm for afternoon delivery. It would be prudent, however, to verify this beforehand by calling the Magome or Tsumago tourist office, but note that only Japanese is spoken.

VISITOR INFORMATION There is a friendly tourist office both at the bus stop and in town at Tsumago and one in Magome, which has an English pamphlet and map. But as no English is spoken, you may want to inquire ahead at the Matsumoto tourist office or even at the Tourist Information Center in Tokyo or Kyoto, where you can pick up a pamphlet called "Kiso Valley." It provides a rough sketch of the five-mile hiking path between the two villages.

The **information office** for Magome itself is at Yamaguchi-mura, Kiso-gun (☎ 0264/59-2336); and for Tsumago, at Nagiso-machi, Kiso-gun (☎ 0264/57-3123). They are open daily from April to November from 9am to 4:30pm, but closed an undecided day of the week.

HIKING FROM MAGOME TO TSUMAGO

Allow about three hours for the hike between Magome and Tsumago, although you can probably do it in two hours. It doesn't matter which town you start from, since either way it's a beautiful walk, tracing the contours of the Kiso Valley and crisscrossing the stream over a series of bridges. The trail is mainly a footpath, although at times it follows a paved road. In any case, the signs are in Japanese, so familiarize yourself with the kanji for **Magome** (123) and **Tsumago** (124). As the trail does go up some steep inclines, be sure to wear your walking shoes. And have fun—this is a great walk!

MAGOME Magome, the southernmost post town, has old inns and souvenir shops that line both sides of a gently sloping road. It takes about 20 minutes to stroll through the town. Halfway up the slope you'll see a museum dedicated to Shimazaki

Toson (1872–1943), a noted novelist and poet who was born in Magome and who set many of his works there.

TSUMAGO Tsumago, the second post town from the south, is in my opinion the more beautiful and authentic. Threatened with gradual decline and desertion after the Chuo Line was constructed in 1911, thus bypassing Tsumago, the town experienced decades of neglect—probably what ultimately saved it. Having suffered almost no modernization in the zeal of the 20th century, Tsumago was a perfect target for renovation and restoration in the early 1970s. In a rare show of insight (I say rare because this has hardly ever happened in Japan), electrical wires, TV antennas, and telephone poles were hidden from sight along the main road. Tsumago looks much as it did back in the days of Edo.

On the main street of Tsumago, be sure to stop off at **Waki-honjin Okuya** (☎ 0264/57-322), an officially appointed inn once serving as a way station for daimyo and court nobles. It was also home of a sake brewery. The present house dates from 1877, rebuilt with *hinoki* cypress trees, which has a special significance for this region. For centuries, all the way through the Edo Period (1603–1867), the people of the Kiso Valley were prohibited from cutting down trees, even if they were on private property. When the Meiji Period dawned and the ban was finally lifted, wealthy landowners were quick to rebuild in a more stately manner. This house, rebuilt in the style of a grand old castle, was visited by Emperor Meiji himself in 1880. Be sure to check out the daimyo's bathtub and toilet. Next door is the **Rekishi Shiryokan,** which serves as a local museum, with displays of rice bowls, hair combs, books with ukiyo-e prints, and other items relating to the Edo Period. Admission is ¥600 ($6) for the two adjoining museums.

Across the lane is the **Tsumagojuku Honjin** (☎ 0264/57-4100), another restored inn where the Daiyo's closest family and other high nobles stayed. In 1830 the Shimizu family had plans drawn up to rebuild their inn, but the renovation was to take 160 years. Family circumstances changed, the heirs moved to Tokyo, and the existing inn fell into ruin. Generations later, an ancestor found the plans and gave them to the township, which built the inn in 1995 following the original plans and using techniques dating from the period. You'd swear it was original—it's very interesting. Admission here is ¥300 ($3), but you can buy a ¥700 ($7) ticket that allows admission to all three museums, which are open daily from 9am to 5pm (closed New Year).

DINING

There are a number of restaurants serving noodles and the like along the main streets of both Magome and Tsumago. One I like is **Tawaraya** (125) (☎ 0264/57-2257), which offers *sansai soba,* a filling bowl of hot buckwheat noodles in soup with mushrooms and mountain vegetables for ¥900 ($9) or two skewers of *gohei* (grilled rice cakes with sauce) for ¥500 ($5) and *anmitsu,* a traditional dessert, for ¥400 ($4). Seating is at tables (wooden slabs with irregular natural edges) or on tatami. The women working here couldn't be nicer. Its open from 10am to 4pm daily from mid-March to mid-November.

9

The Rest of Honshu

In addition to Tokyo, Kyoto, and the Japan Alps, Honshu has numerous other towns and attractions well worth a visit. As the largest of Japan's islands, centrally situated, Honshu is where many of the country's most important historical events took place and is thus the home of many castles, gardens, temples, shrines, and other famous sights linked with the past. Honshu offers enough variety to satisfy the whims of every traveler: from the bustling modern cities of Osaka and Nagoya to the sacred shrines of Ise-Shima National Park and Miyajima; from Kurashiki, with its quaint historic districts, to the religious sanctuaries atop Mt. Koya; from the great ports of Kobe and Hiroshima, with their heavy industries, to the outlying forests and agricultural districts, where the bulk of the country's tea and silk are produced, along with rice and cotton. Little wonder that many travelers to Japan never make it farther than the shores of Honshu.

Honshu is where more than 80% of the Japanese people live. Its climate ranges from snowy winters in the north to subtropical weather in the south. The middle of the island is traversed by Japan's longest river, the Shinano.

1 Nagoya

227 miles W of Tokyo, 92 miles E of Kyoto, 116 miles E of Osaka

Although it's Japan's fourth-largest city, with a population of 2.15 million, Nagoya is a place most foreigners never stop to see. True, it doesn't have the attractions of many of the nation's cities, but it does have a castle originally built by the first Tokugawa shogun, as well as one of Japan's most important Shinto shrines.

You can visit the world-famous Noritake chinaware factory, observe summer cormorant fishing, and visit an open-air architectural museum with structures dating from the Meiji Period. Nagoya, capital of Aichi Prefecture, also serves as the gateway to Toba and Ise-Shima National Park. Incidentally, Nagoya is the birthplace of pachinko, the upright Japanese pinball machine now found in the farthest corners of the islands. Its industries include automobile manufacture, chinaware, shipbuilding, and aircraft construction. Almost completely destroyed during World War II, Nagoya was rebuilt with wide, straight streets, many of which are named.

ESSENTIALS

The **telephone area code** for Nagoya, lying in Aichi Prefecture, is 052.

GETTING THERE **By Plane** If you're arriving at Nagoya International Airport on a domestic or international flight, you can take the airport shuttle bus to the Melsa Meitetsu Bus Center in front of the Sakura Dori exit of Nagoya Station, for ¥750 ($7.50). There are buses that depart every 10 minutes from 6am to 8:35pm daily for the 45-minute ride.

By Train The Shinkansen bullet train takes 2 hours from Tokyo (the Nozomi, only 1¾ hours), 43 minutes from Kyoto, and 1 hour from Shin-Osaka Station.

By Bus The Tomei Highway Bus takes 5 hours and 40 minutes from Tokyo. The Meishin Highway Bus takes 2 hours and 25 minutes from Kyoto and 3 hours from Osaka.

VISITOR INFORMATION Before leaving Tokyo or Kyoto, drop by the Tourist Information Center to pick up a free leaflet called "Nagoya and Vicinity," which has a map of the city and a list of attractions in Nagoya and the surrounding area.

Nagoya itself has one of the better tourist information facilities in Japan. The **Nagoya International Center** is on the third floor of the Nagoya International Center Building, 1-47-1 Nagono (☎ 052/581-0100), a 10-minute walk from the train station. It's open Tuesday through Saturday from 9am to 8:30pm and on Sunday and holidays from 9am to 5pm (closed the second Sunday of February and August). This modern facility has an English-speaking staff, a lounge area with a TV featuring CNN newscasts from the United States, and information on the city, including a free monthly publication called *Nagoya Calendar.* The center also advises foreign residents on how to get a visa, where to find an apartment, and which doctors speak English. Be sure to pick up a city map, as well as a map of the underground shopping arcade radiating out from Nagoya Station. Also available are English-language magazines on Nagoya, such as *Eyes* and *Avenues.*

There's also a **tourist information center** at the central concourse of Nagoya Station (☎ 052/541-4301), open from 9am to 7pm. It has pamphlets and maps of Nagoya. Its staff speaks English but sometimes is not very helpful.

GETTING AROUND Clustered around JR Nagoya Station are the Shinkansen Station, the Meitetsu Bus Terminal, Meitetsu Shin-Nagoya Station, the city bus terminal, and Kintetsu Station, as well as many hotels and a huge underground shopping arcade. The city's downtown area is called Sakae and has many shops, restaurants, and department stores. The easiest way to get around is via the city's subway system, which is simple to use because stations have names written in both English and Japanese, as well as English announcements and digital signs in trains. Probably the most important line for tourists is the Meijo Line, which runs through Sakae. It takes you to both Atsuta Jingu Shrine (stop: Jingu-Nishi) and to Nagoya Castle (stop: Shiyakusho); and if you take this line all the way to the end, you'll end up in Ozone—no kidding!

WHAT TO SEE & DO

Built for his ninth son by Tokugawa Ieyasu, the first Tokugawa shogun of Japan, ✪ **Nagoya Castle** (☎ 052/231-1700), at 1-1 Honmaru, Naka-ku, was completed in 1612 and served as both a stronghold and a residence for members of the Tokugawa family for almost 250 years, until the Meiji Restoration ended Tokugawa rule in 1868. Tokugawa, a shrewd and calculating shogun, forced feudal lords throughout Japan to contribute to the castle's construction, thereby depleting their resources and making it harder for them to stage rebellions.

Although Nagoya Castle was destroyed in World War II, it was rebuilt in 1959 and is almost a carbon copy of the original. Like most reconstructed castles in Japan, this one is made of ferroconcrete, and it even has an elevator up to the fifth floor, where you have fine views of Nagoya and beyond.

The 154-foot donjon houses treasures that escaped the bombing during World War II, including beautiful paintings on sliding doors and screens. On top of the donjon roof are two golden dolphins, thought to protect the castle from dreaded fires. The dolphins each weigh about 2,650 pounds and are made of cast bronze covered with 18-karat-gold scales. The castle is open daily from 9am to 4:30pm, and the entrance fee is ¥500 ($5) for those 12 and over, ¥100 ($1) for children.

East of the castle is **Ninomaru Garden,** one of the few remaining castle gardens in Japan. Besides providing a beautiful setting, it served as an emergency shelter for the lord in case of enemy attack. Stop by the Ninomaru Tea House—it's said that if you drink tea here, five years will be added to your life.

The **Tokugawa Art Museum,** 1017 Tokugawa-cho, Higashi-ku (☎ 052/935-6262), houses thousands of documents, armor, swords, helmets, pottery, lacquerware, and paintings that once belonged to the Tokugawa family. The museum's most famous exhibits are picture scrolls of *The Tale of Genji* (*Genji Emaki*)—but they're displayed only a few weeks a year in autumn (check with the tourist office). Closed during exhibition changes, the museum is open Tuesday through Sunday from 10am to 5pm; the entrance fee is ¥1,000 ($10) for adults, ¥700 ($7) for students, ¥500 ($5) for children.

Because it contains one of the emperor's Three Sacred Treasures, **Atsuta Jingu Shrine** (☎ 052/671-4151) at 1-1-1 Jingu, Atsuta-ku, is revered as one of the three most important shrines in Japan. It enshrines the Kusanagi-no-Tsurugi (Grass-Mowing Sword), and even though the sword isn't on public display, Japanese make pilgrimages here to pay their respects. (The other two sacred treasures are the Sacred Mirror, which is in the Ise Jingu Shrines, and the Jewels, which are kept in the Imperial Palace in Tokyo.)

Atsuta Shrine was founded in the 2nd century and was rebuilt in 1965. According to legend, the Grass-Mowing Sword was presented to an ancient prince named Yamato-Takeru, who used it during a campaign against rebels in eastern Japan. The rebels set a field of grass on fire, and the prince used the sword to mow down the grass, thereby quelling the fire. *Atsuta* means "hot field" in Japanese.

If you like high places, you may be interested in knowing that the **Nagoya TV Tower** (☎ 052/971-8546) was the first such tower in Japan. Since it opened in 1954, more than 28 million visitors have ridden its glass-enclosed elevators to its observation platform, approximately 300 feet above the ground, for a bird's-eye view of the sprawling city. Used jointly by Nagoya's five television stations, the tower is about a two-minute walk from the Sakae subway station in the heart of Nagoya. It's open daily from 10am until 10pm (until 9pm in spring and autumn and until 6pm in winter and on rainy days and Mondays). Admission to the observation platform is ¥700 ($7) for adults and ¥350 ($3.50) for children.

The **Osu Kannon Temple** is in Nagoya's *shitamachi,* or old downtown, and was originally constructed by Shogun Tokugawa Ieyasu in 1612 (rebuilt after the war). The temple itself houses a large collection of sutras, and the area still has a pleasant shitamachi feeling. A flea market is held here twice a month (check with the tourist office). In front of the temple is **Ohsu Uiro** (☎ 052/262-1816), the most famous shop for *uiro.* These rice jelly cakes are a Nagoya specialty, making Ohsu Uiro a good place to take a break.

For centuries Nagoya has been a pottery and porcelain production center, and today the city and its vicinity manufacture 90% of Japan's total export chinaware. The largest chinaware company in Japan is Noritake, known the world over for its fine tableware. Founded in 1904, Noritake now exports to more than a 100 nations around the world. The **Nagoya Noritake Factory,** about a 10-minute walk north of Nagoya Station, offers free tours Monday through Friday at 10am and 1pm. Conducted in English, the tours last about an hour, but you must reserve in advance (☎ 052/561-7114). The tour begins with an excellent film that depicts the history of Noritake and describes the manufacturing and decorating processes involved in making porcelain. After the film ends, you're led on a trip through the various production stages of the Diamond Collection, Noritake's best porcelain line. Unlike most modern-day factories, where work is largely automated, almost all the work here is still done by hand. If you're interested in buying some porcelain, try the two shops next to the plant that sell Noritake ware at reduced prices. Ask your guide to point you in the right direction.

If you're a real Noritake fan, you might want to make a trip to the company's largest store in Japan, located at 2-1 Shinsakae-Machi, Naka-ku (☎ 961-6831). The closest subway station is Sakae. The store is open daily from 9am to 6pm, closed on national holidays.

In addition to its chinaware, Nagoya and its vicinity also rank first in the nation in the production of cloisonné, and the Nagoya International Center has a 14-minute videotape demonstrating its production. You can also visit the **Shippo Industrial Hall** (☎ 052/441-3411) at 119-2 Jubei, Tojima Shippo-cho. Open Wednesday through Monday (closed national holidays) from 9am to 5pm, *Shippo Sangyou Kaikan* is free of charge to the public and contains exhibits of cloisonné ware (*shippo* means cloisonné in Japanese). If you want to see demonstrations of how cloisonné is made, the Industrial Hall can arrange an appointment with one of the area's many cloisonné factories. To reach the Industrial Hall, take the Meitetsu bus from the Meitetsu Bus Terminal (in the Melsa Building, next to Nagoya Station) to the Yasumatsu stop; from there it's a 15-minute walk. Or, from Shin-Nagoya Station, take the Meitetsu Line to Shippo-cho Station; the hall is nearby.

Nearby Attractions

If architecture is your passion, you'll find a lot to delight in at **Meiji Mura** open-air museum (☎ 0568/67-0314). It features more than 50 buildings and structures dating from the Meiji Period (1868–1912). Before Japan opened its doors in the mid-1800s, unpainted wooden structures dominated Japanese architecture. After Western influences began infiltrating Japan, however, stone, brick, painted wood, towers, turrets, and Victorian features came into play. Contained on the grounds of this 250-acre museum are Western homes that once belonged to foreigners living in Nagasaki and Kobe; official government buildings and schools; two Christian churches; a post office; a Kabuki theater; a brewery; and even a prison. Don't miss the front facade and lobby of the original Imperial Hotel in Tokyo, designed by American architect Frank Lloyd Wright.

To get to Meiji Mura, your best bet is to take the Meitetsu Line from the Meitetsu Shin-Nagoya Station to Inuyama (¥520/$5.20 one way) and change there for a direct bus to Meiji Mura (¥380/$3.80 one way). Admission to Meiji Mura is ¥1,500 ($15) for adults, ¥1,000 ($10) for students, ¥600 ($6) for children.

Meiji Mura is open daily from 9:30am to 5pm (to 4pm from November through February).

There are two places near Nagoya where you can watch **cormorant fishing** every night (except during a full moon) in summer. In this ancient Japanese fishing method, trained *ukai* (seabirds) dive into the water in search of ayu, a small Japanese trout. To ensure that the cormorants don't swallow the fish, the birds are fitted with neck rings.

The city of **Gifu** features cormorant fishing on the Nagaragawa River from May 11 to October 15, and you can view the whole spectacle aboard a small wooden boat. To reach Gifu, take the Meitetsu Main Line train from Meitetsu Shin-Nagoya Station to Shin-Gifu Station. From there, switch to a local train or bus heading for Nagarabashi Station. You'll see the ticket office (*Gifu-shi Ukai Kanransen Jimusho*) after exiting the station. Beginning mid-April you can call ahead to reserve your ticket (☎ 0582/62-0104 between 8:45am and 5:15pm). In May, June, and October, tickets cost ¥2,900 ($29) for adults and ¥2,500 ($25) for children; from July to September, tickets are ¥3,300 ($33) for adults and ¥2,900 ($29) for children.

The other site for cormorant fishing is in the town of **Inuyama,** from June 1 to September 30. Take the Inuyama Line of the Meitetsu Railways from Meitetsu Shin-Nagoya Station to Inuyama Yuen Station. From there it's a five-minute walk. Tickets are sold from 9am to 4pm, and the action starts after 6pm. Call ahead to make reservations (☎ 0568/61-0057). Tickets cost ¥2,500 ($25, or ¥2,000/$20 for children 4 to 11) in June and September, and ¥2,800 ($28, or ¥2,300/$23 for children 4 to 11) in July and August.

There are several attractions of interest in **Inuyama City**—come here for the day and top it off with the cormorant fishing described above. Just a 10-minute walk from Inuyama Yuen Station, for example, is **Inuyama Castle,** which was constructed in 1537 and is Japan's oldest castle. Admission is ¥300 ($3), and it's open daily from 9am to 5pm. Another popular activity is to **shoot the rapids** of the Kiso River. Boats depart approximately every 30 or 60 minutes for the one-hour trip, priced at ¥3,400 ($34) for adults and ¥1,700 ($17) for children. For more information, call the Nihon-Rhine Kanko Company (☎ 0574/28-2727).

ACCOMMODATIONS

EXPENSIVE

✪ Century Hyatt

2-43-6 Meieki, Nakamura-ku, Nagoya 450. ☎ **052/541-1234** or 800/233-1234 in the U.S., Canada, and the Caribbean. Fax 052/571-0151. 115 rms. AC MINIBAR TV TEL. ¥24,000–¥30,000 ($240–$300) twin/double; from ¥60,000 ($600) suite. AE, DC, JCB, MC, V. Station: Nagoya (3 minutes).

Excellent location, modern yet warm interiors, comfortable rooms with spacious desks, room extras (like satellite TV), efficient service, and the Hyatt name make this hotel a popular place to stay for the foreign business executive, especially if he or she has brought along a spouse. You can walk underground from the station to the hotel (great when it's raining). I highly recommend this hotel.

Dining/Entertainment: Guests are treated to complimentary welcome drinks or morning coffee in the continental Lounge, while Whizz features international cuisine (described in "Dining," below).

Services: 24-hour concierge, secretarial service, printing service, same-day laundry. **Facilities:** Parking.

Hotel Nagoya Castle

3-19 Hinokuchi-cho, Nishi-ku, Nagoya 451. ☎ **052/521-2121.** Fax 052/531-3313. 239 rms. A/C MINIBAR TV TEL. ¥24,000–¥30,000 ($240–$300) double; ¥24,000–¥35,000 ($240–$350) twin. AE, DC, JCB, MC, V. Subway: Sengencho Station on Tsurumai Line (10 minutes).

The chief attraction at this hotel, just west of Nagoya Castle, is wonderful views of the castle from its higher-priced twins and doubles. If you don't have a room with a view, I think you'll actually find the hotel location rather inconvenient.

Dining/Entertainment: The Crown restaurant features international entertainment, great views, and the revolving Crown Bar. There are Japanese, French, and Chinese restaurants as well, and the coffee shop, Boulogne, serves one of the best breakfast buffets I've seen at ¥2,000 ($20).

Services: Free newspaper, free shuttle bus to/from Nagoya Station.

Facilities: Indoor swimming pool, sauna and gym (fee: ¥3,000/$30), shops, business center.

Nagoya Kanko Hotel

1-19-30 Nishiki, Naka-ku, Nagoya 451. ☎ **052/231-7711.** Fax 052/231-7719. 505 rms. A/C MINIBAR TV TEL. ¥24,000–¥35,000 ($240–$350) double or twin. AE, DC, JCB, MC, V. Subway: Fushimi Station.

Located between Nagoya Station and Sakae, this first-class hotel offers many conveniences in one place, including a variety of restaurants and a shopping arcade. First opened in 1934 and completely renovated in 1985, it has a huge lobby featuring white brick, natural woods, brass, and contemporary glass chandeliers.

Dining/Entertainment: Five restaurants serve French, Japanese, and Chinese cuisine, including the 18th-floor Aurora with its views of the city and an all-you-can-eat buffet (see "Dining," below). There are two bars.

Services: Free newspaper.

Facilities: Shopping arcade, barbershop.

MODERATE

Hotel Castle Plaza

4-3-25 Meieki, Nakamura-ku, Nagoya 450. ☎ **052/582-2121.** Fax 052/582-8666. 262 rms. A/C MINIBAR TV TEL. ¥15,000–¥17,000 ($150–$170) double; ¥16,000–¥18,000 ($160–$180) twin. AE, DC, JCB, MC, V. Station: Nagoya (6 minutes).

Under the same management as the Hotel Nagoya Castle, this hotel has more facilities than you'd expect from a moderately priced establishment, including a dozen restaurants and bars, a travel agency, and a shopping plaza. The swimming pool, sauna, gym, and jogging track can be used for ¥3,000 ($30). The rooms are bright and cheerful, and the most expensive twins have good views of the city, plus a separate entrance foyer and semi-double-size beds.

Hotel Sunroute Nagoya

2-35-24 Meieki, Nakamura-ku, Nagoya 450. ☎ **052/571-2221.** Fax 052/571-2235. 276 rms. A/C MINIBAR TV TEL. ¥13,000–¥15,500 ($130–$155) twin; ¥16,000 ($160) double. AE, DC, JCB, MC, V. Station: Nagoya (3 minutes).

This is one of Nagoya's best and most conveniently located business hotels. A handsome brick building, it features a spacious lobby with an atrium and marbled fountain, and restaurants serving Japanese and Western food. As with many business hotels, the majority of its rooms are singles. Light-colored walls make the simply decorated accommodations bright and pleasant.

Meitetsu Grand Hotel

1-2-4 Meieki, Nakamura-ku, Nagoya 450. ☎ **052/582-2211.** Fax 052/582-2230. 242 rms. A/C MINIBAR TV TEL. ¥18,000–¥25,000 ($180–$250) twin; ¥20,000 ($200) double. AE, DC, JCB, MC, V.

Built in 1967, this hotel is conveniently located right above Meitetsu Station. In addition to its three restaurants, one lounge, and a beer garden open in the summer, it has shops from the basement to the sixth floor. The check-in desk is on the 11th floor. Singles are comfortably decorated with semi-double-size bed, desk, chair, and table, and all rooms have cable TV and minibar. The most expensive twin is a large room featuring an entry foyer, a separate vanity area, semi-double-size beds, and a sitting area with couch, chairs, and table separated from the sleeping area by a glass partition.

Nagoya Miyako Hotel

4-9-10 Meieki, Nakamura-ku, Nagoya 450. ☎ **052/571-3211.** Fax 052/571-3242. 400 rms. A/C MINIBAR TV TEL. ¥18,000–¥23,000 ($180–$230) twin; ¥20,000–¥23,000 ($200–$230) double. Japanese-style rooms, ¥20,000–¥30,000 ($200–$300) for one or two people. AE, DC, JCB, MC, V. Station: Nagoya.

This is one of the best hotels in this price category. As in all Miyako hotels, service is excellent, and all rooms have recently been refurbished. The hotel has an attractive ivory-colored marble lobby; a rooftop beer garden open in summer; Chinese, Japanese, and Western restaurants; and an underground shopping arcade with passageways to the Meitetsu Bus Terminal, Kintetsu Station, and Nagoya Station. Comfortable rooms have wooden furniture, and most singles face an inner courtyard—no view, but the rooms are quiet. Some of the 10 Japanese-style rooms have bathtubs made of cypress. Guests receive a free newspaper.

INEXPENSIVE

Nagoya Daini Washington Hotel

3-12-22 Nishiki, Naka-ku, Nagoya 460. ☎ **052/962-7111.** Fax 052/962-7122. 320 rms (all with bath). A/C TV TEL. ¥11,600–¥13,700 ($116–$137) double or twin. AE, DC, JCB, V. Subway: Sakae (3 minutes).

This hotel is near the restaurants and bars of the Sakae quarter. Unlike most business hotels, which have few facilities, it features three restaurants serving Japanese, Chinese, and Western food, and one bar. Even the cheapest singles manage to maintain a cheerful atmosphere, even though they're small and windowless. Twins and doubles are small but functional, with single, narrow beds, a small writing area, and two chairs. Machines dispense soda and beer.

Nagoya Plaza Hotel

3-8-21 Nishiki, Naka-ku, Nagoya 460. ☎ **052/951-6311.** Fax 052/951-6319. 176 rms (all with bath). A/C MINIBAR TV TEL. ¥10,000–¥11,000 ($100–$110) double; ¥10,500 ($105) twin. All rates include tax and service. AE, DC, JCB, MC, V. Subway: Sakae Station (3 minutes).

Also located in Sakae, this business hotel offers just the basics and is cheap. The decor could use some updating, but the staff is friendly and the location convenient. Rooms come with a desk. The cheapest single is rather bare, with just a bed and wall hooks for clothes. The hotel's one restaurant serves only breakfast, Japanese- or Western-style, with the price running ¥900 ($9).

Nagoya Youth Hostel

1-50 Kameiri, Tashirocho, Chikusa-ku, Nagoya 464. ☎ **052/781-9845.** Fax 052/781-7023. 80 beds. A/C. ¥2,200 ($22) for JYHA members and nonmembers. Sheets ¥200 ($2) extra; breakfast ¥460 ($4.60) extra; and dinner ¥800 ($8) extra. No credit cards. Subway: Higashiyama Koen (10 minutes).

As in most youth hostels, life here is fairly regimented: Check-in is 3 to 9pm, the front doors close at 9pm, lights are out at 10pm, and check-out is 6:30am (7am in winter).

Ryokan Iroha (126)

4-28 Yanagawa-cho, Nakagawa-ku, Nagoya 454. ☎ **052/671-0168.** Fax 052/681-7268. 70 rms (63 with bath). A/C TV TEL. ¥10,000 ($100) twin. JCB, MC, V. Directions: Kanayama Station on the Meijo Line (10 minutes) or a 15-minute taxi ride from Nagoya Station.

In a plain white building, this ryokan is more like a business hotel. Rooms are adequate (though baths are minuscule), and the price is right. Windows open, but ask for a south-side room with clear—not glazed—glass windows. Vending machines in the hall sell juice, coffee, and sodas, and there's a coin-operated laundry. There's a public bath with a view, but for men only. Japanese-style breakfast is ¥800 ($8), and dinner runs ¥1,500 to ¥2,000 ($15 to $20).

Ryokan Meiryu

2-4-21 Kamimaezu, Naka-ku, Nagoya 463. ☎ **052/331-8686.** Fax 052/321-6119. 23 rms (none with bath). A/C TV TEL. ¥8,000 ($80) twin; ¥10,500 ($105) triple. Japanese breakfast ¥600 ($6) extra; Japanese dinner ¥2,200 ($22) extra. AE, V. Subway: Kamimaezu (exit 3, 4 minutes).

A Japanese Inn group member, family-owned for more than 40 years, this concrete-and-wood building is a no-nonsense business accommodation. Most customers are Japanese businessmen, some of whom have lived here for years during the week, commuting home to families on weekends. The men's public bath also has a sauna (they don't have many female guests at this ryokan, but there is a separate public bath in case a lone female makes an appearance).

Youth Hostel Aichi-Ken Seinen-Kaikan

1-18-8 Sakae, Naka-ku, Nagoya 460. ☎ **052/221-6001.** Fax 052/204-3508. 90 beds. A/C. ¥2,800 ($28) JYHA members, ¥3,300 ($33) nonmembers. Breakfast ¥500 ($5) extra; dinner ¥1,000 ($10) extra. No credit cards. Bus: 50 to the Nayabashi stop (3 minutes).

It's worth a try, but this hostel's so centrally located it's usually full. Try to make a reservation one month in advance.

DINING

One of Nagoya's specialties is *kishimen* (white) noodles. It's also famous for *miso nikomi udon*—udon noodles served in a bean-paste soup and flavored with such ingredients as chicken and green onions. There are also fine restaurants serving kaiseki, tempura, and other Japanese cuisine, and I have included two other choices.

AROUND NAGOYA STATION

Nagoya Miyako Beer Garden

4-9-10 Meieki, Nakamura-ku. ☎ **052/571-3211.** Main dishes ¥500–¥2,000 ($5–$20); barbecue course ¥3,900 ($39). No credit cards. May–Aug, daily 6–8pm. BARBECUE/WESTERN/CHINESE.

For outdoor summer dining, head for the Miyako Hotel's beer garden, a five-minute walk from Nagoya Station. A plastic-food display case helps you make your selection—anything from frankfurters to sushi. The barbecue course (strips of beef that you grill at your table) includes all the beer or fruit juice you can consume. If you go the à la carte route, beer starts at ¥500 ($5).

Yamamoto-ya Honten (127)

In the basement of the Horiuchi Bldg., Sakura Dori. ☎ **052/565-0278.** Udon ¥970 ($9.70); udon with chicken ¥1,270–¥1,730 ($12.70–$17.30). No credit cards. Daily 10:45am–7:30pm. UDON NOODLES.

This chain noodle shop, a three-minute walk from Nagoya Station, near the Hotel Castle Plaza, specializes in miso nikomi udon. Its noodles, all handmade, are thick, hard, and chewy and are served in a type of bean paste special to Nagoya. If you like your noodles spicy, you can add a mixture of spices to your food from the large bamboo container on your table. An English-language menu with explanations makes ordering easy. The restaurant also sells its own noodles, if you want to take some home. Another specialty is *Nagoya kochin* (free-range chicken), which is ¥1,730 ($17.30).

If you want to try these noodles in Sakae, there's another shop just a couple of minutes from the Sakae subway station, in the basement of the Chu-Nichi Building (☎ 263-7519), open from 11am to 9pm.

In Sakae

Across the Border

Sakae Sky Bldg., 1-100 Sakae. ☎ **201-4300.** Main dishes ¥800–¥1,800 ($8–$18); beer ¥500 ($5); cocktails ¥800–¥1,000 ($8–$10). AE, MC, V. Sun–Thurs 6pm–1am (kitchen closes at 11pm), Fri–Sat 6pm–2am. Subway: Fushimi Station (5 minutes). TEX/MEX.

This is really a drinking establishment, but you'll feel right at home in this bar-restaurant, where all the staff are foreigners. The last time I was there, an Australian waited on me and the cook was Mexican. The decor is swap-meet eclectic, with drawings and business cards on the walls and ceiling, where patrons have "marked their spot," and a huge screen shows MTV and sports from the United States. Start light with nachos and quesadillas, then dig into southern spareribs or fried chicken, and wash it down with the "best margarita in the world" for ¥800 ($8). A cover charge of ¥500 ($5) for men and ¥300 ($3) for women—special price for foreigners only—is added on Friday and Saturday. Across the Border is on the side street along the Hilton Hotel.

Aurora

Nagoya Kanko Hotel, 1-19-30 Nishiki. ☎ **231-7711.** Lunch buffet ¥2,500 ($25) adults, ¥1,800 ($18) children 6–11; main dishes ¥3,200–¥5,000 ($32–$50). AE, DC, JCB, MC, V. Daily 11:30am–2:30pm and 5–10pm. Subway: Fushimi Station (2 minutes). BUFFET LUNCH/STEAKS/SEAFOOD.

This may be the best deal in town for lunch if you have a large appetite or if you're traveling with youngsters (children under 6 lunch with you for free), because you can have all you want and the choice (a mixture of French and Japanese) is large. In the evening, main dishes of steak and seafood offer less value for money. The panoramic view of Nagoya is a plus.

Kishimentei (128)

Toya Bldg., 3-20-4 Nishiki, Naka-ku. ☎ **951-3481.** Noodles ¥600–¥1,800 ($6–$18). No credit cards. Mon–Sat 11am–8:30pm (last order). Subway: Sakae (5 minutes). KISHIMEN NOODLES.

Kishimentei, a small hole-in-the-wall, has been offering Nagoya's specialty for more than 70 years—kishimen noodles. It even sells packages of noodles in case you want to take some home with you. There's no menu in English, but plastic food is displayed in the window. Meals include kishimen noodles with pork, tempura shrimp, or vegetables.

Torigin Honten (129)

3-14-22 Nishiki. ☎ **973-3000.** Set meals ¥1,400–¥4,800 ($14–$48). AE, DC, JCB, MC, V. Mon–Sat 5–11pm. Station: Sakae (6 minutes). YAKITORI.

In the heart of Nagoya, this 20-year-old casual restaurant with counter, tatami, or table seating is known for its *Nagoya kochi* (free-range chicken). It also serves yakitori, *miso-nabe* (rice cake, tofu, chicken, and vegetable stew), and kamameshi set meals. An amiable staff and a photo menu make it user-friendly; a black-and-white kura-style facade and a raccoon statue at the door make it easy to identify.

Whizz

Century Hyatt, 2-43-6 Meieki. ☎ **541-1234.** Main dishes ¥900–¥3,400 ($9–$34). AE, DC, JCB, MC, V. Mon–Sat 11:30am–2:30pm and 5:30–11:30pm. Closed hotels. INTERNATIONAL.

This is a sophisticated setting with quiet jazz music, a bar/counter perfect for lone diners/drinkers, and booths for romantic tête-a-têtes. Steak, seafood, and pasta are prepared in Thai, French, Chinese, and Japanese style. The daily pasta special at ¥1,500 ($15) is hearty. Foreign businesspeople to young Japanese couples dine here.

Yabaton (130)

3-6-23 Osu. ☎ **241-2409.** Set meals ¥950–¥1,600 ($9.50–$16). DC, MC, V. Tues–Sun 11am–9pm. Directions: From the corner of Wakamiya Dori and Otsu Dori, walk one short block south on Otsu Dori and turn right. TONKATSU.

You'll recognize immediately this everyman's eatery in shitamachi by its white curtains displaying comical pigs dressed like sumo wrestlers. The only thing served is tonkatsu, and Yabaton is famous for it. You'll be asked whether you want yours with *sa-u-zu* (sauce) or miso; the former is thicker and sweeter, but the latter is the specialty here (I ask for both and get away with it). *Donburi,* a breaded and fried pork cutlet on rice, is the cheapest, but recommended is the *hire,* a tender cut with less fat. A Nagoya family I met at Minshuku Sosuke in Takayama introduced me to this place, and I love it.

2 Ise-Shima National Park

289 miles W of Tokyo, 62 miles S of Nagoya

Blessed with subtropical vegetation, small islands dotting its shoreline, and the most revered Shinto shrine in Japan, Ise-Shima National Park merits a one- or two-night stopover if you're anywhere near Nagoya. Located on the Shima Peninsula and covering 200 square miles, this national park has bays and inlets that are the home of the Mikimoto pearl, Japan's famous women divers, and thousands of oyster rafts. Although you could conceivably cover the major attractions on a day's outing from Nagoya, I've included recommended accommodations in case you'd like to take in the sights at a more leisurely pace.

Ise-Shima's major attractions are concentrated in the small towns of Ise, Toba, and Kashikojima, all in Mie Prefecture. Ise, for example, is where you'll find the Ise Jingu Shrines; Toba contains the Mikimoto Pearl Island, with a pearl museum and demonstrations by women divers; and in Kashikojima you can visit the Shima Marineland or take boat trips around Ago Bay, perhaps the most scenic spot in the park.

ESSENTIALS

Ise-Shima National Park lies in Mie Prefecture.

GETTING THERE By Train The easiest way to get to Ise-Shima is from Nagoya on the private Kintetsu Nagoya Line (Kinki Nippon Railway), which departs about every 30 minutes or so from the Kintetsu Station next to the Japan Railways Nagoya Station. It takes about 1 1/2 hours to reach Ise (Ujiyamada Station), about 1 hour and 40 minutes to reach Toba, and 2 hours to reach Kashikojima. A ticket from Nagoya to the end of the line in Kashikojima costs ¥2,970 ($29.70) one-way. There are also Kintetsu lines to the Shima Peninsula from both Kyoto (2 1/4 hours to Toba) and from Osaka's Kintetsu Station in Uehonmachi (2 hours to Toba).

If you're on a Japan Rail Pass, you can also reach Ise-Shima by Japan Railway on several Kaisoku (Rapid) Mie trains a day, but you'll be charged an extra ¥440 ($4.40). JR trains terminate in Toba, so change to the Kintetsu private line there for Kashikojima.

VISITOR INFORMATION Be sure to drop by the Tourist Information Center in Tokyo or Kyoto to pick up the free leaflet "Ise-Shima." It lists train schedules from Osaka, Kyoto, and Nagoya, and gives information on the park's main attractions.

GETTING AROUND Transportation inside Ise-Shima National Park is either by local train or by bus. You might also consider joining a sightseeing tour. Although they're conducted in Japanese only, tours provide a convenient way of seeing the park's far-flung attractions.

WHAT TO SEE & DO

The easiest way to see the sights of Ise-Shima National Park is to start in Ise and work your way down the peninsula to Kashikojima.

ISE

Ise, the northern gateway to Ise-Shima National Park, is famous for the **Ise Jingu Shrines,** also called the Grand Shrines of Ise. The grounds consist of the Outer Shrine, the Inner Shrine, and more than 100 minor shrines.

The **Outer Shrine** *(Geku)* is just a 10-minute walk from either Ujiyamada or Iseshi Station. Founded in 478, it's dedicated to the Shinto goddess of harvest and agriculture. The **Inner Shrine** (*Naiku*) was founded a few centuries earlier and is dedicated to Amaterasu, the sun goddess. Since the shrines are about four miles apart, walk first to the Outer Shrine and then take a bus to the Inner Shrine. Buses run between the two shrines every 10 to 30 minutes; the fare is ¥380 ($3.80), half price for children.

The Ise Jingu Shrines are some of the few Shinto shrines in Japan without any Chinese Buddhist influences. Constructed of plain cypress wood, with thick thatched roofs, they are starkly simple and have no ornamentation except for gold and copper facing on their beams and doors. In fact, if you've come all the way to Shima Peninsula just to see the shrines, you may be disappointed—there's nothing much to see. The shrines are so sacred that no one is allowed close to them—no one except members of the imperial family and high Shinto priests. Both shrines are surrounded by four wooden fences, and we lesser mortals are allowed only as far as the third gate. Because of the fences you can't see much, but that doesn't stop the estimated six million Japanese who come here annually. They come because of what the shrines represent, which is an embodiment of the Japanese Shinto religion itself. The Inner Shrine is by far the more important because it's dedicated to the sun goddess, considered the legendary ancestress of the imperial family. It contains the Sacred Mirror (Yata-no-Kagami), one of the Three Sacred Treasures of the emperor.

According to legend, the sun goddess sent her grandson to Japan so that he and his descendants could rule over the country. Before he left she gave him three insignia—a mirror, a sword, and a set of jewels. As she handed him the mirror, she is said to have remarked, "When you look upon this mirror, let it be as if you look upon me." The mirror, therefore, is considered to embody the sun goddess herself and is regarded as the most sacred object in the Shinto religion. The mirror is kept in the deep recesses of the Inner Shrine in a special casket and is never shown to the public. (The sword is in the Atsuta Shrine in Nagoya, and the jewels are in the Imperial Palace in Tokyo.)

Even though you can't see much of the shrines themselves, they're still the most important stops in Ise-Shima. The Inner Shrine is surrounded by old cypress trees.

Watch how the Japanese stop after crossing the second small bridge on the approach to the shrine to wash and purify their hands and mouth with water from the Isuzu River. Its source lies on the Inner Shrine grounds itself, and it's considered sacred. You'll also see a couple of white royal horses, kept near the shrine for the use of the sun goddess. Perhaps the most amazing thing about the Outer and Inner Shrines is that even though they were founded centuries ago, the buildings themselves have never been more than 20 years old. Every 20 years they are completely torn down and rebuilt exactly as they were on neighboring sites. The present buildings were built in 1993 for the 61st time. No photographs of the shrines themselves are allowed.

Near the Inner Shrine is **Oharai-machi,** an interesting area in which to stroll or have tea or lunch. There are several beautiful, old wooden buildings here, including *kura,* or storehouses. A great place to try the sticky rice cakes for which Ise-Shima is famous is the original shop, **Akafuku** (131). You'll recognize the shop by the *kamado* (huge, red, ginger jar–shaped ceramic cooking stoves) used to heat water for tea in the open entranceway. It has been a tradition to serve complimentary tea to shrinegoers for centuries, and this shop, built in 1887, still does. You pay only for the cakes (¥230/$2.30 for three cakes with tea). First pay for your cakes at the old cash register on the dark-wood counter; then the staff, in dark-blue traditional cloth outfits, will serve you on tatami mats around braziers or benches in the back overlooking the river. Swallows fly in and out to their nests in the eaves. You can also watch the cakes being made. On the first of the month, a specialty cake is made, a different type for each month. Akafuku is open daily from 5am to 5pm.

Ise-Shima Skyline Highway

Near the front entrance of the Inner Shrine are buses that depart for Toba, traveling on the Ise-Shima Skyline Highway. About 10 miles long, it rises up over Mt. Asama, on top of which is **Kongoshoji Temple.** You can get off the bus here, visit the temple, and then catch the next bus on to Toba. Kongoshoji Temple is renowned for the vermilion-painted Moon Bridge, which forms a circle as it reflects in a pond, and for a huge footprint said to be Buddha's. Behind the temple is a pathway lined with poles erected in memory of departed loved ones. The entire ride from the Inner Shrine to Toba takes about 40 minutes and costs ¥1,000 ($10), half price for children.

Toba

Toba's best-known attraction is the **Mikimoto Pearl Island** (☎ 0599/25-2028), just a few minutes' walk from Toba Station and connected to the mainland via a short bridge. This attraction is geared entirely toward tourists, but is still quite enjoyable, especially if you have a weakness for pearls or have ever wondered how they're cultivated. In addition to a pearl museum and a shop, there's a demonstration hall where the processes of culturing pearls and sorting and stringing them are explained in live demonstrations. Most fascinating in my opinion is the **Mikimoto Memorial Hall,** rebuilt with high-tech touches in 1993 to commemorate the 100th anniversary of Mikimoto's cultured pearl success and designed to chronicle (in flawless English) the attempts, failures, and final success of Kokichi Mikimoto to cultivate pearls.

The son of a noodle-shop owner, Mikimoto went to Yokohama as a young man and was surprised to see stalls selling pearls with great success. Mikimoto reasoned that if oysters produced pearls as the result of an irritant inside the shell, why couldn't man introduce the irritant himself and thereby induce oysters to make pearls? It turned out to be harder than it sounded. Oysters used in Mikimoto's experiments kept rejecting the foreign material and dying. It wasn't until 1893, five years after he started his research, that Mikimoto finally succeeded in cultivating his first pearl. In 1905, Mikimoto was able to cultivate his first perfectly round pearl, after which he built what is probably the most successful pearl empire in the world. Mikimoto, who died at the age of 93, was a remarkable man and a real character. His favorite expressions included "Have you anything worth talking about?" and "Make the most of it." Nothing disgusted him more than wastefulness. He once said to Emperor Meiji: "I want to adorn the neck of every woman in the world with a pearl necklace."

As for the **Pearl Museum,** it examines the relationship between humanity and pearls since ancient times. On the second floor you'll find various models made with pearls. The Pearl Pagoda, for example, has 12,760 Mikimoto pearls and took 750 artisans six months to complete, after which it was exhibited at the Philadelphia World Exhibition in 1926. The Liberty Bell, a third the size of the original, has 12,250 pearls and was displayed at the New York World's Fair in 1939.

Also at Mikimoto Pearl Island, women divers, wearing traditional white outfits, demonstrate how women of the Shima Peninsula have dived through the ages in search of abalone, seaweed, and other edibles. At one time there used to be thousands of women divers, known for their skill in going to great depths for extended periods of time. Today's tourist brochures say that there are still 2,500 of these women divers left—but I've seen them only at demonstrations given for tourists. If you happen to see women divers working in earnest, consider yourself lucky. Open daily from 8:30am to 5:30pm (until 5pm from January to July 20, and in September and November; from 9am to 4:30pm in December), it charges ¥1,200 ($12) for adults or ¥600 ($6) for children 6 to 15.

If you have more time in Toba, visit the **Toba Aquarium** (☎ 0599/25-2555), with its 20,000 fish and animals of some 850 species, and the Brazil Maru (☎ 0599/25-3211), a ship, now moored, that took Japanese immigrants to Brazil from 1954 to 1974.

FUTAMIGAURA

If you're at all sentimental, make a trip to Futamigaura, which you can reach by either bus or train from Ise or Toba. There you'll find a pair of large rocks that jut out of the sea not far from shore. Known as the **Wedded Rocks,** they represent man and wife and are joined by a thick braided rope, the same kind you see extended from torii gates at Shinto shrines. The best time to visit the rocks is at dawn: in this Land of the Rising Sun, the spectacle of the sun rising between these two rocks is a favorite among Japanese.

The castle you see on the hill from near the Futami Station is not the former residence of a famous shogun but a replica of Azuchi Castle in Sengoku Jidaimura, a theme park, like the parks that the Daishinto Company has opened in Nikko and Noboribetsu. If you have youngsters with you or if you haven't seen one of these period theme parks elsewhere in Japan, go to one—they're fun! The park reproduces the life of the Sengoku, or Warring States, Period (just before the Edo Period), when local warlords struggled for supremacy. All the staff members are dressed in period costumes and headdress, and there are period adventure dramas, ninja troupe acrobatics, courtesans, and old-fashioned game centers. A pass that includes admission and entrance to all the theaters, galleries, and events is ¥4,300 ($43) for adults and ¥2,700 ($27) for children 5 to 15 (free for children under 5). Admission and one theater ticket is ¥3,000 ($30) for adults and half price for children. The park is open daily from 9am to 5pm (9:30am to 4:30pm from December through March). For details, call the park's public relations department in Tokyo (☎ 03/5802-1777).

KASHIKOJIMA

At the southern end of the Shima Peninsula, the last stop on the Kintetsu Line is Kashikojima. Here you can visit **Shima Marineland,** open daily from 8:30am to 6pm in summer and 9am to 5pm the rest of the year. It describes the fish and plant life of the region and beyond, and also has demonstrations given by women divers. Although explanations are in Japanese only, it's a fun place for children. Entrance is ¥1,000 ($10) for adults, ¥600 ($6) for children.

The main attraction of Kashikojima, however, is its **boat cruises of Ago Bay.** Vessels leave from the boat dock, about a two-minute walk from the train station. The cost of the cruise is ¥1,500 ($15) for adults, half price for children. You'll pass oyster rafts, fishing boats, and many small islands along the way. The trip lasts approximately an hour, with boats departing every hour or so between 8:50am and 3:50pm in the summer. For more information or inquiries about the winter schedule, call the Kintetsu Shima Kanko Kisen Co. (☎ 05994/3-1023).

If you're desperate for a dip in salt water, the most popular beach in the area is **Goza.** The boat from Kashikojima to Goza takes about 25 minutes and costs ¥600 ($6) one-way, passing oyster rafts, their cultivators, and the sweeping mountainous terrain of the region. The boat ride is enjoyable, but I found the beach itself is a bit disappointing after coming all that distance. There are certainly prettier beaches in the world, but this one is okay for a quick fix.

ACCOMMODATIONS

There are resort and hotel establishments throughout the Shima Peninsula that offer wonderful seafood dining. Kashikojima is the best place to go if you want to escape the crowds and relax in a rural setting, while Toba has the most attractions. Not considered as much a resort area as Toba and Kashikojima, Ise has more reasonably priced accommodations.

ISE

Asakichi (132)

109 Nakano-cho, Ise-shi 516. ☎ **0596/22-4101.** 12 rms (3 with bath). A/C TV TEL. ¥10,000–¥20,000 ($100–$200) per person. All rates include two meals. No credit cards. Directions: a 10-minute walk from Isuzugawa Station on the Kintetsu Line or a 10-minute taxi ride from Ise-shi Station.

In a neighborhood of simple older homes, this wooden ryokan was built at the end of the Edo Period. Yukio Ueda, the head of the family, is the 21st generation of Uedas to run the ryokan. Each room is different, and you'll find old and precious details in shoji, woodwork, Meiji-era glass lights, and hanging screens. Views look out over roofs, gardens, and the neighborhood. Walls display autographs and drawings of the many famous Japanese who have stayed here. The ryokan is known for its food, including the seafood and fish specialties of Ise. If you can't sit on the floor, you'll be served at a table; otherwise, you're served in your room on antique lacquer tray tables. The owners plan to open their storehouse of antique tableware as a gallery. Highly recommended.

$ Hoshidekan (133)

2-15-2 Kawasaki, Ise-shi 516. ☎ **0596/28-2377.** 13 rms (none with bath). A/C TV. ¥7,000 ($70) double; ¥9,900 ($99) triple. All rates include tax and service. AE, MC, V. Station: Iseshi or Ujiyama (10 minutes).

Catering to a young traveling crowd, this inexpensive 70-year-old ryokan has several rooms with windows framed with gnarled roots and bamboo (they simply don't make windows like that anymore). This ryokan is run by a group of women who are strong advocates of macrobiotic vegetarian cooking, which they serve in a simple tatami room connected to the ryokan. Open from 11am to 8pm by reservation only, it offers a vegetarian course (Genmai teishoku) for ¥1,000 ($10), vegetarian pilaf for ¥550 ($5.50), and noodles, tempura, tofu dishes, raw wheat beer, and natural raw sake. The women also have a macrobiotic-foods store across the street.

Ise City Hotel (134)

1-11-31 Fukiage, Ise-shi 516. ☎ **0596/28-2111.** Fax 0596/28-1058. 94 rms (all with bath). A/C TV TEL. ¥13,390 and ¥14,420 ($133.90 and $144.20) twin. All rates include tax and service. AE, JCB, MC, V.

Of the business hotels in the area, your best bet is the Ise City Hotel, which opened in 1985 and is right beside the railroad tracks between Ise-shi and Ujiyamada Stations. The adequately sized rooms are clean and cheerful, with flowered wallpaper and tiled bathrooms. All the single rooms feature a semi-double-size bed. Facilities include a Western-looking steak restaurant.

TOBA

Awami (135)

300-7 Ohama-cho, Toba-shi 517. ☎ **0599/25-2423.** Fax 0599/25-2701. 10 rms (5 with bath). A/C TV TEL. ¥8,000–¥9,500 ($80–$95) per person. All rates include two meals and service. No credit cards. Station: Toba (8 minutes).

Fresh and clean, this small ryokan is in a three-story white building. All the rooms are Japanese style and have small sitting areas with windows, some with a view of the bay. In-room baths are minuscule. Toilets are Western style, and public baths are clean and pleasantly decorated. Inquire about room-only rates if you wish to take your meals elsewhere.

✪ Thalassa Shima

Shirahama, Uramura-cho, Toba-shi 517. ☎ **0599/32-1111.** Fax 0599/32-1109. 122 rms (all with bath). A/C MINIBAR TV TEL. Experience Plan (one night, two meals, and a thallasotherapy treatment) ¥33,500 ($335) per person. Resort Plan (two nights, four meals, and two thallasotherapy treatments) ¥60,000 ($600) per person. AE, DC, JCB, MC, V. Directions: From the JR or Kintetsu Toba Station, take the free, 20-minute shuttle bus leaving every hour or half hour.

In a stunningly beautiful setting on the water at the entrance to Ise-Shima Bay, Thalassa Shima is a French-Japanese joint venture into thalassotherapy, consisting of seawater, seaweed, and sea-mud treatments. Thalassotherapy is popular in France, but this modern, striking, and elegant hotel is the first such resort in Japan. I was skeptical that a one-night stay involving a seaweed bath, an underwater-jet treatment, a massage bath, and pressure therapy could make much difference, but I have to admit I left the hotel much more relaxed and feeling beautiful!

Rooms are large, well appointed, and full of amenities, including terry robes, CDs, and complimentary cookies and camomile tea. When you check in, reserve your table at either the French or the Japanese restaurant, with views of the sea, expensive artwork on the walls (including a Chagall), and delicious food. A calorie-control menu is available. Facilities include a doctor; full French thalassotherapy equipment; a pool overlooking the bay; a sauna and Jacuzzi; a lounge/library featuring books, music, and original-version videos; a Shu Uemura esthetic salon; and a shop selling bathing suits and various thalassotherapy products. A great getaway, with prices not much higher than in some ryokan that don't include treatments. French and English are spoken.

KASHIKOJIMA

Ishiyama-So (136)

Yokoyama-jima, Kashikojima Ago-cho, Mie 517-05. ☎ **05995/2-1527.** Fax 05995/2-1240. 10 rms (3 with bath). A/C TV. ¥4,500 ($45) per person room without bath, ¥5,500 ($55) per person room with bath. All rates include Western-style breakfast. AE, MC, V. Directions: Boat from Kashikojima pier, a 2-minute trip.

If you're looking for an inexpensive place to stay, a good choice is the family-run Ishiyama-So, located on a small island just a stone's throw from the Kashikojima pier, which can be reached only via the hotel's own private boat—you pull up right at the ryokan's front door. If you call ahead, they'll even come fetch you at the harbor and lead you to their boat. Although the building itself is concrete, the rooms are tatami and feature a heater and a safe for valuables, among other amenities. Japanese dinners are available from ¥1,500 ($15). You can swim right off the dock here, and footpaths cross the small island. One of the family members here speaks English well.

Shima Kanko Hotel

Ago-cho, Kashikojima, Mie 517-05. ☎ **05994/3-1211.** Fax 05994/3-3538. 202 rms (all with bath). A/C MINIBAR TV TEL. ¥15,000 ($150) semi-double; ¥22,000 ($220) double; from ¥22,000 ($220) twin; from ¥20,000 ($200) Japanese-style rooms for up to four people. Peak season ¥5,000 ($50) extra; weekend ¥3,000 ($30) extra. AE, DC, JCB, MC, V. Station: Kashikojima (free shuttle).

Sitting on a hill above Ago Bay, with its many oyster rafts, this is a resort hotel in the old tradition, boasting impeccable service. Rooms are spacious, and despite periodic updating, retain an old-fashioned atmosphere with their shoji screens and wooden furniture. Some of the twins have a balcony, and rooms facing the bay have a splendid view. There's a pathway leading from the hotel through its garden to its own private dock, where you can sit and watch the pearl cultivators at work on their rafts.

Dining/Entertainment: There are five restaurants, some of them described in "Dining," below. Spring to fall, from 9:30am to 5pm, sit on the terrace of the coffee shop in good weather and enjoy an incredible view.

Services: Free shuttle bus to station.

Facilities: Large outdoor swimming pool, garden, beauty salon.

FUTAMIGAURA

Futamikan

569-1 E, Futami-cho, Watarai-gun, Mie 519-06. ☎ **05964/3-2003.** Fax 05964/2-1224. 43 rms (21 with bath). A/C MINIBAR TV TEL. ¥16,000–¥35,000 ($160–$350) per person. All rates include two meals and service. AE, DC, MC, V. Directions: Walk 20 minutes from Futamigaura Station or take a 20-minute bus ride from Ujiyamada Station.

Futamikan, a grand, traditional Japanese-style inn, has even hosted the imperial family. The oldest part of the ryokan is more than 100 years old and features beautifully carved transoms and sitting alcoves overlooking the garden. Since they didn't make private bathrooms back then, you might prefer rooms in the newer annex; these also have a small balcony—ask for a room on the fifth floor, where you have a sweeping view of the sea. But no matter where you stay, explore. On the second floor of the old building is one of the most beautiful banquet rooms I've ever seen—it has wooden railings outside its sliding glass windows, chandeliers, and 120 tatami mats.

As for the town itself, it's small and peaceful. The famous Wedded Rocks are only a five-minute walk away.

Youth Hostel Taikoji (137)

1659 E, Futami-cho, Watari-gun, Mie 519-06. ☎ **05964/3-2283** or 05964/2-1952 for information in English. 28 beds. ¥1,800 ($18) JYHA members, ¥2,400 ($24) nonmembers. Breakfast ¥500 ($5) extra; dinner ¥800 ($8) extra. No credit cards. Bus: From Futamigaura Station, a 4-minute ride; then a 5-minute walk.

Located in a temple not far from the famous Wedded Rocks, this small youth hostel offers accommodation for only 28 people, with sleeping on futon in tatami rooms. A famous viewing spot for wisteria, in a beautiful, wooded, bird-filled area, is the platform under the trellised wisteria, which blooms in late April or early May. Cherry-tree blossoms litter the walks just before the wisteria blooms.

DINING

La Mer

Shima Kanko Hotel, Kashikojima. ☎ **05994/3-1211.** Reservations required for set dinners. Main dishes ¥5,500–¥8,000 ($55–$80); set dinners ¥22,000–¥29,000 ($220–$290); set lunches ¥6,500–¥13,000 ($65–$130). AE, DC, MC, V. Daily 11:30am–2pm and 5–9pm. FRENCH.

Since Kashikojima is surrounded by water, you can safely assume that the seafood here is fresh and excellent. One of Ise-Shima's most famous restaurants, La Mer has a well-deserved reputation for serving its own delightful recipes created by its well-known chef. The specialty is lobster, served in a Western dining hall with chandeliers, wooden floor, white tablecloths, and tables overlooking the bay and oyster rafts. A fixed-price lobster menu includes abalone, while other meals include steak as well. The small à la carte menu offers main dishes of lobster, shrimp, or beef. Set lunches have beef or seafood as the main dish. If you've never had abalone, this is a great, albeit expensive, place to try it.

Okadaiya (138)

31 Uji-Imazaike-cho. ☎ **0596/22-4554.** ¥400–¥700 ($4–$7). No credit cards. Daily 10:30am–6pm. NOODLES.

Although this purveyor of Ise-Shima's specialty, *Ise udon* (a soft, thick wheat noodle served in a black soy soup with green onions), has been in business for more than 40 years, the shop itself has been remodeled and is bright. It's a five-minute walk from Naiku (Inner Shrine) on Oharai-machi (street). You'll recognize it by the blue-and-white awning, the big wooden sign above it, and the flower pots below it. There's no Roman-lettered menu, but the udon teishoku, which comes with Ise udon, pickles, rice, and vegetables, is a good bet for ¥700 ($7). This is one of the first restaurants to start feeding hungry shrinegoers.

Sushi Kyu (139)

20 Uji Nakanokiri-machi. ☎ **0596/27-0120.** Set meals ¥900–¥5,000 ($9–$50). No credit cards. Daily 11:30am–3pm and 5–9pm. SUSHI/VARIED JAPANESE.

In a 100-year-old *kura* (storehouse or grange), a seven-minute walk from Naiku (Inner Shrine) on Oharai-machi (street), sit on tatami at low tables and look out over the river. Kimono-clad waitresses serve sushi, tempura, and local cuisine (though there's no Roman-lettered menu). The *kyodo-ryori* (local cuisine) with *tekone sushi* (marinated raw fish on vinegared rice) is ¥2,100 ($21) and includes raw fish, pickles, savory egg custard, soup, tofu, and three other side dishes.

3 Kanazawa

386 miles NW of Tokyo, 140 miles NE of Kyoto

On the northwest coast of Honshu on the Sea of Japan, Kanazawa is a gateway to the rugged, sea-swept Noto Peninsula. It was the second-largest city (after Kyoto) to escape bombing during World War II, and some of the old city has been left intact, including a few samurai houses, old geisha quarters, and tiny narrow streets that run crookedly without rhyme or reason (apparently to confuse any enemies foolish enough to attack). Kanazawa is most famous for its Kenrokuen Garden, one of the most celebrated gardens in all of Japan. It's the main reason people come here.

Kanazawa first gained notoriety about 500 years ago, when a militant Buddhist sect joined with peasant fanatics to overthrow the feudal lord and establish its own autonomous government, an event unprecedented in Japanese history. The independent republic survived almost 100 years before it was attacked by an army of Nobunaga Oda, who was trying to unite Japan at a time when civil wars wracked the nation. Kanazawa was subsequently granted to one of Nobunaga's retainers, Maeda Toshie. The Maeda clan continued to rule over Kanazawa for the next 300 years, amassing wealth in the form of rice paddies and encouraging development of the arts. All through the Tokugawa shogunate era, the Maedas remained the second most powerful family in Japan after the Tokugawas themselves and controlled the largest domain in the country. About a million *koku* (equaling five million bushels) of rice were produced here annually. The arts of Kutani ware, Yuzen silk dyeing, and Noh theater flourished—and enjoy success and popularity even today.

ESSENTIALS

The **telephone area code** for Kanazawa, the capital of Ishikawa Prefecture, is 0762.

GETTING THERE **By Train** There are direct trains from Osaka (via Kyoto) and Nagoya that depart hourly; the ride takes almost four hours. From Tokyo, take the Shinkansen to Nagaoka and switch there for a local line to Kanazawa. The trip takes about four hours.

By Bus Buses depart daily from Tokyo's Ikebukuro Station (trip time: 7 hr. 20 min.), Nagoya Station and Kyoto Station (trip time for either: 3 hr. 50 min.).

VISITOR INFORMATION Be sure to pick up the flyer "Kanazawa" at the Tourist Information Center in Tokyo, Kyoto, or Kanazawa.

The **Tourist Information Center** (☎ 0762/32-6200) is in Kanazawa Station. To find it, continue straight out from the wicket along the concourse; it's beyond the JR Information Center, on your right. Open daily from 9am to 6pm, it distributes a map and brochure in English and will also book hotel rooms.

GETTING AROUND Kanazawa's attractions spread south and southeast from the station (take the station's east exit). Kenrokuen Garden, for example, is three-quarters of a mile southeast of Kanazawa Station, easily reached by **bus** (bus information is on the tourist office map). You can also take a bus from the station to the Kosen Pottery Kiln. The Kanazawa Free Pass (¥900/$9) gives unlimited one-day travel on buses. Other attractions can be covered **on foot** or **bicycle** in one day. JR Rental Cycle (☎ 0762/31-5075) in front of the station rents cycles for ¥900 ($9) per day and is open 9am to 6pm.

WHAT TO SEE & DO

Much of Kanazawa's charm lies in the atmosphere of its old neighborhoods. Be sure to wear your good walking shoes, since the best way to explore the city is on your own two feet.

KENROKUEN GARDEN & VICINITY

At one time Kanazawa possessed an impressive castle belonging to the powerful Maeda clan, but it was destroyed by fire in 1881. One of the few structures left standing is the **Ishikawamon** (Ishikawa Gate), which used to be the south entrance to the castle. Looking at how big and grand the gate is, you can appreciate the size of the original Maeda castle.

Just south of Ishikawamon is **Kenrokuen Garden,** Kanazawa's main attraction. The largest of the three best landscape gardens in Japan—the other two are Kairakuen Garden in Mito and Korakuen Garden in Okayama—it's considered by many to be the grandest. Its name can be translated as "a refined garden incorporating six attributes"—spaciousness, careful arrangement, seclusion, antiquity, elaborate use of water, and scenic charm. Ponds, trees, streams, rocks, mounds, and footpaths have all been combined so aesthetically that the effect is spellbinding. Altogether, it took about 150 years to complete the garden. The fifth Maeda lord started construction in the 1670s, and successive lords added to the garden according to their own individual tastes. The garden as we now see it was finished by the 12th Maeda lord in 1822. Only after the Meiji Restoration was the garden opened to the public. Admission is ¥300 ($3), and it's open daily from 7am to 6pm (8am to 4:30pm in winter).

You may want to arrive at dawn or near the end of the day, since the garden is a favorite destination of Japanese tour groups, led by guides who explain everything in detail—through loudspeakers. I don't know how they affect you, but loudspeakers drive me to absolute distraction. On your way to Kenrokuen to beat the crowds, buy a breakfast or a picnic lunch at the lively **Omicho Market,** which has been vending vegetables, fruits, and fresh seafood for hundreds of years. It's a 10-minute walk from the station on the way to the garden.

In the southeast corner of Kenrokuen Park, charging a separate admission of ¥500 ($5), is **Seisonkaku Villa** (☎ 0762/21-0580), built in 1863 by the 13th Maeda lord as a retirement home for his widowed mother. Elegant and graceful, this villa has a distinctly feminine atmosphere, with delicately carved wood transoms and shoji screens painted with various designs. The villa's bedroom is decorated with tortoises painted on the shoji wainscoting (tortoises were associated with long life, and it must have worked—the mother lived to be 84). It's open Thursday through Tuesday from 8:30am to 4:30pm.

Next to Seisonkaku Villa is the **Ishikawa Prefectural Museum for Traditional Products and Crafts** (☎ 0762/62-2020), open Friday through Wednesday from 9am to 5pm. Admission to *Dento Sangyo Koogei Kan* is ¥250 ($2.50). Opened in 1984, it houses locally produced lacquerware, wood carvings, folk toys, pottery, silk, washi (Japanese paper), and hats and baskets made from cypress. Here you can also see the famous Kutani pottery, first produced under the patronage of the Maeda clan in the 1600s. There are also displays of Yuzen dyeing, with its bold and clear picturesque designs. A pamphlet and explanations in English of the various displays make a visit here worthwhile.

South of Kenrokuen Park and not far from Seisonkaku Villa are a few more museums. The **Ishikawa Prefectural Art Museum** (☎ 0762/31-7580), open daily from 9:30am to 5pm and charging a ¥350 ($3.50) admission (more for special exhibitions), houses a small collection of antique Kutani pottery, samurai costumes, and decorative art, most dating from the Edo Period. *Ishikawa-ken Bijutsukan* devotes several rooms to modern and contemporary paintings, sculptures, and other works by local artists, with exhibitions changed monthly. Close by is the **Honda Museum,** which displays samurai outfits, weapons, artwork, and the personal effects of the Honda clan, one of Lord Maeda's chief retainers. *Honda Zoohenkan* is open daily from 9am to 5pm (closed on Thursday from November through February); it charges ¥500 ($5) admission. A third museum, the **Ishikawa Prefecture History Museum** (☎ 0762/62-3236) exhibits artifacts dealing with the history of the prefecture from prehistoric to modern times. Housed in a handsome redbrick building built to stock guns and gunpowder before the turn of the century, *Reikishi Hakubutsukan* contains archeological finds from the region, items from the Edo Period, folkloric objects, and samurai outfits weighing up to 44 pounds. Open daily from 9am to 5pm, the museum charges ¥250 ($2.50) admission.

If you want to limit your selection (because of exhaustion or expense) to one or two, my own personal favorite is the Ishikawa Prefectural Museum for Traditional Products and Crafts.

Nagamachi Samurai District

About a 20-minute walk west of Kenrokuen Garden, the Nagamachi Samurai District is basically just one street, lined with beautiful wooden homes hidden behind gold-colored mud walls. An unhurried stroll in the neighborhood is the main source of entertainment here. One home open to the public is the **Nomura Samurai House,** open daily from 8:30am to 5:30pm (4:30pm in winter) and charging ¥400 ($4) admission, plus an additional ¥200 ($2) to take tea. Its drawing room is of Japanese cypress, with elaborate designs in rosewood, and its shoji screens are painted with landscapes. There's also a small, charming garden containing a miniature waterf all, a winding stream, and stone lanterns.

Shinise Memorial Hall is an old merchant's house, worth a stroll through, expecially since admission is free. It was reconstructed here to depict the life of merchants in the feudal era. It's open Thursday to Tuesday from 9:30am to 5pm.

Another old home in the Nagamachi Samurai District has been converted into a silk center, where you can watch artists at work painting intricate designs on silk. Open Friday through Wednesday from 9am to 11:45 and 1 to 4:30pm, the **Yuzen Silk Center** (☎ 0762/64-2811) charges ¥500 ($5) admission, which includes a gift. A video shows the process of Yuzen dyeing, and a pamphlet in English describes the steps in detail. It can take up to six months to make one kimono of Yuzen hand-painted silk. Unfortunately, children are not allowed at *Saihitsu-an,* and *gaijin* (foreign) children were mentioned in particular.

From the Nagamachi District it's just a few minutes' walk to **Oyama Jinja,** a shrine built in 1599 in honor of the first Maeda lord, Toshiie Maeda. Its three-story gate was designed by a Dutchman in 1875, with stained-glass windows on the third floor.

Other Sights

The Higashi Geisha District, northeast of Korakuen Park, is one of three old entertainment quarters of the city. A walk here reveals wood-slatted facades of geisha houses dating from the 1820s. The **Shima Geisha House** (140) (☎ 0762/52-5675) at 1-13-21 Higashiyama is open to the public. A typical tearoom where merchants as well as men of letters came to watch geisha perform, Shima has changed names through its 150-year history. Inside you'll find rooms allotted to personal use as well as to performing and the display of ordinary artifacts, from combs to cooking utensils. Admission is ¥200 ($2), half price for children, and it's open Tuesday through Sunday 9am to 5pm.

Near the Higashi Geisha quarter is **Tawaraya Ame** (141) (☎ 0762/52-2079), a 160-year-old traditional Japanese candy shop. Located near Hikoso Bridge in a wooden building with white *noren* (curtain), Tawaraya makes two types of candy from rice and barley; sugar is not used in the process. One type is thick (¥2,000/$20 for 750g/1.65 lb. in a wooden bucket); the other resembles honey (¥700/$7 for 300g/

10.5 oz.). The shop is open Monday to Saturday from 9am to 6pm and Sundays and holidays from 10am to 5pm.

If your interest lies in pottery, it's worth a visit to the **Kosen Pottery Kiln** (☎ 0762/41-0902), 20 minutes by bus from Kanazawa Station to the Nomachi stop. *Kutani Kosengama* shows the entire process of producing Kutani ware. Admission is free, and it's open daily from 9am to 4:30pm.

Myoryuji Temple is popularly known as Ninja-dera (or Temple of the Secret Agents) because of its secret chambers, hidden stairways, tunnels, and trick doors. The temple, 20 minutes by bus from Kanazawa Station to the Nomachi-Hirokoji stop and then a five-minute walk, was constructed as an escape route for the Maeda lord in case his castle was attacked. A well at the temple was supposedly connected to the castle via a secret tunnel. You must make a reservation to see it (☎ 0762/41-0888), and you'll probably be able to go the same day you call. Admission is ¥700 ($7). To make sure you don't get lost (which would be quite easy because of all the trick doors), you'll be grouped with other visitors and led by a guide who, unfortunately, describes everything in Japanese only. Tours, given daily from 9am to 4:30pm (until 4pm in winter), last 30 minutes.

If you're in Kanazawa for more than one day, consider taking an outing to Yuwaka Spa, where you'll find the **Edo-Mura Village.** About a 40-minute bus ride from Kanazawa Station, this open-air architectural museum has a collection of some 20 buildings from the Edo Period, including a samurai mansion, farmhouses, and shops. This museum provides unique insight into how the various social classes lived back in the feudal days. Open daily from 8am to 5pm, it charges ¥1,200 ($12) admission and includes a visit to **Danpuen,** a nearby village of country homes with craft displays, including a charcoal kiln.

SHOPPING

The most famous products of Kanazawa are its Kutani pottery, with bright five-color overglaze patterns, and its hand-painted Yuzen silk. Kanazawa also produces toys, lacquerware, and wooden products.

For one-stop shopping, visit the **Ishikawa Prefectural Products Center,** or *Kanko Bussankan* (☎ 0762/22-7788), near Kenrokuen Garden (if you're arriving at Kenrokuen Garden via bus 10, 11, or 12 from Kanazawa Station, you'll get off the bus just a few steps away from the Bussankan). The ground and basement floors sell local products, the second floor is a restaurant, and the third floor houses the Ishikawa Prefectural Museum of Handicrafts, where you can watch artisans produce crafts of the area, including Kutani pottery, Japanese cakes, and lacquerware. Hours are 9am to 6pm (10am to 6pm in winter; closed some Thursdays).

If you walk straight away from the station along the Miyako Hotel street and take the third left, there's a street lined with some interesting shops, among them **Medaka-ya** (☎ 0762/24-4829), which offers cool '20s, '30s, and '40s Japanese memorabilia. It's open Tuesday to Sunday from 10am to 8pm (closed the 25th of the month). Across the street is **Murata** (☎ 0762/65-6318), vending antiques and bric-a-brac. It's open daily 9am to 7pm (closed the first Sunday of the month).

ACCOMMODATIONS

EXPENSIVE

All the rates given below for expensive accommodations are those charged during peak season, which comprises New Year's, Golden Week, July 25 to the end of August, and the month of October. During the off-season, you can expect rates to be ¥1,000 to ¥3,000 ($10 to $30) lower than those given here.

ANA Hotel Kanazawa

16-3 Showa-machi, Kanazawa 920. ☎ **0762/24-6111** or 800/44-UTELL in the U.S. Fax 0762/24-6100. 255 rms. A/C MINIBAR TV TEL. ¥17,000–¥25,000 ($170–$250) double; ¥20,000–¥40,000 ($200–$400) twin. AE, DC, JCB, MC, V.

This sleek, white building soars above Kanazawa Station (use the east exit), and the main reasons to stay here are convenient access to the station and the fact that it's an ANA hotel. Rooms are simple, comfortable, and uncluttered, with everything you'd expect from one of Kanazawa's best hotels.

Dining/Entertainment: There are seven restaurants and bars, including the popular Unkai, serving Japanese specialties; Karin, a Cantonese restaurant; and the elegant C'est la Vie and the Astral Bar on the 19th floor, which offer panoramic views.

Services: Free newspaper.

Hotel Nikko Kanazawa

2-15-1 Hon-machi Kanazawa, Ishikawa 920. ☎ **0762/34-1111** or 800/NIKKO-US in the U.S. and Canada. Fax 0762/34-8802. A/C MINIBAR TV TEL. ¥24,000–¥27,000 ($240–$270) twin; ¥22,000–¥26,000 ($220–$260) double; from ¥47,000 ($470) deluxe rooms; from ¥90,000 ($900) suites. AE, DC, JCB, MC, V.

Successfully designed by a Japanese-French team, the Nikko Kanagawa, just in front of the station, has a French colonial atmosphere, with Oriental art objects like ginger jars on a mantle and Japanese lacquer boxes and rattan chairs stuffed with pillows. Rooms with many amenities (including satellite and bilingual TV) offer wide windows with great views (at 30 stories it's the highest building in Kanazawa). Standard singles have fairly small baths, but those in doubles and twins are large. No-smoking floors and ladies' rooms (with floral spreads and lamps) are featured, as well as Nikko (executive) floors with deluxe accommodations.

Dining/Entertainment: There are seven restaurants and bars, including the whimsical brasserie Garden House decorated with plants under grow lights, French cafe furnishings, and vegetables. Nikko's signature restaurant, Ben-Kay, highlights Japanese interiors at their best.

Facilities: Florist, kiosk, banquet and meeting rooms, parking and (in the adjacent Porte Kanazawa) shopping, fitness club, JAL ticket counter, art exhibition space, and restaurants.

✪ Miyabo (142)

3 Shimo Kakinokibatake, Kanazawa 920. ☎ **0762/31-4228.** Fax 0762/32-0608. 26 rms (25 with bath). A/C MINIBAR TV TEL. ¥13,000–¥30,000 ($130–$300) per person. All rates include two meals and service. AE, DC, JCB, MC, V. Bus: From Kanazawa Station, a 10-minute ride south.

In the heart of the city, Miyabo is a beautiful Japanese-style inn near Katamachi Shopping Street and within walking distance of Kenrokuen. It boasts one of the oldest private gardens in Kanazawa, and part of the ryokan used to be the private teahouse of Kanazawa's first mayor after the feudal age came to an end. Most of the ryokan dates from before World War II, although there is also a newer section. The lowest price is for a room in the newer section, while the top price is for a room with a private view of the garden and more elaborately prepared meals. My favorite room is one that used to be the mayor's tea-ceremony room; named Bunte, with maroon walls, it's secluded from the rest of the ryokan, right in the middle of the garden.

MODERATE

Citymonde

2-10 Hashiba-cho, Kanazawa 920. ☎ **0762/24-5555.** Fax 0762/24-5554. 207 rms. A/C MINIBAR TV TEL. ¥12,000–¥15,000 ($120–$150) double; ¥15,000–¥19,000 ($150–$190) twin. AE, DC, JCB, MC, V. Bus: 10 or 11 to the Hokuriku Daigaku stop; or a 10-minute taxi ride.

Built in 1991, this modern-design hotel has luxury-style accommodations at business-hotel prices. Some rooms, including the more expensive singles, have a view of Kenrokuen with magnificent snow-capped mountains in the background, but even the cheapest singles have nice city views; all singles have semi-double beds. Facilities include souvenir and florist shops, four restaurants, a coffee lounge, and a bar. The light and airy French restaurant, Les Anges, the teppanyaki and Chinese restaurants, and Al Shain's bar on the 14th floor have views of the park and city. The lobby coffee lounge looks out on a pleasant garden.

Kanazawa Castle Inn (143)

10-17 Konohanamachi, Kanazawa 920. ☎ **0762/23-6300.** Fax 0762/65-6365. 136 rms. A/C MINIBAR TV TEL. ¥6,600 ($66) single; ¥11,000 ($110) double or twin. All rates include tax and service. AE, JCB, MC, V.

This practical and attractive business hotel, a three-minute walk from Kanazawa Station, offers simple but cheerful rooms. The bathtubs are miniature, but amenities include TV with 3D controls (for what that's worth). Singles have a semi-double-size bed. An all-you-can-eat breakfast buffet is ¥900 ($9).

INEXPENSIVE

Kanazawa Youth Hostel (145)

37 Suehirocho, Kanazawa 920. ☎ **0762/52-3414.** Fax 0762/52-8590. 100 beds. A/C. ¥2,600 ($26) for Japanese members, ¥3,200 ($32) for foreigners. Breakfast ¥600 ($6) extra; dinner ¥1,000 ($10) extra. No credit cards. Bus: Ride 25-minutes to the Suizokan-mae stop.

Although this youth hostel is a bit far from all the attractions, it still has a nice location. Rooms here are both tatami and Western style; only the Western-style rooms have TV. Nonmembers are not accepted during the busy summer season. There's a coin-operated laundry.

Matsui Youth Hostel (146)

1-9-3 Katamachi, Kanazawa 920. ☎ **0762/21-0275.** 9 rms. A/C. ¥2,800 ($28) for JYHA members, ¥3,400 ($34) for nonmembers. Breakfast ¥600 ($6) extra; dinner ¥1,000 ($10) extra. No credit cards. Bus: 20 to the Katamachi stop.

More centrally located, this youth hostel offers accommodations in tatami rooms, with about six people to a room. There are laundry facilities.

Ryokan Murataya

1-5-2 Katamachi, Kanazawa 920. ☎ **0762/63-0455.** 11 rms (none with bath). A/C TV TEL. ¥8,500 ($85) twin; ¥12,000 ($120) triple. Western breakfast ¥450 ($4.50) extra; Japanese breakfast ¥800 ($8) extra. AE, MC, V. Bus: 20, 21, 22, 30, 31, 32, 40, 41, 44, or 45 from Kanazawa Station to Katamachi-Kingeki-mae (3 minutes).

This ryokan is in the heart of Kanazawa, not far from Katamachi Shopping Street and within walking distance of Kenrokuen. A member of the Japanese Inn Group, it's modern and rather uninteresting from the outside, but comfortable and pleasant inside. All rooms come with heating, among other amenities. There's a coin-operated laundry.

✪ Yogetsu (144)

1-13-22 Higashiyama, Kanazawa 920. ☎ **0762/52-0497.** 5 rms (none with bath). TV. ¥4,500 ($45) per person without meals, ¥6,500 ($65) per person with two meals. All rates include tax and service. No credit cards. Bus: From Kanazawa Station, a 10-minute ride.

This delightful little minshuku is a 20-minute walk east of Kanazawa Station, in the middle of the old Higashiyama district, set aside in the 1820s by the local government as a place where geishas could entertain. Run by a jovial woman, Yogetsu is a 100-year-old house that used to belong to a geisha. The rooms are rather plain, but the quiet, quaint surrounding atmosphere makes up for the lack of decor. Some rooms are air-conditioned.

DINING

Kanazawa's local specialties are known collectively as *Kaga no aji* and consist of seafood such as tiny shrimp and winter crabs, as well as freshwater fish and mountain vegetables.

AROUND KENROKUEN GARDEN

Kinjoro Honten

2-23 Hasibacho. ☎ **0762/21-8188.** Reservations required. Set lunch ¥13,000 ($130); set dinner ¥15,000 ($150). AE, DC, MC, V. Daily 1–3pm and 5–9pm. Directions: Taxi 10 minutes. KAGA.

This 100-year-old ryokan—there are only three exquisite guest rooms (starting at ¥60,000/$600 per person, including two meals)—also serves kaga kaiseki in traditional, garden-view tatami rooms (some with leg wells under tables). My favorite room is *Kiri noma,* with its faded-lacquer-colored walls and beautiful wood-carved transoms. Of course, the sliding doors are changed to correspond with the seasons: reed doors in summer and *washi*-covered (handmade paper) ones in winter. And, of course, you are served a seasonal feast by refined, kimono-clad waitresses. If you can afford it, a delightful experience.

Kinjoro

2-20 Kenrokumachi. ☎ **0762/22-5188.** Set meals ¥1,800–¥5,000 ($18–$50). AE, DC, JCB, MC, V. Fri–Wed 1–7pm. Bus: From Kanazawa Station to Kenrokuen Garden. VARIED JAPANESE/KAGA.

If you can't afford Kinjoro Honten, above, try their traditionally decorated branch located on the second floor of the Ishikawa Prefectural Products Center, near Kenrokuen Garden's main entrance. It offers fixed-price meals, with main dishes consisting of sashimi, tempura, noodles, and other common Japanese dishes, including Kaga cuisine. The most popular set lunch is the local cuisine *Kenroku bento.* Although the menu is in Japanese only, pictures of set meals and a plastic-food display case translate for you.

✪ Miyoshian (147)

1-11 Kenrokumachi. ☎ **0762/21-0127.** Reservations required for dinner, not accepted for lunch. Lunch teishoku ¥1,500–¥3,000 ($15–$30), Kaga cuisine ¥8,000–¥15,000 ($80–$150). No credit cards. Daily 10am–2pm and 4–8:30pm. Directions: Bus or walk to Kenrokuen Garden. KAGA/KAISEKI.

A great place to try the local Kaga cuisine right in Kenrokuen Garden, this 100-year-old restaurant consists of three separate wooden buildings, the best of which is a traditional room extending over a pond. This is where you'll probably dine, seated on tatami with a view of an ancient pond (giant carp swim in the murky waters). In addition to the local Kaga cuisine, you can also order such à la carte dishes as jibuni stew (a chicken-and-vegetable stew eaten primarily in winter) and shrimp sashimi. In the evening, only kaiseki is served, with meals easily costing ¥20,000 ($200).

Katamachi Area

Just east of the Saigawa Ohashi Bridge is an area full of restaurants and drinking establishments, radiating out from Katamachi Shopping Street and Chuo Dori. Nearby Tatemachi Dori is a street lined with boutiques, including Issey Miyake and Kaneko Isao. Here you'll find **Capricciosa** for copious pasta (less than ¥1,600/$16), and **Doutor** for coffee (¥180/$1.80) and hot dogs or sandwiches (¥190 to ¥350/$1.90 to $3.50).

Hamacho (149)

2-27-23 Katamachi. ☎ **0762/33-3390.** Reservations recommended. Set meals ¥5,000–¥8,000 ($50–$80). AE, DC, JCB, MC, V. Mon–Sat 5pm–midnight. Closed hols. Bus: To Katamachi. JAPANESE SEAFOOD.

Hamacho offers seafood and vegetables in season. The menu, written on a blackbo ard but in Japanese only, changes according to what's fresh and available and may include *imo* (Japanese potatoes), freshly picked mushrooms, vegetables, various seafood selections, and sashimi. Just tell Mr. Ishigami, the owner and chief chef, how much you want to spend and he'll do the rest. If there's anything you don't like, be sure to tell him. Sit at the counter, where you can watch the preparation of your set meal, which may include grilled fish or shrimp, noodles, tofu, sashimi, soup, and vegetables.

Kaga Tobi (150)

2-1 Kohrinbo. ☎ **0762/62-0535.** Set lunches ¥850–¥2,500 ($8.50–$25); set dinners ¥3,500–¥8,000 ($35–$80). MC, V. Thurs–Tues 11am–2pm and 5–10pm. Bus: To Kohrinbo. VARIED JAPANESE/KAGA.

This restaurant is easy to find; it's right beside the Tokyu Hotel. To reach the restaurant, walk around the Kohrinbo 109 department store building to the tiny back street flanking a narrow canal. You'll find good and very reasonable set lunches of sashimi, tempura, or eel with side dishes. For Kaga cuisine, order the Shokado bento. The restaurant is crowded with regulars, and they don't treat outsiders very nicely.

Kitama (151)

2-3-3 Katamachi. ☎ **0762/61-7176.** Set meals ¥1,500–¥4,000 ($15–$40). DC, V. Thurs–Tues 11:30am–8:30pm. Bus: To Katamachi. VARIED JAPANESE/KAGA.

Sitting on tatami mats, you'll have a pleasant view of a small moss-covered 100-year-old garden of tiny pines, stone lanterns, and rocks. We ordered the jibuni teishoku with chicken stew, clear soup, pickled vegetables, rice, and hors d'oeuvres. The Kojitsu obento, served in an upright lunch box, features sashimi, small pieces of pork and fish, fried shrimp, a soybean patty, and various seasonal vegetables. From the corner of Katamachi and Chuo Dori (marked Saigawa Dori on the tourist map), walk one block up Chuo Dori and turn right; the restaurant will be on your left.

Zeniya (152)

2-29-7 Katamachi, ☎ **0762/33-3331.** Reservations required. Kaiseki meals ¥15,000–¥30,000 ($150–$300); lunch bento ¥5,000 ($50). AE, DC, JCB, MC, V. Daily 11:30am–2pm and 5–10pm. Closed second and fourth Sun of the month. Bus: From Kanazawa Station to Katamachi, near Saigawa-Ohashi Bridge. KAISEKI.

One of Kanazawa's best-known and most exclusive restaurants, it serves seasonal kaiseki meals of local specialties in cool, elegant surroundings. The presentation of each dish, naturally, is spectacular. Zeniya is tucked away on a small side street, in a traditional Japanese house with a small court entryway.

Around Kanazawa Station

Belle Vue

Kanazawa Miyako Hotel, 6-10 Konohanacho. ☎ **0762/61-2111.** Main dishes ¥2,200–¥6,000 ($22–$60); set dinners ¥3,000–¥10,000 ($30–$100); set lunches ¥1,500–¥3,000 ($15–$30). AE, DC, JCB, MC, V. Daily 11:30am–2pm and 5–10pm. CONTINENTAL.

City views, comfortable cushioned chairs, and chandeliers provide a romantic setting, and piano music serenades on Saturday and Sunday nights at this continental restaurant. A changing menu includes sole, steak, veal, lamb chops, and other seasonal choices. The fixed-price dinners and lunches are very reasonably priced and include appetizers, salad, dessert, and coffee.

Kakitsubata

Kanazawa Miyako Hotel, 6-10 Konohanacho. ☎ **0762/61-2111.** Kaiseki ¥4,000–¥12,000 ($40–$120); set lunches ¥1,500–¥3,000 ($15–$30). AE, DC, JCB, MC, V. Daily 11:30am–2pm and 5–9:30pm. KAISEKI/VARIED JAPANESE.

The simply decorated Kakitsubata serves inexpensive kaiseki, as well as sashimi and fresh seafood, from shrimp and crab to yellowtail. At lunch, eel, sashimi, or tempura set meals and obento lunch boxes are offered on an English-language menu.

Near Higashi

Kotobuki-Ya

2-4-13 Owari-cho. ☎ **0762/31-6245.** Reservations required at least one day in advance. Obento ¥2,500 ($25); set meals ¥7,000–¥12,000 ($70–$120). All prices include service charge. No credit cards. Wed–Mon 11:30am–2pm and 5:30–9:30pm. Directions: Bus heading for Kenrokuen-shita, or taxi 5 minutes. VEGETARIAN.

Specializing in *shojin ryori* (Buddhist vegetarian cooking), Kotobuki-ya is in a 160-year-old merchant's house, which used to be a place where samurai met. Dining here, on beautiful lacquer and pottery tableware, is a wonderful experience. Three generations have been serving shojin ryori in this quiet setting. If you want a private room, you'll have to pay ¥300 ($3) extra per person for obento and ¥800 ($8) for course meals. Two of the rooms have a view of the garden.

4 Osaka

341 miles W of Tokyo; 26 miles SW of Kyoto; 212 miles E of Hiroshima

Although its history stretches back about 1,500 years, Osaka first gained prominence when Hideyoshi Toyotomi built Japan's most magnificent castle here in the 16th century. To develop resources for his castle town, he persuaded merchants from other parts of the nation to resettle in Osaka. During the Edo Period the city became an important distribution center as feudal lords from the surrounding region sent their rice to merchants in Osaka, who in turn sent the rice onward to Tokyo and other cities. As the merchants prospered, the town grew and such arts as Kabuki and Bunraku flourished. With money and leisure to spare, the merchants also developed a refined taste for food.

Nowadays, Osaka, in Osaka Prefecture on the southern coast of western Honshu, is an industrial city with a population of almost 2.8 million, making it the third-largest city in Japan (after Tokyo and Yokohama). With the legacy of merchant beginnings still present, Osakans are usually characterized as being outgoing and

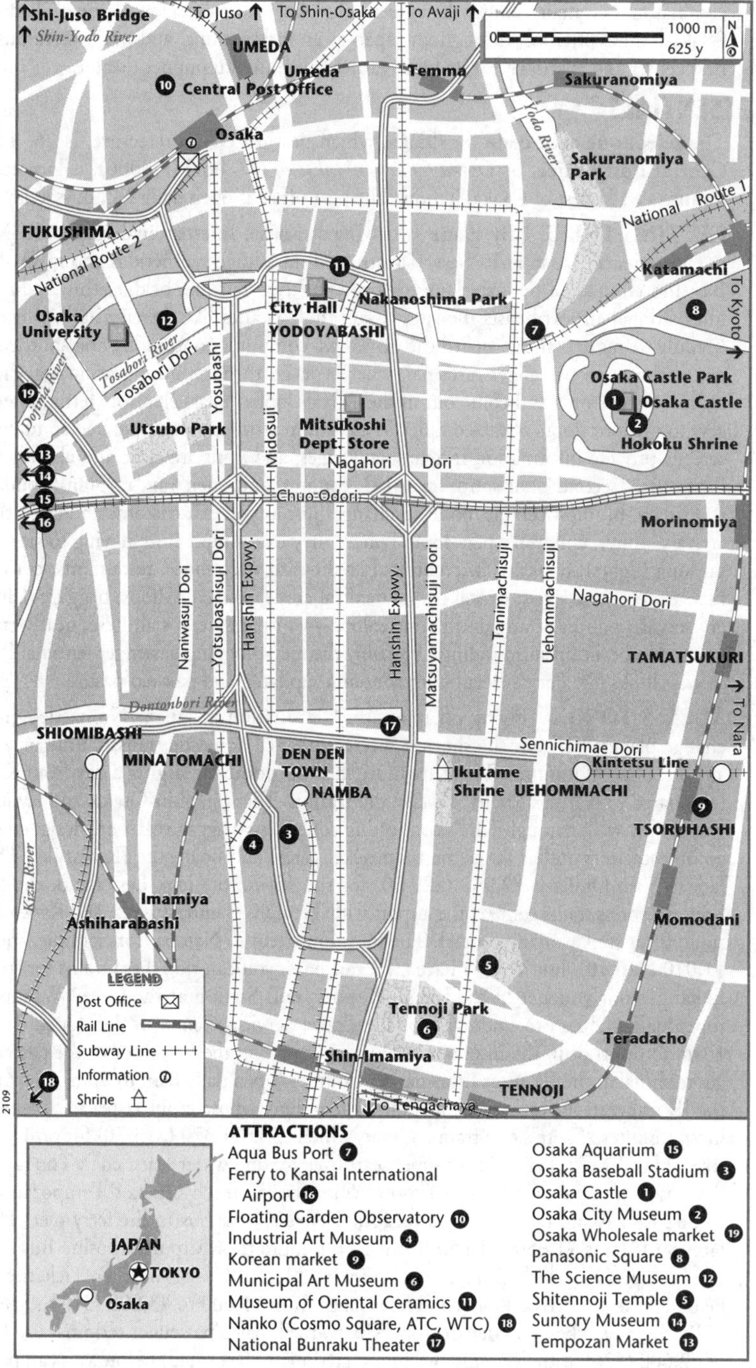

ATTRACTIONS

Aqua Bus Port 7
Ferry to Kansai International Airport 16
Floating Garden Observatory 10
Industrial Art Museum 4
Korean market 9
Municipal Art Museum 6
Museum of Oriental Ceramics 11
Nanko (Cosmo Square, ATC, WTC) 18
National Bunraku Theater 17
Osaka Aquarium 15
Osaka Baseball Stadium 3
Osaka Castle 1
Osaka City Museum 2
Osaka Wholesale market 19
Panasonic Square 8
The Science Museum 12
Shitennoji Temple 5
Suntory Museum 14
Tempozan Market 13

clever at money affairs. An Osakan greeting is "Are you making any money?" Today, Osaka has a reputation throughout Japan as an international and progressive business center and is known for its food, castle, and Bunraku puppet theater.

ESSENTIALS

The **telephone area code** for Osaka, which lies in Osaka Prefecture, is 06. The **Central Post Office,** or *Osaka Chuo Yubinkyoku* (☎ 06/347-8006), is located a minute's walk west of Osaka Station. The post office is open daily 24 hours a day.

GETTING THERE By Plane Arriving at Kansai International Airport (KIX), one experiences Japan at its best. Constructed on a huge synthetic island in Osaka Bay and connected by a six-lane highway and two-rail line bridge, this 24-hour international airport boasts the latest in technology and, like the city itself, is user-friendly. After deplaning, board the driverless, computer-controlled wing shuttle to get to the main passenger terminal, where you go through immigration, baggage claim, and customs and come out in the arrivals lobby. Glass elevators ferry passengers to the four floors of the complex in an atrium setting, touch-operated computer screens provide information in many languages, and signs are clear and abundant. Post office (second floor south, near JAL counter, and open 9am to 5pm Monday to Friday), business center, money exchange (just as you exit customs and enter the arrivals lobby), children's play room (where they can romp before having to sit still on long flights), banks of international credit-card telephones, restaurants, convenience stores, nurseries, dental clinic, medical clinic, souvenir shops, baggage delivery service, police, beauty and barber salons—you name it, it's all here, neatly laid out and in beautiful surroundings. Probably the nicest-looking passenger terminal I've seen, it looks like Paris's Beaubourg Museum, updated and painted pastel.

ACCESS TO KIX Flying off to another destination in Japan? No hassle—just change planes: KIX has the shortest international-to-domestic transfer time of any airport, only 30 minutes. There are more than 60 **domestic flights** a day from KIX (compared to Narita's seven). To take the **train** to Tennoji, Shin-Osaka, and Kyoto, you simply walk through KIX's connecting concourse (baggage carts are designed to go on escalators and as far as the train ticket gates) and board the JR Haruka. The fare to Shin-Osaka is ¥2,930 ($29.30) for the 45-minute trip. Less rapid, the JR Kansai Express trains connect the airport with Tennoji, Namba, Osaka, and Kyobashi stations (as well as many others). The 60-minute trip to Namba, for example, costs ¥1,010 ($10.10). but if you a have a **JR rail pass,** you can ride these trains for free. Exhange your voucher in the Kansai Airport (rail) Station at the Green Window (open daily 5:30am to midnight) or the Travel Services Center or TiS (open daily 10am to 6pm) or in the international arrivals lobby on the first floor of the passenger terminal at the JR West Information Counter (open daily 8am to 9pm). Next to the JR trains in the same station is the Nankai line, whose rapi:t α reaches Namba in 29 minutes. There's one train an hour, which costs ¥1,370 ($13.70) for ordinary reserved or ¥1,670 ($16.70) for super seats (free tea and wider seats, etc.). The rapi:t β stops at more stations and is slower. You can also reach Osaka's Tempozan or Kobe's Port Island by high-speed **jet foil.** Take a shuttle bus to the ferry pier. The fare to Osaka is ¥1,650 ($16.50) for the 38-minute trip. Airport limosine **bus** service connects KIX with Osaka, Kobe, Nara, and Itami (Osaka Airport). Tickets can be bought in the arrival lobby, and fares range from ¥1,000 to ¥3,800 ($10 to $38).

By the way, when you depart from KIX you will pay a passenger terminal use **fee** of ¥2,600 ($26) at the vending machines (credit cards accepted) before you can pass through security check.

By Train Osaka is $2^1/_2$ hours from Tokyo by Shinkansen bullet train. All Shinkansen bullet trains arrive at Shin-Osaka Station, at the city's northern edge. To get from Shin-Osaka Station to Osaka Station and other points south, use the most convenient public transportation, the Midosuji subway line. The subway stop at Osaka Station is called Umeda Station. Japan Railways trains also make runs between Shin-Osaka and Osaka Stations. If you haven't yet turned in your voucher for your Japan Rail Pass, you can do so at Osaka Station's or Shin-Osaka Station's Green Windows between 5:30am and 11pm, or at Osaka Station at the Travel Information Satellite (TiS) on the main floor from 10am to 7pm (until 6pm Sunday and holidays), or at the Shin-Osaka Station TiS on the second floor from 7am to 8pm.

If you're arriving in Osaka from Kobe or Kyoto, remember that commuter lines will deliver you directly to Osaka Station in the heart of the city (unlike the Shinkansen).

By Bus JR night buses depart from both Tokyo (Yaesu exit) and Shinjuku (new south exit) stations every evening, arriving in Osaka the next morning.

VISITOR INFORMATION I find Osaka easier to get around than other large Japanese cities (except Tokyo, which I know because I lived there), because there is lots of signage and information in English.

At the Airport The Kansai Tourist Information Center (☎ 0724/56-6025) is in the north end of the International Arrivals Lobby. It is open 9am to 9pm on weekdays and 9am to 12:30pm Saturdays (closed Sundays and holidays). The multilingual staff can help with general travel information and hotel reservations, and they offer brochures and maps. The Tourist Information Office is in the south end of the International Arrivals Lobby and is open daily from 9am to 9pm. They also offer travel information, but not the Welcome Inn Reservations service.

In Town The Osaka Tourist Information Office (☎ 06/345-2189) is at the east (Midosuji) exit of Osaka Station and is open daily from 8am to 8pm. Its staff speaks English, gives out good maps of the city, and assists in securing hotel rooms. Another tourist office is near the central exits of Shin-Osaka Station, on the third floor (☎ 06/305-3311). Note that if you're arriving by Shinkansen, you'll be up on the fourth floor, so simply go down one flight to the tourist office, which is open daily from 8am to 8pm. Osaka Visitors Information Center (06/774-3077) is at the north exit of JR Tennoji Station and is open daily from 8am to 8pm.

For transportation information, there are information counters in major train stations, where an excellent booklet, *Osaka Traffic Network,* explains in detail how to get around Osaka.

To find out what's going on in Osaka, pick up a copy of *Kansai Time Out,* a magazine with information on sightseeing, festivals, restaurants, and other items of interest pertaining to Osaka, Kobe, and Kyoto. Published monthly (except for the December/January issue), *Kansai Time Out* sells for ¥300 ($3) at bookstores, restaurants, tourist information offices, and places frequented by English-speaking tourists, but is available free at major hotels.

Another source of information available free at the tourist offices and at many hotels is *Meet Osaka,* a quarterly with information on sightseeing, Bunraku, festivals, concerts, and special exhibits and events.

GETTING AROUND Osaka's user-friendly **subway** network is easy to use because all lines are color-coded and the station names are in English (even announcements are in English on many lines). The **Midosuji Line** is the most important one for visitors; it passes through Shin-Osaka Station and then goes to Umeda (close to

Osaka Station), Shinsaibashi, Namba, and Tennoji. There's also a Japan Railways train called the Osaka Kanjo Line, or **JR Loop Line,** which passes through Osaka Station and makes a loop around the city; take it to visit Osaka Castle.

If you prefer to take an **organized tour,** Rainbow Bus (☎ 06/311-2995) has half-day and full-day tours. The Castle, Shrine, and Temple Tour, for example, includes Osaka Castle, Sumiyoshi Taisha Shrine, and Shitennoji Temple, and costs ¥3,240 ($32.40) for the half-day excursion.

CITY LAYOUT

Osaka can be divided into north, south, east, and west districts. In the north, around Shin-Osaka, Osaka, and Umeda stations, are many hotels, restaurants, and shopping districts. In the south is the center of the JR Loop Line, which includes the Shinsaibashi shopping district and a lively eating and entertainment district clustered around a narrow street called Dotonbori. Connecting the two areas is a wide boulevard lined with gingko trees called Midosuji Dori, running from Osaka Station one-way south all the way to Namba Station. Farther south is Den Den Town, Osaka's electronics district. The eastern part of town is more historical, with Osaka Castle and its park and museums. While the west is mostly new and high-tech, Nanko, the new port town, includes a complex of business facilities, and at Tempozan Harbour Village are the aquarium, market place, museums, and ferry terminal. The rivers that cross Osaka cross from east to west. Farther west (outside the city limits) is the new Kansai International Airport, built, like much of the rest of the west, on a synthetic island.

WHAT TO SEE & DO

AROUND OSAKA CASTLE

In the eastern part of the city is one of the most famous castles in Japanese history, **Osaka Castle,** or *Osaka-jo* (☎ 06/941-3044), was first built in the 1580s on the order of Hideyoshi Toyotomi, who requisitioned materials from his feudal generals. The most conspicuous of these materials were huge stones; the largest, 19 feet high and 48 feet long, is known as the "Higo-ishi." Upon its completion, Osaka Castle was the largest castle in Japan, a magnificent structure used by Hideyoshi as a military stronghold against rebellious feudal lords. By the time he died in 1598, Hideyoshi had succeeded in crushing his enemies and unifying Japan under his command.

After Hideyoshi's death, Tokugawa Ieyasu seized power and established his shogunate government in Edo. Hideyoshi's heirs, however, had ideas of their own and, considering Osaka Castle impregnable, they plotted to overthrow the Tokugawa government. In 1615, Tokugawa sent troops to Osaka, where they not only defeated the Hideyoshi insurrectionists but destroyed Osaka Castle. Although the Tokugawas rebuilt the castle, they burned it down in 1868 during the Meiji Restoration, as they made their last retreat.

The present Osaka Castle dates from 1931. Built of ferroconcrete, it's not as massive as the original but is still impressive. Its eight-story donjon, or keep, rises 130 feet and houses a museum with displays relating to the Hideyoshi clan and old Osaka, including armor, fans, and personal belongings. It's open daily from 9am to 5pm, and admission is ¥500 ($5). To reach Osaka Castle, take either the JR Loop Line to Morinomiya or Osakajokoen Station, or the subway to Temmabashi, Tanimachi 4-chome, or Morinomiya Station.

In the castle park is the **Osaka City Museum** (☎ 06/941-7177) displaying articles relating to the history of Osaka, including its early history, when it was known as Naniwa-zu and was a gateway to other Asian cultures. Articles relating to Osaka's merchant history and performing arts history are also on display. Open Tuesday through Sunday from 9:30am to 5pm daily, it charges ¥300 to ¥600 ($3 to $6).

Just a few minutes' walk from the castle is the **O-Kawa River,** one of the many waterways that once served as important transportation avenues back in Osaka's merchant days. Although O-Kawa doesn't look anything like it used to, glass-enclosed boats ply the river throughout the year, departing from a dock close to the castle. Another way to see Osaka is by these water buses; a one-hour round-trip costs ¥1,800 ($18). Boats depart once an hour on the hour from Osaka Castle Pier (10 minutes later from Temmabashi Pier and 20 minutes later from Yodoyabashi Pier), from 10am to 7pm. The trip is beautiful (and therefore crowded) during the cherry-blossom season. For information or reservations, call **Osaka Aqua Bus** (☎ 06/942-5511).

Also just a few minutes' walk from Osaka Castle are the Twin 21 buildings, 2-1-61 Shiromi, easy to spot because they are two identical-looking structures among the several skyscrapers in this business park. On the second floor of the National Tower Building is **Panasonic Square,** a hall filled with electronics of various fields, including communications (such as the TV telephone) and games. Although it's designed for the Japanese (with most things explained in Japanese), there's enough to interest everyone, especially children. A robot, for example, can draw your portrait, while a periscope mounted on the building's roof lets you scan Osaka's panorama. Panasonic Square is open daily from 10am to 6pm, and admission is ¥300 ($3) for adults and ¥200 ($2) for children. For more information, call 06/949-2122.

And if you have plenty of time or are a market buff, the **Korean market** is located around Tsuruhashi Station. Not for the weak-stomached, the market sells all sorts of bizarre edibles, also beautiful Korean dresses and accessories.

The Western District

In Tempozan Harbour Village, an amusement, shopping, and restaurant complex with a breezy leisure atmosphere, the **Osaka Aquarium,** or *Kaiyukan* (☎ 06/576-5500), is one of the world's largest aquariums, encompassing 286,000 square feet and containing 2.9 million gallons of water. It's constructed around the theme "Ring of Fire," which refers to the volcanic perimeter encircling the Pacific Ocean. A visitor tour begins with a video of erupting volcanoes, followed by an escalator ride to the eighth floor. From there, visitors pass through 14 different habitats following a spiraling corridor back to the ground floor, starting with the daylight world above the ocean's surface and proceeding to the depths of the ocean floor. Arctic, Antarctic, tropical, and temperate zones are all represented, in exhibits ranging from the Gulf of Panama and Monterey Bay to the Great Barrier Reef. The walls of the aquarium tank are constructed of huge acrylic glass sheets, imparting a sense of being immersed in the middle of the ocean. Visitors look at 35,000 specimens representing 380 species, including two whale sharks, the largest fish in captivity. Allow about one to two hours to tour the aquarium, avoiding weekends. It's open daily from 10am to 8pm; closed every third Wednesday between December and February and every third Thursday in January and February. Admission is ¥1,950 ($19.50) for adults, ¥900 ($9) for children 7 to 15, and ¥400 ($4) for children 4 to 6. To reach it, take the Chuo subway line to Osaka Port (*Osakako*) Station, from which it's about a five-minute walk.

The **Suntory Museum** is that fantastically modern-looking structure you see nearby. The museum displays art and design from the world around us and has an impressive collection of posters. Its IMAX theater is billed as the world's largest and most advanced 3-D projection system. The Sky Lounge is a great place to view the bay and take a break. Open from 10am to 8pm, it charges ¥950 ($9.50) for entrance to the museum, ¥1,000 ($10) for IMAX, or ¥1,900 ($19) for both.

You can take a bay cruise from Tempozan on the Santa Maria (☎ 06/942-551), a replica of the ships of Columbus's era; inside are displays on the ships and life of the era. A day cruise of the harbor costs ¥1,500 ($15) for adults and ¥750 ($7.50) for children, while a night cruise is ¥2,750 ($27.50) for adults and ¥1,380 ($13.80) for children. Santa Maria Pier is five minutes on foot from Osakako Station.

A newly developed business center in Nanko boasts the beautifully designed Osaka Port Friendship Hall (☎ 06/572-5121), with its wine museum, the Asia and Pacific Trade Center (☎ 06/615-5000, see "Shopping," below), and the World Trade Center (☎ 06/232-1301). While the area is a marvel of ultramodern business, engineering design, and layout, as of this writing access is difficult. You must take a bus from Asashiobashi subway station or a shuttle bus from either JR Osaka (45 minutes) or Nankai Namba Station (30 minutes) until the new subway is completed. In any case, the area is chiefly of import to those interested in Japanese business.

The Northern District

In a modern building designed especially for viewing ceramics in natural lighting and computerized natural-light simulation, the **Museum of Oriental Ceramics Osaka** (☎ 06/223-0055) displays mostly Korean and Chinese ceramics, but includes some Japanese pieces designated National Treasures. Conceived as a showcase for the famed Ataka Collection, the museum is open 9:30am to 5pm Tuesdays through Sundays (closed before and after special exhibits). It's a five-minute walk from Yodoyabashi Station on the Midosuji Line. Admission is ¥500 ($5).

The **Science Museum, Osaka** (☎ 06/444-5656) was designed to enhance mankind's knowledge of the universe and our position in it, and to consider alternatives to unrestrained energy consumption. Exhibits range from hands-on to audiovisual, and there is a library, a computer-controlled planetarium, and an OMNIMAX theater. Located 8 minutes from Higobashi Station or 10 minutes from the JR Fukushima Station, the museum charges ¥400 ($4) plus ¥600 ($6) for either the planetarium or OMNIMAX (discounts for children and students). It's open 9:30am to 6:45pm (OMNIMAX tickets until 4pm) Tuesday through Sunday.

The **Floating Garden Observatory,** or *Kuchu Teien Tenbodai,* is a futuristic observatory 173 meters high. You ride up superfast glass elevators to the observatory, which seems to float between the two towers of the Umeda Sky Building. Not only do you have a view of all Osaka, but there's an interesting display, Dreams of Skygardens, showing human achievements through the ages and dreams of attaining the sky (including the pyramids and extraterrestial structures). Female attendants wear space-age costumes with ocher-colored cone-head hats—no kidding; I thought the price was worth it just to see those costumes. Built on two floors, the observatory has an upstairs area that is an outdoor viewing platform (no umbrellas allowed; someone has already hang-glided off). It costs ¥1,000 ($10) for adults and ¥500 ($5) for those under 13, and is open daily from 10am to 10:30pm. It's a 9-minute walk from either JR Osaka Station or Hankyu Umeda Station.

Around the Tennoji Temple

Shitennoji Temple (☎ 06/771-0066), in the city's southern district, was first built in 593 at the order of Prince Shotoku and is believed to be one of the oldest Buddhist temples in Japan (it was founded more than a decade before Horyuji Temple, outside Nara). Popularly known as Tennoji Temple and considered to represent the birthplace of Buddhism in Japan, it has been destroyed by fire many

Impressions

In trade it is a Chicago. In situation it is a Venice.
—John Foster Fraser, *Round the World on a Wheel,* 1899, on Osaka

times through the centuries; none of the original structures remains. It does have a Treasure House, however, which contains a large collection of religious artwork. Shitennoji is open Tuesday through Sunday from 8:30am to 4pm. The nearest station is JR Tennoji Station or the Shitennoji-mae subway station on the Tanimachi Line. Admission is ¥200 ($2) for adults, ¥120 ($1.20) for children.

Southwest of the temple is **Tennoji Park** (☎ 06/771-8401), where you can visit a zoo, botanical gardens, and the **Municipal Art Museum** (☎ 06/771-4874), with both ancient and modern Asian art (open 9:30am to 5pm Tuesdays through Sundays and charging ¥300/$3). **Tennoji Zoo,** opened in 1915, is home to 1,000 animals, including kiwis, Tasmanian devils, and rare Mongolian gazelles. It's open Tuesday through Sunday from 9:30am to 5pm and charges a ¥500 ($5) admission for those between 16 and 64. If you wish to visit only Tennoji Park, admission here is ¥150 ($1.50) for those between 16 and 64, waived if you're visiting the zoo. The park is open Tuesday through Sunday from 9:30am to 5pm (to 9pm in July and August). To reach Tennoji Park, take the subway or JR Loop Line to Tennoji Station; if your main destination is the zoo, head for Dobutsuen-mae Station.

A Nearby Attraction

Takarazuka is a town northwest of Osaka, but its name is synonymous with the all-female **Takarazuka Troupe.** Founded in 1914 to attract vacationers to Takarazuka, the troupe proved instantly popular with the general public, whose taste turned from traditional Japanese drama to lively Western musicals and entertainment. Performances are held at the Takarazuka Revue Hall most days throughout the year (closed Wednesday), usually at 1pm on weekdays and at 11am and 3pm on weekends and holidays. Tickets range from about ¥3,500 to ¥7,500 ($35 to $75).

Takarazuka Family Land is an amusement park, admission to which is ¥1,200 ($12), half price for children, and includes access to a zoo and botanical garden. The amusement park is open Thursday through Tuesday from 9:30am to 5:30pm. It takes approximately 45 minutes to reach Takarazuka Station from Umeda Station via the private Hankyu Line, followed by an eight-minute walk. For more information, call 0797/86-7777.

SHOPPING

Den Den Town is Osaka's electronics shopping region, similar to Tokyo's Akihabara (*Den* is short for "electric"). There are more than 150 shops here dealing in electrical and electronic equipment, from rice cookers to cassette players and personal computers. Most stores here are open daily from 10am to 7pm. The nearest subway station is either Nipponbashi or Ebisucho.

If you're in the market for dolls or toys, you'll want to visit **Matsuyamachi Street,** located near Tanimachi 6-chome and Nagahoribashi stations. This street is lined with wholesale and retail outlets selling everything from elaborate Japanese dolls to yo-yos. Shops here are open from 9:30am to 5:30pm; some shops are closed different days of the week, so you're always sure to find some open.

Osaka must rank as one of the world's leading cities in underground shopping arcades; **Diamor Osaka** has 73 shops and 16 galleries and is the newest—opened in 1995. The underground **Umeda Chika Center** connects Osaka and Umeda stations to a number of buildings, including the Hanshin and Hankyu department stores,

Hankyu Sanbangai, and the Hankyu Grand Building. They are both so massive and complicated that you'll probably get lost in the maze. Other shopping areas include the underground mall at **Namba** and an aboveground covered shopping street near the Shinsaibashi subway station. Paralleling Midosuji Dori to the east, it runs south all the way past Dotonbori and on to Namba.

The Asia and Pacific Trade Center was designed to increase market accessibility for foreign firms and accentuate trade. International and Japanese companies sell jewelry, leisure goods, gifts, home furnishings, and fashion. While the **International Trade Mart** is a bonded and supposedly uniquely wholesale market, I know an Osaka resident who buys there; especially for jewelry, it may be worth a try.

ACCOMMODATIONS

Like Tokyo, Osaka has a wide range of hotels, from first-class accommodations to business hotels. Most are concentrated around Osaka Station, while most of the rest stretch to the south and around Shin-Osaka Station, but with the development of the west port areas, hotels are now available there, too.

THE NORTHERN DISTRICT

Expensive

ANA Hotel

1-3-1 Dojimahama, Kita-ku, Osaka 530. ☎ **06/347-1112.** Fax 06/348-9208. 500 rms. A/C MINIBAR TV TEL. ¥27,000–¥40,000 ($270–$400) double/twin. AE, DC, JCB, MC, V. Taxi: 5 minutes. Directions: Walk 15 minutes south from Osaka Station.

Opened in 1984, this sleek, white hotel emphasizes running water, greenery, and ample sunlight in its architectural philosophy, evident as soon as you enter the impressive lobby. An inner courtyard stretches up to a skylight on the sixth floor, from which water trickles along extended chains to a pond below; nearby, water trickles over a rock sculpture. Built on the banks of the Dojima River (rooms with river views are best), the ANA offers a guest-relations desk to help with everything from restaurant reservations to sightseeing. Large guest rooms feature bilingual, satellite TV and sightseeing information in English.

Dining/Entertainment: There are five restaurants, a cafe, two bars, and a lobby lounge, as well as an outdoor beer garden open in summer.

Services: 24-hour room service, English-language newspapers delivered twice a day, same-day laundry service.

Facilities: Indoor swimming pool and sauna (fee: ¥3,000/$30), business center.

Hotel Osaka Grand

2-3-18 Nakanoshima, Kita-ku, Osaka 530. ☎ **06/202-1212.** Fax 06/227-5054. 348 rms. A/C MINIBAR TV TEL. ¥21,000–¥28,000 ($210–$280) double or twin. AE, DC, JCB, MC, V. Station: Higobashi (5 minutes).

This is a fine small hotel on the island of Nakanoshima in the heart of Osaka, with a location close to Osaka's Festival Hall that makes it a favorite of concert-goers and musicians. Dating from 1960, it's also one of Osaka's older hotels and has aged gracefully. The small, cozy lobby, with its high ceiling and old decor, evokes a European atmosphere of days gone by. With prices lower than other hotels in this category (and with no facilities outside its restaurants), it offers rooms with radio, clock, TV with bedside control buttons, pot for hot water, and bathroom covered with tile instead of the usual plastic. I prefer the rooms that face the river—although there's little traffic on the river and nothing really to see, it at least conveys a sense of spaciousness.

Dining/Entertainment: The seven bars and restaurants include a popular Western-style dining spot on the 14th floor that offers buffet lunches and dinners.

Services: Same-day laundry service.

✪ Hankyu International Hotel

19-19 Chayamachi, Kita-ku, Osaka 530. ☎ **06/377-2100** or 800/243-1166 in the U.S. and Canada. Fax 06/377-3622. 168 rms and suites. A/C MINIBAR TEL TV. ¥27,000–¥33,000 ($270–$330) single; ¥40,000–¥46,000 ($400–$460) double/twin; from ¥65,000 ($650) suites. All rates include breakfast. AE, DC, JCB, MC, V. Station: Hankyu Umeda or JR Osaka (7 minutes). Taxi: 10 minutes from Shin-Osaka Station.

The dramatic interiors by designer Richard L. Mayhew—from the Renaissance-style, dramatic public spaces to the large modern rooms—are an experience in themselves. The hotel occupies the top ten floors and the first six levels of the 34-story Chayamachi Applause Building. There are two lobbies, featuring Renaissance furnishings worth about ¥100 million; one for those using the hotel's entertainment and reception facilities and one on the 25th floor for overnight guests. Service is at a premium, with a staff of 430. Pampered guests range from Japanese business executives to foreign visitors with ample pocketbooks.

City view rooms have every convenience, from satellite TV and video cassette, CD, and cassette players to magnified, lit mirrors and separate-shower baths. Complimentary soft drinks are hidden in a wood cabinet minibar and there are bedside controls in a pullout panel (no annoying lights).

Dining/Entertainment: Six restaurants (small, beautifully designed, with intimate seating), a cafe, tea lounge, and two bars.

Services: 24-hour room and valet service, secretary service.

Facilities: Library, beauty salon, fitness club with gym, aerobics, massage, sauna, indoor pool (fee ¥5,000/$50), banquet and meeting rooms, parking, two theaters, florist, designer boutiques, heliport.

The Plaza

2-2-49 Oyodo-Minami, Kita-ku, Osaka 531. ☎ **06/453-1111** or 800/223-6800 in the U.S. and Canada. Fax 06/454-0169. 532 rms. A/C MINIBAR TV TEL. ¥24,000–¥40,000 ($240–$400) double or twin. AE, DC, JCB, MC, V. Station: Fukushima, on the JR Loop Line. Bus: Free shuttle bus from Osaka Station (north central exit) to the hotel every 15 minutes.

One of Osaka's first deluxe hotels, the Plaza remains in high standing as a member of the Leading Hotels of the World. Although relatively close to Osaka Station, it's far enough away to be out of the mainstream of human traffic. Further, it has none of the decorating pretentiousness sometimes afflicting modern hotels. Foreigners constitute about 30% of the Plaza's guests. Rooms are large and comfortable. No-smoking rooms are available.

Dining/Entertainment: There are six restaurants, one lounge, and two bars. The Rendezvous French restaurant on the 23rd floor is one of Osaka's best.

Services: 24-hour room service, free newspaper, same-day laundry service, baby-sitting, in-house doctor, free shuttle bus to Osaka Station every 15 minutes.

Facilities: Outdoor swimming pool (free of charge).

Royal Hotel

5-3-68 Nakanoshima, Kita-ku, Osaka 530. ☎ **06/448-1121** or 800/937-5454 in the U.S. Fax 06/448-4414. 1,060 rms. A/C MINIBAR TV TEL. ¥26,000–¥50,000 ($260–$500) double or twin. AE, DC, JCB, MC, V. Subway: Yodoyabashi Station, then a free shuttle bus from near exit 4, with departures every 15 minutes; or Osaka Station north exit, then a free shuttle every 20 minutes.

One of Osaka's most established hostelries, the Royal was first opened more than 58 years ago and remains among the city's largest hotels. Located on Nakanoshima, an island in the middle of the Dojima River, in the heart of Osaka, less than a 10-minute ride from Osaka Station, it has been remodeled and updated. Its rooms sport large windows and bilingual TV with CNN. Foreign guests include businesspeople, airline employees, and diplomats. The mutilingual staff is friendly, courteous, and helpful.

Dining/Entertainment: There are almost two dozen restaurants, the most renowned of which is the Chambord, a French restaurant on the 29th floor with views of the city.

Services: 24-hour room service, free newspapers delivered twice daily, same-day laundry service, baby-sitting.

Facilities: A beautifully designed swimming pool (one of the largest hotel pools in Osaka) and sauna (fee: ¥2,060/$20.60), a shopping arcade with more than 40 boutiques, business center, beauty salon, barbershop, no-smoking floor.

Moderate

$ Hotel Kitahachi

7-16 Doyama-cho, Kita-ku, Osaka 530. ☎ **06/361-2078.** Fax 06/361-7468. 38 rms. A/C MINIBAR TV TEL. ¥10,000–¥12,500 ($100–$125) double; ¥11,000–¥14,500 ($110–$145) twin; ¥18,500 ($185) triple. All rates include service. AE, DC, JCB, MC, V. Station: Osaka.

Kitahachi opened as a ryokan in 1946 and then converted to a Western-style hotel in the early 1980s. Half the rooms at this small, personable hotel are singles with semi-double-size beds, but they're often fully occupied because of their low prices. Twins are usually available. Rooms are larger than those of most business hotels, and they're more tastefully furnished as well. All rooms have double doors to block out corridor noise. At last check, no one here spoke any English—try to have a Japanese make your reservation. There's one cafe for breakfast, and a bar that stays open until 2am.

Hotel New Hankyu

1-1-35 Shibata, Kita-ku, Osaka 530. ☎ **06/372-5101.** Fax 06/374-6885. 947 rms. A/C MINIBAR TV TEL. ¥19,000–¥33,500 ($190–$335) twin; ¥23,000–¥28,000 ($230–$280) double; ¥32,000 ($320) triple. AE, DC, JCB, MC, V.

Shin Hankyu is part of the conglomerate that owns Hankyu Railways, Hankyu department stores, restaurants, and even Takarazuka Family Land. Rooms have cable TV and double-pane windows. Vending machines dispense soda and beer in a simple business-hotel decor. There are 23 bars and restaurants in the hotel and in the neighboring Hankyu complex; and in the Hotel New Hankyu Annex, a few minutes' walk away, guests can use a fitness club with pool and gym for ¥4,000 ($40).

Osaka Tokyu Inn

2-1 Doyama-cho, Kita-ku, Osaka 530. ☎ **06/315-0109.** Fax 06/315-6019. 402 rms. A/C MINIBAR TV TEL. ¥17,000 ($170) double; ¥17,600–¥19,600 ($176–$196) twin. All rates include service charge. AE, DC, JCB, MC, V. Station: Osaka (10 minutes). Directions: Take the underground passageway lined with shops and follow the signs for OGIMACHI until they bring you above ground at the W31 exit.

Part of a nationwide chain, this typical business hotel has a restaurant serving Western food, and its rooms are quiet and clean. The cheapest singles and twins face an inner courtyard with absolutely no view; better are those facing the front, where you can look down on a small and tidy temple and cemetery seemingly out of place among Osaka's office buildings—typical Japan. The hotel is a bit confusing to find, so you may want to stop by the tourist office to get a map showing the way to the hotel.

Shin-Osaka Station Hotel

1-16-6 Higashi-Nakajima, Higashi-yodogawa-ku, Osaka 533. ☎ **06/325-0011.** Fax 06/325-3366. 89 rms. A/C MINIBAR TV TEL. ¥11,000 ($110) double; ¥13,500 ($135) twin; ¥16,000

($160) triple. All rates include tax and service. AE, DC, JCB, MC, V. Directions: Walk from Shin-Osaka Station's central exit and go to the left over the pedestrian bridge over the railroad tracks (2 minutes).

This is one of the newest inexpensive business hotels to open near Shin-Osaka Station. Don't confuse this hotel with the much older, smaller one just in front of it with the exact same name (the older hotel is identified only in Japanese, while the newer one has an English sign). Rooms are small but adequate, with TV with pay video, clock, and hot-water pot with tea. There's one restaurant serving Western food.

Inexpensive

$ Hotel Hokke Club (62)

12-19 Togano-cho, Kita-ku, Osaka 530. ☎ **06/313-3171.** Fax 06/313-4637. 247 rms (none with bath). A/C MINIBAR TV TEL. ¥5,900 ($59) for one person, ¥10,600 ($106) for two people. Breakfast ¥680 ($6.80) extra. All rates include service charge. AE, DC, JCB, MC, V. Station: Osaka. Directions: Take the underground passageway, following signs for OGIMACHI, until you come above ground at the W32 exit.

First opened in 1966, this hotel is one of Osaka's oldest business hotels. Its small but clean and adequate rooms, available in both Western and Japanese style, are without private baths, but there are large, separate public baths for men and women. If you're taking a single, request a corner room, since the other singles face an inner courtyard and are dark. There's one Japanese-style restaurant, and vending machines dispense beer and soft drinks.

$ Shin-Osaka Sen-i City (153)

2-2-17 Nishi-Miyahara, Yodogawa-ku, Osaka 532. ☎ **06/394-3331.** Fax 06/394-3335. 70 rms (12 with bath). A/C MINIBAR TV TEL. ¥9,500 ($95) twin without bath, ¥11,000–¥11,500 ($110–$115) twin with bath. All rates include tax and service charge. AE, DC, JCB, MC, V. Directions: Take the free shuttle bus from Shin-Osaka Station's central exit.

This very simple business hotel, a 10-minute walk northwest of Shin-Osaka Station, is easy to spot with its green-and-blue sign and clock on the top of the building. The lobby is on the sixth floor, and guest rooms are on the sixth and seventh floors. The rooms are a few decades away from being modern, but they're clean, good for the price, and fairly large as far as business hotels go. All the singles and most twins are bathless, but there are public baths. Twins with private bathrooms have Western-style toilets and deep, Japanese-style bathtubs. Shuttle buses bound for Sen-i City depart every 10 minutes or so from the lowest level of Shin-Osaka Station's central exit—turn right out of the station and walk to the end of the row of buses.

The Southern District

Expensive

Nankai South Tower Hotel Osaka

5-1-60 Namba, Chuo-ku, Osaka 542. ☎ **06/646-1111.** Fax 06/648-0331. 548 rms. A/C MINIBAR TV TEL. ¥30,000–¥42,000 ($300–$420) double or twin. AE, DC, JCB, MC, V. Station: Namba (1 minute).

Towering above Namba Station, with a marbled atrium lobby on the sixth floor, this hotel's guest rooms are on floors 14 through 34, with prices based on size and height. Pluses are fax machine outlets and bathroom phones.

Dining/Entertainment: There are 10 restaurants and bars serving French, Chinese, and a wide range of Japanese food, including sukiyaki, sushi, tempura, teppanyaki, and kaiseki. The Sky Lounge on the 36th floor offers breathtaking views of Osaka.

Services: 24-hour room service, free newspapers delivered twice a day, same-day laundry service, baby-sitting room.

Facilities: Fitness center, indoor pool, gym, and sauna (fee: ¥5,000/$50), shopping arcade, business center, travel counter, beauty salon, barbershop, no-smoking floor.

Moderate

D-Hotel

2-5-15 Dotonbori, Chuo-ku, Osaka 542. ☎ **06/212-2995.** Fax 06/211-7462. 12 rms. A/C MINIBAR TV TEL. ¥10,000–¥28,000 ($100–$280) double; ¥20,000–¥23,000 ($200–$230) twin. MC, V. Station: Namba (3 minutes). Directions: Walk to the far west end of Dotonbori Street on the river's south side.

You can stay at this new, postmodern hotel in style for about the same price you'd pay at an unexciting business hotel. A concrete-and-steel structure of interesting design, the D-Hotel offers wooden floors, rubbed copper, and steel-and-glass rooms with great audio systems, including a laser disc player to pop in your own sounds. The large windowed baths have Jacuzzi jets, and the more expensive r ooms have glass-encased personal saunas. Colors are gray and black. A plus is this hotel's great location in the heart of the nightlife area. Complimentary coffee is served in the basement lounge/lobby, and complimentary newspapers are offered. The hotel's restaurant, Dim Sum, which offers a river view, serves Chinese delicacies (from ¥1,000/$10). There's an art gallery and cafe where you may meet some arty types.

Holiday Inn Nankai

2-5-15 Shinsaibashisuji Chuo-ku, Osaka 542. ☎ **06/213-8281** or 800/HOLIDAY in the U.S. and Canada. Fax 06/213-8640. 229 rms. A/C MINIBAR TV TEL. ¥18,000–¥26,000 ($180–$260) double or twin. Children up to 12 stay free in parents' room. AE, DC, JCB, MC, V. Station: Namba (3 minutes).

This hotel has a very convenient location close to Dotonbori and Osaka's nightlife district, right on Midosuji Dori. The lobby is on the fifth floor, and the rooftop pool, open free to hotel guests during July and August, is a plus. There's also an outdoor beer garden on the third floor, open daily from 5 to 9pm from the end of May to the end of August. Four restaurants serve French, Chinese, American, and Japanese cuisine. As with all Holiday Inns, all beds are double size, even those in single rooms, and the rooms are large.

$ Hotel California

1-9-30 Nishishinsaibashi, Chuo-ku, Osaka 542. ☎ **06/243-0333.** Fax 06/243-0148. 54 rms. A/C MINIBAR TV TEL. ¥11,000–¥14,000 ($110–$140) double; ¥13,000–¥14,000 ($130–$140) twin. Sat and hol eves, ¥1,000 ($10) extra. AE, DC, JCB, MC, V. Station: Shinsaibashi (3 minutes).

This place tries to evoke images of sunny California through its use of whites and greens, plants, and brass railings. Rooms are cheerfully decorated with soft pastels and rattan furniture. The Hotel California is conveniently located near America Mura. It has one Western-style restaurant, California Garden, and one American-style bar.

Inexpensive

Ebisu-So Ryokan

1-7-33 Nipponbashi-Nishi, Naniwa-ku, Osaka 556. ☎ **06/643-4861.** 15 rms (none with bath). A/C TV. ¥9,000 ($90) twin; ¥13,500 ($135) triple. AE, MC, V. Station: Ebisucho (from exit 1, 5 minutes) or Nipponbashi, on the Kintetsu Line (10 minutes).

This Japanese-style inn is a member of the Japanese Inn Group, and is more cluttered and run-down than most (it has been an inn for 35 years, and no one speaks English). It reminds me of a small apartment house where young single Japanese often live—a narrow corridor flanked on both sides with 4½- and 6-tatami rooms. I have friends who say they like living in a 4½-tatami room because they can reach everything without having to move. Rooms come with coin-operated TV, fan, and heater, and there's a public bath. The ryokan is near Den Den Town, Osaka's electronics shopping region.

THE EASTERN DISTRICT

Expensive

✪ Miyako Hotel Osaka

6-1-55 Uehommachi, Tennoji-ku, Osaka 543. ☎ **06/773-1111** or 800/336-1136 in the U.S. Fax 06/773-3322. 586 rms. A/C MINIBAR TV TEL. ¥25,000–¥29,000 ($250–$290) double or twin. AE, DC, JCB, MC, V. Station: Uehommachi Station, on the Kintetsu Line; or the Tanimachi 9-chome subway station exit no. 12 (underground passage).

This hotel was designed by the well-known Japanese architect Togo Murano, renowned for his ability to combine Japanese simplicity and tradition with modern efficiency. He was the interior designer as well, reflected in his preferences for light, muted colors and wooden furniture. Chandeliers are in every guest room. He died at the age of 91, so this Miyako Hotel was his last complete architectural achievement.

The service here is excellent. Guest rooms come with all the comforts you'd expect from a first-class hotel, plus lots and lots of added amenities. Room rates are based on size, with the highest rates charged for the executive floors, where guests are treated to free breakfast and cocktails and to the services of an executive desk with a bilingual staff eager to help you with any request. The hotel is conviently attached to the Kintetsu Station, so you can take a direct train from here to either Ise-Shima or Nara.

Dining/Entertainment: The 13 restaurants and bars offer everything from Japanese and Chinese to French cuisine. La Mer is an exclusive, expensive seafood restaurant, while the Ciel Bleu on the 21st floor offers French dishes and a grand view. In the basement are inexpensive restaurants, including Tsuruki Soba, specializing in inexpensive buckwheat noodles.

Services: 24-hour room service, same-day laundry service, English-language newspapers delivered twice a day, a well-equipped and expertly staffed childcare facility.

Facilities: Domestic airport shuttle service (fee: ¥440/$4.40) every 20 minutes; KIX shuttle (fee: ¥1,300/$13) every 30 minutes; in-house video information; business center; drugstore; travel agency; no-smoking floor; health club (fee: from ¥4,000/$40) with exercise gym, racquetball court, sauna, and swimming pool (pool charge: ¥2,500/$25); adjacent department store and post office.

New Otani Osaka

1-4-1 Shiromi, Chuo-ku, Osaka 540. ☎ **06/941-1111.** Fax 06/941-9769. 540 rms. A/C MINIBAR TV TEL. ¥30,000–¥34,000 ($300–$340) twin; ¥31,000–¥38,000 ($310–$380) double; ¥44,000 ($440) triple. AE, DC, JCB, MC, V. Station: Osakajokoen, on the JR Loop Line (3 minutes).

The New Otani Osaka, near Osaka Castle and a business park—with corporate headquarters for KDD, NEC, Sumitomo, and other big companies—has a steady business clientele, while its proximity to Osaka Castle brings in the tourists as well. Everything about this hotel is visually pleasing. The marbled lobby boasts a four-story atrium, with a clever use of mirrors and skylights to give it an added airiness.

Rooms are pleasant and comfortable (windows open). Rates are based on room size and view, with the more expensive rooms providing a view of Osaka Castle.

Dining/Entertainment: Among the hotel's 16 restaurants and bars is the ever-popular Trader Vic's, as well as restaurants serving Chinese, continental, Italian, and Japanese cuisine. The Four Seasons is a piano bar with views of Osaka Castle.

Services: 24-hour room service, free newspaper delivered twice a day, same-day laundry service.

Facilities: Fitness club with indoor and outdoor swimming pools and tennis courts (fee charged), shopping arcade with designer names, business center, travel agency, beauty salon, medical clinic, no-smoking floors.

Moderate

Hotel International House

8-2-6 Uehommachi, Tennoji-ku, Osaka 543. ☎ **06/773-8181.** Fax 06/773-0777. 50 rms. A/C TV TEL. ¥13,500 ($135) twin. All rates include tax and service charge. Closed Dec 29–Jan 3. AE, DC, JCB, MC, V. Station: Uehommachi on the Kintetsu Line (5 minutes); or the Tanimachi 9-chome or Shitennoji-mae subway station (5 minutes).

The International House is a facility used for international seminars, conventions, and meetings. It includes the Hotel International House, used mainly by those attending seminars but also open to the public—try to book well in advance. Rooms are spartan but have everything you need, including a small unit bath with a clothesline. Some 40 of the 50 rooms here are singles, making it a great place to stay for the single traveler. One restaurant serves Western-style foods at very reasonable prices, and there is one bar/cafe. It's managed by the Miyako Hotel Osaka, so service is better than what you'd find at most hotels at these prices.

$ Hotel Osaka Castle

1-1 Tenmabashi-Kyomachi, Chuo-ku, Osaka 540. ☎ **06/942-2401.** Fax 06/946-9043. 122 rms. A/C MINIBAR TV TEL. ¥13,000–¥17,000 ($130–$170) twin; ¥13,000–¥15,000 ($130–$150) double; ¥19,500 ($195) triple. All rates include tax and service. AE, DC, MC, V. Station: Tenmabashi (1 minute).

One gets excellent value for money in this tourist hotel, popular with youth groups and next to the Okawa River and just above Tenmabashi Station. The 7th-floor lobby has a connecting corridor with Matsuzakaya department store. The best rooms face the river and are wonderful when cherry blossoms line the river. Singles have semi-double beds but do not face the river; however, single travelers can ask for a twin at no extra charge. There are three restaurants, and the Castle Café on the ground floor has a ¥480 ($4.80) morning set with coffee, a ham sandwich, boiled eggs, and buttered toast.

The Western District

Expensive

Hyatt Regency Osaka

1-13-11 Nanko-kita, Suminoe-ku, Osaka 559. ☎ **06/612-1234.** Fax 06/614-7800. A/C MINIBAR TV TEL. 500 rms. ¥33,000–¥37,000 ($330–$370) Regency Club single; from ¥85,000 ($850) suites. Extra ¥5,000 for second person and ¥6,000 for second person in Regency Club. AE, DC, JCB, MC, V. Directions: Airport limousine from KIX (fee: ¥1,300/$13). Subway: Bentencho, then free shuttle.

Textural prints and textiles are used to break up the smooth coolness of marble and wood in this five-star hotel situated in Osaka's high-tech Cosmo Square near the Asia and Pacific Trade Center and World Trade Center. (The hotel will become more convenient to downtown once the new line is operating.) Luxurious accommodations are very business-minded, with TV with message-receiving system, two phone lines, voice mail, and dataports for fax and PCs. Regency Club includes continental breakfast, all-day coffee and tea service, evening cocktails, and personal concierge.

Dining/Entertainment: There are 14 restaurants and bars, from poolside to sophisticated to casual, and in summer a beer garden.

Services: Handicapped rooms, no-smoking rooms, baby-sitting.

Facilities: Business center with multilingual services; meeting rooms; children's playground; drugstore; barbershop; photo studio; florist; beauty salon; parking; and fitness center (fee: ¥3,000/$30 or ¥4,000/$40 in summer) with exercise room, sauna, steambath, hot and cold plunge pools, Jacuzzi, indoor lap pool, and outdoor pool (summer).

NEAR KANSAI INTERNATIONAL AIRPORT

Hotel Kansai Airport

1 Senshu-kuko Kita, Izumisano-shi, Osaka 549. ☎ **0721/55-1111,** or 800/NIKKO US. Fax 0721/55-155. 576 rms and suites. A/C MINIBAR TV TEL. ¥26,000–¥30,000 ($260–$300) double; ¥24,000–¥70,000 ($240–$700); suites from ¥85,000 ($850). AE, DC, JCB, MC, V.

If you want to stay close to the airport, this hotel, part of the Nikko Hotels group, is connected directly to the passenger terminal of KIX. More expensive rooms are on the top two executive floors, which offer a private lounge and special services. Every room is completely soundproofed.

Dining/Entertainment: There are seven food and beverage outlets.

Services: 24-hour room service and flight information channel.

Facilities: Business center, banquet and meeting rooms, gift shop, amusement space, parking, pool, sauna, and Jacuzzi.

ELSEWHERE IN OSAKA

Hattori Ryokuchi Youth Hostel (154)

1-3 Hattori-ryokuchi, Toyonaka-shi, Osaka 540. ☎ **06/862-0600.** Fax 06/863-0561. 104 beds. A/C. ¥2,000 ($20) for JYHA members and nonmembers. Breakfast ¥500 ($5) extra; dinner ¥850 ($8.50) extra; sheets ¥100 ($1) extra. No credit cards. Subway: From Umeda Station 45 minutes to Ryokuchi-koen (10 minutes).

This youth hostel, although a bit far from the center of Osaka, is located in Hattori-Ryokuchi Park, which has a swimming pool and an open-air museum of old Japanese farmhouses. The front doors close at 9pm, and lights-out is at 10pm.

DINING

There's a saying among Japanese that whereas a Kyotoite will spend his last yen on a fine kimono, an Osakan will spend it on food. You don't have to spend a lot of money, however, to enjoy good food in Osaka.

Specialties of Osaka include sushi, udon (noodles) with white soy sauce, and *takoyaki* (cooked dumplings made of octopus). It is probably best known, however, for *okonomiyaki*, which literally means "as you like it." Its origins date from about 1700, when a type of thin flour cake cooked on a hotplate was served during Buddhist ceremonies. The cake was filled with a bean paste called miso. It wasn't until this century that it became popular, primarily during food shortages. At first it was a simple dish consisting only of flour, water, and a sauce, but gradually other ingredients, such as pork, egg, and vegetables, were added. Today, Osaka is literally riddled with okonomiyaki restaurants offering very inexpensive dining.

Family-Friendly Restaurants

The Cafe in the Hyatt Regency Osaka *(see p. 378)* For an all-inclusive price of ¥1,750 ($17.50) for children 4 to 10 (adults ¥3,500/$35), The Cafe serves children's favorites with balloons and ice cream every Sunday night.

Kuidaore *(see p. 382)* This establishment pleases parents with its wide variety and little ones with a kid's meal and toy.

THE NORTHERN DISTRICT

Botejyu

Hankyu Sanbangai Bldg., 2nd basement. ☎ **06/374-2254.** ¥650–¥1,500 ($6.50–$15). No credit cards. Daily 11am–9:30pm. Closed third Wed of each month. Station: Osaka (east exit, 2 minutes). OKONOMIYAKI.

One of the best-known okonomiyaki chain restaurants, this informal eatery is in a restaurant mall called Gourmet Museum (if you can find a map here, Botejyu is number 16). I tried the *omu soba,* an omelet filled with cabbage, wheat noodles, and pork and smothered in ketchup and mayonnaise. Cooking is done on a hot griddle right in front of you, and dishes are served on sheets of aluminum foil.

✪ Jidoritei Yakitori Shin Miura

Takimi-koji Village, Umeda Sky Bldg. basement, 1-1-90-B100 Oyodo-naka. ☎ **06/440-5957.** Set meals ¥500–¥1,800 ($5–$18). No credit cards. Mon–Fri 11:30am–1:30pm and 5–9pm; Sat–Sun noon–9:30pm. Station: JR Osaka (9 minutes). YAKITORI.

Takimi-koji Village is a recreated 1920s–30s Japanese town with an old-fashioned sweets shop, barbershop, and restaurants serving fish tongue, okonomiyaki, kushikatsu, and teppanyaki. The village, filled with old tin signs and posters, is a delightful place to dine. One of my favorites is Jidoritei Yakitori Shin Miura, which dishes up yakitori and grilled chicken meals.

Kaen (155)

Steak Ron Bldg., 3rd floor, 1-10-2 Sonnezaki-shinchi. ☎ **06/344-2929.** Reservations required. Set dinners ¥9,000–¥15,000 ($90–$150); set lunches ¥2,500–¥5,000 ($25–$50). AE, DC, JCB, MC, V. Mon–Sat 11:30am–2pm and 5–9pm (last order). Subway: Yotsubashi (2 minutes). FRENCH KAISEKI.

A new form of cuisine: French food presented in the Japanese kaiseki manner. The food is French, but each course is served separately using Japanese plates and dishes, and guests use chopsticks instead of forks. Each plate is chosen to enhance the food, according to color, texture, and the seasons. This refined, modern restaurant serves only set meals, which are changed twice a month. Highly recommended.

Okonomiyaki Madonna

Hilton Plaza, 1-8-8 Umeda. ☎ **06/347-7371.** ¥1,050–¥2,500 ($10.50–$25). AE, DC, JCB, MC, V. Daily 11am–11pm. Subway: Yotsubashisen. OKONOMIYAKI.

At this modern and with-it okonomiyaki restaurant served by a young and friendly staff, ingredients change with the seasons but may include pork, beef, squid, octopus, shrimp, potato, mushroom, or oyster. Fried noodles are also available. Madonna is located across from Victoria Station (see below), in the basement of the Hilton Plaza. Single diners will feel comfortable sitting around a counter watching food being prepared. Very casual.

Le Rendezvous

The Plaza, 2-2-49 Oyodo-Minami. ☎ **06/453-1111.** Reservations required. Main dishes ¥4,500–¥8,000 ($45–$80); set dinners ¥12,000–¥23,000 ($120–$230). AE, DC, JCB, MC, V. Daily 5:30–10pm. Transportation: Free shuttle bus or a 5-minute taxi ride from Osaka Station. FRENCH.

Le Rendezvous is one of the most famous—if not *the* most famous—of Osaka's French restaurants. It receives advice on its creations from internationally known chef Paul Bocuse and was the first of only two Asian restaurants that are members of Traditions et Qualité, a prestigious gastronomical association of French restaurants (the second restaurant is Tour d'Argent in Tokyo). With windows overlooking

Osaka, this small and intimate restaurant serves seasonal dishes that in the past have included such selections as Kobe sirloin and tenderloin steaks, duck, sole stuffed with artichoke and basil, young rabbit leg, and turbot cooked in champagne. Men must wear dinner jackets.

The Southern District

Dotonbori Street, a narrow pedestrian lane flanking the south bank of the Dotonbori River, is lined with restaurants and drinking establishments. The area is expanding to reach Europa Dori and neighboring streets. There are two famous ramen shops, **Kinryu** (☎ 06/211-6202) and **Kamukura** (☎ 06/213-1238), next to each other near Ebisubashi (bridge), where ramen runs about ¥600 ($6). Kinryu (look for the dragon on the building and red noren) is a stand-up bar and open 24 hours. At Kamukura (look for the yellow-and-red sign), open from 11am to 7pm, you can sit down but you'll have to wait. While you are waiting, notice a slot between the two ramen shops where people are lined up. You'll see people putting merchandise won at pachinko in the slot and then a hand handing over cash. Gambling for money in Japan is illegal, but here's a way around the law.

Capricciosa

2-8-110-105 Nambanaka. ☎ **06/631-5155.** Pizza and pasta ¥960–¥2,790 ($9.60–$27.90). No credit cards. Daily 11am–11pm. Station: Namba. ITALIAN.

This chain restaurant has become very popular by serving portions large enough for two (I've never managed to finish a bowl alone) at inexpensive prices in a casual setting with Italian decor and music. Families and students make up the bulk of traffic.

Cirque de Haagen Dazs

2-4-9 Shinsaibashisuji. ☎ **06/212-9235.** Cones and sundaes ¥500–¥1,500 ($5–$15). No credit cards. Daily 11am–11pm (until 2am Sat and hol eves). Directions: Near Ebisubashi (bridge). ICE CREAM.

Well named, the Cirque provides a circuslike experience when stopping for an ice cream here. Downstairs is a merry-go-round, but one you'd perhaps prefer not to put your children on—scantily clad women figurines go round and round and up and down on the poles and (yes) you can ride on them. Upstairs you go through three different doors, each of which has a different theme and is a different musical instrument. In the middle of the room is a revolving platform with themed tables and chairs divided by pink quilted butterfly wings. The women's toilet is a shell with blinking red lights that sings, and the men's urinal moves, so take careful aim. If the decor isn't enough, someone will be tap dancing or miming. By the way, the ice cream is excellent.

Kani Doraku (156)

1-6-2 Dotonbori. ☎ **06/211-1633.** Crab dishes ¥500–¥13,000 ($5–$130); set lunch ¥3,500 ($35); set dinners ¥4,300–¥9,500 ($43–$95). AE, DC, JCB, MC, V. Daily 11am–11pm. Station: Namba. CRAB.

Specializing in *kani* (crab), this restaurant would be difficult to miss because of the huge model crab on its facade (it moves its legs and claws). Part of a chain originating in Osaka a couple of decades ago, there are now more than 55 throughout Japan. Its dishes range from crab-suki and crab-chiri (a kind of crab sukiyaki) and fried crab dishes, to crab croquette, roasted crab with salt, crab salad, crab sushi, and boiled king crab. Located on Dotonbori right beside the bridge over the canal, the restaurant occupies several floors, with some tables offering a view of the water.

Kuidaore (157)

1-8-25 Dotonbori. ☎ **06/211-5300.** Dishes ¥580–¥2,500 ($5.80–$25); set meals ¥980–¥3,500 ($9.80–$35). AE, DC, JCB, MC, V. Daily 11am–10pm. Second-floor pub, daily 4–11pm. Station: Namba. VARIED JAPANESE.

Kuidaore is famous for its clown model outside the front door, which has been beating a drum and wiggling its eyebrows ever since the place first opened in 1949. There's an extensive plastic-food display case, an indication of the wide variety served, including tempura, sashimi, charcoal-broiled beef, shabu-shabu, udon, eel, sukiyaki, yakitori, noodles, and even Western food. Altogether, there are four floors of dining, with prices increasing the higher up you go. On the ground floor is a modern, family-style dining area. From the clown outside to the food inside, this is a great place to bring youngsters; a child's set meal (¥800/$8) includes Groucho Marx faux-nose glasses. On the second floor is a *nomi-ya,* or pub, where you can order a beer, yakitori, and snacks. The fourth floor is for *nabe* (one-pot stews), including shabu-shabu, and the fifth floor is for set meals.

Takoume

1-1-8 Dotonbori. ☎ **06/211-0321.** Oden ¥100–¥1,450 ($1–$14.50). No credit cards. Mon–Sat 5–10pm. Station: Namba (4 minutes). ODEN.

Run by a bunch of no-nonsense women, this shop dates from the Edo Period. There's no English-language menu, so just sit at the counter and point—you can see things boiling in a big pot. There are three set meals: *Take* (¥1,000/$10), *Matsu* (¥2,000/$20), and *Ume* (¥4,000/$40), which give you a variety. *Tamago* (boiled egg) is the least expensive thing to order, while *saezuri* (whale's tongue) is the most expensive and also practically the only thing on the menu that is nonvegetarian. *Hirosu* is tofu and vegetables with an egg-batter coating.

THE EASTERN DISTRICT

$ Fugetsu (158)

2-18 Ajiharacho Tennojiku. ☎ **06/771-7938.** Okonomiyaki ¥550–¥880 ($5.50–$8.80); yakisoba ¥580–¥1,100 ($5.80–$11). No credit cards. Daily 11:30am–10pm (last order). Station: Tsuruhashi. Directions: From the west exit (nishiguchi) go straight, turn right at the second alleyway. OKONOMIYAKI.

There are always lines in this famous okonomiyaki restaurant, where your dinner is cooked at your table. The squid, octopus, and pork yakisoba are among the best I've ever had. Very popular is *butatama,* an okonomiyaki with pork and egg. On the other side of the station is the Korean market, so you may want to combine a lunch here with a stroll through the market.

Kinjokaku

Hotel Osaka Castle, 1-1 Tenmabashi-Kyomachi. ☎ **06/942-2401.** Main dishes ¥650–¥5,000 ($6.50–$50); set lunch (Kinjo teishoku) ¥850 ($8.50). Daily 11am–8:30pm (last order). Station: Tenmabashi. SHANDONG CHINESE.

Classical favorites like sweet-and-sour spareribs, chili prawns, and braised bean curd tempt one from Kinjokaku's English menu. Best, of course, is to come in a group (set meals for groups start at ¥1,000/$10, while ordering à la carte can be expensive).

Miyako

Miyako Hotel, 6-1-55 Uehommachi. ☎ **06/773-1111.** Reservations recommended. Set dinners ¥6,000–¥18,000 ($60–$180); set lunches ¥2,500–¥5,000 ($25–$50). AE, DC, JCB, MC, V. Daily 11:30am–2:30pm and 5–10pm. Station: Uehommachi (on the Kintetsu Line) or Tanimachi 9-chome subway station. KAISEKI/VARIED JAPANESE.

This pleasant restaurant makes choosing what you want to eat easy by offering a tempura counter (I've always felt the only way to eat tempura is as it comes out of the pan), a sushi counter, tables, and private tatami rooms. I had the Hancha course for ¥7,000 ($70) with miso and mushroom soup; steamed meat, vegetables, and chestnut; grilled fish; vinegared tender octopus tendrils; savory crab-egg custard; pickles; and rice topped with crunchy brown rice. While some kaiseki can be so esoteric as to be uneatable, every dish here was delicious. Lunches (tempura set or eel obento) are quite reasonable.

Trader Vic's

New Otani Hotel, 1-4 Shiromi. ☎ **06/941-1111.** Main dishes ¥3,500–¥6,500 ($35–$65); set lunch ¥1,900 ($19). AE, DC, JCB, MC, V. Mon–Sat noon–midnight, Sun and hols 11:30am–midnight. Station: Osakajo-koen (3 minutes). INTERNATIONAL.

This is a great lunch choice for Osaka Castle sightseers. Decorated in Polynesian style typical of Trader Vic's around the world, it offers dining with a view of the castle, the park, and the river. There's a luncheon special for ¥1,900 ($19), served Monday through Saturday until 2:45pm, as well as a lunch menu including hamburgers, club sandwiches, pasta, and other international selections. Dinners offer a wider selection, including salads, a good selection of vegetable side dishes, curries, steaks, seafood, and Chinese dishes. Come for the Sunday champagne brunch, served from 11:30am to 2:45pm, which costs ¥4,500 ($45) for adults, ¥2,000 ($20) for children under 12.

The Western District

Basilico

Hyatt Regency, 1-13-11 Nanko-kita. ☎ **06/612-1234.** Pasta and pizza ¥1,000–¥1,800 ($10–$18); set dinner ¥2,950 ($29.50). AE, DC, JCB, MC, V. Subway: Bentencho, then free shuttle. ITALIAN.

Blue pitchers hold flowers, and jars of pasta and antipasto set the mood in this casual trattoria looking out on a patio. There is a real wood-burning pizza oven, and the antipasto and pasta are homemade.

Marseille

Cosmo Tower, 46th floor, 1-14-6 Nanko-kita. ☎ **06/615-7120.** Main dishes ¥500–¥1,000 ($5–$10); set dinner ¥3,500–¥5,500 ($35–$55); all-you-can-eat lunch buffet ¥890 ($8.90). Lunch buffet includes tax and service. No credit cards. Lunch buffet daily 11am to 2pm and dinner 5–9:45pm. Station: Bentencho; then take a bus.

Though perhaps far from the port that bears its name, this restaurant on the 46th floor offers a great harbor view and an incredibly inexpensive all-you-can-eat lunch buffet (spring rolls, fried chicken, soft drinks). A large wooden boat in the middle of the room serves as the buffet. A great spot for a beer (¥390/$3.90) with a panoramic view.

Sun Tempo

1-5-10 Kaigandori. ☎ **06/577-0009.** Main dishes ¥800–¥1,500 ($8–$15); salad bar ¥1,300 ($13). AE, DC, JCB, MC, V. Daily 11am–10pm. PASTA/SALAD BAR.

Next to the Suntory Museum (see above for directions) in the newly developed waterfront area of Tempozan Harbour Village is this airy wood-and-rattan restaurant with green ironwork grapevine decor. The extensive all-you-can-eat salad bar comes with soup and homemade bread. Pasta, too, is freshly made. Steak and hamburgers are also on the English-language menu.

Osaka After Dark

Bunraku

The **National Bunraku Theater,** 1-12-10 Nipponbashi, Chuo-ku (☎ 06/212-2531), was completed in 1984 and presents traditional puppet theater five times a year, with most productions running for two to three weeks at a time. Tickets usually range from ¥4,200 to ¥5,400 ($42 to $54), and children 6 to 11 are usually charged ¥2,100 to ¥4,200 ($21 to $42). Performances are usually held daily at 11am and 4pm. To find out whether a performance is being held, contact the Osaka Tourist Information Office. The National Bunraku Theater is about a 10-minute walk from the Namba subway station on the Midosuji Line, or a 5-minute walk from Nipponbashi Station on the Kintetsu Line.

The Club & Music Scene

Osaka's liveliest—and most economical—nightlife district radiates out from a narrow pedestrian lane called **Dotonbori,** which flanks the south bank of the Dotonbori River. About a 3-minute walk from Namba Station or less than a 10-minute walk from Shinsaibashi Station, it's lined with restaurants and drinking establishments.

Grand Cafe

2-10-21 Nishi-Shinsaibashi. ☎ **06/213-8637.** Live music charge ¥2,000 ($20) includes one drink.

An airy spot for inexpensive dining, music, and dancing, Grand, near American Mura, has a variable events schedule, but usually live blues on Sundays. If there's no live music, there's no cover. Kirin draft beer goes for ¥500 ($5), as do some cocktails and food (pasta, sandwiches, and salads.) It's cash only, near America Mura, and open Monday to Thursday from 5pm to 3am and Friday and Saturday from 6pm to 5am.

Qoo

Heaven Bldg., 1-4-4 Nambanaka, Naniwa-ku. ☎ **06/649-2017.** Cover charge ¥2,000 ($20), including one drink.

Qoo can get crowded, but even if there are crowds waiting outside, foreigners are let in. The interior is postmodern, with a blue-lit, metal open stairwell, black- and red-clad waiters, and a red-lit bar behind the dance floor. The ninth floor is a mezzanine from which you can watch dancing below; there's an enclosed and somewhat less noisy restaurant, with spotlit fresh flowers "growing" out of the white-tiled floor. Dine on appetizers or such dishes as spaghetti and beef Stroganoff (all under ¥1,500/$15). There are a variety of bars: one for shots, one for mixed drinks, and so on. Beer costs ¥500 ($5) and cocktails ¥500 to ¥1,000 ($5 to $10). Perhaps the best feature is the roof terrace, with its view of the city; aluminum chairs and tables abound for those seeking to cool off. To get there, take exit 5 from the Namba subway station and, with your back to Dotonbori, turn right on the first street before Kabukiza, then left at the signal; the building will be on your right-hand side. Open daily from 8pm to midnight.

A Snack Bar

When I first arrived in Japan, I remember thinking a *sunaku* (written "snack") would be a good place to get a bite to eat. However, in Japan, a *sunaku* is a kind of drinking place with a *mama-san* (female owner or manager), who coddles her clients, who are mostly men. As these are usually places where regulars stop in for afterwork drinks, to become a regular you normally must be introduced by an acquaintance. At most of them you must keep a bottle of whiskey to drink there. The foreign visitor rarely gets a glimpse into the world of *sunaku.* The one I've listed here is run by a friend, who will be happy to welcome foreign visitors.

Tosca

Senju Bldg. basement, 1-6 Senmichimae. ☎ **06/211-1387.** Cover ¥3,000 ($30).

An accomplished pianist and singer, the mama-san at Tosca serves snacks, pours drinks, smiles, and chats from behind the bar, never missing a beat. As the evening wears on, even shy guests take a turn at karaoke, singing to music from words (and corny videos) on a TV screen. The small bar has a convivial atmosphere, and it's a good place to meet other customers. Mama Tosca is friendly and interested in trying out her English, so even lone females will have a relaxed evening here. All drinks cost ¥500 ($5) and the cover charge includes a snack. Tosca is open Monday to Saturday from 7pm to midnight (closed on holidays).

The Bar Scene

Bar Isn't It

Yoshimoto Bldg., 2-5-5 Shinsaibashi-suji. ☎ **06/211-3250.** Live music charge ¥500 ($5).

Part of a chain, this Bar Isn't It is also low on decor, inexpensive (all food and drinks ¥500/$5), and run by *gaijin* (foreigners), who seem to be nicer here than at others—well anyway, they did finally speak to me. Live DJ sounds range from reggae to rock. There's no cover charge unless there's live music (four times a month on Fridays). It's open daily from 6pm to 2am (until 4am Friday and Saturday).

Pig and Whistle

Is Bldg., 2-1-32 Shinsaibashisuji. ☎ **06/213-6911.**

Probably the best-known expatriate bar in Osaka, Pig and Whistle is located a few blocks north of Dotonbori on Europa Dori (nearest station: Shinsaibashi). Still, the majority of customers here are Japanese. Munchies include fish and chips (of course), and there's a dartboard for entertainment. A large draft beer is ¥700 ($7). Open Sunday through Thursday from 5pm to midnight, and on Friday and Saturday from 5pm to 1am. There's also a branch in Umeda (☎ 361-3198).

Pump

2-5-11 Higashi Shinsaibashi. ☎ **06/213-8541.**

Another gaijin hangout, this one has a great music selection: Choose your own from hip-hop and rap to traditional rock. Beer costs ¥500 ($5), and a breakfast of eggs, toast, bacon, and salad goes for ¥800 ($8). After your barhopping is over, come here for breakfast and to await the trains; it's open daily 6pm to 5am (weekends until 7am). Pump is one block south of Europa Mura and in the fourth block west of Midosuji Dori.

Sam & Dave's

Kihachi Bldg., 2-3-12 Shinsaibashisuji. ☎ **06/213-4107.** Cover ¥1,000 ($10).

Dancing to hip-hop or rock is the main attraction in this self-service bar. Good food includes sweet-and-sour chicken, fajitas, hearty salads, and burgers for less than ¥1,500 ($15). Beer is ¥500 ($5) but only ¥300 ($3) between 7 and 9pm. Sam & Dave's is located on Soemon-cho just off of Shinsaibashi Street. It's open 7pm to 2am Monday to Thursday and until 4am and 5am Friday and Saturday respectively.

Solar Beer Garden

Holiday Inn Nankai, 2-5-15 Shinsaibashisuji. ☎ **06/213-8281.**

For outdoor drinking in the summer, head for the Holiday Inn on Midosuji Dori (not far from Dotonbori), where you'll find a beer garden on its third-floor patio. A snack menu includes salad, seafood, yakisoba, and fried shrimp. For those of you who are serious drinkers, ¥1,200 ($12) buys you all you can quaff, while lightweights can order one draft beer for ¥700 ($7). Open June to August, daily from 5 to 9pm.

Wine Bar
Awajiya Bldg., 2-4-5 Shinsaibashisuji. ☎ **06/211-7736.**

Part of a chain that has more than 15 locations in Japan, the Wine Bar serves wine by the glass and is popular with young Japanese. If you get a window seat, you'll have a view of the river and bridge. It's located on the first street paralleling the Dotonbori River to the north, in the same building as Irohanihoheto (described above). Along with wines from France, Germany, and California, it also offers such dishes as chicken, spareribs, salads, gratin, and snacks. There's a table charge of ¥500 ($5); wine costs ¥350 to ¥600 ($3.50 to $6). Open daily from 5pm to 1am (opens at 11am Sundays and holidays and closes at 2am holiday evenings).

5 Kobe

365 miles W of Tokyo, 47 miles W of Kyoto, 19 miles W of Osaka

Blessed with the calm waters of the Seto Inland Sea, Kobe has served Japan as an important port town for centuries. Even today its port is the heart of the city, its raison d'être, and the people of Kobe are proud of their city, content with where they are. One of the first ports to begin accepting foreign traders in 1868, following Japan's two centuries of isolation, this vibrant city of 1.5 million inhabitants is quite cosmopolitan, with 44,000 foreigners living here. There are a number of fine restaurants serving everything from Moroccan to Western, Japanese, Chinese, Korean, and Indian—each immigrant has brought with him or her a rich heritage and cuisine. Also, many steakhouses offer famous Kobe beef. Equally famous is Kobe's wonderful nightlife, crammed into a small, navigable, and rather intimate quarter of neon lights, cozy bars, brawling pubs, and sophisticated nightclubs. As one resident of Kobe told me, "We don't have a lot of tourist sights in Kobe, so we make up for it in nightlife."

But I would add the remarkable character of the people to the attractions of Kobe. On January 24, 1995, Kobe was hit very hard by an earthquake, since dubbed the Great Hanshin Earthquake. Tragically, nearly 5,000 people were killed, and most of Kobe was destroyed. Following this disaster, the people of Kobe are working together to rebuild their city with an intensity of purpose that is to be commended.

Very little of Kobe was not in transition or being rebuilt when I last visited it to update this edition. The mayor of Kobe has declared that it will take three years before Kobe recuperates. Therefore be forewarned: Everything from hotel rates to transportation in this chapter can and probably will change over the next two years. One good reason to visit Kobe now is that it is one of the least expensive places in Japan.

ESSENTIALS

The **telephone area code** for Kobe, lying in Hyogo Prefecture, is 078.

GETTING THERE **By Plane** If you are arriving at Kansai International Airport (KIX), take the shuttle to the ferry pier and the jet foil to Port Island's Kobe City Air Terminal of K-CAT (on your return you can check in here, if you are flying ANA or JAL). There's never any traffic, so the trip across the bay takes 30 minutes. It costs ¥2,200 ($22). Limousine buses to Sannomiya Station cost ¥1,800 ($18). If you want to use your rail pass, JR trains are now fully operational, but check with the tourist information center at KIX for details.

By Train The Shinkansen bullet train takes 3½ hours from Tokyo, 33 minutes from Kyoto, and 13 minutes from Osaka. All Shinkansen trains arrive at Shin-Kobe

Station, about a mile northwest of Sannomiya Station, which is considered the heart of the city. Shin-Kobe Station is linked to Sannomiya Station via a 3-minute subway ride (or a 20-minute walk). If you're arriving from nearby Osaka, Himeji, or Okayama, however, it's easiest to take a local train stopping at Sannomiya Station. Incidentally, there are several terminals in Sannomiya, including stations for Japan Railways (JR), Hankyu, and Hanshin (but the later two were not fully operating as of this writing).

By Bus Buses depart from Tokyo Station's Yaesu south exit for Kobe every night (trip time: 8 hours, 20 minutes).

VISITOR INFORMATION There are **tourist information offices** at Shin-Kobe Station (☎ 078/241-9550) and Sannomiya Station (☎ 078/322-0220), where you can pick up a map, get information, and ask for directions to your hotel. The Shin-Kobe Station office is open Monday through Saturday from 10am to 6pm (until 5:30pm in winter) and on Sunday and holidays from 10am to 5pm. The office at Sannomiya Station is in front of the south exit of the station and is open daily from 9am to 5:30pm. Also in Sannomiya Station is the Kobe City tourist office, open daily 10am to 6pm.

Current information on Kobe's sights, festivals, and attractions appears in a monthly magazine called *Kansai Time Out,* which you can pick up at bookstores, restaurants, and tourist-oriented locations for ¥300 ($3).

GETTING AROUND Squeezed in between hills rising in the north and the shores of the Seto Inland Sea in the south, Kobe stretches some 18 miles along the coastline, but in many places it's less than 2 miles wide. It is made up of many wards (*ku*), such as Nada-ku, Chuo-ku, and Hyogo-ku. The heart of the city lies around the Sannomiya and Motomachi stations in the Chuo-ku ward. It's here you'll find the city's nightlife, its port, its restaurants and shopping district, and most of its hotels. Many of the major streets have names with signs posted in English.

Because the city is not very wide, you can walk to most points north and south of Sannomiya Station. South of Sannomiya Station are the Sannomiya Center Gai covered-arcade shopping street and a flower-lined road leading straight south, toward the port—called, appropriately enough, Flower Road. North of Sannomiya Station are bars and restaurants clustered around narrow streets like Higashimon Street and Kitano-Zaka. About a 10-minute walk west of Sannomiya Station is Motomachi Station, south of which lies Chinatown. The next stop on the JR line from Motomachi Station is Kobe Station, just south of which is Harborland, a pleasant place to stroll. Mosaic, an outdoor restaurant and shopping complex, avoids the mall look through the use of varied architectural and color schemes. By offering a diversity of world goods and foods, it blends with Kobe's international roots.

WHAT TO SEE & DO

SEEING THE PORT I find Kobe's port fascinating. Unlike many harbor cities where the port is located far from the center of town, Kobe's is right there, demanding attention and getting it. For a bird's-eye view of the whole operation, go to the **Port Tower** at Naka Tottei Pier. Opened in 1963, the tower is designed to resemble a Japanese drum, a cylindrical shape with the middle squeezed together. Almost 600 feet tall, its glass-enclosed five-story observatory can be reached by two elevators. It's open Tuesday through Sunday from 10am to 6pm.

Right beside the Port Tower is **Meriken Park,** along with the **Kobe Maritime Museum**, which has a roof shaped like a ship. Open Tuesday through Sunday from 10am to 5pm, the museum has exhibits that recount the history of Kobe's port, as well as ports and harbors around the world. At the push of a button, models of port activities spring to life, along with a spoken commentary in English. A combination ticket for both the Port Tower and the Maritime Museum is ¥700 ($7). If you buy the tickets separately, they're ¥500 ($5) each. The closest station is Motomachi.

Next to Port Tower are boats offering **cruises of the harbor.** Costing ¥1,030 ($10.30), the trip lasts 50 minutes and takes you to Kawasaki and Mitsubishi shipyards, the container yard, Port Terminal, and Port Island. Although the commentary is in Japanese only, it's well worth it. Departures are every hour on the hour from 10am to 4pm on Monday through Saturday, and every 30 minutes on Sunday and holidays and daily in August from 10am to 4:30pm. There are also some midnight cruises. For more information, call ☎ 078/391-8633.

Another interesting way to see the harbor is by taking the computer-controlled **Portliner monorail** from Sannomiya Station out to **Port Island,** an artificial island complete with amusement park, luxury hotel, highrise condominiums, exhibition grounds, and convention halls. This is a great ride even if you don't get off the monorail. It takes about a half hour to make the whole loop around the island, passing bridges, ships, tankers, tugboats, barges, and stacked containers along the way. If you're up to an outing, get off at Shimin Hiroba Station and go to the Portopia Hotel for a meal or a cup of coffee. It's quite an interesting hotel, with a dramatic lobby. From there you can walk to the amusement park.

NEARBY ATTRACTIONS You might also want to travel to **Mt. Rokkosan,** a resort high among the peaks, with hiking, golfing, eating, and relaxation as the major forms of entertainment. Serving mainly as an escape for residents of Osaka and Kobe, it's worth a day's outing if you're here for an extended length of time. More convenient for a quick getaway are the hills directly behind Shin-Kobe Station, with hiking trails through woods and streams. You can reach **Nunobiki Falls** (called Nunobiki-no-taki in Japanese) in less than an hour.

ACCOMMODATIONS

EXPENSIVE

Hotel Okura Kobe

2-1 Hatoba-cho, Chuo-ku, Kobe 650. ☎ **078/333-0111.** Fax 078/333-6673. 489 rms. A/C MINIBAR TV TEL. ¥24,000–¥35,000 ($240–$350) double or twin. AE, DC, JCB, MC, V. Station: Motomachi (10 minutes south).

This majestic 35-story hotel has a grand location right beside Meriken Park and the Port Tower, within easy walking distance of the shopping arcades near Motomachi and Sannomiya Stations. Each elegantly appointed room has all the comforts of a first-class hotel, with the best views afforded by those accommodations facing the harbor. Pick up your phone and someone will answer "Yes, Mr. or Ms. . . . "; I like that kind of service.

Dining/Entertainment: There are eight restaurants and bars, with food ranging from French haute cuisine to Japanese and Chinese.

Services: Free newspaper, same-day laundry service.

Facilities: Daily fully equipped business center; beauty salon; tea-ceremony room; travel agent; Go salon; shopping arcade; and health club (fee: ¥3,000/$30) with gym, indoor and outdoor swimming pools, sauna, and tennis courts.

✪ Kobe Kitano Hotel

3-3-20 Yamamoto-dori, Chuo-ku, Kobe 650. ☎ **078/271-3711.** Fax 078/271-3700. 30 rms. A/C MINIBAR TV TEL. ¥34,000–¥45,000 ($340–$450) double; ¥34,000–¥65,000 ($340–$650) triple. All rates include breakfast. AE, DC, JCB, MC, V. Directions: Taxi 5 minutes from either JR Sannomiya Station or Shin-Kobe Station.

This is one of my favorite hotels in Japan. Built like an English manor house, the Kobe Kitano looks like one of the neighboring foreign houses of 18th-century Kobe; it won the prestigious Kobe Municipal Artist prize for use of architectural space. Interior designer Chikako Nakajima has created a fantasy—you feel as if you're entering the home of some wealthy English family. Over Oriental rugs, a chess game is in progress. Sit at the discreetly placed reception desk to check in, as if you were discussing weekend plans as the guest in a friend's mansion. The perfectly bilingual staff are perspicacious, yet unobtrusive at all times; you don't ask for your key when you return—it's brought to you with a smile. Each elegantly appointed room with mansard ceilings is different; color schemes are rose, ivory, and green. The feeling that you're in a home rather than a hotel is achieved through the use of live plants and real furniture. Nothing is built in: The brass clock on the antique bedside table can be picked up, the mahogany armoire is a piece you'd be proud to own. Five of the rooms have private balconies. An elegant tea service awaits you. Roses are a theme in artwork and coffee-table books. The large window in the bathroom is curtained in lace, the hair dryer has its own padded bag, the towel rack is brass, the terry robes are thick, and the basket of full amenities holds a rose, ribbon, and lace nosegay. Of course, there's bilingual satellite TV. A delicious breakfast of egg, salad, breads, juice, and coffee or tea is complimentary.

Dining/Entertainment: Bistro Vingt-Cinq is an elegant, peach-toned French dining room. The terrace-style cafe Antenor is more casual and a good tea stop if you are sightseeing in Kitano.

Services: Free newspaper, same-day laundry service.

Facilities: Antiques shop.

$ Kobe Portopia Hotel

6-10-1 Minatojima, Nakamachi, Chuo-ku, Kobe 650. ☎ **078/302-1111.** Fax 078/302-6877. 778 rms. A/C MINIBAR TV TEL. ¥16,000 ($160) twin or double. Japanese-style rooms ¥30,000 ($300) for four. AE, DC, JCB, MC, V. Directions: Taxi 15 minutes from Shin-Kobe Station or ride 10 minutes on the Portline monorail from Sannomiya Station.

The most dramatic way to arrive at the Kobe Portopia is via monorail—sleek, tall, and white, this hotel looks like some futuristic ship slicing through the landscape. Inside, it flaunts space and brightness, with waterfalls, fountains, lots of brass, marble, and plants. Its rooms, whose large windows face either the sea or Kobe city (some even have a balcony), are elegantly designed with all the amenities, including bilingual cable TV with CNN.

Dining/Entertainment: There are 15 restaurants, lounges, and coffee shops, including the 31st-floor Alain Chapel—named for its French chef.

Services: Free newspaper, same-day laundry service.

Facilities: Fashion boutiques, indoor and outdoor swimming pools, gym, tennis courts, drugstore.

New Otani Harborland

Harborland, 1-3-5 Higashi Kawasaki-cho, Chuo-ku, Kobe 650. ☎ **078/360-1111** or 800/421-8795 in the U.S. and Canada. Fax 078/360-7799. 235 rms. A/C MINIBAR TV TEL. ¥26,000–¥42,000 ($260–$420) twin; ¥30,000–¥45,000 ($300–$450) double; ¥60,000–¥90,000 ($600–$900) suites. AE, DC, JCB, MC, V. Station: Kosoku Kobe or Kobe.

Located in the newly developed Harborland area, this sleek, modern hotel manages to give the impression of a small, personable hotel despite its size. Attractions for business travelers are room amenities such as multiple phone lines for faxes and telecommunications, cable TV with CNN, in-room pants press, and single rooms with queen-size beds, while deluxe rooms also have CD players, VCRs, and cordless phones. One floor is reserved for ladies only; no-smoking rooms are available; and windows have sun-blocking blinds and can open. Sea views are not more expensive, so ask for one.

Dining/Entertainment: There are three restaurants, including a Japanese restaurant serving sushi and teppanyaki; a tea lounge; and a bar.

Services: Complimentary newspaper.

Facilities: Beauty salon, wedding hall, photo studio, parking, shops, conference rooms, and spa (fee).

MODERATE

Hana Hotel

4-2-7 Nunobiki-cho, Chuo-ku, Kobe 651. ☎ **078/221-1087.** Fax 078/221-1785. 47 rms. A/C MINIBAR TV TEL. ¥8,000 ($80) single; ¥12,000 ($120) double; ¥12,000 ($120) twin. AE, JCB, V. Directions: Walk 2 minutes north from JR Sannomiya Station.

Opened in 1986, the Hana Hotel is a cheerful, airy business hotel, with an accommodating and courteous staff. Hana means flower in Japanese, and that's the motif here, on the wallpaper, the furniture, and everywhere the hotel logo is displayed. A small, personable business hotel with only six rooms on each floor, it has accommodations that are nicely furnished with radio, TV with pay video, alarm clock, hair dryer, and windows that open. There's a coffee shop serving a morning set meal for ¥600 ($6).

Hotel Grand Vista

2-13-7 Kano-cho, Chuo-ku, Kobe 650. ☎ **078/271-2111.** Fax. 078/271-1171. 108 rms. A/C MINIBAR TV TEL. ¥16,000–¥17,000 ($160–$170) double; ¥18,000 ($180) twin. AE, DC, JCB, V. Station: JR Shin-Kobe (5 minutes) and Shin-Kobe subway (2 minutes).

Friendly, native-English-speaking staff greet you at this hotel very conveniently located on the hill behind Shin-Kobe Station and near Kitano. Comfortable rooms have desks with mirrors and city views. A restaurant serves new Italian cuisine, including an inexpensive (¥1,800/$18) lunch buffet from 11:30am to 2pm.

✪ Hotel Tor Road

3-1-19 Nakayamate Dori, Kobe 651. ☎ **078/391-6691.** Fax 078/391-6570. 78 rms. A/C MINIBAR TV TEL. ¥17,000–¥20,000 ($170–$200) double or twin. AE, DC, JCB, MC, V. Directions: On Tor Road just north of Ikuta-shinmichi Dori.

Hotel Tor Road has a marble and dark-wood wainscoted lobby, and the English-style interior is carried into the rooms, which are clean and tastefully decorated with larger-than-usual bath, Oriental rugs, hair dryer, comforter, and bilingual TV and video. Keys slip into a slot by the door to turn on the lights. Twin and deluxe rooms (which are made into triples) have a separate sink area. There are two restaurants—Muffin, for light meals, and a beer hall on the lower level. Complimentary newspapers are provided.

Kobe Washington Hotel

2-11-5 Shimoyamatedori, Chuo-ku, Kobe 650. ☎ **078/331-6111.** Fax 078/331-6651. 218 rms. A/C MINIBAR TV TEL. ¥14,500–¥16,500 ($145–$165) double or twin. All rates include tax and service charge. AE, DC, JCB, MC, V. Directions: Walk 7 minutes northwest of Sannomiya Station, on Ikuta Shinmichi Street.

As part of a nationwide business hotel chain, the Kobe Washington Hotel is a reliable and high-quality place to stay. The rooms are tiny but nicely decorated with modern furniture, and come with TV with pay video, clock, and piped-in music. Panels on the windows slide shut for complete darkness. Three restaurants serve

Japanese and Western food, including shabu-shabu; its ninth-floor restaurant-bar is a steakhouse with views of the city.

INEXPENSIVE

Kobe YMCA Hotel

2-7-15 Kano-cho, Chuo-ku, Kobe 650. ☎ **078/241-7205.** Fax 078/231-1031. 14 rms (all with bath). A/C TV. ¥11,000 ($110) twin. ¥500 ($5) discount for YMCA members. All rates include breakfast, tax, and service charge. No credit cards. Station: Shin-Kobe or Sannomiya (10 minutes).

Sandwiched in between the two Green Hill Hotels, this hotel is used primarily for banquets, weddings (yes, you can get married here at the YMCA), and teaching classes. It has only four single rooms and 10 twins with a bare, dormitory look to them, but they all have a minuscule bathroom, coin-operated TV, and a pot for heating water. Men, women, and families are welcome.

Kobe Tarumi Youth Hostel

5-58 Kaigan Dori, Tarumi-ku, Kobe 651. ☎ **078/707-2133.** 32 beds. ¥2,500 ($25) for JYHA members, ¥3,000 ($30) for nonmembers. Breakfast ¥500 ($5) extra. No credit cards. Station: JR Tarumi (5 minutes).

This is the only youth hostel in Kobe. It doesn't serve dinner, but it has free laundry facilities. It's near the beach, so you need to reserve well in advance for the summer.

DINING

Kobe is famous for its beef, so tender the best cuts virtually melt in your mouth. Unlike countries like Australia and the United States, where cattle graze in open fields, in villages around Kobe cattle are hand-fed barley, corn, rice, bran, molasses, rapeseed oil, and soybean meal. The rumor that cattle are fed beer is untrue—they may, however, get one bottle each as a farewell present just before being sent off to the slaughterhouse. There are only a few head of cattle per household, so each gets a lot of individual attention. For exercise the cattle are used for labor, and after the workout are washed and massaged with water and straw brushes.

With a sizable foreign population, Kobe is also a good place to dine on international cuisine, including Indian and Chinese food. The greatest concentration of Chinese restaurants is in Chinatown, called Nankinmachi by the locals, south of Motomachi Station in the former hot spot of sailor bars and pubs, now a pedestrian lane.

If you are looking for a picnic or simply craving some familiar foods, **Kobe Grocers** (☎ 078/221-2838) at 2-19-2 Nakayamate Dori has a good selection of world foods. It's open from 10am to 7pm Monday through Saturday. **German Home Bakery**, also on Nakayamate Dori (☎ 078/221-1257), has mouthwatering cakes, tortes, breads, and cookies (from ¥300/$3). It's open Thursday to Tuesday from 9am to 6pm.

EXPENSIVE

Alain Chapel

Portopia Hotel, 31st floor, 6-10-2 Minatojima, Port Island. ☎ **078/303-5201.** Reservations recommended. Set dinners ¥10,000–¥18,000 ($100–$180); set lunches ¥6,000 ($60). AE, DC, JCB, MC, V. Tues–Fri 5–9pm and Sat–Sun, hols 11:30am–2:30pm and 5–9pm. FRENCH.

For elegant French dining, Alain Chapel is an excellent choice. In a stately drawing-room setting, this restaurant serves the creations of French chef Alain Chapel. The set meals are popular with the Japanese clientele. If you decide to dine à la carte, you might start with lobster salad and then try either Kobe beef or duck in foie gras.

Average dinner checks, including wine, tax, and service, are generally around ¥17,000 ($170) per person.

Kitano Club

1-5-7 Kitano-cho. ☎ **078/222-5123.** Reservations recommended. Set dinners ¥6,000–¥10,000 ($60–$100); set lunches ¥3,000–¥5,000 ($30–$50). Daily 11:30am–2:30pm and 5:30–10:30pm. Station: Shin-Kobe (10 minutes). FRENCH/CONTINENTAL.

Located on a hill overlooking the city, this well-known restaurant offers dining with a view. It's especially popular with middle-aged Japanese women, who come to take advantage of the daily lunch special, called Queen's Lunch, for ¥3,000 ($30)—and yes, you guys can order it, too. There are also set steak lunches and dinners. The dinner menu also includes sole, turbot, lobster, chicken, filet mignon, and scallops.

Okagawa

1-5-10 Kitano-cho. ☎ **078/222-3511.** Reservations recommended. Tempura course ¥10,000 ($100); shabu-shabu or sukiyaki ¥8,000 ($80); kaiseki ¥12,000 ($120). AE, DC, JCB, MC, V. Daily 11am–9pm. Closed first and third Tues of each month. Station: Shin-Kobe. TEMPURA.

Okagawa occupies a rather new and dignified building up on the bluffs of Kitano. It specializes in tempura, but also serves shabu-shabu or sukiyaki and a kaiseki menu. Although the restaurant is modern, it has latticed wood, shoji screens, and flower arrangements—coolly elegant and emphasizing the Japanese tradition of simplicity. In addition to various tatami rooms, its two tempura counters command good views of the city. A tempura teishoku is available for ¥5,000 ($50).

Vingt-Cinq

Kobe Kitano Hotel, 3-3-20 Yamamoto-dori. ☎ **078/271-0280.** Reservations recommended. Set lunches ¥3,500–¥5,000 ($35–$50); set dinners ¥6,000–¥15,000 ($60–$150). AE, DC, JCB, MC, V. Daily 11:30am–2pm and 5:30–9pm. FRENCH.

Intimate dining at peach-clothed and candlelit tables and nouvelle French set meals are offered at this small restaurant on a calm courtyard. Delicious Japanese seafoods are featured and beautifully presented.

MODERATE

Gaylord

Bacchus Bldg. basement, 1-26-1 Nakayama. ☎ **078/251-4359.** Reservations recommended. Curries ¥1,000–¥2,500 ($10–$25); set dinners ¥3,300–¥5,000 ($33–$50); set lunch ¥800 ($8). AE, DC, JCB, MC, V. Daily noon–3pm and 5–7:30pm. Directions: On Nakayama Dori. INDIAN.

One of Kobe's best-known Indian restaurants, Gaylord belongs to the famous franchise (Bombay, New Delhi, Hong Kong, London, San Francisco, and Los Angeles). The extensive menu includes such delights as shrimp cooked in mild gravy with coconut, marinated lamb pieces cooked in cream and spices, and tandoori fish, chicken, or mutton. Vegetarian selections vary and include saffron-flavored rice with nuts and fruit, Bengal beans cooked in sharp spices, spiced lentils cooked with cream, and spinach and cheese cooked in spices. It's customary to order one dish per person and then share. If you're by yourself, you can order one of the set menus starting at ¥3,000 ($30). The mini-tandoori set, for example, comes with fish and chicken tandoori, shish kebab, Indian bread, salad, chicken curry, a dry vegetable dish (in this case potato and cabbage), rice, and tea or coffee.

Another branch (☎ 078/302-5728) is opposite Shimin Byoin Mae bus stop on Port Island and is open the same hours.

Haishin

2-2-2 Motomachi Dori. ☎ **078/331-4139.** Main dishes ¥800–¥2,500 ($8–$25); set lunch ¥1,000 ($10); set dinners ¥3,000–¥8,000 ($30–$80). DC, JCB, V. Wed–Mon 1:30am–3pm and 4:30–8:30pm. Station: Sannomiya. CHINESE.

A display case outside this restaurant in the heart of Chinatown helps you order. The dishes and food are fairly standard, like chili sauce shrimp or scallops in cream sauce or cashew chicken. Service and interior are a bit more refined than at Poco, listed below. The lunch special, served until 2pm, includes two dishes, soup, and rice.

Iroriya

3-chome Kitano-cho. ☎ **078/231-6777.** Sukiyaki or shabu-shabu ¥5,400 ($54); udon suki ¥3,100 ($31). AE, DC, JCB, MC, V. Daily noon–10pm (last order 9:30pm). Directions: Walk 12 minutes north of Sannomiya Station to Kitano-zaka. SHABU-SHABU/SUKIYAKI.

A rather formal establishment, Iroriya is well known and serves Kobe beef in shabu-shabu and sukiyaki. Take off your shoes at the front entryway, where they'll be whisked out of sight. Then a kimono-clad woman will lead you through this rather large restaurant to your dining table and your own private hearth. All interior artwork is done by the owner of the restaurant. If you don't care for beef, you may wish to order the udon suki, which consists of noodles, seafood, chicken, and vegetables cooked together and eaten straight out of the pot.

✪ Marrakech

Maison de Yamate basement, 1-20-15 Nakayamate-dori. ☎ **078/241-3440.** Reservations recommended for dinner. Main dishes ¥1,500–¥8,500 ($15–$85). No credit cards. Daily 5–11pm, Sat–Sun and hols noon–2pm. Directions: From the intersection with Nakayamate-dori and Kitano-zaka walk north to Pearl Street and turn right; Marrakech is three blocks farther on your right. MOROCCAN.

You won't find a Marrakech in any other city in Japan; it's the only Moroccan restaurant. Since 1985, Elmaleh, the multilingual, friendly owner and chef, has been making from scratch everything from cookies to breads to sauces—even the cashews are home-roasted. A Moroccan interior and music compliment the *tajine du jour,* lamb in lemon sauce, and, of course, couscous. Vegetarian meals can be prepared with advance reservation. Anybody from diplomats to tourists in-the-know eats here.

Raja

2-7-4 Sakaemachi Dori. ☎ **078/332-5253.** Curries ¥1,000–¥1,600 ($10–16); set dinners ¥3,000–¥5,000 ($30–$50); set lunches ¥1,200–¥2,200 ($12–$22). AE, DC, JCB, V. Thurs–Tues 11:30am–2:30pm and 5–9pm. INDIAN.

A few minutes' walk south of Motomachi and just west of Chinatown, this small, popular establishment offers tandoori chicken, seafood, mutton, and vegetable curries.

INEXPENSIVE

Masaya Honten

1-8-21 Nakayamate Dori. ☎ **078/331-4178.** Dishes ¥800–¥4,000 ($8–$40). No credit cards. Daily 11am–midnight. Directions: Walk north of Sannomiya Station on Kitano-zaka. NOODLES.

This well-known noodle restaurant has been dishing out noodles for more than 30 years and is easy to spot by the waterwheel and plastic-food display case outside its front door (there's another display case inside). Since the menu is in Japanese only, make your choice from one of these cases before sitting down. Dishes include tempura with noodles (*tempura soba*) and pork cutlet with noodles (*tonkatsu soba*).

Sukiyaki served with noodles is available for less than ¥4,000 ($40). This is a good place for night owls, since it stays open late.

Mehfil

Ijin Plaza, 2nd floor, 2-12-21 Yamamoto-dori. ☎ **078/271-7579.** Set lunches ¥780–¥2,400 ($7.80–$24); set dinners ¥2,000–¥2,700 ($20–$27). AE, MC, V. Tues–Sun 11am–2:30pm and 6–9:30pm. Directions: On Hunter-zaka in Kitano-cho. INDIAN.

Suresh and Neeta run this casual Indian restaurant with Indian decor and amusingly innocent music videos. The pleasant bilingual staff serves up tasty, spicy, thick curries (I only wish they would be a little larger). Vegetarian and special family meals are on the menu, no doubt for the local Indians who eat here.

$ Old Spaghetti Factory

Harborland, 1-5-5 Higashi Kawasaki-cho. ☎ **078/360-3911.** Set lunch ¥900 ($9); set dinner ¥1,500 ($15). AE, MC, V. Daily 11am–2:30pm and 5–11pm. Station: JR Kobe. SPAGHETTI.

A branch of an American chain, this restaurant, located in a converted warehouse, offers inexpensive spaghetti with a choice of 15 sauces. Weekday lunches include salad and bread, while dinner and weekend lunches also include ice cream and soft drinks—a great deal! From JR Kobe Station, walk to Harborland; the Old Spaghetti Factory is on Kobe Gas Light Street across from Hankyu Department store and next to the sculpture park and old sailing ship.

$ Poco

3-1-2 Motomachi Dori. ☎ **078/331-0284.** Main dishes ¥450–¥650 ($4.50–$6.50). No credit cards. Thurs–Tues 11am–2pm and 5:30–10pm (last order). Directions: Chinatown. CHINESE.

Sample food is under wraps outside this simple Chinese eatery, where the staff speak English. *Mabodofu* (tofu and beef in a spicy ginger sauce), *gyoza,* and *harumaki* (egg roll) are among the standards.

Steakland Kobe (159)

1-8-2 Kitanagasa Dori. ☎ **078/332-1787.** Steaks ¥2,000–¥5,300 ($20–$53); steak set dinner ¥2,600 ($26); set lunch ¥970 ($9.70). No credit cards. Daily 11am–10pm. Directions: On the street facing the north side of Hankyu Sannomiya Station. STEAKS.

If you want to eat teppanyaki steak but can't afford the high prices of Kobe beef, one of the cheapest places you can go is Steakland Kobe. Lunch specials, served from 11am to 3pm, are inexpensive for steak (cooked on the hot plate in front of you), miso soup, rice, Japanese pickles, and a vegetable. More expensive Kobe beef is also available.

Tooth Tooth

Ginryu Bldg. 3-12-3 Kitaganasa Dori. ☎ **078/332-3052.** Main dishes ¥550–¥1,000 ($5.50–$10); set lunch ¥650 ($6.50). No credit cards. Daily 11:30am–midnight. Directions: From Motomachi Station walk along the Port side of the tracks, double back, then take the first right. WESTERN.

You'll find a piano here, which you can play, or, if not, canned classical or Latin—or who knows what mood may strike in this eclectic, youthful cafe with French-style doors open to the street? Pasta and steak are served, as well as homemade cakes. Beer is only ¥400 ($4) and coffee ¥350 ($3.50).

$ Yamada No Kakasi

3-9-6 Sannomiya-cho. ☎ **078/391-0769** or 391-0360. Skewers ¥200 ($2); kakasi course ¥1,600 ($16); kasukatsu teishoku ¥1,000 ($10); set lunch ¥700 ($7). JCB, V. Mon and Wed–Fri 11:30am–3pm and 5–9pm, Sat–Sun and hols 11am–9pm. Station: Motomachi (5 minutes). KUSHIKATSU.

This cozy restaurant is on the western edge of the Sannomiya Center Gai shopping arcade. Narrow and small, it consists of a long counter and some tables in the back.

Gleaming wood and pottery provide a country atmosphere. The man who has been operating this eatery for the past quarter of a century makes 25 different kinds of kushikatsu, depending on the season. Order by the skewer, or the 10-stick "kakasi course." After 5pm (after 3pm on Saturday, Sunday, and holidays), order the kasukatsu teishoku, a complete meal. Your man behind the counter will select the ingredients himself, and since the food is supposed to be eaten hot, he'll serve it one stick at a time. Specialties here are delicately breaded shrimp and garlic, asparagus wrapped in bacon, mushrooms, potatoes with cheese, chicken wrapped in mint leaf, and lotus root. Highly recommended.

KOBE AFTER DARK

Kobe has a wide selection of English-style pubs, bars, expatriate hangouts, and nightclubs. All the establishments below are easily accessible to foreigners and are within walking distance of Sannomiya Station.

THE CLUB & MUSIC SCENE

The Casablanca Club

3-1-6 Kitano-cho, on Yamamoto Dori (also called Ijinkan Dori). ☎ **078/241-0200.**

This dinner club offers dinner (¥4,000/$40), entertainment, and dancing. If you don't eat dinner, there's a one-drink minimum per person. Beer costs ¥700 ($7); cocktails ¥1,000 ($10). The interior is an elegant, cool white, with a grand piano, palm trees, and pictures of Bogart and Bacall. Its open Wednesday to Monday from 5pm to midnight.

Copacabana

2-1-13 Nakayamate Dori. ☎ **078/332-6694.** Cover ¥1,500 ($15).

In the basement of the Akai Fusha-no-Aru Building, on Yamate Kansen Road north of Sannomiya Station (next to Second Chance; see "The Bar Scene," below), this is one of Kobe's most famous entertainment hot spots. It features Brazilian and other Latin American music, but the real draw is probably the almost-nude female dancer who entertains the many sailors who come here. The place is small, with a brightly colored interior. Beer and cocktails go for ¥1,000 ($10). Open Tuesday to Sunday from 6pm to 2:30am.

Kento's

3-10-18 Shimoyamate Dori. ☎ **078/392-2181.** Cover ¥1,800 ($18) plus one-drink and one-food minimum.

With more than 20 locations in Japan, Kento's has been a great hit among the Japanese, with live bands playing oldies but goldies from the 1950s and '60s. It's on Tor Road just north of where it intersects with Ikuta Shinmichi Street (near the Washington Hotel). Snacks go for ¥1,000 ($10) and beer is ¥750 ($7.50). Open daily from 6pm to 2am.

THE BAR SCENE

Acrophobia

Unte bldg. basement, 1-7-10 Nakayamate Dori. ☎ **078/333-6685.**

All drinks are only ¥500 ($5) here, while snacks (tacos, fried chicken) range from ¥400–¥700 ($4–$7). A sign says CASH ON DERIVERY, walls are rust colored, and a 3-D Native American with Day-Glo feathers stares at you from under the black lights. Reggae music and a small wooden dance floor are the main attractions. Open Sunday to Thursday from 7pm to 3am (until 5am Friday and Saturday).

Bar Isn't It?

Algo Bldg., 6th floor, 1-1-8 Shimoyamate Dori. ☎ **078/334-3036.**

Decor? There isn't any, but it's usually packed, so who can see the walls? Can't wait your turn at the bar? Get a beer from the vending machines. All food and all drinks ¥500 ($5). The English DJ was playing Bon Jovi when I was here, and it was full of 20-year-old foreigners—staff and customers. An outside metal staircase provides access, and conversations are struck on landings, but if you've had a bit to drink, find the elevator. Open daily 6pm to 5am.

Gastation

4-21-9 Ninomiya-cho. ☎ **078/251-0082.**

A slick modern interior is the backdrop for this bar, which plays reggae, rock, and occasionally something more metallic. If you've had too much to drink, don't look up at the dummies hanging from the ceiling. All food (chili con carne, nachos, pizza) and all drinks are ¥500 ($5). From the Hunter-zaka and Community Road crossroads, walk west on Community Road and take the second right. Open daily 6pm to 2am (until 5am Friday and Saturday).

J-Attic

Ijinkan Club Bldg., top floor, 4-1-12 Kitano-cho. ☎ **078/222-1586.** A 20% service charge for nonmembers; ¥500 ($5) cover Sat–Sun.

The Attic is crammed with the kinds of things often relegated to the attic and then promptly forgotten—tennis shoes, rackets, football helmets, license plates, and assorted junk. The J is for the owner, a friendly English-speaking fellow nicknamed Jumbo. Even single women will feel comfortable here. Open Wednesday to Monday from 6pm to 2am.

King's Arms

4-2-15 Isobedori. ☎ **078/221-3774.**

This English-style pub is popular with Kobe's foreigners. Located south of Sannomiya Station on Flower Road, it started out in 1950 as an exclusive club for American and British military personnel. After it went public, it became a favorite hangout for sailors and travelers passing through town, and has since mellowed into a cozy and well-established eating and drinking spot catering to all kinds of people, including the businessmen who stop here after work for a drink and a study of the daily newspaper. Its walls are decorated with beer coasters, bills of various currencies from around the world, and business cards of former patrons. Churchill's portrait gazes sternly down upon the bar. While the first floor is for serious drinking, the second floor is for dining. Try the roast beef and Yorkshire pudding (¥5,500/$55) or inexpensive (¥950/$9.50) lunch specials. Beer costs ¥600 ($6) and cocktails are ¥900 ($9). Open daily from 11:30am to 11pm (last food order, 9pm).

Pick up

2-2-7 Yamamotedori. ☎ **078/241-7566.**

Looking to get out of the teeny-bopper crowd, for something more sophisticated? This modern-interior (black chairs and stools complement blond-wood tables and bar), soft-lit cafe-bar plays from soft rock to jazz and soul. From 10am to 5pm, this is a cafe (coffee ¥300/$3); from 6pm to 2am, a bar serving cocktails (¥600/$6), beer (¥500/$5), tofu, steak, and smoked salmon (less than ¥1,000/$10).

Second Chance

Takashima Bldg., 2nd floor, 2-1-12 Nakayamate Dori. ☎ **078/391-3544.**

This all-nighter on Yamate Kansen Road is a small, one-room bar favored by young night owls who don't mind the rather sparse furnishings. I must admit that my own recollections of this place are a bit fuzzy, but I do remember music ranging from the Doors to the Talking Heads. This is where people congregate when the other bars have had the good sense to close down for the night. Snacks like fried rice are under ¥700 ($7) and beer is ¥500 ($5). Open daily from 6pm to 5am.

6 Mount Koya

465 miles W of Tokyo, 124 miles S of Osaka

If you've harbored visions of wooden temples nestled in among the trees, the sacred mountain of Mt. Koya is that Japan. It's all here—head-shaven monks, religious chantings at the crack of dawn, the wafting of incense, temples, towering cypress trees, tombs, and early-morning mist rising above the treetops. Mt. Koya, called Koyasan by the Japanese, is one of Japan's most sacred places and is the mecca of the Shingon Esoteric sect of Buddhism. Standing 3,000 feet above the world, the top of Mt. Koya is home to about 120 Shingon Buddhist temples scattered through the mountain forests. Some 50 of these temples offer accommodations, making it one of the best places in Japan to observe temple life firsthand.

Koyasan became a place of meditation and religious learning more than 1,170 years ago, when Kukai, known posthumously as Kobo Daishi, was granted the mountaintop by the imperial court in 816 as a place to establish his Shingon sect of Buddhism. Kobo Daishi was a charismatic priest who spent two years in China studying Esoteric Buddhism and introduced the Shingon sect in Japan upon his return. Revered for his excellent calligraphy, his humanitarianism, and his teachings, Kobo Daishi remains today one of the most beloved figures in Japanese Buddhist history. When he died in the 9th century, he was laid to rest in a mausoleum on Mt. Koya. His followers believe Kobo Daishi is not dead but simply in a deep state of meditation, awaiting the arrival of the last Bodhisatva (Buddha messiahs). According to popular belief, priests opening his mausoleum decades after his death found his body still warm. Through the centuries many of Kobo Daishi's followers, wishing to be close at hand when the great priest awakens, have had huge tombs or tablets constructed close to Kobo Daishi's mausoleum, and many have had their ashes interred here. Pilgrims over the last thousand years have included emperors, nobles, and common people, all climbing to the top of the mountain to pay their respects. Women, however, were barred from entering the sacred grounds of Koyasan until 1872.

ESSENTIALS

The **telephone area code** for Mt. Koya, lying in Wakayama Prefecture, is 0736.

GETTING THERE **By Train** The easiest way to get to Koyasan is from Osaka. Ordinary express (*kyuko*) trains of the Nankai Line depart from Osaka's Namba Station every half hour and cost ¥1,150 ($11.50) one-way. The trip south takes about 1 hour and 40 minutes. If you want to ride in luxury, take one of the limited-express cars with reserved seats, costing ¥750 ($7.50) extra and taking about 1 hour and 20 minutes. After the train ride (the last stop is called Gokurakubashi), you continue your trip to the top of Mt. Koya by cable car, the price of which is included in your train ticket. For more information, call Nankai Denki Tetsudo (☎ 06/643-1005).

VISITOR INFORMATION At the top of Koyasan is Koyasan Eki Station, where you'll find a booth of the local tourist office, the **Koyasan Tourist Association,** whose main office (☎ 0736/56-2616) is located approximately in the center of Koyasan. At both tourist offices you can pick up a map of Koyasan and book a room in a temple. Both offices are open daily from 8:30am to 5pm, with slightly shorter hours in winter. Mt. Koya's complete address is 600 Koyasan, Koya-cho, Ito-gun, Wakayama Prefecture.

GETTING AROUND Outside the station, you can board a bus following the main street of Koyasan all the way to the Okunoin-mae or Ichinohashi-guchi (also called Ichinohasi) bus stop. It passes almost all the sites along the way, as well as most temples accommodating visitors and the Koyasan Tourist Association's main office.

WHAT TO SEE & DO

The most awe-inspiring and magnificent of Koyasan's many structures and temples, **Okunoin** contains the mausoleum of Kobo Daishi. The most dramatic way to approach Okunoin is from the Ichinohashi-guchi bus stop, where a pathway leads one mile to the mausoleum. Swathed in a respectful darkness of huge cypress trees that form a canopy overhead are monument after monument, tomb after tomb, all belonging to faithful followers from past centuries.

I don't know whether being here will affect you the same way, but I was awestruck by the hundreds of tombs, the iridescent green moss, the shafts of light streaking through the treetops, the stone lanterns, and the gnarled bark of the old cypress trees. Together, they present a dramatic picture representing a thousand years of Japanese Buddhist history. If you're lucky you won't meet many people along this pathway. (Tour buses fortunately park at a newer entrance to the mausoleum at the bus stop called Okunoin-mae. I absolutely forbid you to take this newer and shorter route, since its crowds lessen the impact of this place considerably. Rather, make sure you take the path farthest to the left, which begins near the Ichinohashi bus stop. Much less traveled, it's also much more impressive.) At any rate, be sure to return to the mausoleum at night—the stone lanterns are lit (now electrically), creating a mysterious and powerful effect.

At the end of the pathway is the **Lantern Hall,** which houses about 21,000 lanterns. If you'd like to buy a lantern to dedicate to someone, it costs ¥500,000 to ¥1,000,000 ($5,000 to $10,000). Two sacred fires, which reportedly have been burning since the 11th century, are kept safely inside. The mausoleum itself is behind the Lantern Hall. Buy a white candle, light it, and wish for anything you want. Then sit back and watch respectfully as Buddhists come to chant and pay respects to one of Japan's greatest Buddhist leaders.

As for other things to see, **Kongobuji Temple** (160) is close to the tourist office and is the headquarters of the Shingon sect in Japan. While Kongobuji was originally built in the 16th century by Hideyoshi Toyotomi to commemorate his mother's death, the present building is 150 years old. The entrance fee of ¥350 ($3.50) allows you to wander around the wooden structure. On the temple grounds is a large and magnificent rock garden. Imagine the effort spent in getting those huge boulders to their present site. If it's raining, consider yourself lucky—the wetness adds a sheen and color to the rocks.

Another important site is the **Danjogaran Complex,** an impressive sight with a huge main hall (*kondo*); a large vermilion-colored pagoda (*daito*), which many consider to be Koyasan's most magnificent structure; and the oldest building on Mt. Koya, the Fudodo, which was built in 1198. Next to the complex is the **Reihokan Museum** (161), with such treasures of Koyasan on display as wooden Buddha sculptures, scrolls, art, and implements. It's open daily from April through October from 8:30am to 5:30pm (November through March to 4:30pm). Admission is ¥500 ($5).

A little out of the way from the other sites are the Tokugawa Mausolea, where two Tokugawa shoguns were laid to rest. Visit these only if you have extra time.

ACCOMMODATIONS

Although this community of 6,000 residents has the usual stores, schools, and offices of any small town, there are no hotels here—the only place you can stay is at a temple, and I strongly suggest you do so. Japanese who come here have almost always made reservations beforehand, so you should do the same. You can make one by calling the temple directly or through travel agencies such as JTB. You can also make reservations upon arrival in Koyasan at the Tourist Association offices described above, but that may be a bit risky during peak travel seasons. At last check, the Koyasan Tourist Association indicated that it would make reservations only for those who come in personally to its office.

Prices for an overnight stay, including two vegetarian meals, are the same for all temples on Koyasan and range from ¥9,000 to ¥20,000 ($90 to $200) per person, depending on the room. Tax is extra, and you should bring your own towel and toiletries.

Your room will be tatami and may include a nice view of a garden. Living at the temple are high school students and college students attending Koyasan's Buddhist university; they will bring your meals to your room, make up your futon, and clean your room. The morning service is at 6am. (You don't have to attend, but I recommend that you do.) Both baths and toilets are communal, and meals are at set times. Because the students must leave for school, breakfast is usually served by 7:30am. Incidentally, Buddhist monks are vegetarians, not teetotalers, and because beer and sake are made of rice and grain, they're readily available at the temples for an extra charge. Below are just a few of the dozens of temples open for overnight guests.

Ekoin (162)

☎ **0736/56-2514.** 36 rms (none with bath). ¥9,000–¥15,000 ($90–$150) per person. All rates include two meals. No credit cards. Bus: Okuno-in or Ichinohashi stop.

This 100-year-old temple has beautiful grounds and is nestled in a wooded slope. The place is known for its excellent Buddhist cuisine, and the master priest will give zazen meditation lessons if his schedule permits. Here, 23 rooms have TV and 25 have telephones. Someone here speaks a little English. Reservations must be made at least two days in advance.

Fumonin Temple (163)

☎ **0736/56-2224.** 35 rms (none with bath). TEL. ¥9,000–¥12,000 ($90–$120) per person. All rates include two meals. No credit cards. Bus: Senjuinbashi stop.

Centrally located near the Tourist Association, this temple has a small but beautiful garden created by the same person who designed the garden at Nijo Castle in Kyoto. (Other temples with famous gardens include Hosenin and Tentokuin.) Fifteen rooms have TV.

Ichijoin (164)

☎ **0736/56-2214.** 38 rms (none with bath). ¥9,000–¥25,000 ($90–$250) per person. All rates include two meals. No credit cards. Bus: Keisatsushomai stop.

The head monk's daughter here speaks English, making it a convenient place to book. Some 20 rooms face the garden, which has a waterfall and pond full of carp. Rooms have heating, a plus since Koyasan can be quite cold.

Rengejoin Temple (165)

☎ **0736/56-2231.** 48 rms (none with bath). ¥9,000–¥10,000 ($90–$100) per person. All rates include two meals. No credit cards. Bus: Isshinguchi stop.

This temple is owned by a priest who speaks English, as does his mother, so a lot of foreigners are directed here—it's a good place to meet people. There's also a nice garden, and this is one of the few temples that will probably take you in without a reservation. Sixteen rooms have a TV.

Shojoshinin (166)

☎ **0736/56-2006.** 20 rms (none with bath). ¥9,000–¥12,000 ($90–$120). All rates include two meals. No credit cards. Bus: Ichinohashi-guchi stop.

This temple has a great location at the beginning of the tomb-lined pathway to Okunoin, making it convenient for your late-night stroll to the mausoleum. The present temple buildings date from about 150 years ago, but the temple was first founded about 1,000 years ago. A large wooden structure with rooms overlooking a small garden and pond, it's usually full in August and peak seasons, so make reservations early. About half the rooms have a TV; three-fourths have a telephone.

Tentokuin (167)

☎ **0736/56-2714.** 55 rms (none with bath). ¥8,000–¥15,000 ($80–$150). All rates include two meals. No credit cards. Bus: Honzanmae or Senjuin-bashi stop.

The rooms of this temple, which dates from 1622, have been rebuilt. They all look out onto the garden, which was recognized in the 1930s as one of the most beautiful places in Japan. With a natural mountain background, the garden is of the "borrowed landscaping" type and very lovely. Most of the rooms have TVs, but no telephones. Rates depend on room size and garden view.

7 Himeji

400 miles W of Tokyo, 81 miles W of Kyoto, 54 miles E of Okayama

The main reason tourists come to Himeji is to see its beautiful castle, which embodies better than any other the best in Japan's military architecture.

ESSENTIALS

The **telephone area code** for Himeji, lying in Hyogo Prefecture, is 0792.

GETTING THERE **By Train** About four hours from Tokyo, one hour from Kyoto, and half an hour from Okayama by the Shinkansen bullet train.

By Bus It takes seven hours to travel from the Tokyu Shibuya Bus Terminal in Tokyo to Himeji Station, by night bus (departs 11pm and arrives 6am). You must make a reservation (☎ 03/3499-0739).

VISITOR INFORMATION The **Himeji City Tourist Information Center** (☎ 0792/85-3792) is at a central exit of the station's north side, to the left after you exit from the ticket gate. It's open daily from 9am to 5pm, but foreigners are advised to visit the center between 10am and 3pm, when an English-speaker is available. There's an English-language pamphlet, but the map is useless. Get the Japanese pamphlet (but not the pink hotel map, which is also useless); or better yet, ask at your hotel. I experienced some of the rudest and worst service here of anywhere in Japan. If you're stopping in Himeji only for a few hours to see the castle, deposit your luggage in the coin **lockers** just beside the tourist office or underneath the Shinkansen tracks.

WHAT TO SEE & DO

Himeji Castle

Honmachi. ☎ **0792/85-1146.** Admission ¥500 ($5). Daily 9am–5pm (until 4pm in winter).

Perhaps the most beautiful castle in all of Japan, Himeji Castle is nicknamed "White Heron Castle" in reference to its white walls, which stretch out on either side of the main donjon and resemble a white heron poised in flight over the plain. Whether it looks to you like a heron or just a castle, the view of the white five-story donjon under a blue sky is striking. This is also one of the few castles in Japan that has remained virtually undamaged since its completion centuries ago, surviving even the World War II bombings that laid Himeji city in ruins. Himeji Castle is about a 10-minute walk straight north of the station and is connected to the station by a wide boulevard, Otemae Dori. You can see the castle immediately upon leaving the station.

Originating as a fort in the 14th century, Himeji Castle took a more majestic form in 1581, when a three-story donjon was built by Hideyoshi Toyotomi during one of his military campaigns in the district. In the early 1600s the castle became the residence of Terumasa Ikeda, one of Hideyoshi's generals and a son-in-law of Tokugawa Ieyasu. He remodeled the castle into its present five-story structure. With its extensive gates, three moats, and turrets, it had one of the most sophisticated defense systems in Japan. The maze of passageways leading to the donjon was so complicated that intruders would find themselves trapped in dead ends. The castle walls were constructed with square or circular holes to allow muzzles of guns to poke through; the rectangular holes were for archers. There were also drop chutes where stones or boiling water could be dumped on enemies trying to scale the walls.

On weekends, volunteer guides sometimes hang around the ticket office and are willing to give you a guided tour of the castle for free. It gives them an opportunity to practice their English. Often college students, they can tell you the history of the castle and relate old castle gossip. But even if you go on your own, you won't have any problems learning about the history of the castle, since the city of Himeji has done a fine job of placing English explanations throughout the castle grounds. Allow about 1½ hours here.

Hyogo Prefectural Museum of History

68 Honmachi. ☎ **0792/88-9011.** Admission ¥200 ($2). Tues–Sun 10am–4:30pm.

Just behind Himeji Castle to the northeast is the Hyogo Prefectural Museum of History. If you're coming here from the castle, take the Karamete exit from the castle, follow the circular drive to the right, and then turn left in front of the redbrick building (the city art museum); the history museum is straight ahead. It exhibits materials from prehistoric times to the present day, with many explanations in English. Some of the displays allow hands-on experience, such as traditional Japanese toys and Bunraku puppets with strings you can pull to move eyebrows and other facial features. If you're here on Sunday or a national holiday, you can even try on a samurai period costume (samurai outfits were amazingly heavy). Displays include those devoted to castles in Japan and around the world, children's games of yesteryear, and Shoshazan Enkyoji, a famous temple complex on nearby Enkyo Mountain.

A Nearby Attraction

If you have time for an excursion, board the bus in front of Himeji Station (to the right after exiting from the station's central exit) and ride it for 25 minutes to the last stop, **Shoshazan Enkyoji.** Founded in the Heian Period (12th century), this large complex of temples contains a thousand years of Buddhist history in its precincts, including the Kongo Satta Buddha, sculpted in 1395, and the Yakushido, the oldest surviving structure dating from the Kamakura Period (early 14th century). The easiest way to reach the temple complex from the bus stop (called Shosha) is by ropeway, which costs ¥300 ($3) one-way. There are also horse-drawn carriages available for the same price.

ACCOMMODATIONS

Himeji lacks an adequate supply of good accommodations. In fact, some of the worst hotels I've seen in Japan are in Himeji. Your safest bet is to stick to the recommendations listed below. If you've noticed the large Sungarden Hotel across from the station, the reason it's not included is that *gaijin* (foreigners), except business partners of the owners' Mitsui Corporation, are not welcome.

MODERATE

✪ Claire Higasa

22 Jyunishomae-cho. Himeji 670. ☎ **0792/24-3421.** Fax 0792/89-3729. 60 rms. AC TV TEL. ¥12,000 ($120) twin. Japanese style ¥12,000 ($120) for two; ¥15,000 ($150) for three; ¥18,000 ($180) for four. AE, V. Station: Himeji (5 minutes).

A business hotel (50 single rooms and machines sell soda and noodles) with lots of pluses, Claire's has a lobby with soothing music, pink touches, and flower arrangements. The all-female staff are English-speaking and accommodating; room windows open and have city or castle views; and a pleasant restaurant serves inexpensive Japanese meals. The bathrooms are tiny, but who cares when the large 7th-floor public bath has great castle views?

Himeji Castle Hotel

210 Hojyo, Himeji 670. ☎ **0792/84-3311.** Fax 0792/84-3729. 207 rms. A/C MINIBAR TV TEL. ¥15,000 ($150) double; ¥14,000–¥21,000 ($140–$210) twin. AE, DC, JCB, MC, V. Directions: Take the free shuttle bus from the south (Shinkansen) exit of Himeji Station.

Opened in 1975, this is considered one of Himeji's best tourist hotels. I especially like the cheapest twins—they were made by joining two single rooms together, with beds in one room, a couch in the other, two bathrooms, and two television sets. This could be a lifesaver for couples or friends who have been traveling together a bit too long. Facilities include a restaurant that serves Western-style food.

Himeji Washington

Omizusuji, Himeji 670. ☎ **0792/25-0001.** Fax 0792/25-0133. 149 rms. A/C MINIBAR TV TEL. ¥13,500 ($135) double or twin. AE, DC, JCB, V. Station: Himeji (5 minutes).

Located just off the Omizusuji covered shopping street, the Washington is part of a chain of business hotels. Its lobby is on the second floor, above the Café de Paris, which offers service from 6:30am to midnight, including a morning set meal for ¥800 ($8). The comfortable rooms have eiderdown comforters, bilingual TV, and windows that open. Some of the staff spoke a little English, and all were extremely helpful when I was there. The Japanese restaurant, Ginza, on the 11th floor, is reasonable.

Hotel Sunroute Himeji (168)

195-9 Ekimae-cho, Himeji 670. ☎ **0792/85-0811.** Fax 0792/84-1025. 89 rms (all with bath). A/C MINIBAR TV TEL. ¥11,000–¥13,500 ($110–$135) twin; ¥12,500 ($125) double; ¥15,800 ($158) triple. AE, DC, JCB, V. Directions: Walk 1 minute northeast of Himeji Station's central exit (turn right out of the exit).

The pluses here are convenience to the station and rooms with heavy curtains to shut out any light. Rooms facing the railroad tracks are fitted with double-pane windows to screen out train noises. The hotel's one restaurant serves Japanese food, plus a Japanese/Western-style buffet breakfast for ¥1,000 ($10).

INEXPENSIVE

Hotel Himeji Plaza

158 Toyozawa-cho, Himeji 670. ☎ **0792/81-9000.** Fax 0792/84-3549. 218 rms (50 with toilet only, 168 with bath). A/C TV TEL. ¥12,000–¥13,500 ($120–$135) double or twin with bath.

All rates include tax and service. AE, DC, JCB, MC, V. Directions: 1 minute from the south (Shinkansen) exit.

This business hotel (look for the white building with a clock on top) is inexpensive and close to the station. Rooms, redone in 1994, are bright and cheerful. The windows are glazed but can be opened. There's a coin-operated laundry in the hotel, a public bath and sauna, soda and beer machines, and one Western-style restaurant. The staff is friendly and courteous.

Hotel Okuuchi

3-56 Higashi Nobusue, Himeji 670. ☎ **0792/22-8000.** Fax 0792/85-0306. 315 rms. A/C MINIBAR TV TEL. ¥10,000–¥11,000 ($100–$110) twin; ¥11,000 ($110) double. AE, DC, JCB, MC, V. Directions: Near the Castle Hotel, 10 minutes south of Himeji Station.

Okuuchi has an indoor swimming pool that guests can use for free. The rooms, mostly singles, are small, and most have absolutely no view—if that's important to you, be sure to specify your wishes. The hotel's two restaurants serve Japanese and Chinese cuisine.

DINING

Parallel and to the right of Otemae-Dori, the main drag from Himeji Station to the castle, is a covered shopping arcade called Miyukidori, with lots of restaurants and coffee shops. If you want to get a picnic lunch to eat on the castle grounds, your best bet is to go to the food section in the basement of one of the department stores near the station for an obento. Or, if you must, there's a McDonald's in the Miyuki covered shopping arcade.

Fukutei (169)

75 Kameimachi. ☎ **0792/23-0981.** Set meals ¥1,400–¥3,500 ($14–$35); set lunch obento ¥1,400 ($14). JCB, V. Fri–Wed 11am–9pm. Directions: Walk about 4 minutes from Himeji Station, about halfway down Miyukidori arcade on a side street. VARIED JAPANESE.

This popular restaurant offers a wide assortment of Japanese food, including sashimi, tempura, noodles, eel, and sushi. A great deal is the hearty teishoku obento served until 3pm. It usually includes sashimi, tempura, soup, rice, and pickled vegetables. There's also a mini-kaiseki available for lunch (¥1,400/$14) and dinner (¥3,500/$35). A refuge for shoppers, Fukutei has soothing Japanese instrumental music playing in the background. Fish swim in a black-marble pool in the center of the restaurant, while waiting to be scooped out and put on your table.

$ Minato-an (170)

58 Tatemachi. ☎ **0792/22-1171.** ¥600–¥1,500 ($6–$15). No credit cards. Thurs–Tues 11am–8:30pm. Directions: Walk up Otemae Dori, turn left at 114th Bank. UDON NOODLES.

Across from a tiny neighborhood shrine and located on a corner, this neighborhood restaurant has a plastic-food display case outside. The specialty here is udon noodles served in a wooden bucket, called okeudon. A ¥600 ($6) lunch teishoku is served until 1:30pm. Other noodle dishes include somen, ramen, tempura udon, and curry udon. The menu is in Japanese only, so make your choice from the plastic goodies on display. In any case, no matter what you choose, you're sure to be satisfied—the food here is simple but delicious.

8 Okayama

454 miles W of Tokyo, 136 miles W of Kyoto, 100 miles E of Hiroshima

With the opening of the Seto Ohashi Bridge in the spring of 1988, Okayama Prefecture has leaped into the tourism spotlight. Japanese from all over the country have come to marvel over this bridge, measuring almost six miles in length and connecting

Okayama Prefecture on Honshu island with Sakaide on Shikoku island. Whereas it used to take an hour by ferry to reach Shikoku, the double-decker bridge for trains and cars cuts travel time down to just 15 minutes. For the Japanese, the Seto Ohashi Bridge is one of the most important attractions of Okayama Prefecture and the Seto Island Sea.

For those of you less interested in bridges, Okayama is important for other reasons as well. In Okayama city, there's one of the most beautiful gardens in Japan. In nearby Kurashiki, covered later in this chapter, there's an old sectionof the town that's one of the most picturesque places in the country. And scattered through Okayama Prefecture are so-called International Villas, built by the prefecture especially for foreigners and located primarily in rural areas, with amazingly low rates.

ESSENTIALS

The **telephone area code** for Okayama City, lying in Okayama Prefecture, is 086.

GETTING THERE **By Train** Okayama is a major stop on the Shinkansen bullet line, about 4 hours from Tokyo (3¼ hours by the *Nozomi Super Express*), 1½ hours from Kyoto, and less than 1 hour from Hiroshima.

By Bus There are three overnight buses leaving daily from Shinjuku and Shinagawa stations in Tokyo, arriving in Okayama the next day. There's also express bus service from Osaka.

VISITOR INFORMATION Before leaving Tokyo, stop by the Tourist Information Center and pick up a leaflet called "Okayama and Kurashiki."

The **Okayama Tourist Information Office** (☎ 086/222-2912) is inside the Okayama Station building, near the central exit of the east side (look for the signs). The tourist office window is well marked in English and is open daily from 9am to 6pm. They're well prepared for foreign visitors, with excellent brochures and a map in English.

GETTING AROUND Okayama's sights are all clustered within walking distance of each other and are east of Okayama Station. The easiest way to sightsee is to take a **streetcar** from Okayama Station bound for Higashiyama, and to disembark after about eight minutes at the Shiroshita tram stop. Or take a **bus** from platform 2 to Korakuen-mae. From there, **walk** to the Orient Museum, then Korakuen Garden, Okayama Castle, the Yumeji Art Museum, and the Hayashibara Museum of Art. Allow at least five hours to tour all of these sights.

WHAT TO SEE & DO

Hayashibara Museum of Art

2-7-15 Marunouchi. ☎ **086/223-1733.** Admission ¥300 ($3) adults, ¥200 ($2) children. Daily 9am–5pm.

About a five-minute walk from Okayama Castle, *Hayashibara Bijutsukan* contains relics belonging to the former feudal owners of the castle, the Ikeda clan, including furniture, swords, pottery, lacquerware, Noh costumes, and armor.

✪ Korakuen Garden

1-5 Korakuen. ☎ **086/272-1148**. Admission ¥300 ($3) adults, ¥120 ($1.20) children. Daily Apr–Sept 7:30am–6pm, Oct–Mar 8am–5pm.

Okayama's claim to fame is its Korakuen Garden, considered to be one of Japan's three most beautiful landscaped gardens (the other two are in Kanazawa and Mito). Completed in 1700 after 14 years of work, its 28 acres are graced with a pond, running streams, pine trees, plum and cherry trees, bamboo groves, and tea plantations. The surrounding hills, as well as Okayama's famous black castle, are incorporated into the design of the garden. Its name, Korakuen, means "the garden for taking pleasure later," which has its origins in an old saying: "Bear sorrow before the people; take pleasure after them." This garden differs from most Japanese gardens in that it has large expanses of grassy open areas, a rarity in crowded Japan.

Okayama Castle

2-3-1 Marunouchi. ☎ **086/225-2096.** Admission ¥250 ($2.50) adults, ¥100 ($1) children. Daily 9am–5pm.

Across the river from Korakuen Park and over a footbridge, *Okayamajo* was originally built in the 16th century. Destroyed in World War II and rebuilt in 1966, this unique castle has earned the nickname "Crow Castle" because of its black color, painted deliberately so as to contrast with neighboring Himeji's famous White Heron castle. Like most castles, this one houses swords, samurai gear, and palanquins. Unlike castles of yore, however, this one comes with an elevator that whisks you up to the top floor of the donjon, from which you have a view of the park and the city beyond. If you feel like indulging in whimsical fantasies deserving of children's fairy tales, you can rent paddleboats in the shape of swans or teacups in the river below the castle.

Orient Museum

9-31 Tenzincho. ☎ **086/232-3636.** Admission ¥300 ($3) adults, half price for children. Tues–Sun 9am–5pm.

Oriento Bijutsukan, designed in the style of an Islamic mosque, exhibits about 2,000 items of artwork from the ancient Orient, including pottery, glassware, and metalwork from Asia, Iran, Syria, and ancient Mesopotamia.

Yumeji Art Museum

2-1-32 Hama. ☎ **086/271-1000.** Admission ¥600 ($6). Apr–Nov, daily 9am–6pm; Dec–Mar, Tues–Sun 9am–5pm.

North of Korakuen Park and across the river is *Yumeji-Kyodo Bijutsukan,* dedicated to the works of Takehisa Yumeji. Born in Okayama Prefecture in 1884, Yumeji is sometimes referred to as Japan's Toulouse-Lautrec and is credited with developing the fin de siècle art nouveau movement in Japan. This collection includes some of his most famous works, including watercolors, oils, and woodblock prints.

SHOPPING

A sampling of products and crafts made in Okayama Prefecture can be seen at the **Okayama Prefectural Product Center** (177) (☎ 086/234-2270) at 1-5-1 Omotecho, in front of the Shiroshita streetcar stop. *Okayama-ken Kanko Bussan Centa* is open daily from 10am to 8pm, closed the second Tuesday of every month. It features Bizen pottery, rush-grass mats (*igusa*), wood carvings, colorful wooden masks, spirits, papier-mâché toys, and more.

For general shopping, at Okayama Station there's a large underground shopping arcade called **Ichibangai** with boutiques selling clothing, shoes, and accessories, and across from the station is **Takashimaya,** a department store. In addition, in the heart of the city is the **Omotecho covered shopping arcade,** where you'll find **Tenmaya,** Okayama's largest department store.

ACCOMMODATIONS

EXPENSIVE

Okayama Kokusai Hotel

4-1-16 Kadota Honmachi, Okayama City 703. ☎ **086/273-7311.** Fax 086/271-0292. 177 rms. A/C MINIBAR TV TEL. ¥17,000–¥19,000 ($170–$190) twin; ¥19,000–¥20,000 ($190–$200) double. AE, DC, JCB, MC, V. Taxi: 15 minutes.

This Western-style hotel with a resortlike holiday atmosphere is located above the city on a wooded hill. It has the most psychedelic elevators I've ever seen—lined with fabric of colorful silk threads in wavy patterns. Rooms face city or woods—city views are more dramatic and expensive. Comfortable rooms have refrigerators stocked with everything from beer to "titbits"—which turn out to be nuts. The staff here is friendly and courteous.

Dining/Entertainment: Restaurants serve Japanese, French, and Chinese cuisine, including L'Arc en Ciel on the 13th floor, with panoramic views of the city. There's also a rooftop beer garden with romantic views of the city lights, open from mid-June through August.

Facilities: Outdoor swimming pool, open from mid-July to the end of August.

MODERATE

Culture Hotel

1-3-2 Gankunan-cho, Okayama City 700. ☎ **086/253-2233.** Fax 086/255-1516. 93 rms. A/C TV TEL. ¥14,000 ($140) double or twin; ¥12,000–¥15,000 ($120–$150) Japanese-style rooms. AE, DC, JCB, MC, V. Bus: From platform 9 to Sports Center mae stop. Taxi: 5 minutes.

This is an excellent choice for a modestly priced hotel. It's a rather striking white building, and its lobby uses white bricks in a number of imaginative ways—chipped to form patterns, buckled, or pulled out from the wall in relief. Water from an inside fountain empties into a stream that runs through the lobby lounge to an outside waterfall and small garden. The courteous and friendly staff don't speak much English. Japanese (bean) pillows are a downer. The hotel's one restaurant serves Western-style food.

Hotel Sunroute (171)

1-3-12 Shimoishi, Okayama City 700. ☎ **086/232-2345.** Fax 086/225-6556. 120 rms. A/C MINIBAR TV TEL. ¥9,300–¥13,000 ($93–$130) double or twin; ¥16,000 ($160) triple. Children under 6 stay free in parents' room. AE, DC, JCB, MC, V. Directions: Walk 10 minutes southwest.

This chain business hotel is in a redbrick building. The staff are accommodating. It has two restaurants. Rooms are basic but adequate.

Okayama Plaza Hotel

2-3-12 Hama, Okayama City 703. ☎ **086/272-1201.** Fax 086/273-1557. 85 rms. A/C TV TEL. ¥13,000–¥14,000 ($130–$140) twin; ¥13,000–¥15,000 ($130–$150) double. AE, DC, JCB, MC, V. Bus: Okaden bus from gate 9 to the Yumeiji-kyodo Bijutsukan-mae stop.

Located just north of Korakuen Garden, this hotel has a lobby featuring a gigantic wind chime—glass chandeliers in front of the main door sway in the breeze and make a music of their own. Rooms are large, with semi-double-size beds, but the bathrooms are fairly small. There are also some Japanese-style rooms.

Hotel Maira

8-16 Nishiki-cho, Okayama City 700. ☎ **086/233-1411.** Fax 086/222-5601. 80 rms. A/C MINIBAR TV TEL. ¥13,000 ($130) twin/double. All rates include service charge. JCB. Directions: Next to the Nishigawa (West River), 7 minutes from Okayama station on foot or a few minutes' walk from the Yubinkyoku-mae streetcar stop.

This simple hotel has a lot of pluses for the price, including views and comfortable, clean, and bright rooms with quilt-covered beds. Doubles have a sofa bed. It has a good Italian restaurant, Ambiente, which also serves breakfast (¥1,000/$10).

Washington Hotel

3-6 Honmachi, Okayama City 700. ☎ **086/231-9111.** Fax 086/221-0048. 210 rms (all with bath). A/C MINIBAR TV TEL. ¥13,200 ($132) twin; ¥14,000 ($140) double. AE, DC, JCB, MC, V. Directions: Walk 5 minutes east of Okayama Station on Momotaro Odori.

Opened in 1988, the Washington Hotel has a second-floor lobby. The rooms—of which 167 are singles, all featuring semi-double-size beds—are pleasant, with windows that open and bilingual TV. Toilets are even equipped with bidetlike jets of water, the latest in Japanese technology. Facilities here include a Chinese restaurant, a coffee shop, and a live-music venue in the basement called Kento's, which features tunes from the '50s and '60s.

INEXPENSIVE

Matsunoki (172)

19-1 Ekimotomachi, Okayama City 700. ☎ **086/253-4111.** Fax 086/253-4110. 52 rms (30 with bath). A/C TV TEL. ¥8,000 ($80) twin without bath; ¥10,000 ($100) twin with bath. Breakfast ¥700 ($7) extra; dinner ¥1,300 ($13) extra. No credit cards. Directions: Walk 2 minutes west of Okayama Station, down the street alongside the Tokyu Daiichi Hotel.

The Matsunoki is in three different neighboring buildings (the lobby is in a white one, and rooms without baths are in an annex with a wooden, traditional exterior) and is owned by a friendly family. It has both Japanese- and Western-style rooms. Meals are served in a cheerful communal dining hall. The hotel also runs a karaoke bar next door; it's open from 11am to midnight and charges ¥2,500 to ¥3,500 ($25 to $35).

Youth Hostel Okayama-ken Seinen Kaikan (173)

1-7-6 Tsukura-cho, Okayama City 700. ☎ **086/252-0651.** 65 beds. A/C. ¥2,800 ($28) for JYHA members, ¥3,400 ($34) for nonmembers. Breakfast ¥450 ($4.50) extra; dinner ¥850 ($8.50) extra. No credit cards. Bus: 5 or 15 to the Seinen-kaikan-mae stop.

This hostel's 13 Japanese-style rooms sleep 3 to 10 people per room. There are bicycles for rent, as well as laundry facilities. Ask at the tourist office for an infor-mation sheet.

ELSEWHERE IN OKAYAMA PREFECTURE

INTERNATIONAL VILLAS Although they're not located within the city limits of Okayama, you might consider treating yourself to a few days in the countryside by staying at one of the International Villas. Financed and maintained by the Okayama Prefectural Government, these small country inns are the brainstorm of Okayama's governor, who wished to repay the kindness he received from foreigners during his trips abroad as a youth. Thus, these villas are open only to foreigners, though accompanying Japanese guests are welcome. The cost of staying at one of the villas is only ¥3,000 ($30) per person for nonmembers and ¥2,500 ($25) for members. The cost of a membership card is ¥500 ($5) and is available at check-in at any villa—worth it if you're staying more than one night. Each villa is small, with only a half dozen or so guest rooms, and is outfitted with the latest in bathroom and kitchen facilities. These villas are so well constructed, in fact, that you would easily pay more than twice the rate if they were privately owned. You can cook your own food or visit one of the local restaurants.

There are six International Villas, most in small villages or in rural settings. One of the completed villas, modeled after a traditional soy-sauce warehouse, is located in a mountain village named **Fukiya,** an old copper-mining town that has changed little since the mid-19th century. In **Koshihata** and **Hattoji,** accommodations are in two 19th-century renovated thatched farmhouses, and in **Ushimado** guests stay in a modern open-beamed villa with sweeping views of the Seto Inland Sea—probably the most popular villa for visiting tourists. Also offering great views is the villa on **Shiraishi Island,** which offers beaches, shrines, and accommodations in an airy glass-and-wooden building. In **Takebe,** known for hot springs where visitors can enjoy nine different types of baths, guests stay in an innovative building constructed of wood and designed to resemble a traditional wooden barge. It also has an outdoor hot-spring bath. In short, these villas are remarkable—and maybe other prefectures will take their cue from Okayama and start building inexpensive lodgings.

For more information on the International Villas, telephone or fax 086/34-3311.

DINING

As with all cities in Japan, you won't have any problems finding restaurants in Okayama. Many Japanese restaurants are clustered around Okayama Station, while the best Western-style restaurants are located in the hotels. Okayama's most famous dish is the *Okayama Barazushi,* made of Seto Inland Sea delicacies and fresh mountain vegetables. Traditionally served during festive occasions, it consists of a rice casserole laced with shredded ginger and cooked egg yolk and topped with a variety of goodies, including conger eel, shrimp, fish, lotus root, and bamboo.

EXPENSIVE

✪ L'Arc En Ciel

Okayama Kokusai Hotel, 13th floor, 4-1-16 Kadota Honmachi. ☎ **086/273-7311.** Reservations recommended. Main dishes ¥800–¥3,500 ($8–$35); set dinners ¥5,000 ($50); set lunches ¥1,500–¥4,000 ($15–$40). AE, DC, JCB, MC, V. Daily 11:30am–2pm and 5–10pm. Taxi: 15 minutes. FRENCH.

For relaxed and intimate dining, head for L'Arc en Ciel, located on top of a hill in the Kokusai Hotel, with sweeping views of the city (beautiful at sunset). A la carte dishes include filet of steak and lobster. Dishes here are imaginative and fun—I once had filet of sole in white-cream sauce and was surprised to see it arrive with a small squid and a shrimp, and topped with shredded crab and carrots. Chef Shigeo Yuasa, who learned his craft in France, changes the imaginative menu five times a year.

MODERATE

Gonta-Zushi (174)

1-2-1 Nodaya-cho. ☎ **086/233-4430.** Nigiri Matsu ¥2,000 ($20); sushi set meals ¥1,000 ($10), ¥1,500 ($15), and ¥2,000 ($20). AE, DC, JCB, MC, V. Thurs–Tues 11am–11pm. Directions: Walk 5 minutes through the Ekimae Shotengai covered shopping arcade until you reach a busy street; Gonta-Zushi is across this street. SUSHI.

The prices are reasonable, the food is excellent, and the atmosphere is typical sushi bar, with a long counter and sushi experts dressed in traditional garb. I had the Nigiri Matsu, which came with nigiri-zushi of conger eel, shrimp, squid, sea bream, tuna, and fish from the Seto Inland Sea, plus three *norimaki* (edible seaweed rolled around rice and pickled vegetables). If you order sushi à la carte, it will be served to you on large shiny leaves. Gonta-Zushi is recognizable by its white lanterns hanging in front of the door and green sign.

Petit ("Puchi") Marie (175)

6-7 Nishikimachi. ☎ **086/222-9066.** Main dishes ¥1,500–¥5,000 ($15–$50); set dinner ¥3,000 ($30); set lunch ¥770 ($7.70). No credit cards. Thurs–Tues 11:15am–2:30pm (last order); and 5–9pm (last order). Directions: Walk 5 minutes east. FRENCH.

This tiny one-room establishment is so popular that customers line up outside and dining is on a first-come, first-served basis. The interior is corny, but the food is fun. A beef stew cooked in red wine is popular, as is the very inexpensive set lunch.

Sienna

2-9-11 Maronouchi. ☎ **086/222-4262.** Antipasto ¥400–¥1,000 ($4–$10); set dinners ¥2,200–¥5,200 ($22–$52); set lunches ¥700–¥1,300 ($7–$13). No credit cards. Mon–Sat 11:30am–2pm and 5:30–11pm. Streetcar: Shiroshita. ITALIAN.

To reach this tiny Italian restaurant not far from the castle, from Shiroshita tram stop follow the tracks to the right, take the second left, and go down three blocks—Sienna is across the street on your left. You'll recognize the place by the Italian flag outside. Wicker highback chairs, Italian music, and pasta-filled jars set the mood. Chef-owner Taniguchi's dedication to Italian cuisine makes this a great find. I had the daily pasta (spinach, mushroom, and cream sauce), salad, three kinds of antipasti, freshly made dessert (real *tarte tatin*), and espresso for ¥2,200 ($22).

INEXPENSIVE

Hama-ya

2-1-32 Hama. ☎ **086/272-4322.** ¥350 ($3.50) coffee or tea; ¥650 ($6.50) cake set. No credit cards. Tues–Sun 9am–6pm. Directions: Cross the Horai Bashi (bridge) from Korakuen. COFFEE SHOP.

This is a delightful rest stop from sightseeing, a cafe that serves cakes and tea or coffee, but where you can also browse for souvenirs like prints and postcards. Their specialty is peach candy.

Okabe

1-10-1 Omotecho. ☎ **086/222-1404.** Set meals ¥800–¥1,100 ($8–$11); set lunch ¥700 ($7). No credit cards. Mon–Sat 11:30am–2pm and 5–9pm. Closed national hols. Streetcar: Shiroshita stop. TOFU.

In the heart of town just off the Omotecho covered shopping arcade is a very popular and informal eatery specializing in homemade tofu. It offers a great lunchtime Okabe teishoku for ¥700 ($7), which consists mainly of tofu dishes, along with rice and pickled vegetables. Seating is along one long counter, behind which an army of women scurry to get out orders. This is one of Okayama's best-known restaurants.

Suishin (176)

Dai-ichi Central Bldg., basement. ☎ **086/232-5101.** Rice casseroles ¥700 ($7); most dishes ¥1,500–¥2,500 ($15–$25). AE, DC, JCB, MC, V. Thurs–Tues 11am–9pm. RICE CASSEROLES/FISH/VARIED JAPANESE.

There are lots of inexpensive restaurants in the basement of the Dai-ichi Central Building, across from Okayama Station's east exit. Among them is Suishin, which specializes in *kamameshi* (rice casserole dishes) and fish from the Seto Inland Sea. This is a chain restaurant with headquarters in Hiroshima. Being a great fan of eel dishes, I chose the eel kamameshi, which came laced with bits of conger eel, ginger, and boiled egg yolk, with Japanese pickles on the side. The Japanese menu shows pictures of other dishes served, including eel, tempura, sushi, and (in summer) *hiyashi,* cold shabu-shabu. A simply furnished and popular place, it gets quite busy at lunchtime.

9 Kurashiki

16 miles W of Okayama

If I were forced to select the most picturesque town in Japan, Kurashiki would certainly be a top contender. In the heart of the city, clustered around a willow-fringed canal, is a delightful area of old buildings and ryokan perfect for camera buffs. As an administrative center of the shogunate in the 17th century, Kurashiki blossomed into a prosperous marketing town where rice, sake, and cotton were collected from the surrounding region and shipped off to Osaka and beyond. Back in those days, wealth was measured in rice, and large granaries were built in which to store the mountains of granules passing through the town. Canals were dug so that barges laden with grain could work their way to ships anchored in the Seto Inland Sea. *Kurashiki,* in fact, means "Warehouse Village." It's these warehouses still standing that give Kurashiki its distinctive charm. In addition, Kurashiki is known throughout Japan for its many art museums. The willow-lined canal with all the museums is only a 10-minute walk from Kurashiki Station, reached by walking south on Chuo Dori.

ESSENTIALS

The **telephone area code** for Kurashiki, lying in Okayama Prefecture, is 086.

GETTING THERE **By Train** If you're arriving in Kurashiki by Shinkansen (which takes about 4½ hours from Tokyo and almost 2 hours from Kyoto), you'll arrive at Shin-Kurashiki Station, which is about six miles west of Kurashiki Station and the heart of the city. The local train between the stations runs about every 15 minutes. If you're coming to Kurashiki from the east, it's easier to disembark from the Shinkansen in Okayama and transfer to a local train for the nine-minute ride directly to Kurashiki Station.

By Bus Buses depart from Okayama Station for Kurashiki on a regular basis.

VISITOR INFORMATION In Kurashiki, the **tourist information office** (☎ 086/426-8681) at Kurashiki Station has maps in English, as well as the leaflet "Okayama and Kurashiki" and other brochures, and will point you in the right direction to your hotel. It's on the second floor of the station, near the ticket wicket. There's another tourist information office, called the **Kurashiki-Kan** (☎ 086/422-0542), right on the canal, which also has maps and brochures. It's the only Western-looking wooden building in the area. They are both open daily from 9am to 6pm (5pm in winter).

WHAT TO SEE & DO

BIKAN HISTORICAL AREA

Called the Bikan Historical Area, Kurashiki's old town is small, consisting of a canal lined with graceful willows and 200-year-old granaries made of black-tile walls topped with white mortar. Many of the granaries have been turned into museums, ryokan, restaurants, and boutiques selling hand-blown glass, papier-mâché toys, and mats and handbags made of *igusa* (rush grass).

Street vendors sell jewelry, their wares laid out beside the canal, and healthy young boys stand ready to give visitors rides in rickshaws. "I hear they're imported from Hong Kong," explains a resident, who feels impelled to stop and point out Kurashiki's museums spread out along the canal. He's anxious that I don't miss a thing.

Another Kurashiki resident advises me that because of the crowds that descend upon Kurashiki during the day (about four million tourists come here a year), I should get up early in the morning before the shops and museums open and explore this tiny area while it's still under the magic of the early-morning glow. "Real lovers of Kurashiki come on Monday," he adds, "because that's when most everything is closed and there are less people." But no matter when you come, you're likely to fall under the city's spell. Even rain only enhances the contrasting black and white of the buildings. In other words, one of the most rewarding things to do in Kurashiki is simply to explore.

THE MUSEUMS

Kurashiki Archeological Museum

1-3-13 Chuo. ☎ **086/422-1542.** Admission ¥400 ($4). Tues–Sun 9am–5pm (to 4:30pm Dec–Feb).

In an old granary, *Kurashiki Koko-Kan* houses objects unearthed in the surrounding region. It also has relics of the Incas and Chinese.

Kurashiki Folkcraft Museum

1-4-11 Chuo. ☎ **086/422-1637.** Admission ¥700 ($7). Tues–Sun 9am–5pm (to 4:15pm Dec–Feb).

If you walk along the same side of the canal as the Ohara Museum of Art (see below), rounding the curve to the right you'll come to *Kurashiki Mingei-Kan,* easily identified by its sign in English. With the slogan USABILITY EQUALS BEAUTY, the museum contains folkcrafts not only from Japan but from various other countries as well, giving unique insight into their cultural similarities and differences as reflected in the items they make and use in daily life. There are baskets made of straw, bamboo, willow, and other materials from Taiwan, Hawaii, Mexico, Sweden, Indonesia, England, Portugal, Germany, and Japan, and there are also ceramics, glass, textiles, and woodwork. The displays are housed in three old rice granaries.

Japanese Rural Toy Museum

1-4-16 Chuo. ☎ **086/422-8058.** Admission ¥310 ($3.10). Daily 8am–5pm.

Almost next to the Folkcraft Museum is *Nihon Kyodogangu-Kan,* a delightful and colorful display of traditional and antique toys from all over Japan and from other countries (the United States is represented by a cornhusk doll). Included are miniature floats, spinning tops, masks, and kites—2,000 items in all. A store at the entrance sells toys.

Ohara Museum of Art

1-1-15 Chuo. ☎ **086/422-0005.** Admission ¥800 ($8) allows entry to all galleries. Tues–Sun 9am–5pm.

A highlight of Kurashiki's Bikan Historical Area is its many fine museums, and foremost in this cultural oasis is *Ohara Bijutsukan,* which first opened in 1930 and is located right on the canal. The main building, a two-story stone structure resembling a Greek temple, is small but manages to contain the works of such European greats as Picasso, Matisse, Vlaminck, Chagall, Manet, Monet, Degas, Pissarro, Sisley, Toulouse-Lautrec, Gauguin, Cézanne, El Greco, Renoir, Corot, and Rodin. The founder of the museum, Ohara Magosaburo, believed that people even in remote Kurashiki should have the opportunity to view great works of art.

Other galleries on the museum grounds hold modern Japanese paintings, contemporary Japanese and Western art, ceramics, and woodblock prints, including prints by the famous Japanese artist Shiko Munakata, paintings by Ryusei Kishida, and ceramics by Shoji Hamada.

OTHER ATTRACTIONS

A few minutes' walk from the canal and museums is a complex called **Kurashiki Ivy Square.** Built as a cotton mill by a local spinning company in 1888, this handsome redbrick complex shrouded in ivy has been renovated into a hotel, restaurants, museums, and a few boutiques and galleries selling crafts. It's especially romantic in the evening, when from the end of June to the end of August there's a beer garden in the inner courtyard, open daily from 6 to 9:30pm. Classical music wafts from loudspeakers built into the brick floors of the courtyard.

As for museums at Ivy Square, the **Kurabo Memorial Hall** shows the history of the old spinning company, which was Kurashiki's biggest employer for decades, providing jobs for many young women in the area. Perhaps the most interesting thing to see in this museum is a film made more than 70 years ago showing life at the factory, including the women's dormitory, where many of the single women lived. The tape is located toward the end of the museum and is activated with the push of a button.

Nearby is **Ivy Gakkan,** a museum with a curious mixture of reproductions of the world's famous paintings (perhaps for art students who can't afford trips to see the real thing) and a section devoted to the history of Kurashiki. Interesting here are photographs of the city taken in the early 1900s.

Finally, the **Torajiro Kojima Memorial Hall** contains more Western art of the Ohara collection, as well as paintings by Torajiro Kojima, who went to Europe to purchase most of the pieces in the Ohara museums. The Oriental Room of the Memorial Hall (with its own separate entrance) contains vases, pottery, glass, and some sculpture from ancient Egypt, Iran, Turkey, and other early cultures.

Entrance to Kurabo Memorial Hall, Ivy Gakkan, and Kojima Memorial Hall costs ¥500 ($5) for a combined ticket. Hours for all are 9am to 5pm, but the Torajiro Kojima Memorial Hall is closed on Monday.

Near Ivy Square is the **Kurabo Orchid Center,** which displays 200 different varieties of orchids in every conceivable shape, color, and size. Daily hours here are 9am to 6pm, and admission is ¥300 ($3).

ACCOMMODATIONS

RYOKAN

✪ Ryokan Kurashiki (178)

4-1 Honmachi, Kurashiki 710. ☎ **086/422-0730.** Fax 086/422-0990. 20 rms (9 with bath). A/C TV TEL. ¥18,000–¥20,000 ($180–$200) per person without bath, ¥22,000–¥50,000 ($220–$500) per person with bath. All rates include breakfast and dinner. AE, DC, MC, V. Directions: Bikan Historical Area.

The best place to stay to get a feeling for old Kurashiki is right in the heart of it—in one of the old warehouses, made up of an old mansion and three converted rice-and-sugar warehouses more than 250 years old. Located right on Kurashiki's picturesque willow-lined canal and filled with antiques, this ryokan has long, narrow corridors, nooks and crannies, and the peaceful sanctuary of an inner garden. There's no other ryokan in Japan quite like this one—it's fun simply walking through the corridors and looking at all the antiques. No two rooms are alike, and at the Terrace de Ryokan Kurashiki you can sip ceremonial green tea while looking out over a small garden. Even if you don't stay at this ryokan, you may wish to come treat yourself to tea or coffee, which costs ¥800 ($8). Western-style breakfasts are available.

Tsurugata (179)

1-3-15 Chuo, Kurashiki 710. ☎ **086/424-1635.** 13 rms (10 with toilet only, 3 with bath). A/C TV TEL. ¥16,000–¥39,000 ($160–$390) per person. All rates include Japanese breakfast and dinner. AE, DC, JCB, MC, V. Directions: Bikan Historical Area.

This ryokan, located in a 240-year-old building on the canal, was once a merchant's house and shop selling rice, cotton, and cooking oil. The rooms here have their own toilet, and there are public baths with instructions in English on how to use them, indicating that they're accustomed to foreign guests here. Rustic furniture, gleaming wood, and high ceilings are trademarks of this ryokan.

Tsurugata also maintains its own small restaurant, serving kaiseki, tempura, and sashimi. The kaiseki dinners here are lovely, beautifully arranged on various dishes and as delicious as they look. Open daily from 11:30am to 2:30pm and 5 to 7pm, it's a good place to stop off for lunch. Mini-kaiseki starts at ¥3,000 ($30) for lunch and ¥4,000 ($40) for dinner, while a kaiseki set dinner is ¥7,000 ($70).

MINSHUKU

Kamoi (180)

1-24 Honmachi, Kurashiki 710. ☎ **086/422-4898.** Fax 086/427-7615. 15 rms (none with bath). A/C TV. ¥4,000 ($40) per person without meals; ¥6,000 ($60) per person with breakfast and dinner. All rates include tax and service. No credit cards. Directions: Bikan Historical Area.

Kamoi is a minshuku located on a slope leading toward Tsurugatayama Park and Achi Shrine, right beside the stone torii gate that leads to the shrine. It's popular among young people, and its fourth-floor rooms have good views of the city. Since the owner of this minshuku is also owner and chef of a restaurant (see "Dining," below), you can be assured the food served here is especially good. Although the building was built about a decade ago, it follows an architectural style befitting old Kurashiki. Rooms are simple, with coin-operated TV. Western-style breakfast is served upon request.

Kokumin Ryokan Ohguma

3-1-2 Achi, Kurashiki 710. ☎ **086/422-0250.** 13 rms (2 with bath). A/C TV TEL. ¥4,500–¥5,000 ($45–$50) per person without meals; ¥8,000–¥10,000 ($80–$100) per person with breakfast and dinner. No credit cards. Directions: Across from Kurashiki Station.

If you wish to stay close to the station, the entry to this small establishment with Japanese-style rooms is through a narrow shopping arcade, located to the right of the main road leading from the station (not the more obvious, large arcade, located to the left). The ryokan first opened more than 60 years ago, but the building has been updated. Its tatami rooms are simple but comfortable.

Minshuku Kawakami (181)

1-10-13 Chuo, Kurashiki 710. ☎ **086/424-1221.** Fax 086/424-1237. 11 rms (none with bath). A/C TV. ¥4,500 ($45) per person without meals; ¥6,500 ($65) per person with breakfast and dinner. JCB, MC, V. Directions: Walk from Kurashiki Station to the Bikan Historical Area, about 15 minutes.

Located on a tiny side alley just off the Kurashiki canal and not far from the Japan Rural Toy Museum, this minshuku features simple Japanese-style rooms, with coin-operated TV and air-conditioning.

HOTELS

El Paso Inn

1-9-4 Chuo, Kurashiki 710. ☎ **086/421-8282.** Fax 086/426-6030. 30 rms (all with bath). A/C TV TEL. ¥10,000 ($100) double; ¥11,000 ($110) twin; ¥16,500 ($165) triple; ¥22,000 ($220) quad. All rates include service. AE, JCB, MC, V. Directions: Bikan Historical Area.

Not far from the Ohara Museum of Art, the El Paso Inn, which opened in 1987, appeals mainly to the younger set with its simple, breezy architecture reminiscent of the American Southwest. It features a pleasant, contemporary restaurant with seating under a glass-domed inner courtyard. Rooms are simple, with tiny bathrooms, and those on the third floor facing north have the best view. Most rooms have minibars. There are bicycles available free of charge to hotel guests.

Hotel Kurashiki

1-1-1 Achi, Kurashiki 710. ☎ **086/426-6111.** Fax 086/426-6163. 133 rms. A/C MINIBAR TV TEL. ¥15,000–¥19,000 ($150–$190) twin; ¥20,000 ($200) triple. AE, DC, JCB, MC, V.

If you prefer a place near Kurashiki Station, you can't get any closer than this combination business-tourist hotel, part of the Japan Railways Group. The rooms in this modern, spotless, and attractive hotel are pleasantly decorated with flowered bedspreads and cheerful pastels of green or pink and have nicely tiled bathrooms instead of the usual one-unit cubbyholes of most business hotels. Windows are of double-pane glass to shut out noise, and there are both Japanese and Western restaurants.

✪ Kurashiki Ivy Square Hotel

7-2 Honmachi, Kurashiki 710. ☎ **086/422-0011.** Fax 086/424-0515. 157 rms (83 with bath). A/C MINIBAR TV TEL. ¥11,000–¥13,000 ($110–$130) twin without bath, ¥14,800–¥27,000 ($148–$270) double or twin with bath; ¥14,000–¥20,000 ($140–$200) triple without bath. AE, DC, JCB, MC, V. Directions: Bikan Historical Area.

Another interesting place to stay and a good choice in this price category, this hotel is located in the converted cotton mill on Ivy Square. The rooms have a somewhat stark but country feel, and come with the usual clock and hot water for tea, among other amenities, plus toilet. All doubles are with bath, while triples are without. Much of the architectural style of the old mill has been left intact. The best rooms face a tiny expanse of green grass and an ivy-covered wall. Pleasant restaurants serve Japanese and Western food.

✪ Kurashiki Kokusai Hotel

1-1-44 Chuo, Kurashiki 710. ☎ **086/422-5141.** Fax 086/422-5192. 106 rms. A/C MINIBAR TV TEL. ¥14,000–¥17,000 ($140–$170) double; ¥14,000–¥20,000 ($140–$200) twin. AE, DC, JCB, MC, V. Directions: Next to the Bikan Historical Area on Chuo Dori.

If you prefer to sleep in a bed rather than on a futon, this is Kurashiki's most popular Western-style hotel—and it's easy to see why. This delightful hotel, built in 1963, blends into its surroundings, with black-tile walls set in white mortar. Inside the hotel's lobby are two huge woodblock prints by Japanese artist Shiko Munakata. Commissioned by the hotel, *Great Barriers of the Universe* is his largest piece.

The atmosphere of the hotel is decidedly old-fashioned, which only adds to the charm. If you prefer more modern surroundings, however, ask for a room in the much newer annex, which features mainly twins with slightly upgraded facilities. Located behind the Ohara Museum of Art, its back rooms have a pleasant view of the museum, greenery, and the black-tile roofs of the old granaries. All rooms come with radio, hot-water pot, and tea bags. The more expensive rooms face the back of the hotel and have the most pleasant views.

Dining/Entertainment: There's a pleasant Western-style restaurant, a Japanese-style restaurant with a tempura corner, a bar, and a beer garden in the backyard open from mid-July to the end of August from 5 to 9pm daily.

Services: Free newspaper, same-day laundry service.

Young Inn Kurashiki

1-14-8 Achi, Kurashiki 710. ☎ **086/425-3411.** Fax 086/425-3412. 39 rms (4 with bath). A/C TV. ¥7,000 ($70) twin without bath, ¥11,000 ($110) twin with bath; ¥12,000 ($120) triple without bath. No credit cards. Directions: 1 minute from Kurashiki Station's south exit.

If all the hostelries suggested above are full, you might try a rather different kind of place called Young Inn Kurashiki. A redbrick building, it has a youth-hostel feel and seems more European than Japanese. Painted in bright primary colors, it looks as though it might have been rather chic at one time but has faded somewhat with neglect. Informal, it caters mainly to young people, with two to three beds per room; the beds are arranged on different levels in bunk-bed style. In fact, the three-bed rooms on the fifth floor have to be seen to be believed—the third bed is about 10 feet off the floor, and you have to climb a ladder to reach it. Definitely for the nimble unafraid of heights.

A Youth Hostel

Kurashiki Youth Hostel

1537-1 Mukoyama, Kurashiki 710. ☎ **086/422-7355.** 60 beds. A/C. ¥2,800 ($28) for JYHA members, ¥600 ($6) extra for nonmembers. Breakfast ¥600 ($6) extra; dinner ¥1,000 ($10) extra. No credit cards. Directions: Walk 30 minutes south.

This youth hostel, located in Mukoyama Park, has a policy of accepting card-carrying members only, but has been known to let in unknowing foreign non-members who show up forlornly on their doorstep. What you do with that bit of information is up to you. There is a maximum of six people to a room. Laundry facilities are available.

DINING

All the outlets listed here are in the Bikan Historical Area.

El Greco Coffeehouse

1-1-15 Chuo. ☎ **086/422-0297.** ¥400 ($4) coffee. No credit cards. Tues–Sun 10am–5pm. COFFEE HOUSE.

Next door to the Ohara Museum in an ivy-colored stone building, El Greco is Kurashiki's most famous coffee shop, simply decorated with a wooden floor, wooden tables and benches, vases of fresh flowers, and El Greco prints. It serves coffee, green tea, milk shakes, ice cream, and cake.

$ Kamoi (180)

1-3-17 Chuo. ☎ **086/422-0606.** Set meals ¥1,300–¥2,200 ($13–$22). No credit cards. Tues–Sun 9am–6pm. SUSHI.

This sushi restaurant is run by the man who has a minshuku of the same name. It's located in a 200-year-old rice granary along Kurashiki's willow-fringed canal, across from the Ohara Museum of Art. Inside, the stark-white walls and dark wooden beams are decorated with such antiques as cast-iron teapots, old rifles, gourds, and samurai hats. Since the menu is in Japanese, you can select from the plastic-food display outside the front door. In addition to sushi set meals, there are also eel, and *daikonzushi,* a local rice dish covered with vegetables and seafood and commonly served during festivals. During winter the same dish is served warm and is called *nukuzushi.*

Kiyutei

1-2-20 Chuo. ☎ **086/422-5140.** Main dishes ¥1,000–¥5,500 ($10–$55); steak dinners ¥2,200–¥6,300 ($22–$63). AE, DC, JCB, MC, V. Tues–Sun 11am–9pm (last order at 8:30pm). STEAKS.

Kiyutei is across from the main entrance of the Ohara Museum of Art. Enter through the front gate, pass through the small courtyard, and go into a small room dominated by a counter with cooks grilling steaks, the specialty of the house. Steak dinners, which come with soup, salad, and rice or roll, are available, as well as grilled lobster or salmon, stewed beef with soup, hamburger steak, spaghetti, fried shrimp, and grilled chicken. There's an English-language menu.

Restaurant Ivy

Ivy Square. ☎ **086/422-0011.** Main dishes ¥1,000–¥1,800 ($10–$18); set meals ¥1,800–¥4,000 ($18–$40). AE, DC, JCB, V. Daily 11:30am–9:30pm. WESTERN.

Next to Tsuta (below) in Ivy Square, this Western restaurant is decorated with an ivy theme—even the napkins have vine designs. It also has the high ceiling of the original factory. Set menus range from a minute hamburger-steak course to sirloin or tenderloin steak dinners. A la carte main dishes include beef Stroganoff and sandwiches.

Tsuta

Ivy Square. ☎ **086/422-0011.** Set meals ¥1,000–¥3,800 ($10–$38); kaiseki ¥6,500–¥12,000 ($65–$120). AE, DC, JCB, V. Daily 11:30am–2pm and 5–9:30pm. VARIED JAPANESE.

Tsuta means "ivy" in Japanese, a reference to the fact that the restaurant is in Ivy Square. It serves local Kurashiki specialties, including special rice dishes, fish, obento, sukiyaki, shabu-shabu, and farm products. Set in the converted spinning factory, it has high ceilings and is airy and bright. The most popular dish consists of rice with red beans, sashimi, fried tofu, and vegetables and is called *obento rikyu.*

Wisteria

Kurashiki Kokusai Hotel, 1-1-44 Chuo. ☎ **086/422-5141.** Set dinners ¥6,000–¥12,000 ($60–$120); set lunches ¥1,500–¥3,500 ($15–$35). AE, DC, JCB, MC, V. Daily 11am–2pm and 5–9pm. WESTERN.

For Western dining Wisteria offers a pleasant setting with large windows. Lunch includes such dishes as seafood, salads, spaghetti, sandwiches, and curry, as well as set lunches. The dinner menu includes seafood, roast duck with orange sauce, stewed beef, roast salmon, lobster, and steaks. If it's available, try the *sawara* (a locally caught fish) in mushroom-butter sauce.

10 Matsue

570 miles W of Tokyo, 116 miles NW of Okayama, 251 miles NE of Hakata (Fukuoka)

With a population of about 140,000, Matsue lies near the northern coast of western Honshu in Shimane Prefecture. It's off the beaten track of most foreign tourists, who keep to a southerly route in their travels toward Kyushu. The Japanese, however, are quite fond of Matsue, and a fair number of them choose to spend summer vacation at this pleasant small town. I'll always remember Matsue as the place where the local schoolchildren greet foreigners with "*konnichiwa*" (good afternoon) instead of the usual "*haro*" (hello), testimony to the fact that foreigners are still few and far between.

At last check with the Japan National Tourist Organization, only 1 of the more than 130 group tours organized by foreign tour operators included Matsue in its itinerary of Japan. And yet Matsue, hugging the shores of Lake Shinji, has a number of cultural assets that make a trip here worthwhile.

ESSENTIALS

The **telephone area code** for Matsue, lying in Shimane Prefecture, is 0852.

GETTING THERE **By Train** The easiest way to reach Matsue is from Okayama via a three-hour train ride. There's also one train a day from Hakata Station in Fukuoka.

VISITOR INFORMATION At the Tokyo or Kyoto Tourist Information Center, be sure to pick up the leaflet "Matsue and Izumo-Taisha Shrine."

Upon arrival at Matsue Station, stop off at the **tourist information office,** located to the left after you leave the station by the north exit, and open daily from 9am to 6pm. It has an English-language brochure with a good map of the city. If you have any questions, call the tourist office (☎ 0852/21-4034).

GETTING AROUND Although Matsue's sights are concentrated in one area of town and are easy to find on your own, you may want a "goodwill guide" to show you around, especially if you're going to Izumo-Taisha Shrine. Established by the Japan National Tourist Organization, the goodwill guide network is composed of volunteers with foreign-language abilities who act as guides in their city. All you have to do is pay their entrance fees into museums and sights—and it's nice if you buy them lunch, too. If you wish to have guides (they're always assigned in pairs), apply the day before at the tourist information office before 4pm.

Matsue's attractions lie to the north of the station, and although **buses** run virtually everywhere, you can easily cover the distances on foot.

WHAT TO SEE & DO

MATSUE CASTLE

First built in 1611 and partly reconstructed in 1642, Matsue Castle (☎ 0852/21-4030) was the only castle along this northern stretch of coast built for warfare rather than merely as a residence. It's also one of Japan's few remaining original castles—that is, it's not a reconstruction. Rising up from a hill, with a good view of the city about a mile northwest of Matsue Station, the five-story donjon (which actually conceals six floors to give its warriors a fighting advantage) houses the usual daimyo and samurai gear, including armor, swords, and helmets that belonged to the ruling Matsudaira clan.

Lafcadio Hearn, a European who lived in Matsue in the 1890s, adopted Japanese citizenship, and wrote extensively about Japan and the Japanese, said of Matsue Castle: "Crested at its summit, like a feudal helmet, with two colossal fishes of bronze lifting their curved bodies skyward from either angle of the roof and bristling with horned gables and gargoyled eaves and tilted puzzles of tiles roofing at every story, the creation is a veritable architectural dragon, made up of magnificent monstrosities."

As you walk through the castle up to the top floor, notice the staircase. Although it looks sturdy, it's light enough to be pulled up to halt enemy intrusions. And to think that the castle almost met its demise during the Meiji Restoration, when the ministry of armed forces auctioned it off. Luckily, former vassals of the clan pooled their resources and bought the castle keep. In 1927 the grounds were donated to the city. It's open daily from 8:30am to 5pm (until 6pm in summer); admission is ¥400 ($4), ¥200 ($2) for children.

ATTRACTIONS NEAR THE CASTLE

Just south of Matsue Castle is the **Matsue Cultural Museum** or *Matsue Kyodo-kan* (182) (☎ 0852/22-3958), a white Western-style building erected in honor of Emperor Meiji in 1903. Open daily from 8:30am to 5pm (until 6pm in summer) and charging admission of ¥200 ($2) for adults, half price for children, it displays crafts, utensils, and implements of everyday life from the Meiji Period, beginning in 1868 and extending through the early 1900s. There are old photographs, manuscripts, obento lunch boxes, combs and hairpins, and tea-ceremony objects.

If you walk from Matsue Castle north along its moat, in about five minutes you'll come to a number of attractions. Stop off at **Teahouse Meimei-an** (183) (☎ 0852/21-9863), one of Japan's most renowned and well-preserved thatch-roofed teahouses, which was built in 1779. It's located at the top of a flight of stairs, from which you have a good view of Matsue Castle. For the entrance fee of ¥200 ($2) and an additional ¥350 ($3.50), you can have the bitter Japanese green tea and sweets served to you before moving off to your next destination. It's open daily from 9am to 5pm.

Buke Yashiki (184) (☎ 0852/22-2243), a few minutes' walk from the teahouse, is an ancient samurai house open daily to the public from 8:30am to 5pm (to 6pm in summer). Facing the castle moat, it was built in 1730 and belonged to the Shiomi family, one of the chief retainers of the feudal lord residing in the castle. High-ranking samurai, the Shiomi family lived pretty much like kings themselves, having separate servants' quarters and even a shed for their palanquin. Compared with samurai residences in wealthier regions of Japan, however, this samurai house is considered rather austere. As you walk around it, peering into rooms with their wooden walls slid open to the outside breeze, you'll see furniture and objects used in daily life by samurai during the Edo Period. Admission is ¥250 ($2.50), ¥120 ($1.20) for children. Green tea costs ¥400 ($4).

On the same street as this samurai house are two more attractions. The **Tanabe Art Museum** (185) (☎ 0852/26-2211) is a modern building housing changing exhibits of ceramics and artwork, particularly items used in the tea ceremony; it's open Tues day through Sunday from 9am to 5pm (except days of exhibit changes). *Tanabe Bijutsukan's* admission ranges from ¥500 to ¥750 ($5 to $7.50), depending on the exhibit.

The **Hearn Memorial Hall** or *Hearn Kinenkan* (☎ 0852/21-2147) contains memorabilia of writer Lafcadio Hearn (1850–1904), including his desk, manuscripts, and smoking pipes. The memorial is open daily from 8:30am to 5pm (until 6pm in summer), and admission is ¥250 ($2.50), ¥120 ($1.20) for children.The Japanese are fascinated with this man who married a Japanese, became a Japanese citizen, and adopted the name Koizumi Yakumo. He was one of the first writers to give the Japanese the chance to see themselves through the eyes of a foreigner. His books still provide insight into Japanese life at the turn of the century and are available at all bookstores in Japan with an English section.

Since most Japanese will assume it's out of respect for Hearn that you've come to Matsue, you may want to read one of his books before coming here. His volume *Glimpses of Unfamiliar Japan* contains an essay called "In a Japanese Garden," in which he gives his impressions of Matsue, where he lived for 15 months before moving to Kumamoto to teach English. Near the memorial is **Yakumo Kyukyo** (☎ 0852/23-0714), a Japanese-style house where Hearn lived. Charging ¥200 ($2) admission, it's open Thursday through Tuesday from 9am to 4:40pm (to 4:30pm from December to February).

About a 15-minute walk west of Matsue Castle is **Gesshoji Temple** (186) (☎ 0852/21-6056), the family temple of the Matsudaira clan. It was established back in 1664 by Matsudaira Naomasa, whose grandfather was the powerful Tokugawa Ieyasu. Nine generations of the Matsudaira clan are buried here. The temple is open daily from 8:30am to 5:30pm (to 5pm in winter), and admission is ¥300 ($3).

The most important religious structure in the vicinity of Matsue, however, is **Izumo-Taisha Shrine.** It's a 30- to 40-minute JR train ride from Matsue Station to Izumo and then a 30-minute bus ride (take the *Taisha yuki* bus) costing ¥560 ($5.60). Or take a bus from Matsue-onsen to Taisha-mae stop, which costs ¥750 ($7.50) for the 50-minute trip. The shrine is important because its site is the oldest in Japan. It's probably the most popular attraction in the area, but as with most things in Japan, the present shrine buildings date only from 1744 and 1874. Dedicated to the Shinto deity responsible for medicine and farming, the shrine is constructed in an ancient style, simple and dignified.

SHOPPING

For one-stop shopping for locally crafted goods, visit the **Shimane Souvenir and Handcraft Center** (☎ 0852/22-5758) at 191 Tonomachi, just southeast of Matsue Castle, near the Ichibata department store. In a modern building that resembles the black-and-white structures typical of the region, the *Shimane-ken Bussankanko-kan* has extensive information on the area, including English-language videos about the prefecture (instructions, however, are in Japanese only, so ask someone to help you).

It sells everything from ceramics and furniture to toys and foodstuffs, all products of Shimane Prefecture. It's open daily from 9am to 6pm.

More local products are on sale at the **Matsue Folk Art Center** (☎ 0852/21-5252) at 36 Chidori-cho, located next to the Ichibata Hotel in an area of town called Matsue Onsen. Open daily from 9am to 9pm, the *Matsue Meisan Senta* also features a stage on the third floor where music, dance, and other traditional performing arts shows are given four times every day except in December. The cost is ¥500 ($5). Inquire at the tourist office for current showtimes.

ACCOMMODATIONS

RYOKAN

✪ Horaiso (187)

Tonomachi, Matsue 690. ☎ **0852/21-4337.** Fax 0852/21-4338. 10 rms (2 with bath). A/C TV TEL. ¥15,000–¥22,000 ($150–$220) per person with breakfast and dinner. No credit cards. Taxi: 10 minutes.

Tucked away on a side street not far from Matsue Castle, this 50-year-old ryokan is guarded by a wall, an imposing wooden gateway, and a pine tree. Each room is different and faces an inner courtyard garden. There are small tiled women's and men's baths. The higher rates are for rooms with a private bathroom.

Minami-Kan (188)

14 Suetsugu Honmachi, Matsue 690. ☎ **0852/21-5131.** Fax 0852/26-0351. 10 rms (7 with bath). A/C MINIBAR TV TEL. ¥20,000–¥50,000 ($200–$500) per person. Room in lake house, ¥35,000–¥45,000 ($350–$450). All rates include breakfast and dinner. DC, JCB, MC, V. Taxi: 8 minutes.

Minami-Kan, located off the Kyomise covered shopping arcade in the heart of Matsue, has Japanese-style rooms facing Lake Shinji. Completely remodeled in 1995, rooms are modern. If you want to feel special, stay in one of the two rooms in a separate little house right beside the lake. Minami-Kan is also renowned for its restaurant.

HOTELS

Hotel Ichibata

30 Chidori-cho, Matsue 690. ☎ **0852/22-0188.** Fax 0852/22-0230. 148 rms. A/C MINIBAR TV TEL. ¥13,000 ($130) double; ¥15,000 ($150) twin facing inland; ¥19,000 ($190) twin facing the lake or Japanese-style rooms for two people. AE, DC, JCB, MC, V. Bus: Ride 15 minutes to the Matsue Onsen stop (5 minutes).

Matsue's best-known tourist hotel is the Hotel Ichibata, in a part of town called Matsue Onsen, a hot-spring spa. It's not very conveniently located, but it does have indoor and outdoor hot-spring public baths on the seventh floor, with views over the nearby Lake Shinji. It also has a summertime beer garden on its front lawn, as well as three restaurants. None of the singles or doubles has views of the lake, but all the Japanese-style rooms do, including some combination-style rooms with both beds and tatami area.

Matsue Minami Guchi Hotel (189)

470-1 Asahimachi, Matsue 690. ☎ and fax **0852/27-2000.** 43 rms. A/C MINIBAR TV TEL. ¥4,500 ($45) single; ¥8,000 ($80) twin; ¥7,500 ($75) double. No credit cards. Directions: South exit.

Among the few inexpensive business hotels across the street from the station's south exit is Minimi Guchi, in a white building on the corner. The front desk (on the second floor) is staffed by accommodating clerks. Recently redone in soothing grays, it's a good deal for the price.

Matsue Plaza Hotel (190)

469-1 Asahimachi, Matsue 690. ☎ **0852/26-6650.** Fax 0852/31-0075. 35 rms. A/C TV TEL. ¥7,500 ($75) double or twin.

This business hotel near the Minami Guchi (above) is run-down but cheap. Single rooms are discounted on the weekend. No rooms have a good view, but the top floor is best. All rooms have windows that open.

Matsue Urban Hotel (191)

590-3 Asahimachi, Matsue 690. ☎ **0852/22-0002.** Fax 0852/21-6363. 183 rms. A/C TV TEL. ¥5,300 ($53) single; ¥7,500 ($75) double; ¥9,000 ($90) twin. All rates include tax and service. AE, DC, JCB, MC, V. Directions: 1 minute north.

This hotel is a red building to the right of the Tokyu Inn, visible from the station. Although the 60 single rooms are rather small, with tiny windows, all beds are semi-doubles, and the 10 twins are all corner rooms with large windows. Rooms are pleasant, but large people may have trouble fitting into the tiny tubs. There are two restaurants. The front desk is on the second floor.

If there are two of you and you want to sleep in the same bed, you're welcome to one of the single's semi-double-size beds. You're probably better off, however, moving to the Urban's new annex building next door, which offers rooms with full double beds. The phone number is the same as the one for the main hotel.

Matsue Washington Hotel

Kyobashi, Matsue 690.☎ **0852/22-4111.** Fax 0852/22-4120. 158 rms. A/C MINIBAR TV TEL. ¥13,000 ($130) double; ¥14,000 ($140) twin; ¥18,500 ($185) triple. AE, DC, JCB, MC, V. Taxi: 5 minutes. On foot: 12 minutes.

This is a business hotel that also has some tourist guests. Rooms are basic but clean, and service is friendly. Twin rooms have a river view and are nicer than doubles or singles. Heavy sliding screens block out the light. Rooms may be noisy, with businesspeople returning from the nightlife district, which the hotel borders. On the first floor is a Western-style restaurant, and in the annex a Japanese restaurant, serving shabu-shabu and kaiseki.

Tokyu Inn

590 Asahimachi, Matsue 690. ☎ **0852/27-0109.** Fax 0852/25-1327. 181 rms. A/C MINIBAR TV TEL. ¥14,300–¥17,300 ($143–$173) double or twin. All rates include service. AE, DC, JCB, MC, V. Directions: Across the street from the station's north exit.

Part of a national business hotel chain, the Tokyu Inn offers rooms of adequate size with everything you need. Vending machines dispense beer, coffee, soda, and whiskey. The front desk staff is courteous.

Facilities include the Shangri-La restaurant, which serves both Western and Japanese dishes. It's open from 11am to 2pm and 5 to 9:30pm (the bar is open until 11pm), offering seafood, steaks, spaghetti, tempura, and sandwiches. Japanese-style obento lunch boxes cost ¥1,000 ($10). If you're on a budget or like sitting outside, the Tokyu Inn also has a rooftop beer garden open in summer from 5:30 to 9pm. There's an all-you-can-eat-and-drink menu available at ¥3,800 ($38) for men and ¥2,800 ($28) for women.

DINING

Ginsen (192)

498 Asahimachi. ☎ **0852/21-2381.** Reservations required for kaiseki. Main dishes ¥600–¥3,500 ($6–$35); kaiseki ¥6,000–¥8,000 ($60–$80). No credit cards. Mon–Sat 11am–10pm. Directions: Walk 3 minutes left out of the north exit on the main road. VARIED JAPANESE.

The outside of Ginsen looks like a traditional house, and inside, carp swim in a pond with a waterfall. On the ground floor, tempura, sashimi, and kamameshi are served at counter or tables; upstairs, kaiseki is served in beautiful traditional tatami rooms.

✪ Kaneyasu (193)

Otesemba-cho. ☎ **0852/21-0550.** Reservations not accepted. Dinners average ¥3,000 ($30); lunch teishoku ¥600 ($6). No credit cards. Mon–Fri 11:30am–9pm, Sat 5–9pm. Closed hols. Directions: 2 minutes north. FISH/JAPANESE.

This modest one-counter place with tatami rooms upstairs has good food and is run by motherly bustling women. Behind the Meiji Seimei Building, it has been around for more than 20 years, and most of its customers are local working people, so avoid the noontime rush. It has a great lunch teishoku, which includes a piece of *yakizakana* (grilled fish), vegetable, soup, tofu, rice, and tea. It's served from 10:30am to "whenever"; I came at 3pm and still got the lunch special. Highly recommended.

Yakumoan (194)

308 Kitabori-cho. ☎ **0852/22-2400.** Noodles ¥600–¥2,000 ($6–$20). No credit cards. Daily 9am–5pm. Directions: Between the Buke Yashiki samurai house and the Tanabe Art Museum on the road bordering the castle moat. SOBA NOODLES.

A wonderful place to stop off for lunch if you're sightseeing north of Matsue Castle, this lovely soba shop with a teahouse-like atmosphere is surrounded by bamboo, bonsai, a Japanese garden, and a pond full of prize carp. The noodles here are all handmade. Surrounded by a stone wall with a large wooden entryway, this restaurant has a section that is 200 years old and is a former samurai residence. A plastic-food display case is to the left as you step through the entryway.

11 Hiroshima

554 miles W of Tokyo, 235 miles W of Kyoto, 174 miles E of Hakata/Fukuoka

With a population of approximately one million, Hiroshima looks just like any other up-and-coming city in Japan. Modern buildings, industry, the manufacture of cars and ships—the city is full of vitality and purpose, with a steady flow of both Japanese and foreign business executives in and out of the city.

But unlike other cities, Hiroshima's past is clouded: It has the unfortunate distinction of being the first city ever destroyed by an atomic bomb (the second city, and hopefully the last, was Nagasaki). It happened one clear summer morning, August 6, 1945, at 8:15, when three B-29s approached Hiroshima from the northeast. One of them passed over the central part of the city, dropped the bomb, and then took off at full speed. The bomb exploded 43 seconds later at an altitude of 1,900 feet in a huge fireball, followed by a mushroom cloud of smoke that rose 29,700 feet in the air.

There were approximately 400,000 people living in Hiroshima at the time of the bombing, and about half of them lost their lives. The heat from the blast was so intense that it seared people's skin, while the pressure caused by the explosion tore clothes off bodies and caused the rupture and explosion of intestines and other internal organs. Flying glass tore through flesh like bullets, and fires broke out all over the city. But that wasn't the end of it. Victims who survived the blast were subsequently exposed to huge doses of radioactivity. Even people who showed no outward signs of sickness suddenly died, creating a feeling of panic and helplessness in the survivors. And today, people still continue to suffer from the effects of the bomb, including a high incidence of cancer, disfigurement, scars, and keloid skin tissue.

Impressions

We had found the awesome sight of a Hiroshima that was now even bigger than it had been before the bomb, far richer and more prosperous.

—James Cameron, *Point of Departure,* 1967

In the dying afternoon, I wander dying round the Park of Peace. It is right, this squat, dead place, with its left-over air of an abandoned International Trade and Tourist Fair.

—James Kirkup, "No More Hiroshimas," *These Horned Islands,* 1962

ESSENTIALS

The **telephone area code** for Hiroshima, lying in Hiroshima Prefecture, is 082.

GETTING THERE **By Train** Hiroshima is 4½ hours from Tokyo by Shinkansen bullet train (3 hours and 55 minutes by *Nozomi Super Express*), 2 hours from Kyoto, and 1 hour and 20 minutes from Hakata Station.

By Bus Buses from Tokyo Station reach Hiroshima in 12 hours.

VISITOR INFORMATION Before leaving Tokyo, pick up a copy of the leaflet "Hiroshima and Miyajima" at the Tourist Information Center.

The Hiroshima **city tourist offices** are located at both exits of Hiroshima Station, open daily from 9am to 5:30pm; and in the Rest House at the north end of Peace Memorial Park, open daily from 9:30am to 6pm April through September and from 8:30am to 5pm October through March. Both locations have a brochure and map in English. If you have any questions, call the tourist office (☎ 082/261-1811).

GETTING AROUND The Hondori covered shopping arcade and its neighboring streets, considered the heart of the city, are to the east of Peace Park. Close by is Nagarikawa, Hiroshima's nightlife district.

There are **tram** and **bus** lines running through the city, but you can make the circuit between Shukkei-en Garden, Hiroshima Castle, and Peace Memorial Park **on foot.** Shukkei-en Garden is 15 minutes from Hiroshima Station, Hiroshima Castle is 5 minutes from the garden, and from the castle to the park it's another 15-minute walk, passing the A-Bomb Dome on the way.

SPECIAL EVENTS Hiroshima's most important event is the peace demonstration held here every year on August 6.

WHAT TO SEE & DO

As you walk around Hiroshima today, you'll find it hard to imagine that the city was the scene of such widespread horror and destruction 50 years ago. On the other hand, Hiroshima does not have the old buildings, temples, and historical structures other cities have. But it draws a steady flow of travelers, who come to see Peace Memorial Park, the city's best-known landmark. Hiroshima is also the most popular gateway for cruises of the Seto Inland Sea and for trips to Miyajima, a jewel of an island covered later in this chapter.

PEACE MEMORIAL PARK The main focus of Peace Memorial Park, in the center of the city, is **Peace Memorial Museum** (☎ 082/241-4004). The exhibit begins with a description of the atomic bomb that destroyed the city, the route the American B-29s took to drop the bomb, and the intensity of the blast's epicenter. It then shows in graphic detail the effects of the blast on bodies, buildings, and materials. Most of the photographs in the exhibit are of burned and seared skin, charred remains

Hiroshima

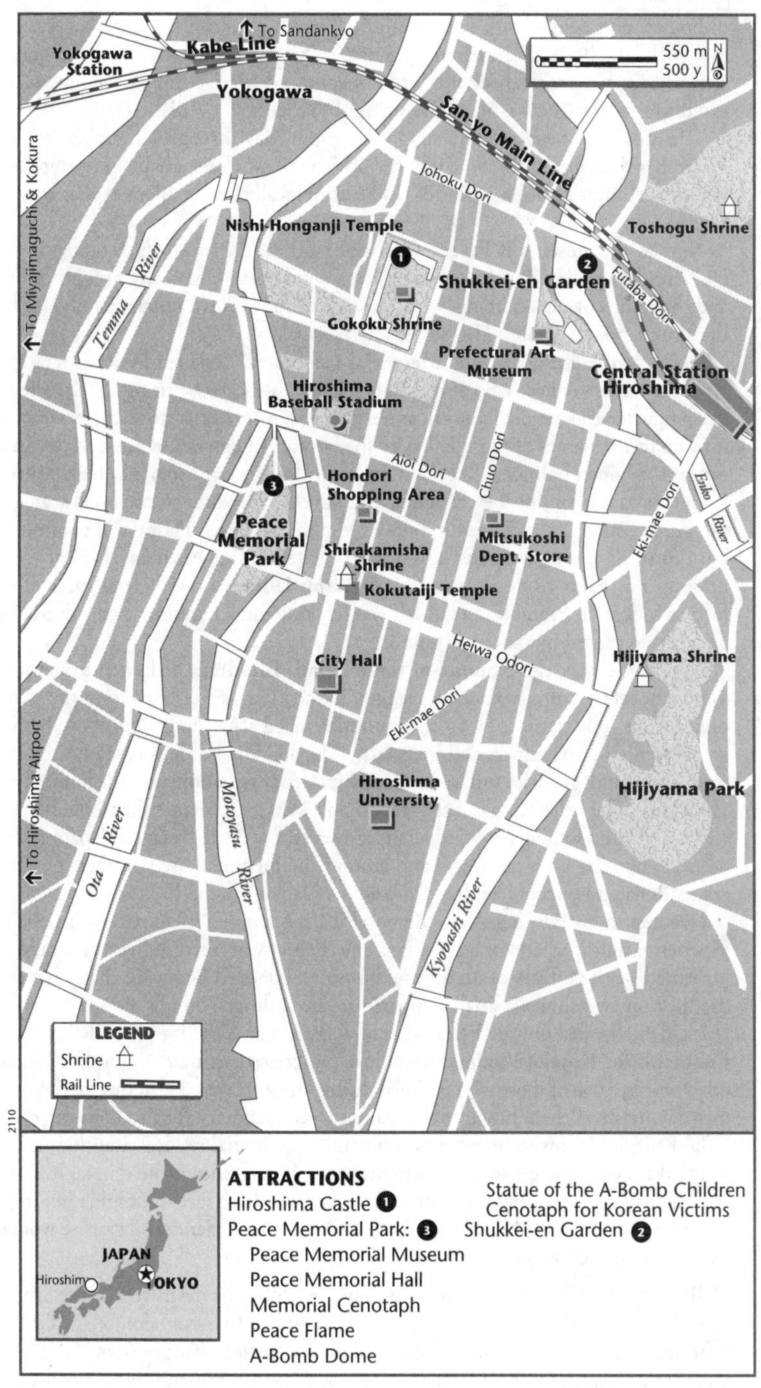
To Sandankyo
Kabe Line
Yokogawa Station
Yokogawa
San-yo Main Line
550 m
500 y
N
To Miyajimaguchi & Kokura
Johoku Dori
Nishi-Honganji Temple
Toshogu Shrine
Temma River
Shukkei-en Garden
Futaba Dori
Gokoku Shrine
Prefectural Art Museum
Central Station Hiroshima
Hiroshima Baseball Stadium
Aioi Dori
Chuo Dori
Hondori Shopping Area
Enko River
Eki-mae Dori
Peace Memorial Park
Shirakamisha Shrine
Mitsukoshi Dept. Store
Kokutaiji Temple
Heiwa Odori
City Hall
Hijiyama Shrine
Eki-mae Dori
To Hiroshima Airport
Hiroshima University
Hijiyama Park
Motoyasu River
Ota River
Kyobashi River
LEGEND
Shrine
Rail Line
2110
JAPAN
Hiroshima
TOKYO
ATTRACTIONS
Hiroshima Castle 1
Peace Memorial Park: 3
Peace Memorial Museum
Peace Memorial Hall
Memorial Cenotaph
Peace Flame
A-Bomb Dome
Statue of the A-Bomb Children
Cenotaph for Korean Victims
Shukkei-en Garden 2

of bodies, and people with open wounds. There's a bronze Buddha that was half melted in the blast, and melted glass and ceramics. There are also some granite steps that show a dark shadow where someone had been sitting at the time of the explosion—the shadow is all that remains of that person.

The museum opens at 9am and closes at 6pm May through November (at 5pm December through April). Note that the ticket window closes a half hour before closing time. Admission fee is ¥50 (50¢). The exhibits all have excellent explanations in English.

Next to the museum is **Peace Memorial Hall,** where two documentaries in English are shown throughout the day on the second floor. One focuses on Hiroshima and the results of the bombing, while the second film takes a more scientific look at the atomic bombs in both Hiroshima and Nagasaki.

North of the museum is the **Memorial Cenotaph,** designed by Japan's famous architect Kenzo Tange (who also designed Tokyo's Akasaka Prince Hotel). Shaped like a figurine clay saddle found in ancient tombs, it shelters a stone chest, which in turn holds the names of those killed by the bomb. An epitaph, written in Japanese, carries the hopeful phrase, "Repose ye in Peace, for the error shall not be repeated." If you stand in front of the cenotaph, you have a view through the hollow arch of the Peace Flame and the Atomic-Bomb Dome. The **Peace Flame** will continue to burn until all atomic weapons vanish from the face of the earth and nuclear war is no longer a threat to humanity. The **A-Bomb Dome** is the skeletal ruins of the former Industrial Promotion Hall—it was left as a visual reminder of the death and destruction caused by the single bomb.

Also in the park is the **Statue of the A-Bomb Children,** dedicated to the war's most innocent victims, who died instantly in the blast or afterward from the effects of radiation. The statue is of a girl with outstretched arms, and rising above her is a crane, symbol of happiness and longevity in Japan. The statue is based on the true story of a young girl who suffered from the effects of radiation after the bombing in Hiroshima. She believed that if she could fold 1,000 paper cranes she would become well again. After folding her 964th crane, however, she died. Today, all Japanese children are familiar with her story, and around the memorial are streamers of paper cranes donated by schoolchildren from all over Japan.

Needless to say, visiting Peace Memorial Park is a rather sobering and depressing experience, but it's perhaps a necessary one. Every concerned individual should be informed of the effects of an atomic bomb and should be aware that what was dropped on Hiroshima is small compared to the hydrogen bombs of today.

Incidentally, just outside Peace Memorial Park, across the Honkawa River, is the **Cenotaph for Korean Victims.** It's a little-publicized fact that 20,000 Koreans (in other words, 10% of those who perished during the war) were killed that fateful summer day, most of them brought to Japan as forced laborers. The monument reads: "The Korean victims were given no funerals or memorial services and their spirits hovered for years unable to pass on to heaven. " It's significant the cenotaph is outside the park—even today, Koreans and their descendants face discrimination in Japan. But I must also add that it was a concerned and conscientious Japanese woman who made sure I saw this monument.

HIROSHIMA CASTLE Originally built in 1593 but destroyed in the atomic blast, Hiroshima Castle was reconstructed in 1958. Its five-story donjon, or keep, is a faithful reproduction of the original one. It's open from 9am to 6pm (5pm from October through March). Inside the castle is a history museum with a collection focusing on Japan's feudal days, with displays of samurai gear, models of old

Hiroshima, and pictures of the past. Entrance to both the museum and the castle is ¥300 ($3).

SHUKKEI-EN GARDEN Near Hiroshima Station, Shukkei-en Garden was first laid out in 1620, with a pond constructed in imitation of a famous lake in China, Si Hu. The garden's name means "landscape garden in miniature." The park is situated on the Ota River and includes streams, ponds, islets, and bridges—a pleasant respite from city traffic. Charging a ¥250 ($2.50) admission, Shukkei-en is open daily from 9am to 6pm (to 5pm from October through March).

THE SETO INLAND SEA Hiroshima is also the usual departure point for day cruises on the Seto Inland Sea. Stretching between Honshu and the islands of Shikoku and Kyushu, the Inland Sea is dotted with more than 3,000 pine-covered islands and islets. Cruises are operated daily from March to the end of November by the **Setonaikai Kisen steamship company** (☎ 082/253-1212), and advance booking is required. One cruise departs from Miyajima daily at 8:30am, with a stop at Hiroshima before heading on to Kure, Yasura, Omishima Island, and Setoda. The round-trip from Miyajima or Hiroshima to Setoda, including lunch, is ¥12,000 ($120). If it's winter or you're simply more interested in a shorter cruise, Setonaikai Kisen also offers a daily cruise throughout the year to the island of Miyajima, with a departure at 11:30am. Cost of the round-trip cruise is ¥7,000 ($70), including lunch.

All the above cruises must be booked in advance, which you can do at several hotels, including the ANA Hotel Hiroshima. More information on these cruises is given in a leaflet called "Inland Sea and Shikoku," available from the Tourist Information Center in either Tokyo or Kyoto.

ACCOMMODATIONS

EXPENSIVE

ANA Hotel Hiroshima

7-20 Nakamachi, Naka-ku, Hiroshima 730. ☎ **082/241-1111** or 800/ANA-HOTELS in the U.S. and Canada. Fax 082/241-9123. 431 rms. A/C MINIBAR TV TEL. ¥17,500–¥21,500 ($175–$215) double; ¥18,500–¥22,500 ($185–$225) twin. AE, DC, JCB, MC, V. Streetcar: 1 to the Chudenmae stop.

The ANA Hotel Hiroshima is on the tree-lined Peace Boulevard (Heiwa Odori), just a five-minute walk from Peace Memorial Park and a seven-minute taxi ride from Hiroshima Station. Its lobby features piano concerts in a marble-and-glass setting. The large, comfortable rooms have bilingual TV and all the amenities you'd expect from a first-class hotel.

Dining/Entertainment: There are seven restaurants and bars, including those serving Japanese, Chinese, and French cuisine and teppanyaki steaks. A rooftop beer garden (open summer months from 5:30 to 9:30pm) and one of the two bars on the 22nd floor featuring live piano music nightly add to the hotel's entertainment.

Services: Free delivery of *Japan Times,* same-day laundry service.

Facilities: Health club with indoor swimming pool, exercise equipment, and sauna (fee: ¥4,000/$40; ¥2,000/$20 for use of the pool alone).

✪ Mitakiso (195)

1-7 Mitaki-cho, Nishi-ku, Hiroshima 733. ☎ **082/237-1402.** Fax 082/237-1403. 10 rms (7 with toilet only, 3 with bath). A/C TV TEL. ¥22,000–¥40,000 ($220–$400) per person. All rates include breakfast, dinner, and service. AE, DC, MC, V. Taxi: 15 minutes.

This is a beautiful traditional Japanese inn, part of which is 70 years old. Its rooms are spread along an exquisite landscape garden with stunted pines, ponds, tiny maple trees, stone lanterns, and meandering streams. The best rooms are elegant and private, with sliding doors that open onto the garden. The least expensive rooms face away from the garden toward the street, but if you're traveling off-season you may be upgraded to a room with a garden view. There are lovely public baths. The ryokan is well known for its excellent cuisine. Its entrance is past a high stone wall and a massive stone lantern. A great place for a splurge.

Rihga Royal Hiroshima

6-78 Motomachi, Naka-ku, Hiroshima 730. ☎ **082/502-1121.** Fax 082/228-5415. 490 rms. A/C MINIBAR TV TEL. ¥19,000–¥28,000 ($190–$280) twin; ¥18,000–¥24,000 ($180–$240) double; ¥50,000 ($500) suite. AE, DC, JCB, MC, V. Streetcar: Kencho-mae stop.

Opened in 1994, the Rihga Royal offers city center convenience (it's next to shopping and restaurants and city hall), an elegant but warm peach-colored lobby, and rooms with flower print quilts and a European feel. Rooms are large and better furnished than most and come with lots of amenities, including bathroom extras like magnified adjustable mirrors, scales, and roomy counter space. Singles and twins have semi-double beds.

Dining/Entertainment: The seven restaurants include the 33rd-floor Sky Buffet Rijo, which serves an all-you-can-eat buffet (¥2,500/$25 for lunch and ¥5,000/$50 for dinner). The Rihga Top is a sophisticated spot for tea (11:30am–5:30pm) or cocktails (5:30pm to midnight). There's also a karaoke bar.

Facilities: Shopping arcade, health clinic, dental clinic, barbershop, beauty salon, and health club (¥3,000/$30 extra) with pool and sauna.

MODERATE

Hiroshima City Hotel

1-4 Kyobashi-cho, Minami-ku, Hiroshima 732. ☎ **082/263-5111.** Fax 082/262-2403. 184 rms. A/C TV TEL. ¥11,000 ($110) double; ¥12,000–¥18,000 ($120–$180) twin; ¥12,000–¥15,500 ($120–$155) Japanese room for two. AE, DC, JCB, MC, V. Directions: Walk 3 minutes from the Minami Guchi exit, straight through the underpass and over the bridge.

If you wish to stick close to Hiroshima Station, this business hotel across from the Century City Hotel (you can see the Century City Hotel's sign from the train station if you look hard enough) is a good bet. Although it opened in the 1970s, it has since been renovated and looks much newer. Half the rooms are singles, and the cheapest are the smallest I've seen (which, in Japan, says quite a lot), but all rooms come with bathroom and TV, and all but two with minibars. If you want a view, ask for a room above the ninth floor. You'll also find vending machines, three restaurants, a cafe, and a bar.

Hiroshima Kokusai Hotel

3-13 Tatemachi, Naka-ku, Hiroshima 730. ☎ **082/248-2323.** Fax 082/248-2622. 76 rms. A/C MINIBAR TV TEL. ¥12,500 ($125) double; ¥12,500–¥16,000 ($125–$160) twin. Japanese room for four ¥20,000 ($200). AE, DC, JCB, MC, V. Streetcar: 1, 2, or 6 to the Tatemachi stop (5 minutes).

Built in 1966, this well-known, established hotel is in the center of Hiroshima, within walking distance of Peace Memorial Park, Shukkei-en Garden, Hiroshima Castle, and the Hondori covered shopping arcade. Rooms are rather crowded in appearance and a bit run-down, but they're comfortable and large. There are Japanese, Chinese, and Western restaurants, and breakfasts are served for ¥1,200 ($12).

Hotel Granvia

1-5 Matsubara-cho, Minami-ku, Hiroshima 732. ☎ **082/262-1111.** Fax 082/262-4050. 440 rms. A/C MINIBAR TV TEL. ¥15,500–¥18,000 ($155–$180) double; ¥17,500–¥30,000 ($175–$300) twin. AE, DC, JCB, MC, V. Directions: North Shinkansen exit.

The Granvia stands beside Hiroshima Station, so it's very convenient. It also offers a no-smoking floor and 12 restaurants and bars, including a high-class okonomiyaki eatery and a good sushi bar. The steakhouse on the 21st floor offers dining with a view. The only drawback is that the Granvia people send their staff to rudeness school.

Hotel Silk Plaza

14-1 Hatchobori, Naka-ku, Hiroshima 730. ☎ **082/227-8111.** Fax 082/227-8110. 231 rms. A/C MINIBAR TV TEL. ¥12,500 ($125) double or twin. AE, DC, JCB, MC, V. Streetcar: 1, 2, or 6 to the Hatchobori stop.

The Hotel Silk Plaza is on Hakushima Dori, near three department stores. A locally owned hotel rather than part of a chain, it attracts foreign tourists with an English-speaking staff that couldn't be more helpful. Single rooms all have semi-double-size beds, but some singles are not recommended, since they are dark and open toward a wall with windows of other guest rooms just two feet away. All rooms are very simple. There are both Western and Japanese restaurants, and a buffet-style breakfast is served for ¥1,000 ($10).

Sera Bekkan (196)

4-20 Mikawa-cho, Naka-ku, Hiroshima 730. ☎ **082/248-2251.** Fax 082/248-2768. 35 rms (all with bath). A/C MINIBAR TV TEL. ¥12,000–¥25,000 ($120–$250) per person. All rates include breakfast and dinner. AE, DC, JCB, MC, V. Streetcar: 1, 2, or 6 to Hatchobori stop.

This modern ryokan is in the city center, just off Namiki Dori. Although the building itself is far from traditional, the rooms are Japanese style, with tatami mats, shoji screens, and a safe for valuables. There are large public baths. Dinner is served in your room (Western-style breakfasts are available). Rates vary depending on the meal you order for dinner and the number of people staying in the rooms.

INEXPENSIVE

Hiroshima Youth Hostel (197)

1-13-6 Ushitashin-machi, Higashi-ku, Hiroshima 732. ☎ **082/221-5343.** 104 beds. A/C. ¥2,000 ($20) per person. Breakfast ¥450 ($4.50) extra; dinner ¥750 ($7.50) extra. All rates include sheets. No credit cards. Bus: To the Ushitashin-machi 1-chome stop (a 15-minute ride; fare: ¥190/$1.90), then an 8-minute walk.

This youth hostel is very easy to find: The bus even announces the youth-hostel stop in English, and from there you'll see signs directing you. Located partway up a hill with good views, it accepts nonmembers. The staff all speak English, and they're enthusiastic about accepting foreigners (reservations in summer a must). Doors close at 9:30pm, but there's bilingual TV in the lounge.

Mikawa Ryokan

9-6 Kyobashi-cho, Minami-ku, Hiroshima 732. ☎ **082/261-2719.** Fax 082/263-2706. 13 rms (none with bath). A/C TV TEL. ¥6,000–¥7,000 ($60–$70) double; ¥9,000 ($90) triple. AE, V. Directions: Walk 7 minutes southwest.

This two-story member of the Japanese Inn Group prefers advance reservations. Rooms are simple tatami and come with coin-operated TV, heater, and air conditioning. Check-in is at 5pm, and the front doors close at 11pm. There's a coin-operated laundry facility.

$ Rijyo Kaikan (198)

1-5-3 Otemachi, Naka-ku, Hiroshima 730. ☎ **082/245-2322.** Fax 082/245-2315. 49 rms (all with bath). A/C TV TEL. ¥4,600–¥4,900 ($46–$49) per person twin. Additional bed ¥2,300 ($23) extra; breakfast ¥700 ($7) extra. No credit cards. Streetcar: 1, 2, or 6 to the Kamiyacho stop.

Located close to the Hondori covered shopping arcade and Peace Memorial Park, this ryokan is intended primarily as lodging for government office employees, but anyone can stay here if room permits. Check-in isn't until 4pm. The rooms are great for the price—bright, white, and cheerful. There are both Japanese and Western restaurants and a self-service cafeteria, Maple, where you can get a cup of coffee for only ¥200 ($2). If you want to stay here, it's best to make a reservation six months in advance.

DINING

EXPENSIVE

Atago

7-20 Nakamachi. ☎ **082/241-1111.** Reservations recommended. Set dinners ¥5,000–¥15,000 ($50–$150); set lunches ¥2,500–¥6,000 ($25–$60). AE, DC, JCB, MC, V. Daily 11:30am–2:30pm and 5–10pm. Streetcar: 1 to Chuden-mae. TEPPANYAKI.

This teppanyaki steak restaurant, next to the ANA Hotel on Peace Boulevard, is convenient if you're visiting the Peace Memorial Museum. It's strikingly modern with its marble tables and geometric lines, but kimono-clad waitresses bring drinks while chefs prepare steak and seafood before your eyes.

Castle View

ANA Hotel, 22nd floor, 7-20 Nakamachi. ☎ **082/241-1111.** Reservations recommended. Set dinners ¥8,000–¥14,000 ($80–$140); set lunches ¥2,500–¥5,500 ($25–$55). AE, DC, JCB, MC, V. Daily 11:30am–2:30pm and 5–10pm. Streetcar: 1 to Chuden-mae. FRENCH.

This restaurant is named for the view you'll have of the castle, but you have to look pretty hard to find it. Still, you do have a fine view of the city. A small, elegant restaurant decorated in gold and light pink, with comfortable chairs and a single rose on each table, this establishment offers steaks and seafood and a variety of other main courses on its seasonal menu.

MODERATE

✪ Kanawa (199)

On the Motoyasu River. ☎ **082/241-7416.** Reservations recommended. Main dishes ¥500–¥2,500 ($5–$25); set dinners ¥7,000–¥15,000 ($70–$150); set lunches ¥3,000–¥4,000 ($30–$40). AE, DC, JCB, MC, V. Mon–Sat 11am–2pm and 5–10pm. Streetcar: 1 to Chuden-mae. OYSTERS.

There are 10,000 rafts cultivating oysters in Hiroshima Bay, with a yearly output of 30,000 tons of shelled oysters. Needless to say, oysters are a Hiroshima specialty, and this houseboat moored on the Motoyasu River just off Peace (Heiwa) Boulevard not far from Peace Memorial Park is one of the best places to enjoy them. Although winter is the best time for fresh oysters, the owner of this restaurant has his own oyster rafts and freezes his best stock in January so that he's able to serve excellent oysters even in summer. This floating restaurant has been here more than 30 years, and dining is in tatami rooms with views of the river. The English-language menu lists oysters cooked about any way you like or can imagine. A la carte dishes include the popular baked oyster in its shell with lemon, tempura oyster, or oyster soup. If you feel like indulging, order one of the set meals that feature just oysters cooked in various ways, including in the shell, fried, in soup, and steamed.

Kushinobo (200)

2-18 Shintenchi. ☎ **082/245-9300.** Reservations recommended. Skewers ¥140–¥500 ($1.40–$5); set dinners ¥2,200–¥5,000 ($22–$50); set lunches ¥1,000 ($10). AE, DC, JCB, MC, V. Daily 11:30am–2pm and 5–10pm. Streetcar: 1, 2, or 6 to Hatchobori. KUSHIYAKI.

This is a lively, crowded restaurant with two floors of counter seating, where food on skewers is cooked before your eyes. There's a friendly "rub elbows with the locals" kind of atmosphere. Japanese knickknacks decorate the walls. While skewered offerings start as low as ¥140 ($1.40), expect to pay at least ¥3,000 ($30) for dinner with drinks. I had the *Kushinobo-gozen* with 10 skewers of vegetables, meat, and seafood, plus fresh vegetables, rice, soup, and dessert. You'll recognize the place by the shrine lanterns outside displaying the name and its rust-colored and wood exterior. There's a menu in English.

Le Train Blue

Kokusai Hotel, 3-13 Tatemachi. ☎ **082/248-2323.** Set dinners ¥3,000–¥8,000 ($30–$80); set lunches ¥800–¥2,500 ($8–$25). AE, DC, JCB, V. Daily 11:30am–midnight. Streetcar: 1, 2, or 6 to the Tatamachi. WESTERN.

This is Hiroshima's only revolving restaurant, making a full turn every hour. It's fashioned after the dining car of a train (supposedly the *Orient Express*), and each table is placed beside the window, making for privacy with a view. Reasonably priced, Le Train Blue's à la carte menu lists steak, seafood, lamb, veal, and duck; but the best bargain is the weekly set lunch. You can also come here just for a drink; cocktails are ¥850 ($8.50), and beer starts at ¥650 ($6.50). By the way, the chef speaks English.

Unkai

ANA Hotel, 5th floor, 7-20 Nakamachi. ☎ **082/241-1111.** Main dishes ¥2,000–¥3,500 ($20–$35); set dinners ¥5,000–¥15,000 ($50–$150); set lunches ¥1,800–¥4,500 ($18–$45). AE, DC, JCB, MC, V. Daily 11:30am–10pm. Streetcar: 1 to Chuden-mae. VARIED JAPANESE.

Another convenient restaurant if you're visiting Peace Memorial Park, Unkai overlooks a garden of stunted pine trees, azalea bushes, neatly arranged stones, and a pond full of golden carp—said to resemble Shukkei-en Garden in miniature. There's an English-language menu here, with such à la carte choices as tempura shrimp, abalone in butter served in its own shell, sashimi, rice porridge, and even the head of red snapper boiled in soy sauce. There are also set meals for such fare as shabu-shabu, tempura, kaiseki, and red-snapper sashimi. Teishoku lunches are served until 2pm, including noodles (¥850/$8.50), or for bigger appetites, obento lunch boxes (¥3,200/$32 and ¥5,500/$55).

INEXPENSIVE

$ Anderson Kitchen

7-1 Hondori. ☎ **082/247-2403.** Set meals ¥950–¥3,000 ($9.50–$30). DC, JCB, MC, V. Daily 7:30am–8:30pm. Closed second or third Wed of every month. Streetcar: 1, 2, or 6 to the Kamiyacho. INTERNATIONAL.

This restaurant, located on a corner of the Hondori covered shopping arcade not far from Peace Memorial Park, is a popular cafeteria on the second floor above its own bakery with the same name. There are several counters specializing in different types of food—for example, salads and sandwiches, fried dishes such as grilled chicken, desserts—while one counter sells drinks. Just pick up a tray and select the items you want. You pay at the end of each counter.

Caspi

Hotel Silk Plaza, 2nd floor, 14-1 Hatchobori. ☎ **082/227-8111.** Set dinners ¥1,800–¥4,900 ($18–$49); set lunches ¥900 ($9). AE, JCB, MC, V. Daily 11am–2:30pm and 5–8:30pm (last order). Streetcar: 1, 2, or 6 to the Hatchobori stop. WESTERN.

This simple restaurant serves a great bargain set lunch. Its menu changes daily, but when I was last there the special consisted of soup, salad, pork cutlet with vegetables, and coffee, with unlimited portions of salad.

Edosawa

13-13 Hachobori. ☎ **082/221-5428.** Nabe ¥1,500–¥2,500 ($15–$25). Daily 11:30am–1:30pm and 5–10pm. Streetcar: 1, 2, or 6 to the Hatchobori stop. CHANKO RYORI.

This restaurant, near the Silk Plaza Hotel, serves *chanko ryori,* the one-pot stews (*nabe*) served to sumo wrestlers. Recognize it by its white-and-black sign outside and a display case with plastic food and sumo wrestler dolls. Decor is sumo photos and noren. Dining is in private tatami rooms where you cook your large-portioned nabe, ususally with seafood or chicken, noodles, and vegetables at your own table.

Masui

14-13 Hatchobori. ☎ **082/227-2983.** Set meals ¥900–¥4,000 ($9–$40); lunch teishoku ¥750 ($7.50). No credit cards. Thurs–Tues 11am–8:45pm. Closed second Tues of every month. Streetcar: 1, 2, or 6 to Hatchobori. STEAKS/SHABU-SHABU/SUKIYAKI.

A very inexpensive, popular restaurant serving beef dishes, Masui is near Chugoku Bank, which is close to the Silk Plaza Hotel in the middle of town. Individual small servings of shabu-shabu or sukiyaki, for example, start at only ¥900 ($9). This two-story restaurant is especially crowded during lunchtime, when it churns out plate after plate of teishoku specials. The ¥750 ($7.50) teishoku gets you a hamburger patty, ham, omelet, pork cutlet, and rice, but if that's too expensive you can forgo the hamburger and get the tonkatsu teishoku for ¥350 ($3.50).

$ Okonomi-Mura (201)

5-13 Shin-tenchi. ☎ **082/241-8758.** Set dinners ¥700–¥1,100 ($7–$11). No credit cards. Daily 11am–9pm, but some stalls stay open to 1am. Streetcar: 1, 2, or 6 to the Hatchobori. OKONOMIYAKI.

Although the people of Osaka claim to have made okonomiyaki popular among the masses, the people of Hiroshima claim to have made it an art. In any case, *okonomiyaki* is a kind of Japanese pancake, filled with cabbage, meat, and other fillings. Whereas in Osaka the ingredients are all mixed together, in Hiroshima each layer is prepared separately, which means that the chefs have to be quite skilled at keeping the whole thing together. The best place in town to witness these short-order cooks at their trade is here. Its name means "okonomiyaki village," and that's what it is—three floors of individual stalls, each dishing out okonomiyaki (the food still remains a dish for the masses). I recommend Chii-chan (☎ 082/249-8102) on the second floor, who stays open until 1am and has an English-language menu. Chii-chan and his all-girl staff sell between 200 and 500 okonomiyaki a day!

All stalls offer basically the same menu—just sit down at one of the counters and watch how the chef first spreads pancake mix on a hot griddle, then follows it with a layer of cabbage and bean sprouts, bacon, and then an egg on top. If you want, you can have yours with udon (thick white noodles) or soba (thin yellow noodles). Helpings are enormous. You'll find the place just off the Hondori shopping arcade. Highly recommended, it's one of Hiroshima's most beloved establishments.

Suishin (176)

6-7 Tatemachi. ☎ **082/247-4411.** Main dishes ¥1,000–¥2,700 ($10–$27); kamameshi (rice casseroles) ¥750 ($7.50). AE, DC, JCB, MC, V. Thurs–Tues 11:20am–10pm (last order 9pm). Streetcar: 1, 2, or 6 to Tatemachi. RICE CASSEROLES.

This is the main shop of a locally owned restaurant chain specializing in *kamameshi* (rice casseroles). First opened in 1950, this chain now has five locations in Hiroshima alone. The main shop, in the middle of town, has five floors of dining, and though the decor is rather simple, this place is very popular for its rice casseroles topped with such Hiroshima delicacies as oysters, mushrooms, sea bream, sea eels, shrimp, and chestnuts. It sells about 800 kamameshi per day, a number that swells to as many as 2,000 on Sunday. To deal with the demand, the restaurant owner invented his own conveyor-belt oven, which can cook 180 kamameshi in an hour. Other dishes include oysters, eel, globe fish, flatfish, and sardines. Lunch specials change daily. There are also take-out boxes of seafood and vegetables, making this a good place to buy your picnic lunch.

12 Miyajima

8 miles NW of Hiroshima

Easily reached in about 45 minutes from Hiroshima, Miyajima is a treasure of an island only 1.2 miles off the mainland in the Seto Inland Sea. No doubt you've seen pictures of its most famous landmark—a huge red torii, or shrine gate, rising up out of the water. Erected in 1875 and made of camphor wood, it's the largest torii in Japan, measuring more than 53 feet tall, and guards Miyajima's main attraction, Itsukushima Shrine.

Miyajima is one of the most scenic spots in Japan—known as one of the three most beautiful—an exceptionally beautiful island held sacred since ancient times. In the olden days no one was allowed to do anything so human as to give birth or die on the island, with the result that both the pregnant and the ill were quickly ferried across to the mainland. Even today there's no cemetery on Miyajima. Covered with cherry trees illuminating the island with snowy petals in spring, as well as with maple trees emblazoning it in reds and golds in autumn, Miyajima is home to tame deer that roam freely through the village and to monkeys that swing through the woods. It's a delightful island on which to stroll around—but avoid coming on a weekend.

ESSENTIALS

The **telephone area code** for Miyajima, lying in Hiroshima Prefecture, is 0829.

GETTING THERE The easiest way to get to Miyajima is from Hiroshima. You can travel from Hiroshima by JR **train, streetcar,** or **bus,** all of which deposit you at Miyajimaguchi, from which it's just a 10-minute ferry ride to the island of Miyajima. If you have a Japan Rail Pass, you can ride free on the JR **ferry,** which leaves from the pier right in front of the train station. Or you can take a direct ferry (not JR) from Hiroshima, which arrives at Miyajima 23 minutes later and costs ¥1,440 ($14.40).

VISITOR INFORMATION Before leaving Tokyo or Kyoto, drop by the Tourist Information Center for a copy of "Hiroshima and Miyajima."

In Miyajima stop off at the **Tourist Information Office** (☎ 0829/44-0008), located in the JR ferry terminal. Open every day from 8:30am to 7:30pm, it has a brochure in English with a map. For ¥300 ($3) you can rent a radio guide that describes in English 20 places of interest noted on a companion map—a great convenience!

WHAT TO SEE & DO

Miyajima's major attraction, **Itsukushima Shrine** is less than a 10-minute walk from the ferry pier along a narrow street lined with souvenir shops and restaurants. Founded back in 592 to honor three female deities, the wooden shrine is built out over the water so that when the tide is in it appears as though the shrine is floating. A brilliant vermilion, it contrasts starkly with the wooded hills in the background and the blue of the sky above, casting its reflection in the waters below. The majority of the buildings are thought to date from the 16th century, preserving the original style of 12th-century architecture, but they have been repaired repeatedly through the centuries. Most of the buildings of the shrine are closed, but from sunrise to sunset daily (usually 6:30am to 6pm in summer and to 5pm in winter) and for ¥300 ($3), you can walk along the 770-foot covered dock that threads its way past the outer part of the main shrine and the oldest Noh stage in Japan. From the shrine you have a good view of the red torii standing in the water. If you're lucky you might get to see bugako put on for one of the many tour groups that pass through. An ancient musical court dance, *bugako* was introduced to Japan centuries ago from India through China and Korea. The costume of the dancer is orange, matching the shrine around him.

Incidentally, I should also add that if you happen to see Itsukushima Shrine when the tide is in and it's seemingly floating on water, you should consider yourself very lucky indeed. Most of the time the lovely shrine is floating above nothing more glamorous than mud. That's when a little imagination comes in handy.

As you exit from the shrine, you'll find the **Miyajima Museum of Historic Treasures,** which contains replicas of national treasures (the real ones are safely locked away), old books, armor, and household items. Perhaps of more interest is the **Miyajima Municipal History and Folklore Museum,** a few minutes' walk from the shrine. This one has explanations in English to guide you through the 150-year-old house, which once belonged to a wealthy merchant. Open daily from 8:30am to 4:30pm, it features farm equipment, water jars, cooking objects, carved-wood boxes, furniture, and items used in daily life. Admission is ¥250 ($2.50).

Other attractions on Miyajima include an **aquarium;** 1,750-foot-high **Mount Misen,** the largest peak on the island and easily reached by cable car (¥1,500/$15 round-trip) from Momijidani Park; and **beaches** for swimming.

ACCOMMODATIONS

Higashiya (202)

5-8-3 Miyajima 739-05. ☎ **0829/44-2151.** Fax 0829/44-2150. 30 rms (all with bath). A/C MINIBAR TV TEL. ¥12,000–¥20,000 ($120–$200) per person. Off-season discounts available. All rates include breakfast, dinner, and service. AE, DC, JCB, MC, V.

This is an ordinary ryokan by the looks of the Westernized lobby. But it's conveniently located on the main street of town, a five-minute walk from the ferry; also, the owner speaks English and is very helpful. Some rooms have a great view of the bay (they're more expensive), while others have mountain views. Rooms are discounted off-season, especially in the calm of winter.

✪ Iwaso Ryokan (203)

Momijidani, Miyajima, Saeki-gun 739-05. ☎ **0829/44-2233.** Fax 0829/44-2230. 40 rms (30 with bath). A/C MINIBAR TV TEL. ¥20,000–¥40,000 ($200–$400) per person. Cottage, ¥35,000–¥50,000 ($350–$500) per person. All rates include two meals and service charge. AE, JCB, V.

A 15-minute walk from the ferry pier, this is the most famous ryokan on the island, and with a history spanning more than 130 years, it was also the first ryokan to open on Miyajima. It's highly recommended for a splurge, with the price dependent on the room, its view, and the meals you select. There are four price levels of dinners, and Western breakfasts are served on request. The newest part of the ryokan was built in 1981, and though some of its newer rooms have very peaceful and relaxing views of a stream and woods, I prefer the rooms dating from about 50 years ago (they have more individuality). But if you really want to go all out and live in style, there are also a couple of separate cottages more than 70 years old that are exquisitely decorated and come with old wooden tubs. You can open your shoji screens here to see maples, a gurgling brook, and woods, all in utter privacy. You'll be treated like royalty here, but of course you have to pay for it.

Jukeiso (204)

Miyajima, Saeki-gun 739-05. ☎ **0829/44-0300.** Fax 0829/44-0388. 13 rms (all with bath). A/C MINIBAR TV TEL. ¥18,000 ($180) per person. All rates include breakfast, dinner, and service. AE, DC, JCB, MC, V.

If you're looking for a smaller ryokan that's a bit more moderately priced, this is a good choice. Although it's a hike from the ferry pier (about a 20-minute walk), it sits on a small hill and affords some pleasant views of Miyajima. In addition, the owner here speaks English. The ryokan was started some 50 years ago by his grandmother, though the present building is much more modern. All but two of the rooms are Japanese tatami rooms. Western breakfasts are available on request. On the fourth floor is a French restaurant with nice views.

Miyajima Grand Hotel

Miyajima, Saeki-gun 739-05. ☎ **0829/44-2411.** 55 rms (all with bath). A/C MINIBAR TV TEL. ¥15,000–¥50,000 ($150–$500) per person. Weekday and winter discounts. All rates include two meals. AE, JCB, MC, V. Directions: Free shuttle bus service from the ferry pier.

This modern building looks like a hotel rather than a ryokan, and while 27 of its rooms are Japanese-style tatami rooms, it also has 20 combination rooms with both twin beds and separate tatami areas, as well as eight Western-style rooms. The Grand is a typical modern ryokan. Western breakfasts are served on request.

Pension Miyajima

796 Miyajimacho. ☎ **0829/44-0039.** Fax 0829/44-2773. 7 rms (all with bath). TEL TV. ¥14,000 ($140) double; ¥19,500 ($195) triple; ¥24,000 ($240) quad. All prices include breakfast. AE, DC, MC, V.

A European-style pension with wood wainscoting and classical music playing, Pension Miyajima, seven minutes from the ferry pier, offers both futon and beds. There's a tiny restaurant in the entrance (open from 11:30am to 2pm and serving okonomiyake for ¥480 to ¥1,000/$4.80–$10), and a lovely dining room with a piano where breakfast and French dinner (¥3,000 to ¥5,000/$30 to $50) are served. The owner is the chef and speaks English. In this family-friendly establishment, little ones stay with you for only ¥1,000 ($10), and child's meals (¥1,500/$15) can be ordered.

DINING

Fujitaya (205)

☎ **0829/44-0151.** Anagomeshi teishoku ¥2,300 ($23). No credit cards. Daily 11am–5pm. ANAGOMESHI.

This pleasant restaurant is located a 20-minute walk from the ferry pier, on the right side of the road leading toward Mt. Misen and Daishoin as you exit from Itsukushima Shrine. It has a history of more than 80 years; but although the building itself is recent, a traditional atmosphere is created with a wooden ceiling, shoji lamps, and a back courtyard with a maple tree, moss-covered rocks, and water running from a bamboo pipe into a pool carved into a flat rock. Fujitaya serves only *anagomeshi* (barbecued conger eel on rice), available with side dishes (such as pickled vegetables), soup, and tea. It closes when no *anago* is available.

Heike (206)

Miyajima. ☎ **0829/44-0300.** Reservations recommended for evening. Set meals ¥1,800–¥5,000 ($18–$50). Daily 11am–2:30pm and 6–9pm. VARIED JAPANESE.

This restaurant at the bottom of the stairs below Jukeiso Ryokan has great views of the bay, the Otorii, and Tohoto Pagoda from large, open tatami rooms. The tempura teishoku with various tempura-fried dishes, rice, pickles, savory custard, soup, salad, and fruit costs ¥2,500 ($25). Try the fried-oyster set meal, the Miyajima-gozen, for ¥3,500 ($35).

Tonookajaya (207)

Omachi, Miyajima. ☎ **0829/44-2421.** Reservations not accepted. Main dishes ¥550–¥730 ($5.50–$7.30). Daily 10am–5pm (until 6pm in summer). NOODLES.

Sit inside or out at this tiny shop next to the five-storied pagoda, a 10-minute walk from the ferry. The *ryuzan matsu* (Pinus thumbergii), a 200-year-old pine tree that has been trained to grow 30 meters on either side of the trunk, is in front of the shop and makes for interesting scenery. The shop serves mostly *udon* (thick wheat noodles) but also offers *omochi chikara* (stickly rice cakes) and *amazake* (a sweet rice porridge without sugar). Beer starts at ¥350 ($3.50).

Shikoku 10

The smallest of Japan's four main islands, Shikoku is also one of the least visited by foreigners. That's surprising considering the natural beauty of its rugged mountains, its mild climate, and its most famous monuments—88 sacred Buddhist temples. It's the wish of many Japanese to make a pilgrimage to all 88 temples at least once in their lifetime as a tribute to the great Buddhist priest Kobo Daishi, who was born in Shikoku in 774 and who founded the Shingon sect of Buddhism. Many Japanese make the trip upon retirement.

Such a pilgrimage has been popular since the Edo Period, in the belief that a successful completion of the tour exonerates Buddhist followers from rebirth. It used to take several months to visit all 88 temples on foot, and even today you can see the pilgrims making their rounds dressed in white—only now they go by bus, which cuts traveling time down to two weeks.

SEEING SHIKOKU

I suggest that you visit Shikoku on your travels through southern Japan. You could, for example, travel through Honshu to Kyushu and from Kyushu start back north via Shikoku, or vice versa. Ferries connect Shikoku to Beppu on Kyushu Island, as well as to Tokyo, Osaka, Kobe, and Hiroshima on Honshu Island. In fact, for centuries the only way to reach Shikoku was by boat, but the completion of one of the longest bridges in the world changed all that. Opened in 1988, the Seto Ohashi Bridge measures 5.83 miles from shore to shore and connects Kojima on Honshu with Sakaide on Shikoku. Those of you aboard the Shinkansen, therefore, need change trains only in Okayama for trains bound for either Takamatsu or Matsuyama on Shikoku.

1 Takamatsu

496 miles W of Tokyo, 44 miles S of Okayama

The second-largest populated town on Shikoku, Takamatsu is on the northeastern coast of the island, overlooking the Seto Inland Sea. Takamatsu means "high pine," and the city served as the feudal capital of the powerful Matsudaira clan from 1642 until the Meiji Restoration in 1868. Takamatsu's most famous site is Ritsurin Park, one of the most outstanding gardens in Japan.

What's Special About Shikoku

Buddhist Temples

- A total of 88 sacred temples ringing the island—a visit to all of them is Japan's most popular pilgrimage.

Architectural Highlights

- Matsuyama Castle, built almost 400 years ago.
- Shikoku Mura Village, an open-air museum of 21 houses and buildings dating from the Edo Period.
- Dogo Onsen Honkan, a three-story wooden bathhouse built in 1894 and one of the most delightful public bathhouses in the country.
- Kompira Grand Playhouse, Japan's oldest Kabuki theater.

Parks

- Ritsurin Park, laid out in the 1600s and one of Japan's most outstanding landscaped gardens.

ESSENTIALS

The **telephone area code** for Takamatsu, lying in Kagawa Prefecture, is 0878.

GETTING THERE **By Plane** Flying time is 1 hour and 10 minutes from Tokyo, 1 hour from Fukuoka, and 2 hours and 10 minutes from Sapporo. There are also flights from Nagoya (1 hour) and Osaka (45 minutes), as well as from Seoul (1½ hours).

By Train Trains depart from Okayama approximately twice an hour, reaching Takamatsu in one hour.

By Bus Buses depart from Tokyo Station nightly, reaching Takamatsu in about 11 hours.

By Boat Hydrofoils connect Takamatsu with Osaka in 2 hours and 10 minutes.

VISITOR INFORMATION If you want some detailed information on Shikoku, be sure to drop by the Tourist Information Center in Tokyo or Kyoto for a leaflet called "Inland Sea and Shikoku."

The **Takamatsu City Information Office** (☎ 0878/51-2009) is located just outside the train station and is open every day except New Year's from 9am to 5pm. Stop here for an English-language map of the city and directions to your hotel. They have a useful brochure, "Your Traveling Companion Kagawa."

If you are in need of a home culture fix or planning to stay in the area, head for the **I-Pal Kagawa** (☎ 0878/37-5901) in Chuo Park, where magazines and newspapers in many languages are on stands and CNN is on the tube. Information on cultural activities in the area is also available. Open Tuesday to Sunday from 9am to 6pm.

GETTING AROUND The Takamatsu train station is on the coast of the Seto Inland Sea, only a few minutes' walk from the pier where ferries depart for Honshu and Shodo islands. All the hotels and restaurants listed below, as well as Ritsurin Park, are located south and southeast of the train station. Chuo-dori Street is the town's main avenue and runs south from the train station past Ritsurin Park, passing the Takamatsu Grand Hotel, the Tokyu Inn, and the Rihga Hotel Zest on the way.

Buses and **trams** depart from in front of the train station. The tram station, called Kotoden Chikko Station, is across the street from the train station, next to the Takamatsu Grand Hotel.

WHAT TO SEE & DO

The main attractions of Takamatsu are spread out in the city but are easily reached by bus, tram, or train from the train station.

THE TOP ATTRACTIONS

RITSURIN PARK Ritsurin Park (☎ 0878/33-7411) was once the summer retreat of the Matsudaira family. Work on the park began in the 1600s and took about 100 years to complete. Using the backdrop of adjacent Mt. Shiun in a principle known as "borrowed landscaping," the park incorporates the mountain into its overall design. Basically, the garden can be divided into two parts: a traditional, classical southern garden and a modern northern garden with wide grassy lawns.

The **southern garden** holds the most interest for visitors. Arranged around the prescribed 6 ponds and 13 scenic mounds, it represents what is called a strolling garden, in which each bend of the footpath—indeed, every new step—brings another perspective into view, another combination of rock, tree, and mountain. The garden is absolutely exquisite, and when I was there a mist was rolling off Mt. Shiun, lending a mysteriousness to the landscape. After all, what better fits the image of traditional Japan than mist and pine trees? Altogether, there are 1,500 pine trees and 500 cherry trees in Ritsurin Park, which you should tour in a counterclockwise fashion to appreciate fully the changing views.

Also in the park are a museum of local folk art and handcrafts, a zoo, and a shop where local products of Kagawa Prefecture are sold, including kites, masks, wood carvings, umbrellas, fans, and bamboo vases. Be sure to stop off at the park's teahouse for a cup of frothy green tea. Called Kikugetsu-tei, the teahouse dates from feudal days. There's a separate entrance charge to Kikugetsu-tei of ¥310 ($3.10); a cup of ceremonial tea costs another ¥340 ($3.40).

Ritsurin Park is open daily from sunrise to sunset, approximately 7am to 5pm in winter and 5:30am to 7pm June through August. The admission fee is ¥310 ($3.10). The park is about 10 minutes from Takamatsu train station by bus or tram—the tram stop is called Ritsurin-Koen. If you have a Japan Rail Pass, you might even consider going by JR train traveling in the direction of Tokushima; get off at Ritsurin-koen Kita Guchi, which is near the north entrance to the park.

SHIKOKU MURA VILLAGE Shikoku Mura Village (☎ 0878/43-3111) is an open-air museum of 21 Shikoku houses dating from the Edo Period. The houses, which are picturesquely situated on the slope of Yashima Hill, include thatch-roofed homes of farmers and fishermen, a 150-year-old rural Kabuki stage, a tea-ceremony house, and sheds for pressing sugar and for producing paper out of mulberry bark. There's also a suspended bridge made of vines, a familiar sight in Shikoku as a means for crossing the island's many gorges and ravines—if you look closely, however, you'll see that this one is reinforced by cables.

It takes at least an hour to stroll through the village, which is open daily from 8:30am to 4:30pm (to 5pm in summer). The admission fee is ¥500 ($5). I heartily recommend this village if you have not had the opportunity to see similar villages in Takayama or Kawasaki, since they convey better than anything else rural life in Japan in centuries past. Shikoku Mura Village is about a 20-minute tram ride from the Kotoden Chikko tram station. You can also get there by JR train traveling in the direction of Tokushima. The station for both is called Yashima.

OTHER ATTRACTIONS

From Yashima Station, close to Shikoku Mura Village, you can take a cable car to the top of Yashima Plateau, where you'll find **Yashimaji Temple,** 84th of Shikoku's 88 sacred temples. Yashima is also famous as the site of a 12th-century battle between the rival clans of Taira and Minamoto as they fought for control over Japan. The Minamoto clan eventually won and established its shogunate court in Kamakura.

The **Takamatsu City Museum of Art** (*Takamatsu Bijutusukan*), 10-4 Konyamachi (☎ 0878/23-1711), is about a 10-minute walk south of Takamatsu Station. Walk along Chuo-dori past the Hyogomachi covered shopping arcade, and turn left a couple of blocks later onto Bijutsukan Dori. The museum features a permanent exhibition of postwar Japanese art, as well as changing exhibitions of Japanese and Western artists. Cost of the permanent exhibit is ¥200 ($2), and the museum's hours are 9am to 4:30pm Tuesday through Sunday (until 6:30pm on Friday).

If you are interested in historical battles or in the literary piece *Heike Monogatari* written in the Kamakura Period, a trip to the wax museum Heike Story History Hall (☎ 0878/23-8400) is in order. *Heike Monogatari Rekishikan* exhibits the story of the battle on Shikoku Island between the Hei and Gen clans through some 300 wax figures, great costumes, and sound. The last diaorama of an automated blind *biwa* (lute) player shows the tradition of chanting the poetic-form Heike. Cost is a bit steep: ¥1,200 ($12). It's open daily from 9am to 5:30pm. Take the Kotoden bus to Asahimachi-mae stop; then it's a three-minute walk.

If you're spending several days in Takamatsu, there are several attractions in the surrounding countryside worthy of your attention. **Shodo Island** (*Shodoshima*) is the second-largest island in the Seto Inland Sea and is easily reached from the ferry pier close to the Takamatsu train station in about an hour. Most visitors come to Shodo Island to see its natural wonders, including Kankakei Gorge, which measures 3.7 miles long; a monkey park with more than 1,300 wild monkeys; and Shihozashi Lookout, with its panoramic views of the Inland Sea. Shodo also contains a miniature replica of Shikoku's 88 sacred temples, located so close together on this small island that a pilgrimage on foot here takes only five days or so. An extensive network of public buses crisscrosses the island, but if you're on a tight schedule, you may wish to join one of the full- or half-day sightseeing tours available. More information on Shodo Island can be obtained by calling the Shodoshima Tourist Office (☎ 0879/62-1111).

One of the best historical side trips you can take is to **Kotohira,** home of Kotohiragu Shrine as well as the oldest Kabuki theater in Japan. It takes about an hour to reach Kotohira by train from Takamatsu Station, but that isn't the end of it—the shrine itself is at the top of 785 granite steps. If that's too much for you, you can hire porters who will take you only to the main gate (called Omon in Japanese), which is reached after climbing 365 steps. The cost of riding in one of these palanquins is ¥5,000 ($50) one-way and ¥6,500 ($65) if you're carried back down.

At any rate, the long trek up to Kotohiragu Shrine begins by exiting from the Kotohira train station's only exit, taking a left after passing under the first torii gate, and then turning right on a narrow, shop-lined street. Presently you'll reach the first flight of stairs. If you're making a detour to the Kabuki theater (described below), turn left after the 22nd step, from which the theater is only a three-minute walk away; otherwise, continue climbing upward—you should reach the main shrine after a 30-minute workout. You'll be rewarded with a sweeping view of the surrounding countryside, as well as the shrine itself. Popularly known as Kompira-San, Kotohiragu

Shrine was originally founded in the 11th century but has been rebuilt many times, with the main shrine buildings re-erected about 100 years ago.

Since you're in the vicinity, I highly recommend a visit to **Kompira Grand Playhouse** (208), known as *Kompira O-Shibai* in Japanese. Open Wednesday through Monday from 9am to 5pm and charging an admission fee of ¥300 ($3), it is stunning in its simplicity and delightful in its construction. Since there was no electricity in 1835, when it was built, the sides of the hall are rows of shoji screens and wooden coverings, which could be opened and closed to control the amount of light reaching the stage. Notice the tatami seating, the paper lanterns, and the revolving stage, which was turned by eight men in the basement. You can also tour the various makeup and dressing rooms behind the stage. Actual Kabuki plays are staged once a year in April, but as you may well imagine, tickets are hard to come by.

Kobo Daishi is said to have been born at **Zentsu-ji** (number 75 of the 88 temples), and here you visit a circular tunnel underground, which is pitch black, symbolizing the darkness of the human mind. Walk along by feeling the wall (painted—so they tell us—with mandalas, angels, and lotus flowers to guide you) with your left hand. You are supposed to come out cleansed. It does take an act of faith to walk into the unknown in total darkness. It is 40 minutes by JR express train or one station farther than Kotohira to Zentsu-ji Station and a 25-minute walk from the station.

ACCOMMODATIONS

RYOKAN

Hotel Kawaroku

1-2 Hyakken-machi, Takamatsu 760. ☎ **0878/21-5666.** Fax 0878/21-7301. 63 rms (all with bath). A/C MINIBAR TV TEL. ¥12,000–¥15,000 ($120–$150) twin; ¥10,000–¥30,000 ($100–$300) per person in Japanese-style room, including two meals. Discounts in winter. AE, DC, JCB, MC, V. Station: Takamatsu (10 minutes south).

First opened as a ryokan more than a 100 years ago, this place was destroyed during an air raid in World War II; it's now a modern structure with 45 Japanese-style and 18 Western-style rooms, all with a safe and the usual amenities. It's close to the Mitsukoshi department store and several shopping arcades in the heart of the city. The Western-style rooms are white, bright, and clean, while the Japanese-style rooms are simply furnished and have the wonderful smell of tatami. Le Bon 6, the hotel's one restaurant, serves French cuisine (described in detail in "Dining," below); if you want Japanese food, it will be served in your room.

✪ Tokiwa Honkan (209)

1-8-2 Tokiwa-cho, Takamatsu 760. ☎ **0878/61-5577.** 24 rms (17 with bath). A/C MINIBAR TV TEL. ¥12,000–¥21,000 ($120–$210) per person. All rates include breakfast and dinner. Tram: Kawaramachi Station (2 minutes).

This traditional Japanese ryokan has a delightful inner courtyard reminiscent of those found around teahouses, with a pond, dwarf pine trees, golden carp, stone lanterns, wooden passageways, and vermilion railings. The ryokan is topped with a donjon, making it look like a shogun's castle. Built in 1954, the ryokan originally catered to foreigners, but it now receives only about 20 foreign guests a year. A little more than half the rooms are equipped with a private bathtub, but public baths are on each floor. There are also large communal baths separate for men and women.

HOTELS

Rihga Hotel Zest

9-1 Furujinmachi, Takamatsu 760. ☎ **0878/22-3555.** Fax 0878/22-7516. 133 rms. A/C MINIBAR TV TEL. ¥14,160 ($141.60) double; ¥15,860–¥28,325 ($158.60–$283.25) twin. All rates include tax and service. AE, DC, JCB, MC, V. Station: Takamatsu (7 minutes south).

Located almost directly across the street from the Tokyu Inn on Chuo-dori Street, a seven-minute walk south of Takamatsu Station, this beige-brick hotel features three restaurants serving Japanese, Chinese, and French cuisine, as well as a bar. There's no room service here, but the in-room minibar is well stocked. Rooms on the ninth floor have been nicely remodeled but are not more expensive, so ask for one.

Royal Park Hotel

1-3-11 Kawara-machi, Takamatsu 760. ☎ **0878/23-2222.** Fax 0878/23-2233. 50 rms. A/C MINIBAR TV TEL. ¥18,000–¥20,000 ($180–$200) double; ¥20,000–¥22,000 ($200–$220) twin. AE, DC, JCB, MC, V. Tram: Kawaramachi (4 minutes north).

Built in 1989, this sleek, art deco–style hotel, a five-minute taxi ride from Takamatsu Station, offers beautiful design from the lobby lounge to the rooms. Blond wood, faux-marble sinks, and soft pastels set the tone for rooms, which have TV with pay video among other amenities. Singles are larger than standard and have semi-double beds. Slip your key into the slot next to the door to turn on lights. South-facing rooms have the best views. Services include a free newspaper. There are three restaurants, one serving teppanyaki.

Takamatsu Grand Hotel

1-5-10 Kotobuki-cho, Takamatsu 760. ☎ **0878/51-5757.** Fax 0878/21-9422. 136 rms. A/C MINIBAR TV TEL. ¥13,000 ($130) double; ¥13,000–¥21,000 ($130–$210) twin. AE, DC, JCB, MC, V. Station: Takamatsu.

In terms of location, price, and view, this is one of the best deals in town. A striped building on Chuo-dori, it's quite near Takamatsu Station, the main artery for trains to the rest of Shikoku and for ferries from Honshu and Kyushu, and on the edge of Tamamo Park, formerly the site of Takamatsu Castle and now an oasis of pine trees, three-story turrets, moats, and a classical garden. Both the lobby on the third floor and the Yashima Sky Restaurant on the seventh floor command sweeping views of the park. The higher-priced rooms facing the park have the nicest views. There are seven bars and restaurants and a shopping arcade in the hotel complex.

DINING

Takamatsu is known throughout Japan for its *sanuki udon*—thick white noodles made from wheat flour. With Takamatsu as the center of this industry, there are as many as 400 sanuki manufacturers and more than 2,000 noodle shops in Kagawa Prefecture. It has been estimated that about 10% of the population eats sanuki noodles every day, a percentage that's about five times higher than in any other area of Japan. Takamatsu also has a fresh supply of fish from the Seto Inland Sea.

EXPENSIVE

Le Bon 6

Hotel Kawaroku, 1-2 Hyakken-machi. ☎ **0878/21-5666.** Main dishes ¥2,500–¥6,000 ($25–$60); set meals ¥6,500 and ¥8,800 ($65 and $88), set lunches ¥1,000–¥3,500 ($10–$35). AE, DC, JCB, MC, V. Daily 11:30am–1:30pm and 5–8:30pm. FRENCH.

This is one of Takamatsu's best-known French restaurants. The Japanese chef here studied and worked for many years in both France and Belgium and, representing Japan, won a gold medal in 1982 at a world food contest held in Luxembourg. The emphasis at this restaurant is on food rather than on decor, and the menu includes seafood, beef, and lamb dishes. The chef takes special pride in his creations for the set meals, which change monthly. These dishes are so beautifully arranged you almost hate to eat them. If you're on a budget, consider coming for one of the set lunches.

MODERATE

Milano No Okazuyasan

Egou Bldg., 11-14 Kamei-cho. ☎ **0878/37-1782.** Main dishes ¥980–¥1,600 ($9.80–$16); pasta ¥750–¥1,000 ($7.50–$10); set meals ¥2,200–¥7,400 ($22–$74). No credit cards. Daily 11am–9pm. Tram: Kawaramachi (3 minutes). NORTHERN ITALIAN.

Hospitable chef-owner, Mr. Takeda, speaks some English and has created an Italian atmosphere with red-and-green tablecloths and Italian pottery and music. An English-language menu (with charming mistakes like "castard pudding maid from fresh cream") features baked scampi or broiled chicken with olive oil, garlic, and red pepper. Don't miss the homemade bread, also the homemade pasta and desserts. Finish with a cappuccino (¥380/$3.80).

Tenkatsu (210)

7-8 Hyogomachi. ☎ **0878/21-5380.** Reservations required. Dishes ¥300–¥2,500 ($3–$25); set lunches ¥800–¥1,000 ($8–$10); set dinners ¥1,000–¥8,000 ($10–$80). AE, DC, JCB, MC, V. Daily 11am–10pm. Directions: Walk 10 minutes south of Takamatsu Station on Chuo-dori, turn right at the Hyogomachi covered shopping arcade, and go through the arcade; the restaurant will be immediately on your left. TEMPURA/SUSHI.

This well-known tempura and sushi restaurant is in a modern-looking building with a plastic-food display case and a window where passersby can watch a chef prepare sushi. Inside the restaurant are tatami mats and tables, but I suggest sitting at the counter, which encircles a large pool filled with fish, mainly flatfish. As customers order, fish are swooped out of the tanks with nets—they certainly couldn't be fresher, in fact, still quivering even though sliced for sashimi. Although the menu here is in Japanese only, there are pictures accompanying some of the tempura and sushi courses. A specialty of the house is wine, served every month with something different in it. In March, for example, it's peach blossoms; in April, cherry blossoms.

INEXPENSIVE

$ Hansuke (211)

9-10 Hyogomachi. ☎ **0878/51-5653.** Skewer ¥100 ($1). No credit cards. Mon–Sat 11:30am–1pm and 4–10pm. Closed national hols. Station: Takamatsu (10 minutes south). YAKITORI.

This yakitori-ya, just around the corner from the Tokyu Inn in the Hyogomachi shopping arcade, has been in operation for more than 30 years, making it one of the oldest yakitori shops in town, if not the oldest. Simple and cheap, it's a greasy spoon in the true sense of the word; the grill looks as if it's been here from the beginning. The yakitori, however, is excellent, as is the *kabayaki* (filet of eel ¥1,500/$15). The real specialty of Hansuke, however, is its namesake, *hansuke,* which according to the shop owner means "heads of eel stuck on a skewer." Both I and the Japanese I was with thought it was one of the most unappetizing sights we had ever seen, but in a spontaneous burst of adventure we decided to try it. I don't want to spoil your own experience by telling you what it was like, but be prepared for lots of bones.

Kanaizumi (212)

Daikumachi. ☎ **0878/21-6688.** Set meals ¥680–¥3,000 ($6.80–$30). AE, JCB, MC, V. Daily 10:30am–9:30pm. Station: Takamatsu (15 minutes). SANUKI UDON.

A bit classier than your usual noodle shop, it's easily recognizable from the outside by a huge red paper lantern hanging in front of the restaurant and a front window where sanuki noodles are being made by hand. Although the menu is in Japanese, pictures accompany each set meal, which comes with noodles and a combination of various vegetables and meats. You can also order a bowl of noodles without side dishes for just ¥400 ($4). I had *niku-nabe udon* (¥1,000/$10), a bowl of noodles, leeks, thin slices of beef, and (ultra-chewy) rice cake (*mochi*) in hot broth. I dipped each morsel first into a mixture of raw egg, just as one does with sukiyaki. Be prepared for slippery noodles and the good-natured slurping of a noodle shop.

✪ Maruichi (213)

1-4-13 Tokiwa-cho. ☎ **0878/61-7623.** Main dishes ¥100–¥750 ($1–$7.50); course meal ¥2,000 ($20). No credit cards. Mon–Sat 5–11pm. Tram: Kawaramachi Station (1 minute). YAKITORI.

Although a drinking establishment, it's also a great place for an inexpensive meal. Cozy and friendly, it's decorated with colorful kites, heavy wooden beams, and a stone floor. An English-language menu lists octopus sashimi, *kimchee* (Korean spiced cabbage) with pork, mushrooms with melted cheese, salads, and, of course, yakitori. An evening of eating, drinking, and merriment here should cost about ¥2,000 ($20) per person. Maruichi is easy to spot from the outside by its huge red lantern and circle (*maru*) with a horizontal line (*ichi*) through it.

Zaigoudon-Waraya

91 Yashima-Nakamachi. ☎ **0878/43-3115.** Sanuki udon ¥400–¥2,300 ($4–$23). No credit cards. Daily 10am–7:30pm. Tram: Kotoden Yashima Station (10 minutes). SANUKI UDON NOODLES.

Another noodle restaurant you might want to try, especially if you're going to Shikoku Mura Village, it's located just below the village in a 100-year-old thatched house (look for the waterwheel). It features handmade noodles, with the combination udon and tempura dish especially popular.

2 Matsuyama

496 miles W of Tokyo, 120 miles E of Takamatsu, 132 miles SW of Okayama

Although Matsuyama is Shikoku's largest town, with a population of more than 440,000, it has the relaxed atmosphere of a small town. Located on the island's northwest coast, Matsuyama features one of Japan's best-preserved feudal castles and what I consider to be the most delightful public bathhouse in the country.

ESSENTIALS

The **telephone area code** for Matsuyama, lying in Ehime Prefecture, is 0899.

GETTING THERE **By Plane** Flights connect Matsuyama with Tokyo, Osaka, Nagoya, Fukuoka, Sapporo, Kagoshima, and Hiroshima.

By Train The easiest way to reach Matsuyama is by train from Okayama on Honshu island, with 11 departures daily; the trip takes 2 hours and 30 minutes. There are also 10 trains a day from Takamatsu, and the trip takes less than $2^1/_2$ hours.

By Bus Buses depart daily from Tokyo's Tokyo Station and Shinjuku Station, reaching Matsuyama 11 hours later.

By Boat Matsuyama is also linked to various ports on Honshu and Kyushu islands, including Kobe (trip time: 8 hr.), Osaka (10 hr.), Beppu (4 hr.), and Hiroshima (1 hr.). Buses departing from Matsuyama Port (Matsuyama Kanko Ko) reach Matsuyama Station in about 30 minutes.

VISITOR INFORMATION Information on how to reach Matsuyama and places of interest can be obtained in a leaflet called "Inland Sea and Shikoku," available at the Tourist Information Center in either Tokyo or Kyoto.

The **Matsuyama City Tourist Information Office** (☎ 0899/31-3914) is inside the Matsuyama JR Train Station and is easy to find because of its sign in English. Open daily from 8:30am to 5:15pm, it has an excellent pamphlet with a map in English. *What's Going On* is a free English-language guide to the city sponsored by the Matsuyama International Center. Pick it up for events, English-language church services, club outings, and so on.

GETTING AROUND Matsuyama Station is in the west end of town, and most points of interest spread to the east. **Streetcars** depart from the front of the station to such places as Dogo Spa and the Okaido Shopping Arcade, a covered pedestrian passageway lined with restaurants and shops, considered to be the heart of the city. Matsuyama Castle lies just northwest of Okaido, less than 1 1/2 miles from the train station. Many **buses** and **commuter trains** bound for the suburbs depart from Matsuyama City Station, called Shi-eki in Japanese, which is linked to Matsuyama (JR Train) Station by streetcar.

WHAT TO SEE & DO

THE TOP ATTRACTIONS

Right in the heart of the city, **Matsuyama Castle** (☎ 0899/21-4873) crowns the top of Katsuyama Hill. It was built by feudal lord Kato Yoshiakira about 385 years ago, later falling into the hands of the powerful Matsudaira family. Like most structures in Japan, Matsuyama Castle has suffered fire and destruction through the ages, but unlike many other castles (such as those in Osaka and Nagoya), this one is the real thing. There's only one entrance, a pathway leading through a series of gates that could be swung shut to trap attacking enemies. The three-story donjon houses a museum of armor and swords from the Matsudaira family. Surrounding the castle is a park, and if you're feeling energetic you can walk through the park to the castle in about 15 minutes. Otherwise, the easiest way to reach the castle is to take the streetcar to the Ichibancho stop, walk five minutes north, and then take a chair lift and a cable car on the east side of Katsuyama Hill. A ticket for ¥750 ($7.50) includes the round-trip ride to the top of the hill and entrance to the castle; otherwise, admission is ¥350 ($3.50). The castle is open daily from 9am to 5pm.

Dogo Spa (*Dogo Onsen*), with a 3,000-year history, claims to be the oldest hot-spring spa in Japan. Located in the northeast part of the city, about a 20-minute tram ride from Matsuyama Station (take streetcar no. 5 to the Dogo Onsen stop), Dogo Spa can accommodate about 9,000 people in 62 hotels and ryokan, which means that the narrow streets resound at night with the slap of thongs as vacationers go to the various bathhouses in yukata.

Most of the hotels and ryokan in Dogo have their own *onsen* (hot-spring bath), but I suggest, no matter where you stay, that you make at least one trip to **Dogo Onsen Honkan** (☎ 0899/21-5141), a wonderful three-story public bathhouse built in 1894. A wooden structure with shoji screens, tatami rooms, creaking wooden stairways, and a white heron topping the crest of the roof, it's as much a social institution as it is a place to soak and scrub. On busy days as many as 4,000 people will pass through its front doors. The water here is transparent, colorless, tasteless, and alkaline. The hottest spring water coming into the spa is 120°F; the coolest, 70°F. But don't worry—the waters are mixed to achieve a comfortable 108°F.

Bathing, however, is just a small part of the experience here. Most people come to relax, socialize, and while away an hour or more, and I suggest that you do the same. Although you can bathe for as little as ¥280 ($2.80), it's worth it to pay extra for the privilege of relaxing on tatami mats in a communal room on the second floor, dressed in a rented yukata (kimono), drinking tea from a lacquered tea set, and eating Japanese sweets. If the weather is fine, all the shoji screens are pushed open to let in a breeze, and as you sprawl out on the tatami, drinking your tea and listening to the clang of the streetcar and the clatter of wooden shoes, you can almost imagine that you've somehow landed in ancient Japan. To my mind the whole scene resembles an old woodblock print that has suddenly sprung to life.

Cost of the bath, yukata, sweets, and tea is ¥620 ($6.20). Use of a smaller and therefore more private bath and lounging area where tea and sweets are also served costs ¥980 ($9.80). And if you really want to splurge, you can rent your own private tatami room on the third floor, which also comes with tea, sweets, and yukata, for ¥1,240 ($12.40).

Connected to the spa is another building, built in 1899 for the imperial family, and you can take a tour of its rooms for ¥210 ($2.10). The spa is open from 6:30am (which is the arrival time of the first streetcar) until 11pm, but you must enter by 10pm. The ticket window for sweets, yukata, and tea closes at 9pm.

After your bath, you may want to visit **Ishiteji Temple,** about a 10-minute walk east of Dogo Onsen Station. Built in 1318, it's the 51st of Shikoku's 88 sacred temples and, with its blend of Chinese and Japanese styles, is a good example of architecture of the Kamakura Period. Notice the many straw sandals hanging on the temple gate. They're placed there by older Japanese in hopes of regaining new strength in their legs. There are, incidentally, seven other temples in Matsuyama that belong to the sacred 88, but Ishiteji is the most important and popular.

Crafts & Culture

Matsuyama is famous for several crafts, one of which is Iyo Kasuri, a cotton cloth dyed with Japanese indigo and worn traditionally as working attire by farm housewives. It was originated in the early 1800s by a woman named Kana Kagiya. If you're interested in seeing firsthand how this cloth is produced, then and now, you can visit **Mingei Iyo Kasuri Kaikan** (214), Kumanodai 1165 (☎ 0899/22-0405), a small factory you can reach by bus (no. 61 or 62) from Matsuyama JR Station. It displays the processes of dyeing, machine weaving, and hand-weaving the blue cloth. Open daily from 8am to 5pm, it charges a small admission fee of ¥50 (50¢). You can even dye your own handkerchief for an extra ¥1,000 ($10). A shop sells Kasuri pillowcases, purses, clothing, hats, and bolts of cloth.

Another product of Ehime Prefecture is Tobe pottery, called Tobe-yaki in Japanese. Noted for its thick white porcelain painted with cobalt-blue designs, Tobe pottery is produced in the town of Tobe, which you can reach by bus in about 40 minutes from Matsuyama Shi-eki. There are several kilns open to the public, the best known of which is **Umeno-Seito-jo** (215)(☎ 0899/62-2311), open Tuesday through Sunday from 8am to 5pm; closed the second Sunday of the month and for a few days in mid-August. Founded back in 1882 and now in its fourth generation of ownership by the Umeno family, it employs more than 100 people. You can watch all the artisans except those who do the actual painting of the designs—the technique is a closely guarded secret. Inside the shop, be sure to check out the bargain corner, where pieces with slight imperfections go for about half price. Another place you can shop for Tobe-yaki is at the **Tobe-yaki Kanko Center** (216) (☎ 0899/62-2070), open daily from 8am to 6pm. At both places you can try your hand in a workshop.

If you don't have time to visit the places where Kasuri cloth and Tobe-yaki are made, you can see both at the **Ehime Prefectural Products Hall** or *Ehime no Bussan* (217) (☎ 0899/41-7584), Ichibancho 4-chome, not far from the ANA Hotel at the

Kencho-mae tram stop. Open Monday through Friday from 8:30am to 5pm and on Saturday from 8am to noon, it sells Ehime Prefecture products, including foodstuffs (such as sweets and honey), Tobe pottery, Kasuri cloth, masks, bamboo vases, lacquerware, cultivated pearls, and dolls. The dolls are shaped in an oval and are known as the princess doll, made in the image of Empress Jingu, who came to Dogo Spa in the 2nd century when she was pregnant.

If you're interested in the performing arts, the **Ehime Prefectural Convention and Cultural Hall** (☎ 0899/23-5111), designed by Kenzo Tange, has frequent concerts, dramas, and other performances. Check with your hotel or the tourist office for information on current productions.

And finally, if you're a devoted fan of Japanese swords and samurai armor, head straight for the hydrofoil that will whisk you to **Omishima** in about an hour. Here, on this unpretentious and rather neglected island, is Japan's most important sword and armor collection. As much as 80% of Japan's national treasure of swords and armor is kept at the shrine here, just as it has been for centuries. Many of the pieces were donated by the owners themselves, including armor once worn by Yoritomo Minamoto 800 years ago. You can also see the armor worn by female warrior Tsuruhime, a kind of Japanese Joan of Arc.

Nearby Attractions

If you have time for a side trip around Ehime Prefecture, I strongly recommend an excursion to the village of **Uchiko,** which has some fine old homes and buildings dating back to the Edo Period and the turn of the century. Whereas about 70% of Matsuyama was destroyed during World War II, Uchiko was left intact, and a tiny part of the old city is a living memorial to the days of yore. Even the 20-minute express train ride from Matsuyama JR Station is enjoyable as you weave through valleys of wooded hills past grape, mikon orange, persimmon, rice, and tobacco farms. Signs from the station direct you to Yokaichi, the old part of town. Note that most museums and buildings in Uchiko are closed on Monday.

Your first stop is **Uchikoza** (218), which is a Kabuki theater built in 1916. Be sure to pick up an English-speaking guide and map, *The Uchiko*, here. Uchikoza was recently restored and though it's not as grand as the one near Takamatsu (described earlier in this chapter), it's a good example of how townspeople used to enjoy themselves years ago. It features a revolving stage and many windows that can be opened and closed to control the amount of light reaching the stage. Buy a ¥850 ($8.50) ticket here, which allows admission to the theater and other sights listed below, all of which are open from 9am to 4:30pm Tuesday through Sunday.

Farther along the main street is the **Historic Folkways, Business and Livelihood Museum,** which you will recognize immediately as two figures kneeling in a Taisho-era pharmacy chat with you, the client. The museum uses wax figurines and authentic artifacts to show various scenes of merchant life, such as a restaurant. Other places of interest in Yokaichi include **Machi-ya Shiryokan** and **Kamihagatei House,** old homes that have been restored and opened to the public. Built in 1894, Kamihaga House is especially grand, having once belonged to a merchant who made his fortune by exporting wax. During the Edo Period, Uchiko gained fame as a center of candlemaking and wax production, used both for lighting and for the styling of elaborate hairdos.

Today, only one man carries on this wax-making tradition, a man named Omori, who represents the sixth generation of candlemakers. Following the same techniques as those developed by his ancestors 200 years ago, he even collects his own haze berries (a kind of sumac) and makes his candles by hand. His workshop is open to the public Tuesday through Sunday from 9am to 5pm, where you can observe him at work.

ACCOMMODATIONS

RYOKAN

Funaya (219)

1-33 Dogo Yunomachi, Matsuyama 790. ☎ **0899/47-0278.** Fax 0899/43-2139. 54 rms (all with bath). A/C MINIBAR TV TEL. ¥25,000–¥50,000 ($250–$500) per person double. All rates include breakfast, dinner, and service charge. AE, DC, JCB, MC, V. Tram: Dogo Onsen (5 minutes).

This is where the imperial family stays on visits to Dogo. Everything about this ryokan—from the spacious, softly colored lobby design to the hushed rustling of kimono—says class. Completely redone in 1993, the ryokan is still very traditional; the history of the ryokan itself goes back 360 years. The lobby and many of its rooms look out onto a garden. Some 41 of the ryokan's rooms are tatami, 2 are furnished with twin beds, and 10 combine beds and tatami areas. Facilities include an indoor pool (open May through October), a Jacuzzi, two saunas, two large indoor baths, and two outdoor baths. The seventh and eighth floors of the annex are club floors, where the best and most expensive rooms, with their own private onsen baths, are located. If you just want to experience it, have tea in the Taisho-era anteroom, where the imperial family has stayed.

Luna Park

5-19 Sagitani-cho, Dogo, Matsuyama 790. ☎ **0899/31-1234.** Fax 0899/33-3198. 86 rms (all with bath). A/C MINIBAR TV TEL. ¥13,000–¥20,000 ($130–$200) per person. All rates include breakfast, dinner, and service charge. AE, DC, JCB, MC, V. Tram: Dogo Onsen (5 minutes).

New and clean, this ryokan features a rooftop bath and indoor baths, both of which reputedly have healing spa waters. The rates depend on the type of meal you order, on whether it's a holiday or weekend, and on the number of people per room, but are reasonable for the rooms' size and facilities. Rooms are both Western and Japanese style. In-room baths are the tiny module ones, so I recommend the public baths. The owner's son, who is the manager here, speaks English, and is enthusiastic about foreign guests. Dine in tatami rooms. Facilities include a bar, shopping arcade, and video-games corner.

HOTELS

Expensive

Ana Hotel

3-2-1 Ichiban-cho, Matsuyama 790. ☎ **0899/33-5511.** Fax 0899/21-6053. 333 rms. A/C MINIBAR TV TEL. ¥14,000–¥18,000 ($140–$180) double; ¥15,000–¥30,000 ($150–$300) twin. AE, DC, JCB, MC, V. Tram: Kencho-mae (2 minutes).

Matsuyama's premier hotel is in the heart of the city, just south of Matsuyama Castle and not far from the Okaido covered shopping arcade. It's only a five-minute walk to the cable car going up to the castle, and streetcars heading for Dogo pass right in front of the hotel. Built in 1979, the hotel is spacious and cheerfully decorated, and offers 55 boutiques on four floors (including one selling Tobe-yaki). Rooms are large and well appointed.

Dining/Entertainment: There are six restaurants, bars, and lounges. The Unkai (Japanese) and the Castle Grill (seafood and steaks) restaurants are described in "Dining," below. There's a 14th-floor bar next to the Castle Grill for after-dinner drinks, and a rooftop beer garden.

Services: Free newspaper, same-day laundry service.

Facilities: Shopping arcade.

Moderate

Hotel Sunroute

391-8 Miyatacho, Matsuyama 790. ☎ **0899/33-2811.** Fax 0899/33-2763. 110 rms (all with bath). A/C TV TEL. ¥11,000–¥16,500 ($110–$165) double/twin; ¥19,000–¥20,000 ($190–$200) triple. AE, DC, JCB, MC, V. Station: Matsuyama (3 minutes).

This redbrick building, opened in 1986, is part of a nationwide chain of business hotels. Its rooms are reasonably priced and feature double-pane windows to shut out noise. The best views are from those rooms on the top floors facing east—they offer a glimpse of the distant castle. On the hotel's roof is a covered beer garden, open April to September, daily from 5:30 to 9pm—rain or shine. After paying an initial charge of ¥2,800 ($28), you can eat and drink as much as you like.

Kokusai International Hotel

1-13 Ichiban-cho, Matsuyama 790. ☎ **0899/32-5111.** Fax 0899/45-2055. 80 rms. A/C MINIBAR TV TEL. ¥9,000–¥21,000 ($90–$210) double or twin. AE, DC, JCB, MC, V. Tram: Ichiban-cho (3 minutes).

Small, pleasant, and not far from the ANA Hotel, this medium-priced hotel features rooms with radio, clock, and large windows that let in lots of light. Even single rooms here have double beds, and some rooms have views of Matsuyama Castle. Yoshicho, the hotel's Japanese restaurant, serves kushikatsu, sashimi, sukiyaki, and tempura, while the hotel's Western restaurant offers sandwiches, fish, beef curry, spaghetti, and set meals, as well as teppanyaki steaks. There's also a Chinese restaurant, Tohkalin. A lobby shop offers a daily-necessities corner.

Taihei Business Hotel (220)

3-3-15 Heiwa Dori, Matsuyama 790. ☎ **0899/43-3560.** Fax 0899/32-2525. 140 rms (all with bath). A/C TV TEL. ¥9,000 ($90) double; ¥11,000–¥12,000 ($110–$120) twin; ¥15,000 ($150) Japanese-style room for three. Buffet breakfast ¥500 ($5) extra. No credit cards. Tram: Teppo-cho (3 minutes).

This rather interesting establishment is located at the northern base of Katsuyama Hill. Unlike the plastic, impersonal atmosphere of most business hotels, this one has blond wood, quilts, and soft colors. The effect is cozy and pleasant, and the rooms are great for the price. Breakfast buffets, as well as set dinners starting at ¥1,000 ($10), are served in a cheerful dining area. There are public baths and saunas for men and women. Four rooms are combination tatami and Western style. An annex built in 1991 has more expensive rooms; all those facing the back look out on the mountain greenery. A fax corner from which you can send faxes is handy.

A Youth Hostel

Matsuyama Shinsen-en Youth Hostel (221)

22-3 Dogohimezuka Otsu, Matsuyama 790. ☎ **0899/33-6366.** Fax 0899/33-6378. 70 beds. A/C. ¥3,200 ($32) Japanese; ¥2,650 ($26.50) non-Japanese. Breakfast ¥500 ($5) extra; dinner ¥900 ($9) extra. No credit cards. Tram: Dogo Onsen (8 minutes).

Its convenient location in Dogo Onsen Spa makes this a popular youth hostel among young Japanese. Facilities include bicycles for rent and a coin-operated laundry. The place is spotlessly clean. There's a wood-burning stove in the lobby/living room, and rackets are available near the tennis courts.

DINING

Castle Grill

ANA Hotel, 3-2-1 Ichiban-cho. ☎ **0899/33-5511.** Reservations recommended. Main dishes ¥1,600–¥6,000 ($16–$60); set lunch ¥1,800 ($18); set dinners ¥3,500–¥6,000 ($35–$60).

AE, DC, JCB, MC, V. Mon–Sat 11:45am–2:30pm and 5:30–9:30pm; Sun and hols 11:45am–9:30pm. Tram: Kencho-mae. SEAFOOD/STEAKS.

A good choice for variety and convenience (located close to the castle and the shopping arcades), this romantic Western restaurant sports candles and flowers on each table and a view of a European-style castle, Bansuiso Mansion, built by a former lord and lit at night. After dinner, retire to the Blue Bell Lounge next door, with more views of the city and live entertainment.

Goshiki

3-5-4 Sanbancho. ☎ **0899/33-3838.** Set meals ¥900–¥4,500 ($9–$45); some from ¥400 ($4). No credit cards. Daily 11am–8:30pm (last order). Tram: Kencho-mae. SOMEN NOODLES.

This local-foods restaurant with plastic-food display cases outside is on the same street as the central post. You can purchase some noodles here as well. It's a good place to try hot or cold *somen,* a local noodle dish. The Yozushi set offers somen with shrimp, egg, mushroom, and tofu, plus rice balls (delicately seasoned with mikon), *yakoten* (fried fish cake), and pickles seved in beautiful lacquer dishes. The menu has photos, and the traditionally clad waitresses are helpful.

Shinhamasaku (222)

4-6-1 Sanbancho. ☎ **0899/33-3030.** Set meals ¥1,000–¥10,000 ($10–$100). No credit cards. Daily 11am–3pm and 4:30–8:30pm. Tram: Shi-eki-mae (8 minutes). VARIED JAPANESE.

This modern restaurant, located near the Matsuyama Central Post Office, serves fresh seafood from the Seto Inland Sea and other local specialties, as well as shabu-shabu, kamameshi, and crab and eel dishes. The menu is in Japanese only, but there's a display of food. Popular is the *seiro bento* with tempura, which includes about 20 different bite-size morsels, all served in a wooden box. Kaiseki sets start at ¥4,000 ($40).

Sushimaru

2-3-2 Nibancho. ☎ **0899/41-0447.** Set meals ¥800–¥2,500 ($8–$25). AE, DC, MC, V. Daily 11am–9pm. Tram: Ichiban-cho. SUSHI.

Located just off (east) of the Okaido shopping arcade, Sushimaru has a display case outside. A popular lunch is served from 11am to 2pm, which includes sushi and soup for ¥850 ($8.50).

Unkai

ANA Hotel, 3-2-1 Ichiban-cho. ☎ **0899/33-5511.** Reservations recommended. Set meals ¥1,000–¥12,000 ($10–$120). AE, DC, JCB, MC, V. Mon–Sat 11:45am–2:30pm and 5–9:30pm; Sun and hols 11:45am–9:30pm. Tram: Kencho-mae. VARIED JAPANESE.

This restaurant offers a variety of food, including sukiyaki, shabu-shabu, tempura, and sashimi. Although the menu is in Japanese only, there are pictures accompanying most of the set meals. *Inaka ryori* is a local dish (¥3,000/$30). The restaurant overlooks a small garden with a stream that's lit up at night.

Kyushu

11

The southernmost of Japan's four main islands, Kyushu offers a mild climate, such hot-spring spas as Beppu and Ibusuki, beautiful countryside, national parks, and warm, friendly people. Historians believe that Japan's earliest inhabitants lived on Kyushu before gradually pushing northward, and according to Japanese legend it was from Kyushu that the first emperor, Jimmu, began his campaign to unify Japan. Kyushu is therefore considered to be the cradle of Japanese civilization. And because Kyushu is the island closest to Korea and China, it has served through the centuries as a point of influx for both people and ideas from abroad, including those from the West.

SEEING KYUSHU

Most of Kyushu's towns are along the coast, which means that you can visit most cities and attractions by circling the island by train. You might, for example, wish to start out in Fukuoka, where its Hakata Station is the terminus for Shinkansen bullet trains from Tokyo. From there you can head south to Kagoshima, stopping at Beppu and Miyazaki along the way. From Kagoshima, consider taking the bus to Chiran to visit its famous samurai gardens and continuing by bus onward to Ubusuki, Kyushu's southernmost tip. From there, take the train northward along Kyushu's western coast to Kumamoto, where you can take a side trip to Mt. Aso in the middle of the island. Nagasaki is easily reached by train from Kumamoto, and you can complete your tour of Kyushu by taking a bus from Nagasaki to the mountain resort of Unzen. Complete your circuit of the island by returning to Fukuoka and boarding the Shinkansen bullet train bound for Honshu.

1 Fukuoka

730 miles W of Tokyo; 281 miles W of Hiroshima

With a population of 1.2 million, Fukuoka is Kyushu's largest city and serves as a major international and domestic gateway to the island.

During Japan's feudal days, Fukuoka was actually divided into two distinct towns separated by the Nakagawa River. Fukuoka was where the samurai lived, since it was the castle town of the local feudal lord. Merchants lived across the river in Hakata, the commercial

What's Special About Kyushu

Hot-Spring Spas

- Beppu, with its 168 public bathhouses; open-air sand bathing; Takegawara bathhouse, built in the late 1800s; and Suginoi Palace, one of the largest bathhouses in Japan.
- Ibusuki, located on the southern tip of Kyushu and famous for its open-air sand bathing, the huge indoor Jungle Bath, and its tropical climate.
- Unzen, a resort town with hot sulphur springs 2,385 feet high in the mountains.

Castles

- Kumamoto Castle, originally constructed in the 1600s and now containing a museum.

Natural Spectacles

- The Hells of Beppu, boiling ponds created by volcanic activity.
- Mt. Aso, the largest crater basin in the world.
- Mt. Sakurajima, an active volcano in southern Kyushu.

Gardens

- Suizenji in Kumamoto, famous for its miniature reproductions of well-known landmarks along the old Tokaido Highway, including a miniature Mt. Fuji.
- Iso Garden in Kagoshima, laid out more than 300 years ago and used by former lords for poetry-composing parties.
- Six samurai gardens in Chiran, laid out in the 18th century.

Dining

- Kumamoto's local specialties, including grilled tofu, fish and taro with bean paste, lotus root, and *basashi* (raw horse meat).
- The internationally influenced cuisine of Nagasaki, including a sponge cake with Portuguese origins, and *Shippoku,* dishes native to Nagasaki that show Chinese, Japanese, and European influences.
- The *satsuma* cuisine of Kagoshima, which includes fish, pork, and chicken dishes unique to southern Kyushu.

Shopping

- Ningyo clay dolls of Hakata.
- Damascene and pearls, specialties of Kumamoto.
- Oshima pongee, a type of Japanese silk produced in Kagoshima.
- Satsuma pottery, first brought to Kyushu by Korean potters almost 400 years ago.

center of the area. Both cities were joined in 1889 under the common name of Fukuoka. Fukuoka's main train station, however, is in Hakata and is therefore called Hakata Station.

In the 13th century, Fukuoka was selected by Mongol forces under Kublai Khan as the best place to invade Japan. The first attack came in 1274, but the Japanese were able to repel the invasion. Convinced the Mongols would attack again, the Japanese built a 10-foot-high stone wall along the coast. The second invasion came in 1281. Not only did the Mongols find the wall impossible to scale, but a typhoon blew in and destroyed the entire Mongol fleet. The Japanese called this gift from heaven "divine wind," or *kamikaze,* a word that took on a different meaning during World War II, when young Japanese pilots crashed their planes into American ships in a last-ditch attempt to win the war.

As an industrial and business center of Kyushu, Fukuoka is not considered much of a destination on the tourist circuit. However, you may find yourself making a one-night stopover here after an international flight or a day's train ride from Tokyo.

ESSENTIALS

The **telephone area code** for Fukuoka, lying in Fukuoka Prefecture, is 092. An **international post office** is located next to Hakata Station.

GETTING THERE **By Plane** International direct flights from Pusan, Seoul, Taipei, Hong Kong, Honolulu, Beijing, Shanghai, Colombo, Guam, Saipan, Singapore, Kuala Lumpur, Sydney, Manila, Bangkok, Denpasar, London, Cairns (Australia), and Dailan (China). The Fukuoka Airport Subway now connects the airport with Hakata Station in five minutes. Domestic flights connect Fukuoka with Tokyo in 1½ hours.

By Train Fukuoka's Hakata Station is the last stop on the Shinkansen bullet train from Tokyo, about 6 hours away (5 by *Nozomi Super Express*); Hiroshima is 1½ hours away.

By Bus Night buses depart from Shinjuku Station, arriving in Tenjin in 14 hours.

VISITOR INFORMATION Before leaving Tokyo or Kyoto, drop by the Tourist Information Center to pick up a leaflet called "Fukuoka." It lists the major sights of the city. The **Fukuoka Tourist Information Office** (☎ 092/431-3003) is in Hakata Station (Hakata deguchi). Open from 9am to 7pm, it has maps and a pamphlet in English. For Fukuoka Prefecture information, go to the **Fukuoka Information Center** (☎ 092/725-9100) at 1-1-1 Tenjin, Chuo-ku, in the Across Building. It's open daily from 10am to 8pm (closed 2nd and 4th Monday of the month).

GETTING AROUND Although Hakata Station is the terminus for the Shinkansen bullet train, with most of Fukuoka's hotels clustered nearby, the heart of Fukuoka is an area called **Tenjin,** which serves as the business center for the city. It's also home to several department stores, a large underground shopping arcade, coffee shops, and restaurants. Less than a 10-minute walk from Tenjin is **Nakasu,** Fukuoka's largest nightlife district, with lots of bars, restaurants, and small clubs. As a port town, Fukuoka's seaside has always been important, but recently several areas have been developed for tourism, notably Momochi Seaside Park (Fukuoka Hawks baseball stadium, a waterfront promenade extending onto the ocean, and Fukuoka Tower), Bayside Place (ferry terminal and aquarium), and Uminonakamichi (Seaside Park and Marine World).

By Subway The easiest method of transportation is the subway. One convenient subway line, for example, runs from Hakata Station to Tenjin (the third stop), passing Nakasukawabata on the way, the stop for the Nakasu nightlife district. This same line will also take you to Ohori-Koen Park and Fukuoka Airport.

By Bus The city's two bus terminals are located in Tenjin and at Hakata Station.

By Train Whereas Hakata Station serves as the terminus for the Shinkansen and Japan Railways trains departing for the rest of Kyushu, Tenjin has its own station, called the Nishitetsu Fukuoka Station. This is where you board the train if you're going to Dazaifu.

WHAT TO SEE & DO

Shofukuji Temple is just a five-minute walk northwest of Hakata Station. Thought to be the oldest Zen Buddhist temple in Japan, it was founded in 1195 by a priest named Eisai, who introduced Zen and tea seeds into Japan after studying four years in China.

Located about 15 minutes on foot from Hakata Station is **Sumiyoshi-jinja Shrine.** With 400-year-old buildings, it's one of Kyushu's oldest Shinto shrines and is dedicated to the guardians of seafarers. As it's favored by the Japanese as a good place for wedding ceremonies, you may be lucky and witness a traditional wedding in progress.

Near the Gofuku-machi subway stop is **Hakata Machiya Folklore Museum,** housed in Meiji Era buildings that were moved to the sight. It displays folkcrafts, and artisans demonstrate their techniques. Open daily from 10am to 6pm, it charges ¥200 ($2) admission.

Near the Ohori-Koen subway stop you'll find **Ohori-Koen Park,** built on part of the outer defenses of the former Fukuoka Castle. Laid around a lake said to be a copy of Xi Hu in China, and dotted with small islands connected with bridges, it's a perfect place to relax with a picnic lunch. On the south side of the park is a traditional Japanese garden—constructed in 1984.

The nearby **Fukuoka City Art Museum** (☎ 092/714-6051), in the southeastern part of the park facing the lake, contains modern and Buddhist art, tea-ceremony utensils, ancient weapons, and armor. *Fukuoka Shiritsu Bijutsukan* is open Tuesday through Sunday from 9:30am to 5:30pm. Admission is ¥200 ($1.80).

If you have time, the most popular thing to do in Fukuoka is to take a side trip to **Dazaifu Temmangu Shrine,** which you can reach in 35 minutes by taking the Nishi Nippon Tetsudo Line (called Nishitetsu for short) from Nishitetsu Fukuoka Station in Tenjin. Trains depart every 30 minutes; take the express for Futsuka-Ichi and change there for Daizai Station. Dazaifu Temmangu Shrine was established in 905, although the present main hall dates from 1590. It's dedicated to the god of scholarship, which is one reason why the shrine is so popular—high school students flock here to pray that they pass the tough entrance exams into universities. Planted with lots of plum trees, camphor trees, and irises, the extensive grounds surrounding the shrine can be explored on a rented bicycle.

ESPECIALLY FOR CHILDREN The **Fukuoka City Children's Science and Culture Center,** 2-5-27 Maizuru, Chuo-ku (☎ 092/771-8861), is five floors of educational, fun things to do for youngsters and their parents, too. Sit in a jet cockpit and pilot, through video simulation, your own jet. Videos put you in space or underwater. You may be small and have to avoid giant people stepping on you or catch yourself from falling into a hippo's mouth. Among the many hands-on exhibits are: a solar-powered robot that you can guide by moving a light source; wooden orchestras that you can play; an explanation of how gears work; a helicopter children can "fly"; a real weather station; an explanation and simulation of an earthquake; and tide pool dioramas. There's also an extensive library and computer database. Entrance to the center is free; however, the ground-floor planetarium show costs ¥200 ($2) for adults, ¥100 ($1) for children 6 to 11 (free for children under 6). You can reach the center by taking the subway to Akasaka Station; from there it's a five-minute walk. The center is open Tuesday through Sunday from 9am to 5pm, closed the last day of the month.

Uminonakamichi (Seaside Park and Marine World) is home to 7,000 species, and dolphins and sea lions put on a show. Open daily from 9:30am to 5:30pm (until 5pm in winter), it charges ¥1,500 ($15) for adults, ¥1,100 ($11) for high school and junior high students, ¥750 ($7.50) for elementary school students, and ¥500 ($5) for preschoolers. To reach Uminonakamichi, take a JR local train from Hakata Station to Uminonakamichi or ferry across the bay from Hakata Pier Municipal Ferry Landing.

ACCOMMODATIONS

EXPENSIVE

ANA Hotel Hakata

3-3-3 Hakata-ekimae, Hakata-ku, Fukuoka 812. ☎ **092/471-7111.** Fax 092/472-7707. 354 rms. A/C MINIBAR TV TEL. ¥12,000–¥18,000 ($120–$180) single; ¥23,000 ($230) double; ¥21,000–¥32,000 ($210–$320) twin; ¥27,000 ($270) Japanese-style suites for two to three people. AE, DC, JCB, MC, V. Directions: Walk 4 minutes from Hakata Guchi, Hakata Station.

This modern first-class hotel has a spacious lobby and bright and comfortable rooms with large bathroom. Japanese-style suites have all the modern conveniences.

Dining/Entertainment: There are six food and beverage outlets.

Services: Free newspaper, same-day laundry service.

Facilities: Health club with pool, sauna, and exercise equipment (fee: ¥7,000/$70); shopping arcade.

Hakata Miyako Hotel

2-1 Hakata-eki Higashi, Hakata-ku, Fukuoka 812. ☎ **092/441-3111.** Fax 092/481-1306. 269 rms. A/C MINIBAR TV TEL. ¥11,000–¥16,000 ($110-$160) single; ¥18,000–¥21,000 ($180–$210) double or twin; ¥22,000 ($220) Japanese-style rooms for two. AE, DC, JCB, MC, V. Directions: In front of the Shinkansen bullet train exit of Hakata Station (Chikushi Guchi).

With the good name and legendary service of the Miyako hotel chain behind it, this hostelry has well-appointed rooms (some with bilingual TV). The hotel's six Japanese-style rooms, used most often as waiting rooms before wedding ceremonies and receptions held at the hotel, have cypress bathtubs.

Dining/Entertainment: French restaurant Starlight features live piano music, Shikitei specializes in Kyoto-style dishes, and Le Marché Brasserie and Le Marché Brasserie features all-you-can-eat (¥1,500 to ¥2,500/$15 to $25) and all-you-can-drink (¥1,000/$10). There's also a cocktail lounge, a bar, and a lobby tea lounge, from which you can watch the busy station traffic.

Services: Free newspaper, same-day laundry service.

Facilities: Beauty parlor, souvenir shop, medical clinic.

Il Palazzo

3-13-1 Haruyoshi, Chuo-ku, Fukuoka 810. ☎ **092/716-3333.** Fax 092/724-3330. 62 rms. A/C MINIBAR TV TEL. ¥13,000 ($130) single; ¥21,000 ($210) twin; ¥22,000 ($220) double; ¥14,000–¥50,000 ($140–$500) Japanese-style rooms. AE, DC, JCB, MC, V. Subway: Nakasukawabata Station (8 minutes). Bus: 68 to Miniami Shinchi (4 minutes).

Il Palazzo is the only hotel listed not near Hakata Station. I've included it because it's a marvel of modern design and *the* place to stay for artists, designers, or those in or interested in related fields. Winner of the American Institute of Architects 1991 Honor Award and the Fukuoka Urban Beautification Award, it's the work of Italian architect Aldo Rossi and Japanese interior designers Shigeru Uchida and Ikuyo Mitsuhashi. Rooms, even singles, are large for Japan, and the marble bath is divided by a large glass plate, so that the wet area (shower/bathtub) is separate from the dry area (sink and toilet). While rooms come with all the usual amenities (bedside clock, hair dryer, desk area, and yukata), none of it is usual in design. Staying here is like taking a vacation in itself. A twin suite I could easily move into has a wet bar, sofa area, and free-standing desk in the living area. There are seven Japanese-style rooms.

Dining/Entertainment: There is one restaurant, Ristorante, serving Italian cuisine; four bars (each interesting and each designed by a different well-known international designer); and the Crossing Hall, which features events from fashion shows to blues concerts.

Services: Free newspaper.

Moderate

Chisan Hotel Hakata (223)

2-8-11 Hakata-ekimae, Hakata-ku, Fukuoka 812. ☎ **092/411-3211**. Fax 092/473-8323. 286 rms. A/C MINIBAR TV TEL. ¥7,500–¥8,000 ($75–$80) single; ¥10,000 ($100) double; ¥14,000–¥16,000 ($140–$160) twin. AE, DC, JCB, MC, V. Directions: Walk 7 minutes from the Hakata Guchi exit of Hakata Station, straight ahead on the right-hand side.

This light-tiled triangular building is an efficient and dependable business hotel with good service and a friendly staff. The best rooms are the higher-priced twins. Located in the curve of the hotel's front facade, they offer large rounded windows and lots of space. The hotel's one restaurant serves a buffet breakfast of Japanese and Western food for ¥1,000 ($10).

Clio Court

5-3 Hakataeki-Chuogai, Hakata-ku, Fukuoka 812. ☎ **092/472-1111.** Fax 092/474-3222. 199 rms. A/C MINIBAR TV TEL. ¥9,000–¥13,000 ($90–$130) single; ¥10,000–¥15,000 ($100–$150) double; ¥11,000–¥19,000 ($110–$190) twin. AE, DC, JCB, MC, V. Directions: Next to the Shinkansen exit.

A chic lobby, featuring lots of chrome, mirrors, and white marble, and art deco–style rooms make this medium-priced hotel stand out. Few of the rooms have the same interior design—they're the creation of well-known female architect Rei Kurokawa. Rooms are large; even the bathrooms are roomy. The cheapest rooms, however, don't have any windows, and since there are no single rooms per se, single travelers are assigned to twin or double rooms at rates slightly less than for double occupancy.

Restaurants in the hotel serve French, Chinese, and Japanese cuisine. In the basement is an interesting setup called Clio Seven, which is essentially one large room divided into seven different bars and restaurants, including a sushi bar, a yakitori-ya, and an English-style pub. Clio Seven is open Monday through Saturday from 5pm to 1am, on Sunday and holidays until midnight.

Hotel Centraza Hakata

4-23 Hakataeki-Chuogai, Hakata-ku, Fukuoka 812. ☎ **092/461-0111.** Fax 092/461-0171. 198 rms. A/C MINIBAR TV TEL. ¥10,500 ($105) single; ¥15,000–¥19,000 ($150–$190) double; ¥16,000–¥20,000 ($160–$200) twin. AE, DC, JCB, MC, V. Directions: In front of the Shinkansen exit.

This hotel has a spacious and marbled second-floor lobby, and all rooms have semi-double or double beds. There's a small outdoor swimming pool, and in the basement is Gourmet City, with approximately a dozen restaurants.

Mitsui Urban Hotel (224)

2-8-15 Hakata-ekimae, Hakata-ku, Fukuoka 812. ☎ **092/451-5111.** Fax 092/451-5105. 310 rms. A/C MINIBAR TV TEL. ¥14,000 ($140) double or twin. All rates include service charge. AE, DC, JCB, V. Directions: Next to the Chisan Hotel.

This business hotel, part of a nationwide hotel chain, was built more than a decade ago but still looks relatively new. The rooms are small but have large windows and contain everything you need.

Inexpensive

Hakata Business Hotel

2-16-3 Hakata-eki-mae, Fukuoka 812. ☎ **092/431-0737.** Fax 092/414-5526. 37 rms (all with bath). A/C TV TEL. ¥6,200–¥7,000 ($62–$70) single; ¥10,000 ($100) double or twin; ¥13,500 ($135) Japanese-style room for three people. V. Directions: Walk 3 minutes from the Hakata exit.

Perhaps unexciting, still this convenient business hotel has everything you need: clean minibath, clock, yukata, hot water and green tea, windows, and pay TV. The twins and doubles have semi-double-size beds. A coffee shop on the ground floor serves breakfast for ¥600 ($6).

Toyo Hotel

1-9-36 Hakata-eki Higashi, Hakata-ku, Fukuoka 812. ☎ **092/474-1121.** Fax 092/474-0591. 274 rms (all with bath). A/C MINIBAR TV TEL. ¥7,500 ($75) single; ¥10,000 ($100) double; ¥12,000–¥16,000 ($120–$160) twin. Extra person plus ¥2,000 ($20). Rates include tax and service charge. AE, DC, JCB, MC, V. Directions: Walk 2 minutes north of the Shinkansen exit.

All beds in this comfortable business hotel are semi-doubles, and the sofa in the twin rooms can be made into an extra bed. Some of the lower-floor twins face another building, making them rather dark. Ask for a room higher up; those facing north have the best view. Since this is a Japanese businessman's hotel, don't be too surprised to find vending machines selling magazines of questionable taste. Some English is spoken.

YOUTH HOSTELS

Dazaifu Youth Hostel (225)

1-18-1 Sanjo, Dazaifu 818-01. ☎ **092/922-8740.** 30 beds. A/C. ¥3,000 ($30) for JYHA members and foreigners, ¥3,500 ($35) for nonmembers. Breakfast ¥800 ($8) extra; dinner ¥1,000 ($10) extra. No credit cards. Directions: See directions for Dazaifu Temmangu Shrine.

This two-story hostel is a 12-minute walk from Dazaifu Station in Dazaifu, home of the famous Dazaifu Temmangu Shrine. Sleeping is on futon in tatami rooms only. There are kitchen facilities and coin-operated laundry machines. Foreign visitors pay the JYHA price with or without a card.

DINING

Gourmet City

Hotel Centraza basement, 4-23 Hakataeki-Chuogai. ☎ **092/461-0111.** Reservations not required. ¥700–¥2,500 ($7–$25). No credit cards. Daily 11am–11pm. Directions: 1 minute from the Shinkansen exit. WESTERN/JAPANESE.

For inexpensive dining close to the station, try Gourmet City, with approximately a dozen establishments offering everything from sushi, Chinese food, and steaks to ice cream and beer. Restaurants are chic and well designed, with plastic-food displays and lunch specials priced mostly under ¥1,500 ($15).

Gyosai (226)

3-30-26 Hakata-ekimae. ☎ **092/471-9327.** Reservations not required. ¥1,000–¥2,500 ($10–$25); lunch teishoku ¥580 ($5.80). JCB. Mon–Sat 11:30am–1:30pm and 5–11pm. Directions: Walk 7 minutes from the Hakata exit. SASHIMI/SEAFOOD.

Specializing in Japanese seafood, this restaurant is located across the street from the Chisan Hotel (its sign says OKI DOKI). Actually, it's one of four Gyosai restaurants in Fukuoka—two are in the Tenjin shopping area, and another one is located not far from Hakata Station. (There's even a Gyosai in Boston.) You can get a plate of assorted sashimi here for ¥2,000 ($20). The menu is in Japanese only, but they understand some English. The very reasonable lunch teishoku, served from 11:30am to 1:30pm, consists of fried and raw fish, vegetables, pickles, soup, and rice.

✪ Ristorante Il Palazzo

Il Palazzo Hotel, 3-13-1 Haruyoshi, Chuo-ku. ☎ **092/716-3333.** Reservations not required. Main dishes ¥800–¥1,600 ($8–$16); set dinners ¥4,000–¥8,000 ($40–$80); set lunches ¥1,500–¥3,500 ($15–$35). AE, DC, JCB, MC, V. Daily 7:30am–2pm and 5:30–9pm. Directions: See Il Palazzo Hotel. ITALIAN/CONTINENTAL.

High ceilings and quince wood paneling of a rich, dark color provide an elegant setting. Ristorante Il Palazzo has no outside view, as it faces one of the hotel's interior/exterior walkways. But the center marble-and-steel kitchen provides theater as you watch chef Hiroshi Yamada, who trained in Europe for eight years, prepare French-influenced Italian cuisine with his own creative touches. Each dish is a delight to behold as well as to taste, as Yamada designs his presentations with an eye to color and form. Antipasti include fresh basil, tomato, and mozzarella on toast; salmon aspic terrine; aubergine (eggplant) caviar; and smoked ham and caviar. A favorite is the mouth-watering Three Pastas: saffron clam risotto, fettucini pesto, and four-cheese ravioli in red sauce, each different, each delectable. For dessert, six different homemade tarts and cakes are thinly sliced and arranged with fruit and sorbet. The pasta di giorno, a daily selection of pasta, together with soup, salad, bread, and coffee, is a reasonable and delicious lunch.

For evening entertainment in Fukuoka, I'd dine here and then barhop Il Palazzo's four lush-interiored bars.

Shikitei

Hakata Miyako Hotel, 2-1 Hakata-eki Higashi. ☎ **092/441-3111.** Reservations not required. Set dinners ¥3,500–¥10,000 ($35–$100); set lunches ¥1,500–¥3,800 ($15–$38). AE, DC, JCB, MC, V. Daily 11:30am–2pm and 5–9:30pm. Directions: See Hakata Miyako Hotel. KYOTO CUISINE/LOCAL DISHES.

With the Miyako chain's most famous hotel located in Kyoto, it's not surprising Shikitei specializes in Kyoto-style dishes. Set meals include sashimi, tempura, shabu-shabu, and sukiyaki. Kyoto kaiseki selections start at ¥5,000 ($50). During lunch there are also obento lunch box specials.

Tsukushino

ANA Hotel Hakata, 3-3-3 Hakata-ekimae. ☎ **092/471-7111.** Reservations recommended. Kaiseki ¥8,000–¥16,000 ($80–$160); Hakata ryori ¥8,000 ($80); set lunches ¥1,200–¥8,000 ($12–$80). AE, DC, JCB, MC, V. Daily 11:30am –10pm. Directions: See ANA Hotel. VARIED JAPANESE/LOCAL SPECIALTIES.

Tsukushino, with its 15th-floor city views, is designed to resemble a village lane. Overhanging eaves and traditional tiled roofs extend from the ceiling, and in the center of the restaurant is a glass-enclosed courtyard with raked gravel and bushes. *Mizutaki,* a Fukuoka specialty of chicken boiled in light broth with various Japanese vegetables and tofu, is recommended. Kaiseki offerings change twice a month. There are also shabu-shabu, sashimi dishes, and a separate tempura counter. Lunch specials, served until 2pm, are more reasonable. Most popular is the Tsukushino obento lunch box for ¥2,700 ($27), which includes sashimi, boiled vegetables, and lots more.

SHOPPING

You don't have to venture far from Hakata Station to go shopping. In fact, the **Izutsuya department store** (closed Wednesday) is located right above the station itself. Incidentally, on top of the department store is a rooftop beer garden open May through August from 5 to 10pm. Radiating out from the station are underground shopping arcades. **Deitos** is located under the Shinkansen tracks and is composed of various souvenir shops selling cakes, woven handbags, and Hakata's famous clay ningyo dolls.

Another large shopping area is in Tenjin, third stop on the subway line from Hakata Station. There's a huge underground shopping mall here, called **Tenjin Chikagai,** which stretches some 1,300 feet north to south. There are also many boutiques, department stores, specialty shops, coffee shops, and restaurants in the area.

2 Beppu

762 miles SW of Tokyo, 116 miles SE of Fukuoka

Some 12 million people come to Beppu every year to relax and rejuvenate themselves, and they do so in a number of unique ways. They sit in mud baths up to their necks, they bury themselves in hot black sand, they soak in hot springs, and on New Year's they bathe in water filled with floating orange peels. With more than 3,000 hot springs spewing forth 130,000 tons of water daily, and a total of 168 public bathhouses, Beppu is one of Japan's best-known spa resorts.

Bathing reigns supreme here—and I suggest that you join in the fun. After all, visiting Beppu without enjoying the baths would be like going to a famous restaurant with your own TV dinner. Beppu itself, not a very large town, is situated on Kyushu's east coast in a curve of Beppu Bay. It's bounded on one side by the sea and on the other by steep hills and mountains. Steam rises everywhere throughout the city, escaping from springs and pipes and giving the town an otherworldly appearance. Indeed, eight of the hot springs look so much like hell that that's what they're called—Jigoku, the Hells. But rather than a place most people try to avoid, the Hells are a major tourist attraction. In fact, everything in Beppu is geared toward tourism, and if you're interested in rubbing elbows with Japanese on vacation, this is one of the best places to do so.

ESSENTIALS

The **telephone area code** for Beppu, lying in Oita Prefecture, is 0977.

GETTING THERE **By Plane** The nearest airport is Oita, an hour's bus ride away; ANA flights from Tokyo's Haneda airport take about 1 1/2 hours.

By Train From Tokyo, go by Shinkansen to Kokura, then transfer to a limited express bound for Beppu; the trip takes 7 or 8 hours. There are also two trains an hour from Hakata Station in Fukuoka, taking 2 1/2 hours.

BY BUS From Osaka to Beppu, the bus trip takes 10 hours.

BY FERRY Ferries make daily runs to Beppu from Osaka, Hiroshima, Kobe, Shikoku, Matsuyama, and Yuwatahama (¥1,740/$17.40 one way).

VISITOR INFORMATION The Tourist Information Center in Tokyo and Kyoto has a free leaflet called "Beppu and Vicinity," with information on this area of Kyushu, as well as on transportation within it.

Once in Beppu, be sure to stop by the **Beppu Tourist Information Office** (☎ 0977/24-2838), which is located at Beppu Station and opens daily from 9am to 5pm. You can pick up brochures with such useful information as what to see in the area, which local buses to take, the opening and closing hours for the major sights, and a map of the city. If you are a foreigner, the station tourist office will try to get you to go to the **Foreign Tourist Information Service** (☎ 0977/23-1119), about a three-minute walk from Beppu Station, on the second floor of the Frosen Building. It's operated by English-speaking volunteers, some of whom are nice and some of whom have some answers to your questions, while others should have stayed at home. It's open from 10am to 4pm Monday through Saturday.

GETTING AROUND The easiest ways to get around Beppu are **bus** and **taxi.** If you plan on doing a lot of sightseeing by bus, there's a one-day bus pass with the strange name of "My Beppu Free," which nonetheless costs ¥900 ($9) and allows unlimited travel on Kamenoi Company buses within the city. The Yufuin Wide Pass can be used to go to African Safari and Yufuin, as well as around town, and costs ¥1,600 ($16). A city bus visits all the sights and costs ¥130 ($1.30) each time you board, or buy a ¥300 ($3) ticket, which allows you to get on and off as many times as you like.

WHAT TO SEE & DO

TAKING THE BATHS There are many kinds of springs and baths with various mineral contents that help in ailments from rheumatism to skin disease. If all you want is a quick dip in a hot-spring bath in between train rides, you have no farther to go than **Eki-mae Onsen,** which is just a minute's walk from Beppu Station's main exit and which also features a Jacuzzi. It charges ¥100 ($1). If you have a specific ailment, call the hot-springs section of the tourist office (☎ 0977/21-1111) to ask which baths would help you most. Otherwise, if you're simply here for the experience of the baths, there are two I particularly recommend:

✪ **SUGINOI PALACE** Most of the Japanese inns, hotels, and even private homes are tapped into Beppu's hot springs, but Suginoi Palace is one of the most fantastic baths in all of Japan, and also one of the largest. Two separate bathing areas are housed in what look like airplane hangars, one for men and one for women. Filled with lush tropical plants and pools of various sizes and temperatures, one of the baths features a benevolent-looking Buddha sitting atop a giant fish bowl full of carp, while the other boasts a large red torii gate of Shinto shrines. If you come two days in a row you can see both baths, as men and women alternate facilities daily. The baths also feature a steam room, a sauna, a Korean-style heated floor upon which you can lie down and relax, and a pit with hot sand in which to bury yourself.

The baths are open to the public daily from 9am to 10pm at a cost of ¥1,800 ($18). If you're staying at the Suginoi Hotel, you can use the baths daily (8am–10pm) for free. In addition to its huge bathhouses, the Suginoi Palace offers an outdoor waterfall and pond filled with greedy carp (buy some fish food and you'll see what I mean—they almost jump out of the water in their feeding frenzy). There's also a small landscaped garden, a beautiful display of bonsai plants, a play area with amusement-park rides for children, and bowling lanes. There's even a variety show, with two performances daily. (*Note:* The variety show is included in the admission price to the baths, but occasionally big-name entertainers appear and admission prices go up whether or not you attend the show. To avoid having to pay extra, it might be prudent to check the price.)

The **Suginoi Museum,** which charges a separate admission fee of ¥500 ($5), has a valuable collection of samurai armor, Japanese antique weapons, toilet sets, ceramics, lacquerware, religious artifacts, clocks, and other items dating from the Edo Period. Ask for someone to show it to you.

Aqua-Beat is a $5 million extension of the Suginoi bathing experience, a waterpark with six slides (great fun!), children's pools, simulated wave pool and artificial beach, outdoor onsen, sound-and-light show, and Jacuzzi. Indoors it's a constant 30 degrees centigrade, but all you have to wear is your bathing suit because your entrance ticket is exchanged for a bar-coded locker key wrist band, with which you can dine and rent equipment, and so on. When you depart, feed it into the machines to get your bill and exit ticket. Open 10am to 10pm daily, it costs ¥2,800 ($28) for adults, ¥1,700 ($17) for high school students, and ¥1,100 ($11) for children. (Aqua-Beat is not free to hotel guests.) You can buy a joint entrance to Suginoi Palace and Aqua-Beat which costs ¥3,600 ($36), ¥2,800 ($28), and ¥1,500 ($15). If you've been or are going to Ocean Dome in Miyazaki, skip Aqua-Beat—it's not as good.

By the way, much of the Suginoi complex's heating, electricity, and air-conditioning is run by geothermal energy.

A HOT-SAND BATH One of the unique things you can do in Beppu is take a bath in hot sand, and one of the best places to do it is at the **Takegawara Bathhouse.** Built in 1879, it's one of the oldest public baths in the city. The inside of the building resembles an ancient gymnasium. Bathing areas are separate for men and women, and are dominated by a pit filled with black sand. The attendants are used to foreigners here and will instruct you to strip, wash yourself down, and then lie down in a hollow they've dug in the sand. You should bring your own towel, which you should use to cover your vital parts. An attendant will then shovel sand on top of you and pack you in until only your head and feet are sticking out. I personally didn't find the sand all that hot, but it is relaxing as the heat soaks into your body. You stay buried for 10 minutes, contemplating the wooden ceiling high above and hoping you don't get an itch somewhere. When the time is up, the attendant will tell you to stand up, shake off the sand, and then jump into a bath of hot water. The cost of this bathing experience is ¥650 ($6.50), and daily hours are 8am to 9pm (the regular baths are open from 6am to 10pm).

Open-air sand baths are also offered at **Beppu Beach** or *Shoningahama*, reportedly good for muscle pain, rheumatism, and neuralgia. You keep on your yukata for the burial here, and the experience costs ¥600 ($6). Daily hours are 9am to 4pm (shorter hours in winter). You can reach Beppu Beach via bus 20 or 26, departing from the main exit on the east side of Beppu Station; you can also reach it on a local commuter train to Daigoku Station.

THE HELLS As for sightseeing, you might as well join everyone else and go to the Hells. These Hells are boiling ponds created by volcanic activity. Six of them are clustered close together in the Kannawa area, within walking distance of each other, and can be toured in about an hour or so. One ¥2,000 ($20) ticket allows entrance to all eight Hells; otherwise, the separate entrance fee to each one is ¥400 ($4), free for children under 6. You can also join a 2½-hour tour of the Hells for ¥3,540 ($35.40), including admission to the Hells, but it's conducted in Japanese only. Take the bus from the Kitahama Bus Center from 8:30am to 3:40pm. Each Hell has its own attraction. Umi Jigoku, or Sea Hell, is the color of sea water. Chinoike Jigoku, the Blood-Pond Hell, is blood-red in color because of the red clay dissolved in the hot water. Yama Jigoku features animals living in its hot spring, and Oniyama Jigoku is where crocodiles are bred. Tatsumaki Jigoku, or Waterspout Hell, has one of the largest geysers in Japan, and with a temperature of 221°F it's hotter than any other hot spring in Beppu.

TAKASAKIYAMA MOUNTAIN On Beppu's southern border, about a 15-minute bus ride from Beppu Station, rises Takasakiyama Mountain. Its peak is home to more than 2,000 monkeys, which come down every day to feed, returning to their home by late afternoon. They wander freely among the visitors, and humans are advised not to challenge them by looking directly into their eyes. Admission to this attraction is ¥500 ($5), free for children under 6, and daily hours are 8:30am to 5pm in winter, 8am to 5:30pm in summer.

YUFUIN MINGEI MURA If you have extra time or won't have the chance to see another folk village in Japan, you may want to visit the Yufuin Mingei Mura, a folkcrafts village with admission of ¥610 ($6.10), plus ¥950 ($9.50) for the Kotohin or Ceramics Museum. There are demonstrations of ceramics, paper making, woodworking, and knife making, plus a museum. It's all open from 8:30am to 5:30pm daily. There's a pleasant Japanese restaurant here too, where you eat on tatami overlooking the garden and surrounded by antiques in an old farm house.

ESPECIALLY FOR CHILDREN

African Safari is a 370-acre drive-through nature park with a road that winds through bare grassland. Animals are allowed to roam in their own restricted areas, separated by fences so that they don't eat each other. Humans are confined to their cars or special buses. Entrance to the park is ¥2,200 ($22), for adults, ¥1,200 ($12) for children 4 to 11. Best, however, is to pay the extra ¥950 ($9.50) for adults, ¥720 ($7.20) for children 4 to 11, for the caged bus featuring slots of food for the various animals so that you can watch them eat at close range. The park, which features 1,300 animals belonging to 69 different species, is open daily from 9am to 5pm (9:30am to 4pm from November 16 to March 15).

To reach African Safari, take bus no. 41 or 43 from Beppu Station. The trip takes about 50 minutes. Incidentally, the bus passes through an interesting part of Beppu called Myoban, where you'll notice a number of straw huts along the side of the road. These huts are built above hot springs and protect the formation of white powderlike sulphur deposits, called *yunohana* in Japanese. You can buy the powder and add it to your bath at home for an instant hot-spring experience. Located here is the Beppu City Souvenir Shop, which has all the products of Kyushu, as well as basket and ceramic demonstrations. It's open from 8am to 6pm daily. You can also take an outdoor hot-springs bath here for ¥600 ($6) daily from 8:30am to 8pm.

ACCOMMODATIONS

EXPENSIVE

✪ Kannawaen (227)

Kannawa, Beppu 874. ☎ **0977/66-2111.** 17 rms (4 with bath). A/C TV TEL. ¥20,000–¥35,000 ($200–$350) per person. Rates include breakfast, dinner, and service charge. No credit cards.

If it's peace and quiet you're searching for, this is a wonderful 110-year-old ryokan hidden away a 15-minute taxi ride from Beppu Station on a lushly landscaped hill not far from the Hells. It actually consists of six separate houses spread around its grounds, and its tatami rooms with shoji screens look out onto carefully tended gardens, hot springs, bamboo, streams, bonsai, stone lanterns, and flowers. This is the perfect place to escape the crowds and to relax in an open-air bath set among rocks and trees. Most rooms don't have a private bathroom, but the beauty of the surrounding countryside more than makes up for it. I highly recommend this place. Note that this place is cash only—not even traveler's checks.

Incidentally, if the ryokan itself is too expensive for you, you can come here just to use its sky blue open-air bath, open to the public for ¥500 ($5). Since it's close to the Hells, you might want to come here after battling the crowds.

Suginoi Hotel

Kankaiji, Beppu 874. ☎ **0977/24-1141.** Fax 0977/21-0010. 583 rms. A/C MINIBAR TV TEL. ¥19,000–¥37,000 ($190–$370) single; ¥15,000–¥24,000 ($150–$240) double; ¥17,000–¥20,000 ($170–$200) triple. All rates are per person and include breakfast and dinner. AE, DC, JCB, MC, V. Bus: To the Suginoi Palace stop. Taxi: 8 minutes.

Probably the best-known hotel in Beppu, it's famous for gigantic baths. A huge complex situated on a wooded hill, with a sweeping view of the city and sea below, it's a lively and noisy hotel filled with good-natured vacationers. In other words, if you like being in the middle of the action, this is the place for you. The hotel is divided into two wings: Honkan and Hana. Both Western- and Japanese-style rooms are available, but Western-style rooms face inland and are slightly cheaper. Some combination-style rooms, featuring both beds and a separate tatami area, are also available, with fantastic views of the sea. All rooms are modestly furnished and come with a safe for valuables, among other amenities.

Dining/Entertainment: Some 10 restaurants include the Shangrila, which serves Western food, and the Silver Hat, a Japanese restaurant. There are also coffee shops, tea lounges, and the Hana Bar, which offers great views and cocktails (¥1,000/$10).

Facilities: Suginoi Palace, with huge baths; Suginoi Museum; Aqua-Beat; two 24-hour, guests-only baths; landscaped garden; children's amusement park; karaoke; bowling alley; shopping arcade; games room; beauty salon; outdoor swimming pool.

MODERATE

Nippaku Hotel

3-12-26 Kitahama, Beppu 874. ☎ **0977/23-2291.** Fax 0977/23-2293. 72 rms (32 with bath). A/C TV TEL. ¥9,500 ($95) twin without bath, ¥10,500 ($105) twin with bath. Rates include tax and service. AE, DC, JCB, MC, V. Directions: Walk 10 minutes from the main exit.

They're used to foreigners at this reasonably priced tourist hotel, and the front-desk staff speaks English. Rooms are nicely but modestly furnished; those at the back are less noisy. Facilities include a restaurant and hot-spring public baths. Both Japanese- and Western-style rooms are available.

✪ Sakaeya (228)

Ida, Kannawa, Beppu 874. ☎ **0977/66-6234.** Fax 0977/66-6235. 13 rms (7 with bath). A/C MINIBAR TV TEL. ¥4,000 ($40) without bath; ¥5,000–¥6,000 ($50–$60) with bath; ¥8,000 ($80) without bath, including breakfast and dinner; from ¥15,000 ($150) with bath, including breakfast and dinner. All rates per person. Rates higher during holiday periods. No credit cards. Taxi: 10 minutes.

This is one of the best places to stay near the Hells, and the oldest minshuku in the city. The oldest rooms date from the Meiji Period (1868–1912) and feature old radiators heated naturally from hot springs. Another relic is the stone oven in the open courtyard, which uses steam from hot springs for cooking (many older homes in Beppu still use such ovens). Use of the oven is free in case you want to cook your own meals; there's also a modern kitchen you can use. Your dinner will be steamed, and the *kotatsu* in the dining room is steam heated. Most of the rooms, all Japanese style, have sinks, and all come with cotton yukata. This establishment is popular with young Japanese, especially during Golden Week at the beginning of May and during New Year's.

Tenjuso (229)

Minami-soencho 6 Kumi, Beppu 874. ☎ **0977/23-0131.** Fax 0977/25-8455. 14 rms (9 with bath). A/C TV TEL. ¥8,000 ($80) per person; ¥10,000–¥30,000 ($100–$300) per person, including breakfast and dinner. No credit cards. Taxi: 5 minutes.

A reasonably priced ryokan, this traditional inn is more than 60 years old (but was remodeled in 1994). In a residential neighborhood, it seems hidden from the rest of the world. Each tatami-style room is different, and some have private baths, but in any case you'll want to try the hot-spring public bath and outdoor bath. The more expensive rooms have a bathroom and a view of the sea, and there are two Western-style twins.

INEXPENSIVE

Beppu Youth Hostel

Kankaiji 2, Beppu 874. ☎ **0977/23-4116.** Fax 0977/22-0086. 100 beds. A/C. ¥2,800 ($28) for JYHA members. Breakfast ¥450 ($4.50) extra; dinner ¥850 ($8.50) extra. No credit cards. Bus: 14 from Beppu Station to the Suginoi Palace (a 20-minute ride); then a 4-minute walk.

You must have a JYHA card to stay at this youth hostel close to the Suginoi Hotel. Since you have to fork out money for the bus ride, you're better off staying at Kagetsu, described above. In any case, there are both tatami rooms and bunk beds, and facilities include hot-spring baths and a coin-operated laundry.

Green Business Hotel (230)

1-3-11 Kitahama, Beppu 874. ☎ **0977/25-2244.** Fax 0977/25-2236. 53 rms (all with bath). A/C TV TEL. ¥4,500 ($45) single; ¥6,000 ($60) double; ¥8,000 ($80) twin. Breakfast ¥650 ($6.50) extra. Hot-springs tax ¥150 ($1.50). No credit cards.

This relatively new business hotel over a game parlor has larger rooms than those of the average business hotel. Rooms come with coin-operated TV and radio, and those facing the front of the hotel even come with tiny balcony. It's a two-minute walk from Beppu Station.

Kagetsu

Tanoyucho 7-22, Beppu 874. ☎ **0977/24-2355.** Fax 0977/23-7237. 10 rms (all with bath). A/C TV TEL. ¥3,500 ($35) single; ¥6,300 ($63) double; ¥6,500 ($65) twin. No credit cards. Directions: Walk 1 minute from the main exit (turn left out of the station).

Kagetsu probably offers the best deal in all of Beppu—the room rate is about the lowest I've come across in my travels through Japan. Even more astonishing is that each of the rooms, both Western and Japanese style, comes with its own private bathroom and central heating. And as if that weren't enough, the Takayamas give out free tickets to the local public bath, even though their own water is supplied from the natural hot springs. The owners couldn't be nicer. No meals are served, but there are plenty of restaurants in the area. I wish every city had a Kagetsu.

Kokage

8-9 Ekimaecho, Beppu 874. ☎ **0977/23-1753.** Fax 0977/23-3895. 14 rms (10 with bath). A/C TV TEL. ¥4,000 ($40) single; ¥6,000 ($60) twin without bath, ¥7,000 ($70) twin with bath; ¥9,000 ($90) triple without bath, ¥11,500 ($115) triple with bath. Rates include tax. Breakfast ¥800 ($8) extra; Japanese dinner ¥1,800 ($18) extra. AE, DC, MC, V. Directions: Walk 2 minutes from the main exit.

In operation for more than 20 years, this minshuku is run by a friendly older gentleman who speaks a few words of English and is a member of the Japanese Inn group. There are nine Japanese-style rooms, one combination room with bed and tatami area, three twin rooms, and one double room. Rooms are old and a bit worn, but they're furnished with kimono, towels, hot water for tea, and coin-operated heater and air conditioner. There's a public hot-spring bath, and meals are served in a homey dining room with a cluttered but interesting collection of hanging lamps and clocks. In the lobby you'll find a KDD international phone for use with credit cards. The owners will fit you out in wedding kimono and take your picture with your camera, if you like.

DINING

Amamijaya (231)

1-4 Jissoji. ☎ **0977/67-6024.** Reservations not required. ¥450–¥650 ($4.50–$6.50). No credit cards. Thurs–Tues 10am–10pm. NOODLES.

In addition to fugu, another specialty of Beppu is flat noodles. A 15-minute walk from the cluster of six Hells, Amamijaya, which means "Sugar Tea House," serves noodles made by hand by the owner. Filled with local crafts and toys hanging on its walls, this inexpensive shop offers *dangojiro* (flat noodles and vegetable soup), *yaseiuma* (a sweet dish of flat noodles covered with powdered soybeans and sugar), *mochi* (Japanese rice cake), and *zosui* (rice porridge with plums), among other dishes.

Jin (232)
1-15-7 Kitahama. ☎ **0977/21-1768.** Reservations not required. Main dishes ¥300–¥2,500 ($3–$25); set meals ¥2,500–¥5,000 ($25–$50). No credit cards. Daily 5pm–midnight. Directions: Walk 5 minutes. GRILLED FOODS.

If you're looking for a quick, inexpensive dinner near the train station, you'll find plenty of them in and around the main exit. Jin is one of these, easily reached by walking from the station straight down the shop-lined street under the awnings all the way to the end. Jin is on the right, across the street from the Tokiwa department store. It's a lively robatayaki featuring grilled foods, including skewered meats and vegetables and fish.

Yakiniku no. Bungo (233)
4-15 Shinminatomachi. ☎ **0977/21-0780.** All-you-can-eat ¥1,500 ($15). No credit cards. Daily noon–10pm. Directions: Walk 10 minutes from the boat port or take bus 20 or 26 to Shinminatomachi stop (3 minutes). JAPANESE GRILL.

This family-style restaurant probably has the best deal in town. For ¥1,500 ($15), you can choose from more than 20 meat and vegetable items you grill yourself at your table. If that isn't enough, there's also salad, soup, curry, rice, somen noodles, jello, fruit, and dessert. Beer starts at ¥500 ($5). If it's really busy, like on a Sunday, they may ask you to leave after an hour or so; otherwise, dig in for the marathon eat.

3 Mount Aso

31 miles E of Kumamoto, 835 miles SW of Tokyo

In the center of Kyushu, between Beppu and Kumamoto, is the **Mt. Aso National Park,** encompassing two groups of mountains, volcanic Mt. Aso and Mt. Kuju, as well as grasslands, forests, and hot springs. Although Mt. Kuju is the largest mountain on the island, the chief attraction of the park is Mt. Aso: It possesses the largest crater basin in the world. Measuring 11 miles from east to west, almost 15 miles from north to south, and 74½ miles in circumference, Mt. Aso must have been one mighty mountain before blowing its stack—larger even than Mt. Fuji. Today five volcanic cones sit in the Mt. Aso crater basin. One of them, Nakadake, is still active, constantly spewing forth high-temperature gas and sulfurous fumes. Every once in a while it even explodes (the latest eruption occurring in 1979).

ESSENTIALS

The **telephone area code** for Mt. Aso, lying in Kumamoto Prefecture, is 0967 or 09676, depending on the area.

GETTING THERE **By Train** Aso Station is 1 hour from Kumamoto and 2½ hours from Beppu.

By Bus The most popular and pleasant route is by bus along the 186-mile-long Trans-Kyushu Highway, which links Beppu with Mt. Aso, Kumamoto, and Nagasaki. Sightseeing buses departing several times daily from both Kumamoto and Beppu are operated by the Kyushu Kokusai Kanko Bus Company. A timetable for buses departing from both Beppu and Kumamoto is provided in the leaflet "Kumamoto and Mt. Aso," available at the Tourist Information Centers in Kyoto and Tokyo. The buses pass through rice paddies, tobacco and wheat fields, and bamboo groves, and skirt around waterfalls, streams, and hot springs. They all stop at Aso Station and allow 60 to 90 minutes for sightseeing at Mt. Aso's West Station (*Aso-san Nishi*). If you want to spend more time, buy a one-way ticket to Mt. Aso, and then take one of the local buses back down to Aso Station.

GETTING AROUND There are several resort towns at Mt. Aso circling Nakadake, the most famous and only active volcanic cone in the region, including Aso, Takamori, and Aso-Shimoda. If you're interested in going to the top of Nakadake, the approach is from Aso Station in Aso. From Aso Station you can board a **bus** for the 40-minute ride to Aso West Station (Asosan Nishi), from which you can take a **ropeway** to the top of the crater. There are nine buses daily running both ways between Aso Station and Aso West Station. The last bus departs Aso West Station at 5pm, but you'd be wise to check on this.

THE SIGHTS

The natural beauty of the region is the main attraction here, and the volcano is the centerpiece. At the base of Nakadake at Aso West Station is the **Mt. Aso Volcanic Museum,** open daily from 9am to 5pm. The entrance fee is ¥820 ($8.20), and the highlights are two cameras that have been placed on the walls of the active volcanic cone so that you can see the latest activity. There are also two 15-minute films depicting Mt. Aso National Park during the various seasons.

Yumei Kobo (☎ 0967/294-1600) at 759 Higashihiki-no-mizu is a crafts center offering shopping for Kumamoto regional products with a twist: You can watch and/or make yourself blown glass, pottery, or wax resist dye (*roketsu zome*) cloth (each about ¥2,000/$20). Ask the driver for the Yumei Kobo bus stop (it's in front of the center); then, when you've finished, get back on the bus to continue to Aso. The center is open daily from 9am to 7pm.

Also in Aso is Japan's only folk song museum, **Japan International Doyo Museum** (☎ 0967/7-2577), at Kuginomura 869-14. Folk artists from all over Japan perform here daily at 10:30am, 1pm, and 3pm, and there's also a museum. Entrance is ¥1,000 ($10).

If you want to take a hot-springs bath, you can do so at Greenpia Hotel (see below for directions) for ¥300 ($3).

ACCOMMODATIONS

IN MT. ASO NATIONAL PARK

Aso No Tsukasa Villa Park Hotel

Kurokawa, Aso-machi, Aso-gun 869-22. ☎ **0967/34-0811.** Fax 0967/34-0816. 139 rms (102 with bath). A/C MINIBAR TV TEL. ¥13,000–¥36,000 ($130–$360) per person. All rates include breakfast, dinner, and service. AE, DC, JCB, MC, V. Directions: Walk 10 minutes from Aso Station.

The price differences are reflected in room size, furnishings, and meals. The cheapest rooms have no private bathroom, while the most expensive ones feature a wooden tub. Most of the rooms are Japanese style, but there are also combination rooms with a bedroom, a living room, and a separate tatami area, large enough for the whole family. Facilities include hot-springs baths, tennis courts, an outdoor pool, horses for rent, and a botanical garden. In 1991 the Cure Resort Eaux Mar was added, with an indoor pool and hot-springs baths, sauna, and Jacuzzi. Hotel guests can use the facilities for the day for ¥2,000 ($20), while others pay ¥2,800 ($28). Its restaurant, Papiyon, features local beef from the Aso area, known as Higo beef.

Aso Youth Hostel (234)

922-2 Bochu, Aso-machi, Aso-gun 869-22. ☎ **0967/34-0804.** 60 beds. ¥2,500 ($25) for JYHA members and nonmembers. Breakfast ¥450 ($4.50) extra; dinner ¥750 ($7.50) extra. No credit cards. Directions: Walk 15 minutes from Aso Station.

This two-story concrete youth hostel offers just the basics of beds and laundry facilities. There are vending machines and telephones in the halls. All the rooms are Japanese style.

Pension Village

Not far from Aso, near a small town called Uchinomaki, are a dozen or so Western-style pensions, collectively called "Pension Mura" by the locals (Pension Village). Pensions differ from minshuku in that their rooms contain beds instead of futon, but they are also small, family-run affairs with only a handful of rooms. Rooms in all the pensions here average about ¥7,500 ($75) per person, including breakfast and dinner.

Pension Aso No Tokei-Dai

Otohime Pension Mura, Aso-machi, Aso-gun 869-22. ☎ **0967/32-2236.** Fax 0967/32-3429. 9 rms (1 with bath). A/C. ¥7,500 ($75) per person. Rates include breakfast and dinner. AE, JCB, MC, V. Taxi: 5 minutes from Uchinomaki Station.

The owner of this modern pension speaks some English and will refer you to one of the other nearby pensions if his place is full. If you call from the station, someone from the pension will come pick you up.

In Aso-Shimoda

Greenpia

Kuginomura Hisaishi, Minami-Aso 869-14. ☎ **09676/7-2131.** Fax 09676/7-2130. 68 rms (all with bath). A/C MINIBAR TV Tel. ¥9,500 ($95) per person double; ¥8,600 ($86) per person triple. Rates include breakfast and dinner. DC, JCB, MC, V. Taxi:10 minutes from Aso-Shimoda.

The name Greenpia may bring to mind a hotel filled with kids' number one enemy—green peas. Actually, however, this resort hotel is cool for kids and active parents, too. On the large sloping grounds there are horseback riding, croquet, roller skating, putter golf, go-carting, bobsledding, Ping-Pong, mountain biking, video games, and tennis (each of which has a separate charge, for example: ¥1,030/$10.30 per person per hour for tennis). There's a free children's playground, and barbecue/picnic areas, too. Children, who are served a special meal, stay for ¥3,000 ($30), but if your little ones eat and sleep with you, there's no charge. Cuisine is Japanese, but for French cuisine add ¥3,000 ($30). All rooms have a great view of the Aso mountain range, and all the Western-style rooms have a balcony. Facilities include the fifth-floor sky bar Cookoo, a coffee shop called Canary, and the dining room, Robin. The hot-springs baths have floor-to-ceiling windows, great views, and a hedge for discretion, plus a great rest area with large-screen TV and lounge chairs. Make reservations six months in advance for the summer.

Minami Aso Kokumin Shukusha (235)

Choyoson. ☎ **0967/67-0078.** 23 rms (none with bath). TV. ¥6,700–¥7,700 ($67–$77) per person. Rates include breakfast, dinner, and tax. No credit cards.

Near Aso-Shimoda is a People's Lodge, with rates lower than the National Vacation Village described above. There are only three buses daily from Aso-Shimoda Station, so it might be best to take a taxi (a 15-minute ride). All the rooms have balconies, some with splendid views, and come with coin-operated TV, yukata, sheets, and futon. Not far from the lodge is a picturesque open-air bath beside a pounding waterfall, where men and women bathe together.

Dining

Ofukuro Kan (Mother's Kitchen)

Ozawa Higashi Kuginomura 869-14. ☎ **09676/7-0848.** Main dishes ¥400–¥800 ($4–$8). No credit cards. Taxi: 7 minutes from Shimoda.

In a modern building with high windows overlooking ancient burial mounds, rice paddies, and the Aso mountains, Mother's Kitchen features all homemade cooking and handmade pottery dishes. Leave your shoes at the door, choose a dish from the pictures, pay, and then sit down; they'll bring you your meal (tea and water self-service). The Ofukuro Teishoku (¥800/$8) consists of lightly vinegared rice with mountain vegetable, tofu, udon, and salad. You can try your hand at making udon (wheat noodles), *konaku* (a kind of savory jelly), or *odango* (a kind of cake).

4 Kumamoto

804 miles W of Tokyo, 118 miles S of Fukuoka

ESSENTIALS

The **telephone area code** for Kumamoto, lying in Kumamoto Prefecture, is 096.

GETTING THERE **By Train** Trains depart from Fukuoka's Hakata Station several times an hour, reaching Kumamoto in about 1 1/2 hours.

By Bus In addition to express buses that travel between Hakata Station and Kotsu Center in Kumamoto, there are overnight buses from Osaka, Kyoto, Kobe, and Nagoya.

Located roughly halfway down Kyushu's western side, Kumamoto boasts a fine castle and a landscaped garden, both from the first half of the 17th century. Once one of Japan's most important castle towns, Kumamoto today is a progressive city with a population of 626,000. In an effort to attract both domestic and foreign enterprises, the city is planning a technopolis—a technological research city—to be built close to its airport. With other technopolises being planned for such cities in Kyushu as Kagoshima, Oita, and Miyazaki, the island has given itself a nickname: Silicon Island.

VISITOR INFORMATION The leaflet "Kumamoto and Mt. Aso," distributed by the Tourist Information Center in Kyoto and Tokyo, contains information on how to get to Kumamoto and places of interest in the city.

The **tourist information center,** open daily from 9am to 5:30pm, is in front of Kumamoto Station (☎ 096/352-3743). It has a good English map and brochure of the city and is staffed by helpful English-speakers.

GETTING AROUND Kumamoto Station is not in the city's downtown section, but it's easy to get there by streetcar no. 2, which departs from in front of the station. Downtown is northeast of Kumamoto Station, centered around several covered shopping streets called **Shimotori** and **Sunroad Shinshigai,** which are located to the south and southeast of Kumamoto Castle. There are many shops, bars, and restaurants in the area. Nearby is **Kotsu Center,** from which all buses in the city depart, and the location of several business hotels listed below.

By Streetcar The no. 2 streetcar, which departs from Kumamoto Station and passes Kotsu Center, will also take you to both the castle (stop: Kumamoto-jo-mae) and the Suizenji Garden (stop: Suizenji-Koen-mae).

WHAT TO SEE & DO

Completed in 1607, ✪ **Kumamoto Castle** is massive—it took seven years to build. It was constructed under the direction of Kato Kiyomasa, a great warrior who fought alongside Tokugawa Ieyasu in a battle in 1600 and who was rewarded for his loyalty with land in what is today Kumamoto. To make the castle walls impossible for enemies to scale, they were built with curves and topped with an overhang. Furthermore, the castle was built atop a hill and had three main buildings, 49 towers, 29 gates, and 18 two-story gatehouses. Passing into the possession of the Hosokawa family in 1632, the castle remained an important stronghold for the Tokugawa shogunate throughout its 250 years of rule, particularly in campaigns against powerful and independent-minded lords in southern Kyushu.

Much of the castle was destroyed in 1877 during the Seinan Rebellion led by Saigo Takamori, a samurai who was unhappy with the new policies of the Meiji government in which ancient samurai rights were rescinded. Saigo led a troop of samurai in an attack on the castle and its imperial troops. The battle raged for 53 days before government reinforcements finally arrived and quelled the rebellion. When the smoke cleared, most of the castle lay in smoldering ruins, ravaged by fire.

The castle was reconstructed in 1960 of ferroconcrete, and although it's not nearly as massive as before, it's still quite impressive. The interior houses a museum with elaborately decorated palanquins, armor of feudal lords, swords, former possessions of both Kato Kiyomasa and the Hosokawa family, and artifacts from the Seinan Rebellion. There are also displays of such locally made products as pottery and toys. Open daily from 8:30am to 5:30pm (to 4:30pm in winter), it charges an admission of ¥200 ($2) for the castle grounds. If you want to go inside the castle, it costs ¥300 ($3) more. An English earphone guide costs ¥200 ($2).

Not far from the castle are four museums worth seeing. The **Gyobu Tei** is a 300-year old house that was moved near the castle. It was the home of Lord Gyobu and has period furnishings. It charges ¥300 ($3). The **Kumamoto Prefectural Art Museum,** or *Kumamoto Kenritsu Bijutsukan* (☎ 096/352-2111), displays fine art, as well as replicas of burial tombs that have been excavated in the prefecture. In the same area, the prefecture has opened the **Kumamoto Prefectural Art Museum Annex** (☎ 096/351-8411), a new branch that has larger spaces to display bigger works of art. It also has changing exhibits and displays traveling shows. If you happen to be here in March, around the Hino Matsuri, a wonderful collection of the dolls will be on display. Nearby is the **Kumamoto Municipal Museum** (☎ 096/324-3500), housing collections devoted to the humanities and the natural and physical sciences. *Kumamoto Shiritsu Hakubutsukan* also contains a planetarium. Each of these museums is open Tuesday through Sunday from 9am to 4:30pm.

Laid out in 1632 by the Hosokawa family, **Suizenji Garden** wraps itself around a cold spring–fed lake. Incorporated into the garden's design are famous scenes in miniature from the 53 stages of the ancient Tokaido Highway, which connected Kyoto and Tokyo. The 53 stages were also immortalized in Hiroshige's famous woodblock prints. Most recognizable is cone-shaped Mt. Fuji. The park is small—almost disappointingly so. One wishes it stretched on and on. To assuage disappointment, stop off at the 400-year-old thatch-roofed teahouse beside the pond, transported from the imperial grounds in Kyoto. Inside, ceremonial green tea is served while you sit and contemplate the view. If you want to sit on tatami inside the teahouse, it costs ¥520 ($5.20). If you're content sitting outside at a table under the shelter of trees, it costs ¥420 ($4.20). Entrance to the park is ¥200 ($2) between 7:30am and 6pm (8am and 5pm in winter); after that, it's free, but only the main gate remains open. If you want to do some moon gazing, this is the place.

Although it's located on the outskirts of Kumamoto, about 30 minutes by bus from Kotsu Center, if you're at all interested in handcrafted items used in everyday life from various countries around the world, you'll enjoy the **Kumamoto International Folk Art Museum,** or *Tatsuda machi-Kamitatsuda* (☎ 338-7504). This museum displays furniture, pottery, weavings, toys, and other handcrafted items from such diverse countries as India, Peru, Greece, Korea, Mexico, Egypt, and Japan. As items used in everyday life both now and in former times, many of them are rustic but beautifully made. The museum is open Tuesday through Sunday from 9am to 4pm and charges an admission of ¥350 ($3.50). If you're going by bus, get off at the Sannomiya bus stop.

SHOPPING

One of Kumamoto's most famous products is its damascene, in which gold and silver are inlaid on an iron plate to form patterns of flowers, bamboo, and other designs. Originally used to adorn armor, damascene today is used on such accessories as jewelry and tie clasps. Another Kumamoto product is the Yamaga lantern, made of gold paper and used during the Yamaga Lighted Lantern Festival, held in August. Other products include Amakusa pearls, pottery, toys, and bamboo items.

A wonderful place to see Kumamoto Prefecture's products and learn how they are made is the **Kumamoto Traditional Crafts Center** (236) (☎ 096/324-4930) at 3-35 Chiba-jo next to Kumamoto Castle. The center's second floor has handmade craftwork from all over the prefecture, along with displays on how the items are made. Although explanations are in Japanese only, the displays are often self-explanatory. Displays include toys, furniture, wooden rice barrels, damascene, and kitchen knives sharp enough to chop through bone. Entrance here is ¥190 ($1.90) and worth every yen. The first floor of the Traditional Crafts Center is free and serves as a gallery where locally made products are sold. The center is open Tuesday through Sunday from 9am to 5pm.

Another place selling local products is the **Display Hall of Kumamoto Products** (237) on the third floor of the Sangyo Bunka Kaikan Building, downtown next to the Kotsu Center. The *Kumamoto-ken Bussankan,* open daily from 10am to 6pm (except on the second and fourth Mondays of the month), sells pottery, toys, knives, paper lanterns, damascene, Amakusa pearls, spirits, and confectioneries.

ACCOMMODATIONS

EXPENSIVE

Kumamoto Castle Hotel

4-2 Joto-cho, Kumamoto 860. ☎ **096/326-3311.** Fax 096/326-3324. 185 rms. A/C MINIBAR TV TEL. ¥8,000–¥14,000 ($80–$140) single; ¥15,500–¥24,000 ($155–$240) twin; ¥16,000–¥20,000 ($160–$200) double; ¥30,000–¥50,000 ($300–$500) Japanese-style rooms for two. AE, DC, JCB, MC, V. Streetcar: 2 to the Shiyakusho-mae.

This tall brick hotel is located just east of Kumamoto Castle, with some rooms offering good views of the castle grounds. A subdued, quiet, and conservative hotel, it's popular with middle-aged Japanese and has rooms with the usual TV (Japanese only) and hot-water pot with tea.

Dining/Entertainment: Four restaurants in the hotel serve Western, French, and Chinese cuisine, including the Loire on the 11th floor, with views of the castle.

Services: Same-day laundry service.

Hotel New Otani Kumamoto

1-1-13 Kasuga-cho, Kumamoto 860. ☎ **096/326-1111** or 800/421-8795 in the U.S. and Canada. Fax 096/326-0800. 138 rms. A/C MINIBAR TV TEL. ¥8,000–¥12,000 ($80–$120) single; ¥18,000–¥22,000 ($180–$220) double or twin. AE, DC, JCB, MC, V.

Opened in 1992, this luxury hotel, with affordable rates, has everything: next-to-the-station convenience, the name of the respected New Otani Hotels, and the latest in design and amenities. The gracious lobby features a silk-thread mural behind the front desk. The staff of 150 are perspicacious, and many speak English. Rooms feature a corner sofa and large coffee table, plus a generous minibar counter/desk area. All come with hair dryer, bilingual TV, individual reading lights with dimmer switches, window blinds to block light, double-pane windows, message light and bedside controls, the latest air-conditioning system, windows that open, massage shower heads, and such little extra touches as hangers with nonslip pads. Single rooms have queen-size beds. No-smoking rooms are available.

Dining/Entertainment: There are four restaurants and a bar, including a Japanese steakhouse serving Kobe beef and seafood. The coffee shop, Il Fontana, has a breakfast buffet with a fresh fruit and vegetable "wagon" for ¥1,600 ($16) and floor-to-ceiling windows that look out on the bustling station's front.

Services: Complimentary newspaper, room service (6am to midnight).

Facilities: Variety shop, florist, business center with bilingual staff.

MODERATE

Ark Hotel

5-16 Joutou-machi, Kumamoto 860. ☎ **096/351-2222.** Fax 096/326-0909. 222 rms. A/C MINIBAR TV TEL. ¥6,800–¥8,200 ($68–$82) single; ¥12,000–¥22,000 ($120–$220) twin; ¥14,000 ($140) double. AE, DC, JCB, MC, V. Streetcar: 2 to Shiyakusho-mae.

If you want to stay close to the castle, this is a great choice. It opened in 1992 and has an interesting design with lobby bamboo garden. Room colors are relaxing and carry out the flower theme of the hotel. Singles have double beds, and rooms on the seventh to ninth floors have views of Tsuboigawa (the river) and the castle. Other features are a hair dryer, a handy key that fits into a slot by the door and turns on lights, and a phone in the bath. Facilities include a tea-ceremony room and two restaurants.

Chisan Hotel Kumamoto

4-39 Karashimacho, Kumamoto 860. ☎ **096/322-3911.** Fax 096/356-5229. 201 rms. A/C MINIBAR TV TEL. ¥7,500 ($75) single; ¥12,000 ($120) double; ¥12,500–¥13,500 ($125–$135) twin. AE, DC, JCB, MC, V. Streetcar: 2 to the Karashimacho stop.

Part of the Chisan hotel chain, the lobby is pleasantly decorated with marble, brass railings, and stained glass, and the rooms are simple but tasteful. The hotel's one restaurant, decorated with flower prints, serves Western and Japanese food.

Kotsu Center Hotel

3-10 Sakuramachi, Kumamoto 860. ☎ **096/354-1111.** Fax 096/354-1120. 111 rms. A/C MINIBAR TV TEL. ¥5,700–¥8,500 ($57–$85) single; ¥13,000–¥15,500 ($130–$155) double/twin; ¥16,500 ($165) triple. AE, DC, JCB, MC, V.

This hotel is located right in the Kotsu Center itself, with a third-floor lobby buzzing with activity from Japanese group tours. There are French and Szechuan restaurants, and from May through August there's a rooftop beer garden open daily from 5 to 9pm. Rooms are basic but comfortable. The lowest-priced single rooms don't have windows and aren't recommended.

Maruko Hotel

11-10 Kamitori-cho, Kumamoto 860. ☎ **096/353-1241.** Fax 096/353-1217. 39 rms. A/C MINIBAR TV TEL. ¥6,500 ($65) single; ¥12,000 ($120) twin; ¥16,500 ($165) triple. AE, DC, JCB, MC, V. Streetcar: 2 to Torichosuji (walk 8 minutes through the Kamitori shopping arcade).

A member of the Japanese Inn group, this hotel is in the heart of the city, just off the Kamitori covered shopping arcade, and is owned and managed by a petite, gracious woman who is happy to receive foreign guests. Forty of its rooms are Japanese tatami rooms, with a pleasant sitting alcove next to large windows. There are also a couple of Western-style rooms and a couple of combination rooms with both beds and tatami. Both Western and Japanese meals are available, with breakfast for ¥1,000 ($10) and dinner from ¥3,000 to ¥6,000 ($30 to $60).

INEXPENSIVE

$ Guest House Higoji

4-39-31 Kasuga-machi, Kumamoto 860. ☎ **096/352-7860.** Fax 096/354-9812. 7 rms (none with bath). A/C. ¥3,100 ($31) per person, ¥5,650 ($56.50) per person, including tax, breakfast, and dinner. No credit cards. Taxi: 5 minutes.

Staying at this charming inn on a hill, with a small garden and a view of all Kumamoto, is just like staying in the home of the Babas, the older couple who run it. A huge sake jar and *jizaikagi* (fireplace hooks) decorate the entranceway, and guests are gathered around an irori (traditional Japanese fireplace) for tea. You'll eat grilled foods around the irori in winter, and in summer you'll eat outside under the cherry tree and wisteria. The inn has an album of photos and letters from guests who obviously had a wonderful visit. The Babas are kind to children. If you call from the station, they'll come to get you (except in the evening, when they may be too busy). Facilities include TV, laundry machines, bath/shower rooms, and Western toilets. Highly recommended.

Kumamoto Shiritsu Youth Hostel (238)

5-15-55 Shimazaki-machi, Kumamoto 860. ☎ **096/352-2441.** Fax 096/353-1215. 64 beds. A/C. ¥1,500 ($15) for JYHA members and nonmembers. Air-conditioning or heating ¥200 ($2) extra; sheets ¥150 ($1.50) extra; breakfast ¥400 ($4) extra; dinner ¥600 ($6) extra. No credit cards. Bus: A-9 from Kotsu Center to the Kuriyama Youth Hostel Mae.

Located in a residential area, this youth hostel has 32 beds for women and 32 beds for men. The man in charge here speaks English.

Kumamoto Station Hotel (239)

1-3-6 Nihongi, Kumamoto 860. ☎ **096/325-2001.** Fax 096/325-2900. 60 rms A/C TV TEL. ¥6,000 ($60) single; ¥10,600 ($106) double or twin; Japanese-style rooms ¥13,400 ($134) for two, ¥16,800 ($168) for three. Rates include tax and service charge. Breakfast ¥600 ($6) extra. No credit cards. Directions: Walk straight out of Kumamoto Station, cross the first bridge, then turn immediately right; the hotel is the first building on the right, beside a small river.

This is your best bet if you want to stay in a business hotel within walking distance of Kumamoto Station. It has simple rooms refurbished in 1993, a small restaurant/coffee shop, and an English-speaking staff.

Tokyu Inn

7-25 Shinshigai, Kumamoto 860. ☎ **096/322-0109.** Fax 096/322-3050. 138 rms (all with bath). A/C MINIBAR TV TEL. ¥7,100–¥7,300 ($71–73) single; ¥10,300–¥20,000 ($103–$200) double/twin. AE, DC, JCB, MC, V. Streetcar: 2 to the Karashimacho stop.

This business hotel is across the street from the Kotsu Center, right next to the Sunroad Shinshigai covered shopping arcade. Its rooms are small but contain everything you need, including cotton kimono. There's a Western as well as a yakinuku restaurant, and vending machines dispensing pop and beer.

DINING

Kumamoto's specialties include *dengaku* (delicacies such as fish, taro, and tofu coated with bean paste and grilled at a fire), *karashi renkon* (lotus root that has been boiled, filled with a mixture of bean paste and mustard, and then deep-fried), and *basashi* (raw horse meat that's sliced thin and then dipped in soy sauce flavored with ginger or garlic).

Expensive

Loire

Kumamoto Castle Hotel, 4-2 Joto-cho. ☎ **096/326-3311.** Reservations recommended. Set dinners ¥3,800–¥10,000 ($38–$100); set lunches ¥1,200–¥5,000 ($12–$50). AE, DC, JCB, MC, V. Daily 11:30am–2pm and 5–10pm. Streetcar: 2 to Shiyakusho-mae. FRENCH.

This restaurant overlooks Kumamoto Castle and is a convenient place for lunch if you're visiting the castle or the Kumamoto Traditional Crafts Center. The menu is short, offering primarily seasonal set meals of seafood and beef dishes.

Senbazuru

New Otani Hotel, 1-1-13 Kasuga. ☎ **096/326-1111.** Set lunchs ¥1,600–¥5,000 ($16–$50); set dinners ¥5,000–¥15,000 ($50–$150). AE, DC, JCB, MC, V. Daily 11:30am-2:30pm and 5–9:30pm. VARIED JAPANESE.

Next to Kumamoto Station, Senbazuru is a beautifully furnished, highly refined restaurant with tatami rooms. Its low tables have a well underneath, for those errant legs that don't want to bend. Kimono-clad women serve you, kneeling to open and close the shoji to your private room—a sign of grace and respect. Every room is named after a flower, and each room's interior matches its name. Kobe beef shabu-shabu, tempura, and *moriawase* (a selection of sashimi) are offered.

Moderate

Ginnan

Kumamoto Castle Hotel, 4-2 Joto-cho. ☎ **096/326-3311.** Reservations not required. Set dinners ¥2,800–¥10,000 ($28–$100); set lunch from ¥1,000 ($10). AE, DC, JCB, MC, V. Daily 11:30am–2pm and 4:30–9:30pm. Streetcar: 2 to Shiyakusho-mae. TEMPURA/SEAFOOD.

Another good choice for dining in the vicinity of the castle and the Kumamoto Traditional Crafts Center is the Castle Hotel's Japanese restaurant. A fish tank at this restaurant's entrance displays shrimp, flatfish, and eels happily swimming around, unaware of their impending fate, and the Japanese menu has pictures of its offerings, of which the tempura set dinner is the most popular.

✪ Gozan (240)

Taigeki Kaikan Bldg. basement, 4-1 Tedorihoncho. ☎ **096/351-2869.** Dishes ¥300–¥3,800 ($3–$38). AE, JCB, V. Daily 5–midnight. Streetcar: Toricho stop. JAPANESE CROSSOVER.

Don't miss this surreal mix of ancient Japanese and avant-garde interior, food, and waiters. Basically a beer hall (with beers from around the world), Gozan is like no other I've ever seen. New Age/kabuki music plays in the background of noisy eaters. A volcano in the middle of the room erupts in lit optic fibers, while plastic bamboo mixes with tile roofs and faux mud walls. Foods range from basashi to Kumamoto steak and agedashi tofu. Beer starts at ¥400 ($4). Come here just to check out the decor—even the bathrooms are interesting, with wooden grates under which spigots spout up water as if by magic when you approach. A ¥3,500 ($35) set meal allows you to drink all you want for an additional ¥1,300 ($13) for men and ¥1,000 ($10) for women.

Senri (241)

Suizenji Garden. ☎ **096/381-1415.** Reservations recommended. Set dinners from ¥4,500 ($45); set lunches ¥1,600–¥2,000 ($16–$20). No credit cards. Daily 11am–9pm. Streetcar: 2 to Suizenji-Koen-mae. LOCAL SPECIALTIES/VARIED JAPANESE.

You can try Kumamoto's local dishes at this restaurant right in Suizenji Garden, which is a good place to stop off for lunch or dinner while visiting the famous garden. Although the menu is in Japanese only, there's a pamphlet available with pictures. Teishoku set lunches include eel, river fish, tempura, and basashi. Along with your choice of main dish are side dishes of a vegetable, soup, rice, and tea. Dinners include the same items as in the lunch teishoku, plus extra dishes. Dining is in small tatami rooms, located to the right after you enter the front door. The choice rooms face the garden.

INEXPENSIVE

Aoyagi (242)

1-2-10 Shimotori. ☎ **096/353-0311.** Reservations not required. Set meals ¥1,200–¥2,500 ($12–$25); kaiseki ¥4,000 ($40). AE, JCB, MC, V. Daily 11:30am–10pm. Streetcar: 2 to the Torichosuji; then walk through the Shimotori shopping arcade. VARIED JAPANESE/LOCAL SPECIALTIES.

Everyone in Kumamoto knows this restaurant, located in the downtown area just off the Shimotori shopping arcade. It has a plastic-food display case outside its front door, showing dishes of sushi, tempura, basashi, and kamameshi (rice casseroles). You can also take out box lunches of sushi for ¥1,100 ($11) and up. There are four floors of dining.

Beer Garden

Kotsu Center Hotel, 3-10 Sakuramachi. ☎ **096/354-1111.** Reservations not required. Main dishes ¥300–¥500 ($3–$5). No credit cards. Daily 5–9pm. Closed Sept–Apr. VARIED.

If the weather's warm and your main interest is drinking beer outdoors, head for the roof of this conveniently located beer garden at the Kotsu Center bus depot. It has its share of fake palm trees and Astro-turf, but it also offers panoramic views of the city. Beer starts at ¥450 ($4.50), and snacks include grilled chicken, sausage, french fries, *edamame* (soybeans), and other fare.

$ Goemon (243)

1-7-3 Shimotori. ☎ **096/354-2266.** Reservations not required. ¥200–¥600 ($2–$6); set dinners ¥800–¥1,500 ($8–$15). No credit cards. Daily 5pm–2am. Streetcar: 2 to Torichosuji. VARIED JAPANESE/LOCAL SPECIALTIES.

Located downtown near the Shimotori shopping arcade, this is technically a drinking establishment, but it serves a variety of inexpensive dishes and is popular with a lively crowd, especially on weekends. A la carte dishes of dengaku, flatfish, sashimi, green-tea noodles, and much more are offered, as well as set meals. The menu is in Japanese only, but there's a plastic-food display case. This establishment has a rustic feel to it, and although it's tatami seating, some of the tables have leg wells underneath for your feet. Take off your shoes at the front door and deposit them in a locker, just as you would at a bathhouse.

Kimura-so (244)

Suizenji Garden. ☎ **096/384-1864.** Reservations not required. Fried carp ¥650 ($6.50); set meal ¥2,500 ($25). No credit cards. Thurs–Tues 11am–9pm. Streetcar: 2 to Suizenji-Koen-mae. CARP.

Just a few steps away from Senri (described above), and also located in Suizenji Garden, this restaurant features inexpensive dining outside in a pavilion built over a pond, with a partial view of the garden. Carp is its specialty, which you can have raw or fried. Also on the menu are grilled shrimp, eel, tonkatsu, and basashi.

5 Nagasaki

825 miles W of Tokyo, 95 miles SW of Fukuoka

Nagasaki lies on the northwest coast of Kyushu. Unlike Kumamoto, Kagoshima, or many other well-known cities in Japan, Nagasaki does not have a castle or famous landscaped garden. Rather, Nagasaki's charm is much more subtle, lying in the city itself. Many people in Japan—including foreign residents—consider Nagasaki one of the country's most beautiful cities. It's a town of hills rising from the harbor, of houses perched on terraced slopes, of small streets, distinctive neighborhoods, and of people extremely proud of their city. Without a doubt, it's one of Japan's most livable cities.

Perhaps to the untrained foreign eye, Nagasaki may look like any other modern Japanese town, but there's no other city in Japan quite like it. In a nation as homogeneous as Japan, Nagasaki from a historical perspective is its most cosmopolitan city, with a unique blend of outside cultures interwoven into its architecture, food, and festivals. Centuries ago, Nagasaki's bay, sheltered by islands, made it a natural as a safe place to anchor ships. It opened its harbor to European vessels in 1571 and became a port of call for Portuguese and Dutch ships. Chinese merchants moved here and set up their own community. Along with traders came St. Francis Xavier and other Christian missionaries, primarily from Portugal and Spain, who found many converts among the Japanese in Nagasaki. And during Japan's more than 200 years of isolation, only Nagasaki was allowed to conduct trade with outsiders and thus served as the nation's window on the rest of the world. Even today Japanese come to Nagasaki for a dose of the city's intermingled cultures.

ESSENTIALS

The **telephone area code** for Nagasaki, lying in Nagasaki Prefecture, is 0958.

GETTING THERE **By Train** Trains depart Hakata Station in Fukuoka approximately every half hour, with travel time of approximately two hours. From Tokyo, take the Shinkansen bullet train to Hakata Station and transfer there for a train to Nagasaki; travel time is 8 to 9½ hours, depending on the type of train and connections.

VISITOR INFORMATION Information on Nagasaki and its attractions is given in "Nagasaki and Unzen," a leaflet available at the Tourist Information Center in Tokyo and Kyoto.

At Nagasaki Station the **Nagasaki City Office of Tourist Information** (☎ 0958/22-1954 or 23-3631) maintains an information window, located just past the ticket-gate exit, which distributes maps in English. It's open daily from 8am to 7pm. An even better map, however, is available just across the street from the train station in the office of the **Nagasaki Prefecture Tourist Federation** (☎ 0958/26-9407), on the second floor of the Ken-ei Bus Terminal. This office can provide information on all of Nagasaki Prefecture, including Unzen.

GETTING AROUND Along with Kobe and Sapporo, Nagasaki is one of Japan's most navigable cities, and there are lots of signs in English pointing the way to attractions. Nagasaki Station is not considered the downtown part of the city. Rather, most nightspots, shops, and restaurants are located southeast of the station, clustered around an area that contains Shianbashi Dori, Kanko Dori Street, and the Hamanomachi shopping arcade. Peace Park and its museum on the atomic bomb are located north of Nagasaki Station.

By Streetcar The easiest way to get around the city is by streetcar. Four lines run through the heart of the city, and most stops are written in English. The streetcars are ancient one-wagon affairs, retired to Nagasaki from other cities that considered them too slow and old-fashioned. And yet in Nagasaki, streetcars have their own lanes of traffic, so that during rush hour they're usually the fastest things on the road. It costs a mere ¥100 ($1) to ride one; pay at the front when you get off. You can also buy a ¥500 ($5) ticket at major hotels that allows unlimited rides for one day on the city's streetcars. If you're buying individual tickets, you're allowed to transfer to another line only at Tsukimachi Station. Otherwise, you must buy a separate ticket each time you board a streetcar.

On Foot You can also get around Nagasaki easily on foot, certainly the most intimate way to experience the city and its atmosphere. You can walk from the Hamanomachi shopping district to Glover Garden, for example, in 15 to 20 minutes, passing Chinatown, Dejima, and the Dutch Slope on the way. Shianbashi Dori, located just off the streetcar stop of the same name, is just a few minutes' walk from the Hamanomachi shopping arcade.

By Bus Nagasaki also has buses, but destinations are in Japanese only, and who knows where the heck they're going? Stick to the streetcars.

WHAT TO SEE & DO

All of Nagasaki's major attractions are connected with the city's diversified and sometimes tragic past. The city is perhaps best known as the second city—and, we hope, the last city—to be destroyed by an atomic bomb.

NISHIZAKA HILL After Nagasaki opened its port to European vessels, Christian missionaries came to the city to convert the Japanese to Christianity. Gradually, however, the Japanese rulers began to fear that these Christian missionaries would try to exert political and financial influence through their converts. Who wasn't to say that conversion to Christianity was just the first step toward colonialization? So in 1587 the shogun Hideyoshi Toyotomi officially banned Christianity. In 1597, 26 Christians (20 Japanese and 6 foreigners) were arrested in Kyoto and Osaka, marched through the snow to Nagasaki, and crucified on Nishizaka Hill as examples of what would happen to offenders. Through the ensuing years, there were more than 600 documented cases of Christians being put to death in the Nishizaka area. In 1862 the 26 martyrs were named saints by the pope. Today, on Nishizaka Hill, about a three-minute walk from Nagasaki Station, there's a monument dedicated to the saints with statues of the 26 martyrs carved in stone relief. There's also a small museum housing artifacts relating to the history of Christianity in Japan, as well as ashes of three of the saints. Perhaps most amazing about the history of Christianity in Japan is that the religion was practiced secretly by the faithful throughout Japan's isolation policy, surviving more than 200 years underground without the benefits of a church or clergy.

DEJIMA When the Tokugawa shogunate adopted a national policy of isolation in the 1630s, only Nagasaki was allowed to remain open as a port of trade with foreigners. Since the Portuguese and Spaniards were associated with the outlawed Christian religion, only the Dutch and the Chinese were allowed to continue trading. The Dutch were confined to a tiny man-made island called Dejima, and the only people allowed to cross the bridge into the Dutch community were Japanese prostitutes and traders.

Today, Dejima is little more than a streetcar stop, having long ago become part of the mainland in the city's land reclamation projects. If you're interested, however, the **Nagasaki Municipal Dejima Museum** (reached by taking streetcar no. 1 to the Dejima stop) houses materials relating to the Dutch during their seclusion on the island. It's free and is open Tuesday through Sunday from 9am to 5pm. Behind the museum is a model of how the island used to look when the Dutch lived there.

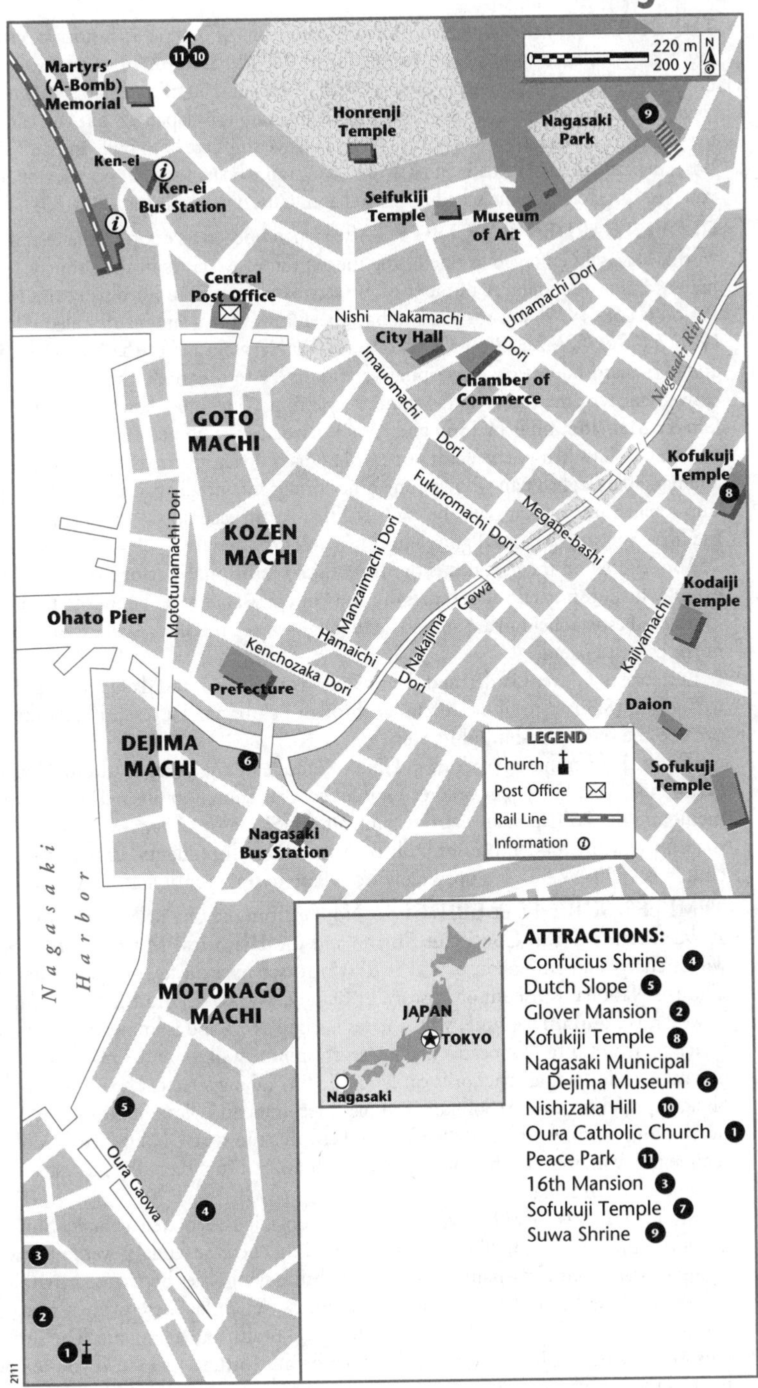

220 m
200 y
N
Martyrs' (A-Bomb) Memorial
11 10
Honrenji Temple
Nagasaki Park
9
Ken-ei
Ken-ei Bus Station
Seifukiji Temple
Museum of Art
Central Post Office
Nishi Nakamachi
Umamachi Dori
City Hall
Dori
Chamber of Commerce
Imauomachi
Dori
Nagasaki River
GOTO MACHI
Kofukuji Temple
8
Fukuromachi Dori
Megane-bashi
KOZEN MACHI
Mototunamachi Dori
Manzaimachi Dori
Kodaiji Temple
Gowa
Ohato Pier
Hamaichi
Nakajima
Kajiyamachi
Kenchozaka Dori
Dori
Prefecture
Daion
DEJIMA MACHI
6
LEGEND
Church
Post Office
Rail Line
Information
Sofukuji Temple
Nagasaki Bus Station
Nagasaki Harbor
MOTOKAGO MACHI
JAPAN
TOKYO
Nagasaki
ATTRACTIONS:
Confucius Shrine 4
Dutch Slope 5
Glover Mansion 2
Kofukuji Temple 8
Nagasaki Municipal Dejima Museum 6
Nishizaka Hill 10
Oura Catholic Church 1
Peace Park 11
16th Mansion 3
Sofukuji Temple 7
Suwa Shrine 9
5
Oura Gaowa
4
3
2
1
2111

THE PORT If you're interested in seeing the results of Nagasaki's history as a trading port, walk to nearby Ohato Port Terminal (☎ 0958/26-6236) or take streetcar no. 1 to the Ohato stop. There you can board a boat for a 50-minute trip through the town's modern harbor. The never-ending commentary is in Japanese, but you can see for yourself the Mitsubishi shipyards, where massive ships are both built and repaired. Boats depart daily at 11:40am and 3:15pm, with more boats added in peak season, but you'd be wise to check the schedule beforehand. Cost of the cruise is ¥900 ($9).

GLOVER GARDEN & VICINITY After Japan opened its doors to the rest of the world, Nagasaki emerged as one of the more progressive cities in the country, with many foreign residents. A number of Western-style houses built during the Meiji Period (1868–1912) still survive and have been moved to a large park called Glover Garden (☎ 0958/22-8223) on a hill overlooking Nagasaki and the harbor. The stone and clapboard houses have sweeping verandas, Western parlors, the most modern conveniences of the time—and Japanese-style roofs. The most famous house is the **Glover Mansion,** built in 1863 and romanticized as the home of Madame Butterfly, the fictitious heroine of Verdi's opera. Thomas Glover, married to a Japanese, was a remarkable Englishman who, among other things, financially backed and managed ship-repair yards in Nagasaki, brought the first steam locomotive to Japan, opened the first mint in Japan, sold guns and ships, and exported tea.

Also located on the grounds is the **Nagasaki Traditional Performing Arts Museum,** which displays floats and dragons used in Nagasaki's most famous festival, the Okunchi Festival, held in autumn. The highlight of the museum is an excellent film of the colorful parade.

Entrance to Glover Garden and the museum is ¥600 ($6), and daily hours are 8am to 5:45pm (8:30am to 5pm December through February). To reach it, take streetcar 5 to the Oura Tenshudoshita stop.

Within a few minutes' walk from Glover Garden are the **Oura Catholic Church** (☎ 0958/23-2628), Japan's oldest Gothic wooden church, built in 1865 to commemorate the 26 Christian martyrs, and **Dutch Slope** or *Oranda-zaka,* a cobbled road lined with wooden houses built by former Dutch residents. Entrance to the church is ¥250 ($2.50). It's open daily from 8am to 6pm (until 4:45 in winter).

TEMPLES, SHRINES & BRIDGES Not far from the Oura Church mentioned above are the colorful **Confucius Shrine** and the **Historical Museum of China,** which charges an admission of ¥515 ($5.15) to see its artifacts, on loan from the Chinese National Museum of History in Beijing. Nagasaki's most famous temple, however, is **Sofukuji Temple,** which dates back to 1629 and is known for its Ming Dynasty architecture. It's located about a seven-minute walk from the Hamanomachi downtown shopping district or is easily reached by taking streetcar no. 1 or 4 to the Shokakujishita stop. From Sofukuji Temple, I recommend a pleasant 20-minute walk north along narrow streets to **Kofukuji Temple,** the first Obaku-Zen Buddhist temple in Japan, founded by a Chinese priest in 1629. From there the nearest streetcar stop is Kokaidomae.

Although the Okunchi Festival has Chinese roots, it's celebrated at **Suwa Shrine,** a Shinto shrine that was built to promote Shintoism when the feudal government was trying to stamp out Christianity. Today, the shrine symbolizes better than anything else the spiritual heart of the Japanese community. When Japanese women turn 33 and men turn 40, they come here to pray for good health and a long life. The shrine sells fortunes in English. If you're satisfied with your fortune, keep it. If you're not, tie it to the branch of a tree and the fortune is conveniently negated. Suwa Shrine is a few minutes' walk from the Suwa Jinja-mae streetcar stop, reached by streetcar no. 3 or 4.

In addition to the temples described above, the Chinese also left their mark on Nagasaki with the construction of several bridges. Most famous of these is the so-called **Megane-bashi,** or **Spectacles Bridge,** named after the reflection the two-arched bridge casts in the water. I wouldn't know, however, because I've never seen the Nakashima River larger than a trickle. It does occasionally flood, as in 1982, when it wiped out several old bridges. These have now been reconstructed, along with a promenade complete with benches and children's playgrounds. Since it's only a five-minute walk from the Hamanomachi shopping arcade, you might wish to come here with some take-out sushi and enjoy a picnic. The Megane-bashi, by the way, was built in 1634 by a Chinese Zen priest named Mozi of Kofukuji Temple. It's the oldest stone-arched bridge in Japan and is one of Nagasaki's most photographed objects. The nearest streetcar stops are Nigiwai-bashi and Kokaidomae on lines 3, 4, and 5.

PEACE PARK On August 9, 1945, at 11:02am, American forces dropped an atomic bomb over Nagasaki, three days after they had dropped a bomb over Hiroshima. Exploding 1,600 feet above ground, it destroyed about a third of the city, killed an estimated 75,000 people, and injured 75,000 more. Today, Nagasaki's citizens are among the most vigorous peace activists in the world, and Peace Park, located north of Nagasaki Station, serves as a reminder of that fateful day and a warning about the destructiveness of the atomic bomb. Every year on the anniversary of the bombing, a peace demonstration is held in Peace Park.

Next to Peace Park is a museum, the **Nagasaki International Cultural Hall** (popularly called the **Atomic Bomb Museum**) (☎ 0958/44-1231). It contains objects, photos, and artifacts showing the devastation caused by the atomic bomb. It's by no means pleasant, but something every concerned individual should see. The International Cultural Hall is open daily from 9am to 6pm April through October, closing an hour earlier November through March. The entrance fee is ¥50 (50¢). Located in the basement of the same building, but containing an entirely different kind of collection, is the **Nagasaki Municipal Museum,** which charges ¥100 ($1) admission. It features artifacts relating to the Edo Period and Japanese Christianity. Peace Park can be reached by streetcar no. 1 or 3; disembark at the Matsuyama stop.

SHOPPING

Locally made Nagasaki products include cultured pearls and coral objects. A convenient place to shop for Nagasaki products is the **Local Products Hall,** or *Nagasaki-ken Bussankan,* across the street from Nagasaki Station on the second floor of the Ken-ei Bus Terminal. Look for the sign outside that says NAGASAKI PREFECTURE TOURIST FEDERATION.

Another famous product of Nagasaki is its castella *(kasutera),* a spongecake with Portuguese origins. Japanese visitors to Nagasaki can't leave without buying castella for co-workers and friends back home. There are cake shops throughout the city, and the most famous is **Fukusaya** (☎ 0958/21-2938) at 3-1 Fundaiku-machi, not far from the Hamanomachi shopping arcade. Fukusaya is located in a 200-year-old building and has a history stretching back even further. Notice the bat symbol on the packaging, noren, and outside lights. In Chinese lore, bats equal happiness. Castella are still sold by the old Japanese weight of *kin* (1 kin = 80g) and cost ¥1,400 ($14) per kin. It's open daily from 8:30am to 8pm.

ACCOMMODATIONS

Nagasaki has very reasonably priced hotels. The busiest time of the year is in May, when Nagasaki is brimming with busloads of schoolchildren who come here on class excursions.

EXPENSIVE

Hotel New Nagasaki

14-5 Daikoku-machi, Nagasaki 850. ☎ **0958/26-8000.** Fax 0958/23-2000. 149 rms. A/C MINIBAR TV TEL. ¥23,000 ($230) double or twin. AE, DC, JCB, MC, V.

One of Nagasaki's deluxe hotels, the Hotel New Nagasaki has a convenient location right next to the train station. Its marble lobby is light and airy, and rooms have cable TV. Many rooms also have connections for fax machines.

Dining/Entertainment: Seven restaurants range from Western to Chinese and Japanese, including a Kobe steakhouse. There's one bar.

Service: Free newspaper, same-day laundry service.

Facilities: Fitness club, indoor swimming pool, sauna (fee: ¥2,000/$20), florist.

Majestic Hotel

2-28 Minami Yamate-machi, Nagasaki 850. ☎ **0958/27-7777.** Fax 0958/27-6112. 23 rms. A/C MINIBAR TV TEL. ¥19,000–¥27,000 ($190–$270) twin; ¥23,000 ($230) double; ¥35,000 ($350) suite. AE, DC, JCB, MC, V. Streetcar: 1 to Tsukimachi, then 5 to Oura Tenshudoshita.

The Majestic is a charming, small, four-floor hotel designed like a little jewel. The beautifully appointed rooms have seven variations of decor, including country, which has wooden floors, light-oak furnishings, and even footed bathtubs. There are no singles. Bathrooms are larger than average, with marble or tile, bathrobes, and a laundry rope (a blessing if you've been on the road). Bayside terrace rooms have a balcony, and the bath has a window that can be opened onto the bedroom and the view. I love this getaway because I feel as though I'm at home instead of among the crowds of tour buses, as is so often the case in Japan.

Dining/Entertainment: One tiny European-style restaurant/bar is cozy and feels like your own place.

Services: Complimentary newspaper.

Nagasaki Tokyu Hotel

1-18 Minamiyamate-machi, Nagasaki 850. ☎ **0958/25-1501.** Fax 0958/23-5167. 218 rms. A/C MINIBAR TV TEL. ¥11,000–¥12,000 single ($110–$120); 20,000 ($200) double; ¥19,000–¥25,000 ($190–$250) twin. AE, DC, JCB, MC, V. Streetcar: 1 to Tsukimachi, then 5 to Oura Tenshudoshita.

The lobby of this hotel, located near Glover Garden, is sparsely furnished (bare white walls and stained-glass windows). It reminds me of the inside of a church—fitting with Nagasaki's history. Comfortable rooms have a tiny balcony and bilingual TV. Since rates are based on room size rather than view, ask for a room facing Glover Garden. The manager speaks English and is accommodating.

Dining/Entertainment: French food is served in the Glover restaurant, along with views of the harbor. Ohura features both Japanese and Chinese cuisine, and there's one bar.

Services: Free newspaper.

Facilities: Souvenir shop.

Park Side Hotel

14-1 Heiwa-machi, Nagasaki 852. ☎ **0958/45-3191.** Fax 0958/46-5550. 61 rms. A/C MINIBAR TV TEL. ¥12,000 ($120) single; ¥18,000 ($180) double; ¥19,000–¥23,000 ($190–$230) twin. AE, DC, JCB, MC, V. Streetcar: 1 or 3 to the Matsuyama.

This pleasant and small hotel located next to Peace Park is a favorite with long-term guests, both because they enjoy its quiet location and because they can jog early in the morning in the park. The Western-style restaurant has big windows overlooking the greenery of the park, which is ablaze with cherry blossoms in spring. There's also a teppanyaki restaurant. Rooms, with semi-double-size beds and double-pane windows, are well appointed in light wood and soft colors. Special touches include a pull-out bedside control panel (so that the clock nightlight doesn't keep you awake) and minibars hidden behind beautiful wooden doors. Bathrooms feature soft-peach tiling and bidet/toilets.

✪ **Sakamoto-ya** (245)

2-13 Kanaya-machi, Nagasaki 850. ☎ **0958/26-8211.** Fax 0958/25-5944. 17 rms (15 with bath). A/C MINIBAR TV TEL. ¥15,000–¥25,000 ($150–$250) per person. Rates include breakfast, dinner, and service charge. AE, DC, JCB, MC, V.

If you want to sleep in a ryokan, this beautiful 90-year-old ryokan (Nagasaki's oldest), a five-minute walk southeast of Nagasaki Station, is right in the heart of the city and is a wonderful place to stay. Most of the rooms have a Japanese-style bathtub made of wood, as well as artwork on the walls. The best room is the Pine Room (Matsu No Ma), which even has its own private little garden. Rates here vary according to the room and the meals served. You may order a shippoku dinner, a Nagasaki specialty consisting of a variety of dishes showing European and Chinese influences, for ¥5,000 ($50) more. Western breakfasts are also served on request.

MODERATE

Hamilton

7-9 Maruyama-machi, Nagasaki 850. ☎ **0958/24-1000.** Fax 0958/27-8111. 87 rms. A/C MINIBAR TV TEL. ¥8,000–¥11,000 ($80–$110) single; ¥14,500–¥16,000 ($145–$160) double; ¥20,000–¥22,000 ($200–$220) twin; ¥26,000–¥28,000 ($260–$280) triple. AE, DC, MC, V. Streetcar: 1 to Shokakuji-shita.

This medium-range tourist hotel gives excellent value for money, with large comfortably furnished rooms decorated in English style, double beds in the singles, and lots of amenities, like rental PCs, fax outlets, and cable TV with 20 channels. It's conveniently located on Shianbashi Street and features Club Carlton, a bar/restaurant offering a vast selection of beers.

Holiday Inn

6-24 Doza-machi, Nagasaki 850. ☎ **0958/28-1234** or 800/HOLIDAY in the U.S. Fax 0958/28-0178. 87 rms. A/C MINIBAR TV TEL. ¥8,500–¥11,000 ($85–$110) single; ¥15,000–¥18,000 ($150–$180) double; ¥16,000–¥20,000 ($160–$200) twin. Children under 12 stay free in parents' room. AE, DC, JCB, MC, V. Streetcar: 1 to Kanko Dori.

This hotel is conveniently located just off Kanko Dori, close to the Hamanomachi shopping arcade in the heart of the city. You can walk from the hotel to most sites, including Glover Mansion and Sofukuji and Kofukuji Temples. All rooms have double-, queen-, or king-size beds. Some rooms face a wall one foot away; if you are claustrophobic, specify a room with a view. The hotel's restaurant serves Japanese cuisine. There's also a cocktail bar.

Hotel New Tanda

2-24 Tokiwa-machi, Nagasaki 850. ☎ **0958/27-6121.** Fax 0958/26-1704. 161 rms. A/C MINIBAR TV TEL. ¥8,100–¥9,900 ($81-$99) single; ¥13,600–¥18,300 ($136–$183) double; ¥16,200–¥19,200 ($162-$192) twin; ¥19,800 ($198) triple. AE, DC, JCB, MC, V. Streetcar: 1 to Tsukimachi, then 5 to Shimin Byoin.

This brick hotel is located at the bottom of Dutch Slope, about a seven-minute walk to either Glover Garden or the Hamanomachi shopping district. Popular with foreign visitors, it has one Western-style restaurant, a bar, and a combination pub/restaurant. In summer there's a rooftop beer garden, where you can look out over the harbor. Room rates are based on location, view, and furnishing.

Hotel Station Royal Ajisai 246

7-3 Daikoku-machi, Nagasaki 850. ☎ **0958/22-2222.** Fax 0958/22-9608. 82 rms. A/C TV TEL. ¥7,000 ($70) single; ¥10,000–¥14,000 ($100-$140) double/twin; ¥18,000 ($180) triple; ¥24,000 ($240) Japanese-style rooms for four. AE, DC, MC, V.

This modern brick building across the street from Nagasaki Station is a cross between a business and a tourist hotel. It's locally owned by a Japanese who has eight hotel properties in Nagasaki, and its rooms come with just the basics, including double-pane windows to shut out train traffic. The most expensive twins are large corner rooms with big windows that open onto a balcony and offer sweeping views. The best deal, however, is a large Japanese-style room with two beds plus a separate tatami area—good for a family, a large group, or the entertaining of friends. The hotel has one coffee shop with a ¥1,000 ($10) set breakfast and one Japanese restaurant.

Nagasaki Grand Hotel

5-3 Manzai-machi, Nagasaki 850. ☎ **0958/23-1234.** Fax 0958/22-1793. 18 rms. A/C MINIBAR TV TEL. ¥9,000 ($90) single; ¥14,000 ($140) double; ¥15,000–¥23,000 ($150–$230) twin; ¥20,000 ($200) Japanese-style rooms for two. AE, DC, JCB, MC, V. Streetcar: 1 to Hamanomachi.

This fine older hotel is conveniently located near the Hamanomachi shopping district. Its rooms are soothingly decorated in soft pastels, windows open, and some have balconies. The single rooms have narrow beds. There are eight Japanese-style rooms. The hotel has two restaurants, one Western, one Japanese.

Nagasaki Washington Hotel

9-1 Shinchi-machi, Nagasaki 850. ☎ **0958/28-1211.** Fax 0958/25-8023. 177 rms. A/C MINIBAR TV TEL. ¥8,000–¥8,300 ($80–$83) single; ¥15,000 ($150) double; ¥16,000–¥17,500 ($160–$175) twin. AE, DC, JCB, MC, V. Streetcar: 1 to the Tsukimachik.

This chain hotel is located on the edge of the city's tiny Chinatown, about a two-minute walk from the Hamanomachi shopping district. The rooms in this 10-story brick building are slightly more expensive than those in the average business hotel, but the rooms are large. Panels in the windows can be closed for complete darkness. The hotel's 10th-floor restaurant, with views of the city, specializes in steaks. There's also a coffee shop and Japanese restaurant.

INEXPENSIVE

Dejimanoki Pub and Pension

10-16 Dejima-machi, Nagasaki 850. ☎ **0958/22-6833.** Fax 0958/22-8197. 10 rms (all with bath). A/C TV TEL. ¥5,000 ($50) per person twin; ¥4,500 ($45) per person triple. Breakfast ¥500 ($5) extra. No credit cards. Streetcar: 1 from Nagasaki Station to Tsukimachi; then a 1-minute walk.

This five-floor, no-frills pension has a pub/cafe on the ground floor serving snacks from ¥500 ($5). Ms. Ano, the congenial owner, speaks English. Rooms are basic and come with pay TV and minuscule bathrooms. All the rooms have a small balcony. It's located next to the Historical Museum.

Fumi

4-9 Daikoku-machi, Nagasaki 850. ☎ **0958/22-4962.** 5 rms (none with bath). A/C TV TEL. ¥4,300 ($43) per person. No credit cards.

This minshuku is across the street from Nagasaki Station and behind the Ken-ei Bus Terminal, so the location is perfect. No meals are served here, but Fumi is convenient to nearby restaurants. All the rooms are Japanese style, and there's a public bath. You'll be treated like family by these extremely kind people. No wonder the place is a bit run-down—I know from both personal and reader experience that the owners are generous to guests. The gift my daughter received certainly cost more than they charged.

Mifune Inn

1-1 Chikugo-machi, Nagasaki 850. ☎ **0958/22-0233.** Fax 0958/22-6451. 17 rms (all with bath). A/C TV TEL. ¥5,000 ($50) single; ¥9,500 ($95) double; ¥10,500 ($105) twin. Japanese-style breakfast ¥600 ($6) extra. No credit cards. Directions: Walk 3 minutes.

Part of the Welcome Inn group, the Mifune Inn, located just up the hill from Nagasaki Station, is adequate and convenient. Rooms are basic, and the minuscule bathrooms could use extra elbow grease. Some English is spoken.

Minshuku Tanpopo

21-7 Hoeicho, Nagasaki 852. ☎ **0958/61-6230.** 12 rms (none with bath). A/C TV. ¥4,000 ($40) single; ¥7,000 ($70) twin; ¥10,500 ($105) triple. Breakfast ¥500 ($5) extra; dinner ¥1,500 ($15) extra. AE, V. Free parking. Station: Urakami JR (15 minutes).

Located in a four-story concrete building situated about halfway between Nagasaki Station and the Peace Park on the east side of the Urakami River, this minshuku offers simple tatami rooms at very reasonable rates, pay TV, and laundry facilities. If you let the owners know you're coming and call from the station, they'll pick you up. The Minshuku Tanpopo is a member of the Japanese Inn group.

Nagasaki Kenritsu Youth Hostel (247)

1-1-16 Tateyama-cho, Nagasaki 850. ☎ **0958/23-5032.** 132 beds. A/C. ¥2,800 ($28) for JYHA members and nonmembers, with breakfast. No credit cards.

A 12-minute walk southeast of Nagasaki Station, this is the most conveniently located youth hostel in Nagasaki, and you don't have to be a youth hostel member to stay here. There are laundry facilities.

Nagasaki Nanpoen Youth Hostel

320 Hamahira-cho, Nagasaki 850. ☎ **0958/23-5526.** 26 beds. A/C TV. ¥2,600 ($26) for JYHA members, ¥3,200 ($32) for nonmembers. Breakfast ¥450 ($4.50) extra; dinner ¥750 ($7.50) extra. No credit cards. Bus: To the Hamahira-cho stop, a 6-minute ride.

This small youth hostel, which sleeps guests on futons, is located up on a hill northeast of Nagasaki Station. The night view is beautiful.

Sansui-so (248)

2-25 Ebisu-machi, Nagasaki 850. ☎ **0958/24-0070.** Fax 0958/22-1952. 30 rms (all with bath). A/C TV TEL. ¥6,000 ($60) per person without meals; ¥10,000 ($100) per person with breakfast and dinner. DC, JCB, V. Directions: Walk 6 minutes southeast.

The lobby of this reasonable Japanese-style accommodation features huge fish tanks with 30-year-old carp swimming about. The dining room is tatami style. A few of the rooms are Western style, and all have coin-operated TV. Facilities include a public bath and a laundry machine.

Uragami-Ga-Oka Youth Hostel

26-27 Joei-machi, Nagasaki 850. ☎ and fax **0958/47-8473.** 56 beds. ¥3,000 ($30) for JYHA members, ¥4,000 ($40) for nonmembers. Breakfast ¥500 ($5) extra; dinner ¥900 ($9) extra. No credit cards. Streetcar: 1 or 3 to Ohashi (4 minutes).

This youth hostel, open to both members and nonmembers, is located one streetcar stop north of Peace Park. Its public bath offers a great view of the city, and facilities include laundry machines.

DINING

Nagasaki's most famous food is actually a whole meal of various courses with Chinese, European, and Japanese influences. Called *shippoku,* it's a feast generally shared by a group of four or more people and includes such dishes as fish soup, sashimi, and fried, boiled, and vinegared seasonal delicacies from land and sea. Another Nagasaki specialty is *champon,* a thick Chinese noodle usually served in soup.

Nagasaki's nightlife district centers on a small street near Hamanomachi known as Shianbashi Dori, which begins just off the streetcar stop of the same name and is easily recognizable by its neon arch of a bridge and palm trees. Lined with pink plastic flowers, this street shimmers with the lights of various drinking establishments and yakitori-ya, which are often the cheapest places to go for a light dinner.

EXPENSIVE

Fukiro (249)

146 Kami Nishiyama-machi. ☎ **0958/22-0253.** Reservations required at least one week in advance. Set dinners ¥9,000–¥17,000 ($90–$170); set lunch ¥5,000 ($50). DC. Daily 11:30am–10pm. Closed twice a month. Streetcar: 3 or 4 to Suwa Jinjamae. SHIPPOKU/KAISEKI.

This elegant old wooden restaurant is on a small cliff not far from Suwa Shrine. In a building 180 years old, it specializes in shippoku served in private tatami rooms, as well as kaiseki. Set meals start at ¥9,000 ($90), but there's virtually no limit to how high they can go. When making your reservation, it's best to state how much you wish to pay. The chef will go from there.

Kagetsu (250)

Maruyama-cho. ☎ **0958/22-0191.** Reservations required at least a week in advance. Lunch obento ¥4,950 ($49.50); shippoku or kaiseki set meals ¥15,000–¥20,000 ($150–$200) dinner, including tax and service charge. DC, JCB, V. Daily noon–7:30pm. Closed some Mon. Streetcar: 1 or 4 to Shianbashi. SHIPPOKU/KAISEKI.

A wonderful but very expensive place to try shippoku, Kagetsu was first established in 1618 and is one of Japan's longest-running restaurants. The oldest part of the present building is about 350 years old. A wooden structure set back from the road, which is the center of Nagasaki's night scene of sailors' bars and strip cabarets, Kagetsu is an oasis of dignified old Japan, with kimono-clad waitresses shuffling down wooden corridors and serving guests in tatami rooms. Formerly a geisha house, it even has a stone-floored room designed for a table and chairs where foreign patrons could be entertained.

Behind the restaurant is a 300-year-old garden. I'll never forget my evening stroll here as a half moon rose above gnarled, stunted pines. The back of the restaurant, consisting mainly of glass, was all lit up, so that I could see into a multitude of private tatami rooms all on different levels. Guests were seated on the floor on cushions, and women in kimonos were playing the gracious hostess, pouring drinks and laughing behind their hands, and from the eaves outside the restaurant hung lighted lanterns. If it hadn't been for the fact that the men wore business suits, I would have sworn it looked exactly like a woodblock print of old Japan.

Needless to say, this restaurant is very popular and sometimes is booked up to a full month in advance. There must be at least two of you if you want to eat shippoku or kaiseki.

Moderate

Dejima Restaurant

Grand Hotel, 5-3 Manzai machi. ☎ **0958/23-1234.** Reservations not required. Set lunches ¥1,000–¥2,500 ($10–$25); set dinners ¥5,000–¥8,000 ($50–$80). AE, DC, JCB, MC, V. Daily 11am–9pm. Streetcar: 1, 3, or 4 to Hamanomachi (4 minutes). WESTERN/SHIPPOKU.

If sitting on the floor puts your legs to sleep, you can enjoy a shippoku meal in Western surroundings at this hotel restaurant, which has set meals of steak, fish, daily specials, and shippoku. The last consists of swordfish in diced soybean sauce, various seasonal hors d'oeuvres, minced veal soup, fresh seafood, brisket of pork, seafood and vegetable fritter, chicken hollandaise, cold beef, Chinese pilaf, dessert,and coffee.

Hamakatsu (251)

6-50 Kajiya-machi. ☎ **0958/26-8321.** Reservations not required. Main dishes ¥500–¥800 ($5–$8); shippoku set meals ¥2,800–¥15,000 ($28–$150). AE, DC, JCB, MC, V. Daily 11:30am–8:30pm (last order). Streetcar: 1 or 4 to Shianbashi stop. SHIPPOKU.

The furabara shippoku (¥2,800/$28) set meal is for one person; the others are for two or more. Set meals are served on the second floor; the first floor is devoted to inexpensive à la carte dishes of both Japanese and Chinese origin. Although the menu is in Japanese and changes seasonally, there are some photos. Included are such items as steamed dumplings, tofu dishes, cold chicken, raw beef, and chili shrimp.

✪ Obinata

3-19 Funadaiku-machi. ☎ **0958/26-1437.** Reservations not required. Pastas and main dishes ¥1,000–¥3,300 ($10–$33); pizza ¥900–¥1,500 ($9–$15). AE. Mon–Sat 5–11pm (last order). Streetcar: 1 or 4 to the Shianbashi stop; then a 1-minute walk. ITALIAN.

One of my favorite restaurants, Obinata has a warm, earthy feel to it, due perhaps to its heavy wooden beams, large bouquets of flowers, candelabra, and classical music playing softly in the background—an oasis of old Europe in the heart of Kyushu. It's located behind the Fukusaya castella shop, just off the nightlife street called Shianbashi Dori. The atmosphere is cozy, and the service is a delight. The menu in Italian lists such main dishes as steak, ossobuco, spaghetti, lasagne, and pizza. Dishes are creative and fun, the restaurant's own interpretations. Expect to pay about ¥6,000 ($60) if you go all out and order an appetizer, main dish, and wine (there's a wide selection of Bordeaux, Moselle, and Rhine wines), but you can eat more cheaply if you stick to pastas.

Ohura

Tokyu Hotel, 1-18 Minamiyamate-machi. ☎ **0958/25-1501.** Reservations not required. Shippoku ¥3,800–¥9,000 ($38–$90); set lunches ¥1,800–¥3,000 ($18–$30); set dinners ¥3,000–¥6,000 ($30–$60). AE, DC, JCB, MC, V. Daily 11:30am–2:30pm and 5–9:30pm (last order). Streetcar: 5 to Oura Tensudoshita. JAPANESE/CHINESE.

A pleasant and quiet place to stop for a meal if you're visiting Glover Garden, this restaurant serves shippoku (colorful pictures depict the various courses available) and Japanese and Chinese selections, including tempura, fried sweet-and-sour chicken, shredded pork with green pepper, and assorted fried noodles Nagasaki style.

Sakura House

6-15 Kajiya-machi. ☎ **0958/26-0229.** Reservations not required. Main dishes ¥1,000–¥2,500 ($10–$25); set dinners ¥2,500–¥7,700 ($25–$77); set lunches ¥1,500–¥2,500 ($15–$25). AE, DC, JCB, MC, V. Daily 11:30am–-10:30pm (last order). Streetcar: 1 or 4 to Shianbashi; then a 3-minute walk. WESTERN/FRENCH.

Although it's one of Nagasaki's newer trendy restaurants, it resembles a much older establishment from the 1930s or '40s. Decorated with half-paneled walls, wooden floors, and a wooden bar counter, it's located close to Hamanomachi and not far from Hamakatsu, described above. Its menu lists soups, salads, seafood, chicken, duck, beef, pork, and lamb selections. Since it calls itself a restaurant/bar, you can also come here for just a drink and listen to background music (jazz, swing, or soft rock).

Tokiwa

Nagasaki View Hotel, 2-33 Oura-machi. ☎ **0958/24-2211.** Reservations not required. Set lunches ¥1,350–¥8,000 ($13.50–$80); set dinners ¥1,800–¥8,000 ($18–$80). AE, DC, JCB, MC, V. Daily 11:30am–2pm and 5–10pm. Streetcar: 5 to Oura Kaigan. SASHIMI/TEMPURA/KAISEKI.

If you're hungering for raw fish, it doesn't come any fresher than at this conveniently located restaurant between Hamanomachi and Glover Garden. Tokiwa features a wooden counter surrounding a pool filled with live fish. When its number is up, a fish is scooped out of the water and then prepared right before your very eyes. Sometimes the fish is gutted and fileted, with only the head, heart, and skeleton left intact, so that the sashimi can be arranged around the alive and still-quivering creature and delivered to the customer's table. Barring that, you might opt for one of the lunch teishoku, which range from sashimi teishoku to tempura teishoku.

INEXPENSIVE

Bharata

2-10 Yasaka St., Aburaya-machi. ☎ **0958/24-9194.** Reservations not required. Curries ¥1,000–¥1,100 ($10–$11); set meals ¥1,600–¥4,200 ($16–$42). AE, DC, JCB, MC, V. Tues–Fri 11:30am–3pm and 5–10pm, Sat–Sun 11:30am–10pm. Streetcar: 1 or 4 to Shianbashi. INDIAN.

A craving for hot and spicy food can be satisfied at Bharata, located close to the Hamanomachi shopping arcade just off Kajiya-machi Street on the second floor of a brick building. An inexpensive establishment with modest decor, it serves Indian food: Curry dishes of beef, chicken, *kofta* (meatballs), shrimp, and fish include Indian bread or pilaf, chutney, and salad. Vegetarian thali offers various small dishes for ¥1,600 ($16), while the Bharata course (¥4,200/$42) features a glass of wine and six meat and vegetable dishes. The owners couldn't be nicer.

Fan Fan

5-36 Yorozuya-machi. ☎ **0958/27-3976.** Reservations not required. Main dishes ¥550–¥1,200 ($5.50–$12). No credit cards. Mon–Sat 7:30pm–2am. WESTERN.

Fan Fan, just off the Hamanomachi covered shopping street, is a jazz club/restaurant/hangout. Popular with local foreigners, Fan Fan has two rooms, each with a long wall lined with records and CDs—a great collection of jazz, blues, and rock. The owner, Ryuichi Tsuchiyama, speaks some English and makes you feel welcome. On Saturdays, live jazz groups play. Occasionally, there is a cover charge if a group from Tokyo is scheduled. The place has an extensive list of whiskeys, gins, vodkas, and beers from ¥800 ($8); such dishes as spaghetti go for ¥900 ($9).

✪ Gohan (252)

2-32 Aburayamachi. ☎ **0958/25-3600.** Lunch teishoku ¥700 ($7); obento ¥1,500 ($15); set dinner ¥4,000 ($40). No credit cards. Mon–Sat noon–2pm and 6–11pm (last order 9pm). Closed hols. Streetcar: 1 to Shokakujishita.

The owner-chef, Tsunehiro Yoshimura, who speaks English, is also a musician, so you'll hear interesting music to go with a creative meal. The wood and soft ocher interior is authentically old; salvaged beams and pieces from five different houses are re-created here. Add to that hip waiters, counter seating (watch the chef at work) or tatami with leg wells (garden views), and a handwritten menu changing daily. You'll eat slowly as dishes are brought to you one after the other. The dinner set is enormous, and mine included sashimi, boiled fish and vegetables, crayfish, shrimp/bread gratin, and bamboo. Service is on original dishes by Keisuke Iwata, a potter of some renown and a lot of talent. Very highly recommended.

Kouzanrou (253)

12-2 Shinchi-machi. ☎ **0958/21-3735.** Reservations not required. Champon ¥700–¥900 ($7–$9); main dishes ¥800–¥2,000 ($8–$20); set lunches ¥2,200 ($22). No credit cards. Daily 11am–9pm (last order at 8:30pm). Streetcar: 1 to the Tsukimachi or Kanko Dori stop; then about a 5-minute walk. CHINESE.

A popular Chinese restaurant located in the heart of Nagasaki's small Chinatown, it serves a mostly Chinese clinetele, and its most popular dish is champon. If you order such à la carte dishes as spring rolls, champon, or sweet-and-sour pork, most of which are under ¥1,200 ($12), you'll dine in the restaurant's simply furnished ground-floor dining area of tables and chairs. If you order a set meal (¥3,300 to ¥10,000/$33 to $100) and there are two or more in your party, you can sit upstairs in private tatami rooms. Kouzanrou is so successful it has an annex on the same street, and between the two they sell 300 to 500 bowls of champon a day. A smaller, very modern shop right next to the Nagasaki train station, the annex also offers champon and is open daily from 11am to 9pm.

Shikairo

4-5 Matsugae-cho. ☎ **0958/22-1296.** Reservations not required. Champon ¥900 ($9); set meals ¥3,000–¥20,000 ($30–$200). DC, JCB, MC, V. Daily 11:30am–3pm and 5–9:30pm (last order at 8pm). Streetcar: 5 to Oura Kaigan. CHINESE.

If you're interested in eating champon Chinese noodles, this is the restaurant that created them. First opened back in 1899, it moved into its present building in 1973. Located close to the Tokyu Hotel and Glover Garden, it's a large white building topped with a rounded dome and offering four floors of dining. It can accommodate as many as 1,500 people, and caters to large groups and receptions. Knowing where to go for a meal would be confusing if it weren't for the ground-floor welcoming committee eager to point the way. Come to think of it, however, you might still be confused, because the numbers for floors in the elevator are written in *kanji* only. Assuming that you do eventually end up in the right dining hall, you'll find yourself in a large and noisy room surrounded by lots of other hungry souls. There are more than 40 items on the English menu, including barbecued pork, braised shark fin with shredded meat, chicken with bamboo shoots and onion, fried noodles, and, of course, champon. If you order à la carte, expect to spend ¥2,000 to ¥3,000 ($20 to $30) per person.

Yagura-Sushi (254)

Hamanomachi. ☎ **0958/22-1813.** Sushi teishoku ¥800 ($8). No credit cards. Fri–Wed 9am–8:30pm. Streetcar: 4 or 5 to Hamanomachi. SUSHI.

To find this place in the Hamanomachi covered shopping arcade near Megane-bashi, look for its traditional-looking storefront, with a window showing the sushi experts at work and a sign in English saying TRY OUR DELICIOUS SUSHI FOR ONE. There's a small dining area; most people you'll see standing in line, however, are waiting for take-out orders, with lunch boxes starting at ¥620 ($6.20). This is a good place to buy a picnic lunch, and you can eat it near Megane-bashi bridge.

6 Unzen

41 miles SE of Nagasaki

Unzen Spa is a small resort town 2,385 feet above sea level in the pine-covered hills of the Shimabara Peninsula. Because of its high altitude and cool mountain air, its great scenery and hot sulfur springs, Unzen became popular in the 1880s as a summer resort for American and European visitors, who came from Shanghai, Hong Kong, and Singapore to escape the oppressive humid summer heat. They arrived in Unzen by bamboo palanquin from Obama, seven miles away. The fact that there were foreigners here explains why Unzen has one of Japan's oldest golf courses, dating from 1913.

ESSENTIALS

The **telephone area code** for Unzen, lying in Nagasaki Prefecture, is 0957.

GETTING THERE **By Bus** The easiest way to get to Unzen is by Ken-ei Bus from Nagasaki. Buses leave about every hour or so from the Ken-ei Bus Terminal across the street from Nagasaki Station. The ride takes about two hours and costs ¥1,700 ($17) one way, or ¥3,150 ($31.50) round trip.

VISITOR INFORMATION Before leaving Tokyo or Kyoto, be sure to stop by the Tourist Information Center to pick up the free leaflet "Nagasaki and Unzen," which describes places of interest in Unzen and the Shimabara Peninsula.

In Unzen, the **Information Center** (☎ 0957/73-3434) is located in the heart of Unzen Spa not far from the Hells. Open daily from 9am to 5pm, it has a rudimentary but adequate map in English of Unzen and the surrounding area. Nearby is the **Unzen Visitor's Center,** with natural history displays of the national park and robot camera views. It's open Friday through Wednesday from 9am to 6pm (until 5pm in winter).

WHAT TO SEE & DO

In 1934 the area around Unzen became **Unzen National Park,** named after what was thought to be an extinct volcano, Mt. Unzen. In 1991, however, Mt. Unzen erupted, killing several dozen people on its eastern slope. Unzen Spa, on the opposite side, was untouched and remains the area's most popular resort town.

Unzen Spa literally bubbles with activity as sulfurous hot springs erupt into surface cauldrons of scalding water in an area known as **the Hells,** or *Jigoku.* Indeed, in the 1600s these cauldrons were used for hellish punishment as some 30 Christians were boiled alive here after Christianity was outlawed in Japan. Today, Unzen Spa has more than 30 solfataras and fumaroles. The Hells are a favorite hangout of huge black ravens, and the barren land has been baked a chalky white through the centuries. There are pathways leading through the hot springs where sulfur vapors rise thick to veil pine trees on surrounding hills. Old women in bonnets sell eggs that have been boiled in the hot springs for ¥50 (50¢) apiece. They also sell corn on the cob for ¥350 ($3.50) an ear.

I like Unzen Spa because it's small and navigable. It consists basically of just a few streets with hotels and ryokan spread along them, a welcome relief if you've been spending a few hectic weeks rushing through big cities and catching buses and trains. Only 1,700 people live here, and from the town a number of hiking paths wind into the tree-covered hills. If you feel like taking an excursion, buses leave about every hour for **Nitta Pass,** about a 20-minute ride away. The fare is ¥700 ($7) round trip. From Nitta Pass you can take a ropeway up higher to **Mt. Myoken** for a better view

(¥1,000/$10 round trip), but the best thing to do in my opinion is to take the footpath that runs from Nitta Pass and skirts the mountain along a tree-shaded path. The first 15 or 20 minutes of the walk is fairly easy, and that's all you may care to exert yourself. If you're ready for some real climbing, however, continue along the path for another half hour or so, where it leads starkly uphill to the summit of **Mt. Fugen,** Unzen's highest peak at 4,462 feet above sea level and the peak that erupted in 1991. There, on a clear day, you'll be rewarded with splendid views of other volcanic peaks as far away as Mt. Aso in the middle of Kyushu. Also on Mt. Fugen is Fugen Shrine, which is about a 20-minute hike from the peak. Allow at least two hours for the hike from Nitta Pass to Mt. Fugen and back.

For sports, you can play golf at Japan's oldest **public golf course** (☎ 0957/73-3368), open daily from 8am to 5pm. Total charge for the nine-hole course, including greens fees, tax, and caddy, is ¥9,570 ($95.70) on weekdays and ¥12,320 ($123.20) on weekends and holidays. There's also a shorter nine-hole course (good for beginners) charging ¥2,900 ($29). Unzen Spa also has **public tennis courts,** which are free—your only obligation is to rake the dirt court when you finish playing.

For a varied bathing experience, try the **Unzen Spa House** ☎ 0957/73-3131), where you can enjoy indoor and outdoor baths, sauna, cold baths, a waterfall massage, a hydro-massage, Jacuzzi, and a swiming pool. Open daily from 10am to 6pm, it costs ¥1,500 ($15) for the day.

Keep in mind that, as with many resort areas in Japan, Unzen tends to be crowded during Golden Week in early May, during New Year's, and in July and August. The best times of year are late April to June, when the azalea bushes are in glorious bloom, and in late October and early November, when the maple leaves turn brilliant reds.

ACCOMMODATIONS & DINING

With the exception of the inexpensive accommodation listed at the end of this section, all the ryokan and hotels listed here are within an easy walk of bus stops along the route followed by the bus from Nagasaki. Tell the bus driver where you're staying, and he'll drop you off at the nearest stop.

EXPENSIVE

Kyushu Hotel

320 Unzen, Obamacho, Minami-Takaki-gun 854-06. ☎ **0957/73-3234.** Fax 0957/73-3733. 89 rms. A/C MINIBAR TEL TV. ¥18,000–¥40,000 ($180–$400) per person. Rates include breakfast and dinner. AE, DC, JCB, MC, V.

The Kyushu Hotel is a 75-year-old ryokan, with a view of a lovely garden from the renovated, luxurious lobby. The staff, some of whom speak English, are very gracious. This is the best place to stay for viewing the nearby hills. About 20 rooms overlook the hills, and if you choose to dine Western, the restaurant Cowbell has a view of them, too. Most of the rooms combine tatami with Western sitting areas, and all have a TV with adult video. Baths feature bidet/toilets and a separate sink-toilet area. Facilities include indoor and outdoor hot-springs baths, and a lobby lounge and souvenir shop.

✪ Miyazaki Ryokan (255)

320 Unzen, Obamacho, Minami-Takaki-gun 854-06. ☎ **0957/73-3331.** 106 rms. A/C MINIBAR TV TEL. ¥20,000–¥30,000 ($200–$300) per person. Rates include breakfast, dinner, and service charge. AE, DC, JCB, MC, V.

One of the largest Japanese inns in Unzen, this modern ryokan with traditional service overlooks a gracefully manicured garden, with hills and sulfur vapors rising in the background. When you arrive, you'll be served green tea and sweets here by graceful women in kimono. In addition to Japanese-style tatami rooms, there are also combination rooms with twin beds and a separate tatami area. The meals served are excellent. Breakfasts (Western style, if desired) are served in a communal dining area, but dinners are served in guest rooms in true ryokan fashion. Room prices are the same regardless of which direction the rooms face, so I'd advise securing one that faces the hot springs and wooded hills rather than the village. The views from these rooms are among the best in Unzen. The ryokan has a large marble hot-spring bath overlooking a rock-lined outdoor bath separated by traditional ocher walls roofed with glazed tiles and covered by a bamboo roof. Elegance and taste reign. Shy about bathing with others? Make a reservation at no extra charge for the private family bath. Try the peaceful tatami area with Go tables, huge flower arrangements, and a dispenser of cool *mugi cha* (wheat tea) for after-bath relaxing.

Unzen Kanko Hotel

320 Unzen, Obamacho, Minami-Takaki-gun 854-06. ☎ **0957/73-3263.** Fax 0957/73-3419. 59 rms. TV TEL. ¥9,000 ($90) single; ¥14,000–¥70,000 ($140–$700) double or twin; ¥27,000–¥45,000 ($270–$450) Japanese-style rooms; ¥22,000 ($220) combination rooms. AE, DC, JCB, MC, V.

If you're the least bit romantic, you won't be able to resist staying at this old-fashioned mountain lodge, built in 1935 of stone and wood and covered in ivy. The rooms are rustic and old-fashioned too, with heavy ceiling-to-floor curtains tied back to reveal a balcony, brass doorsills, a high ceiling, and wooden beams. There are 49 Western-style rooms, eight newer Japanese-style tatami rooms, and two combination rooms that come with both bed and tatami area.

Dining/Entertainment: Even if you don't stay at the hotel, you may want to come here for a meal. The dining hall is large, with wooden paneling and wooden floors, white tablecloths, and flowers on each table. Open for lunch from noon to 1:30pm and for dinner starting at 6pm, with last orders taken at 8pm, it serves set menus of both Japanese and Western selections. Lunch sets for ¥1,800 and ¥3,000 ($18 and $30) are offered, and you can make a reservation for a Japanese obento for ¥1,500 ($15). A la carte items include filet mignon and lobster or inexpensive spaghetti (¥900/$9). Also on the hotel grounds is a tempura restaurant called Gyo En, located just to the right as you enter the hotel's cedar-lined driveway. A small house with one room for dining, it's open daily from 6 to 8:30pm, with set meals ranging from ¥5,000 to ¥15,000 ($50 to $150). Reservations are required.

Facilities: Hot-spring sulfur baths, billiard tables. The hotel also has a couple of rackets you can use in case you want to swing at balls down at the public tennis courts.

MODERATE

Kaseya Ryokan (256)

Unzen, Obamacho, Minami-Takaki-gun 854-06. ☎ **0957/73-3321.** Fax 0957/73-3322. 13 rms (none with bath). A/C TV TEL. ¥8,000–¥12,000 ($80–$120) per person. Rates include breakfast, dinner, and service charge. No credit cards.

This economically priced ryokan, dating back to 1909, has been totally remodeled. All rooms are Japanese style and are simply decorated, with a high ceiling and flower arrangements in each room. There are three communal public sulfur baths, one each for men and for women, and a smaller bath for families. Western-style breakfasts can be requested, if it's not busy. It's a member of the Welcome Inn group.

INEXPENSIVE

Seiunso Kokumin Shukusha (257)

500-1 Unzen, Obamacho, Minami Takaki-gun 854-06. ☎ **0957/73-3273.** Fax 0957/73-2698. 52 rms (none with bath). TV TEL. ¥5,900–¥6,900 ($59–$69) per person, including two meals; ¥3,400–¥4,400 ($34–$44) per person with no meals. All rates include service charge. No credit cards.

Formerly a youth hostel, this place still offers the least expensive accommodations in Unzen Spa. The lower-priced rooms are in an annex. Because it's about a 20-minute walk from the spa, the staff will pick up guests if they telephone from the bus stop in Unzen. Some rooms have a balcony, but the view from other rooms is no less grand. All rooms have coin-operated TV. There's a hot-spring public bath here and also laundry facilities. You should try to make reservations four months in advance for New Year's and August, the most crowded times of the year.

7 Kagoshima

927 miles SW of Tokyo, 197 miles S of Fukuoka,123 miles S of Kumamoto, 214 miles SW of Beppu

With a population of more than half a million, Kagoshima is a city of palm trees, flowering trees and bushes, wide avenues, and people who are like the weather—warm, mild-tempered, and easygoing. Because of its relative isolation at the southern tip of Japan, far away from the capitals of Kyoto and Tokyo, Kagoshima through the centuries has developed an independent spirit that has fostered a number of great men and accomplishments. Foremost is the Shimazu clan, a remarkable family that for 29 generations (695 years) ruled over Kagoshima and its vicinity before the Meiji Restoration in 1868. Much of Japan's early contact with the outside world was via Kagoshima, first with China and then with the Western world. Japan's first contact with Christianity occurred in Kagoshima when St. Francis Xavier landed here in 1549. Although he stayed only 10 months, he converted more than 600 Japanese to Christianity.

By the mid-19th century, as the Tokugawa shogunate began losing strength and the confidence of the people, the Shimazu family was already looking toward the future and the modernization of Japan. In the mid-1850s the Shimazus built the first Western-style factory in the country, employing 200 men to make cannons, glass, ceramics, land mines, ships, and farming tools. In 1865, while Japan's doors were still officially closed to the outside world and all contact with foreigners was forbidden, the Shimazus smuggled 19 young men to Britain so that they could learn foreign languages and technology. After these men returned to Japan, they became a driving force in the Meiji Restoration and the modernization of Japan.

Another historical figure who played a major role during the Meiji Restoration was Takamori Saigo, who was born in Kagoshima Prefecture. A philosopher, scholar, educator, and poet, he helped restore Emperor Meiji to power, but because he was also a samurai he subsequently became disillusioned when the ancient rights of the samurai class were rescinded and the wearing of swords was forbidden. He led a force of samurai against the government in what is called the Seinan Rebellion, but was defeated. He then withdrew to Shiroyama in Kagoshima, where he committed suicide in 1877. Today, Saigo has many fans among the Japanese, and on Shiroyama Hill you can visit the cave where he committed suicide.

ESSENTIALS

The **telephone area code** for Kagoshima, lying in Kagoshima Prefecture, is 0992. An **international post office** is located in the Nishi Kagoshima Station.

GETTING THERE **By Plane** Kagoshima's international airport connects Kyushu with Hong Kong and Korea, while domestic flights give easy access to Tokyo (flight time: 1 hr. 40 min.), Nagoya (flight time: 1 hr. 25 min.), Osaka (flight time: 1 hr. 10 min.), Sapporo (2 hrs. 30 min.), and Hiroshima (flight time: 1 hr. 10 min.).

By Train Travel time is 12 hours from Tokyo, 8 hours from Osaka, and about 4 hours from Fukuoka. All trains passing through Kagoshima make two stops, at both Kagoshima Station and Nishi Kagoshima Station. Be sure to check which station your hotel is closest to, so that you know which to get off at.

By Ferry There's ferry service daily from Osaka, arriving in Kagoshima the next day (travel time: 15 hrs.), costing ¥10,000 ($100).

VISITOR INFORMATION Information on Kagoshima is given in "Southern Kyushu," a leaflet distributed by the Tourist Information Centers in Tokyo and Kyoto.

In Kagoshima there are **tourist information centers** at both Nishi Kagoshima Station (☎ 0992/53-2500) and Kagoshima Station (☎ 0992/22-2500), as well as at the airport. The centers are open daily from 8:30am to 6pm. The staffs speak English and have good maps in English. The **Kagoshima Prefectural Tourist Office** is located in the Sangyo Kaikan Building, 9-1 Meizancho (☎ 0992/23-5771); here you can obtain information on the city as well as the prefecture, including Kirishima National Park, Ibusuki, and Chiran.

GETTING AROUND The downtown section of Kagoshima is the area between Nishi Kagoshima and Kagoshima stations, with Tenmonkan-Dori (a covered shopping arcade) serving as the heart of the city. You can walk from one station to the other in less than 30 minutes, but there's also a streetcar connecting the two.

If you think you'll be doing a lot of traveling by streetcar, you might want to invest in a one-day pass for ¥500 ($5), valid for travel on Kagoshima's two tram lines and on City View and Kagoshima City buses. Passes can be purchased at the tourist office in Kagoshima Station, Nishi Kagoshima Station, and on Kagoshima City buses and trams. The City View buses look like old-time trams, have English announcements, and stop at all the tourist sights (all listed here except Sakurajima). Each time you get off, you pay ¥160 ($1.60). An all-day pass (¥500/$5) allows you to get on and off as many times as you like and also use the trams. Although you can get on at any one of the sights, the loop starts at Nishi-Kagoshima Station and operates between 9am and 5pm daily.

WHAT TO SEE & DO

With ties to Naples, Italy, as its sister city, Kagoshima bills itself as the "Naples of the Orient." That's perhaps stretching things a bit too far, but Kagoshima is balmy most of the year, and it even has its own Mt. Vesuvius—**Mt. Sakurajima,** an active volcano across Kinko Bay, which continuously puffs steam into the sky and occasionally covers the city with fine soot and ash. In 1914, Sakurajima had a whopper of an eruption and belched up three billion tons of lava. When the eruption was over, the townspeople were surprised to discover that the flow of lava had been so great that it blocked the 1,666-foot-wide channel separating the volcano from a neighboring peninsula. Sakurajima, which had once been an island, was now part of the mainland.

Magnificent from far away and impressive if you're near the top, Sakurajima can be visited by a ferry that leaves every 15 minutes from a pier close to Kagoshima Station. It takes 10 minutes to reach Sakurajima. Oddities of Sakurajima include the fact that its rich soil produces the world's largest radishes, averaging about 37 pounds but sometimes weighing in at 80 pounds, and the world's smallest oranges, only 1.2 inches in diameter. There are walking paths through lava fields close to Sakurajima's ferry pier, but because Sakurajima is sparsely populated, with only limited public transportation, you might want to join a tour operated by Japan Railways that visits lava fields and lookouts around the volcano in 1³/₄ hours. JR buses depart twice daily from the ferry dock on Sakurajima. The price of the tour is ¥1,700 ($17), but it's free if you have a Japan Rail Pass. There's also an all-day (six-hour) JR Kagoshima City Tour, including Sakurajima, which costs ¥4,000 ($40) and leaves from Nishi Kagoshima Station. For departure times, check with JR Kyushu (☎ 0992/47-5244). Kagoshima Municipal Transportation Bureau (☎ 0992/53-2500) runs a city tour twice a day. The 3¹/₂ hour tours costs ¥2,500 ($25).

Whereas Sakurajima, rising dramatically out of the bay, is Kagoshima's best-known landmark, **Iso Garden** (☎ 0992/47-1551) is its most widely visited attraction. These gardens of the Shimazu clan, laid out more than 300 years ago, incorporated Sakurajima and Kinko Bay into the design scheme. Open daily from 8:30am to 5:30pm (to 5pm in winter), with an admission fee of ¥800 ($8), Iso Garden features a particularly idyllic spot where the 21st lord of the Shimazu family held famous poem-composing garden parties. Guests seated themselves on stones beside a gently meandering rivulet and were requested to have completed a poem by the time a cup filled with sake came drifting by on the tiny brook. Ah, those were the days!

Also in Iso Garden is **Goten,** one of Lord Shimazu's villas, which is now open to the public daily from 9am to 4:30pm (until 4pm in winter). There are tours of the 25 rooms, 8 of which face the garden, every 20 minutes at a cost of ¥800 ($8). Rooms contain furnishings and artifacts pertaining to the family. A tea ceremony is included in the price of the tour. A joint ticket for Goten and Iso is ¥1,400 ($14).

Next to Iso Garden, and included in its entrance fee, is the **Shokoshuseikan Museum,** built in the mid-1850s as Japan's first modern factory. It houses about 300 items relating to the almost 700-year history of the Shimazu clan, including palanquins used to carry lords to Edo (present-day Tokyo), everyday items the family used, and photographs. I find the photographs showing the Shimazu family dressed in Western-style fashions particularly interesting. The museum shop is particularly good.

Another museum worth visiting is the **City Art Museum,** or *Kagoshima Shiritsu Bijutsukan* (☎ 0992/24-3400), which has a collection of contemporary paintings by artists born in Kagoshima Prefecture, including Seiki Kuroda, Takeji Fujishima, and Wada Eisaku. A small selection of paintings by Western artists is also displayed, as well as pottery, glass, bronzes, and other works of art. The permanent exhibition is small, but special exhibitions are also held here. It's open Tuesday through Sunday from 9am to 5pm; admission is ¥200 ($2). It's located in the heart of the city, between the two train stations; the nearest streetcar stop is Asahi Dori. Only a few minutes' walk away from the City Art Museum, and with the same hours, is the **Kagoshima Prefectural Museum of Culture** or *Reimeikan* (☎ 0992/22-5100). One of the finest prefectural museums in the country, it was built on the former site of Tsurumaru Castle, of which only the moat remains. The museum traces the history of the people of Kagoshima over the last 40,000 years, with exhibits devoted to topography and natural history, archeological finds, and the society and culture of old Satsuma. Admission here is ¥260 ($2.60).

Near Nishi-Kagoshima Station is the **Museum of the Meiji Restoration** (☎ 0992/39-7700). Housed in a modern building, it uses dioramas, holograms, artifacts, and hands-on exhibits to explain the history of the Meiji period, and its heros and heroines. A display called "Satsuma Women" pays tribute to the women of Kagoshima, who helped pave the way into the modern era. The cost is ¥300 ($3), and it's open Wednesday through Monday from 9am to 5pm.

NEARBY ATTRACTIONS

If you have an extra morning or afternoon, I suggest taking an excursion to **Chiran,** a small village 19 miles south of Kagoshima. Surrounded by wooded hills and rows of neatly cultivated tea plantations, it's one of the 102 castle towns that once bordered the Shimazu kingdom during the Edo Period. Although the castle is no longer standing, six old gardens and samurai houses have been carefully preserved by descendants. There are three types of gardens here: the miniature artificial hill style, in which a central pond symbolizes the sea and rocks represent the mountains; the "dry" garden, in which the sea is symbolized not by water but by white sand that is raked to give it rippling movements of water; and the "borrowed landscape" garden, in which surrounding mountains and scenery are incorporated into the general garden design. Although the gardens are small, they are exquisite and charming. Notice, for example, how the tops of hedges are cut to resemble rolling hills, blending with the shapes of mountains in the background.

The six gardens open to the public are indicated by a white marker in front of each entry gate. All six can be visited for ¥310 ($3.10), and it should take about an hour to see them all. Pay the entry fee for all six at the first garden you visit; you'll be given a pamphlet containing a map and a description of the gardens in English.

Chiran can be reached in about 75 minutes from Yamagataya Bus Station, next to the Yamagataya department store in downtown Kagoshima.

SHOPPING

If you're interested in shopping in Kagoshima, **local products** include *oshima pongee,* Japanese silk made into such items as clothing, handbags, and wallets; *shochu,* an alcoholic drink made from such ingredients as sweet potatoes and drunk either on the rocks or mixed with boiling water; furniture, statues, and chests made from *yaku* cedar; and Satsuma pottery—probably Kagoshima's most famous product. It has been produced in the Kagoshima area for more than 380 years, first by Korean potters brought here to practice their trade. Satsuma pottery comes in two styles, black and white. White Satsuma pottery is more elegant and was used by former lords; the black pottery, on the other hand, was used by the townspeople in everyday life.

Another good place to shop for local items is the **Display Hall of Kagoshima Products** in the Sangyo Kaikan Building, 9-1 Meizancho (☎ 0992/25-6120). Open Monday through Friday from 8:30am to 5pm and on Saturday until 12:30pm, this one-room shop is located in Kagoshima's downtown and sells such goods as tinware, handmade knives, Satsuma pottery, glassware, oshima pongee, yaku cedar, shochu, and other items from Kagoshima Prefecture.

There are many Satsuma pottery factories in the Kagoshima area. Most easily accessible is **Kinko Togei** (☎ 0992/61-1019) at 2-2-3 Taniyamako, where you can observe production of Satsuma pottery and purchase from the showroom. The factory will ship your purchases home. Open daily from 8:30am to 5:15pm, it can be reached by train or tram from Nishi Kagoshima Station. If you're going by train, get off at Sakanoue Station; from there it's either a 20-minute walk or a 5-minute taxi ride. If you want to go by streetcar, get off at Taniyama Station; from there it's a 10-minute taxi ride.

ACCOMMODATIONS

EXPENSIVE

✪ Shigetomiso (258)

31-7 Shimizu-cho, Kagoshima 890. ☎ **0992/47-3155.** 8 rms. A/C MINIBAR TV TEL. ¥20,000–¥40,000 ($200–$400) per person. Rates include breakfast, dinner, and service. AE, DC, JCB, MC, V. Taxi: 5 minutes from Kagoshima Station.

One of Kagoshima's most beautiful ryokan, this was once a villa for the ruling Shimazu clan. Spreading along a gentle slope of a hill in a profusion of flowering plants, with a garden and a waterfall, this enchanting ryokan overlooks the bay in a storybook setting. Its oldest rooms date from the 1820s, and through the decades a number of stories, myths, and legends have arisen to add to their mystique. One room, for example, is said to have belonged to the lord's mistress; here you can see a wooden pillar marred by tiny holes—apparently made by the mistress as she stabbed it with her hairpin, out of frustration caused by the lord's too-infrequent visits. Another room is colored a unique reddish tinge, derived from the blood of pigs brought from Okinawa. There's a closet where the clan could hide during attack, and the ceiling of one hallway was constructed deliberately low to thwart downward blows of enemy swords. In more recent history, the James Bond movie *You Only Live Twice* has a sequence filmed in one of the ryokan's rooms. In short, the whole ryokan is a museum in itself and contains antiques that once belonged to the Shimazu family. All rooms come with private bathroom, peace, and tranquillity. Highly recommended if you can afford it.

You can also eat lunch here from 11:30am to 2pm. The cuisine, *okaribayaki,* is supposed to be a legacy from fuedal lords' hunting trips. In any case, it's grilled or barbecued and costs ¥3,000 ($30) for a course meal.

$ Shiroyama Kanko Hotel

41-1 Shinshoin-cho, Kagoshima 890. ☎ **0992/24-2211.** Fax 0992/24-2222. 398 rms. A/C TV TEL. ¥10,000–¥13,000 ($100–$130) single; ¥18,000 ($180) double; ¥18,000–¥24,000 ($180–$240) twin. AE, DC, JCB, MC, V. Taxi: 15 minutes from either station. Bus: City View.

Kagoshima's foremost hotel, the Shiroyama Kanko Hotel sits 353 feet high atop the wood-covered Shiroyama Hill and commands a fine view of the city below and Sakurajima across the bay. Rooms are pleasant and comfortable, although the singles are slightly small. The best rooms face the volcano.

Dining/Entertainment: Dining includes Western (formal and casual), Japanese, Chinese, and a summer beer garden.

Facilities: Indoor swimming pool, sauna, and fitness gym (fee: ¥1,300/$13); shops selling locally made souvenirs (silk pongee, Satsuma pottery, yaku cedar, confectioneries, Satsuma-age); wedding hall; bakery; beauty salon; travel agency.

MODERATE

Kagoshima Sun Royal Hotel

1-8-10 Yojiro, Kagoshima 890. ☎ **0992/53-2020.** Fax 0992/55-0186. 280 rms (260 with bath). A/C MINIBAR TV TEL. ¥15,500 ($155) twin with bath; ¥18,700 ($187) double; from ¥16,500 ($165) Japanese style for two. AE, JCB, MC, V. Bus: 16 to Jungle Park.

This hotel is located in Kamoike, a neighborhood of modern buildings and wide avenues. It's a bit far from the center, but city buses departing from Nishi Kagoshima reach the hotel in 20 minutes. All the double, twin, and Japanese-style rooms face the sea and have a balcony. The cheapest singles come without bathtub or shower but with toilet and sink. I personally prefer the Japanese-style rooms with tatami sitting alcoves beside the balcony. There's a great *onsen* (hot-spring bath) on the 13th floor, separated for men and women. You can look out over Mt. Sakurajima as you bathe. Restaurants include the Phoenix Sky Lounge on the 13th floor, serving Western food and boasting a view of the sea, and a Japanese restaurant where kaiseki and local dishes are served.

Kagoshima Tokyu Hotel

22-1 Kamoike Shinmachi, Kagoshima 890. ☎ **0992/57-2411.** Fax 0992/57-6083. 206 rms. A/C MINIBAR TV TEL. ¥7,800–¥10,000 ($78–$100) single; ¥15,000–¥23,000 ($150–$230) twin; ¥17,000 ($170) double. AE, DC, JCB, MC, V. Bus: 10 from Nishi Kagoshima Station to the Noukyo Kaikan-mae stop.

This first-rate medium-priced hotel, also located in the new section of town, Kamoike, is built right on the waterfront, with a good view of the volcano. Its twins and doubles face the water, and each has a veranda, great for sitting out in the morning and watching the sun rise over Sakurajima. Singles (without balcony) all face inland. There's an outdoor swimming pool open during the warmer months (usually from about May to September) and two outdoor Jacuzzis, fed by natural hot springs and open year-round, plus a child's pool that's heated in winter. The hotel has three restaurants.

$ Urban Port Hotel

15-1 Ogawacho, Kagoshima 892. ☎ **0992/39-4111.** Fax 0992/39-4112. 102 rms. A/C MINIBAR TV TEL. ¥7,200–¥7,700 ($72–$77) single; ¥9,500 ($95) double; ¥14,000 ($140) twin. AE, JCB, MC, V. Directions: Walk 5 minutes from Kagoshima Station. Streetcar: Sakurajima Sanbashi Dori.

Close to Kagoshima Station, the ferry to Sakurajima, and the morning market, this new and well-equipped tourist/business hotel offers excellent value for price. All the clean and bright rooms have views of either city and mountains or sea from large windows, plus lots of amenities like bidet/toilets and hair dryers. Standard single rooms have semi-double beds. There is a business center, a restaurant/bar serving Western food, and a full health club with swimming pool, whirlpool bath, workout gym, and aerobics classes. Hotel guests are charged ¥2,000 ($20) to use the health club, but the manager told me that guests could show him this guidebook and get in for free.

INEXPENSIVE

Business Hotel Gasthof

7-3 Chuo-cho, Kagoshima 890. ☎ **0992/52-1401.** Fax 0992/52-1405. 41 rms (all with bath). A/C TV TEL. ¥5,000–¥5,800 ($50-$58) single; ¥8,000–¥10,000 ($80–$100) twin; ¥12,000 ($120) triple. Rates include tax and service. Breakfast ¥500 ($5) extra. No credit cards. Directions: Walk 3 minutes from Nishi Kagoshima Station.

Although this inexpensive hotel looks rather uninteresting from the outside, the lobby is quite another story. It reminds me of some forgotten pawnshop, with its glass cases packed with antiques (some several centuries old), old knives, ceramics, and pottery, as well as its fish tanks. More likely than not, two small dogs will greet you. The location is convenient, the rooms and baths have been freshly redone, and the addition of antiques in some rooms is a nice touch. A good place for families—the owners are very nice to children. A shop off the lobby offers juice, bread, slippers, underwear, magazines, and even some antiques. Downstairs, in Kitchen Market, are a karaoke bar and yatai-style restaurants and bars.

Nakazono Ryokan

1-18 Yasui-cho, Kagoshima 892. ☎ **0992/26-5125.** Fax 0992/26-5126. 10 rms (none with bath). A/C TV. ¥4,000 ($40) single; ¥7,600 ($76) twin; ¥10,500 ($105) triple. Rates include tax and service. Breakfast ¥1,500 ($15) extra; dinner ¥2,500 ($25) extra. AE. Streetcar: To Shiyakusho-mae.

A member of the Japanese Inn group, this simple ryokan has a convenient location a 5-minute walk from Kagoshima Station and offers laundry facilities and tatami rooms with coin-operated TV. You can use the refrigerator, and the baths are open 24 hours. The owners are nice.

Sakurajima Youth Hostel (259)
Hakama-goshi, Kagoshima 891-14. ☎ **0992/93-2150.** 90 beds. A/C. ¥2,300 ($23) for JYHA members and nonmembers. Heating and air-conditioning charges ¥200 ($2) extra; breakfast ¥450 ($4.50) extra; dinner ¥700 ($7) extra. No credit cards. Directions: Take the ferry to Sakurajima; then a 5-minute walk from the pier.

This youth hostel is on the slope of the Sakurajima volcano, making it a great place for a holiday. There's a sports facility and public hot springs near the hostel, and if you're really adventurous, you can even bathe in the sea. There are laundry facilities.

DINING

While in Kagoshima, be sure to try its local dishes, known as *Satsuma* cooking (Satsuma was the original name of the Kagoshima area). This style of cooking supposedly has its origins in food cooked on battlefields centuries ago, but if that's the case it has improved greatly since then.

EXPENSIVE

Sky Lounge
Shiroyama Kanko Hotel, 41-1 Shinshoin-cho. ☎ **0992/24-2211.** Reservations recommended for a sea view. Main dishes ¥1,500–¥3,500 ($15–$35); set dinners ¥7,000–¥12,000 ($70–$120); set lunches ¥2,500–¥3,500 ($25–$35). AE, DC, JCB, MC, V. Daily 11am–11:30pm. Taxi: 15 minutes from either station. Bus: City View to Shiroyama. WESTERN.

For Western dining with a view, you can't beat this restaurant, located high above the city. It's especially wonderful at dusk as the lights come on below and Sakurajima slowly fades into darkness. The restaurant's à la carte selections include grilled shrimp, sole filet, lobster thermidor, green-pepper steak, veal cutlet, spaghetti, and sandwiches.

MODERATE

$ Ajimori (260)
13-21 Sennichicho. ☎ **0992/24-7634.** Set meals ¥2,000–¥10,000 ($20–$100); set lunch ¥550–¥680 ($5.50–$6.80). No credit cards. Daily 11:30am–2pm and 5:30–9pm (last order). Streetcar: Izuro Dori. SATSUMA KUROSHABU.

This 20-year-old establishment serves *Satsuma Kuroshabu,* a Kagoshima specialty made from the pork of a small black pig, more tender than regular pork. The lightest, best-tasting tonkatsu I've ever had is here. The Kuroshabu you cook yourself at your table and, like regular shabu-shabu, it's dipped in a boiling broth to cook and then in raw egg or sauce if (like me) you prefer. Portions are generous. There is tatami, table, and counter seating and a take-out window for box lunches.

Kumasotei (261)
6-10 Higashisengoku-cho. ☎ **0992/22-6356.** Reservations not required. Satsuma set meals ¥4,500–¥20,000 ($45–$200); kaiseki set meals from ¥2,000 ($20) lunch and ¥4,000 ($40) dinner. AE, DC, JCB, MC, V. Daily 11am–2:30pm and 5–10pm. Streetcar: Tenmonkan-Dori. LOCAL SPECIALTIES.

A good place to try local Satsuma dishes is this well-known restaurant, located in the city center. It reminds me more of a private home or ryokan, since dining is in individual tatami rooms. If there isn't a crowd, you'll probably have your own private room; otherwise, you'll share. The main menu is in Japanese, but there's a smaller menu in English that features Satsuma specialties, including *Satsuma-age* (ground fish that has been deep-fried), *torisashi* (raw chicken, and not as bad as it sounds), *tonkotsu* (pork that has been boiled for several hours in shochu and brown sugar—absolutely delicious), *zakezushi* (rice that has been soaked in sake all day and then mixed with such things as vegetables and shrimp), bonito baked with salt, *awameshi* (rice mixed with wheat), and *Satsume-jiru* (miso soup with chicken and locally grown vegetables). *Kibinago* is a small fish belonging to the herring family, caught in the waters around Kagoshima. A silver color with brown stripes, it's often eaten raw and arranged on a dish to resemble a chrysanthemum. This restaurant also serves kaiseki.

INEXPENSIVE

✪ Noboruya (262)

2-15 Horie-cho. ☎ **0992/26-6697.** Reservations not required. Noodles ¥900 ($9). No credit cards. Mon–Sat 11am–7pm. RAMEN NOODLES.

This popular, inexpensive 40-year-old restaurant in the center of town is Kagoshima's best-known ramen, or noodle, shop. Since only one dish is served, there's no problem ordering. A big bowl of ramen comes with noodles (made fresh every day) and slices of pork, and is seasoned with garlic. You also get pickled radish (supposedly good for the stomach) and tea. As you eat your ramen at the counter, you can watch women peeling garlic and cooking huge pots of noodles over gas flames. A great place to soak in local atmosphere. Every time I eat here, the kind women make me a sack of hot yams, boiled egg, and mikan orange, and give me a photo of Sakurajima to take away with me.

$ Satsuma (263)

27-30 Chuo-cho. ☎ **0992/52-2661.** Reservations recommended. Main dishes ¥500–¥1,000 ($5–$10); set meals ¥600–¥3,000 ($6–$30). No credit cards. Tues–Sun 10am–3pm and 5–11pm. LOCAL SPECIALTIES.

This tiny, modestly priced restaurant serving Satsuma food has a large red lantern and white curtains outside its door. A cozy establishment near Nishi Kagoshima Station, it has room for only about 18 people at a beautiful cherry-wood counter or in a wood-and-tatami room, which has a well under the low table for legs unaccustomed to sitting tailor fashion. Run by a wonderfully generous woman, who serves delicious torisashi, kibinago, Satsuma-jiru soup, Satsuma-age, and tonkotsu.

8 Ibusuki

31 miles S of Kagoshima

At the southern tip of the Satsuma Peninsula, Ibusuki (pronounced "*ee*-boo-ski") is southern Kyushu's most famous hot-spring resort. With a pleasant average temperature of 64.5°F, it's a region of lush vegetation, flowers, and palm trees—and, of course, hot springs.

ESSENTIALS

The **telephone area code** for Ibusuki, lying in Kagoshima Prefecture, is 0993.

GETTING THERE **By Train** It takes one hour from Kagoshima by train.

By Bus It takes 1½ hours by bus from Kagoshima's Yamagataya Bus Center in the heart of the city, near the Asahi Dori tram stop. You can also join a sightseeing bus tour from Kagoshima, with stops in Chiran and other points along the way. See the Kagoshima section for more information.

VISITOR INFORMATION Be sure to get the leaflet "Southern Kyushu" from the Tourist Information Center in Tokyo or Kyoto.

Upon arrival in Ibusuki, stop by the **tourist information counter** (☎ 0993/22-4114) at Ibusuki Station to pick up a map. There's also a bilingual brochure available with a brief rundown of sightseeing attractions in the area around Ibusuki. The information counter is open daily from 9am to 7:30pm.

GETTING AROUND The town of Ibusuki is spread along the coast, and there are public buses that run through the main streets. The town isn't large, and taxis are readily available.

WHAT TO SEE & DO

SPA BATHS The most popular thing to do is to have yourself buried up to your neck in hot black sand, and the best place to do this is at **Surigahama Public Beach,** located about five minutes from Ibusuki Station by bus. After paying ¥710 ($7.10), you'll be supplied with a yukata cotton kimono and towel. Change into the yukata in the changing room and then walk down to the beach. One of the women there will dig you a shallow grave. Lie down, arrange your yukata so that no vulnerable areas are left exposed, and then lie still while she piles sand on top of you. It's quite a funny sight, actually, to see nothing but heads sticking out of the ground. Bodies are heated by hot springs that surface close to the ground before running into the sea. It's best to go when the tide is low so that you can get closer to the sea. The water is alkali saline, a hot 185°F, and helps with gastrointestinal troubles, neuralgia, and female disorders. After your sand bath, go indoors for a hot-spring bath. The Surigahama sand baths are open every day from 8:30am to 9pm (to 8pm in winter). Other hot-spring and sand baths are found in the spa hotels spread along Ibusuki's six-mile-long beach.

THE SIGHTS To visit the area surrounding Ibusuki, it's best either to join a tour group (conducted in Japanese only) or to rent a car. Public bus lines are neither extensive nor frequent. Popular destinations include **Nagasakibana Point,** Kyushu's southernmost point and the location of a bird and animal park with variety shows; and **Lake Ikeda,** Kyushu's largest lake. It has a depth of 820 feet, not to mention gigantic eels. Some of these eels weigh 33 pounds and measure about 6 feet in length. If you're interested in seeing these creatures, go to the souvenir shops along the lake, which have some on display in big tanks.

Another destination is **Kaimon Natural Park,** located at the foot of Mt. Kaimon. The 18-hole Ibusuki Golf Course is here; greens fees are ¥13,000 to ¥21,000 ($130 to $210). Now you know why golf in Japan is a luxury sport. For more information on golfing, call the golf course (☎ 0993/32-3141).

ACCOMMODATIONS

EXPENSIVE

✪ Hotel Hakusuikan (264)

Chirinosato, Ibusuki 891-04. ☎ **0993/22-3131.** 192 rms (28 with toilet only, 154 with bath). A/C MINIBAR TV TEL. ¥15,000–¥45,000 ($150–$450) per person. Rates include breakfast, dinner, and service charge. AE, DC, JCB, MC, V. Taxi: 5 minutes from Ibusuki Station.

A long driveway lined with pine trees sets the mood for this modern and elegant Japanese ryokan on the beach, with perhaps the most beautiful baths I've seen. Soak in hot springs waters in a (reproduction) Edo Period (1603–1867) bathing area made of cypress wood and stone, with pools of varying temperatures, a rotenburo (outdoor hot springs pool), and a period steam room. You can also take in hot-sand baths and a summer outdoor pool. Expect excellent service and beauty. Its resortlike setting is further enhanced by a gallery, two restaurants, a bar, and a practice golf course.

Although the majority of rooms are Japanese-style tatami rooms, there are also Western-style twins and combination rooms with both beds and separate tatami areas. The best rooms have their own balcony and a Japanese-style deep tub made of hinoki cypress, while the least expensive rooms are in an older building and come with toilet only. Breakfasts are Western or Japanese buffets. This is a very pleasant place to stay and a perfect getaway.

Ibusuki Iwasaki Hotel

3755 Juni-cho, Ibusuki 891-04. ☎ **0993/22-2131.** Fax 0993/24-3215. 56 rms. A/C MINIBAR TV TEL. ¥13,000–¥22,000 ($130–$220) single or double; ¥16,000 ($160) Japanese-style rooms for two. Rates include breakfast, dinner, and service charge. AE, DC, JCB, MC, V. Taxi: 5 minutes from Ibusuki Station.

This self-contained resort on 125 acres of lush tropical grounds with pleasant walking trails throughout is very popular with Japanese tour groups. All the rooms (Western and Japanese) have either a full or partial view of the sea and a balcony. The best rooms, in my opinion, also have views of the wonderful garden. The Japanese-style rooms are located in an older building with a less magnificent view. Nights at the Iwasaki Hotel are nice, with the sound of the waves and of the frogs croaking in the lotus pond.

Dining/Entertainment: The hotel has six restaurants and one night club.

Facilities: Outdoor swimming pools, sauna, tennis courts, bowling arcade, shopping arcade, rental bicycles, private beach, and huge hot-spring baths with view of the bay. Reduced greens fees for the Ibusuki Golf Course.

✪ Shusuien (265)

5-27-27 Yunohama, Ibusuki 891-04. ☎ **0993/23-4141.** Fax 0993/24-4992. 50 rms. A/C MINIBAR TV TEL. ¥24,000–¥63,000 ($240–$630) per person. Rates include breakfast, dinner, and service. 10% discount for children, and children under 7 stay free in parents' room. AE, DC, JCB, MC, V. Taxi: 5 minutes from Ibusuki Station.

If you want to stay in a ryokan, Shusuien, renowned for both its excellent service and its cuisine. In annual competitions held by Japanese travel agencies in which 100 top accommodations are rated, Shusuien has consistently won first prize for its cooking and has been in the top ten for its service. Although small, it employs a staff of 120. This is a good place to stay if you want to be pampered and don't want to spend your holidays with group tours of jovial vacationers. The most expensive rooms face the sea, have their own balcony, and are higher up. The less expensive rooms face inland and have no balcony. Needless to say, this ryokan is elegant yet refined in its setting. Used to foreign businessmen, it serves Western-style breakfasts on request.

Dining/Entertainment: It has one bar and one restaurant, Shimazu-han, where you can try its award-winning cuisine even if you don't stay here, and after eating you can try the baths.

Services: Free newspaper.

Facilities: Souvenir shop, hot-springs bath with sauna, outdoor pools, and complimentary mineral water.

MODERATE

Hotel Kairakuen

5-26-41, Yunohama, Ibusuki 891-04. ☎ **0993/22-3121.** Fax 0993/22-3885. 53 rms (all with bath). A/C TV. ¥8,000–¥18,000 ($80–$180). Rates include breakfast, dinner, and service. Children stay for half price, and children under 7 stay free in parents' room. JCB. Taxi: 5 minutes from Ibusuki Station.

This inexpensive combination hotel-ryokan is located right next to the Surigahama sand baths on the beach. The majority of its rooms are Japanese-style tatami rooms, though there are also two Western-style rooms and two combination rooms with both beds and tatami areas. Although the hotel's building is old and a bit run-down, the price is right. The best rooms are those that face the sea, and the absolute best room is no. 408, which is located on a corner of the building; it has lots of windows and features both beds and a tatami area, making it perfect for families. All rooms have a private bath with water directly from the hot springs, and rooms facing the sea have a window above the tub so that you can look out on the water as you bathe. Dinner is served in your room, while Japanese breakfasts are served in a communal dining area.

INEXPENSIVE

Ibusuki Kokumin Kyuka-son (266)

Higashikata, Shiomi-cho, Ibusuki 891-04. ☎ **0993/22-3211.** 65 rms (7 with bath). A/C TV TEL. ¥3,700–¥4,800 ($37–$48) per person without bath, ¥5,500 ($55) per person with bath. Breakfast ¥1,000 ($10) extra; dinner ¥2,500–¥5,000 ($25–$50) extra. No credit cards. Bus: Shuttle buses depart from in front of Ibusuki Station after every train arrival.

This National People's Village is located right at the water's edge and offers reasonably priced accommodations. Tennis courts, rental bikes, and hot-spring baths make this a very popular place to stay, especially during the summer vacation months of July and August, on New Year's, in March during spring vacation, and in May during school trips. Otherwise, you can probably get a room here. Rooms are basic; some that face the sea have a balcony. Eight of the rooms are Western style. You can reach the village by the village's own bus, recognizable by three circles of green, red, and blue, which is the symbol of National People's Villages; it's a 10-minute taxi ride from Ibusuki Station.

DINING

✪ Chozyuan (267)

Kaimon-cho, Tosenkyo. ☎ **0993/22-3155.** Reservations not required. Noodles ¥500 ($5). No credit cards. May–June, daily 10am–7pm; July–Aug, daily 9am–9pm; Sept–Apr, daily 10am–5pm. Bus: 8 departures daily from Ibusuki Station, a 30-minute ride. SOMEN NOODLES.

If you're adventurous, try this fun restaurant in the countryside. Serving as a lunch stop for some of the organized tours of the area (including the Kagoshima-to-Ibusuki bus tour described in the previous section), it specializes in somen, or cold noodles. Seating is under a pavilion beside a man-made waterfall, so you eat to the accompaniment of running water and Japanese traditional music playing in the background. In the middle of your table is a large round container with water swirling around in a circle. When you get your basket of noodles, dump them into the cold water; then fish them out with your chopsticks, dip them in soy sauce, and enjoy. There are also four set menus, which come with such things as grilled trout, vegetables, and soup. You can also try carp sashimi.

$ Shimazu-Han

Hotel Shusuien, 5-27-27 Yunohama. ☎ **0993/23-4141.** Reservations required for dinner, recommended for lunch. Set lunches ¥3,500–¥5,500 ($35–$55). AE, DC, JCB, MC, V. Daily 11am–2pm and 5:30–9pm. Taxi: 5 minutes from Ibusuki Station. JAPANESE.

This is probably the best place in town to have lunch: Meals here are a pleasure, served in 18 private tatami rooms, each designed like a private house on a village lane.

Tableware is chosen with care to match both the seasons and the food displayed. Dishes are served in courses rather than all at once. The menu is in Japanese only; both meat and fish dishes are featured, as well as Japanese box lunches, obento. Be sure to order a cup of plum shochu (*ume shu*)—it's the best shochu I've ever had. After your meal take a complimentary bath; how civilized!

9 Miyazaki

897 miles SW of Tokyo, 252 miles SE of Fukuoka, 78 miles W of Kagoshima

With a population of 295,000, Miyazaki is one of the largest and most important cities in southern Kyushu and serves as the government seat of Miyazaki Prefecture. Yet Miyazaki feels isolated and somewhat neglected by the rest of Japan. Tokyo seems far away, and most foreigners who happen to land at Kagoshima's international airport tend to head north for Kumamoto, missing Miyazaki altogether. Japanese honeymooners, who a decade ago favored Miyazaki over most other domestic destinations, are now flocking to the shores of Hawaii and Australia.

And yet Miyazaki is a perfect place to relax, swim in the Pacific Ocean, get in some rounds of golf, and savor some of the local delicacies. Temperatures here are the second warmest in Japan, after Okinawa, and flowers bloom throughout the year. You won't see many foreigners here, and the natives will treat you warmly and kindly. If you want to unwind and pamper yourself for a few days, Miyazaki is a good place to do it. And if you have the energy for sightseeing, Miyazaki Prefecture offers some historical and natural attractions.

ESSENTIALS

The **telephone area code** for Miyazaki, lying in Miyazaki Prefecture, is 0985.

GETTING THERE By Plane There are daily flights into Miyazaki from most major Japanese cities. The city is 1½ hours from Tokyo, 1 hour from Osaka, and 40 minutes from Fukuoka. The airport is a 15-minute ride from the center of town.

By Train From Tokyo, take the Shinkansen bullet train to Kokura and transfer there to a limited express (trip time: approximately 11 hr.). There are direct trains from Hakata Station in Fukuoka (6 hr.), Beppu (3 hr.), and Kagoshima (2 hr.).

By Bus Eight buses depart daily from Fukuoka for Miyazaki (trip time: almost 5 hr.). There are also buses from Kagoshima and Kumamoto.

VISITOR INFORMATION For pamphlets on the city in English, stop off at the **tourist information center** at either the airport (☎ 0985/51-5114) or JR Miyazaki Station. The airport office is open daily from 7am to 8:30pm, while the train station information center is open daily from 9am to 1pm and 2pm to 5:15pm.

For detailed information on Miyazaki Prefecture, drop by the **prefectural tourist office** or *kanko kyokai* (☎ 0985/25-4676), located just off Higashi (East) Tachibana-dori at 2-7-18 Tachibana-dori. Open Monday through Friday from 9am to 5:15pm, it has information on Aya, Aoshima, Udo Shrine, and other attractions.

GETTING AROUND The main street in town is Tachibana-dori Street, lined with shops, department stores, and restaurants. Many buses serving other parts of town, as well as Miyazaki Prefecture, make stops along this main thoroughfare. There's also a large bus terminal south of the Oyodo River close to Minami Miyazaki Station.

Although all the sights listed below are accessible by public transportation, they are quite spread out. You may, therefore, want to join an **organized tour,** even though it will be conducted in Japanese only. At least it gets you to each destination, and you won't have to worry about time schedules and bus stops. A tour operated by Miyazaki Kotsu Bus Company (☎ 0985/52-2200) departs at 8:50am daily from the bus terminal near Minami Miyazaki Station and visits Miyazaki Shrine, Heiwadai Park, an amusement park for children, Aoshima Island, Horikiri Pass, Cactus Park, and Udo Shrine. The "A" tour lasts seven hours and costs ¥4,630 ($46.30).

WHAT TO SEE & DO

The most important shrine in town is **Miyazaki Shrine,** dedicated to the first emperor of Japan, Emperor Jimmu, who was the first leader of the Yamoto courts. Peacefully surrounded by woods and cedar trees and about a 15-minute bus ride from Tachibana-dori Street, the shrine is built from cedar and is austerely plain. Be sure to visit the nearby **Miyazaki Prefectural Museum,** open Tuesday through Sunday from 8:30am to 5pm. *Miyazaki-ken Sogo Hakubutsukan* houses collections of ancient clay images, stone implements, ancient pottery, and folkloric items.

Archeological digs in Miyazaki Prefecture have unearthed a multitude of ancient burial mounds and clay figures known as *haniwa.* Replicas of these ancient mounds and haniwa clay figures can be seen in **Haniwa Garden,** most easily reached by taxi in about 15 minutes from Miyazaki Station. Approximately 400 of these clay figures have been placed between trees on mounds covered with moss. I especially like the haniwa with the simple face and body and the O-shaped mouth; it's said to represent a dancing woman. A one-room exhibition house displays some items found in ancient burial mounds, and if you want you can buy a small clay replica to take home with you.

Haniwa Garden is located in a large park called Heiwadai Park, in which you'll also find the **Tower of Peace.** It has a pedestal built with stones donated from countries around the world, and was constructed with the help of volunteers; it was finished—ironically enough—in 1940.

Also an hour's bus ride from Miyazaki is **Aya,** a village of about 7,300 people known for its production of traditional handcrafts. It boasts five kilns, a glass-blowing factory, at least a dozen wood-carving shops, two bamboo-craft makers, and three weaving shops. A recently constructed crafts center displays and sells the products of these establishments.

Next to the crafts center is **Aya Castle,** a reproduction of the original Aya Castle built 650 years ago. Made of fir trees, the castle is tiny compared to most in Japan and contains a few artifacts, such as samurai uniforms and swords. Because both the castle and the crafts center are small and located an hour away from Miyazaki, I suggest you visit Aya only if you have a special interest in crafts or have no other chance to see a Japanese castle. Both the crafts center and castle are located about a 10-minute walk from the center of Aya town, on top of a peaceful wooded hill. Hours are 9am to 4:30pm daily; the entrance fee is ¥500 ($5).

One of the most famous sights associated with Miyazaki is **Aoshima,** a tiny island less than a mile in circumference and connected to the mainland via a walkway. Although Aoshima is located about 25 minutes south by train from Miyazaki Station, it's considered part of Miyazaki city. There's a small vermilion shrine on the island, and the beaches nearby are the most popular among the people of Miyazaki for swimming in July and August.

✪ **Seagaia** is a convention and resort complex set in a vast national reserve pine forest along 10 kilometers of unspoiled coast line. A free shuttle bus loops to all facilities (including hotels) in Seagaia. Facilities too numerous to list here include the **Phoenix Country Club,** with a 27-hole course (greens fees ¥25,000 to ¥30,000/$250 to $300); the 18-hole **Tom Watson Golf Course** (greens fees ¥16,000 to ¥21,000/

$160 to $210); two **tennis clubs** (fees ¥1,500 to ¥15,000 for two hours); a zoo; an amusement park; a bowling alley; rental cycles; a 43-story-high **observation platform** accessed by view elevators (¥500/$5); and **Ocean Dome,** the largest all-weather indoor water park (8,790 square meters of water surface), with a high-tech teflon retractable roof to let in natural sunlight (Miyazaki is the sunniest place in Japan). This synthetic tropical paradise (a constant 30°C) features a white sand beach, waves, adventure rides, restaurants and shops, water slides, and daily shows (including a dramatic night show with dancing, exhibition surfing, and an excellent water screen laser light show). No need to wear more than your swim suit, as your wristband key can be used to charge. Admission to Ocean Dome is ¥4,200 ($42) for those over 18, ¥3,100 ($31) for children 12 to 17, and ¥2,000 ($20) for children 4 to 11 (free for children under 4). Twilight admission (after 4pm) is lower, and if you want to enter the observation deck only, you pay ¥600 to ¥1,200 ($6 to $12) depending on age. The Water Crush, Adventure Theater, and Lost World attractions are an additional ¥600 ($6) each. The Ocean Dome is open from 9am to 10pm daily (closed once a month for maintenance).

ACCOMMODATIONS

EXPENSIVE

Ocean 45

Hamayama Yamazaki-cho, Miyazaki 880. ☎ **0985/21-1133.** Fax 0985/21-1134. 753 rms. A/C MINIBAR TV TEL. ¥19,000–¥32,000 ($190–$320) single; ¥30,000–¥32,000 ($300–$320) double or twin; suites and Japanese rooms from ¥68,000 ($680). AE, DC, JCB, MC, V. Bus: Direct bus from Miyazaki Station (¥430/$4.30) or Miyazaki Airport (¥800/$8).

The most relaxing and luxurious place to stay in Miyazaki is Seagaia's crowning jewel, Ocean 45, rising 43 floors above the natural greenery of the Hitotsuba Coast. From the elegant 11-story, 3-mezzanine atrium lobby to the spacious rooms equipped with lots of extras (bathroom phones, 31-channel TV plus videogames, safe, shower plus bath), this hotel is a pleasure to stay in. All the rooms have magnificent views of the sea. The only detraction is a 10:30am checkout time.

Dining/Entertainment: Eight restaurants, seven bars and lounges, disco, and karaoke.

Facilities: All the Seagaia facilities, plus sports club (¥2,000/$20 extra), conference rooms, business center, baby-sitting service, travel agency, library, mah-jongg and Go salon, video room, convenience store, gallery, automatic cash dispensers, cooking school, free parking, and handicapped-accessible facilities and rooms.

Sun Hotel Phoenix

3083 Hamayama Shioji, Miyazaki 880-01. ☎ **0985/39-3131.** Fax 0985/39-6496. 296 rms. A/C MINIBAR TV TEL. ¥11,000–¥13,000 ($110–$130) single or double; ¥17,500–¥33,000 ($175–$330) twin; ¥18,500–¥30,000 ($185–$300) Japanese-style rooms for two. AE, DC, JCB, MC, V. Directions: See Ocean 45.

Built about 15 years ago, the Sun Hotel Phoenix is less highrise and less expensive than the Ocean 45, with higher prices charged for rooms facing the sea. Western-style rooms are roomy.

Dining/Entertainment: Restaurant Sky Blue, on the ninth floor, has unobstructed views of the Pacific, pine woods, and the golf course below. There are also a sushi bar, a cocktail lounge, and a coffee shop.

Facilities: All the Seagaia facilities.

Moderate

Hotel Phoenix

2-1-1 Matsuyama, Miyazaki 880. ☎ **0985/23-6111.** Fax 0985/26-4535. 117 rms. A/C MINIBAR TV TEL. ¥12,000–¥13,000 ($120–$130) double or twin. AE, DC, JCB, V. Taxi: 5 minutes from Miyazaki Station.

This hotel, located right beside the Oyodo River in town, has some rooms with river views (they cost slightly more). There's a small outdoor pool open in July and August; unfortunately, this is located right outside the lobby's window, so there's no hiding those extra pounds. A beer garden on the roof, open May to mid-September, daily from 5:30 to 10pm, has a great view of the river, city, and the hills beyond. Beer starts at ¥600 ($6). There's also a Western restaurant, a Japanese restaurant, and a cocktail bar.

Miyazaki Oriental Hotel

2-10-22 Hiroshima, Miyazaki 880. ☎ **0985/27-3111.** Fax 0985/28-4250. 102 rms. A/C MINIBAR TV TEL. ¥6,000 ($60) single; ¥9,300 ($93) double; ¥11,000 ($110) twin. JCB, V.

In this business hotel close to the station, rooms seem a bit old and could use some cheerful renovations, but prices are reasonable. Rates with meals are also available. There's someone at the front desk who speaks English. The hotel's one restaurant serves inexpensive Chinese food and is well known.

Seaside Hotel Phoenix

3083 Hamayama Shioji, Miyazaki 880-01. ☎ **0985/39-1111.** Fax 0985/39-1639. 196 rms (all with bath). A/C MINIBAR TV TEL. ¥10,000 ($100) single; ¥15,000–¥26,000 ($150–$260) twin; ¥16,000–¥28,000 ($160–$280) Japanese style for two. AE, DC, JCB, V. Directions: See Ocean 45.

The oldest and least expensive of the Seagaia hotels, the Seaside offers both Japanese- and Western-style rooms and restaurants. Guests can use Seagaia facilities.

Inexpensive

Aoshima Kokumin Shukusha (268)

2-12-36 Aoshima, Miyazaki 889-22. ☎ **0985/65-1533.** Fax 0985/65-1120. 57 rms (5 with bath). A/C TV TEL. ¥5,000 ($50) without bath; ¥6,200 ($62) with bath. No credit cards. Train: 25 minutes to Aoshima Station (3 minutes).

If you're a sun worshipper, you may want to stay at this public lodge located right next to tiny Aoshima Island. All its rooms face the ocean, and the beach for swimming is only a five-minute walk away. Popular with Japanese families, this Kokumin Shukusha is heavily booked during New Year's, Golden Week in May, and July and August, so make reservations early. Rates including breakfast and dinner start from ¥2,000 ($20) extra, and there are photos to help you choose your meal plan.

Cottage Himuka

3083 Hamayama Shioji, Miyazaki 880-01. ☎ **0985/32-5131.** 54 rms. A/C MINIBAR TV TEL. ¥5,000 ($50) per person quad or a room for eight. AE, DC, JCB, MC, V. Directions: See Ocean 45.

In Seagaia, these clean, bright, and practical apartments with cooking facilities are a great deal for families and groups. Note, however, that the rate is based on sleeping capacity; thus, if you're a party of eight, you'll pay ¥40,000 ($400), or ¥5,000 ($50) per person. Ground-floor apartments are best, in my opinion, because they have terraces off sliding glass doors. There's a convenience store on the grounds, and in summer an outdoor pool (no charge).

DINING

Miyazaki's subtropical climate is conducive to the growth of a number of vegetables and fruits, including sweet pumpkins, oranges, cucumbers, green peppers, shiitake mushrooms, and chestnuts. Especially popular is *shochu,* made from sweet potatoes, buckwheat, or corn.

The two restaurants listed below specialize in imaginative dishes made with locally grown vegetables, fruit, and other produce. They are located close together just off Tachibana-dori Street, about a 15-minute walk from Miyazaki Station.

Gyosantei (269)

Shokokaikan Bldg. basement, Higashi 1-chome. ☎ **0985/24-7070.** Reservations not required. Set lunches ¥1,000–¥1,500 ($10–$15); set dinners ¥4,000–¥7,500 ($40–$75). JCB, V. Mon–Sat 11:30am–2pm and 5–10pm. LOCAL SPECIALTIES.

Although the stairwell doesn't look like much, this is an attractive restaurant with wooden floors, tatami mats, leg wells under the tables, and waitresses dressed in kimono. Notice the two little mounds of salt on either side of the restaurant's door—they symbolize purification. Just as in the olden days, there's a split length of bamboo inside the leg well on which to rest your stockinged feet, and the menu is written on a scroll. For local food, try the *Himukazen* (facing the sun) course, which changes according to what's in season and what the cook decides to create, but it always includes as its main dish a pumpkin filled with chicken and radish and topped with hard-boiled egg yolk, with a raw yolk plopped on top (which nevertheless slowly cooks from the heat)—meant to resemble the sun. Side dishes might include salmon rolled inside Japanese radish, raw flying fish served with freshly grated *wasabi* (horseradish), fried prawn with dried mushrooms used as a coating instead of flour, or Miyazaki melon. It's truly a restaurant of culinary surprises, making dining here a pleasure.

✪ Sugi no Ko (270)

Tachibana-dori 2-1-4. ☎ **0985/22-5798.** Reservations not required. Set lunches ¥1,000–¥2,500 ($10–$25); set dinners ¥4,000–¥10,500 ($40–$105). AE, DC, JCB, MC, V. Mon–Sat 11:30am–1:30pm and 4–11pm. LOCAL SPECIALTIES.

The owner of this two-floor restaurant creates all his own dishes and has even produced two books of his recipes and advice. The dining area displays haniwa dolls and other crafts of Miyazaki Prefecture, and there are also private tatami rooms. The English-language menu offers the Miyazaki Gyuu Teishoku with Miyazaki beef seasoned with soy sauce and served with four different sauces, vegetables, soup, rice, and fruit. Asahigani crab is a local specialty.

12

Northern Japan—Hokkaido

Because so many of Japan's historical events took place in Kyoto, Tokyo, and other cities in southern Honshu, most tourists to Japan never venture farther north than Tokyo. True, northern Japan does not have the temples, shrines, gardens, and castles of southern Japan, but it does have spectacular scenery. Matsushima, about three hours north of Tokyo, is considered one of Japan's most scenic spots, with pine-covered islets dotting its bay. Farther north is Hokkaido, the northernmost of Japan's four main islands.

HOKKAIDO

Hokkaido's landscape is strikingly different from that of any other place in Japan. With more than 30,000 square miles, Hokkaido makes up about 21% of Japan's total land mass and yet has only 5% of its population. In other words, Hokkaido has what the rest of Japan doesn't—space. Considered the country's last frontier, Hokkaido didn't begin opening up to development until after the Meiji Restoration in 1868, when the government began encouraging Japanese to migrate to the island. Even today, Hokkaido has a frontier feel to it, and many young Japanese come here to backpack, ski, camp, and tour across the countryside on motorcycles or bicycles. There are dairy farms and silos and broad, flat fields of wheat, corn, potatoes, and rice. Then the land puckers up to craggy and bare volcanoes, gorges, and hills densely covered with trees. There are clear spring lakes, mountain ranges, rugged wilderness, wild animals, and rare plants. About 7% of Hokkaido is preserved as national and prefectural parks.

With winters that are long and severe, Hokkaido has its main tourist season in August, when days are cool and pleasant, with an average temperature of 70°F. And while the rest of the nation is under the deluge of the rainy season, Hokkaido's summers are usually bright and clear. In winter, ski enthusiasts flock to slopes near Sapporo and to resorts such as Daisetzusan National Park. And February marks the annual Sapporo Snow Festival, with its huge ice and snow sculptures.

The people of Hokkaido are considered to be as open and hearty as the wide expanse of land around them. Hokkaido is also the home of the Ainu, the native inhabitants of the island. Not much is known about their origins, but the Ainu arrived in Hokkaido approximately 800 years ago. It's not even clear whether they're

What's Special About Hokkaido

Natural Spectacles

- Mt. Hakodate, reached by cable car and famous for its night view of Hakodate.
- Lake Toya, a typical caldera lake, boasting a depth of 590 feet.
- Active volcanoes, including Mt. Usu and Showa-Shinzen.
- Sounkyo Gorge, with rock walls rising almost 500 feet and a series of waterfalls.
- Akan National Park, with its breeding grounds of red-crested cranes.

Hot-Spring Spas

- Noboribetsu, one of Japan's most famous hot-spring resorts.
- Toyako Onsen, on the shores of Lake Toya and featuring the magnificent Sun Palace Hotel, complete with indoor and outdoor baths, swimming pool, and waterslides.
- Akanko Onsen in Akan National Park.

Regional Food and Drink

- Sapporo Beer, produced in Sapporo since 1876.
- Hokkaido local products, including hairy crab, corn on the cob, and potatoes.
- Genghis Khan, a dish of mutton and vegetables that you barbecue at your own table.

Asian or Caucasian, but they're of different racial stock than the Japanese. They are round-eyed and light-skinned, and Ainu males can grow thick beards and mustaches. Traditionally the Ainu lived as hunters and fishermen, but after Hokkaido opened up to development they were gradually assimilated into Japanese society, taking Japanese names and adopting the Japanese language and clothing. Like Native Americans, they were often discriminated against and their culture was largely destroyed. Today, there are an estimated 15,000 Ainu still living in Hokkaido. Some of them earn their living from tourism, selling Ainu wood carvings and other crafts, as well as performing traditional dances and songs.

SEEING HOKKAIDO

Public transportation around Hokkaido is by train and bus. In addition to regular bus lines, there are sightseeing buses linking national parks and major attractions. Although they're more expensive than trains and regular buses, they offer unparalleled views of the countryside. Keep in mind that bus schedules fluctuate with the seasons, as some lines don't run during the snowy winter months.

If you plan to do a lot of traveling in Hokkaido and you're not traveling by Japan Rail Pass, you can purchase a special pass issued by Japan Railways that allows unlimited travel on its trains and buses in Hokkaido. The **Shuyuken Pass** can be purchased anywhere in Japan except Hokkaido; it includes a round-trip ticket between Hokkaido and another island. The price depends on departure point. The pass departing from Tokyo costs ¥39,760 ($397.60) for adults and ¥29,360 ($293.60) for students. The **Hokkaido New Wide Pass** is for unlimited travel in Hokkaido—but does not include travel to and from Hokkaido—and can be purchased anywhere in Japan. The five-day pass costs ¥13,320 ($133.20) for adults and ¥10,340 ($103.40) for students, while the 10-day pass costs ¥21,360 ($213.60) for adults and ¥16,930 ($169.30) for students.

Because distances are long and traffic is rather light, Hokkaido is one of the few places in Japan where driving your own car is actually recommended. Because it's expensive, however, it's economical only if there are several of you. Rates for one day of car rental begin at ¥8,000 ($80) for the first 220 kilometers (136 miles), and each additional day costs ¥5,600 ($56) for 100 kilometers (62 miles). Car-rental agencies are found throughout Hokkaido, as well as at Chitose Airport outside Sapporo.

Incidentally, travel to Hokkaido by land is generally via Shinkansen bullet train from Ueno or Tokyo Station in Tokyo to Morioka, followed by limited express from Morioka to Aomori on the northern tip of Honshu Island. For centuries the only way to continue from Aomori to Hokkaido was by boat, but the opening of the Seikan Tunnel (in 1988) now allows the entire trip to be made by train. Whereas the ferry ride to Hakodate, on Hokkaido, used to take four hours, the train ride by tunnel takes less than three hours—45 minutes of which is in the tunnel. At any rate, the entire trip from Tokyo to Hakodate via train should take about eight hours. The fastest way to reach Hokkaido, of course, is to fly.

As for the best route through Hokkaido, the first stop is usually Hakodate, a convenient one-night stopover. From there you can board a local train bound for Sapporo, stopping off at Shikotsu-Toya National Park along the way. After spending a few days in Sapporo, take the train to Kamikawa and transfer there to a direct bus to Sounkyo Onsen in Daisetsuzan National Park. From Sounkyo Onsen you can then continue your trip by taking a bus to Rubeshibe, transferring there to a train to Bihoro. From Bihoro, sightseeing buses depart for Akan National Park, where you can then spend the night at Lake Akan. From Akan you may wish to return to Tokyo by plane from Kushiro Airport.

1 Matsushima

234 miles NE of Tokyo

Because the trip to Hokkaido is such a long one, the most pleasant way to travel is to break up the journey with an overnight stay in Matsushima in northern Honshu. Matsushima means "Pine-Clad Islands," and that's exactly what this region is. More than 200 pine-covered islets and islands dot Matsushima Bay, giving it the appearance of a giant pond in a Japanese landscape garden. Twisted and gnarled pines sweep upward from volcanic tuff and white sandstone, creating bizarre and beautiful shapes. Matsushima is so dear to Japanese hearts that it's considered one of the three most scenic spots in Japan (the other two are Miyajima in Hiroshima Bay and Amanohashidate on the north coast of Honshu)—and was so designated about 270 years ago in a book written by a Confucian philosopher of the Edo government. Basho (1644–94), the famous Japanese haiku poet, was so struck by Matsushima's beauty that it's almost as though he were at a loss for words when he wrote: "Matsushima, Ah! Matsushima! Matsushima!"

ESSENTIALS

The **telephone area code** for Matsushima and Sendai, both lying in Miyagi Prefecture, is 022.

GETTING THERE **By Train** From Tokyo you can take the Tohoku Shinkansen from Ueno or Tokyo Station to Sendai, which will take from $1^{3}/_{4}$ to $2^{1}/_{2}$ hours, depending on the number of stops. In Sendai, change to the JR Senseki Line—it's well marked in English, so you shouldn't have any difficulty changing trains in

Sendai. It takes about 25 minutes by express train to reach Matsushima Kaigan Station.

By Boat A popular way to get to Matsushima is to take the Senseki train line from Sendai only as far as Hon-Shiogama (about 18 minutes by express). From there you can catch a sightseeing boat to Matsushima Kaigan Pier.

VISITOR INFORMATION Before leaving Tokyo, be sure to stop by the Tourist Information Center for a free leaflet called "Sendai, Matsushima, and Hiraizumi." It has a map of Matsushima Bay and tells of attractions in and around Matsushima.

Upon arrival in Matsushima, stop off at one of the **Matsushima Tourist Association Offices,** located at both Matsushima Kaigan train station and at Matsushima Kaigan Pier (☎ 022/354-2618). You can pick up a brochure with a map in English and get directions to your hotel. Daily hours for both are 8:30am to 5pm (until 4:30pm in winter). The train station and pier are about a 10-minute walk apart.

SPECIAL EVENTS The **Tanabata Festival** is held from August 6 to 8 in Sendai, and the **Toronagashi Festival** takes place August 15 and 16 in Matsushima.

GETTING AROUND All of Matsushima's major attractions are within walking distance of both the train station and the pier, and you can cover the whole area on foot in half a day of leisurely sightseeing.

WHAT TO SEE & DO

Arriving in Matsushima by **sightseeing boat** is a good introduction to the bay, as you pass pine-covered islands and oyster rafts along the way. Board the boat in Hon-Shiogama for the 50-minute trip to Matsushima Kaigan Pier, which costs ¥1,400 ($14), ¥700 ($7) for children. Unfortunately, the commentary is in Japanese only (a good time to break out the Walkman unless you've become oblivious to noise by now). And believe it or not, a couple of the boats are shaped like a huge peacock and a dragon. Boats leave from both Hon-Shiogama and Matsushima Kaigan piers about every half hour between 8am and 4pm in summer, but only once an hour in winter. If you're going in the off-season, be sure to check the schedule (☎ 022/362-2431).

Even if you don't arrive by boat, you might still want to take a boat trip in the bay. Regular sightseeing boats make 50-minute trips around the bay and back and charge ¥1,400 ($14), ¥700 ($7) for children. You can also charter one of the smaller motorboats—which, judging by the number of them leaving the pier every few minutes, seems to be the most popular way to see Matsushima. Charter motorboats cost ¥4,000 ($40) for a tour lasting 20 minutes, ¥6,000 ($60) for 40 minutes, and ¥15,000 ($150) for two hours. You can see more of the islands on these smaller craft than you can on the regular sightseeing boats.

In addition to the boat trips, there are four spots spread around Matsushima that are historically considered the best for viewing Matsushima's islands. These spots are called Otakamori, Tomiyama, Tamonzan, and Ogidani. The closest is **Ogidani,** a 10-minute taxi ride away from the pier. I personally don't think it's worth the time or effort to make it to each of these four lookouts. You can get as much a feel for Matsushima's beauty simply by visiting the more easily accessible attractions listed below. If you feel like hiking to a lookout, **Sokanzan Lookout** is about a 30-minute hike from Matsushima Kaigan Pier and offers a panoramic view of the region.

Matsushima's best-known structure is **Zuiganji Temple** (271), the most famous Zen temple in the northern part of Japan. Located just a few minutes' walk away from Matsushima Kaigan Pier, its entrance is shaded by tall cedar trees. On the right side

Impressions

An Ainu woman on Hokkaido went up to my friend and asked him indignantly: "What is it that is peculiar about us? Why do Japanese people look at us as if we were freaks?" She had tattooed round her lips and chin an enormous blue mustache, and a blue beard.

—Alexander Campbell, *The Heart of Japan,* 1962

of the pathway leading to the temple are caves and grottoes dug out by priests long ago. Adorned with Buddhist statues and memorial tablets, they were used for practicing zazen (sitting meditation). Zuiganji Temple was founded in 1606 by the order of Date Masamune, the most powerful and important lord of northern Honshu. Unifying the region known as Tohoku, Date built his castle in nearby Sendai, and today almost all sites in and around Sendai and Matsushima are tied to the Date family. It took hundreds of workers six years to build the temple, which was constructed in the *shoin-zukuri* style typical of the Momoyama Period and served as the family temple of the Date clan.

An adjoining treasure hall, the **Seiryuden** displays items belonging to the temple and the Date family, while the main hall contains elaborately carved wooden doors, transoms, and painted sliding doors—and at last check this was one of the few temples that still allowed flash photography (in its outer corridor). Admission for both the Seiryuden and Zuiganji Temple is ¥600 ($6). Hours vary according to the season: The longest hours are from April to September, when it's open daily from 8am to 5pm; in winter, from 8am to 3:30, 4, or 4:30pm.

Next to Zuiganji Temple (to the left if you're facing Zuiganji) is **Entsuin** (272), a lesser-known temple also built more than 300 years ago by the Date clan. Open daily from 8am to 5pm throughout the year and charging a ¥300 ($3) admission, it features a small rock garden, a beautiful rose garden, and a small temple housing an elaborate statue of Lord Date Mitsumune, grandson of Lord Date Masamune, who founded the Sendai fief. Depicted here on horseback, Mitsumune was reportedly poisoned and died at the tender age of 19. The statues surrounding him represent retainers who committed ritual suicide to follow their master into death. The statues and small temple are located at the back of the temple grounds, past the rose garden. Tour groups seem to bypass this temple, making it a peaceful retreat away from the crowds that sometimes descend on Matsushima.

Under the supervision of Zuiganji Temple is **Godaido,** a small wooden worship hall on a tiny island not far from the pier. Connected to the mainland by a short bridge, its grounds are open night and day and are free, but there's not much to see. The hall's interior is open to the public only every 33 years. (It won't be open again until August 20, 2005.) Godaido is often featured in brochures of Matsushima, making this delicate wooden temple one of the town's best-known landmarks.

Kanrantei, the "Water-Viewing Pavilion," is just a short walk from the pier. A simple wooden teahouse, it was used by generations of the Date family for such aesthetic pursuits as viewing the moon and watching the ripples on the tide. Originally it belonged to warlord Hideyoshi Toyotomi as part of his estate at Fushimi Castle near Kyoto, but he presented it to the Date family at the end of the 16th century. Kanrantei is open daily from 8am to 5pm (8:30am to 4:30pm in winter). The entrance fee is ¥200 ($2). For an additional ¥300 ($3), you can drink ceremonial green tea while sitting on the teahouse tatami and contemplating the bay, its islands, and the boats carving ribbons through the water. After drinking your tea, wander through the small museum, which contains artifacts belonging to the Date family. I found particularly interesting a screen painted long ago showing Matsushima—even then there were boats winding between the islands. Who knows? Maybe the motorboats of today will someday look quaint and old-fashioned to generations hence.

Just a couple of minutes beyond Kanrantei on the southern edge of Matsushima is **Ojima,** a small island once used as a retreat by priests. At one time, there used to be many caves with carvings of scriptures, Buddhist images, and sutras, but today the island and its remaining stone images and structures are rather neglected and forgotten. There's no fee, no gate, and the island never closes. It's a nice quiet spot to sit and view the harbor. Because it was a Buddhist retreat, women were forbidden to enter Ojima until after the Meiji Restoration in 1868.

At the other end of Matsushima is **Fukuurajima,** another island connected to the mainland, this time by a long red concrete bridge with orange-colored railings. It's a botanical garden of sorts, with several hundred labeled plants and trees, but mostly it's unkempt and overgrown—which comes as a surprise in cultivated Japan. It takes less than an hour to walk completely around the island. Between the hours of 8am and 6pm (4pm in winter), you must pay ¥150 ($1.50) admittance.

The **Matsushima Orgel Museum** (☎ 022/353-3600) is located a 15-minute walk along the sea from Matsushima Kaigan Station. The museum displays an entire museum—the Belgium National Music Box Museum—which was bought and shipped lock, stock, and barrel from Bruges, Belgium. The music boxes on exhibit are priceless, some owned by kings or nobles, some designed for theaters, shows, exhibitions, cafes, or train stations. There are also phonographs, player pianos, harmoniums, the earliest dating back to 1905, and demonstrations with explanations in Japanese (some signs are in English). Admission is ¥1,200 ($12) for adults, ¥800 ($8) for children 13 to 18, ¥500 ($5) for children 6 to 12. It's open daily from 9am to 5:30pm.

ESPECIALLY FOR CHILDREN

Next to Ojima is an aquarium called **Marine Pia,** open daily from 9am to 5pm and charging ¥1,400 ($14) for adults, ¥700 ($7) children 6 to 11, and ¥350 ($3.50) children 3 to 5 (☎ 022/354-2020). Marine Pia has penguins, turtles, crocodiles, octopuses, sea otters, moray eels, sea lions, and ocean sunfish. This place appeals mainly to kids, who also enjoy the aquarium's miniature train, carousel, and monorail.

ACCOMMODATIONS

Because this is a tourist town, accommodations in Matsushima are not cheap, especially during the peak months of May through November. For the Tanabata Festival, held from August 6 to 8 in Sendai, and the Toronagashi Festival, held August 15 and 16 in Matsushima, rooms are usually fully booked six months in advance. Rates are generally lower during the off-season months (from December through April). Almost all accommodations here are in ryokan, which means you're generally expected to take your dinner and breakfast there. Because Matsushima tends to be expensive, I've included some inexpensive accommodations in nearby Sendai at the end of this section. If you stay there, you could make a day trip to Matsushima, only 25 minutes away.

EXPENSIVE

Hotel Sohkan

1-1 Aza Hama, Isozaki, Matsushima-cho, Miyagi-gun 981-02. ☎ **022/354-2181.** Fax 022/354-6118. 134 rms. A/C MINIBAR TV TEL. ¥15,000–¥27,000 ($150–$270) per person Western style; ¥15,000–¥50,000 ($150–$500) per person Japanese style. Rates include breakfast, dinner, and service charge. Off-season discount available. AE, DC, JCB, MC, V. Taxi: 5 minutes from the boat pier.

Despite the "hotel" in its name, this is a modern and comfortable ryokan located on the edge of Matsushima. Catering mainly to Japanese groups, it offers a koto concert in the early evening in its lobby, played by a woman in a traditional kimono. Although the majority of rooms are Japanese style, there are also a few Western-style rooms available that can sleep up to four people. You have your choice of Japanese or Western breakfast and dinner.

Dining/Entertainment: In addition to Japanese, Chinese, and Western restaurants, there's also a karaoke bar, in which people from the audience stand up and sing a variety of songs while accompanied by taped instrumental music. It's a fun place to watch Japanese enjoying themselves.

Facilities: Public baths, outdoor pool (in summer), tennis, a 210-foot-high observation tower (¥400/$4).

Matsushima Century Hotel

8 Aza Senzui, Matsushima, Matsushima-cho, Miyagi-gun 981-02. ☎ **022/354-4111.** Fax 022/354-4191. 192 rms. A/C MINIBAR TV TEL. ¥17,000–¥36,000 ($170–$360) per person in peak season, ¥12,000–¥40,000 ($120–$400) per person in winter. Rates include breakfast, dinner, and service charge. AE, DC, JCB, MC, V. Directions: Walk 10 minutes from Matsushima Kaigan or 3 minutes from the pier.

This glittering white hotel is a cool oasis conveniently located in the middle of town. It's a sleek place appealing especially to the young. Approximately half the rooms are Japanese style, and all these face the bay and have a balcony. The Western-style rooms, sunny and cheerful and decorated in pastels and white, face only inland and have no balcony.

Dining/Entertainment: The bar charges a ¥2,700 ($27) cover, including one free drink. La Saison is a good place to come for lunch or dinner. Open from 11:30am to 2pm and from 6 to 9pm, this Western seafood restaurant is decorated with white latticed wood and ferns. You can order such dishes as sole, fried shrimp, seafood brochette, bouillabaisse, and fondue à la carte, or set lunches starting at ¥2,600 ($26).

Facilities: Outdoor swimming pool, modern public baths, sauna—all overlooking the bay.

Taikanso (273)

10-76 Aza Inuta, Matsushima-cho, Miyagi-gun 981-02. ☎ **022/354-2161.** Fax 022/353-3431. 239 rms (all with bath). A/C MINIBAR TV TEL. ¥16,500–¥35,000 ($165–$350) per person in Western- and combination-style rooms; ¥20,000–¥35,000 ($200–$350) per person in Japanese-style rooms. Rates include breakfast, dinner, and service charge. AE, DC, JCB, MC, V. Taxi: 5 minutes from Matsushima Kaigan Station.

Accommodating 1,500 people, Taikanso sprawls atop a plateau surrounded by pine-covered hills and offers the best view in town. Both Western- and Japanese-style rooms are available. Rates vary according to the season and whether your room faces the sea or the wooded mountains (which are also quite nice), and whether your room has tatami or beds. All the Japanese-style rooms face the sea. Combination-style rooms have both beds and a tatami area.

Dining/Entertainment: The hotel has a nightclub with floor shows nightly. Restaurants include a noodle shop, with noodle dishes starting at ¥1,000 ($10); a Japanese seafood restaurant that serves sashimi and tempura, ranging in price from about ¥1,500 to ¥2,500 ($15 to $25); and a seventh-floor Western restaurant, called Shiosai, with probably the best view in town of both Matsushima Bay and the surrounding pine-covered hills. It's worth the 30-minute walk from Matsushima's pier just for the view.

Facilities: Public baths overlooking island-studded bay, outdoor swimming pool.

MODERATE

Hotel Daimatsuso

Koen-mae, Matsushima Kaigan Eki, Matsushima, Miyagi-gun 981-02. ☎ **022/354-3601.** Fax 022/354-6154. 41 rms (4 with toilet only, 29 with bath). A/C MINIBAR TV TEL. ¥8,000 ($80) single or double; ¥9,000 ($90) per person with breakfast and dinner in a room without a view, ¥10,000–¥15,000 ($100–$150) per person with breakfast and dinner in a room with a view. AE, DC, JCB, MC, V. Directions: Walk 5 minutes from Matsushima Kaigan Eki.

Relatively inexpensive but a bit run-down, rooms here come with safe, yukata, and hot water for tea. Seaside rooms have a small balcony. Some of the mini, built-in bath units are so small as to be troublesome if you're not tiny yourself. There are a few mountainside rooms, which are cheaper but look out on another building next door and are not recommended. Dinner is taken in your room. There's a karaoke bar on the ground floor.

✪ Matsushima Kanko Hotel (274)

Matsushima Kaigan Pier, Matsushima-cho, Miyagi-gun 981-02. ☎ **022/354-2121.** 28 rms (7 with bath). MINIBAR TV TEL. ¥10,000–¥30,000 ($100–$300). Rates include breakfast, dinner, and service charge. JCB, V. Directions: Walk 1 minutes from Matsushima Kaigan Pier or 10 minutes from Matsushima Kaigan Station.

This is the best choice if you want to stay in an old-fashioned ryokan. It's popularly called Matsushima-jo, which means Matsushima Castle. Indeed, as Matsushima's oldest ryokan (built about 100 years ago), it does rather resemble a castle with its sloping tiled roof, white walls, and red railings. Inside, it's airy and delightful, with old wooden banisters polished from decades of human hands. Its walls are decorated with woodblock prints worth a small fortune by famous artists Hiroshige, Utamaro, and others, as well as photographs of stern-faced Japanese who have stayed here in the past. Keep in mind that rooms come only with fans, not air-conditioning, and tend to be drafty in winter; and communal toilets are Japanese style. Still, for a romantic, this is the place. Rooms on the third floor have views of the water. It has a convenient location directly behind the Godaido worship hall. The public bath mixes underground salt water with tap water.

INEXPENSIVE

Pairamatsushima-Okumatsushima Youth Hostel

89-48 Minami Akasaki Aza, Nobiru Narusei-cho, Monoo-gun. ☎ and fax **022/588-2220.** 21 rms (2 with bath). A/C. ¥3,500 ($35) for JYHA members, ¥4,500 ($45) for nonmembers. Breakfast ¥600 ($6) extra; dinner ¥1,000 ($10) extra. MC, V. Directions: Senseki Line from Matsushima Kaigan Station to Nobiru Station (15 minutes).

This two-story hostel, located in a pretty wooded area, was completely remodeled in 1994. There are Japanese- and Western-style rooms, which come with a sink; and two rooms have a bath. Facilities include tennis, rental bicycles, and a coin-operated laundry.

Sendai

Japanese Inn Aisaki

5-6 Kitame-machi, Aoba-ku, Sendai 980. ☎ **022/264-0700.** Fax 022/227-6067. 16 rms (2 with bath). A/C TV TEL. ¥8,400 ($84) twin without bath, ¥11,000 ($110) twin with bath; ¥15,000 ($150) triple with bath. Breakfast ¥800 ($8) extra; dinner ¥1,700 ($17) extra. AE, MC, V. Directions: Walk 12 minutes from Sendai Station.

A Note on Japanese Symbols

Many hotels, restaurants, and other establishments in Japan do not have signs giving their names in English letters. As an aid to the reader, appendix C lists the Japanese symbols for all such places described in this guide. Each set of symbols has a number, which corresponds to the number that appears inside an oval next to the establishment's boldfaced name in the text. Thus, to find the Japanese symbols for, say, **Matsushima Kanko Hotel** (274), refer to number 274 in the appendix.

A member of the Japanese Inn group, this simple inn is behind the Central Post Office. Originally opened in 1868, today the concrete building offers both Western- and Japanese-style rooms with bilingual cable TV. Coin-operated laundry facilities are available.

Sendai Chitose Youth Hostel

6-3-8 Odawara, Aoba-ku, Sendai 980. ☎ **022/222-6329.** Fax 022/265-7551. 50 beds. ¥2,500 ($25) for JYHA members, ¥3,200 ($32) for nonmembers. Breakfast ¥500 ($5) extra; dinner ¥900 ($9) extra. No credit cards. Bus: 10 minutes from Seibu Department Store to the Miya-machi Ni-chome stop (3 minutes).

This is the closest youth hostel to Sendai Station (a 20-minute walk), located in a quiet neighborhood. All rooms are tatami style, and meals are hearty. Facilities include rental bicycles and coin-operated laundry machines.

Sendai-Dochuan Youth Hostel

31 Kitayashiki, Onoda, Taihaku-ku, Sendai 982. ☎ **022/247-0511.** 40 beds. ¥2,600 ($26) for JYHA members, ¥3,200 ($32) for nonmembers. Breakfast ¥680 ($6.80) extra; dinner ¥1,000 ($10) extra. No credit cards. Subway: From Sendai Station to Youth Hostel stop (8 minutes).

This hostel seems more like a hotel, offering both beds and futon accommodations. Facilities include bicycles for rent and coin-operated laundry machines.

Sendai Onai Youth Hostel

1-9-35 Kashiwagi, Aoba-ku, Sendai 981. ☎ **022/234-3922.** 21 rms. ¥2,300 ($23) for JYHA members, ¥3,000 ($30) for nonmembers. Breakfast ¥450 ($4.50) extra; dinner ¥850 ($8.50) extra. No credit cards. Bus: 15 minutes from Platform 24 of Sendai Station (2 minutes).

Rental bicycles and vegetarian meals are available at this small youth hostel offering Japanese-style accommodations. There are facilities for preparing your own meals.

Youth Hostel Sendai Akamon

61 Kawauchi-Kawamae-cho, Aoba-ku, Sendai 980. ☎ **022/264-1405.** Fax 022/223-5129. 70 beds. ¥2,300 ($23) for JYHA members, ¥3,000 ($30) for nonmembers. Breakfast ¥400 ($4) extra; dinner ¥750 ($7.50) extra. No credit cards. Bus: 15 minutes from Sendai Station.

This youth hostel is located near the Hirose River, offering hiking opportunities. Its rooms are Japanese style.

DINING

Donjiki Chaya (275)

Entsuin-mae, Matsushima. ☎ **022/354-5855.** Noodles ¥350–¥650 ($3.50–$6.50). No credit cards. Summer, daily 9am–4:30pm, Winter, Sat–Sun and hols 9am–4pm. Directions: 5 minutes from Matsushima Kaigan Station or the pier. NOODLES/ODANGO.

This noodle shop is a convenient place for a light, inexpensive lunch. Built about 300 years ago, it is easy to spot because of its thatched roof. It offers tatami seating and sliding doors pushed wide open in the summertime. In addition to noodles, it also serves *odango*—pounded rice balls covered with sesame, red-bean, or soy sauce. *Donjiki* means "everyone gathered together for a meal."

Shiosai

Taikanso Hotel, 7th floor, 10-76 Aza Inuta. ☎ **022/354-2161.** Reservations recommended for lunch, required for dinner. Main dishes ¥1,200–¥2,000 ($12–$20); set dinners ¥6,000 ($60); set lunches ¥2,000 ($20). Daily 11:30am–3pm and 6–9pm. Directions: See Taikanso Hotel. JAPANESE/WESTERN.

A new chef has given the food a boost in this restaurant with the best view in town. I still remember very clearly sitting at a table close to the floor-to-ceiling windows overlooking Matsushima, while the sun set, the lights gradually began to glimmer below in the twilight, and the live piano music played in the background. It's very romantic (even when your dining partner is a 3-year-old!). Main dishes range from seafood to Japanese dishes. Set dinners are large and include an appetizer, fish and meat courses, bread, salad, and dessert. The set lunch is an even better bargain.

2 Hakodate

557 miles NE of Tokyo, 177 miles SW of Sapporo

The southern gateway to Hokkaido, Hakodate is about as far as you can get in a day if you're arriving in Hokkaido from Tokyo by train. Not a destination in and of itself, Hakodate makes a good one-night stopover because it has one nighttime attraction and one early-morning attraction, which means that you can easily see a little of the city before setting out for your next destination.

ESSENTIALS

The **telephone area code** for Hakodate, lying in Hokkaido Prefecture, is 0138.

GETTING THERE **By Train** From Tokyo, take the Shinkansen bullet train to Morioka (trip time: 3½ hr.); then transfer to direct train for Hakodate (trip time: about 4 hr.). There's also a night train that departs Tokyo around 7pm, arriving in Hakodate the next morning at 6:30am. Hakodate is about four hours by train from Sapporo, Hokkaido's largest town.

VISITOR INFORMATION Before leaving Tokyo or Kyoto, be sure to pick up a flyer called "Southern Hokkaido" at the Tourist Information Center. Its strolling tours include Hakodate's old Western-looking buildings, constructed back in the days when the town first opened as an international port.

The Hakodate **tourist office** (☎ 0138/23-5440) is just to the right after you exit from the Hakodate train station. Open from 9am to 7pm (to 5pm in winter), the office has information and an excellent map of Hakodate written in English.

WHAT TO SEE & DO

Hakodate is probably most famous for its night view from atop **Mt. Hakodate,** which rises 1,100 feet just 1¾ miles southwest of Hakodate Station. Few vacationing Japanese spend the night in Hakodate without taking the cable car to the top of this lava cone, which was formed by the eruption of an undersea volcano. From the peak, the lights of Hakodate shimmer and glitter like jewels spilled on black velvet. You can reach the foot of Mt. Hakodate via a five-minute streetcar ride from Hakodate Station to the stop named Jyujigai. From there you can take the cable car to the top for ¥1,200 ($12) round trip. From mid-April to mid-October, it runs every 10 minutes from 9am to 10pm, with shorter hours during the cold winter season. On the peak is an informal restaurant where you can indulge in a drink or snack while admiring the spectacular view, as well as the usual souvenir shops.

The next morning, visit the **morning market** before taking the train out of town. The market spreads out just south of the train station and is open Monday through Saturday from about 5am to noon. Walk around and look at the variety of food for sale, especially the hairy crabs for which Hokkaido is famous.

ACCOMMODATIONS

EXPENSIVE

Hakodate Kokusai Hotel

5-10 Otemachi, Hakodate 040. ☎ **0138/23-5151.** Fax 0138/23-0239. 340 rms. A/C MINIBAR TV TEL. ¥10,000–($100-$150) single; ¥20,000–¥30,000 ($200–$300) double or twin; ¥23,000–¥26,000 ($230–$260) Japanese style for two. AE, DC, JCB, MC, V. Directions: Walk 5 minutes.

Although located in a part of town full of junkyards and roads with potholes, this is the city's most expensive hotel. It has both Japanese- and Western-style rooms in two parts, an older hotel and the new annex. The most expensive twins and doubles are deluxe rooms larger than standard rooms and facing the busy harbor. The twins have semi-double-size beds.

Dining/Entertainment: On the eighth floor are Matsumae, a Japanese restaurant, and Vue Mer, a Western restaurant—both with good views of the harbor. There is also a casual restaurant serving Western and Chinese food, a coffee shop, and a bar.

Facilities: Shopping arcade, beauty salon, wedding hall.

Harborview Hotel

14-10 Wakamatsu-cho, Hakodate 040. ☎ **0138/22-0111.** Fax 0138/23-0154. 190 rms. A/C MINIBAR TV TEL. ¥17,000–¥18,000 ($170–$180) double; ¥20,000–¥22,000 ($200–$220) twin. AE, DC, JCB, MC, V.

This tall brick building, located just to the right as you exit from Hakodate Station, is one of the city's newest hotels. Despite its name, none of its 190 rooms squarely faces the harbor, though those closest to the waterfront do afford views of the water. Rooms are small but pleasant. Since room rates are based on room size, ask for a room on one of the top floors, where you have a view of the whole city.

Dining/Entertainment: On the 13th floor are both a bar (open from 6pm to 1am) and a Western restaurant. There are also Japanese and Chinese restaurants and a coffee shop.

✪ Wakamatsu Ryokan (276)

1-2-27 Yunokawa-cho, Hakodate 042. ☎ **0138/59-2171.** Fax 0138/59-3316. 36 rms. A/C MINIBAR TV TEL. ¥27,000–¥61,000 ($270–$610) per person high season; ¥25,000–¥51,000 ($250–$510) per person off-season. Rates include breakfast and dinner. AE, DC, JCB, MC, V. Taxi: 15 minutes. Bus: From Gate E to Yunokawa Onsen.

A family affair, the 110-year-old Wakamatsu has been run by four generations of Nakazawas. Mr. Nakazawa selects the freshest ingredients daily—even buying the squid from the boats in front of the ryokan—and cooks and arranges them with care. Mrs. Nakazawa, always in kimono, is the superbly gracious hostess. The epitome of a Japanese ryokan, from its exquisite cuisine to its traditional and costly interiors, Wakamatsu is a favorite of the imperial family. Located in the Yunokawa Onsen area, where the salty hot springs are reputedly as good for you to drink as to soak in, all the rooms here face the sea (my room was 10 yards from the shore). Handmade paper shoji, *hinoki* (cedar) wood baths (including the redone public bath with views of the sea and the outdoor bath), burl wood and stone flooring, and twisted wood transoms are some of the traditional and lovely details. It's definitely worth the splurge. There is also a restaurant here serving lunch from 11:30am to 2pm, with meals from ¥5,000 ($50); and dinner from 5:30 to 8pm, with meals from ¥10,000 ($100).

Inexpensive

$ Niceday Inn

9-11 Ote-Machi, Hakodate 040. ☎ **0138/22-5919.** Fax 0138/23-4178. 6 rms (none with bath). ¥3,000 ($30) per person for foreigners. Directions: Across from the Kokusai Hotel.

The Saitos, the kindly couple who run this inn, speak English. No meals are served, but restaurants are nearby. The inn offers both Japanese- and Western-style rooms and a chance to feel at home in a Japanese family. Many foreigners staying here have had a warm welcome.

DINING

Bay Restaurant and Market

11-5 Toyokawa-cho. ☎ **0138/22-1300.** Dinner buffet ¥2,500 ($25) adults, ¥1,500 ($15) children 4–12; lunch buffet ¥1,500 ($15) adults, ¥1,000 ($10) children 4–12. AE, DC, JCB, MC, V. Daily 11am–3:30pm and 5–10pm (shorter hours in winter). Directions: Walk 10 minutes south. SMORGASBORD.

This is my favorite restaurant among the several in the renovated brick warehouses along the waterfront. It's an airy locale, with exposed ceiling beams, brick walls, and simple but hip furniture. It serves an all-you-can-eat buffet of chicken and hamburgers and a big salad bar at lunch; the dinner smorgasbord is similar and adds curry, soba, rice dishes, and lots of seafood. There's also a raw-seafood bar where you can choose from the fresh seafood on display and then specify whether you want it grilled, fried, or even simply raw. There are tables outside by a canal for dining in fine weather.

Matsumae

Hakodate Kokusai Hotel, 8th floor, 5-10 Otemachi. ☎ **0138/23-5151.** Reservations not required. Set dinners ¥3,500–¥12,000 ($35–$120); set lunches ¥700–¥2,800 ($7–$28). AE, DC, JCB, MC, V. Daily 11:30am–9:30pm (last order). Directions: See Kokusai Hotel. JAPANESE SEAFOOD.

Matsumae is a Japanese seafood restaurant offering good views of the harbor and a variety of dishes, from sashimi to tempura to broiled flatfish and squid. There are also lots of Hokkaido specialties, such as spring salmon, crab, and shrimp. An English-language menu makes ordering easy. Special lunch teishoku, served until 2pm, may include tempura or fried fish in addition to side dishes.

Vue Mer

Hakodate Kokusai Hotel, 5-10 Otemachi. ☎ **0138/23-5151.** Main dishes ¥1,200–¥3,500 ($12–$35); set dinners ¥5,000–¥9,000 ($50–$90). AE, DC, JCB, MC, V. Daily 5pm–12:30am (last order). Directions: See Kokusai Hotel. FRENCH/WESTERN.

For Western food, try the Kokusai Hotel's premier restaurant, the Vue Mer, which has a great view and an extensive wine and cocktail menu. It's the perfect place to come for a late dinner—you might want to come here after an evening stroll atop Mt. Hakodate. Its à la carte menu lists seafood, steaks, and pastas.

3 Sapporo

731 miles NE of Tokyo, 177 miles NE of Hakodate

Sapporo is one of Japan's newest cities. A little more than a century ago, it was nothing more than a scattering of huts belonging to Ainu and Japanese families. All of Hokkaido, in fact, was a vast wilderness, largely unsettled, rich in timber and land. With the dawning of the Meiji Period, however, the government decided to colonize

Sapporo

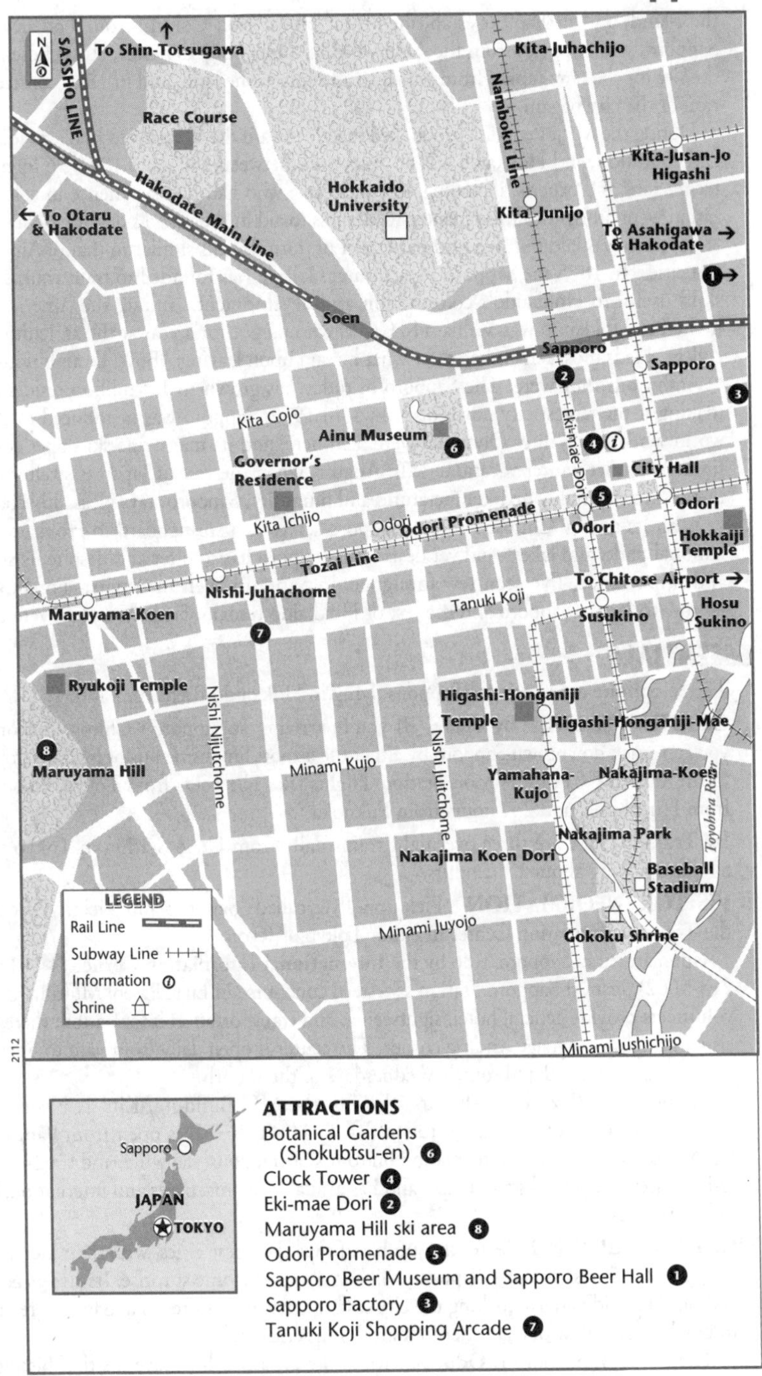
SASSHO LINE
To Shin-Totsugawa
Race Course
Hokkaido University
Hakodate Main Line
To Otaru & Hakodate
Soen
Kita-Juhachijo
Namboku Line
Kita-Jusan-Jo Higashi
Kita-Junijo
To Asahigawa & Hakodate
Sapporo
Sapporo
Kita Gojo
Ainu Museum
Eki-mae Dori
City Hall
Governor's Residence
Kita Ichijo
Odori
Odori Promenade
Odori
Odori
Hokkaiji Temple
Tozai Line
Nishi-Juhachome
Maruyama-Koen
To Chitose Airport
Tanuki Koji
Susukino
Hosu Sukino
Ryukoji Temple
Nishi Nijutchome
Higashi-Honganiji Temple
Higashi-Honganiji-Mae
Maruyama Hill
Minami Kujo
Nishi Juitchome
Yamahana-Kujo
Nakajima-Koen
Toyohira River
Nakajima Park
Nakajima Koen Dori
Baseball Stadium
Minami Juyojo
Gokoku Shrine
Minami Jushichijo
LEGEND
Rail Line
Subway Line
Information
Shrine
2112
Sapporo
JAPAN
TOKYO
ATTRACTIONS
Botanical Gardens (Shokubtsu-en) 6
Clock Tower 4
Eki-mae Dori 2
Maruyama Hill ski area 8
Odori Promenade 5
Sapporo Beer Museum and Sapporo Beer Hall 1
Sapporo Factory 3
Tanuki Koji Shopping Arcade 7

the island, and in 1869 it established the Colonization Commission. The area of Sapporo, which comes from the Ainu word meaning "big, dry river," was chosen as the site for the new capital from which to administer the land, and in 1871 construction of the city began.

During the Meiji Period, Japan looked eagerly toward the West for technology, ideas, and education, and Hokkaido was no exception. Between 1871 and 1884, 76 foreign technicians and experts, including 46 Americans, who had had experience in colonization were brought to this Japanese wilderness to aid in the island's development.

Sapporo was laid out in a grid pattern of uniform blocks similar to that of American cities. In 1875 the Sapporo Agricultural College was founded to train youths in skills useful to Hokkaido's colonization and development. Among the Americans invited to Hokkaido was William S. Clark, who taught for a year at the agricultural college. He is most remembered for what he said upon leaving: "Boys, be ambitious."

Ambitious they were. The Sapporo of today has grown to 1.7 million residents, making it the largest city north of Tokyo. In 1972, Sapporo was introduced to the world when the Winter Olympics were held here, and its many fine ski slopes continue to attract winter vacationers. In August, when the rest of Japan is sweltering under uncomfortably high temperatures and humidity, Sapporo stays pleasantly cool.

With its nearby Chitose Airport, Sapporo serves as a springboard to Hokkaido's national parks and lakes. And yet despite all Sapporo has to offer and despite its size and importance, I've seen few foreigners in Sapporo even in August. For most visitors to Japan, Sapporo and the rest of Hokkaido remain virtually undiscovered.

ESSENTIALS

The **telephone area code** for Sapporo, lying in Hokkaido Prefecture, is 011.

GETTING THERE **By Plane** If you're arriving at Sapporo's Chitose Airport, you can reach downtown Sapporo by either the airport limousine bus or by train from Japan Railways' Chitose Airport Station. Flights take 1½ hours from Tokyo, 2 hours from Hiroshima, and 2½ hours from Fukuoka.

By Train There are three overnight trains daily from Ueno Station in Tokyo to Sapporo, taking about 17½ hours.

VISITOR INFORMATION Pick up a flyer called "Sapporo and Vicinity" from the Tourist Information Center in either Tokyo or Kyoto.

Upon arrival in Sapporo, stop by the **International Information Corner** (☎ 011/213-5062), just off Sapporo Station's western concourse in Lilac Paseo. Multilingual volunteers provide general hotel, sightseeing, and transportation information; there's also an English-language reading corner. The center is open daily from 9am to 5pm, but closed the second and fourth Wednesdays of the month.

In addition, **Plaza i,** on the first floor of the MN Building, Kita 1, Nishi 3, Chuo-ku, across from the clock tower (☎ 011/211-3678), is open from 9am to 5:30pm daily. It provides information on tourist attractions, daily life, and transportation; offers guidebooks and maps; and has available fax machines and international public phones.

GETTING AROUND After the jumble of most Japanese cities, with their incomprehensible address systems, Sapporo will come as a welcome surprise. Its streets are laid out in a grid pattern, making the city easy to navigate. Addresses in Sapporo refer to blocks that follow one another in logical, numerical order.

The center of Sapporo is **Odori,** or Main Street, a tree-lined avenue that bisects the city into north and south sections. North 1st, therefore, refers to the street one block north of Odori, as well as the entire block to the north of that street. Addresses in Sapporo are generally given by block. N1 W4, for example, is the address for the Sapporo Grand Hotel and means that it's located a block north of Odori and four blocks west of West 1st Street. (West 1st Street runs along the west bank of the Soseigawa River, while East 1st Street runs along the east bank.) If you want to be more technical about it, the entire, formal address of the hotel would read N1-jo W4-chome. "Jo" runs from north to south, while "chome" goes from east to west. Street signs are in English. Most of Sapporo's attractions and hotels lie south of Sapporo Station.

Transportation in Sapporo is via **bus,** three **subway** lines, and one **streetcar** line. Sapporo is also easy to cover **on foot.** You can, for example, walk south from Sapporo Station to Odori Park in less than 10 minutes and on to Susukino, Sapporo's nightlife district, in another 7 or 8 minutes.

SPECIAL EVENTS Sapporo's annual **Snow Festival** is held from the first Wednesday in February to the following Sunday. Its mammoth snow and ice sculptures attract visitors from around the world.

WHAT TO SEE & DO

A STROLL AROUND SAPPORO One of the first things you should do in Sapporo is simply walk around. Starting from Sapporo Station, take the street leading directly south called **Eki-mae Dori** (which is also West 4). This is one of Sapporo's main thoroughfares and takes you through the heart of the city. Four blocks south of the station, turn left on N1, and after a block you'll find Sapporo's most famous landmark, **Clock Tower.** This Western-style wooden building was built in 1878 as a drill hall for the Sapporo Agricultural College (now Hokkaido University). The large clock at the top was made in Boston and was installed in 1881. In summer it attracts tourists even at night; they hang around the outside gates just to listen to it strike the hour. Inside the tower is a local-history museum with some old photographs of Sapporo and displays outlining the city's development. Although the explanations are in Japanese only, the museum is free and is open Tuesday through Sunday from 9am to 4pm (closed national holidays).

If you continue walking one block south of the Clock Tower, you'll reach **Odori,** a wide boulevard stretching almost a mile from east to west. In the middle of the boulevard is a wide median strip that has been turned into a park with trees, flower beds, and fountains. This is where much of the Sapporo Snow Festival is held in early February, when packed snow is carved to form statues, palaces, and fantasies. One snow structure may require as much as 300 six-ton truckloads of snow, brought in from the surrounding mountains. The Snow Festival also displays intricate ice carvings, done with so much attention to detail that it's almost a crime the carvings must melt. First begun in 1950 to add a bit of spice and life to the cold winter days, the Snow Festival now features about 150 large and small snow statues and draws about 2.2 million visitors a year.

Odori Park is also the scene of the **Summer Festival,** celebrated with beer gardens set up the length of the park from mid-July to mid-August and open every evening beginning at 5pm. Various Japanese beer companies set up their own booths and tables under the trees, while vendors put up stalls selling fried noodles, corn on the cob, and other goodies. Live bands serenade the beer drinkers under the stars. It all resembles the cheerful confusion of a German beer garden, which isn't surprising, considering that Munich is one of Sapporo's sister cities (Portland, Oregon, is another one).

From Odori Park you can continue your walk either above or below ground. Appreciated especially during inclement weather and during Hokkaido's long cold winters are two underground shopping arcades. Underneath Odori Park from the Odori subway station all the way to the TV tower in the east is **Aurora Town,** with its boutiques and restaurants. Even longer is **Pole Town,** 1,300 feet of shops, almost 100 in all. Pole Town extends from the Odori subway station south all the way to Susukino, Sapporo's nightlife amusement center, where you can find many restaurants and pubs (refer to "Dining," below). Before reaching Susukino, however, you may want to emerge at **Sanchome** (you'll see escalators going up), where you'll find more shopping at the Tanuki-koji covered shopping arcade.

Backtracking now toward the station, you should make your last stop the **Botanical Garden,** or *Shokubutsu-en,* the entrance to which is at N3 W8. Open Tuesday through Sunday from 9am to 4pm (10am to 3pm in winter), it has 5,000 varieties of plants arranged in marshland, herb, and alpine gardens, a greenhouse, and other sections. With lots of trees and grassy lawns, it's a good place for a summer afternoon picnic. Admission is ¥400 ($4). In winter, only the greenhouse is open.

OTHER THINGS TO SEE

Although it's not within easy walking distance of Sapporo Station, you should make the **Sapporo Beer Museum** part of your sightseeing itinerary. The museum is directly east of Sapporo Station, about 10 minutes by bus. Sapporo Beer is famous throughout Japan, and the brew has been produced here ever since the first factory opened in 1876. Tours are held daily throughout the year, with the first tour starting at 8:40am and the last at 4:40pm during peak summer months. You must make reservations beforehand (☎ 011/731-4368). Although tours are conducted in Japanese only, a few of the guides speak English, so ask whether it's possible to have an English interpreter at the time you make your reservation. Free of charge, tours last approximately an hour.

The Sapporo Beer Company, the fourth-largest beer producer in the world, recently opened the **Sapporo Factory** (☎ 011/207-5000) in a 114-year-old unused brick warehouse. The huge complex houses 147 restaurants (from Mexican to German) and shops (from record stores to designer boutiques), including nine Sapporo Beer products restaurants and shops, among them the Budoshu Wine Bar. The center features a four-floor atrium with a waterfall and pond. Most restaurants and shops are open daily from 10am to 9pm. The Cure House (open Monday to Friday from 1pm to midnight and Saturday, Sunday, and holidays from 11am to midnight) has 50 kinds of pools, Jacuzzis, and hot-spring baths, and charges ¥1,800 ($18). There is also a fitness center, and you can even stay here at the Hotel Clubby.

A shuttle bus departs every 10 minutes from in front of the Seibu department store near Sapporo Station and stops at both the Sapporo Beer Museum and the Sapporo Factory. The fare is ¥190 ($1.90) for adults, ¥100 ($1) for children.

If you have time, you should also consider visiting **Nopporo Forest Park,** or *Nopporo Shinrin Koen,* where you'll find a 330-foot tower (built in 1970 to commemorate Hokkaido's centennial) and two other attractions. The **Historical Museum of Hokkaido** houses collections detailing Hokkaido's development from prehistoric to modern times (including Ainu artifacts). Admission to *Kaitaku Kinenkan* is ¥300 ($3), and hours are 9am to 4:30pm Tuesday through Sunday; closed national holidays. The **Historical Village of Hokkaido** is an open-air museum of historical houses, including homes, farmhouses, a school, a hostel, and a shrine. *Kaitaku-no-Mura* has the same hours as the Historical Museum and charges ¥600 ($6) admission. You can reach Nopporo Park via the JR bus from Sapporo Station in 50 minutes.

SKIING The slopes around Sapporo offer skiing from early December to late April. Since you can fly directly to Sapporo from many cities in Japan, it's a popular winter destination. The **Teine Olympia Ski Grounds** are about an hour from Sapporo by bus. This was the site of the alpine, bobsled, and toboggan events in the Sapporo Winter Olympic Games of 1972. Other skiing areas within 30 minutes of Sapporo are **Mt. Moiwa, Mt. Arai,** and **Maruyama.** Most sites provide ski-rental equipment for approximately ¥3,500 ($35) per day, but keep in mind that sizes are generally smaller than in the West.

ACCOMMODATIONS

Because the 1972 Winter Olympics were held in Sapporo, the city has a large selection of fine hotels in various price categories. Sapporo's heaviest tourist season is during summer and during the annual Snow Festival held in early February. If you plan to attend the Snow Festival, book your hotel room at least six months in advance. At other times during the year you should have no problem finding a room, but it's always wise to make a reservation in advance. During winter (excluding the time of the Snow Festival), some upper- and medium-priced hotels lower their room rates, sometimes by as much as 40%. That should come as welcome news to you ski enthusiasts. Be sure to ask for a discount.

EXPENSIVE

ANA Hotel Sapporo (Zenniku Hotel) (277)

N3 W1, Chuo-ku, Sapporo 060. ☎ **011/221-4411.** Fax 011/222-7624. 412 rms. A/C MINIBAR TV TEL. ¥27,000 ($270) double; ¥24,000–¥35,000 ($240–$350) twin. AE, DC, JCB, MC, V. Directions: Walk 5 minutes southeast.

This gleaming white hotel, rising high in Sapporo's skyline, has the kind of rooms travelers can appreciate: five lamps in its larger rooms so that you don't have to read in the dark, bilingual TV sets that swivel and have pay video, an extra phone in the bathroom, and two layers of curtains for complete darkness.

Dining/Entertainment: Top of Sapporo, on the 26th floor, is a French restaurant with views of the city. Chinese and Japanese restaurants are on the 25th floor, also with views of the city. After dinner, retire to the sky lounge, Sapporo View, where there's nightly piano music.

Services: Same-day laundry service.

Century Royal Hotel

N5 W5, Chuo-ku, Sapporo 060. ☎ **011/221-2121.** Fax 011/231-2538. 305 rms. A/C MINIBAR TV TEL. ¥26,000 ($260) double; ¥26,000–¥41,000 ($260–$410) twin. AE, DC, JCB, MC, V. Directions: Next to Sapporo Station.

The Century Royal Hotel's excellent location is its main selling point. Another is its revolving restaurant on the 23rd floor. Rooms come with fax and word-processor outlets and windows with double panes to shut out noise. Foreign businesspeople stay here.

Dining/Entertainment: Rondo, a revolving restaurant on the 23rd floor, offers one of the best dining views in the city. The Century also has a Japanese restaurant serving Hokkaido specialties, two coffee shops, and a bar.

Services: Same-day laundry service.

Facilities: Gift and souvenir shops, florist.

✪ Hotel Arthur

S10 W6, Chuo-ku, Sapporo 064. ☎ **011/561-1000.** Fax 011/521-5522. 229 rms. A/C MINIBAR TV TEL. ¥23,000 ($230) double; ¥25,000–¥35,000 ($250–$350) twin; from ¥45,000 ($450) suite. AE, DC, JCB, MC, V. Subway: Namboku Line to Nakajima-koen (5 minutes).

I love this European-feeling, art deco–decor hotel, located near Nakajima-koen park in a quiet section of town. The staff is courteous and the service excellent, and I like being near the park for the joy of green space. (By the way, two interesting Meiji Period buildings, Hasso-an and Hoheikan, the old town hall now used for wedding ceremonies, are located in the park.) Westside rooms have city views with snow-capped mountain backdrops; eastside rooms have park views. Guest rooms are done in soft pastels—even the sheets are pink—and come with an extra phone in the tiled bathroom (real bathtubs, not mini-units), yukata, hot water for tea and coffee, hair dryers, and bilingual cable TV. Standard singles feature semi-double-size beds; deluxe singles have double beds. There's a staff of 250 to pamper guests.

Dining/Entertainment: The hotels boast three restaurants, a coffee lounge, and two bars.

Services: Complimentary newspaper.

Facilities: Florist, souvenir shop, beauty parlor, photo studio, convention rooms, parking.

Monterey

N4 E1, Chuo-ku, Sapporo 060. ☎ **011/232-7111.** Fax 011/242-2424. 250 rms. A/C MINIBAR TV TEL. ¥16,000–¥20,000 ($160–$200) double; ¥23,000–¥40,000 ($230–$400) twin. AE, JCB, MC, V. Directions: Walk 10 minutes east.

You can see this English-style building from the train as you arrive at Sapporo Station. Built in 1994, it has an interior that carries out the English theme. Rooms are comfortably furnished, doubles have queen-size beds, and bathrooms are large for the price. The hotel appeals to young Japanese.

Dining/Entertainment: There are three restaurants—Chinese, Japanese, and Teppanyaki—plus a coffee shop.

Facilities: Souvenir and convenience shop, wedding hall, conference rooms.

Sapporo Grand Hotel

N1 W4, Chuo-ku, Sapporo 060. ☎ **011/261-3311.** Fax 011/231-0388. 571 rms. A/C MINIBAR TV TEL. ¥24,000–¥25,000 ($240–$250) double; ¥24,000–¥29,000 ($240–$290) twin. AE, DC, JCB, MC, V. Directions: Walk 6 minutes south.

This dignified hotel, with 60 years of excellent service, is usually where VIPs stay when they come to Sapporo. Rooms in the newer annex are very chic, with contemporary furniture and bilingual TV with pay video. There are large desks with lots of working space, semi-double-size beds in the single and twin rooms, and tiled bathrooms with marble-topped counters. Rooms in the older part of the hotel are also very nice and have been updated.

Dining/Entertainment: The hotel has an exceptional French restaurant, a beer hall, several bars, two Japanese restaurants, a Chinese restaurant, a tea lounge, and a coffee shop.

Services: Same-day laundry service.

Facilities: Shopping arcade, sauna, obento shop.

Moderate

Chisan Hotel Sapporo Shinkan

N2 W2, Chuo-ku, Sapporo 060. ☎ **011/222-6611.** Fax 011/222-6617. 162 rms. A/C MINIBAR TV TEL. ¥14,000 ($140) double; ¥18,000 ($180) twin. All rates include service charge. AE, DC, JCB, MC, V. Directions: Walk 5 minutes south.

This pleasant business hotel opened in 1984—don't confuse it with the older Chisan, just a 30-second walk away (with rooms that are outdated and less cheerful, making the newer annex a much better deal). The rooms here come with dark wood furniture, and panels close over the windows for darkness. The hotel has one Japanese restaurant.

Nakamuraya Ryokan (278)

N3 W7, Chuo-ku, Sapporo 060. ☎ **011/241-2111.** Fax 011/241-2118. 30 rms (all with bath). A/C MINIBAR TV TEL. Rates for foreign guests (without meals) ¥7,000 ($70) per person. Breakfast ¥1,500 ($15) extra; dinner ¥3,000 ($30) extra. AE, JCB, MC, V.

If you want to stay in a ryokan, this is a modern and comfortable Japanese inn located next to the entrance of the Botanical Garden, a seven-minute walk southwest of Sapporo Station. All rooms are Japanese style and come with TV and clock. Although rooms have their own tub, you might want to take advantage of the hot-springs public baths here. This ryokan is a member of the Japanese Inn Group, so if you make a booking in advance and mention the Japanese Inn Group, you'll receive a much lower rate as a foreigner. There's a cafeteria serving curry, soba, and udon.

Washington Hotel 1

N4 W4, Chuo-ku, Sapporo 060. ☎ **011/251-3211.** Fax 011/241-8238. 434 rms. A/C TV TEL. ¥17,000–¥18,000 ($170–$180) double or twin. Rates include tax and service charge. AE, DC, JCB, MC, V.

The cheaper and older of the two Washington hotels, across from Sapporo Station, this one has a lobby on the second floor, up the escalator. I don't advise the cheapest singles unless you hate sunshine, since they have no windows and are extremely dark. Slightly more expensive are those that face a rather drab inside courtyard, but at least you have a window. Why not splurge and go for one of the best singles inthe house, which are larger and face toward the outside? Rooms that face the station have double-pane windows to shut out noise. Vending machines in the hallways dispense beer, snacks, and soft drinks; there are also Western and Japanese restaurants.

INEXPENSIVE

Sapporo House Youth Hostel

N6 W6, Kita-ku, Sapporo 001. ☎ **011/726-4235.** 124 beds. ¥2,700 ($27) for JYHA members and nonmembers. Breakfast ¥510 ($5.10) extra; dinner ¥900 ($9) extra. No credit cards. Directions: From Sapporo Station, turn right out of the south exit, walk three blocks, and then turn right again; the hostel is just beyond the railroad tracks, on the right.

The sign outside this white concrete building—the closest youth hostel to Sapporo Station—is in Japanese only, but look for the sign with YH on it. Sleeping accommodations are both beds and futon, but in dormitories. Even in August they often have space.

Sapporo Miyagaoka Youth Hostel

N1 14-chome Miyanomori, Chuo-ku, Sapporo 064. ☎ **011/611-9016.** 52 beds. ¥3,500 ($35) for JYHA members or nonmembers. Breakfast ¥450 ($4.50) extra. No credit cards. Open July–Sept. Subway: Subway to Maruyama Koen stop; transfer there to the bus for Sogogrando-mae stop.

This youth hostel is open only in summer, from July 1 through September. It's near a park with tennis courts, west of the city. Make a reservation three months in advance.

Sapporo Shiritsu Lions Youth Hostel

N1 18-chome Miyanomori, Chuo-ku, Sapporo 064. ☎ **011/611-4709.** 80 beds. ¥3,050 ($30.50) for JYHA members, ¥3,650 ($36.50) for nonmembers. Breakfast ¥450 ($4.50) extra; dinner ¥850 ($8.50) extra. Subway: To Maruyama Koen, transfer there to the bus.

Not far from the Miyagaoka Youth Hostel, above, this hostel is also located near Maruyama Koen Park.

DINING

Hokkaido's specialties include crab, corn on the cob, potatoes, Genghis Khan (also spelled "Jingisukan"), Chinese noodles, salmon, and Ishikari Nabe. Genghis Khan is a dish of mutton and vegetables that you grill yourself, while Ishikari Nabe is a stew of salmon and other Hokkaido vegetables, also cooked at your table. As for Western food, your best bet is to dine in one of the many fine restaurants in Sapporo's top hotels.

Sapporo is famous for its ramen (Chinese noodles), and the most popular place to eat them is on a tiny, narrow street in Susukino popularly known as **Ramen Yokocho.** Located just one block east of the Susukino subway station before you get to the Hotel Sunflower, it's an alleyway of noodle shop after noodle shop—16 in all. It doesn't matter which one you choose—just look to see where there's an empty seat. The shops are all very small affairs consisting of a counter and some chairs. Most are open from 11:30am to 4pm, and their closed days are staggered, so you're sure to find some open. Noodles generally begin at ¥700 ($7) for a steaming bowlful.

EXPENSIVE

Grand Chef

Grand Hotel, N1 W4. ☎ **011/261-3311.** Reservations not required. Set dinners ¥5,000–¥10,000 ($50–$100); set lunches ¥2,000–¥7,000 ($20–$70). AE, DC, JCB, MC, V. Daily 11:30am–2:30pm and 5–10pm. FRENCH.

This excellent French restaurant a six-minute walk south of Sapporo Station is elegantly and cheerfully decorated in pink, white, and gray, and specializes in Hokkaido food cooked Western style. The menus change annually but always include selections of seafood, such as scallops, sole, or salmon, as well as steak, lamb, chicken, and duck.

21 Club

Hotel Arthur, 25th floor, S10 W6. ☎ **011/561-1000.** Reservations recommended. Main dishes ¥2,500–¥12,000 ($25–$120); set dinners ¥8,000–¥15,000 ($80–$150); set lunches ¥1,500–¥8,000 ($15–$80). AE, DC, JCB, MC, V. Daily 11am–2pm and 5–10pm. Directions: See Hotel Arthur. TEPPANYAKI.

The 21 Club—a sleek, elegant spot that carries out the hotel's art-deco decor—is the highest point in Sapporo at which you can dine. The views of the city, Nakajima-koen park, and the Toyohira River are stunning. The "21 Club" course lunch for ¥2,100 ($21) is a great deal, consisting of grilled beef, vegetables, salad, pickles, rice, soup, dessert, and tea or coffee. Relax in the sophisticated bar-lounge before your dinner for a cocktail or after your meal for tea or coffee. This is the kind of place where you're asked whether you want milk or lemon with your tea, and then whether you want your milk hot or cold. Even if you're not a tea drinker, you'll appreciate the subtlety. This is a great place to come to for a drink—cocktails start at ¥800 ($8) and beer at ¥700 ($7). There's an extensive list of wines—the hotel has six wine advisers! This has to be the best place to watch the summer fireworks put on every year over the Toyohira River by the Hokkaido newspaper companies.

MODERATE

Kurumaya

ANA Hotel, 25th floor, N3 W1. ☎ **011/221-0608.** Reservations not required. Main dishes ¥900–¥6,000 ($9–$60); set dinners ¥4,800–¥12,000 ($48–$120); set lunches ¥1,000–¥3,500 ($10–$35). AE, DC, JCB, MC, V. Daily 11:30am–9:30pm. VARIED JAPANESE.

If you want to dine in elegant surroundings with a view of the city, try this Japanese restaurant on the 25th floor of the ANA Hotel. The Japanese menu includes a shabu-shabu and broiled Matsuzaka beef with Japanese peppers, as well as tempura, sashimi, salmon, noodles, rice porridge, and kaiseki.

Sky Restaurant Rondo

Century Royal Hotel, 23rd floor, next to Sapporo Station, N5 W5. ☎ **011/221-2121.** Reservations recommended Sun and hols. Main dishes ¥1,600–¥8,000 ($16–$80); set dinners ¥5,500–¥13,000 ($55–$130); set lunches ¥1,300–¥3,500 ($13–$35). AE, DC, JCB, MC, V. Daily 11:30am–11pm. WESTERN.

This revolving restaurant, conveniently located near Sapporo Station atop the Century Royal Hotel, makes a complete turn every hour and has an English-language menu complete with photos. Tables are all located at windows so that everyone gets the best view in the house. Even if you don't eat here, it's a good place to come on a fine clear day for a cup of coffee or an evening cocktail. The varied menu includes spaghetti, sandwiches, curry rice, grilled half chicken, pork chops, steak, crab gratin, and lobster gratin. Cocktails start at ¥800 ($8), but there's a ¥500 ($5) table charge after 9pm.

INEXPENSIVE

✪ Hyosetsu-no-Mon (279)

S5 W2. ☎ **011/521-3046.** Reservations recommended. Set meals ¥5,000–¥12,000 ($50–$120). Daily 11am–11pm. KING CRAB.

A well-known restaurant that specializes in giant king crab caught in the Japan Sea north of Hokkaido, Hyosetsu-no-Mon is in Sapporo's Susukino nightlife district. Its menu (in English with photos) is easy enough—it consists almost entirely of king crab dishes, which comes in a variety of styles. Set courses include a cooked crab, sashimi, crab soup, crab tempura, and vegetables. You can also order à la carte fried king crab claws, deep-fried king crab, tempura king crab, grilled king crab, and crabmeat chowder. This establishment is filled with Japanese tourists on holiday in Hokkaido and is great fun. You sit on the floor here to eat your meal in a dining hall reminiscent of old Kabuki theaters. There are two floor shows nightly (5:40pm and 7:40pm). The show starts off with a classical dance, followed by contemporary and folk dances, and costs only ¥815 ($8.15) in addition to dinner.

Round Midnight

Hotel Arthur, S10 W6. ☎ **011/561-1000.** Dim sum ¥150–¥500 ($1.50–$5); set lunches ¥1,200–¥2,000 ($12–$20); set dinner ¥7,000 ($70); all-you-can-eat ¥3,300 ($33). AE, DC, JCB, MC, V. Directions: See Hotel Arthur. DIM SUM/CHINESE.

A sophisticated interior, with live foreign entertainment nightly (8 to 9:30pm) and excellent service, this is the kind of restaurant I like. Set lunches of dim sum are tasty, and a dinner set includes chicken wrapped in leaves and artfully prepared by the chef at your table. But the best deal is the all-you-can-eat meal with 30 dishes to order from—it's brought to your table (no standing in those tacky buffet lines). Chili sauce shrimp, spring rolls, cashew chicken, and scallops are some favorites.

✪ Sapporo Bier Garten

N6 E9. ☎ **011/742-1531.** Reservations not required. Main dishes ¥440–¥4,000 ($4.40–$40); all-you-can-eat Genghis Khan ¥3,300 ($33). AE, DC, JCB, MC, V. Garden, June–Aug, daily 5–9pm. Beer hall, daily 11:30am–9pm. Taxi: 5 minutes from Sapporo Station. GENGHIS KHAN.

I can't imagine going to Sapporo without dropping by the Sapporo Bier Garten, which is spread out under broad-leafed acacia trees. If it's winter or early in the day, you can dine in the Sapporo Beer Hall, an old ivy-covered brick building built in

1889 as the Sapporo brewery. The interior is also brick, with a wood floor and wood beams, making for a very congenial atmosphere. I personally prefer the second floor, where you dine underneath a huge old mash tub once used in brewing beer. The specialty of the house is Genghis Khan, which you cook yourself on a hot skillet at your table. The best deal in the house is the King Viking, which for ¥3,300 ($33) gives you as much Genghis Khan and as much draft beer as you can consume in a two-hour period. Draft beer starts at ¥470 ($4.70) for a small mug.

Suntory Beer Benizakura Garden

Sumikawa 389-769, Minami-ku. ☎ **011/582-4411.** Reservations not required. Main dishes ¥500–¥1,300 ($5–$13); all-you-can-eat Genghis Khan ¥2,800 ($28). JCB, MC, V. Daily 11:30am–9pm. Subway: Nanboku Line to Makomanai Station; then a 5-minute taxi ride. Take one of the Suntory shuttle buses that run between Makomanai Station and the beer garden every 30 minutes. GENGHIS KHAN.

Not to be outdone by the Sapporo beer company, Suntory opened its own beer garden in 1985, on the south edge of town. Although the restaurant itself is bright and airy, you can also dine outside by the lotus pond in fine weather. Be sure to wander through the gardens, which extend back behind the restaurant and consist of ponds and a waterfall. Suntory beer starts at ¥470 ($4.70). For ¥2,800 ($28), you can eat all the Genghis Khan and drink as much beer as you want in a two-hour period. Mild or spicy sauces for dipping morsels of mutton and vegetables are available.

Taj Mahal

S1 W2. ☎ **011/231-1168.** Reservations not required. Curries ¥700–¥1,980 ($7–$19.80); set dinners ¥1,700–¥5,500 ($17–$55); set lunches ¥720–¥1,650 ($7.20–$16.50). AE, DC, JCB, V. Daily 11am–10pm (last order). Subway: Odori Station. INDIAN.

The main shop of this Indian restaurant is near Odori and the Mitsukoshi department store. In addition to its tandoori and kebabs are chicken, lamb, fish, seafood, and vegetable curries (no pork or beef is served). Lunch specials are served until 3pm, but not on Sundays or holidays. The selection is wide and the service friendly.

Taj Mahal also has branches at N2 W3, near the Grand Hotel, about a five-minute walk from Sapporo Station, and at the Sapporo Factory.

4 The National Parks of Hokkaido

Much of Hokkaido's wilderness has been set aside in national parks. Of these, Shikotsu-Toya, Daisetsuzan, and Akan National Parks are the best known, offering a wide range of activities from hiking to skiing to bathing at hot-spring resorts. There are many spas, called *onsen* in Japanese.

SHIKOTSU-TOYA NATIONAL PARK

If you have only a couple of days to spare to visit a national park in Hokkaido, go to Shikotsu-Toya National Park, the closest to Sapporo and therefore the easiest for the short-term visitor. It's also the first national park you'll reach if you've entered Hokkaido via train to Hakodate. This 381-square-mile national park encompasses lakes, volcanoes, and the famous hot-spring resorts of Toyako Spa and Noboribetsu Spa. In the village of Shiraoi, a museum and village commemorate the native Ainu and their culture.

Be sure to pick up a copy of "Southern Hokkaido," put out by the Tourist Information Center in either Tokyo or Kyoto. It lists places of interest throughout the national park. As for traveling to and within the park, there's a bus from Sapporo that goes directly to Toyako Spa on Lake Toya. From Toyako Spa (or Toyako

Onsen—*onsen* means "spa") you can then proceed by bus to Noboribetsu and then back to Sapporo; from Noboribetsu you can also take a train to Shiraoi and back to Sapporo. There are also Japan Railways trains that run directly from Hakodate to Toya Station (from Toya Station it's a 15-minute bus ride to Lake Toya), and on to Noboribetsu, Shiraoi, and Sapporo.

TOYAKO ONSEN

Hugging the shores of Lake Toya, Toyako Spa is a small resort town with a sprinkling of ryokan, souvenir shops, and not much more. However, you don't come here for Toyako Spa itself, but for **Lake Toya,** the shining blue jewel of Shikotsu-Toya National Park. Surrounded on all sides by hills, Lake Toya is almost perfectly round. It's a typical caldera lake—that is, a lake that has formed within the collapsed crater of an extinct volcano. Approximately 590 feet deep, Lake Toya is invitingly clear and cool and never freezes over even in the dead of winter. In the middle of the lake are four thickly wooded islets, casting mirror images of themselves in the water below.

Most people stay in Toyako Onsen only one night. It's enough time to relax and do the few things the place has to offer. If you happen to stay two nights, you'll find your ryokan deserted after checkout time until the next crowd arrives at check-in time.

Essentials

The **telephone area code** for Toyako Onsen is 0142.

GETTING THERE If you're arriving by train from Sapporo (about two hours) or from Hakodate (a little over two hours), you'll arrive at Toya Station, about 4¹/₂ miles from Toyako Onsen. Since there is no train station in Toyako Onsen, you should transfer at Toya Station to a bus bound for the Toyako Onsen bus terminal, or you can take a taxi from Toya Station to Toyako Onsen for about ¥2,000 ($20).

You can also reach Toyako Onsen directly by either Donan or Jotetsu Bus Company from Sapporo. The trip takes 2¹/₂ hours and costs ¥2,550 ($25.50) one way.

VISITOR INFORMATION The Toyako Onsen **tourist association** (☎ 0142/75-2446) is down the hill toward the lake, about a minute's walk away from the bus terminal. It's open daily from 9am to 5pm and offers an English-language pamphlet with a map of Lake Toya.

GETTING AROUND The spa is so small that you shouldn't have any difficulty finding your way around. **On foot** is the best way to get around town, which stretches along one main road following the curve of the lake. **Buses** for Showa-Shinzan and Takinoue Camp depart from the bus terminal, so inquire there about the schedule. Buses aren't very frequent.

What to See & Do

The most popular thing to do is take a **boat ride** across the clear lake to a couple of the islands in the middle. (Recently added to the fleet is a boat that looks like a castle. Sure to delight children, it leaves on the hour and is the same price as other boats.) Charging ¥1,100 ($11), the boat pulls into two small docks, the first at an island where there are some deer and winding footpaths, the second at another island where there's a natural history museum (which, unfortunately, has explanations in Japanese only and is therefore of little interest to foreign visitors). If you decide to disembark at either of these islands, you can catch the next boat in about a half hour. If you stay on the boat for the entire trip, it takes about an hour. Along the shore of Toyako Spa are also several docks where you can rent rowboats and paddleboats.

If it's August and hot, the temptation to simply jump into the lake and cool off will be almost too hard to resist. You may be astonished to learn, however, that there are no swimming facilities in Toyako Onsen itself. In fact, hardly any lakes in Hokkaido allow swimming because they are considered too cold and dangerous for humans. Desperate for a swim, I once took a bus ride 20 minutes around the lake to **Takinoue Camp** (☎ 0142/66-2121), one of the few places where swimming is allowed. There's a small sandy beach here and a few parents playing with their children, making it a good place to jump in and play, too. Incidentally, you can also camp here for ¥300 ($3) per person (¥200/$2 for children). There are even tents for rent at ¥850 ($8.50) that sleep five people, but you must have your own sleeping bag and camping supplies.

The huge **public baths** of the Sun Palace Hotel, located on the edge of Toyako Spa (see "Accommodations," below), are open to the general public every day from 10am to 4pm (and only to hotel guests after 4pm). They feature a huge indoor pool filled with hot-spring water and complete with artificial waves and even water slides. You wear your swimming suit here, but there are also hot-spring bathing facilities (separate for men and women) that include saunas. Incidentally, the swimming pool also has an outdoor area where you can sun yourself. If you've never been to one of Japan's huge public baths, it's worth the ¥2,000 ($20) entry fee, which becomes ¥2,500 ($25) on Sundays and public holidays and during summer vacation. Hotel guests use the facilities for free.

There are two very active volcanoes on the shores of Lake Toya not far from Toyako Spa. **Mt. Usu,** which towers over the tiny spa, erupted in August 1977, blanketing 80% of Hokkaido in volcanic ash and dumping enough ash on Toyako Onsen itself that the people literally had to dig their way out of it. Chronicling Mt. Usu's eruption is the **Abuta Volcano Science Museum** (*Abuta Kazan Kagaku-kan*) (☎ 0142/75-4400), conveniently located right above the Toyako Onsen bus terminal. Open daily from 9am to 5pm and charging ¥600 ($6) for admission (half price for children under 12), it depicts the 1977 eruption with photographs and lava-rock displays. Although explanations are in Japanese only, a pamphlet is available in English setting forth the important facts. The most interesting aspect of the museum is the "experience room," which seats 350 people around a large panoramic model of Lake Toya and Mt. Usu. During the experience, a rumbling begins directly below you and seats shake and shimmy, approximating what it must feel like to experience a volcano. Following is a film (again, in Japanese only) showing the Usu eruption, the evacuation of Toyako Onsen, and the ashes covering the town. The whole experience emphasizes Japan's volcanic origins and how its people have always lived in the shadows of volcanoes and earthquakes.

The other famous volcano in the vicinity is **Showa-Shinzan,** which first erupted in 1945. Before then it was nothing more than a flat farm field. Over two years, however, the ground began to rise, volcanic eruptions shook the area, and lava rose, resulting in the fledgling volcano. Showa-Shinzan still spouts billowing clouds of smoke. If you're interested in getting a close-up view, you can reach Showa-Shinzan by buses that depart from the Toyako Onsen bus terminal. A small museum at the foot of the volcano documents its birth. You can also catch a glimpse of the volcano from afar if you take the boat ride out onto Lake Toya.

One other thing worth mentioning is the nightly **fireworks** displays put on by the town of Toyako Onsen from the end of April (just before Golden Week) through October. The show begins at about 8:40pm, when fireworks are set off from boats in the lake.

Accommodations

The best rooms in town are those that face the lake, with its picturesque islands. Of course, these rooms are also the most expensive. This being a resort town for the Japanese, accommodations are largely in Japanese-style inns, where you're expected to take your dinner and breakfast. The busiest tourist season is from May to October; rates are generally higher during these months.

Hotel New Toyako (280)

Aza Toyako-Onsen-machi, Abutacho, Abuta-gun 049-57. ☎ **0142/75-2818.** Fax 0142/75-4067. 16 rms (2 with bath). TV TEL. ¥7,000–¥10,000 ($70–$100) per person, including breakfast, dinner, and service charge; ¥5,000–¥6,000 ($50–$60) per person, room only. No credit cards. Directions: From the bus terminal, walk 1 block downhill toward the lake; it's near the tourist office.

This combination business hotel–minshuku is run-down and offers basic rooms, including a dozen Japanese-style rooms, two twins, and one double. Only the twin rooms have a private bath (but the plumbing in mine didn't work).

Manseikaku (281)

Aza Toyako-Onsen-machi, Abutacho, Abuta-gun 049-57. ☎ **0142/75-2171.** Fax 0142/75-2271. 246 rms. A/C MINIBAR TV TEL. Summer, ¥16,000–¥32,000 ($160–$320) per person. Off-season, ¥13,000–¥30,000 ($130–$300) per person. Rates include breakfast, dinner, and service charge. AE, DC, JCB, MC, V. Directions: Take a local bus to the Chuo Dori bus stop in front of the hotel; or a 15-minute walk from the bus terminal.

Another first-class hotel in town, this large, handsome brown-brick building is at the water's edge. Rooms are modern and comfortable, and some even come with their own balcony. Most of the rooms are Japanese-style tatami. There are also Western-style rooms with beds, but most of these rooms face inland. Combination rooms, on the other hand, with both beds and a tatami area, are lakeside. Breakfast is served buffet style, and for dinner you have a choice of a Japanese meal served in your room or a Western-style buffet in the hotel's European restaurant.

Dining/Entertainment: There's a European-style restaurant, two coffee shops, a disco, and a karaoke bar (where guests sing along to their favorite tunes).

Facilities: Tennis court, indoor pool, large indoor and outdoor public baths. A women's bath on the eighth floor features a small outdoor hot-spring bath (called *rotenburo* in Japanese), which, if you ask me, would be a perfect spot from which to watch the fireworks. Right beside the hotel is a boat dock where you can rent paddleboats and take charter motorboats around the lake.

Park Hotel

Aza Toyako-Onsen-machi, Abutacho, Abuta-gun 049-57. ☎ **0142/75-2445.** Fax 0142/75-3918. 280 rms (all with bath). MINIBAR TV TEL. Summer, ¥14,000–¥22,000 ($140–$220) per person. Off-season, ¥11,000–¥18,000 ($110–$180) per person. All rates ¥4,000 ($40) higher on Sat. Rates include breakfast, dinner, and service charge. AE, DC, JCB, V. Directions: From the bus terminal, walk 1 block toward the lake and then turn right.

This waterfront hotel boasts an outdoor rooftop pool, Jacuzzi, public baths with water views and *hinoki* (cedar) wood, sauna, sundecks, a game room, bowling lanes, and a bar with laser shows. Half the rooms facing the water have a veranda of sorts; the other rooms have windows only. Since the hotel's Western-style rooms—all twins—face only inland, the Japanese rooms here are better by far.

Dining/Entertainment: The Park has one Japanese restaurant and another serving Asian and Western food, a tea lounge, a coffee shop, and a disco.

Facilities: Shopping arcade.

Impressions

Japan is a great people. Her masons ply with stone, her carpenters with wood, her smiths with iron, and her artists with life, death, and all the eye can take in.

—Rudyard Kipling, *From Sea to Sea,* 1889

Showa-Shinzan Youth Hostel (282)

103 Sobetsu-onsen, Sobetsu cho, 052-01. ☎ **0142/75-2283.** 67 beds. ¥3,500 ($35) for JYHA members, ¥4,300 ($43) for nonmembers. Breakfast ¥550 ($5.50) extra; dinner ¥900 ($9) extra. No credit cards. Bus: From the Toyako Onsen bus terminal to the Showa-Shinzan Toza-an Guchi stop, an 8-minute ride.

Located at the foot of the Showa-Shinzan volcano, this is the closest youth hostel to Toyako Onsen. In addition to rental bicycles and laundry facilities, it also has hot-spring baths, for which there's an obligatory ¥100 ($1) charge. All rooms, freshly remodeled in 1993, are tatami style.

Sun Palace Hotel

Aza Toyako-Onsen-machi, Abutacho, Abuta-gun 049-57. ☎ **0142/75-4126.** Fax 0142/75-2875. 426 rms. A/C MINIBAR TV TEL. Summer, ¥17,000–¥26,000 ($170–$260) per person. Off-season, ¥10,000–¥20,000 ($100–$200) per person. Rates include breakfast, dinner, and service charge. AE, DC, JCB, MC, V. Directions: Take a right out of bus terminal and walk 20 minutes; or take a local bus to the Sun Palace bus stop in front of the hotel.

This is the most elaborate and conspicuous hotel in Toyako Onsen, isolated on the edge of town on the shores of the lake. Make sure to take one of the buses from Toya Station that go all the way to the hotel, or take a taxi from the bus terminal. Its lobby features a spectacular light fixture made of gold-colored twisted metal sheets that rise to the ceiling. With the largest public bath in town, including water slides and other attractions for children, this is a good family hotel that appeals widely to both adults and kids. Rooms, all facing the lake, come in Japanese and Western style. The main thing you're paying for at this hotel is its public facilities.

Dining/Entertainment: Another reason to choose this hotel is its elaborate buffets serving Chinese, Japanese, and Western food. Both breakfast and dinner are served in a fancy, chandeliered dining room with floor-to-ceiling windows affording great views. There's also a coffee shop, an outdoor beer garden (in summer), and a bar.

Facilities: Huge public baths (both inside and out), large indoor pool.

✪ Takatsu Ryokan (283)

Aza Toyako-Onsen-machi, Abutacho, Abuta-gun 049-57. ☎ **0142/75-3088.** 10 rms (2 with bath). MINIBAR TV TEL. ¥8,000–¥10,000 ($80–$100) per person. Rates include breakfast, dinner, and service charge. No credit cards. Directions: Turn left out of the bus terminal and walk across the bridge.

If you want to stay in Toyako Onsen but can't afford a hotel on the lake's edge, you might try this very clean ryokan, which is located a block inland. No English is spoken, but the proprietress says she gets by, and the staff is very kind. All rooms are Japanese style except for one twin.

Toyako Onsen Hotel

Aza Toyako-Onsen-machi, Abutacho, Abuta-gun 049-57. ☎ **0142/75-2222.** 76 rms (36 with bath). MINIBAR TV TEL. Summer, ¥12,000–¥25,000 ($120–$250) per person. Off-season, ¥8,000–¥18,000 ($80–$180) per person. Rates include breakfast, dinner, and service charge. AE, JCB, V. Directions: From the bus terminal, walk 1 block toward the lake and then turn right, about a 20-minute walk.

At this somewhat older ryokan, the only facilities for guests are rather nice public baths, and rooms that were recently renovated with new wallpaper and tatami mats. The big plus here is that all rooms facing the lake have a balcony, perfect for watching the fireworks. All rooms have a toilet, and a few have a tub as well. Although 15 Western-style rooms are available, none of them faces the lake; a few combination rooms (with both beds and a tatami area), however, do have lake views.

Dining

✪ Boyotei

36-12 Toyako Onsen-machi. ☎ **0142/75-2311.** Reservations not required. Set lunches ¥1,400–¥7,000 ($14–$70). No credit cards. Spring–autumn, daily 10am–10pm. Winter, daily 10am–9pm. Directions: From the bus terminal, walk 1 block downhill toward the lake and turn right. WESTERN.

Not far from the tourist office, this is a rather interesting-looking cafe set back from the town's main road behind an overgrown garden. A wooden sign hanging outside over the sidewalk says KAFE RESTAURANT. Opened more than 45 years ago, before the large hotels across the street were built to block the view, it now seems rather hidden and forgotten. The interior looks as if it hasn't changed much over the decades and is filled with knickknacks. A good, cozy place for a morning coffee, lunch, or an evening drink, it even has some tables and chairs outside. The menu includes pork chops, hamburger steak, fried salmon, macaroni chicken gratin, macaroni crabmeat gratin, beef curry, spaghetti, and sandwiches. There are also set lunches and dinners. Various kinds of coffees start at ¥400 ($4), and beer starts at ¥600 ($6). The restaurant even has Guinness.

Ragtime

144 Aza. ☎ **0142/75-4224.** Main dishes ¥500–¥700 ($5–$7). No credit cards. Daily 10am–10pm. Directions: From the bus terminal, walk 1 block downhill and cross the river. WESTERN.

Although the food in this tiny coffeehouse makes no claims to haute cuisine, the price is right for spaghetti, curry, and pilaf, and the owners couldn't be nicer. The views make it a good place to have lunch or even take a drink and watch the fireworks in summer. As you might have guessed from the name, recorded jazz music sets the atmosphere.

Sendoan

Wakasaimo, 2nd floor. ☎ **0142/75-2782.** Reservations not required. Set meals ¥1,200–¥3,000 ($12–$30). No credit cards. May–Oct, daily 11am–7pm (last order). Winter, daily 11am–6pm (last order). Directions: From the bus terminal, walk 1 block downhill toward the lake, turn left, and cross the bridge; the restaurant is immediately to your right. JAPANESE.

This pleasant and attractive modern restaurant is on the water's edge, just west of the main boat dock (to the left if you're facing the lake). You sit on tatami beside huge windows overlooking the lake. The menu is in Japanese only, but there are photos, or you can make your selection from the plastic-food display case. This is primarily a tempura and soba restaurant, with a variety of other selections as well. Set meals include shrimp tempura, salmon teishoku, obento lunch box, and tempura soba. By the way, Wakasaimo is a souvenir shop named for the specialty cake of Toyako Onsen, which is made from white beans.

NOBORIBETSU SPA

Famous for the variety of its hot-water springs, Noboribetsu Spa (called **Noboribetsu Onsen** in Japanese) is one of Japan's best-known spa resorts. It boasts 11 different types of hot water and gushes 10,000 tons a day. With temperatures ranging between 113°F and 197°F, the waters contain all kinds of minerals, including sulfur, salt, iron, and gypsum, and are thought to help relieve such disorders as high blood pressure, rheumatism, arthritis, eczema, and even constipation. Noboribetsu's name comes from the Ainu word meaning "white muddy river."

Essentials

The **telephone area code** for Noboribetsu Onsen is 0143.

GETTING THERE Noboribetsu Onsen is about a 15-minute bus ride from the town of Noboribetsu and its Noboribetsu Station, which is where you'll arrive if you come by train. Noboribetsu Station lies on the main train line that runs between Hakodate and Sapporo, about 2½ hours from Hakodate, 45 minutes from Toya Station, and 1 hour and 10 minutes from Sapporo. There are also direct buses from Sapporo and Toyako Onsen to Noboribetsu Onsen.

VISITOR INFORMATION The **tourist office** (☎ 0143/84-3311) is on Noboribetsu Onsen's main street just a minute north of the bus depot. It's open daily from 9am to 6pm. There's a pamphlet and map in English, but you may not encounter anyone here who speaks English. Luckily, the town is so small that you shouldn't have any problem getting around. The busiest tourist season is May to October and during New Year's, which is when hotel rates are at their highest.

What to See & Do

Although all the spa hotels and ryokan have their own taps into the spring water, the most famous hotel bath in town is at the **Daiichi Takimotokan,** a monstrous bathing hall with more than a dozen pools containing different mineral contents at various temperatures. It's an elaborate affair with hot-spring baths both indoors and out, a Jacuzzi, saunas, steam rooms, and waterfall massage (this is one of my favorites—you simply sit under the shooting water and let it pummel your neck and shoulders).

The baths are separate for men and women, but there's an indoor pool with mixed bathing, so be sure to bring your swimsuit. My only complaint is that the workers cleaning the walls and floors of the bathhouses are men, a couple of whom were none too discreet in their stares. The Japanese women paid them no attention, so I guess others are supposed to do the same. At any rate, visiting the baths here is the best favor you can do yourself while in Noboribetsu. If you're staying at the Daiichi Takimotokan hotel, you can use the baths free of charge at any time. Otherwise, the baths are open to the public daily from 9am to 3pm (that is, you must enter by 3pm). The charge is ¥2,000 ($20).

To get an idea of what all this hot water looks like, visit **Hell Valley,** or *Jigokudani,* at the north edge of town past the Daiichi Takimotokan hotel. A volcanic crater 1,485 feet in diameter, the huge depression is full of bubbling and boiling water and rock formations of orange and brown. If you walk along the concrete path that winds along the left side of the crater (called Hell Valley Promenade) and follow it as it swings farther to the left, you'll soon see a picnic area with a narrow footpath that leads off to the right through lush woods. If you follow it for about 10 minutes, you'll come to a lookout point over a large pond of hot bubbling water called Ohyunuma (the lookout is across the highway). If you want to take a different route back, follow the path that leads to the right just as you recross the highway. This pathway, called Funamiya Promenade, traces the backbone of several ridges all the way back into town, passing a number of small stone deities on the way.

Another attraction is **Lake Kuttara.** It's an unspoiled caldera lake a few miles from Noboribetsu Onsen and ranks as the second clearest in Japan (the clearest is considered to be Masshu in Akan National Park). Because the water is very cold, swimming is forbidden, but you can rent rowboats. The water is beautiful, and wooded hills rise on all sides.

There's also a small restaurant at Lake Kuttara where you can eat ramen, tempura, soba, and trout. Unfortunately, there are only three buses a day that come here from Noboribetsu Onsen, leaving the spa at 9:30am, 11am, and 3:50pm. Each bus makes a 20-minute stop at the lake before returning to Noboribetsu Onsen. If this isn't enough time for you, you might want to take the early bus to the lake and return on a later one. Be sure to check on the latest schedule. Buses run from about June 1 to October 22 only.

Incidentally, you'll also see advertisements for a bear park and Ainu village attraction. The best thing about this place is the trip via ropeway—the bear park occupies one of the tallest hills around. The 100 or so bears, however, are crowded together in a concrete pen, and the Ainu "village" is mainly for souvenirs. I personally think you're better off spending your money elsewhere.

If you find yourself at Noboribetsu Station with some time on your hands, you might want to check out the **Noboribetsu Marine Park** (☎ 0143/83-3800), about 10 minutes from the station on foot. While it's in the European castlelike building, Castle Nixe, visible from the station, the attraction curiously mixes Danish and Roman themes. Opened in 1990, it is one of the largest aquariums in northern Japan. Admission is ¥2,200 ($22), and it's open daily from 9am to 8pm (until 5pm in winter).

Basically a nice place for a walk is **Tenkaen Chinese Park,** whose centerpiece is a five-story pagoda. Take an elevator to the top to view the ocean or mountains. Have tea in the Chinese Tea House or eat in one of the Chinese restaurants. There are interesting Chinese performances of acrobatics and music, for example, and a nice Chinese products shop (but the prices are Japanese). Open daily from 9am to 5pm (from 8:30am to 9pm in July and August), the park charges ¥1,800 ($18) admission for adults (¥1,000/$10 for children). There's a free shuttle bus from Noboribetsu Station.

ESPECIALLY FOR CHILDREN A visit to **Noboribetsu-Date Historic Village,** or *Jidai-mura,* is like taking a stroll through history. There are acres of shops, restaurants, theaters, and amusements, all with early Edo-era themes. The 350-member staff and some 80 performers are dressed in kimono and headdresses of the period. See Ninja warriors fighting in the streets busy with local merchants hawking their wares in this re-creation of how it must have been. Watch *oiran* courtesans dance in a theater of the period. It's fun for the whole family, and if you haven't seen another historic village elsewhere in Japan, it's definitely worth a visit. General admission is ¥2,000 ($20); admission plus three attractions is ¥3,000 ($30); and admission plus all attractions is ¥3,500 ($35); Open daily from 9am to 5pm (until 4pm in winter), Jidai-mura can be reached by bus from Noboribetsu Station; take the bus for the onsen and get off at Jidai-mura.

Accommodations

As with many Japanese resorts, hotel and ryokan rates depend on the season, and in some cases even the day of the week. Weekend rates are generally higher, especially May to October and during New Year's.

Akashiya Youth Hostel (284)

Noboribetsu Onsen 059-05. ☎ **0143/84-2616.** 55 beds. ¥3,000 ($30) for JYHA members, ¥3,800 ($38) for nonmembers. Breakfast ¥600 ($6) extra; dinner ¥1,000 ($10) extra. No credit cards.

Just a couple of minutes' walk from the bus terminal, this youth hostel accommodates guests in both beds and tatami. It features a hot-spring bath and laundry facilities.

Daiichi Takimotokan

Noboribetsu Onsen 059-05. ☎ **0143/84-2111.** Fax 0143/84-2202. 401 rms (340 with bath). MINIBAR TV TEL. ¥16,000–¥30,000 ($160–$300) per person; ¥2,000 ($20) less off-season; ¥3,000 ($30) extra Sat. Rates include breakfast, dinner, and service charge. AE, DC, JCB, MC, V. Directions: Walk from the bus terminal, beside Hell Valley, for about 5 minutes.

Because of its large bathing hall with the various pools, this is Noboribetsu Onsen's best-known ryokan. It first opened 135 years ago and today is a large, modern hotel. Guests are entitled to use the pools free anytime, night or day. Only eight of the ryokan's rooms are Western style; the rest are Japanese-style tatami. As with most first-class ryokan in Hokkaido's resort areas, rooms come with fan (only 72 rooms have air-conditioning). The newer wing has a shopping arcade, coffee shop, disco, pub, and snack, karaoke, and piano bar.

Grand Hotel

Noboribetsu Onsen 059-05. ☎ **0143/84-2101.** Fax 0143/84-2543. 261 rms (all with bath). A/C MINIBAR TV TEL. ¥13,500–¥16,000 ($135–$160) per person; ¥2,000 ($20) extra Sat. Rates include breakfast and dinner. AE, DC, JCB, MC, V.

Rivaling Daiichi Takimotokan in terms of size, facilities, and comfort is the Grand Hotel, spread along the slope of a hill just above the bus terminal. You can stay here without taking meals if there are two or more in your party; however, the price is practically the same. This hotel sports a nice public bath; though not as large as Takimotokan's, it's more elegant. The men's section has baths both indoors and outdoors, complete with waterfall and Roman goddess statues. As for the women's section, there's an outdoor pool but no goddesses. There are saunas for both sexes. The hotel was remodeled in 1993; the rooms, lobby, and baths have been slicked up, and there are now four bars, a shopping arcade, and a restaurant.

Kikusui (285)

Noboribetsu Onsen 059-05. ☎ **0143/84-2437.** Fax 0143/84-3302. 9 rms (none with bath). TV. ¥11,000 ($110) double; ¥13,500 ($135) triple. With breakfast and dinner ¥8,200 ($82) per person double; ¥7,200 ($72) per person triple. No credit cards. Bus: From Noboribetsu Station to the Chugaku-mae stop; then a 5-minute walk.

Although it's a bit far from Noboribetsu Onsen, you might consider staying here if you're on a budget. The simple minshuku is run by a family that also manages the adjoining temple, and the husband of the owner is a Buddhist monk. Since this minshuku doesn't have a hot-spring bath (they do have regular public baths, however), you'll have to hike into town (about 30 minutes) to Takimotokan if you want the real thing. (Complimentary tickets to the hot springs are offered.) Note that these two minshuku are located on the route of the bus that travels between Noboribetsu Station and Noboribetsu Onsen, so if you're coming from the train, there's no need to go all the way to the spa. Buses are infrequent, so check the schedule. Personally, I like this area's isolation—and the rooms here are spotless.

✪ Kiyomizu-Ya Oyado

173 Noboribetsu Onsen 059-05. ☎ **0143/84-2145.** Fax 0143/84-2146. 44 rms (all with bath). TV TEL. ¥8,000 ($80) per person, ¥15,000–¥30,000 ($150–$300) per person with breakfast and dinner. AE, DC, JCB, MC, V.

This reasonably priced and very friendly ryokan, located above Noboribetsu Onsen's main street, a 10-minute walk from the bus terminal, is a member of the Japanese Inn Group. The owner, Mr. Iwai, speaks English very well and can answer your questions regarding Noboribetsu and the surrounding area. Rooms are Western or Japanese in style, or a combination of the two. Room rates depend on the type of room and your food order (in winter, your room will be upgraded and you'll pay less).

The menu changes four times a year; it offers delicious food by an excellent chef—more food than I could eat. There are two public baths, one of *hinoki* (cedar) wood, plus an outdoor bath, a lobby coffee shop, a bar, and a karaoke spot (where you can sing to your favorite tunes). The staff will pick you up at the station if you let the hotel know of your arrival time in advance.

Ryokan Hanaya

Noboribetsu Onsen 059-05. ☎ **0143/84-2521.** Fax 0143/84-2240. 21 rms (5 with bath). MINIBAR TV TEL. ¥10,000–¥12,000 ($100–$120) twin; ¥15,000–¥18,000 ($150–$180) triple. Japanese or Western breakfast ¥1,000 ($10) extra; dinner ¥2,000 ($20) extra. AE. Bus: From Noboribetsu Station to the Hanaya-mae stop.

This simple two-story ryokan is at the edge of Noboribetsu Onsen, about a five-minute walk from the bus terminal (if you're arriving by bus, get off before reaching the bus terminal—ask the bus driver to let you know where). A member of the Japanese Inn Group, it has hot-spring public baths and an outdoor bath, and serves meals in your room. The owner speaks English.

Takimoto Inn

76 Noboribetsu Onsen 059-05. ☎ **0143/84-2205.** Fax 0143/84-2645. 47 rms (all with bath). TV TEL. ¥12,000 ($120) per person; ¥1,000 ($10) extra high season and Sat. Rates include breakfast, dinner, and service charge. AE, DC, JCB, V.

Across the street from Daiichi Takimotokan, this small, comfortable, and moderately priced Western-style hotel's main advantage is that you can use Daiichi Takimotokan's famous baths for free. All the rooms are twins or triples and are fairly basic, with a small bathroom and TV with pay video.

Youth Hostel Ryokan Kanefuku (286)

Noboribetsu Onsen 059-05. ☎ **0143/84-2565.** Fax 0143/84-2073. 30 beds. ¥2,500 ($25) for JYHA members, ¥3,500 ($35) nonmembers. Breakfast ¥600 ($6) extra; dinner ¥850 ($8.50) extra. No credit cards.

Located a few minutes farther out of town than the other hostels listed here, this youth hostel is slightly cheaper. Unfortunately, there's no hot-spring bath here—only baths with water of the regular kind. There are laundry facilities.

Dining

Poplar Restaurant

Takimoto Inn. ☎ **0143/84-2205.** Reservations not required. Main dishes ¥750–¥2,500 ($7.50–$25). AE, DC, JCB, V. Daily 11am–2pm. WESTERN.

If you find yourself looking for a place to stop for lunch, or a draft beer, or coffee, try this restaurant, which serves inexpensive Western dishes. The Japanese menu with pictures lists such choices as beefsteak, pork chops, hamburger steak, fried shrimp, fried scallops, sandwiches, curry rice, shrimp gratin, and spaghetti. The restaurant is a five-minute walk from the bus terminal, near Hell Valley.

Tokumitsu

29 Chuo-dori. ☎ **0143/84-2079.** Reservations not required. Main dishes ¥800–¥1,800 ($8–$18). Daily 11am–2pm and 4:30pm–1am. SUSHI/TEMPURA/UDON.

On the main street, across from the tourist association office—a two-minute walk from the bus terminal—this is a friendly, local hangout where you'll be served good, reasonably priced dishes while sitting at the counter or on tatami. You'll recognize it by the maroon *noren* (curtain) outside and the plastic-food display, which will help you to order. Chiraishi sushi (raw fish served over a bed of rice) or unagi (eel) are ¥1,500 ($15), and tempura is only ¥1,300 ($13). Tokumitsu stays open late as a nightcap spot for locals and tourists alike.

DAISETSUZAN NATIONAL PARK

Although I find it difficult to rank nature in terms of beauty, there are some who maintain that Daisetsuzan National Park is the most spectacular of Hokkaido's parks. With its tall mountains covered with fir and birch trees and sprinkled with wildflowers, its river gorge laced with waterfalls and hiking trails throughout, Daisetsuzan National Park is the perfect place to come if you've been itching to get some exercise in relatively unspoiled countryside. Lying in the center of Hokkaido, this national park, Japan's largest, contains three volcanic mountain groups, including the highest mountain in Hokkaido, Mt. Asahi, at 7,513 feet. Hiking in summer and skiing in winter are the primary pursuits of the region.

SOUNKYO ONSEN

Nestled at the very edge of Sounkyo Gorge, Daisetsuzan's most famous natural attraction, Sounkyo Onsen is the perfect base for exploring the national park. Although the town itself is rather unattractive, with its cluster of souvenir shops and unimaginative buildings, its soothing hot springs and magnificent scenic backdrop make coming here worthwhile. In addition, Sounkyo Onsen serves as the starting point for bicycle trips along Sounkyo Gorge and for the cable-car trip to the top of a neighboring peak. Sounkyo is one of my favorite places in all of Hokkaido.

Essentials

The **telephone area code** for Sounkyo Onsen is 01658.

GETTING THERE The only way to reach Sounkyo Onsen by public transportation is by bus. If you're coming from Sapporo, take the train as far as Kamikawa (2½ hours), then transfer to a bus for a 30-minute ride that will take you directly to Sounkyo. There are also buses connecting Sounkyo Onsen with Asahigawa (2 hours) and Rubeshibe (1½ hours).

VISITOR INFORMATION The **tourist information office** (☎ 01658/5-3350) is located inside the bus terminal on the right-hand side. Some English is spoken, but note that the window is not marked in English. Maps of the village are in Japanese only, but the staff can point you in the direction of your ryokan or even make ryokan reservations for you (in person). They also have a brochure in English describing the national park and its attractions. The office is open daily from 10am to 5:30pm (until 4:30pm November through April). In any case, the village is so tiny you won't have any difficulty getting around.

SPECIAL EVENTS From the first to the last Saturday in February, Sounkyo Onsen puts on the **Sounkyo Ice Fall Festival.** The river itself is used to create huge ice sculptures, slides, and structures which are lit up at night. The multicolored ice forms are beautiful when lit; during the festival, there are fireworks over them at 8pm every weekend. In the summer, there's the **Keikoku Hi Matsuri,** the Fire Festival, which highlights the Ainu culture. It's held on July 24th and 25th every year.

What to See & Do

The **Sounkyo Gorge** is a river valley hemmed in on both sides by rock walls rising almost 500 feet high. Almost perpendicular in places, the gorge extends for about 12 miles, offering spectacular views with each bending curve. The best way to see the gorge is on a bicycle, which you can rent from stalls beside the bus terminal and a number of other places for ¥1,500 ($15) a day. There's a designated route you're supposed to follow (maps provided), and altogether the trip to the end of the route and back should take no longer than 2½ hours.

The first part of the trip by bicycle is unfortunately on a sidewalk next to a highway strung with cars. The highway winds along a rushing river past a couple of waterfalls until finally disappearing into a dark tunnel—which is where I'm convinced it belongs anyway. At this point the gorge belongs to cyclists and hikers and becomes quite narrow. You then pass through a tunnel yourself and emerge at the turning point of your trip where you'll find—what else?—souvenir shops, soda machines, and vendors selling corn on the cob. This is where tour buses pull in for a quick look.

If you're interested in hiking, or even if you're not, take the cable car from Sounkyo Onsen to the lofty peak of **Kuro-dake Mountain.** The trip takes seven minutes and costs ¥1,500 ($15) round-trip. From the cable-car station, walk a few minutes farther up the mountain, where you'll come to a chair lift. This costs ¥500 ($5) one way and takes 15 minutes, swinging you past lush forests of fir and birch. At the end of the lift, where the hiking paths begin, there's a hut where you sign your name and give your route so that tabs can be kept on people who are on the mountain. If you're not feeling overly ambitious, you can hike an hour and reach the peak of Kuro-dake, 6,500 feet high, where if the weather is clear you'll be rewarded with views of the surrounding mountain ranges.

If you feel like taking a day's hike, there's a circular path along the top of mountain ridges that you can hike in about seven hours. And if you're really into hiking and wish to carry your backpack with you, a popular route is to walk from the Sounkyo chair lift over Mt. Asahi, Hokkaido's tallest mountain, and on to another chair lift that will take you down to Asahidake Onsen, a spa where you can spend the night. This trip takes 8 to 10 hours, so set out early. Be sure to pick up a map showing the hiking trails. It's in Japanese only, but since the trails are also marked in Japanese only, having an English map wouldn't do you much good. The hiking path isn't considered that strenuous, but you do need sturdy walking shoes. If you're going for just a short hike, tennis shoes are fine. The tops of the mountains are really beautiful here, covered with wildflowers and alpine plant life. It would be a shame to come to Sounkyo and not spend a few hours amid its lofty peaks.

From November to May the mountains become a skier's haven, especially for beginners (advanced skiiers won't find the slopes here challenging). Although you can rent skis up on the mountain at the cable-car station, keep in mind that your feet may be too big. Skis and boots rent for ¥3,500 ($35) and up. A day's cable-car and chair-lift ticket cost ¥3,200 ($32) at last check. The lift operations vary according to the month, but are open daily from about 8 or 9am to 4 or 4:30pm in winter and from 6am to 7pm in summer. The lifts shut down entirely for two weeks beginning in mid-February for maintenance work.

If you have time to kill, you might also consider dropping in on the **Sounkyo Museum Daisetsuzan National Park.** Its explanations are in Japanese only, but you'll see some aerial reliefs of the area, stuffed animals, butterflies, insects, and birds. Admission is ¥200 ($2) for adults, half price for children. The museum is open daily from 8:30am to 5pm.

Accommodations

If you want to stay here in August, make reservations in advance. Incidentally, most families who live here run several operations that might include a ryokan, an adjoining restaurant, and a souvenir shop. The army of college-age Japanese you see working in the area come from other parts of Japan to work in Sounkyo for the summer. They may not know a lot about the area, but most of them speak some English.

Grand Hotel (287)

Sounkyo 078-17. ☎ **01658/5-3111.** Fax 01658/5-3302. 200 rms (all with bath). MINIBAR TV TEL. ¥10,000–¥50,000 ($100–$500) per person winter; ¥20,000–¥50,000 ($200–$500) summer. Rates include breakfast, dinner, and service charge. AE, DC, JCB, MC, V. Directions: A 2-minute walk from bus terminal.

Situated beside the highway that runs through Sounkyo Gorge, this older hotel was recently renovated. The lobby, with its marbled pillars and white walls, is cheerful though a bit overdone; the public spa is quite nice, with large windows, white tile, and stone. There are also outdoor baths, separated for men and women. Higher rates are for top-floor rooms with views of the surrounding mountain ranges.

Kitagawa (288)

Sounkyo 078-17. ☎ **01658/5-3515,** or 5-3231. 12 rms (none with bath). TV TEL. ¥6,500 ($65) per person. Rates include breakfast, dinner, and service charge. No credit cards.

Less than a three-minute walk from the bus terminal, this clean and pleasant minshuku offering Japanese-style accommodations attracts mainly young Japanese. Located above a souvenir shop and restaurant of the same name, it has both a coin-operated laundry and hot-spring baths.

Mountview Hotel

Sounkyo 078-17. ☎ **01658/5-3011.** Fax 01658/5-3010. 98 rms (all with bath). MINIBAR TV TEL. Summer, ¥12,000–¥25,000 ($120–$250) per person. Winter, ¥5,000 ($50) discount. Rates include breakfast, dinner, and service charge. AE, DC, JCB, MC, V.

Built in 1983, this ryokan—a two-minute walk from the bus terminal—has 69 Western-style rooms and 28 Japanese-style rooms, a souvenir shop, a bar, a games corner, and of course, hot-spring baths. Meals, served in a dining room, are either Western or Japanese. Breakfast is a smorgasbord buffet. The guest rooms are new, clean, and bright; they have safes, TV with remote control, hot water for tea, and minuscule baths. Lower floors have no view, but seventh-floor rooms have a view of the gorge, so you might want to ask for one of these when making a reservation.

Onozuka (289)

Sounkyo 078-17. ☎ **01658/5-3308.** 5 rms (none with bath). TV. ¥6,500 ($65) per person. Rates include breakfast, dinner, and service charge. No credit cards.

This simple minshuku, a three-minute walk from the bus terminal, has all Japanese-style rooms, and its own hot-spring baths, as well as a coffee shop on the ground floor. Western-style breakfasts are available if ordered the night before.

Pension Milky House

Sounkyo 078-17. ☎ **01658/5-3737.** Fax 01658/5-3404. 60 rms (none with bath). TV TEL. Summer, ¥8,950 ($89.50) per person. Winter, ¥7,360 ($73.60) per person. Rates include breakfast, dinner, tax, and service charge. JCB.

The owners of this pension—which is spread among several buildings, a five-minute walk from the bus terminal—are friendly. Dining is Japanese only, in a pleasant dining room. There are coin-operated laundry facilities and public hot-spring baths. The in-room TVs are coin operated.

Pension Yukara (290)

Sounkyo 078-17. ☎ **01658/5-3216.** 7 rms (none with bath). TV TEL. ¥9,000 ($90) per person. Rates include breakfast, dinner, and service charge. AE, DC, JCB, MC, V. Closed Nov–Mar.

The spotlessly clean, white, bright, and cute style of this pension, a six-minute walk from the bus terminal, is meant to appeal to young Japanese girls. Its rooms include both twins and tatami rooms, and they're decorated with pastel-colored wallpaper and lots of pink. There's a coin-operated laundry here, but the drawback to this place is that it doesn't have a hot-spring bath—just regular bath water. Breakfast and dinner are Western style. Since the owners run a ski lodge elsewhere, the pension is closed November through March.

Sounkyo Prince Hotel Choyotei

Sounkyo 078-17. ☎ **01658/5-3241.** 271 rms (all with bath). MINIBAR TV TEL. Summer, ¥20,000–¥27,000 ($200–$270) per person. Off-season, ¥10,000–¥27,000 ($100–$270) per person. Rates include breakfast, dinner, and service charge. AE, DC, JCB, MC, V.

This hotel (which, by the way, is not a member of the Prince Hotel Group) offers the most expensive accommodations in town and boasts a good view of the gorge from its location atop a ridge, an eight-minute walk from the bus terminal. Both Japanese-style and combination rooms are available, pleasant and elegantly simple, with minibar, safe for valuables, and TV with adult video. The higher rates are charged for rooms with views of the gorge. Facilities include a modern, comfortable lobby with views of a rock garden, an electronic-games room, a souvenir shop, noodle and sushi counters, and public baths on the top floor overlooking the gorge.

Sounkyo Youth Hostel (291)

Sounkyo 078-17. ☎ **01658/5-3418.** 95 beds. ¥2,850 ($28.50) for JYHA members and nonmembers. Breakfast ¥650 ($6.50) extra; dinner ¥1,030 ($10.30) extra. No credit cards.

Located on top of a hill above the city, a ten-minute walk from the bus terminal, past the Taisetsu hotel, this hostel offers both beds and futon. Unfortunately, it doesn't have hot springs, but it does have a public bath and laundry facilities.

Taisetsu Hotel

Sounkyo 078-17. ☎ **01658/5-3211.** 230 rms (200 with bath). A/C MINIBAR TV TEL. Summer, ¥16,500–¥22,000 ($165–$220) per person. Off-season, ¥11,000–¥22,000 ($110–$220) per person. Rates include breakfast, dinner, and service charge. AE, DC, JCB, MC, V.

Just across the street from the Sounkyo Prince Hotel Choyotei, this large white hotel on a hill above the town is another great place to stay, especially if you can get a room on a top floor facing the gorge. Rates depend on the size of your room and its view. The most expensive rooms face the gorge, while the cheapest rooms have a toilet but no bath. Western breakfasts are available on request. Most rooms are tatami, but two Western-style rooms are also available. The hot-spring public baths here are large and consist of several different pools. As is often the case, however, the men's bath commands a better view than the women's bath.

Dining

Yama (292)

Sounkyo 078-17. ☎ **01658/5-3522.** Reservations not required. Main dishes ¥500–¥1,000 ($5–$10). No credit cards. VARIED.

This small restaurant, a five-minute walk from the bus terminal, has only a Japanese menu, but the "*ranch seto,*" a set lunch, is a good deal at ¥800 ($8). The set lunch changes daily; mine was fried pork, octopus, rice, pickles, salad, soup, and tea. Yama also makes obento (box lunches) for a picnic; if you want one, ask your hotel or pension to order it the day before. At this local hangout there are lots of games and puzzles, such as Rubik's Cubes and other mind bogglers, which you can play to while away the time. You'll recognize the place by the white *noren* (curtain) outside and the name in neon.

AKAN NATIONAL PARK

Spreading through the eastern end of Hokkaido, Akan National Park features volcanic mountains, dense forests of subarctic primeval trees, and three caldera lakes, including Lake Akan.

Because Akan National Park lies at the eastern extremity of Hokkaido, you may wish to fly back to Tokyo. Kushiro Airport is 1 hour and 20 minutes away by bus from Akanko Onsen. The plane trip from Kushiro to Tokyo takes about 1 ½ hours.

AKANKO ONSEN

The best place to stay in the park is at Akanko Onsen, a small hot-spring resort on the edge of Lake Akan. It makes a good base from which to explore both the Akan National Park and the Red-Crested Crane National Park nearby. As for Akanko Onsen itself, it's small, and walking is the best way to get around. It consists primarily of one main street that snakes along the lake, with ryokan and souvenir shops on both sides.

Essentials

The **telephone area code** for Akanko Onsen is 0154.

GETTING THERE Since there's no train station at Akanko, transportation to the resort town is by bus from Kushiro or Bihoro. A bus from Kushiro to Akanko costs ¥2,490 ($24.90) one way. Bihoro is approximately five hours from Sapporo by train. If you're coming from Sounkyo, take the JR train from Kamikawa to Bihoro directly. In addition to regular buses that run from Bihoro to Akanko (¥2,040/$20.40 one way), there are also sightseeing buses (¥5,490/$54.90) that take in the most important sights along the way, offering the best way to see the national park.

VISITOR INFORMATION If you have any questions concerning Akan National Park itself, drop by the **visitor's center,** with displays (unfortunately in Japanese only) of natural wonders pertaining to the park.

You can also stop at the **tourist association** (☎ 0154/67-2254), located just a minute's walk from the Akanko Onsen bus terminal in the direction of the lake. You can pick up a pamphlet in English about Akan National Park here and make reservations for hotels, ryokan, and minshuku. It's open daily from 9am to 6pm. There's also a small tourist window next to the boat pier where you buy tickets for boat rides on Lake Akan.

What to See & Do

Your sightseeing in Akan National Park should begin before reaching Akanko Onsen, which lies in the southern part of the park. The best way to see the national park, if you're not renting a car, is to board an **Akan sightseeing bus** in Bihoro, which is north of the park. That way, you'll travel all the way through the park and see the most important natural wonders. The bus trip takes five hours, making stops at several scenic spots along the way, including Kussharo and Mashu Lakes. Kussharo is one of Japan's largest mountain lakes, while Mashu is considered to be one of the most beautiful. A deep crater lake with the clearest water in Japan, Mashu was called "lake of the devil" by the Ainu because no water flows either into it or out of it. Surely Mashu is one of Japan's least-spoiled lakes: Because of the steep, 660-foot-high rock walls ringing the lake, it has remained inaccessible to humanity (the bus stops at two observation platforms high above the water). The bus trip costs ¥5,590 ($55.90) and is called the Panorama Course. At last check, buses departed from Bihoro three times daily. In winter, only one bus departs daily. Be sure to check departures ahead of time, since bus schedules change. In addition to sightseeing buses, there are also regular, direct buses that travel between Bihoro and Akan in about 70 minutes. For more information, call 0152/3-4181.

As for things to do in Akanko, the most popular activity is to take a boat cruise around **Lake Akan.** Lake Akan is famous for its very rare spherical green weed, called *marimo.* It's a spongelike ball of duckweed that grows to two to five inches in diameter. Found in only a few places in the world, marimo is formed when many separate and stringy pieces of weed at the bottom of the lake roll around and eventually come together to form a ball. The ball grows larger and larger until sooner or later it breaks apart, whereby the whole process starts over again. On your boat cruise you'll make a stop at a small island on the lake where a marimo museum has been set up, consisting of duckweed in a few tanks, together with explanations of how they're formed. Supposedly, when the sun shines the marimo rises to the surface of the water, giving Lake Akan a wonderful green shimmer. However, the only marimo I ever saw was in the museum's tanks and in tanks of souvenir shops around town—even though the sun was shining. Perhaps you'll have better luck. The boat trip takes 1½ hours and costs ¥1,300 ($13).

While you're out on your boat trip, you'll notice two cone-shaped volcanoes, **O-Akandake** to the east and **Me-Akandake** to the south. Both are popular destinations for hikers. O-Akandake is dormant, and it's about a 4½-hour hike to the summit from Akanko Onsen. Me-Akandake, the highest mountain in the Akan area, is active and is covered with primeval forests of spruce and fir. There's a trail leading to Me-Akandake from the west end of the town, and it takes about six hours to reach the top, from which you have panoramic views of the surrounding area.

A shorter hike follows a trail to **Mt. Hakutozan,** from which you also have a good view of the town and lake. It takes about 20 minutes to reach Akan's skiing area and another 30 minutes to reach Mt. Hakutozan, a grassy and moss-covered knobby hill that remains slightly warm throughout the year because of thermal activity just below the surface. The woods of birch and pine here are beautiful, and what's more, you'll probably find yourself all alone.

Incidentally, behind the park's visitor's center, described earlier, is a catwalk leading through marshy woods and connecting with a trail that terminates on the lake's shore. Here you'll find some bubbly hot-mud ponds, a grassy area good for picnics, and a rock-enclosed hot spring that empties right into the lake.

If you're in Akan in the winter, you may want to take advantage of its artificial snow atop the town's one skiing hill, with two runs that are good for beginners. The season runs from about the end of November until April 5.

If you haven't seen any Ainu dances yet, you might want to pay a visit to **Ainu Kotan Village** (☎ 0154/67-2727), which is a souvenir-shop-lined street leading to a thatch-roofed lodge where you can see Ainu performing traditional dances. Costing ¥1,000 ($10) for adults, half price for children, shows are performed several times a day. You can also visit the **Seikatsu Kinen Kan** here, built like an Ainu home and displaying various utensils.

By the way, since Akanko Onsen is a hot-spring spa, it would be a shame to come all this way and not partake of its waters. If you're staying somewhere that doesn't have hot springs, you can visit the public hot springs, called **Marimo Yu,** located across the street from the main boat dock. Open daily from 9am to 10pm, it charges ¥250 ($2.50) admission.

Red-crested cranes are the official birds of Hokkaido, and south of Akan is a breeding ground for these graceful and beautiful creatures. **Tancho-zuru Shizen Koen (Red-crested Crane Natural Park)** (☎ 0154/56-2219) is a marshy area set aside for breeding and raising the crane. Open throughout the year, daily from 9am to 6pm (to 4pm in winter), it charges ¥300 ($3) for visitors to observe the birds behind high mesh fences. You'll be surprised at how large these birds actually are. The crane park is 1¼ hours by bus from the Akanko Onsen bus terminal; get off at the Tsuru-koen stop. By the way, this is the same bus that goes from Akanko to Kushiro Airport. The bus makes a 15-minute stop at this park, which is enough time to take a quick look at the birds before continuing on to the airport.

If you happen to be in Akan in the winter, you'll have the extra delight of visiting **Tancho-no-Sato** (☎ 0154/66-2331), private grounds where red-crested cranes court, mate, and live in the winter months from November to March. This is the best place to photograph the birds in action. It's a 42-minute bus ride from Akanko Onsen bus terminal.

Accommodations

Akan Grand Hotel (293)

Aza Akankohan, Akancho, Akan-gun 085-04. ☎ **0154/67-2531.** Fax 0154/67-2754. 221 rms (all with bath). MINIBAR TV TEL. ¥11,000–¥27,000 ($110–$270) per person. Rates include breakfast, dinner, and service charge. AE, DC, JCB, MC, V.

This white hotel on the lake's edge, a 15-minute walk from the bus terminal, offers rooms with prices based upon view, meal, and season. Both Japanese-style tatami rooms and combination Japanese- and Western-style rooms are available. Rooms are modern and clean. The public baths here are fairly unusual and have a large fish tank built into the wall. An annex opened in 1994 features rooms with views. The annex's baths, also with lake views, includes a *rotenburo* (outdoor bath), Jacuzzi, cedar tub, sauna, steam room, and waterfalls.

Akan View Hotel

Aza Akankohan, Akancho, Akan-gun 085-04. ☎ **0154/67-3131.** Fax 0154/67-3139. 228 rms (all with bath). MINIBAR TV TEL. Summer, ¥7,000–¥17,000 ($70–$170) per person. Rates include breakfast, dinner, and service charge. AE, DC, JCB, MC, V.

Despite its name, this is one of the few hotels without a view of the lake. It's back from the waterfront, more inland than the other hotels, a six-minute walk from the bus terminal. Most of its rooms are Western-style twins, though 28 Japanese-style rooms are also available. Rates are based upon season. One of the best things about this hotel is that it has large indoor pools, one for swimming laps and one with slides for children, as well as the usual hot-spring baths, open 24 hours. Even if you're not staying at the hotel, you can use the facilities for ¥700 ($7) Monday through Saturday from 7:30am to 9pm and ¥1,000 ($10) on Sunday and holidays. Other facilities include tennis courts, a coin-operated laundry, and bicycles for rent. Although none of the rooms has a view of the water, the best rooms, in my opinion, are those that face east, toward some woods and a creek.

Angel Youth Hostel (295)

Aza Akankohan, Akancho, Akan-gun 085-04. ☎ **0154/67-2309.** Fax 0154/67-2954. 90 beds. ¥2,600 ($26) for JYHA members, ¥3,600 ($36) for nonmembers. Breakfast ¥600 ($6) extra; dinner ¥1,000 ($10) extra. No credit cards.

Angel's building is in good shape, and the owners are friendly enough. This hostel is a bit far out of town (a 15-minute walk from the bus terminal), but if you call from the bus terminal, someone will come to pick you up. There are also bicycles for rent here, making it easy to get back and forth to town. The place has its own hot-spring bath and laundry facilities.

Hotel Akankoso

Aza Akankohan, Akancho, Akan-gun 085-04. ☎ **0154/67-2231.** Fax 0154/67-2593. 92 rms (all with bath). MINIBAR TV TEL. Summer, ¥15,000–¥35,000 ($150–$350) per person. Off-season, ¥8,000–¥18,000 ($80–$180) per person. Rates include breakfast, dinner, and service charge. AE, DC, JCB, MC, V. Directions: Walk 5 minutes from bus terminal.

Located right next to the boat dock on the water's edge, this small hotel has a variety of Japanese-style rooms, as well as combination rooms, the best of which face the lake. The hotel's large communal hot-spring baths on the fifth floor are nicely laid out in brick and have views of the lake. Originally opened in 1933, the Akankoso is where all the VIPs stay. A daily show in the lounge from 8pm to 11pm features topless dancers and ¥3,500 ($35) all-you-can-drink course.

✪ Hotel Ichikawa (294)

Aza Akankohan, Akancho, Akan-gun 085-04. ☎ **0154/67-2011.** 110 rms (98 with bath). MINIBAR TV TEL. ¥10,000–¥23,000 ($100–$230) per person. Rates include breakfast, dinner, and service charge. AE, DC, JCB, MC, V.

Located right on the water's edge, an eight-minute walk from the bus terminal, this ryokan is very reasonably priced, and the front-desk personnel are friendly and accommodating. One advantage to staying here is Shigeru Dameon Takada, a young Japanese man whose family owns the ryokan and who speaks very good English. He told me he'd be very happy to help foreigners with any questions they might have regarding Akan—which could be quite useful, since hardly anyone in Akan speaks English. He's solved quite a few problems since I first wrote this. Rooms are Japanese or Western style, rates are based on season and meals, and rooms on the top (sixth) floor command the best views. The hot-spring public baths on the second and third floors are very modern and include a Jacuzzi, a sauna, and an outdoor bath. If you're here in summer, be sure to take the hotel's pontoon boat for a two-hour sunset cruise on the lake, complete with barbecue dinner and a glass of wine for ¥5,000 ($50) per person. The hotel can make arrangements for fishing, waterskiing, canoeing, and snow skiing and will even tailor day trips to other lakes and hiking destinations to your own desires. Ask about packages that include air fare from Tokyo.

Minshuku Kiri (296)

Aza Akankohan, Akancho, Akan-gun 085-04. ☎ and fax **0154/67-2755.** 9 rms (none with bath). TV. ¥5,500 ($55) per person. Rates include breakfast, dinner, tax, and service charge. No credit cards.

This minshuku is across the street from the Hotel Ichikawa, an eight-minute walk from the bus terminal. Look for the wooden sign hanging above the door with the English written very small. The nine Japanese-style rooms here are simple, with coin-operated TV. The bathtubs here are wooden, and the water is from hot springs.

New Akan Shangrila Hotel

Aza Akankohan, Akancho, Akan-gun 085-04. ☎ **0154/67-2121.** Fax 0154/67-3339. 360 rms (all with bath). MINIBAR TV TEL. Summer, ¥15,000–¥30,000 ($150–$300) per person. Off-season, ¥8,000–¥15,000 ($80–$150) per person. Rates include breakfast, dinner, and service charge. AE, DC, JCB, MC, V.

Situated in a shady spot beside Lake Akan, a five-minute walk from the bus terminal, this hotel winds along the curve of the lake in a series of wings built at various stages in the past 20 years. The newest remodeling has rooms featuring bay windows looking out on shade trees and the lake beyond, as does the Annex Crystal. Both Japanese-style and Western-style rooms are available. Personally, I always feel lost in a popular tourist hotel like this.

Dining/Entertainment: A restaurant has good views of the lake, and there's a coffee shop, bar, and disco.

Facilities: Souvenir shops; large public hot-spring baths, including *rotenburo* (outdoors) overlooking the lake.

Appendix

A Glossary

Needless to say, it takes years to become fluent in Japanese, particularly in written Japanese, with its thousands of *kanji,* or Chinese characters, and many *hiragana* and *katakana* characters. Knowing just a few words of Japanese, however, not only is useful but will delight the Japanese people you meet during your trip.

Everyday Expressions

Good morning	**Ohayo gozaimasu**
Good afternoon	**Konnichiwa**
Good evening	**Konbanwa**
Good night	**Oyasuminasai**
Hello	**Haro (or Konnichiwa)**
Good-bye	**Sayonara (or Bye-bye!)**
Excuse me, I'm sorry	**Sumimasen**
Thank you	**Domo arigatoo**
You're welcome	**Dooitashimashite**
Please (go ahead)	**Doozo**
Yes	**Hai**
No	**Iie**
Foreigner	**Gaijin**
Japanese person	**Nihonjin**
Japanese language	**Nihongo**
American person	**Amerikajin**
English language	**Eigo**
Do you understand?	**Wakarimasu ka?**
I understand	**Wakarimasu**
I don't understand	**Wakarimasen**
Just a minute, please	**Chotto matte kudasai**
How much is it?	**Ikura desu ka?**
Where is it?	**Doko desu ka?**
When is it?	**Itsu desu ka?**
Expensive	**Takai**
Cheap	**Yasui**
I like it	**Suki desu**

Numbers

1	Ichi	12	Juuni
2	Ni	20	Nijuu
3	San	30	Sanjuu
4	Shi	40	Shijuu (*or* yonjuu)
5	Go	50	Gojuu
6	Roku	60	Rokujuu
7	Shichi (*or* nana)	70	Nanajuu
8	Hachi	80	Hachijuu
9	Kyuu	90	Kyuuju
10	Juu	100	Hyaku
11	Juuichi	1,000	Sen

General Terms

Fusuma Sliding paper doors

Gassho-zukuri Roofs built at steep angles, usually thatched and found in regions with heavy snowfalls

Geta Wooden sandals

Haori A short coat worn over a kimono.

Jinja Shinto shrine

Kotatsu A heating element placed under a low table (which is covered with a blanket) for keeping one's legs warm; used in place of a heater in traditional Japanese homes

Minshuku Inexpensive lodging in a private home; the Japanese equivalent of a European pension

Nomi-ya A drinking establishment

Ryokan Japanese-style inn

Shitamachi Old downtown area of Tokyo

Shoji White paper sliding windows

Tatami Rice mats

Tera (*or* **dera**) Temple

Tokonoma A small, recessed alcove in a Japanese room used to display a flower arrangement, scroll, or art object

Torii Entrance gate of a Shinto shrine, consisting usually of two poles topped with one or two crossbeams

Yukata A cotton kimono worn for sleeping

Zabuton Floor cushions

Menu Terms

Ayu A small river fish; a delicacy of western Japan

Basashi Raw horse meat; a specialty of Kyushu

Champon Nagasaki-style Chinese noodles, served usually in soup

Chu-hai Shochu *(see below)* mixed with soda water and flavored with syrup and lemon

Dengaku Lightly grilled tofu (*see below*) coated with a bean paste

Dojo A small, eel-like river fish

Fugu Putterfish (also known as blowfish or globefish)

"Genghis Khan" Mutton and vegetables grilled at your table

Gohan Rice

Gyoza Chinese fried pork dumplings
Jibuni A winter stew of chicken and vegetables; a specialty of Kanazawa
Kaiseki A formal Japanese meal consisting of many courses and served originally during the tea ceremony
Kamameshi A rice casserole topped with seafood, meat, or vegetables
Kushiage (*also* **kushikatsu** *or* **kushiyaki**) Deep-fried skewers of chicken, beef, seafood, and vegetables
Kyo-ryoori (*also* **Kyo-ryori**) Kyoto-style cuisine, including Kyo-kaiseki
Maguro Tuna
Makizushi Sushi (see below) vegetables, and rice rolled inside dried seaweed
Miso A soybean paste, used as a seasoning in soups and sauces
Miso-shiru Miso soup
Mochi Japanese rice cake
Nabemono A single-pot dish of chicken, beef, pork, or seafood, stewed with vegetablesNattoFermented soybeans
Nikujaga A beef, potato, and carrot stew, flavored with sake (see below) and soy sauce; popular in winter
Oden Fish cakes, hard-boiled eggs, and vegetables, simmered in a light broth
Okonomiyaki A thick pancake filled with meat, fish, shredded cabbage, and vegetables or noodles, often cooked by diners at their table
Ramen Thick, yellow Chinese noodles, served in a hot soup
Sake Rice wine
Sansai mountain vegetables, including bracken and flowering fern
Sashimi Raw seafood
Shabu-shabu Thinly sliced beef quickly dipped in boiling water and then dipped in a sauce
Shippoku A variety of dishes of Chinese, European, and Japanese origin; a specialty of Nagasaki
Shochu Japanese whiskey, made from rice, wheat, or potatoes
Shojin-ryoori Japanese vegetarian food, served at Buddhist temples
Shoyu Soy sauce
Shumai Steamed Chinese pork dumplings
Soba Buckwheat noodles
Somen Fine white wheat vermicelli, eaten cold in summer
Sukiyaki A Japanese fondue of thinly sliced beef cooked in a sweetened soy sauce with vegetables
Sushi (*also* **nigiri-zushi**) Raw seafood placed on top of vinegared rice
Tempura Deep-fried food coated in a batter of egg, water, and wheat flour
Teppanyaki Japanese-style steak, seafood, and vegetables cooked by a chef on a smooth, hot tableside grill
Tofu Soft bean curd
Tonkatsu Deep-fried pork cutlets
Udon Thick white wheat noodles
Unagi Grilled eel
Wasabi Japanese horseradish, served with sushi
Yakisoba Chinese fried noodles, served with sautéed vegetables
Yakitori Charcoal-grilled chicken, vegetables, and other specialties, served on bamboo skewers
Yudofu Tofu simmered in a pot at your table

B A List of Japanese Symbols

Tokyo

1. Tokyo YWCA Sadowara Hostel
東京ＹＷＣＡ砂土原ホステル
2. Shimizu Bekkan
しみず別館
3. Sushiko
寿司幸
4. Kinsen
金扇
5. Ginza Daimasu
銀座大増
6. Kushi Colza
串コルザ
7. Ohmatsuya
大松屋
8. Shabusen
しゃぶせん
9. Suehiro
スエヒロ
10. Sushi Sei
寿司清
11. Atariya
当り屋
12. Donto
どんと
13. Tamura
田村
14. Tentake
天竹
15. Edogin
江戸銀
16. Sushi Dai
寿司大
17. Hayashi
はやし
18. Inakaya
田舎屋
19. Zakuro
ざくろ
20. Takamura
篁
21. Fukuzushi
福鮨
22. Hassan
八山
23. Shabu Zen
しゃぶ禅
24. Ganchan
がんちゃん
25. Ichioku
一億
26. Torigin
鳥ぎん
27. Genrokusushi
元禄寿司
28. Kakiden
柿伝
29. Tsunahachi
つな八
30. Irohanihoheto
いろはにほへと
31. Negishi
ねぎし
32. Tonki
とんき
33. Mugitoro
むぎとろ
34. Kuremutsu
暮六つ
35. Komagata Dojo
駒形どうじょう
36. Chinya
ちんや
37. Daikokuya
大黒屋
38. Keyaki
欅
39. Namiki
並木藪
40. Izu'ei
伊豆栄
41. Kandagawa
神田川
42. Yabu Soba
やぶそば
43. Kappa Tengoku
かっぱ天国
44. Hakusuke
百助
45. Lupin
ルパン
46. Yagura Chaya
櫓茶屋

47. Anyo
あんよ
48. Volga
ボルガ

Kamakura

49. Miyokawa
御代川
50. Monzen
門前
51. Kayagi-ya
茅木屋
52. Nakamura-an
中村庵
53. Raitei
擂亭

Hakone

54. Ryuguden
龍宮殿
55. Ichinoyu
一の湯

Atami

56. Hotel New Akao
ホテルニューアカオ
57. Kiunkaku
起雲閣
58. Kyotei
京亭

Shimoda

59. Haji
はじ

Dogashima

60. Ginsuiso
銀水荘
61. Kaikomaru
海晃丸

Kyoto

62. Hotel Hokke Club
ホテル法華クラブ
63. Kinmata
近又
64. Ryokan Rikiya
力弥
65. Rokuharaya
六波羅屋
66. Myokenji Temple
妙顕寺
67. Myorenji Temple
妙蓮寺
68. Izusen
泉仙
69. Misogi-gawa
禊川
70. Izumoya
いづもや
71. Tagoto
田ごと
72. Bio-Tei
びお亭
73. Ganko Sushi
がんこ寿司
74. Gontaro
権太呂
75. Musashi
むさし
76. Omen
おめん
77. Zu Zu
厨厨
78. Hyotei
瓢亭
79. Mikaku
みかく
80. Minoko
美濃幸
81. Isobe
いそべ
82. Okutan
奥丹
83. Chorakukan
長楽館
84. Goemonjaya
五衛ェ門茶屋
85. Koan
高庵
86. Nakamuraro
中村楼
87. Kodaiji Rakusho Tea Room
洛匠
88. Zenrinji Temple
永観堂　禅林寺
89. Tanakaya
田中弥
90. Taku Taku
磔磔
91. Suishin Honten
酔心本店

NARA

92. Furuichi
古市
93. Kikusuiro
菊水楼
94. Harishin
はり新
95. Yugayama
ゆがや満

TAKAYAMA

96. Asunaro
あすなろ
97. Hida Gasshoen
飛騨合掌苑
98. Kinkikan
金亀館
99. Ryokan Hishuya
飛州屋
100. Seiryu
清龍
101. Hachibei
八兵衛
102. Kakusho
角正
103. Bandai Kado Mise
萬代角店
104. Sara
沙羅
105. Suzuya
寿々屋
106. Jizakaya
地酒屋
107. Kofune
小舟

SHIRAKAWA-GO

108. Seikatsu Shiryokan
生活資料館
109. Myozenji
明善寺
110. Doburoku Matsuri no Yakata
どぶろく祭りの館
111. Juemon
十右ェ門
112. Magoemon
孫右ェ門
113. Nodaniya
のだにや
114. Otaya
大田屋
115. Yosobe
よそべえ
116. Irori
いろり
117. Kitanosho
基太の庄

MATSUMOTO

118. Matsumoto Mingei-kan
松本民芸館
119. Hotel Ikyu
一休
120. Suminoe
住の江
121. Kajika
かじか
122. Shikimi
しき美

MAGOME & TSUMAGO

123. Magome
馬籠
124. Tsumago
妻籠
125. Tawaraya
俵屋

NAGOYA

126. Ryokan Iroha
旅館いろは
127. Yamamoto-ya Honten
山本屋本店
128. Kishimentei
きしめん亭
129. Torigin Honten
鳥銀本店
130. Yabaton
矢場とん

ISE-SHIMA NATIONAL PARK

131. Akafuku
赤福
132. Asakichi
麻吉
133. Hoshidekan
星出館
134. Ise City Hotel
伊勢シティホテル
135. Awami
阿波海
136. Ishiyama-So
石山荘

137. Youth Hostel Taikoji
ユースホステル太江寺
138. Okadaiya
岡田屋
139. Sushi Kyu
すし久

Kanazawa

140. Shima Geisha House
志摩
141. Tawaraya Ame
俵屋あめ
142. Miyabo
みやぼ
143. Kanazawa Castle Inn
キャッスルイン金沢
144. Yogetsu
陽月
145. Kanazawa Youth Hostel
金沢ユースホステル
146. Matsui Youth Hostel
松井ユースホステル
147. Miyoshian
三芳庵
148. Tozan
東山
149. Hamacho
浜長
150. Kaga Tobi
加賀鳶
151. Kitama
きたま
152. Zeniya
銭屋

Osaka

153. Shin-Osaka Sen-i City
センイシティホテル
154. Hattori Ryokuchi Youth Hostel
服部緑地ユースホステル
155. Kaen
花宴
156. Kani Doraku
かに道楽
157. Kuidaore
くいだおれ
158. Fugetsu
風月

Kobe

159. Steakland Kobe
ステーキランドKOBE

Mt. Koya

160. Kongobuji Temple
金剛峯寺
161. Reihokan Museum
霊宝館
162. Ekoin
恵光院
163. Fumonin Temple
普門院
164. Ichijoin
一乗院
165. Rengejoin Temple
蓮華定院
166. Shojoshinin
清浄心院
167. Tentokuin
天徳院

Himeji

168. Kotel Sunroute Himeji
ホテルサンルート姫路
169. Fukutei
福亭
170. Minato-an
三七十庵

Okayama

171. Hotel Sunroute Okayama
ホテルサンルート岡山
172. Matsunoki
まつのき旅館
173. Youth Hostel Okayama-ken Seinen Kaikan
ユースホステル岡山県青年会館
174. Gonta-Zushi
権太寿し
175. Petit ("Puchi") Marie
プチマリエ
176. Suishin
酔心
177. Okayama Prefectural Product Center (Okayama-ken Kanko Bussan Senta)
岡山県物産センター

Kurashiki

178. Ryokan Kurashiki
旅館くらしき
179. Tsurugata
鶴形
180. Kamoi
カモ井

181. Minshuku Kawakami
民宿かわかみ

Matsue

182. Matsue Cultural Museum (Matsue Kyodokan)
松江郷土館
183. Teahouse Meimei-an
明々庵
184. Buke Yashiki
武家屋敷
185. Tanabe Art Museum
田部美術館
186. Gesshoji Temple
月照寺
187. Horaiso
蓬莢荘
188. Minami-Kan
皆美館
189. Matsue Minami Guchi Hotel
松江南口ホテル
190. Matsue Plaza Hotel
松江プラザホテル
191. Matsue Urban Hotel
松江アーバンホテル
192. Ginsen
銀扇
193. Kaneyasu
かねやす
194. Yakumoan
八雲庵

Hiroshima

195. Mitakiso
三瀧荘
196. Sera Bekkan
世羅別館
197. Hiroshima Youth Hostel
広島ユースホステル
198. Rijyo Kaikan
鯉城会館
199. Kanawa
かなわ
200. Kushinobo
串の坊
201. Okonomi-Mura
お好み村

Miyajima

202. Higashiya
ひがしや
203. Iwaso Ryokan
岩惣旅館
204. Jukeiso
聚景荘
205. Fujitaya
ふじたや
206. Heike
平家
207. Tonookajaya
塔之岡茶屋

Takamatsu

208. Kompira O-shibai
金毘羅大芝居
209. Tokiwa Honkan
常盤本館
210. Tenkatsu
天勝
211. Hansuke
半助
212. Kanaizumi
かな泉
213. Maruichi
まるいち

Matsuyama

214. Mingei Iyo Kasuri Kaikan
民芸伊予かすり会館
215. Umeno-Seito-jo
梅野清陶所
216. Tobe-yaki Kanko Center
砥部焼観光センター
217. Ehime Prefectural Products Hall (Ehime no Bussan)
愛媛の物産
218. Uchikoza
内子座
219. Funaya
ふなや
220. Taihei Business Hotel
ビジネスホテル泰平
221. Matsuyama Shinsen-en Youth Hostel
松山神泉園ユースホステル
222. Shinhamasaku
新浜作

Fukuoka

223. Chisan Hotel Hakata
チサンホテル博多

224. Mitsui Urban Hotel
三井アーバンホテル
225. Dazaifu Youth Hostel
太宰府ユースホステル
226. Gyosai
魚菜

Beppu

227. Kannawaen
神和苑
228. Sakaeya
サカエ屋
229. Tenjuso
天寿荘
230. Green Business Hotel
グリーンビジネスホテル
231. Amamijaya
甘味茶屋
232. Jin
仁
233. Yakiniku no Bungo
焼肉のぶんご
234. Aso Youth Hostel
阿蘇ユースホステル
235. Minami Aso Kokumin Shukusha
南阿蘇国民宿舎

Kumamoto

236. Kumamoto Traditional Crafts Center
熊本県伝統工芸館
237. Display Hall of Kumamoto Products (Kumamoto-ken Bussankan)
熊本県物産館
238. Kumamoto Shiritsu Youth Hostel
熊本市立ユースホステル
239. Kumamoto Station Hotel
熊本ステーションホテル
240. Gozan
五山
241. Senri
泉里
242. Aoyagi
青柳
243. Goemon
五右衛門
244. Kimura-so
きむら荘

Nagasaki

245. Sakamoto-ya
坂本屋
246. Hotel Station Royal Ajisai
ホテルステーションロイヤルあじさい
247. Nagasaki Kenritsu Youth Hostel
長崎県立ユースホステル
248. Sansui-so
山水荘
249. Fukiro
富貴楼
250. Kagetsu
花月
251. Hamakatsu
浜勝
252. Gohan
御飯
253. Kouzanrou
江山楼
254. Yagura-Sushi
矢倉寿司

Unzen

255. Miyazaki Ryokan
雲仙宮崎旅館
256. Kaseya Ryokan
かせや旅館
257. Seiunso Kokumin Shukusha
青雲荘国民宿舎

Kagoshima

258. Shigetomiso
重富荘
259. Sakurajima Youth Hostel
桜島ユースホステル
260. Ajimori
あぢもり
261. Kumasotei
熊襲亭
262. Noboruya
のぼる屋
263. Satsuma
さつま

Ibusuki

264. Hotel Hakusuikan
ホテル白水
265. Hotel Shusuien
秀水園
266. Ibusuki Kokumin Kyuka-son
指宿国民休暇村
267. Chojuan
長寿庵

Miyazaki

268. Aoshima Kokumin Shukusha
青島国民宿舎
269. Gyosantei
魚山亭
270. Sugi no Ko
杉の子

Matsushima

271. Zuiganji Temple
瑞巌寺
272. Entsuin
円通院
273. Taikanso
大観荘
274. Matsushima Kanko Hotel
松島観光ホテル
275. Donjiki Chaya
どんじき茶屋

Hakodate

276. Wakamatsu Ryokan
若松

Sapporo

277. Zennikku Hotel
全日空ホテル
278. Nakamuraya Ryokan
中村屋旅館
279. Hyosetsu no Mon
氷雪の門

Shikotsu-Toya National Park

280. Hotel New Toyako
ホテルニュー洞爺湖
281. Manseikaku
万世閣
282. Showa-Shinzan Youth Hostel
昭和新山ユースホステル
283. Takatsu Ryokan
多佳津旅館
284. Akashiya Youth Hostel
あかしやユースホステル
285. Kikusui
菊水
286. Youth Hostel Ryokan Kanefuku
ユースホステル旅館金福

Daisetsuzan National Park

287. Grand Hotel
グランドホテル
288. Kitagawa
北川
289. Onozuka
おのづか
290. Pension Yukara
ペンションユーカラ
291. Sounkyo Youth Hotel
層雲峡ユースホステル
292. Yama
やま

Akan National Park

293. Akan Grand Hotel
阿寒グランドホテル
294. Hotel Ichikawa
ホテル市川
295. Angel Youth Hostel
エンジェルユースホステル
296. Minshuku Kiri
民宿桐

Index

FROMMER'S COMPLETE TRAVEL GUIDES

(Comprehensive guides to sightseeing, dining, and accommodations, with selections in all price ranges from deluxe to budget)

Acapulco/Ixtapa/Taxco, 2nd Ed.
Alaska, 4th Ed.
Arizona '96
Australia, 4th Ed.
Austria, 6th Ed.
Bahamas '96
Belgium/Holland/Luxembourg, 4th Ed.
Bermuda '96
Budapest & the Best of Hungary, 1st Ed.
California '96
Canada, 9th Ed.
Caribbean '96
Carolinas/Georgia, 3rd Ed.
Colorado, 3rd Ed.
Costa Rica, 1st Ed.
Cruises '95-'96
Delaware/Maryland, 2nd Ed.
England '96
Florida '96
France '96
Germany '96
Greece, 1st Ed.
Honolulu/Waikiki/Oahu, 4th Ed.
Ireland, 1st Ed.
Italy '96
Jamaica/Barbados, 2nd Ed.
Japan, 3rd Ed.
Maui, 1st Ed.
Mexico '96
Montana/Wyoming, 1st Ed.
Nepal, 3rd Ed.
New England '96
New Mexico, 3rd Ed.
New York State '94-'95
Nova Scotia/New Brunswick/Prince Edward Island, 1st Ed.
Portugal, 14th Ed.
Prague & the Best of the Czech Republic, 1st Ed.
Puerto Rico '95-'96
Puerto Vallarta/Manzanillo/Guadalajara, 3rd Ed.
Scandinavia, 16th Ed.
Scotland, 3rd Ed.
South Pacific, 5th Ed.
Spain, 16th Ed.
Switzerland, 7th Ed.
Thailand, 2nd Ed.
U.S.A., 4th Ed.
Utah, 1st Ed.
Virgin Islands, 3rd Ed.
Virginia, 3rd Ed.
Washington/Oregon, 6th Ed.
Yucatan '95-'96

FROMMER'S FRUGAL TRAVELER'S GUIDES

(Dream vacations at down-to-earth prices)

Australia on $45 '95-'96
Berlin from $50, 3rd Ed.
Caribbean from $60, 1st Ed.
Costa Rica/Guatemala/Belize on $35, 3rd Ed.
Eastern Europe on $30, 5th Ed.
England from $50, 21st Ed.
Europe from $50 '96
Greece from $45, 6th Ed.
Hawaii from $60, 30th Ed.
Ireland from $45, 16th Ed.
Israel from $45, 16th Ed.
London from $60 '96
Mexico from $35 '96
New York on $70 '94-'95
New Zealand from $45, 6th Ed.
Paris from $65 '96
South America on $40, 16th Ed.
Washington, D.C. from $50 '96

FROMMER'S COMPLETE CITY GUIDES

(Comprehensive guides to sightseeing, dining, and accommodations in all price ranges)

Amsterdam, 8th Ed.
Athens, 10th Ed.
Atlanta & the Summer Olympic Games '96
Bangkok, 2nd Ed.
Berlin, 3rd Ed.
Boston '96

Chicago '96
Denver/Boulder/Colorado Springs, 2nd Ed.
Disney World/Orlando '96
Dublin, 2nd Ed.
Hong Kong, 4th Ed.
Las Vegas '96
London '96
Los Angeles '96
Madrid/Costa del Sol, 2nd Ed.
Mexico City, 1st Ed.
Miami '95-'96
Minneapolis/St. Paul, 4th Ed.
Montreal/Quebec City, 8th Ed.
Nashville/Memphis, 2nd Ed.
New Orleans '96
New York City '96
Paris '96
Philadelphia, 8th Ed.
Rome, 10th Ed.
St. Louis/Kansas City, 2nd Ed.
San Antonio/Austin, 1st Ed.
San Diego, 4th Ed.
San Francisco '96
Santa Fe/Taos/Albuquerque '96
Seattle/Portland, 4th Ed.
Sydney, 4th Ed.
Tampa/St. Petersburg, 3rd Ed.
Tokyo, 4th Ed.
Toronto, 3rd Ed.
Vancouver/Victoria, 3rd Ed.
Washington, D.C. '96

FROMMER'S FAMILY GUIDES

(Guides to family-friendly hotels, restaurants, activities, and attractions)

California with Kids
Los Angeles with Kids
New York City with Kids
San Francisco with Kids
Washington, D.C. with Kids

FROMMER'S WALKING TOURS

(Memorable strolls through colorful and historic neighborhoods, accompanied by detailed directions and maps)

Berlin
Chicago
England's Favorite Cities
London, 2nd Ed.
Montreal/Quebec City
New York, 2nd Ed.
Paris, 2nd Ed.
San Francisco, 2nd Ed.
Spain's Favorite Cities
Tokyo
Venice
Washington, D.C., 2nd Ed.

FROMMER'S AMERICA ON WHEELS

(Guides for travelers who are exploring the USA by car, featuring a brand-new rating system for accommodations and full-color road maps)

Arizona and New Mexico
California and Nevada
Florida
Mid-Atlantic

FROMMER'S SPECIAL-INTEREST TITLES

Arthur Frommer's Branson!
Arthur Frommer's New World of Travel, 5th Ed.
Frommer's America's 100 Best-Loved State Parks
Frommer's Caribbean Hideaways, 7th Ed.
Frommer's Complete Hostel Vacation Guide to England, Scotland & Wales
Frommer's National Park Guide, 29th Ed.
USA Sports Traveler's and TV Viewer's Golf Tournament Guide
USA Sports Minor League Baseball Book
USA Today Golf Atlas

Frommer's Best Beach Vacations

(The top places to sun, stroll, shop, stay, play, party, and swim, with each beach rated for beauty, swimming, sand, and amenities)

California
Carolinas/Georgia
Florida
Hawaii
Mid-Atlantic from New York to Washington, D.C.
New England

Frommer's Bed & Breakfast Guides

(Selective guides with four-color photos and full description of the best inns in each region)

California
Caribbean
Great American Cities
Hawaii
Mid-Atlantic
New England
Pacific Northwest
Rockies
Southeast States
Southwest

Frommer's Irreverent Guides

(Wickedly honest guides for sophisticated travelers and those who want to be)

Amsterdam
Chicago
London
Manhattan
New Orleans
San Francisco

Frommer's Driving Tours

(Four-color photos and detailed maps outlining spectacular scenic driving routes)

Australia
Austria
Britain
Florida
France
Germany
Ireland
Italy
Scandinavia
Scotland
Spain
Switzerland
U.S.A.

Frommer's Born to Shop

(The ultimate travel guides for discriminating shoppers from cut-rate to couture)

Great Britain
Hong Kong
London
New York

Frommer's Food Lover's Companions

(Lavishly illustrated guides to regional specialties, restaurants, gourmet shops, markets, local wines, and more)

France
Italy